Lurie's Worlds, 1970–1980

LURIE'S WORLDS 1970–1980

by Ranan R. Lurie

THE UNIVERSITY PRESS OF HAWAII
Honolulu

MANUFACTURED IN THE UNITED STATES OF AMERICA

Library of Congress Cataloging in Publication Data

Lurie, Ranan R 1932–
Lurie's worlds, 1970–1980.

1. World politics—1965–1975—Caricatures and cartoons. 2. World politics—1975–1985—Caricatures and cartoons. 3. American wit and humor, Pictorial. I. Title.
D849.5.187 320.9'047'0207 80–15526
ISBN 0–8248–0731–6
ISBN 0–8248–0723–5 (pbk.)

To Danielle

CONTENTS

As shown above, on the opening pages for 1970 through 1979 appear portions of an extended interview with Ranan R. Lurie by the Publishers—his reflections on the art of political cartooning and his reactions to certain international leaders of the decade.

Color insert follows page 52.

FOREWORD

But each for the joy of working,
And each in his separate star,
Shall draw the Thing as he sees it,
For the God of Things as They Are.

Rudyard Kipling
When Earth's Last Picture is Painted (1892)

It takes no prophet to foretell that Lurie's caricatures will be reproduced again and again in the history books of the twenty-first century, for no graphic artist has ever done more revealing caricatures of today's world leaders, or more trenchant cartoons of the many problems that face them.

He stands today as the most influential political cartoonist of the free world.

Thomas Nast (1840–1902) was the first full-time, professional American caricaturist–cartoonist who specialized as a political analyst. Since then, thousands of cartoonists have been employed by newspapers on a regular basis to inform, mold, and sharpen the public's view of political and social issues.

But only very few can compare with Nast. One thinks of Art Young (1866–1943), John J. McCutcheon (1870–1949), Jay Darling, "Ding," (1876–1962), Rollin Dirby (1875–1972). And one also thinks of Conrad, Oliphant, Bill Mauldin, and Herblock (Herbert Block). But who one thinks of first today is Ranan Lurie.

Lurie's work appears in 45 countries and is published in 400 newspapers, with a combined circulation of 62 million. The work of no other graphic artist has ever been so regularly seen by so many people in so many different lands. What are the artistic qualities which explain Lurie's extraordinary popularity with this prodigious international mass audience?

The Lurie style is bold and harsh to the point of brutality. No reader can flip over an editorial page which features a Lurie cartoon. It immobilizes his vision—it smacks him square in the eye. And as the reader's eyes come to rest on the cartoon, the point of the cartoon penetrates his mind as swiftly as a well-directed missile. There's this double whammy—both visual and intellectual—in every Lurie cartoon.

"Art reveals nature by interpreting its intentions and formulating its desires. The great artist [wrote Amiel] is the simplifier." Most of what passes as "editorial opinion" in our newspapers today leaves the ordinary reader confused or baffled. Perhaps the issues are too complex, and the solutions, too complicated for the ordinary citizen to understand. On the other hand, many newspaper editorials today exude an inky fog of political rhetoric and abstractions. A Lurie cartoon that addresses itself to the issues covered by one of these muddled editorials generally has the power to clarify it, and illuminate the heart of its matter.

Every art has its limitations. The political cartoonist is inescapably the slave of symbols. No cartoonist has so far found better symbols for the U.S.A. than "Uncle Sam" or the American Eagle. Every cartoonist in the West tends to show the USSR as a bear; Great Britain as John Bull or a lion; China as a dragon, and so on. Few cartoonists have found a better symbol for a floundering "Administration" than a sinking ship, or for "Peace" than a dove, or for "War" than cannons or missiles. And those two absurd party symbols (invented by Thomas Nast), the Democratic donkey and Republican elephant, have served America's and Europe's cartoonists for a century.

Albeit a cartoonist is, in one sense, slave of these hackneyed symbols, he is also—if he is successful—their master. He uses them only when no symbol he himself can imagine will do as well. And even when he does use them, he puts his own brand on them, thus making them his slaves. A Lurie Uncle Sam, for example, is like no other any cartoonist has ever drawn: Uncle Sam becomes more than a symbol —he becomes a "personality." His stature, in relation to other figures in the cartoons, his expressions of satisfaction or pain, confidence or puzzlement, delight or dismay, mirror with humor and accuracy the perceptions the American people have at any given moment of the country's dominant mood.

The qualities of Lurie as an artist, however, are to be fully found in his caricatures of the great and the near-great. (And of those greats who grate on everyone's nerves.) First, his caricatures are excellent likenesses. There is no doubt that Lurie could have been a first-rate portrait artist. Secondly, Lurie's caricatures reveal the profundity of his own belief in humanity.

Despite the exaggerations and distortions of their features, emphasized by the classical cartoonist device of attaching big heads to small bodies, Lurie's caricatures never depict his "victims" as less than human. It has been the centuries-old temptation of caricaturists to satirize their enemies or those of whom they disapprove by giving them the characteristics of beasts—birds, monkeys, rats, pigs, and so on. Lurie's caricatures never lose sight of the truth that humans, for all their stupidity, selfishness, greed, barbarianism and cruelty, are nevertheless not beasts; but are what is quite a different—and more terrible—thing: rational beings who have, of their own free will, chosen to do irrational or evil deeds for profit, pleasure, or power.

Consider how, without drawing a line that suggests that Arafat is not as human or even as intelligent as, say, Begin or Sadat, Lurie manages to give the P.L.O. leader's wide and toothy smile the allure of the gaping mouth of the great white shark in "Jaws." Certainly no cartoonist has better caught the slack-lipped, blank-eyed Carter expression of bewilderment as one of his policies goes down the drain, or his mildly fanatical, squint-eyed grin, as he announces a new policy, so destined to follow the last one into the dust bin of history.

In an introduction to a 1973 book of cartoons by Lurie, Thomas Griffith, then editor of *Life* magazine, wrote, "I think that Lurie is only beginning to get the recognition he deserves in the front rank of American cartoonists." Since then, that recognition has certainly come to him.

In becoming an American, he has chosen to exercise the larger part of that influence by interpreting America to itself and to the world. America, a nation of immigrants, has been exceedingly fortunate one more time. For Lurie has the greatest gift of the artist: to make us see ourselves as others see us, and to show us "Things as They Are."

Clare Boothe Luce

PREFACE

It was indeed a fascinating moment: here we stood, President Lyndon B. Johnson, my wife Tamar, and myself in the midst of his ranch in Austin, Texas, staring at a tree and listening to what it had to say.

We were LBJ's guests, and in one of his frenzies, he invited us to join him in his Lincoln convertible, indicating that he wanted us to hear something "unusual." Then, driving eighty miles per hour on the wrong side of the narrow road, he brought us to a long line of homely looking trees, and suddenly he stopped next to one of them. He opened his side door and nodded an invitation with his cowboy hat to come and join him. We did, and the President thrust his hand through the leaves of the tree, pressed some unseen button, and a man's voice, delivered off a recorded tape, started to describe to us LBJ's youth on this very ranch.

Here we were on this dusty spring afternoon in Texas, listening to LBJ describe in his own sentimental voice his personal past, his personal deeds. And listening to that tape with a lot of concentration and affection was LBJ himself, looking at the tree with a shine in his eyes that I swear was no more, no less than a sentimental tear.

I have yet to meet with any leader who is not vain. I am not saying this in a derogatory way—my personal belief is that vanity and ego are essential to the drive that pushes a human to become a leader, as a trunk is essential for the elephant to shower itself. The only question that we, mortals, must ask ourselves in each case is whether that inevitable vanity is accompanied by a reasonable share of foresight, wisdom, assertiveness, and personal dignity befitting a real leader.

Nevertheless, the leader's conceit becomes an integral part of the political cartoonist's arsenal; and the cartoonist uses it against a leader when the disproportion between vanity and achievements triggers the political pundit's attention.

I assume that I sounded quite redundant to my students of the University of Hawaii. I could not repeat enough times the function of the political cartoonist: to reduce into graphics an analysis of a political situation—and, whenever possible, develop a conclusion or even a projection of events to come. The humor, the drawing of the metaphor, the caricature, and the facts incorporated in that cartoon are only wheels that are supposed to deliver the cargo—the message, the analysis, and/or the projection. The wisdom of the cartoon is its crown. A good cartoon, like good wine, should become better with the passing of years—as a matter of fact, it should be tested by the years. Did the cartoon, at the time of drawing, identify the bubbling history correctly? Did it evaluate facts properly? Did it gallop ahead of its readers and anticipate for them the forthcoming curves of political, economic, and military things to be?

Some time ago, I had lunch with Tom Winship, the *Boston Globe*'s editor-in-chief, and he challenged me point-blank: "How can a political cartoon that you, Ranan, like to see as a graphic political analysis compare with the written political analysis of an editorial? After all, in the written editorial, I can present my views point by point, describing to my readers most of the pros and cons of the given subject whereas the cartoon can incorporate only one basic conclusion."

I remember how I over-sweetened my coffee while searching for the right words to answer the good and valid question effectively: "You and I, Tom, are like boxers. You, the writer, will win your fight by scoring points. I, the cartoonist, must win by a knock-out."

The successful political cartoonists of today can be divided into two groups: the entertainers and the analysts. With some stretched humorist's license, I equate the comparison between these kinds of cartoonists with a comparison between Bob Hope and Jeremiah, one of the biblical prophets. Hope tries to amuse his audience with a gag, while Jeremiah penetrates the hearts and minds of his audience with parables and instant analyses of history.

Of course, it is easier to create a cartoon in which the entertaining humor becomes its final destination. It is far more complex to create the analytical cartoon, which may and should use humor as a vehicle that will lead its readers to the real, important final destination of a political cartoon: the reduction of complex events into one graphic capsule.

I believe the modern political cartoon has a mission to fulfill. It seems that fewer readers can afford the time or patience to read systematically long, gray editorials, at a time where it becomes more and more important for the regular citizen—who also happens to be the regular voter—to understand the background of events that will determine his own life. The ratio of readers who read the editorial cartoon to the readers who actually read the same page's editorials is overwhelmingly in favor of the former group. It would be unfair professionally to waste these seven to nine precious seconds the reader invests in the cartoon by not including in that piece of entertaining graphics the ingredients of political know-how. Let us include in the ice cream of entertainment the vitamins of knowledge.

The seventies was the decade of political maturity for Americans: Watergate, the truth of Vietnam, the energy crisis, economic deterioration, and blows to human dignity created by both the Iranians who kidnapped our diplomats, and the Russians, who digested with pleasure their small, weak neighbor, Afghanistan.

The constitution arms us with the first amendment to combat the frustration of these events; it grants us the right to know. Without knowing a problem we will never be able to find a solution for it. While we are blessed with the protection of the first amendment—and every one of us is entitled to know—not always do we devote our energies to utilize that granted prerogative. In many dictatorial societies the citizens are denied important knowledge and fair analysis because of constrictions and the mental brutality of tyrants who rule those unfortunate societies. We who are blessed by living in the freest and most advanced society man ever experienced should be careful not to reach almost parallel results as tyrannical states through sheer laziness on the part of the public and the would-be analysts who are supposed to open the doors of comprehension to their readers.

The political cartoonist is the modern minute man. He or she should react and alert the public at a cartoon's notice. The cartoonist should remember that this ammunition is limited, and any cartoon that does not hit the enemy, which is political ignorance, is wasted, scarce ammunition. In this day and age, we simply cannot afford such a luxury.

RANAN R. LURIE

Lurie's Worlds, 1970–1980

1970

Lurie: ON THE INDEPENDENT CARTOONIST

I think cartoonists have almost completely escaped the kinds of restraints that are imposed on news writers. Of course, the key question is: What is your status at the newspaper that you are working for? Because if you are really no more than an editorial illustrator who is not expected to think, just to obey, then you are nothing more than an extension of your editor's brain and you will have to accept all of the restraints editors will transfer to you.

I have found that the truly independent guys in our profession are the syndicated columnists and the syndicated cartoonists. Quite a few excellent staff cartoonists simply adopt the colors of their newspaper for better or for worse, for liberalism or conservatism, simply as a survival mechanism. The syndicated columnist or cartoonist could not, even if he wanted to, adapt to two, three, or four hundred newspapers. He becomes very independent, as he should be and as the First Amendment hopes he will be.

The cartoonist in this country has never been sued successfully by anyone. This fact gives him a strong edge over the writer. Also we have the tools of caricature and of nuance. You cannot be libelous for drawing Nixon, for instance, with a sarcastic or conniving smile, whereas if you wrote the word "conniving" you could perhaps be sued. The political cartoon is still the most unchallenged forum for opinion in the media. And the better the artist you are, the better you understand how to deliver the image of the politician through your cartoon, and the more you can penetrate his character without being penalized by his supporters or he himself.

I am constantly asked whether I am a "conservative" or a "liberal." I am for conservative causes when they are correct and effective and against them when they are not, and I feel the same about liberal causes. This approach makes some eyebrows rise with a question mark or fold into a frown—why is he not a member of any team? I do belong to a team. My team is made up of those columnists who applaud wise, moral political moves, who remove the mask from corruption and stupidity—whether political or economic—and who turn the limelight onto a leader's incompetence.

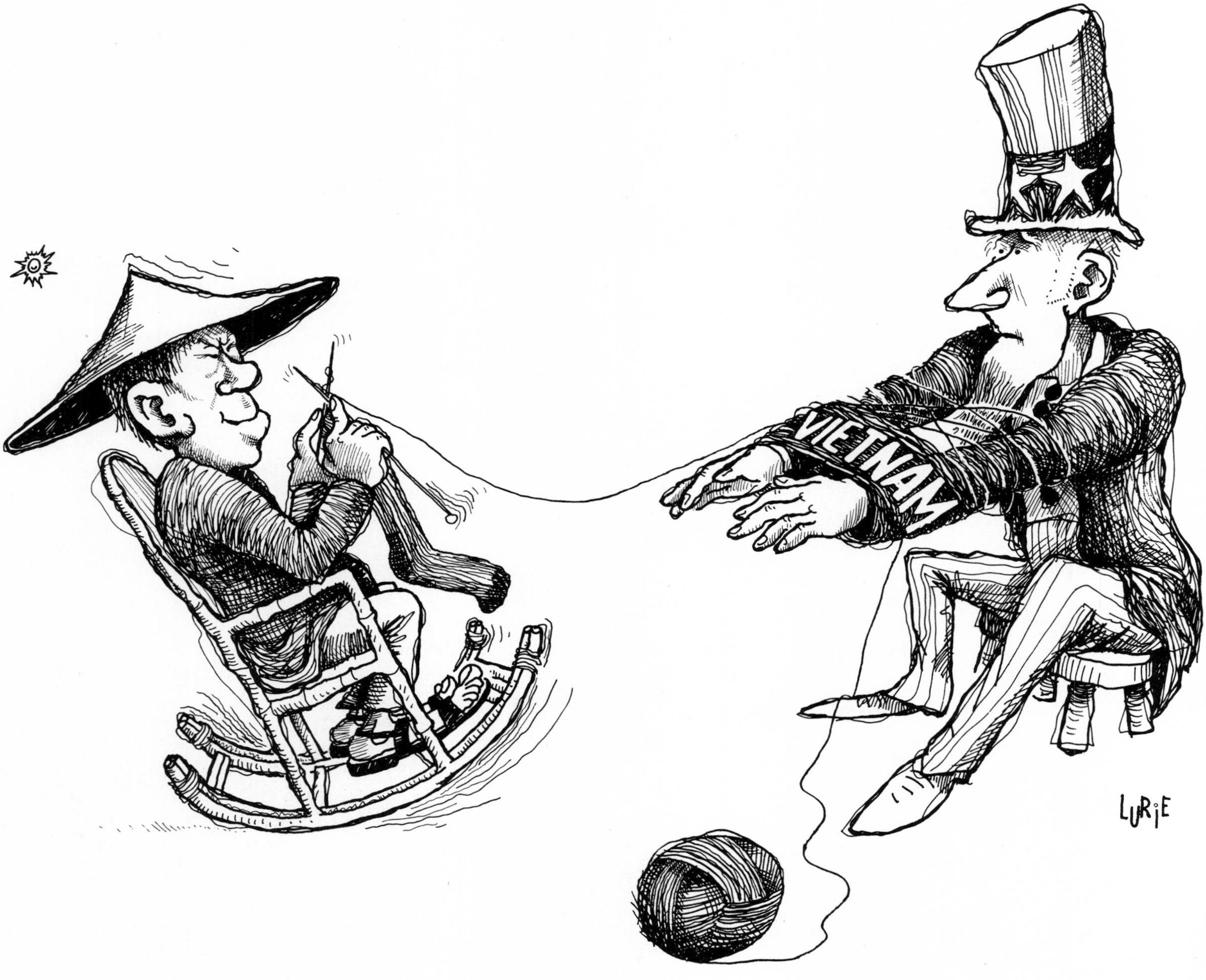
VIETNAM
LURIE

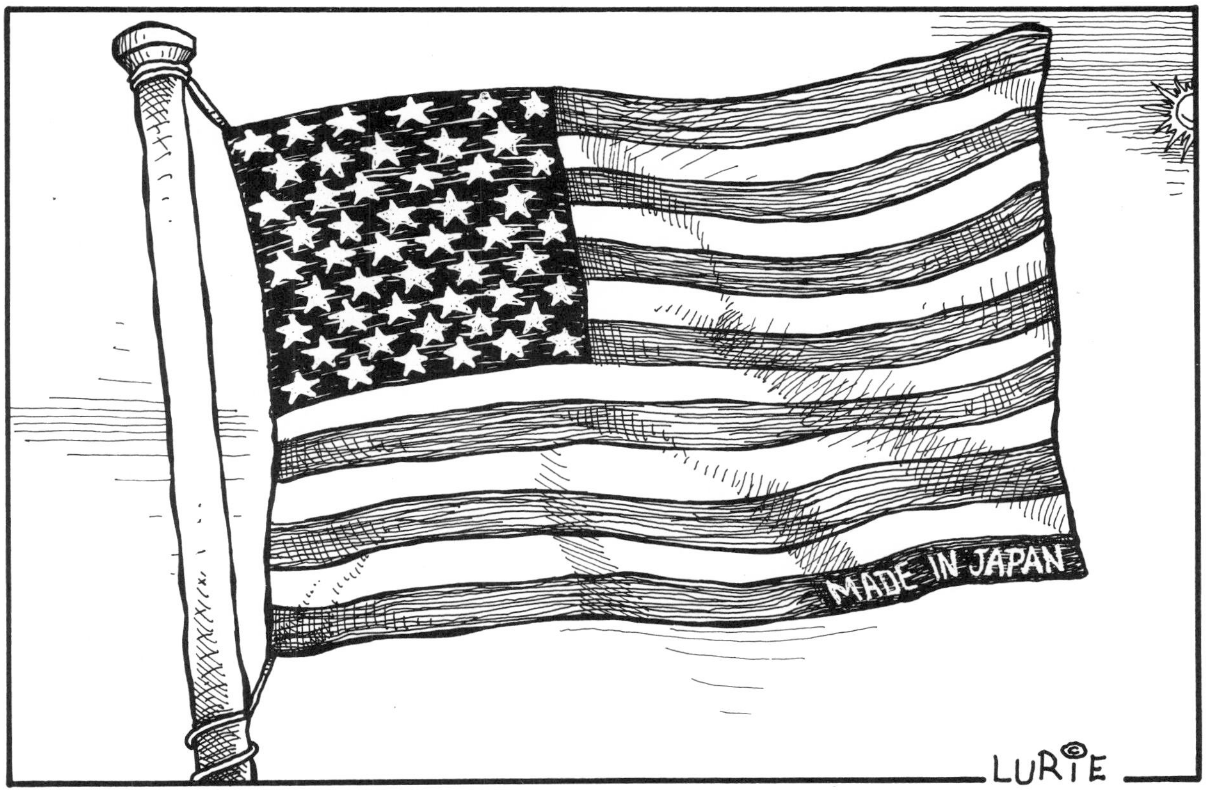
MADE IN JAPAN
LURIE

THE TEXTILE PROBLEM

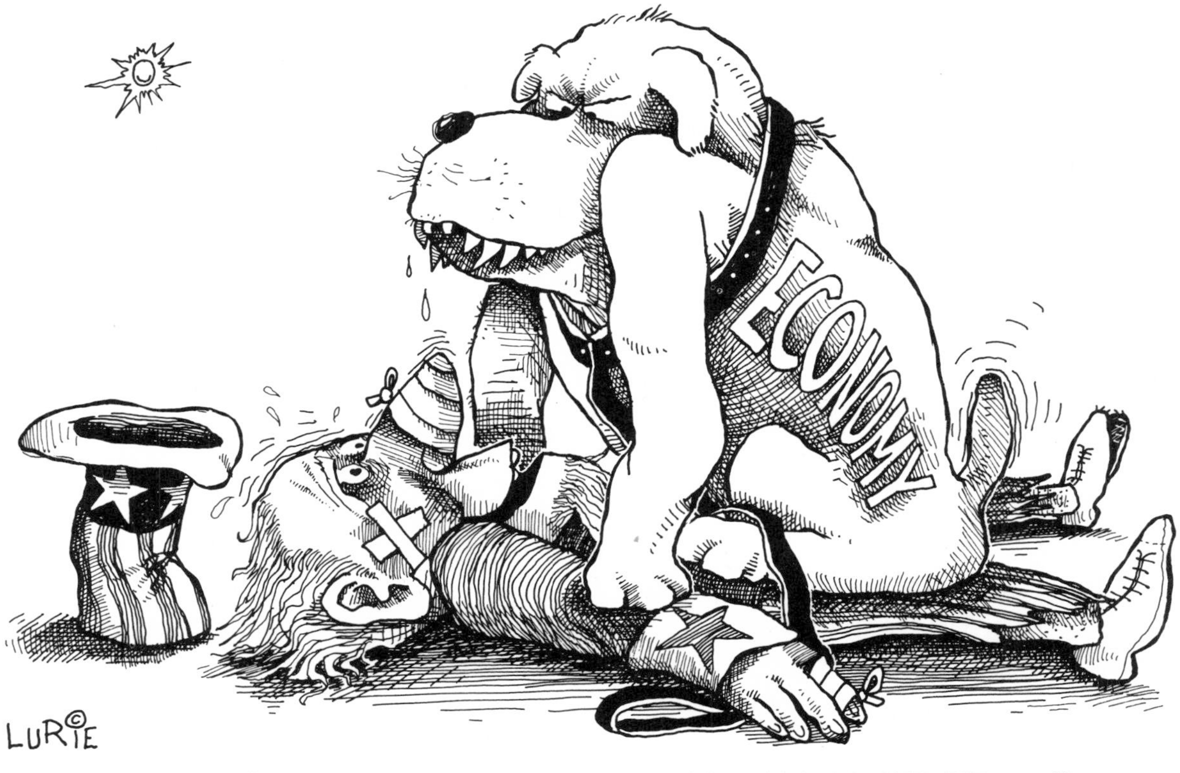
ECONOMY
LURIE

"NOW THAT YOU'VE LEARNED TO SIT, LET'S CONTINUE . . ."

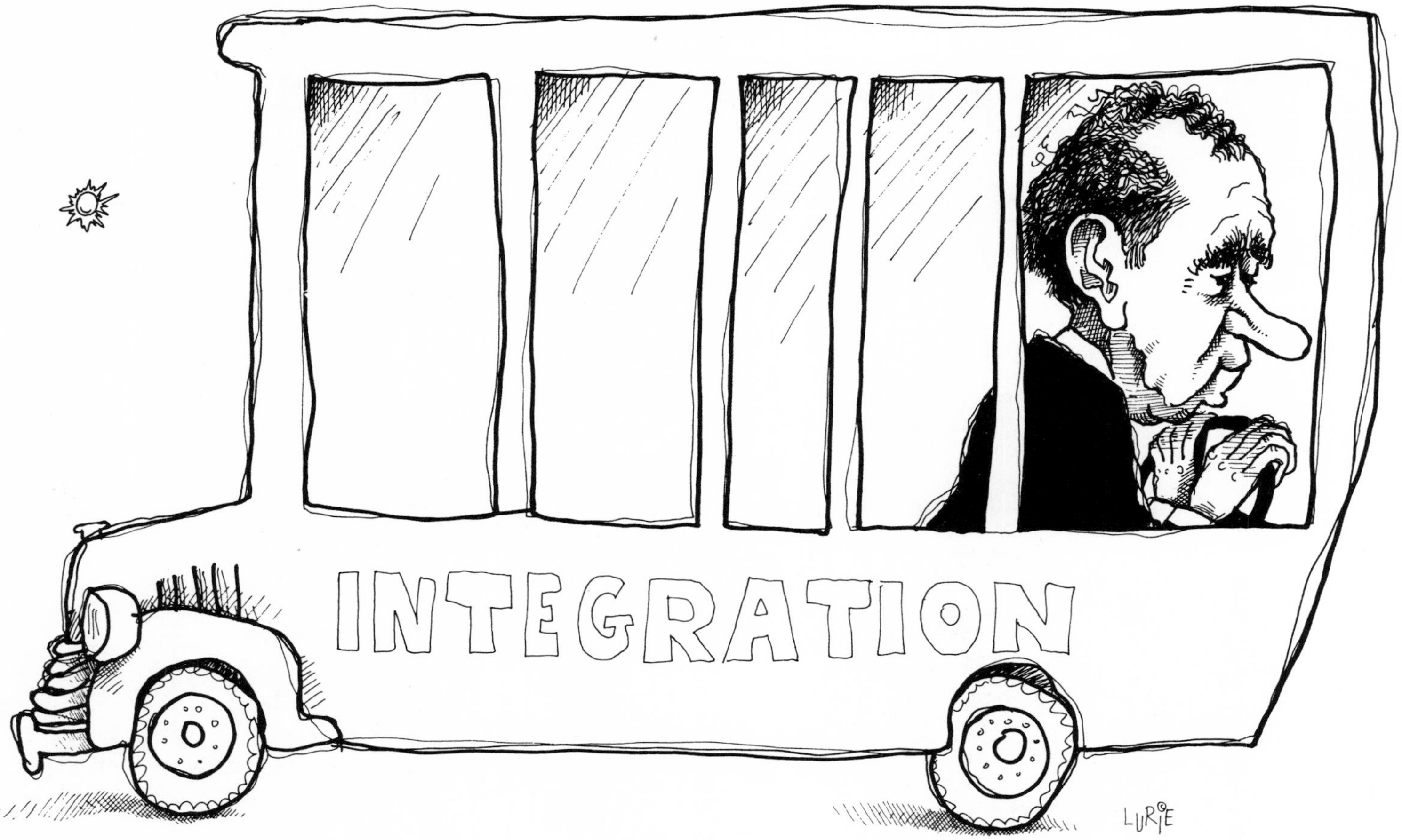
INTEGRATION
LURIE

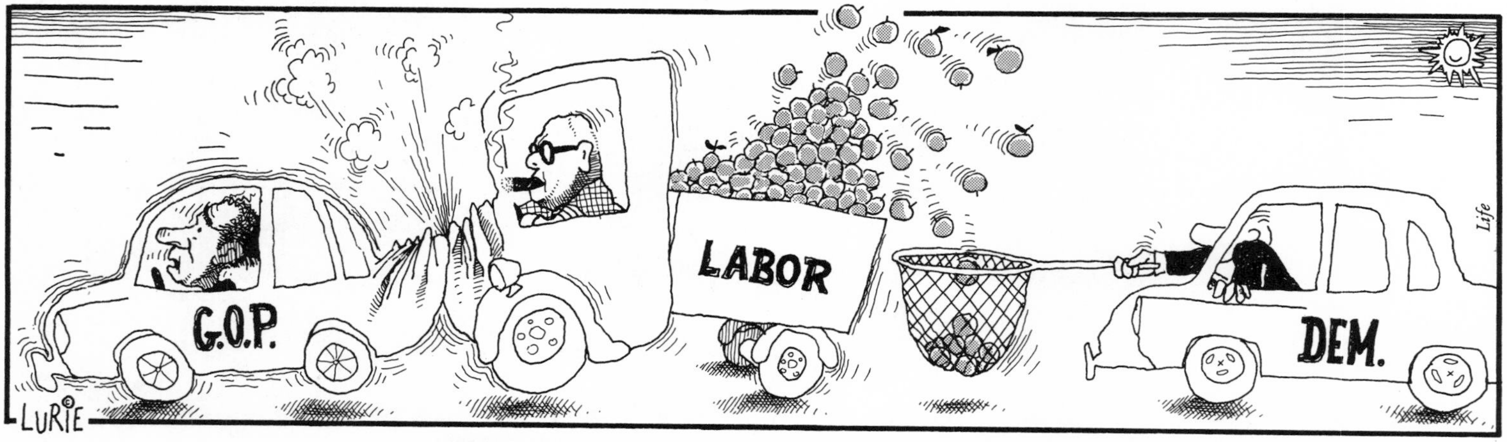
G.O.P.
LABOR
DEM.
Life
LURIE

"SHE LOOKS BETTER AS THE YEARS GO BY"

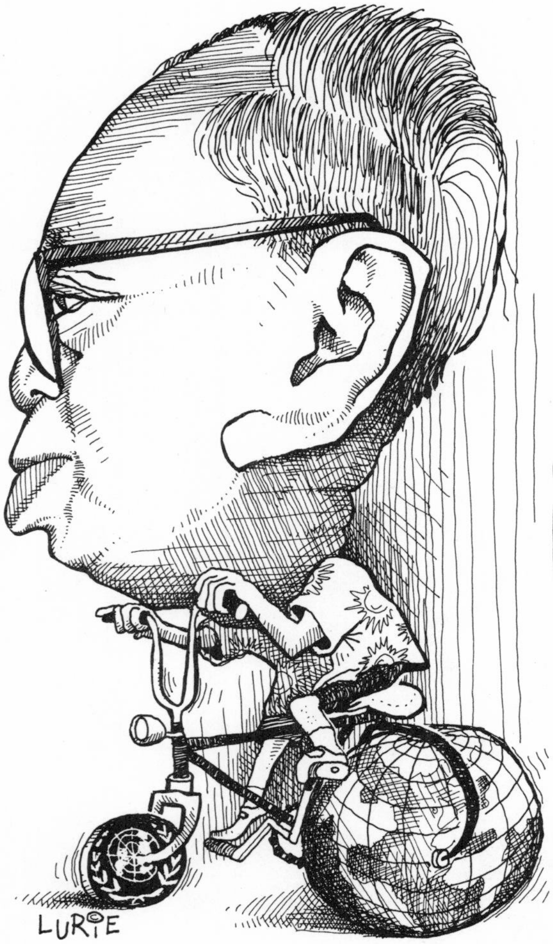
LURIE

U Thant

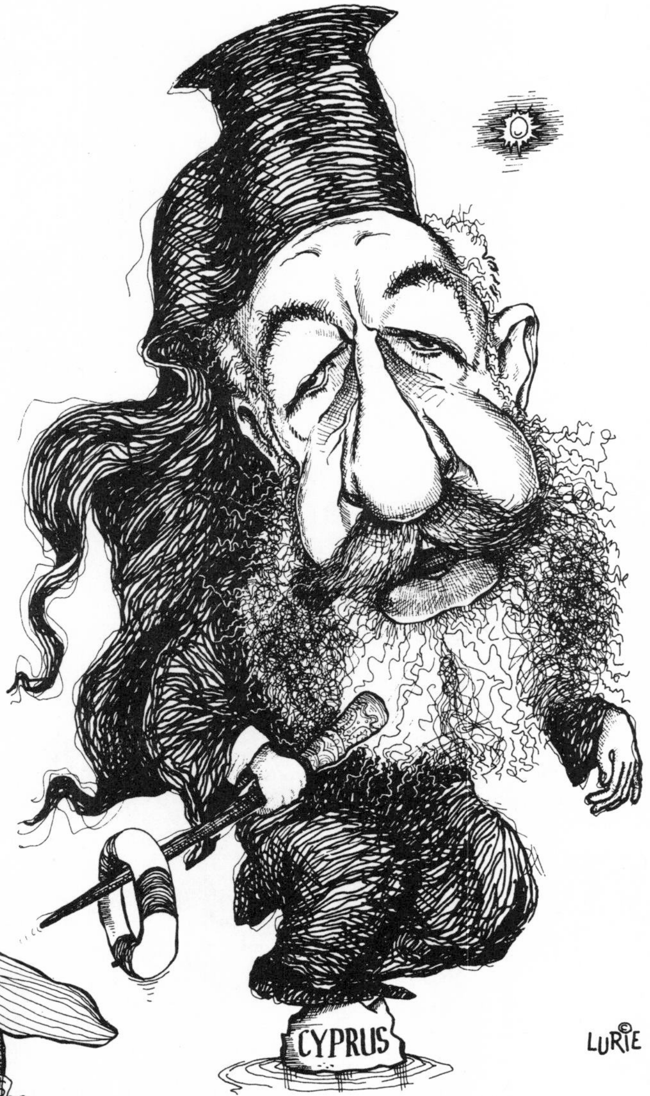
CYPRUS
LURIE

Archbishop Makarios
President of Cyprus

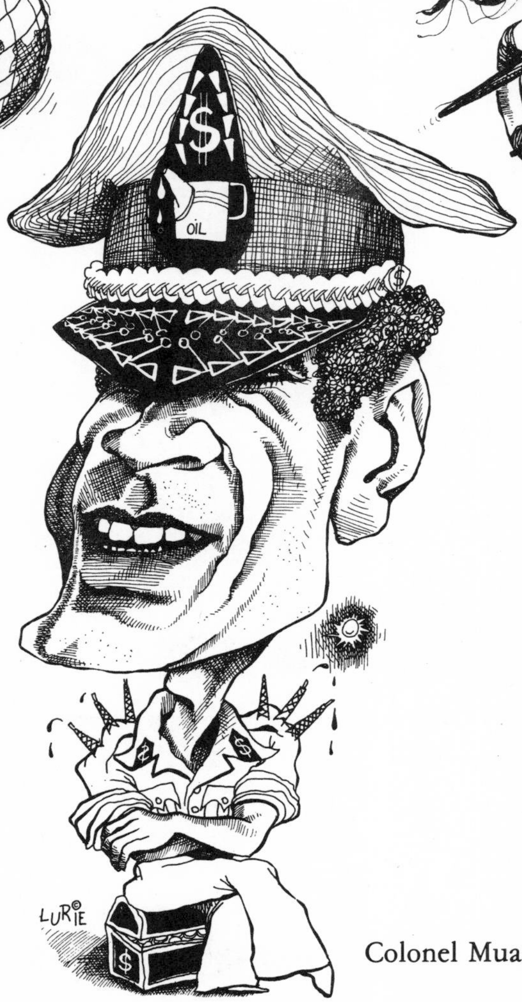
$
OIL
LURIE

Colonel Muaamer el Qaddafi

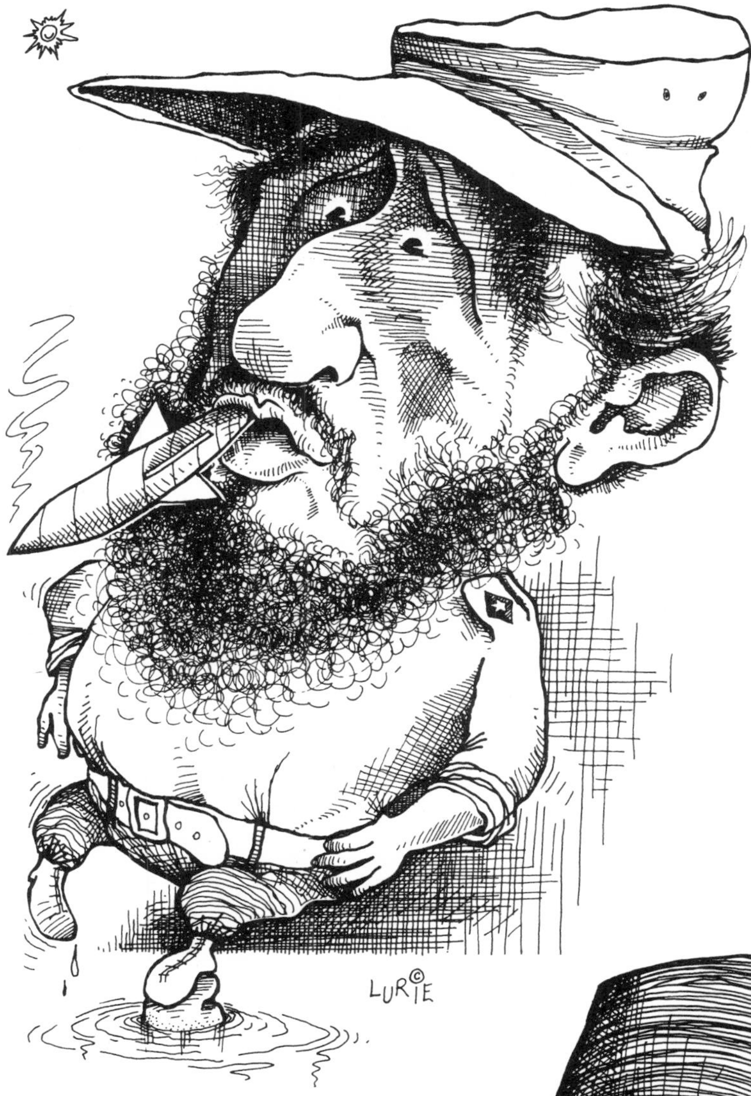
LURIE

Fidel Castro

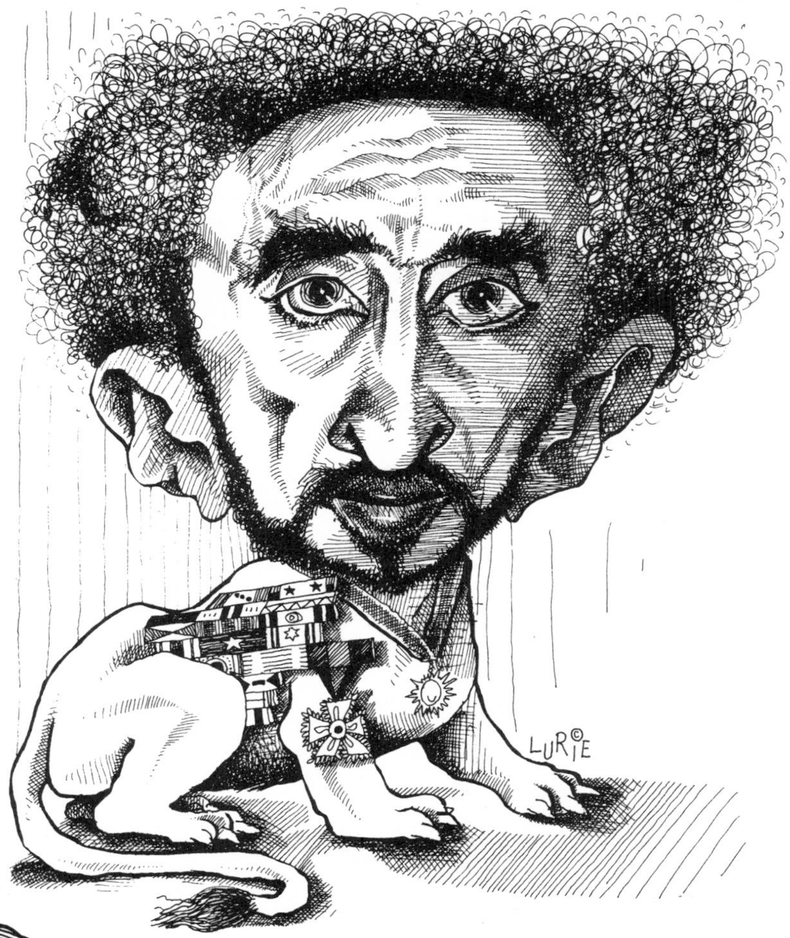
LURIE

Haile Selassie

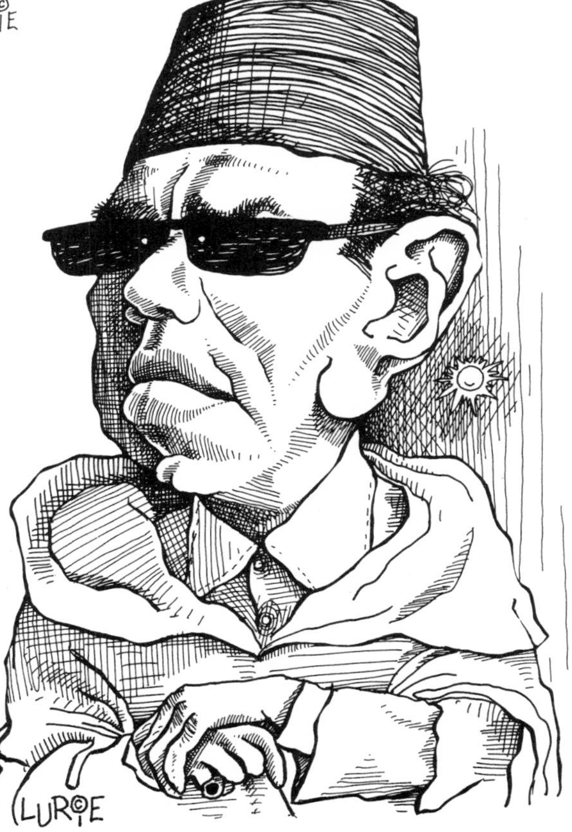
LURIE

King Hassan
of Morocco

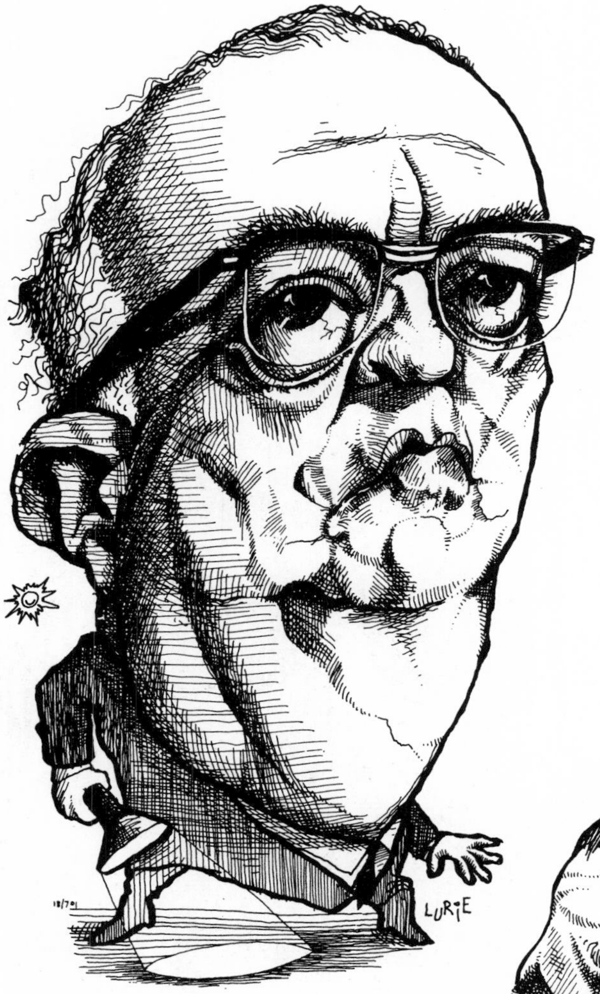
LURIE

J. Edgar Hoover

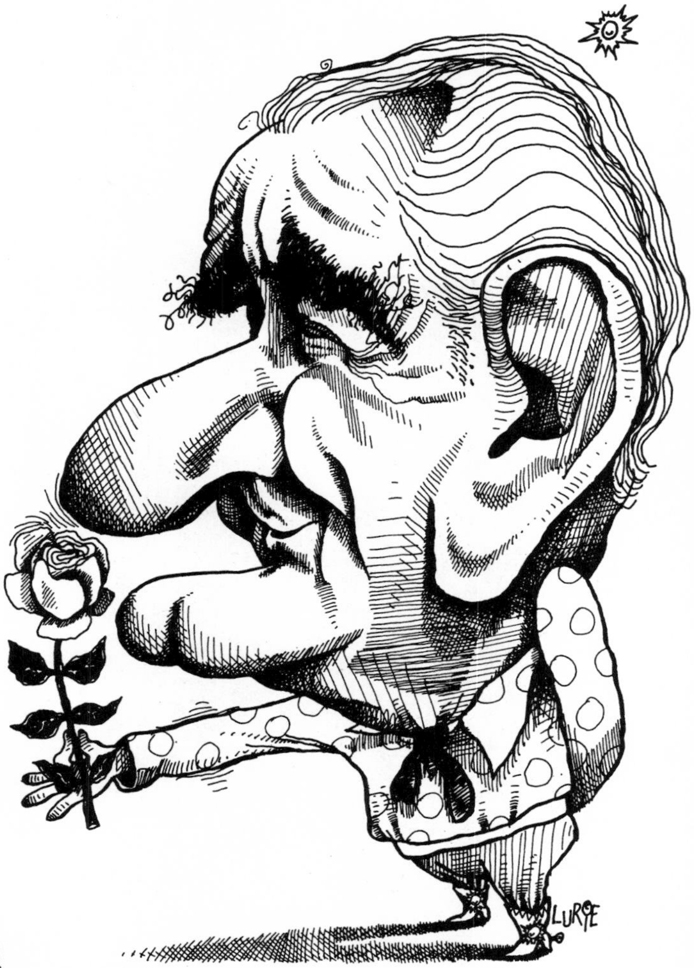
LURIE

LBJ

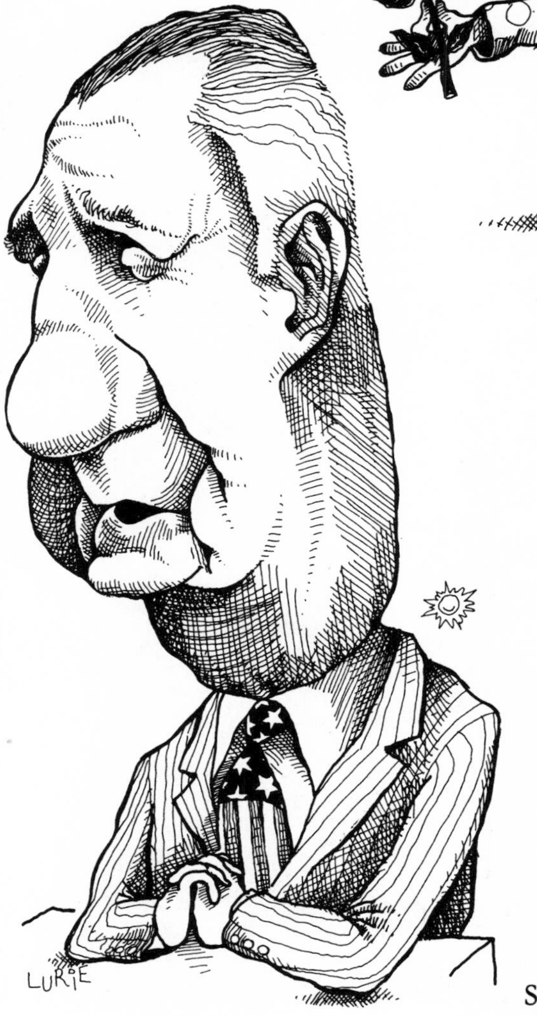
LURIE

Spiro Agnew

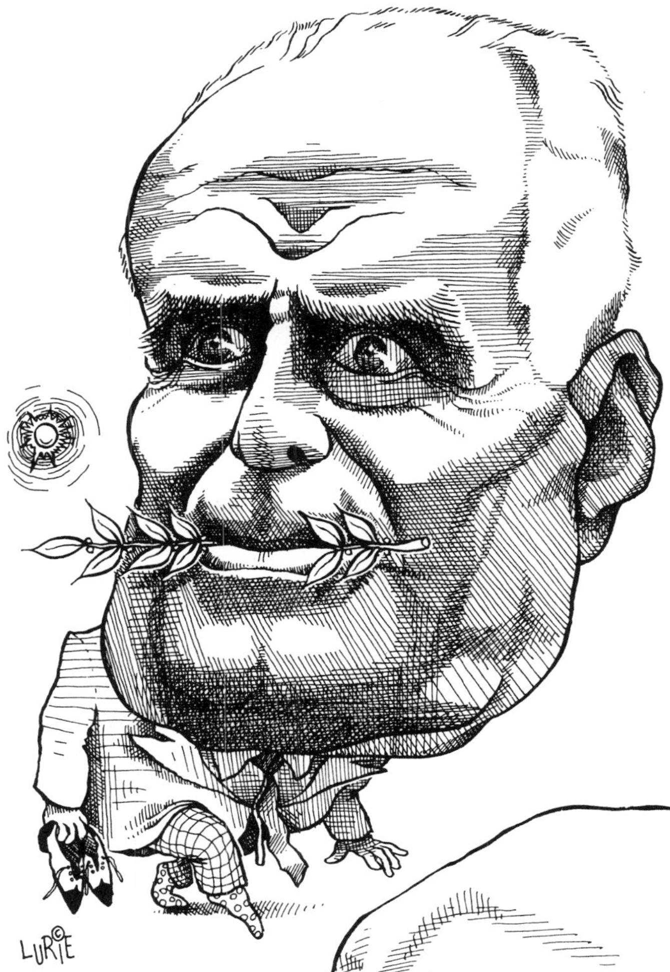
LURIE

President
Habib Bourguiba
of Tunisia

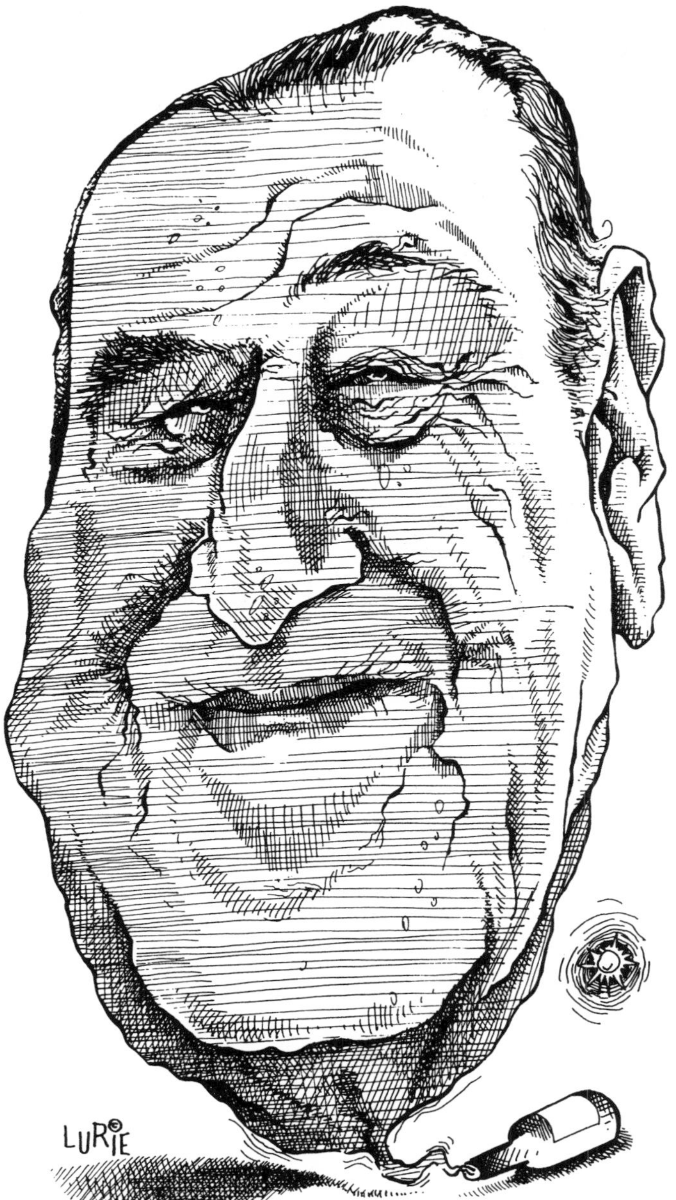
LURIE

Juan Peron

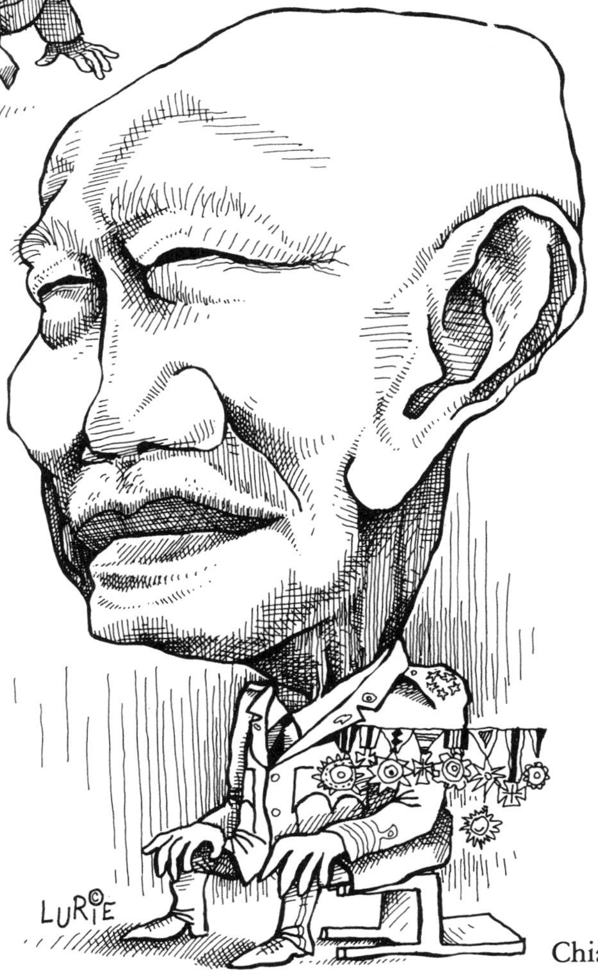
LURIE

Chiang Kai-shek

1971

Lurie: ON RICHARD NIXON AND THE MEDIA

It has been said that my cartoons regarding Nixon's hold on the media seem less barbed than my other cartoons of him. Maybe. If it's true, the reason was that accusing the President of the United States of such a thing at that time would have seemed somewhat paranoiac, and no one likes to be considered paranoid. In the media we were treating it very gingerly. We were not sure about it. It was a thing that was hard to prove.

When Watergate exploded—the burglary, the cover up, the tapes, and so on—the media situation seemed less important. But I believe the media are always extremely careful not to point a finger at themselves. What I mean is, if Nixon really was trying to castrate the media, the job of the media was to jump at him and to bark as loud as possible. If we didn't bark as loud as possible, we failed to justify our function.

I was affected by these restraints. For instance, I drew a very big cartoon for the *Wall Street Journal* attacking Nixon, and the *Journal* editor called me, very bewildered, and said that he had got 52 condemning letters from readers attacking the *Journal,* which by the way was using my cartoons for the first and last time. The 52 letters asked how dare the *Journal* attack the beloved president. It's bad taste, etc., etc.

A week later, the *New York Times Week in Review* published a huge cartoon of mine attacking Nixon. Horrified, the editor of the *Review* called me and said "Ranan, we got 52 letters from readers condemning the cartoon and the *Times* for attacking our President in such a vicious way." I asked him very innocently, "What difference does it make?" And his answer was, "I really don't like to get such letters to the editor." In brief, the *New York Times* and the

Wall Street Journal took these letters very seriously. And as we know now there was a letter campaign organized by the Nixon administration, which had learned that newspapers are vulnerable to readers' letters. It bombarded the newspapers anytime there was something that didn't please Nixon. We newspaper people are, for better or for worse, human. Our subconscious also works and functions in situations where we know that a move of ours may cause friction; we may just think twice before we make that move.

I am sure that the letter campaign eliminated or weeded out at least a certain percentage of articles, commentaries, and cartoons that would have attacked him more aggressively, as he deserved.

Nixon or his administration used the Skinner Theory in handling newspaper people, or, to simplify, they used the carrot-and-stick system. They created an atmosphere of confrontation if you ever attacked Nixon. On the other hand, if there was anything that Nixon was pleased about, you were singled out for reward. For instance, I drew a cartoon that commended one of Nixon's actions: a peace dove playing the role of a stork bringing back the POWs from Vietnam. Herb Klein, then press aide to Nixon, sent me a letter asking for the original. I replied, "Herb, I never give originals, but I'll be delighted to send a print of that cartoon." Herb said, "Terrific. Send the print, just autograph it nicely, and that will do the job." I did and got a beautiful letter from Nixon that said, and I'm quoting here, "Now I can boast of yet another Lurie original." So, I have a great collectors' item: Herb Klein's letter to me; the copy of my letter to him saying, "No originals. I'll give you a print if you want"; the letter from Nixon thanking me for the "original"; and the original itself all under one glass.

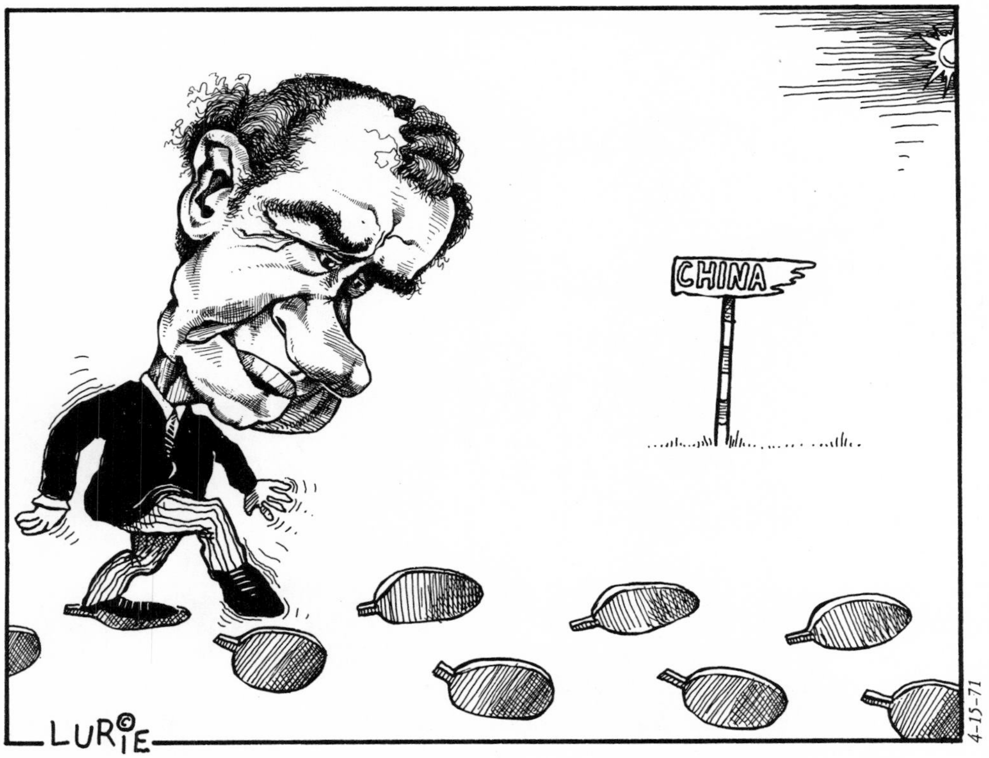
CHINA
LURIE
4-15-71

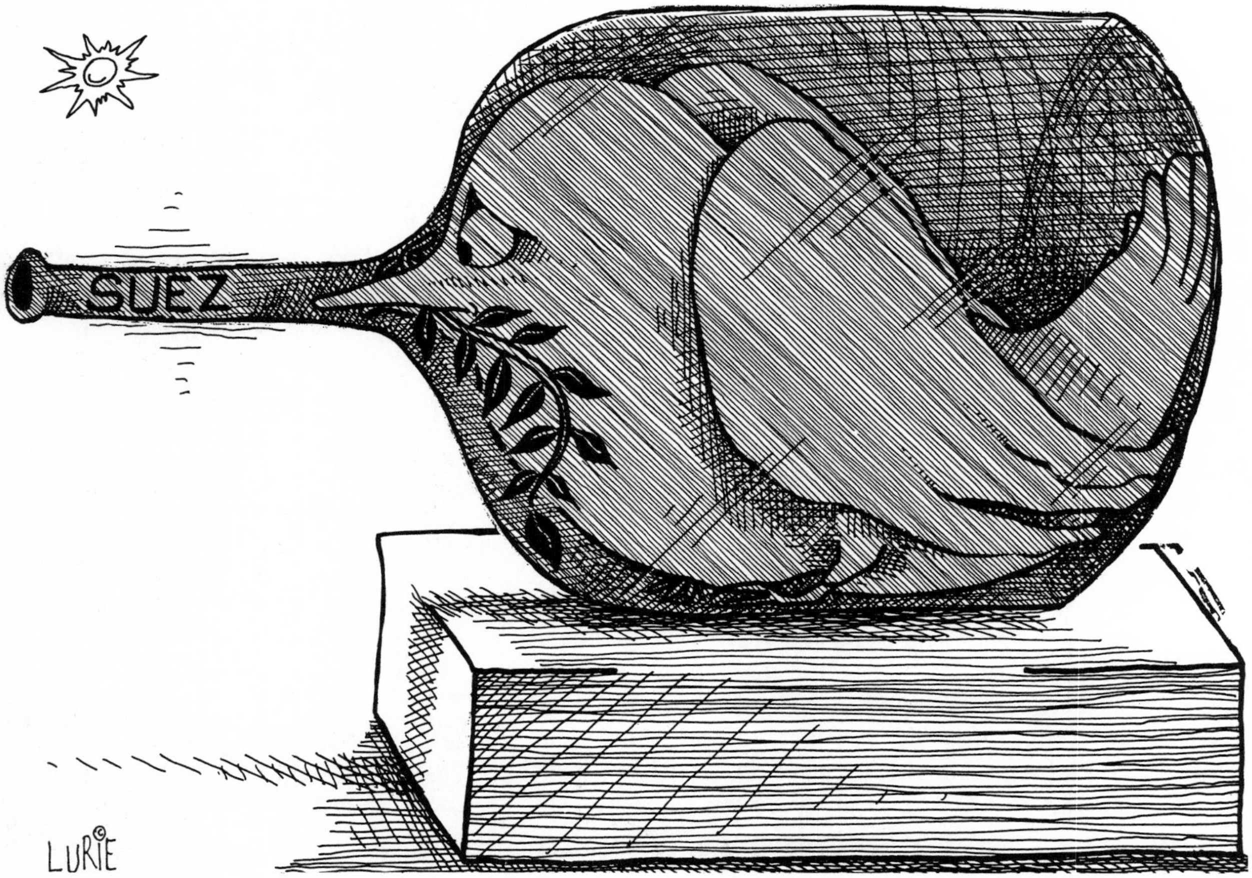
SUEZ
LURIE

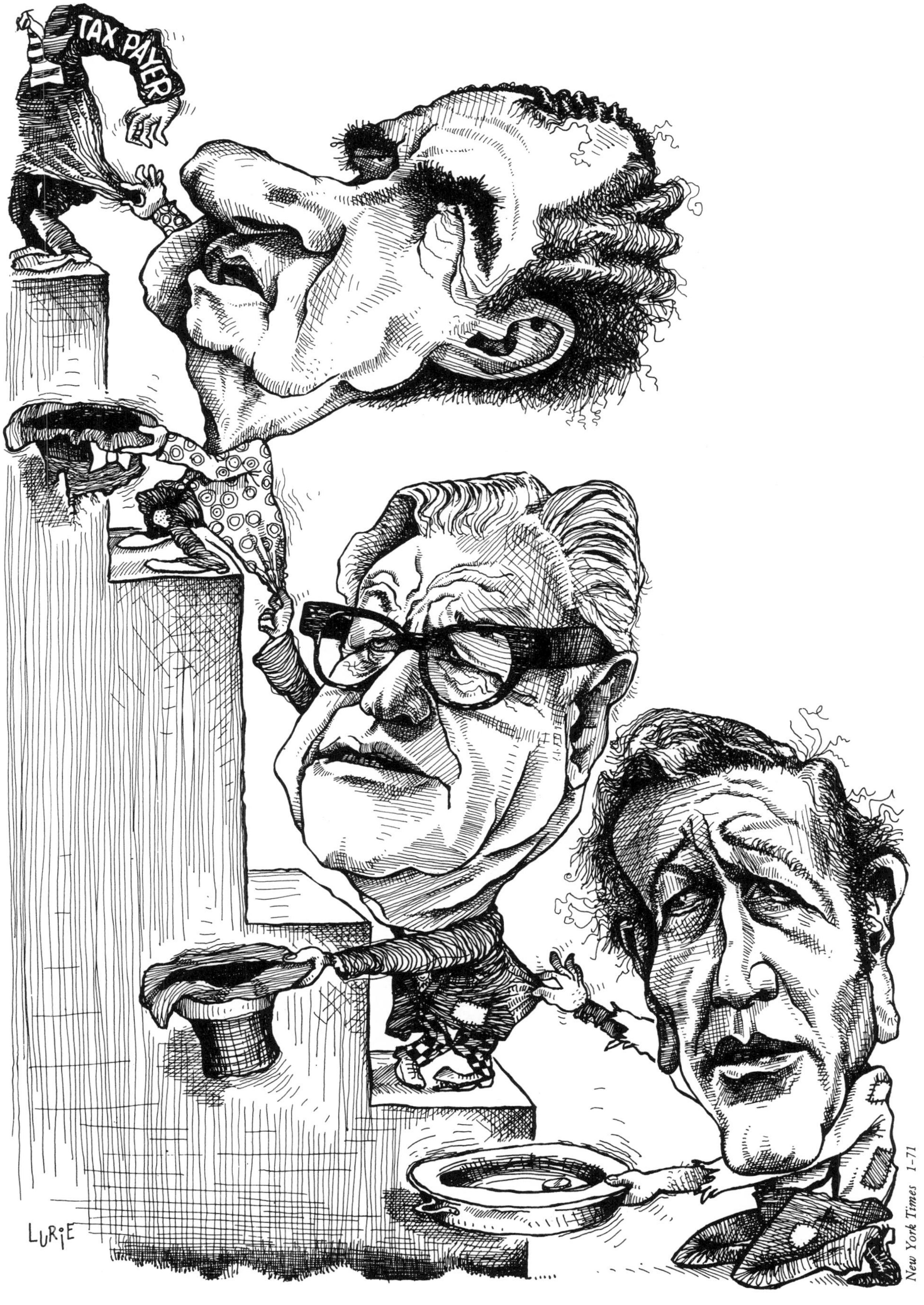
TAX PAYER
LURIE
New York Times 1-71

U.S. MILITARY AID

MIDDLE-EAST PEACE TALKS

$ $ $

SAM 3

LURIE

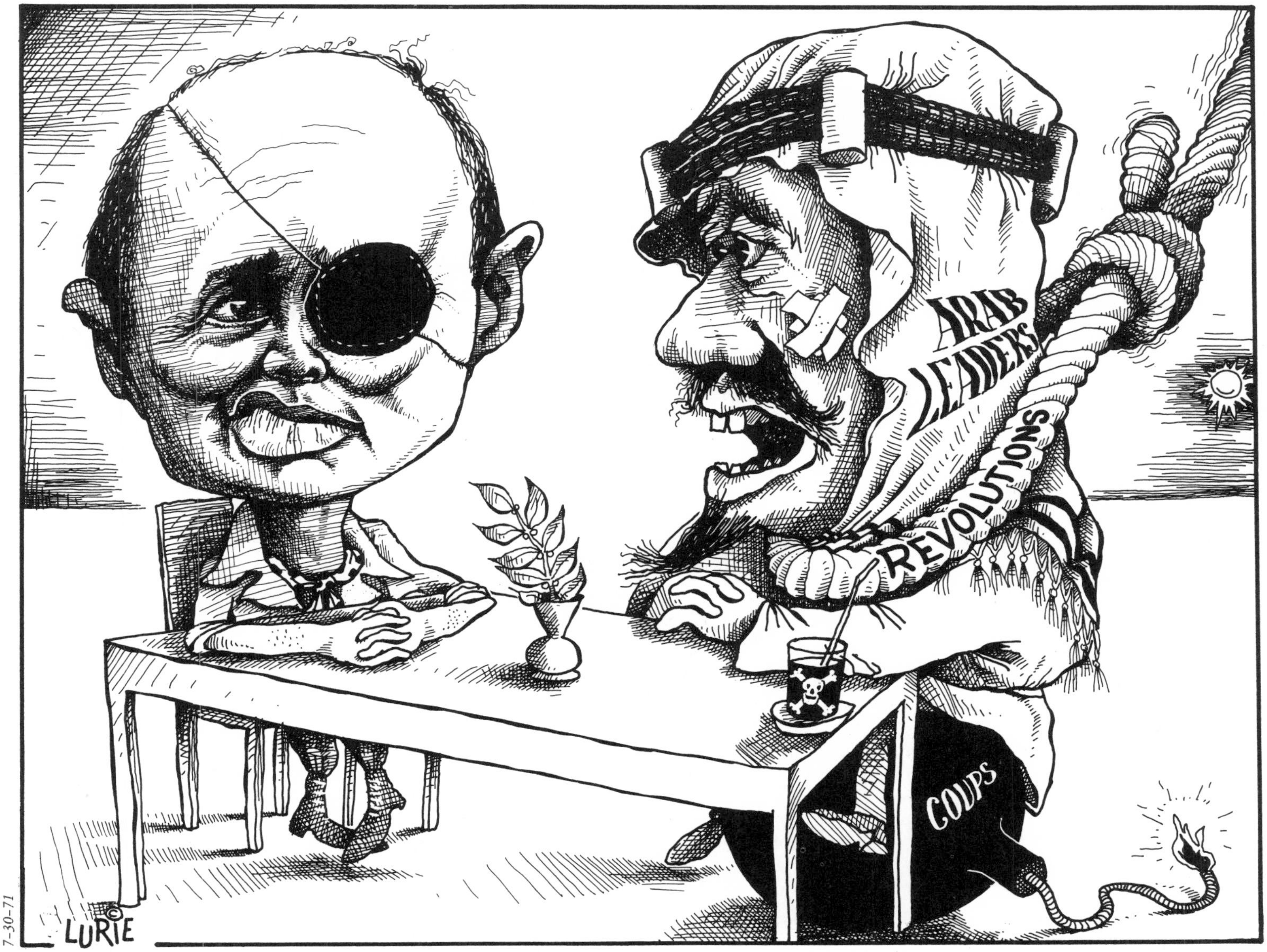
ARAB LEADERS
REVOLUTIONS
COUPS
LURIE
7-30-71

"ACCEPT MY TERMS—AND I'LL BE YOUR FRIEND FOR THE REST OF MY LIFE"

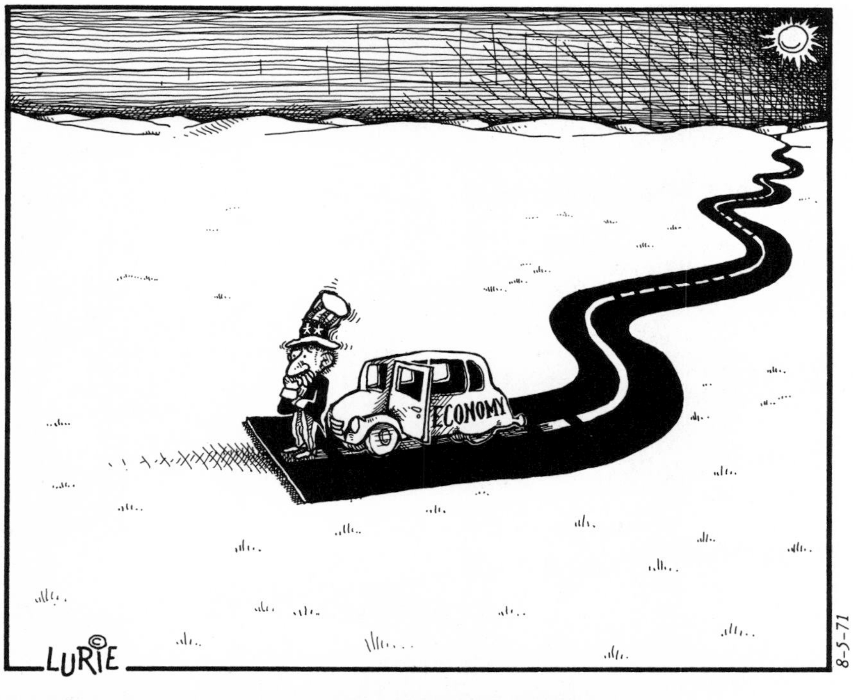
ECONOMY
LURIE ©
8-5-71

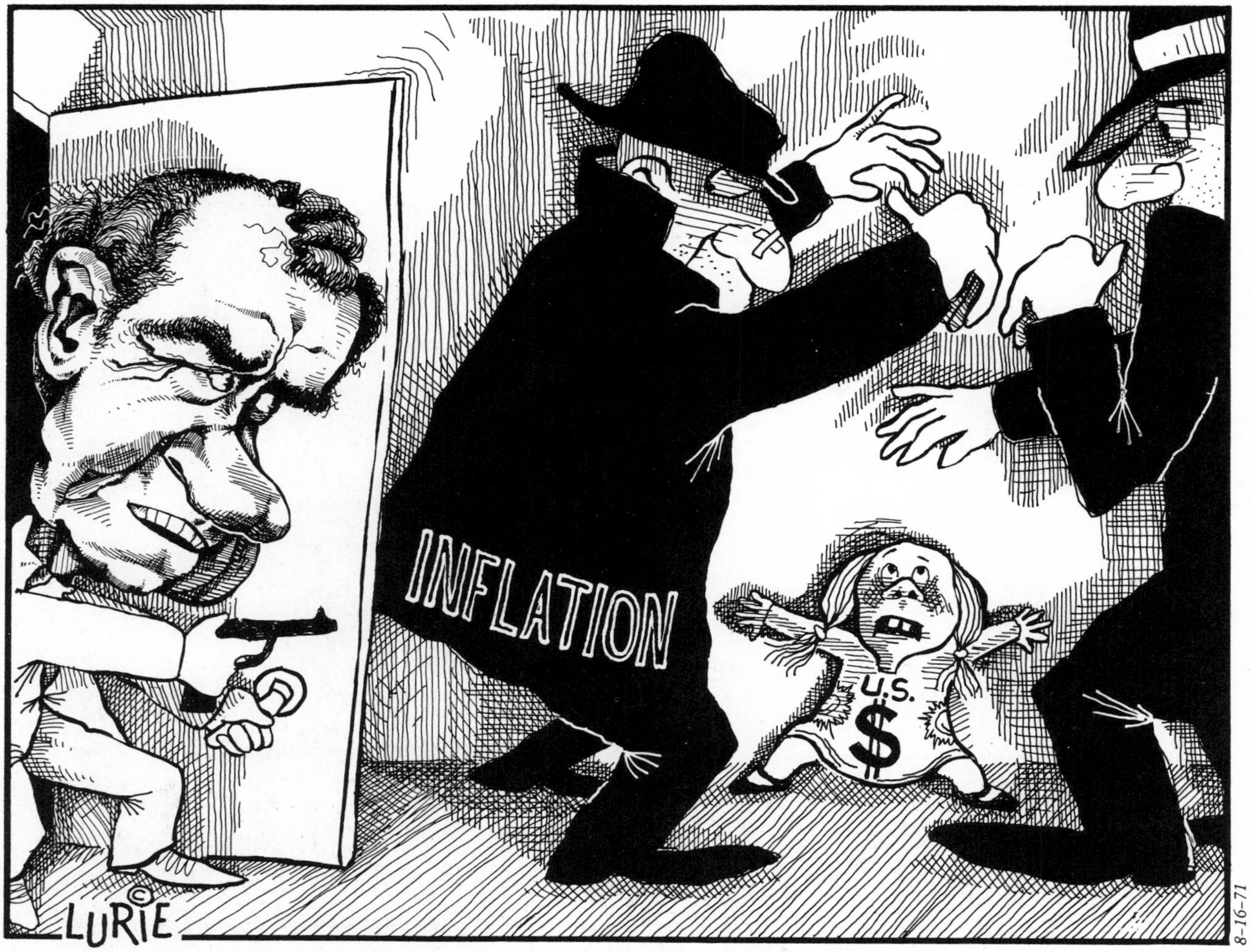
INFLATION
U.S.
$
LURIE ©
8-16-71

"FREEZE!"

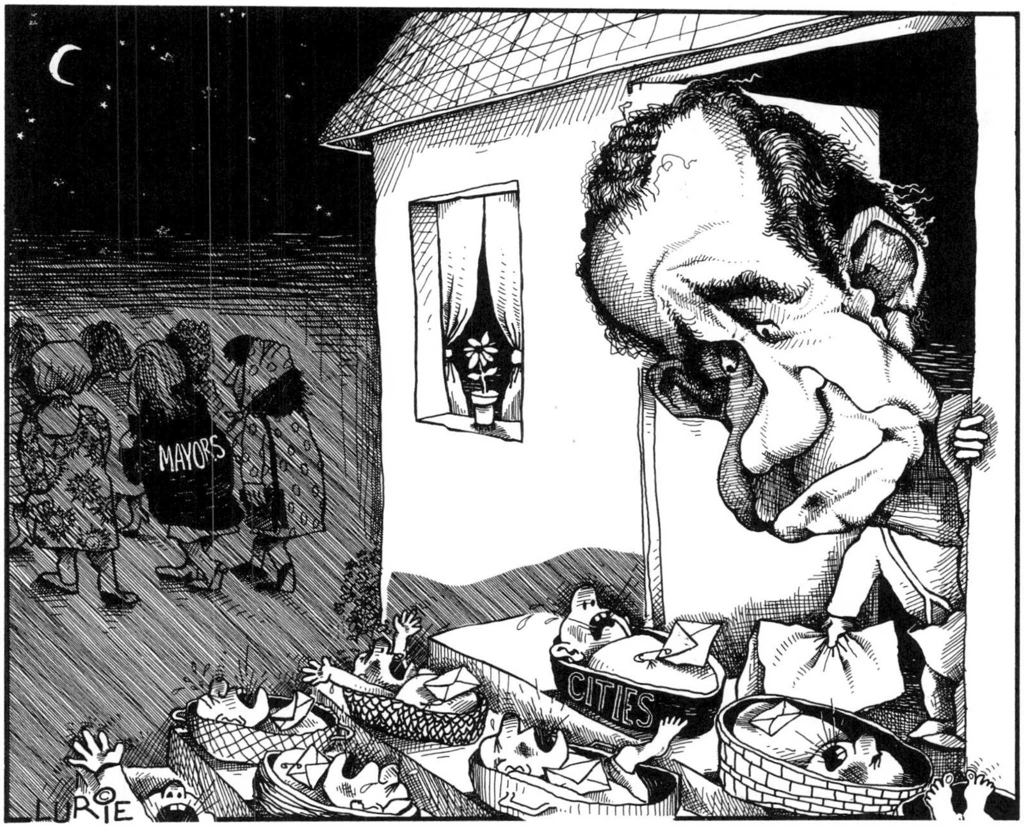
MAYORS
CITIES
LURIE
8-6-71

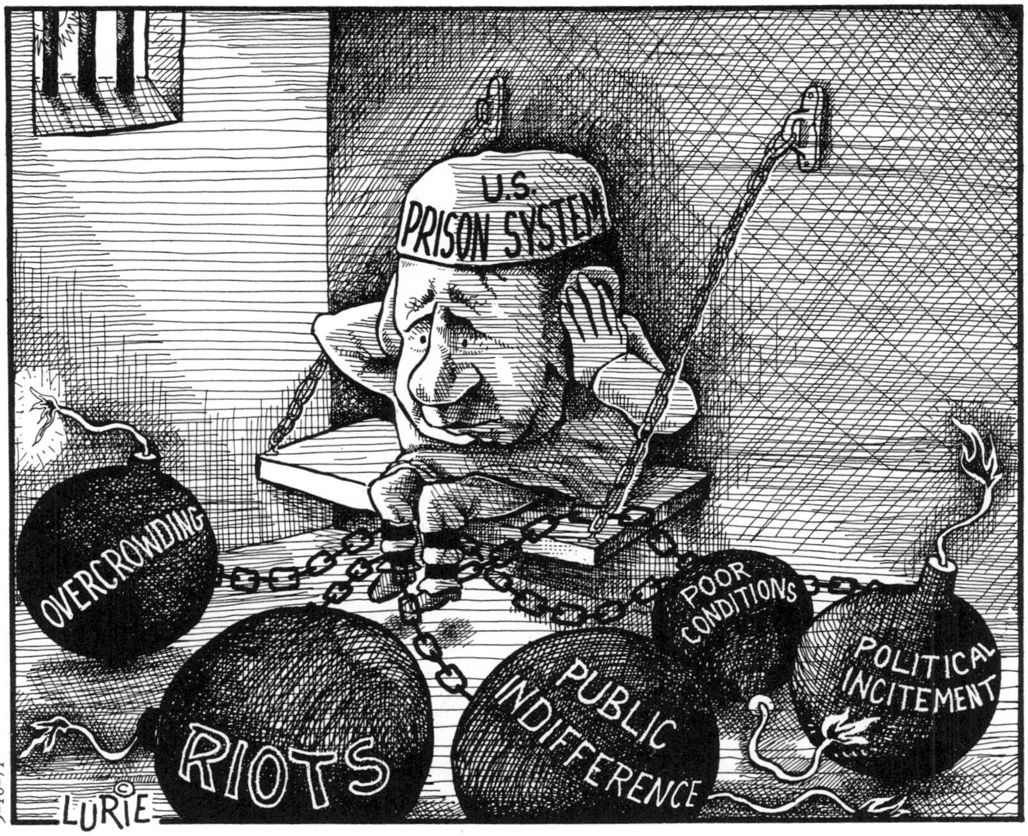
U.S. PRISON SYSTEM
OVERCROWDING
RIOTS
PUBLIC INDIFFERENCE
POOR CONDITIONS
POLITICAL INCITEMENT
LURIE
9-16-71

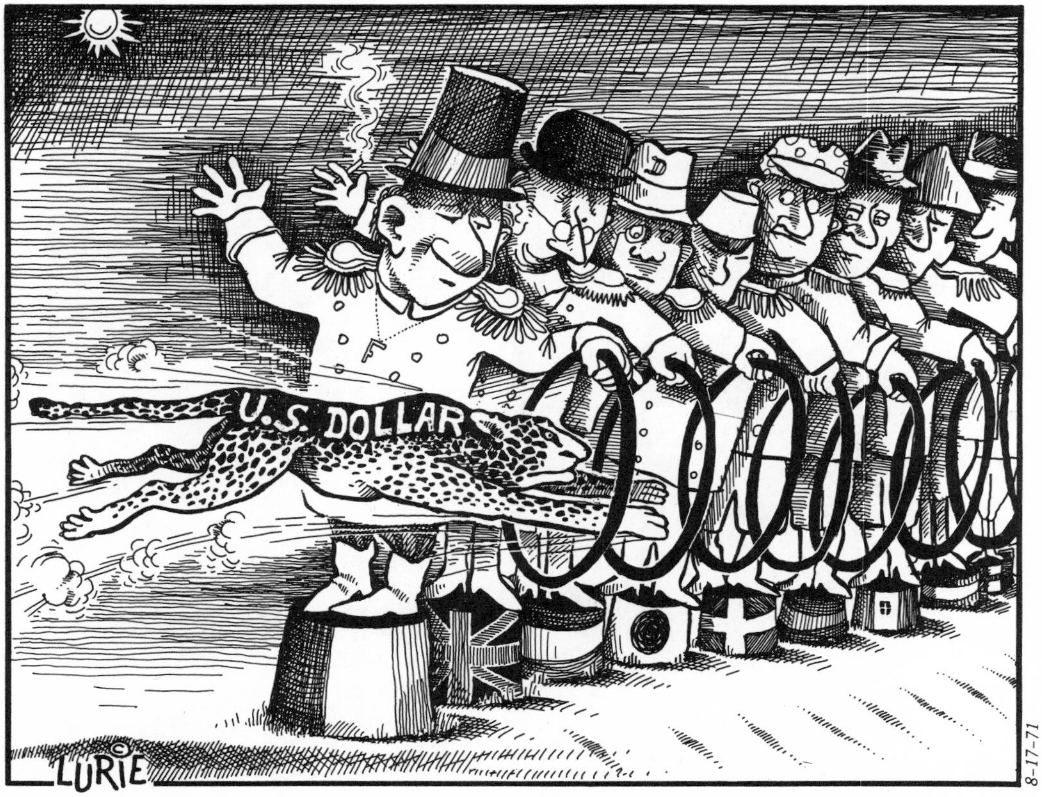
U.S. DOLLAR
LURIE
8-17-71

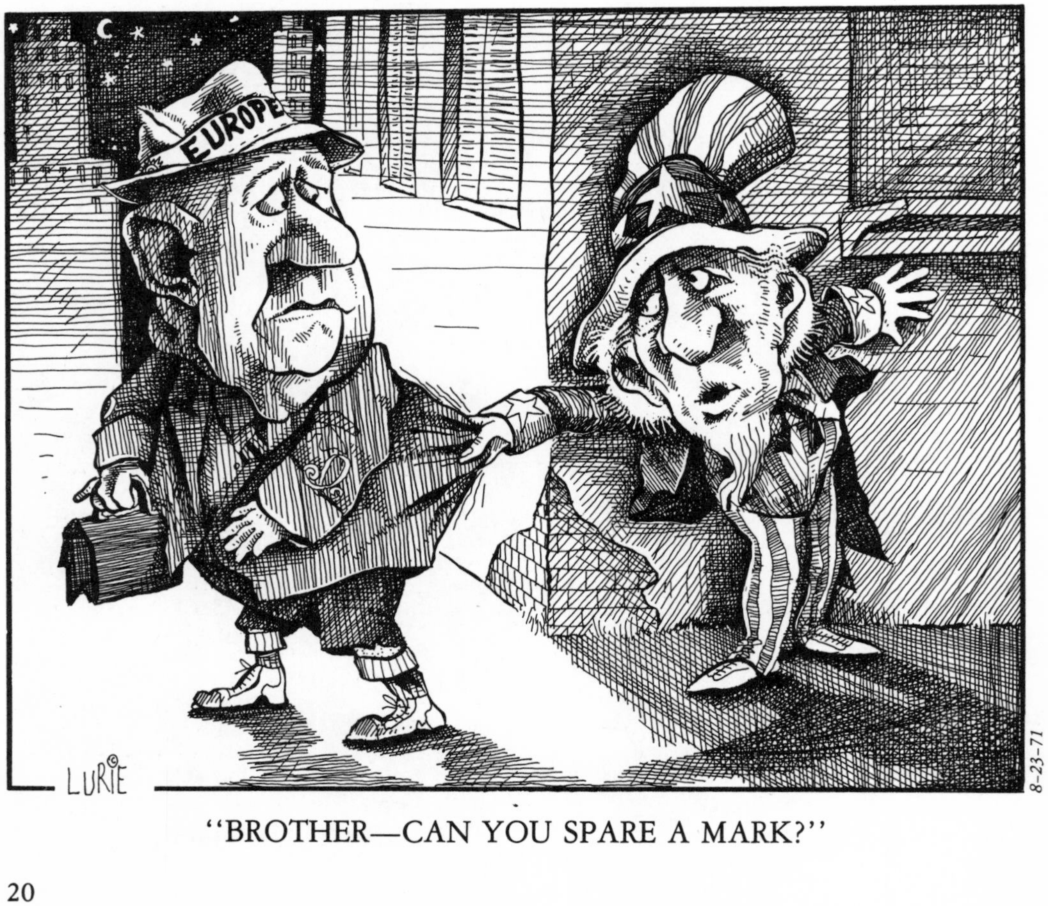
EUROPE
LURIE
8-23-71

"BROTHER—CAN YOU SPARE A MARK?"

NORTH IRELAND
EMPIRE
LURIE
9-9-71

OFFICIAL LIE DETECTOR
GOVERNMENT PROPERTY
STATE DEPARTMENT
LURIE
9-3-71

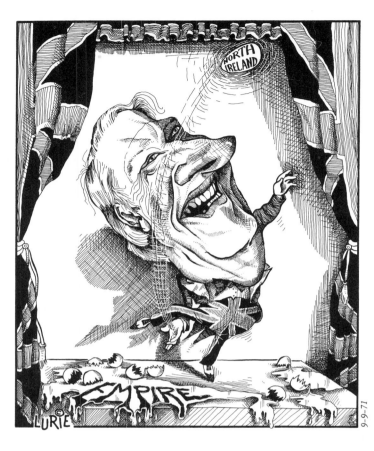

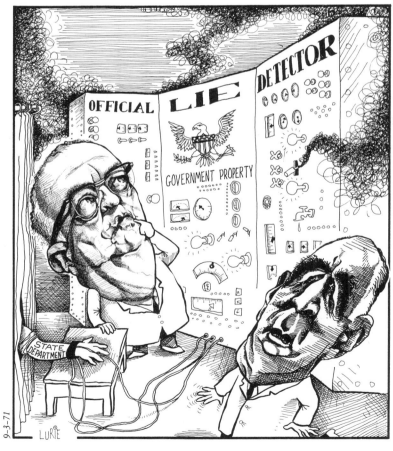

"CAREFUL, EDGAR—
THE LOAD IS TREMENDOUS!"

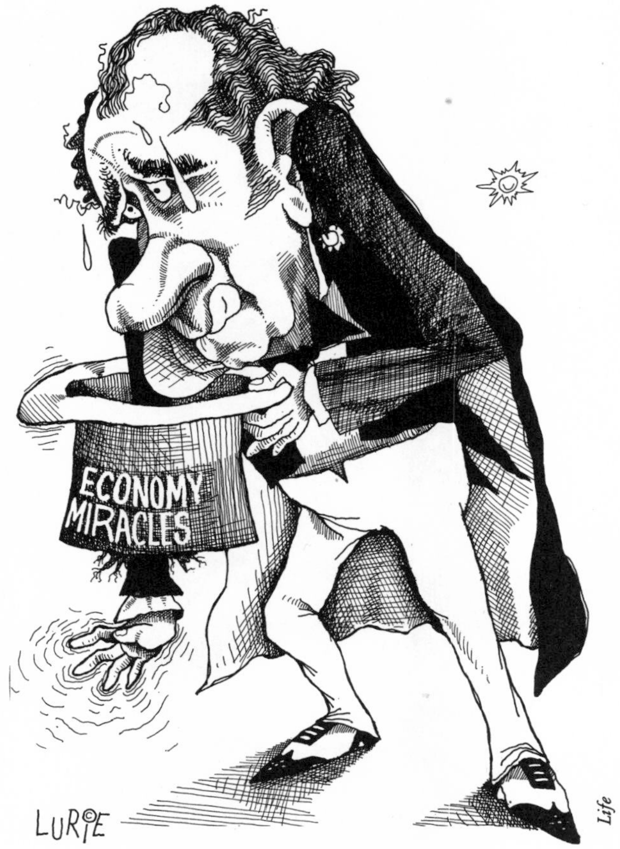
ECONOMY
MIRACLES
LURIE
Life

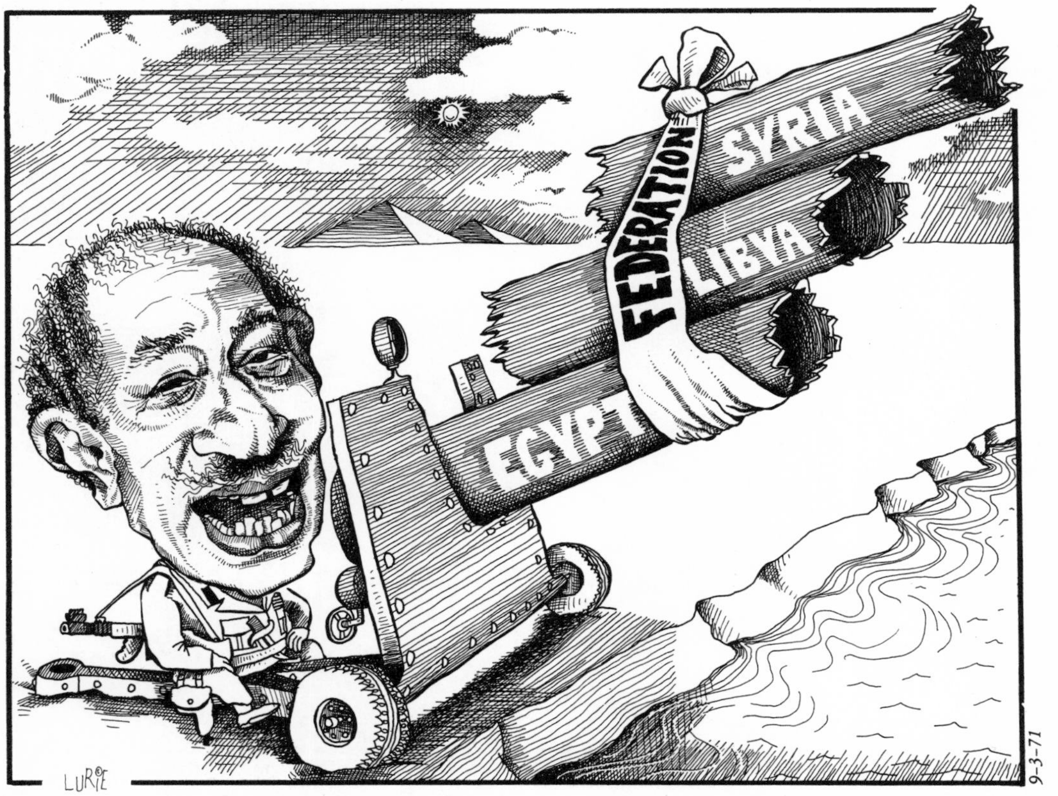
SYRIA
FEDERATION
LIBYA
EGYPT
LURIE
9-3-71

''WE'RE MUCH STRONGER NOW''

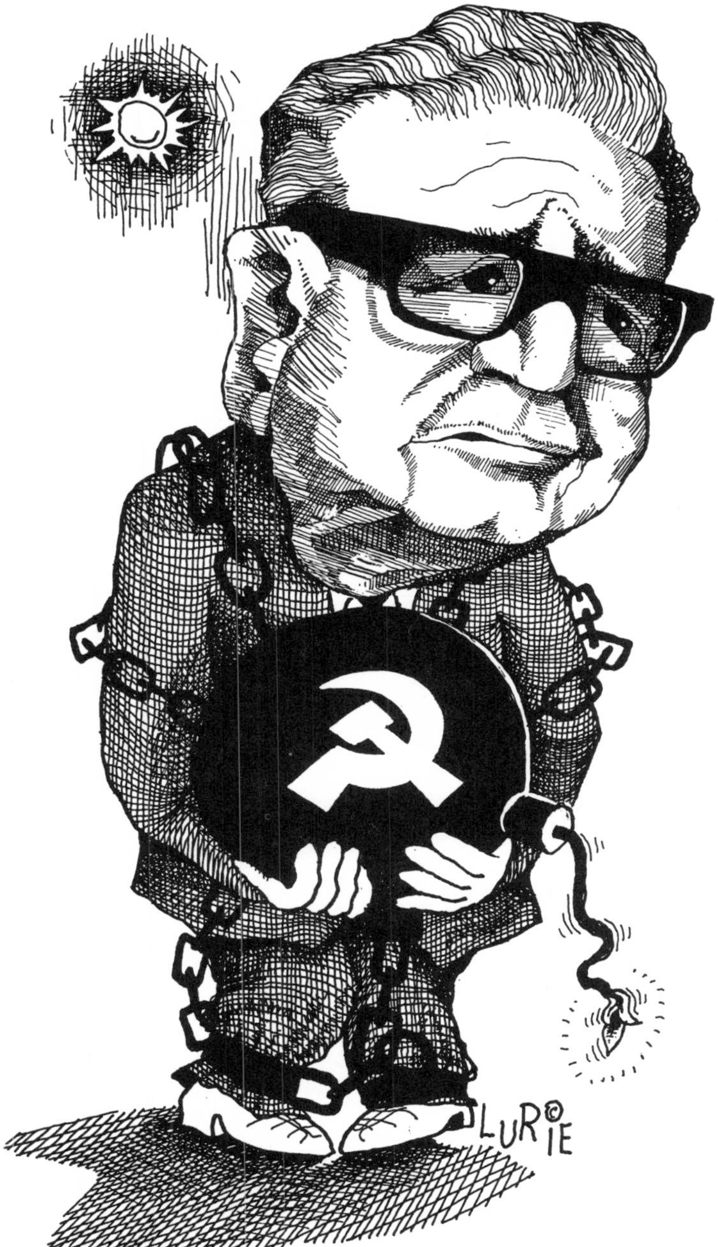
LURIE

Allende

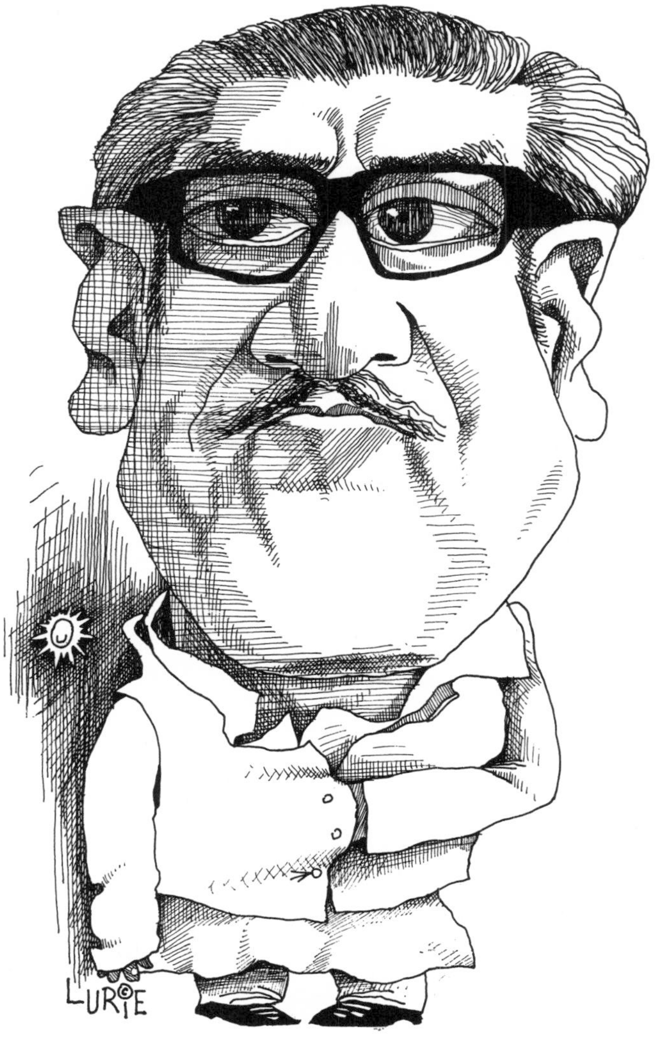
LURIE

Sheikh Rahman

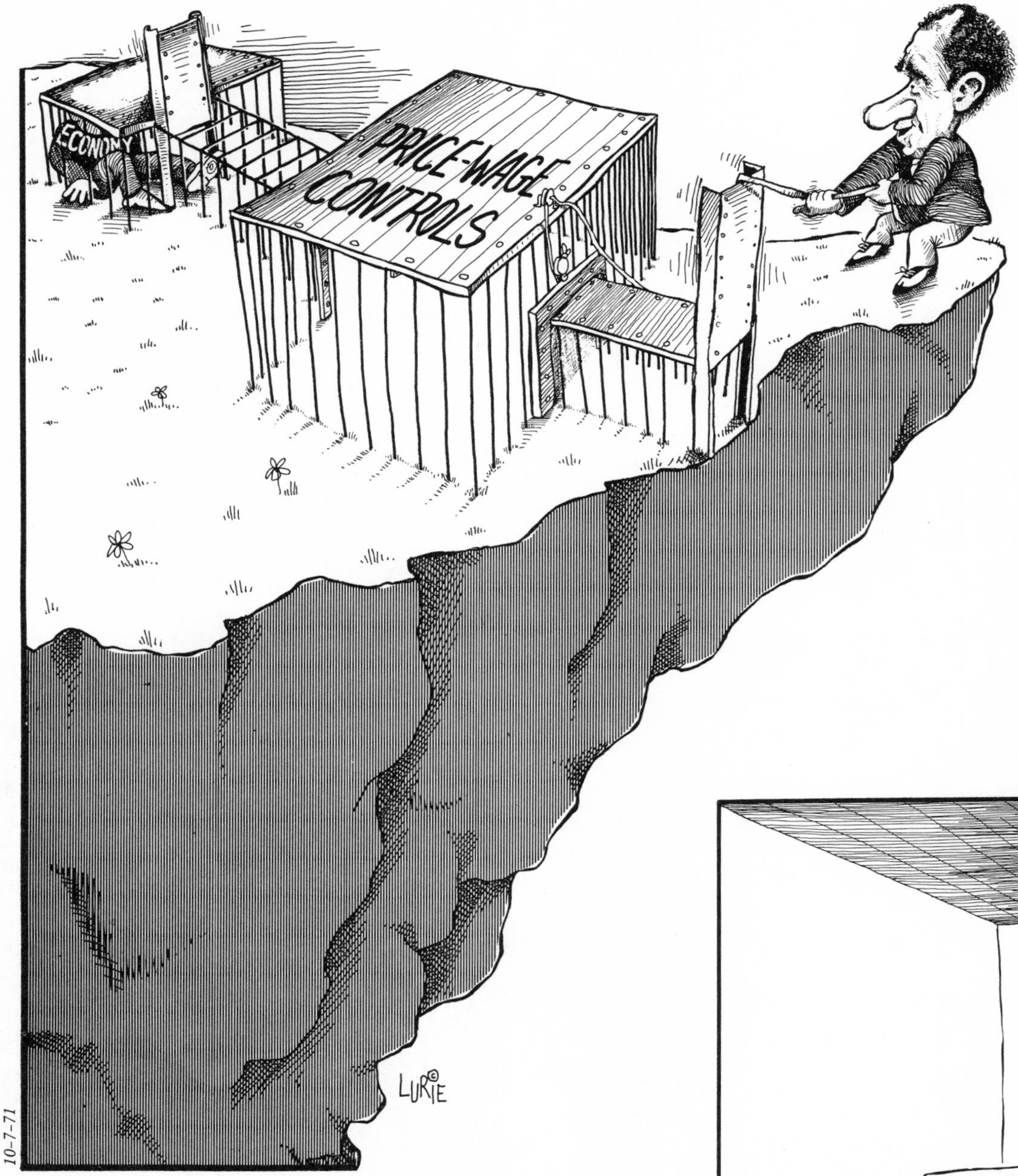
ECONOMY
PRICE-WAGE CONTROLS
LURIE
10-7-71

''YOU'RE FREE—
BUT BETTER WATCH OUT!''

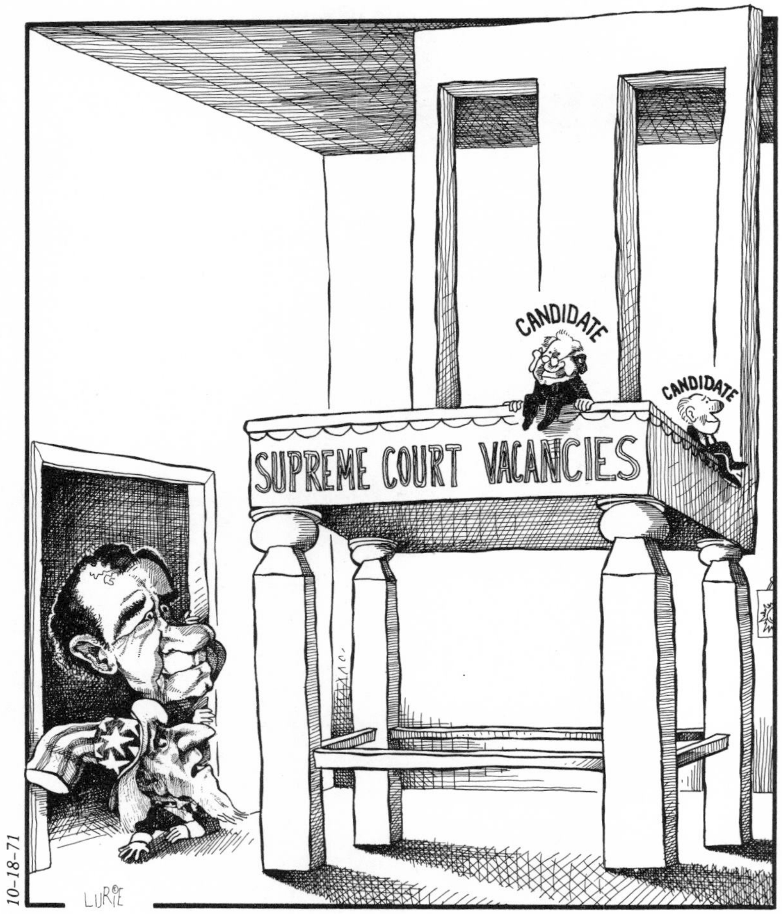
CANDIDATE
CANDIDATE
SUPREME COURT VACANCIES
LURIE
10-18-71

''COULDN'T YOU FIND BIGGER ONES?''

10-6-71

KISSINGER

CHINA

LURIE

25

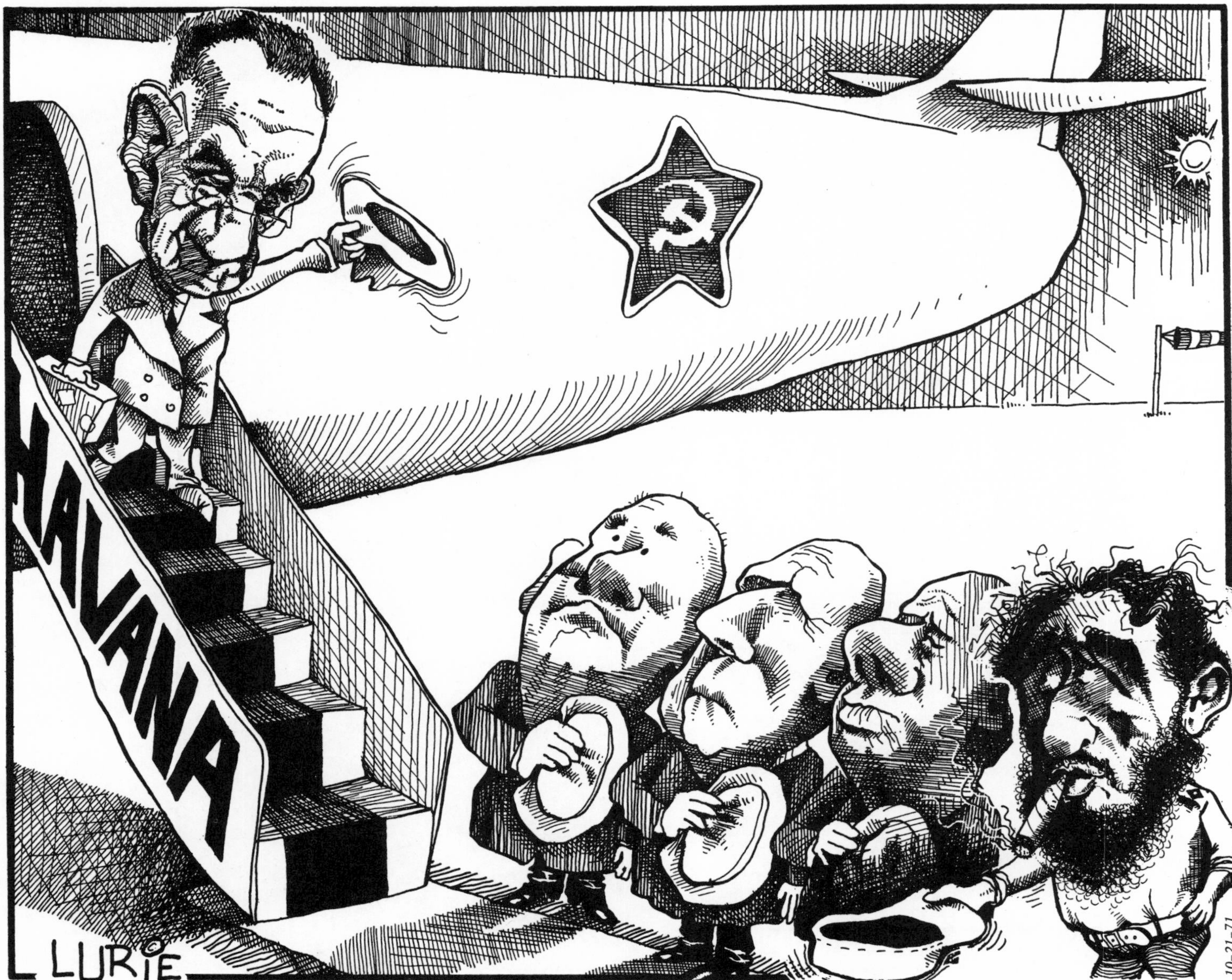
HAVANA
LURIE

10-21-71

MATERNITY
U.N.
LURIE
10-26-71

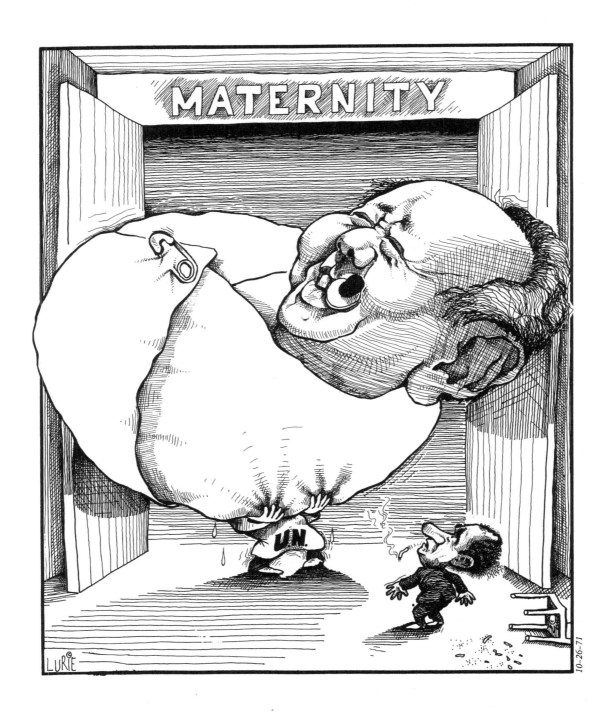

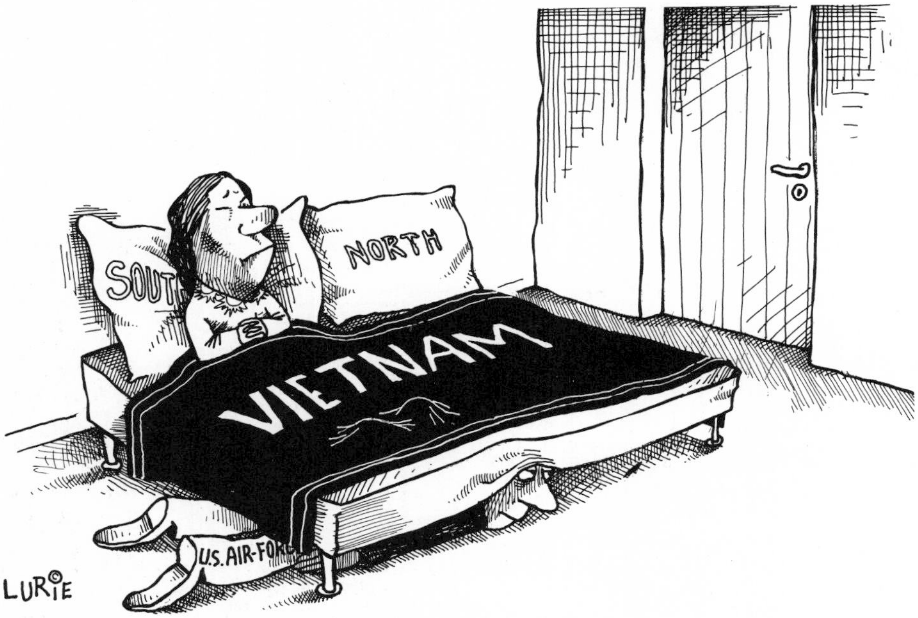
SOUT
NORTH
VIETNAM
U.S. AIR-FOR
LURIE

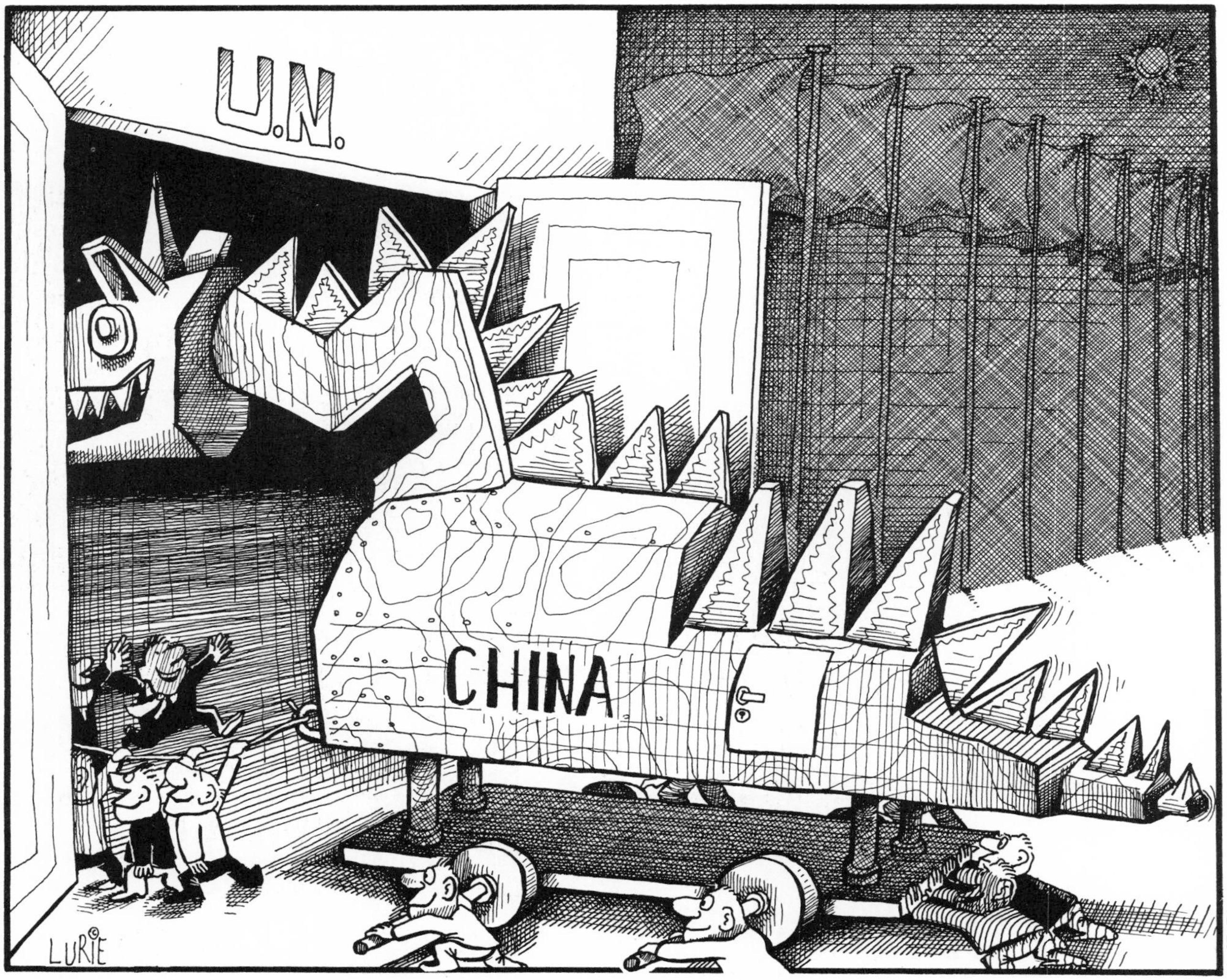
U.N.
CHINA
LURIE
10-27-71

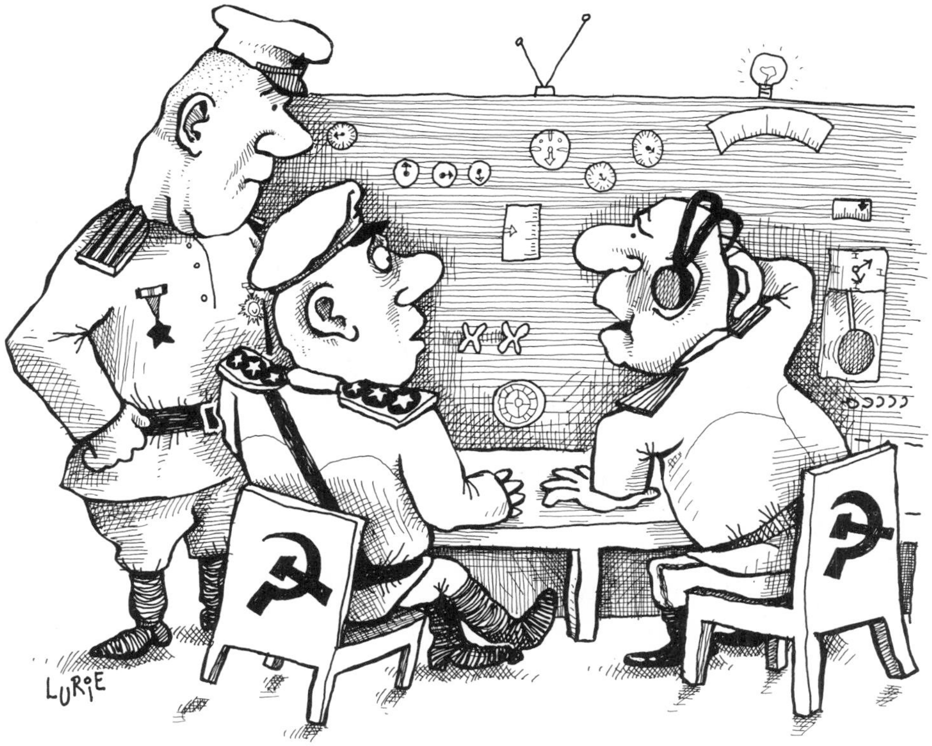
LURIE

''OUR MACHINE ON THE MOON HAS ASKED THEM FOR POLITICAL ASYLUM''

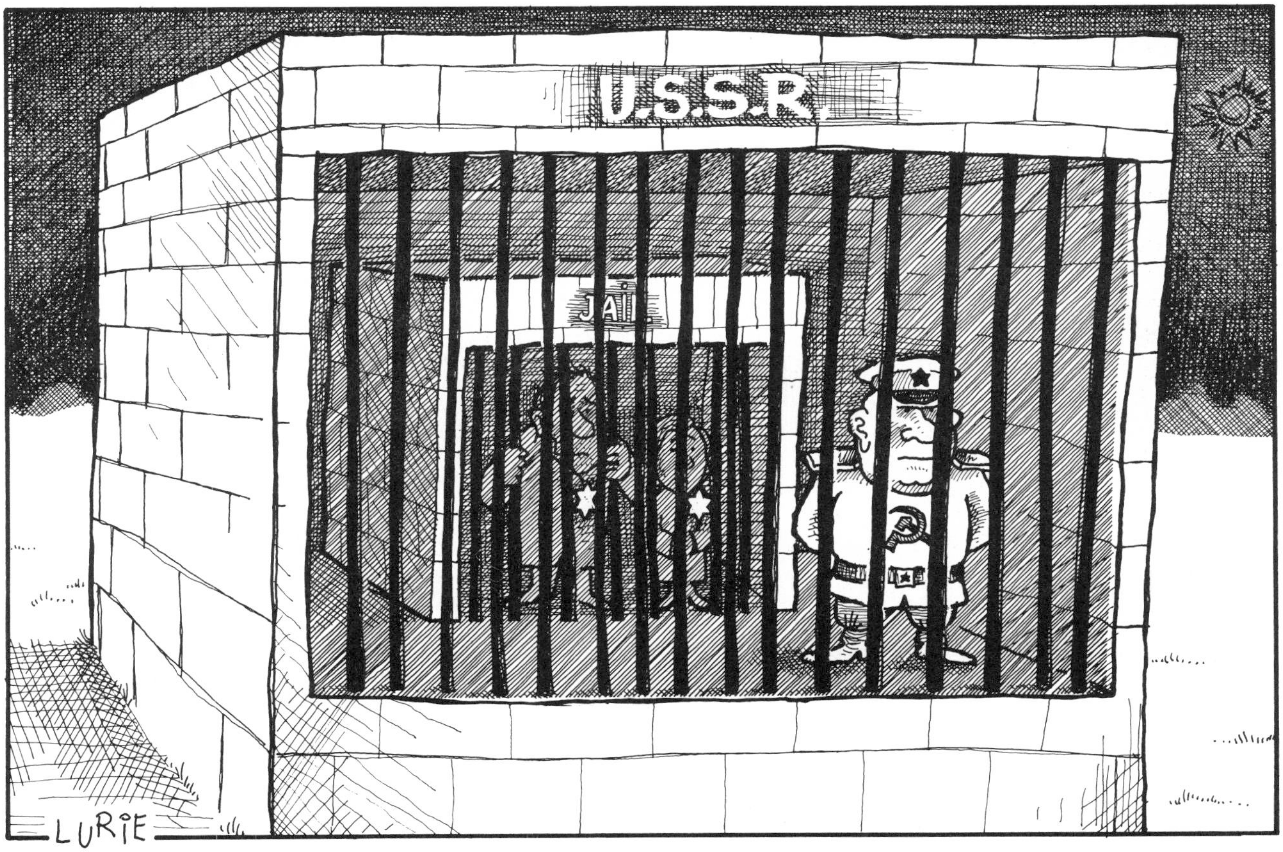
U.S.S.R.
JAIL
LURIE

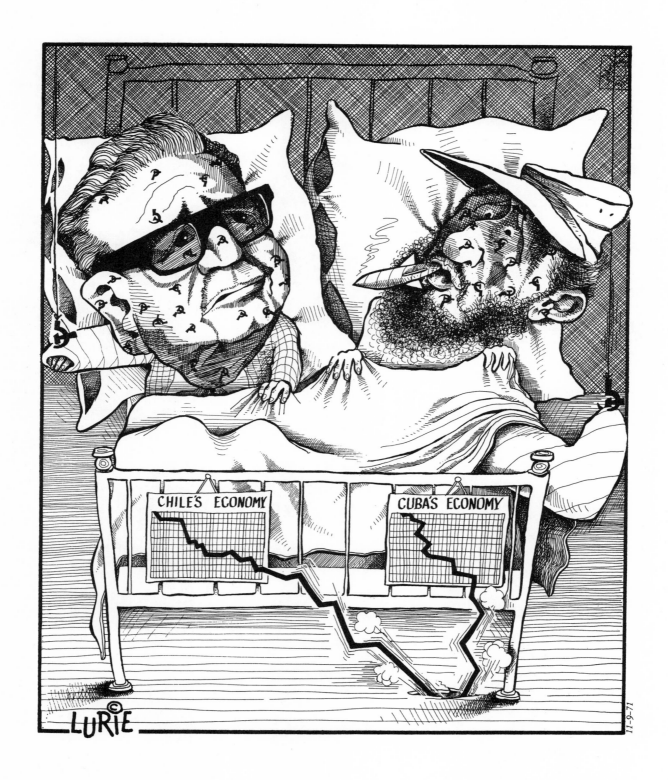

CHILE'S ECONOMY

CUBA'S ECONOMY

LURIE

11-9-71

30

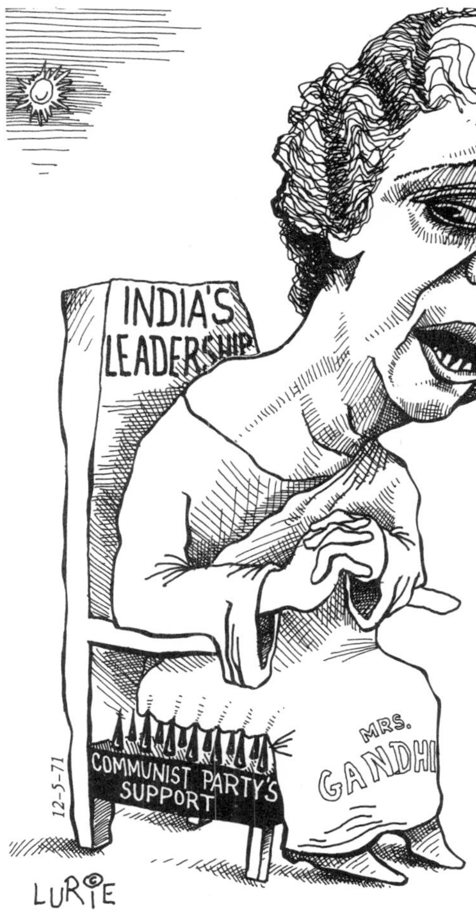
INDIA'S LEADERSHIP
COMMUNIST PARTY'S SUPPORT
MRS. GANDHI
12-5-71
LURIE

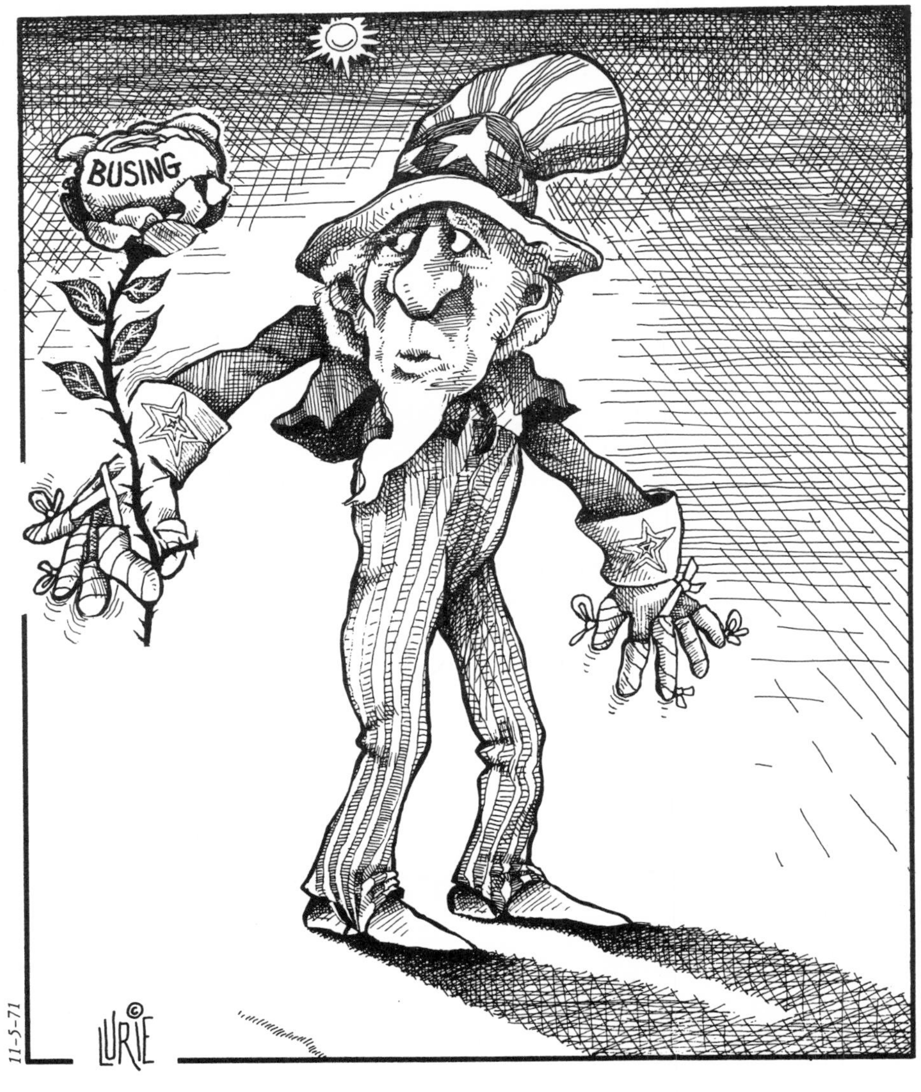
BUSING
11-5-71
LURIE

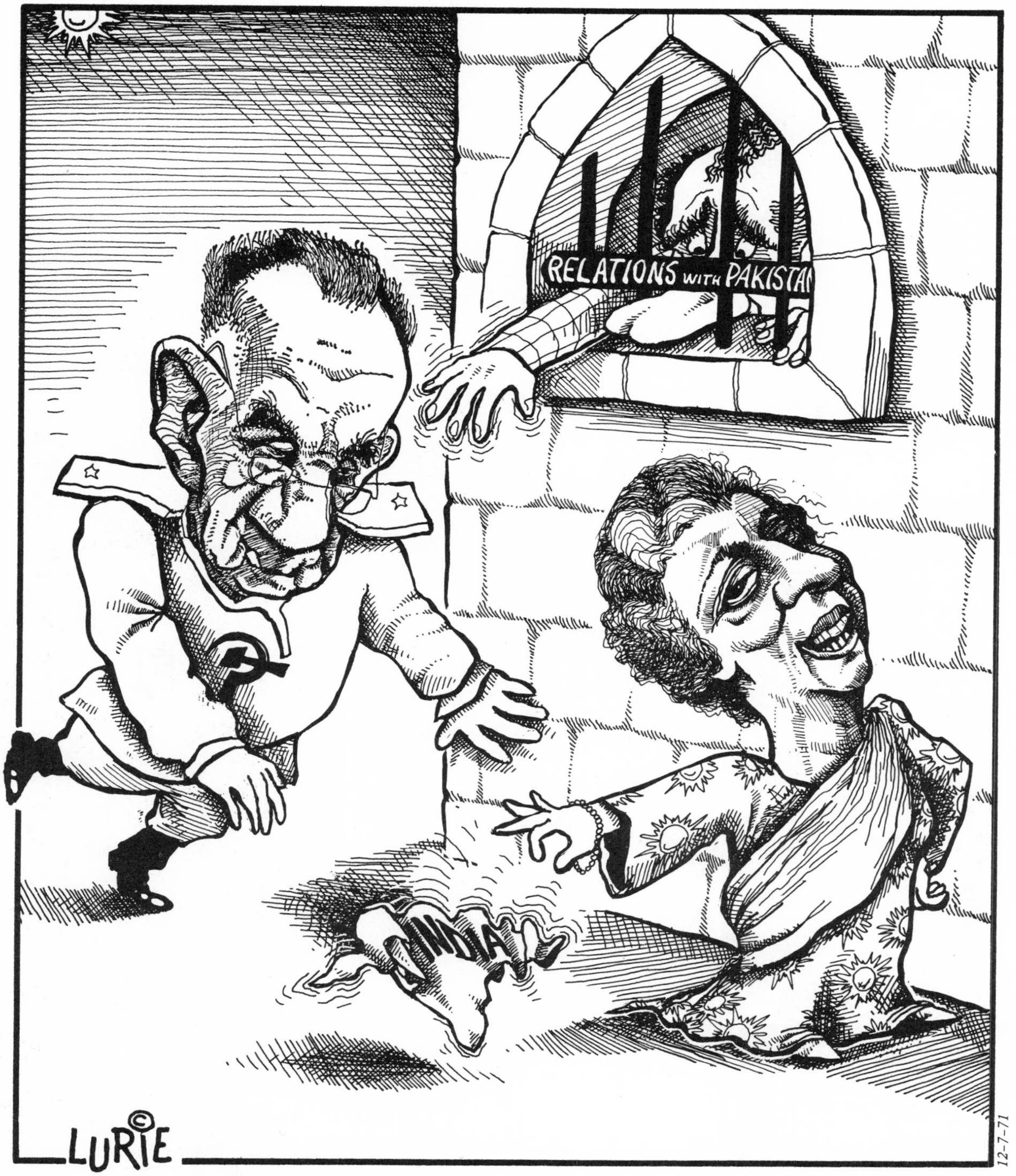
RELATIONS WITH PAKISTAN
INDIA
LURIE ©
12-7-71

''BECAUSE IT'S THERE''

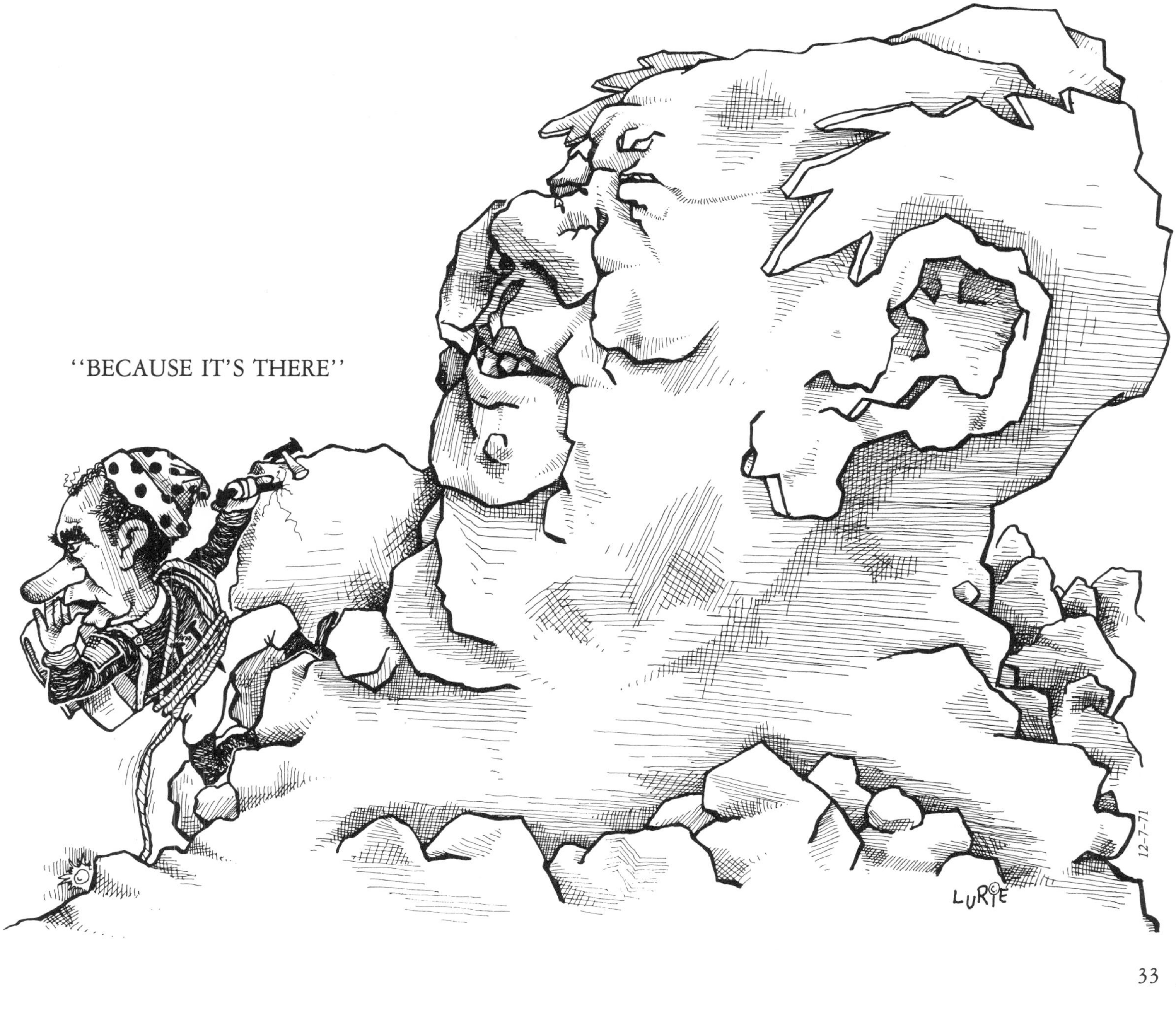
12-7-71
LURIE

1972

Lurie: ON THE UNFUNNY EVENT

When I was teaching a course, The Philosophy of Political Cartooning, my main theme was the five steps in making a good cartoon. I call them the pentathlon of political cartooning. First, deciding the message; second, rendering the metaphor or parable; third, drawing the facial caricature; fourth, use of humor/satire; fifth, exercising journalistic sense—finding the right timing and subjects, anticipating the news.

Regarding the use of humor/satire, a cartoon should be either humorous or satirical, not both. With tragic events such as My Lai or Kent State you obviously use the satirical approach, not to provoke laughter but to show the cruelty, the unnecessary cruelty of such events. With My Lai, for instance, satire would have to dramatize the idiotic, fanatic, cold-blooded murder of men, women, and children. The intent is to expose, to show by means of a dramatic metaphor, the grim event. Such terrible subjects do have to be handled by the cartoonist—you cannot escape them. You select the kind of humor/satire befitting the situation. There is no subject that is, can or should be inappropriate for the political cartoon. I must emphasize: The political cartoonist is in an absolutely different profession from that of a comic-strip cartoonist or gag cartoonist. The political cartoonist must handle unfunny events, and that is one of the important differences that distinguishes political cartooning from all other forms of cartooning.

I do not consider humor—especially in the case of political cartooning—as an end in itself. Humor is simply one of the things that helps deliver the main theme of a cartoon. Once you get the reader laughing, you have the reader's attention. You and he are in the same boat in that moment. Once you have him in the boat your job is to carry him to your message.

I am relentlessly devoted to reporting the facts behind the facts. The facts you will find on the front page. What those facts actually mean you should find in the editorials and political cartoons. The political cartoon is like the good ole Indian scout who rode before the cavalry and reported what was ahead.

A political cartoonist is a kind of instant historian who reports what an Agnew really is, what a Nixon really is, what a Carter really is. His or her job is to report a good Carter on one issue, a negligent Carter on another. Every leader has his better points and worse points, and we should identify them as we find them.

THE VOTER
DEM
IT&T SCANDAL
LURIE©

ITT
3-8-72
LURIE©

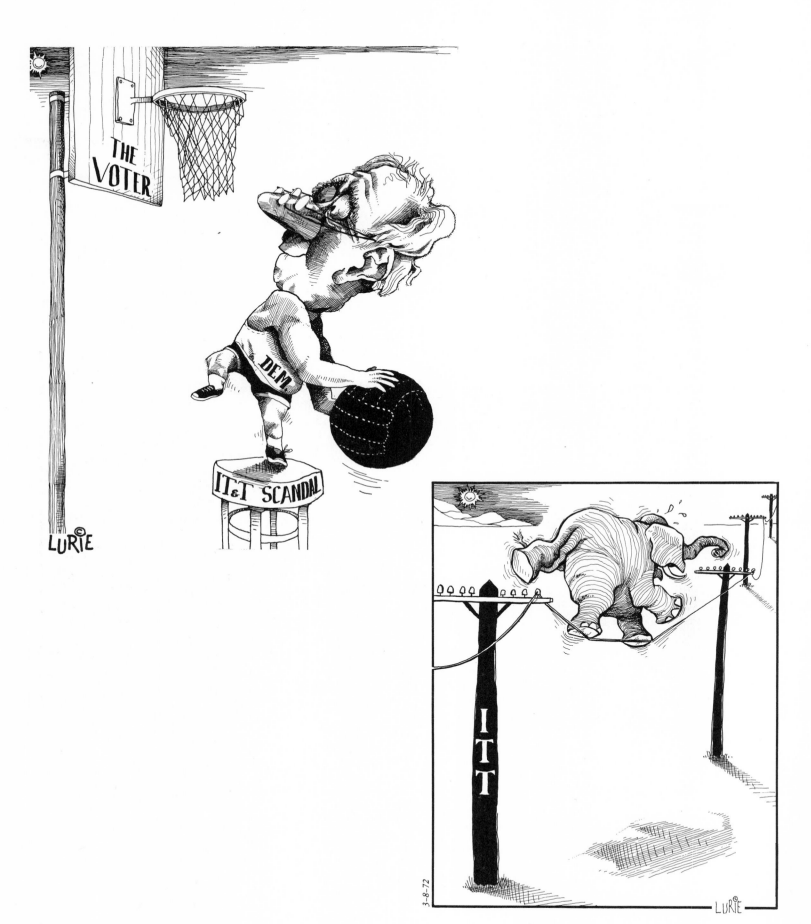

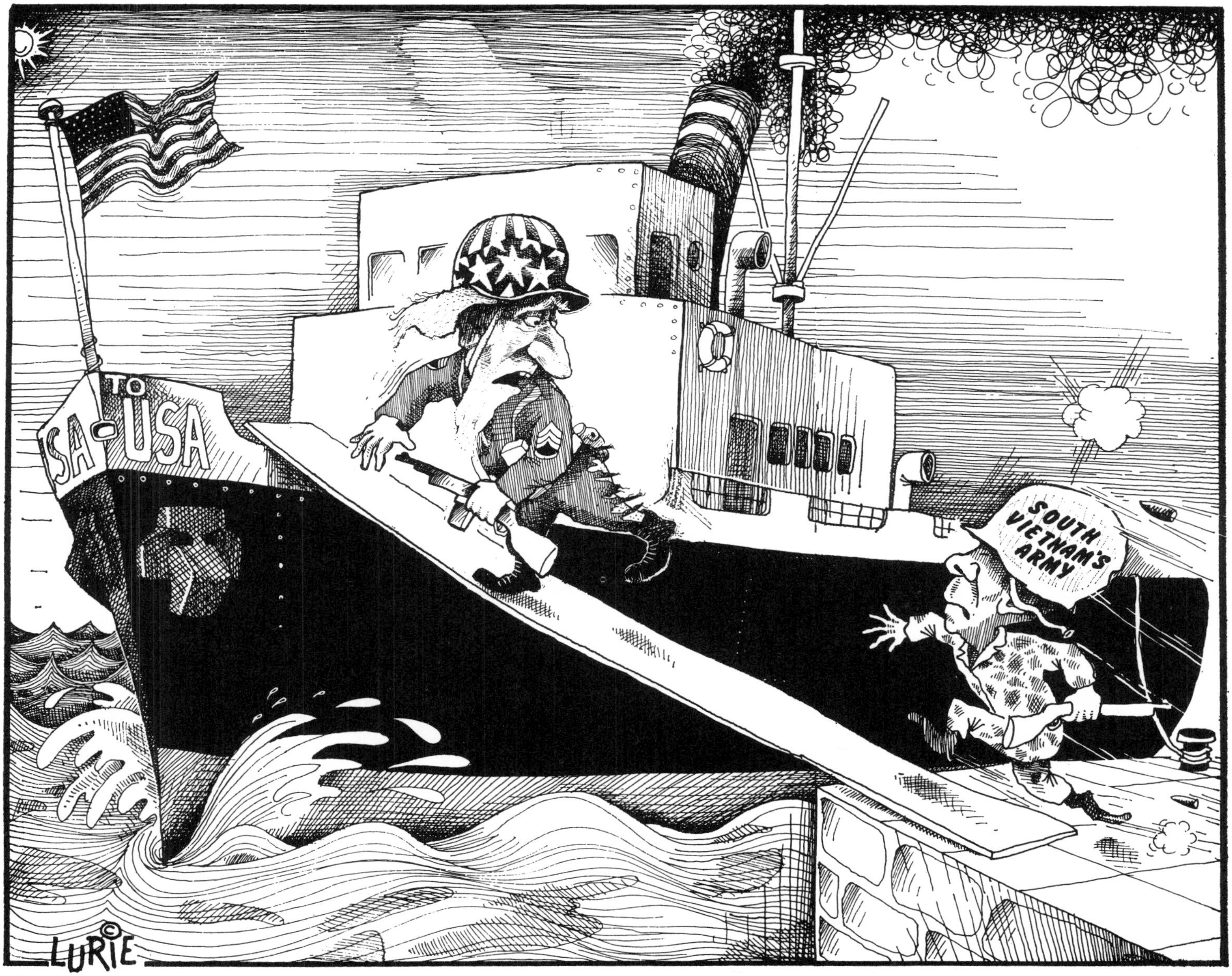

TO
USA
USA
SOUTH VIETNAM'S ARMY
LURIE©

"NO, NO—YOU'RE SUPPOSED TO STAY!"

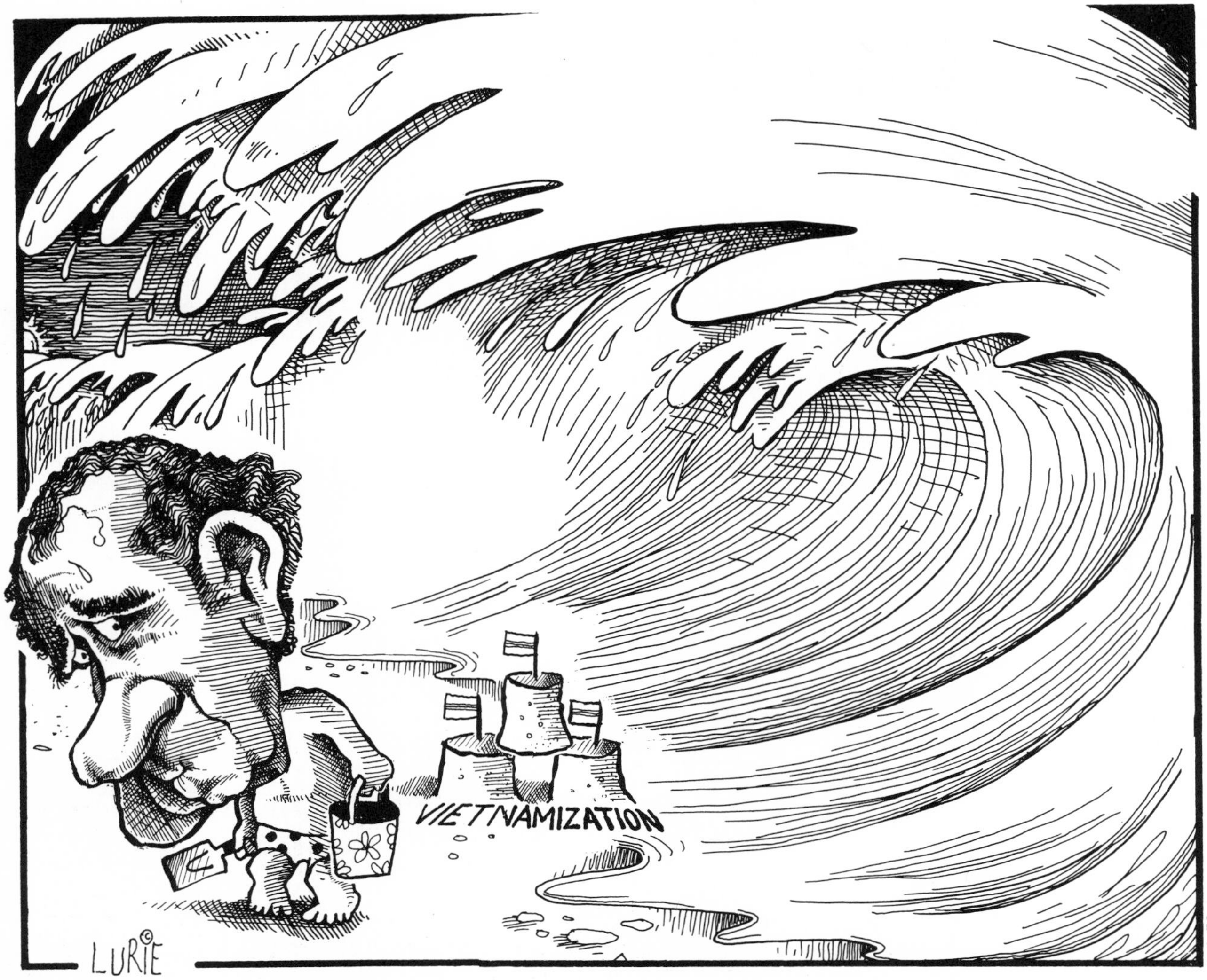
VIETNAMIZATION
LURIE©
5-2-72

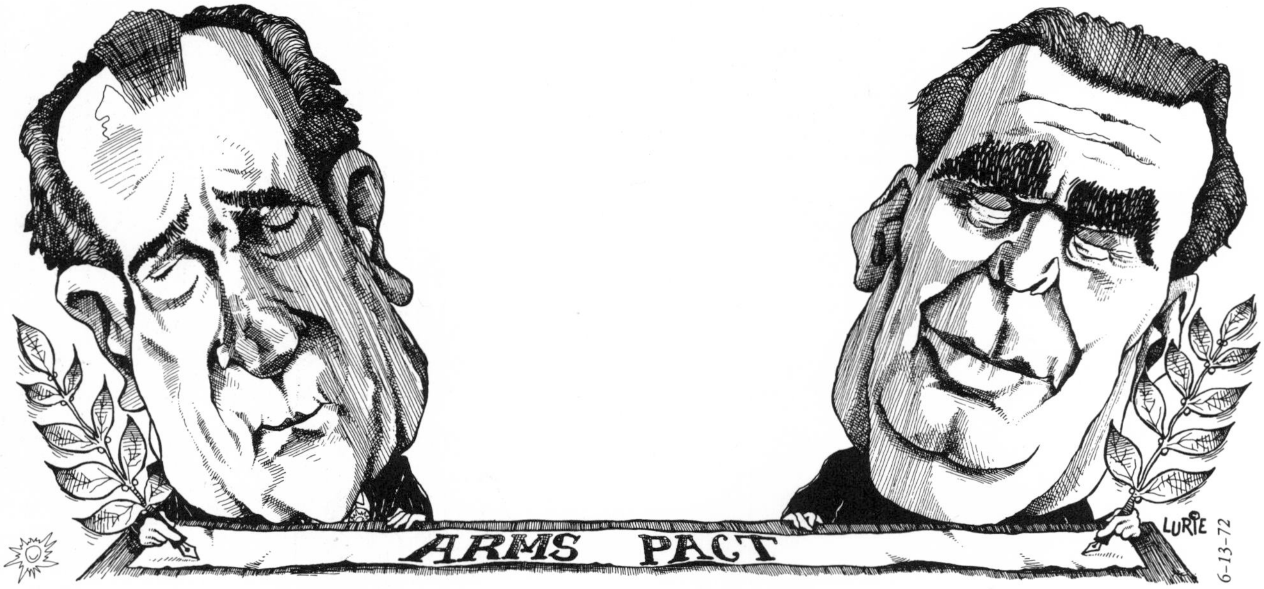
ARMS PACT
LURIE©
6-13-72

ARMS PACT

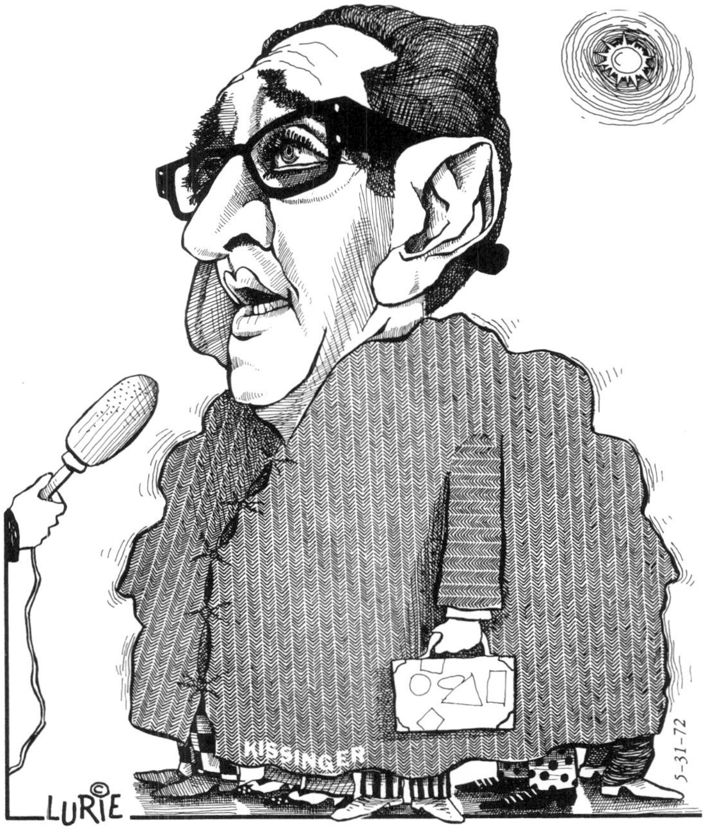
KISSINGER
LURIE
5-31-72

"NO, THERE WERE NO SECRET DEALS."

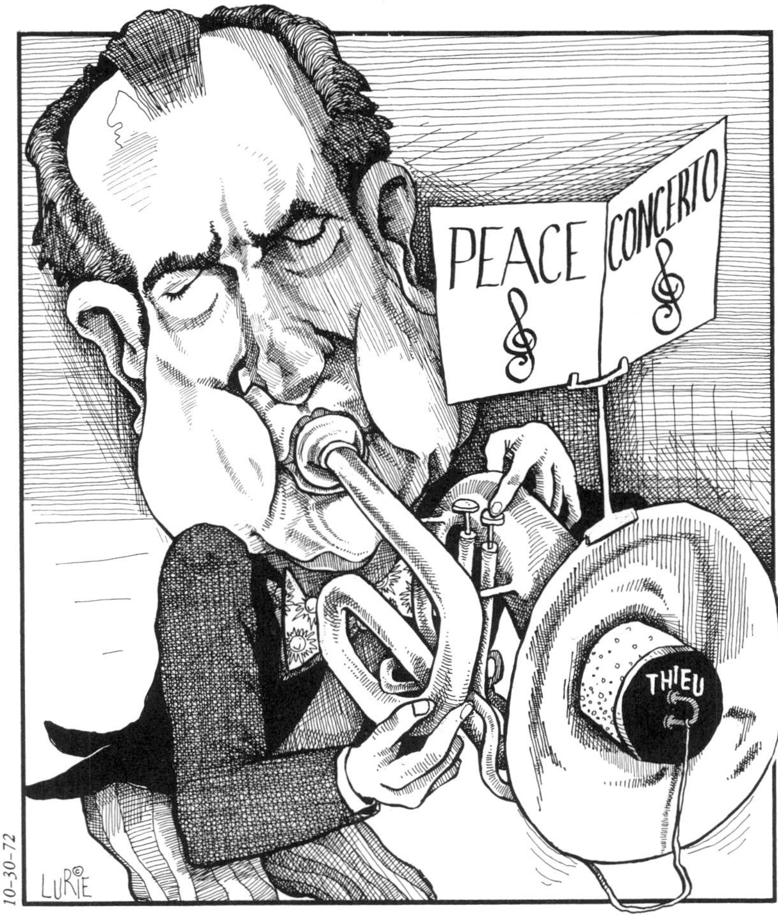
PEACE
CONCERTO
THIEU
LURIE
10-30-72

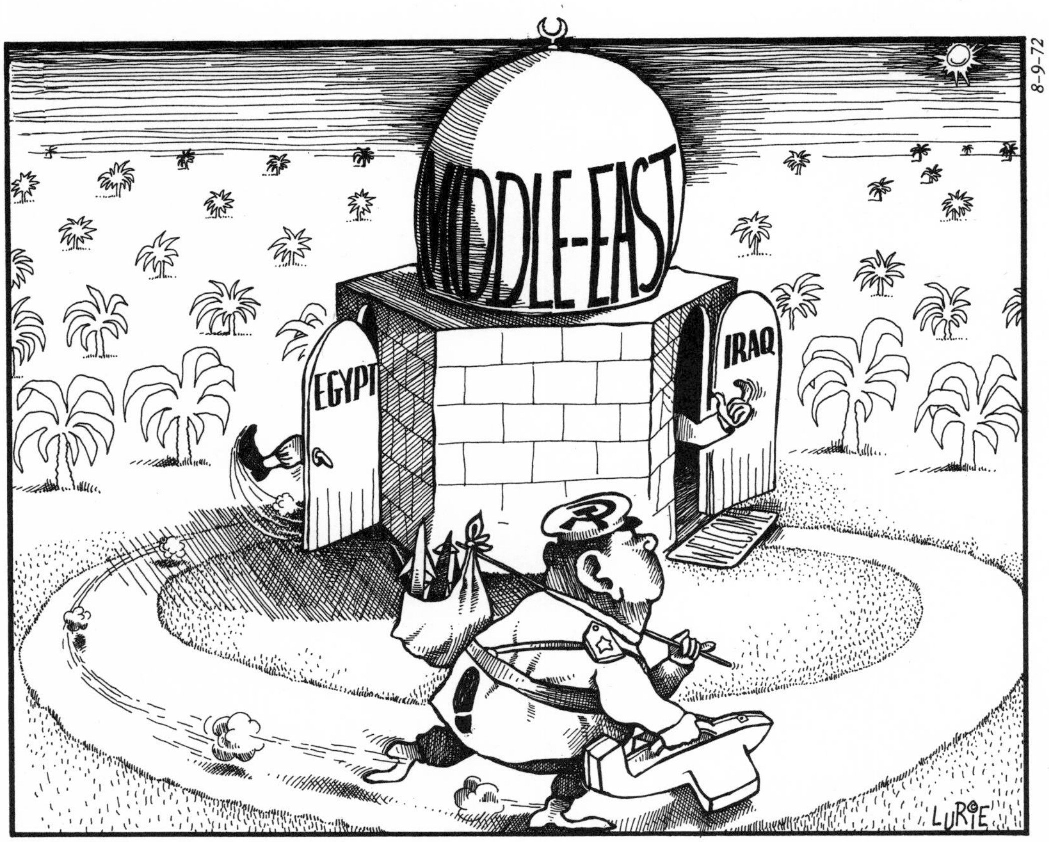
8-9-72
MIDDLE-EAST
EGYPT
IRAQ
LURIE

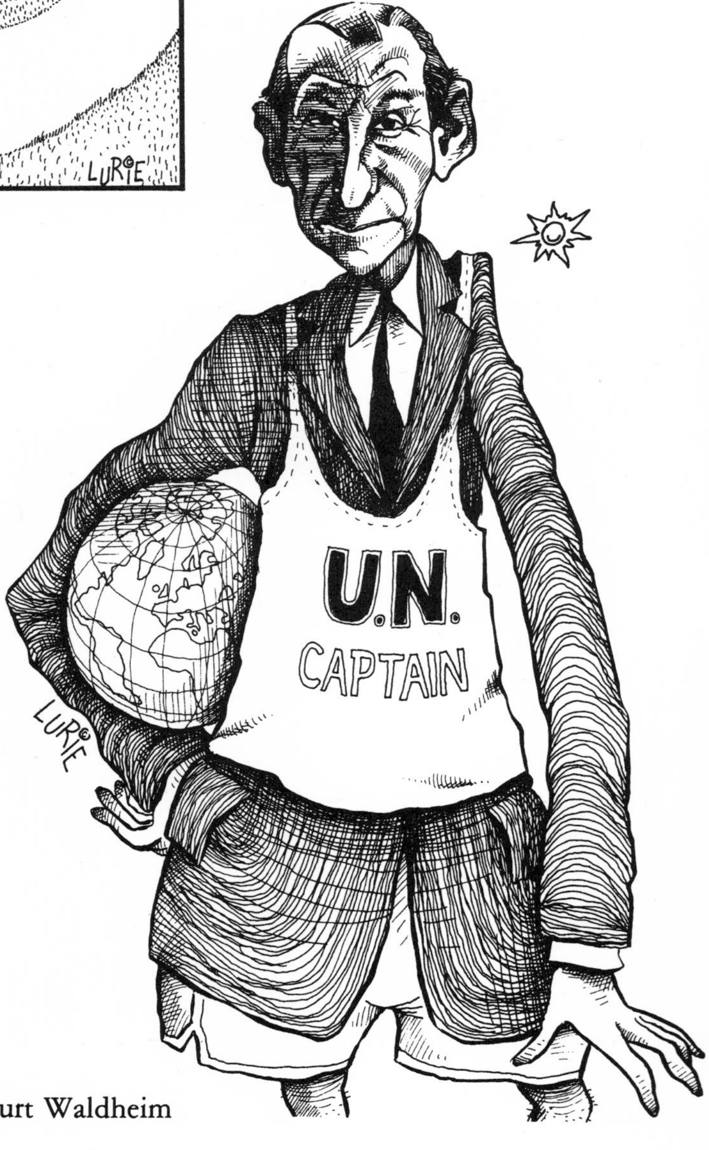
U.N.
CAPTAIN
LURIE

Kurt Waldheim

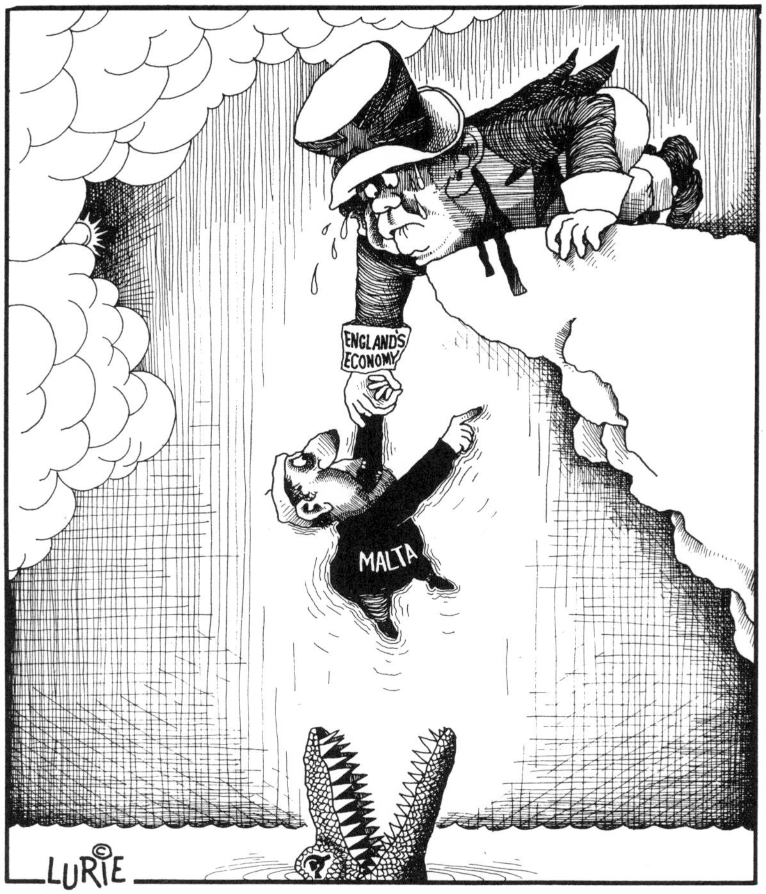
ENGLAND'S ECONOMY
MALTA
LURIE ©

"I COMMAND YOU TO LEAVE!"

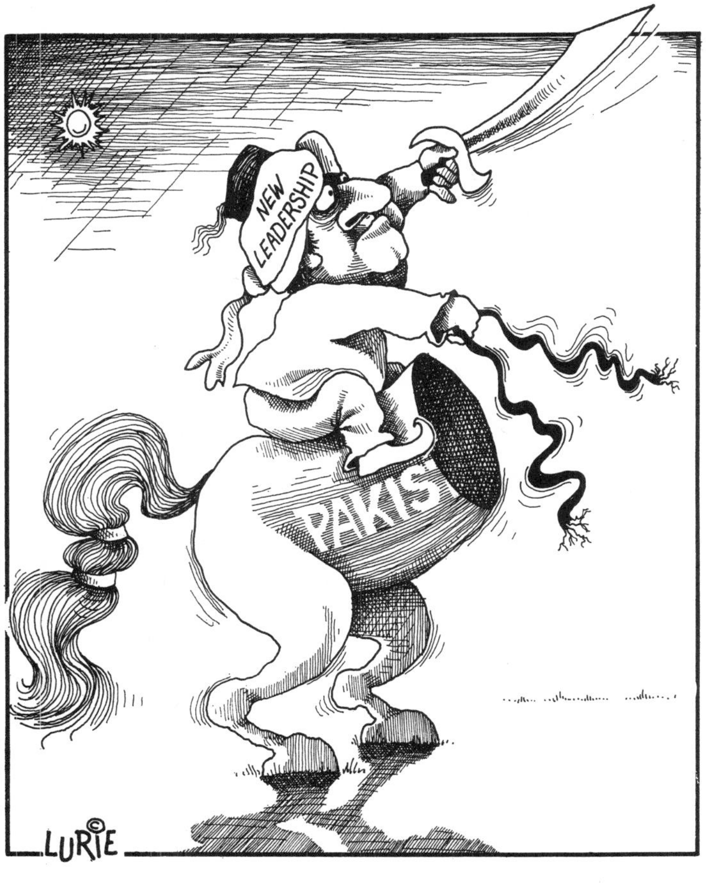
NEW LEADERSHIP
PAKIS
LURIE ©

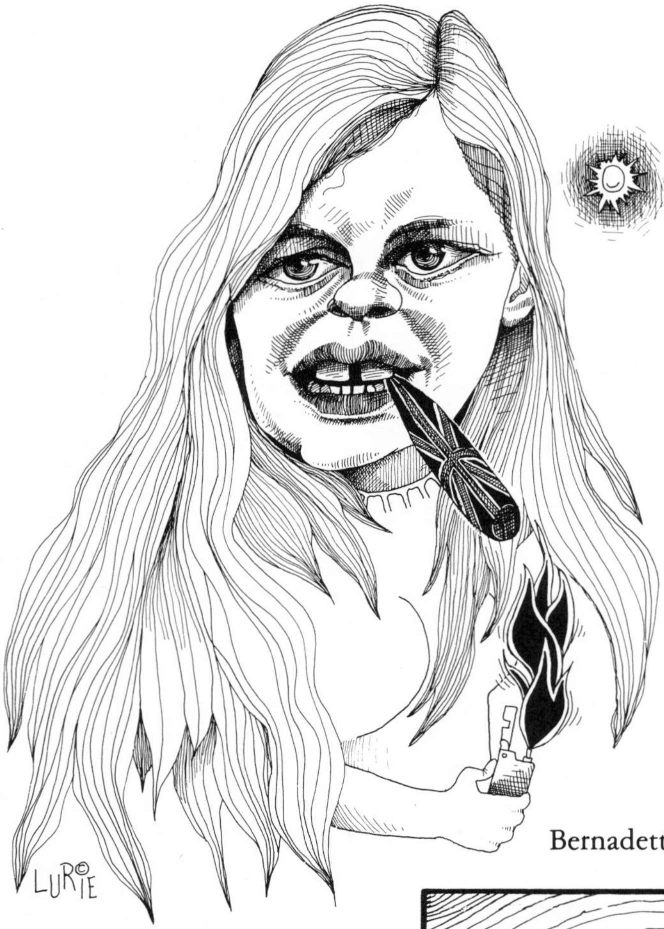
LURIE

Bernadette

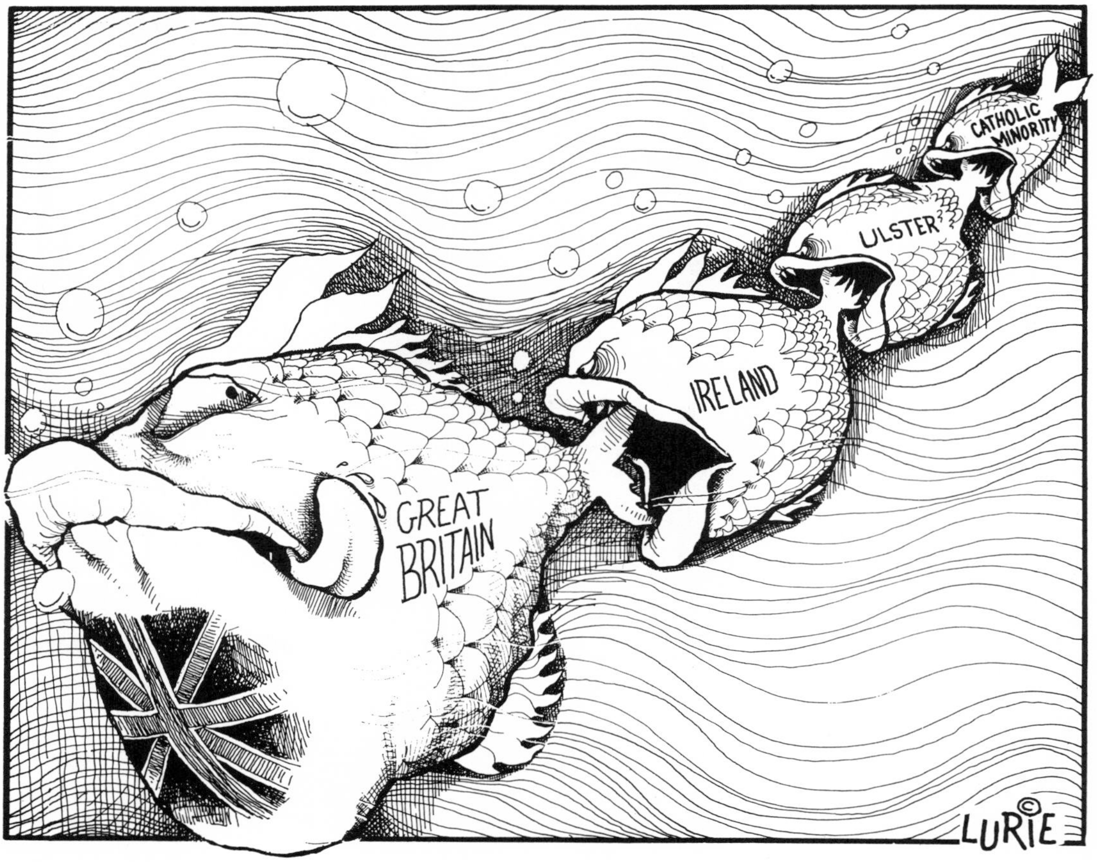
CATHOLIC MINORITY
ULSTER?
IRELAND
GREAT BRITAIN
LURIE

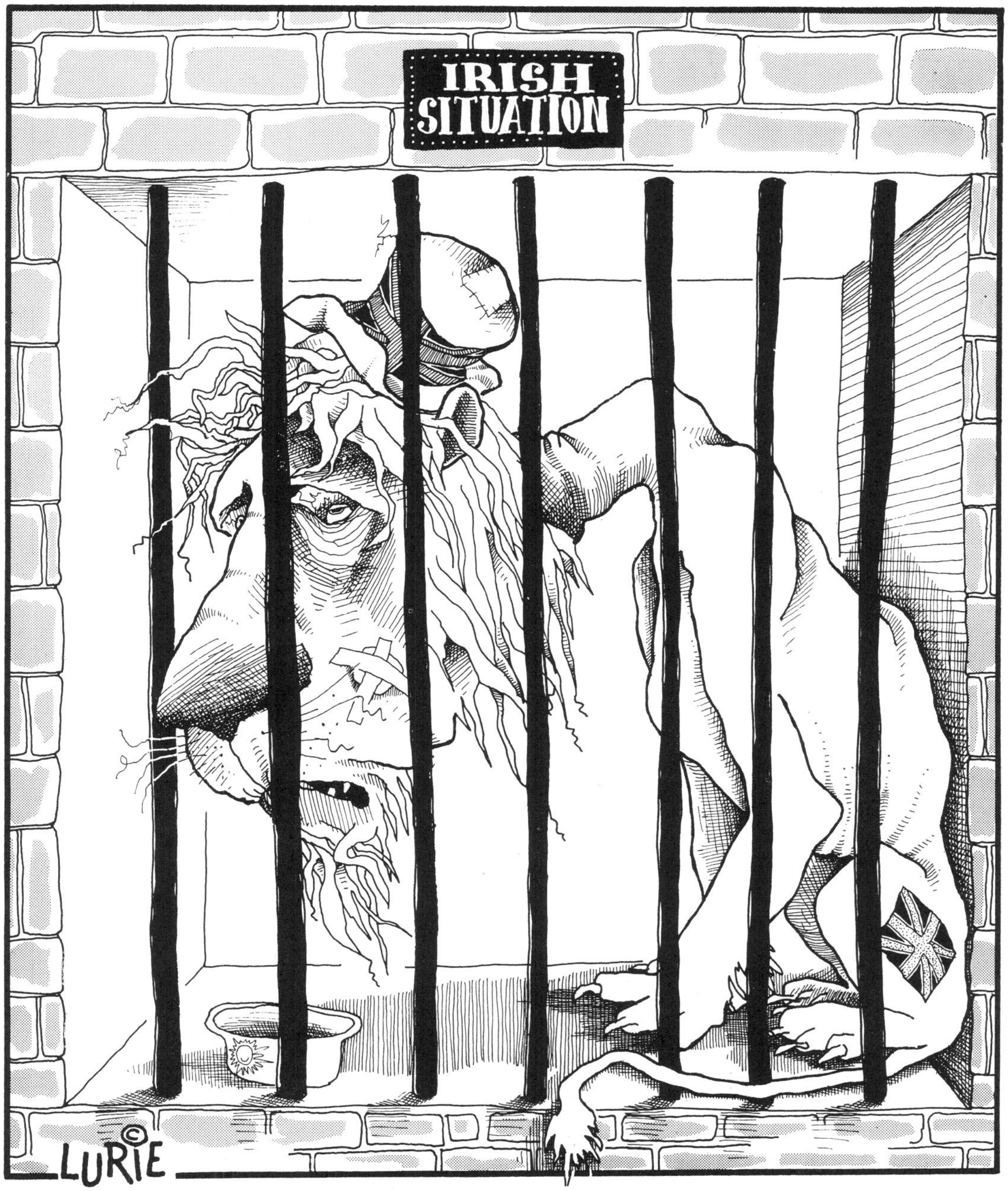
IRISH
SITUATION
LURIE ©

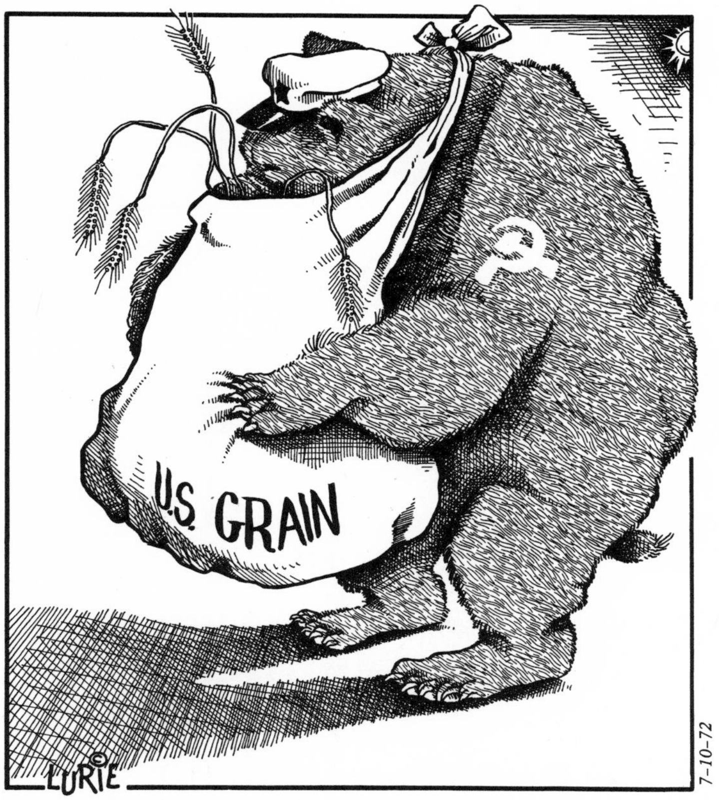
U.S. GRAIN
LURIE
7-10-72

A MUZZLE

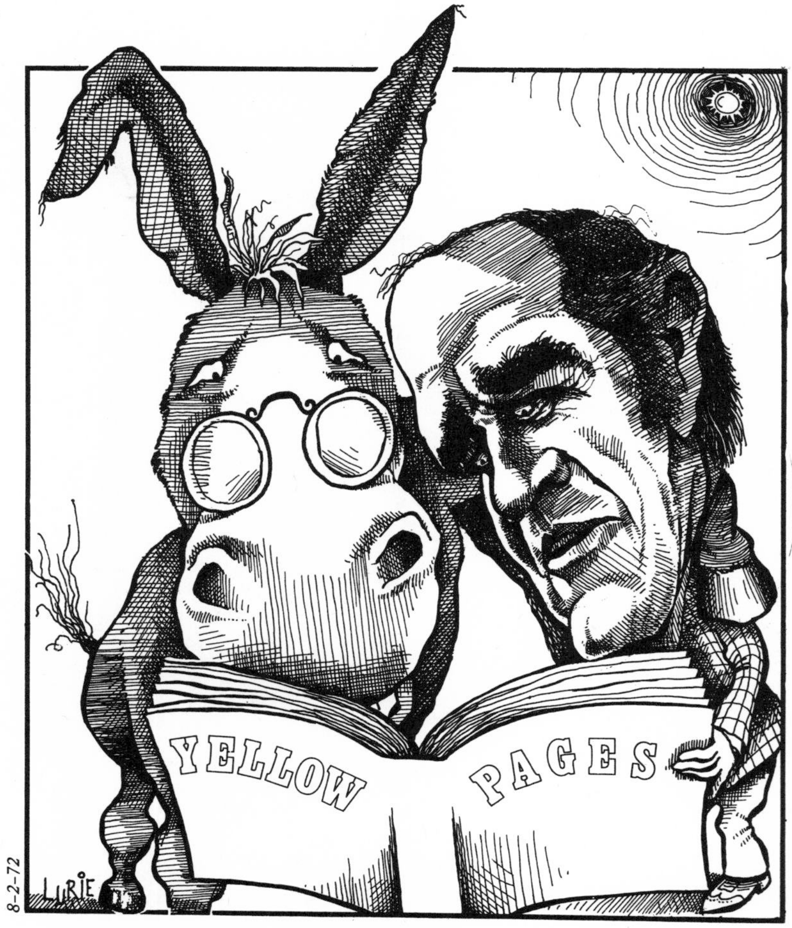
YELLOW PAGES
LURIE
8-2-72

LOOKING FOR A RUNNING MATE

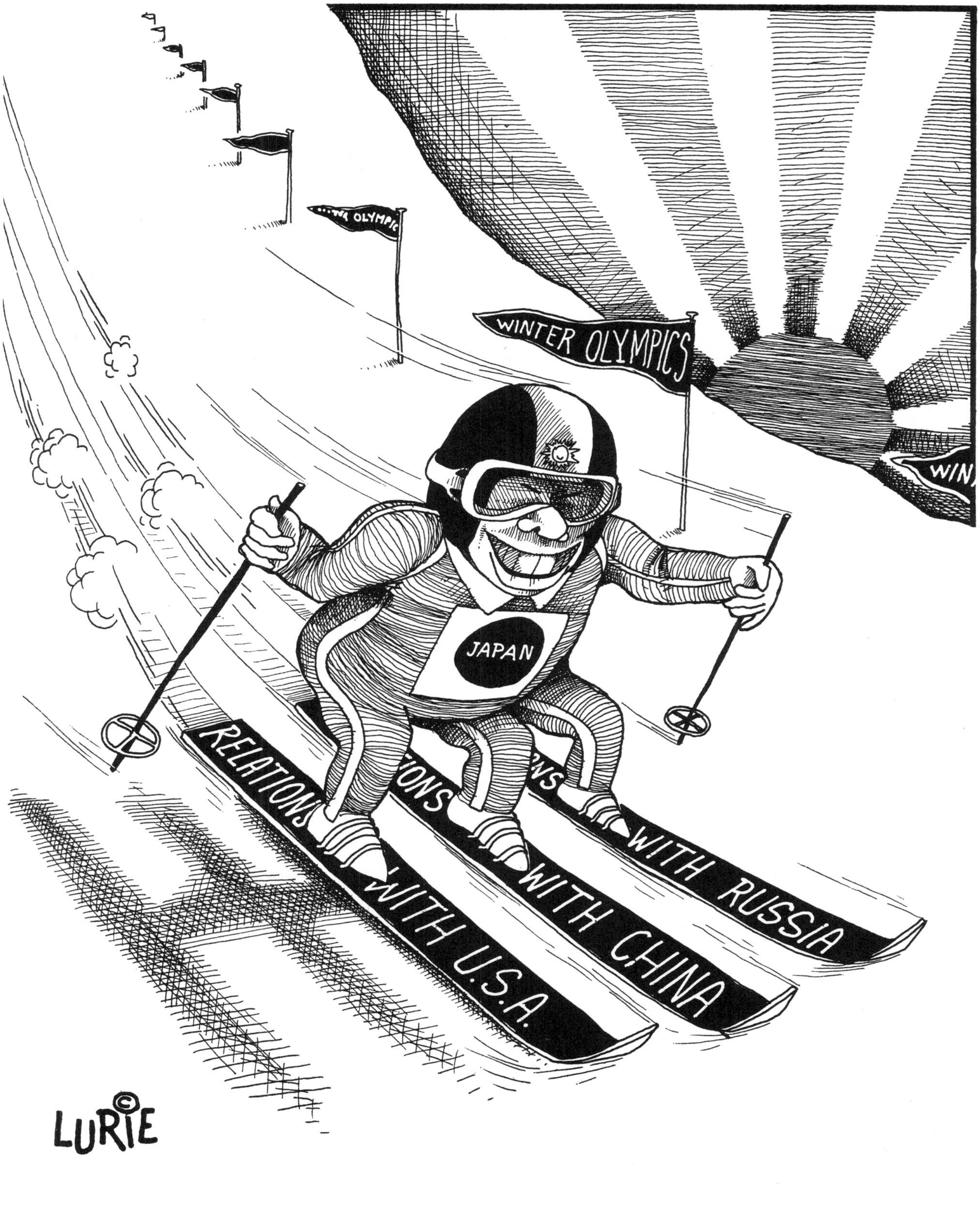
WINTER OLYMPICS
JAPAN
RELATIONS WITH U.S.A.
WITH CHINA
WITH RUSSIA
LURIE

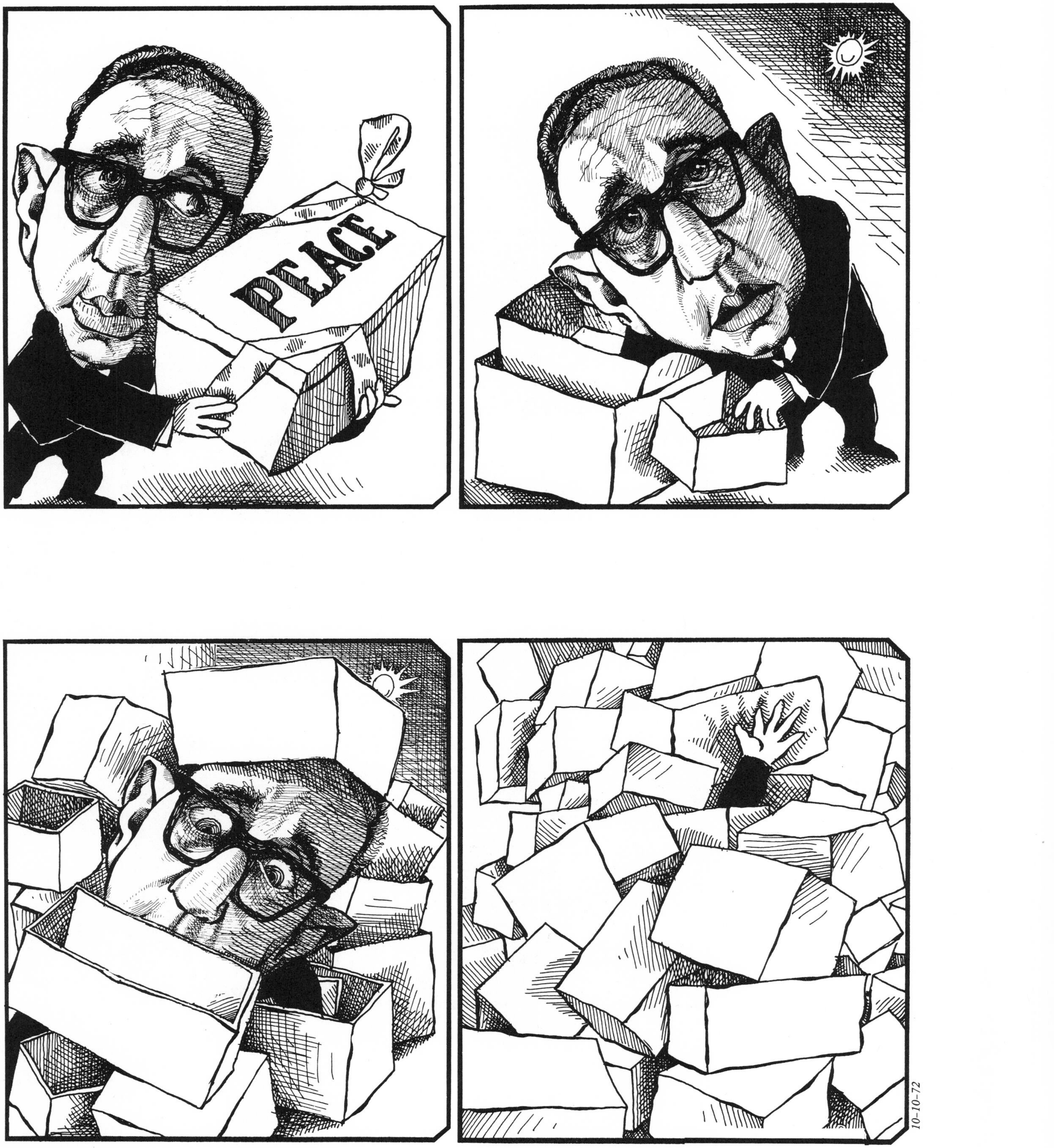
PEACE
10-10-72

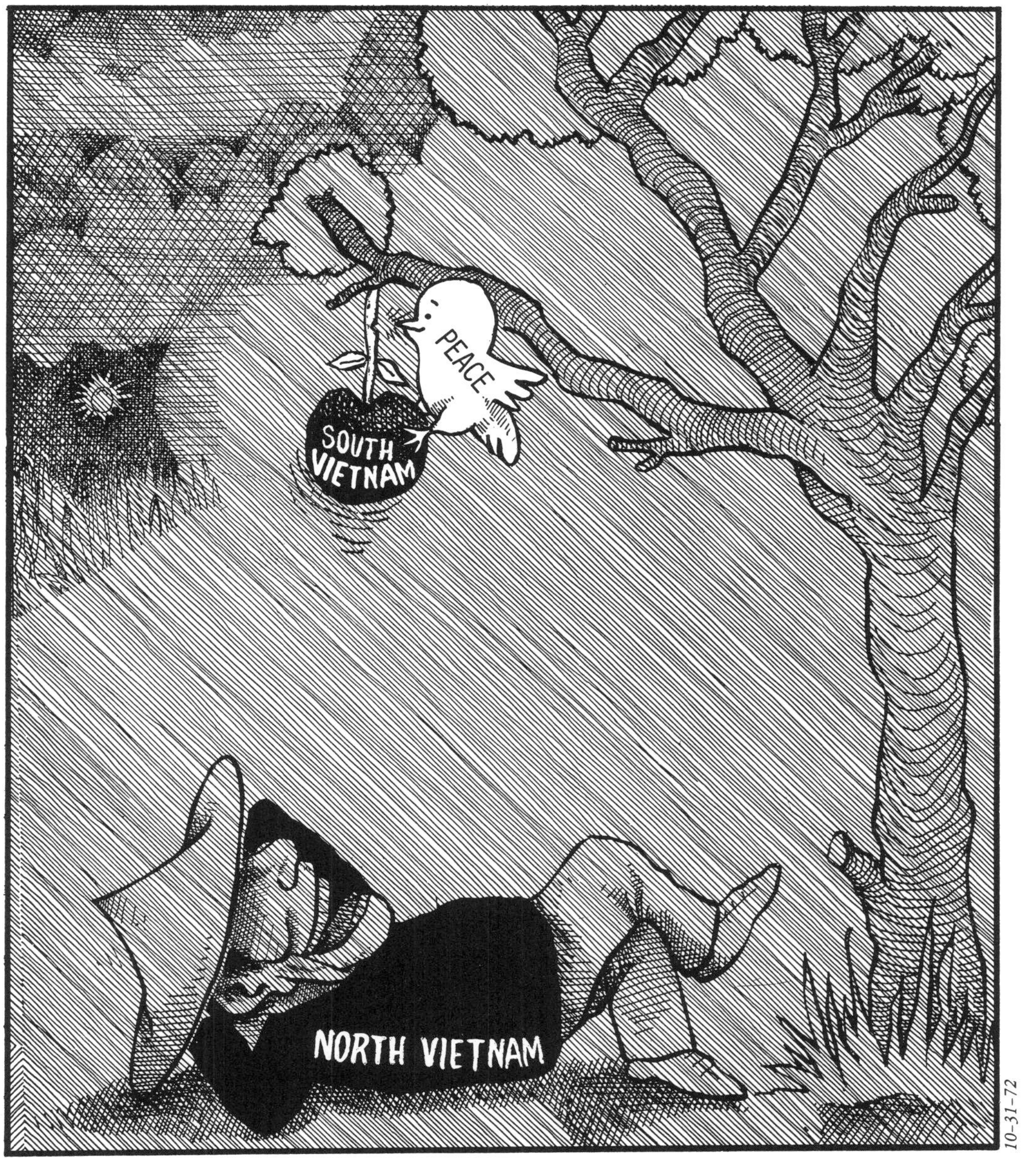
PEACE
SOUTH VIETNAM
NORTH VIETNAM
10-31-72

PRESS
PRESS
PRESS
PRESS

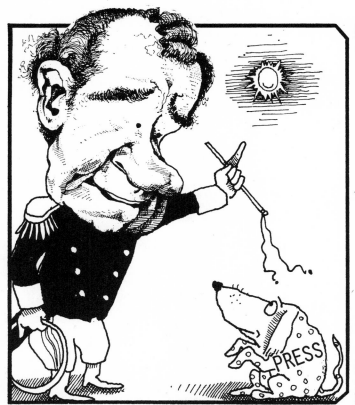

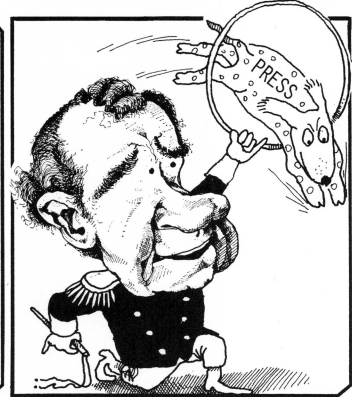

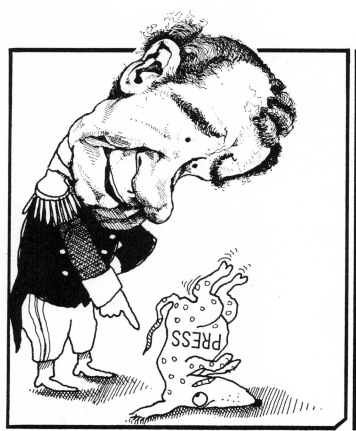

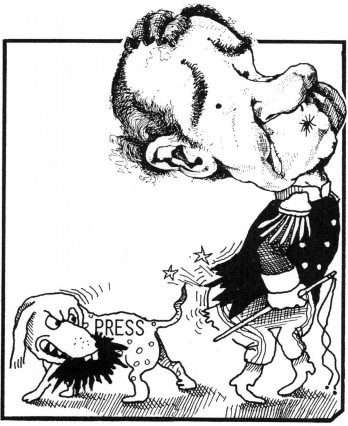

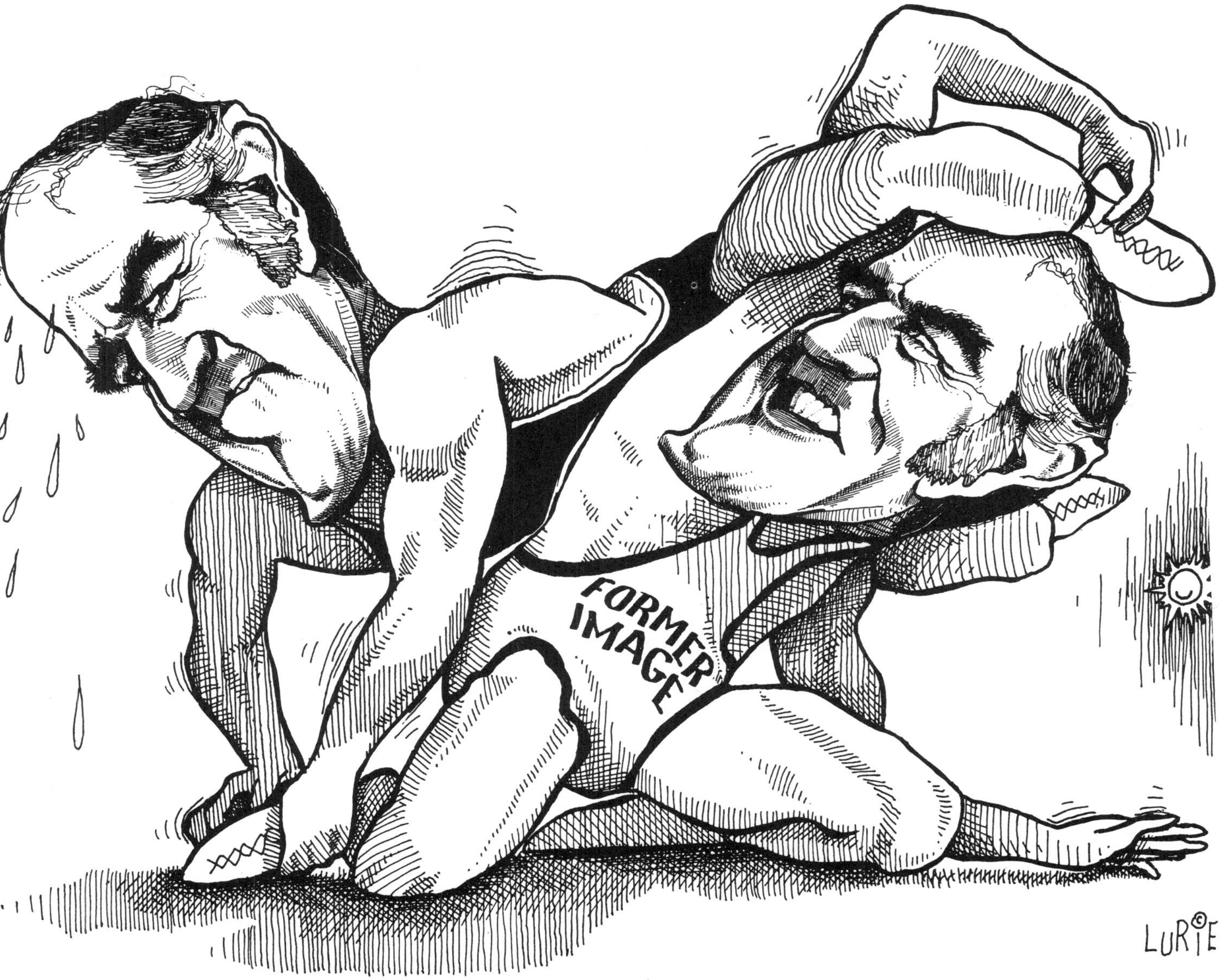
FORMER IMAGE
LURIE

Time 10-2-72

THE REAL CAMPAIGN FIGHT

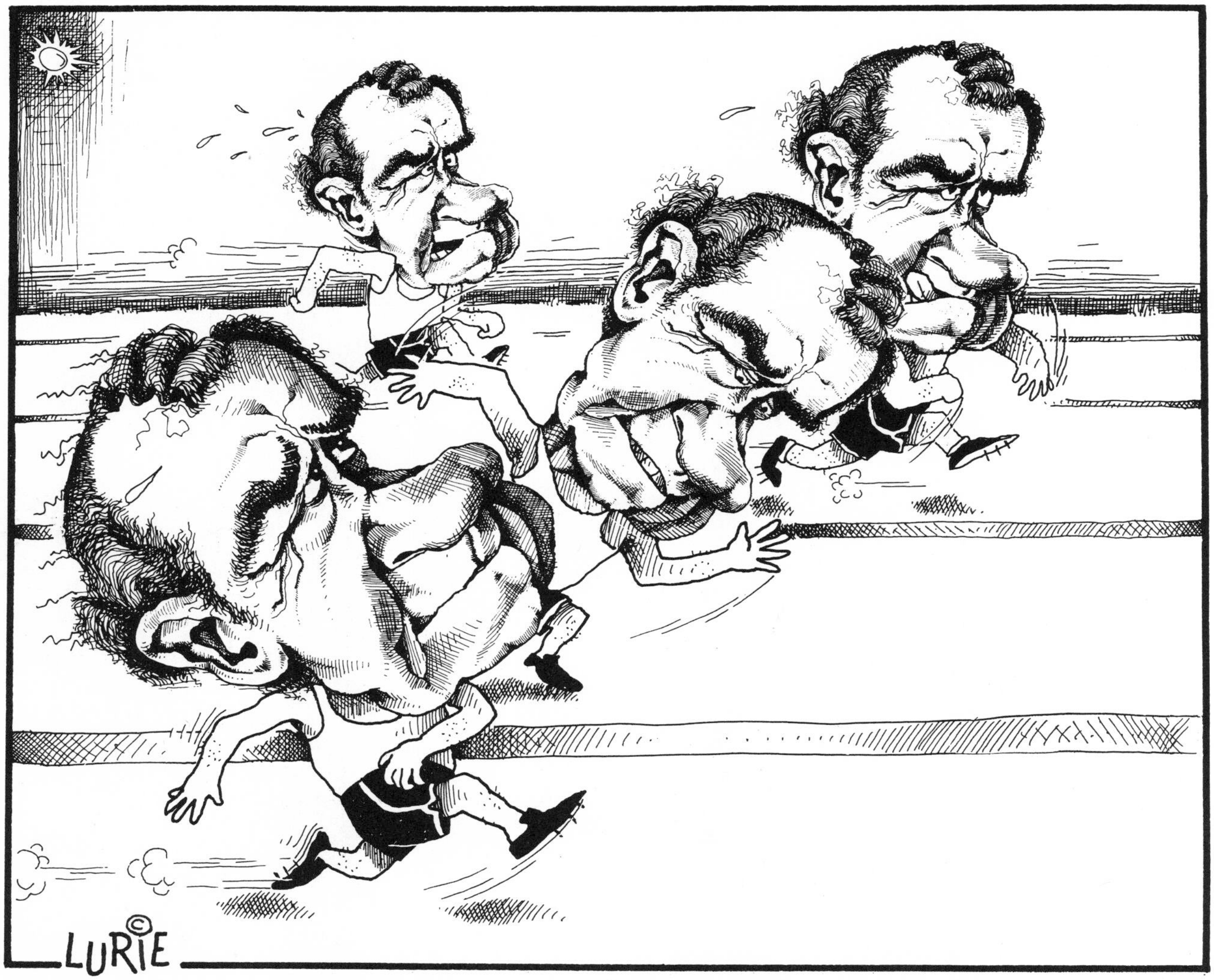
LURIE

G.O.P. PRIMARY RACES

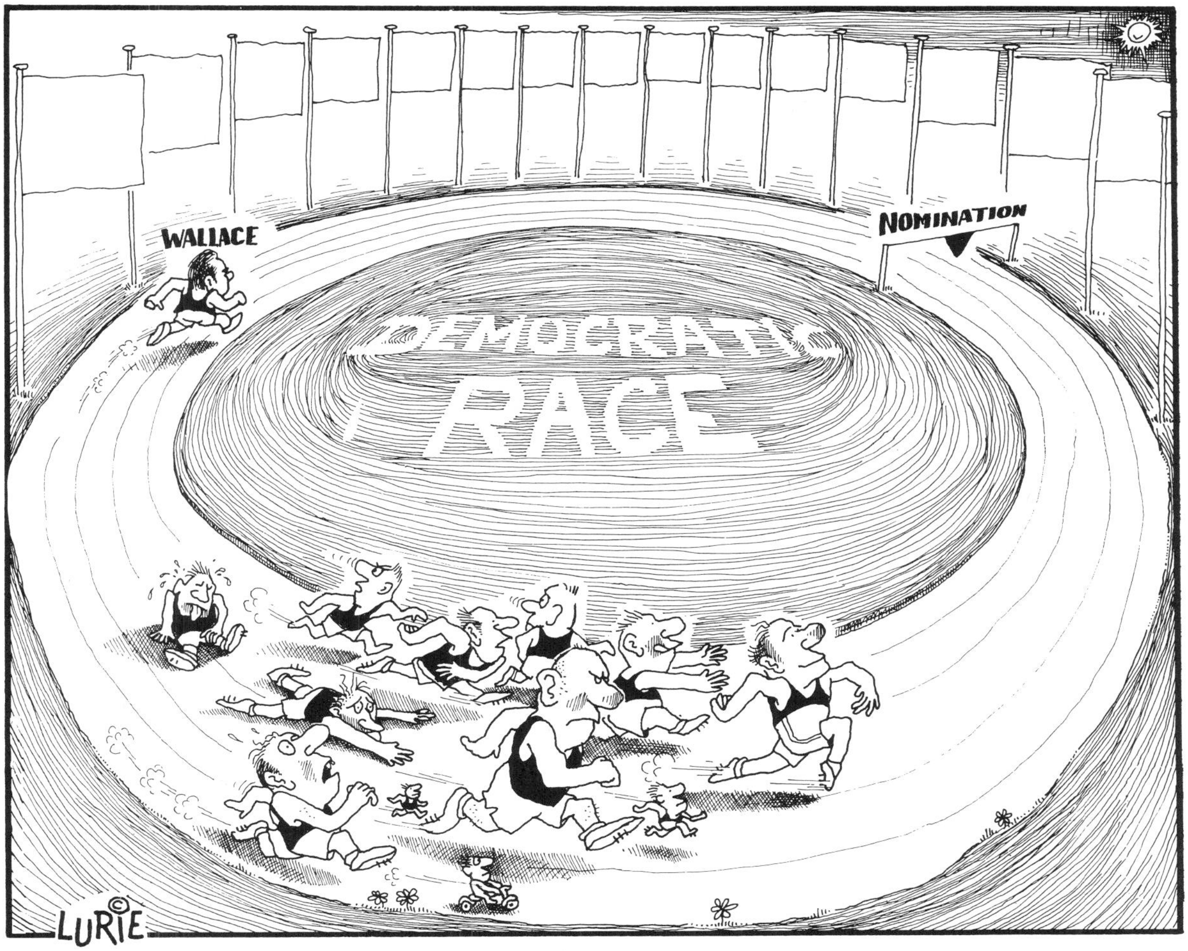
WALLACE
NOMINATION
DEMOCRATIC RACE
LURIE©

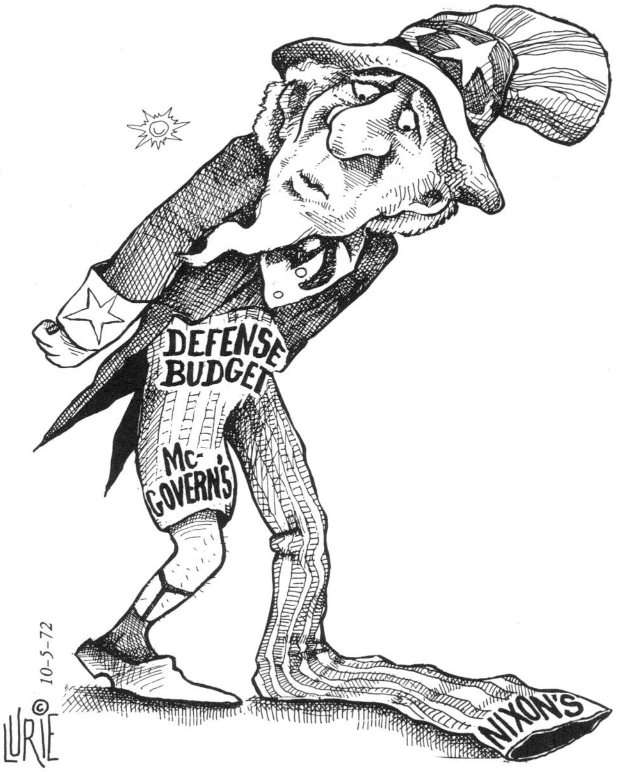
DEFENSE BUDGET
Mc-GOVERN'S
NIXON'S
10-5-72
LURIE©

PLATE 1.

As I was analyzing the racial prejudice of the southern states still fresh with confrontations against the civil rights movements, my eye was attracted to the shape of a horse which those states seem to form on a map. The idea took shape in a short time: I painted that horse lily white, representing the traditional white bias against blacks, and drew George Wallace leading and riding that horse. Then I added to my *Life* cover other politicians that were also catering to the white South in their search for potential votes.

PLATE 2.

The very early seventies also included early flirtations between Russia and China. From a purely geo-political, military standpoint, I believe that perhaps the best thing that happened to the West was the deterioration of relations between the two Communist giants. The real proportions of this blooming animosity and the restraining influence the rift had on Soviet Russia, have not yet been digested and granted the rightful importance they deserve in contemporary history. When I painted this oil-on-canvas cartoon, however, I tried to capture the duplicity of the flirtation between Brezhnev and Mao Tse-tung by emphasizing the steel gun barrels, the predominant consideration in this flirtation, and understating the plastic-looking olive branches.

PLATE 3.

The decade began with a Middle East confrontation that neither Israelis nor Egyptians know how to categorize. Was it a small war or a big lengthy battle? Contemporary historians, in the meantime, have used the expression "war of attrition." Nasser, with the very close aid of Soviet advisors, weapons, and ammunition, was hammering back at the Israelis with whatever he could throw at them in the form of Soviet artillery. For the Soviets it was a great opportunity to re-establish their military presence in the Middle East. The fact that the Israelis were retaliating with their usual devastating efficiency and spreading total destruction on Egyptian canal cities, towns, and refineries did not bother the Russians a bit, and they continued to entice Nasser into suicidal confrontations with the Israelis. This cartoon, done in acrylic, appeared almost simultaneously in *Life* magazine and its French counterpart, *Paris-Match*.

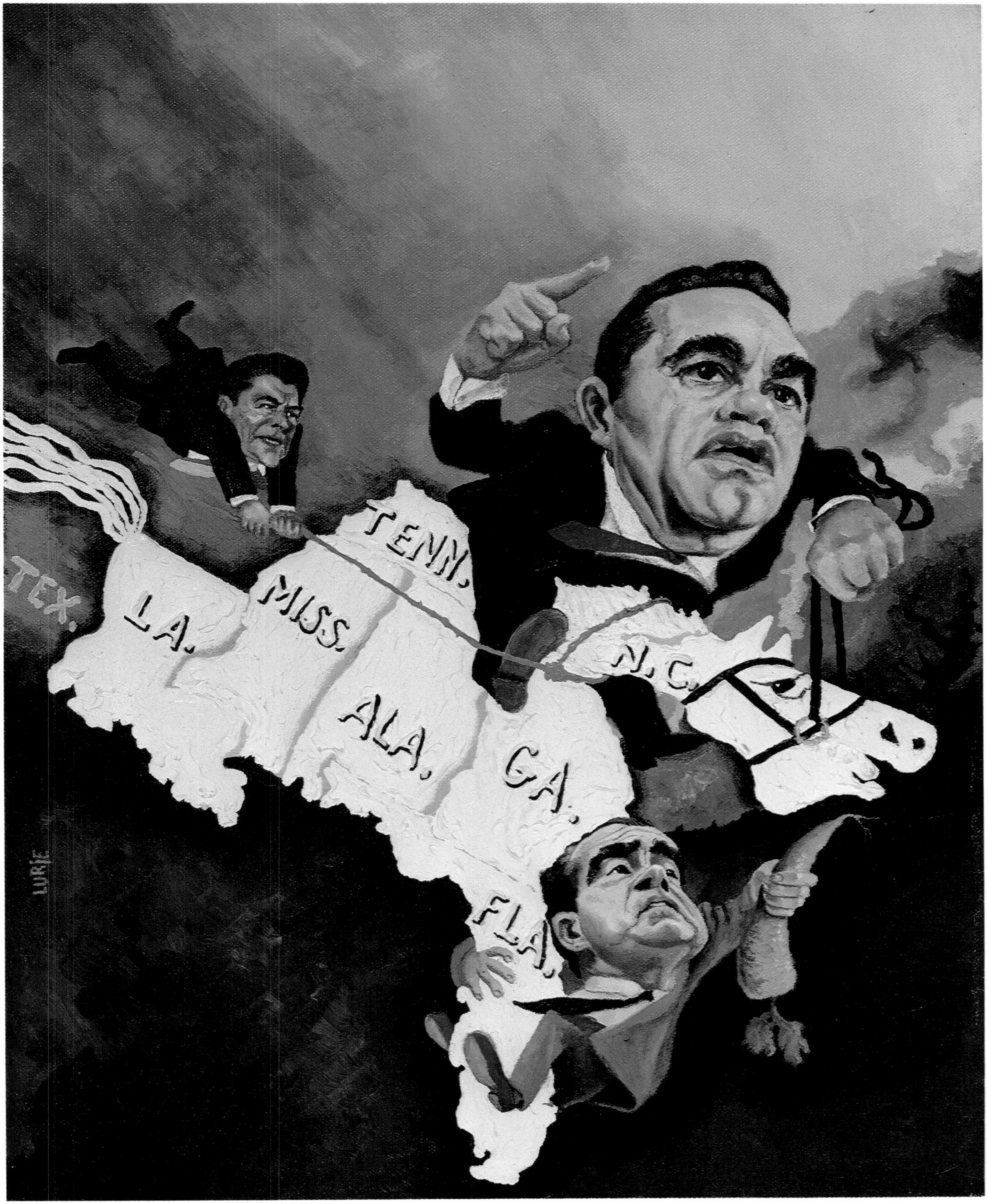
TEX.
LA.
MISS.
TENN.
ALA.
GA.
N.C.
FLA.
LURIE

PLATE 1.

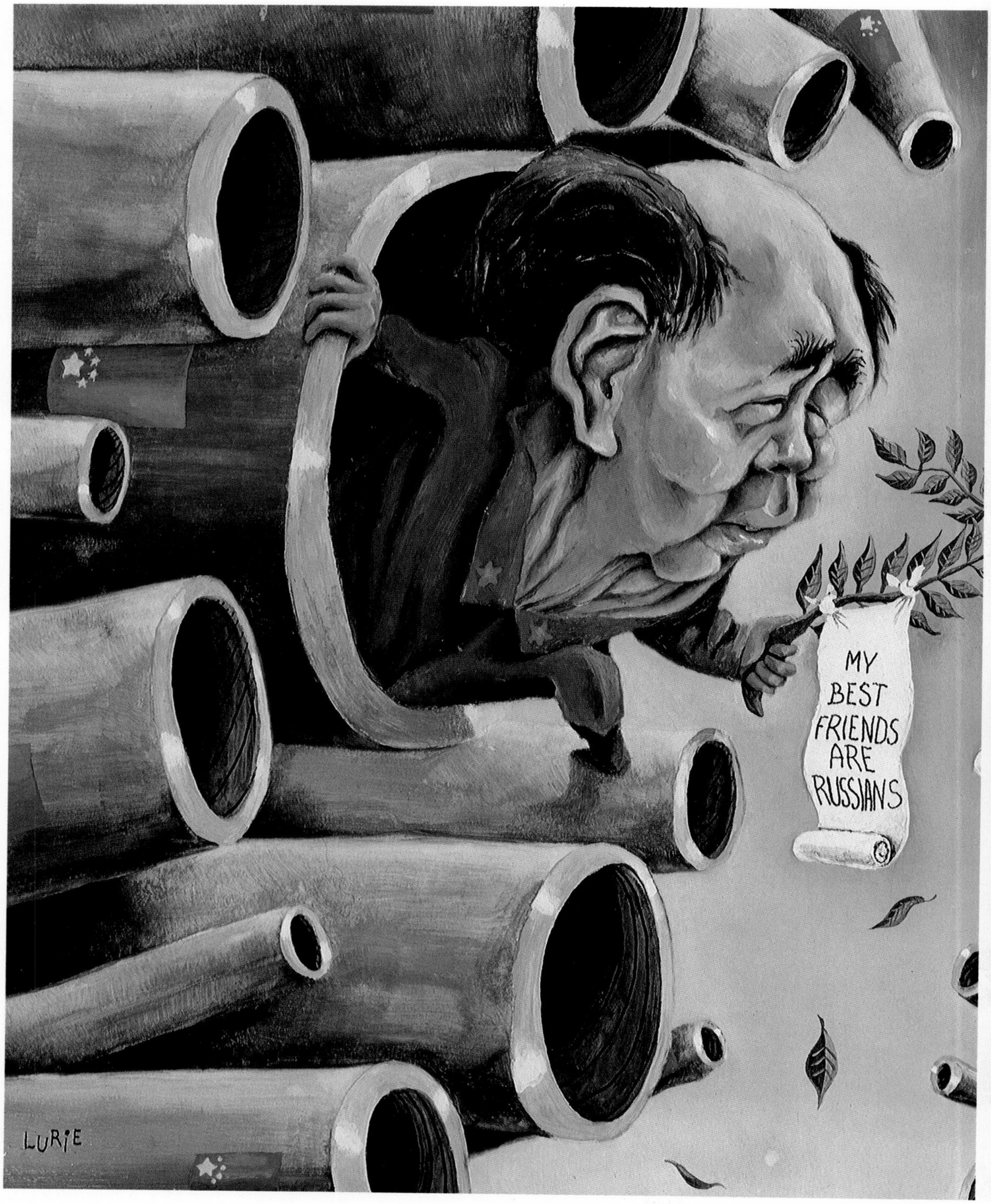
MY BEST FRIENDS ARE RUSSIANS
LURIE

PLATE 2.

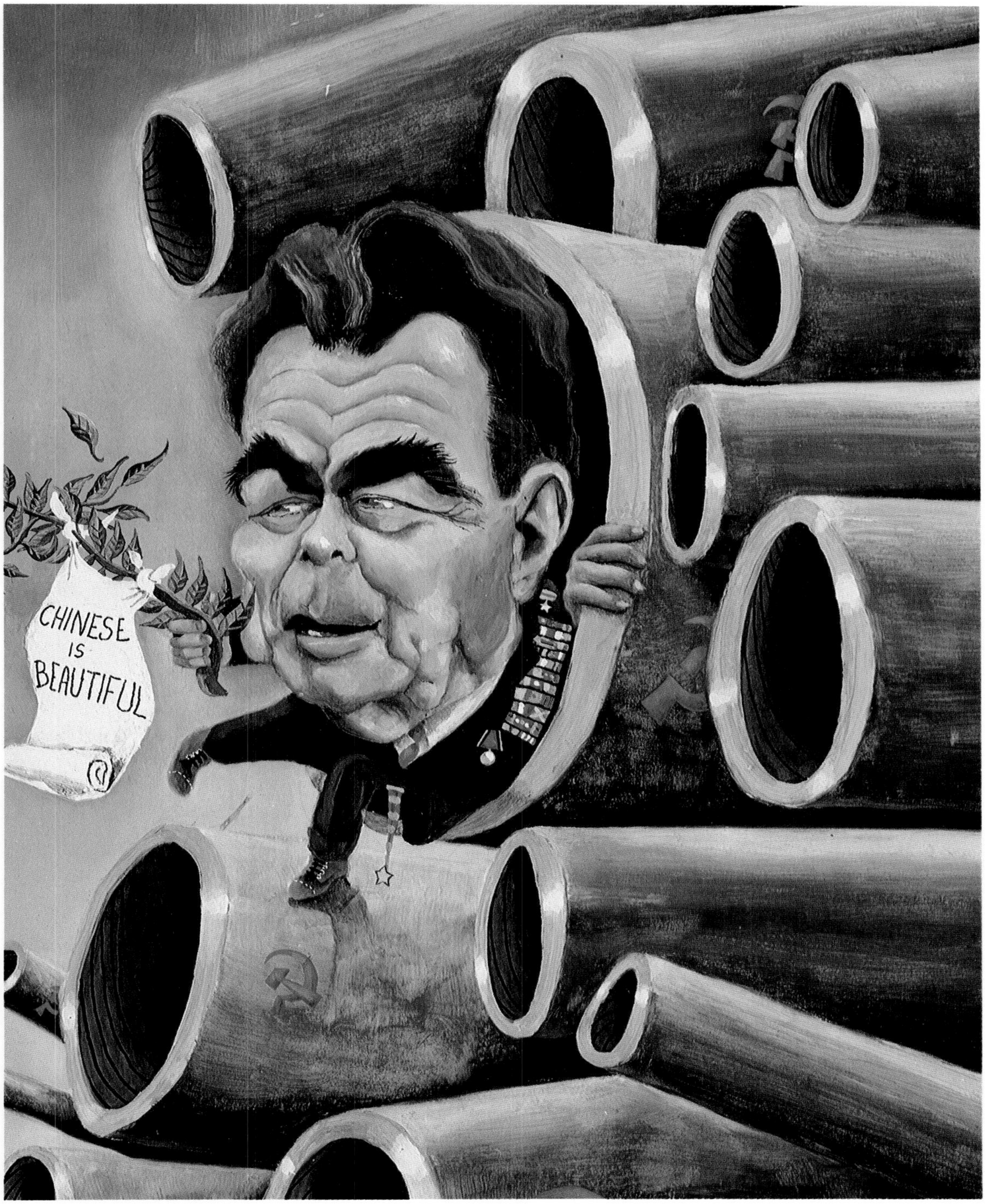
CHINESE
IS
BEAUTIFUL

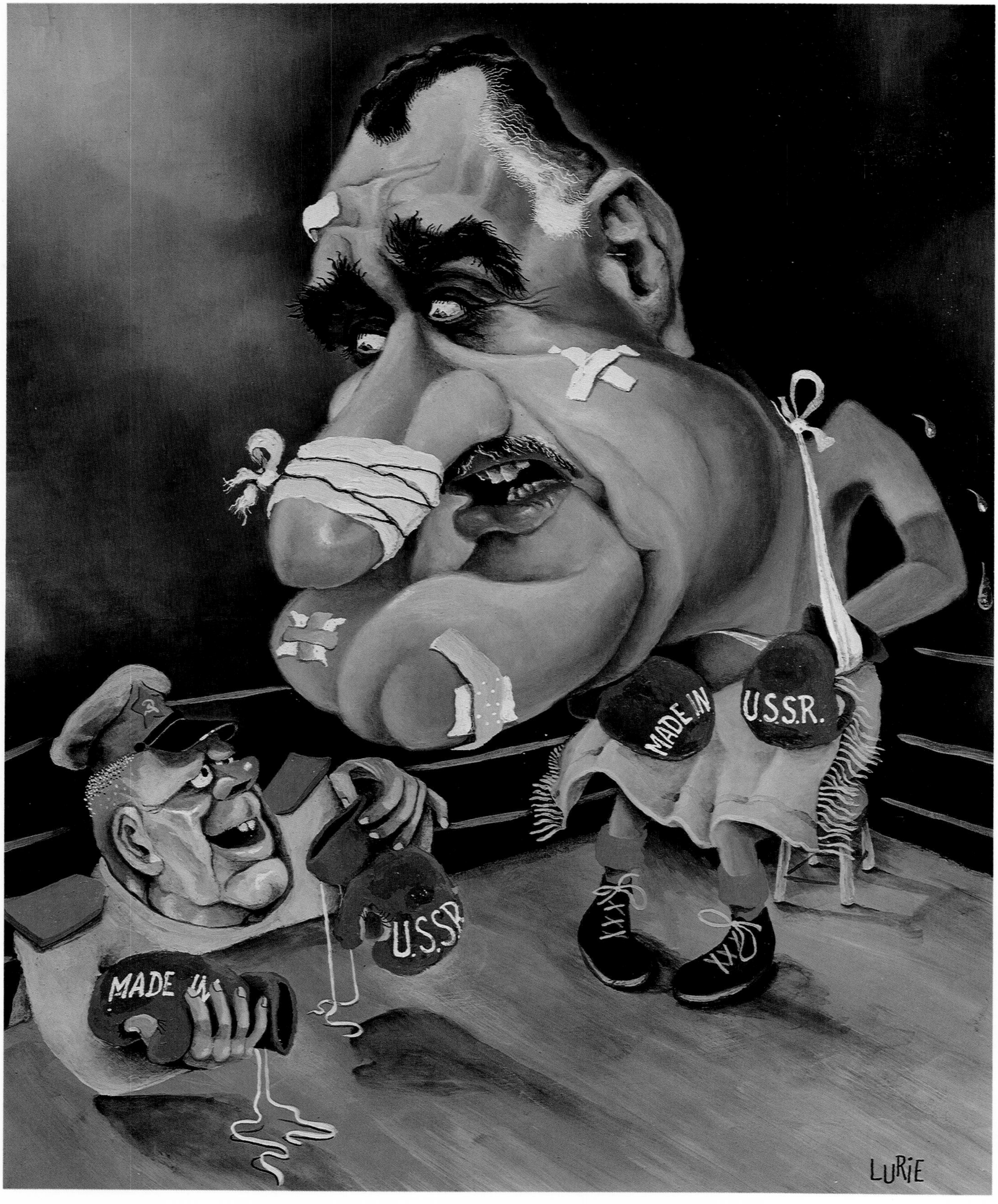
MADE IN
U.S.S.R.
U.S.S.R.
MADE IN
LURIE

PLATE 3.

UNITED STATES OF AMERICA
KISSINGER
LURIE

MAESTRO IS BACK!

TET OFFENSIVE
SLEEPING PILLS
LURIE

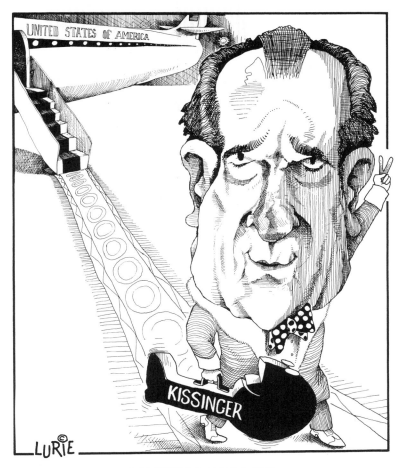

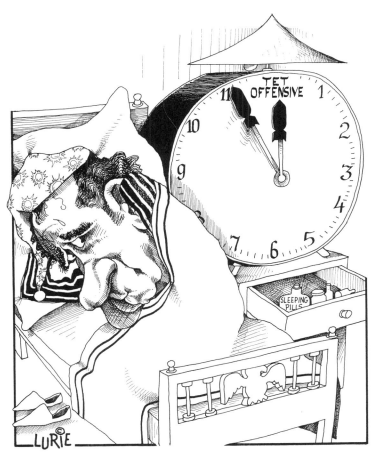

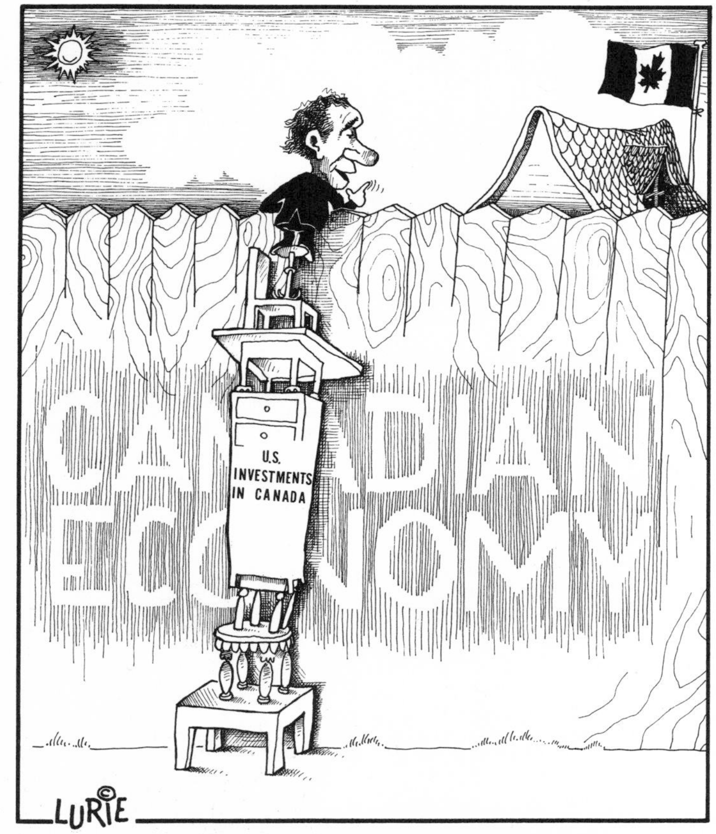
CANADIAN
ECONOMY
U.S.
INVESTMENTS
IN CANADA
LURIE

''FOR PRIVACY, TRUDEAU,
YOU'LL NEED A HIGHER FENCE''

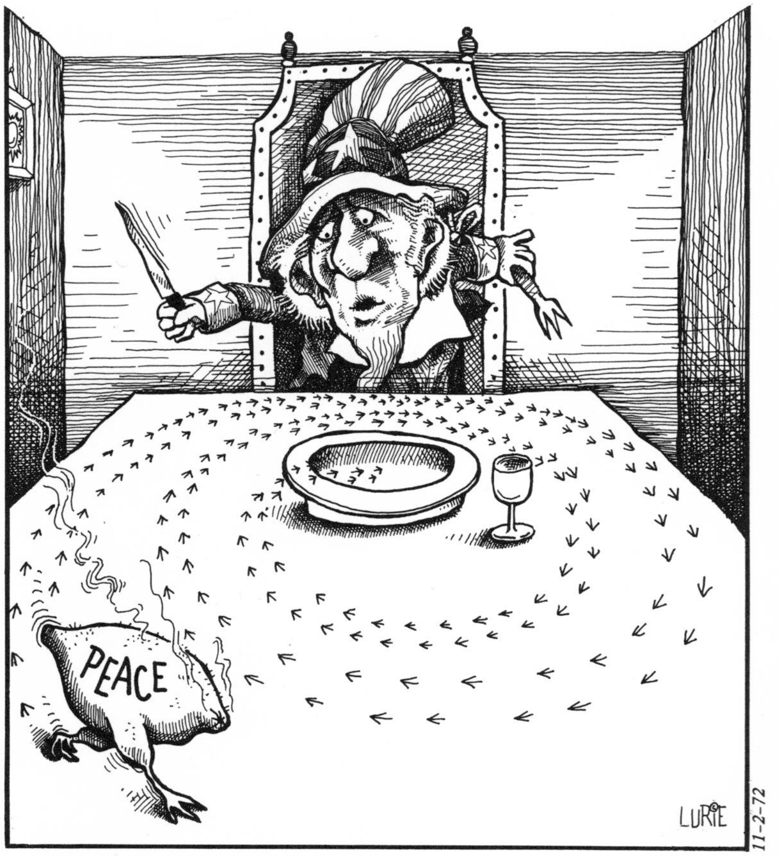
PEACE
LURIE
11-2-72

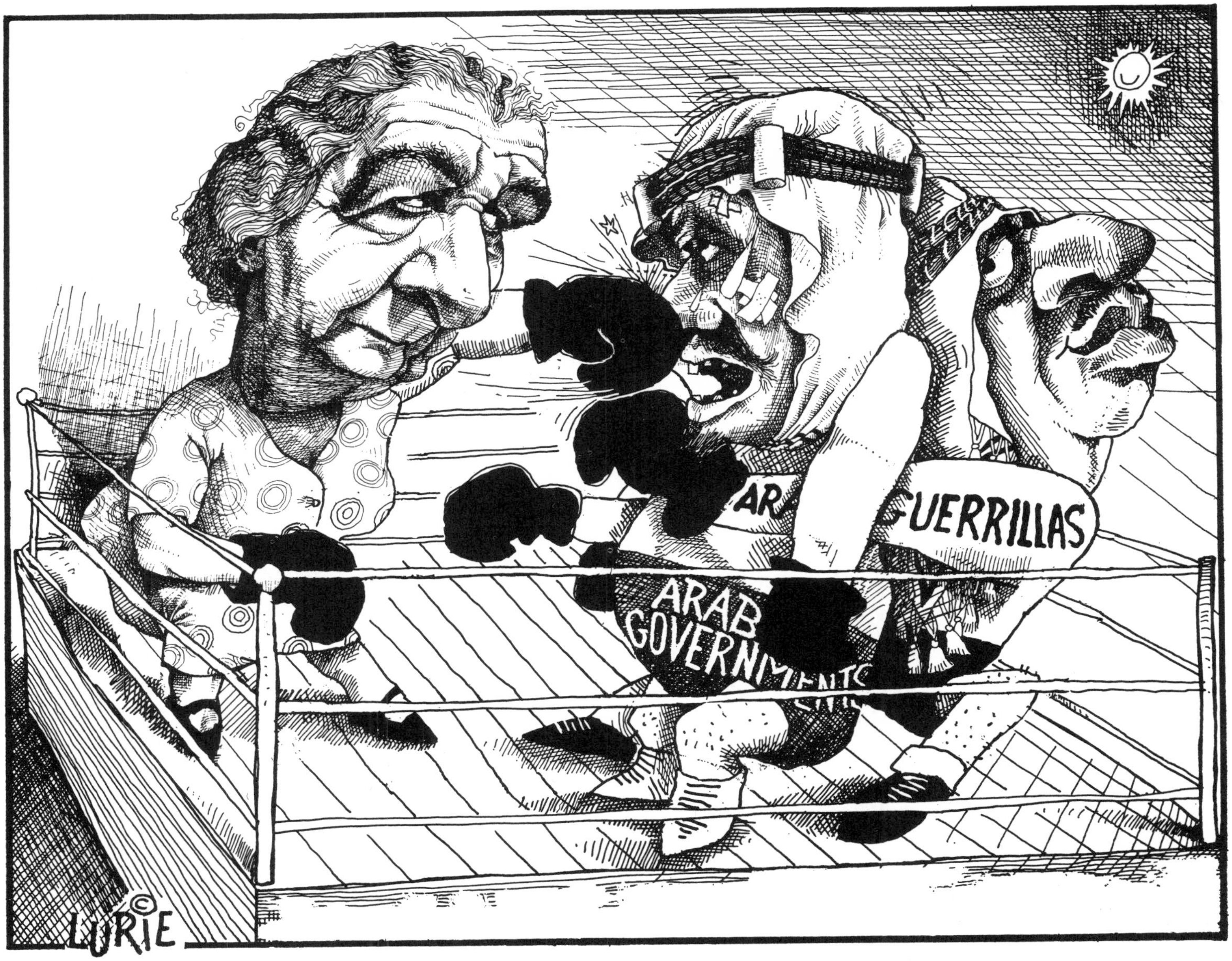
ARA
GUERRILLAS
ARAB GOVERNMENTS
LURIE ©

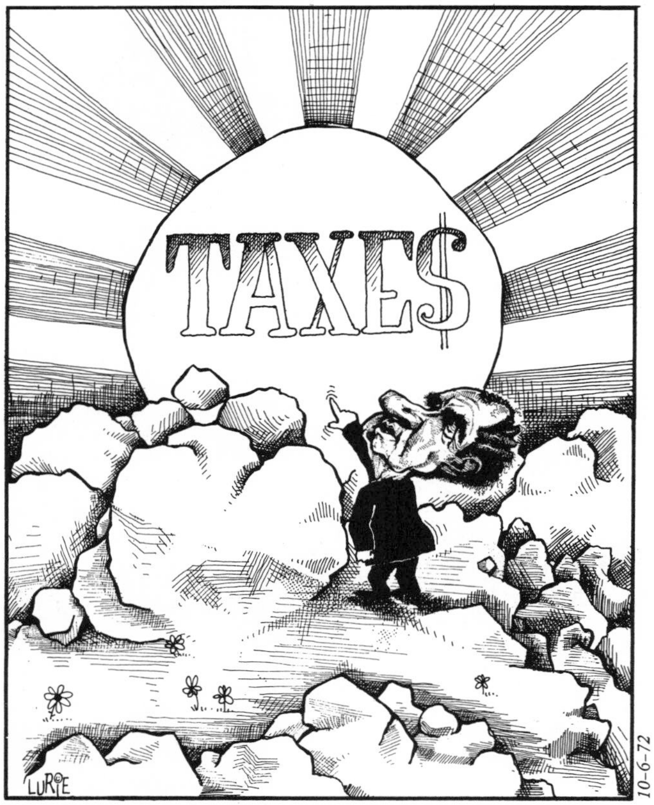
TAXE$
LURIE
10-6-72

"I COMMAND YOU NOT TO RISE!"

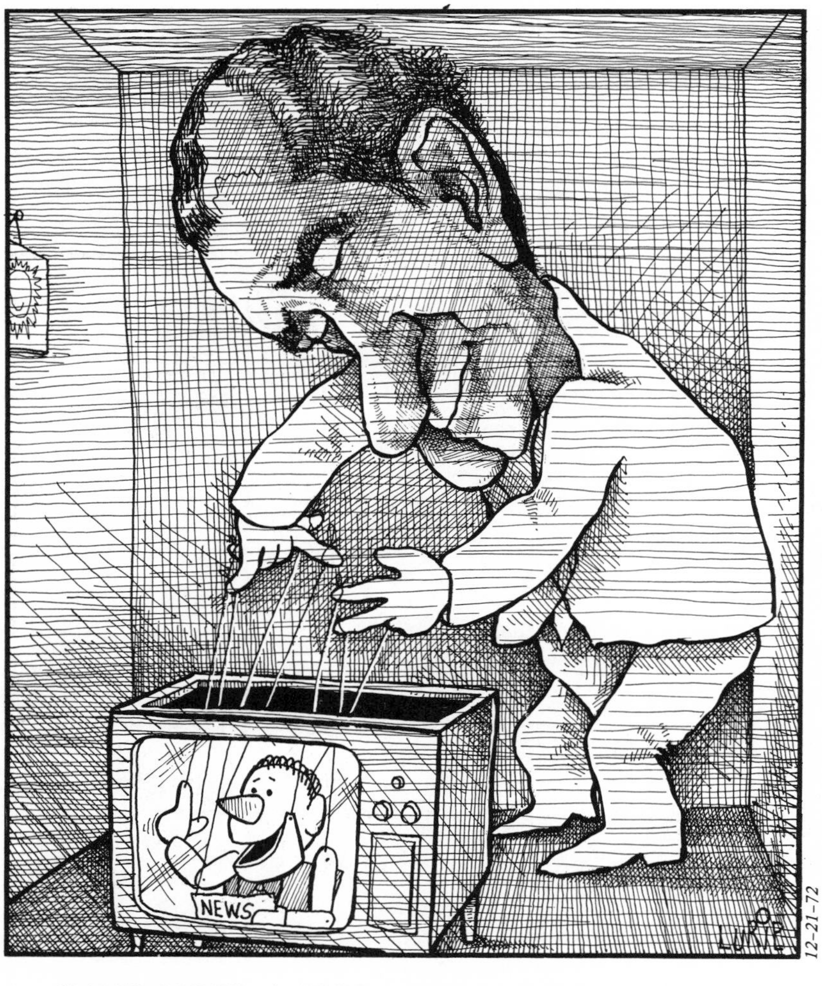
NEWS
LURIE
12-21-72

"AND NOW, A WORD FROM OUR SPONSOR"

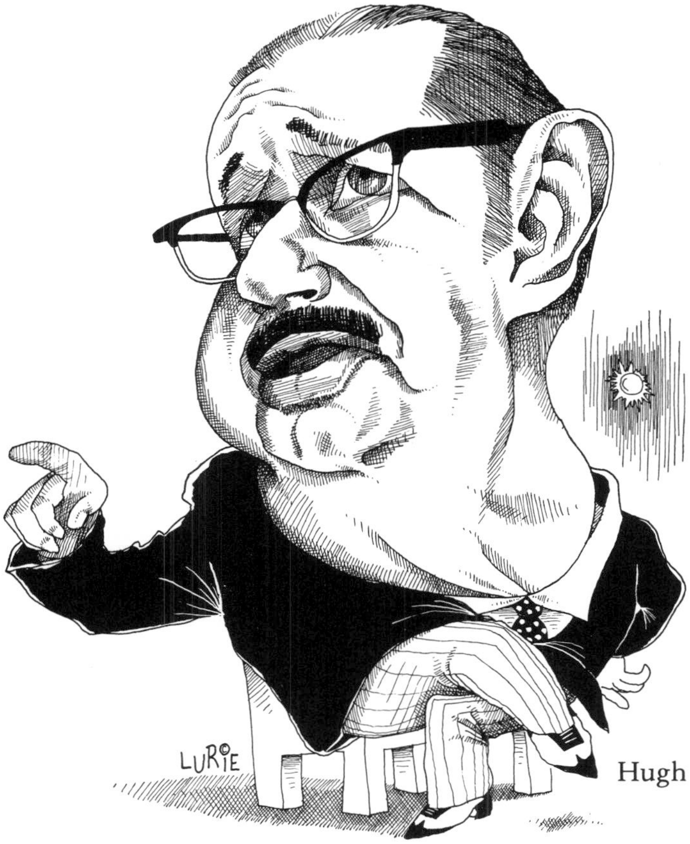
LURIE

Hugh Scott

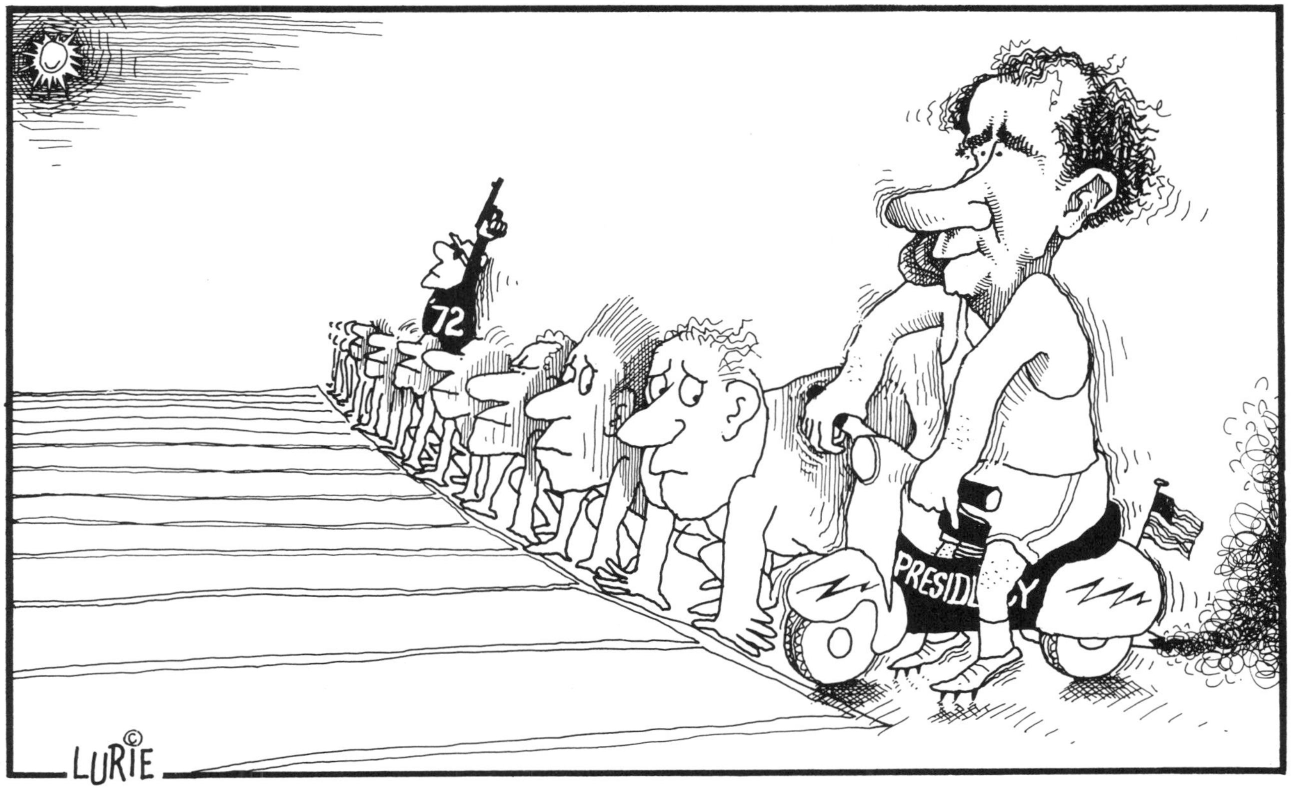
72
PRESIDENCY
LURIE ©

Life

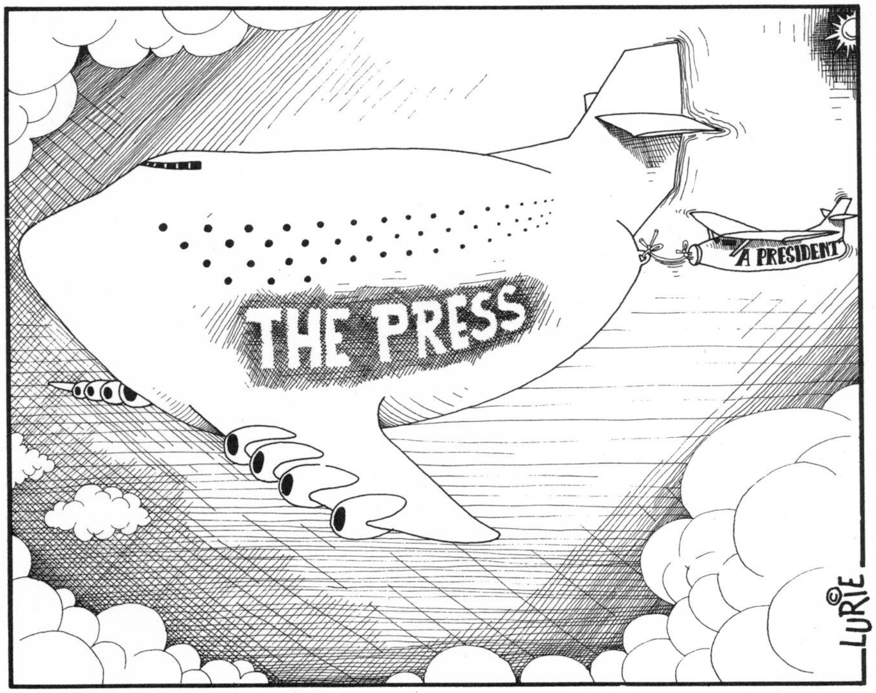
THE PRESS
A PRESIDENT
LURIE

CHINA HERE WE COME

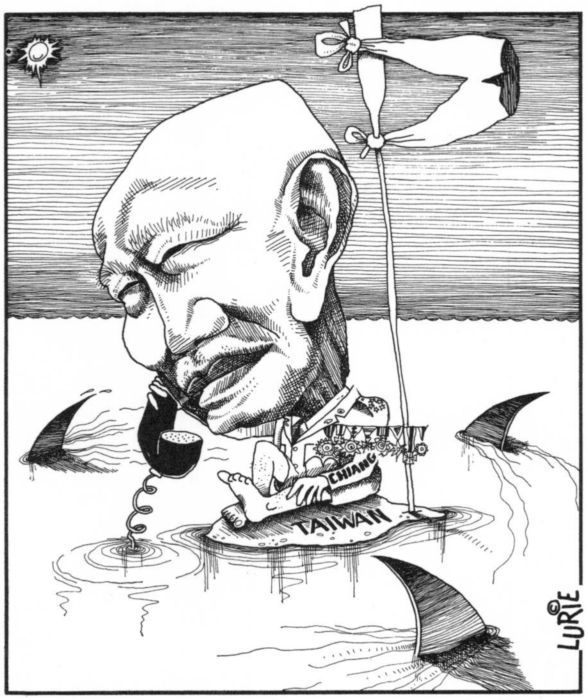
CHIANG
TAIWAN
LURIE

"CONGRATULATIONS—YOU WERE ELECTED TO STAY IN POWER"

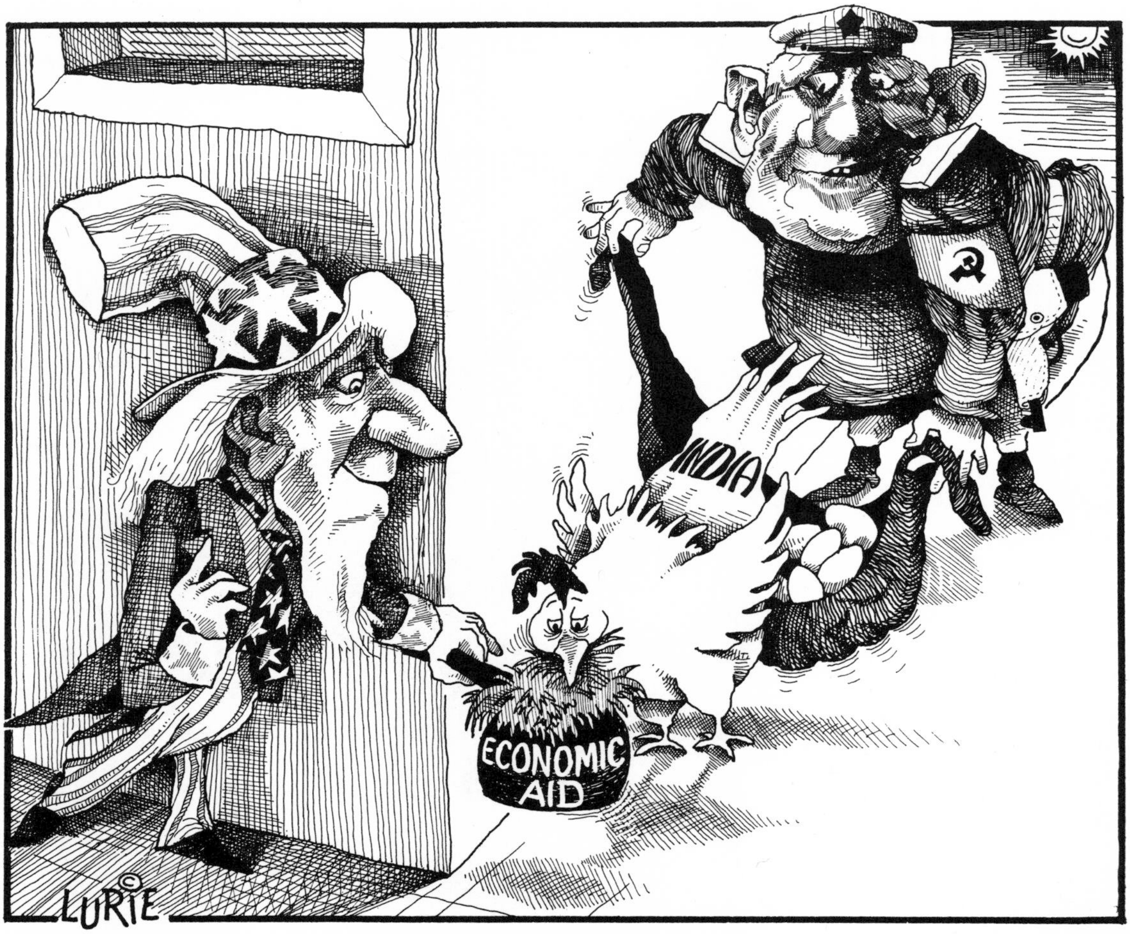
INDIA
ECONOMIC AID
LURIE

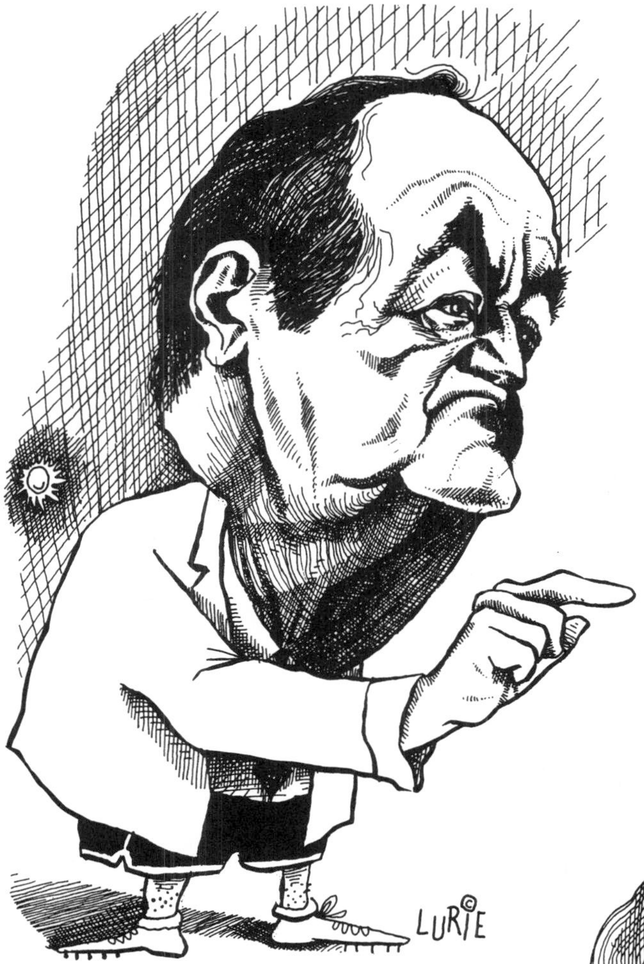
LURIE

Hubert H. Humphrey

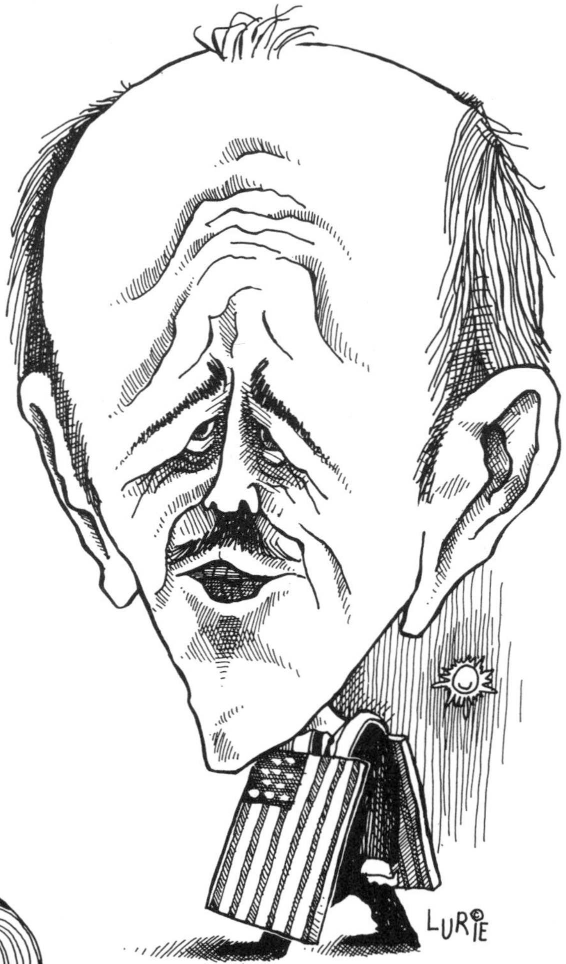
LURIE

John Schmitz
American Party Nominee

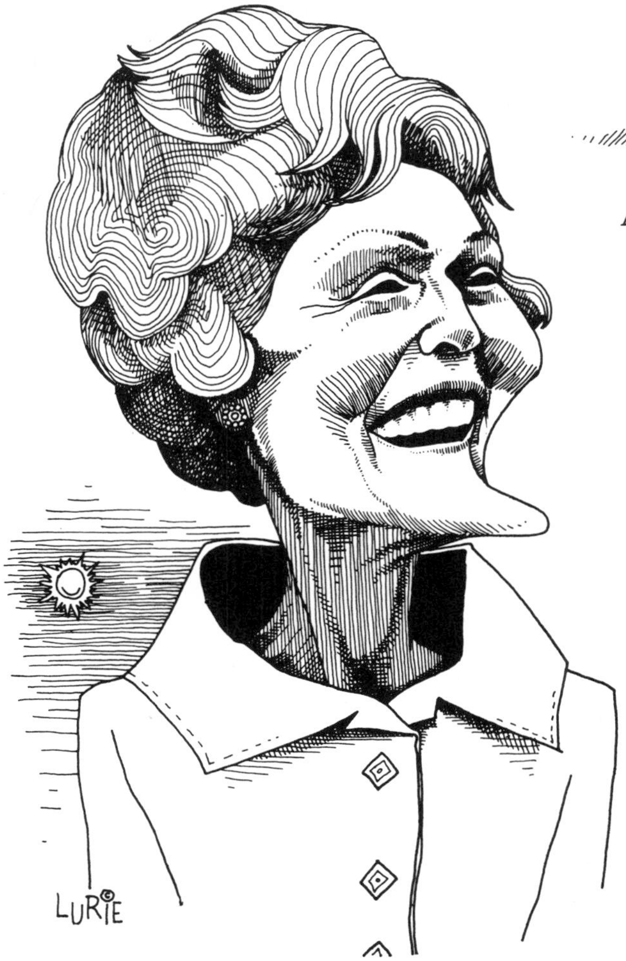
LURIE

Pat

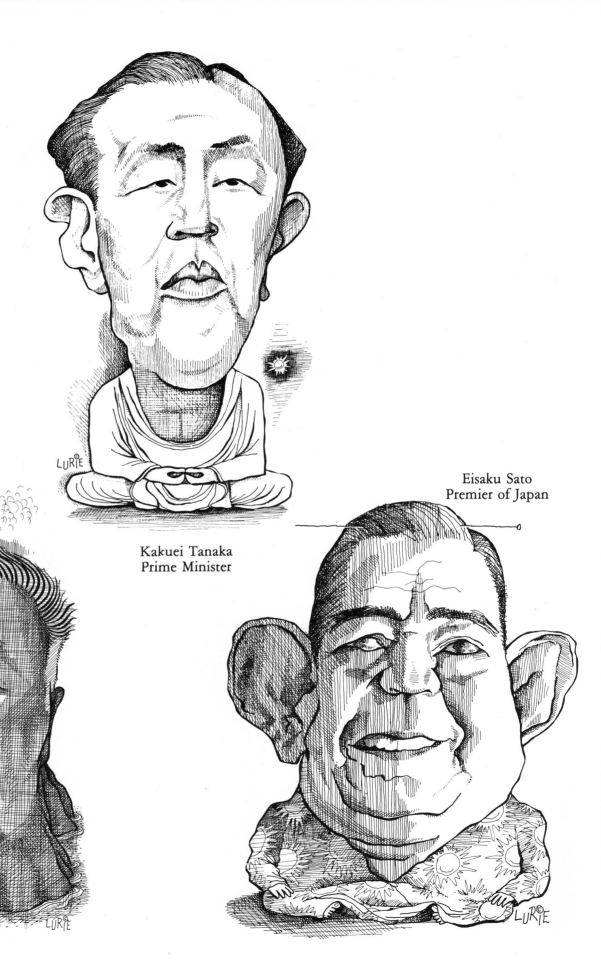

Masayoshi Ohira
Foreign Minister

Kakuei Tanaka
Prime Minister

Eisaku Sato
Premier of Japan

60

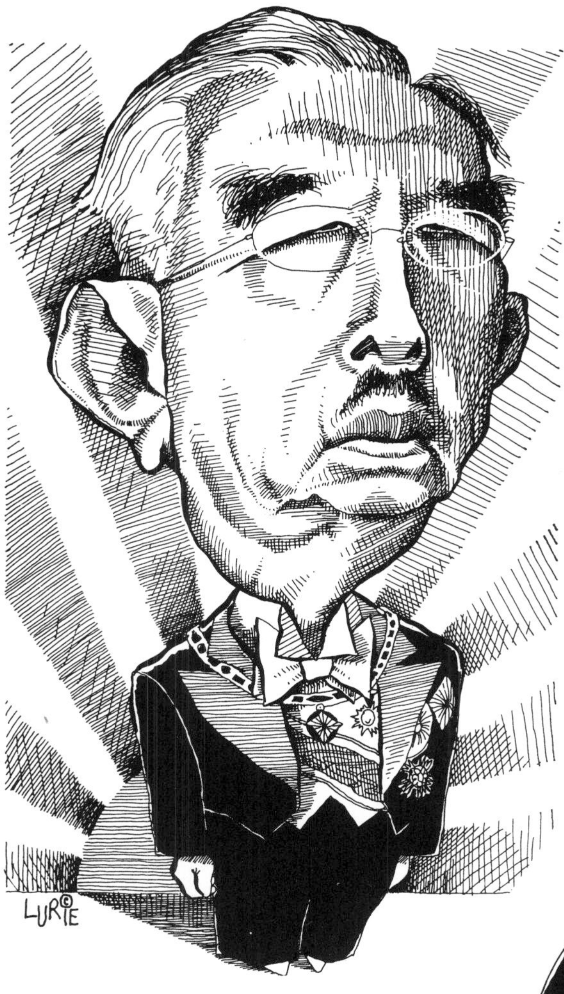
LURIE

Emperor Hirohito

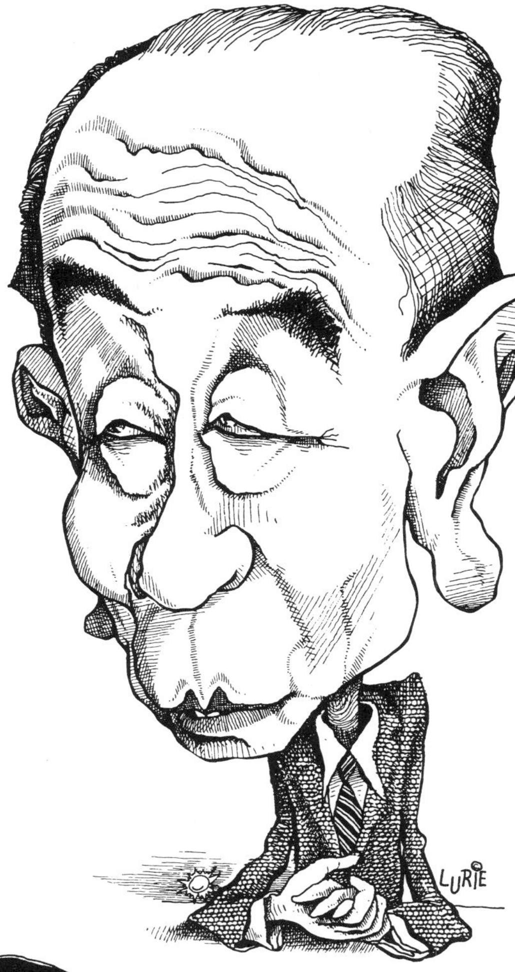
LURIE

Takeo Fukuda

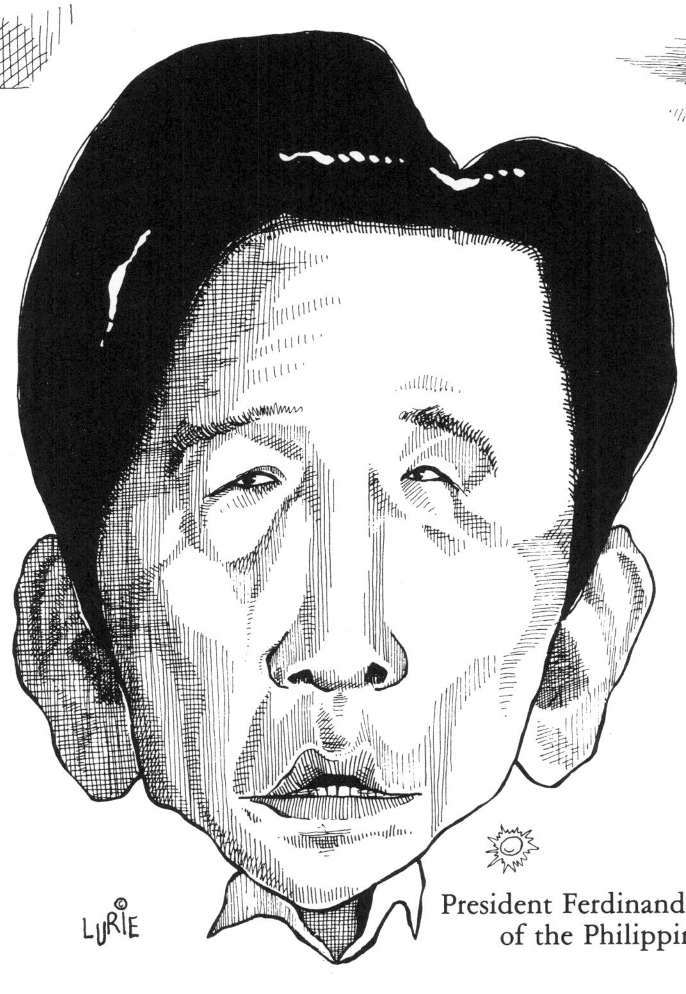
LURIE

President Ferdinand Marcos
of the Philippines

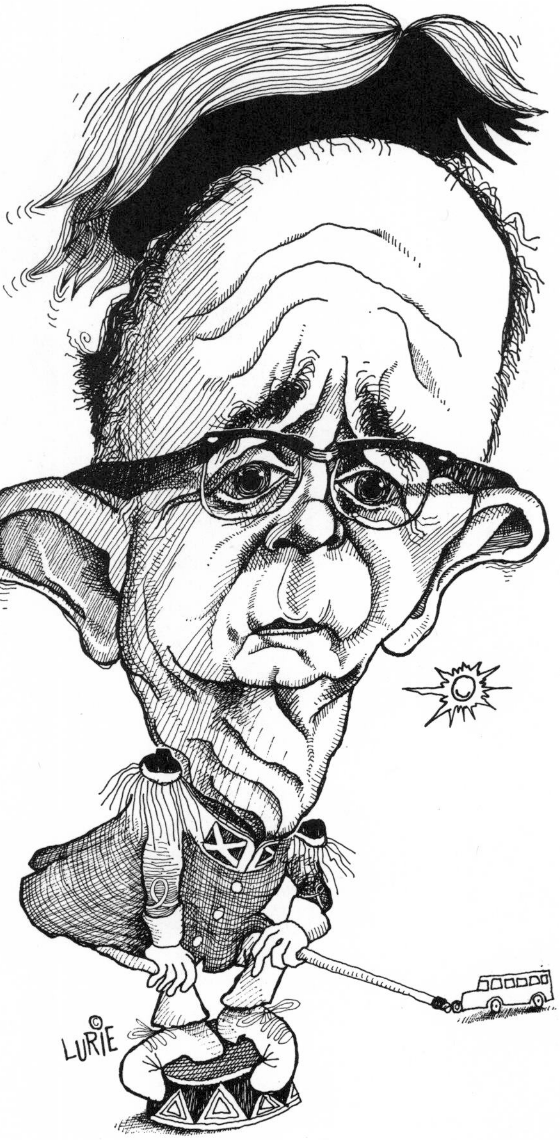
LURIE

Maddox

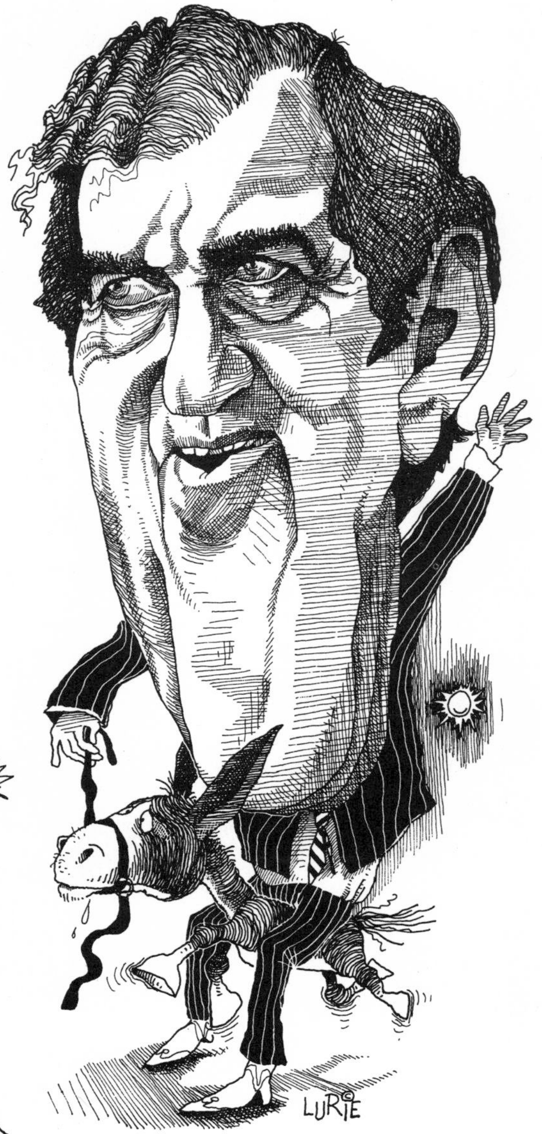
LURIE

Muskie

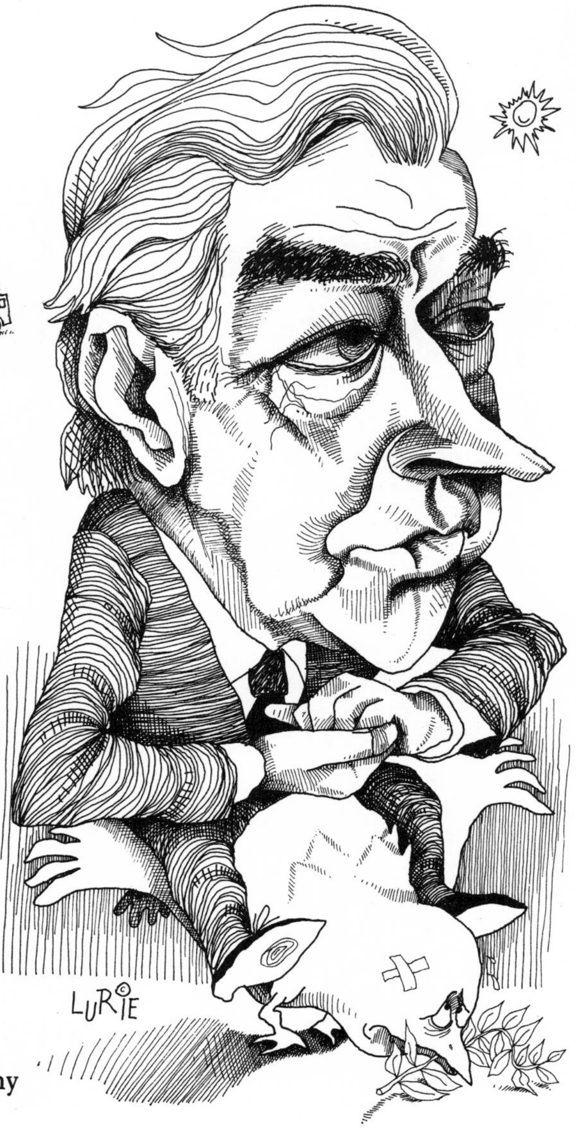
LURIE

McCarthy

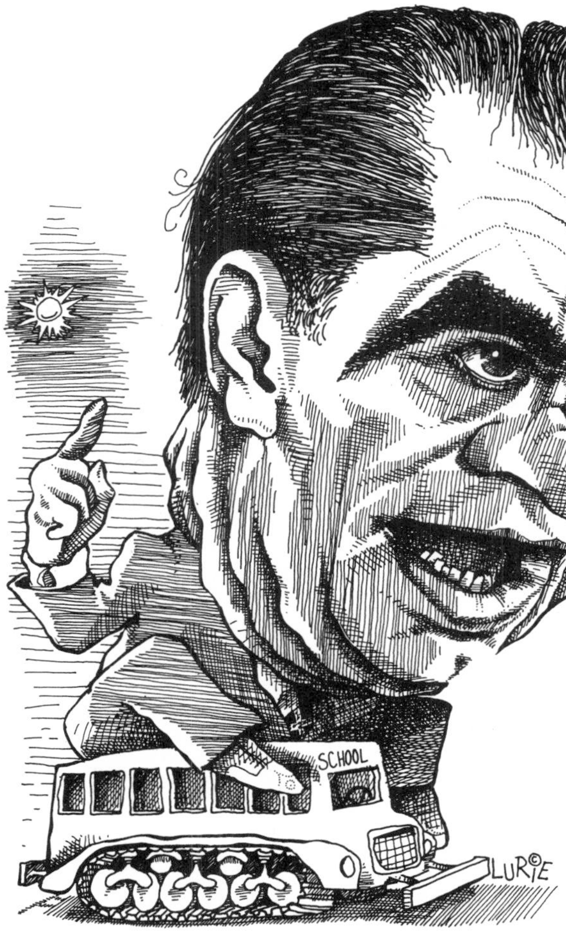
SCHOOL
LURIE

Governor George Wallace

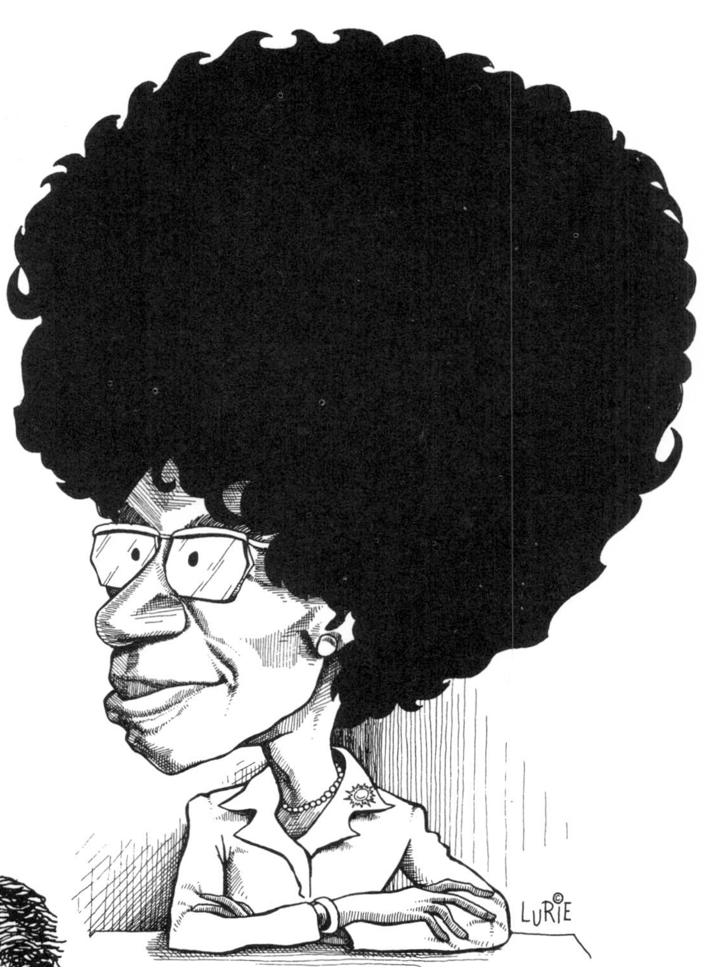
LURIE

Shirley Chisholm

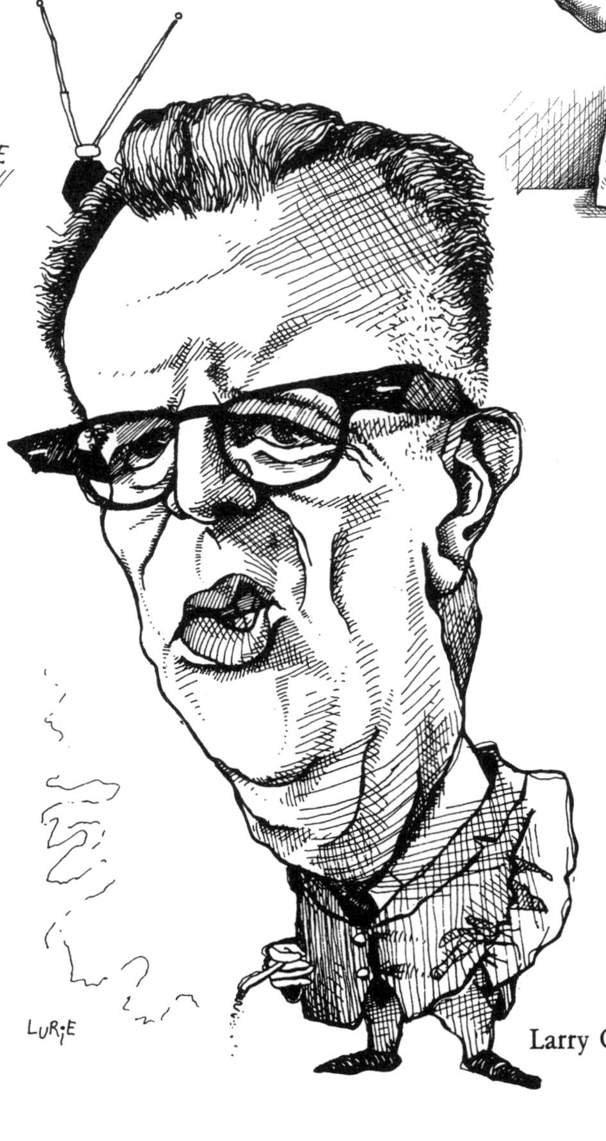
LURIE

Larry O'Brien

PAKISTAN
LURIE

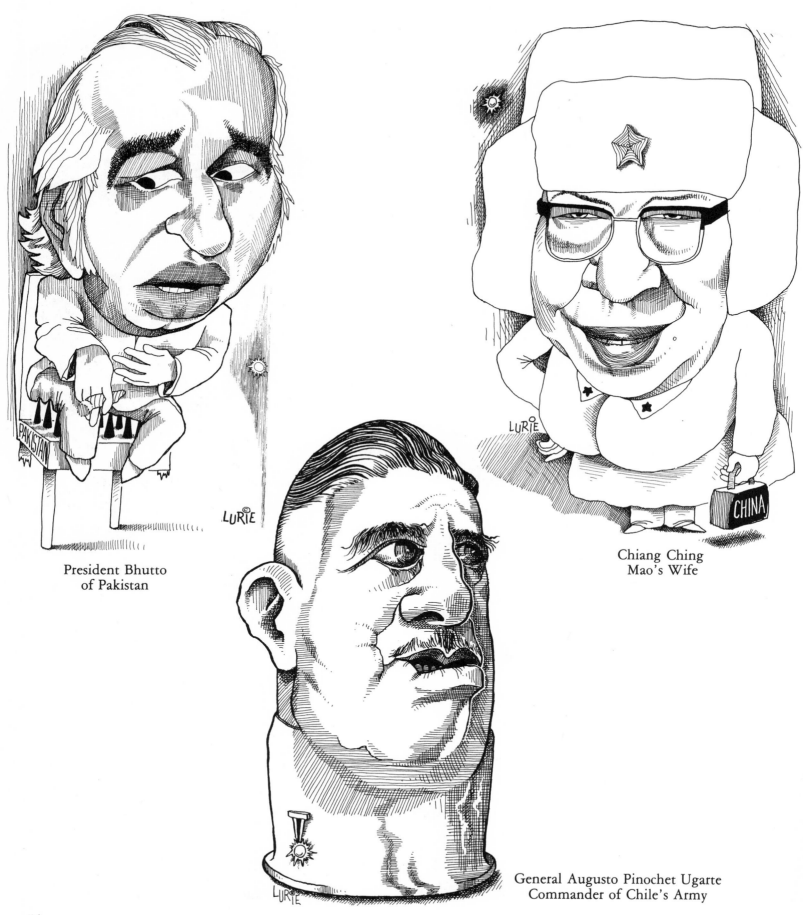

President Bhutto
of Pakistan

LURIE
CHINA

Chiang Ching
Mao's Wife

LURIE

General Augusto Pinochet Ugarte
Commander of Chile's Army

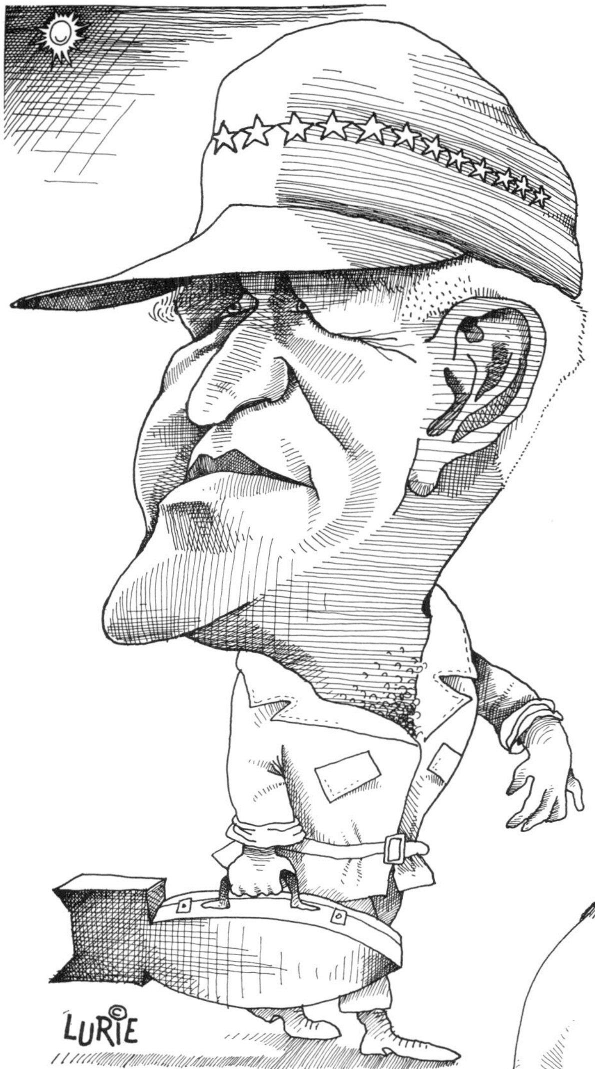
LURIE

General Creighton W. Abrams, Jr.

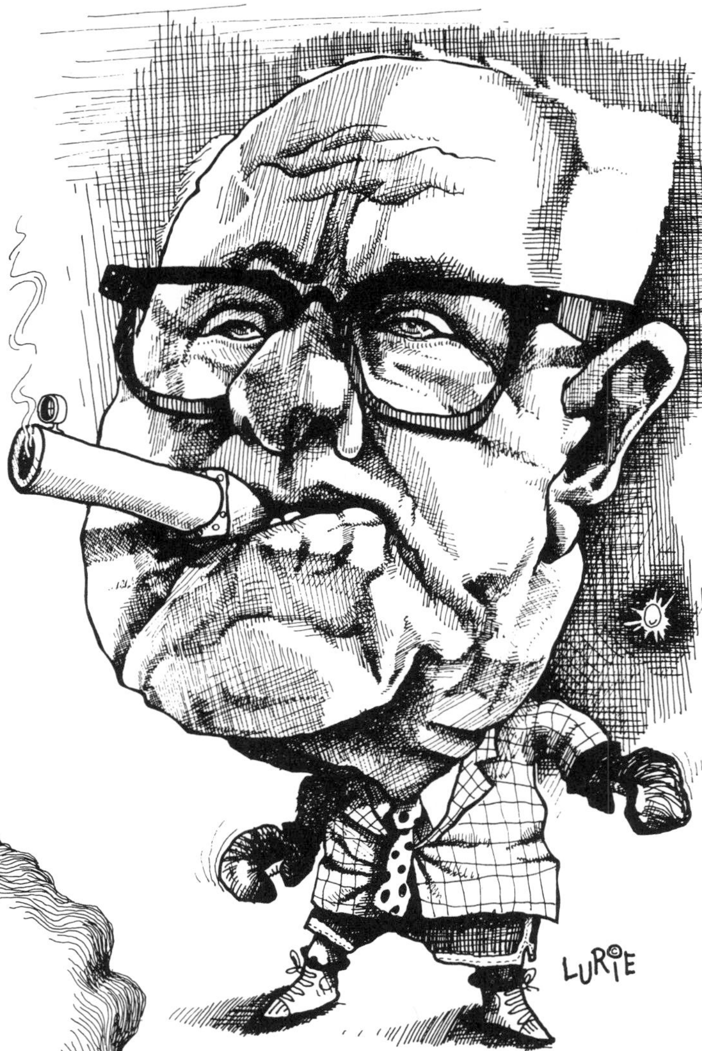
LURIE

George Meany

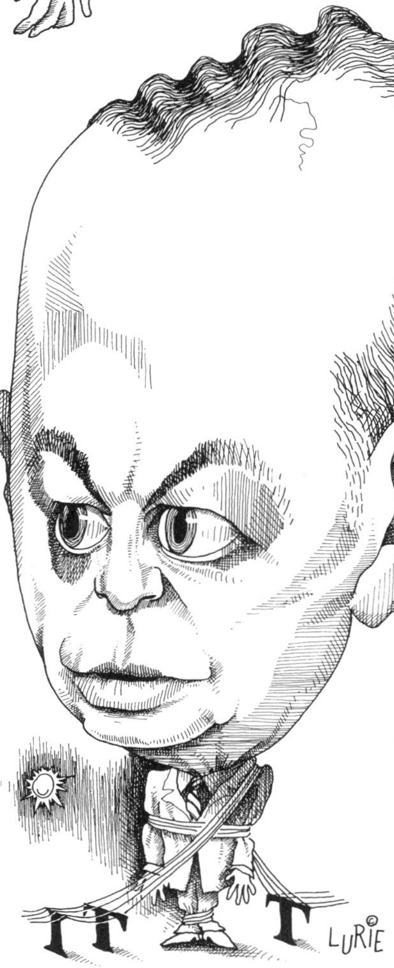
ITT
LURIE

Richard Kleindienst

1973

Lurie: ON GOLDA MEIR

"The wisdom and perception I see in your cartoons, Ranan, seem the natural result of accumulation of knowledge that was passed from generation to generation, for the last thousand years, in your family.

"Your family has produced some of the greatest thinkers and scholars of Judaism. They, however, did it in writing—and you do it in drawing."

Golda Meir
(when Prime Minister of Israel)

Golda Meir reminded me of a friend I had who decided to start dieting. The end result was that my friend ate everything that all of us ate but added a few pieces of cabbage. When she took office her personality and the fact that she was a woman impressed everyone so much that society treated her without any kind of discrimination. She had all of the qualities of a good leader, male or female. She was better than her male contemporaries because, in addition to the qualities they all share, she had that female intuition that gives great women the added dimension that some male leaders lack.

She was a closed person. I feel you could not penetrate the layers and layers of preconceived ideas. She followed a plastic route. She simply knew only the highways of her thoughts; she never knew how to take a short cut.

Golda Meir was convinced that the Jewish people are different from other nations simply because they survived the impositions and the cruelties that other nations have inflicted on the Jewish people for 2,000 years. She could not adapt to the new situation of a young, free, strong, independent Israel which now had a lot of say in Middle Eastern affairs. She did not know the art of manipulation and how to adjust to new circumstances, both especially important in the Mideast.

Once I was invited by then Secretary of State Rogers to come to his headquarters in the State Department in Washington. His spokesman, McClusky, wrote me a letter saying that the Secretary saw some new ideas reflected in my cartoons and would like to analyze them with me. I had a two-hour meeting with the Secretary, and he brought up some very interesting complaints about the methods used by some Israeli diplomats that he found troubling. He asked

my opinion about the matter. A short time later I visited Israel and Golda Meir, who knew about my meeting with Secretary Rogers. Her big black 1961 Dodge arrived to pick me up at my hotel and take me to Jerusalem. She was waiting for me and we sat for a whole hour. During that hour I delivered the exact wording and my interpretations of what the Secretary of State had said. She listened very closely, examining me very carefully—and I can vouch that that woman knew how to listen. When you talked to her, she looked at you as if inviting more and more information. Eventually you felt—at least I felt—completely drained, without her ever having to question or press. The very atmosphere of her personality, her charm, and her politeness and firmness simply invited every bit of information that I could give her.

Even after about 40 or 45 minutes of my talking, she continued to stare at me. I took the initiative and said, "Mrs. Golda Meir, I gave you everything that I have here." I knew that Rogers wanted me to deliver that information to her, and I'm sure he told it to me simply because I was an unofficial go-between. I said to her, "We have a point or two or three of Rogers that does make sense. What is your opinion about it?" She looked at me and said, "Ranan, you are still young. You are a different kind of Jew. You are a several-generation Israeli. You don't know these people. Rogers is a natural anti-Semite. Whatever he says, whatever he thinks, came out of his tradition, his background, and his natural inbred dislike for Jews. That is the way we should treat his comments and analysis." And those were her final words about the concepts that Rogers was concerned about. I sensed a hermetically closed door. She then switched to more personal subjects and the tone changed completely.

NORTH VIETNAM

SOUTH VIETNAM

THIEU

LURIE

1-18-73

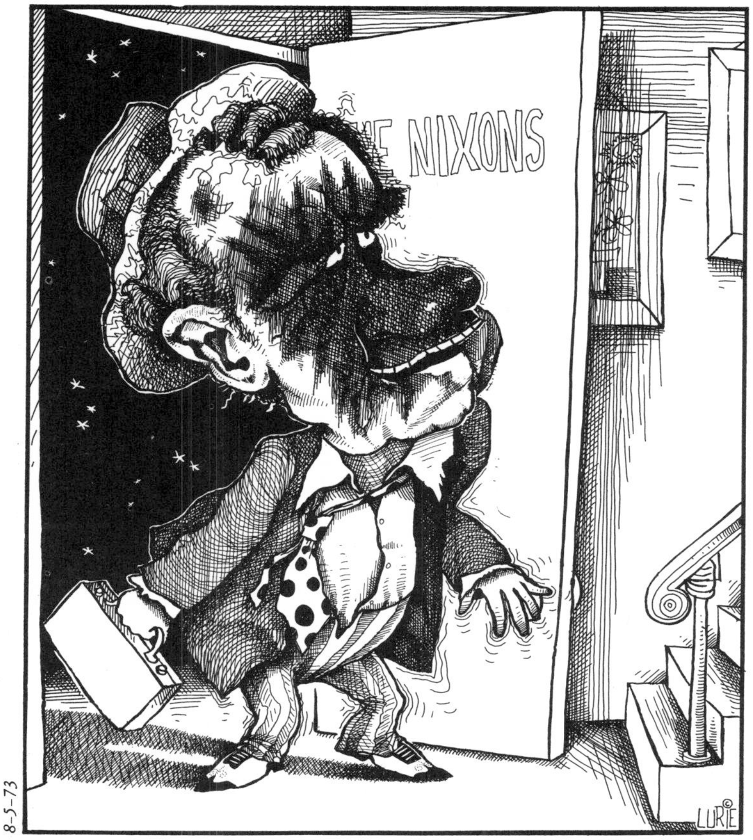
NIXONS
8-5-73
LURIE

"YOO HOO PAT—HAD A GOOD DAY IN OFFICE—LOST ONLY CAMBODIA!"

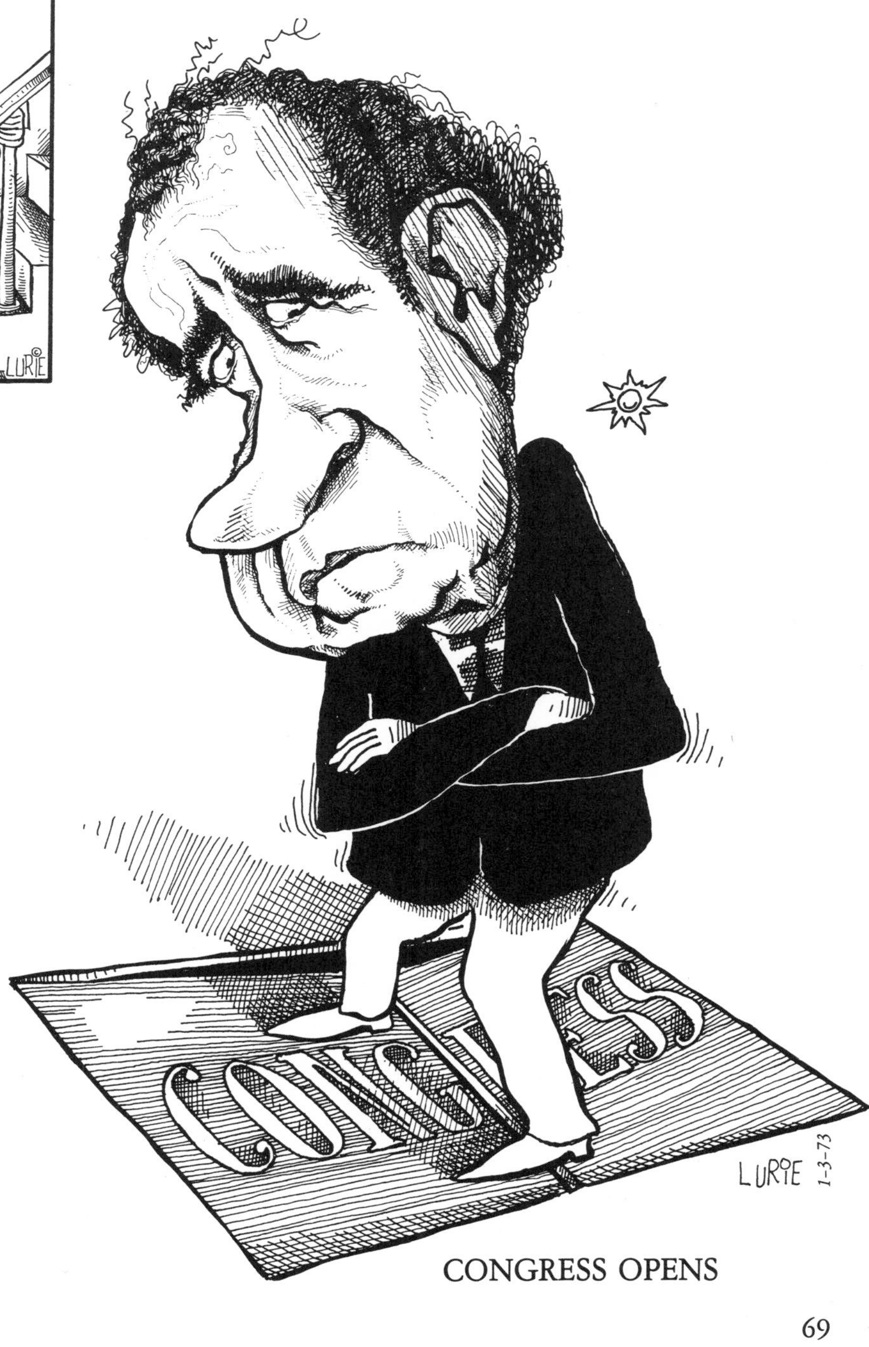
LURIE
1-3-73

CONGRESS OPENS

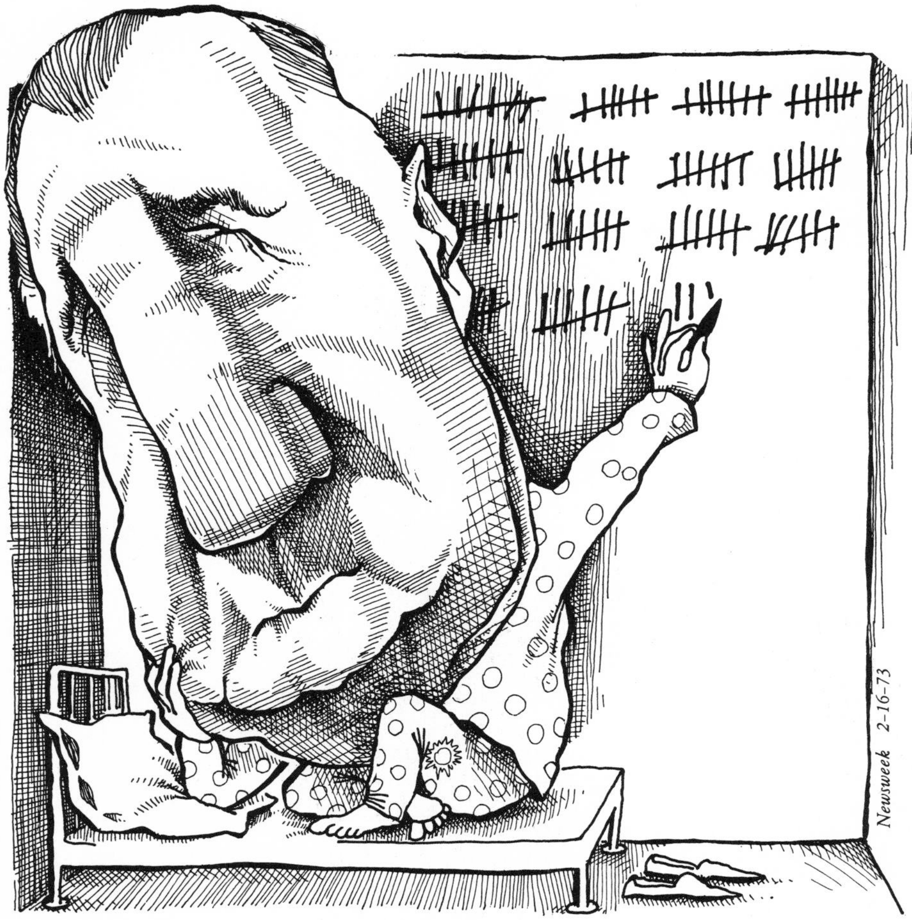
Newsweek 2-16-73

FOUR MORE YEARS

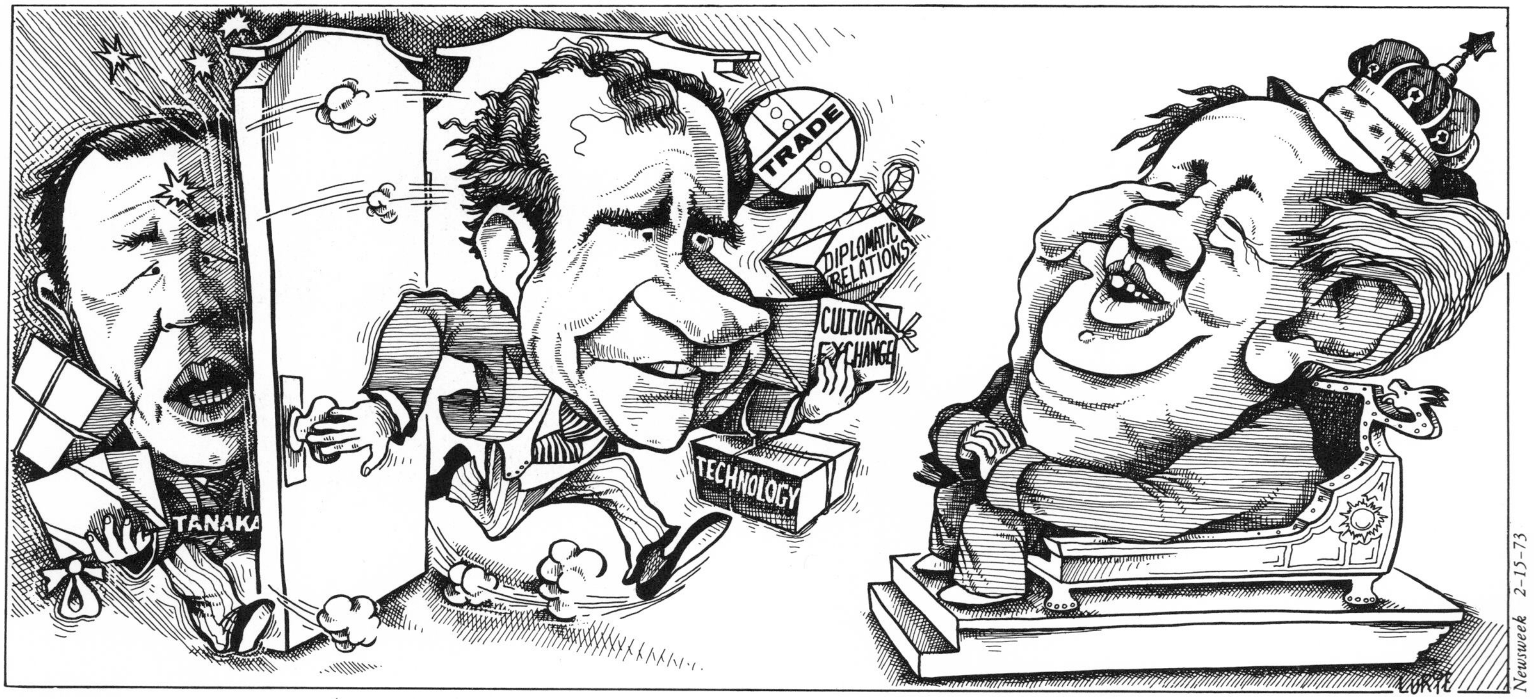
TANAKA
TRADE
DIPLOMATIC RELATIONS
CULTURAL EXCHANGE
TECHNOLOGY
LURIE
Newsweek 2-15-73

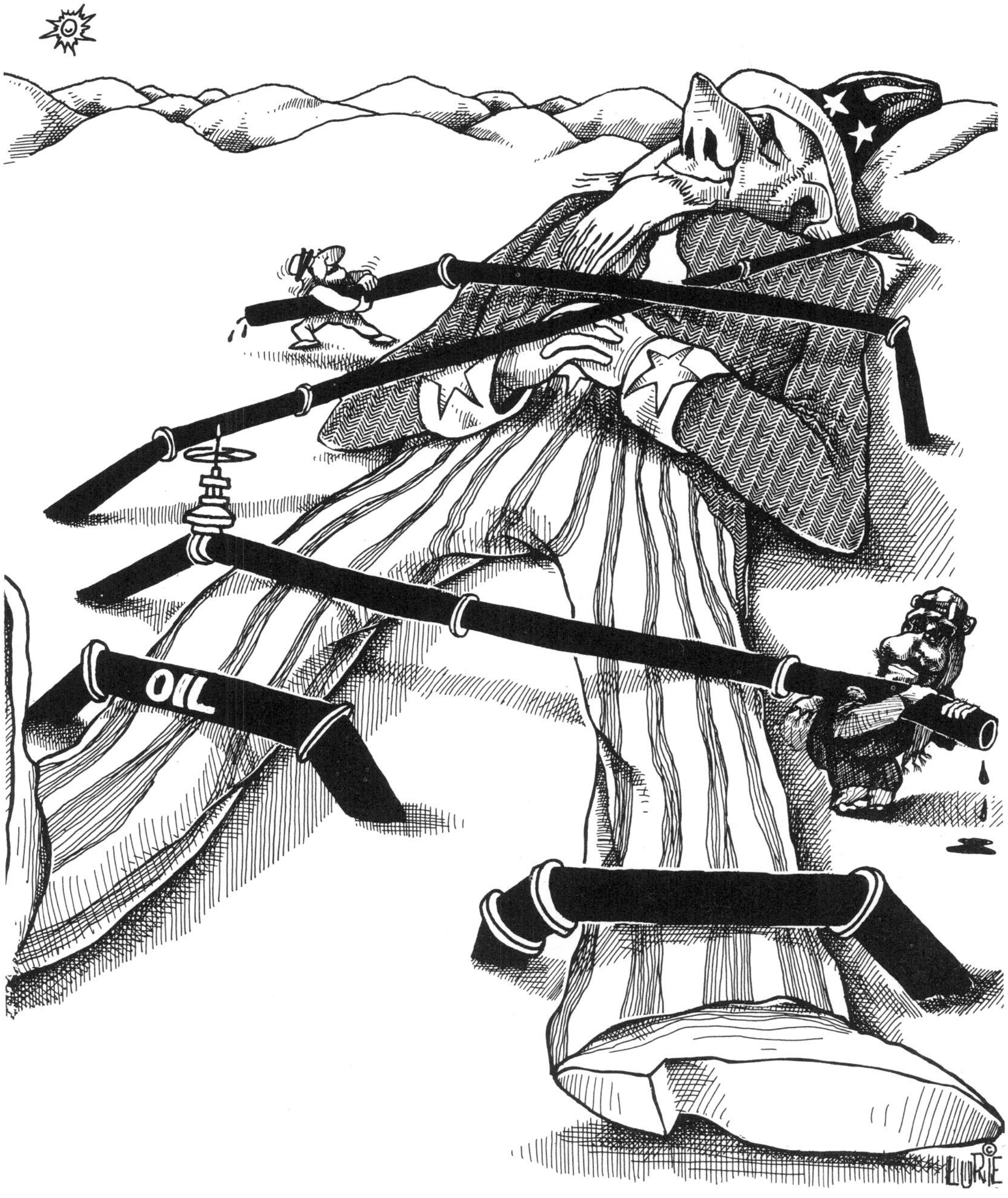
OIL
LURIE ©
4-4-73

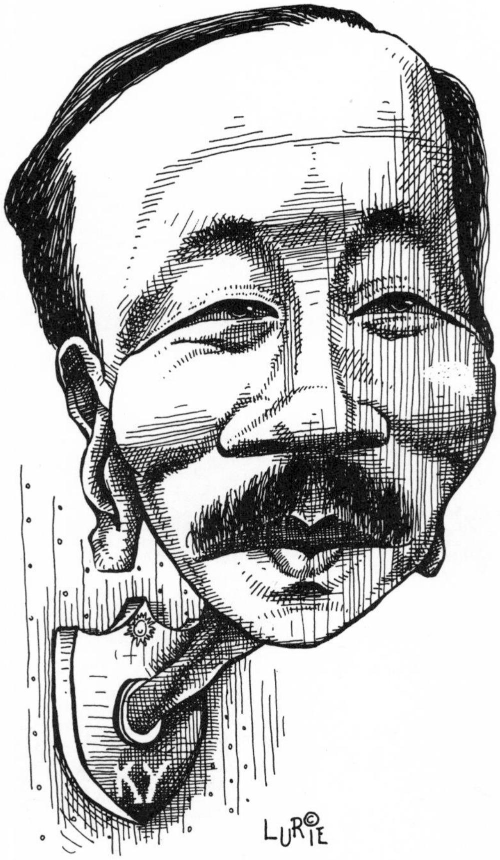
KY
LURIE©
Former Vice President
Nguyen Cao Ky
of South Vietnam

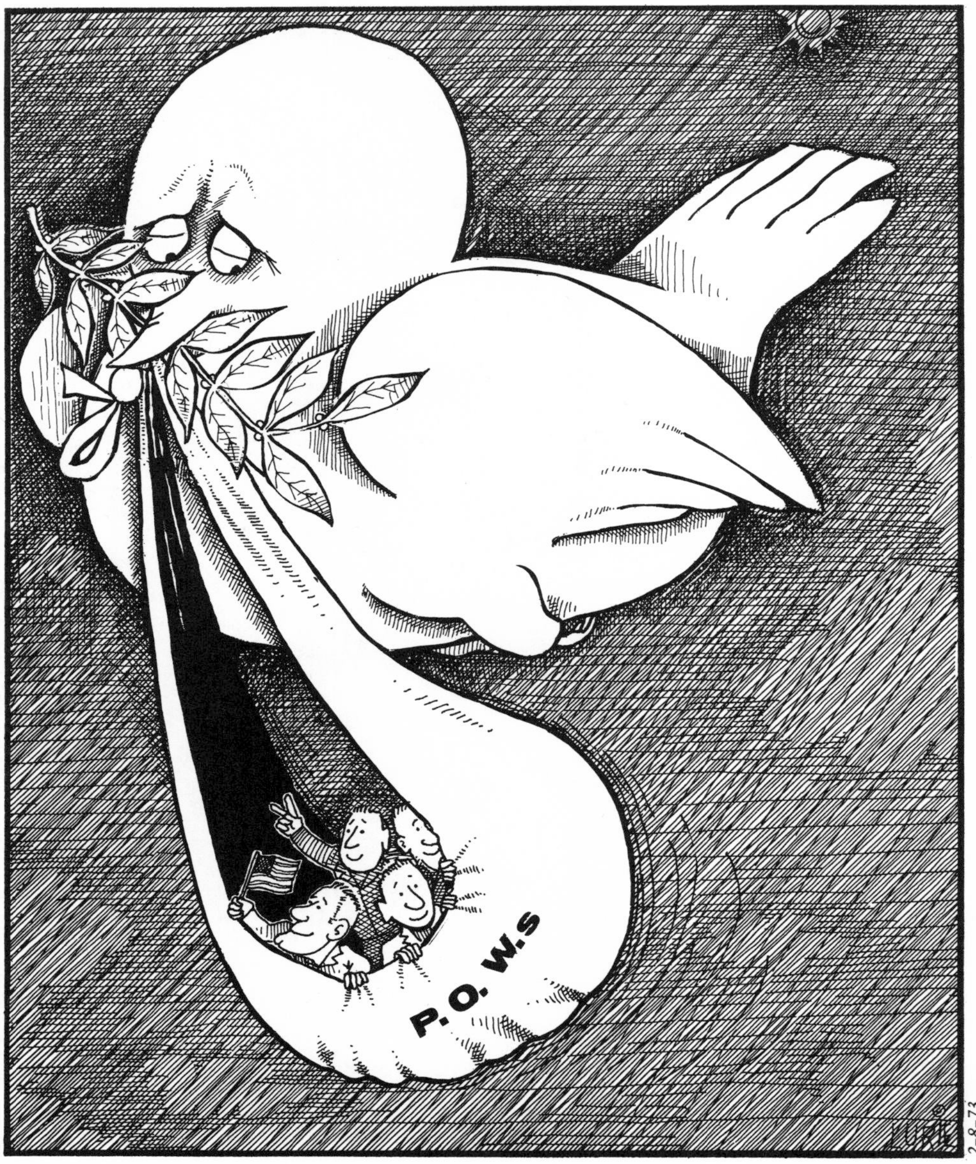
P.O.W.s
LURIE©
2-8-73
REBORN

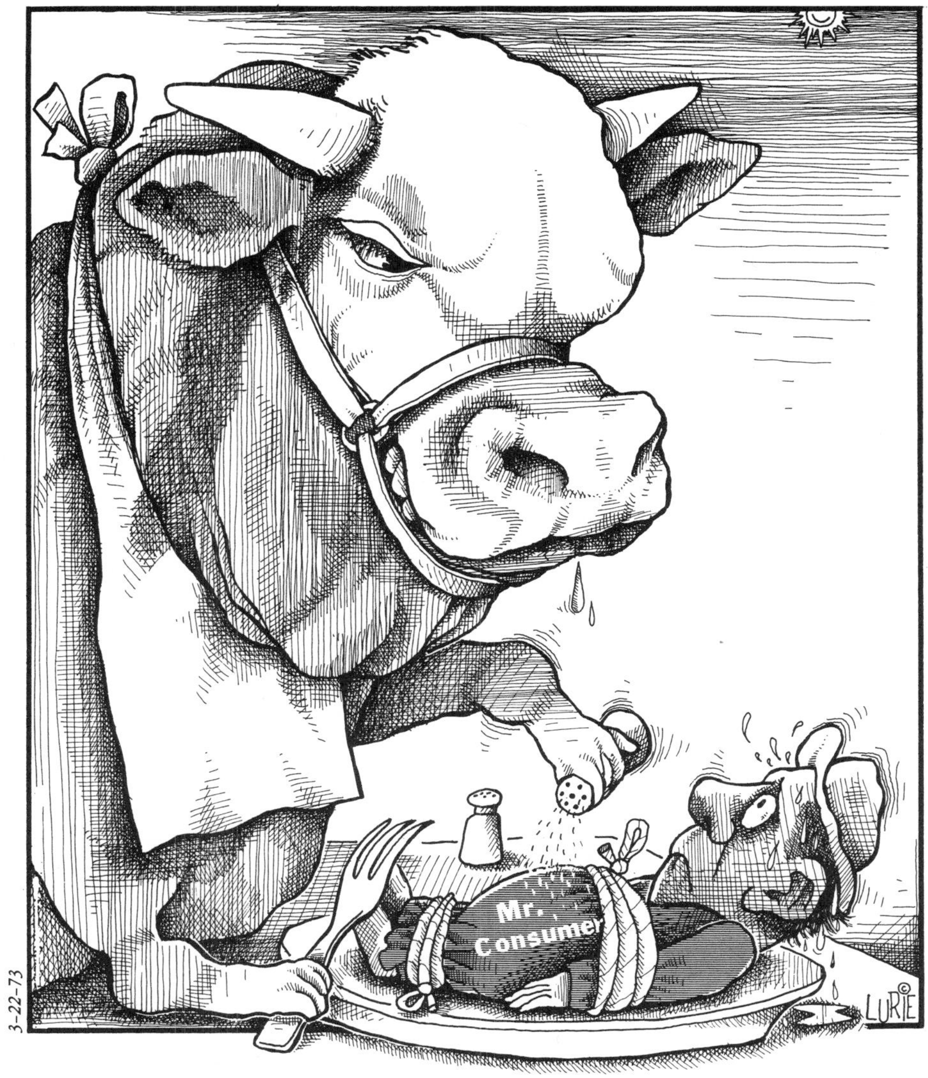

Mr.
Consumer
LURIE©
3-22-73

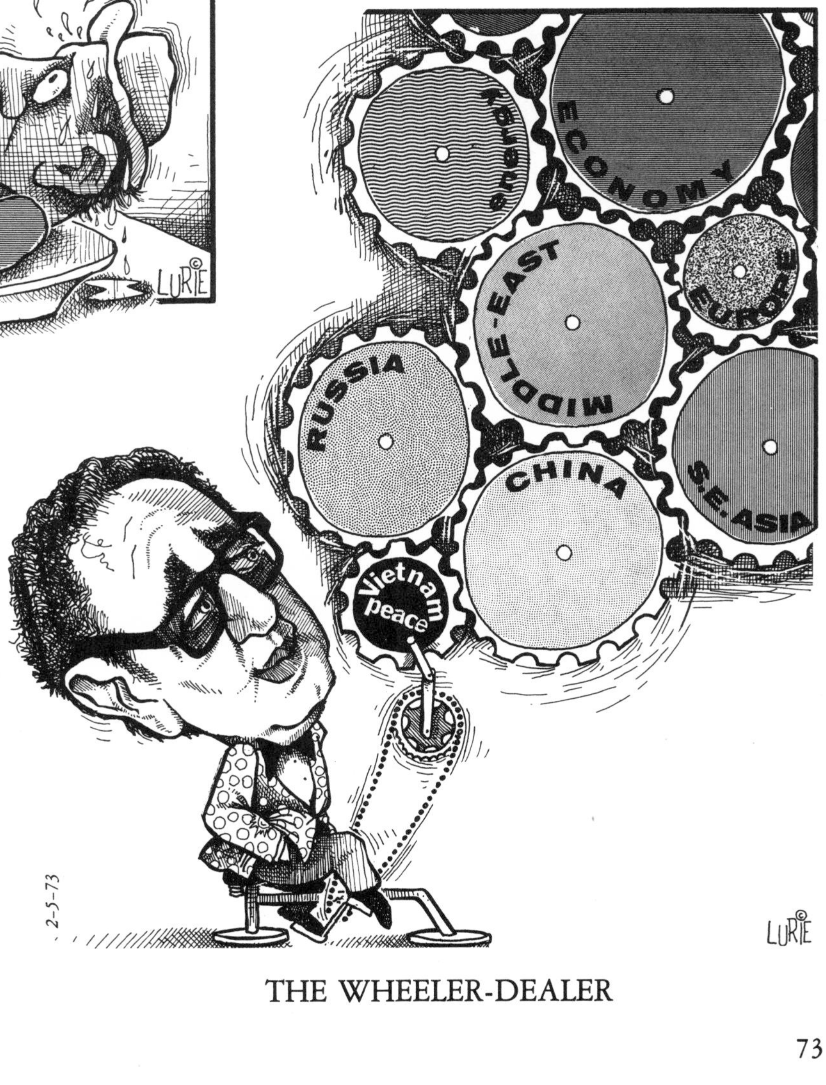

ECONOMY
energy
MIDDLE-EAST
EUROPE
RUSSIA
CHINA
S.E. ASIA
Vietnam
peace
LURIE©
2-5-73

THE WHEELER-DEALER

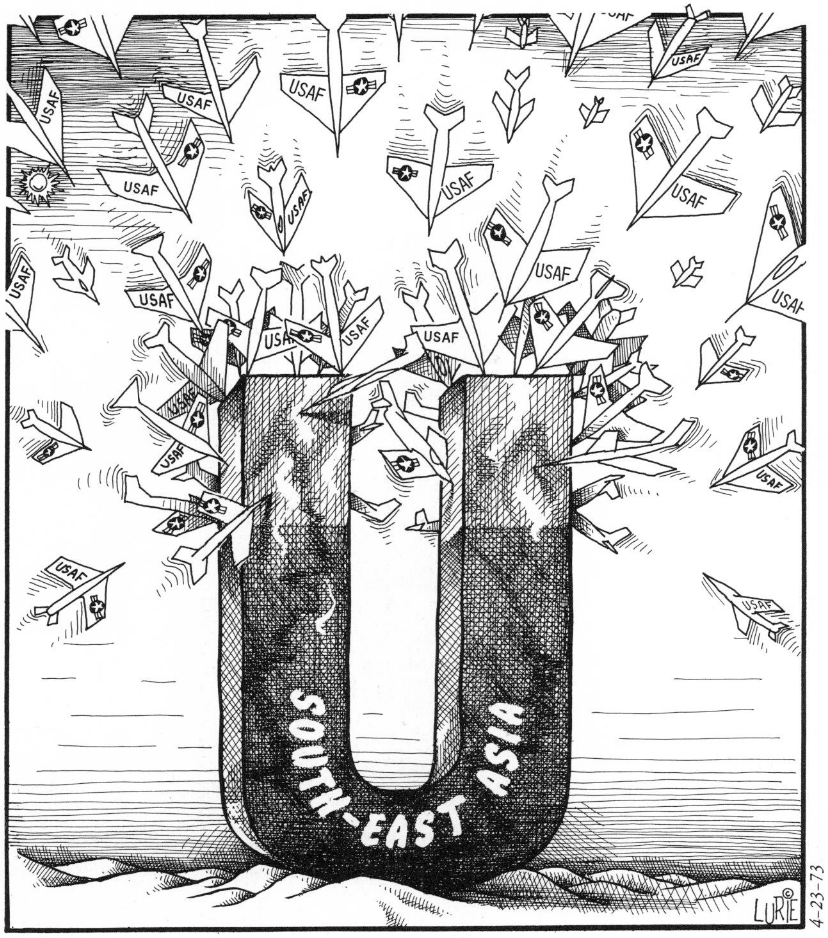
USAF
SOUTH-EAST ASIA
LURIE©

4-23-73

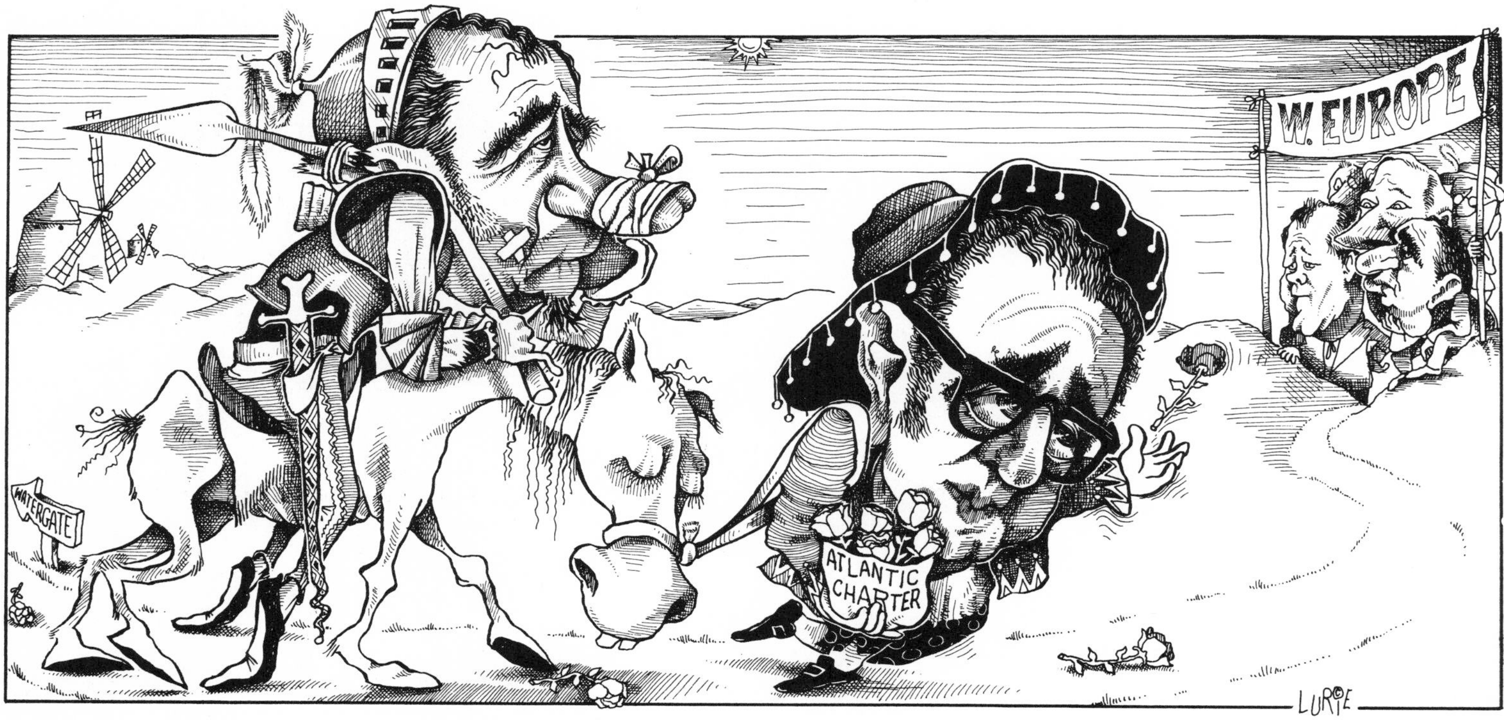
W. EUROPE
WATERGATE
ATLANTIC CHARTER
LURIE©

Newsweek 5-17-73

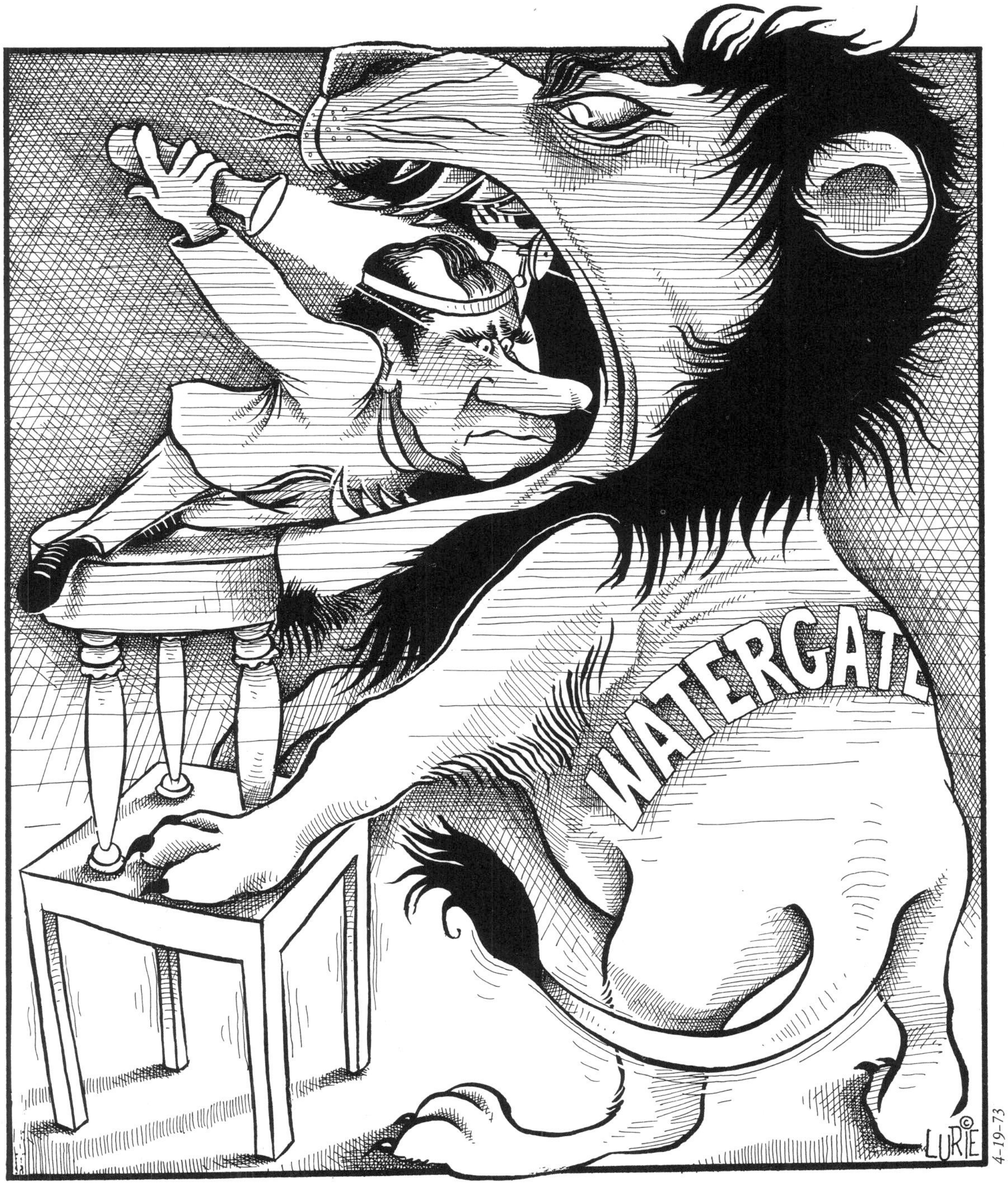
WATERGATE
LURIE ©
4-19-73

W. EUROPE
U.S.
U.S.
U.S.
4-25-73
LURIE

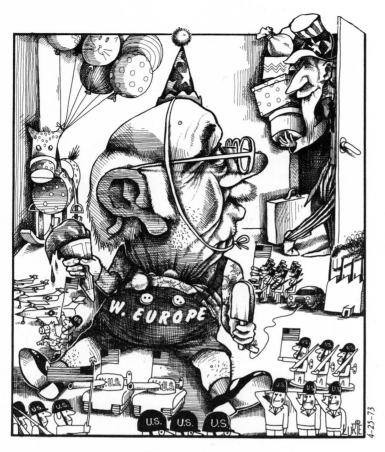

"HI UNCLE—
WHAT DID YOU BRING ME THIS TIME?"

IGNORANCE
COMPLICITY
WATERGATE
4-27-73
LURIE

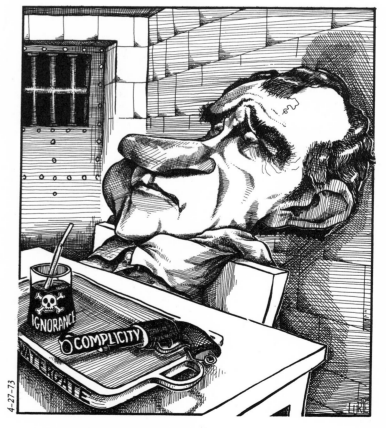

TOUGH POLITICAL CHOICE

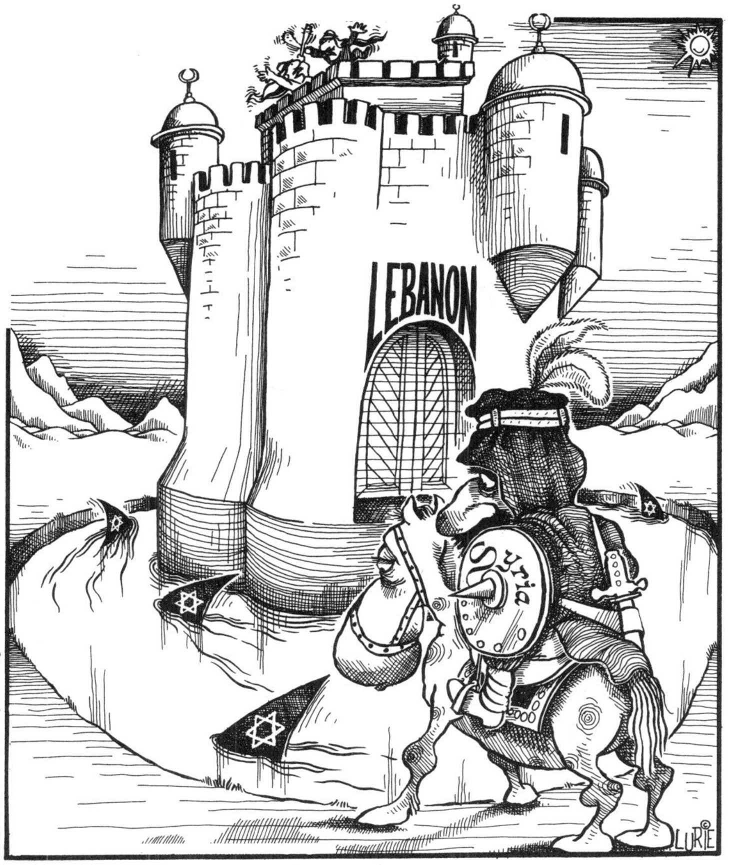
LEBANON
Syria
LURIE

New York Times 5-11-73

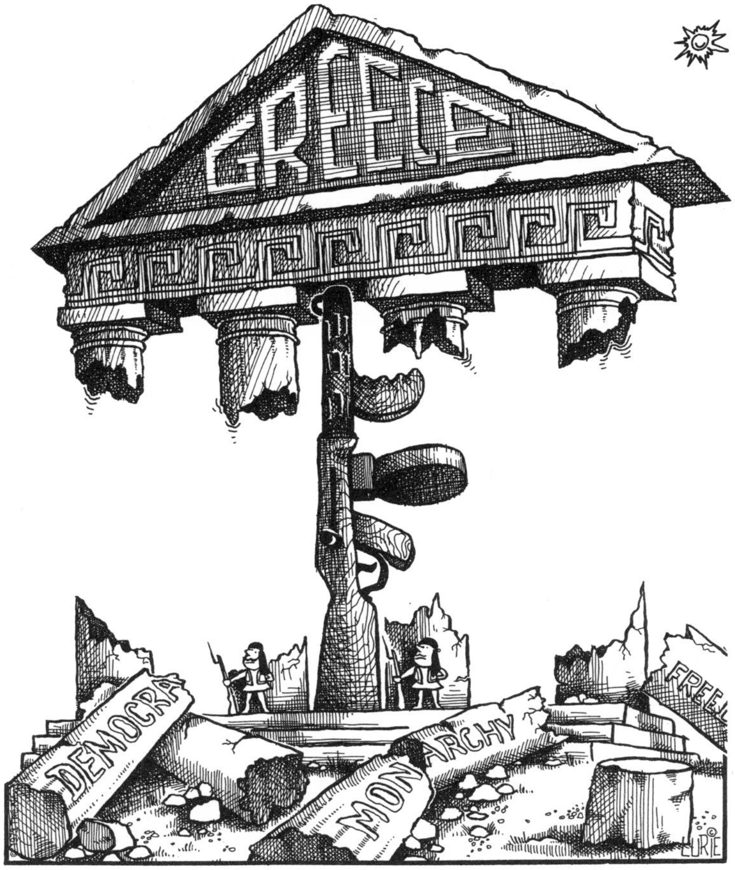
GREECE
DEMOCRA
MONARCHY
LURIE

6-4-73

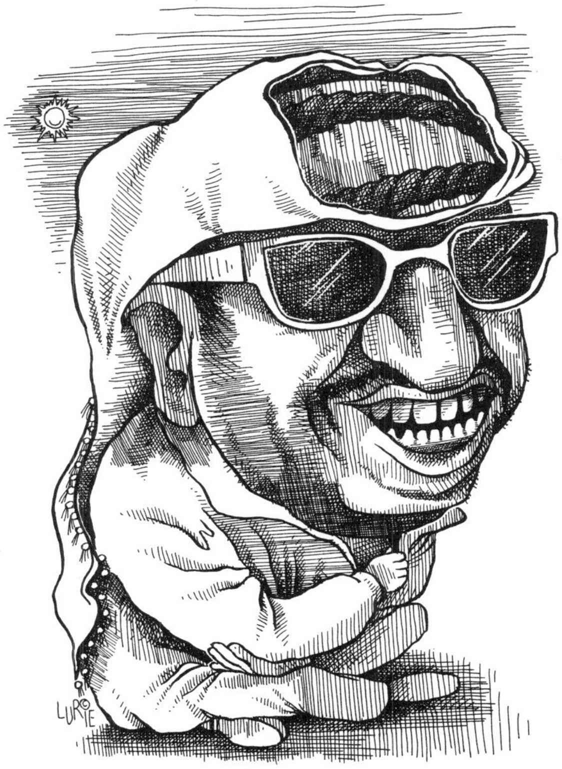
LURIE

Yasir Arafat, Al Fatah Chief

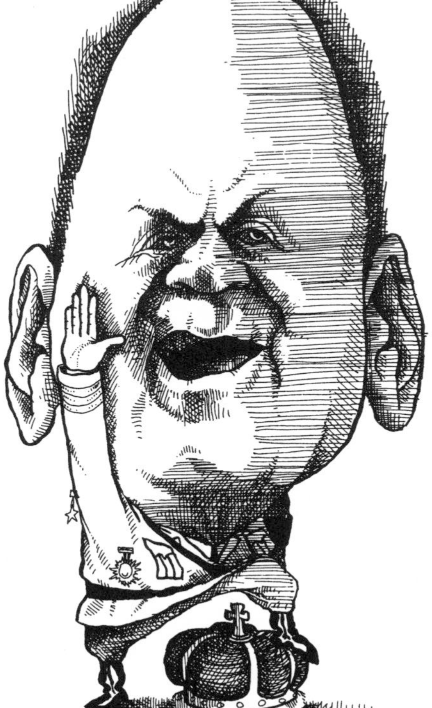
LURIE

Premier Papadopoulos of Greece

CHINESE
SUMMIT
USSR
SUMM
LURIE
6-20-73

9-6-73
EHRLICHMAN
LURIE

FALL FASHIONS

LURIE
Newsweek 6-19-73

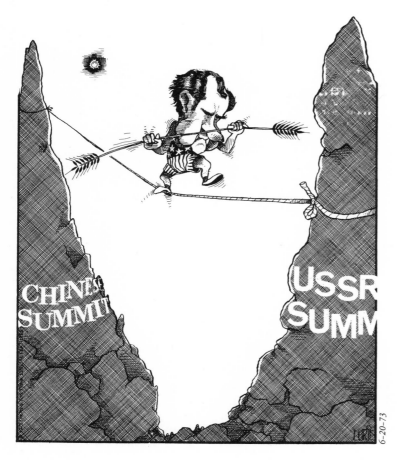

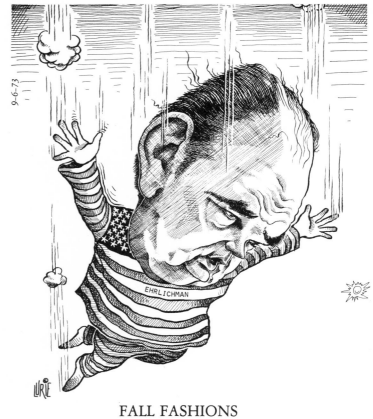

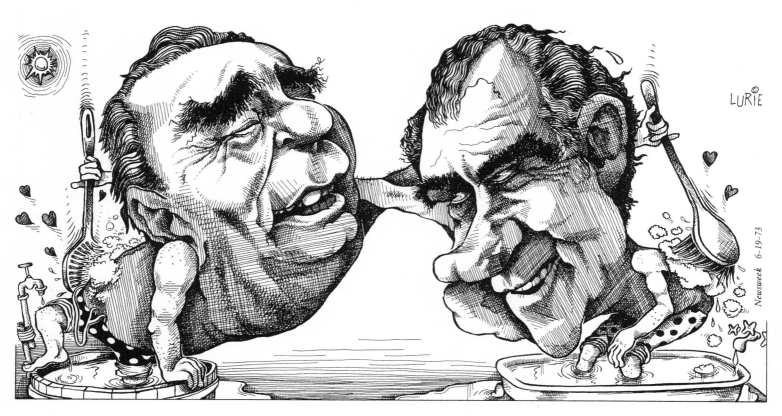

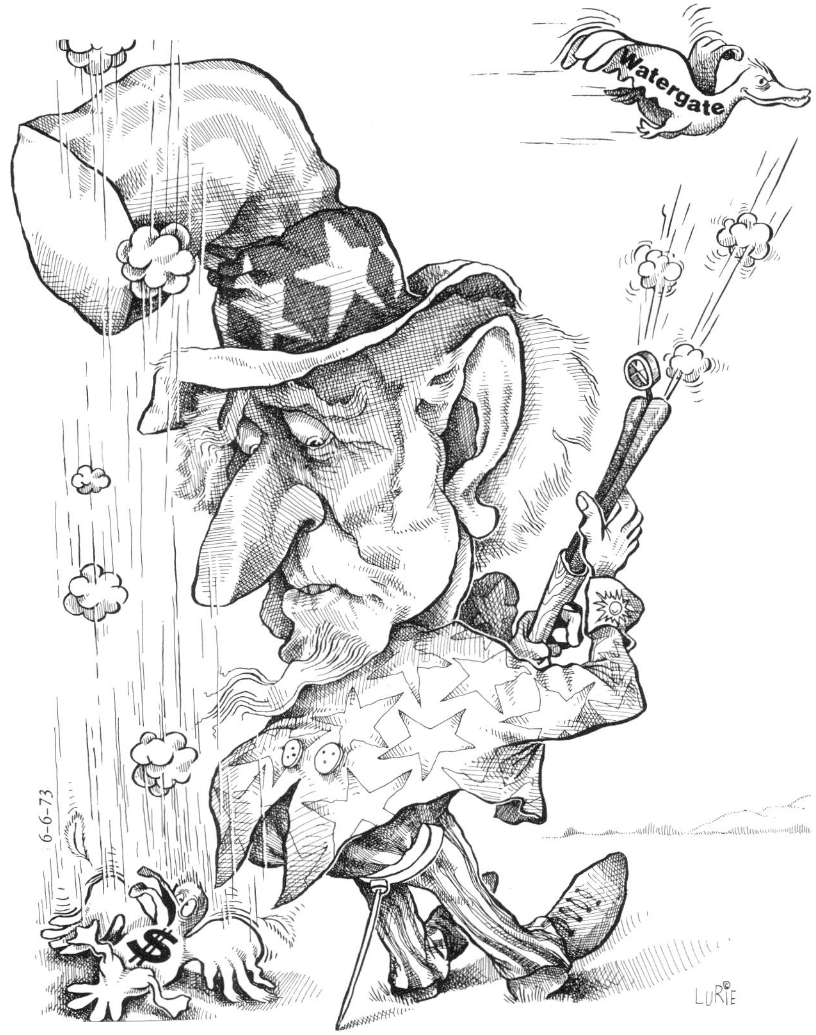
Watergate
6-6-73
LURIE

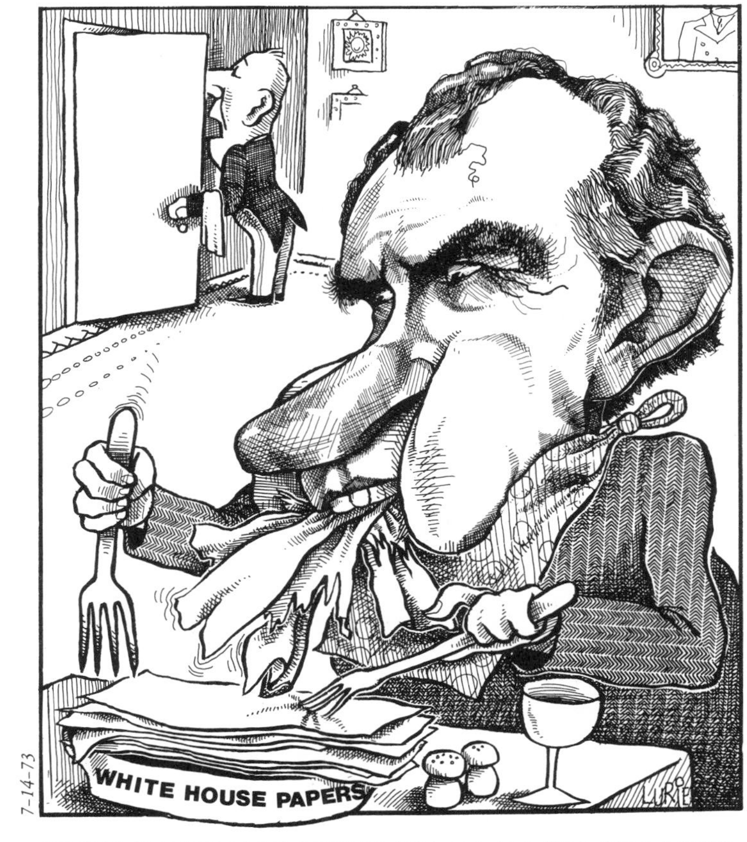
7-14-73
WHITE HOUSE PAPERS
LURIE

"THE PRESIDENT WILL BE GLAD TO SEE YOU, SENATOR ERVIN, AFTER LUNCH"

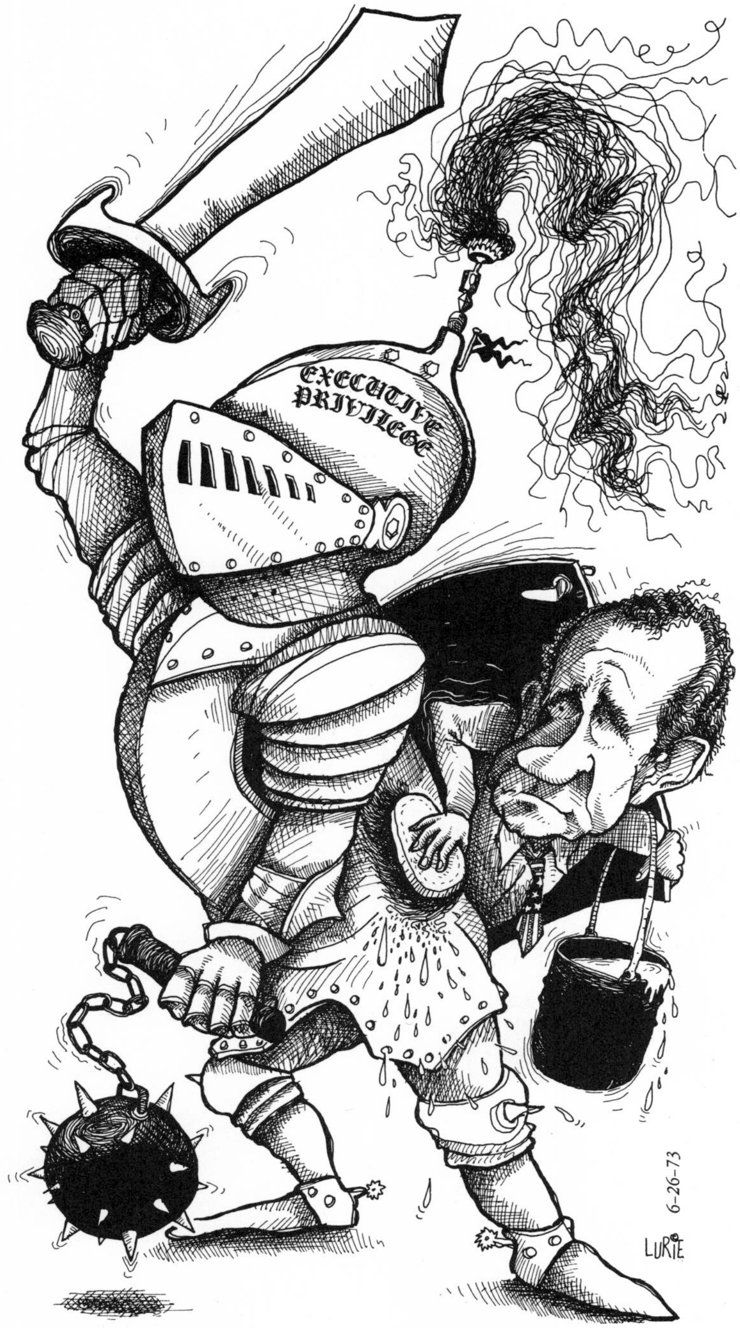
EXECUTIVE PRIVILEGE
6-26-73
LURIE

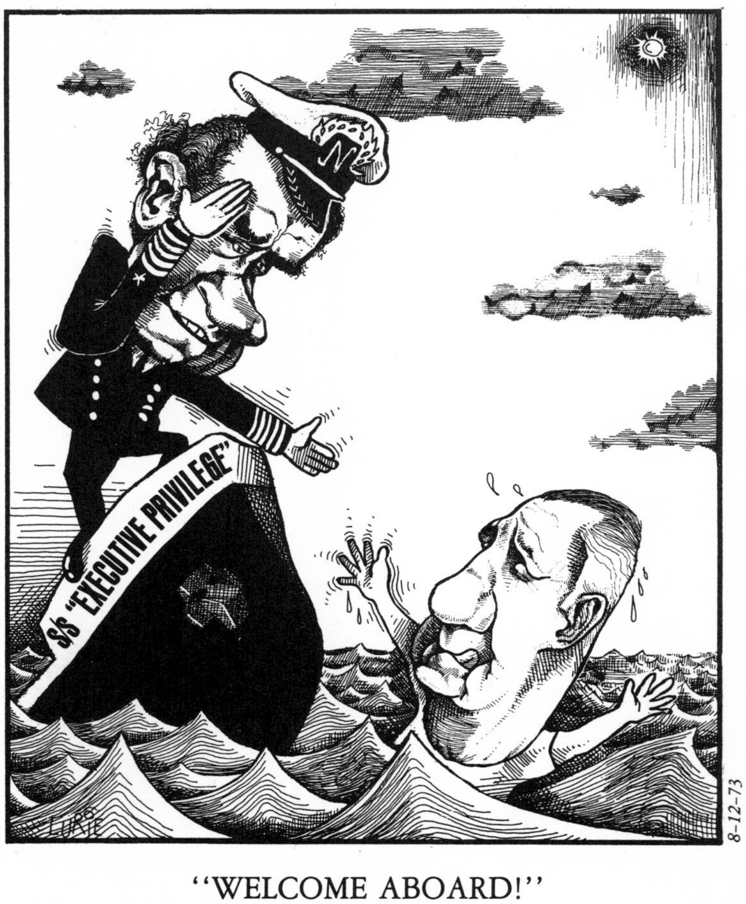
S/S "EXECUTIVE PRIVILEGE"
LURIE
8-12-73

''WELCOME ABOARD!''

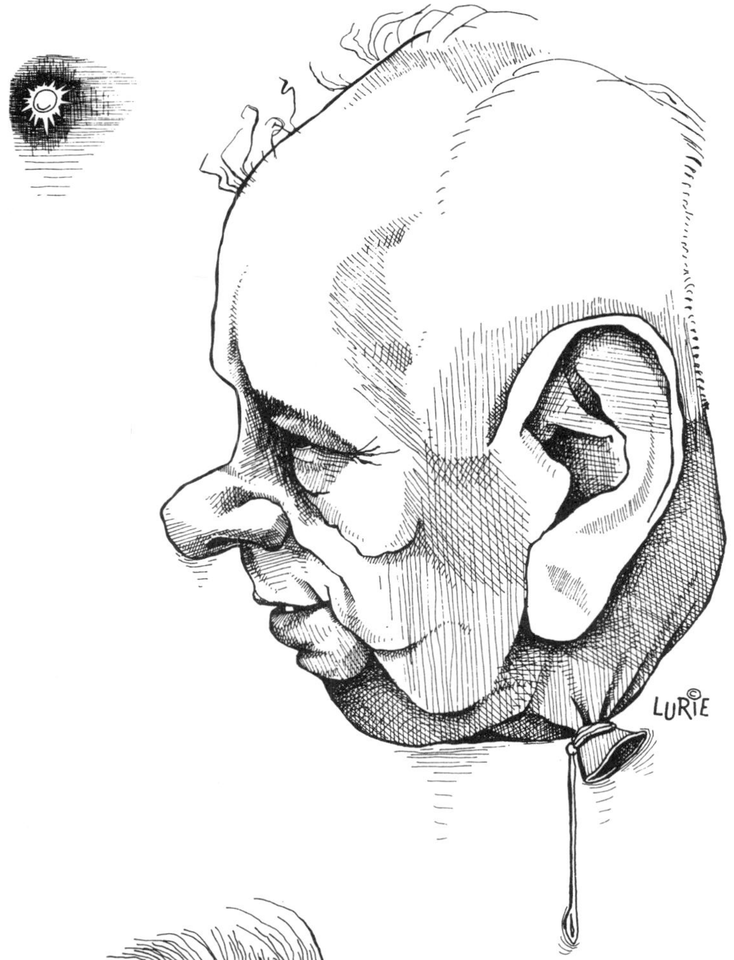
LURIE

Nikolai Podgorny
Soviet President

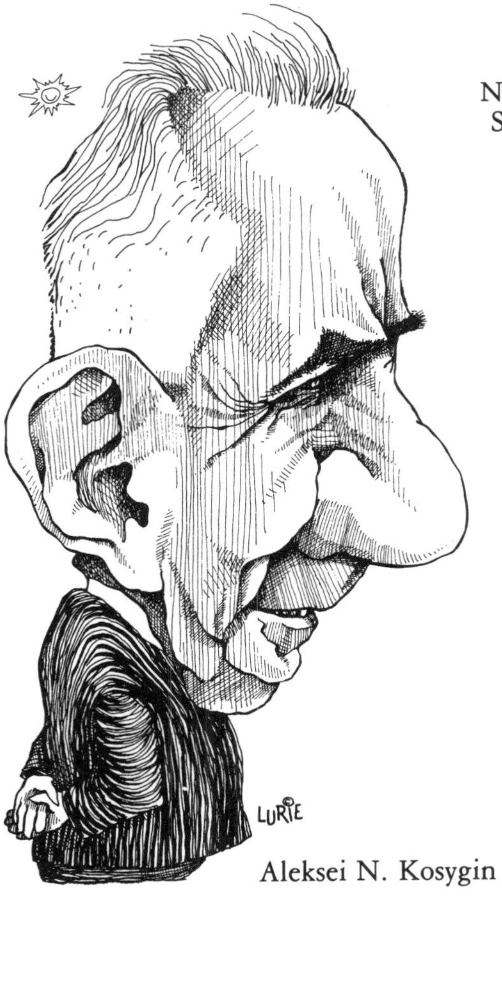
LURIE

Aleksei N. Kosygin

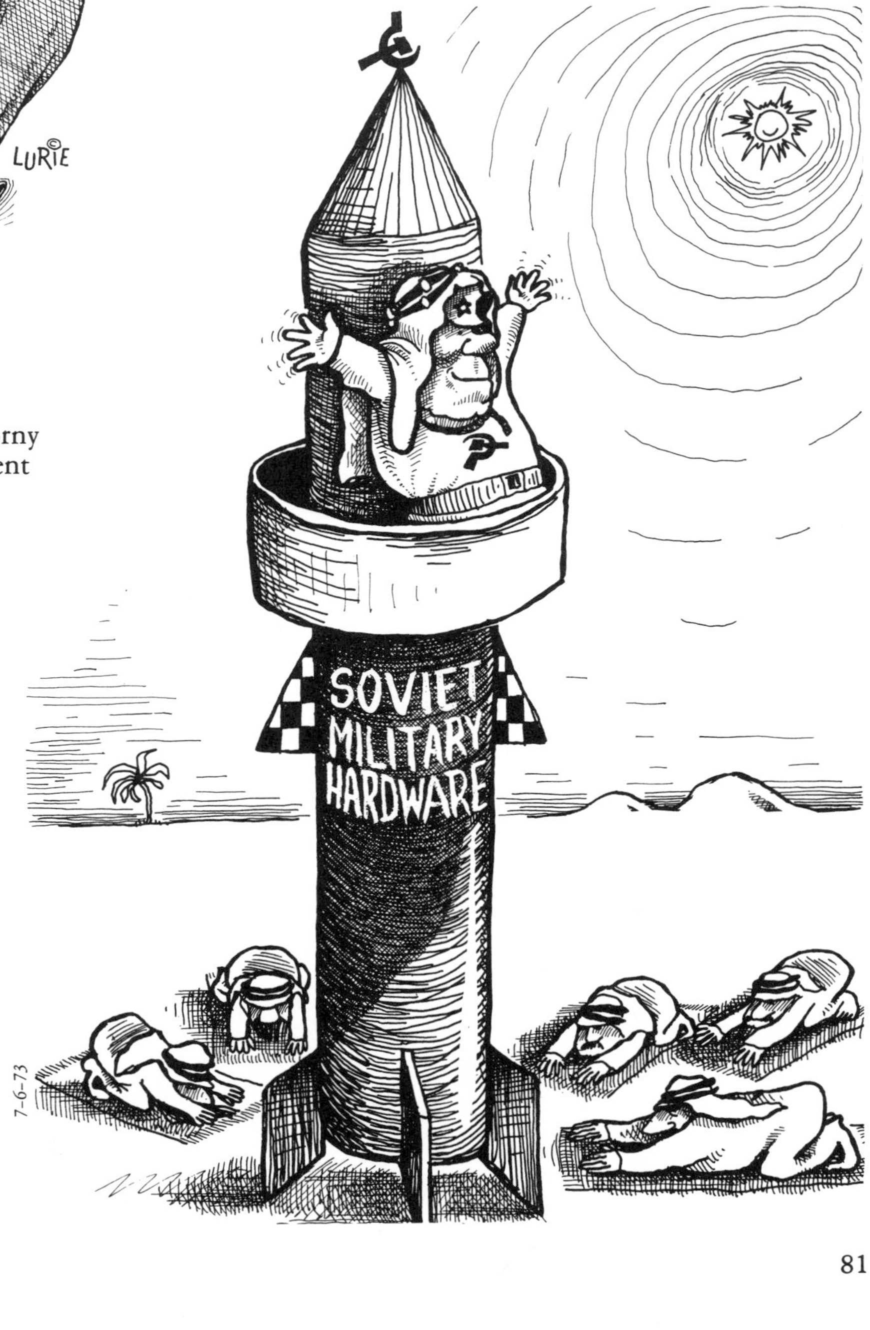
SOVIET
MILITARY
HARDWARE
7-6-73

1.
LAW & ORDER
2.
LAW & ORDE
3.
8-22-73

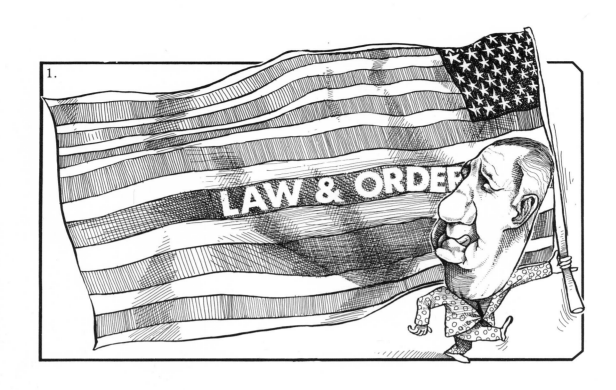

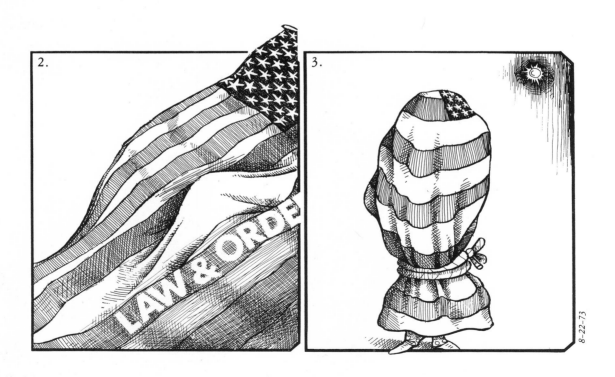

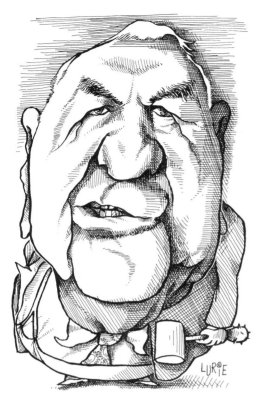

Senator Sam J. Ervin, Jr.

"GOOD MORNING, MR. PRESIDENT"

83

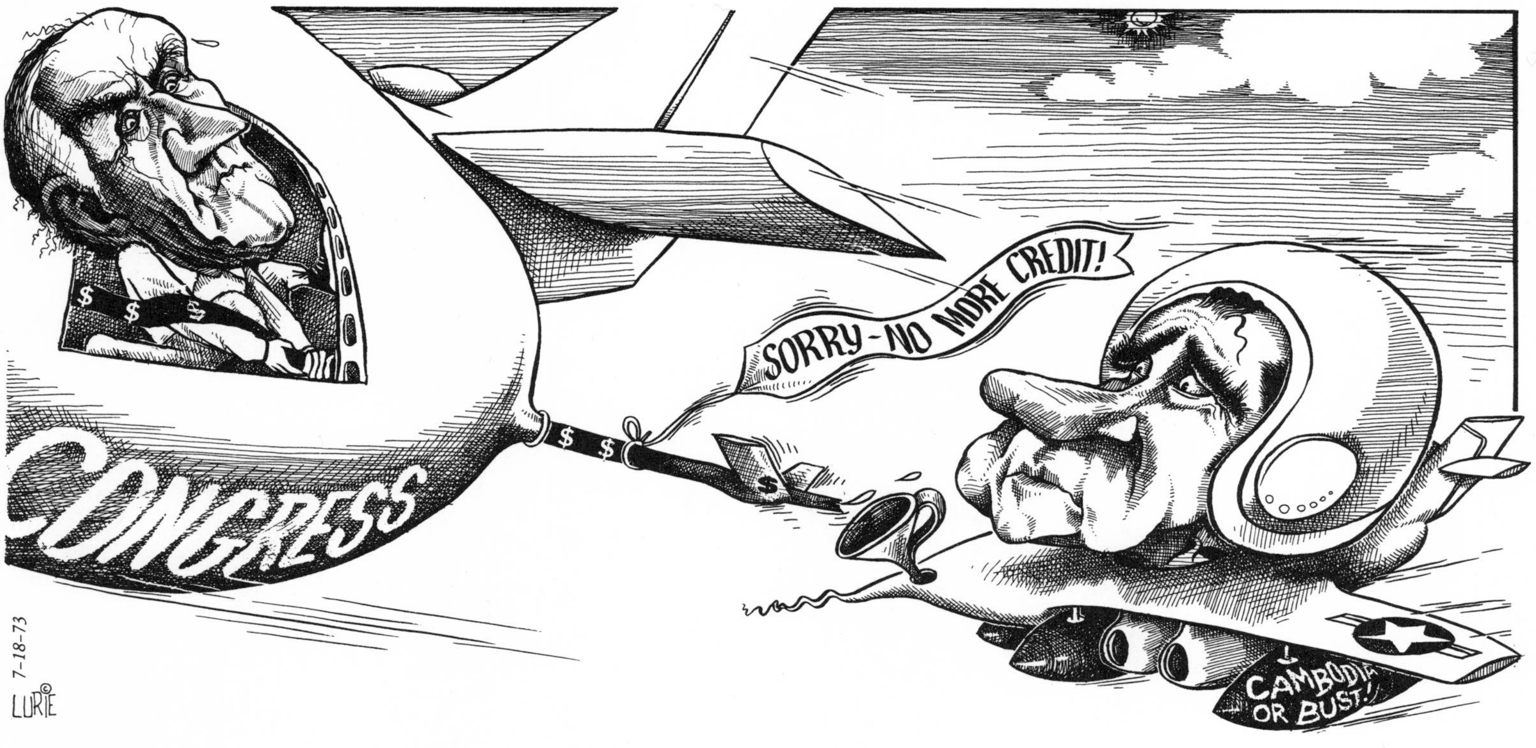
CONGRESS
SORRY-NO MORE CREDIT!
CAMBODIA OR BUST!
LURIE

7-18-73

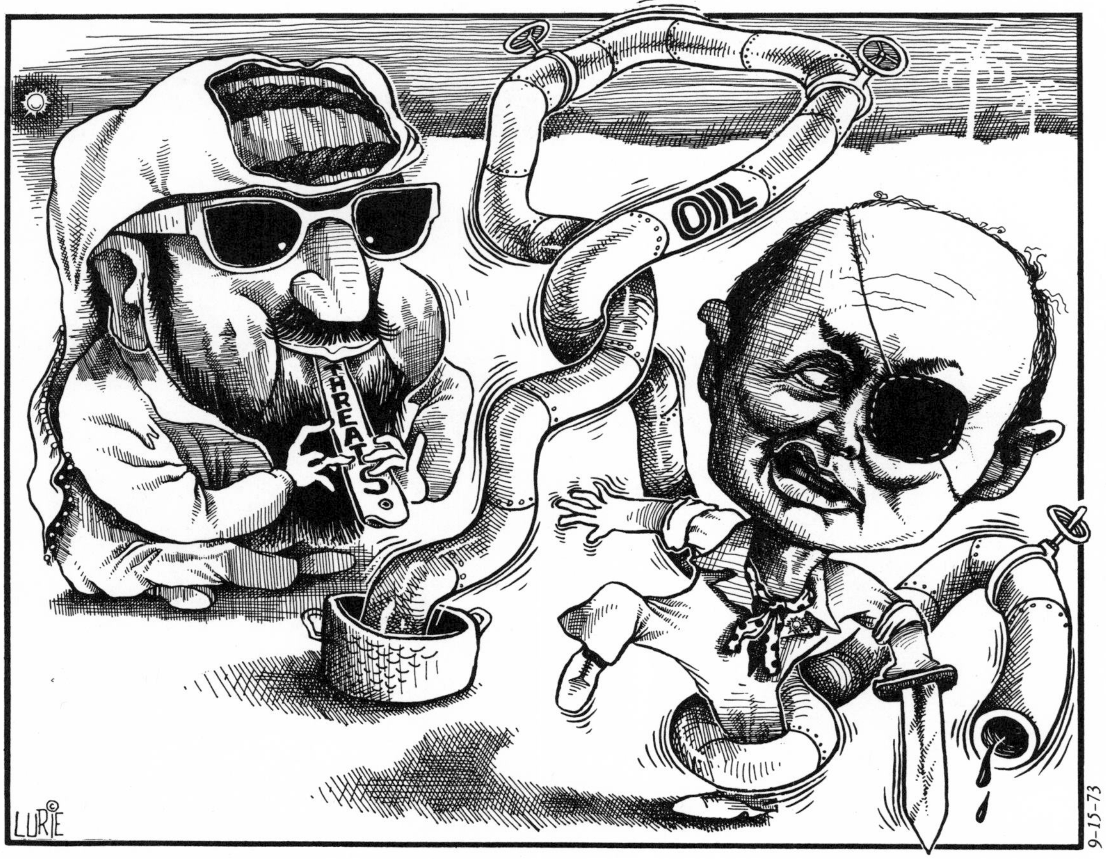
OIL
THREATS
LURIE

9-15-73

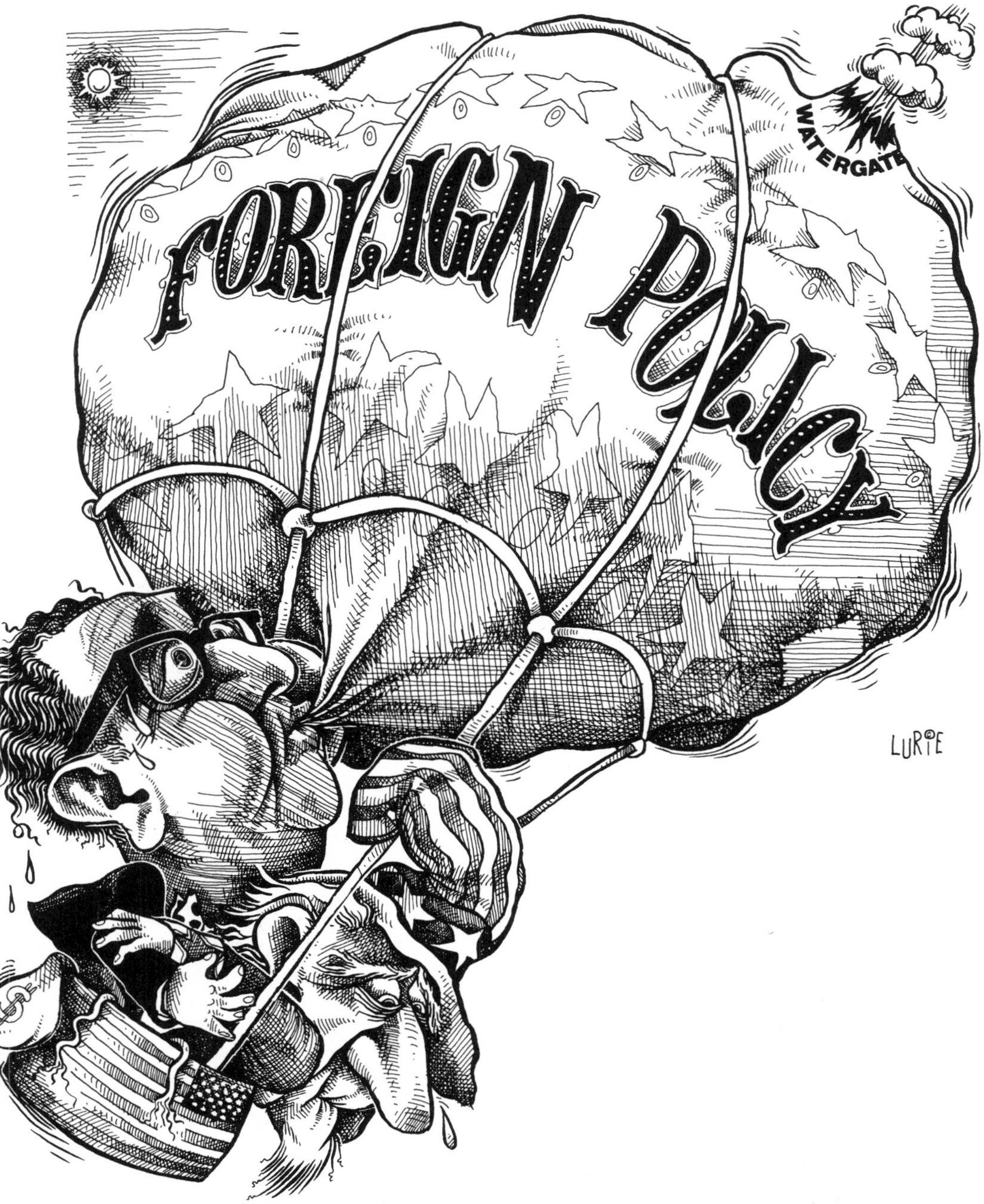
FOREIGN POLICY
WATERGATE
LURIE

Newsweek 8-1-73

CREDIBILITY
CREDIBILITY
CREDI
CREDIBILITY
8-15-73

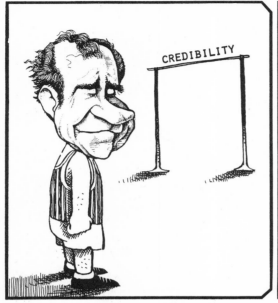

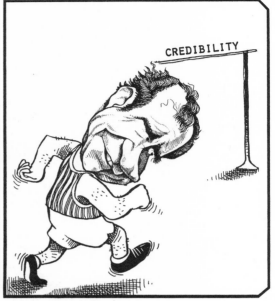

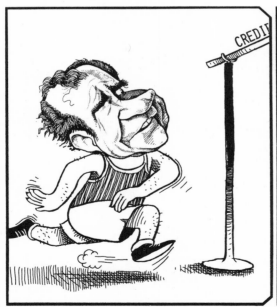

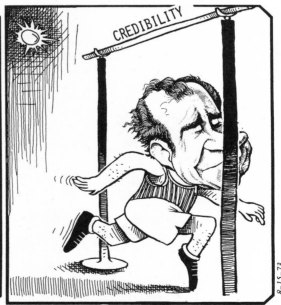

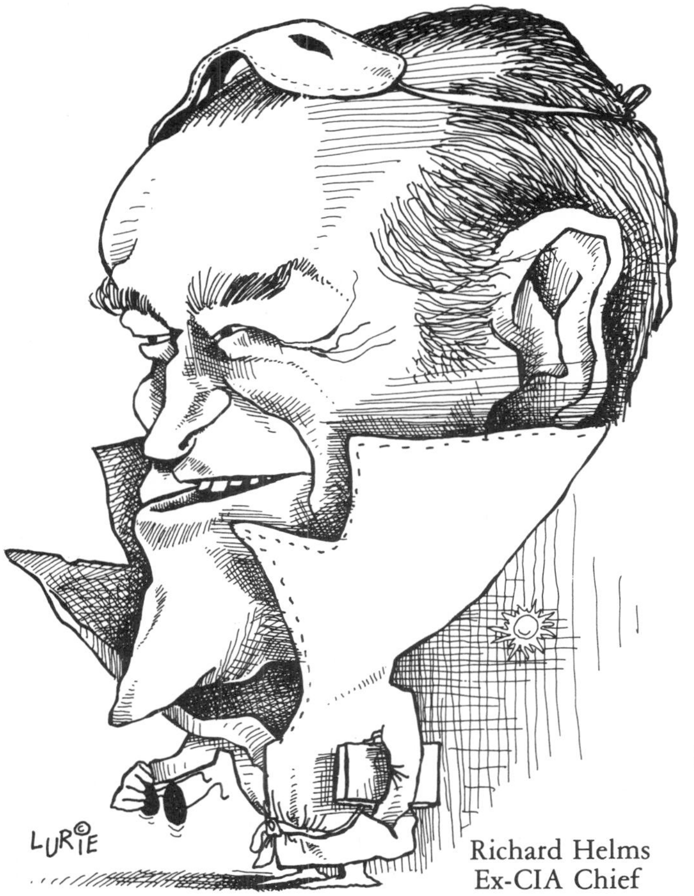

Richard Helms
Ex-CIA Chief

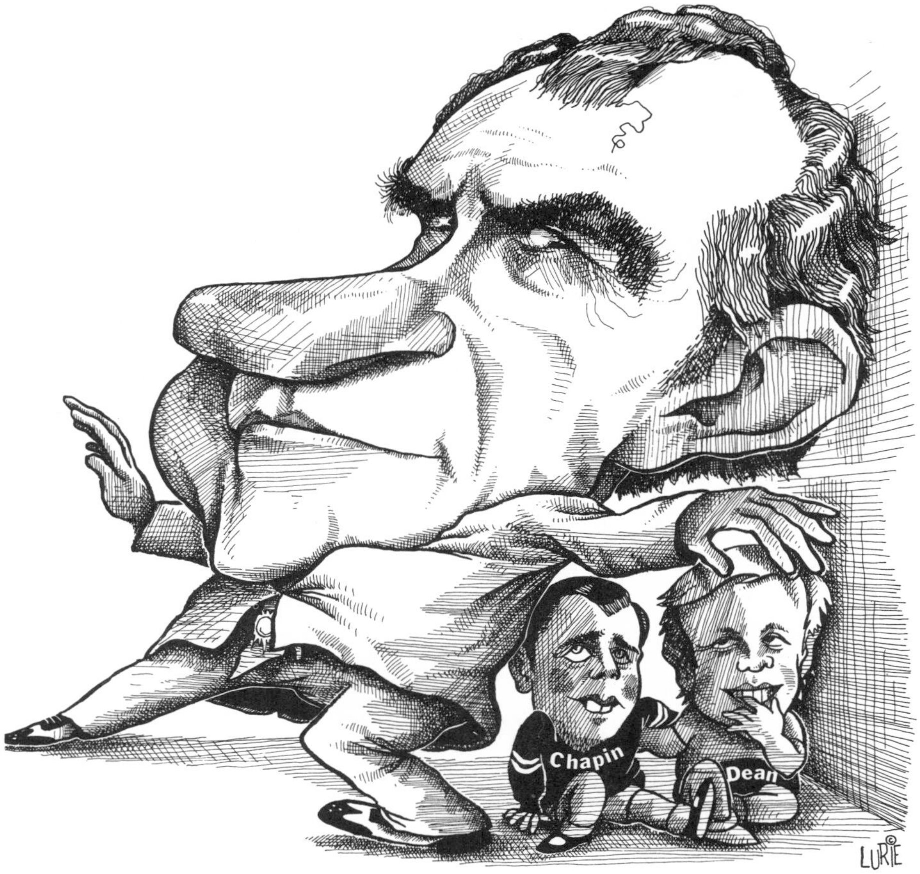
Chapin
Dean
LURIE

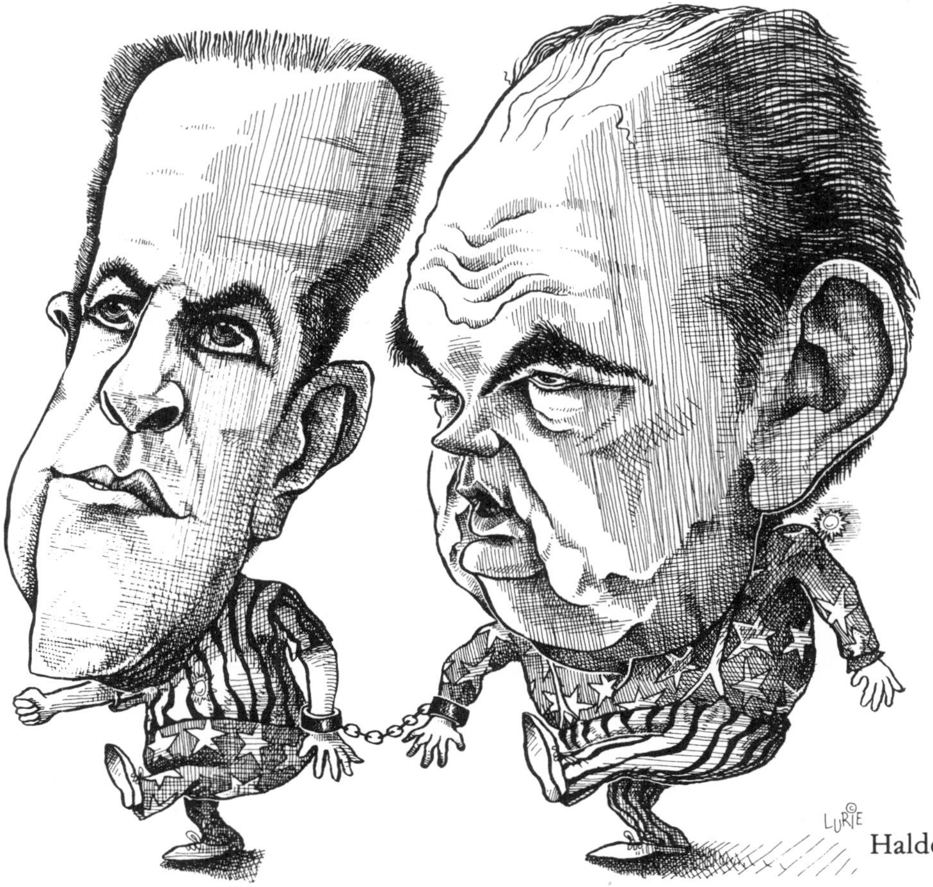

Haldeman & Ehrlichman

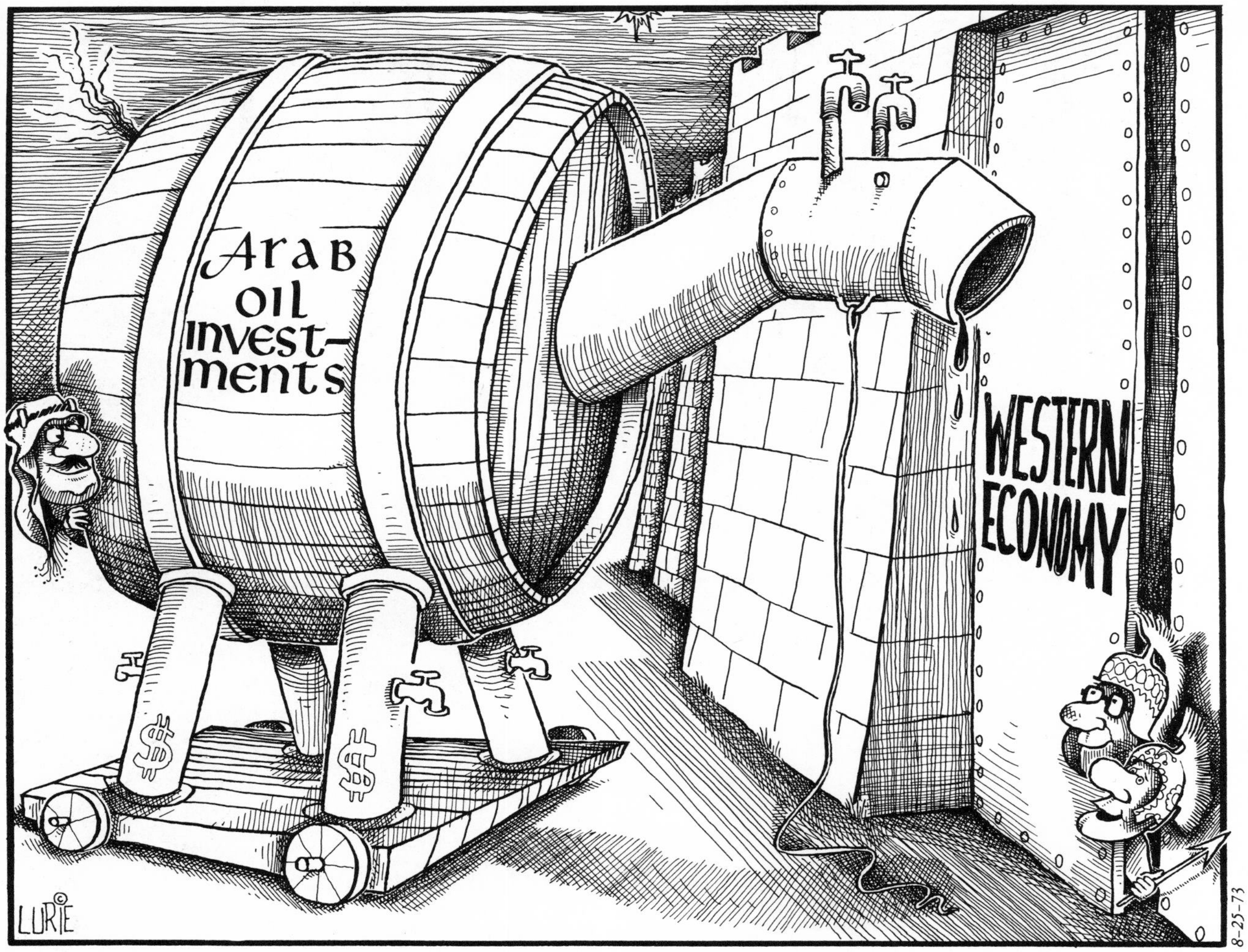
Arab oil invest-ments
$
$
WESTERN ECONOMY
LURIE©
8-25-73

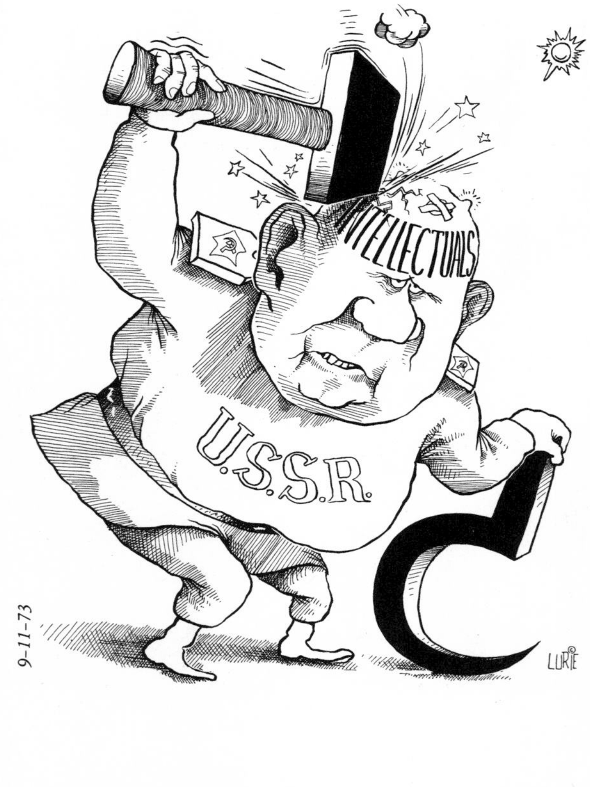
INTELLECTUALS
U.S.S.R.
9-11-73
LURIE©

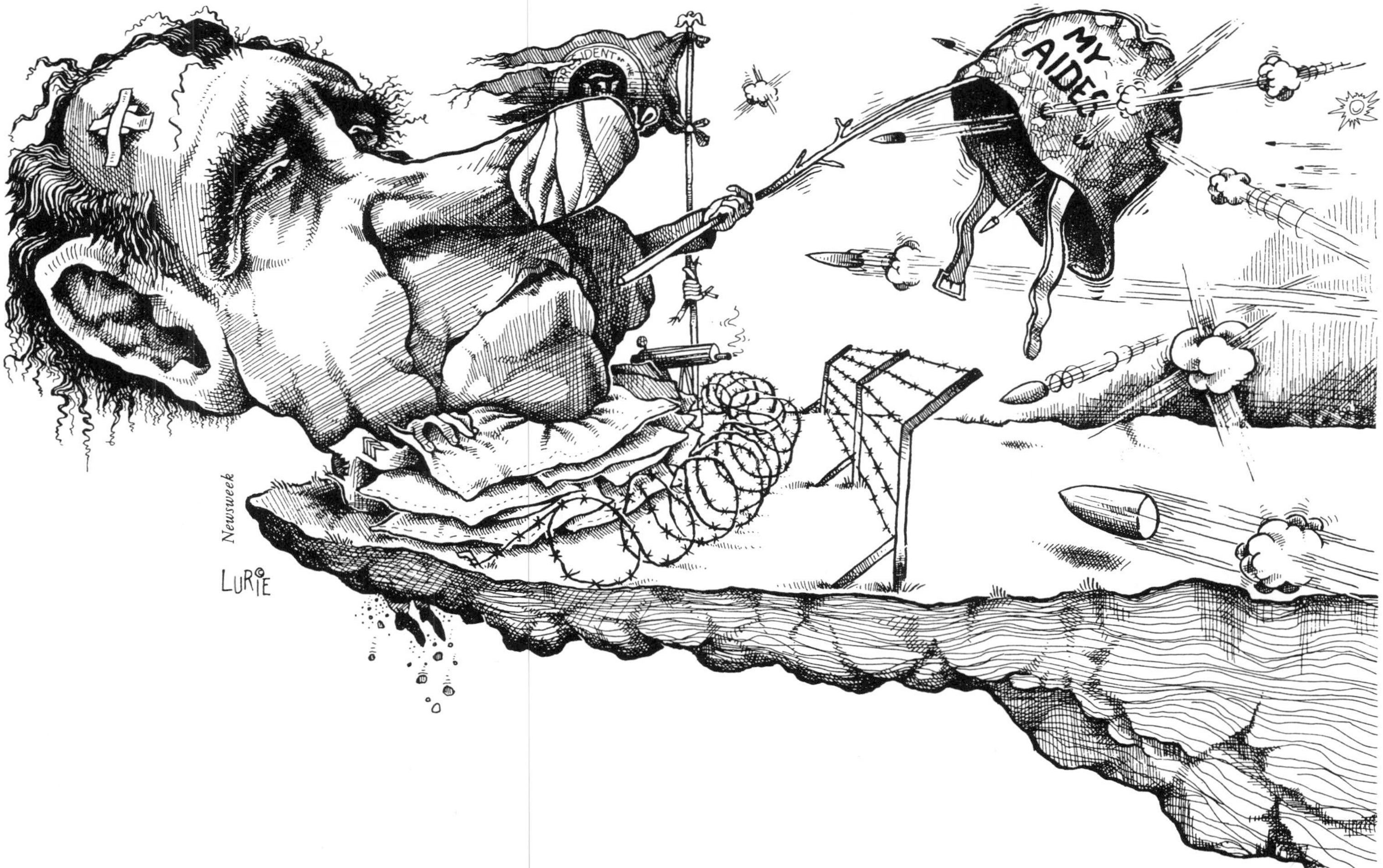
MY AIDES
Newsweek
LURIE

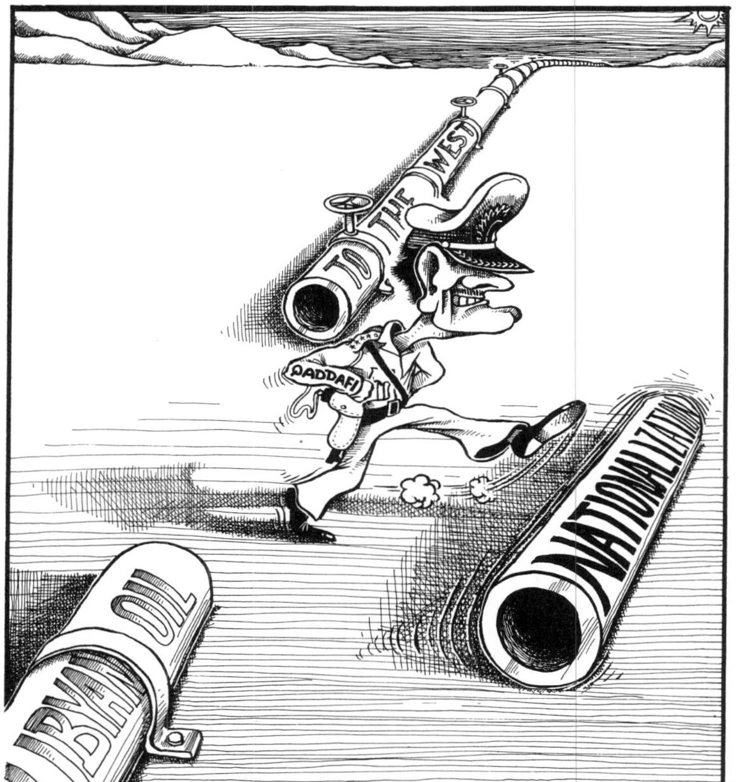
TO THE WEST
QADDAFI
LIBYAN OIL
LURIE
9-5-73

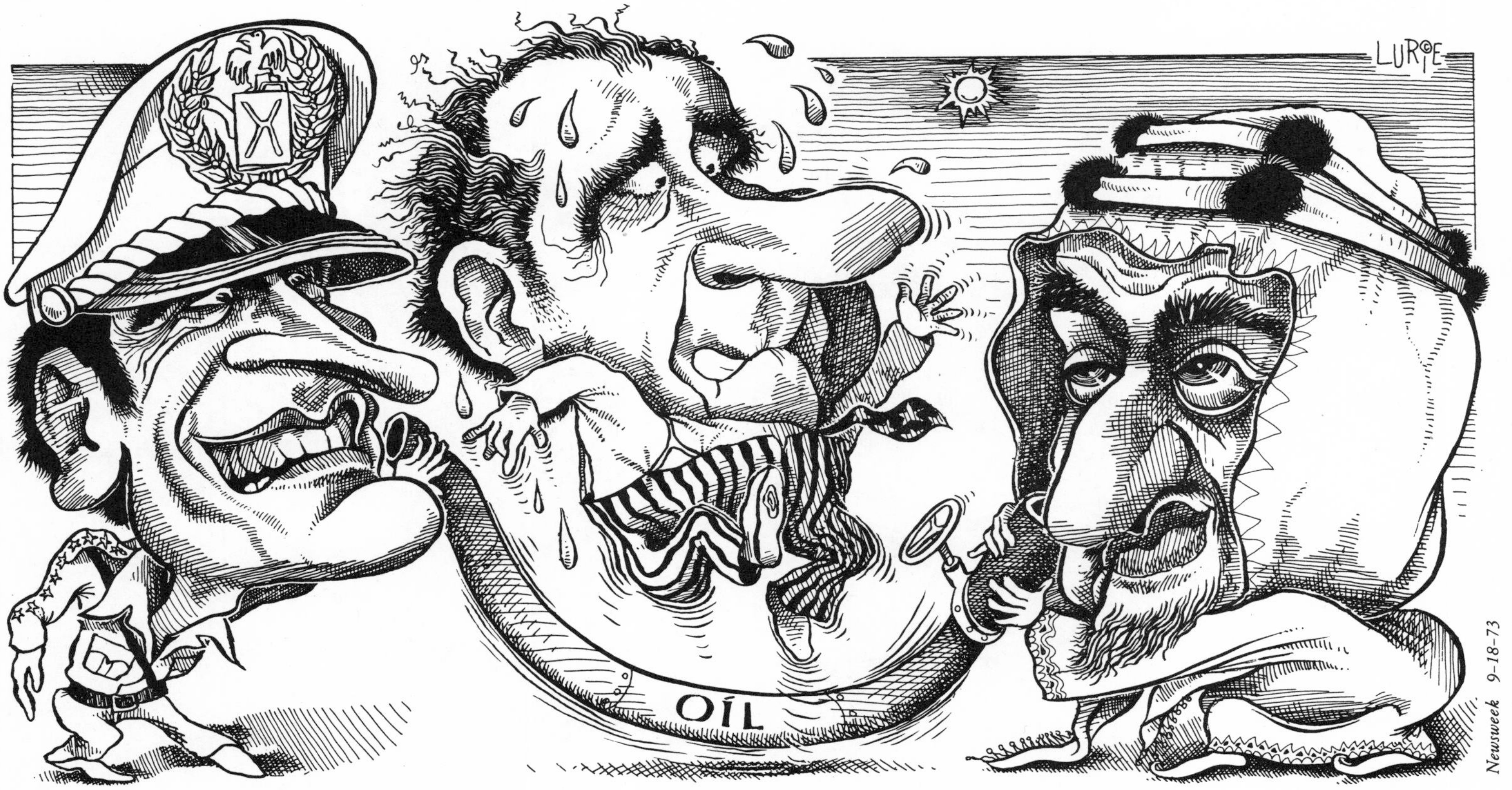
LURIE
OIL
Newsweek 9-18-73

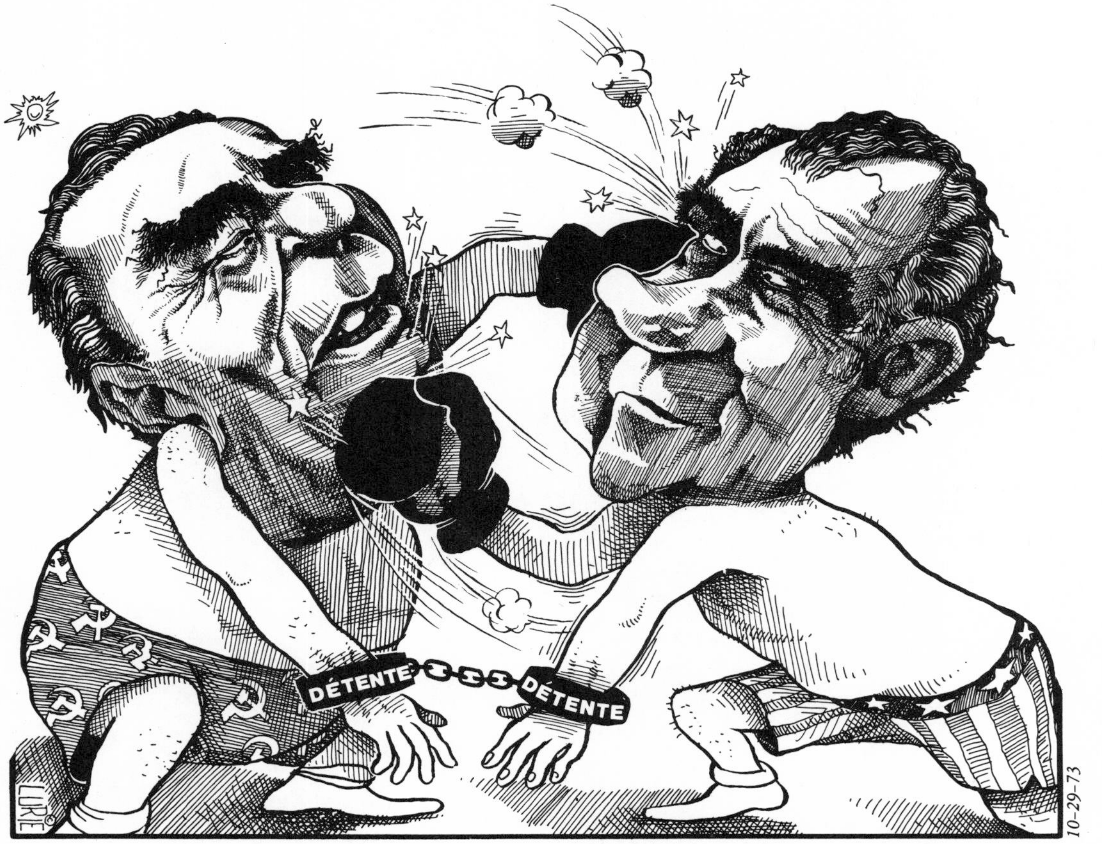
DÉTENTE
DÉTENTE
LURIE
10-29-73

VIVA NON-ALIGNED!
3rd WORLD
VIVA INDEPENDENCE!
3rd WORLD
DRAMA
PATHOS
CRY
HANDS
MOUTH
SINCERETY
9-12-73

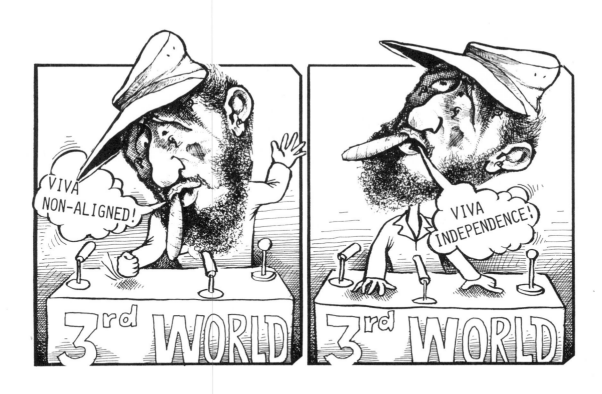

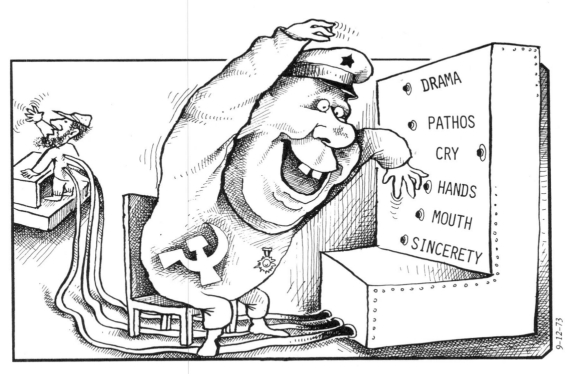

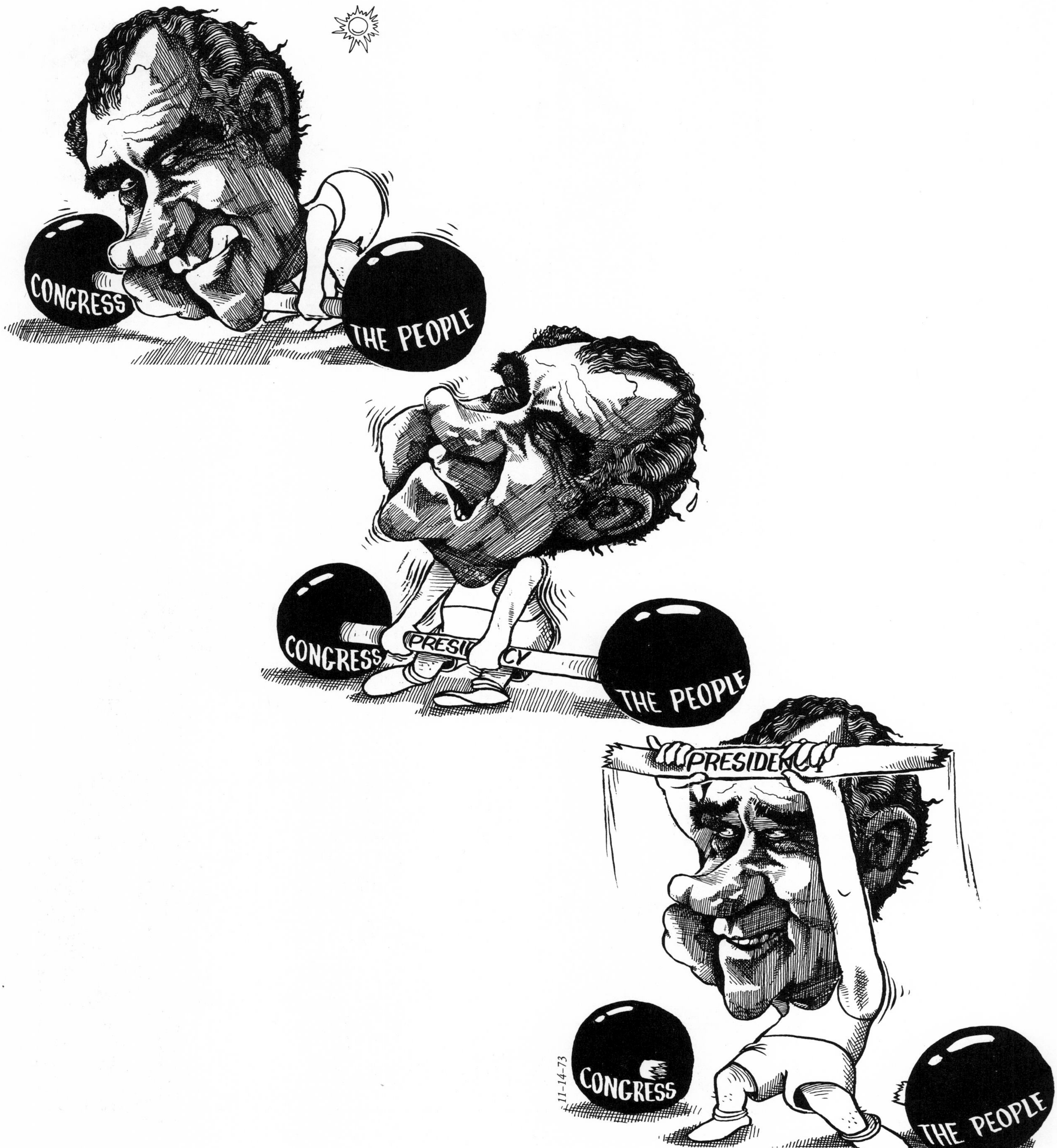
CONGRESS
THE PEOPLE
CONGRESS
PRESI
CY
THE PEOPLE
PRESIDEN
11-14-73
CONGRESS
THE PEOPLE

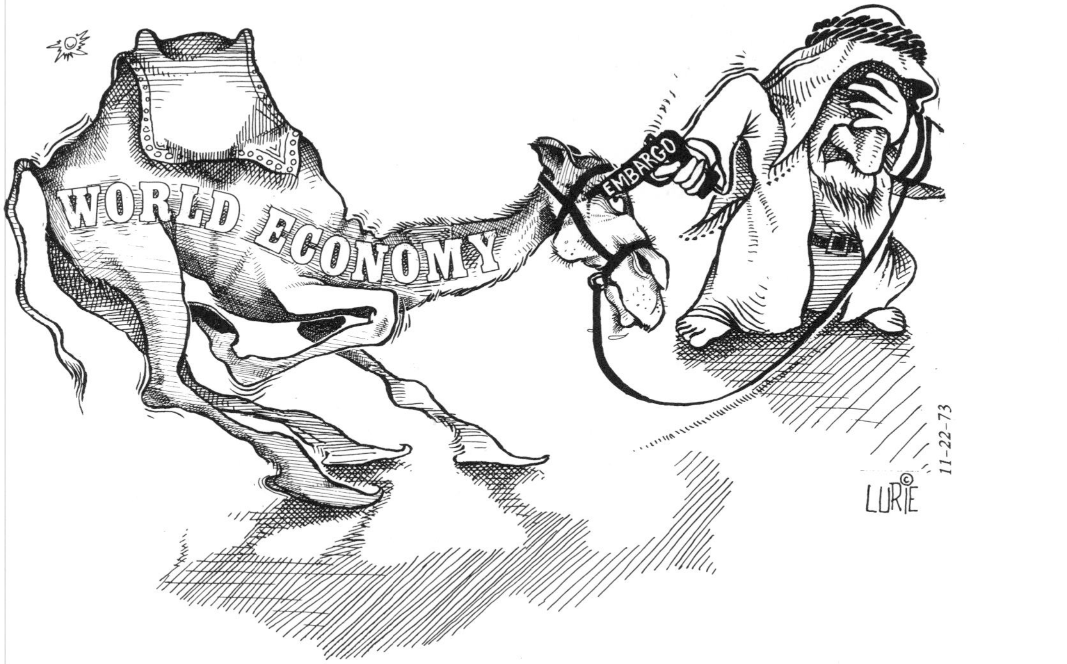
WORLD ECONOMY
EMBARGO
11-22-73
LURIE ©

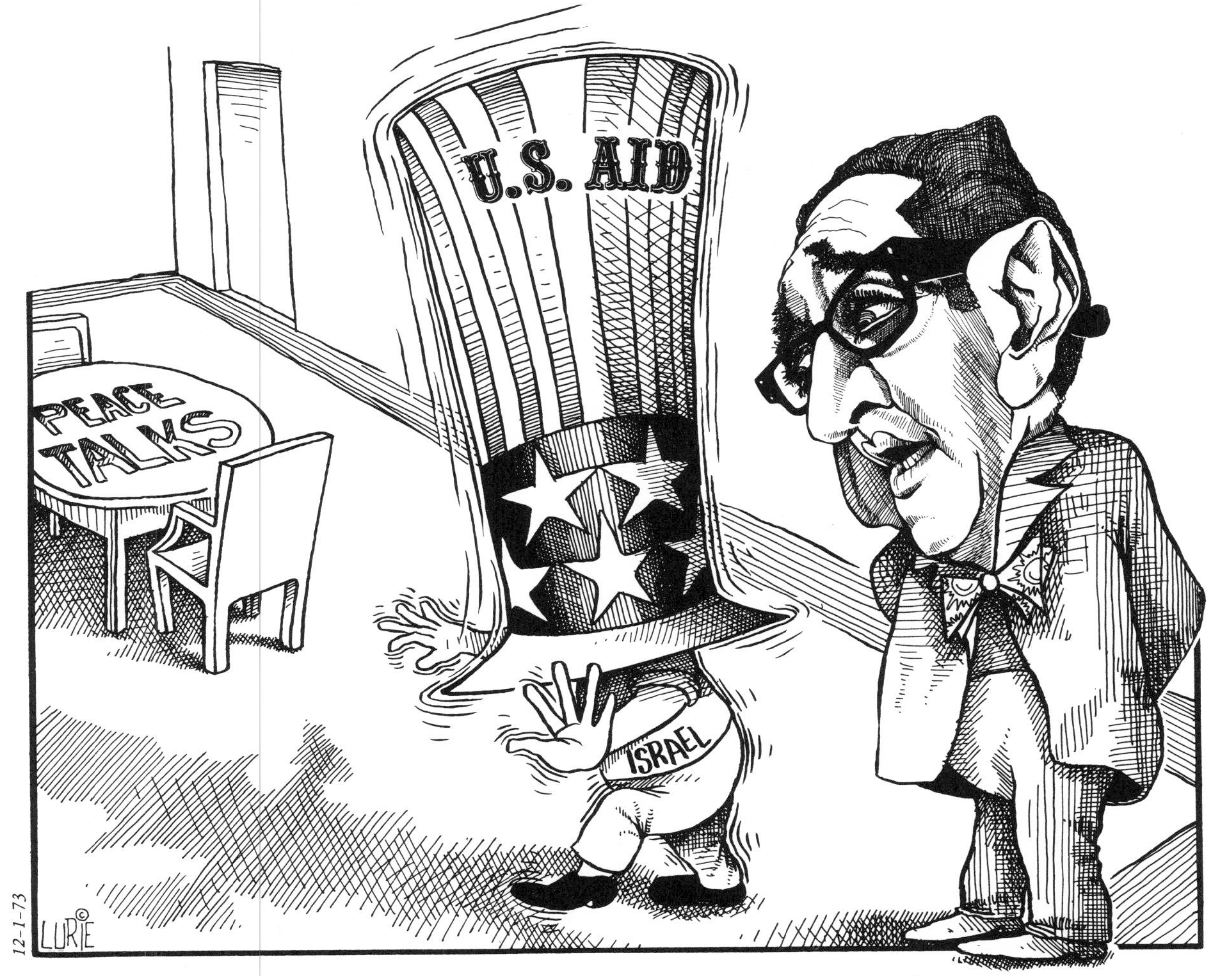
U.S. AID
PEACE TALKS
ISRAEL
12-1-73
LURIE ©

"WARM . . . WARM . . . WARMER . . ."

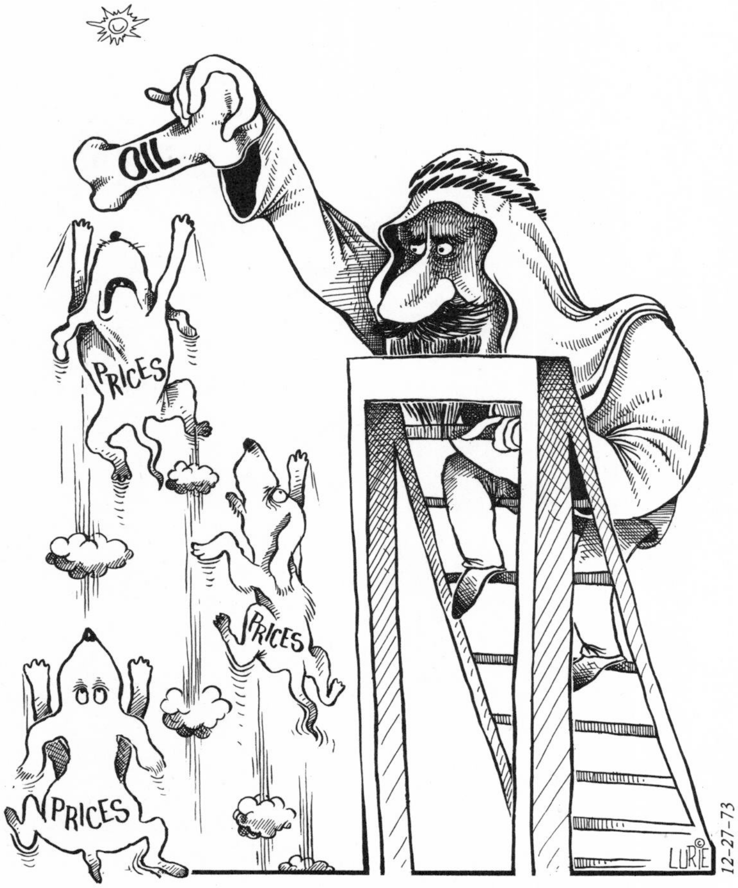
OIL
PRICES
PRICES
PRICES
LURIE

12-27-73

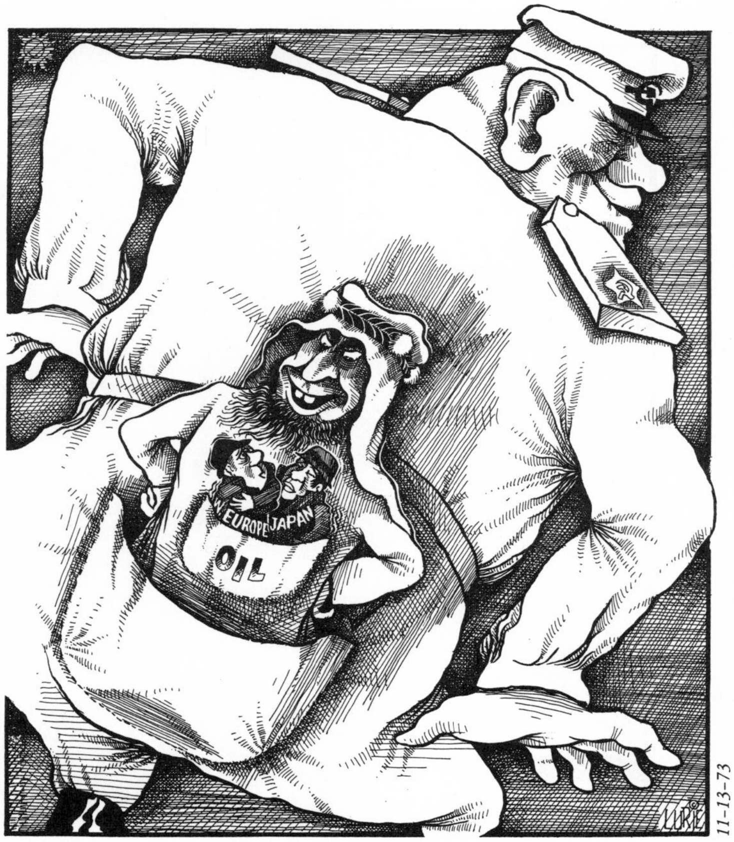
EUROPE
JAPAN
OIL
LURIE

11-13-73

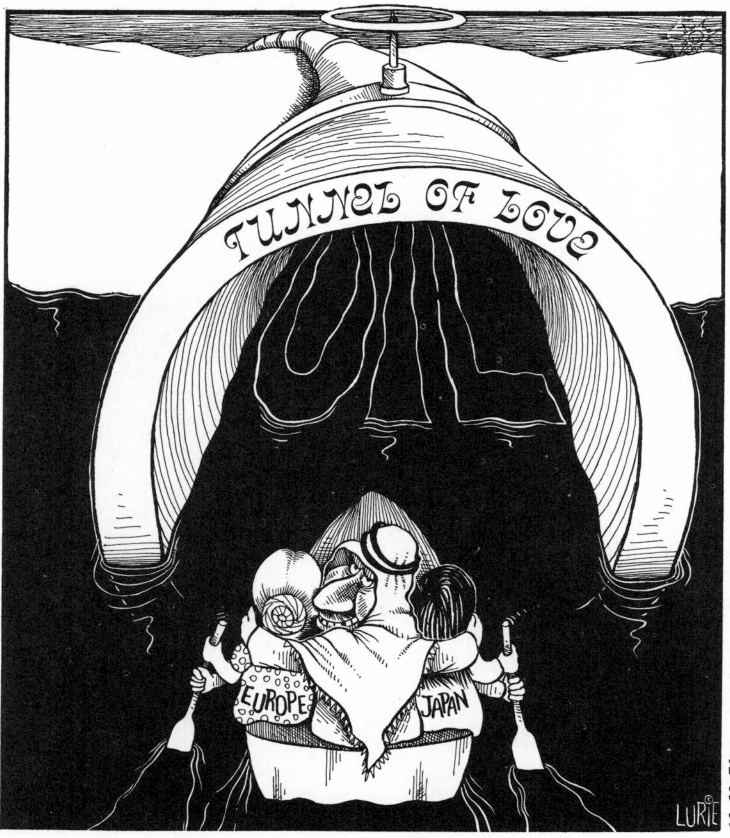
TUNNEL OF LOVE
OIL
EUROPE
JAPAN
LURIE

12-29-73

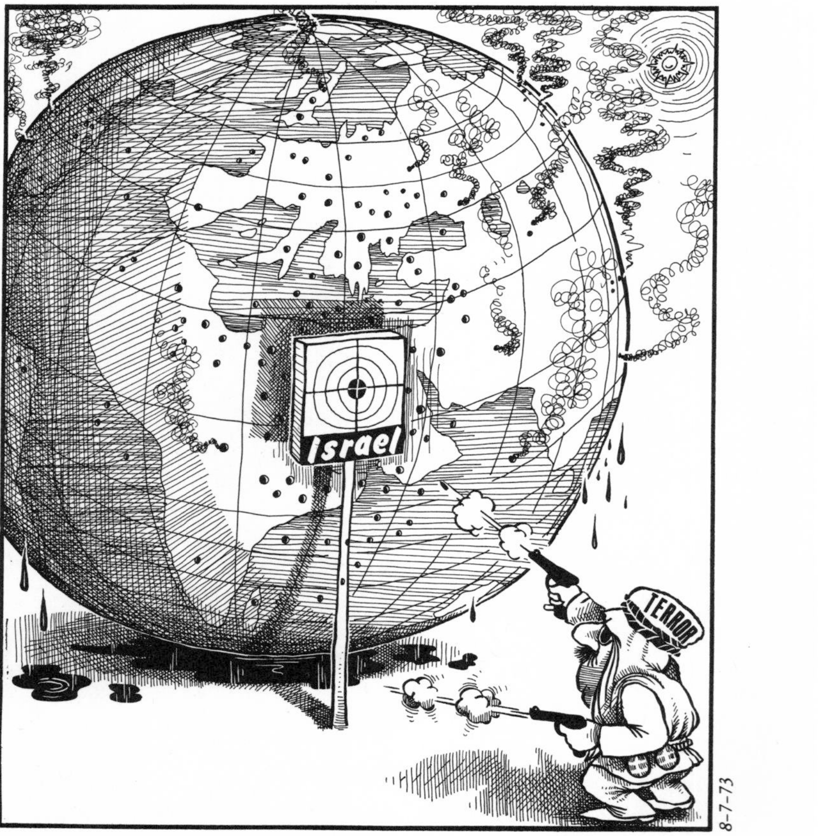
Israel
TERROR

8-7-73

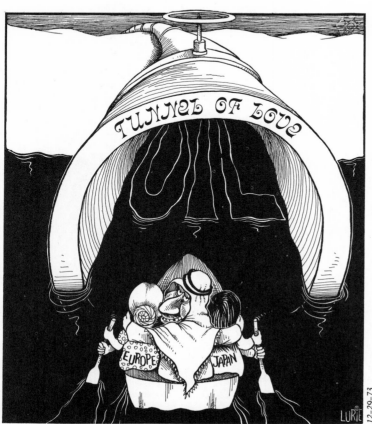

TAPES
WATERGATE
Z Z Z Z Z Z Z Z Z Z Z Z Z Z Z Z Z
SCANDALS
SCANDALS
SCAND
SCANDAL
SCANDAL
SCANDALS
SCANDALS
SCANDALS
SCANDAL
SCANDALS
SCANDAL
SCANDALS
12-5-73

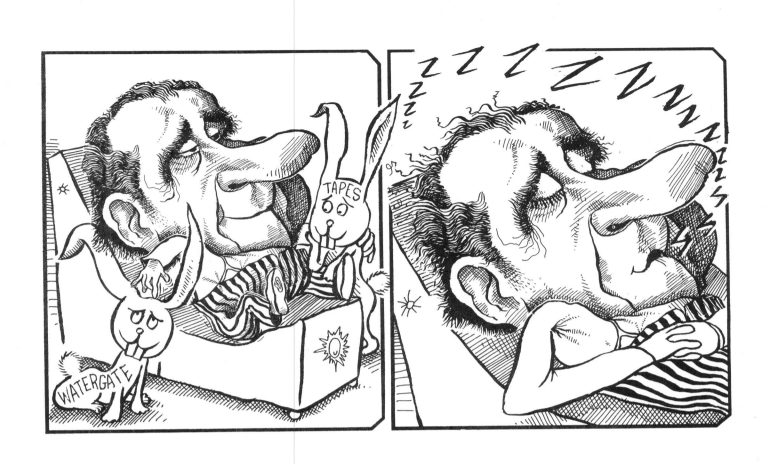

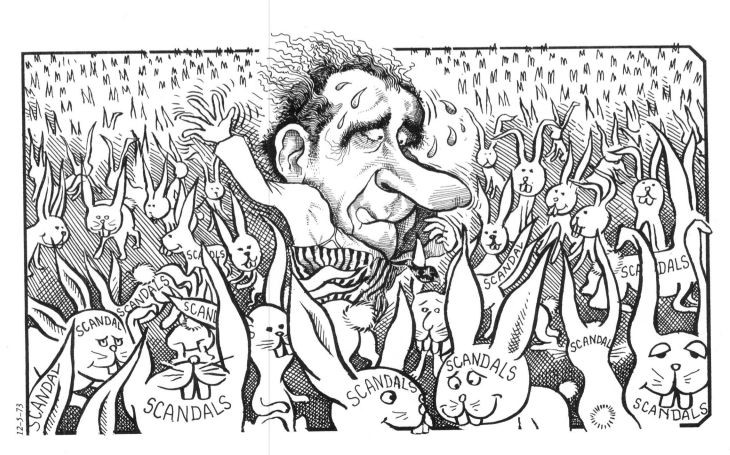

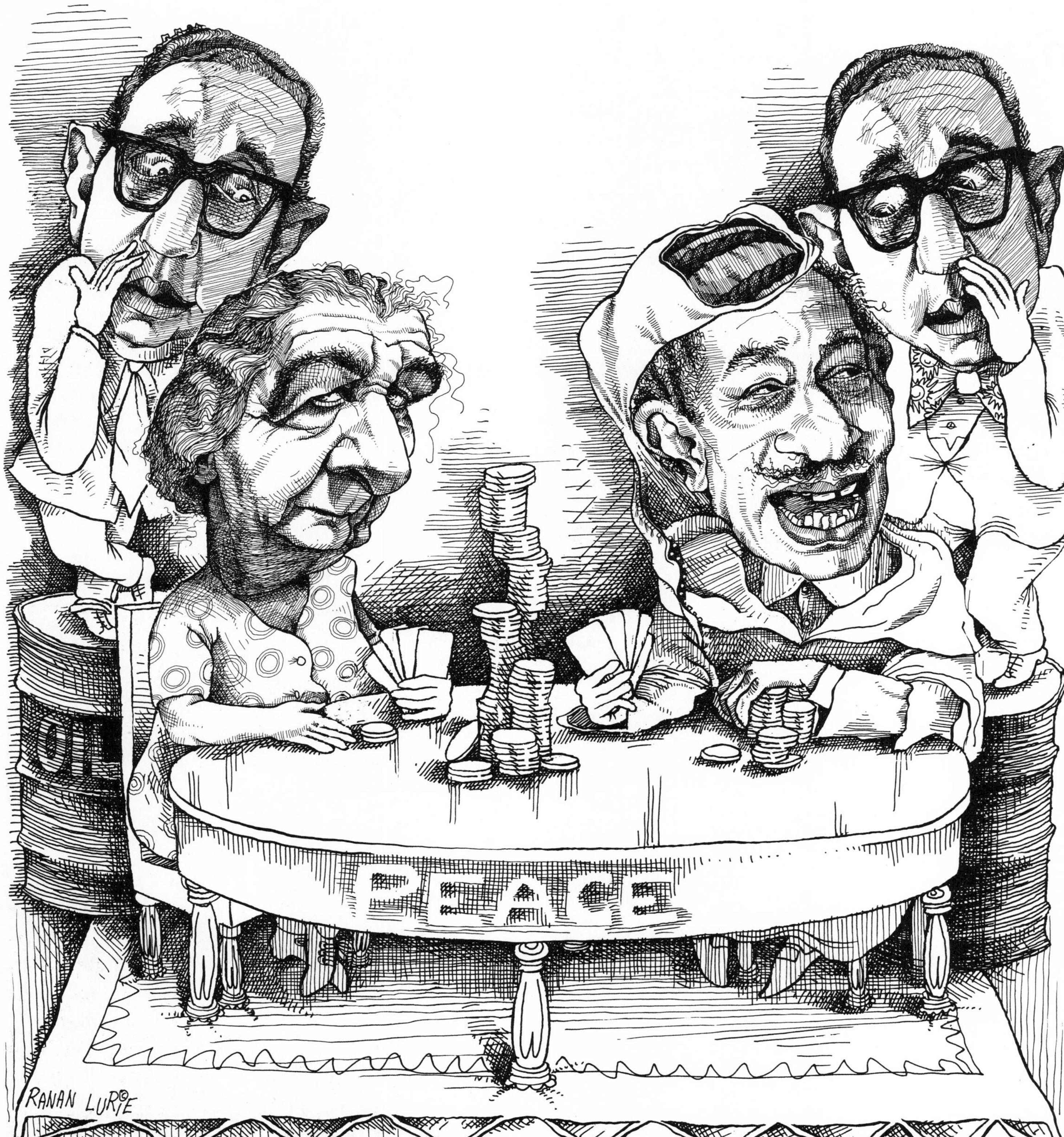
OIL
PEACE
RANAN LURIE©

International Newsweek 12-13-73

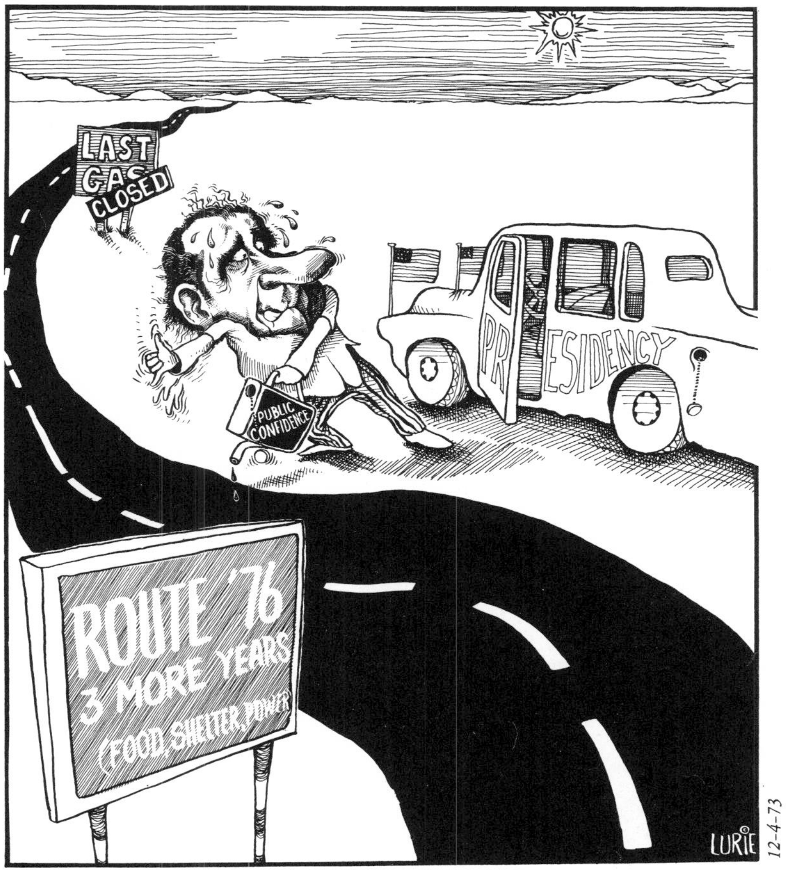
LAST GAS CLOSED
PUBLIC CONFIDENCE
PRESIDENCY
ROUTE '76
3 MORE YEARS
(FOOD, SHELTER, POWER
LURIE
12-4-73

SUNDAY DRIVER

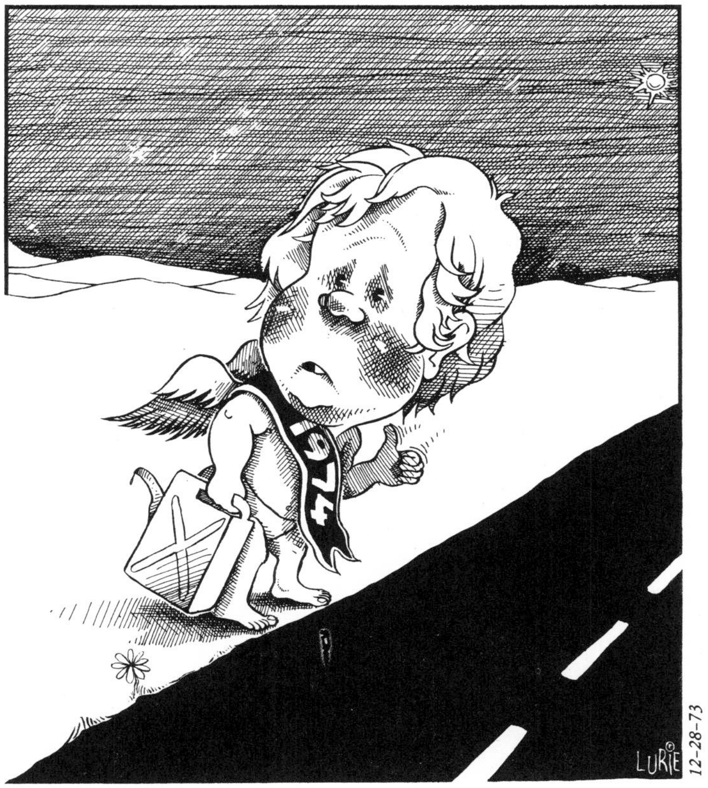
1974
LURIE
12-28-73

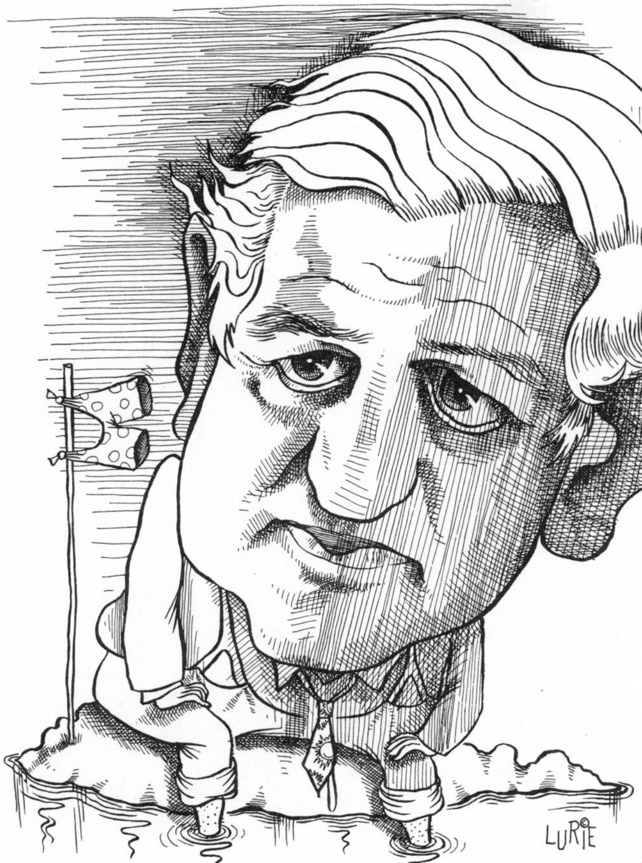
LURIE

Norman Kirk
Prime Minister of New Zealand

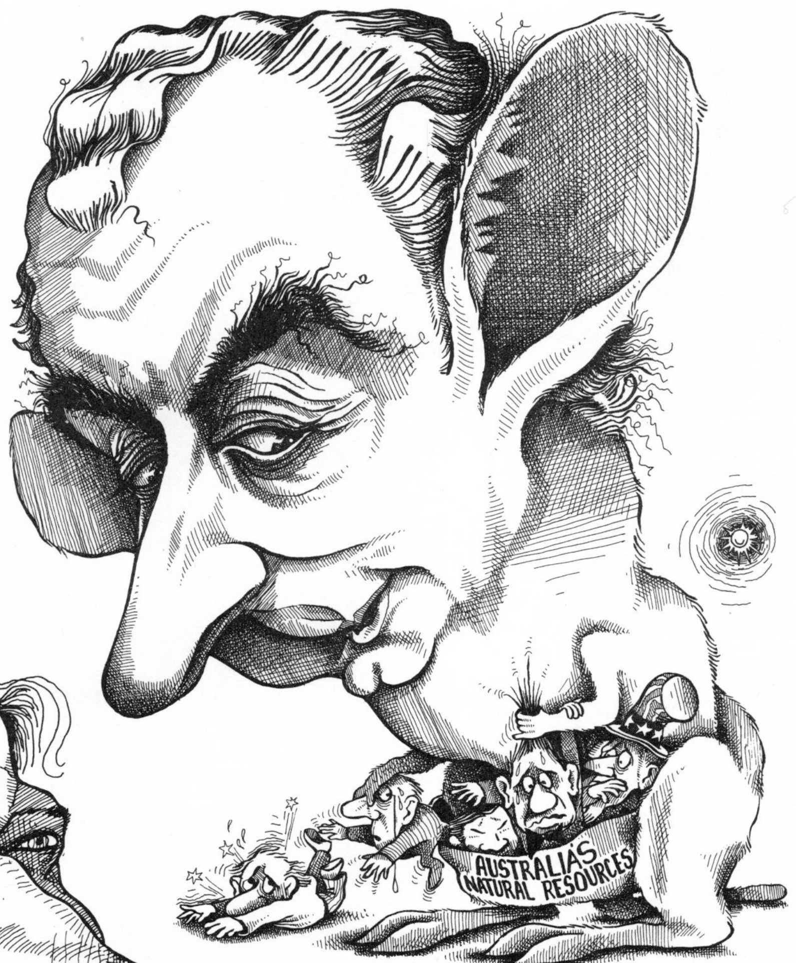
AUSTRALIAS
NATURAL RESOURCES

Gough Whitlam
Australia's Premier

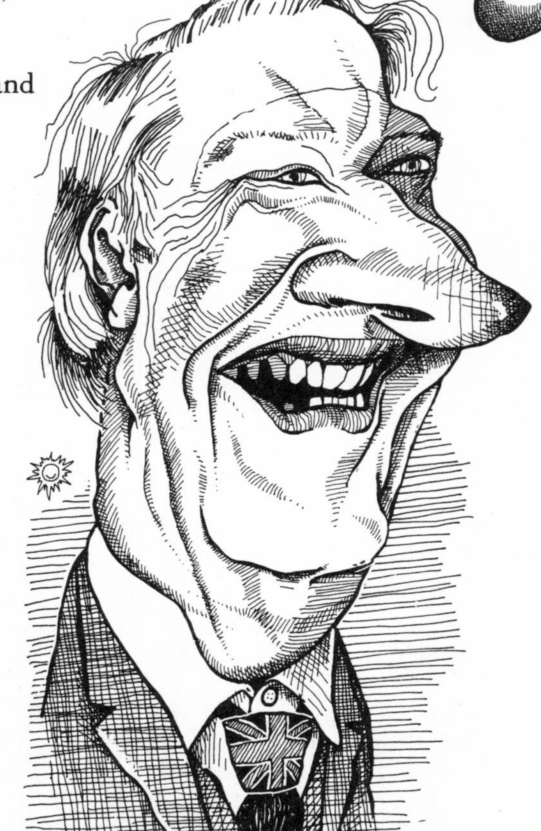
LURIE

Edward Heath
Prime Minister of the United Kingdom

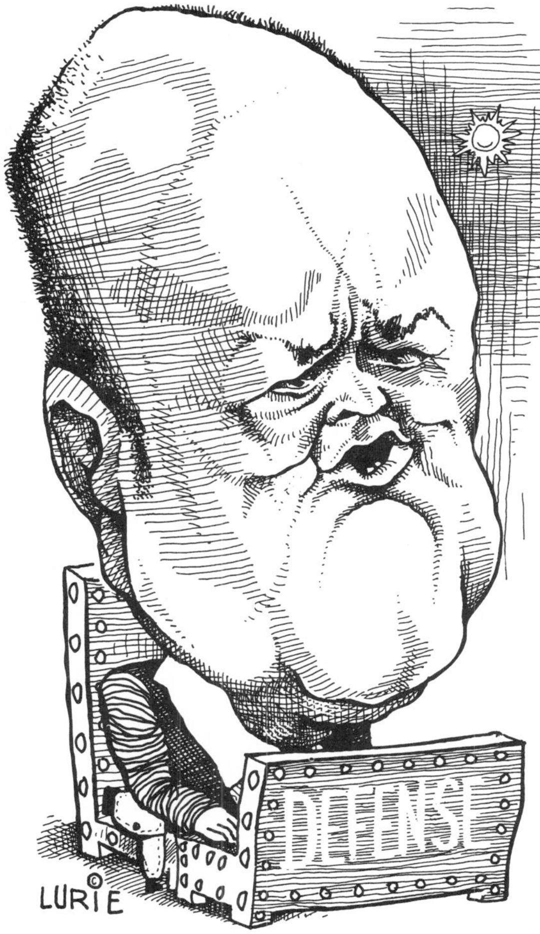
DEFENSE
LURIE

Melvin Laird

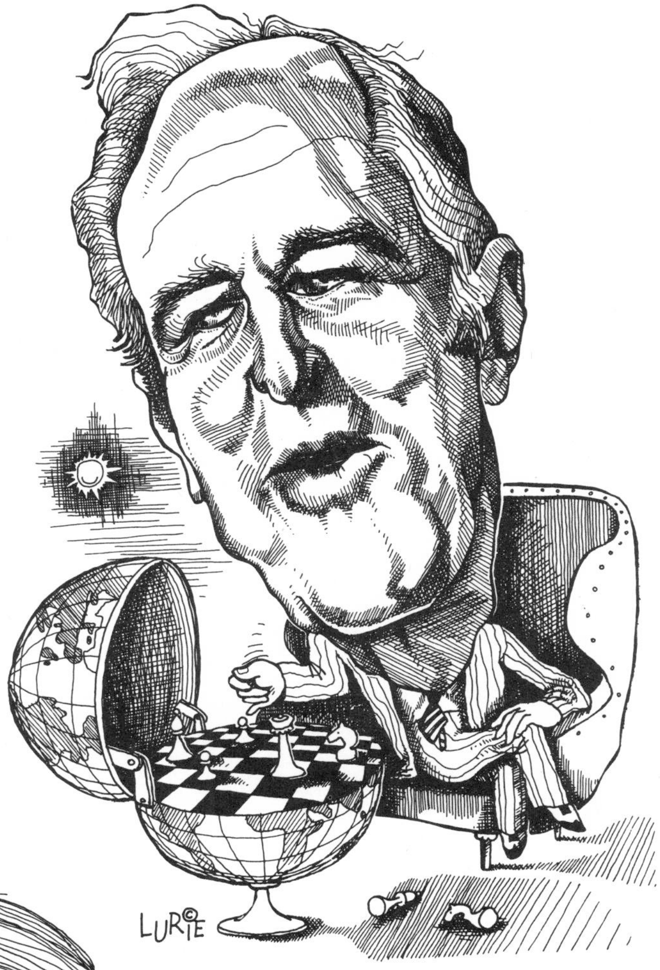
LURIE

William P. Rogers

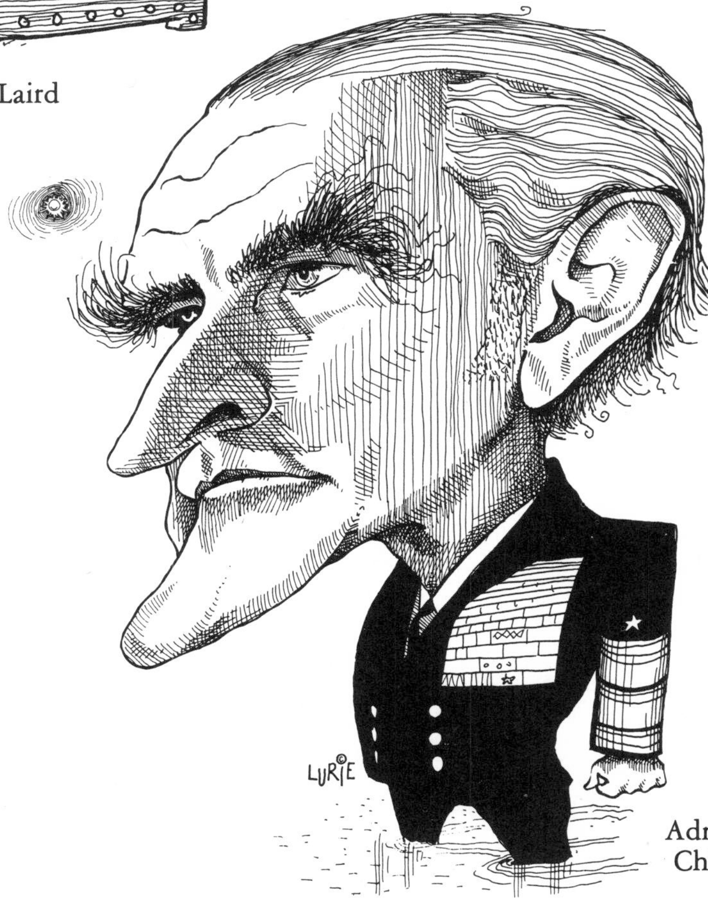
LURIE

Admiral Elmo Zumwalt, Jr.
Chief of Naval Operations

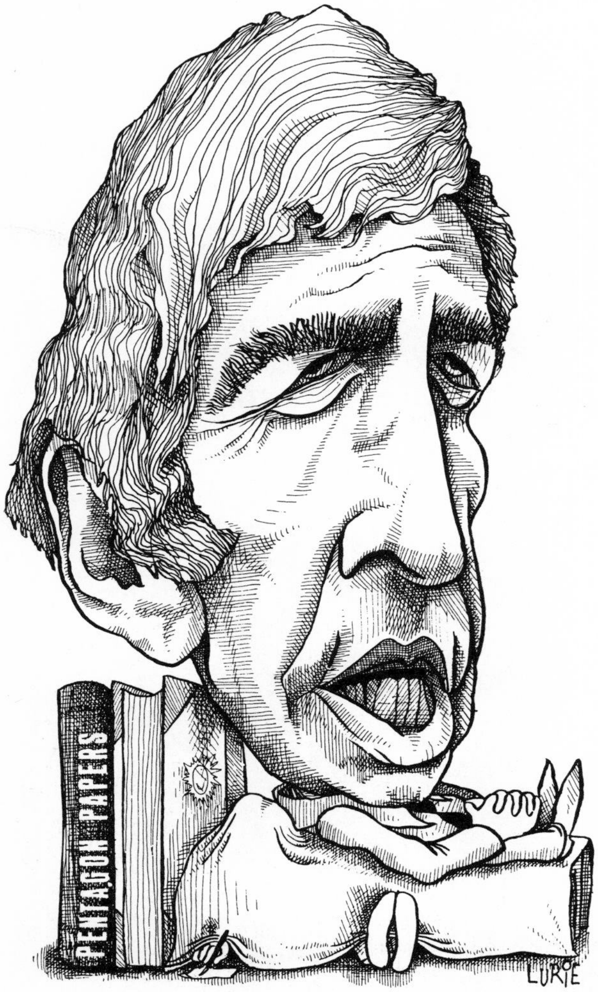
PENTAGON PAPERS
LURIE

Daniel Ellsberg

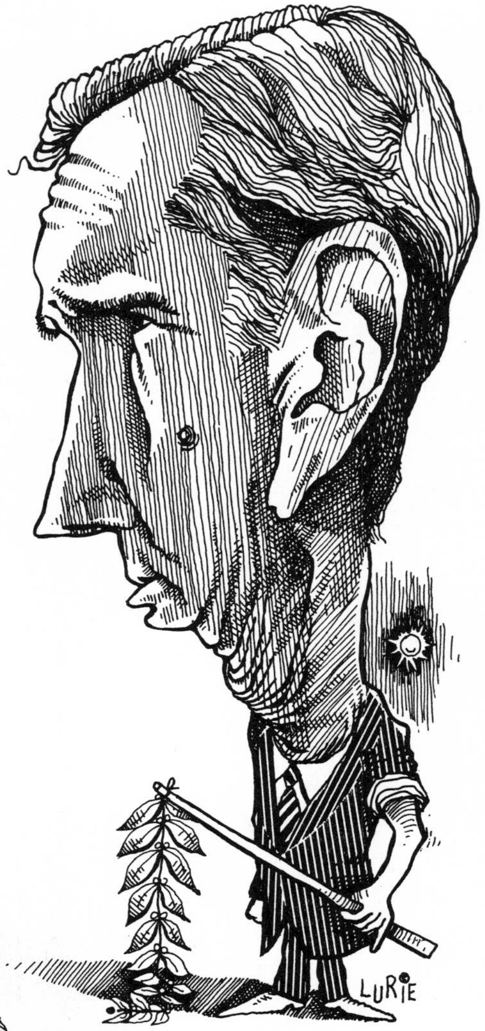
LURIE

Ramsey Clark

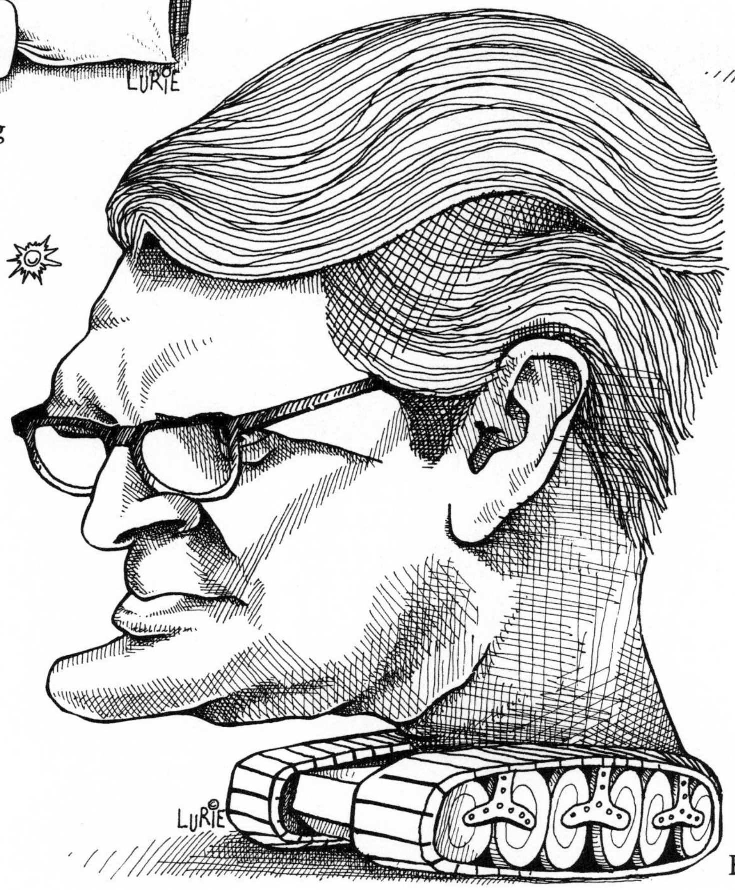
LURIE

Elliot Richardson

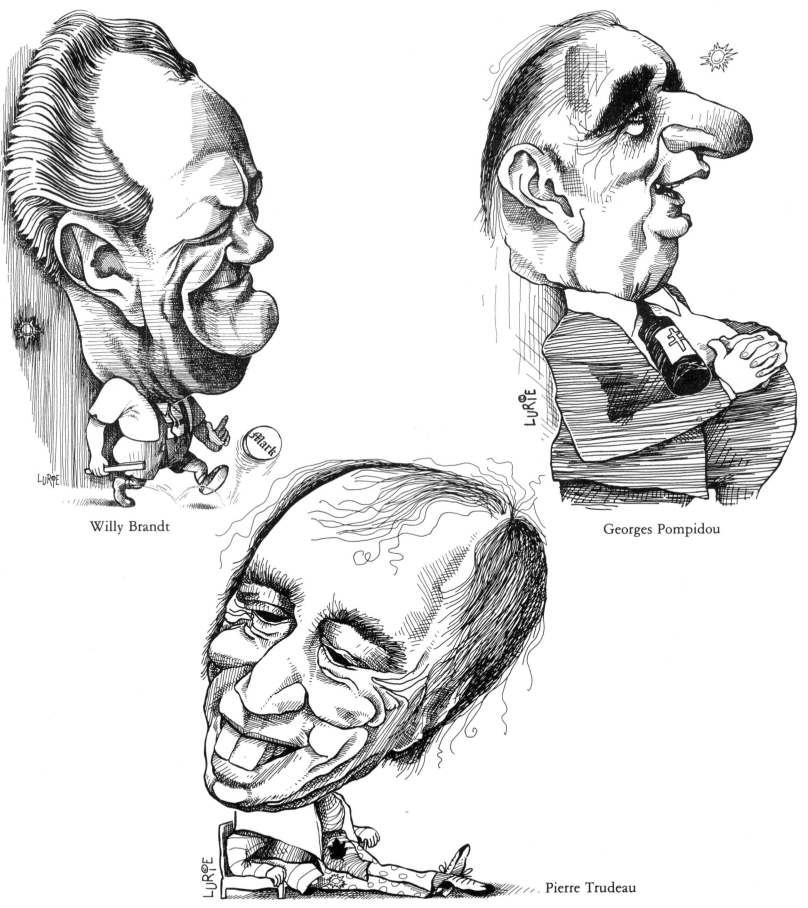

Willy Brandt

Georges Pompidou

Pierre Trudeau

101

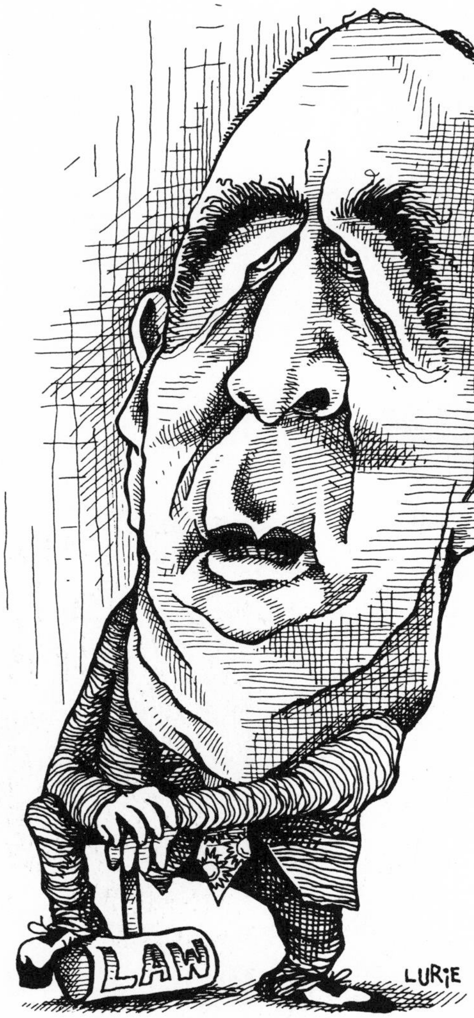
LAW
LURIE

John Mitchell

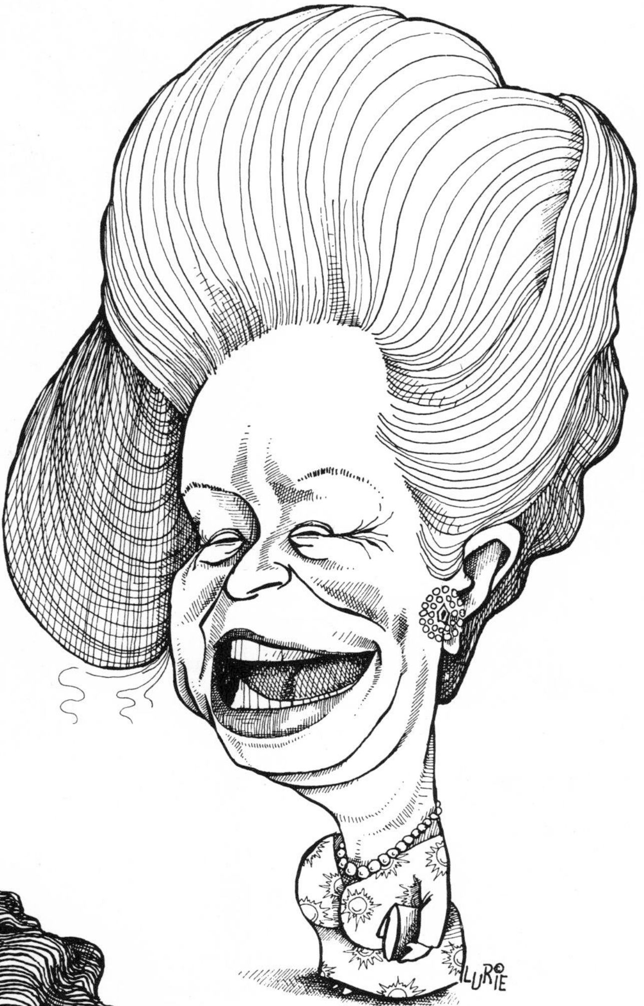
LURIE

Martha Mitchell

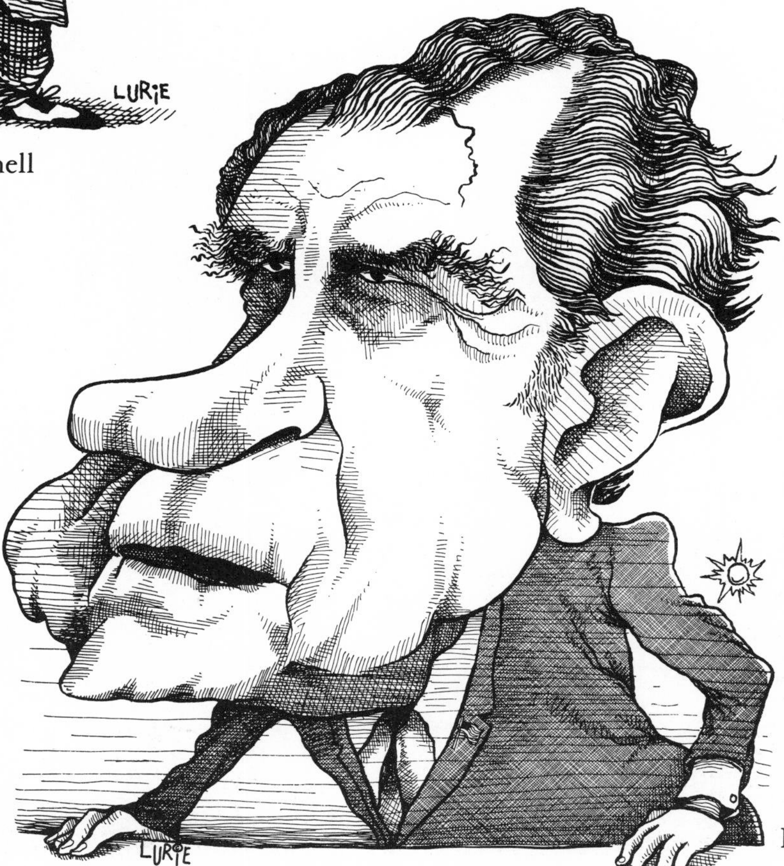
LURIE

President Richard M. Nixon

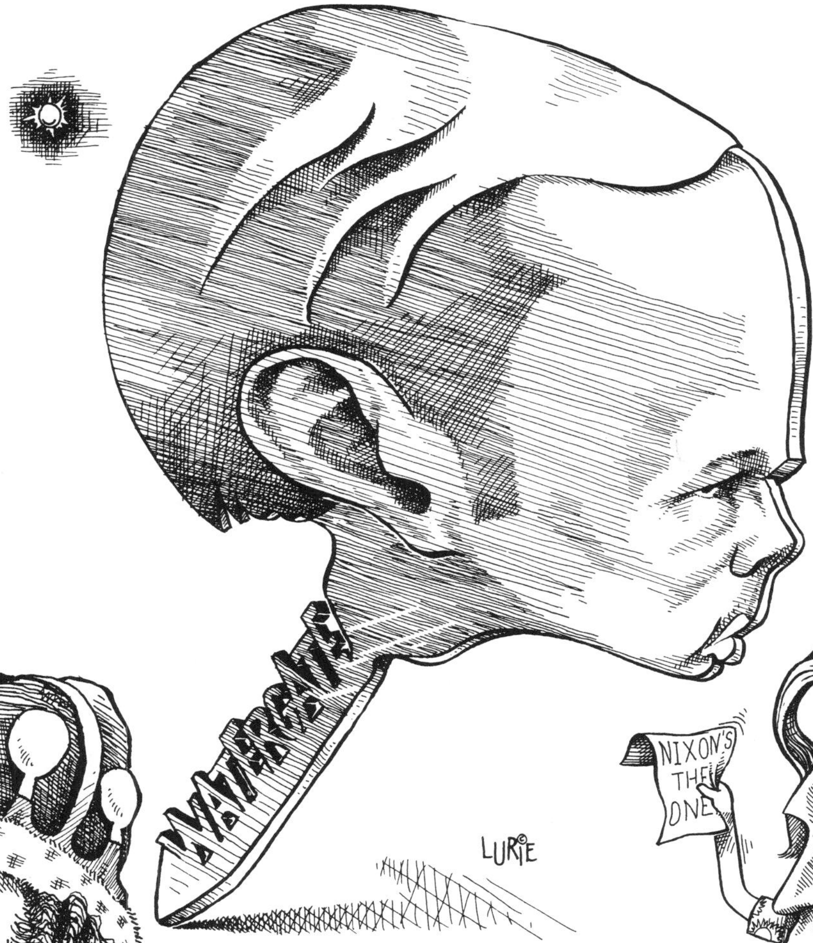
LURIE

John Dean

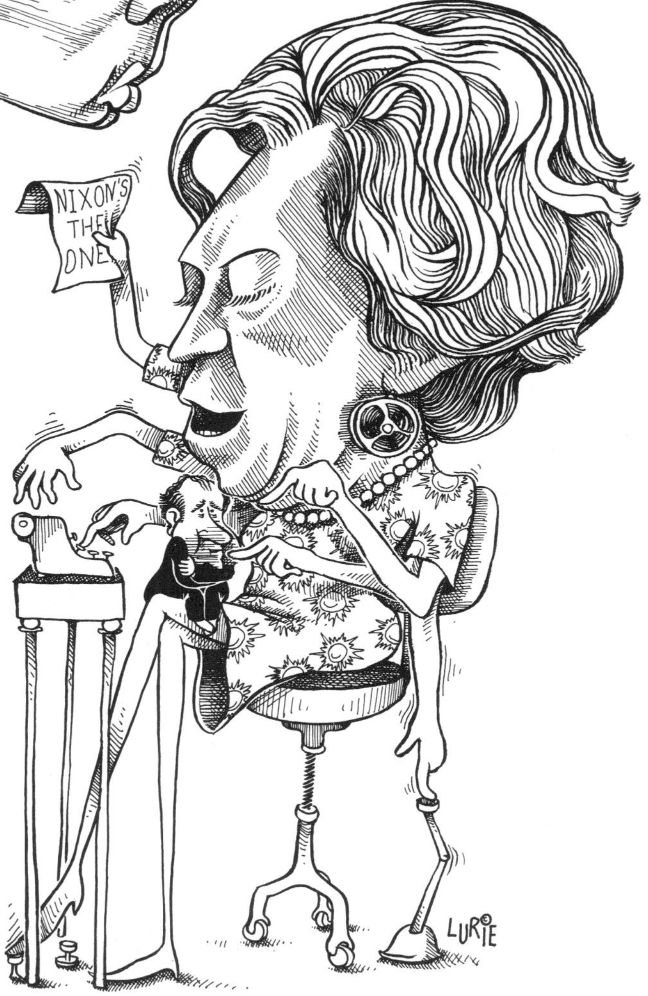
NIXON'S
LURIE

Rose Mary Woods
President Nixon's Secretary

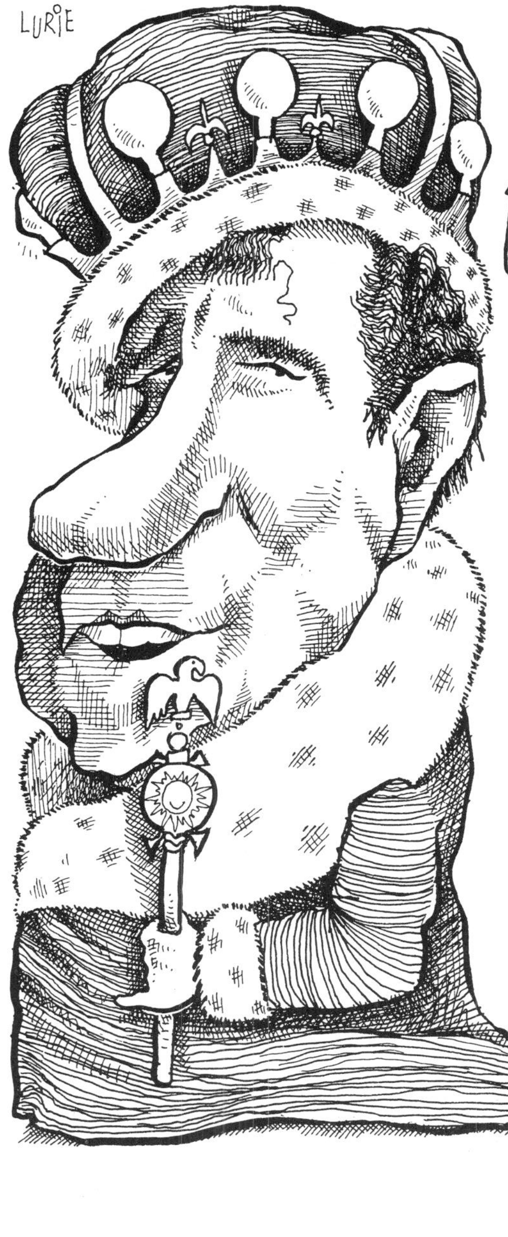
LURIE
WATERGATE

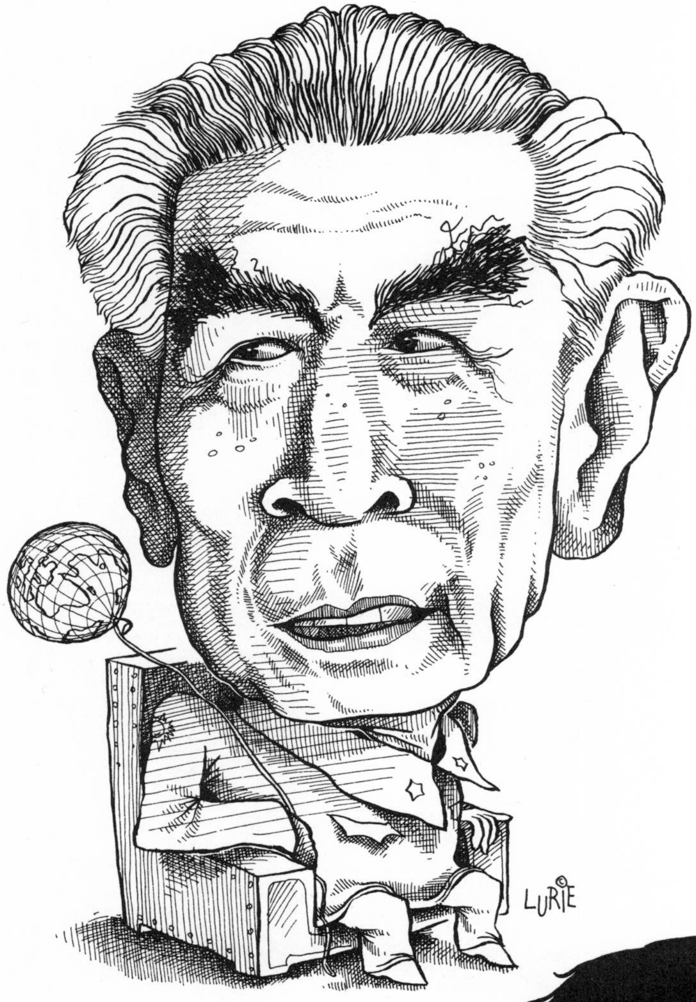
LURIE

Premier Chou En-lai

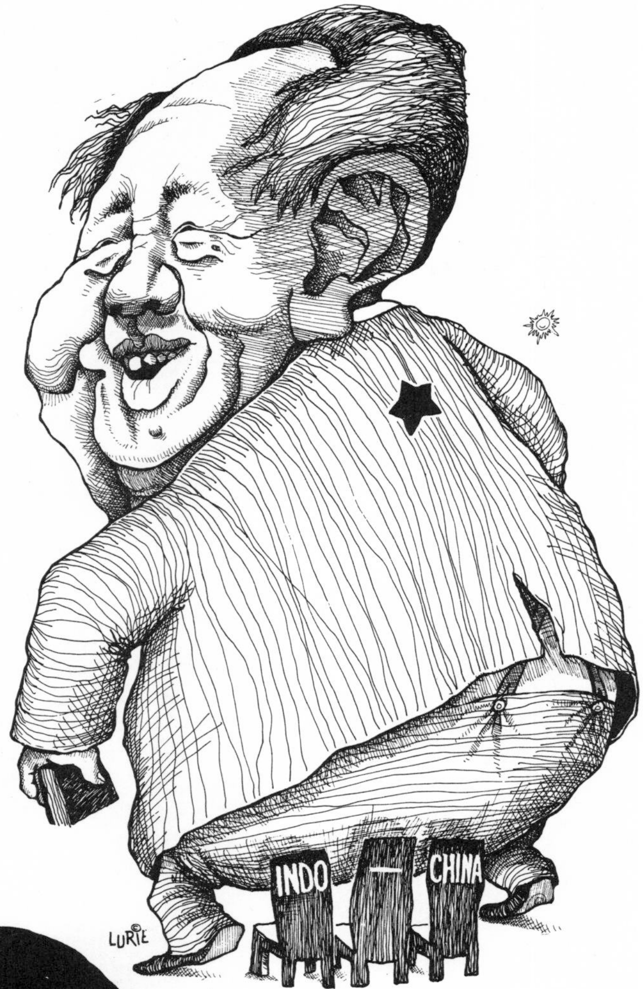
INDO
CHINA
LURIE

Mao Tse-tung

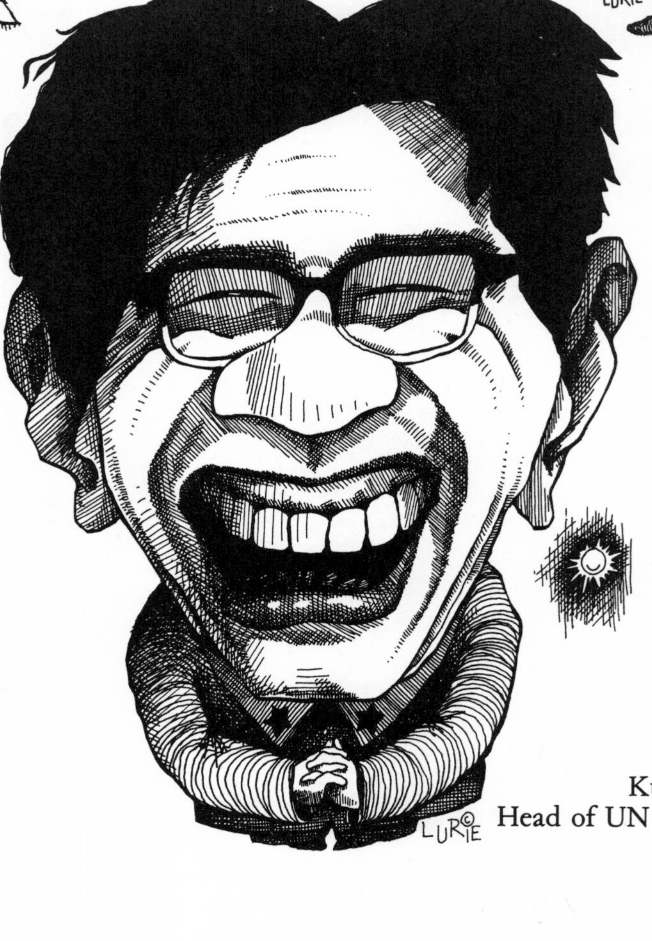
LURIE

Kuan Hua
Head of UN Chinese Delegation

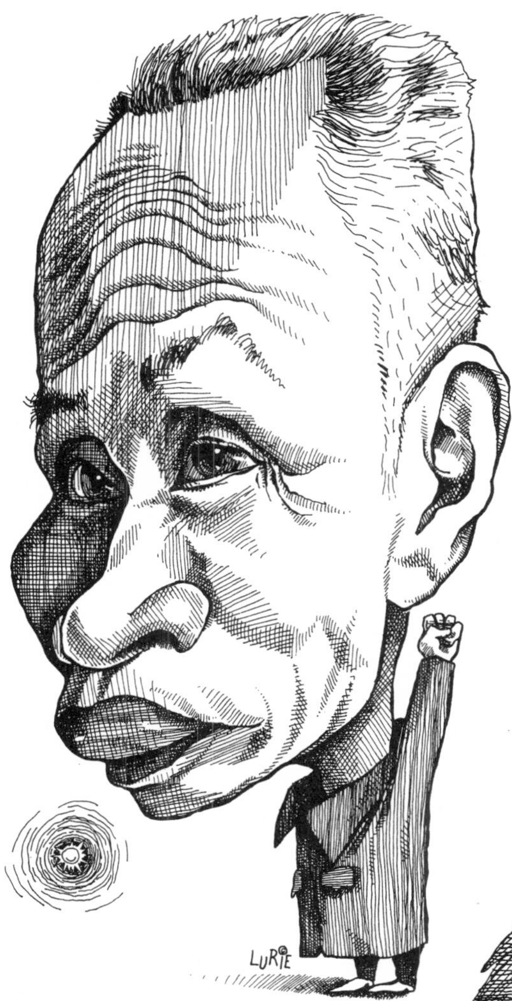
LURIE

Pham Van Dong

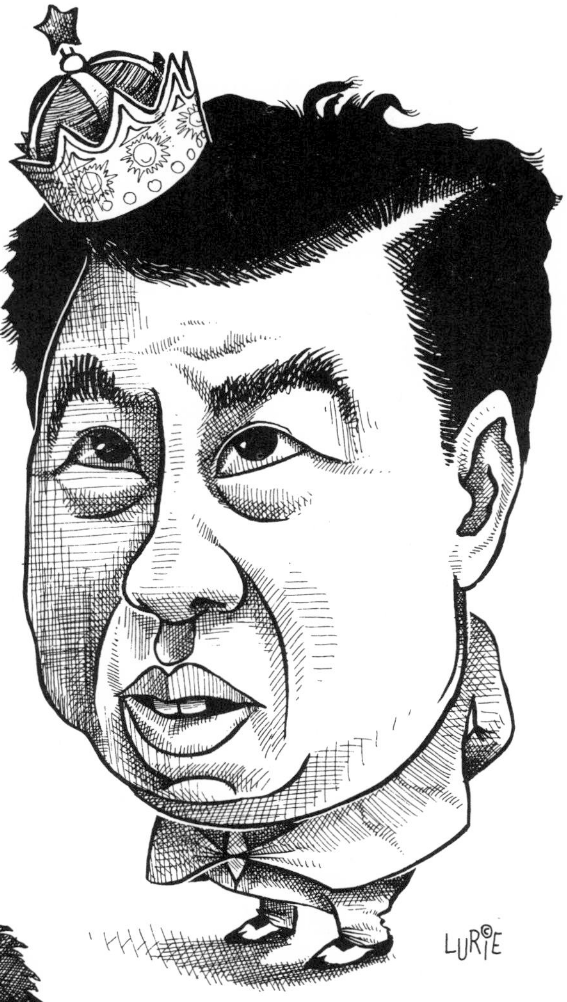
LURIE

Exiled Prince
Norodom Sihanouk
of Cambodia

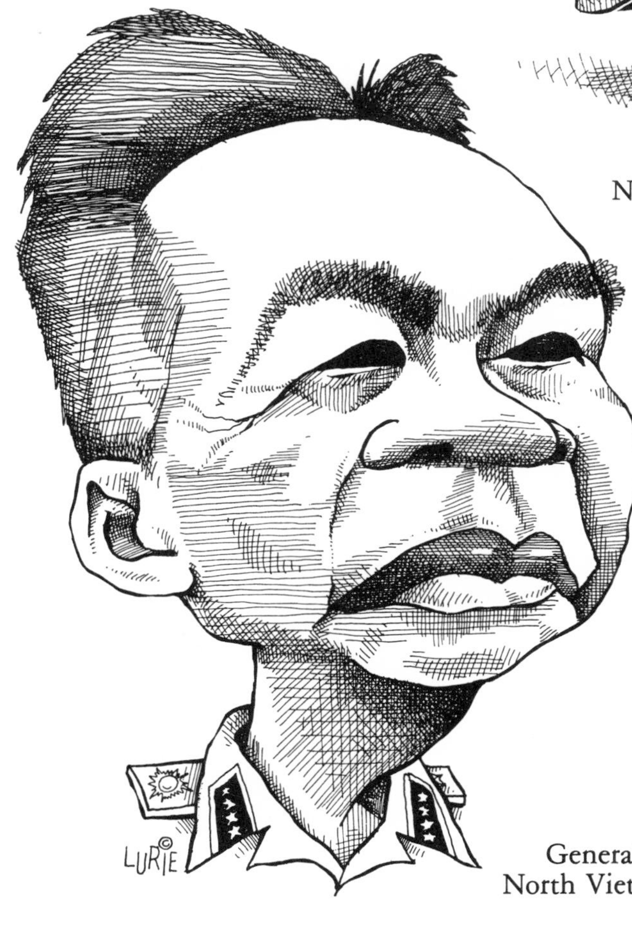
LURIE

General Vo Nguyen Giap
North Vietnam Defense Minister

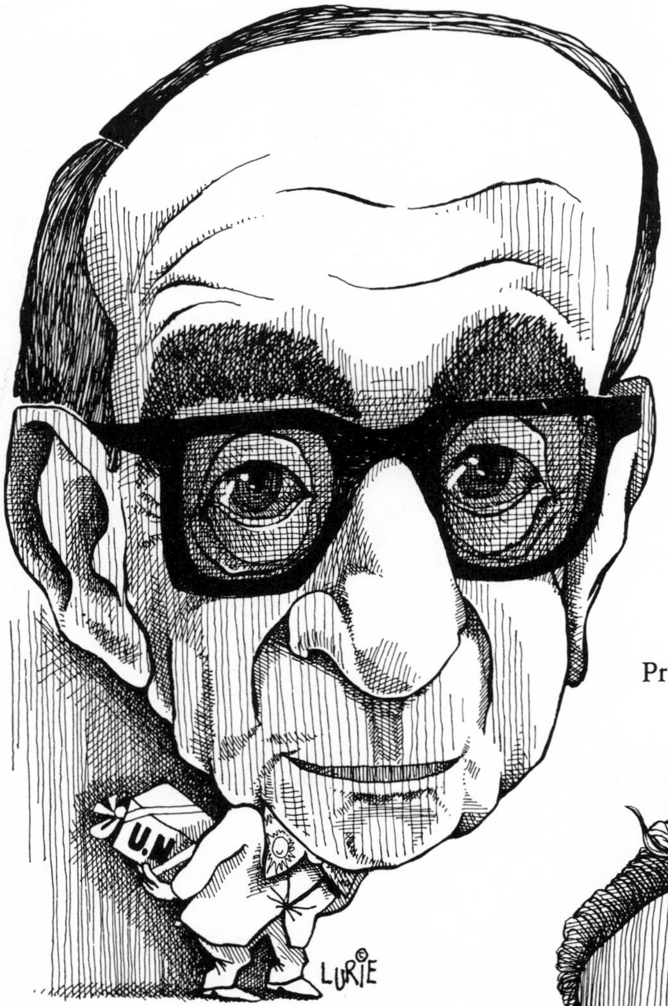
U.N
LURIE

Scali
Our Man in the UN

Abba Eban

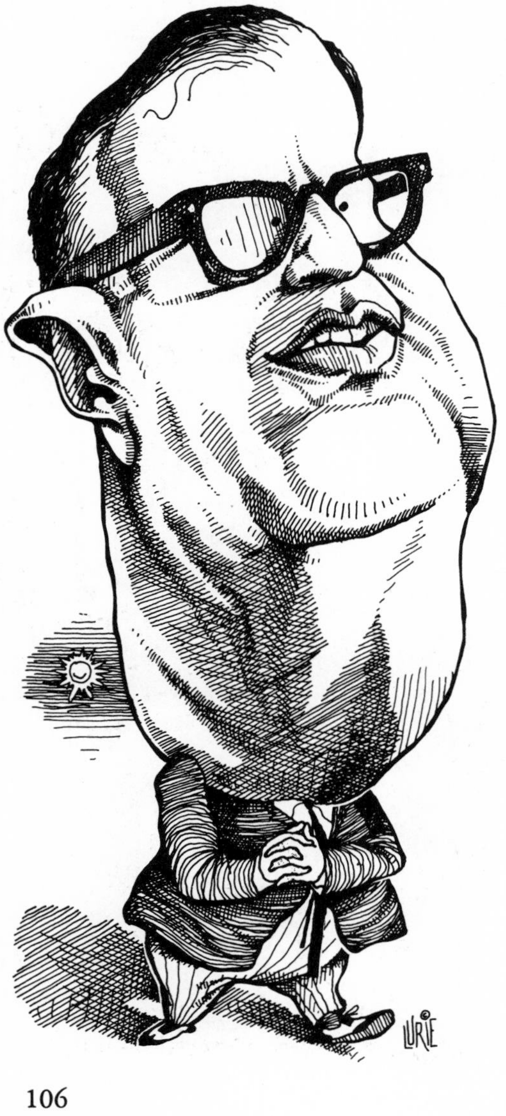
LURIE

President Boumediene
of Algeria

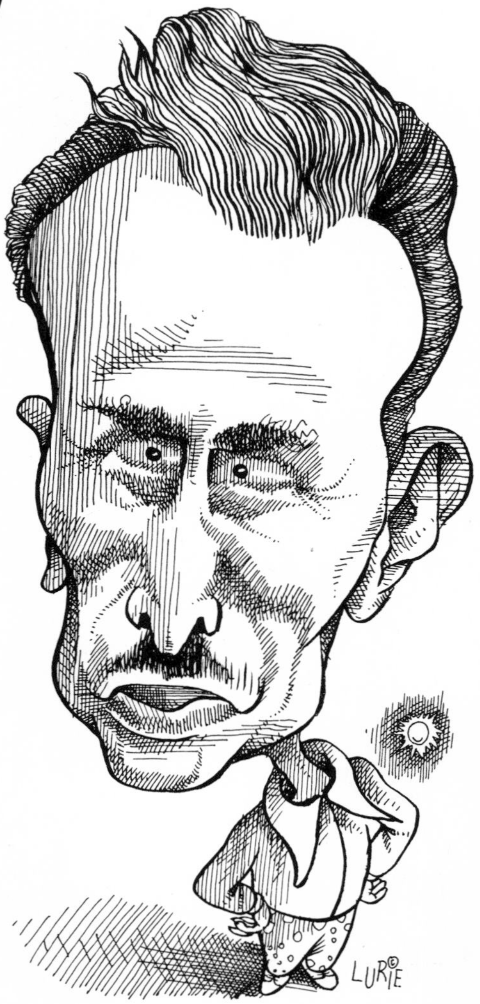
LURIE

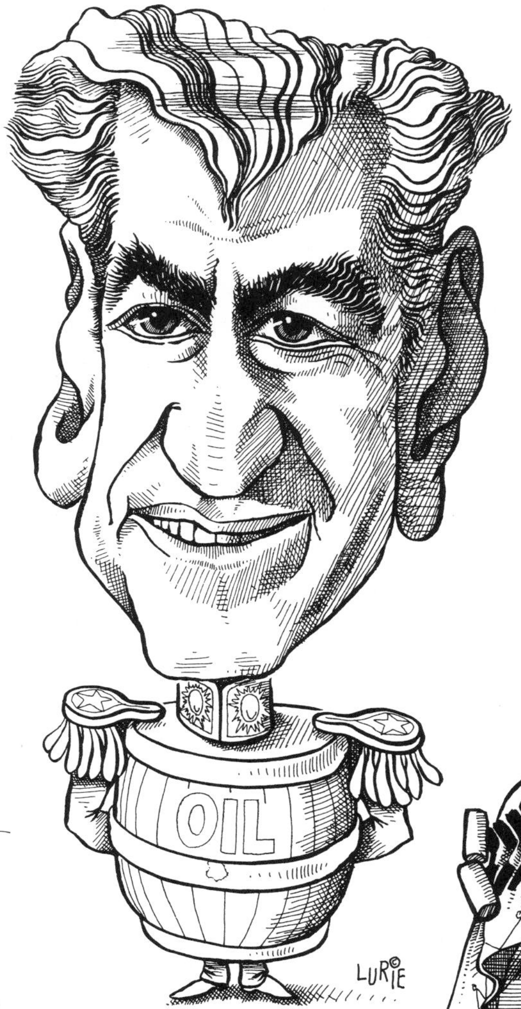
OIL
LURIE

Shah of Iran,
Mohammed Riza Pahlevi

Sheik Sabah of Kuwait

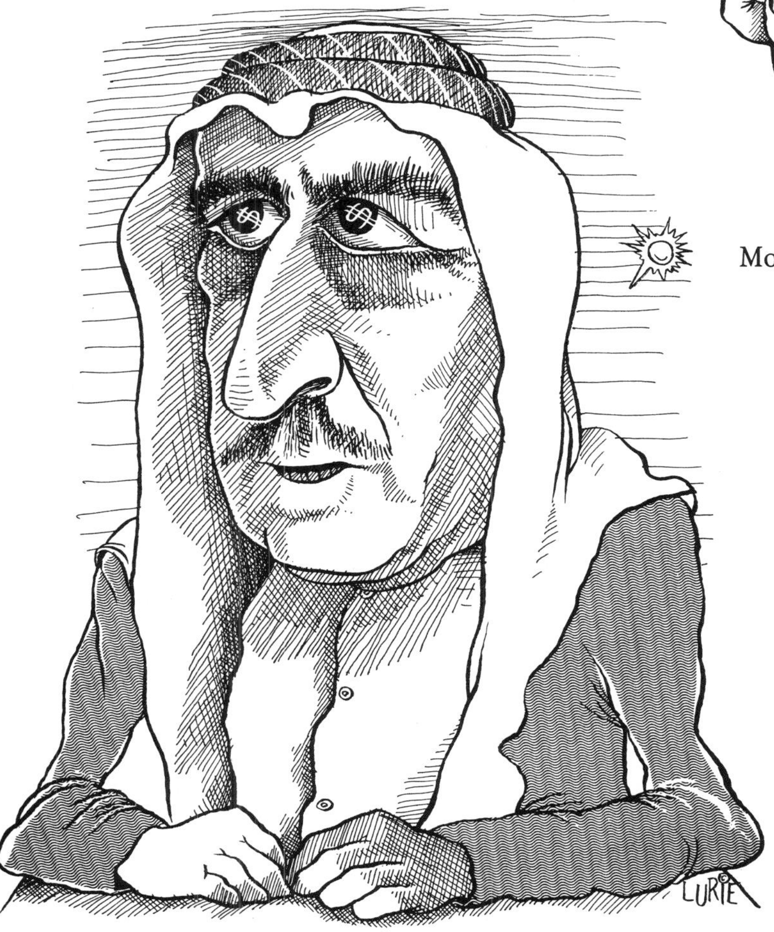
LURIE

Ahmed Zaki Al-Yamani
Saudi Arabian Oil Minister

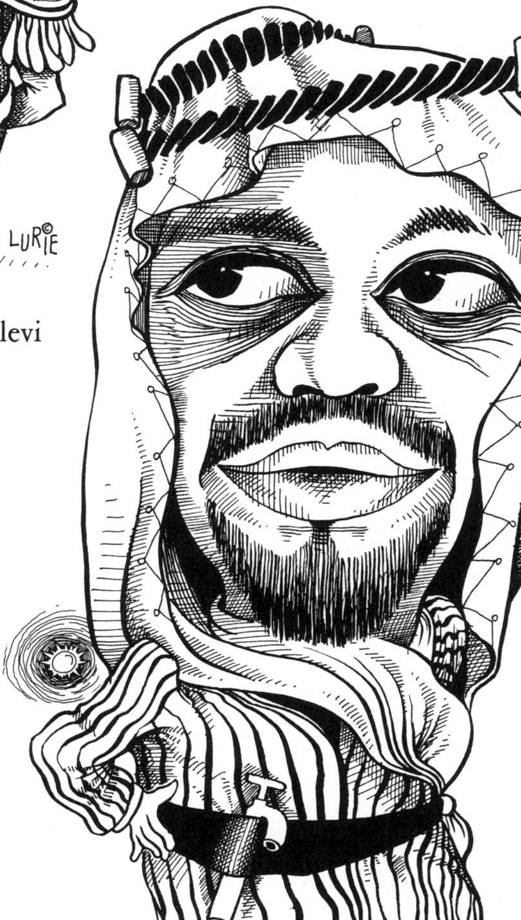
LURIE

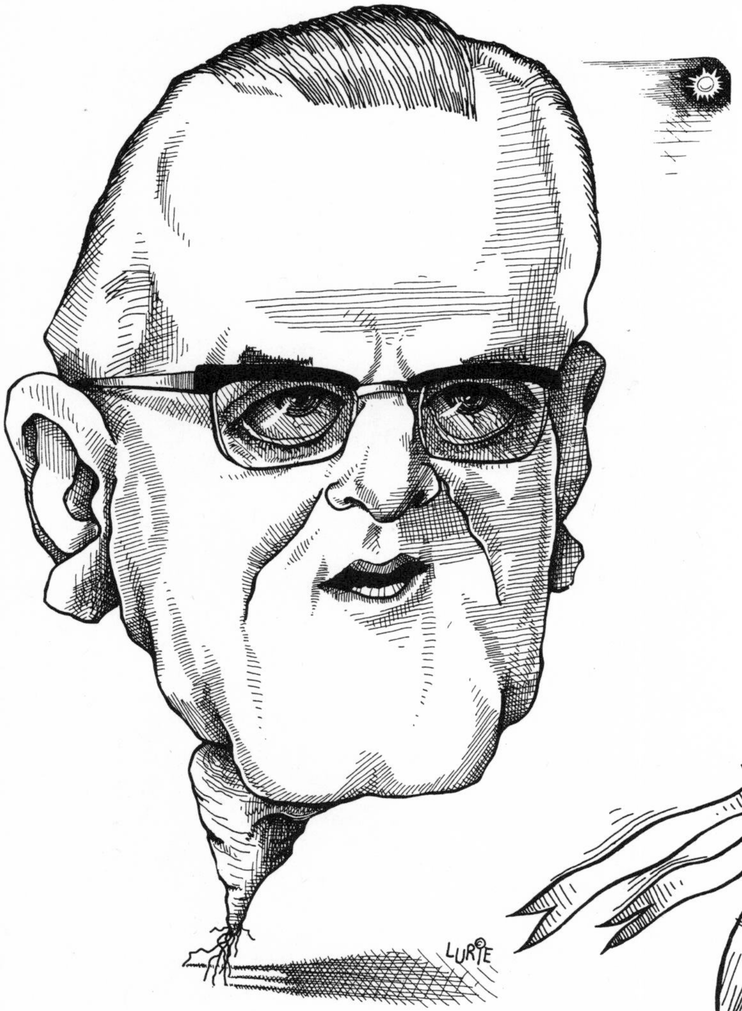
LURIE

Earl Butz

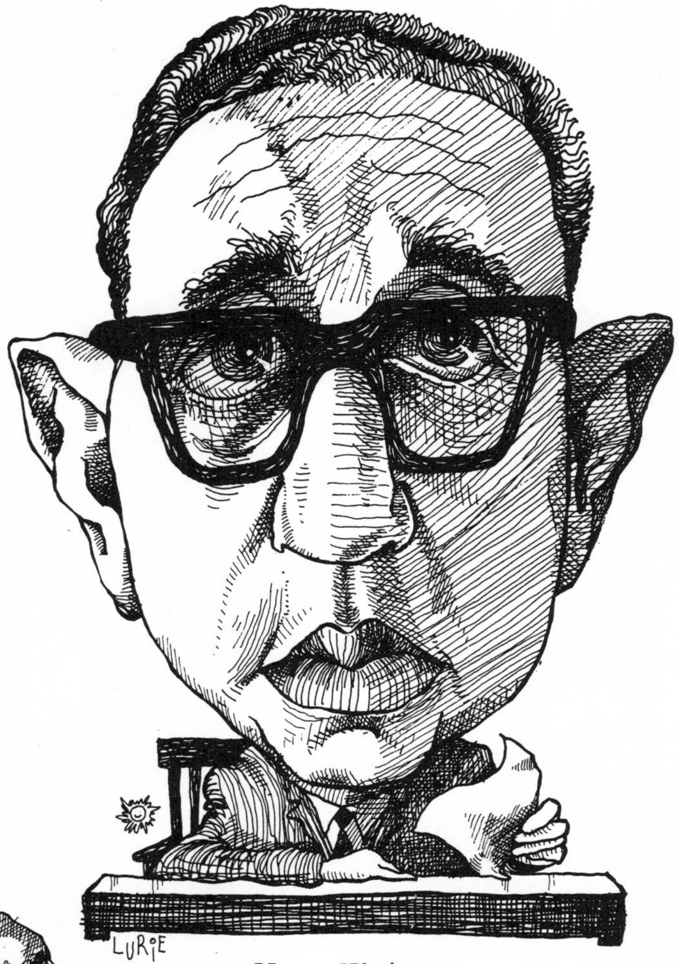
LURIE

Henry Kissinger

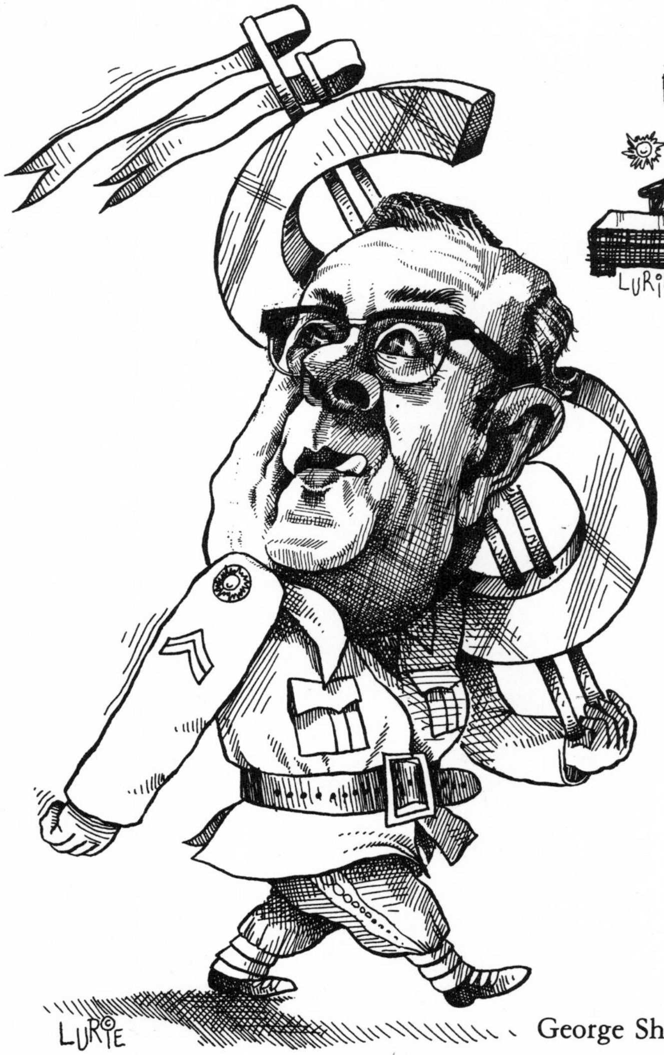
LURIE

George Shultz

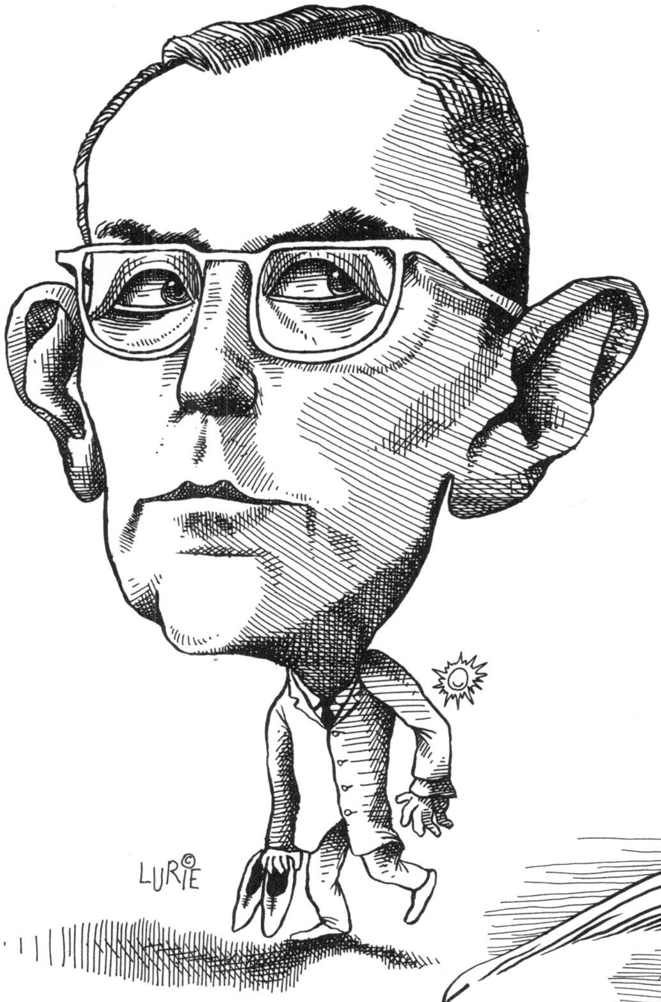
LURIE

William Colby
CIA Director

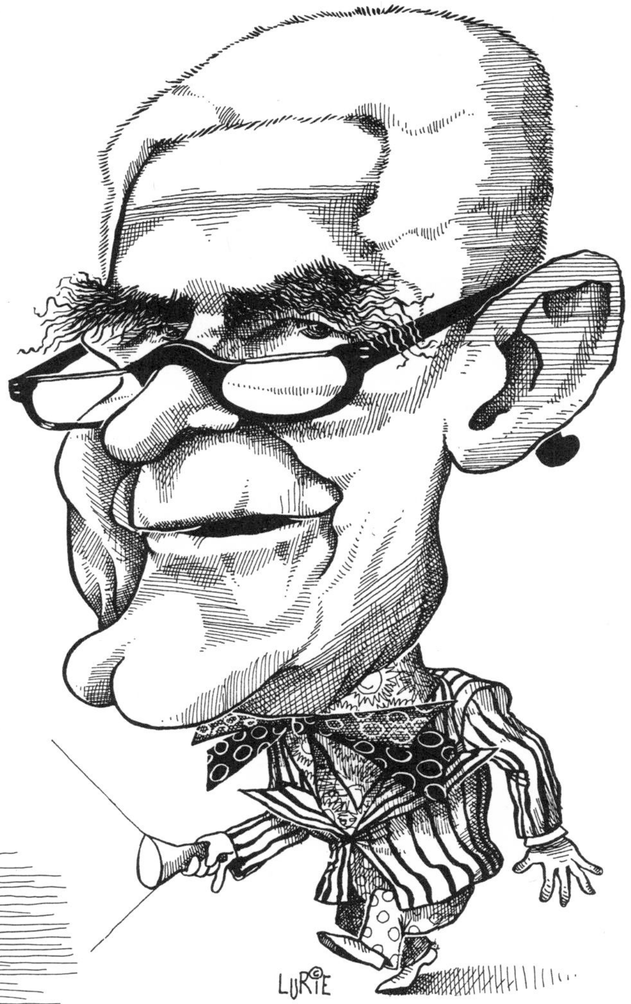
LURIE

Archibald Cox
Special Watergate Prosecutor

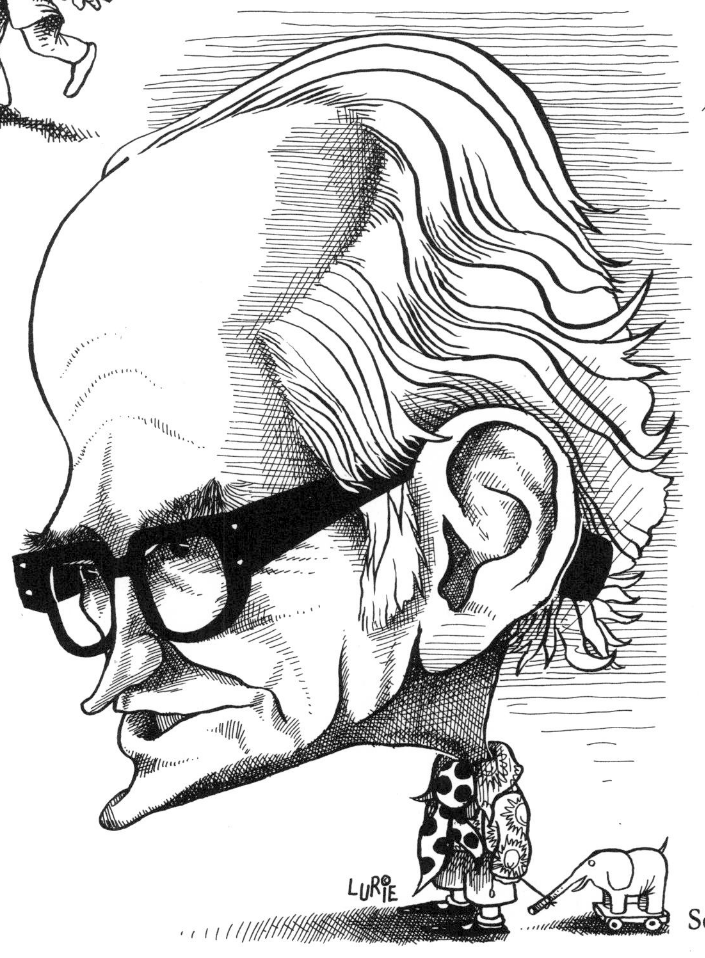
LURIE

Senator Barry Goldwater

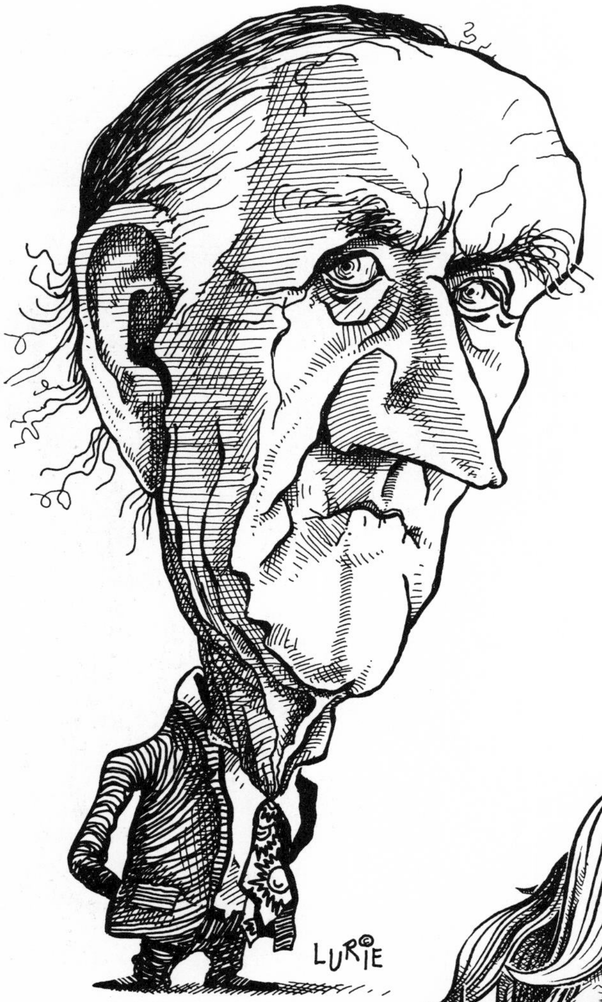
LURIE

Senator Mike Mansfield

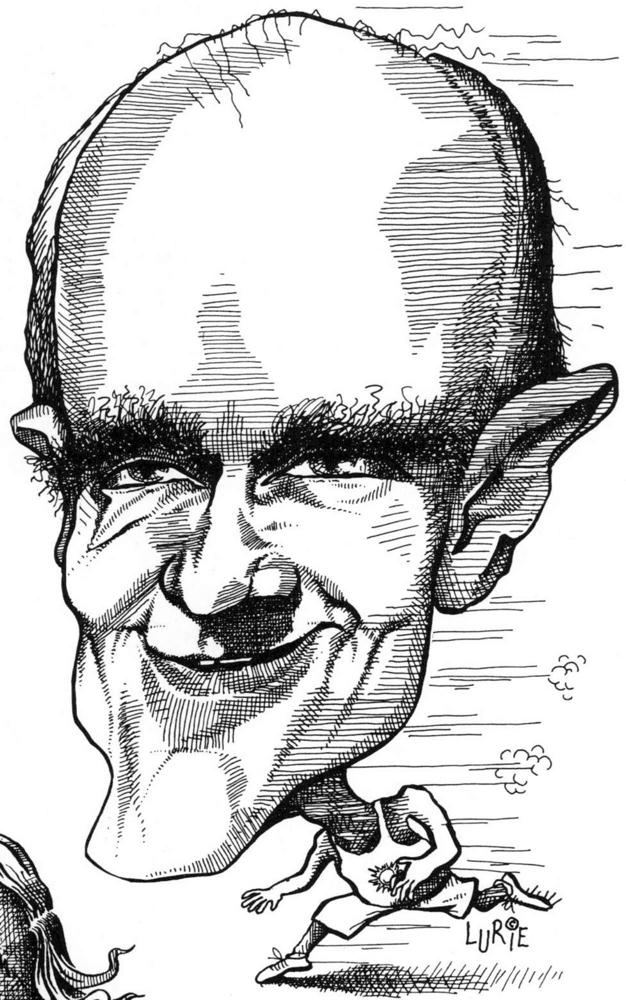
LURIE

William Proxmire

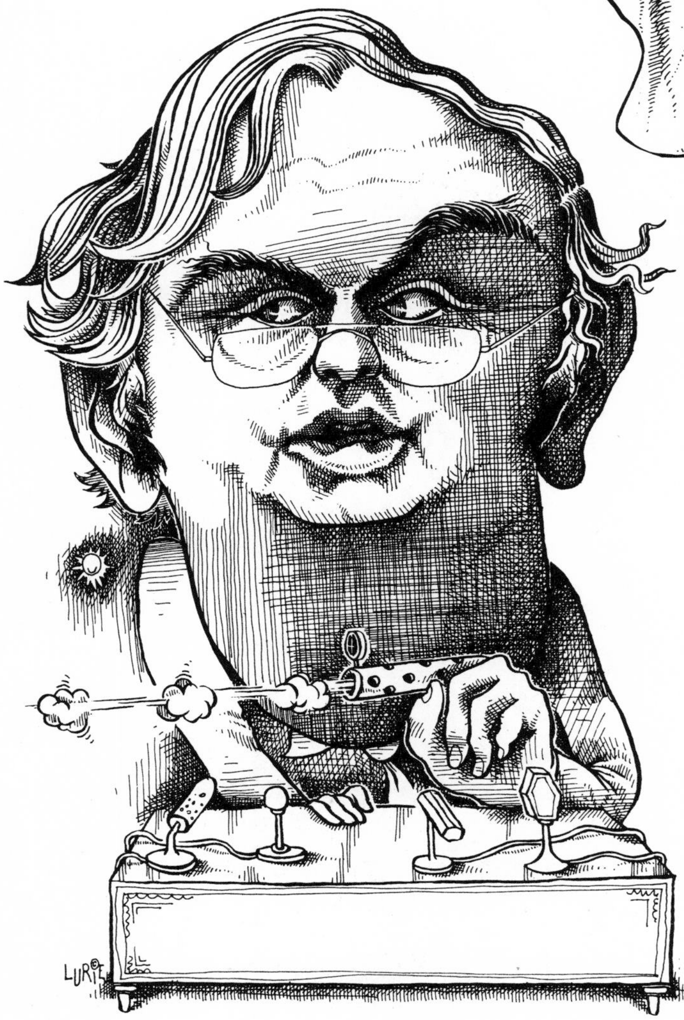
LURIE

Senator Lowell P. Weicker

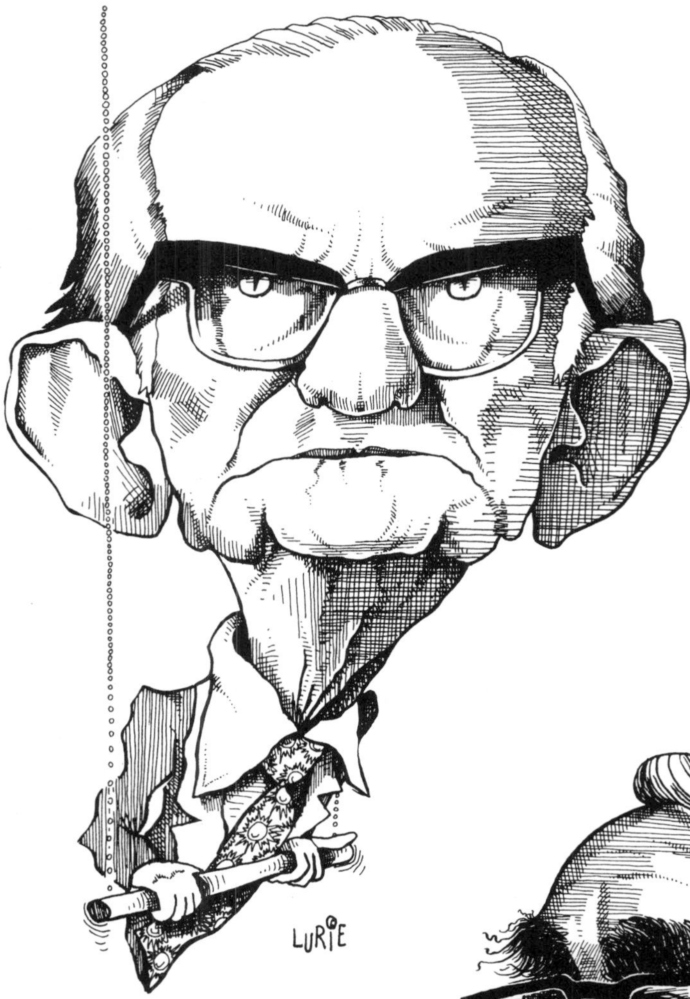
LURIE

Senator John Stenniss

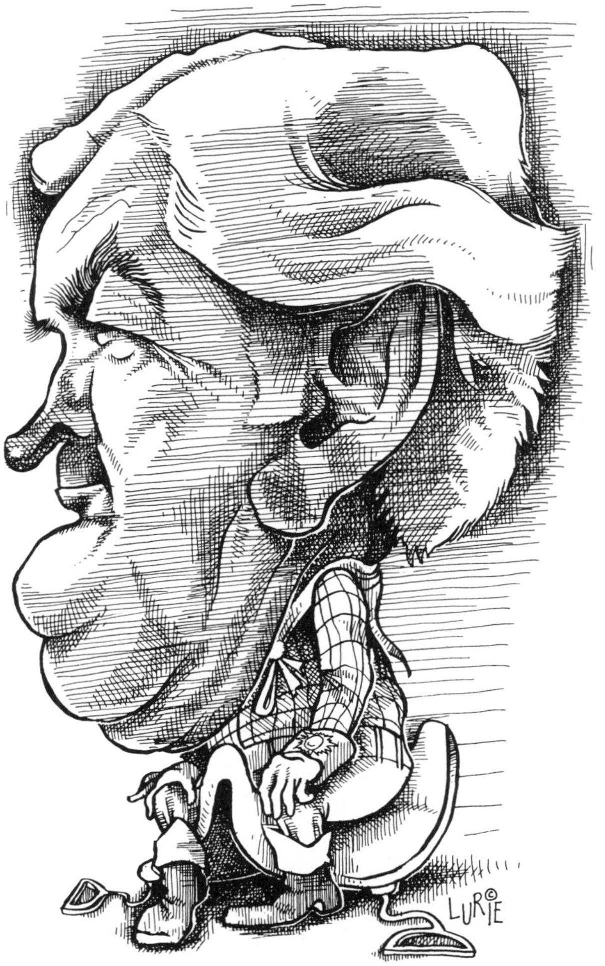
LURIE

John Connally

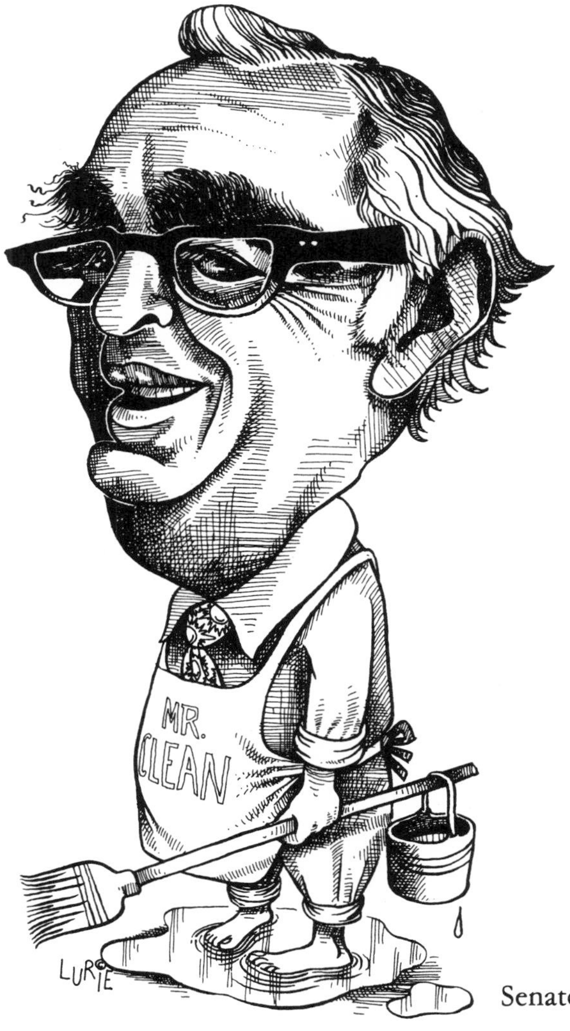
MR.
CLEAN
LURIE

Senator Abe Ribicoff

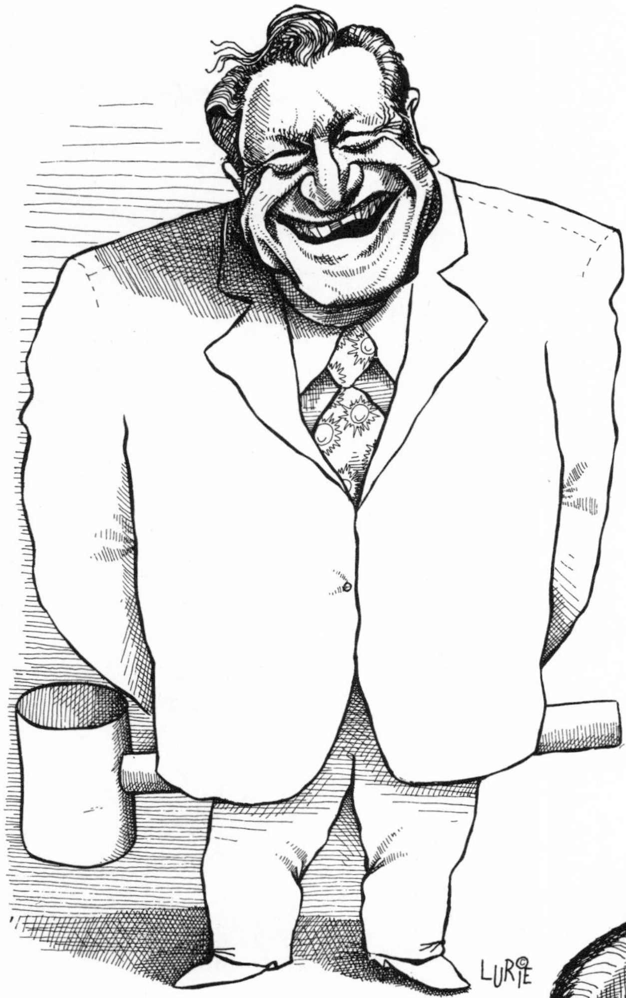
LURIE

Governor
Nelson Rockefeller

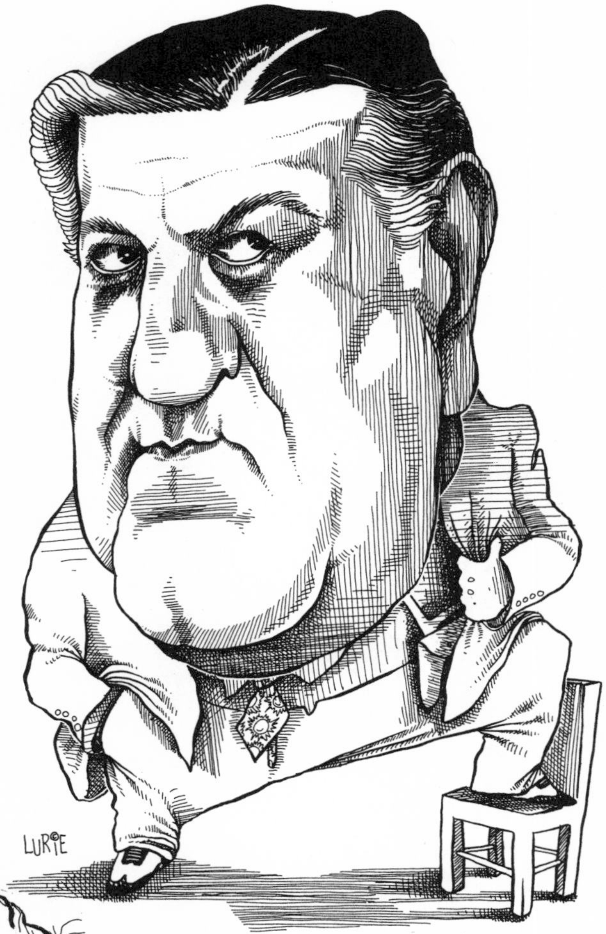
LURIE

Mayor Rizzo
of Philadelphia

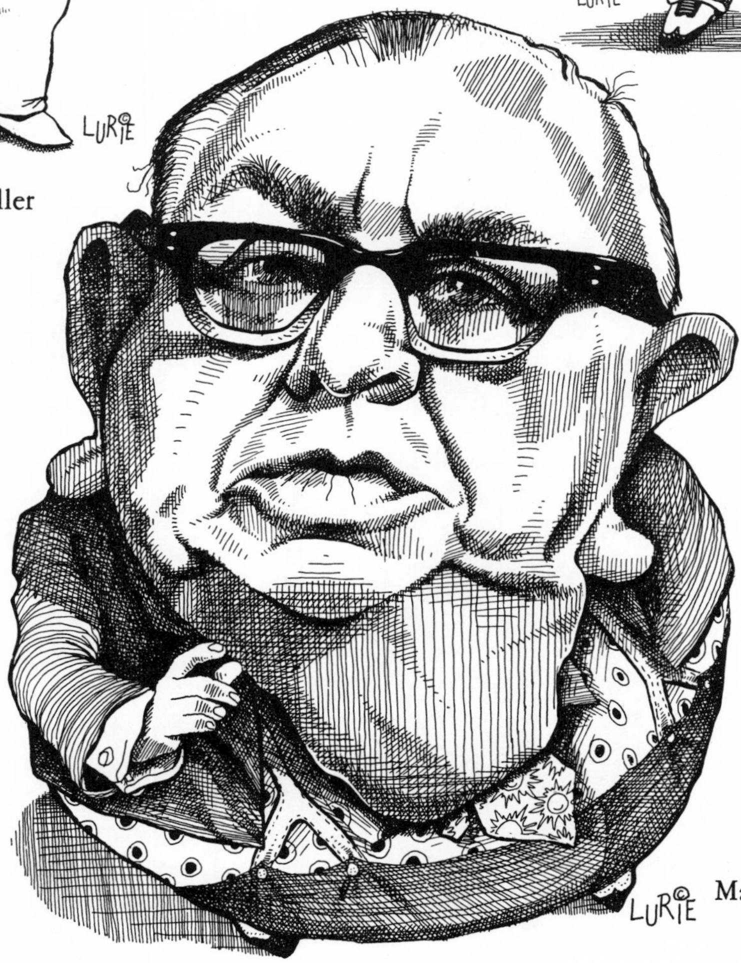
LURIE

Mayor Richard Daley
of Chicago

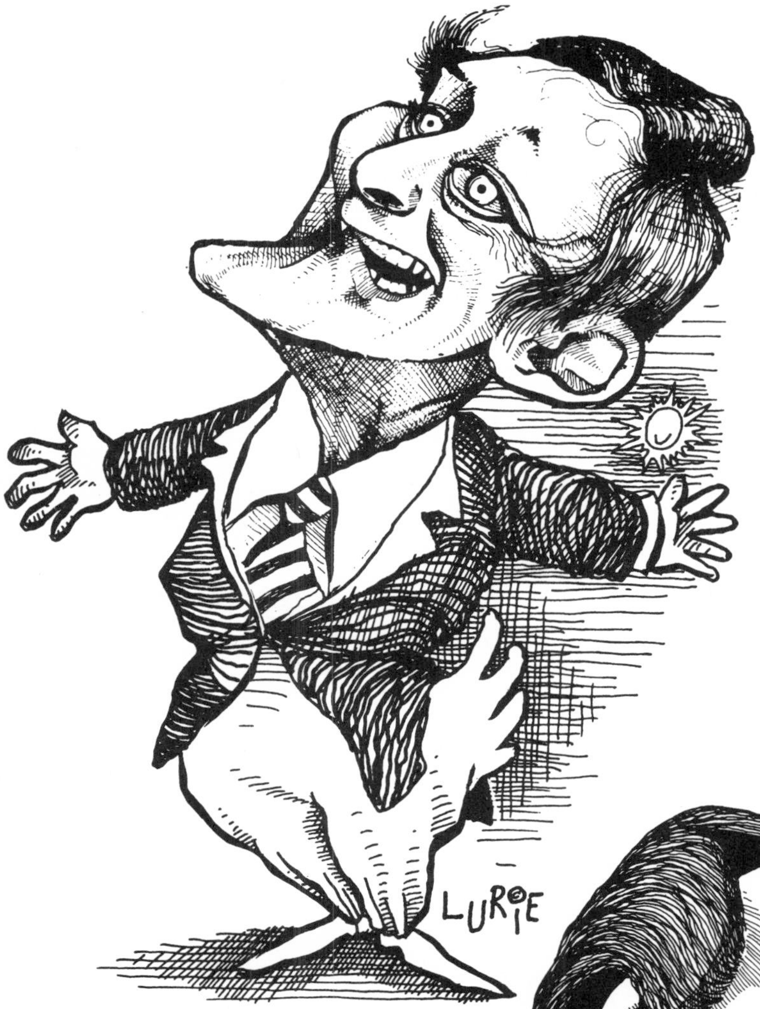
LURIE

Senator Birch Bayh

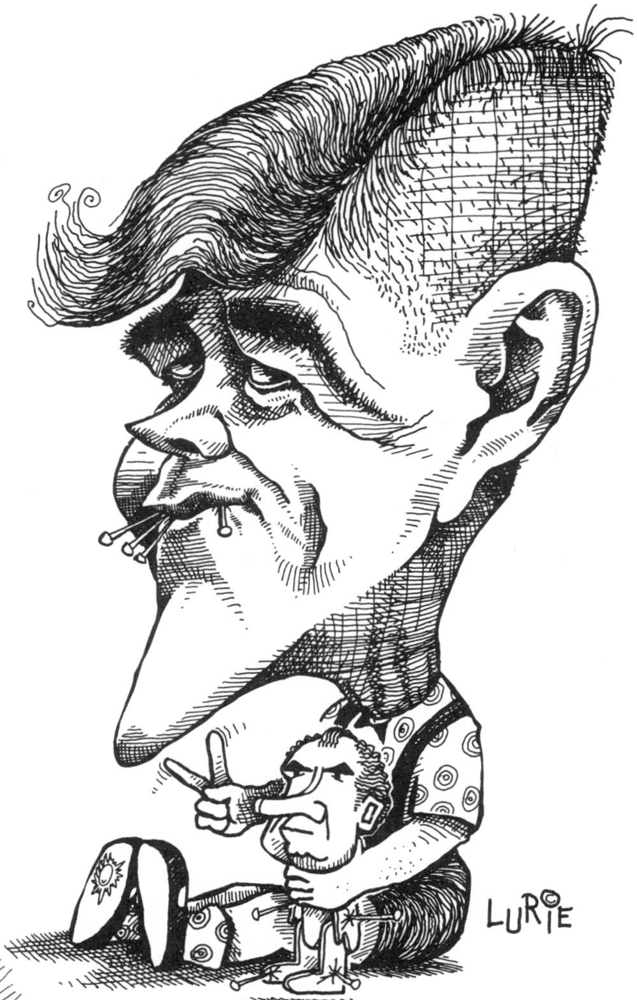
LURIE

Representative
Paul McCloskey, Jr.

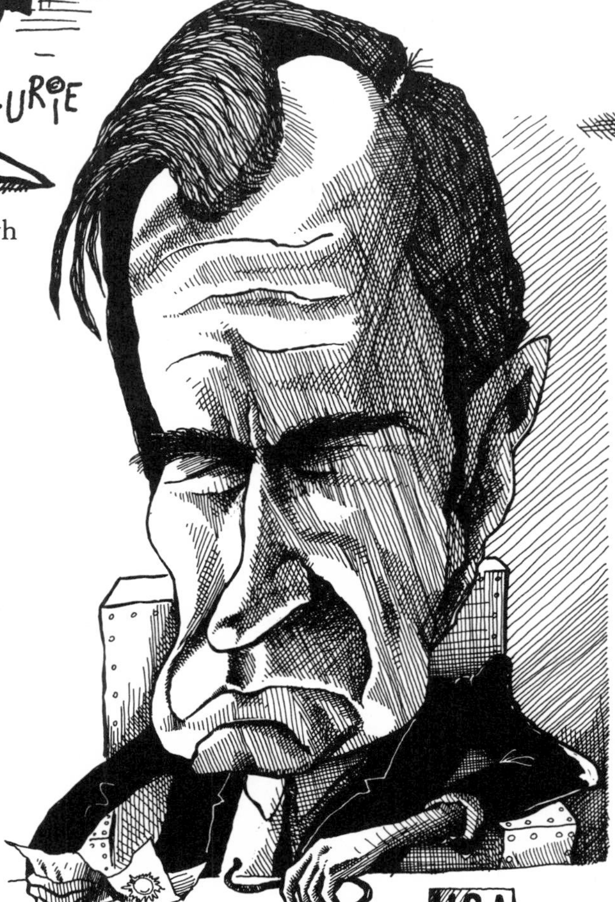
LURIE
U.S.A

George Bush

1974

Lurie: ON HENRY KISSINGER

The most sophisticated politician whose actions I followed during the seventies was Henry Kissinger—it was like watching a master chess player make his moves. However, my favorite cartoon of him is the one entitled "Strip Poker" in which he looks somewhat like a loser.

No one could pull as many tricks out of his hat as Henry Kissinger. The miracles he managed to execute—relations with China, the beginnings of a peace between Egypt and Israel, and many other negotiations in different parts of the world—will make him the most famous politician in the seventies. He is a truly professional politician who knows how to manipulate power, and as such he is a delight to a political cartoonist.

Once I was sitting with him in his private chambers in Washington when the phone rang. It was Mr. Dinitz, then Israeli ambassador to Washington. Kissinger informed the Ambassador that he was sitting for an interview and caricature with me. The Ambassador said something that made Kissinger look very serious and then he answered, "No, I am not committing suicide—just sitting for a cartoonist."

Kissinger had a special affinity for the international language of the media, the political cartoon. With his sixth sense, he felt its unique capacities and managed to maintain a carefully planned, friendly relationship with us. But you could not help feel that he petted you carefully, the way he would a dangerous Doberman.

Lurie: ON SPIRO AGNEW

Vice President Agnew invited me to the White House for a so-called friendly chat. And that conversation convinced me that Agnew was simply bad—a bad person. All kinds of little unpleasant quirks, all kinds of nasty comments showed me his almost fascist mentality. I felt sure that he was capable of anything—absolutely anything.

He invited me to the White House specifically to ask why I drew him with such a big neck. When he asked this question I answered in a very naive way, "Because Mr. Vice Pres-ident, you *do* have a very big neck." This answer hurt him somewhat; I could tell that he took pride in his macho appearance. Of course, he is a fairly big, fairly handsome man, and is in good shape—although as you can see from my cartoons he could afford to lose a few pounds here and there.

There I was, sitting with the Vice President of the United States, who pulled off his tie and opened his shirt to show me the size of his collar. He did this to prove that he wasn't fat.

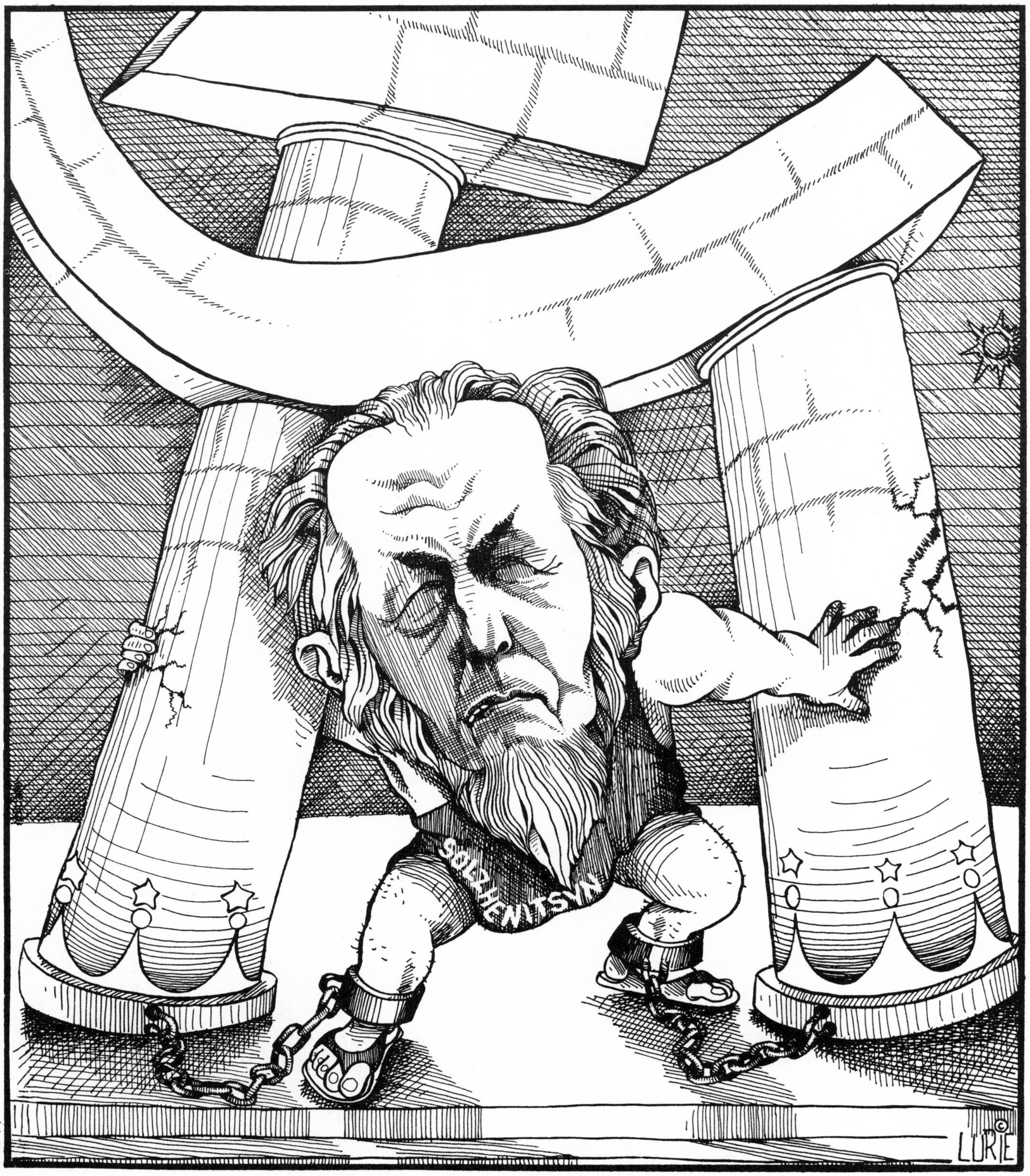
SOLZHENITSYN
LURIE ©

1-12-74

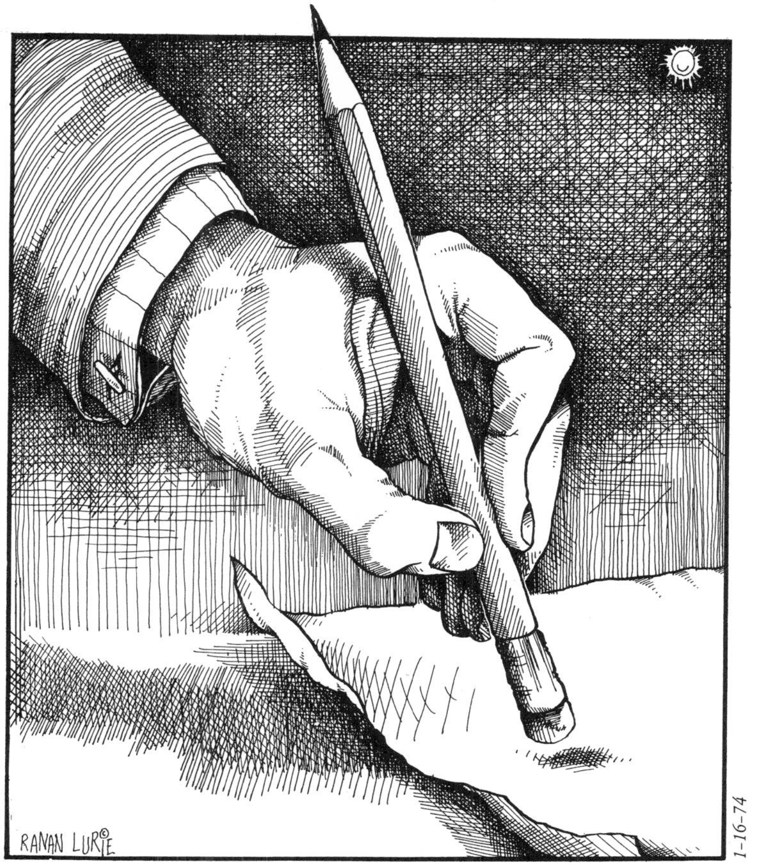
RANAN LURIE©
1-16-74

PRESIDENTIAL SIGNATURE

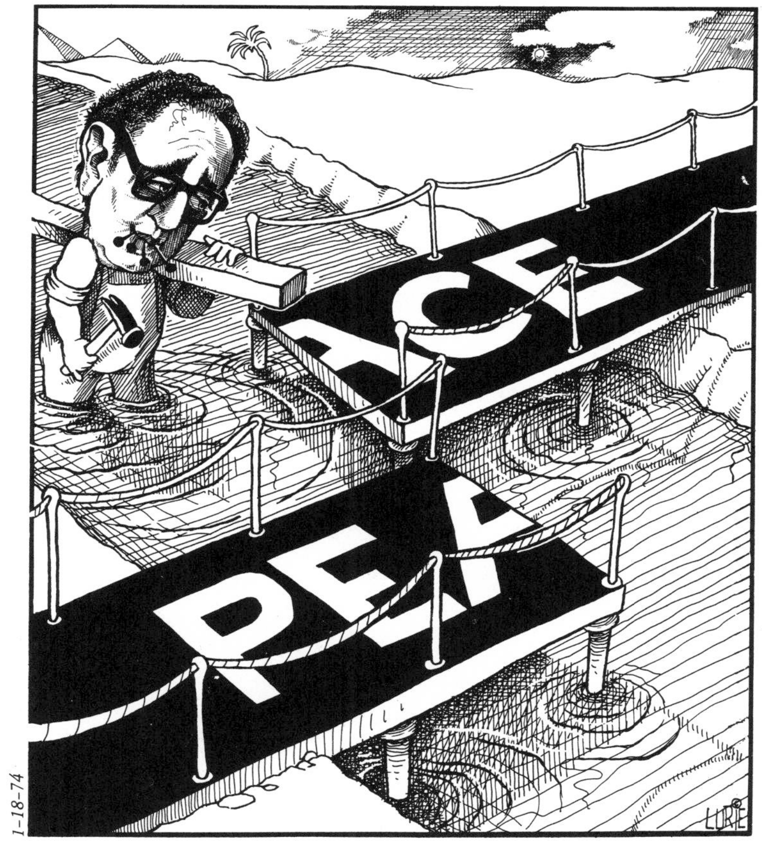
ACE
PEA
1-18-74
LURIE©

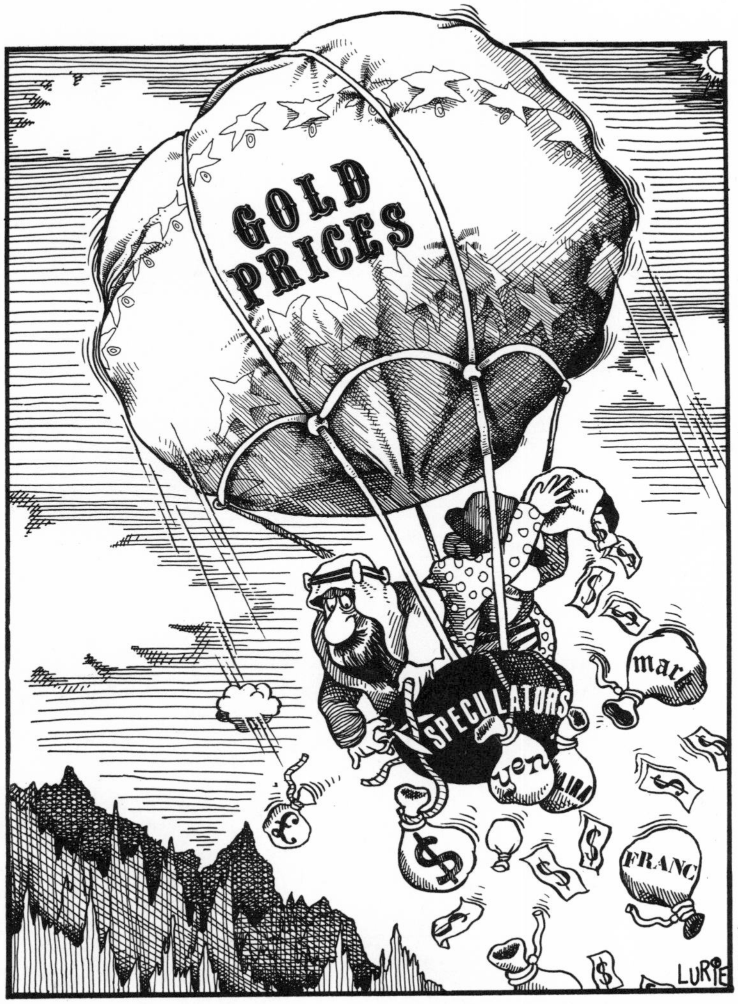
GOLD PRICES
SPECULATORS
mar
yen
LIRA
FRANC
LURIE
2-28-74

UP UP AND AWAY!

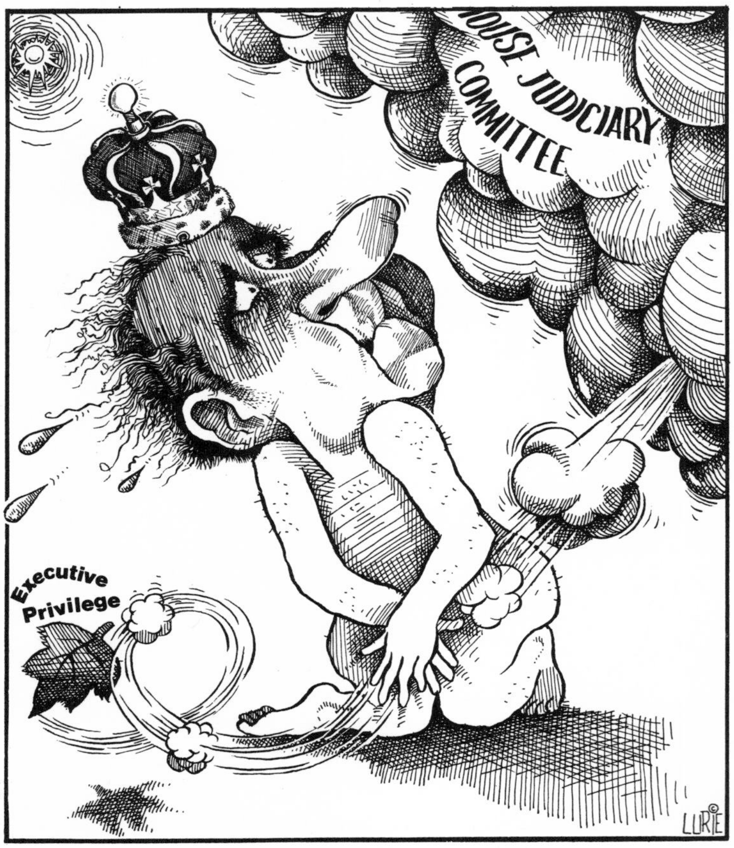
OUSE JUDICIARY COMMITTEE
Executive Privilege
LURIE
2-12-74

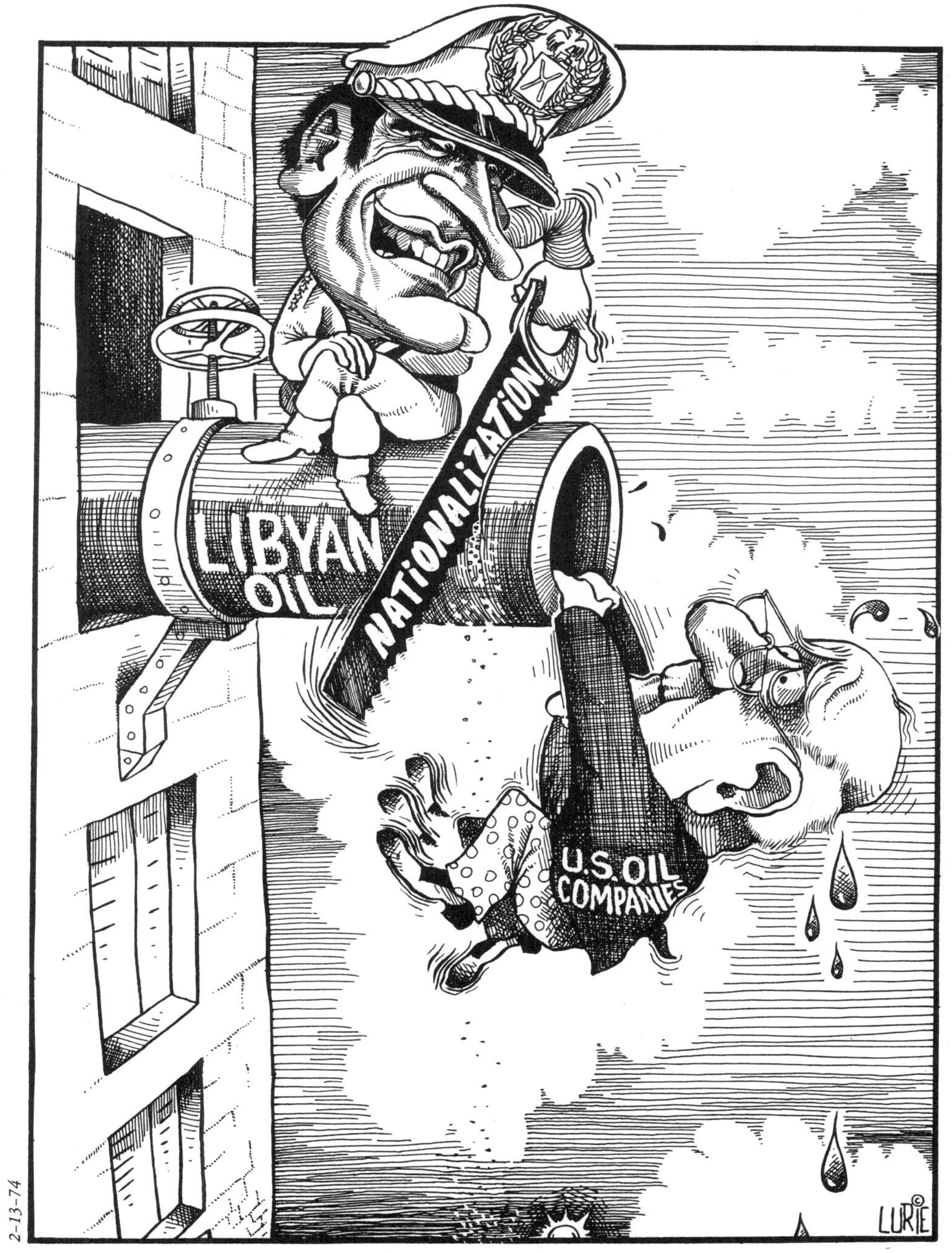
LIBYAN OIL
NATIONALIZATION
U.S. OIL COMPANIES
LURIE
2-13-74

"RELAX—I'M GIVING YOU YOUR FAIR SHARE"

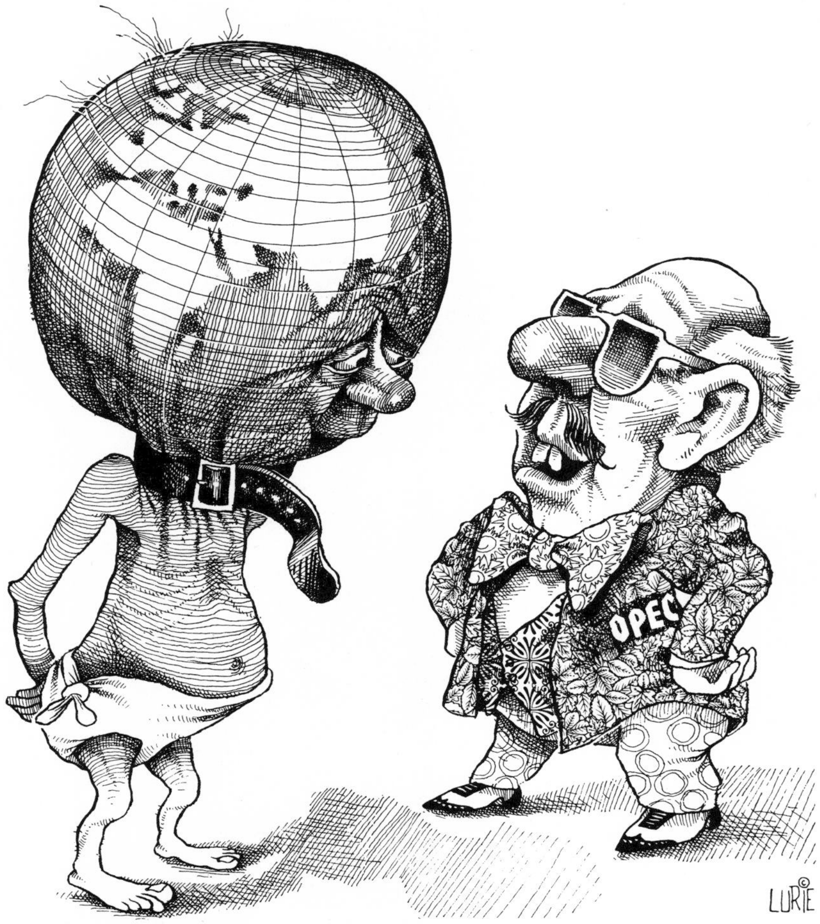
OPEC
LURIE

"THAT'S TOO BAD, YOU'LL SIMPLY HAVE TO TIGHTEN YOUR BELT."

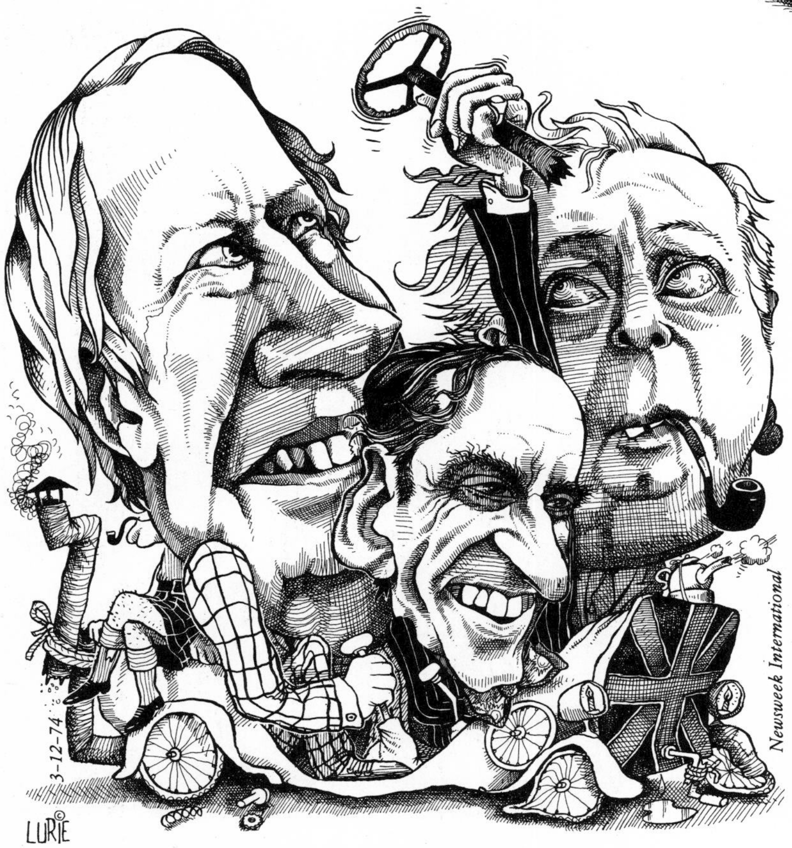
3-12-74
Newsweek International
LURIE

BRITAIN: STARTING THE BIG DRIVE

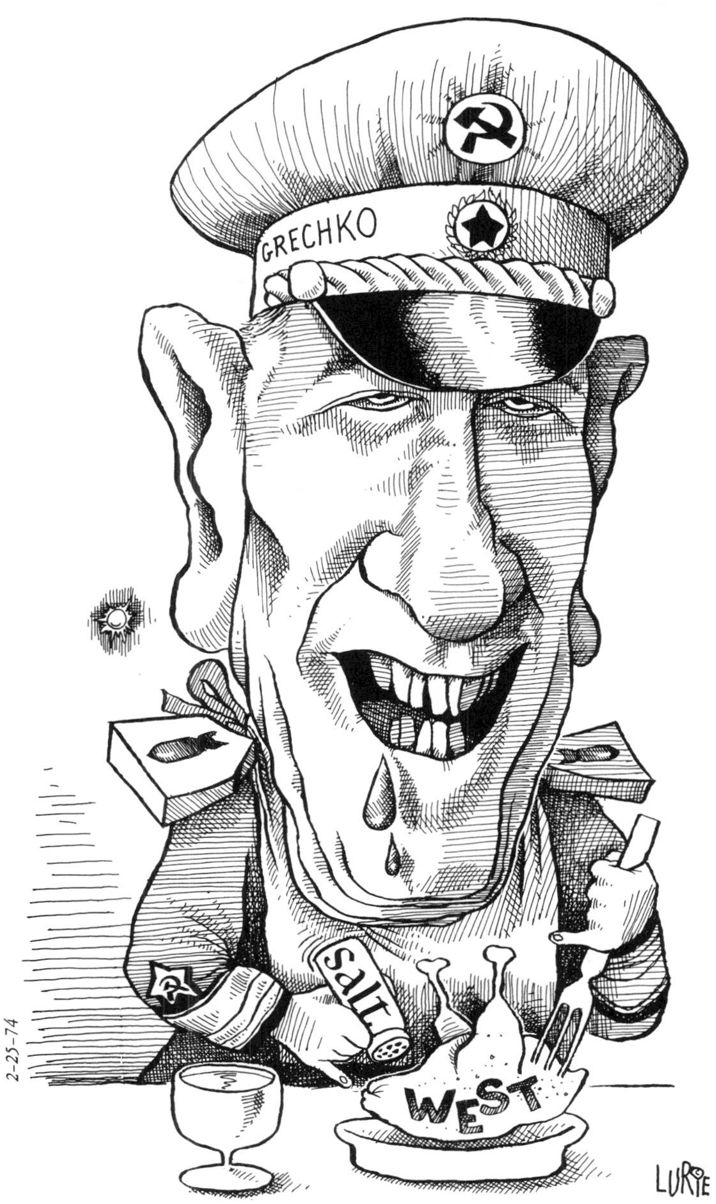
GRECHKO
SALT
WEST
2-25-74
LURIE

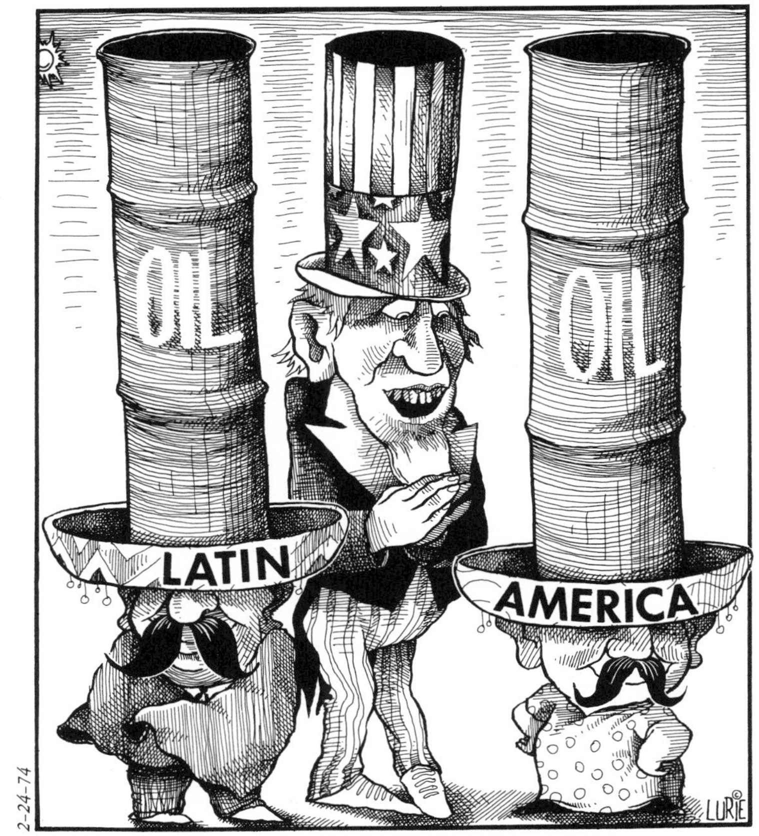
OIL
OIL
LATIN
AMERICA
2-24-74
LURIE

"YES! FROM NOW ON WE ARE EQUAL!"

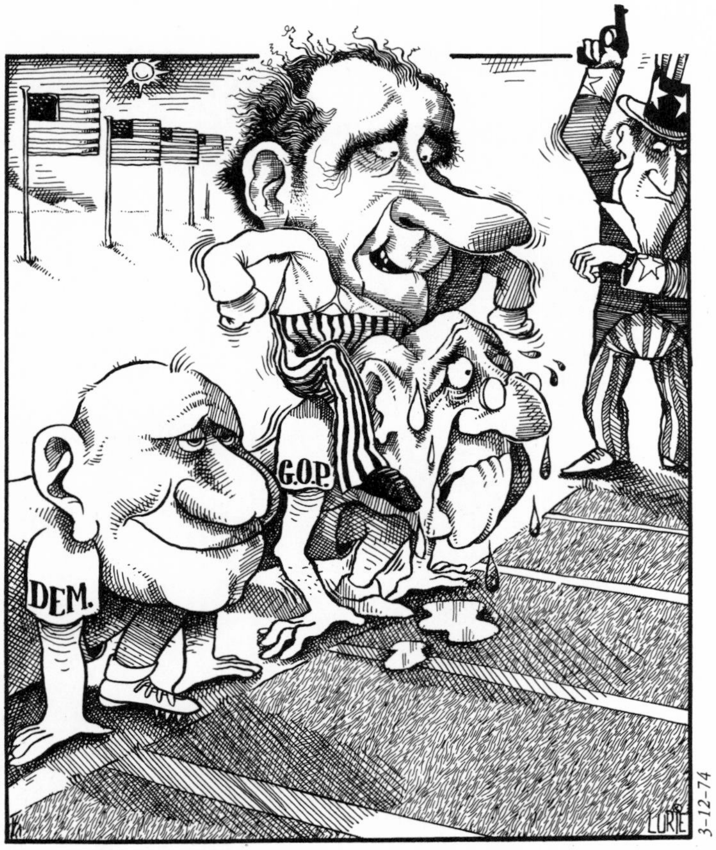
DEM.
G.O.P.
LURIE
3-12-74

"LET'S GET 'EM!"

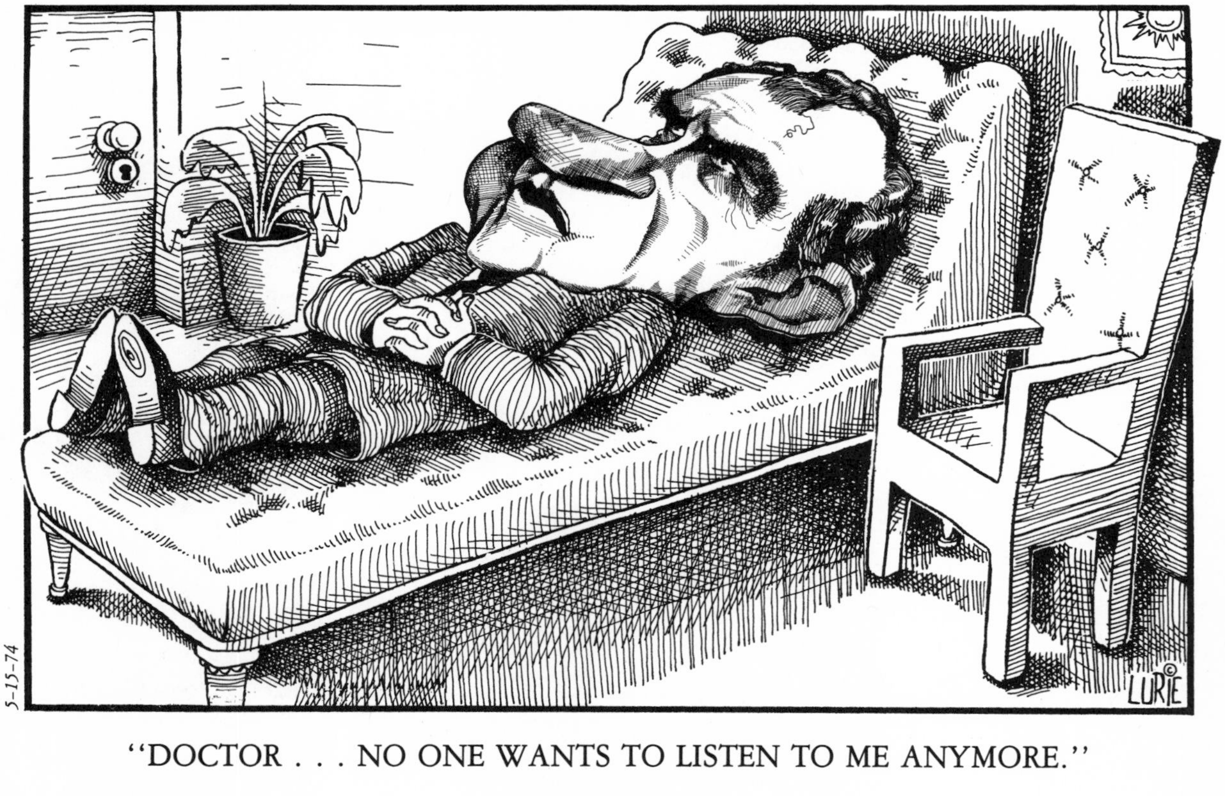
LURIE
5-15-74

"DOCTOR . . . NO ONE WANTS TO LISTEN TO ME ANYMORE."

EUROPE
LURIE©

3-21-74

"WAIT . . . I'VE CHANGED MY MIND!"

WESTERN
LEADERSHIP
WESTERN
LEADERSHIP
LURIE©

5-10-74

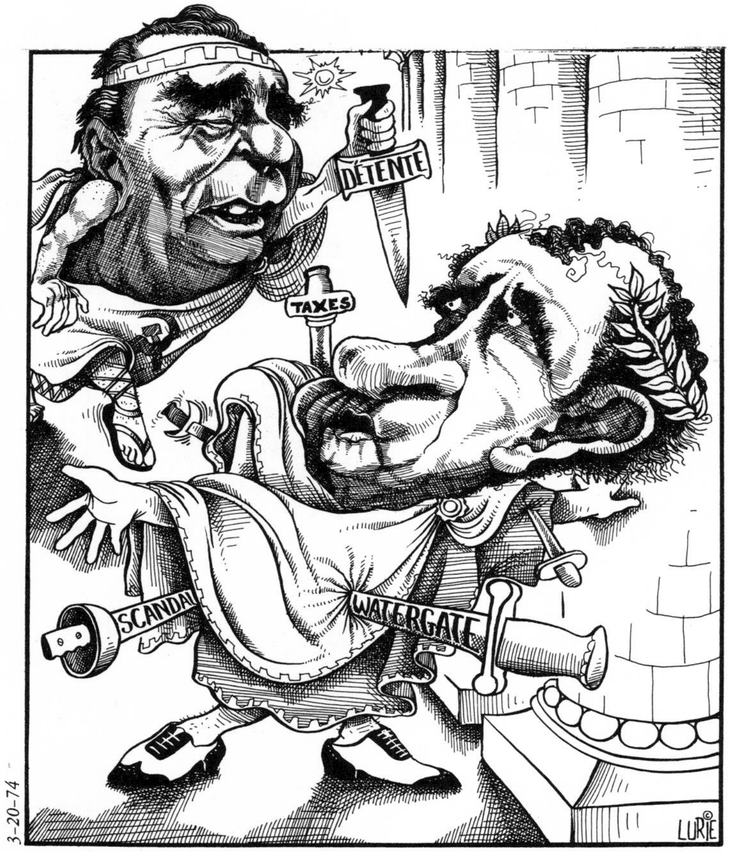
DÉTENTE
TAXES
SCANDAL
WATERGATE
3-20-74
LURIE©

"ET TU, BREZHNEV?"

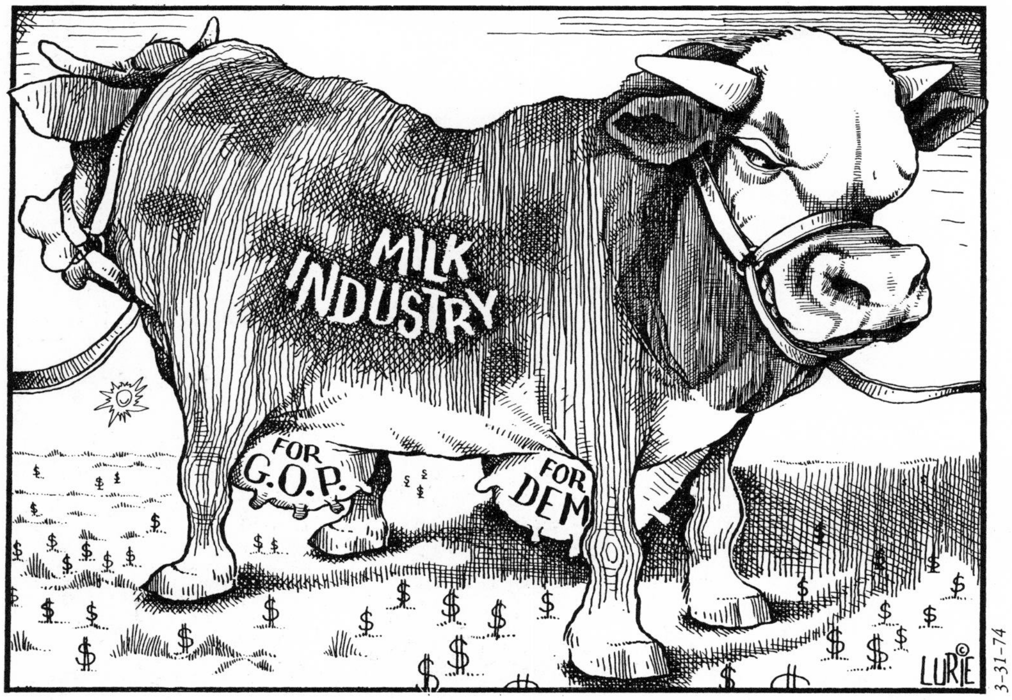
MILK INDUSTRY
FOR G.O.P.
FOR DEM
3-31-74
LURIE©

AN EQUAL OPPORTUNITY EMPLOYER

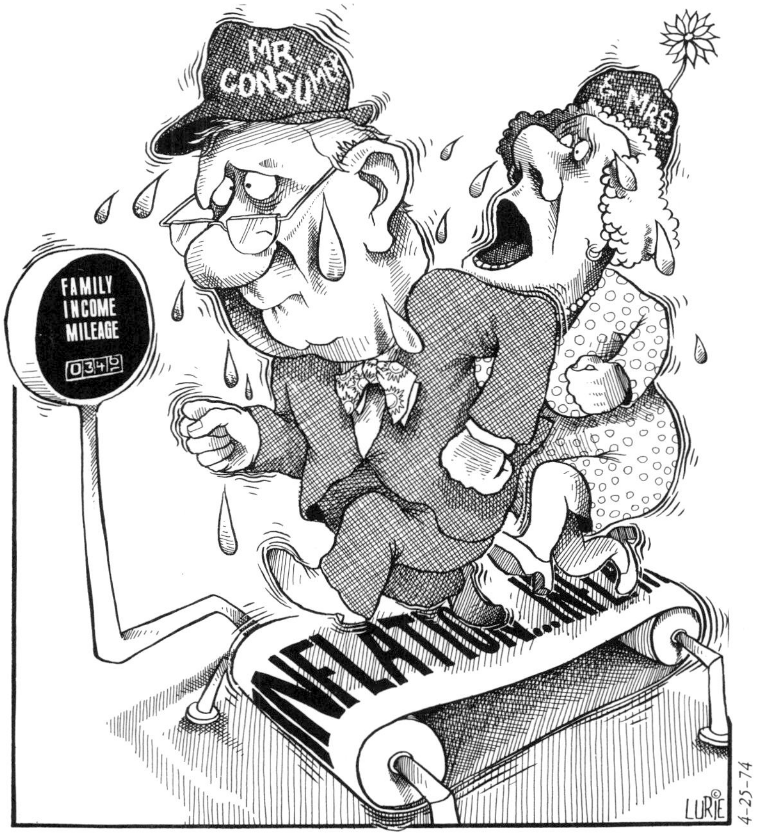
MR. CONSUME
& MRS
FAMILY
INCOME
MILEAGE
INFLATION
LURIE
4-25-74

"WHEN WILL WE ARRIVE, HARRY?"

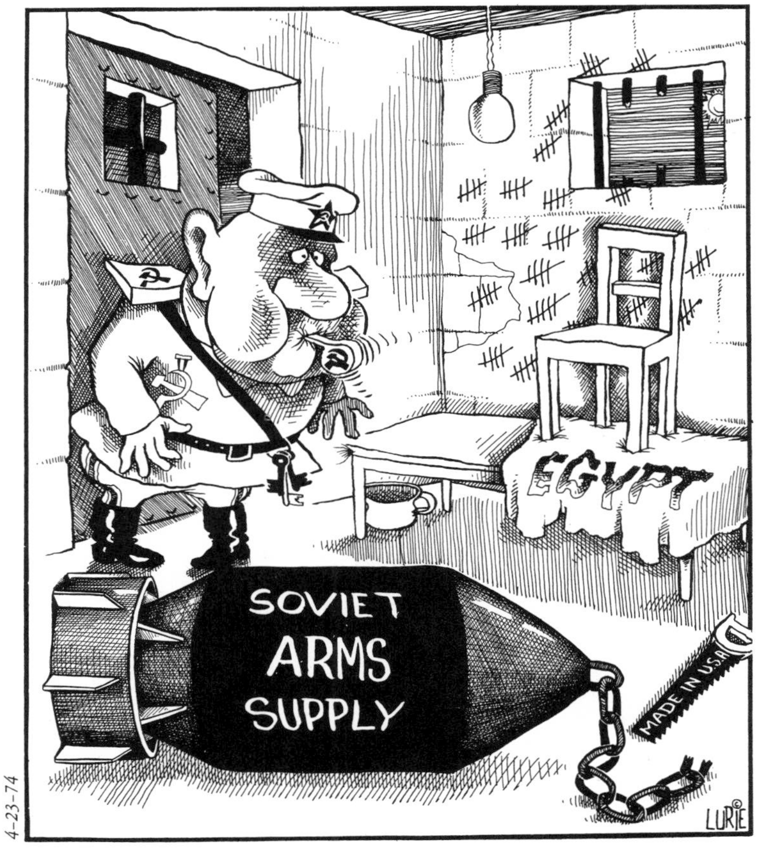
EGYPT
SOVIET
ARMS
SUPPLY
MADE IN USA
4-23-74
LURIE

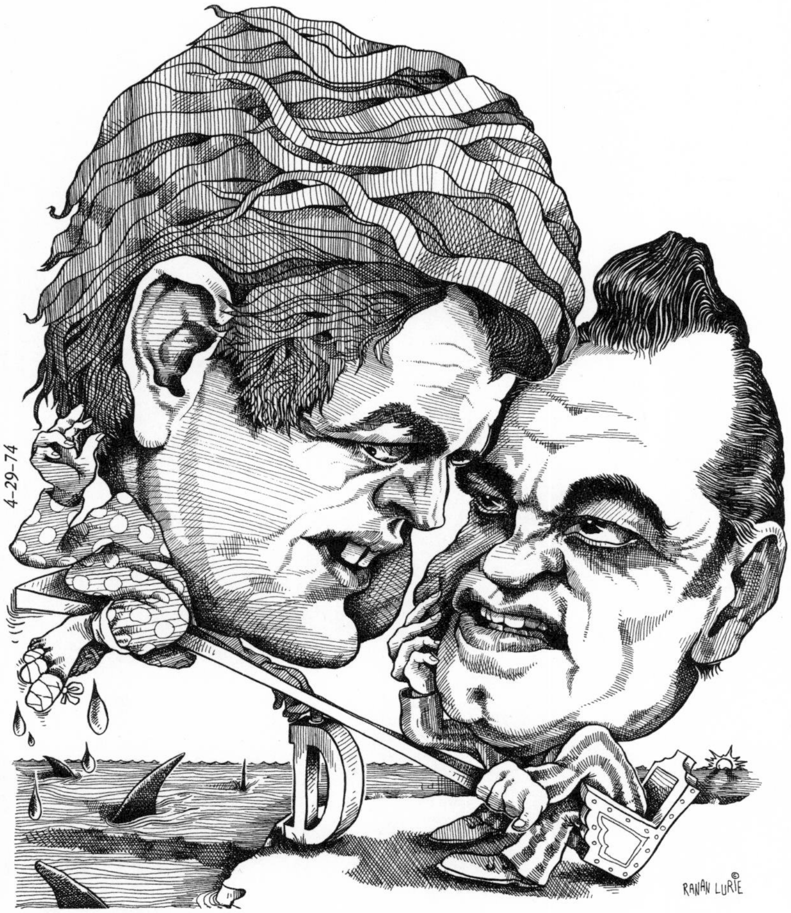
4-29-74
D
RANAN LURIE©

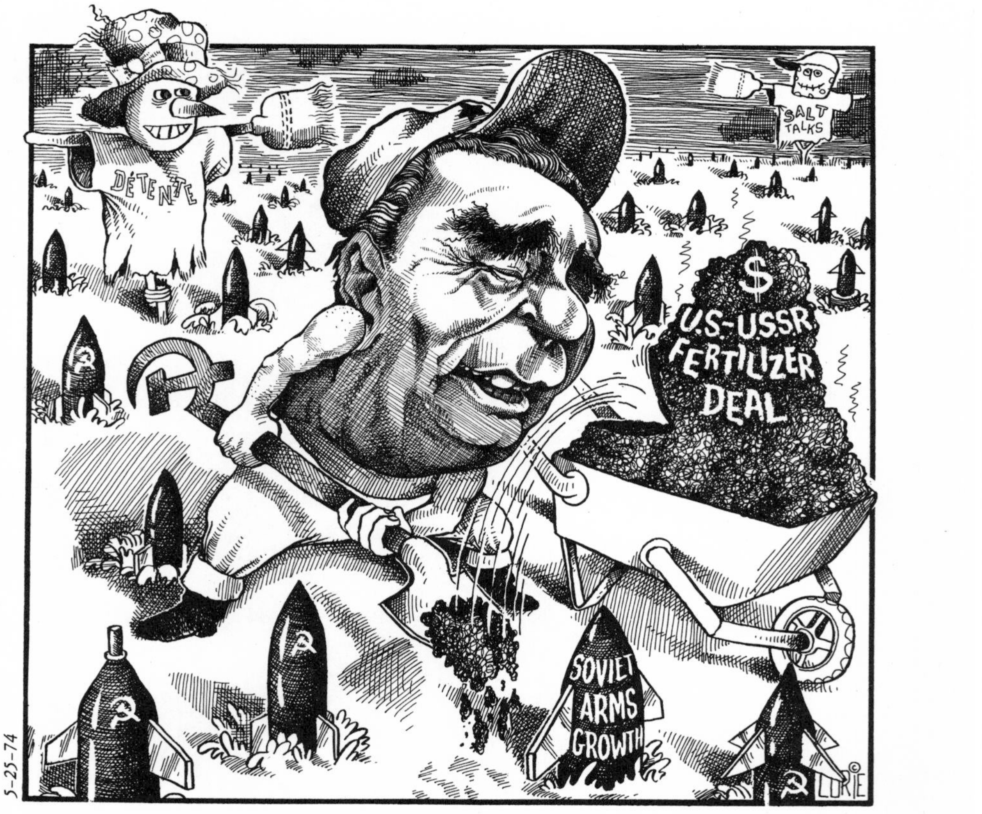
DÉTENTE
SALT TALKS
$
U.S.-USSR FERTILIZER DEAL
SOVIET ARMS GROWTH
5-25-74
LURIE©

PALESTINIAN TERROR

SYRIAN-ISRAELI NEGOTIATIONS

EGYPTIAN-ISRAELI NEGOTIATIONS

5-17-74

LURIE

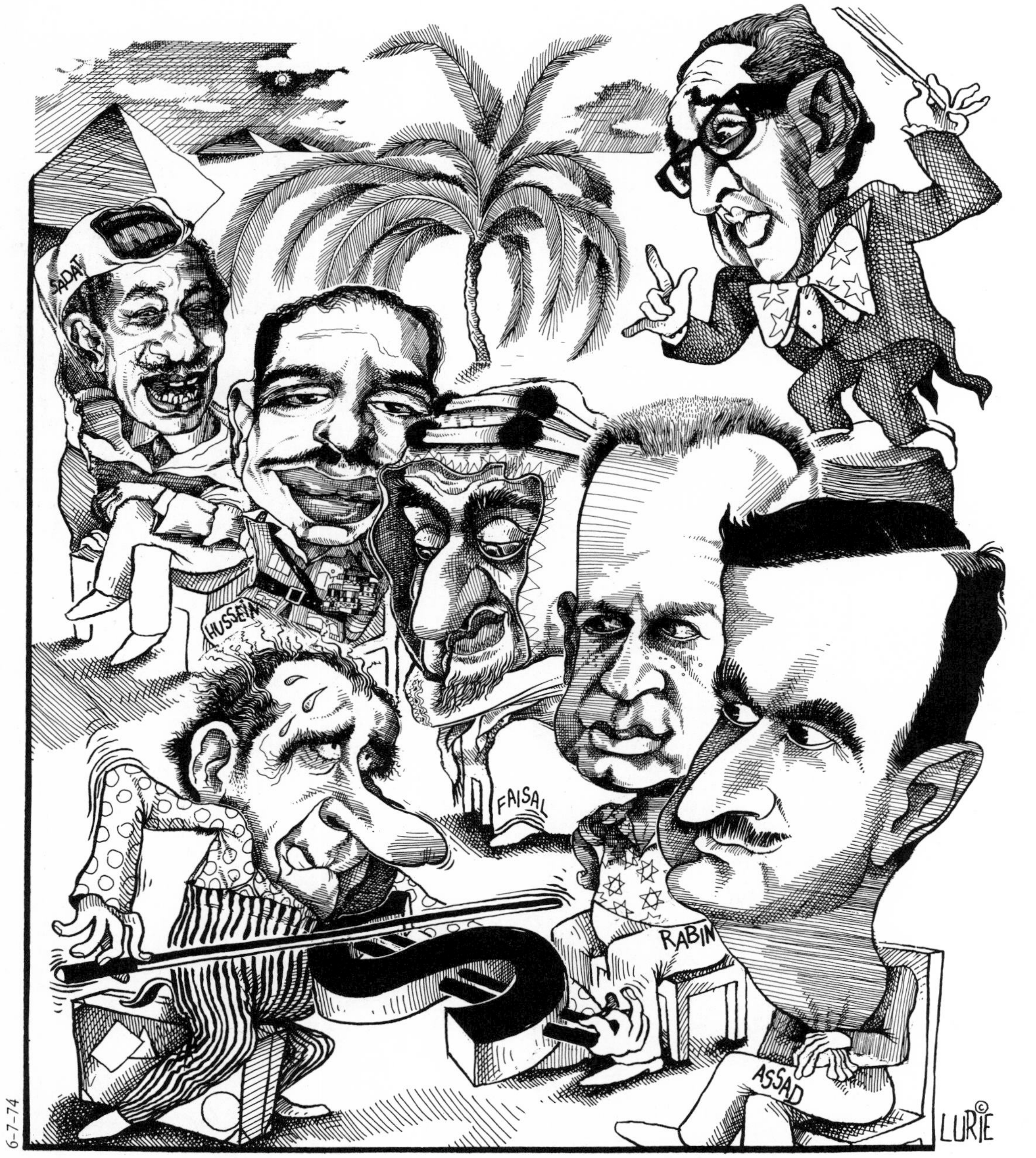

SADAT
HUSSEIN
FAISAL
RABIN
ASSAD
6-7-74
LURIE©

6-1-74

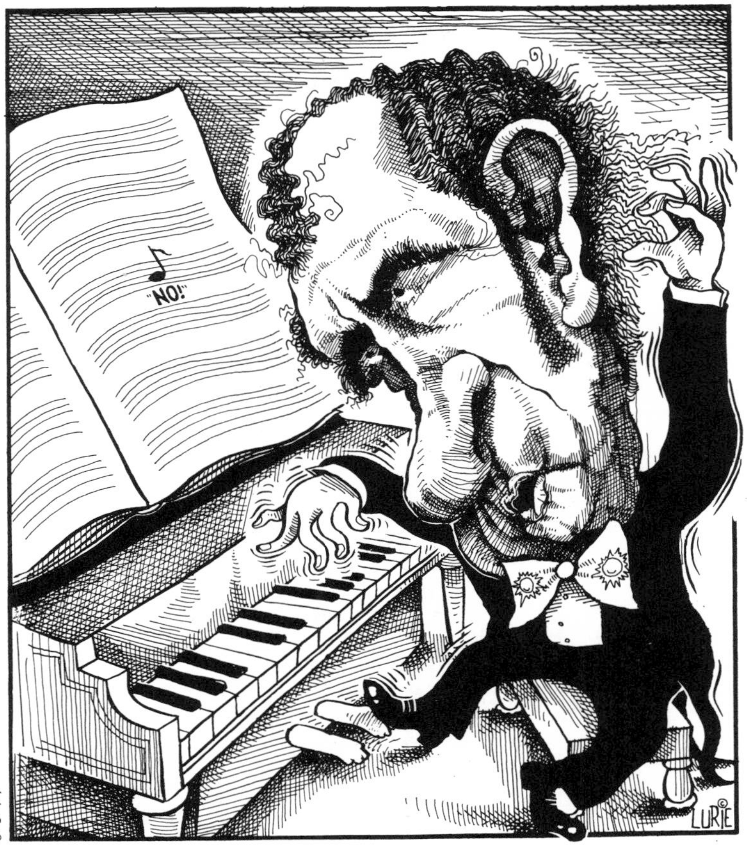
"NO!"
LURIE©

SUBPOENA CONCERTO

6-20-74

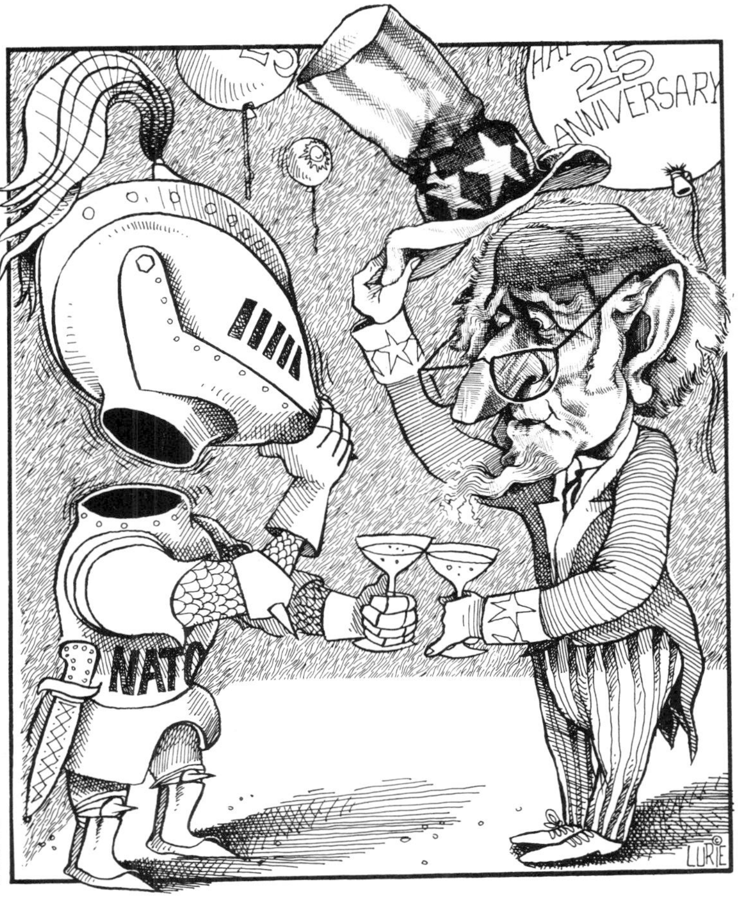
HA
25
ANNIVERSARY
NATO
LURIE©

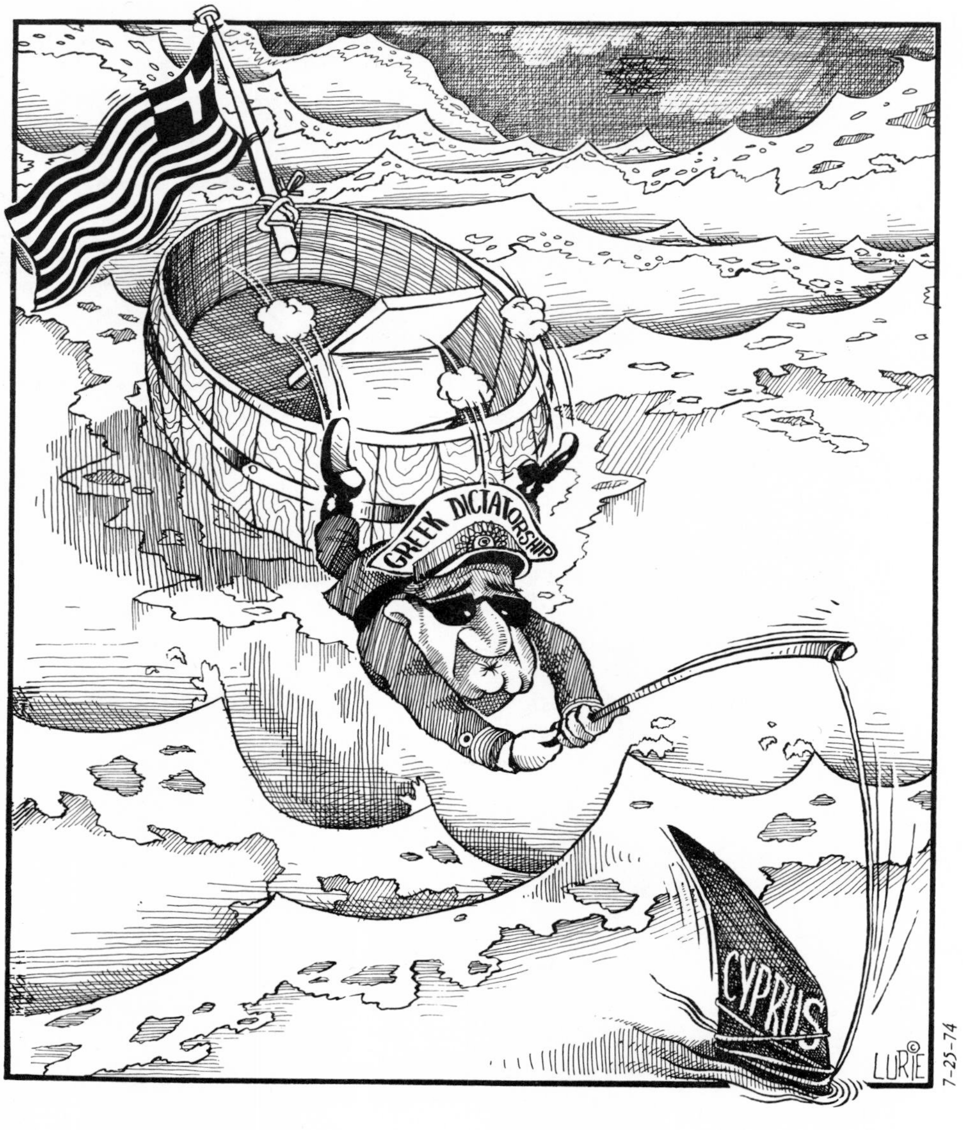
GREEK DICTATORSHIP
CYPRUS
LURIE©
7-25-74

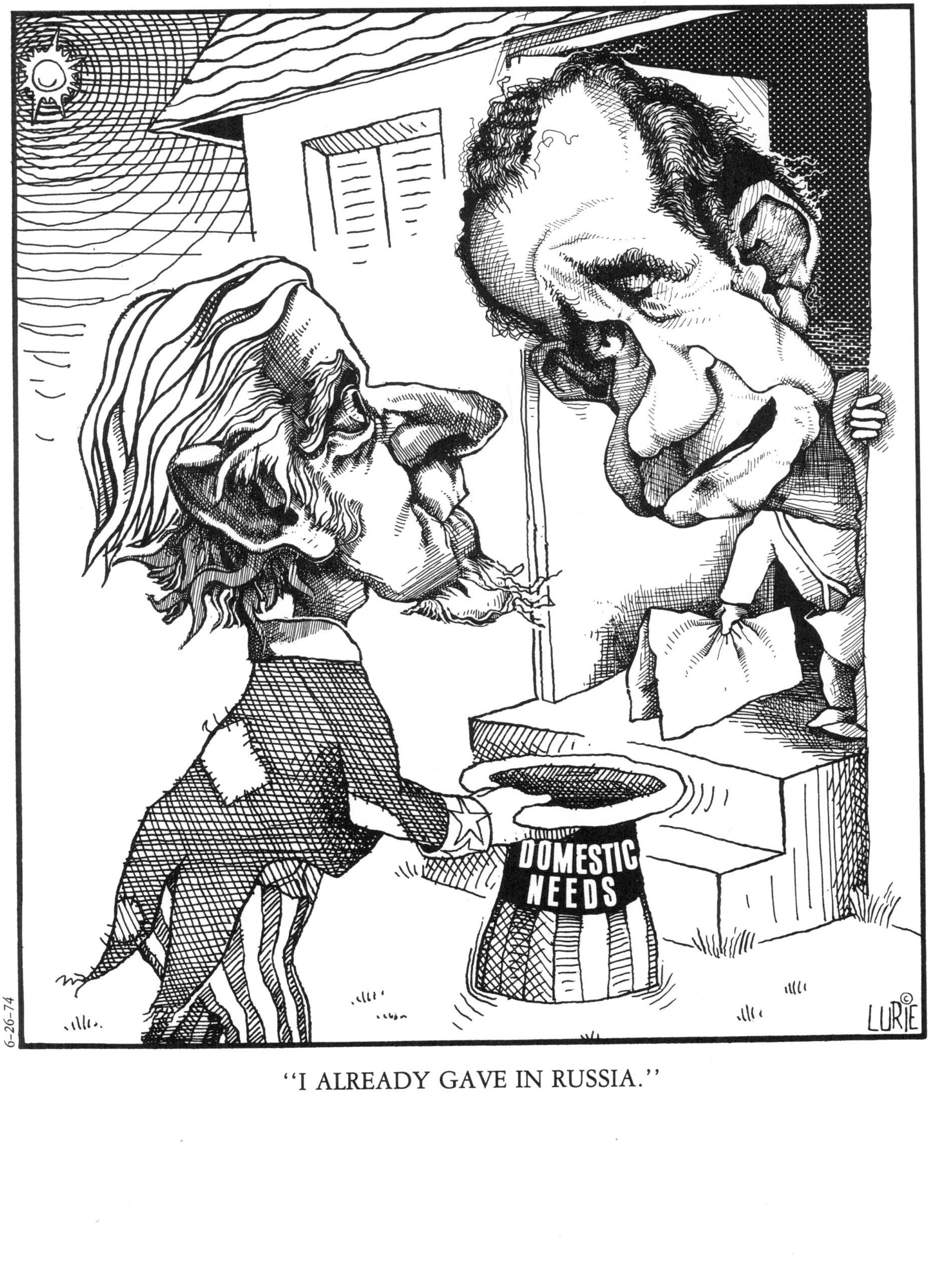
DOMESTIC NEEDS
LURIE ©

6-26-74

"I ALREADY GAVE IN RUSSIA."

JUDICIARY COMM
THE HOUSE
SENATE
LURIE ©
7-31-74

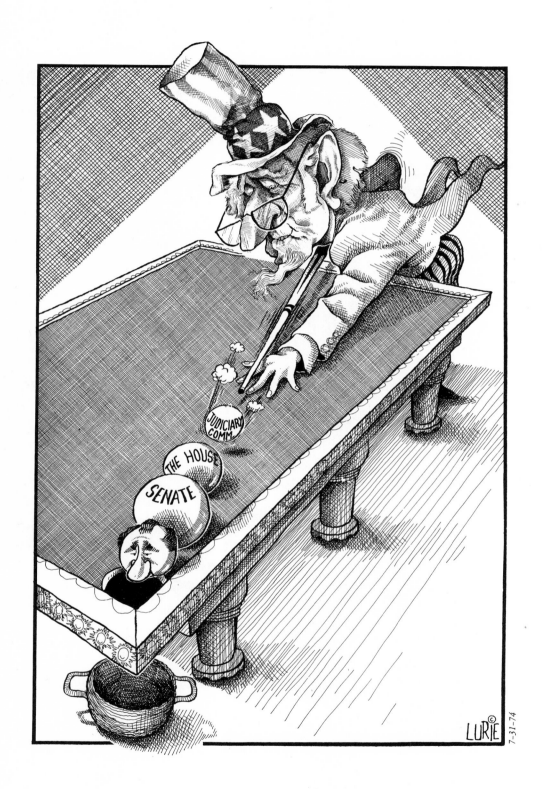

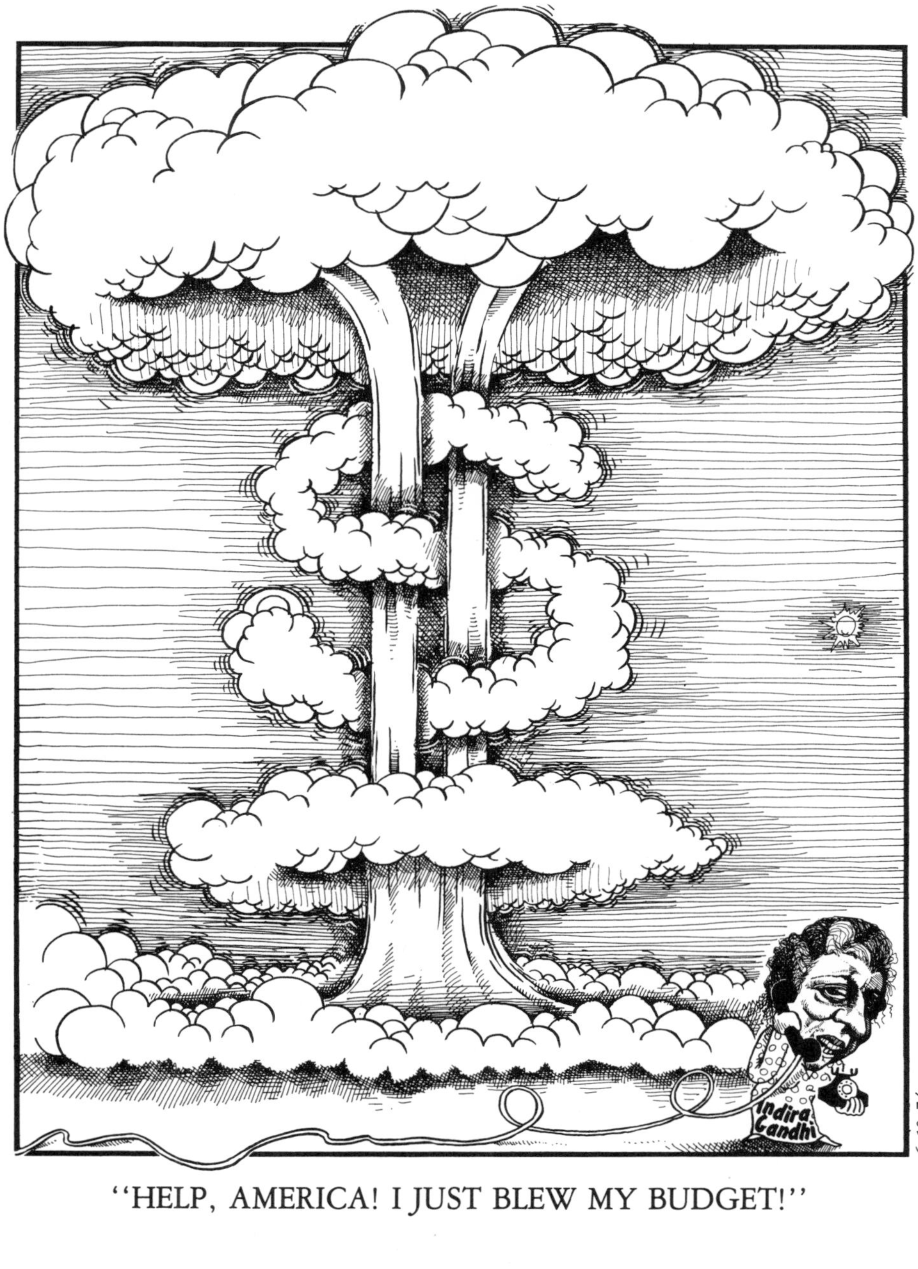
Indira Gandhi
6-19-74

''HELP, AMERICA! I JUST BLEW MY BUDGET!''

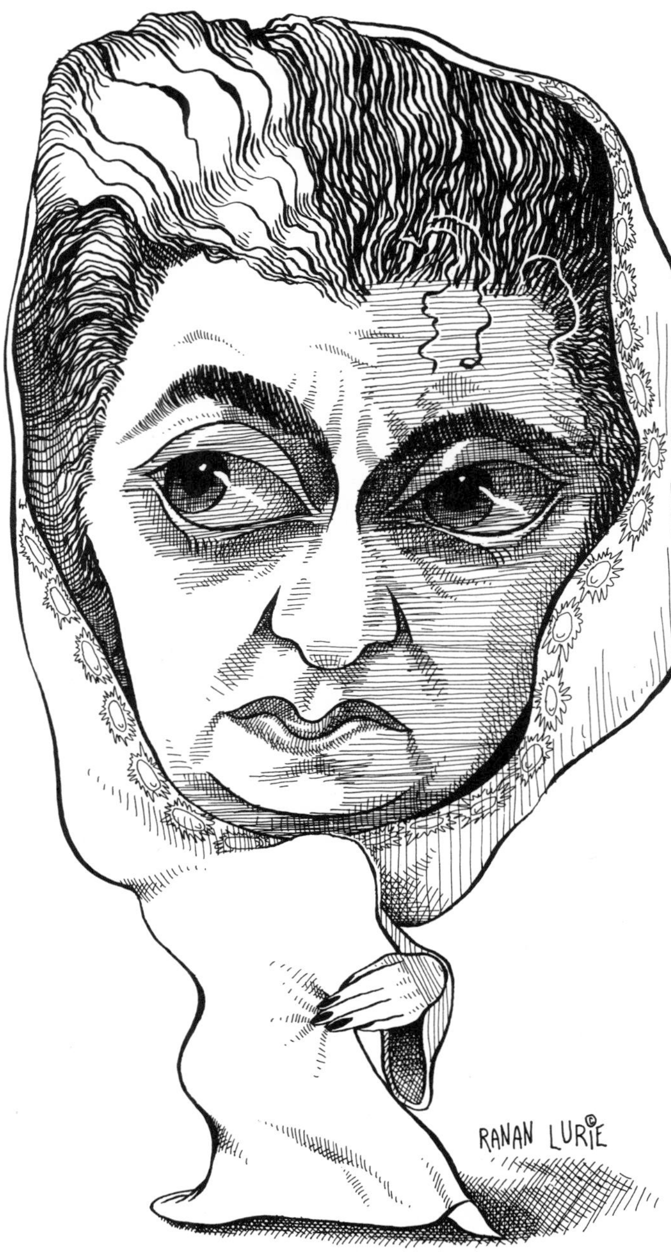
RANAN LURIE

Prime Minister Indira Gandhi
of India

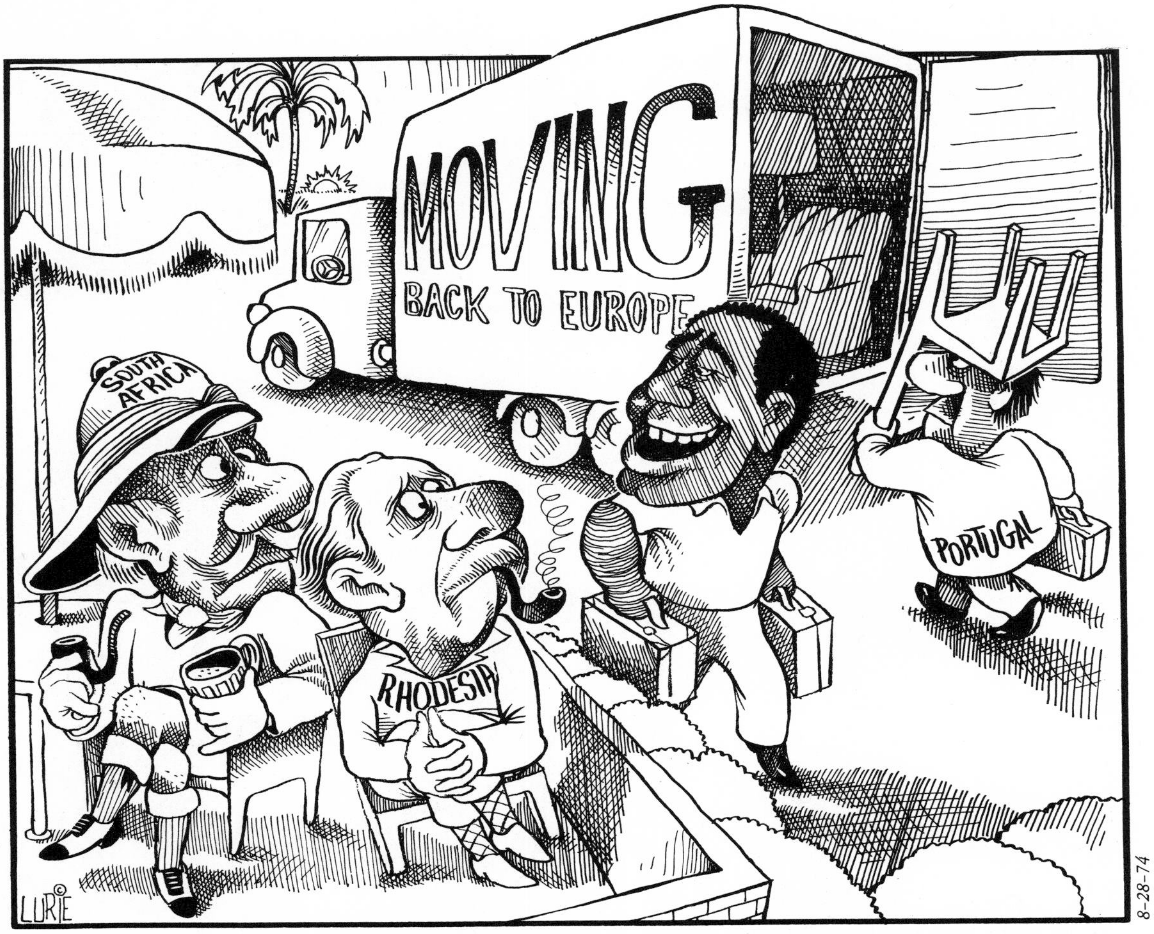
MOVING
BACK TO EUROPE
SOUTH AFRICA
RHODESIA
PORTUGAL
LURIE ©
8-28-74

"THERE GOES THE NEIGHBORHOOD!"

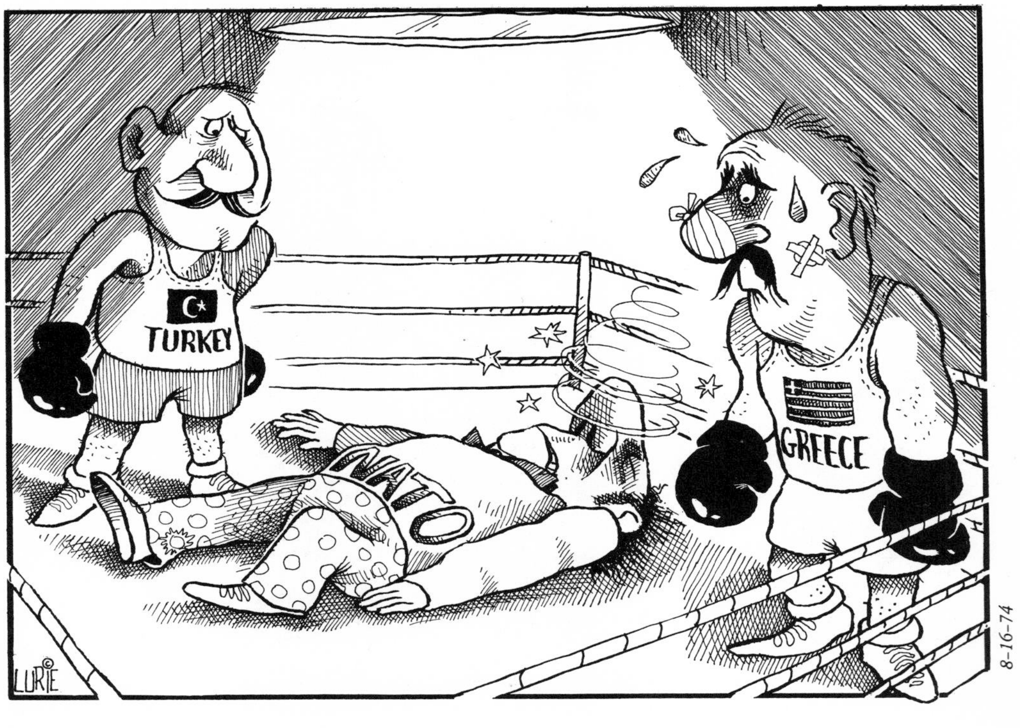
TURKEY
GREECE
LURIE ©
8-16-74

8-12-74
LURIE

TURKEY
GREECE
CYPRUS
LURIE
8-1-74

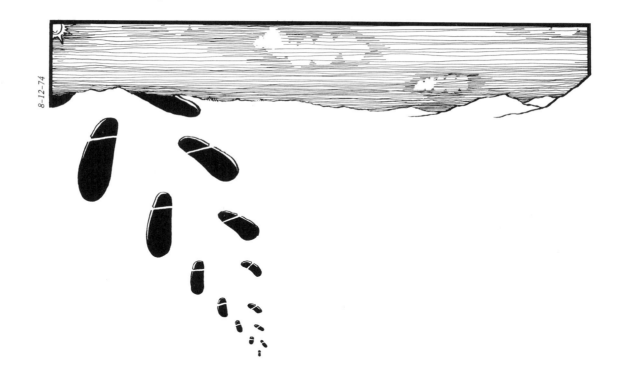

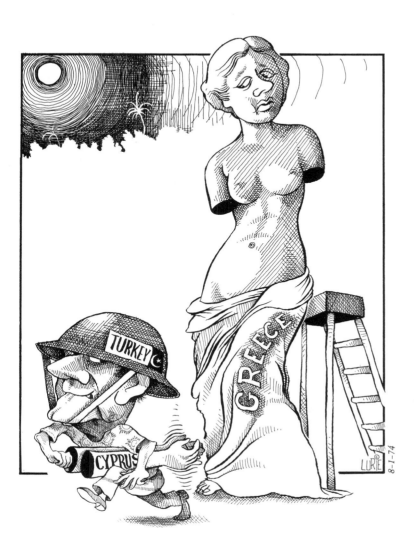

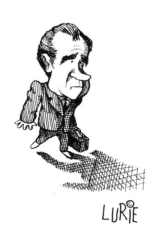

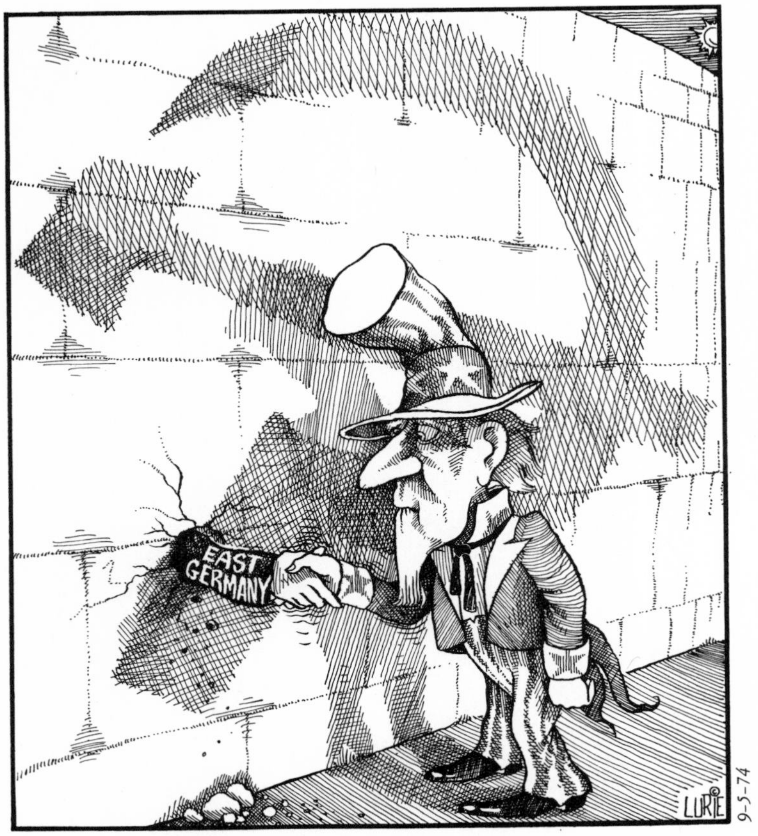
EAST GERMANY
LURIE
9-5-74

DIPLOMATIC BREAKTHROUGH

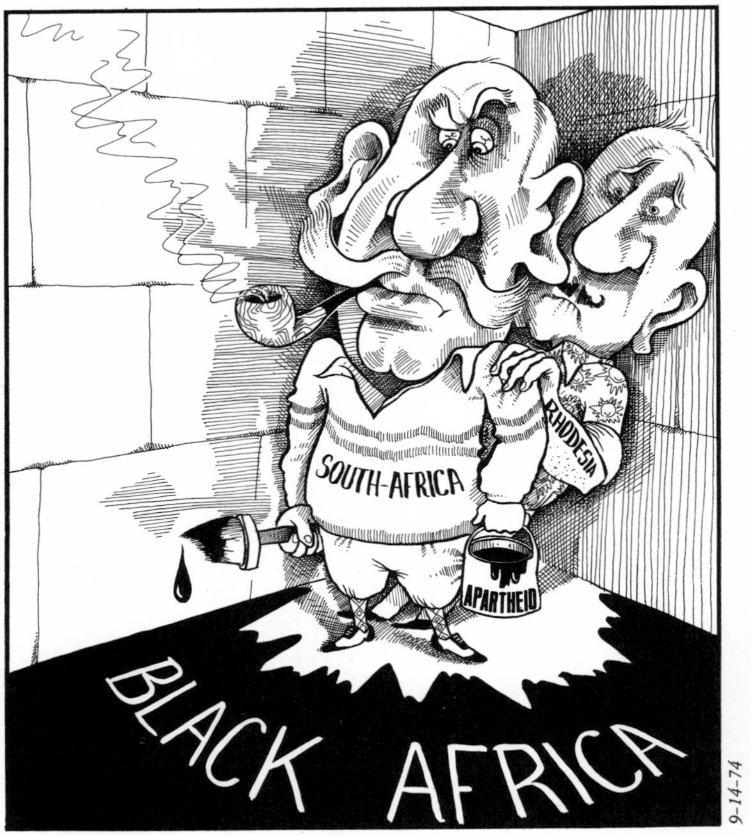
SOUTH-AFRICA
RHODESIA
APARTHEID
BLACK AFRICA
9-14-74

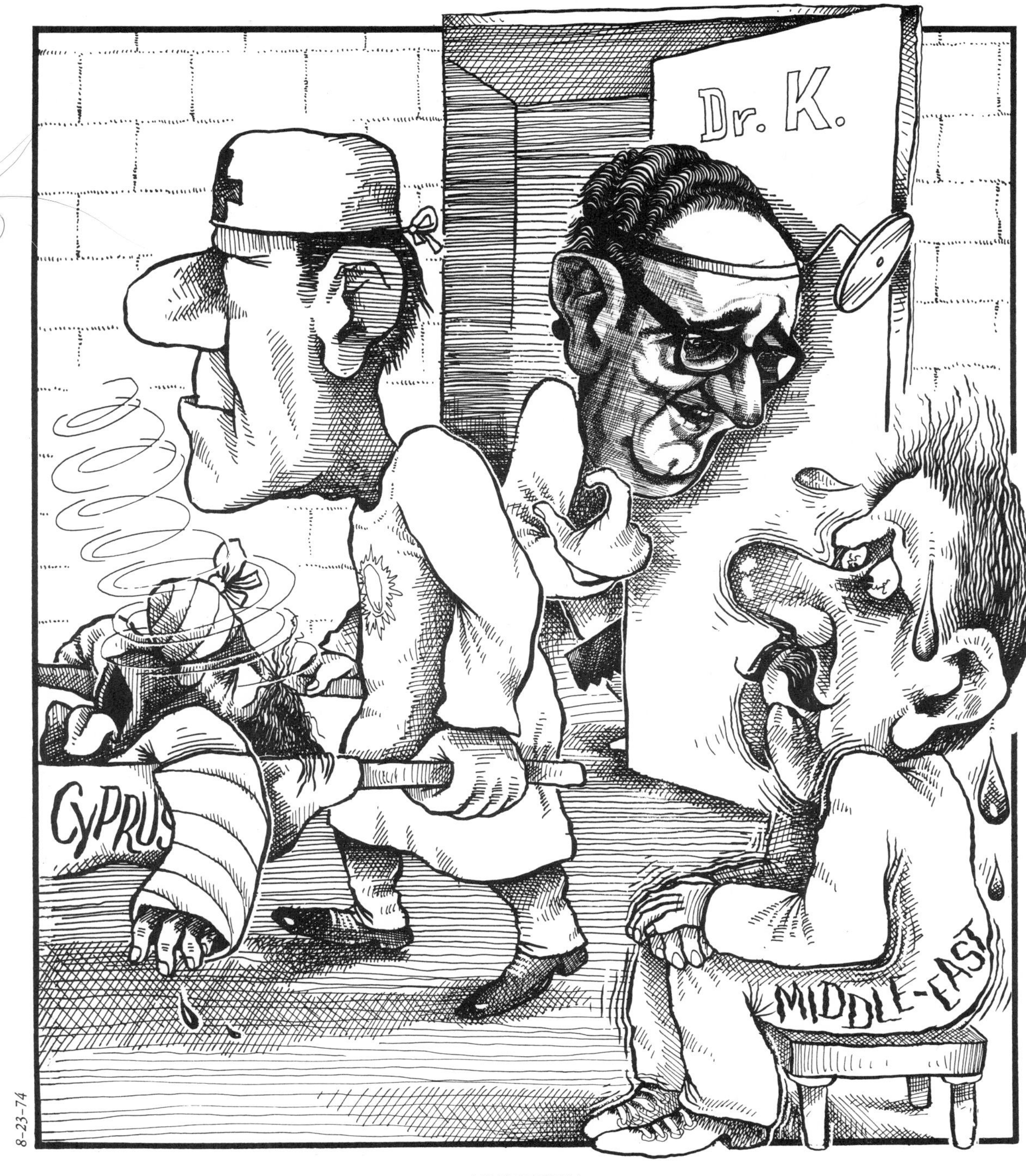
Dr. K.
CYPRUS
MIDDLE-EAST
8-23-74

"NEXT"

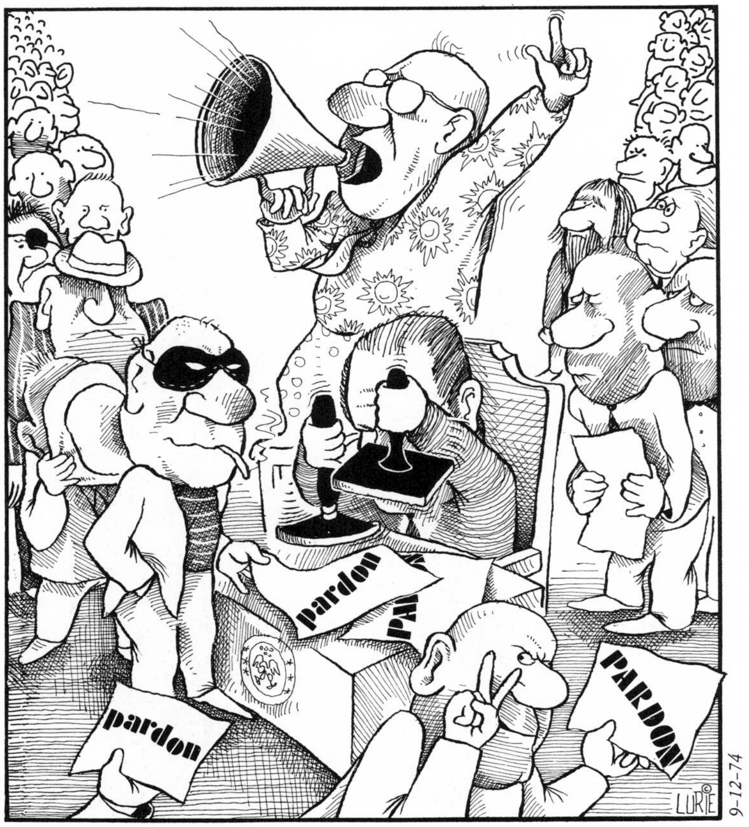
pardon
PARDON
pardon
LURIE
9-12-74

"PLEASE, PLEASE! THE PRESIDENT HAS ONLY TWO HANDS!"

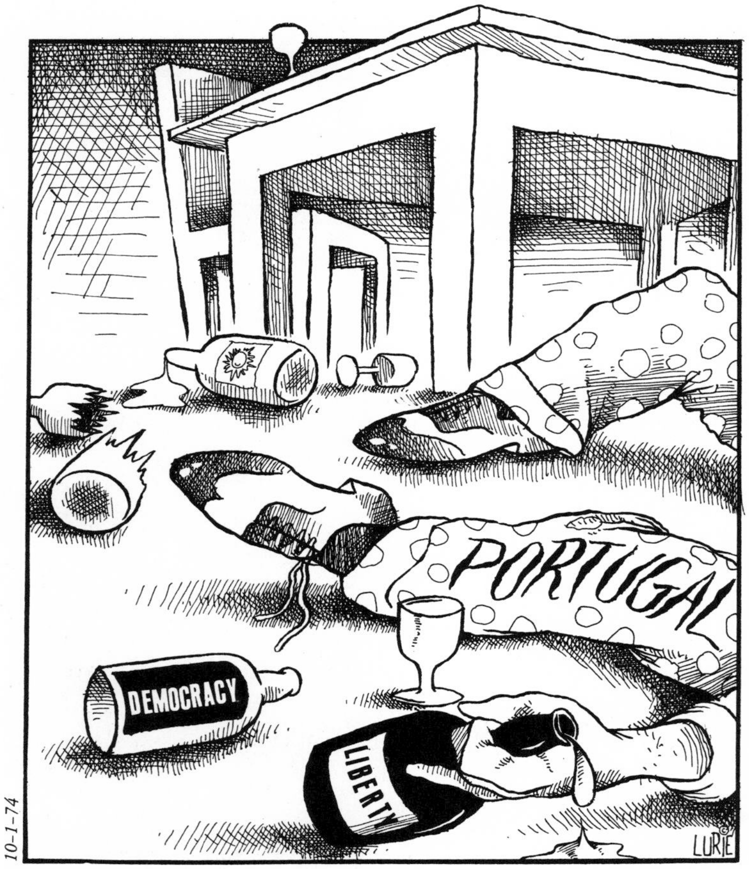
PORTUGAL
DEMOCRACY
LIBERTY
LURIE
10-1-74

INTOXICATED

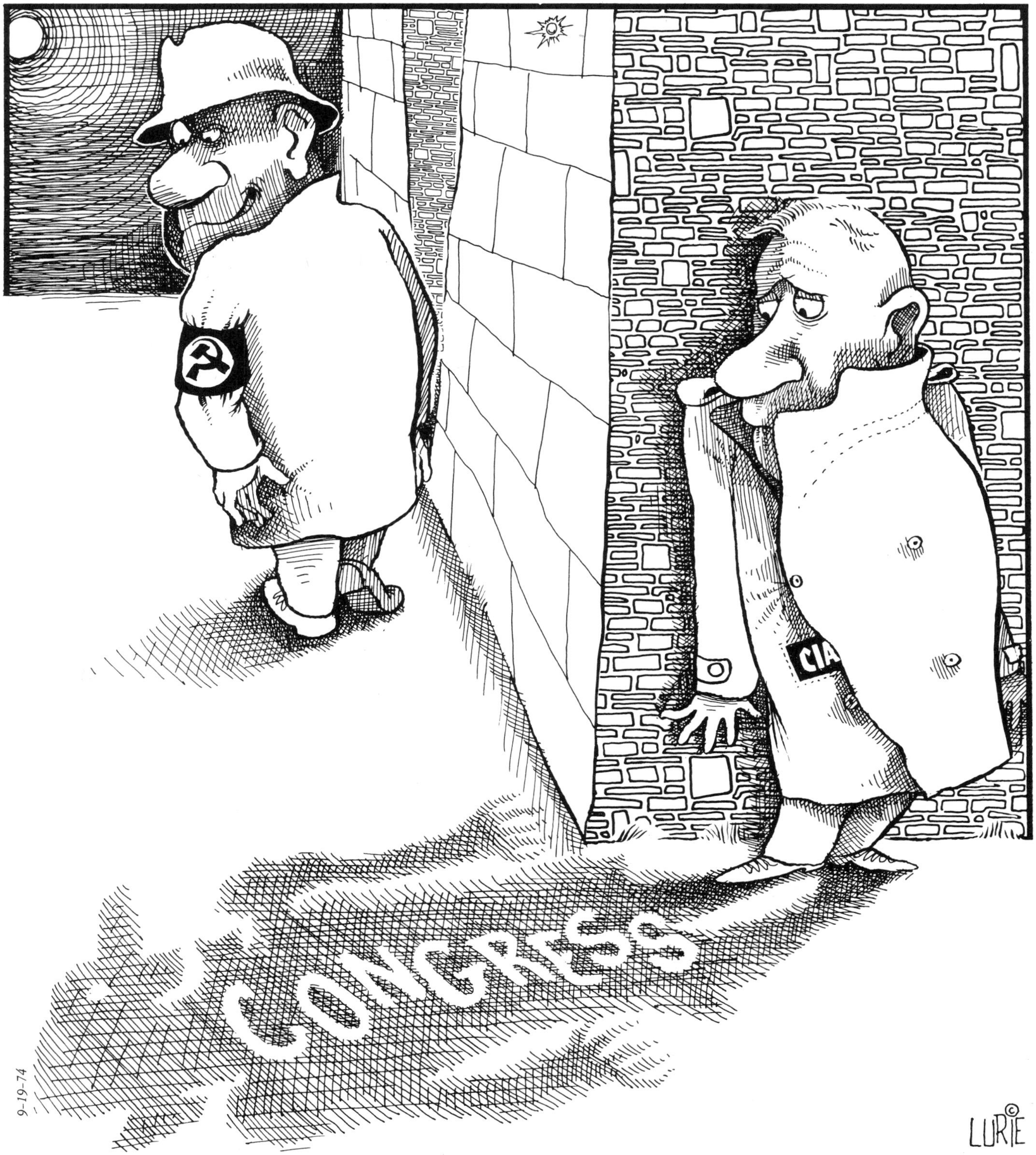
CIA
CONGRESS
9-19-74
LURIE©

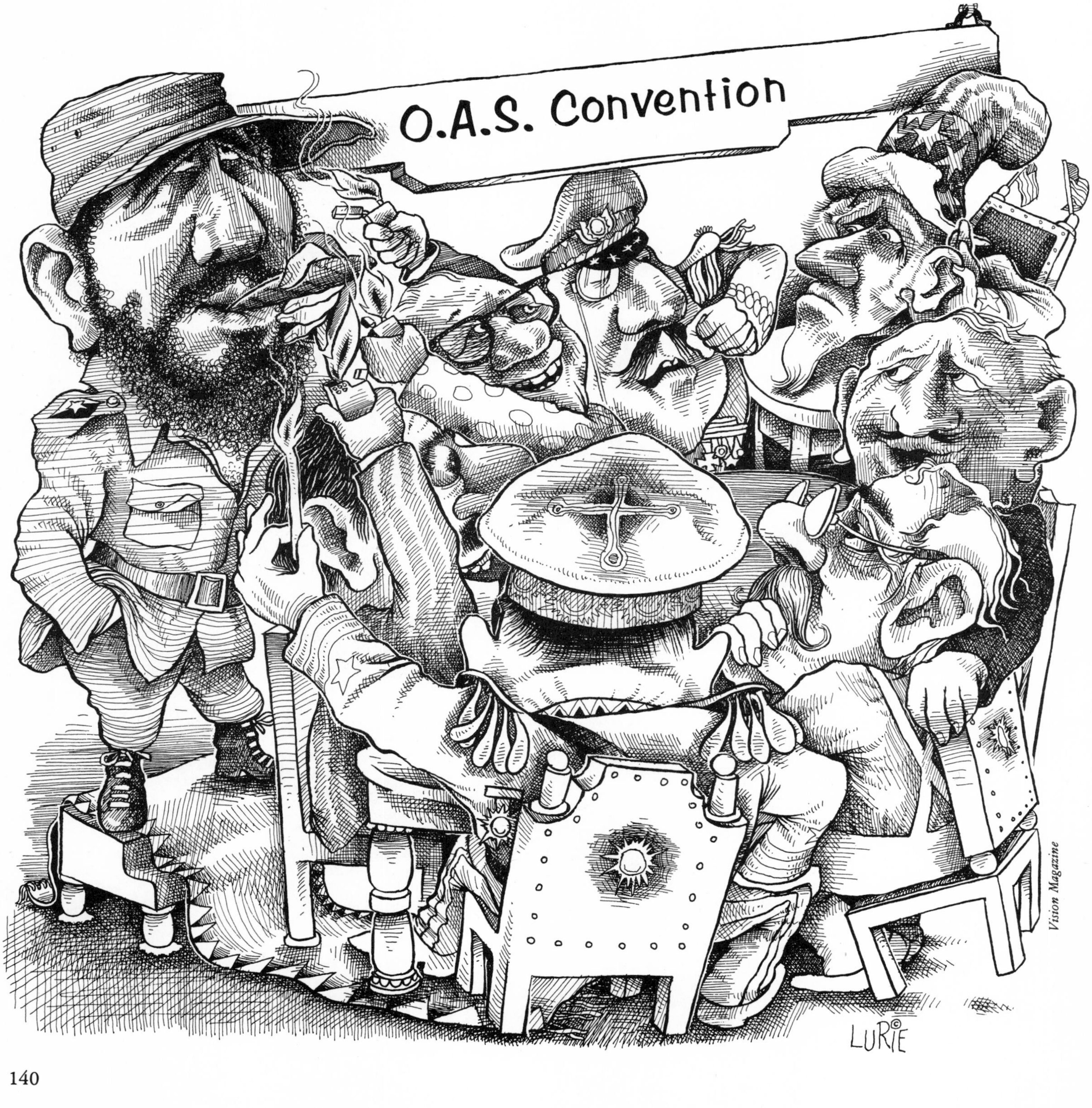
O.A.S. Convention
LURIE©
Vision Magazine

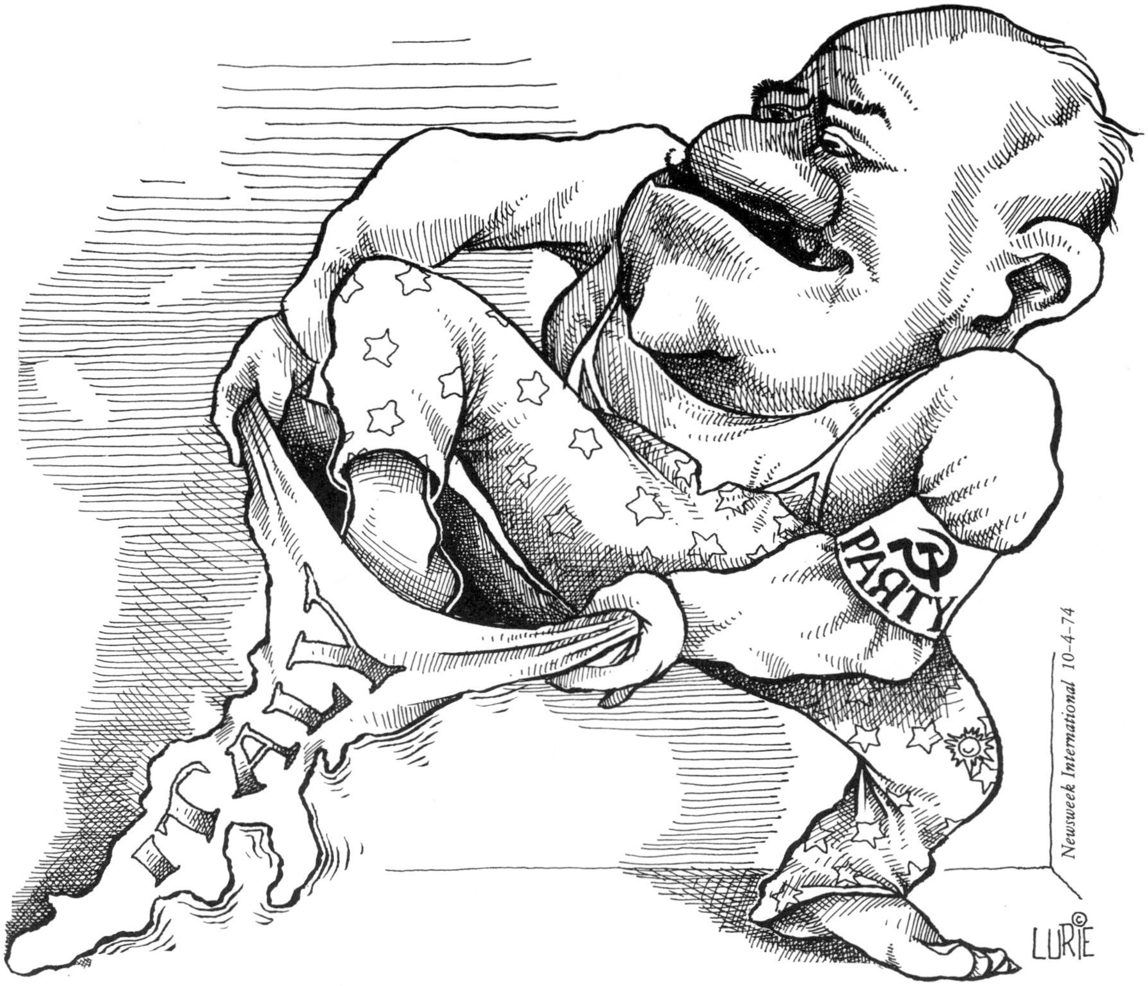
PARTY
ITALY
LURIE©
Newsweek International 10-4-74

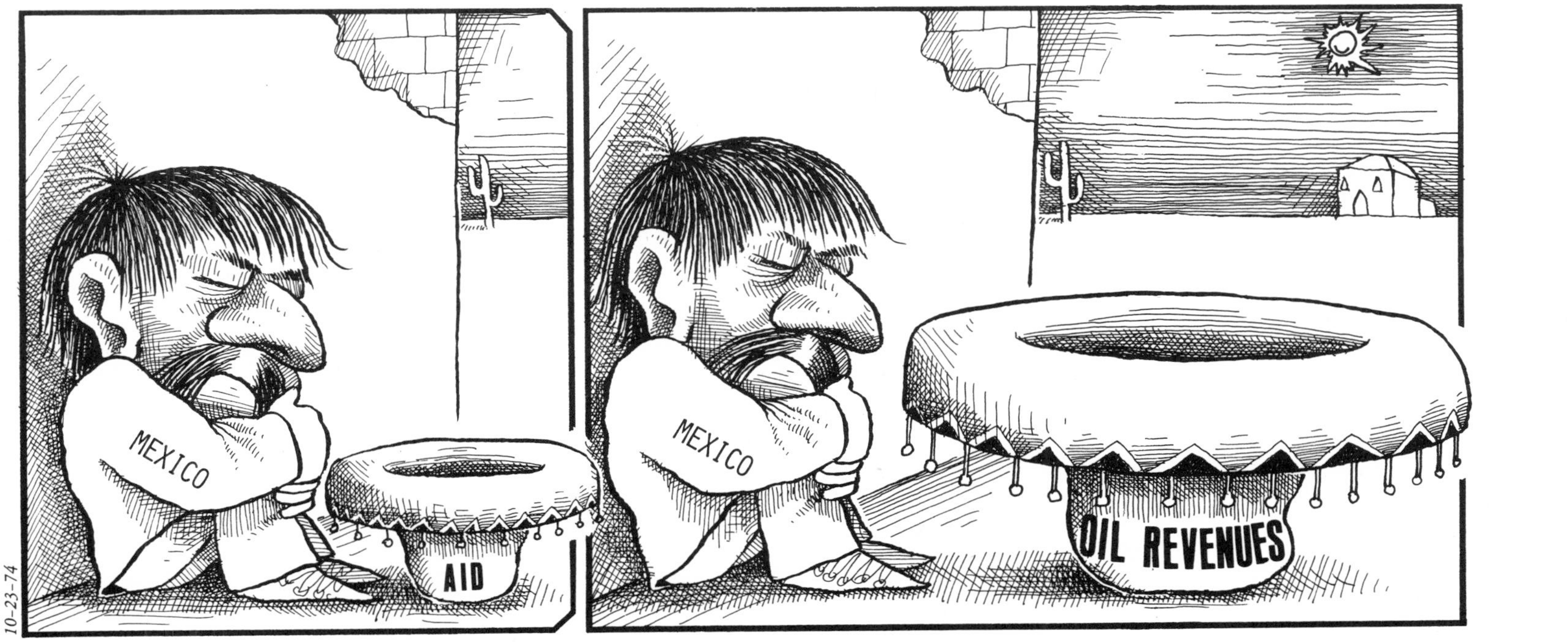
MEXICO
AID
MEXICO
OIL REVENUES
10-23-74

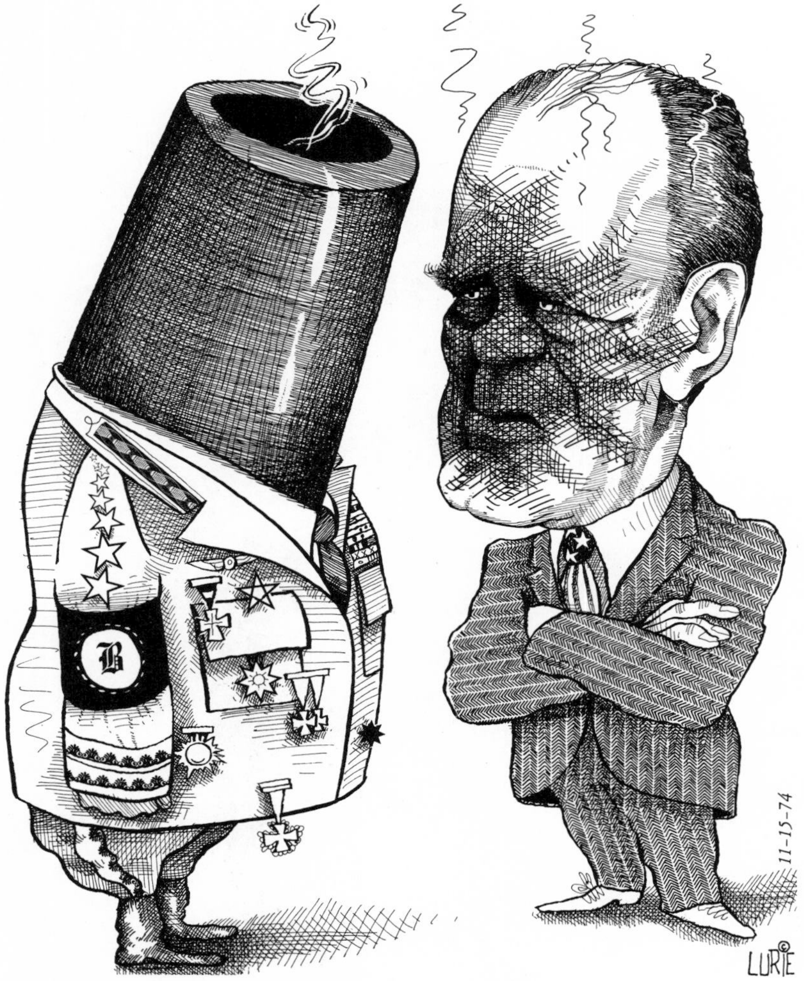

B
11-15-74
LURIE

"I WISH YOU'D KEEP YOUR BIG MOUTH SHUT, GENERAL BROWN!"

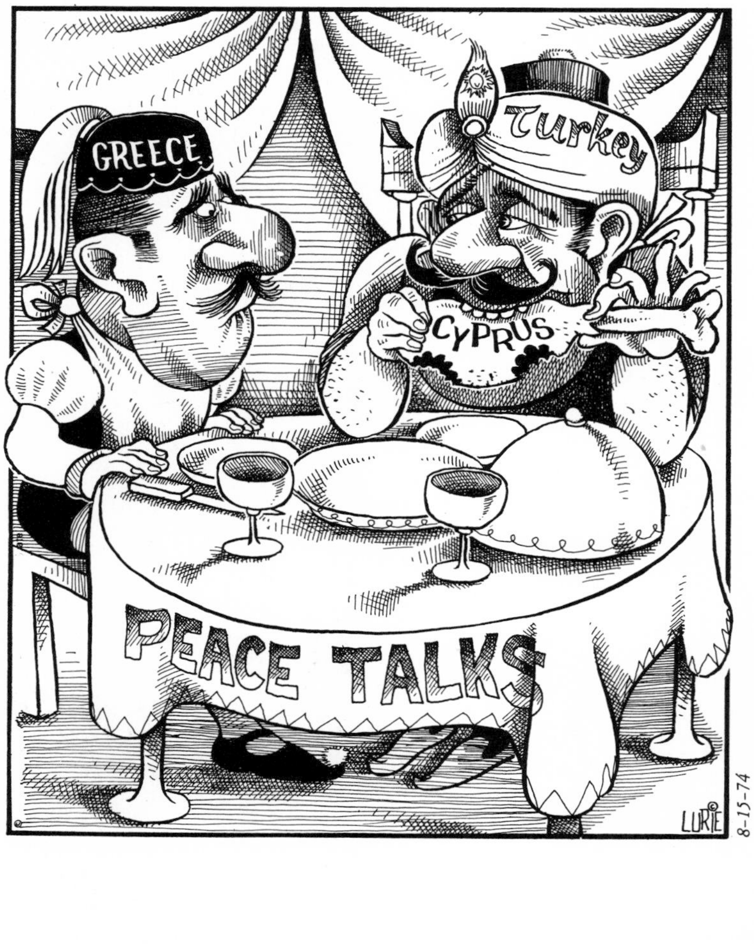

GREECE
Turkey
CYPRUS
PEACE TALKS
8-15-74
LURIE

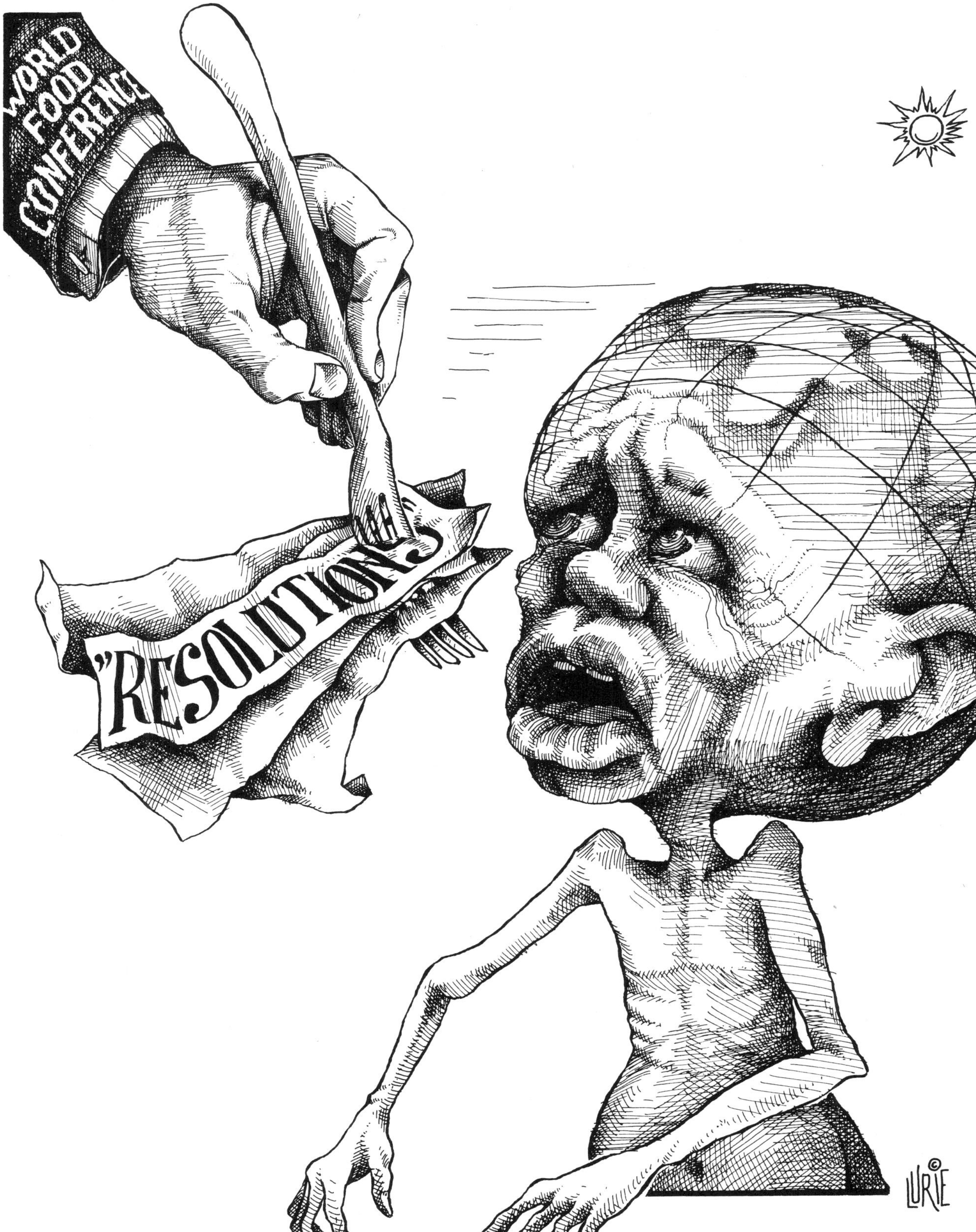
WORLD FOOD CONFERENCE
"RESOLUTIONS"
LURIE ©

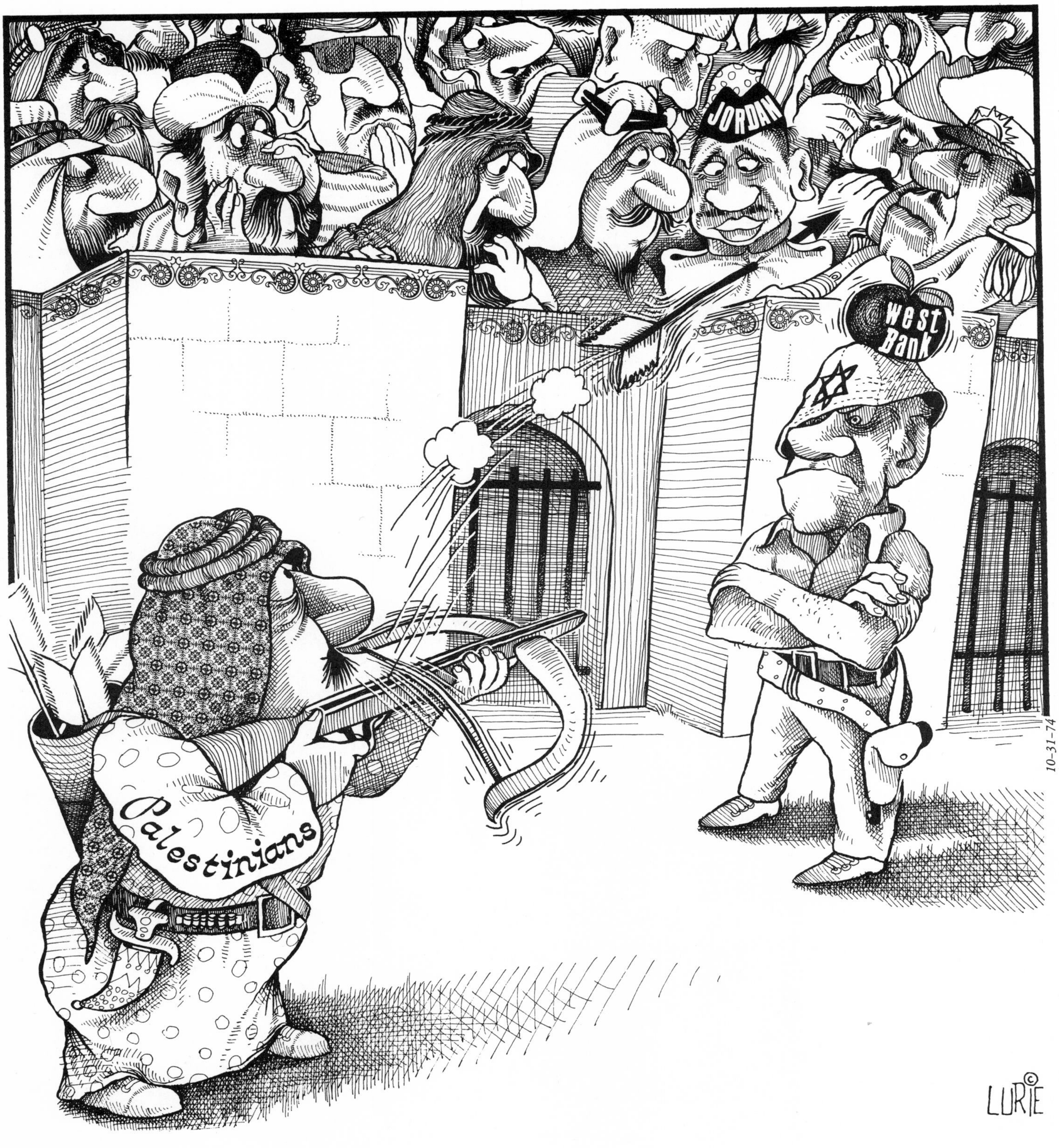
JORDAN
West Bank
Palestinians
10-31-74
LURIE©

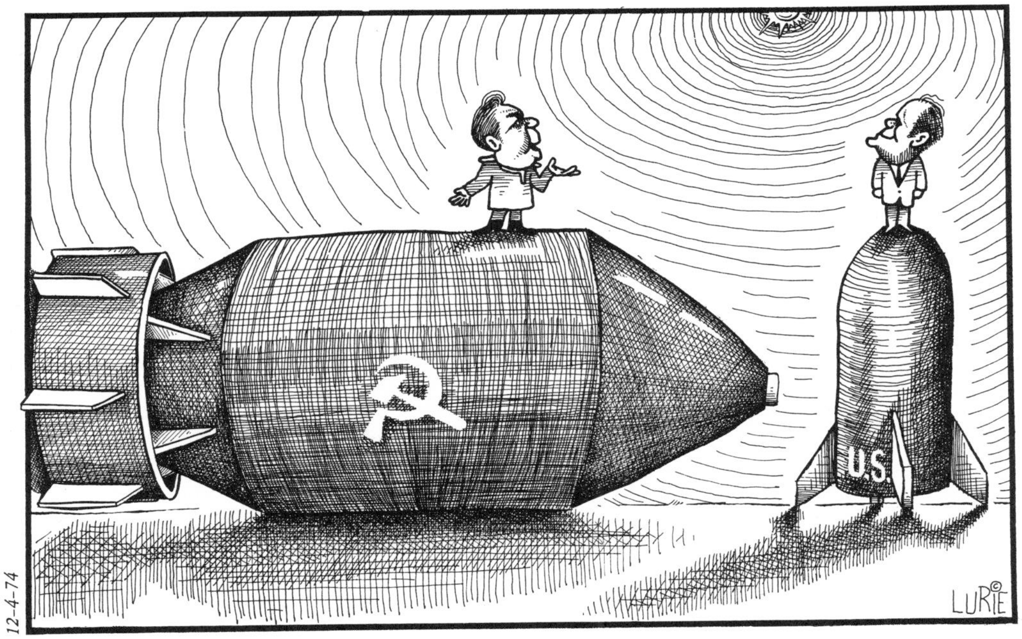
U.S.
LURIE

"I TOLD YOU, GERALD—OUR MIGHT IS
OF THE SAME HEIGHT!"

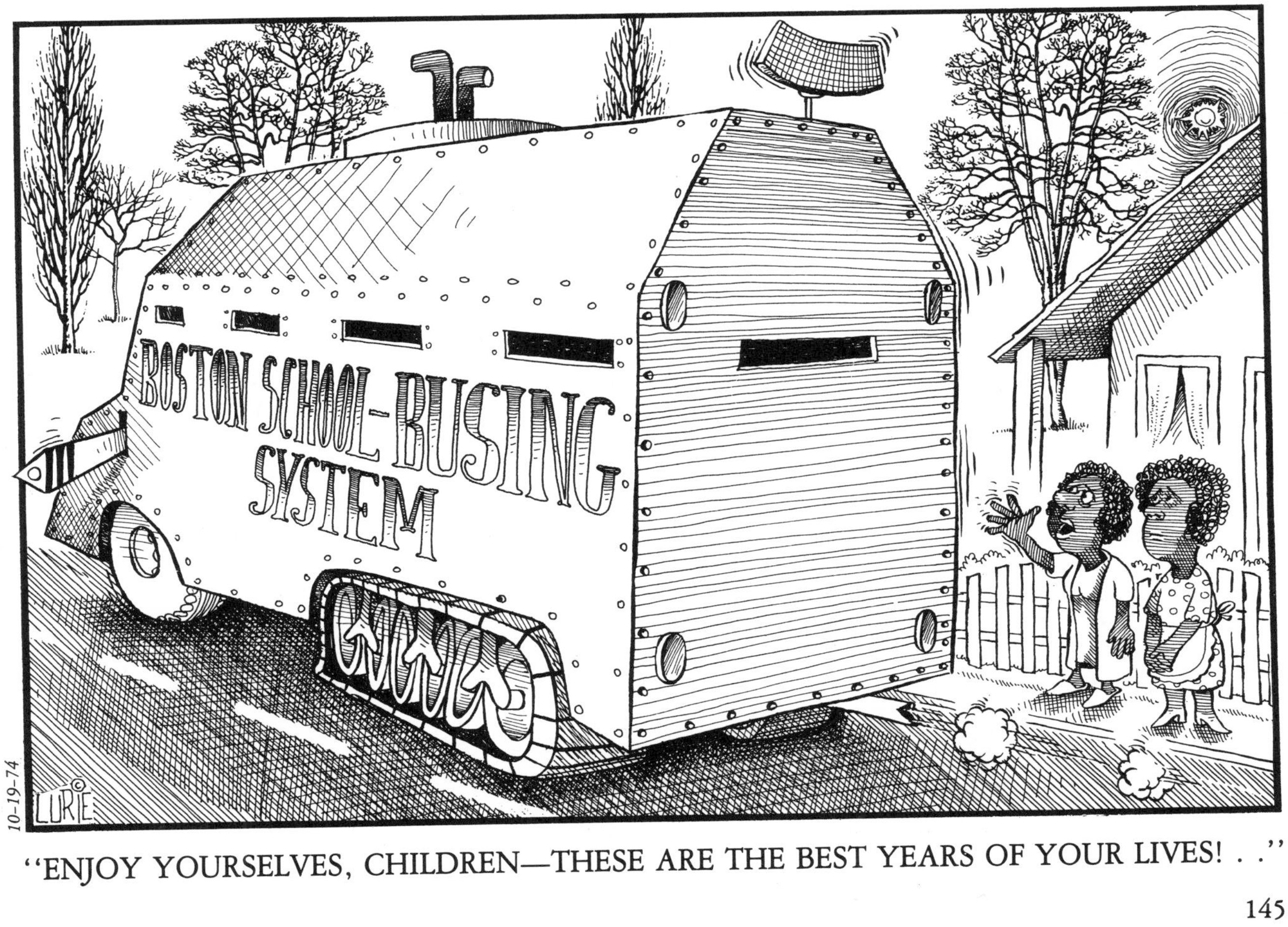
BOSTON SCHOOL-BUSING
SYSTEM
LURIE

"ENJOY YOURSELVES, CHILDREN—THESE ARE THE BEST YEARS OF YOUR LIVES! . ."

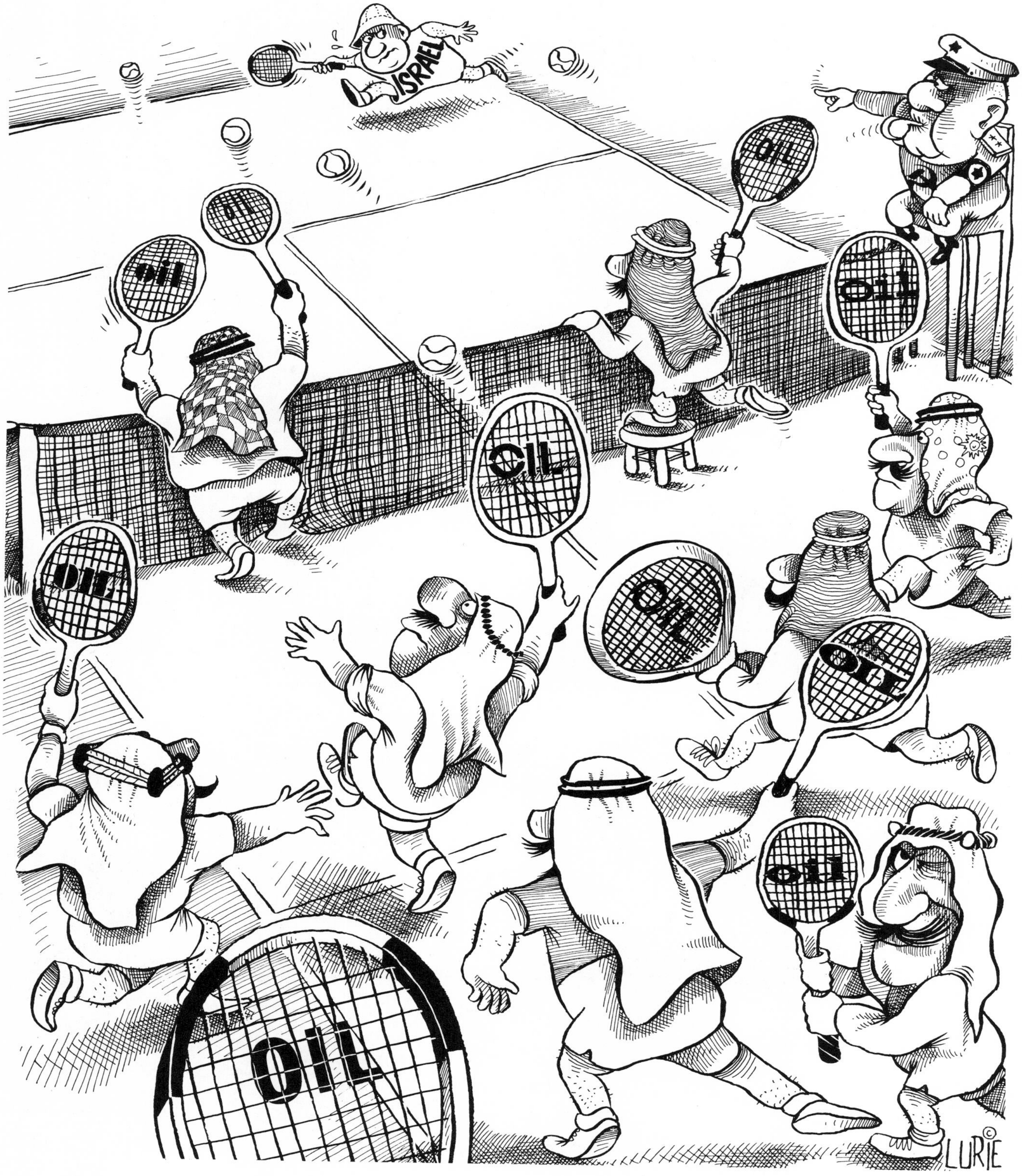
ISRAEL
OIL
OIL
OIL
OIL
LURIE

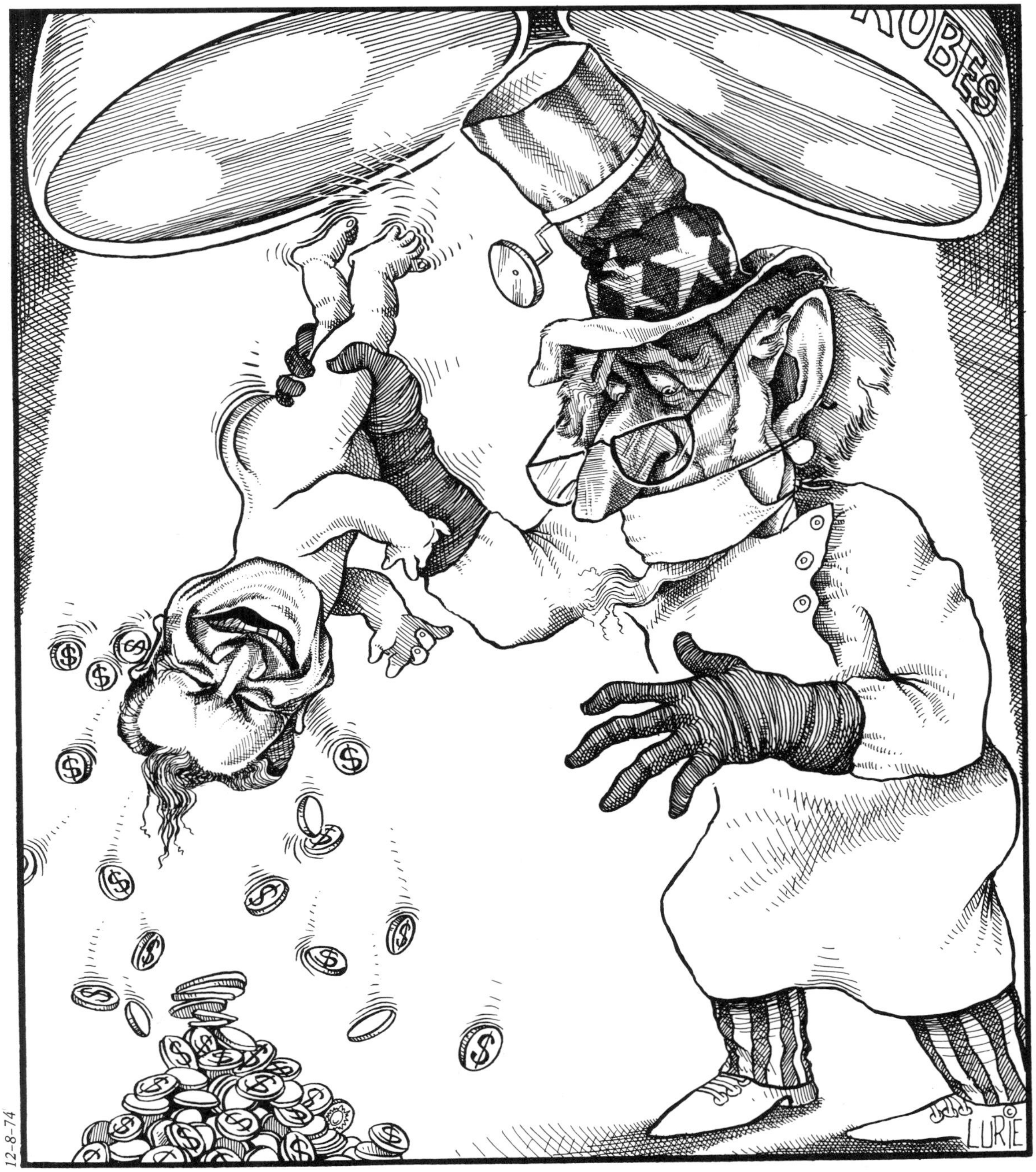
ROBES
LURIE

12-8-74

A VICE PRESIDENT IS BORN

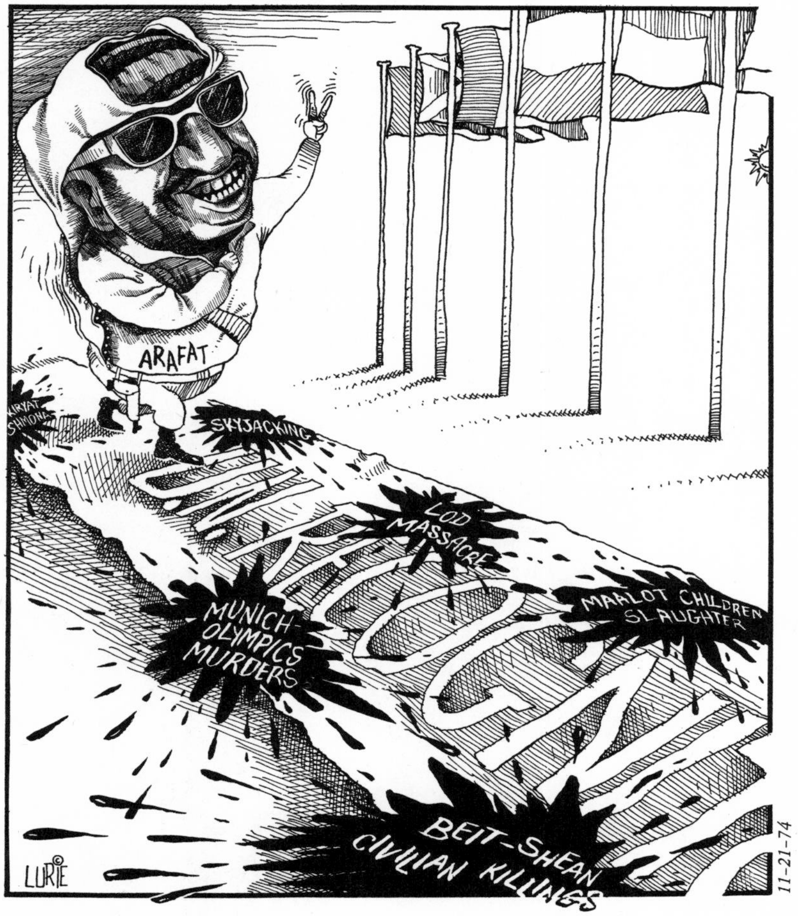
ARAFAT
SKYJACKING
LOD MASSACRE
MUNICH OLYMPICS MURDERS
MAALOT CHILDREN SLAUGHTER
BEIT-SHEAN CIVILIAN KILLINGS
LURIE
11-21-74

THE RED CARPET

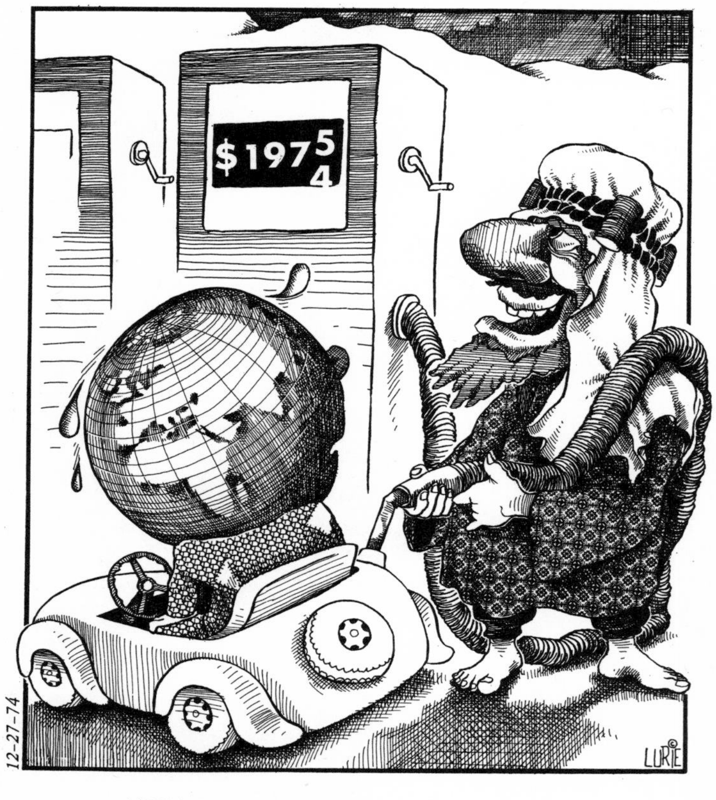
$197 5/4
12-27-74
LURIE

"HAP-P-P-Y-Y-Y NEW YEAR!"

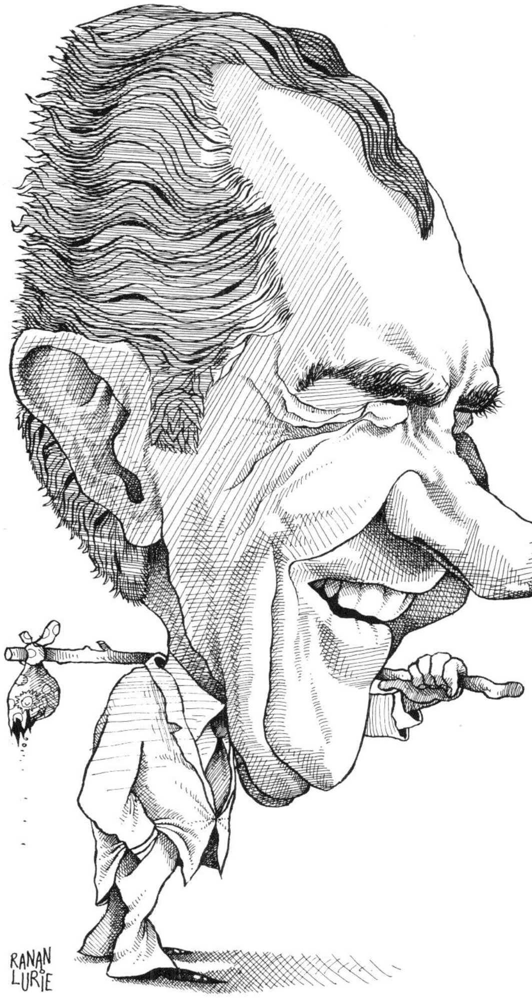
RANAN LURIE

President Richard M. Nixon

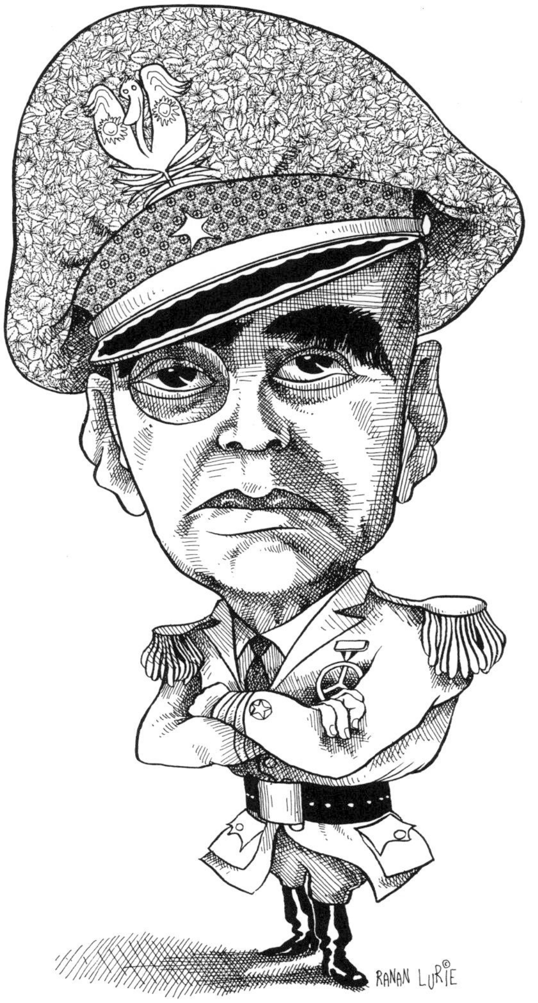
RANAN LURIE

General Antonio de Spinola
New Ruler of Portugal

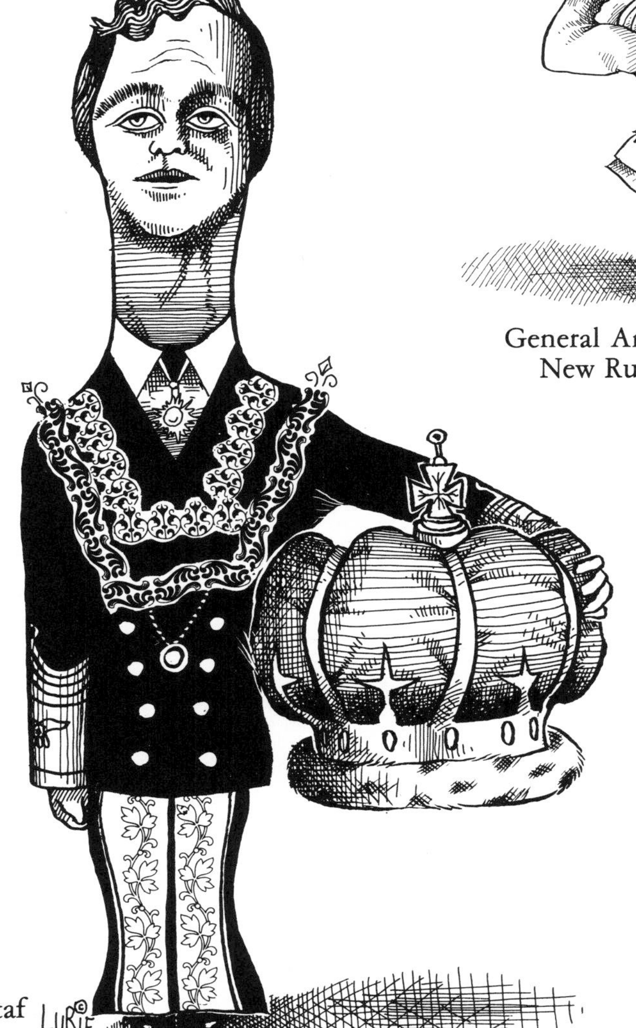
LURIE

King Carl XVI Gustaf
of Sweden

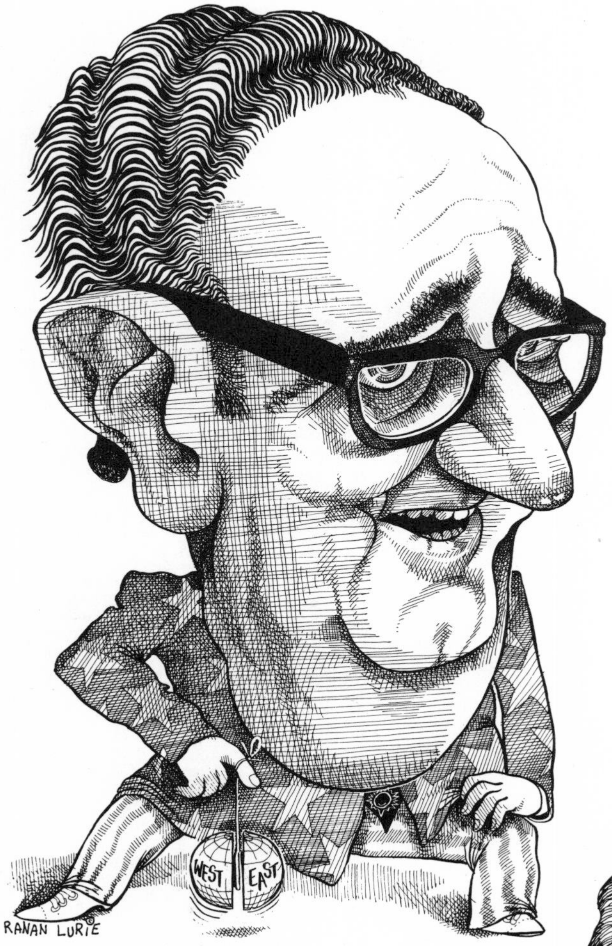
WEST
EAST
RANAN LURIE

Henry Kissinger

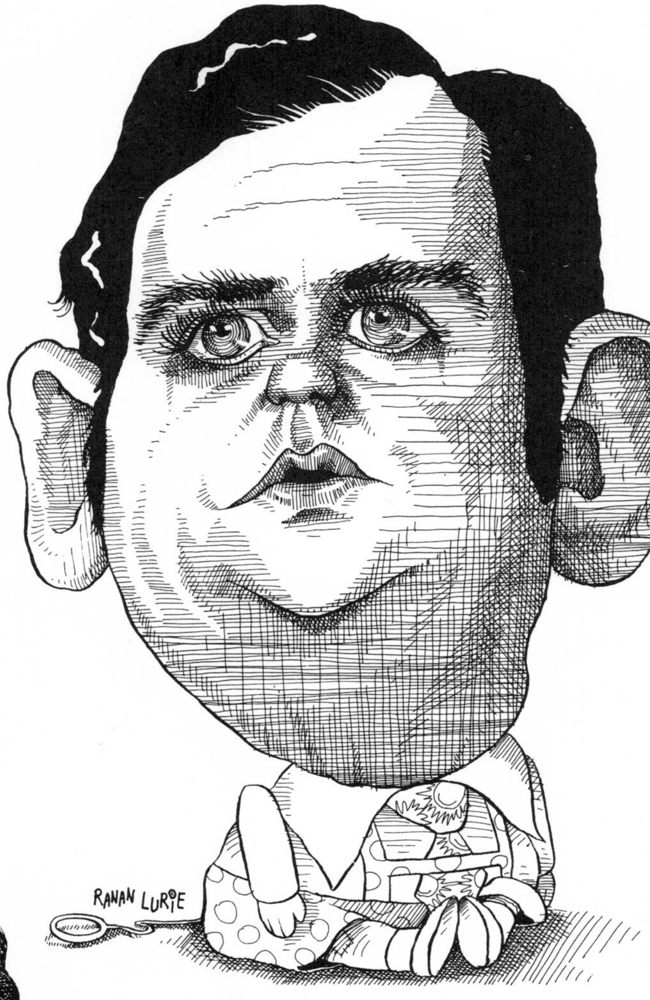
RANAN LURIE

Ronald Ziegler
President Nixon's Spokesman

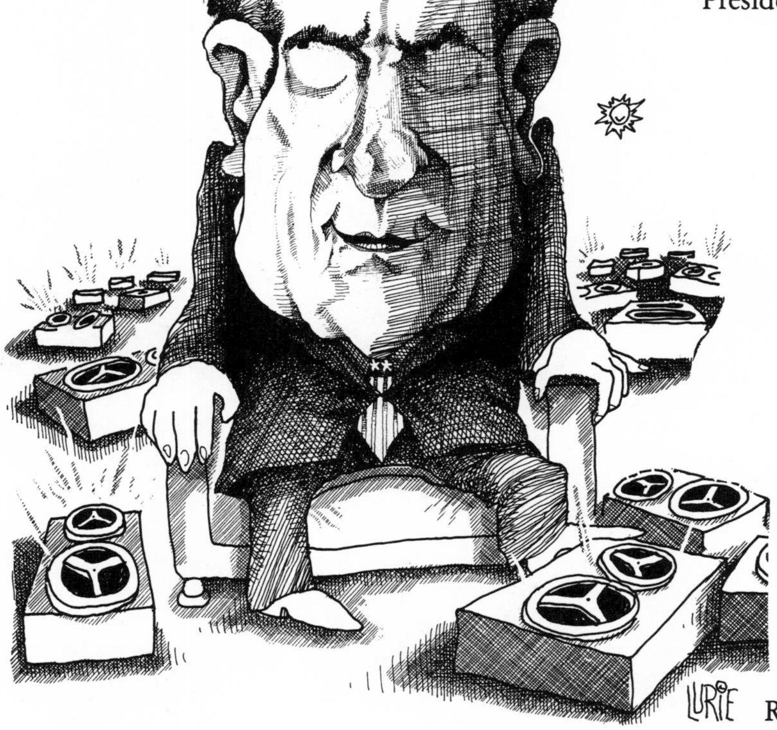
LURIE

Retired President Nixon

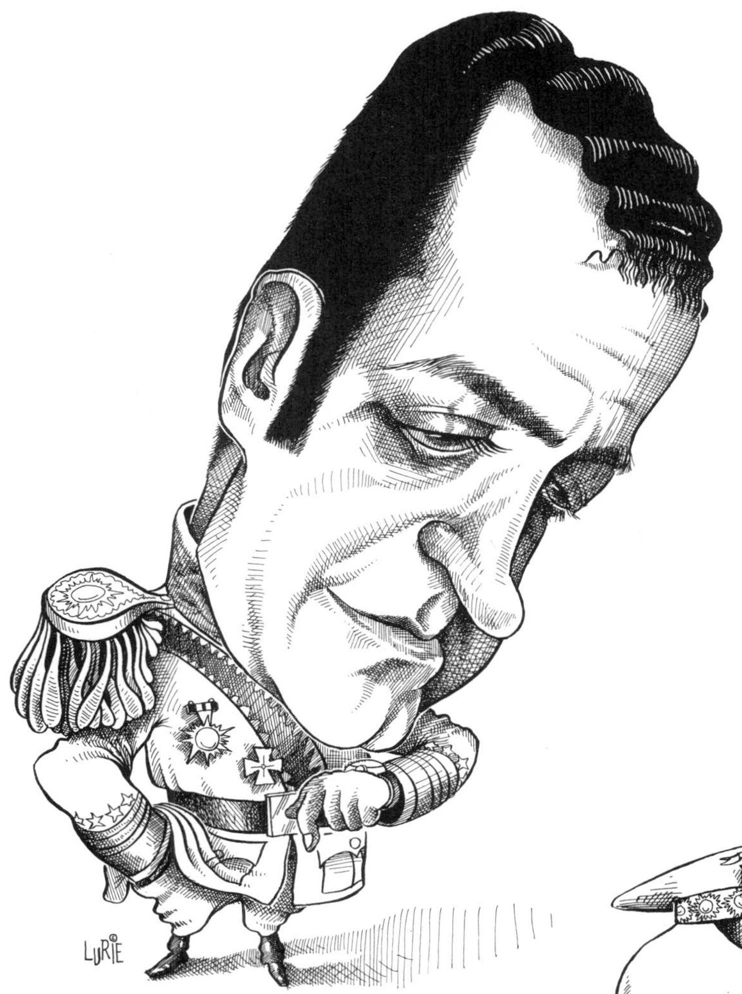
LURIE

Prince Juan Carlos de Borbòn
of Spain

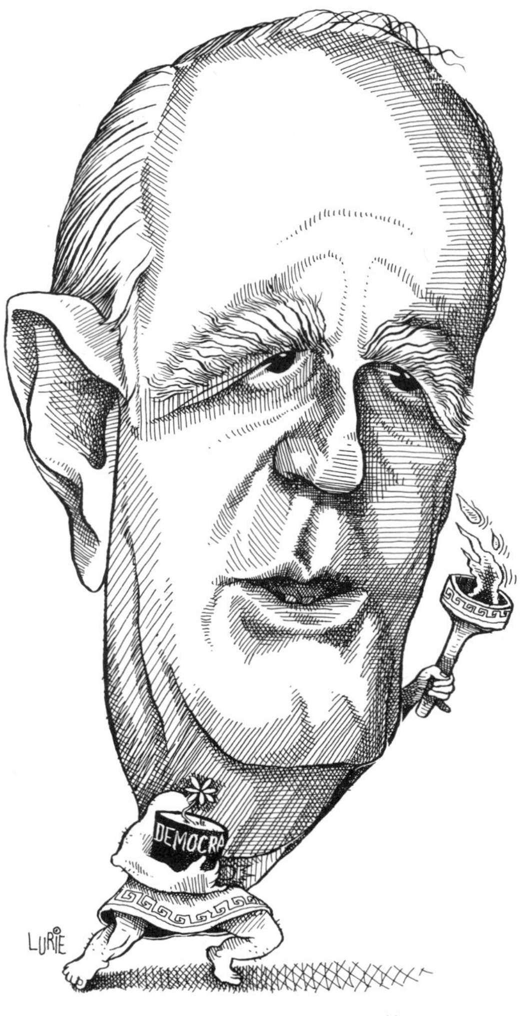
DEMOCRA
LURIE

Constantine Caramanlis
Premier of Greece

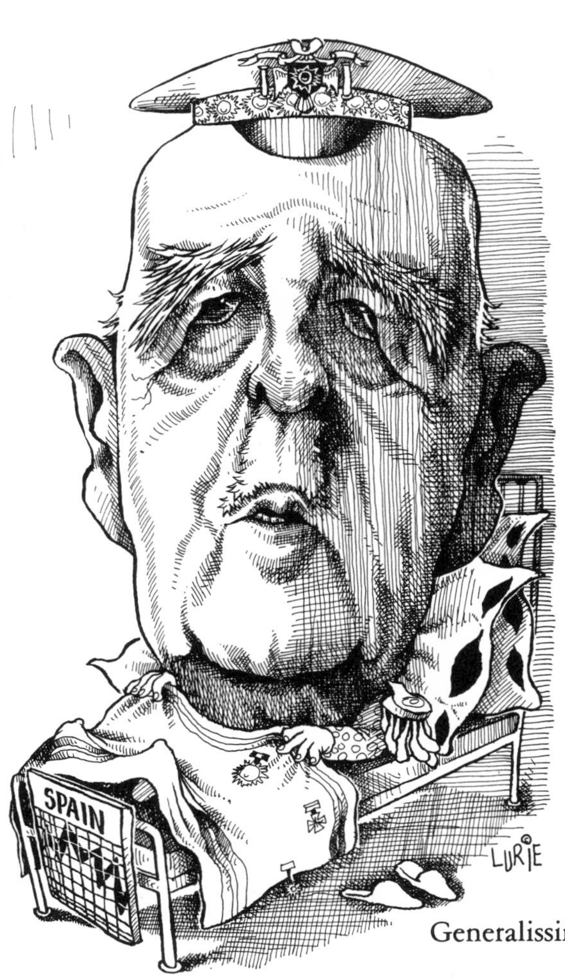
SPAIN
LURIE

Generalissimo Francisco Franco Bahamonde
Ruler of Spain

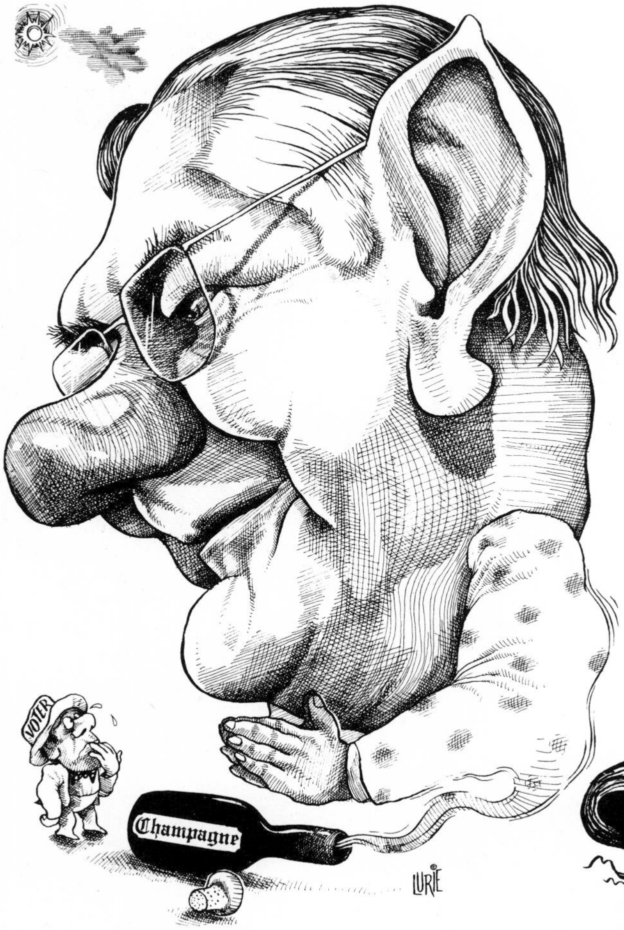
VOTER
Champagne
LURIE

Congressman Wilbur Mills
Chairman of the Ways and Means Committee

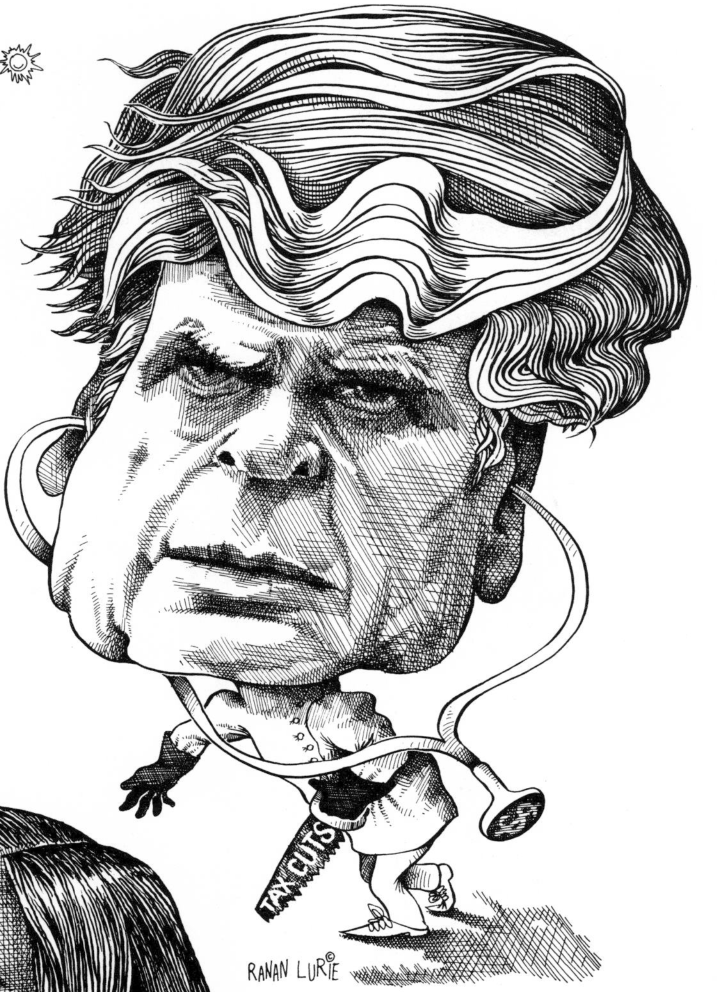
TAX CUTS
RANAN LURIE

Representative Al Ullman
Chairman of the House
Ways and Means Committee
Designate

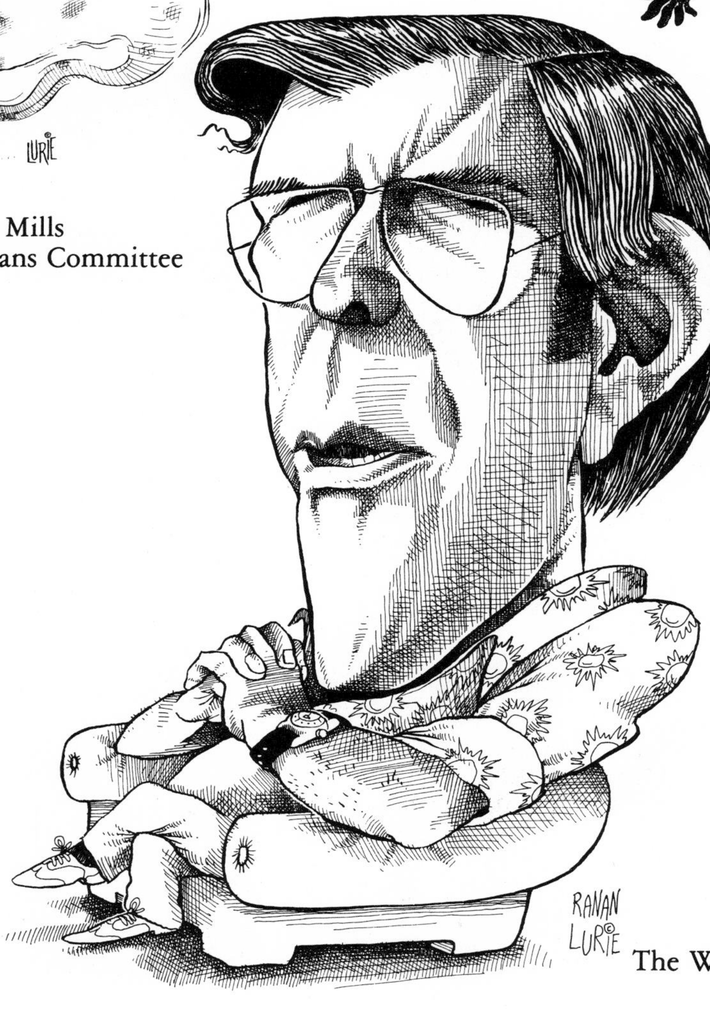
RANAN
LURIE

Donald Rumsfeld
The White House Chief of Staff

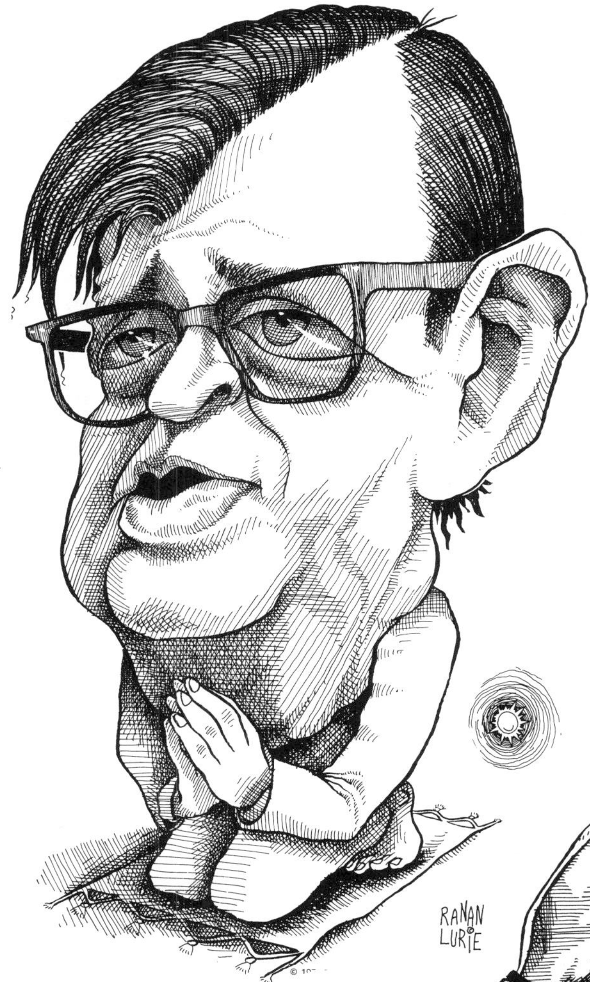
RANAN
LURIE

Charles W. Colson
President Nixon's Former Aide

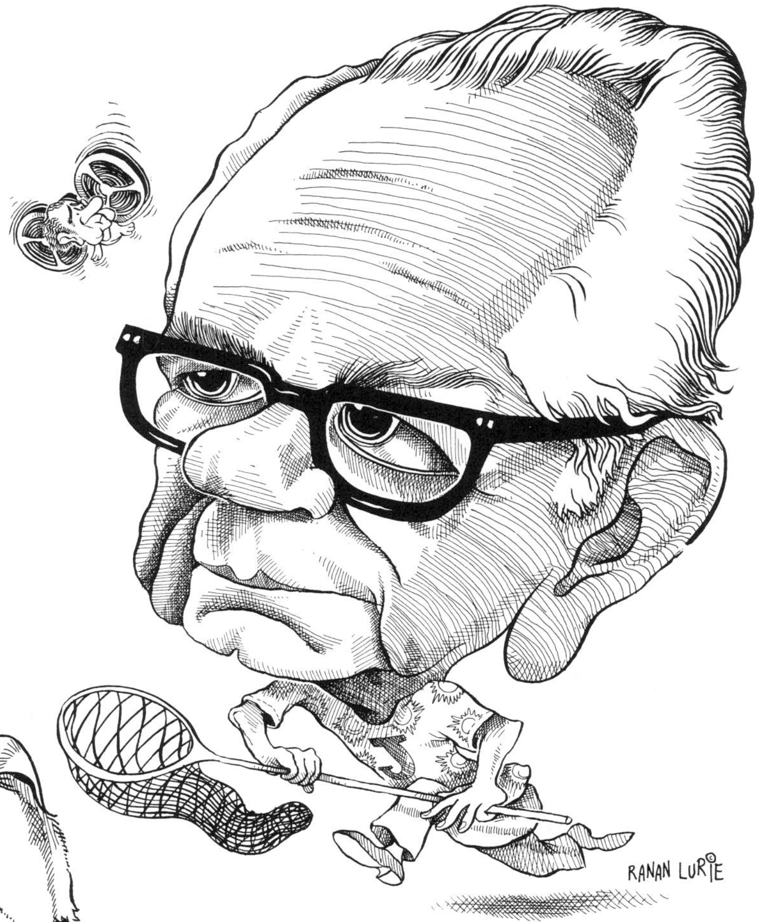
RANAN LURIE

Leon Jaworski
Watergate Special Prosecutor

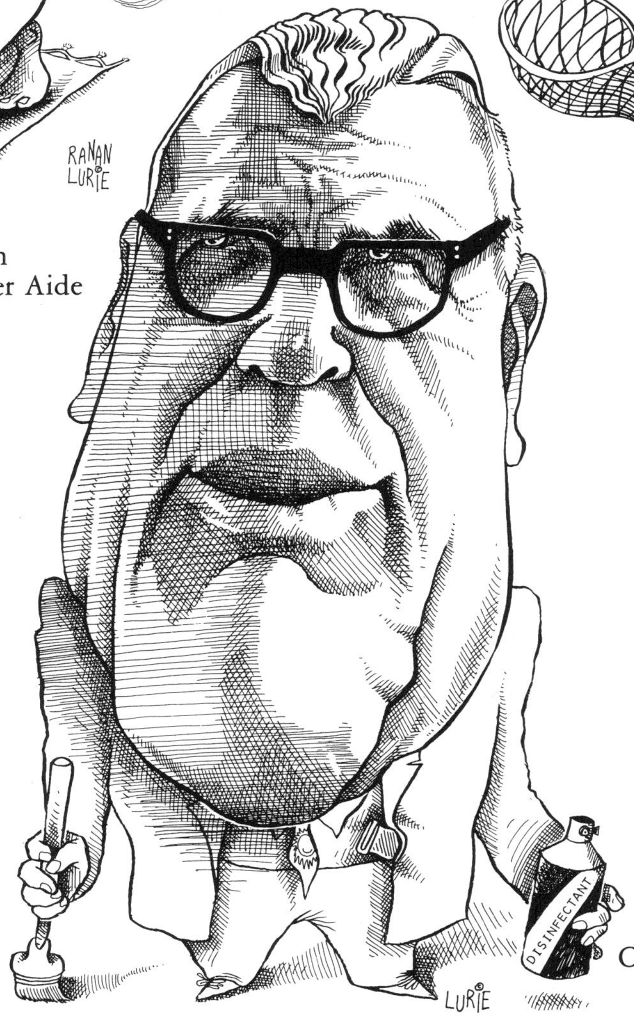
DISINFECTANT
LURIE

Clarence M. Kelly
F.B.I. Director

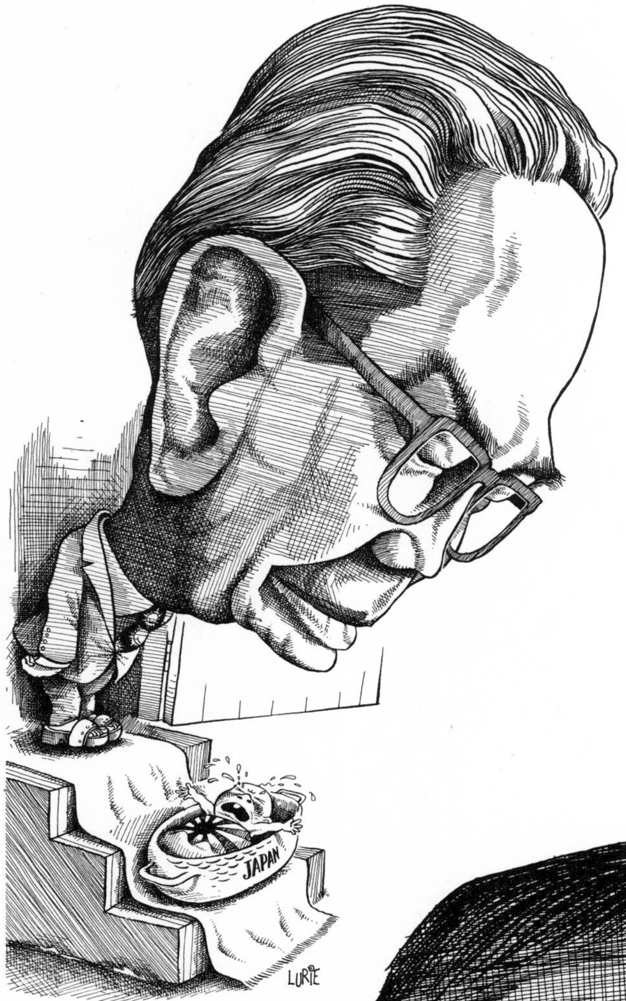
JAPAN
LURIE

Takeo Miki
Japan's Prime Minister

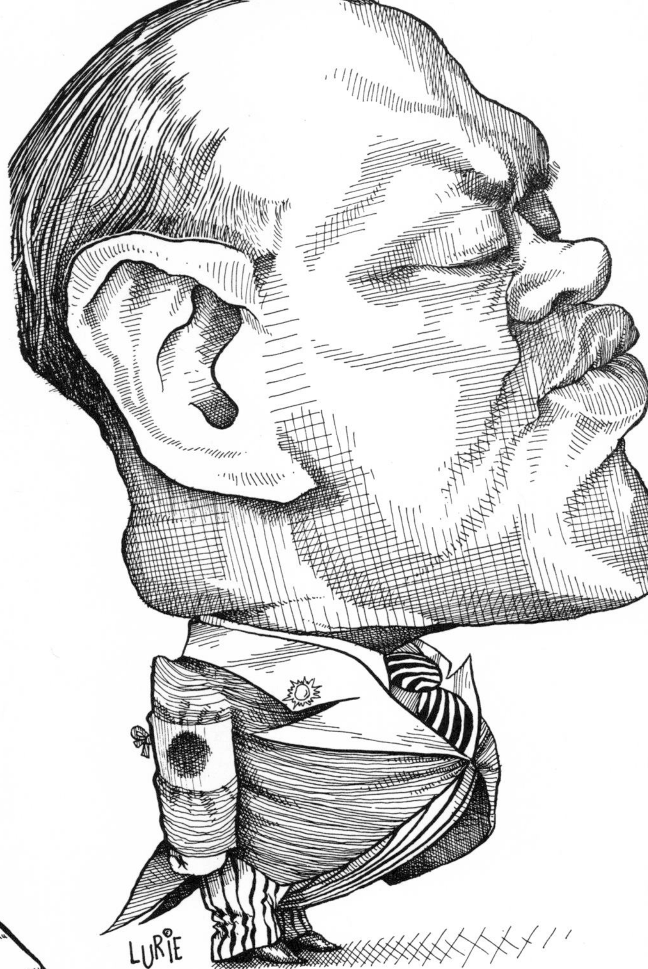
LURIE

Kakuei Tanaka
Japan's Former Prime Minister

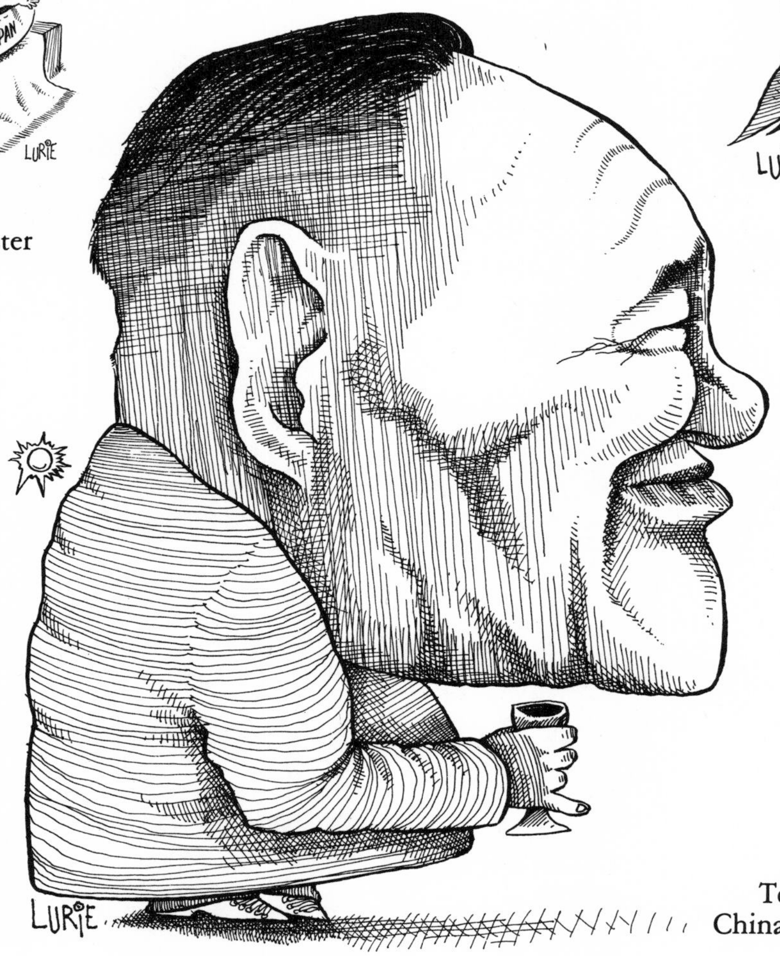
LURIE

Teng Hsiao-ping
China's Deputy Premier

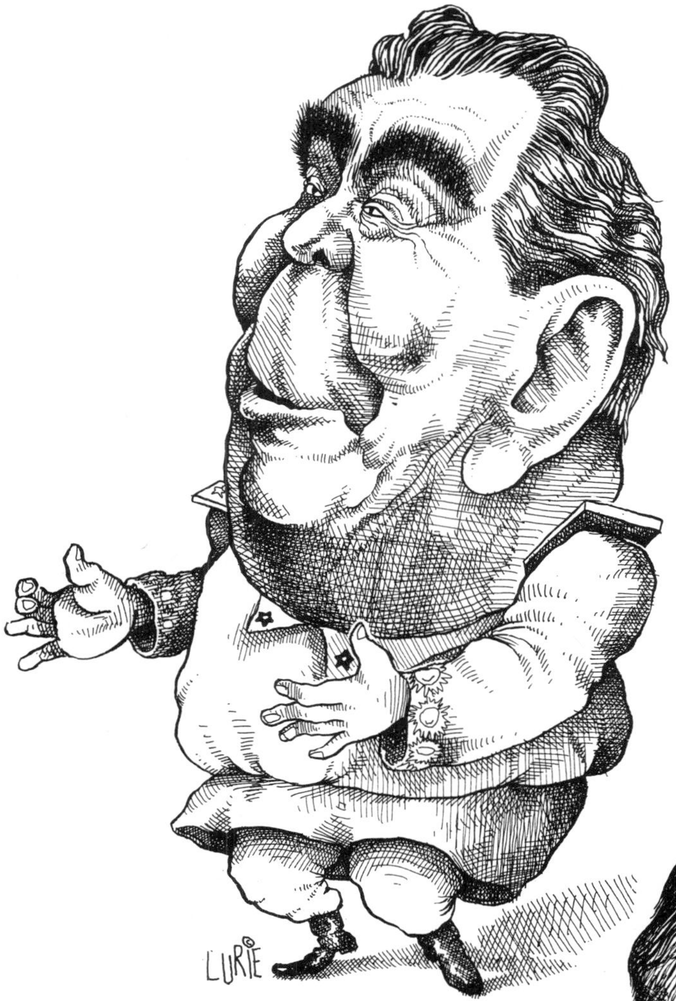
LURIE

Leonid Brezhnev

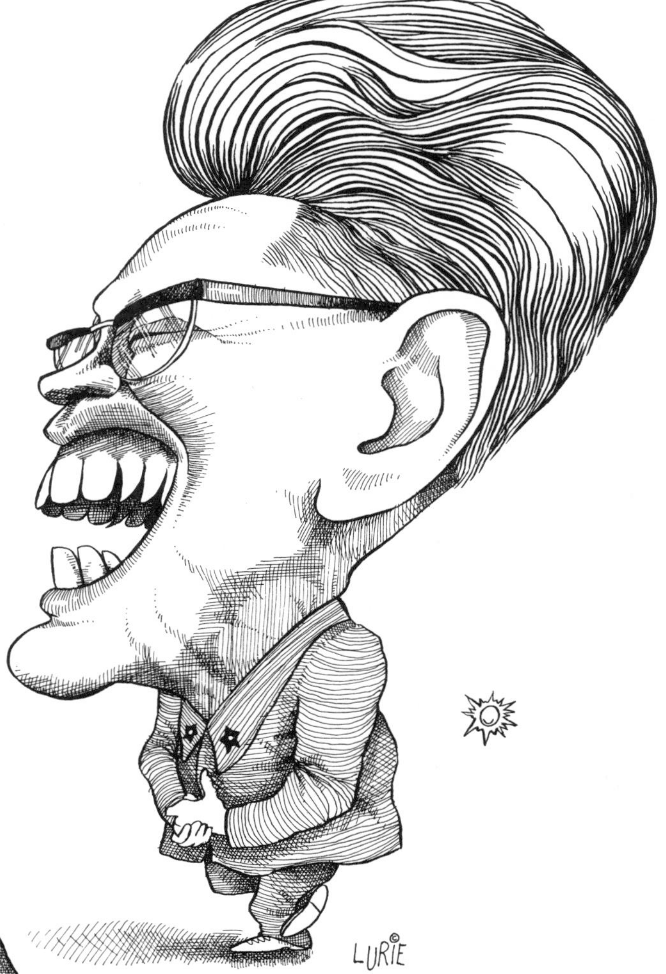
LURIE

Chiao Kuan-hua
China's Foreign Minister

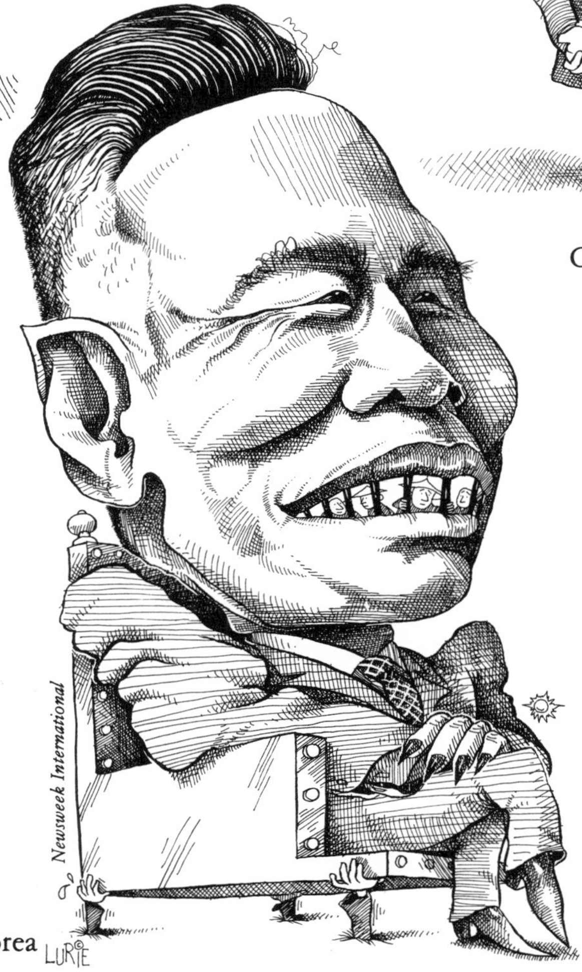
Newsweek International
LURIE

Chung Hee Park
President of South Korea

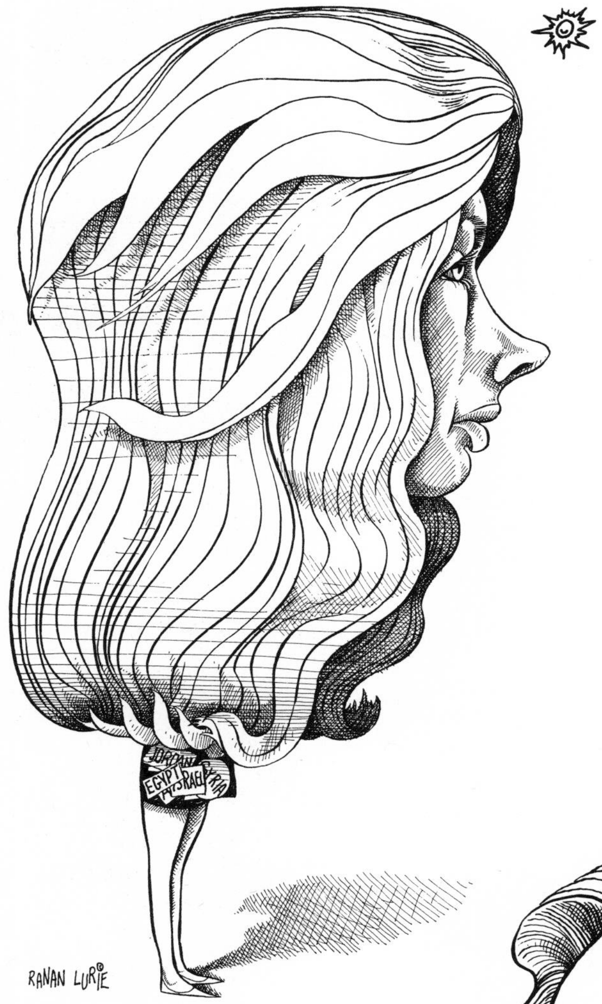
RANAN LURIE

Mrs. Henry Kissinger

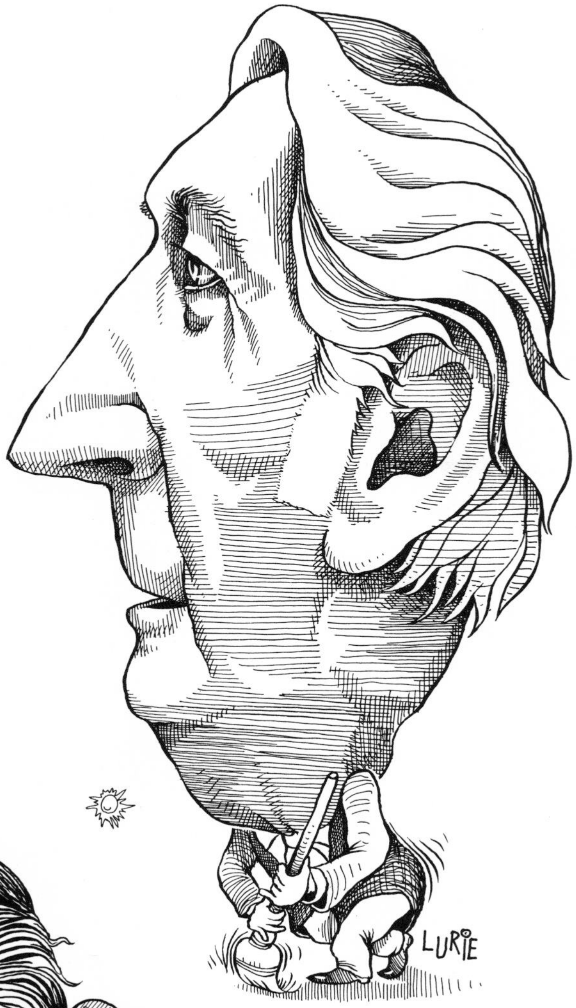
LURIE

Peter W. Rodino, Jr.
Chairman of the House
Judiciary Committee

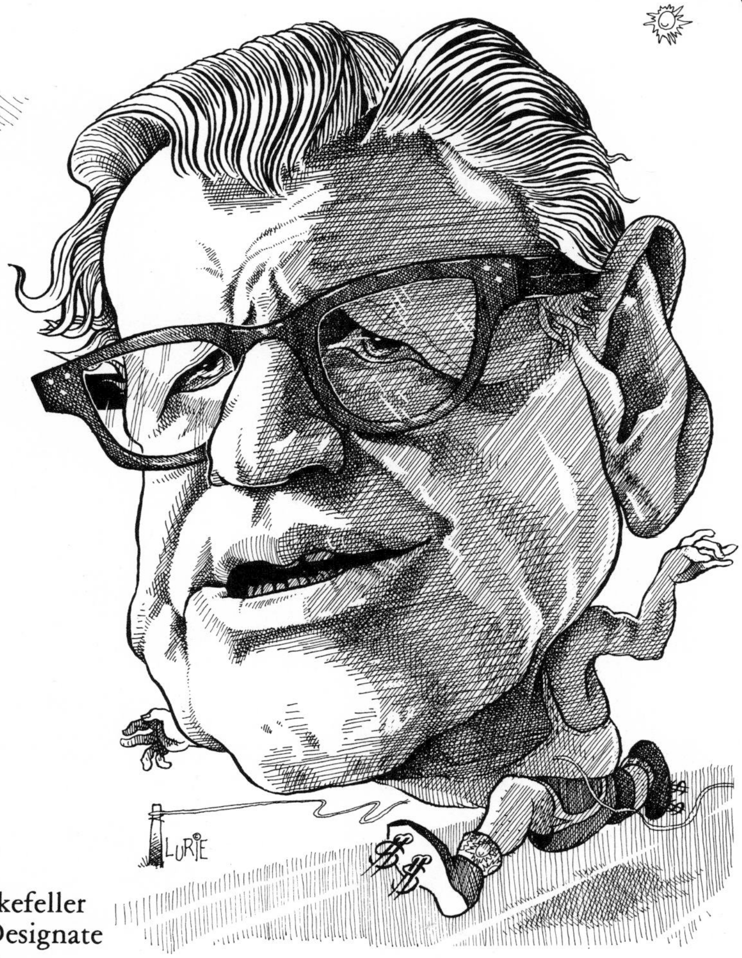
LURIE

Nelson A. Rockefeller
Vice President Designate

RANAN LURIE

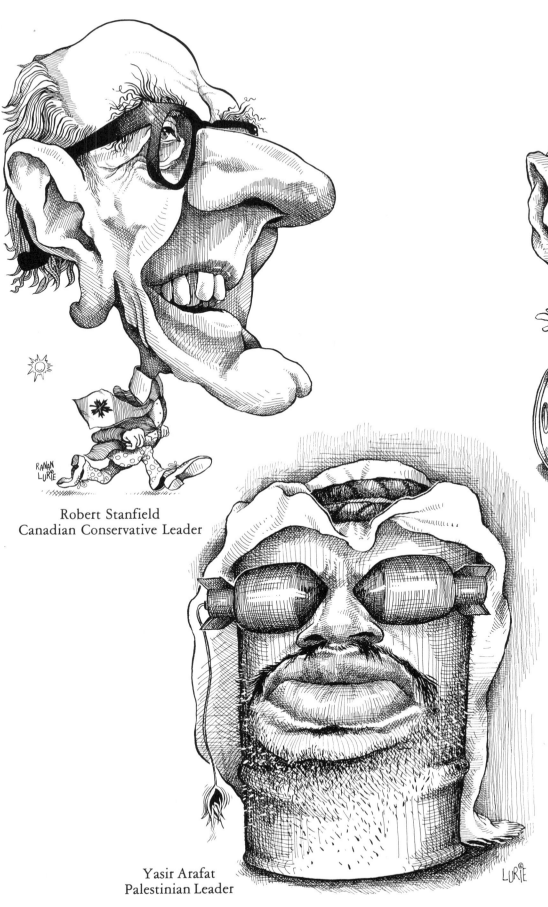

Robert Stanfield
Canadian Conservative Leader

OIL
LURIE

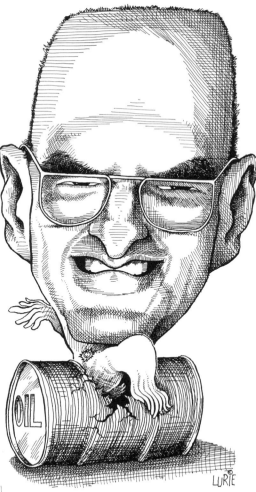

President Luis Echeverria Alvarez
of Mexico

LURIE

Yasir Arafat
Palestinian Leader

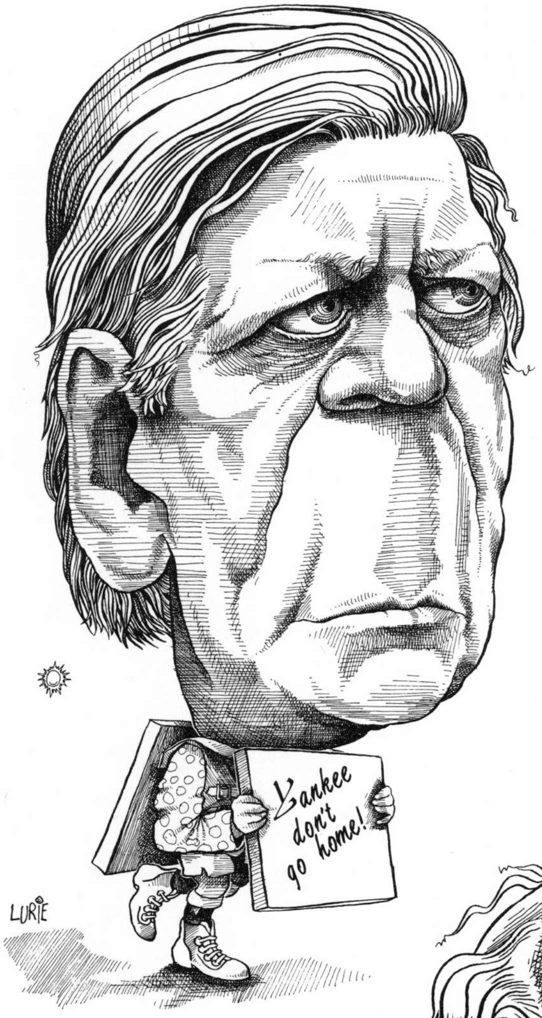
Yankee don't go home!
LURIE

Helmut Schmidt
West German Chancellor

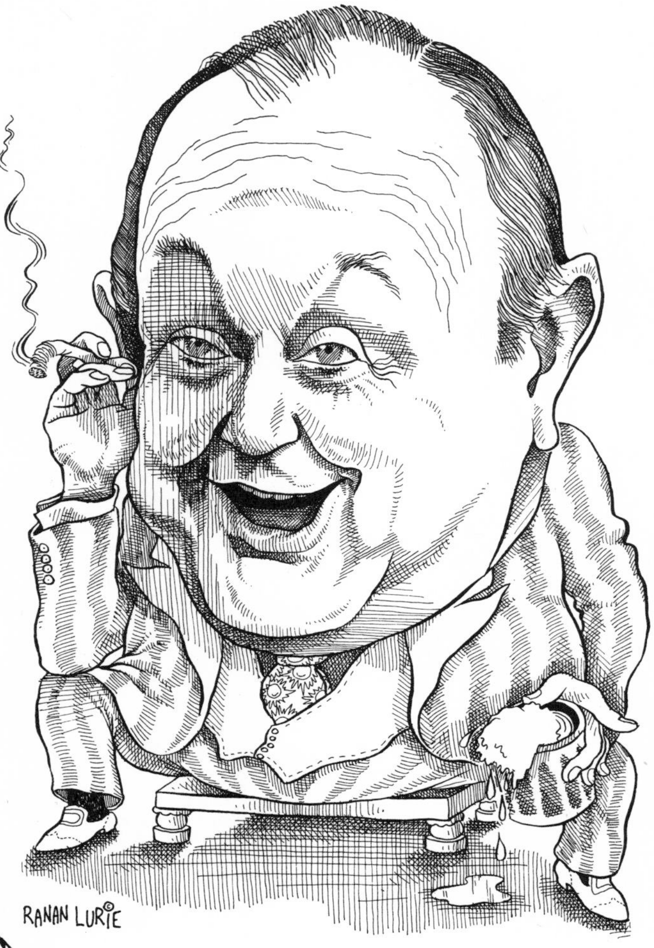
RANAN LURIE

Hans-Dietrich Genscher
Germany's Foreign Minister

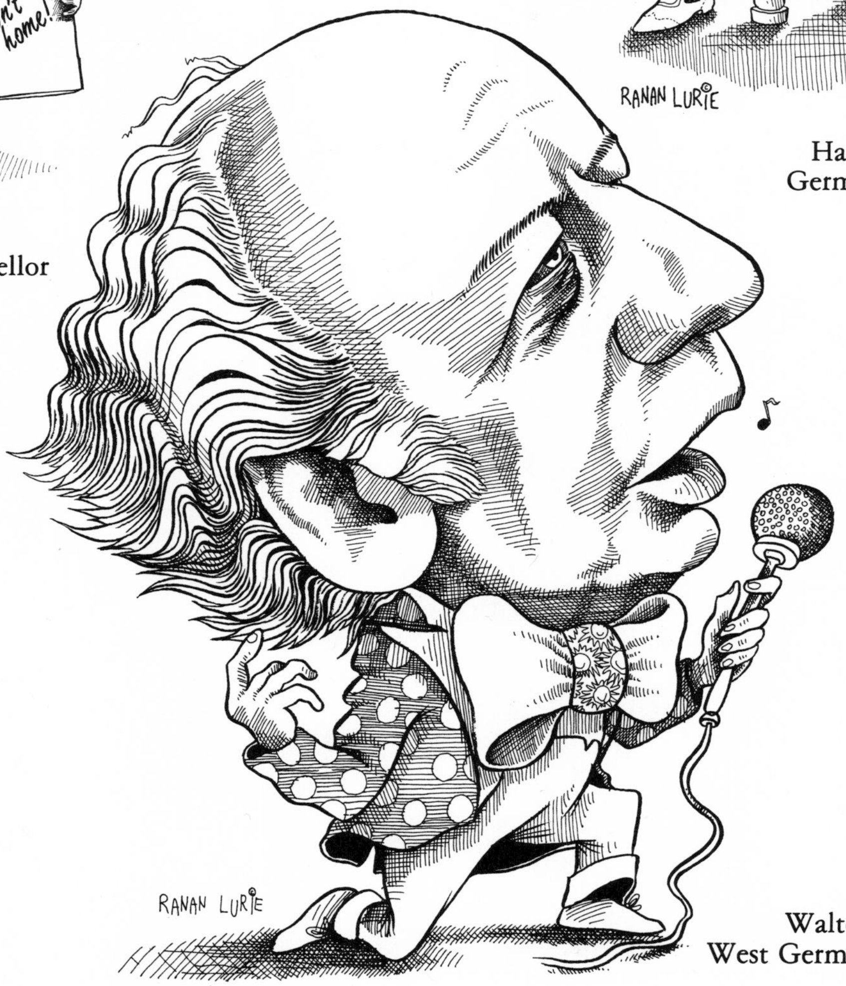
RANAN LURIE

Walter Scheel
West Germany's President

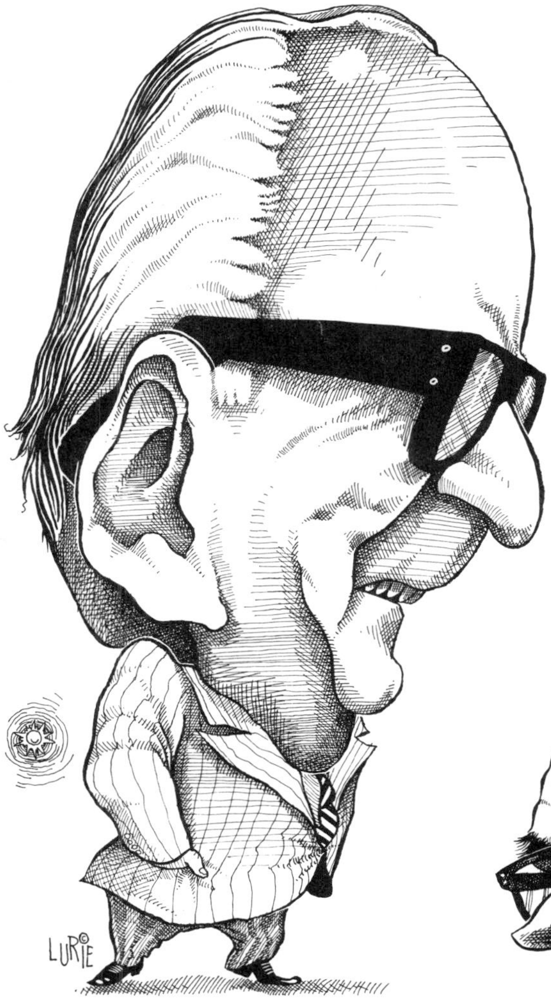
LURIE

Mariano Rumor
Premier of Italy

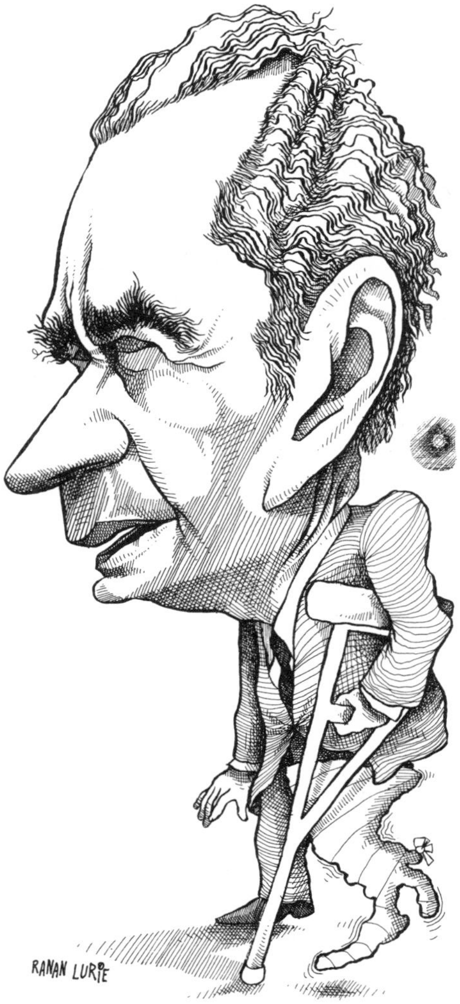
RANAN LURIE

Aldo Moro
of Italy

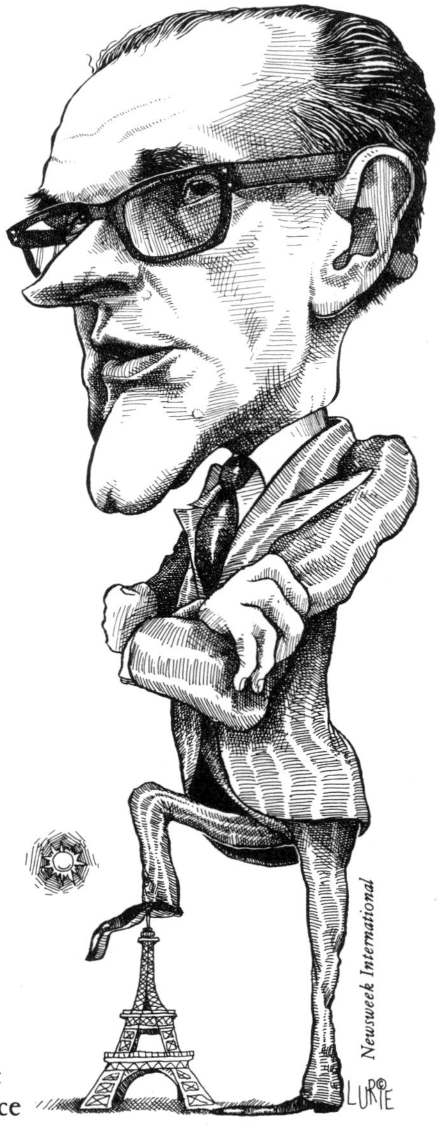
Newsweek International
LURIE

Jacques Chirac
Premier of France

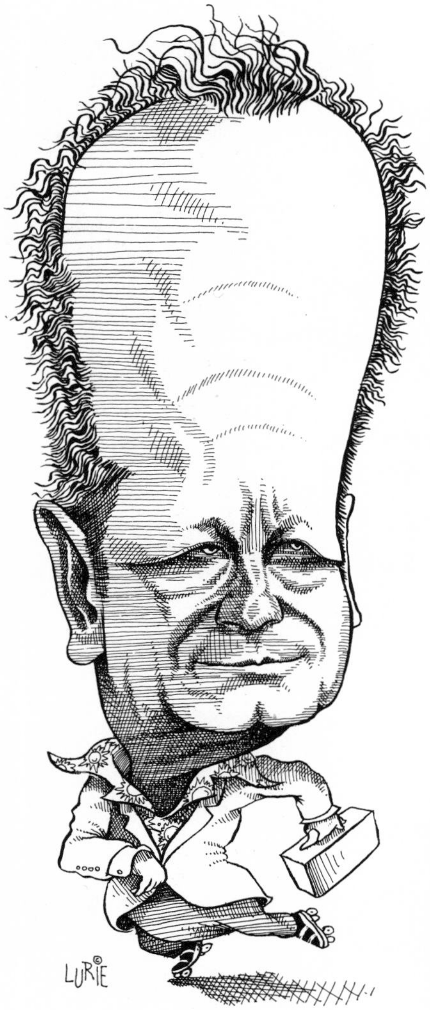
LURIE

Yigal Allon
Israeli Deputy Premier

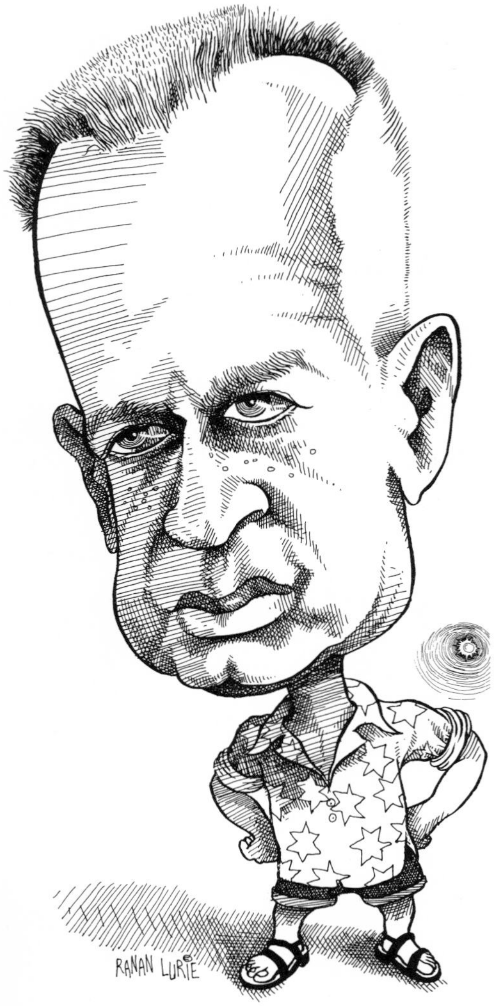
RANAN LURIE

Yitzhak Rabin
Prime Minister Designate of Israel

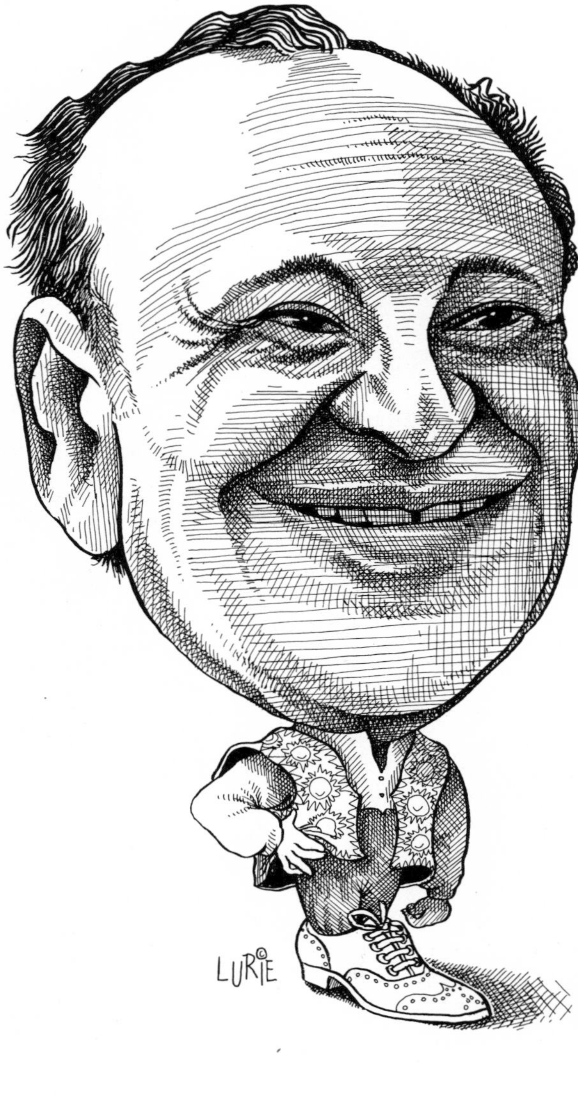
LURIE

Glafkos Clerides
Cypriot President

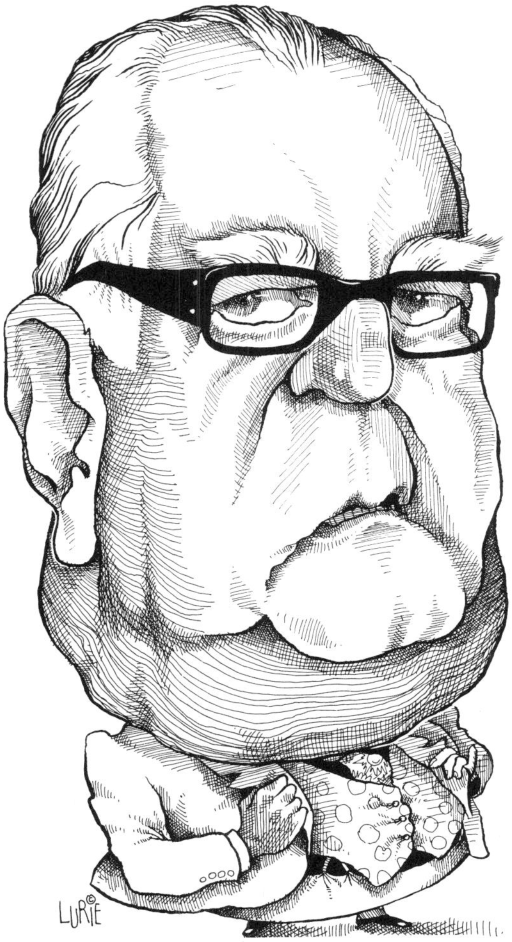
LURIE

John Vorster
South Africa's Prime Minister

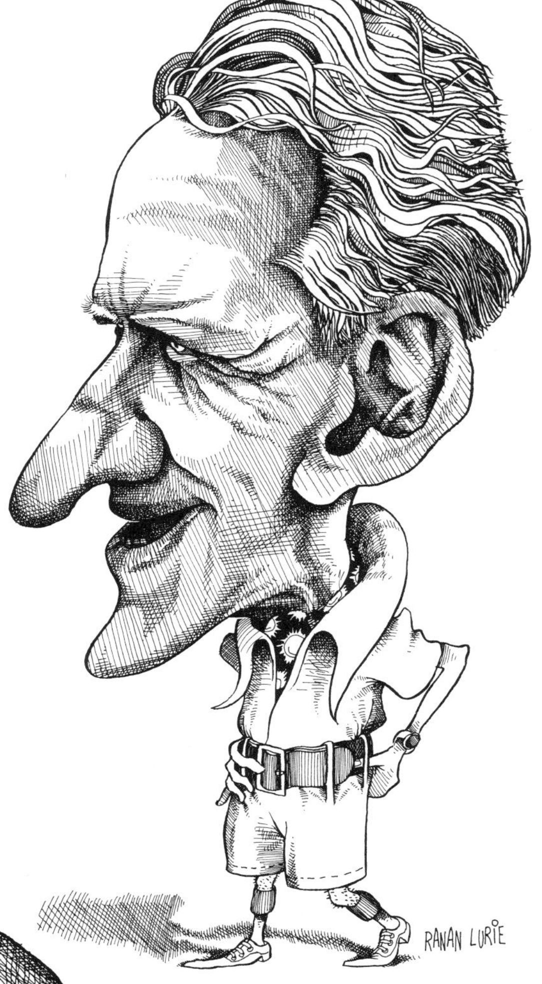
RANAN LURIE

Ian Smith
Prime Minister of Rhodesia

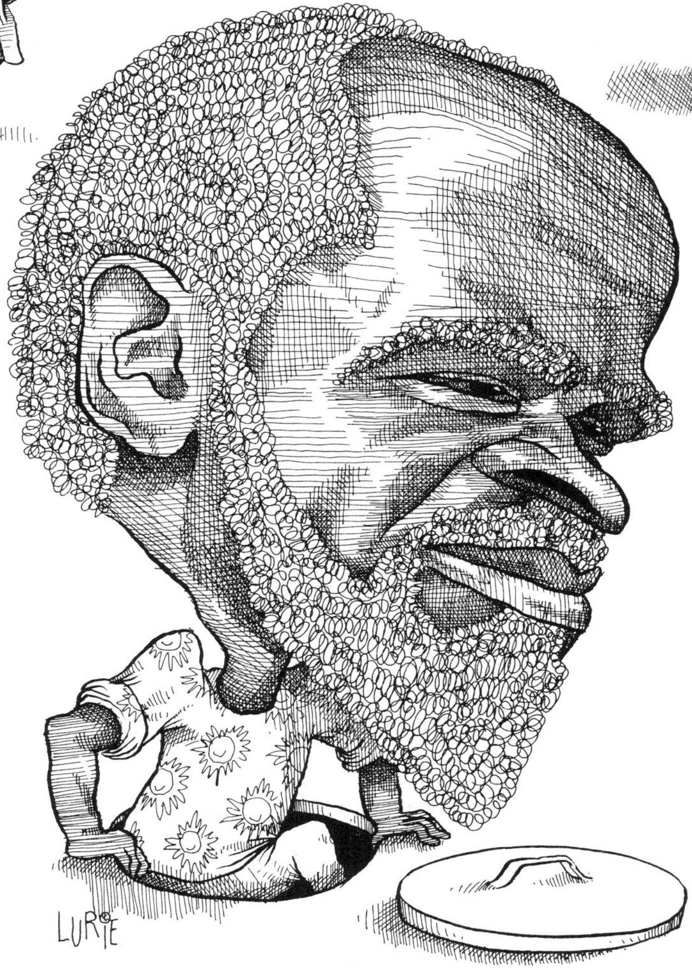
LURIE

Frelimo Leader Machel
of Mozambique

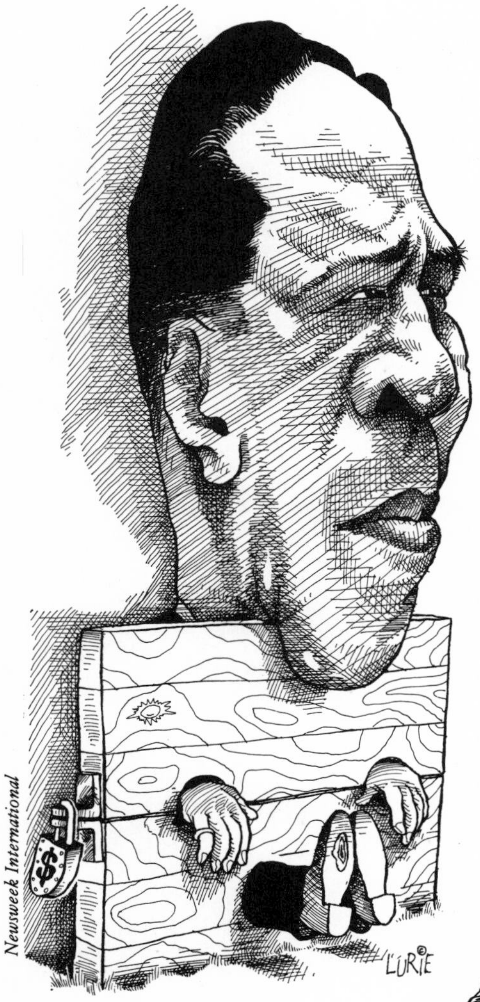
Newsweek International
LURIE

Nguyen Van Thieu
President of South Vietnam

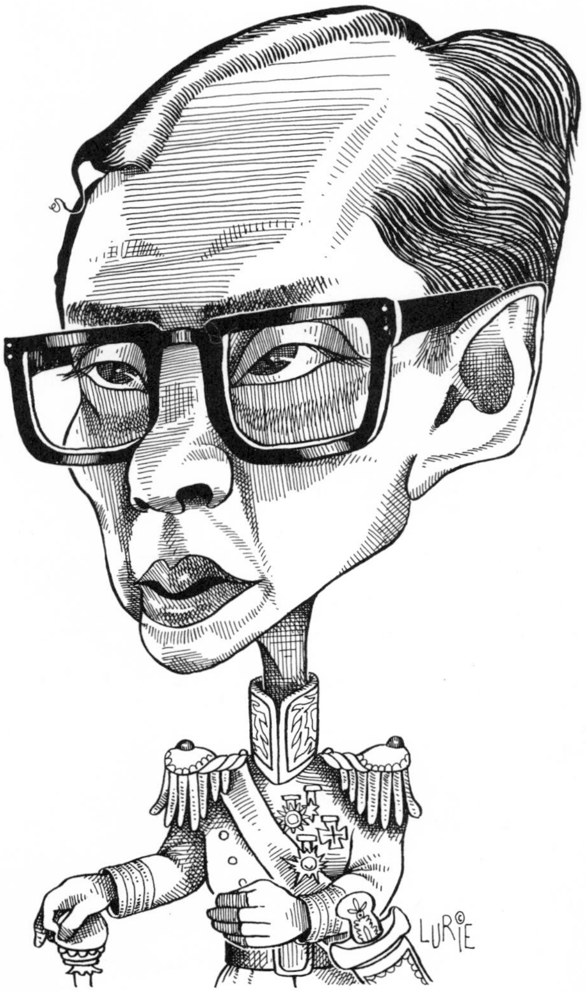
LURIE

King Bhumibol
of Thailand

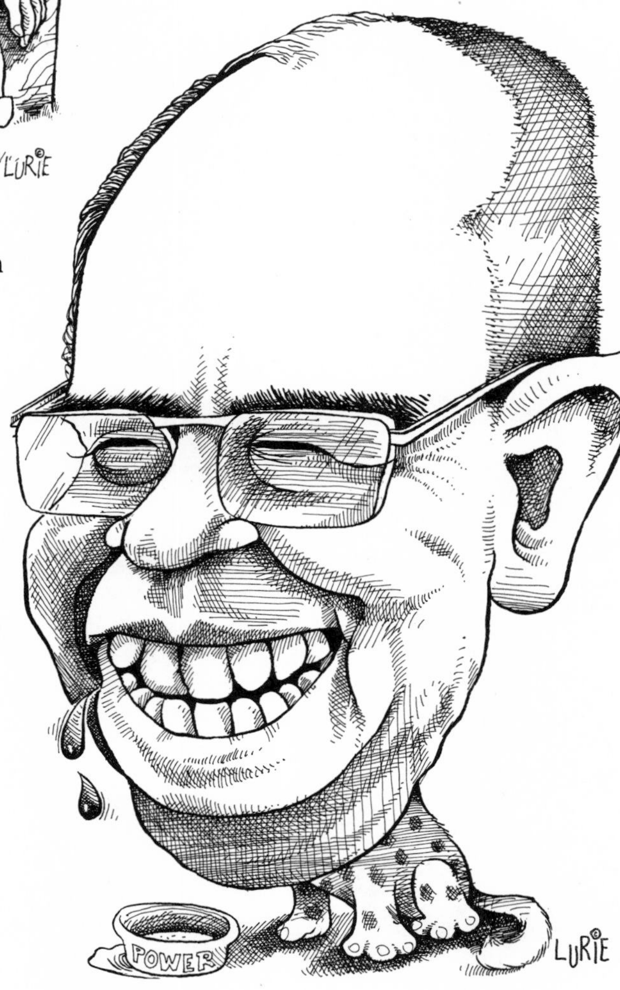
POWER
LURIE

Prime Minister Abdul Razak
of Malaysia

P
LURIE

Maria Estela Martinez de Peron
Acting President of Argentina

MADE IN
LURIE

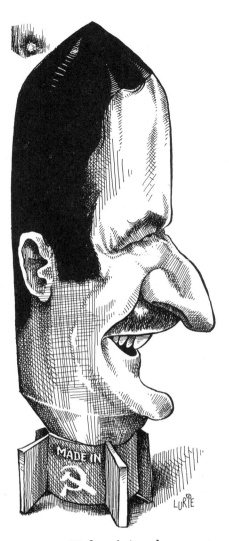

Hafez-al-Assad
Syria's President

RANAN LURIE

Aleksandr Solzhenitsyn

1975

Lurie: ON UNCLE SAM

When I draw a person or symbol, whether it's Uncle Sam, Nixon, or Carter, I never draw them as being always bad or good. I draw them according to what the issue is. When Uncle Sam is tough, my Uncle Sam will look tough. When in a political situation he is vacillating or worried or making an unwise move, I'll not caricature him as an unwise Uncle Sam; instead I will draw him and his suits and his hat so as to suggest this disposition. Chances are, if he's a tough Uncle Sam, his cylindrical hat will be erect and straight. If he's a defeated Uncle Sam, his hat probably will be sticking out backwards, somehow suggesting the tail of a dog stuck between its hind legs. An aggressive Uncle Sam would probably have his hat storming forward. All these little symbols and details are supposed to build a general attitude that will describe what that specific Uncle Sam is doing—was he successful? was he a failure?

I personally not only like but love Uncle Sam very much. And I think it's a figure we should support. It's our own figure; it's our own national symbol. And since Lurie's Opinion is not a propaganda bureau, I try to show things as they are.

My feeling is that most Americans do identify with the image that I have described, especially when they are misled by presidents, when they are suffering due to economic pressures, or being manipulated by Russian bears or Chinese dragons or even their own president.

Abroad America still projects a much stronger figure than we imagine. When other nations compare the Soviet system, let's say, in which Russians couldn't dream of saying anything anti-Soviet in a Soviet newspaper, to our system in which American cartoonists joke and criticize everything from A to Z, from a president to an Uncle Sam, we look very good and very strong. The image of the bewildered, sometimes desperate, sometimes confused Uncle Sam becomes, oddly enough, a symbol that wins respect for America.

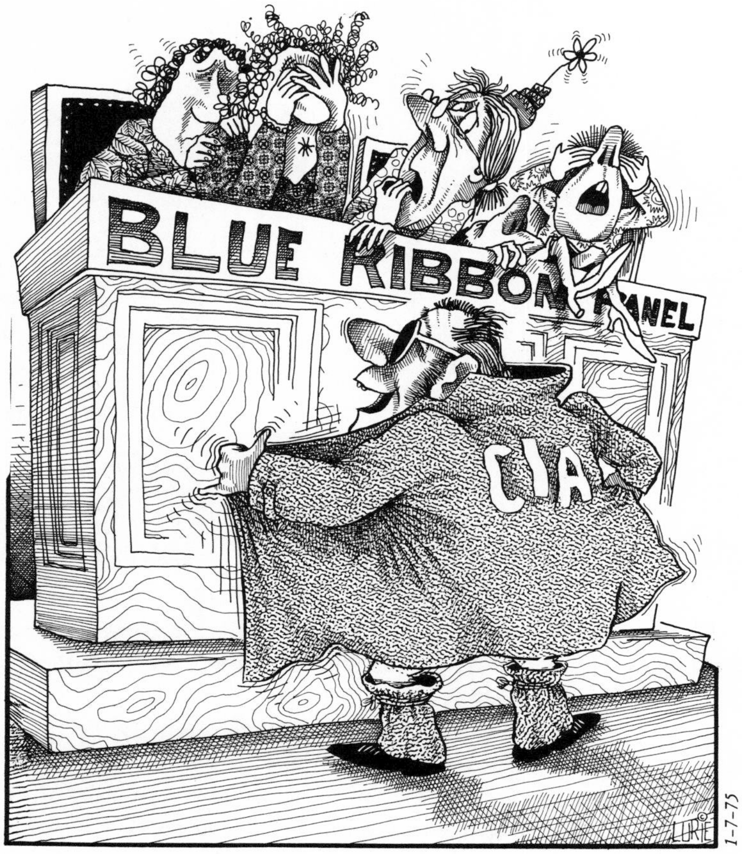
BLUE RIBBON PANEL
CIA
LURIE
1-7-75

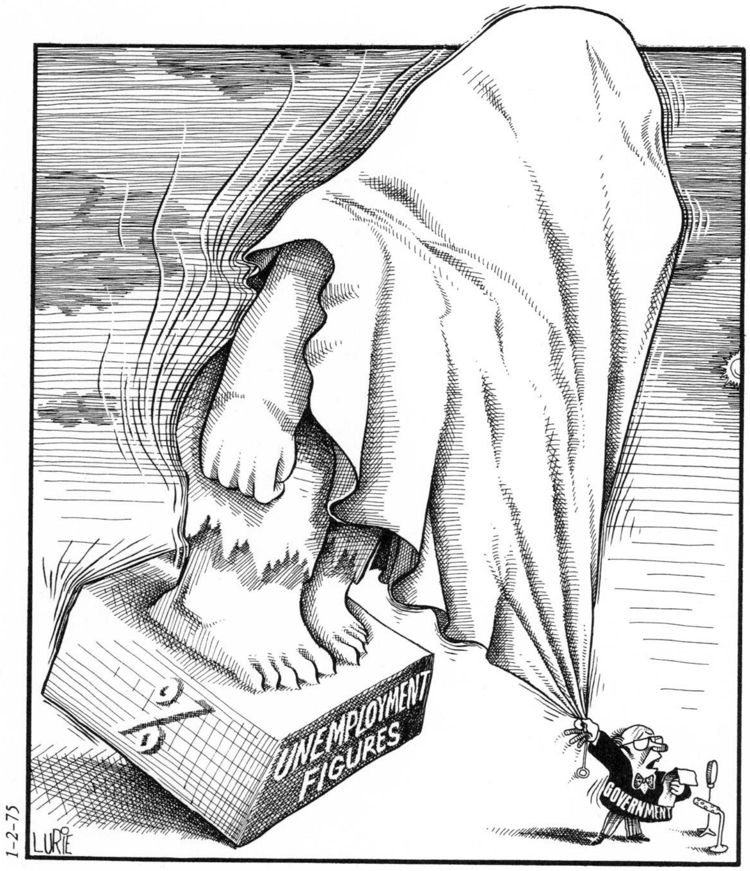
UNEMPLOYMENT FIGURES
GOVERNMENT
LURIE
1-2-75

"AND NOW, THE UNVEILING"

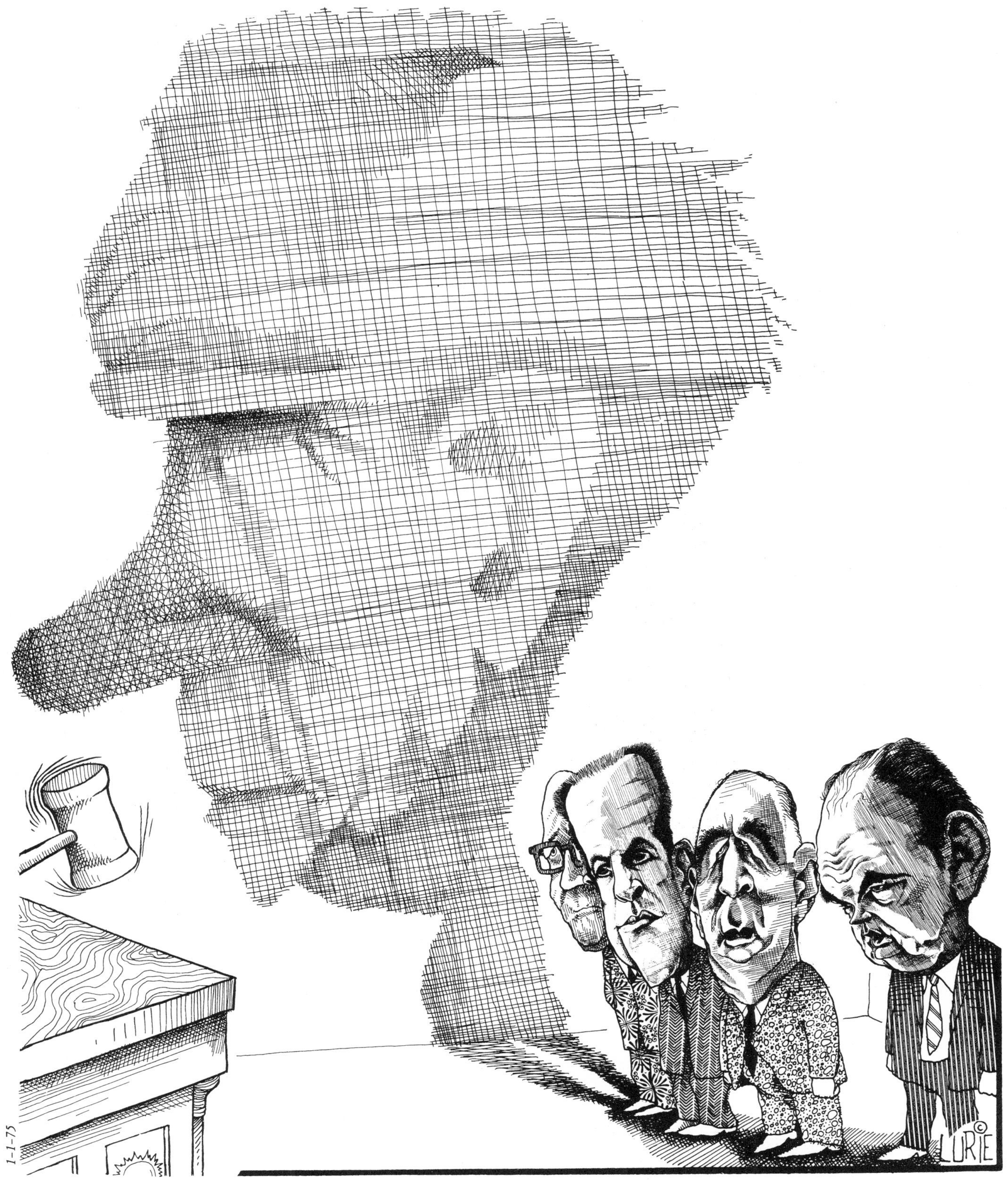
1-1-75
LURIE ©
"GUILTY!"

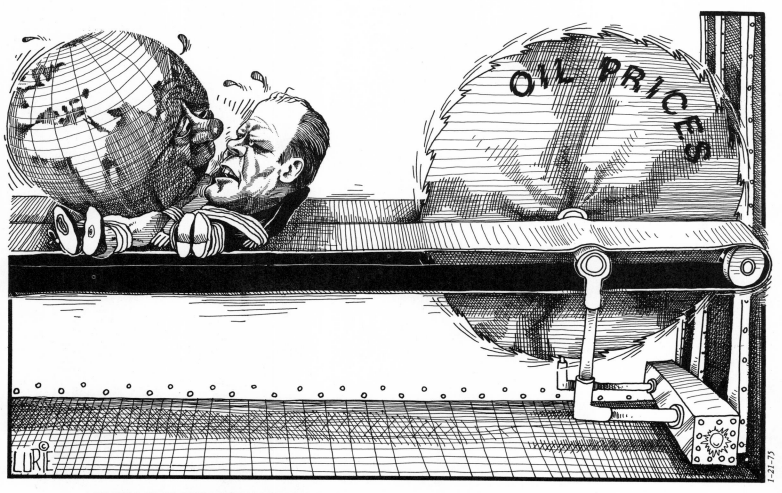

"LET ME EMPHASIZE: I'LL USE FORCE *O N L Y* IF WE'LL BE *STRANGULATED!*"

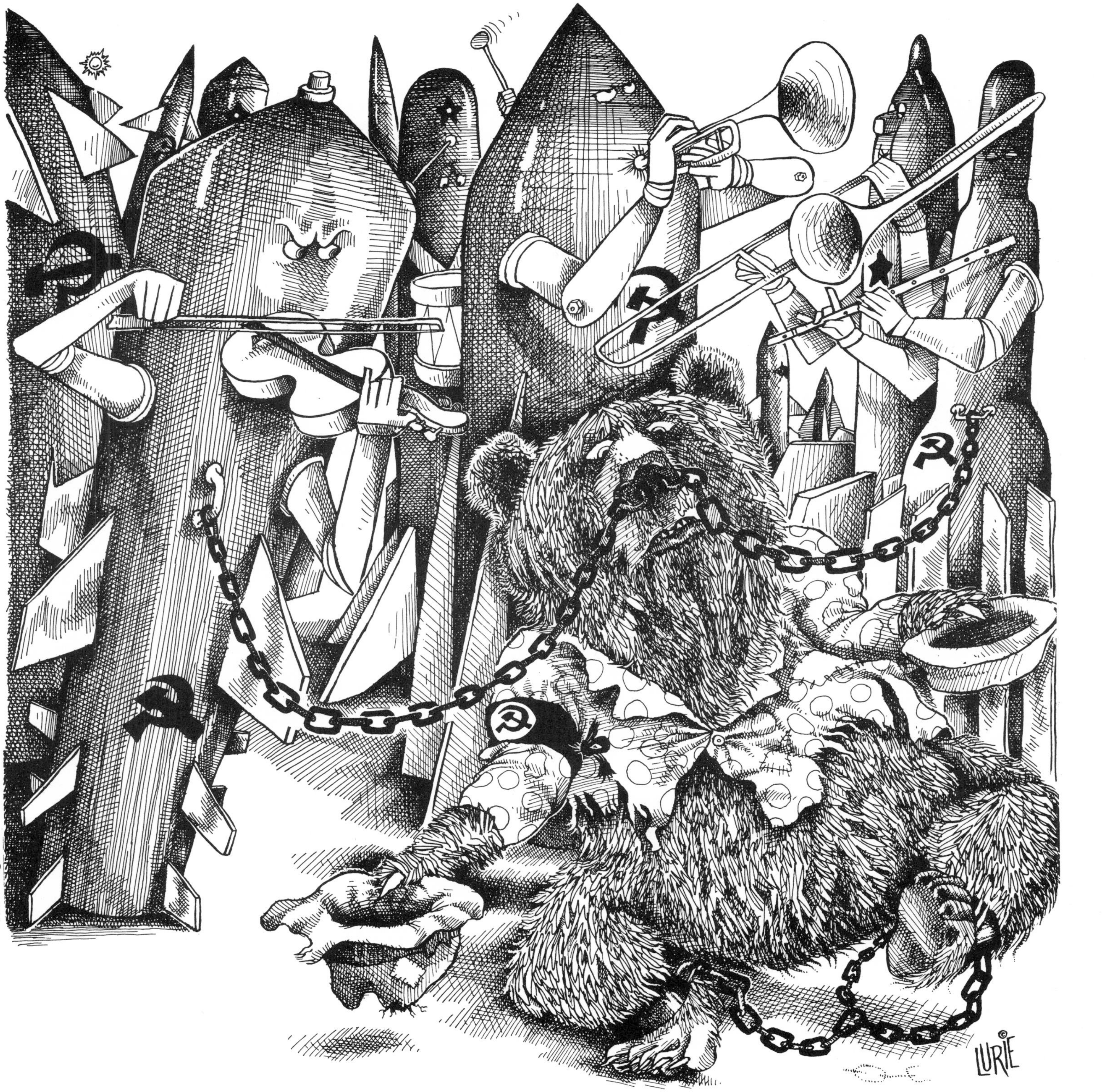
LURIE ©

Vision Magazine 1-11-75

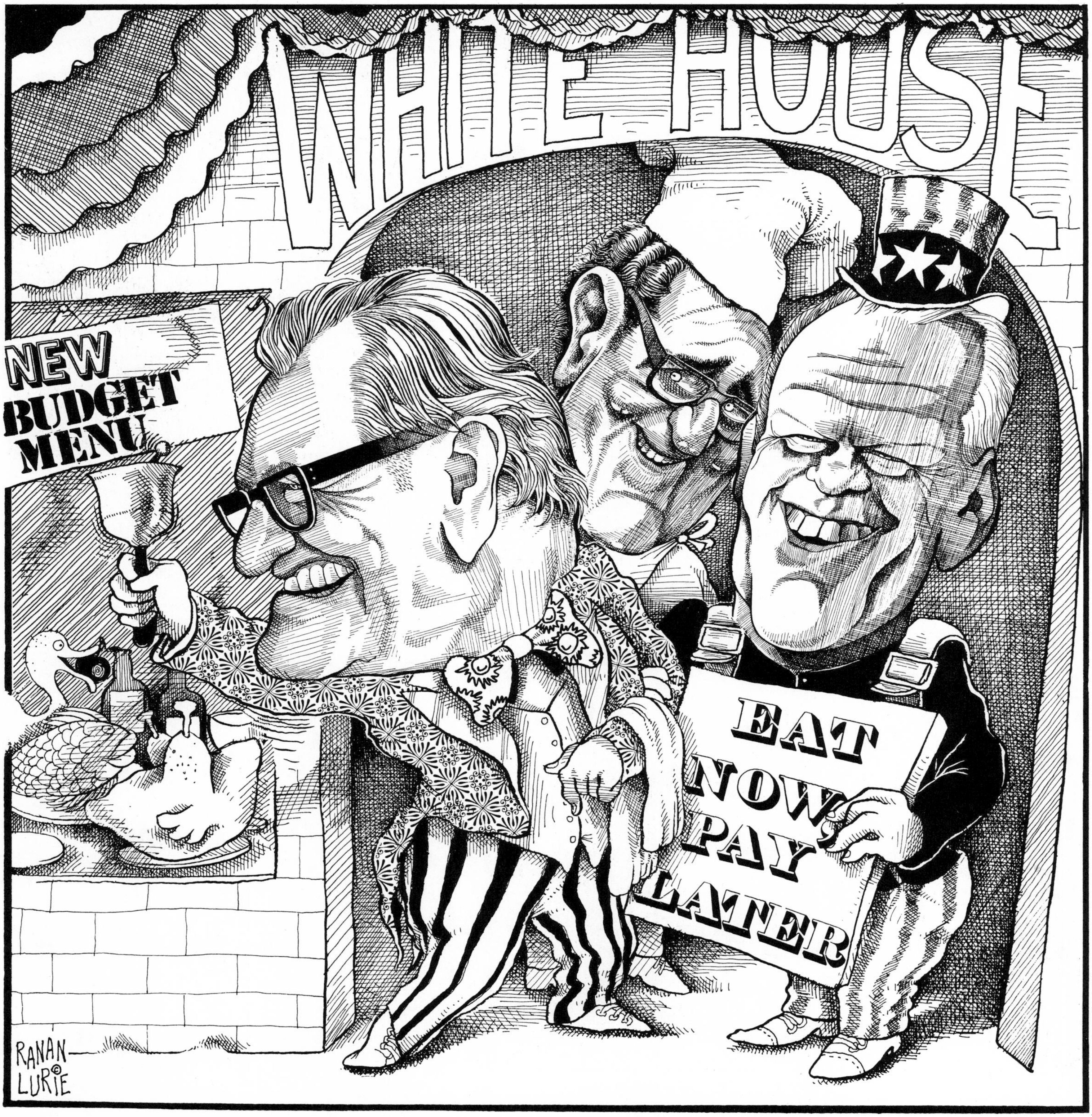
WHITE HOUSE
NEW BUDGET MENU
EAT NOW, PAY LATER
RANAN LURIE ©

Vision Magazine 2-6-75

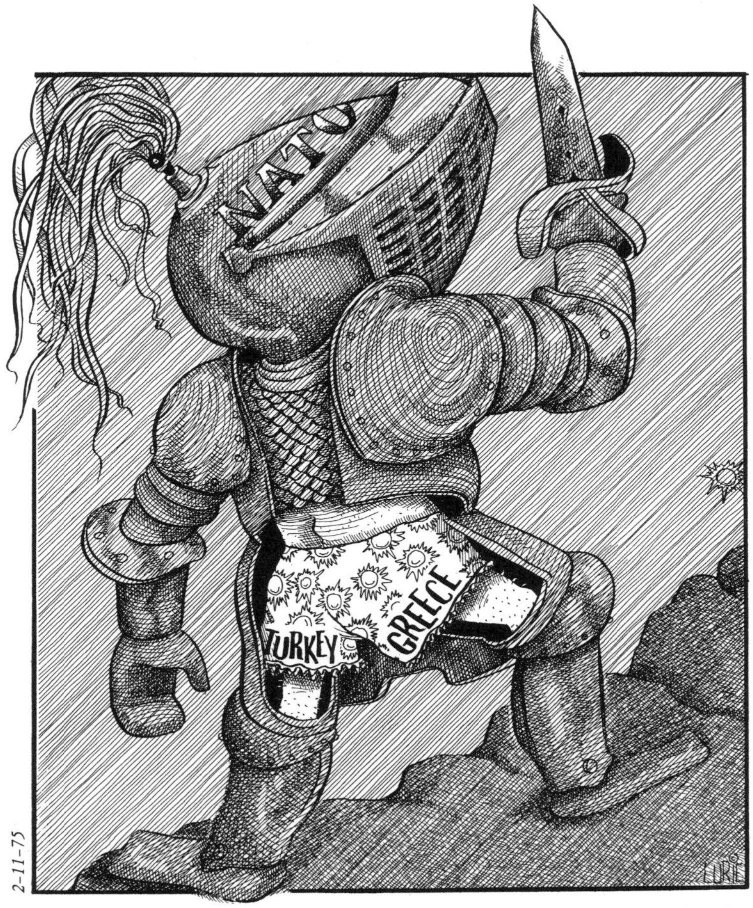

NATO
TURKEY
GREECE
2-11-75
LURIE

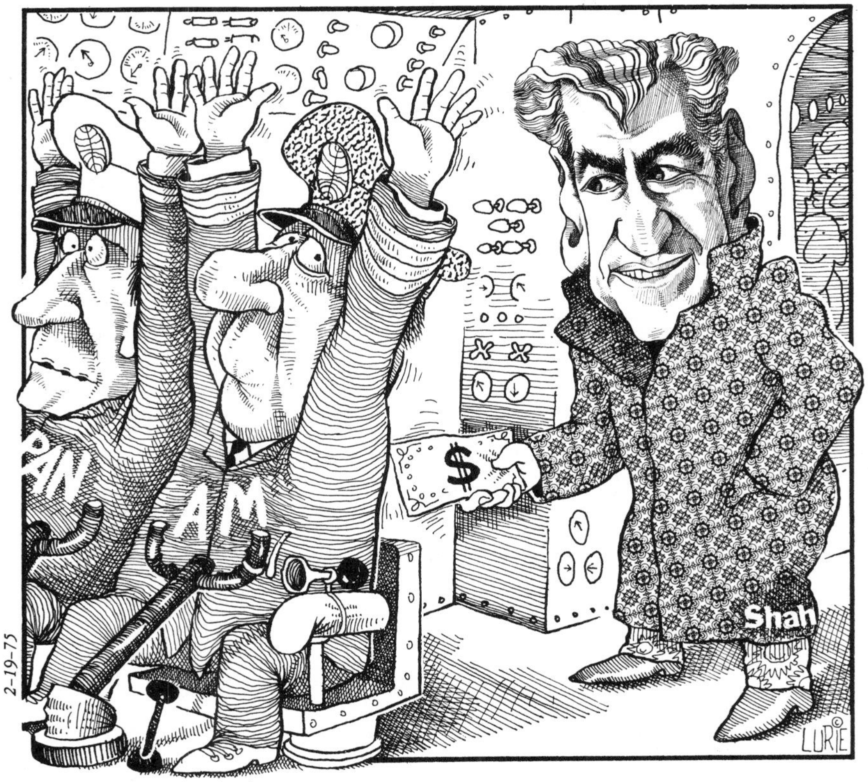

PAN
AM
$
Shah
2-19-75
LURIE

HIJACKED

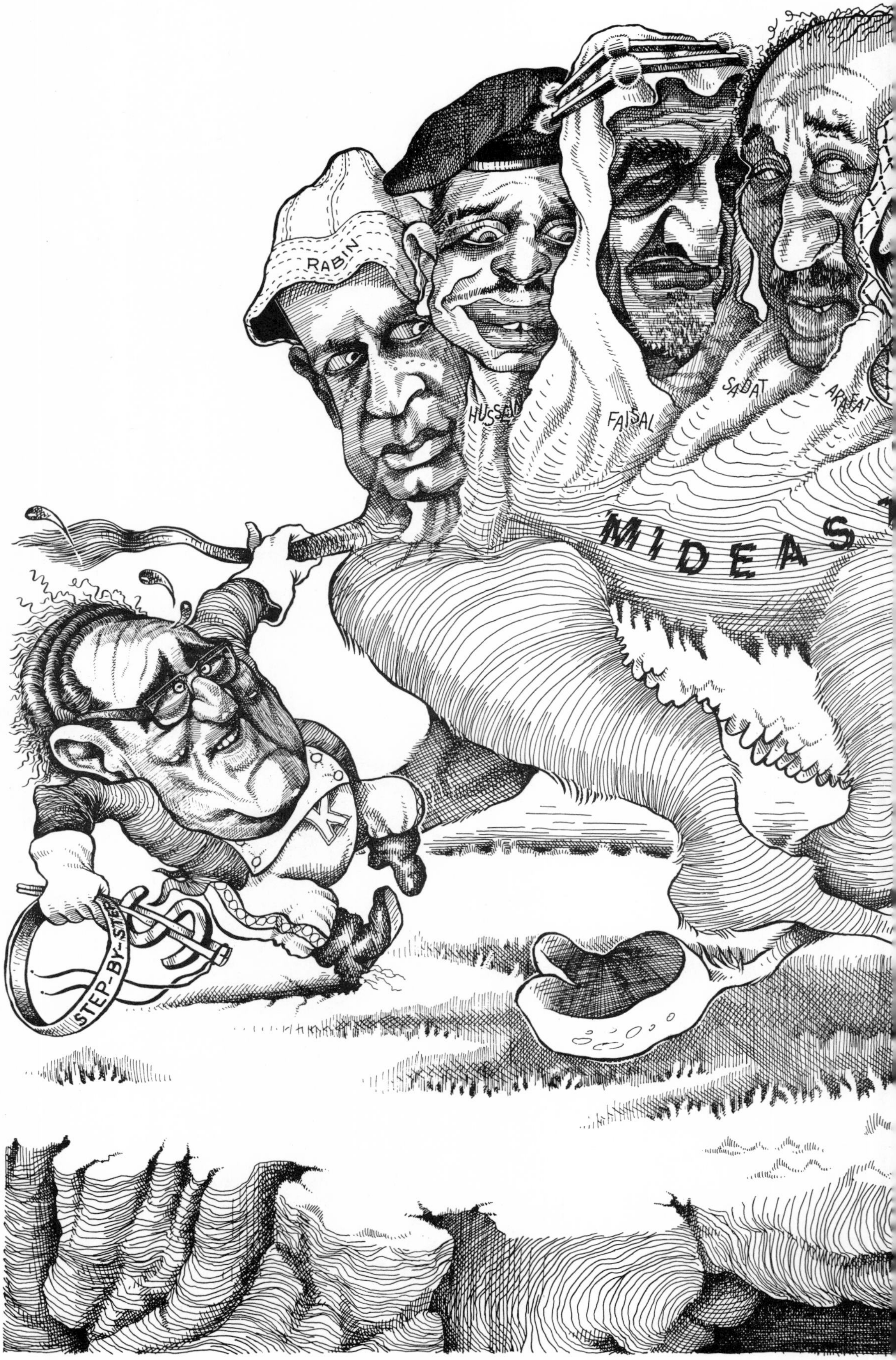

RABIN
HUSSEIN
FAISAL
SADAT
ARAFAT
MIDEAS
K
STEP-BY-STEP

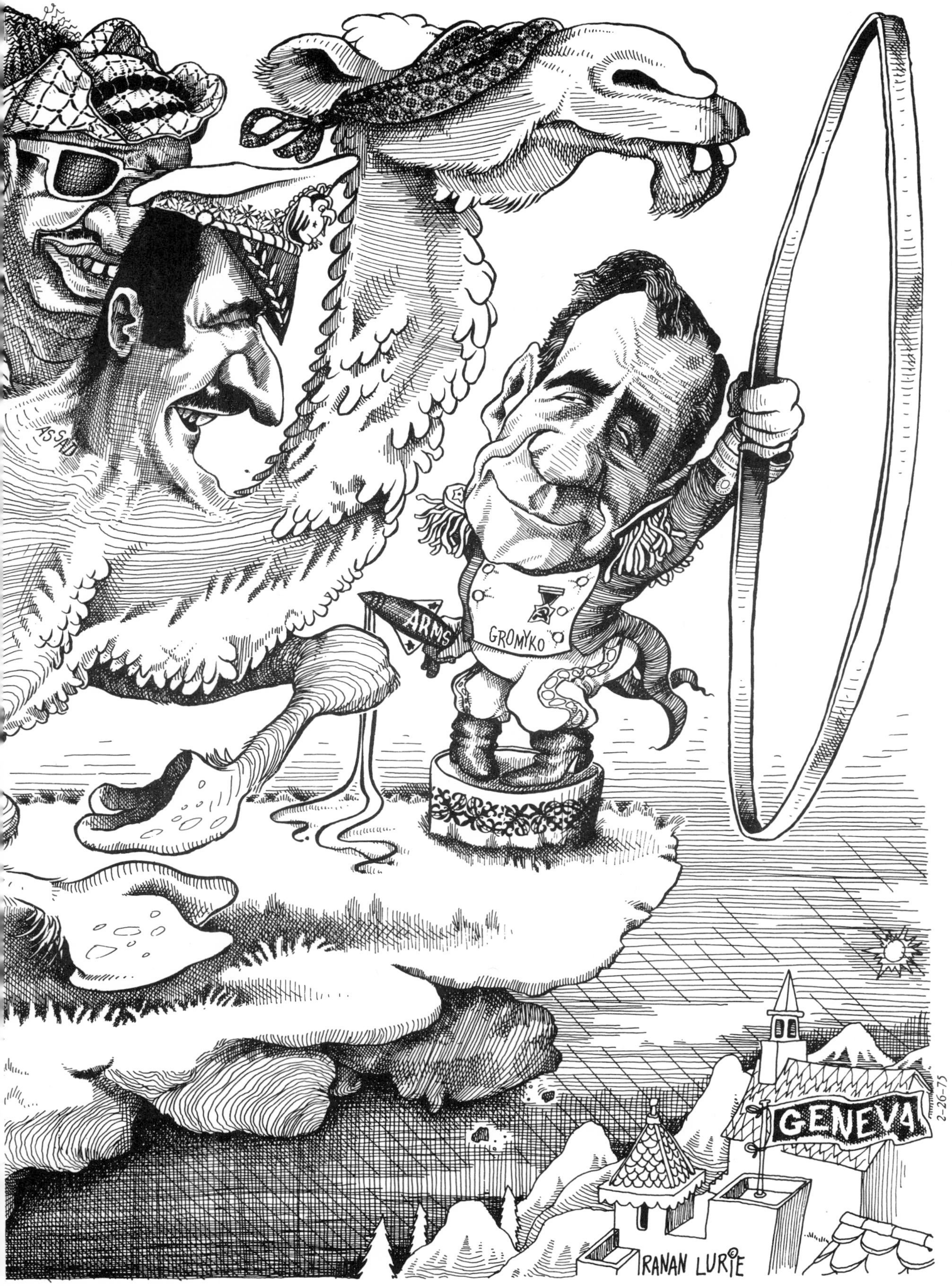
ASSAD
ARMS
GROMYKO
GENEVA
2-26-75
RANAN LURIE

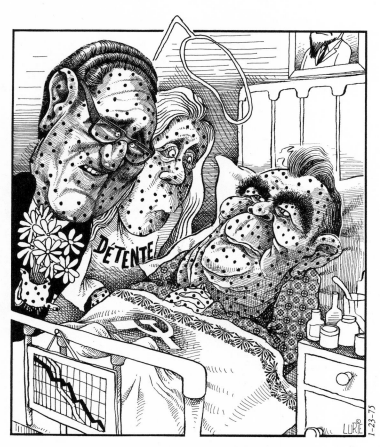

"GEE WHIZ, LEONID—WE SURE HOPE
YOUR ILLNESS ISN'T SERIOUS!"

"WHAT A SLUMP . . .
THE MAFIA HAS LAID OFF
SIX MORE JUDGES IN NEW JERSEY!"

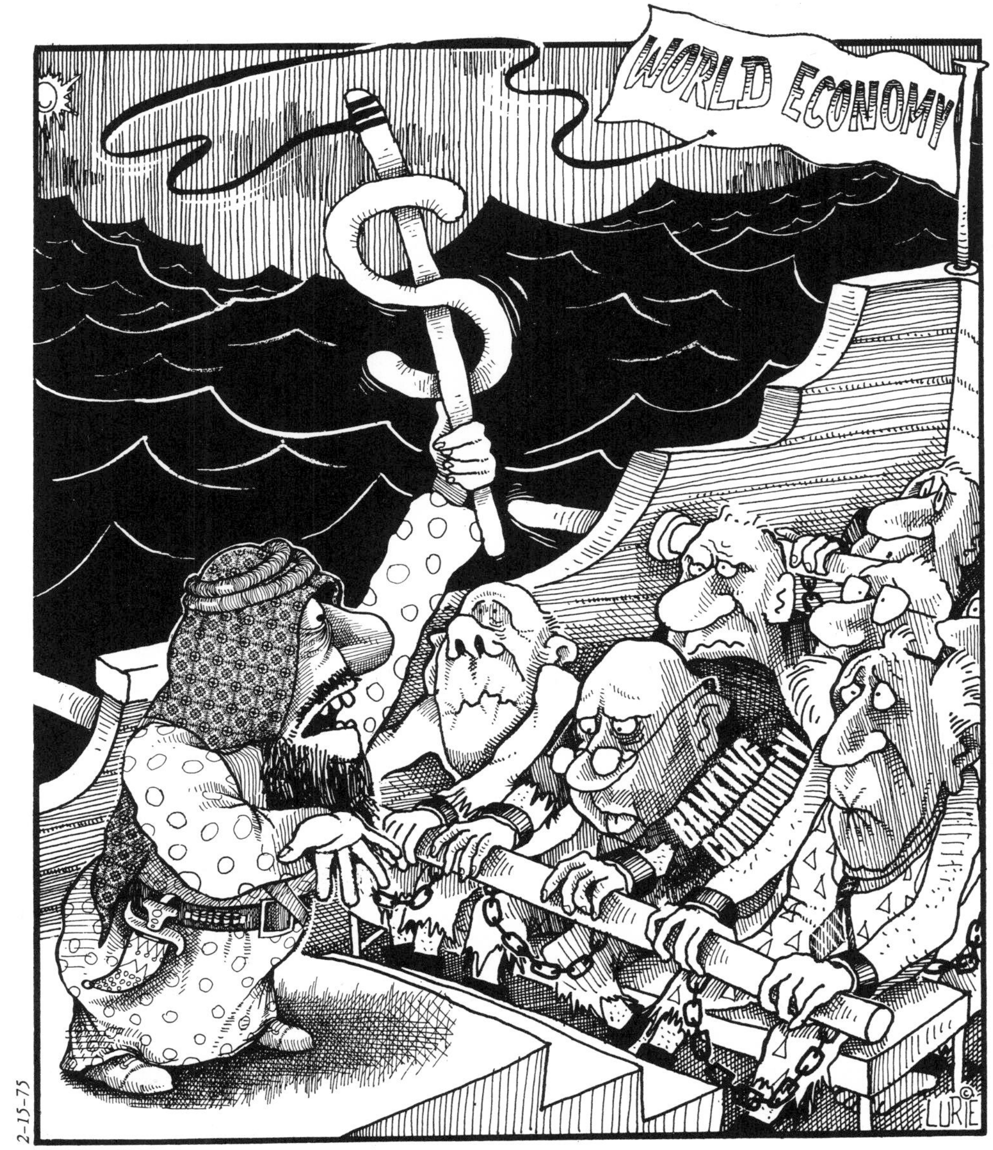
WORLD ECONOMY
BANKING COMMUNITY
2-15-75
LURIE

"C'MON NOW—WE'RE ALL IN THE SAME BOAT!"

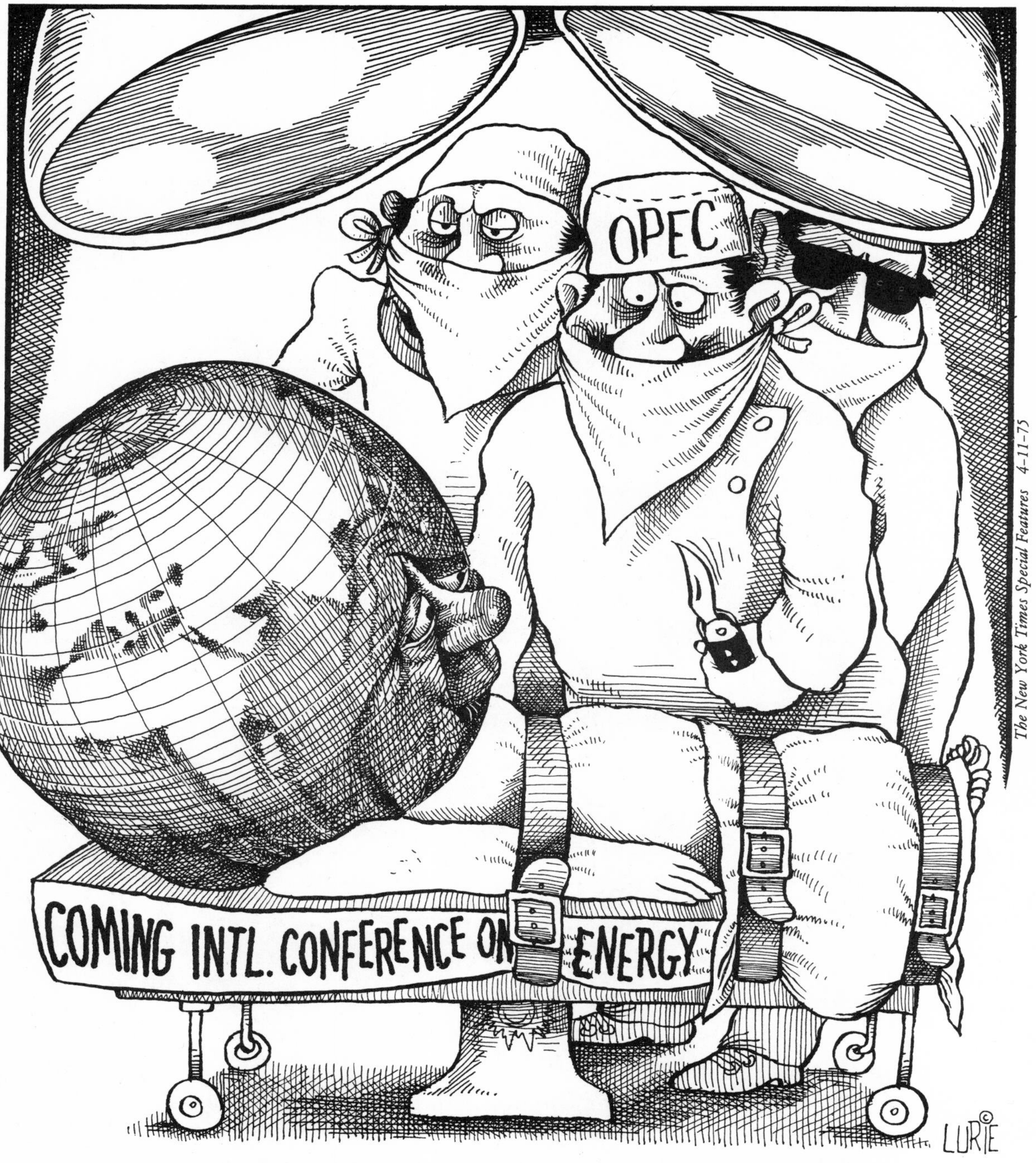
OPEC
COMING INTL. CONFERENCE ON ENERGY
The New York Times Special Features 4-11-75
LURIE ©

"IT'S NOT AN OPERATION, DUMMY—IT'S A HOLDUP!"

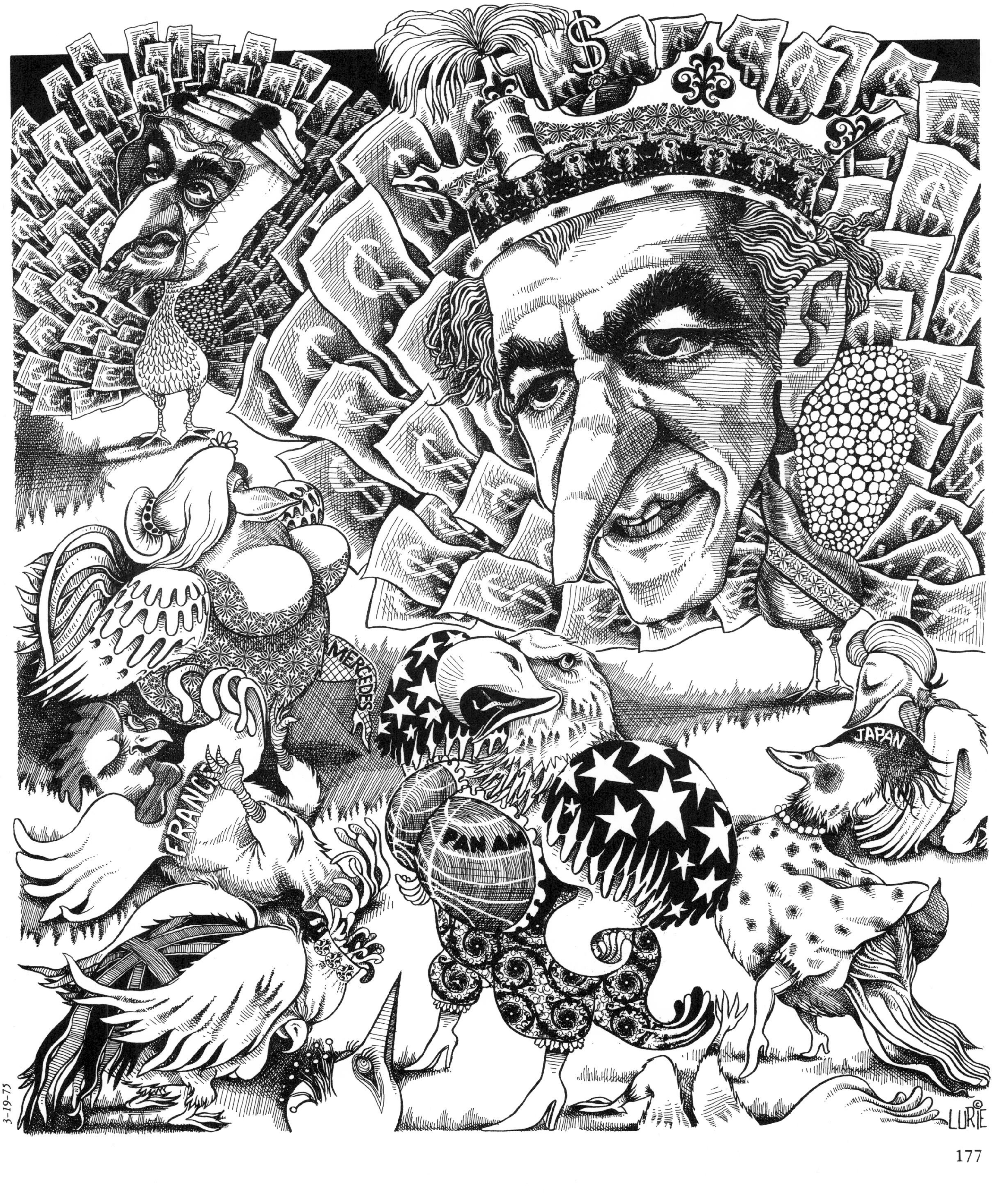
MERCEDES
FRANC
PAN AM
JAPAN
LURIE ©

3-19-75

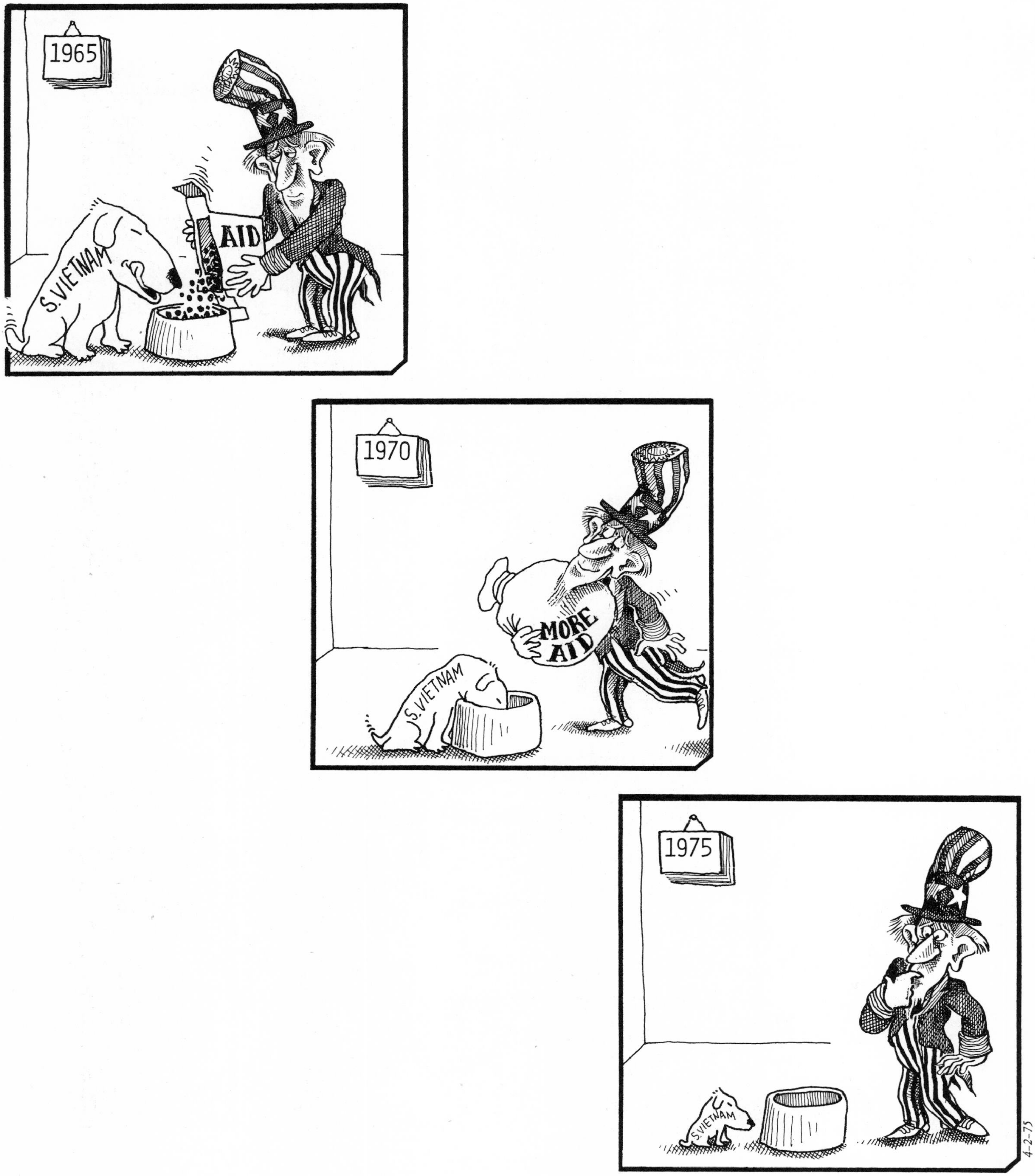
1965
AID
S.VIETNAM
1970
MORE AID
S.VIETNAM
1975
S.VIETNAM
4-2-75

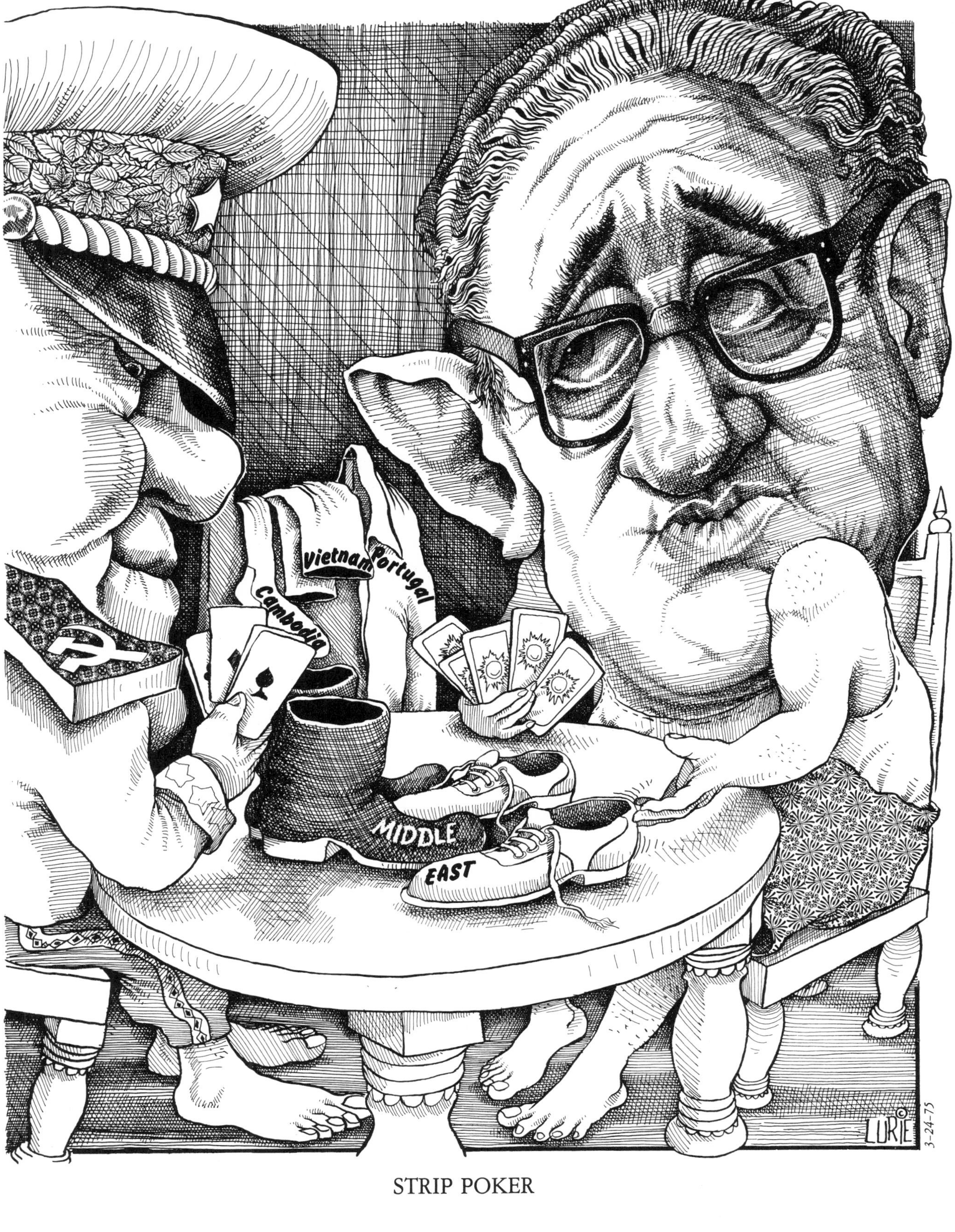
Vietnam
Portugal
Cambodia
MIDDLE
EAST
LURIE
3-24-75

STRIP POKER

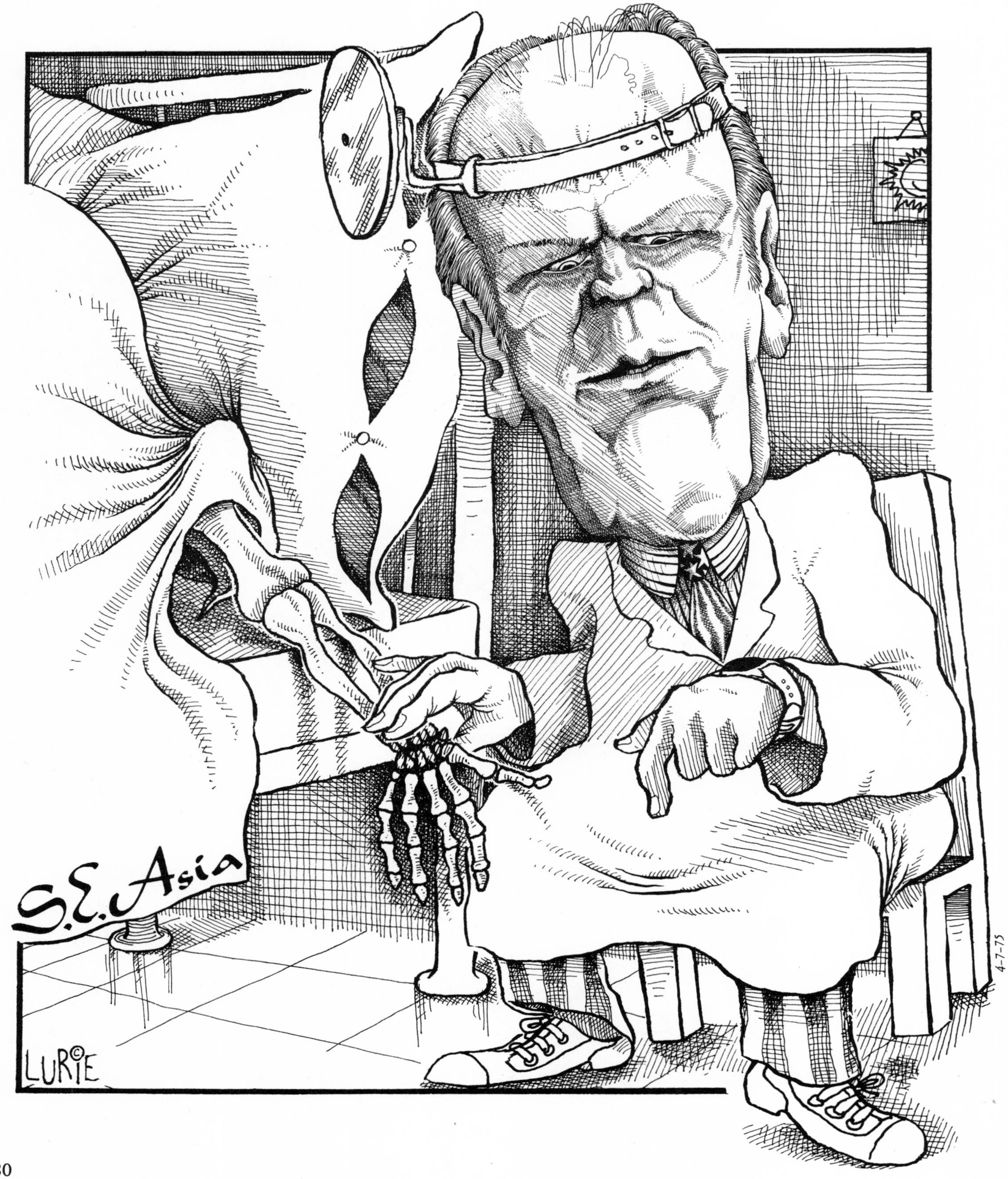
S.E. Asia
LURIE ©
4-7-75

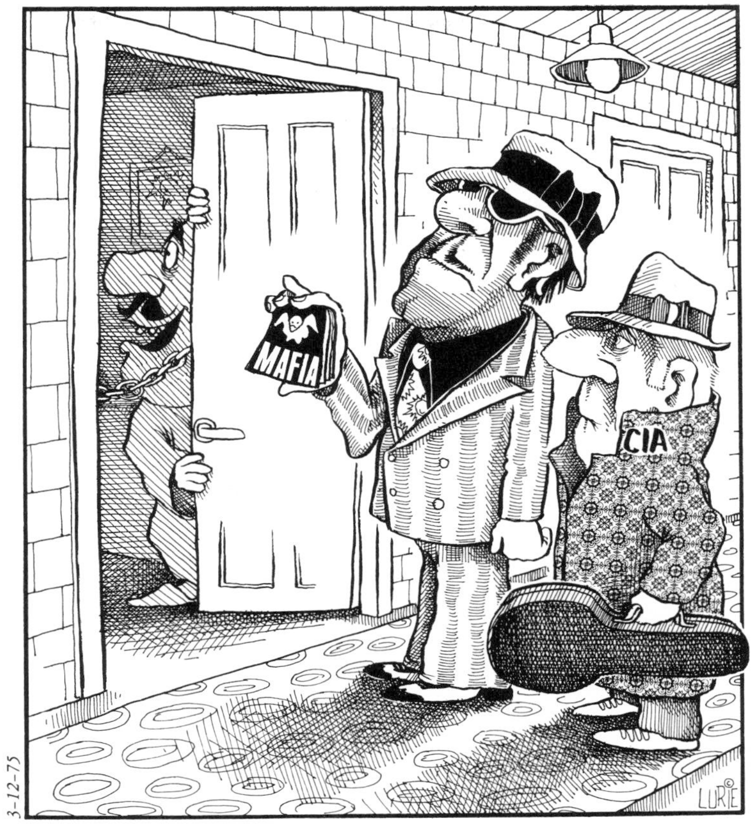
MAFIA
CIA
3-12-75
LURIE©

"IT'S O.K., MANUELA—
IT'S THE AMERICAN AUTHORITIES!"

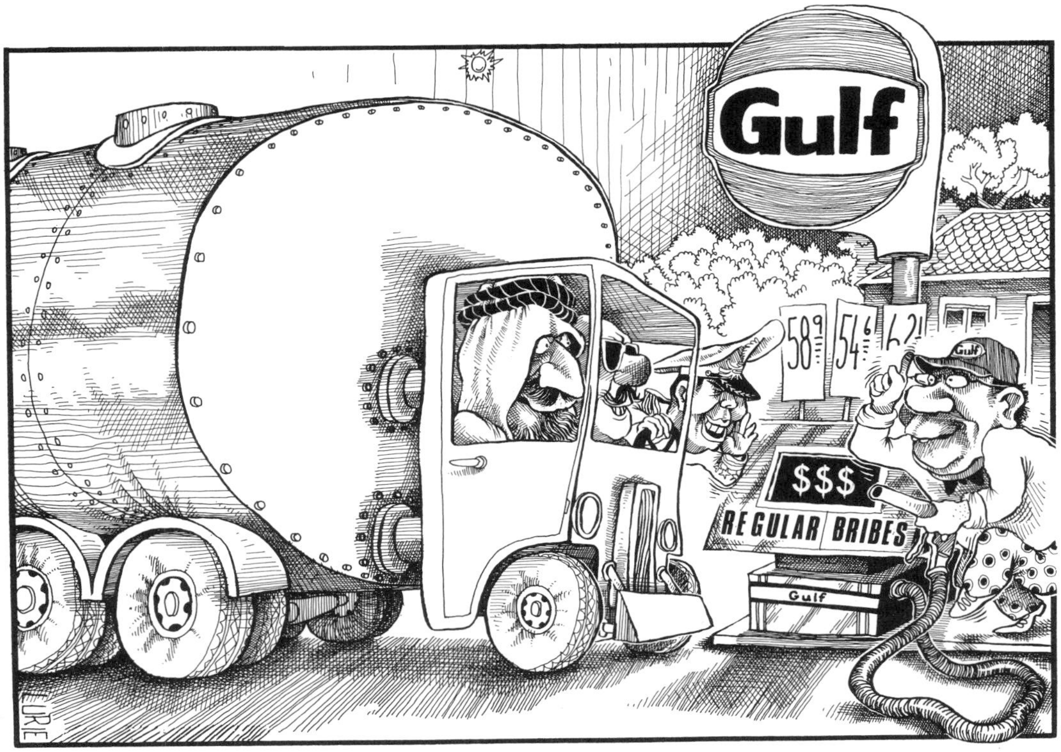
Gulf
$$$
REGULAR BRIBES
Gulf
LURIE
5-22-75

"FILL 'ER UP!"

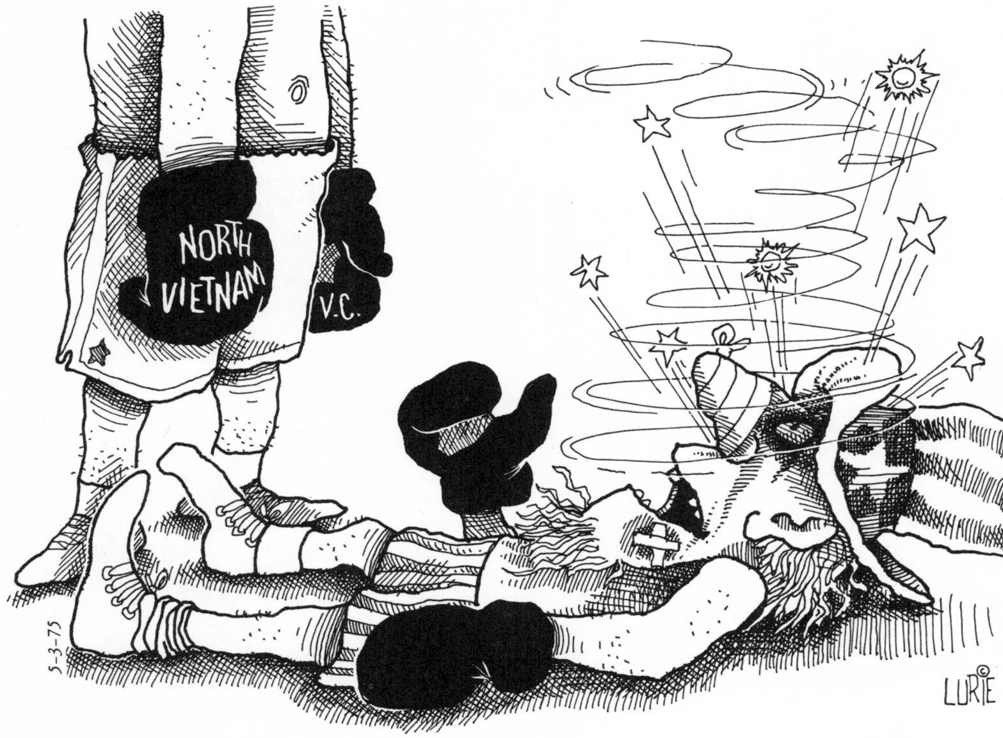
NORTH VIETNAM
V.C.
5-3-75
LURIE

"NOW, OF COURSE, YOU'LL BE NEEDING AMERICAN AID."

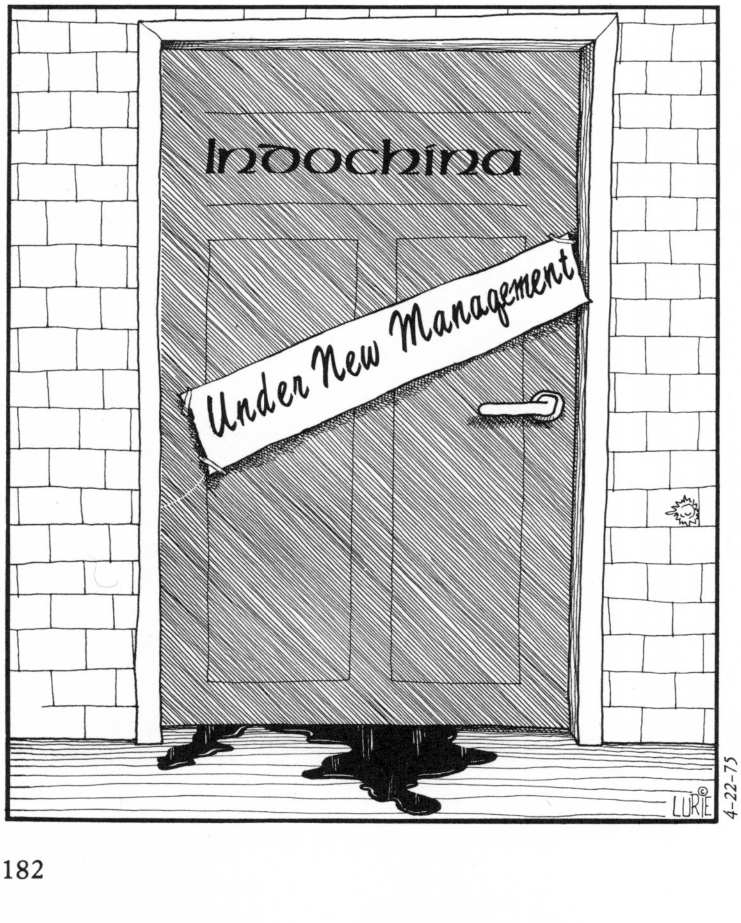
Indochina
Under New Management
4-22-75
LURIE

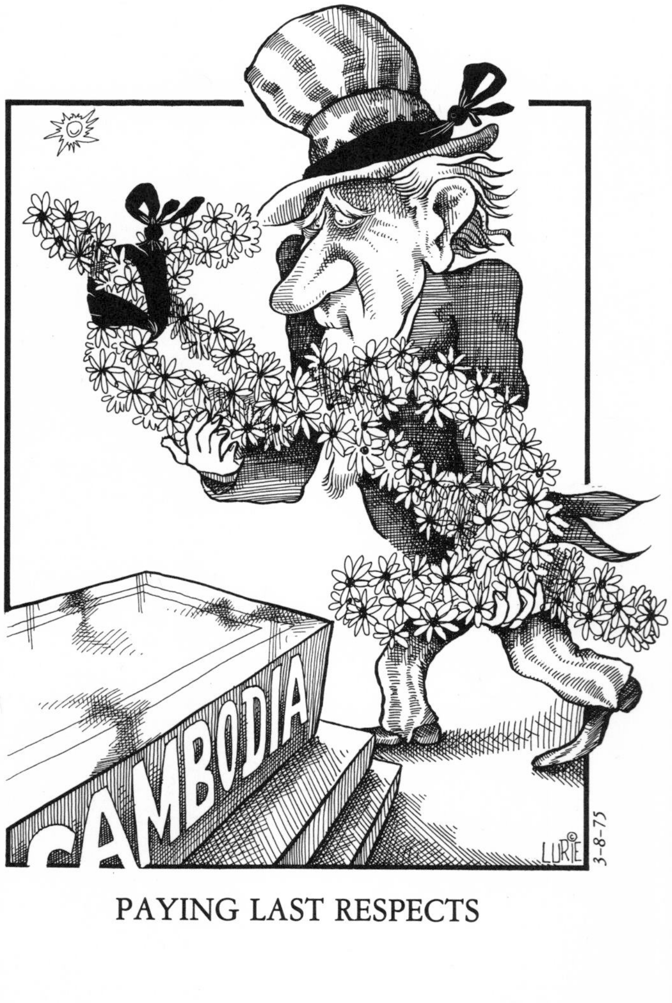
CAMBODIA
LURIE
3-8-75

PAYING LAST RESPECTS

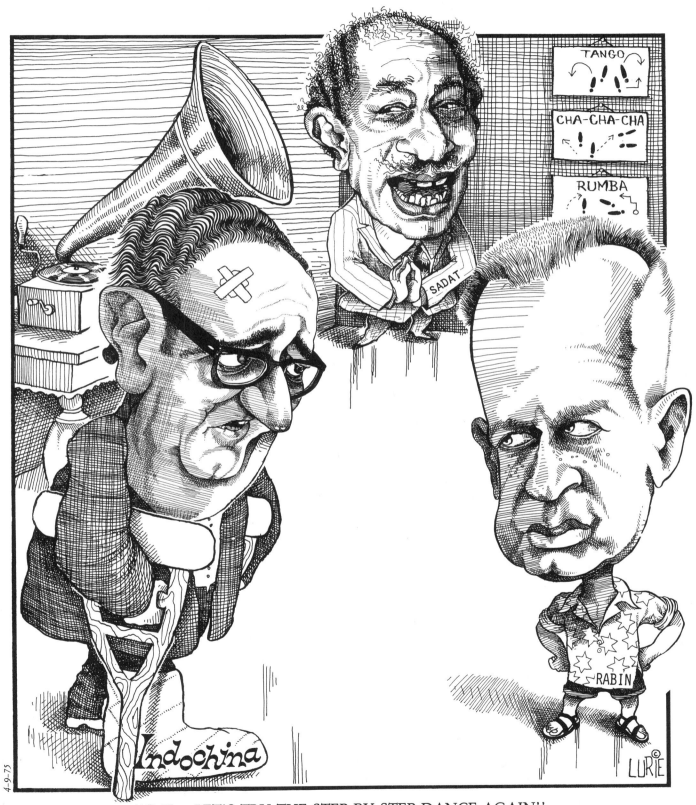

TANGO

CHA-CHA-CHA

RUMBA

SADAT

RABIN

Indochina

4-9-75

LURIE

"O.K.—LET'S TRY THE STEP-BY-STEP DANCE AGAIN"

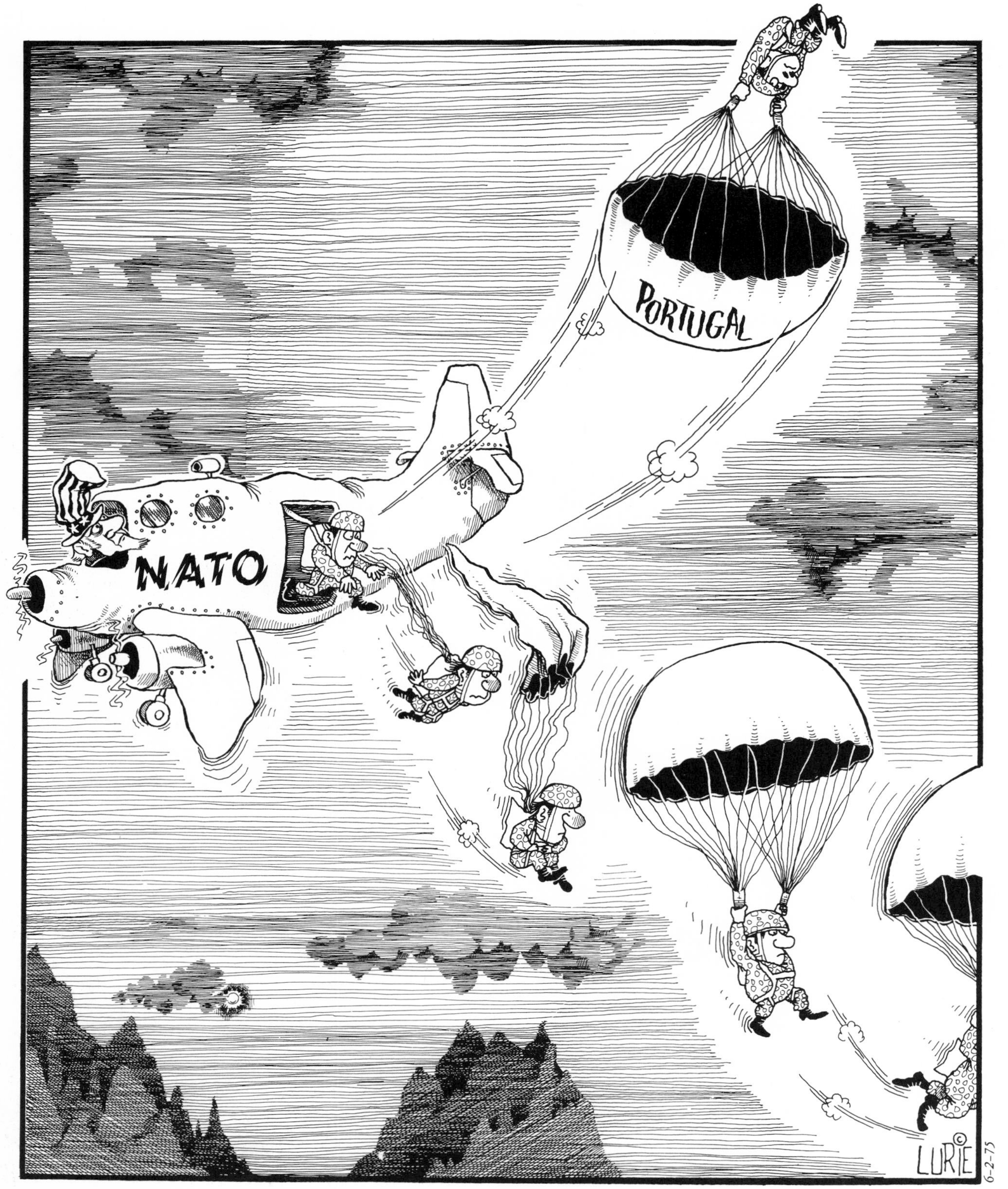
PORTUGAL
NATO
LURIE ©
6-2-75

SUMMER MANEUVERS

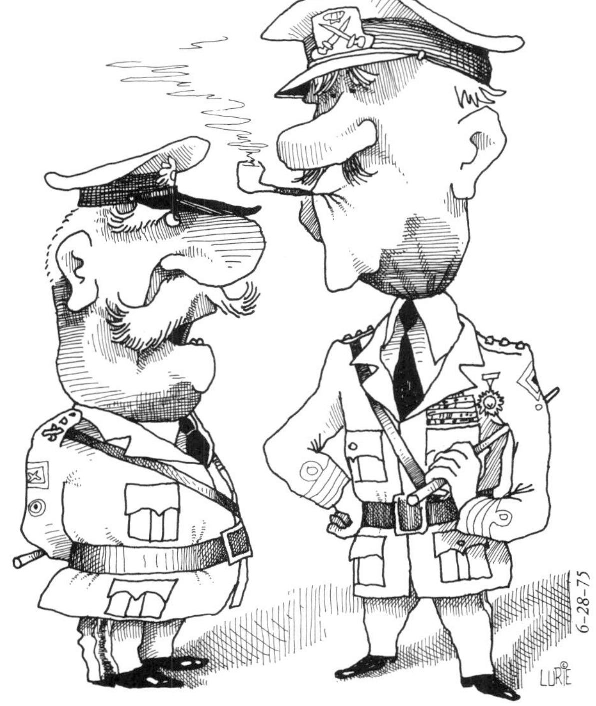
6-28-75
LURIE

"I SAY—WHO'S THE IDIOT
WHO PROMOTED AMIN
TO SERGEANT?!"

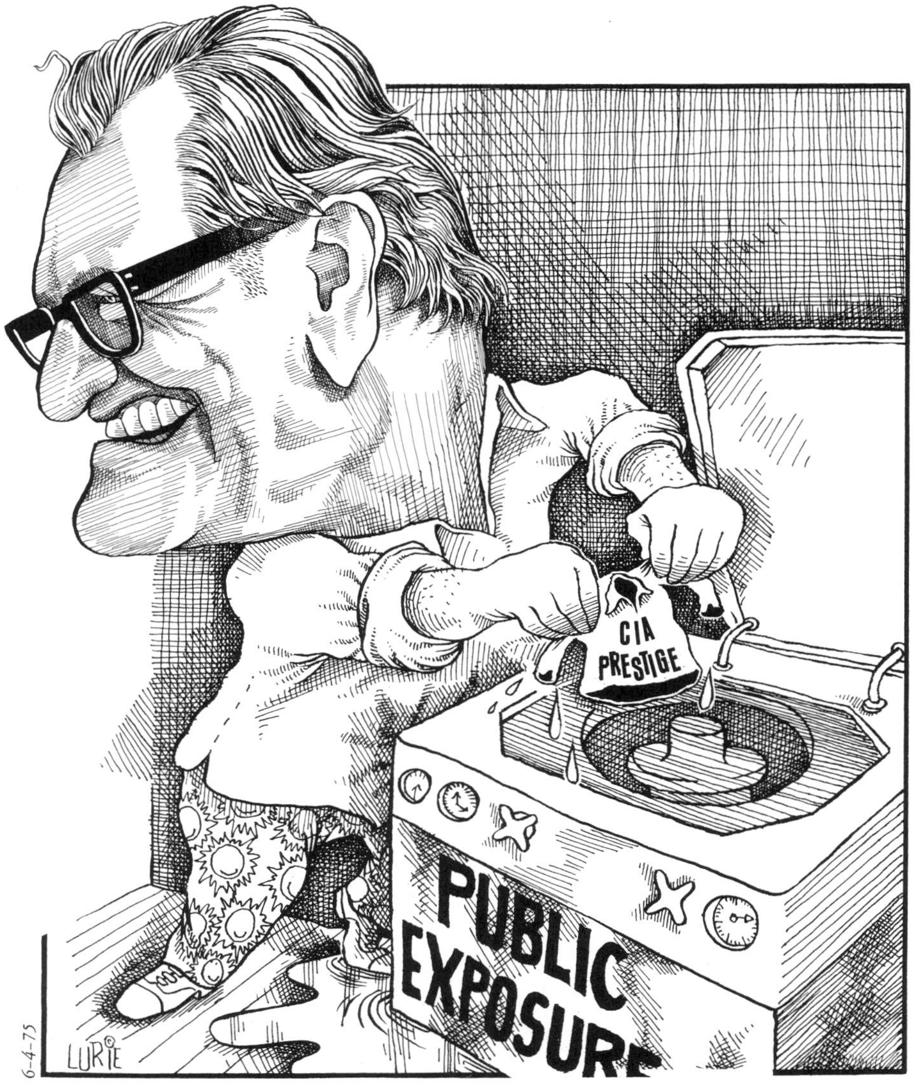
CIA
PRESTIGE
PUBLIC
EXPOSUR
6-4-75
LURIE

"SEE HOW CLEAN IT CAME OUT?!"

INDIA IS THE WORLD'S LARGEST DEMOCRACY!
LURIE©
6-30-75

"O.K., CHILDREN, REPEAT AFTER ME . . ."

HELSINKI SUMMIT
LURIE©
7-19-75

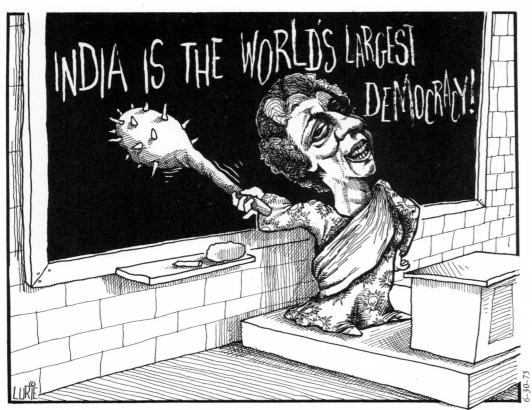

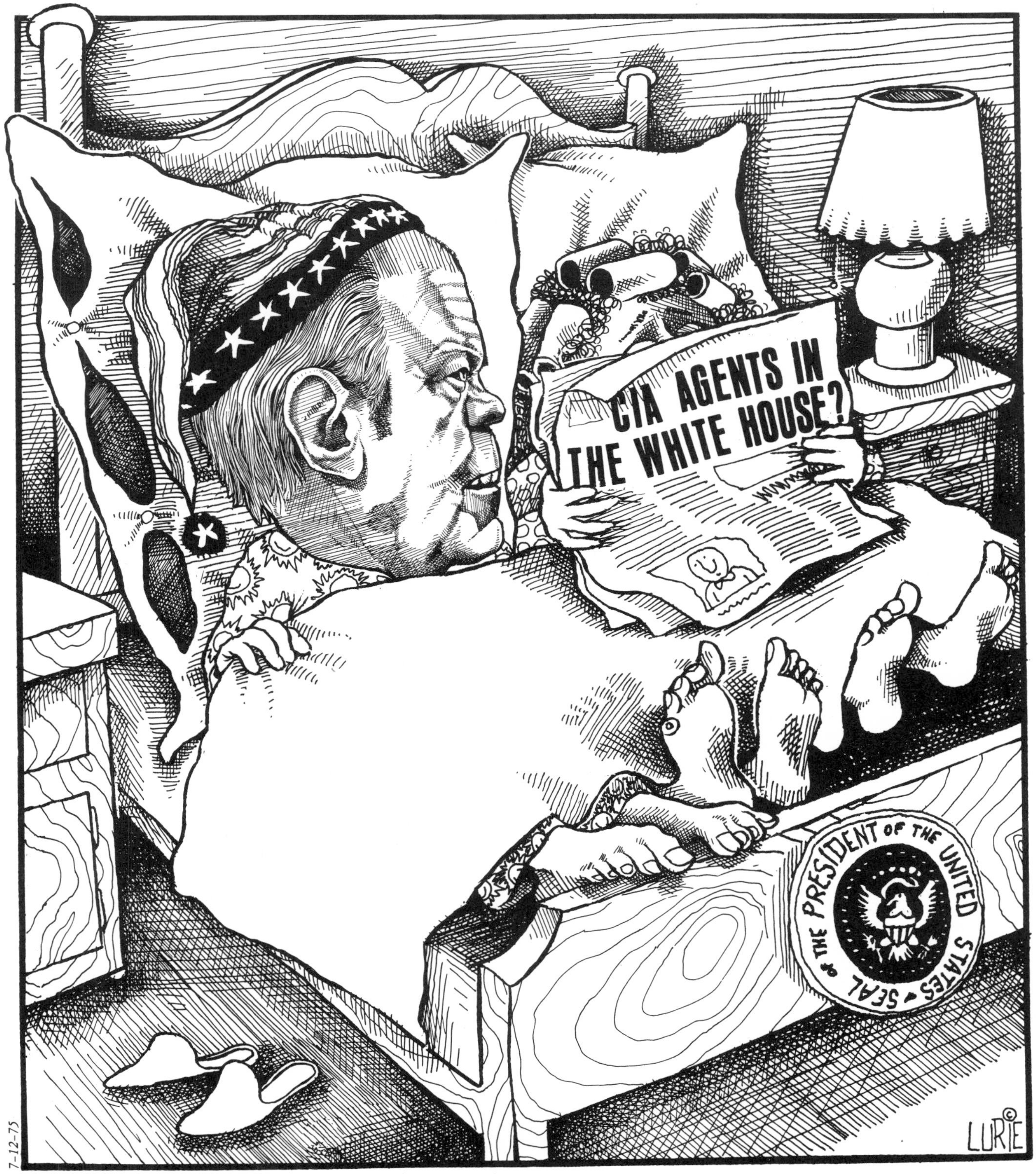
CIA AGENTS IN THE WHITE HOUSE?
SEAL OF THE PRESIDENT OF THE UNITED STATES
LURIE ©
7-12-75

"DON'T BELIEVE A WORD OF IT, BETTY!"

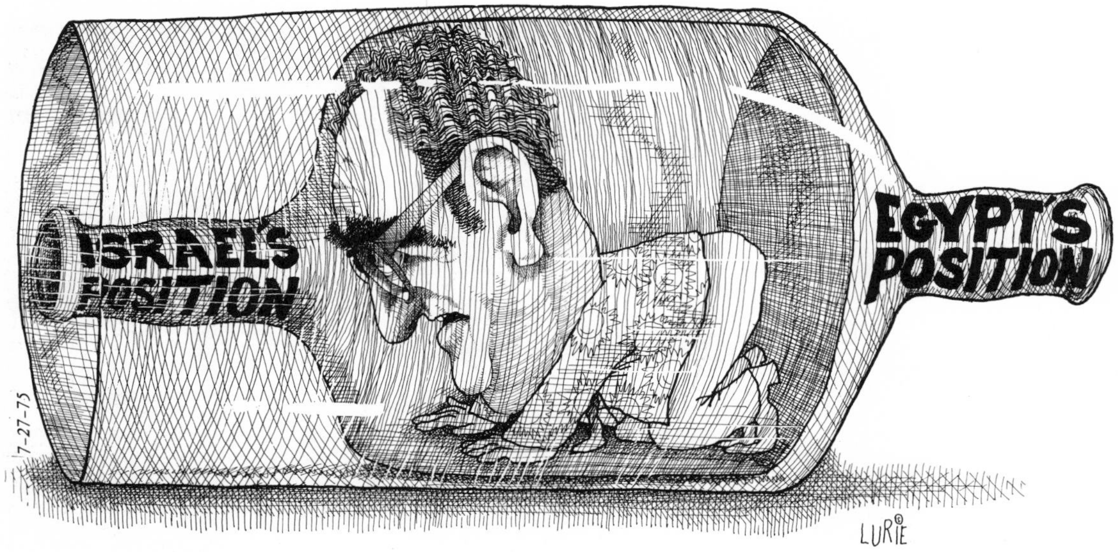
ISRAEL'S POSITION
EGYPT'S POSITION
7-27-75
LURIE

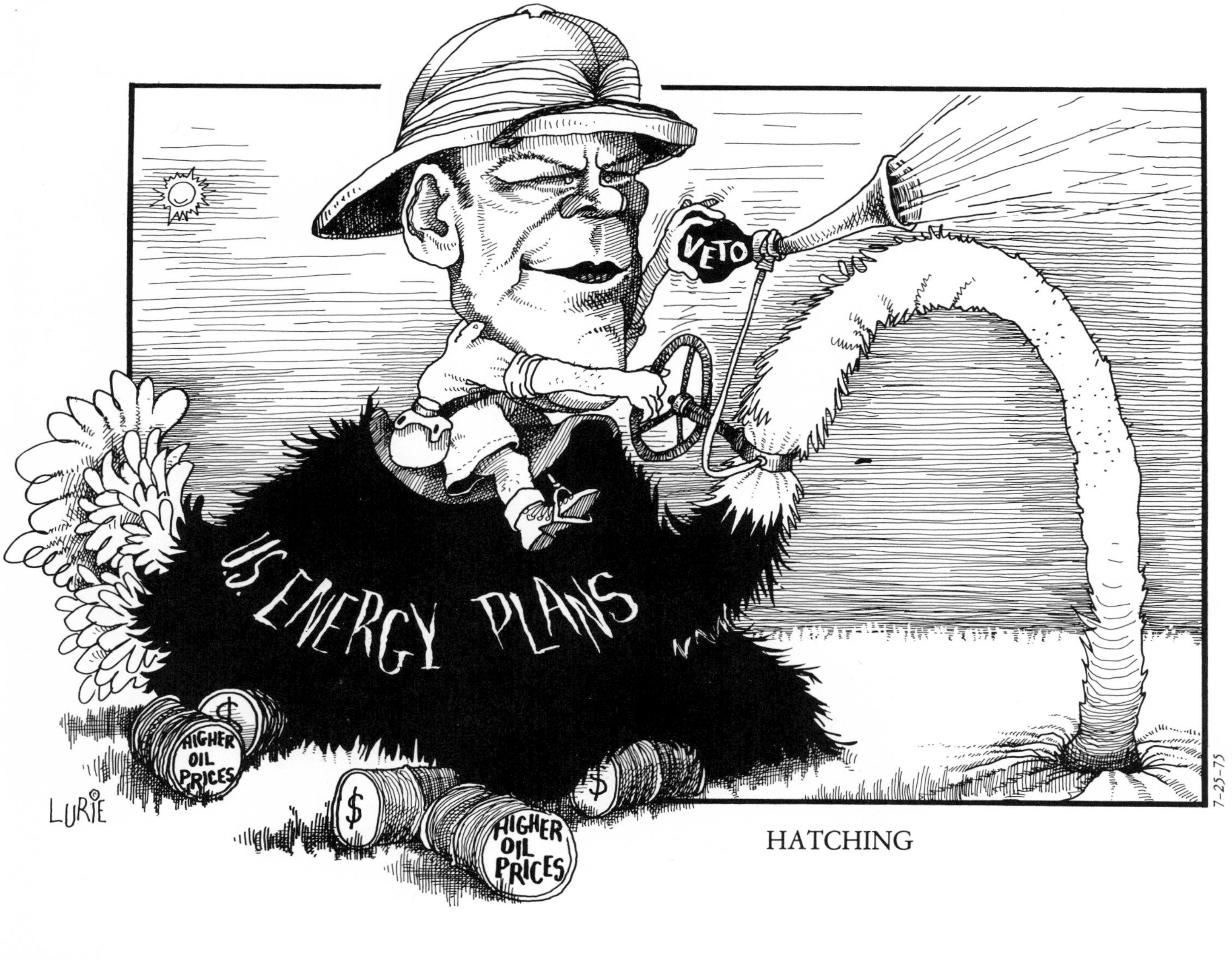
VETO
U.S. ENERGY PLANS
HIGHER OIL PRICES
$
HIGHER OIL PRICES
LURIE
7-25-75

HATCHING

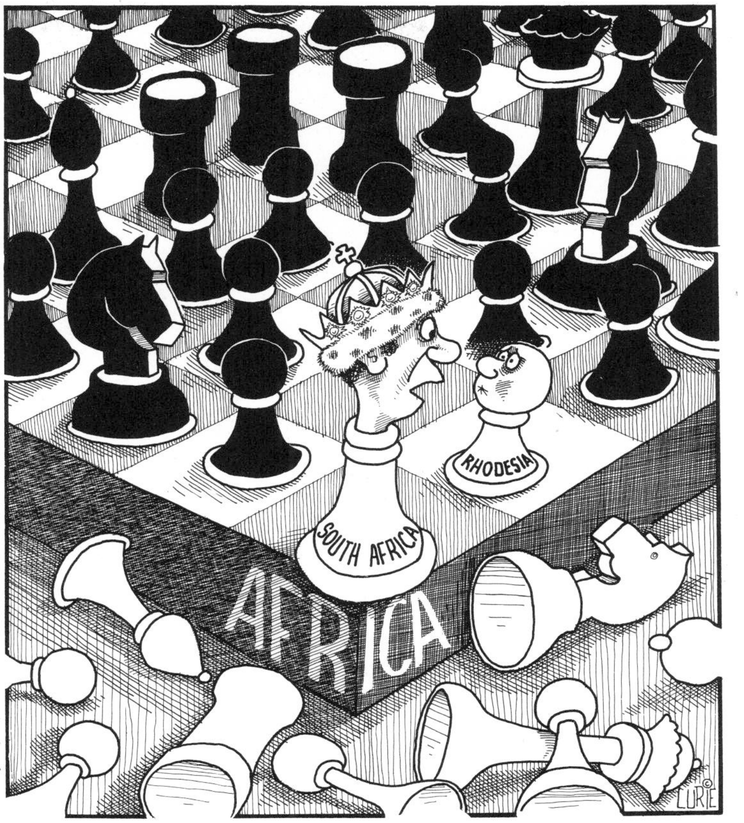
RHODESIA
SOUTH AFRICA
AFRICA
8-19-75
LURIE ©

"PLAN W H A T STRATEGY?"

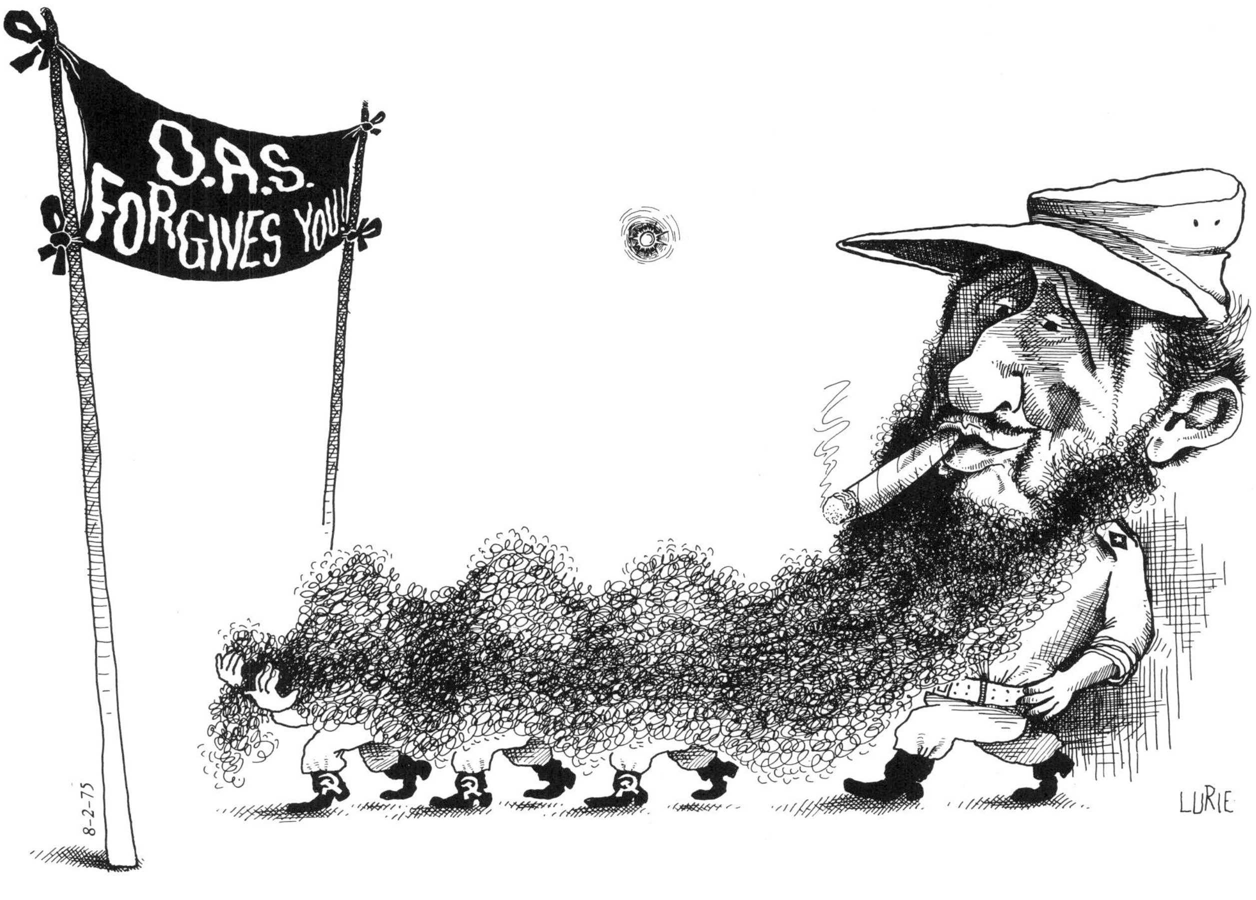
O.A.S. FORGIVES YOU!
8-2-75
LURIE

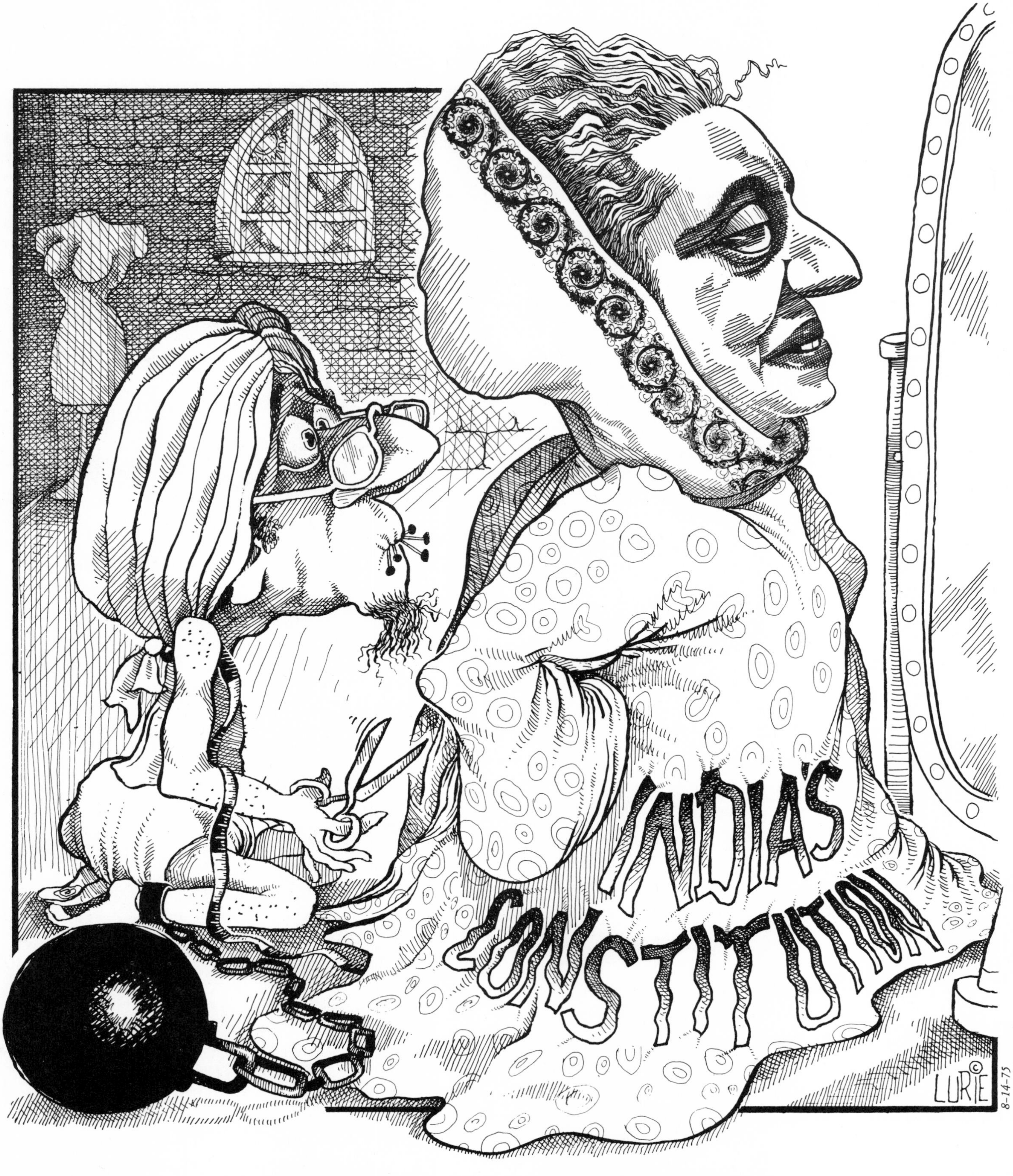
INDIA'S
CONSTITUTION
LURIE ©
8-14-75

"BETTER SHAPE IT TO FIT MY FIGURE, BUSTER!"

EGYPT
ISRAEL
LURIE
The New York Times Special Features 8-31-75

THE WINNERS

MIDEAST PEACE BENEFITS
SADAT
RABIN
MIDEAST PEACE BENEFITS
8-26-75

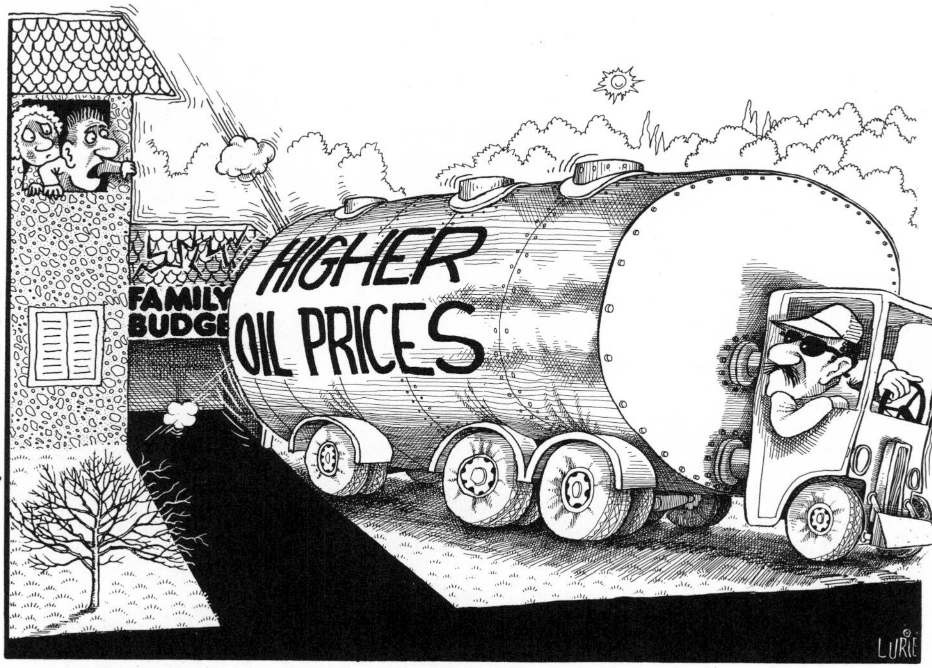
HIGHER
OIL PRICES
FAMILY
BUDGE
LURIE

The New York Times Special Features 9-13-75

"WELL I'LL BE DARNED—
HE'S TRYING TO PARK IN OUR GARAGE!"

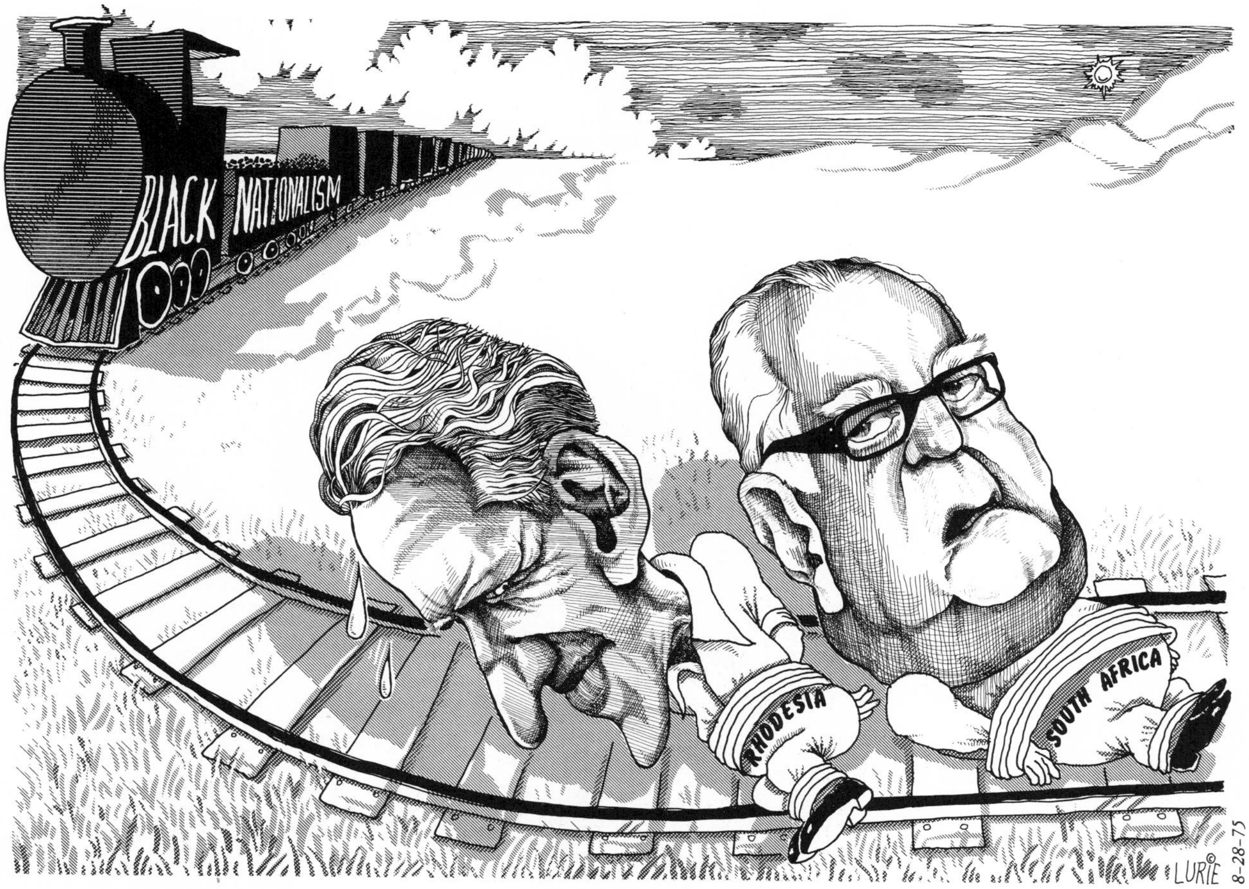
BLACK
NATIONALISM
RHODESIA
SOUTH AFRICA
LURIE

8-28-75

"AT LEAST I'LL LEARN FROM YOUR EXPERIENCES!"

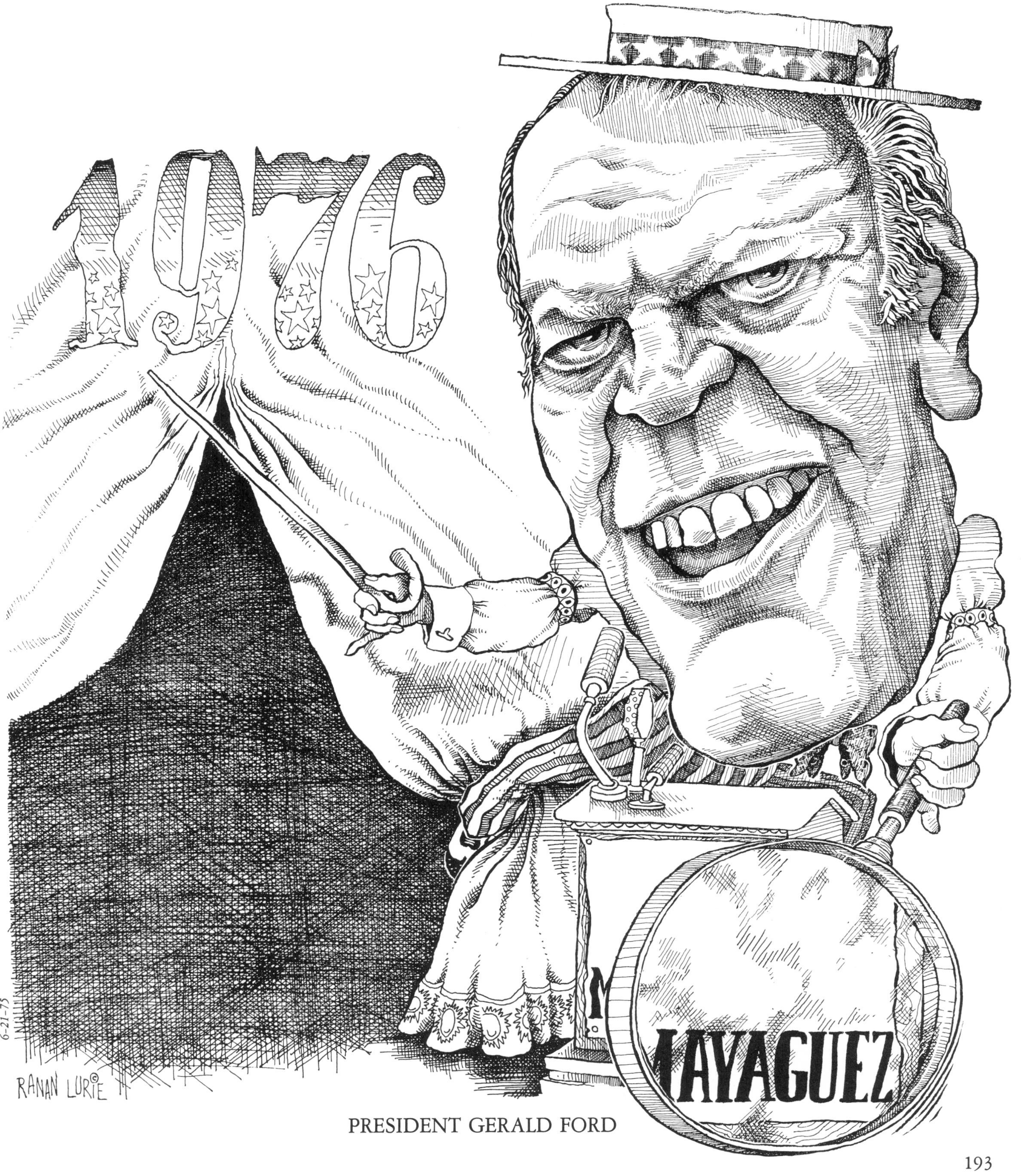
1976
MAYAGUEZ
6-21-75
RANAN LURIE

PRESIDENT GERALD FORD

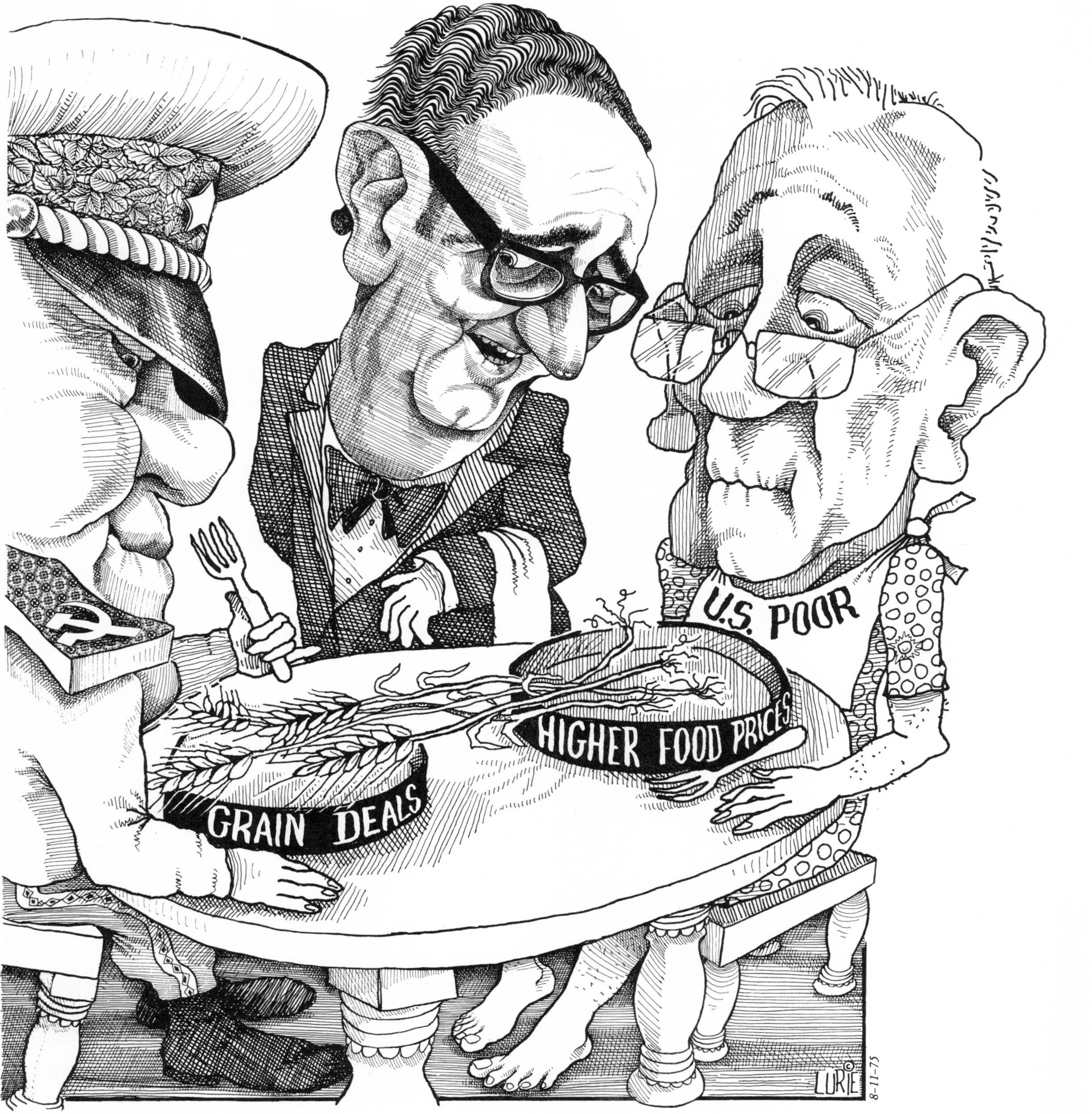
U.S. POOR
HIGHER FOOD PRICES
GRAIN DEALS
LURIE ©
8-11-75

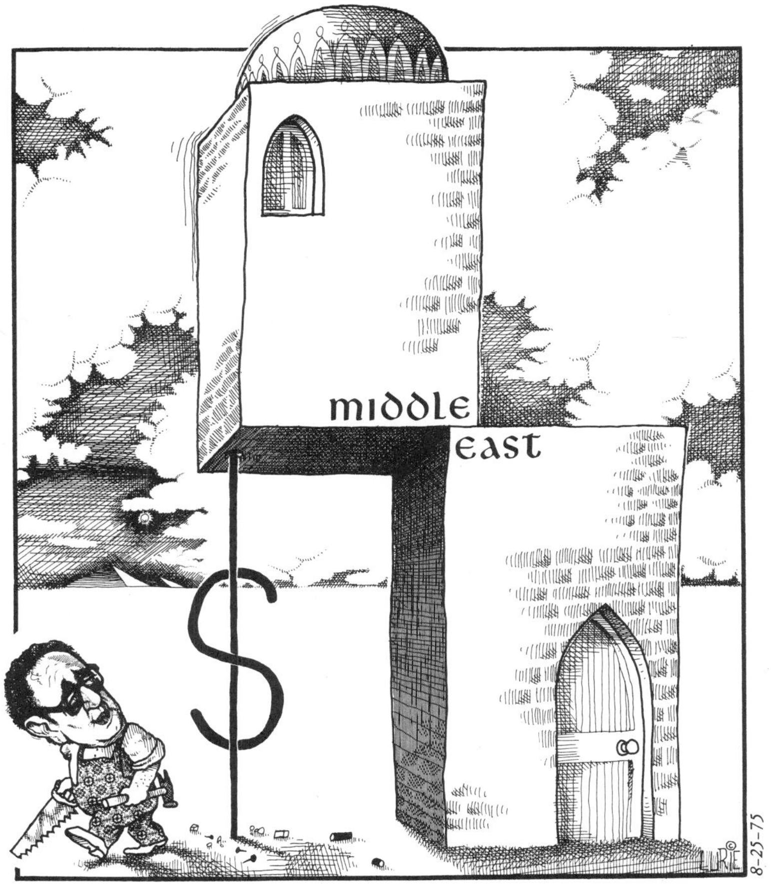
MIDDLE
EAST
LURIE©
8-25-75

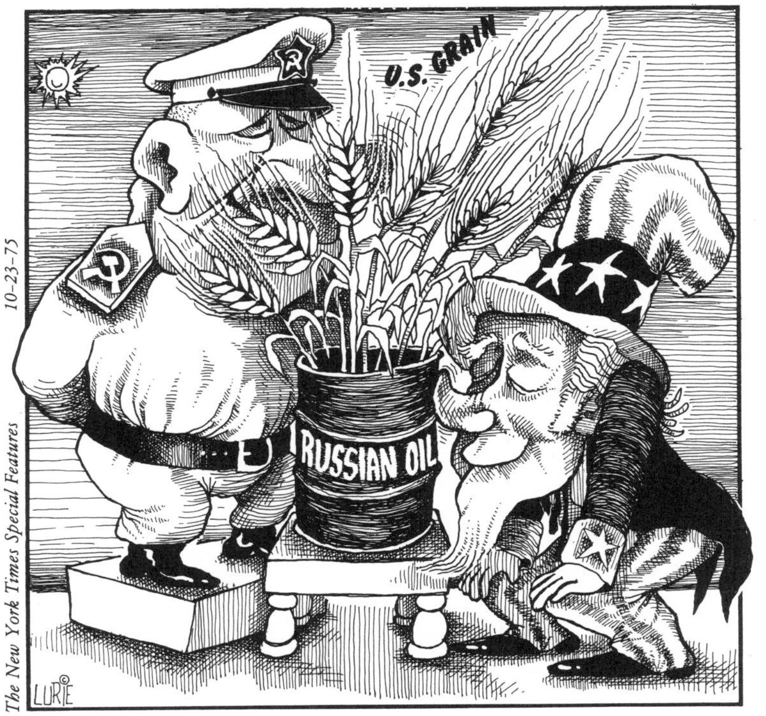
U.S. GRAIN
RUSSIAN OIL
LURIE©
10-23-75
The New York Times Special Features

"AHHHHH . . . NICE SMELL!"

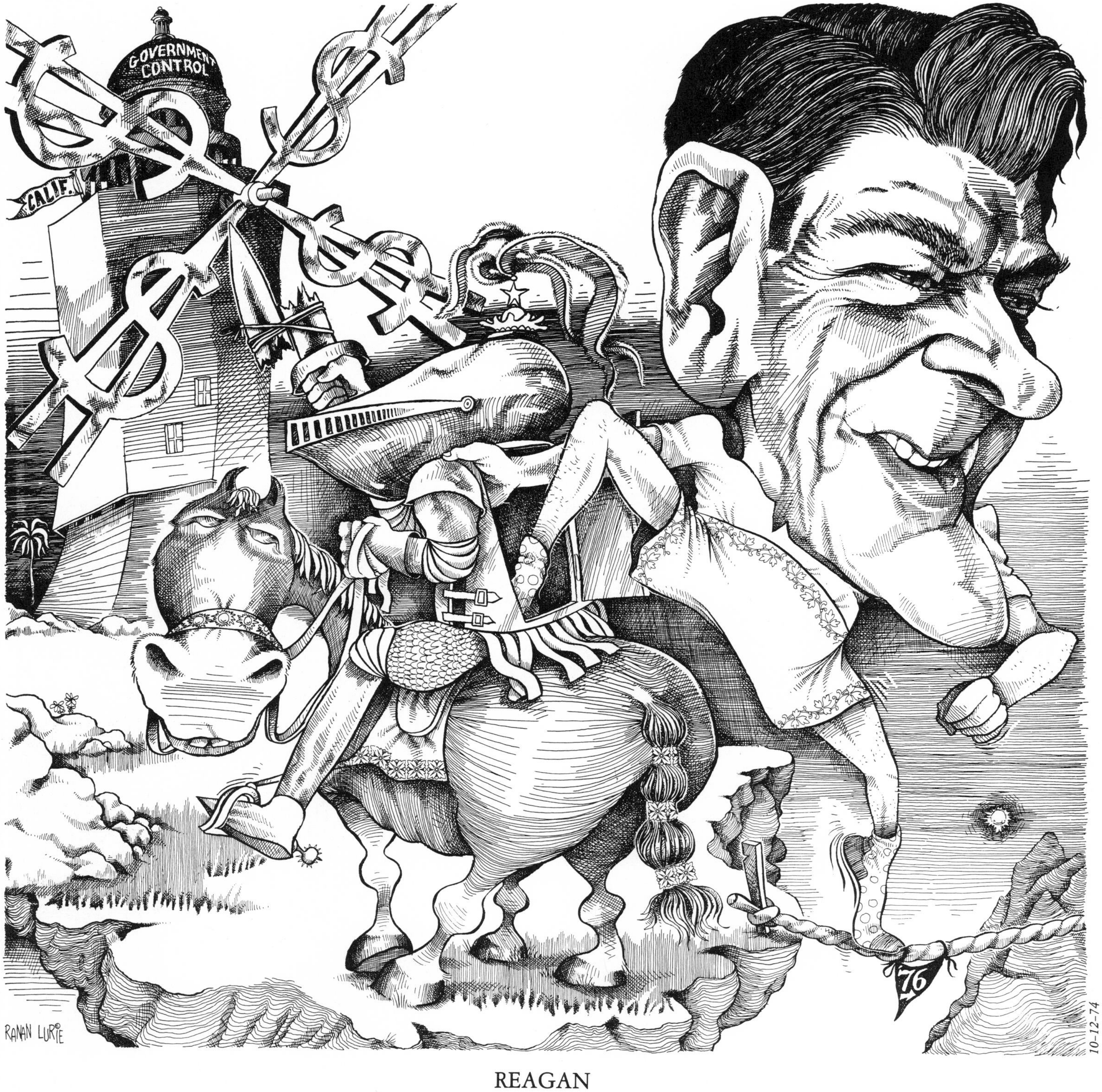
GOVERNMENT CONTROL
CALIF.
76
RANAN LURIE
10-12-74

REAGAN

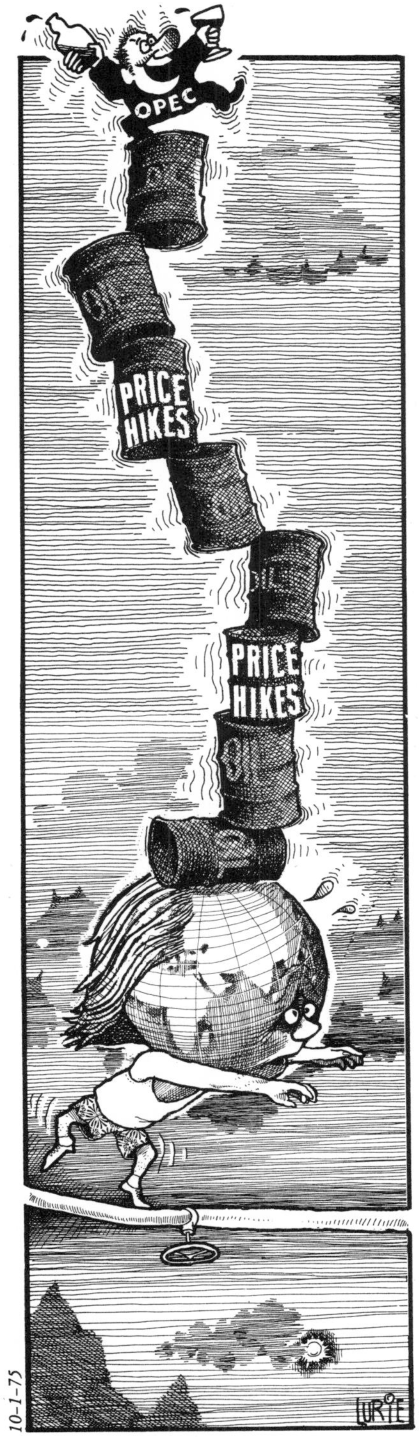
OPEC
PRICE HIKES
PRICE HIKES
10-1-75
LURIE

"WE'RE ON TOP . . .
WE'RE ON TOP!"

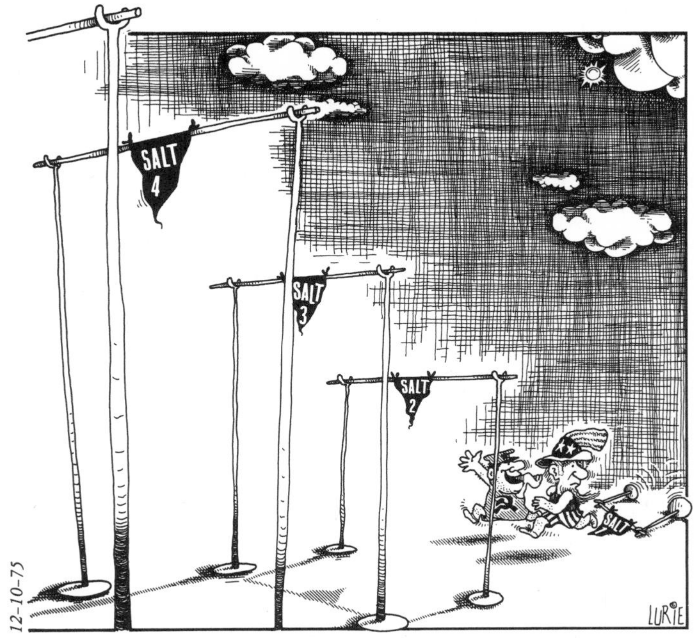
SALT 4
SALT 3
SALT 2
12-10-75
LURIE

"DON'T DESPAIR—
THE OTHERS MIGHT BE EASIER!"

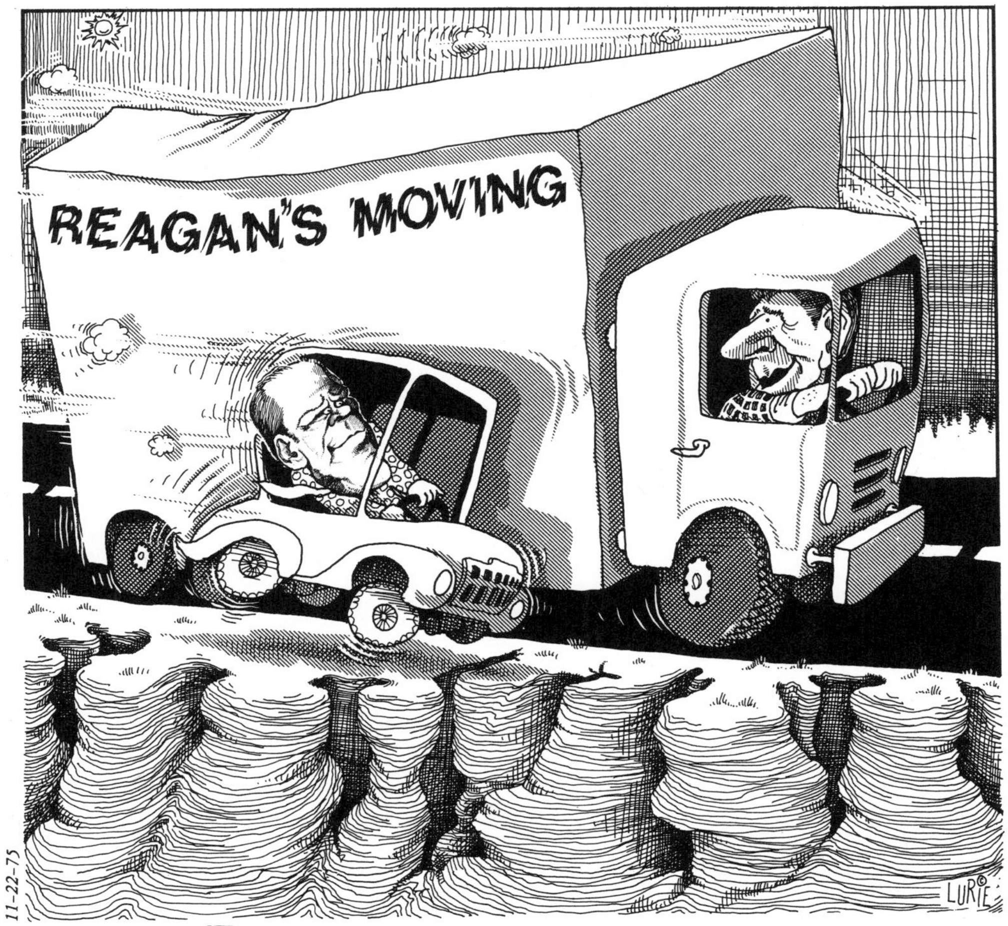
REAGAN'S MOVING
11-22-75
LURIE

"SQUEEZE RIGHT! SQUEEZE RIGHT!"

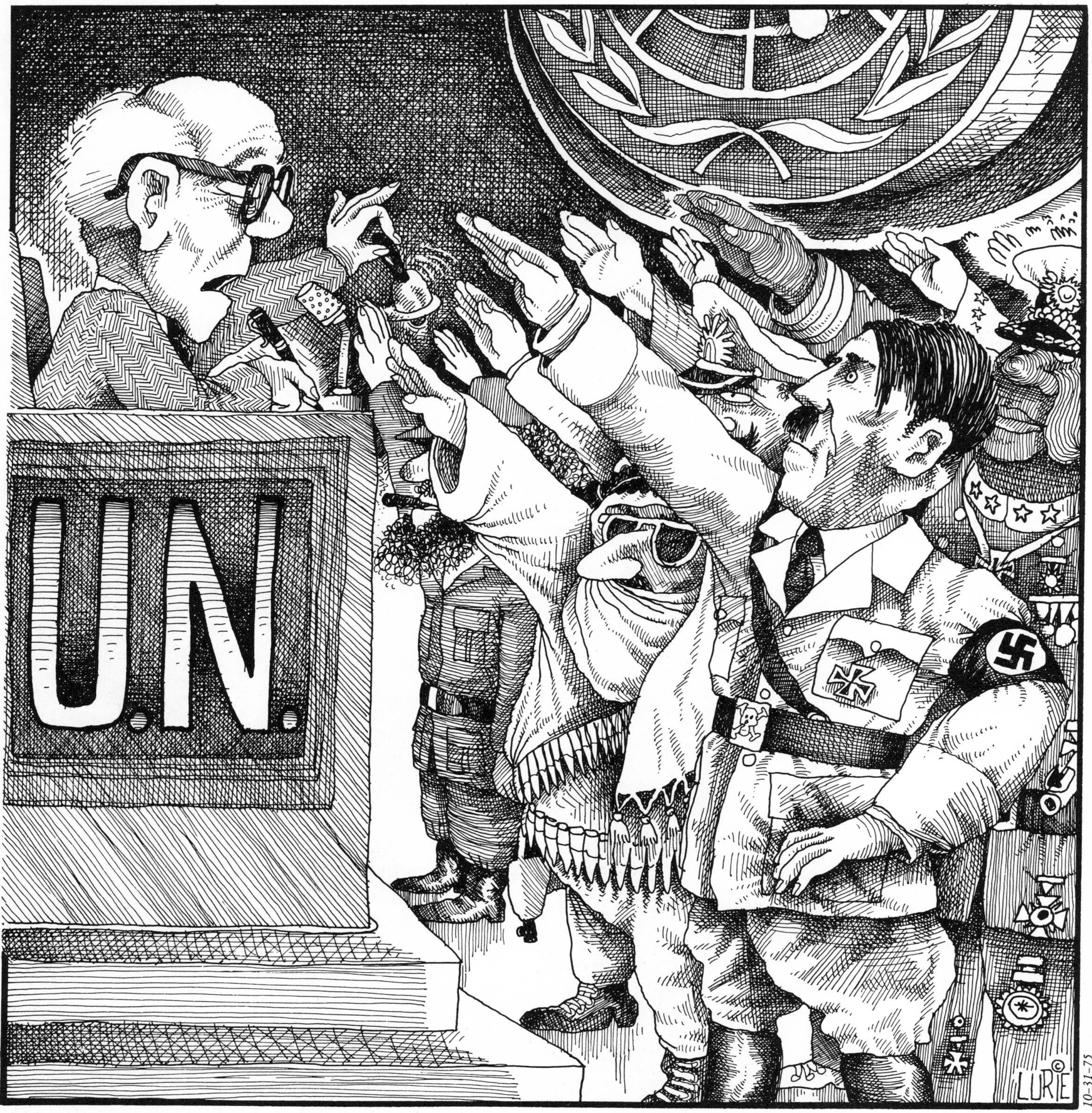
U.N.
LURIE ©
10-31-75

"ALL THOSE CONDEMNING ZIONISM RAISE THEIR HANDS."

The New York Times Special Features 11-15-75

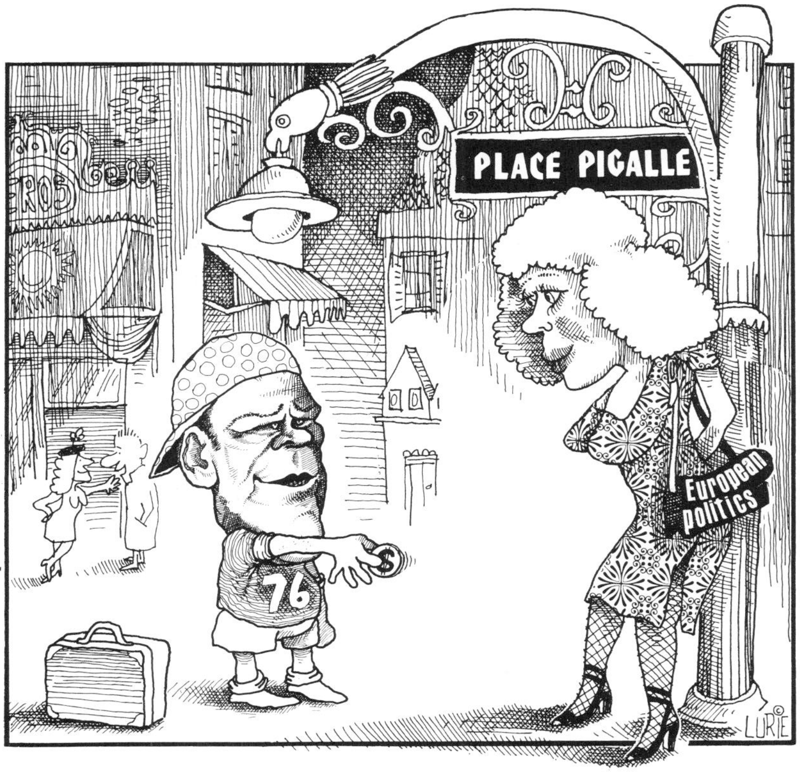
PLACE PIGALLE
76
European politics
LURIE

"I WAS SENT TO GAIN EXPERIENCE."

10-30-75

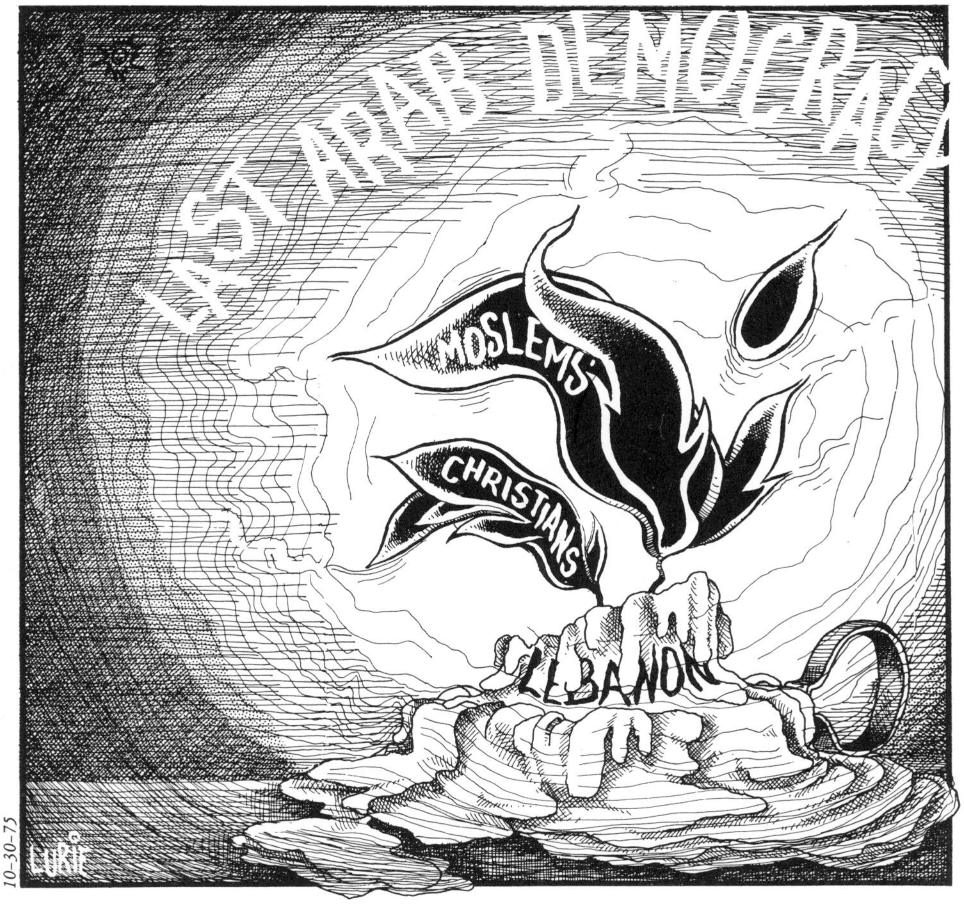
LAST ARAB DEMOCRAC
MOSLEMS
CHRISTIANS
LEBANON
LURIE

CUBA
U.S.
ANGOLA
(TRESPASSING
WELCOMED!)
12-20-75
LURIE

"IMPERIALIST!"
"COLONIALIST!"

NORTH
VIETNAM
SOUTH
VIETNAM
The New York Times Special Features 12-2-75
LURIE

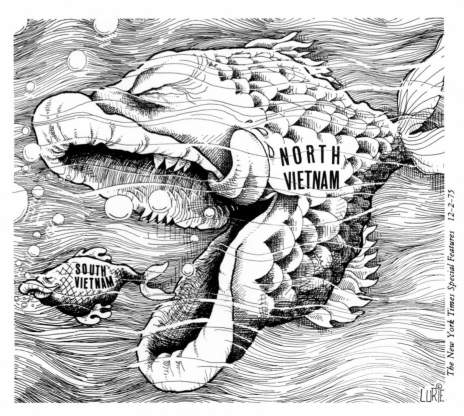

UNIFICATION

United States Ave.
SADAT
RABIN
10-29-75
LURIE©

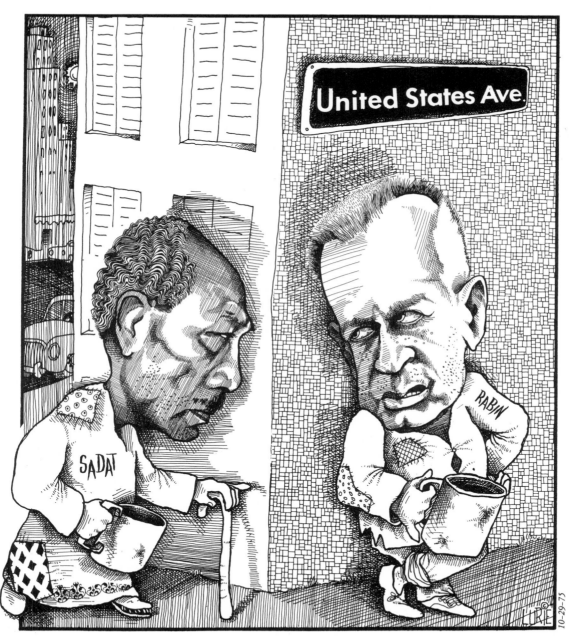

"SHOVE OFF, BUSTER—THIS IS MY CORNER!"

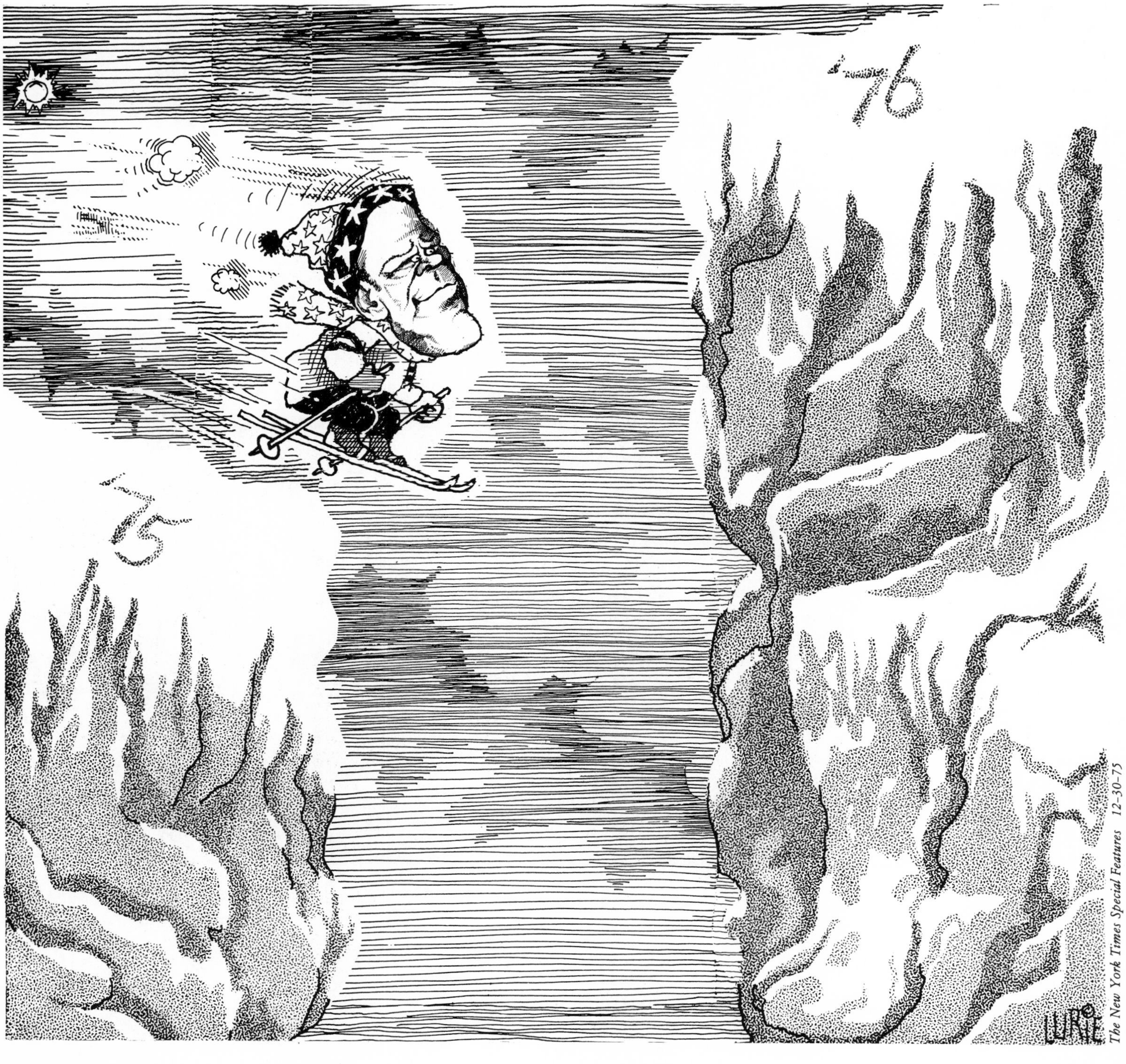
'76
'75
LURIE
The New York Times Special Features 12-30-75

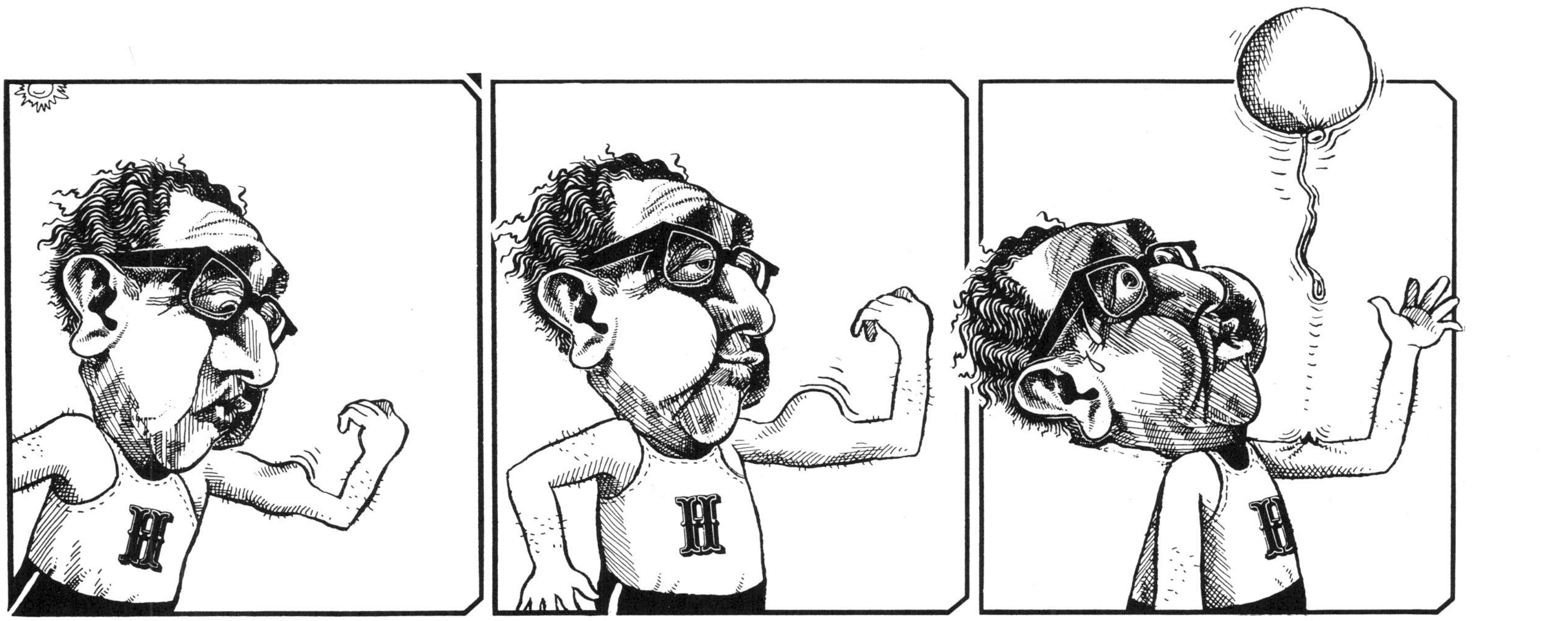

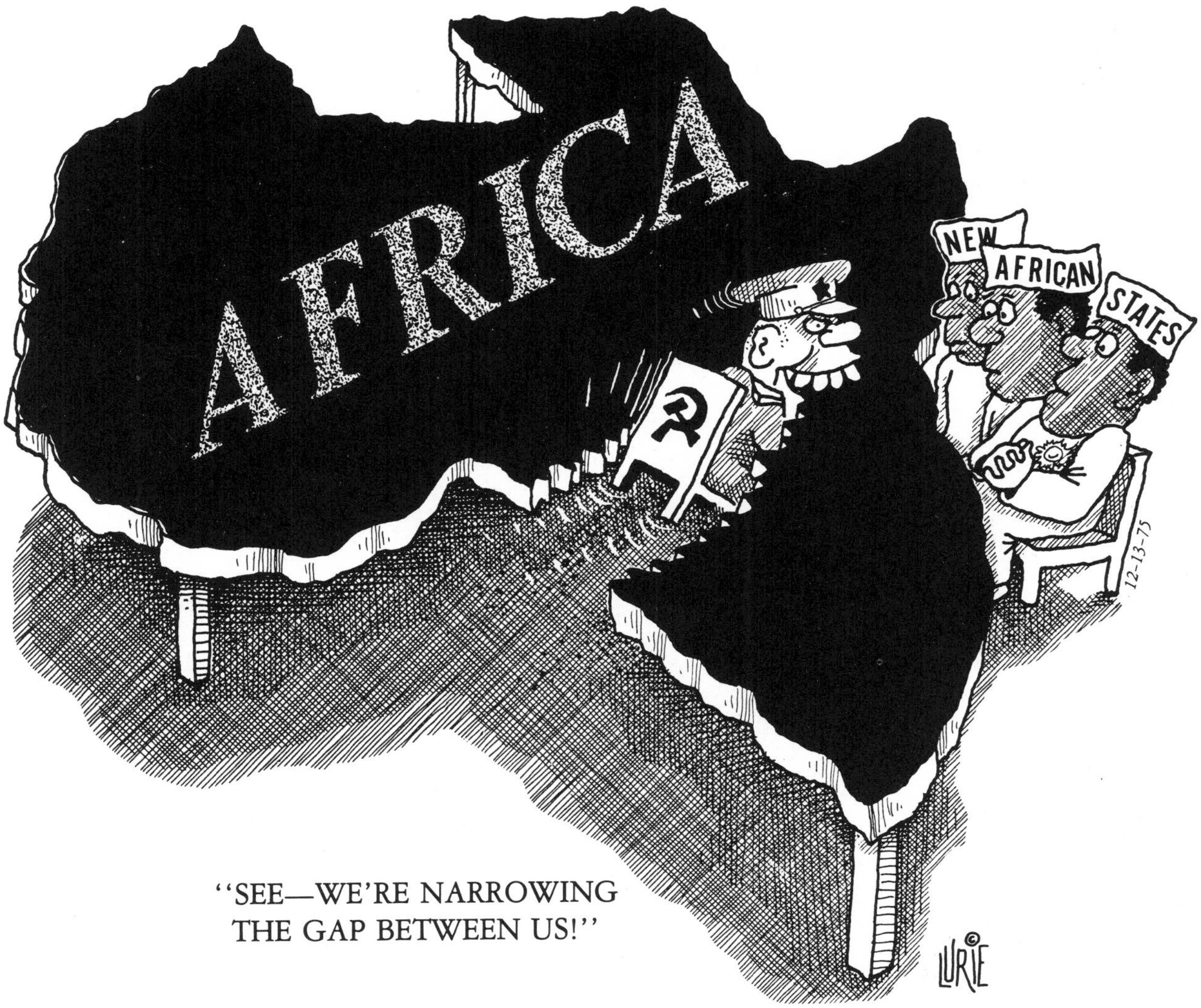
AFRICA
NEW
AFRICAN
STATES
12-13-75
LURIE

"SEE—WE'RE NARROWING
THE GAP BETWEEN US!"

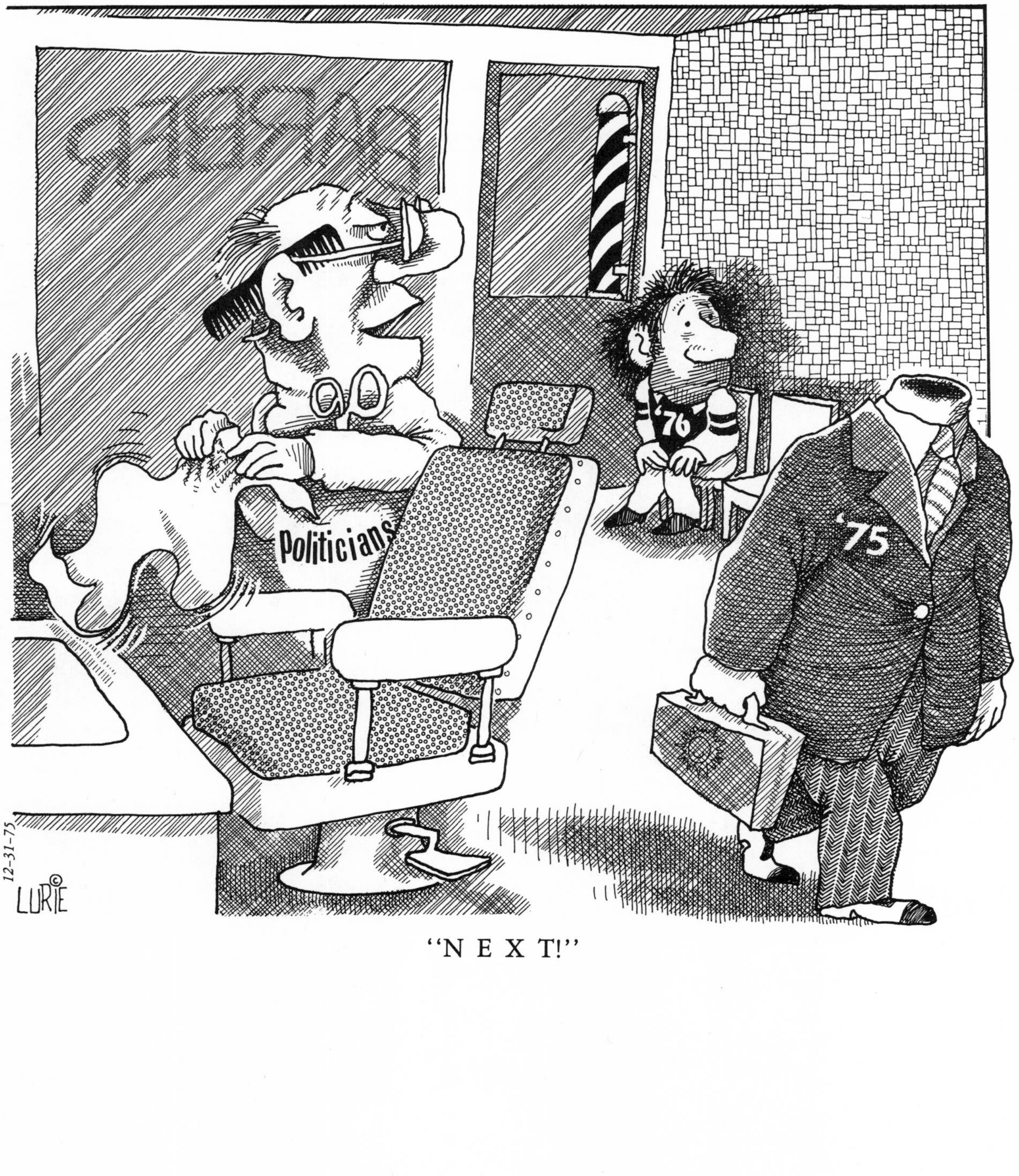
Politicians
'76
'75
12-31-75
LURIE ©

"N E X T!"

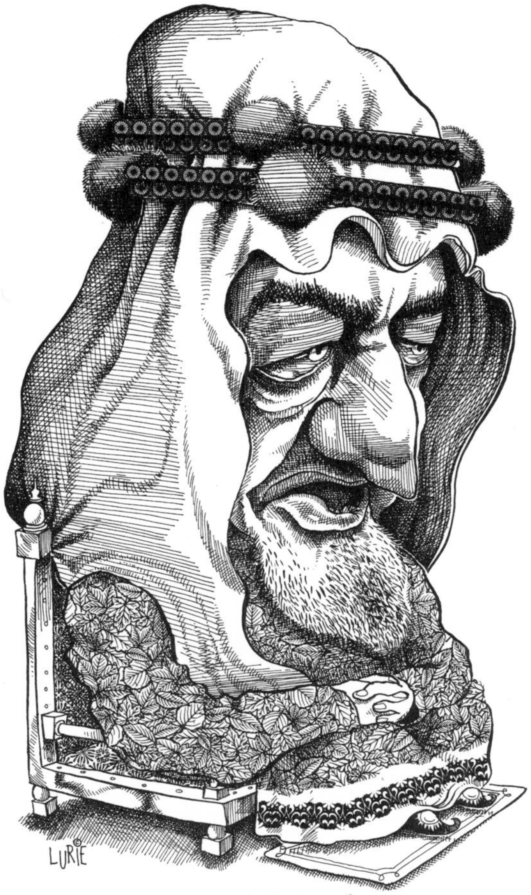
LURIE

King Faisal Abdel Aziz
al Saud Al Faisal
of Saudi Arabia

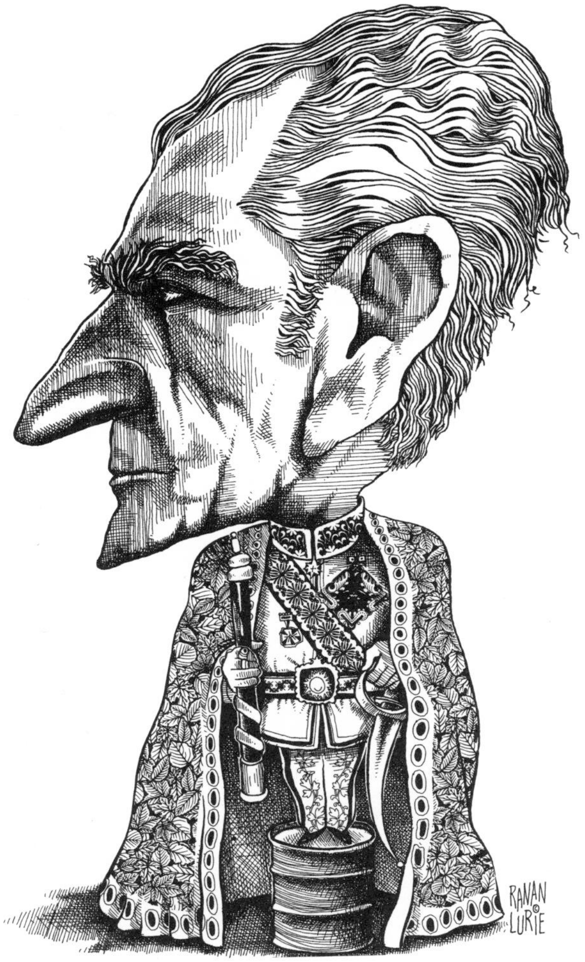
RANAN
LURIE

Shah of Iran
Mohammed Riza Pahlevi

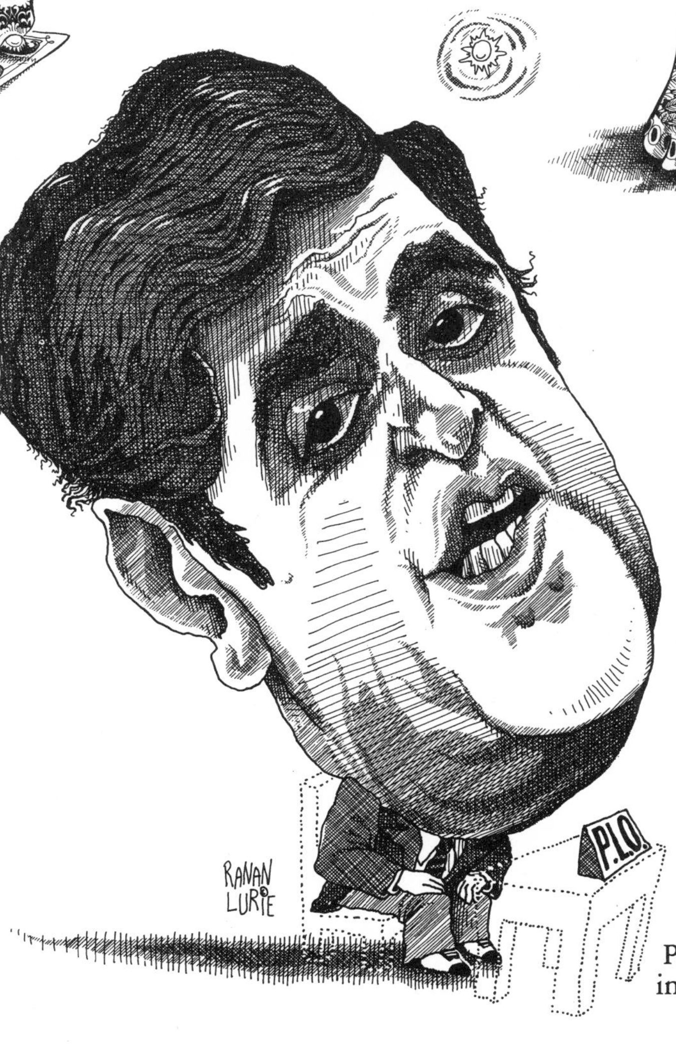
P.L.O.
RANAN
LURIE

Basel Amin Aql
P.L.O. Representative
in the Security Council

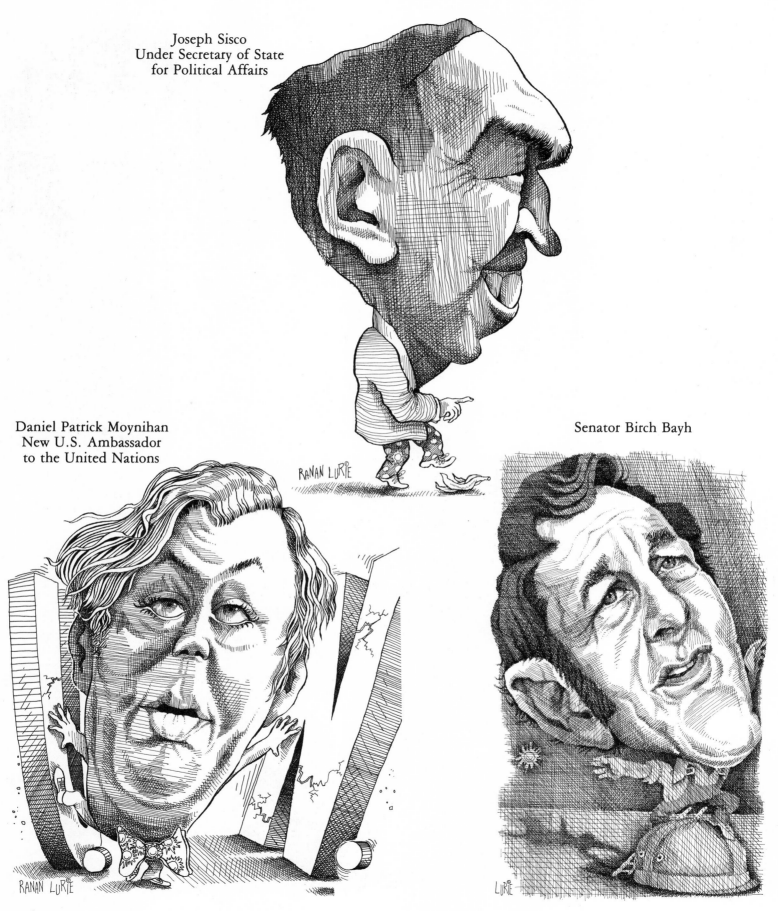

Joseph Sisco
Under Secretary of State
for Political Affairs

RANAN LURIE

Daniel Patrick Moynihan
New U.S. Ambassador
to the United Nations

RANAN LURIE

Senator Birch Bayh

LURIE

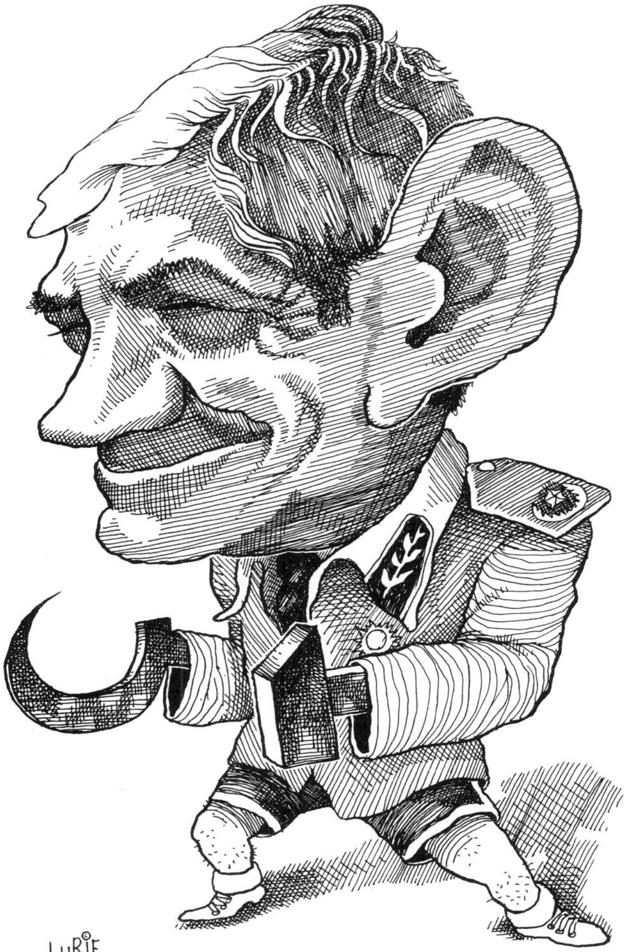

Otelo Saraiva de Carvalho
Portugal's Security Chief

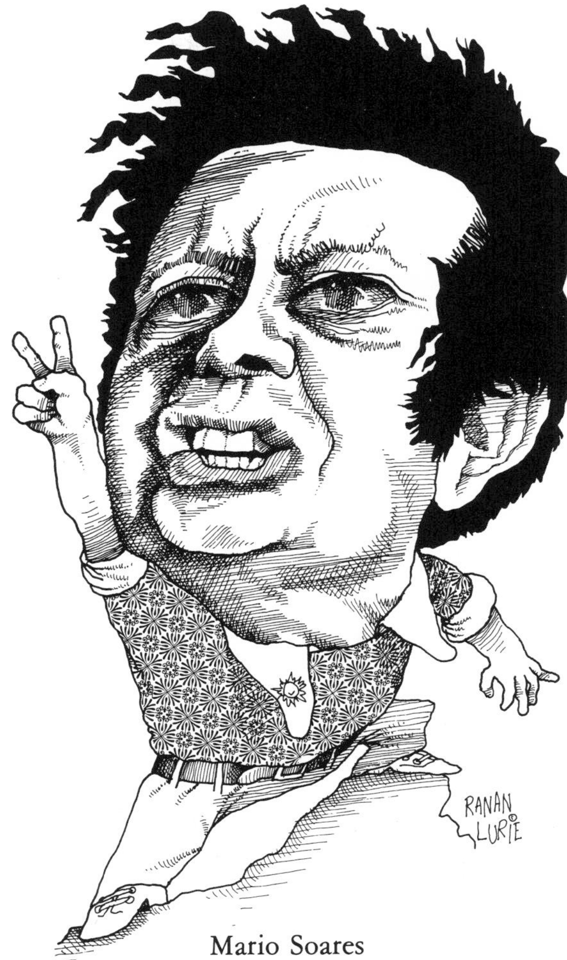
RANAN LURIE

Mario Soares
Portugal's Socialist Party Leader

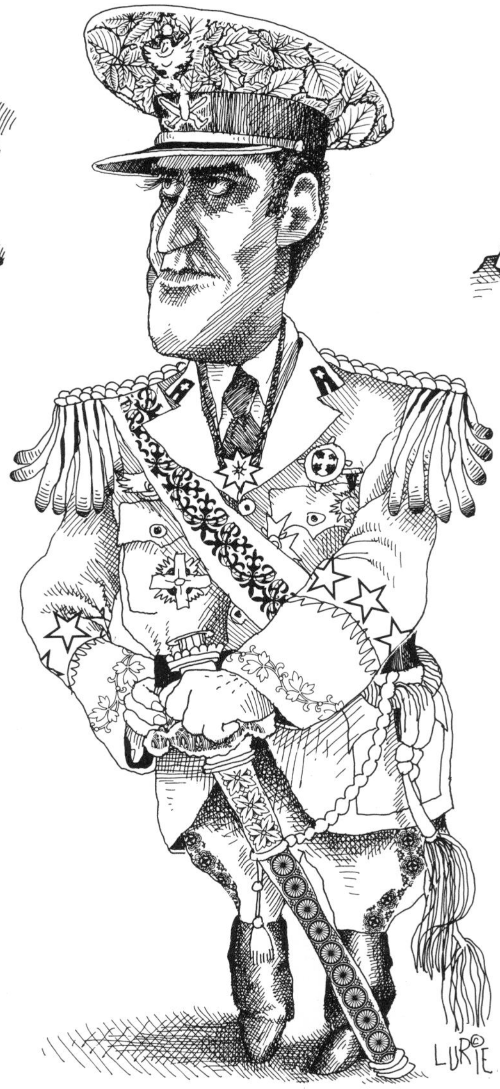
LURIE

Prince Juan Carlos de Borbòn
New Ruler of Spain

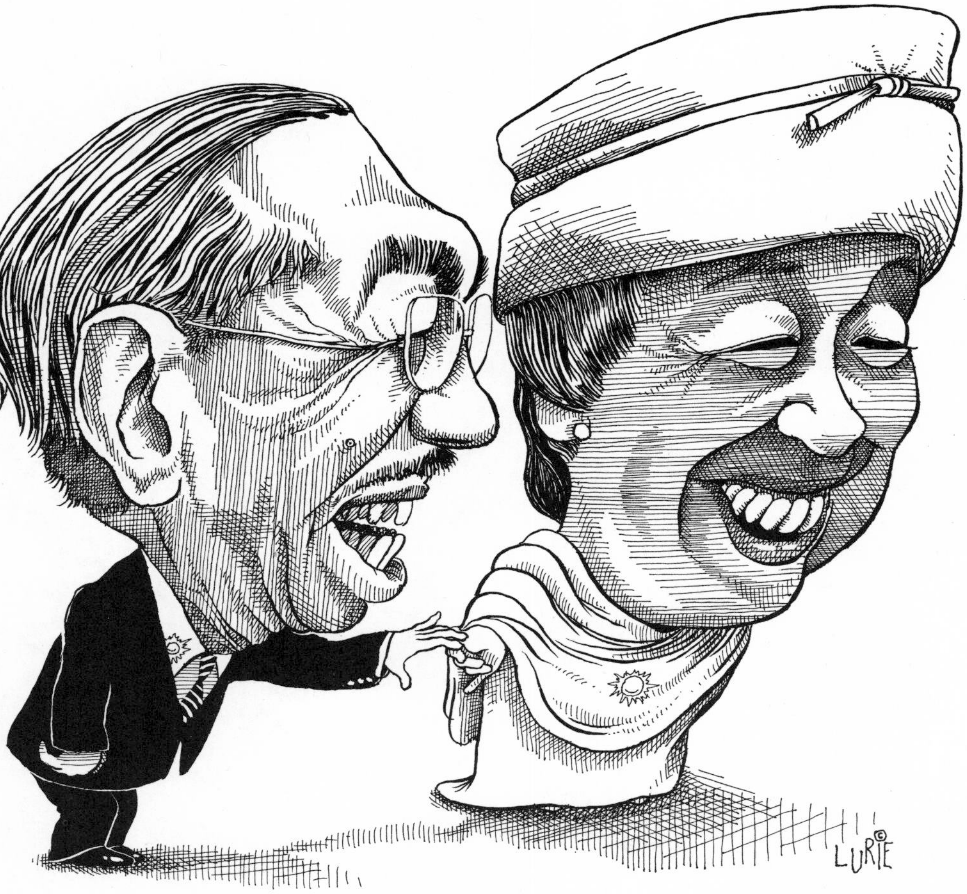
LURIE©

Emperor Hirohito and Empress Nagako of Japan

President Kim Il Sung
of North Korea

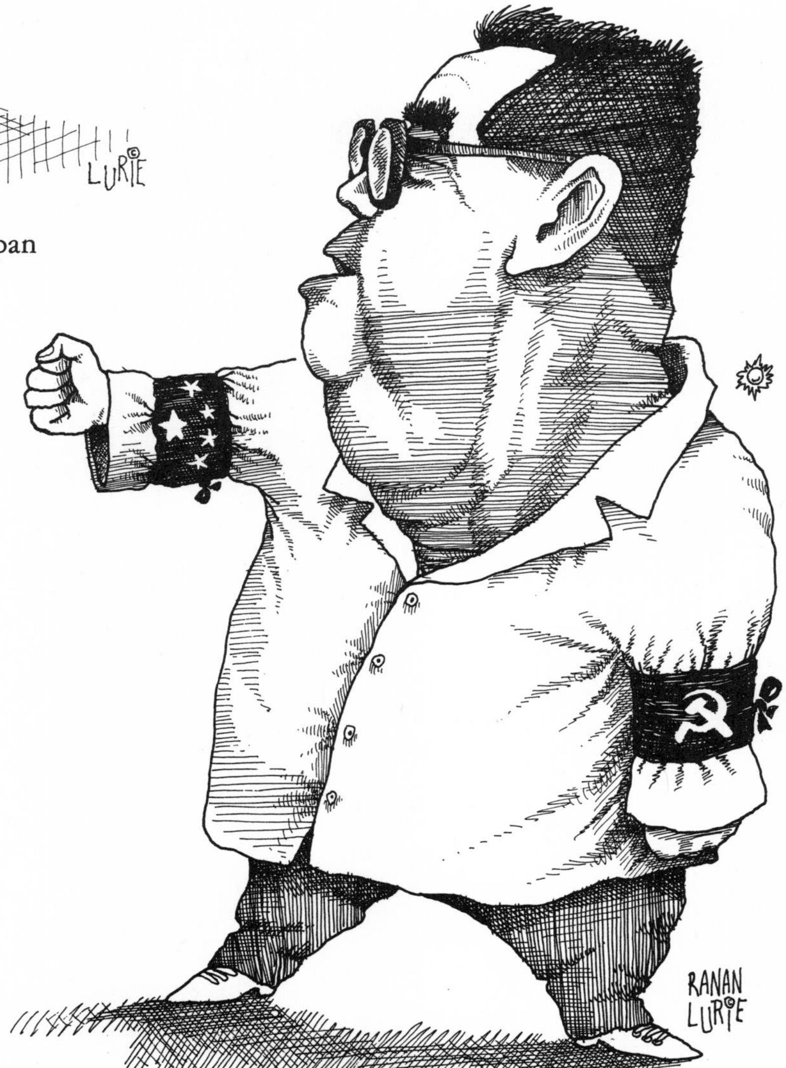
RANAN
LURIE

MAO
LURIE
Dom Mintoff
Malta's Prime Minister

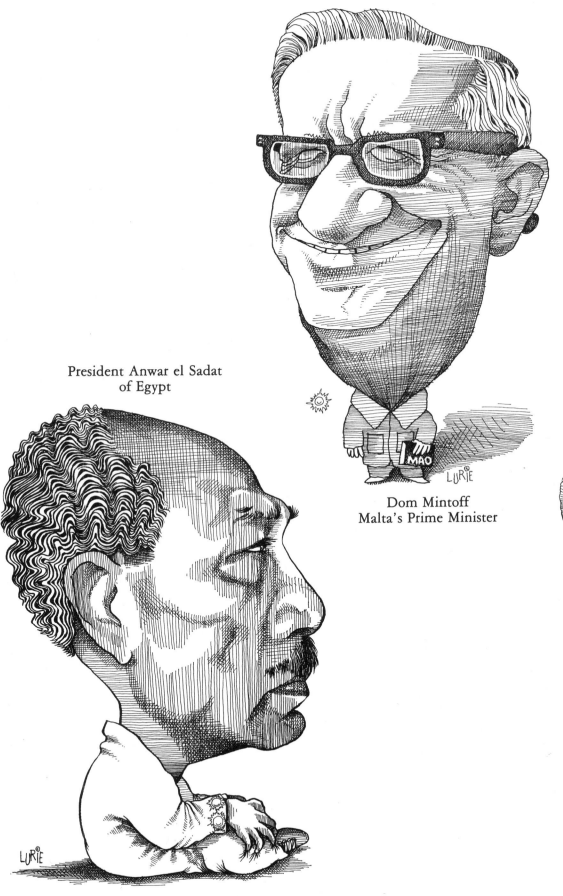

President Anwar el Sadat
of Egypt

LURIE

Shimon Peres
Defense Minister of Israel

RANAN LURIE

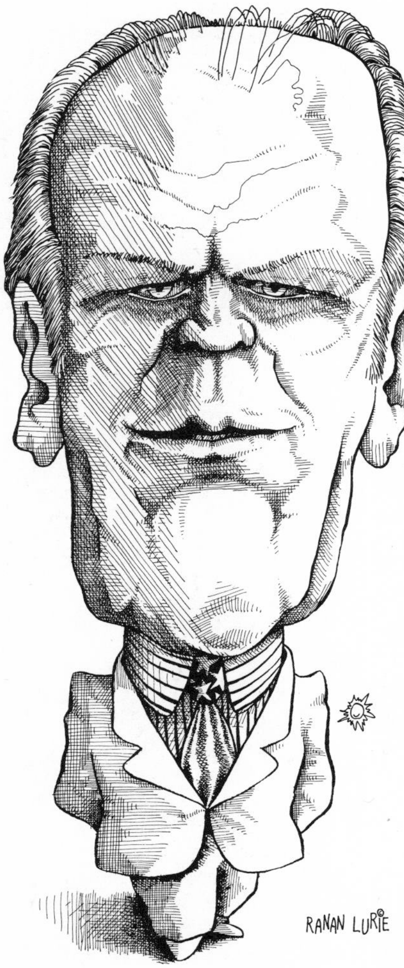
RANAN LURIE

Mr. President

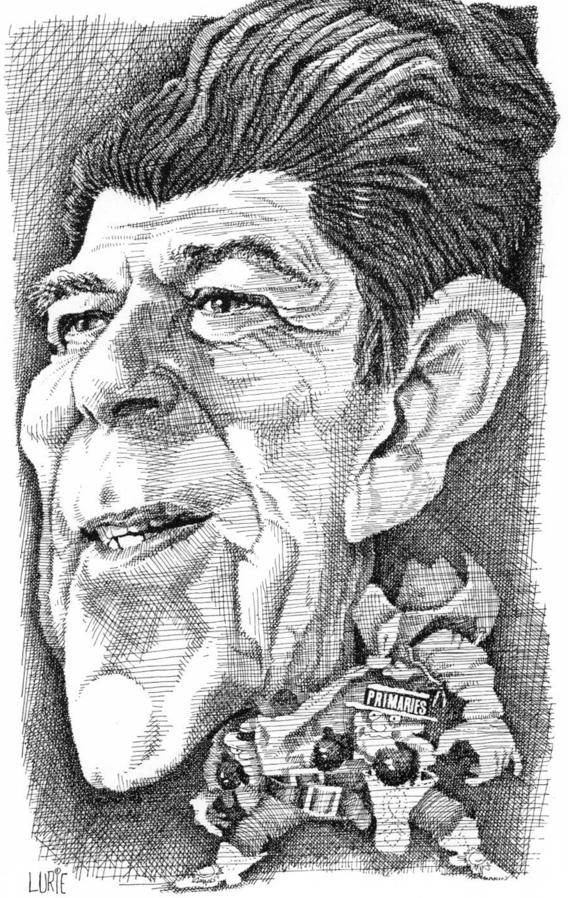
PRIMARIES
LURIE

Ronald Reagan
Presidential Candidate

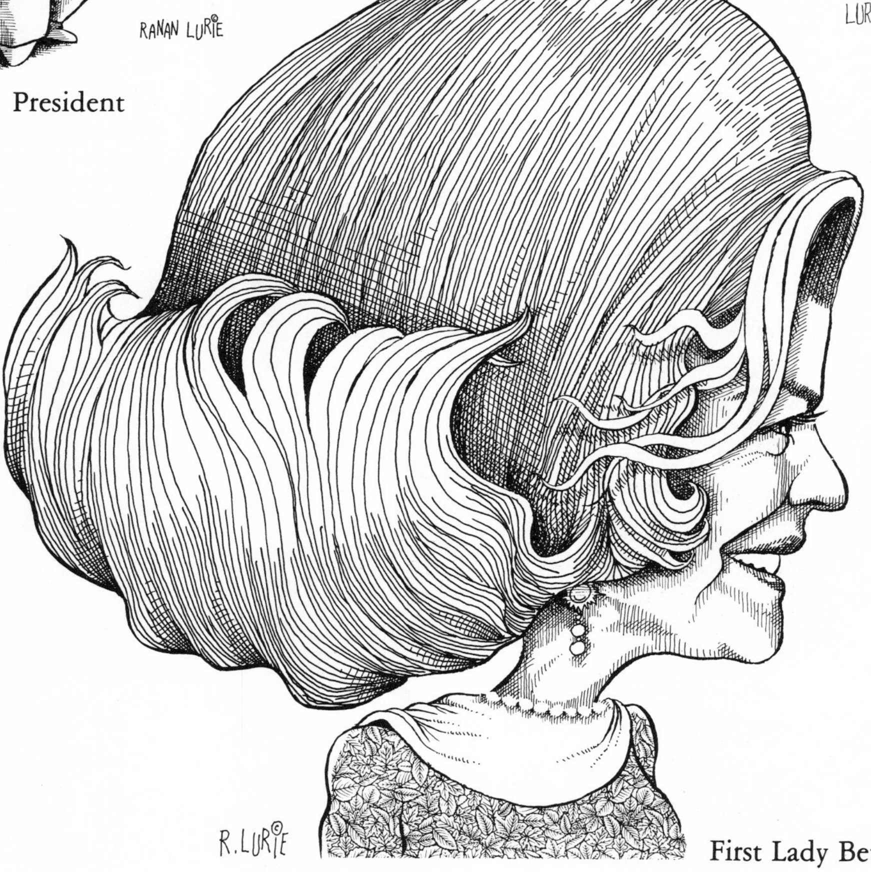
R. LURIE

First Lady Betty Ford

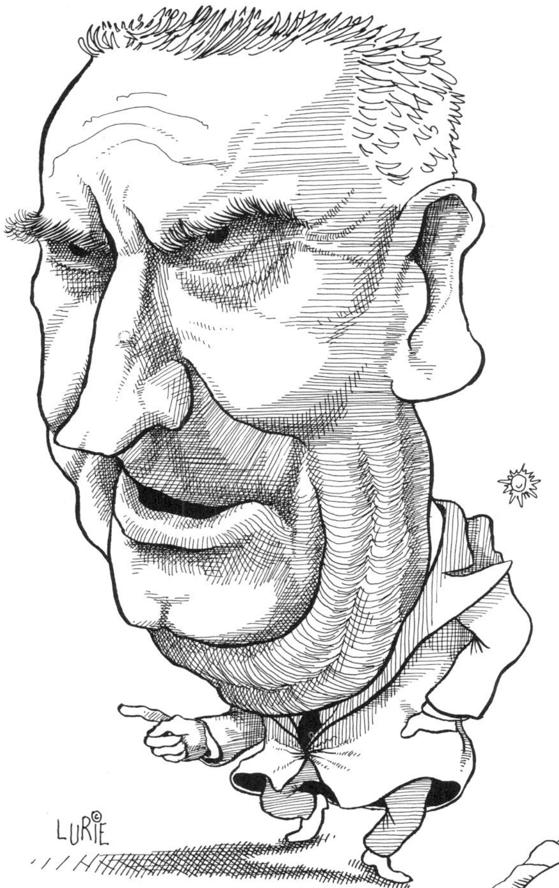
LURIE

Edward Gierek
of Poland

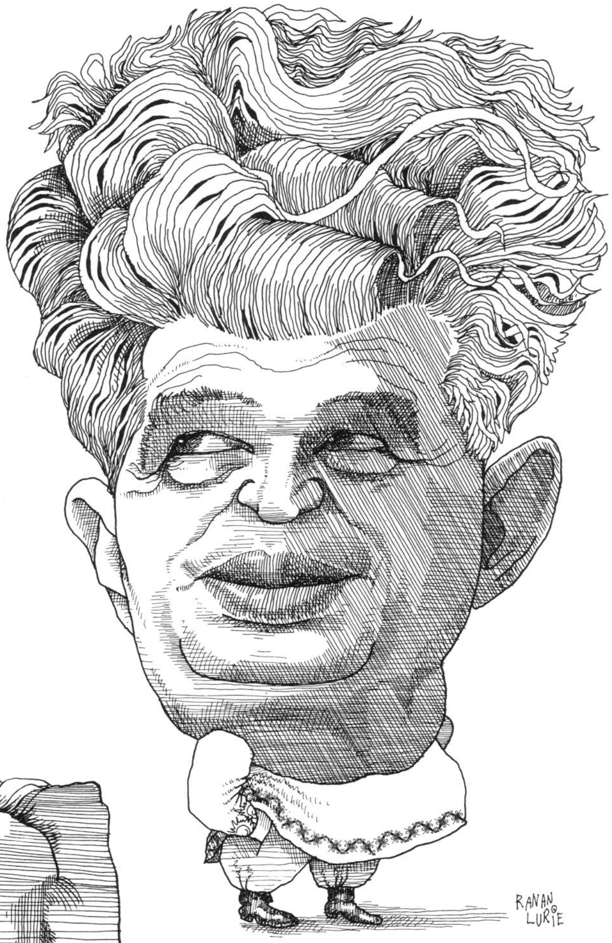
RANAN
LURIE

President Nicolae Ceausescu
of Rumania

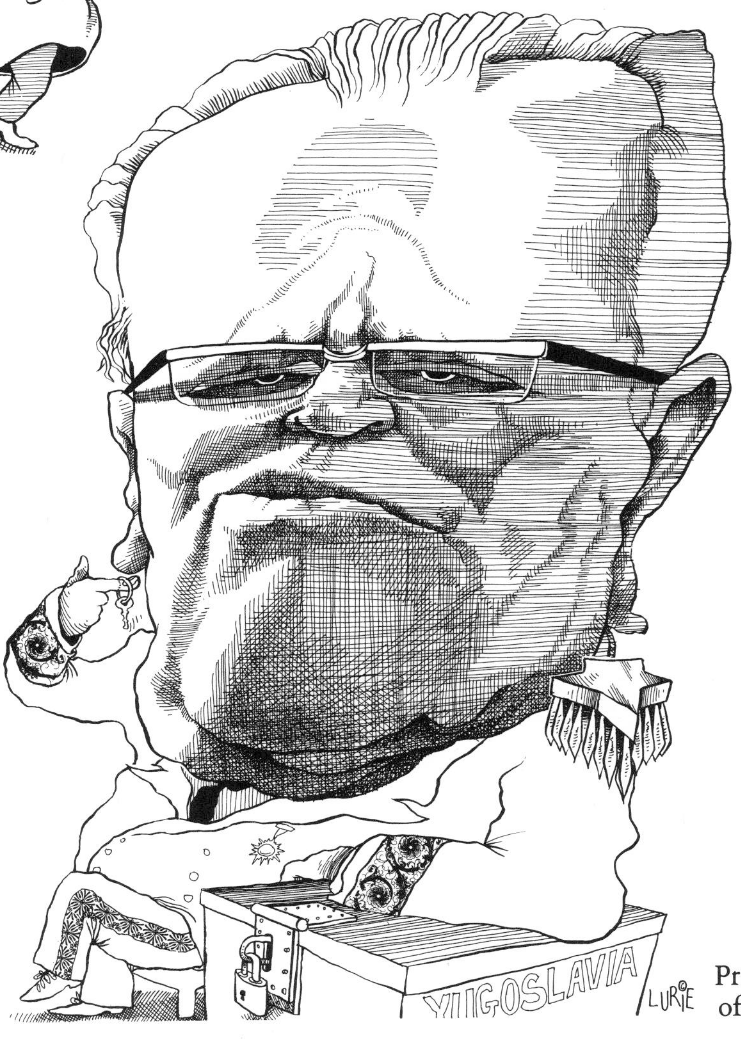
YUGOSLAVIA
YUGOSLAVIA
LURIE

President Tito
of Yugoslavia

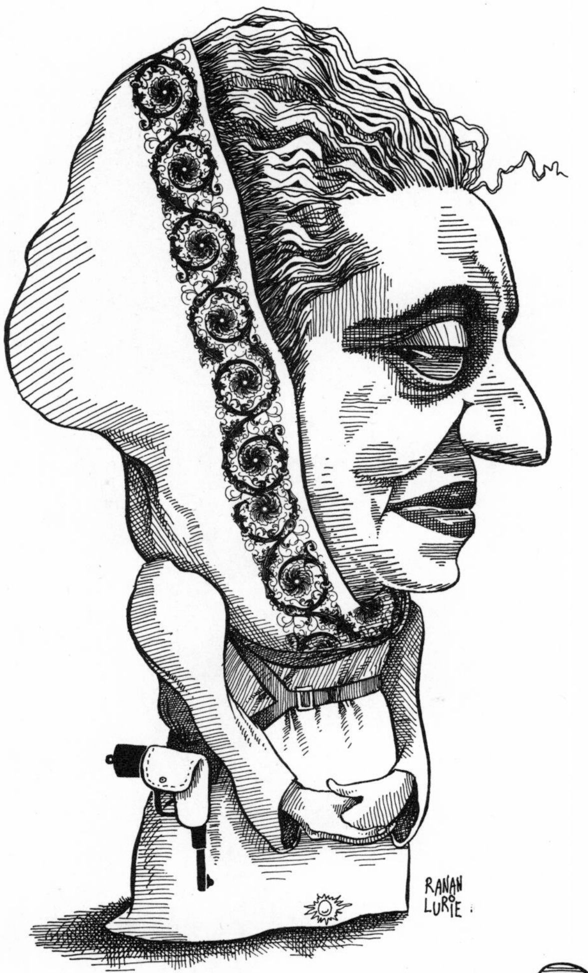
RANAN LURIE

Indira Gandhi
Dictator of India

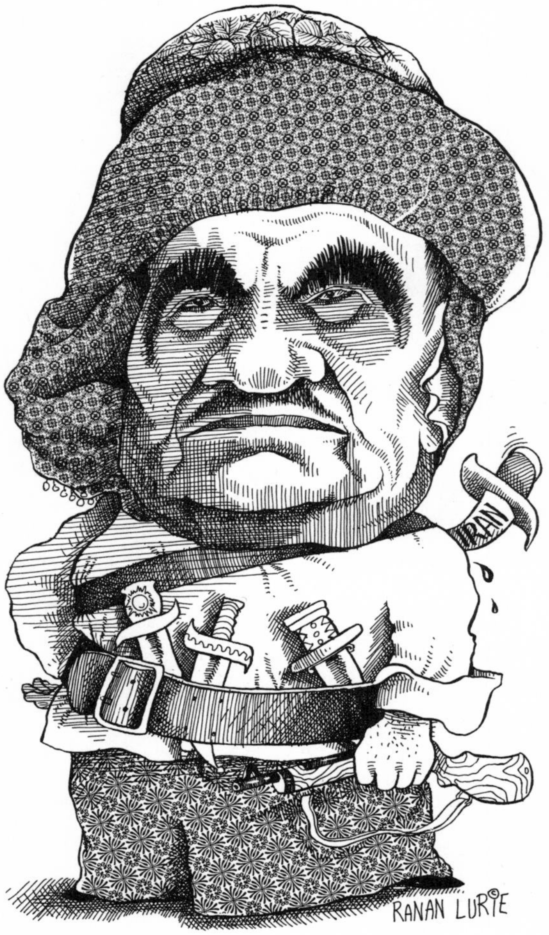
RANAN LURIE

General Mustafa Al-Barzani
Kurdish Leader

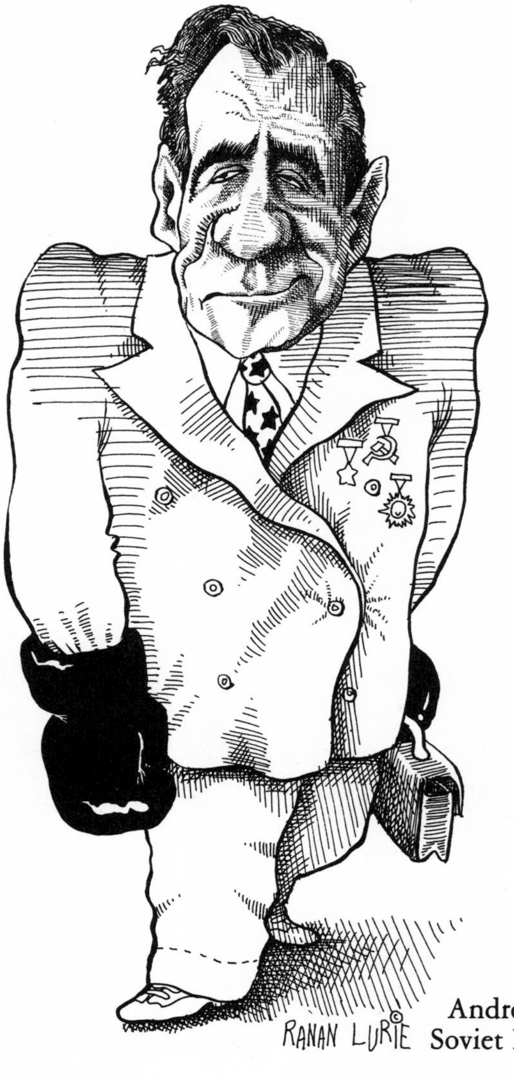
RANAN LURIE

Andrei A. Gromyko
Soviet Foreign Minister

RANAN LURIE

Richard Helms
Former CIA Chief

LURIE

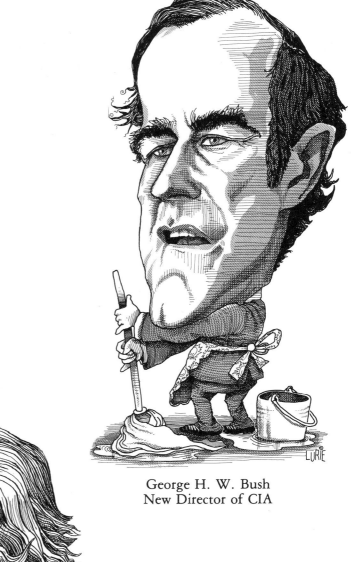

George H. W. Bush
New Director of CIA

1976
RANAN LURIE

Senator Henry Jackson

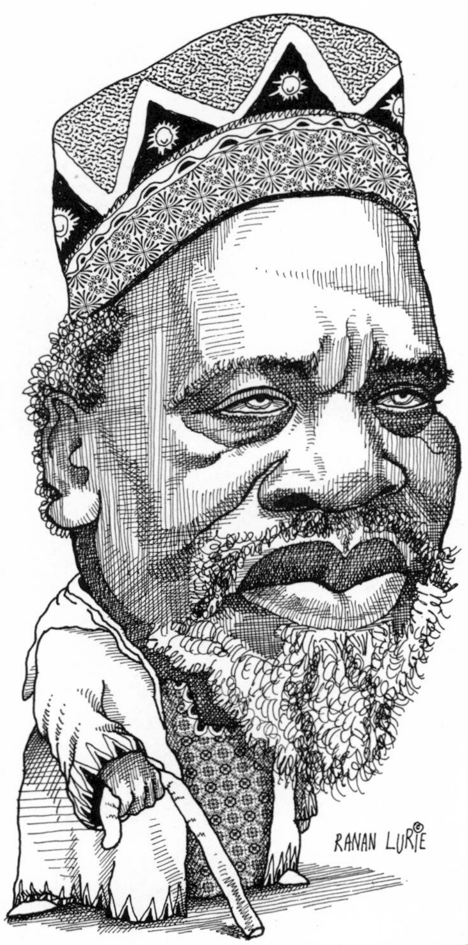
RANAN LURIE

President Jomo Kenyatta
of Kenya

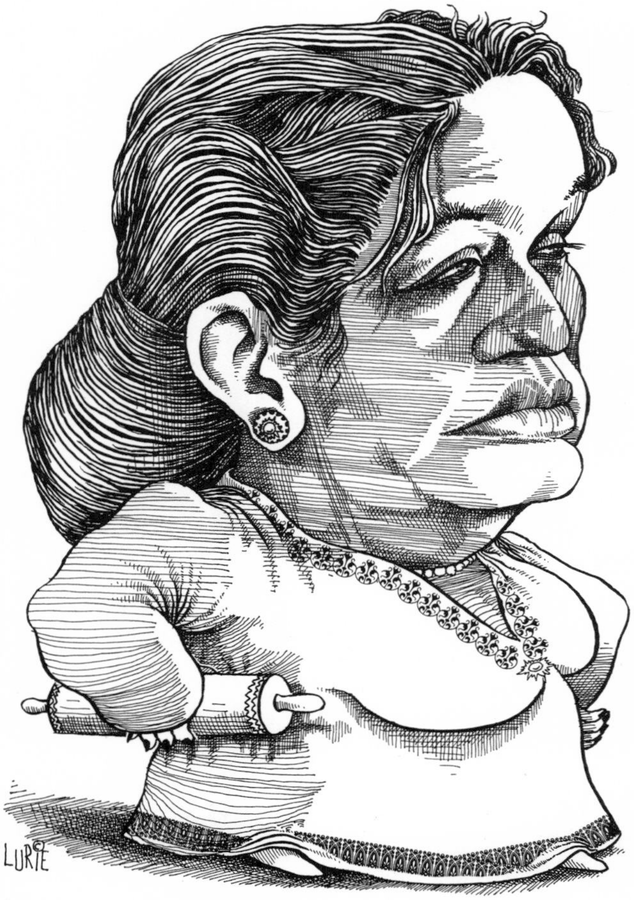
LURIE

Sirimavo Bandaranaike
Prime Minister of Sri Lanka

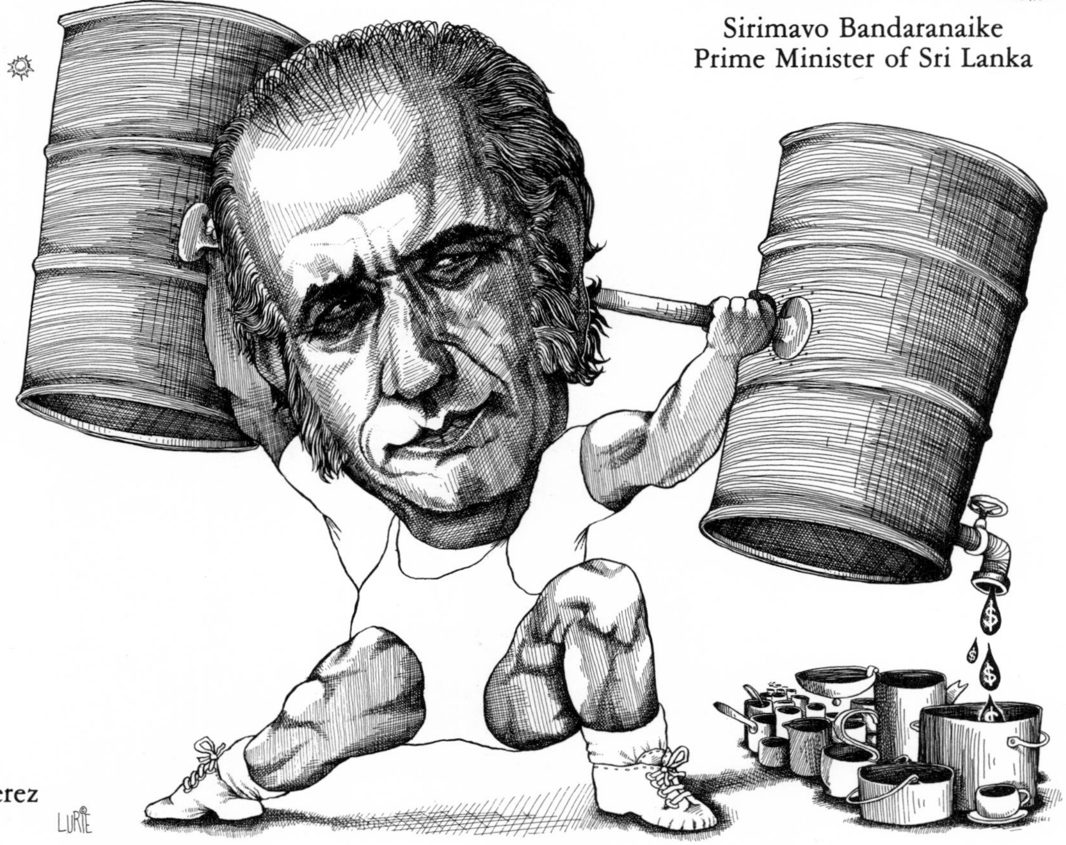
LURIE

President Carlos Andres Perez
of Venezuela

LURIE
UN

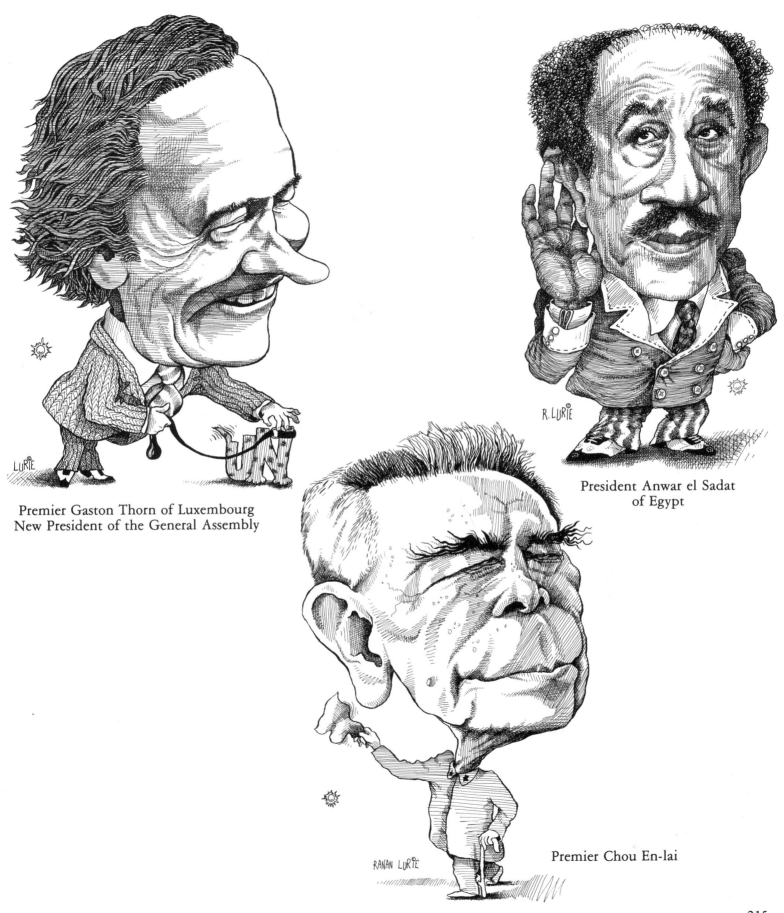

Premier Gaston Thorn of Luxembourg
New President of the General Assembly

R. LURIE

President Anwar el Sadat
of Egypt

RANAN LURIE

Premier Chou En-lai

1976

Lurie: ON CARICATURE

When I was part of a group of American political cartoonists visiting Russia, we were invited to the editorial board meeting of *Crocodile* magazine, the biggest satirical magazine in the world—circulation of about 6 million. We were treated very nicely. We had some coffee and tea and cookies, and the chairman of the board eventually asked, through an interpreter, ''Any questions?'' I raised my hand and asked, ''Why don't we have any caricatures of Soviet leaders in Russian papers? I see from your newspapers that you can do wonderful caricatures of other people, including Uncle Sam and American presidents.'' A crowd of people immediately gathered around the editor-in-chief to come up with the proper answer—it looked like a football team trying to work out its strategy. They came to a conclusion and the chairman, through his interpreter, said with a very serious face, ''Mr. Lurie, you do caricatures of leaders when they make mistakes. Thank goodness our Communist leaders really don't make mistakes. Therefore, we have no need for drawing caricatures.'' Period.

A caricature is really a portrait with an exclamation mark. A cartoon extends and exaggerates the facts to an absurdity so that the viewer can see things, once and for all, in black and white. We try to eliminate the grey areas as much as possible. This results in some kind of natural, funny exaggeration.

Some presidents help cartoonists by their deeds more than others. Nixon, God bless him, really made life easy for cartoonists. Coming basically from a middle-class, Quaker background, he built imperial dreams which were such a fertile ground for funny ideas that good cartoons sprang out everywhere.

Lurie: ON SYMBOLS FOR OPEC

Sooner or later we are going to have to come up with an appropriate OPEC symbol, a person who will represent OPEC the same way that Uncle Sam represents the United States. In all fairness, drawing OPEC only as an Arab is not right since OPEC includes important non-Arab countries such as Nigeria and Venezuela. We will have to find a single symbol to represent several major nationalities that comprise OPEC. At this moment, the Arabs are the dominant figures in OPEC so perhaps the Arab kaffiyeh will command the scene for the next few years.

The New York Times Special Features 1-1-76

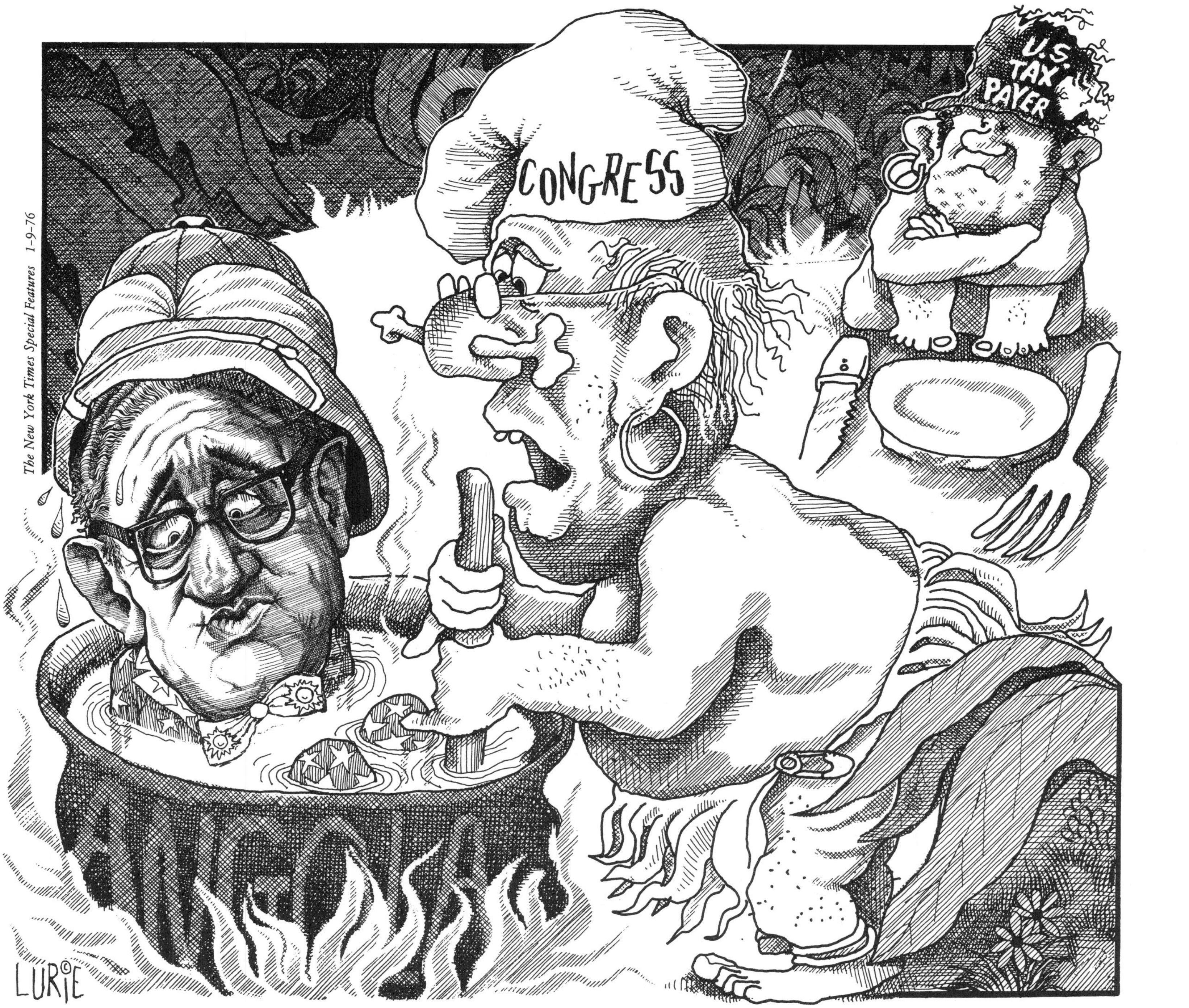
CONGRESS
U.S. TAX PAYER
The New York Times Special Features 1-9-76
LURIE

"SORRY, BUT BIG CHIEF WANTS YOU WELL-DONE!"

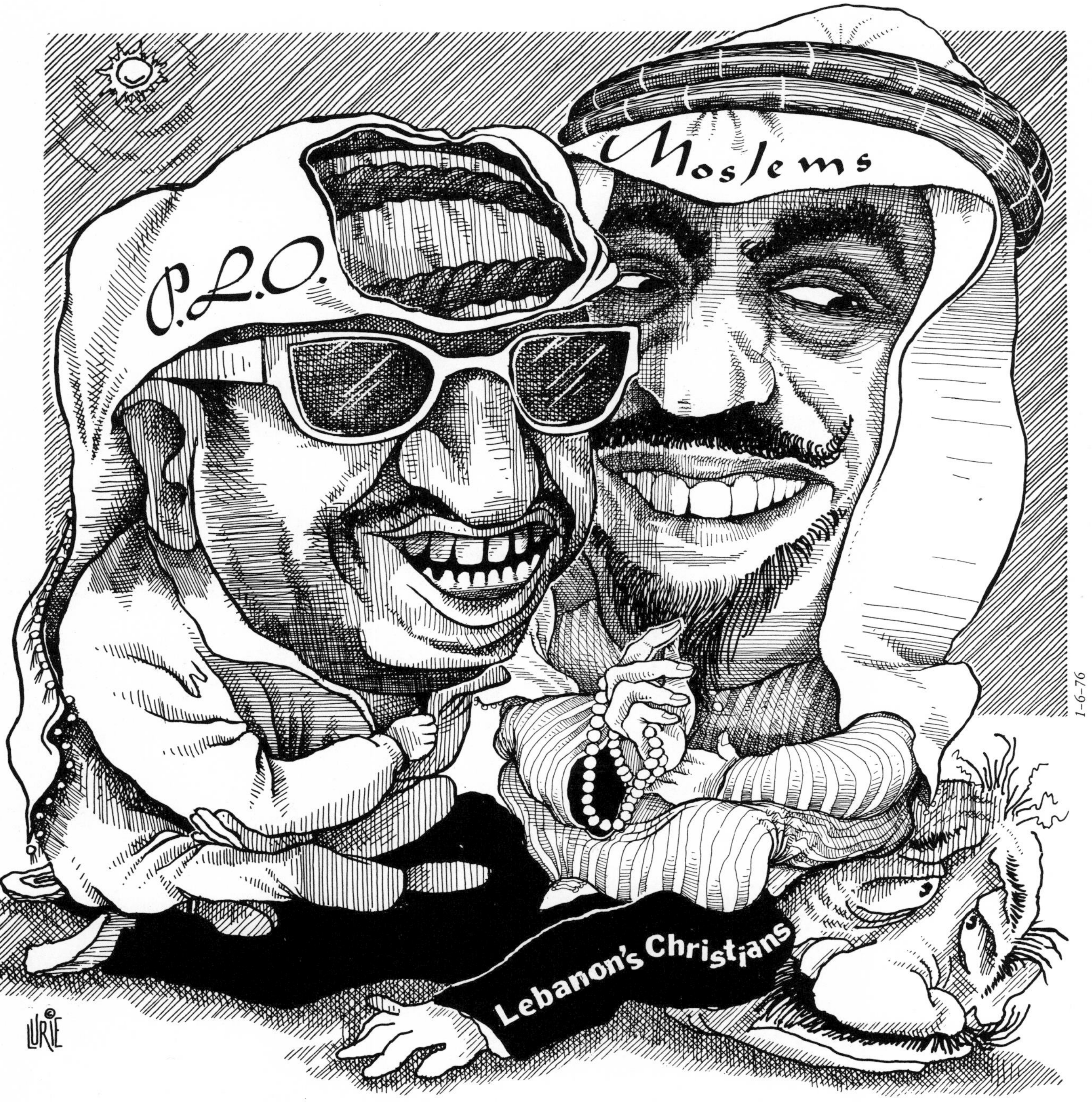

Moslems
P.L.O.
Lebanon's Christians
1-6-76
LURIE

"SEE HOW SITTING DOWN TOGETHER SOLVES OUR DIFFERENCES?!"

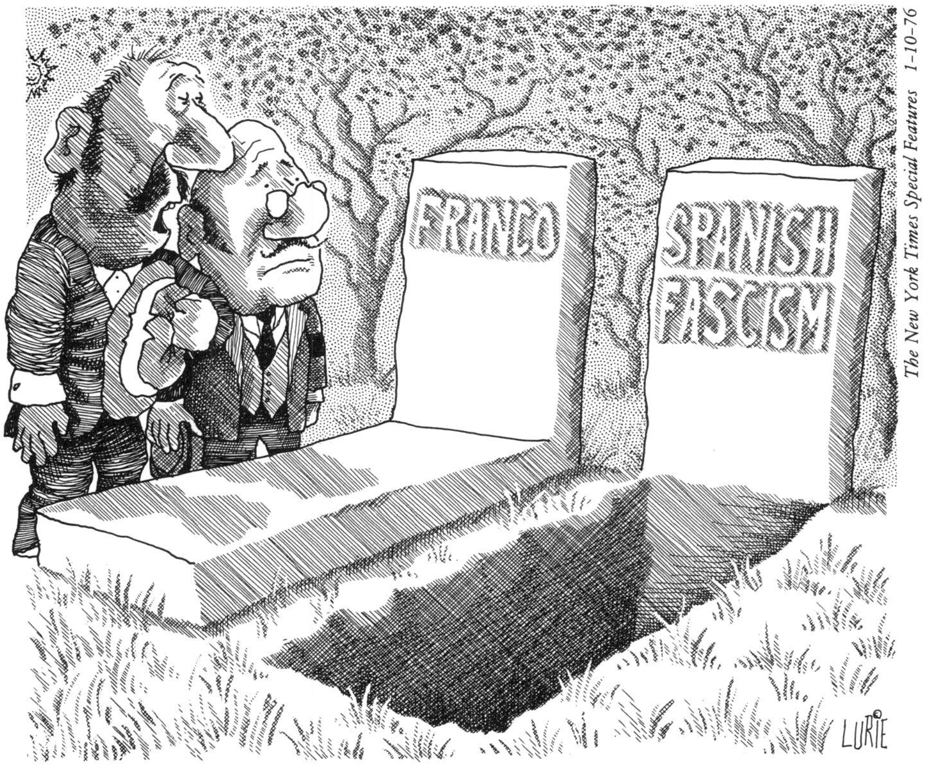
The New York Times Special Features 1-10-76
FRANCO
SPANISH FASCISM
LURIE

"IT'LL BE A NICE REUNION."

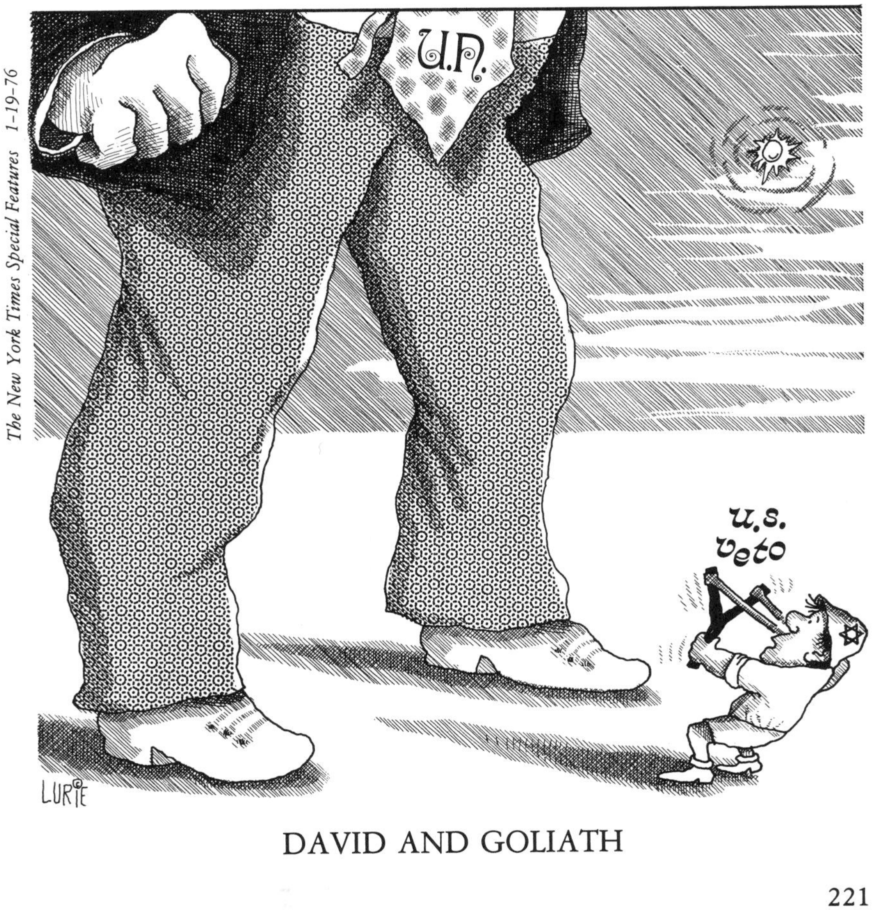
The New York Times Special Features 1-19-76
U.N.
U.S. veto
LURIE

DAVID AND GOLIATH

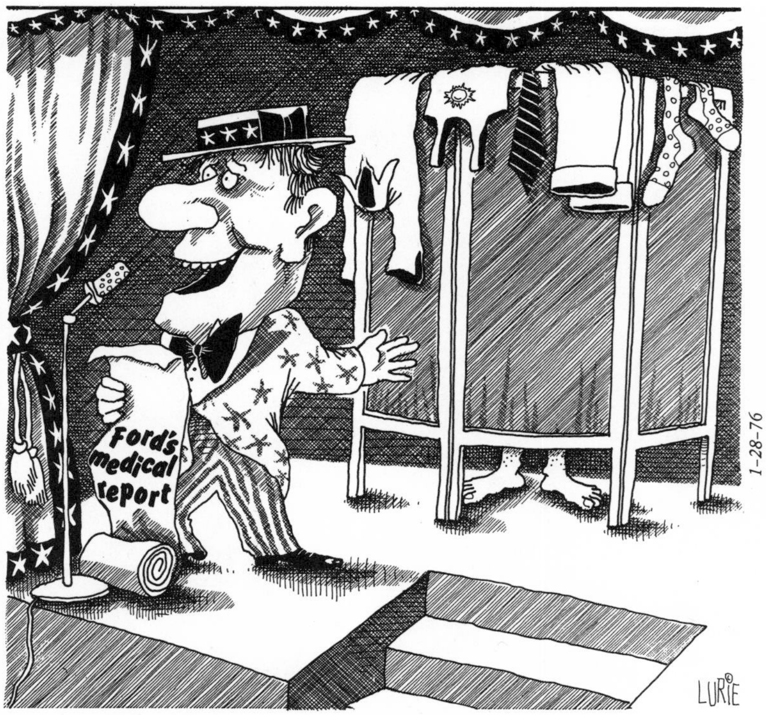
Ford's medical report
1-28-76
LURIE

"LADIES AND GENTLEMEN—
THE PRESIDENT OF THE UNITED STATES!"

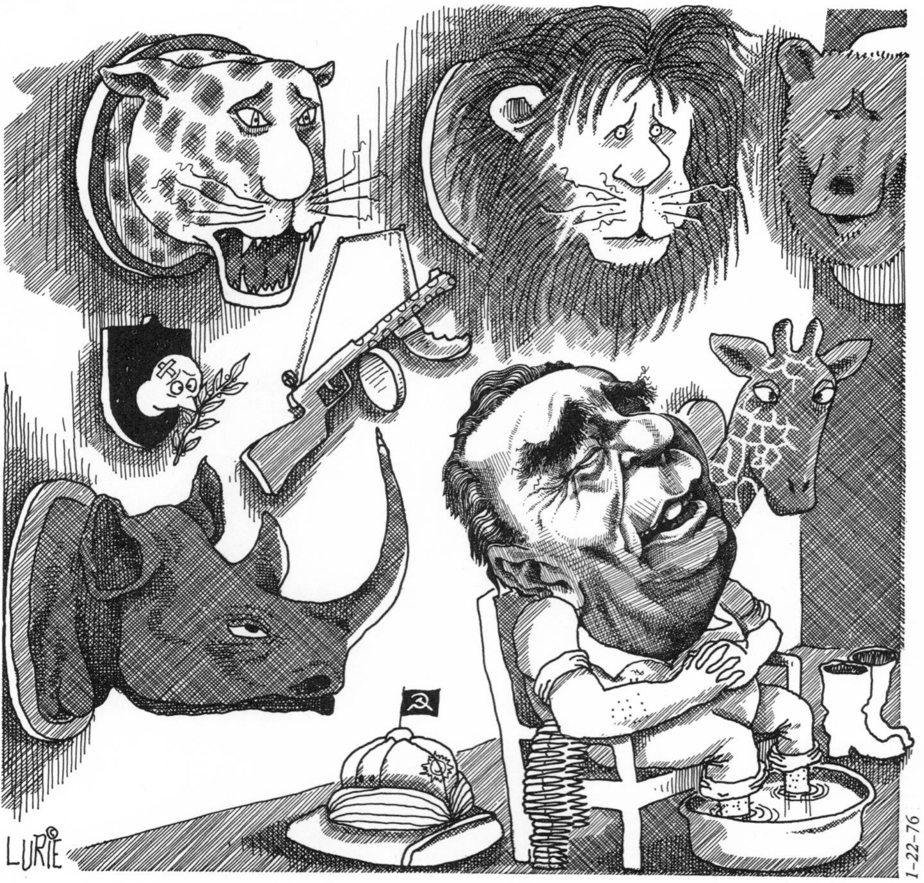
LURIE
1-22-76

BACK FROM THE ANGOLA SAFARI

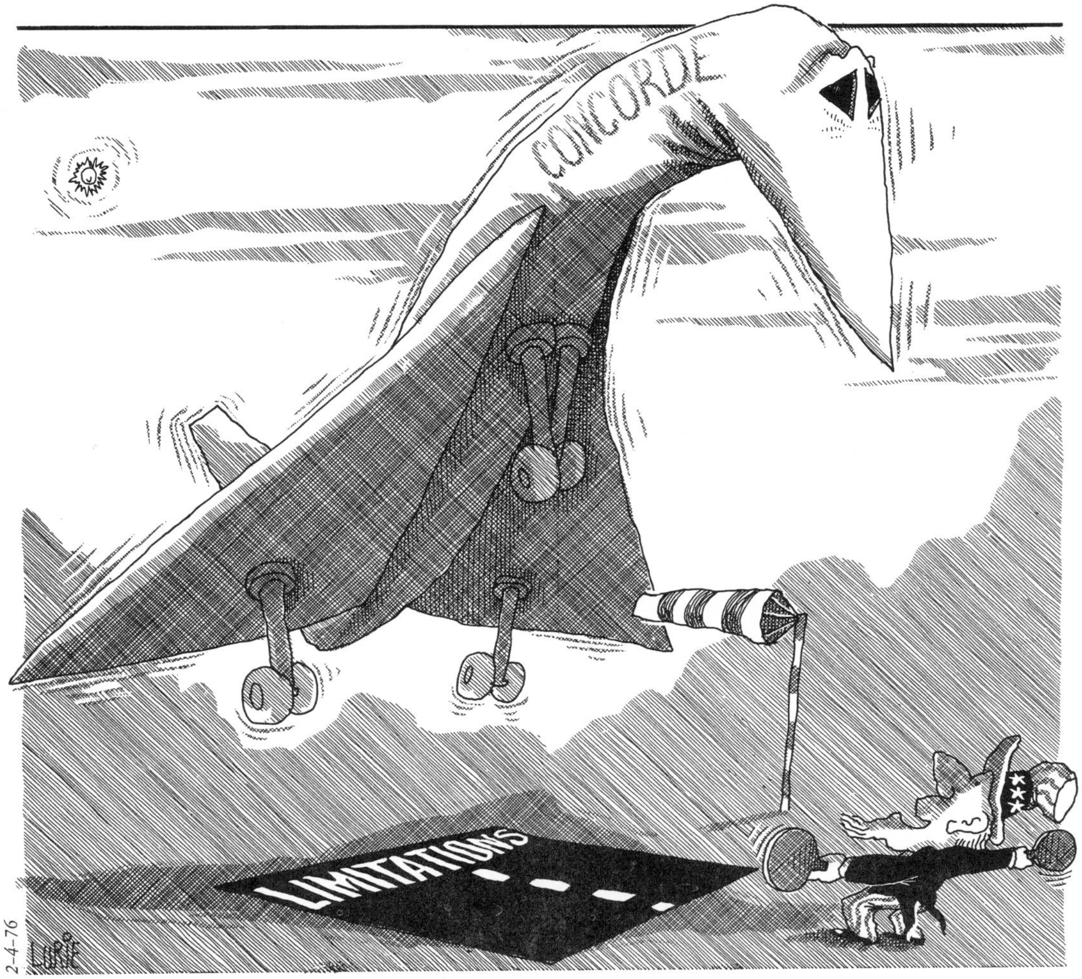
CONCORDE
LIMITATIONS
2-4-76
LURIE

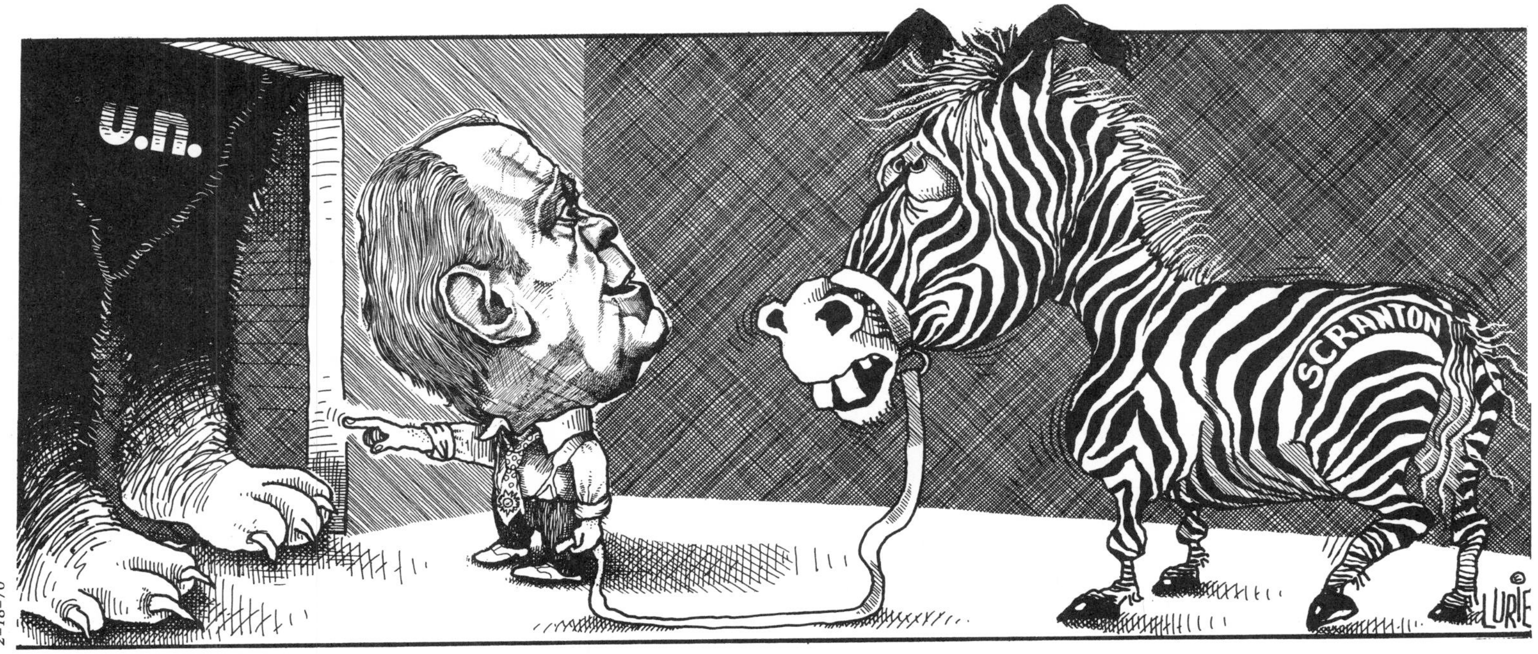
U.N.
SCRANTON
2-18-76
LURIE

"GET 'EM, TIGER!"

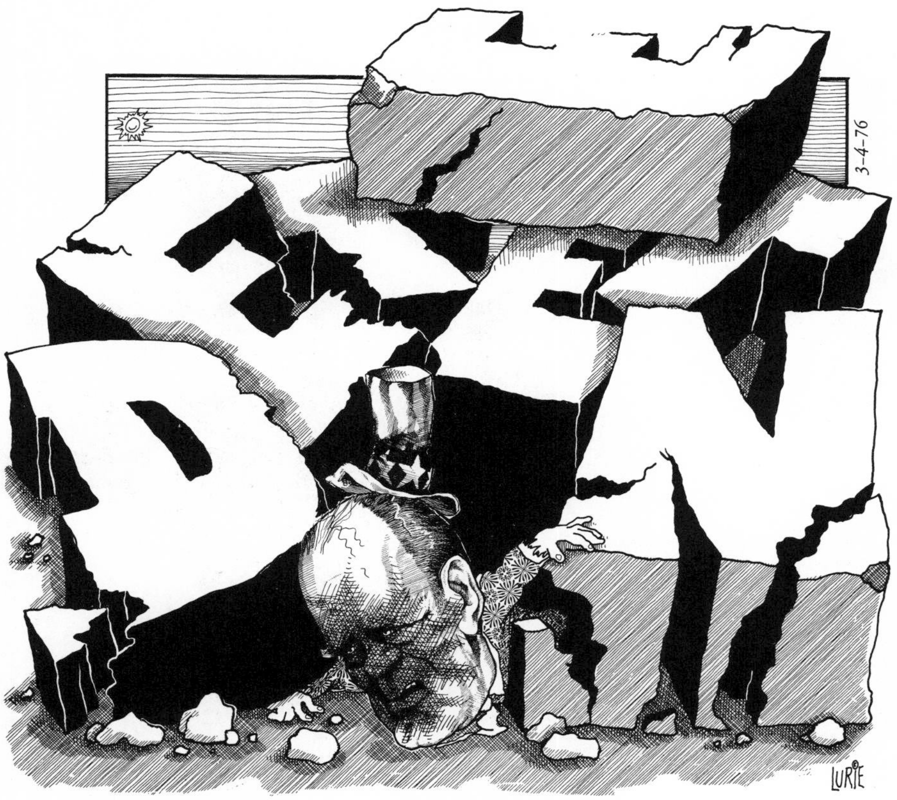
3-4-76
LURIE

"I DON'T USE THE WORD 'DETENTE' ANYMORE!"

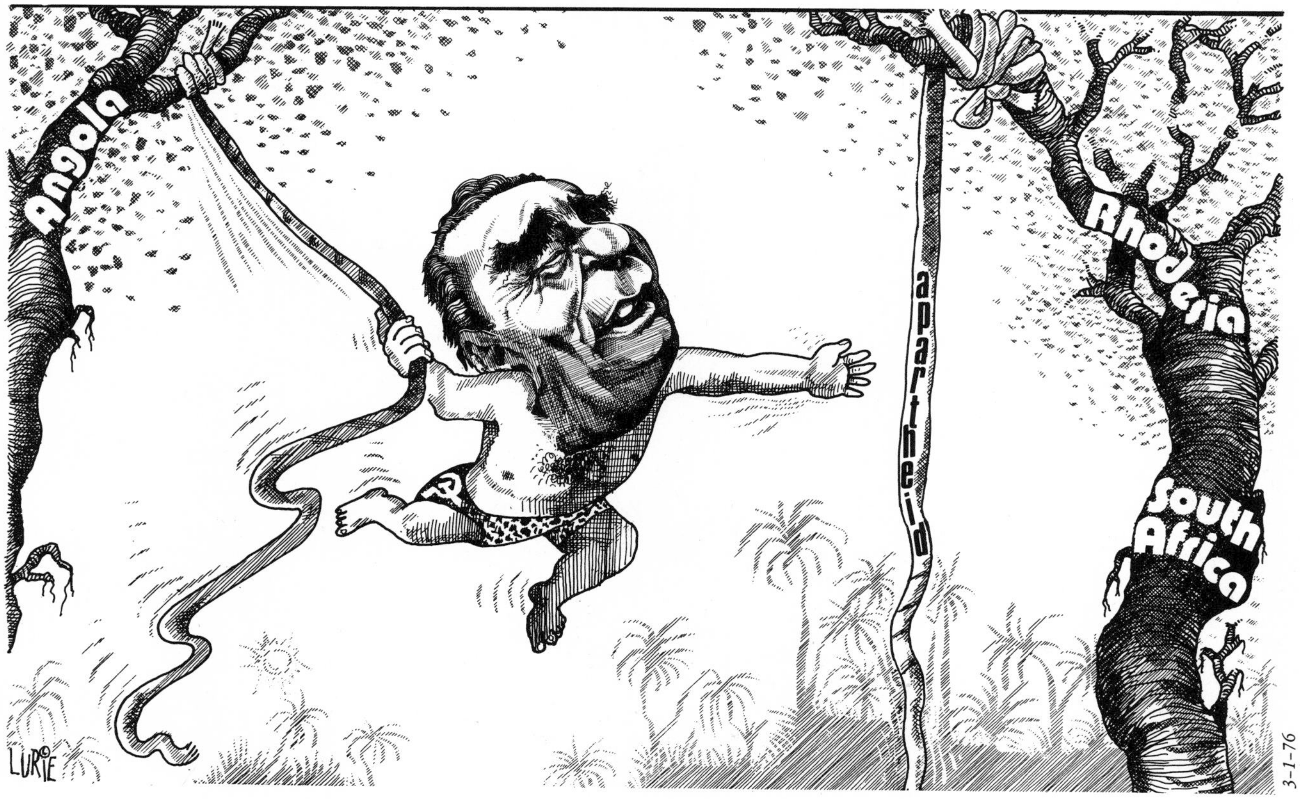
Angola
apartheid
Rhodesia
South Africa
LURIE
3-1-76

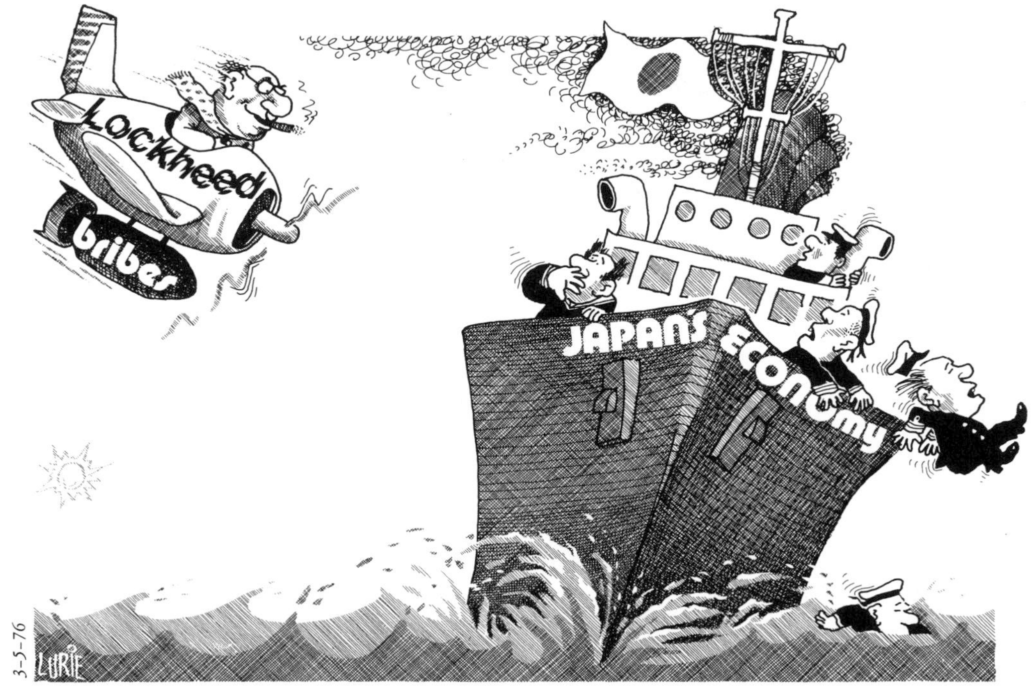
Lockheed
bribes
JAPAN'S ECONOMY
3-5-76
LURIE

KAMIKAZE, INC.

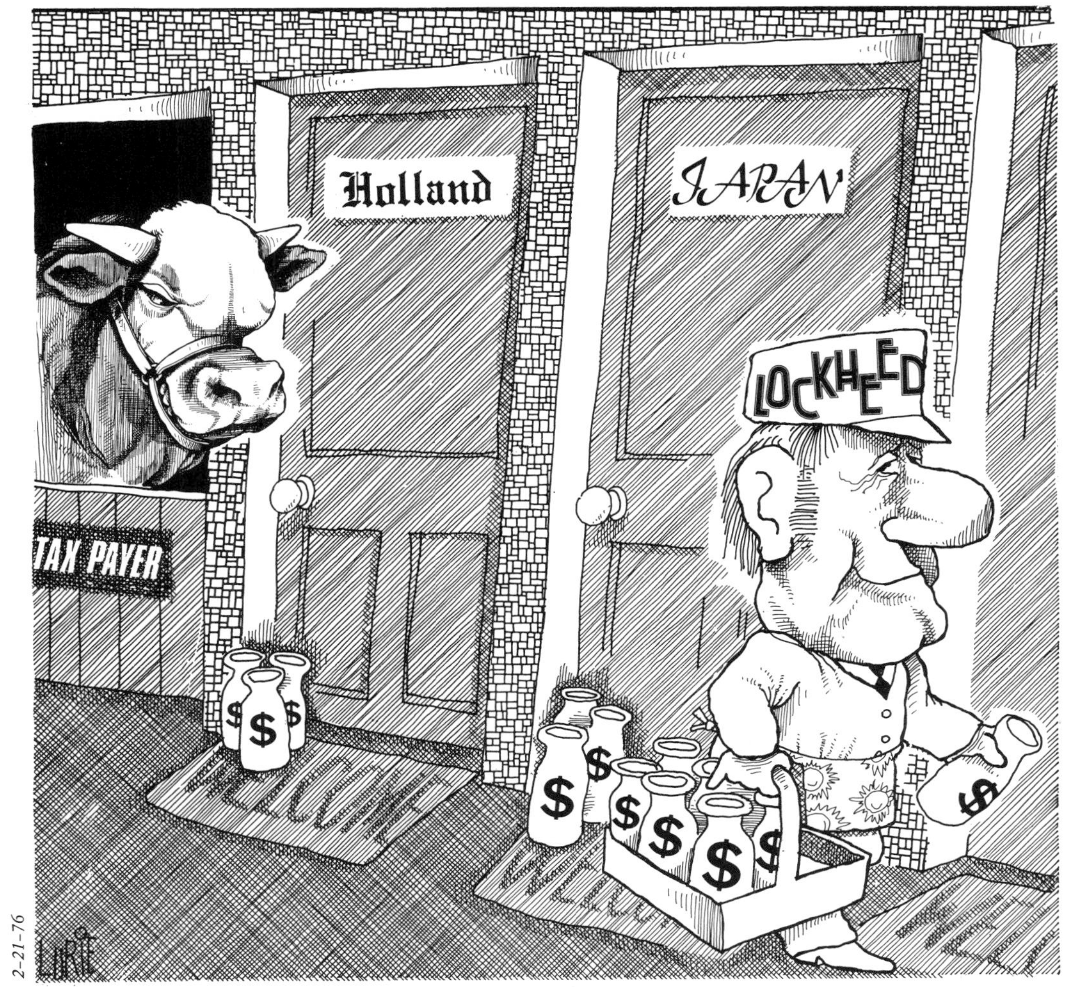
Holland
JAPAN
LOCKHEED
TAX PAYER
WELCOME
2-21-76
LURIE

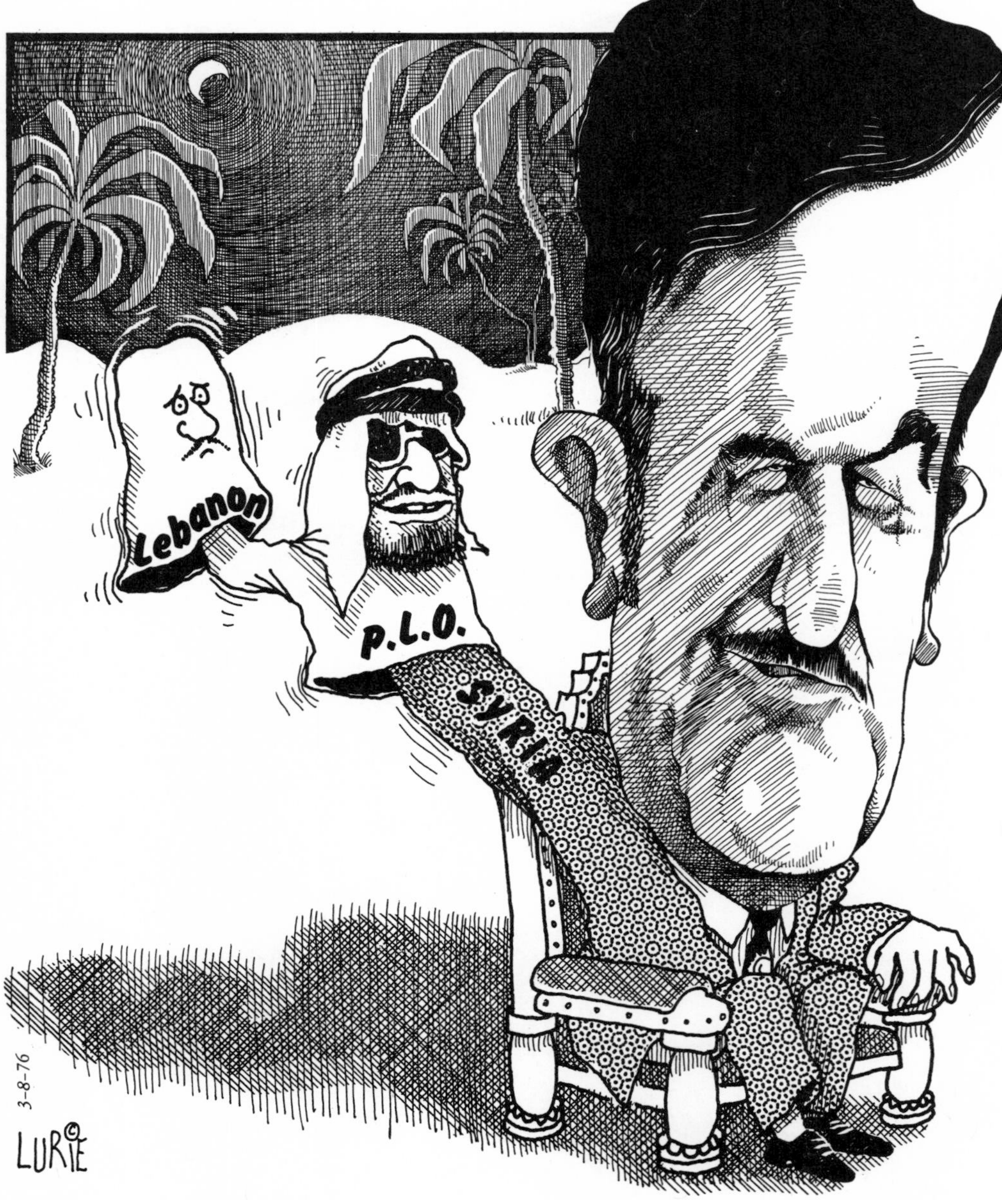
Lebanon
P.L.O.
SYRIA
3-8-76
LURIE

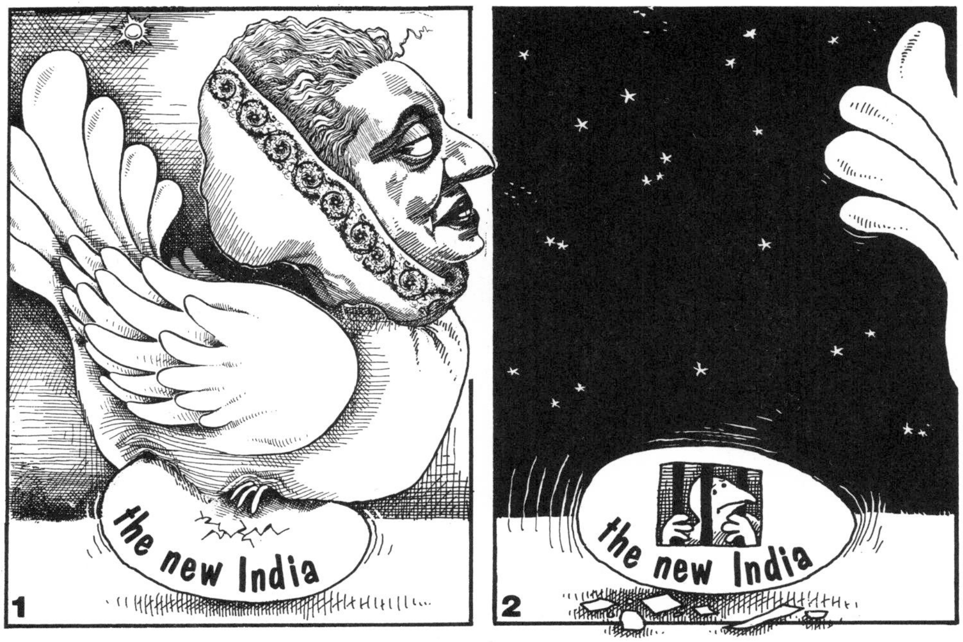
5-9-76
1
the new India
2
the new India

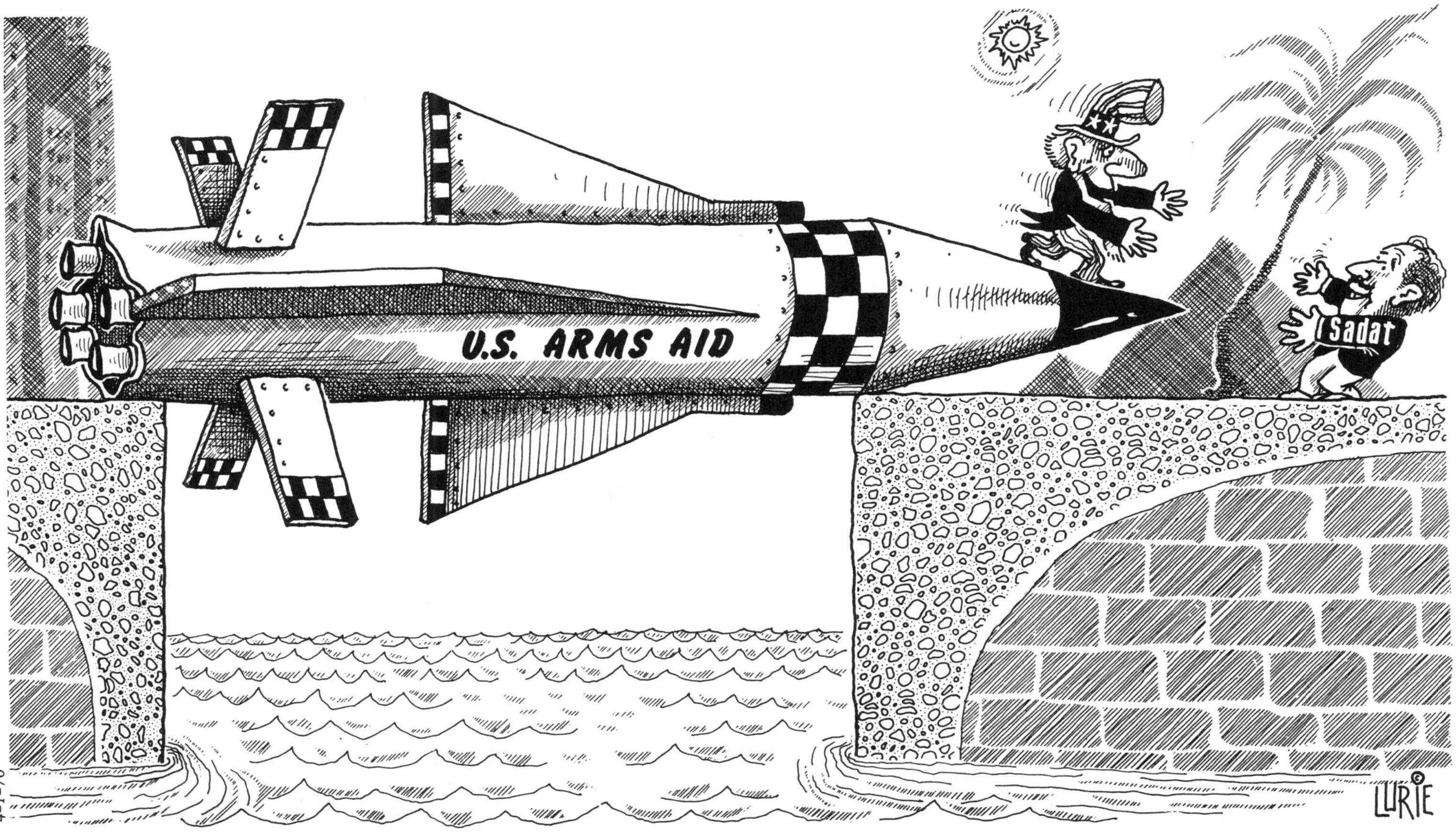
4-1-76
U.S. ARMS AID
Sadat
LURIE

FRIENDSHIP BRIDGE

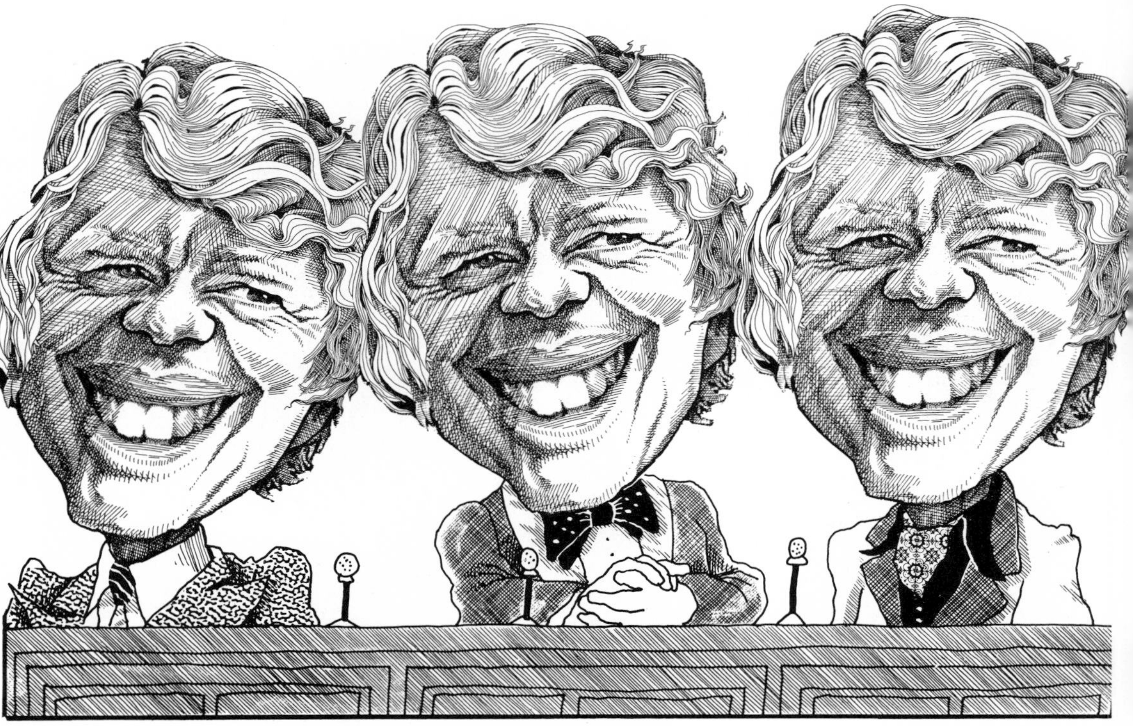

WILL THE *REAL* JIMMY CARTER

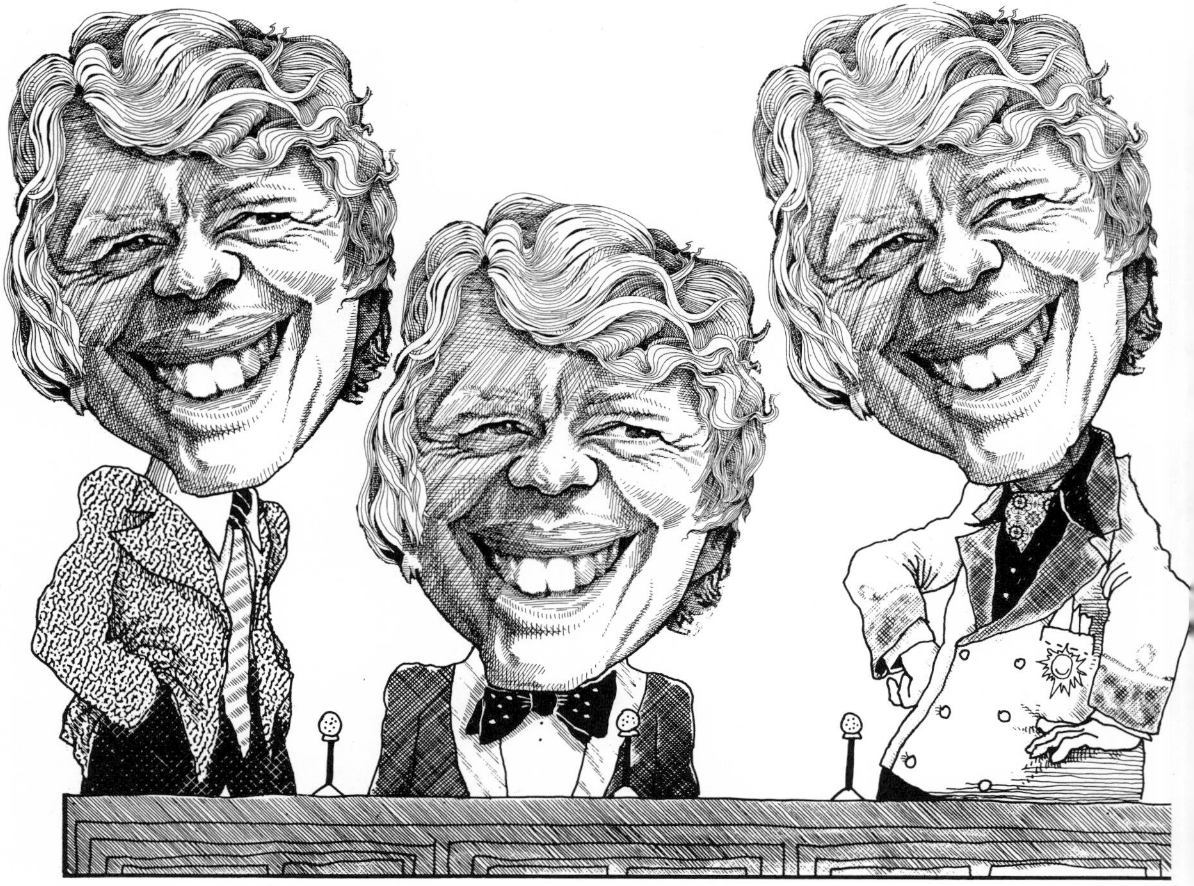

PLEASE STAND UP.''

LURIE

4-13-76

229

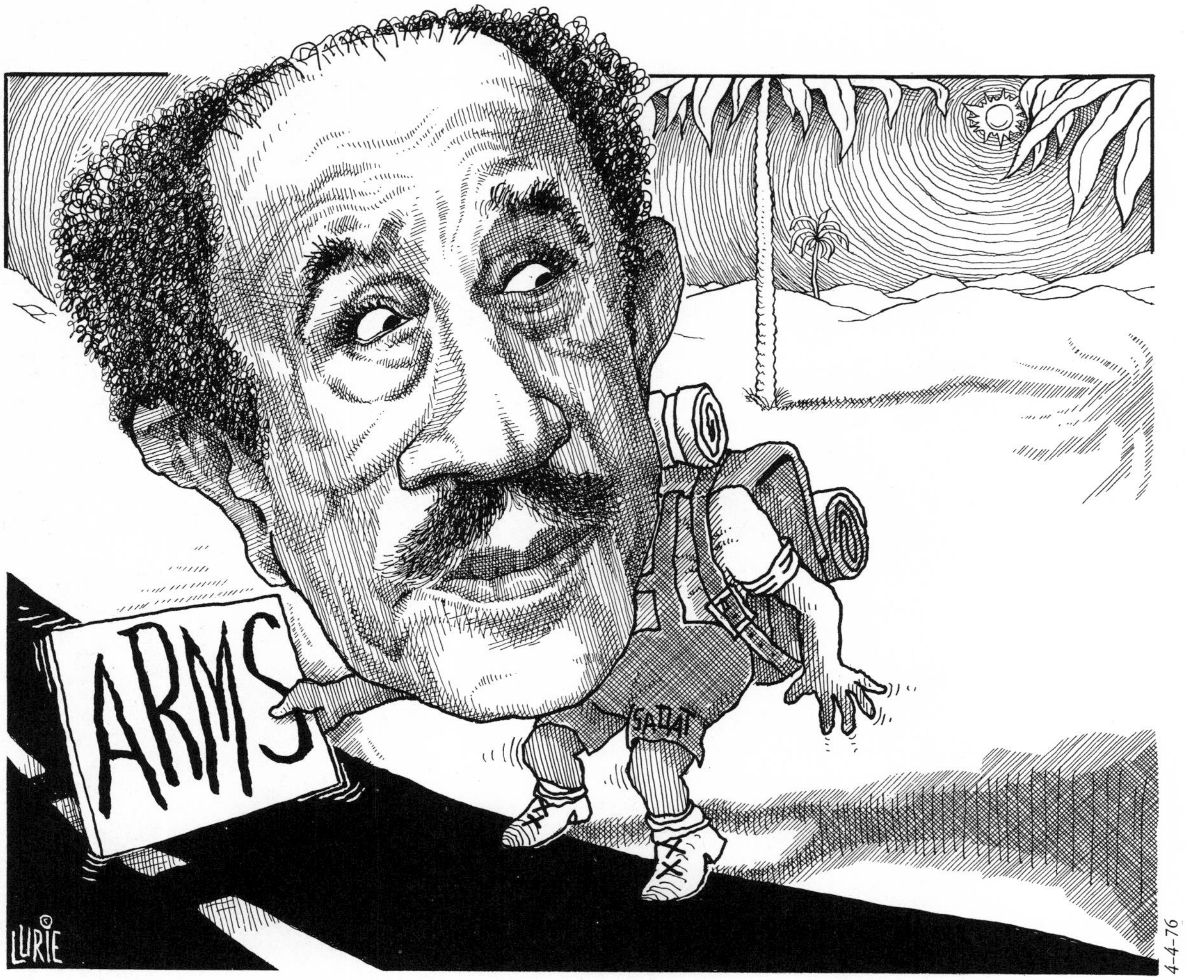
ARMS
SADAT
LURIE
4-4-76

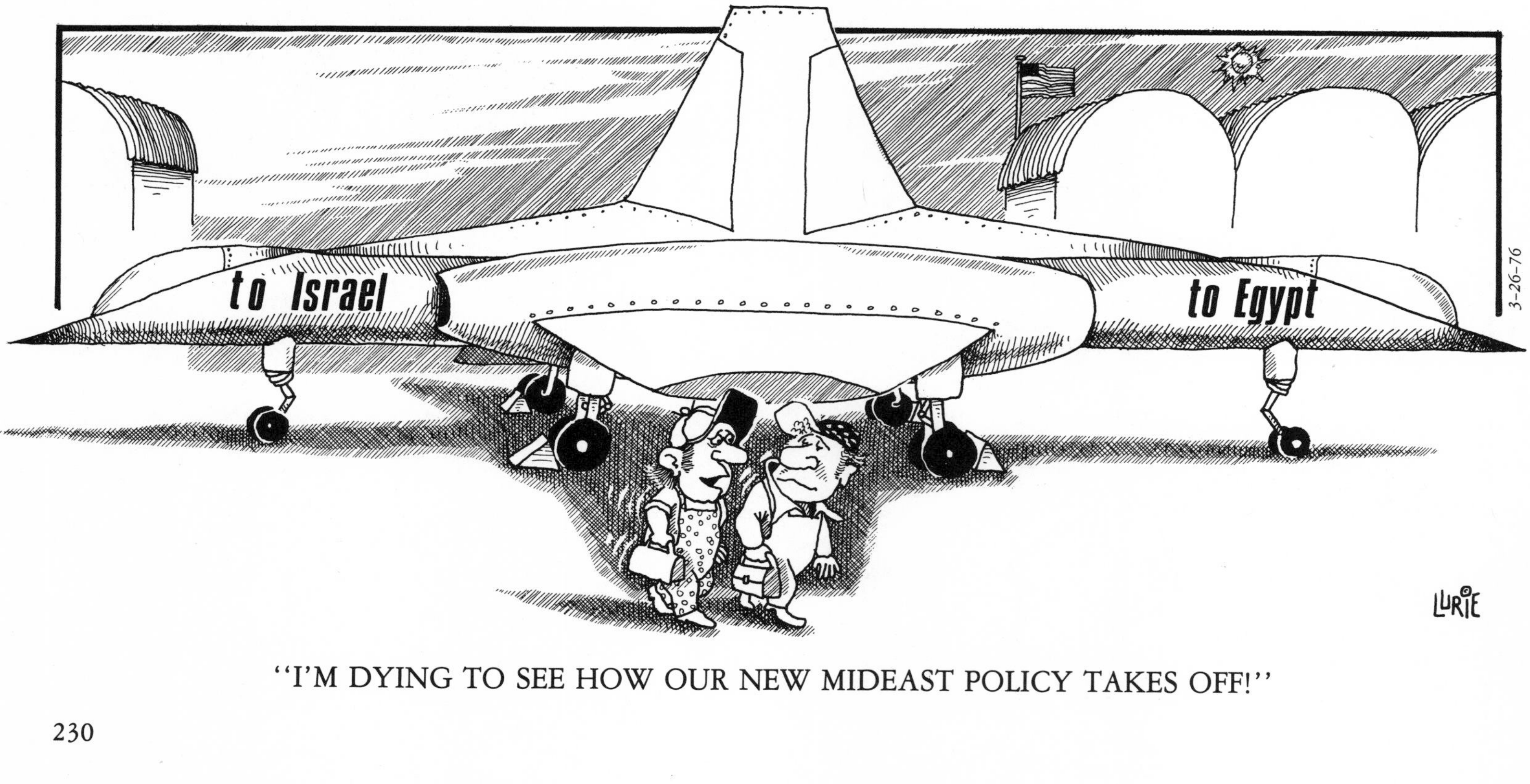
to Israel
to Egypt
3-26-76
LURIE

"I'M DYING TO SEE HOW OUR NEW MIDEAST POLICY TAKES OFF!"

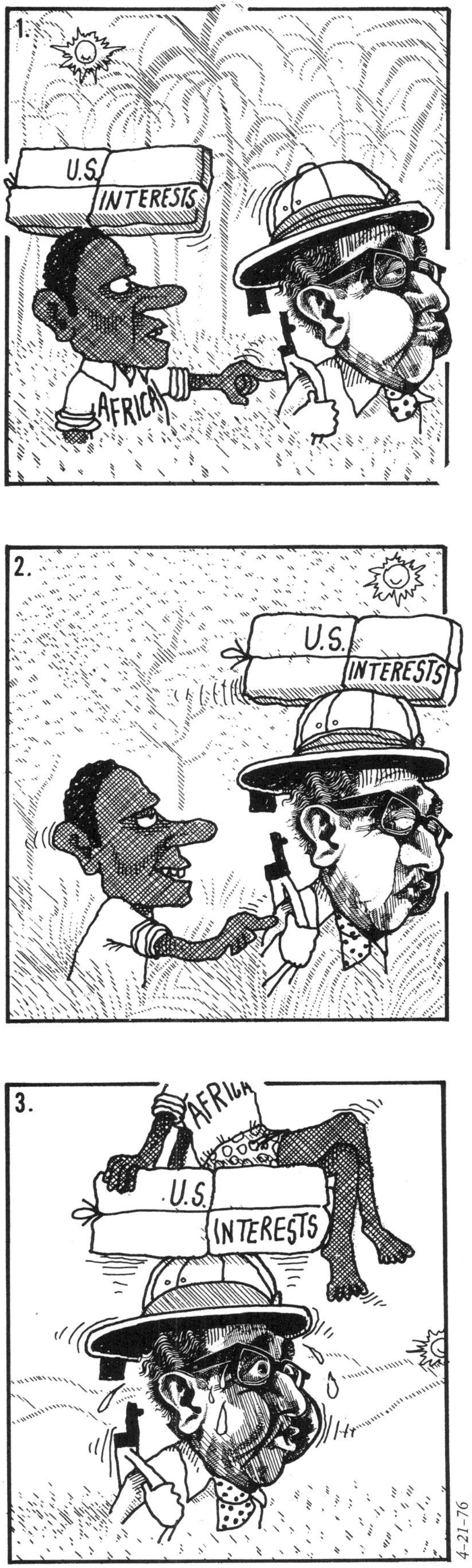
1.
U.S.
INTERESTS
AFRICA
2.
U.S.
INTERESTS
3.
AFRICA
U.S.
INTERESTS
4-21-76

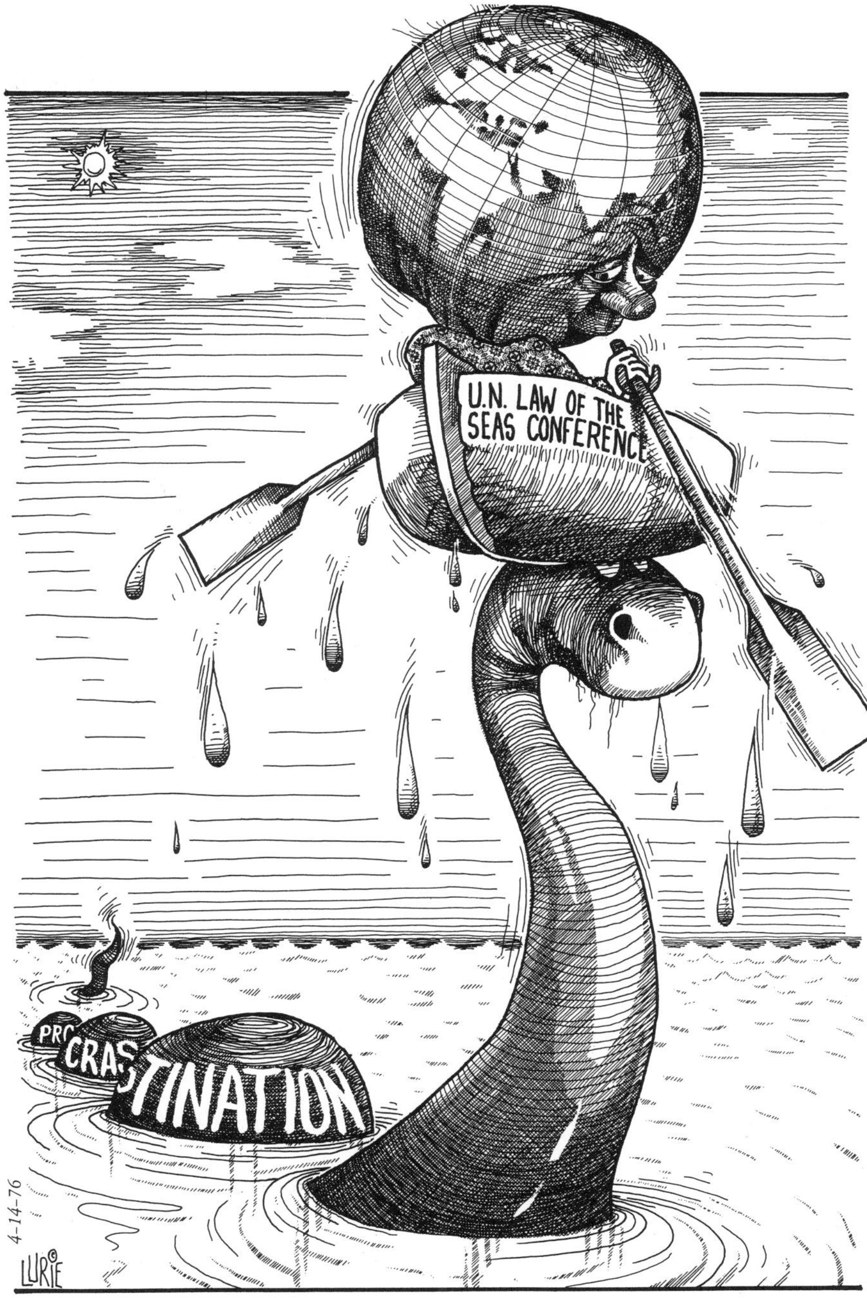
U.N. LAW OF THE SEAS CONFERENCE
PRO
CRAS
TINATION
4-14-76
LURIE ©

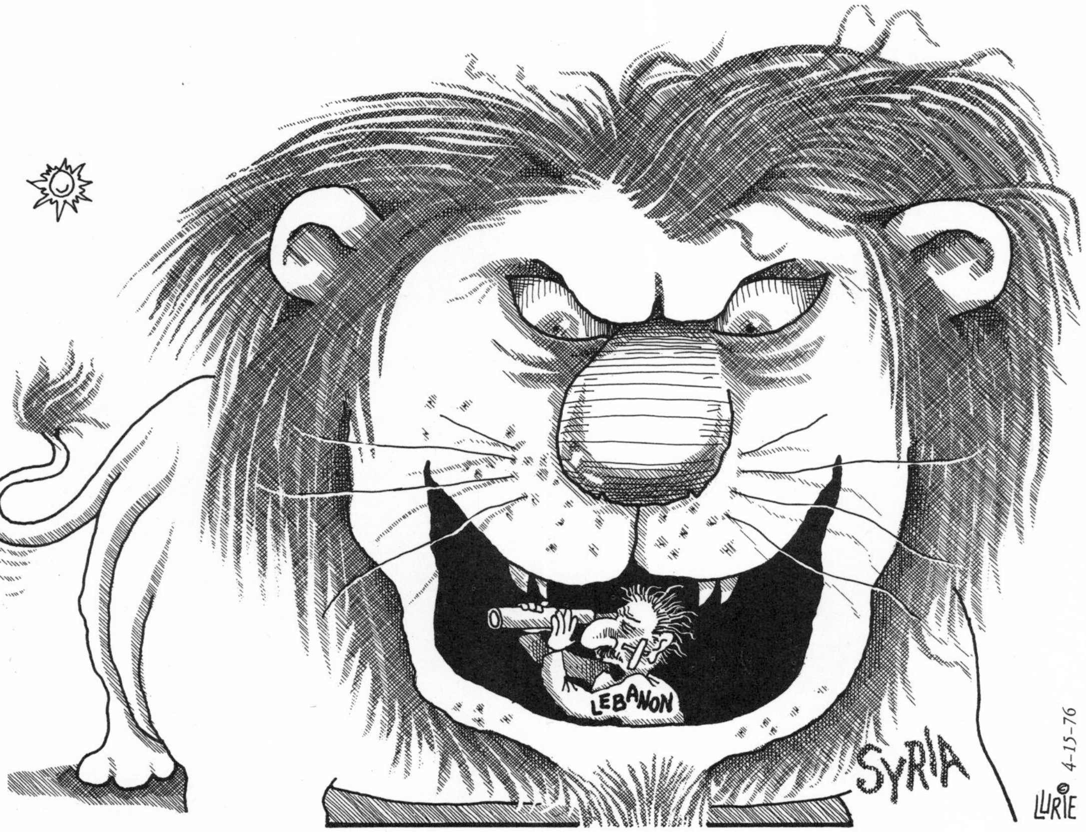
LEBANON
SYRIA
4-15-76
LURIE

''HOW COME I DON'T SEE THE SYRIANS?''

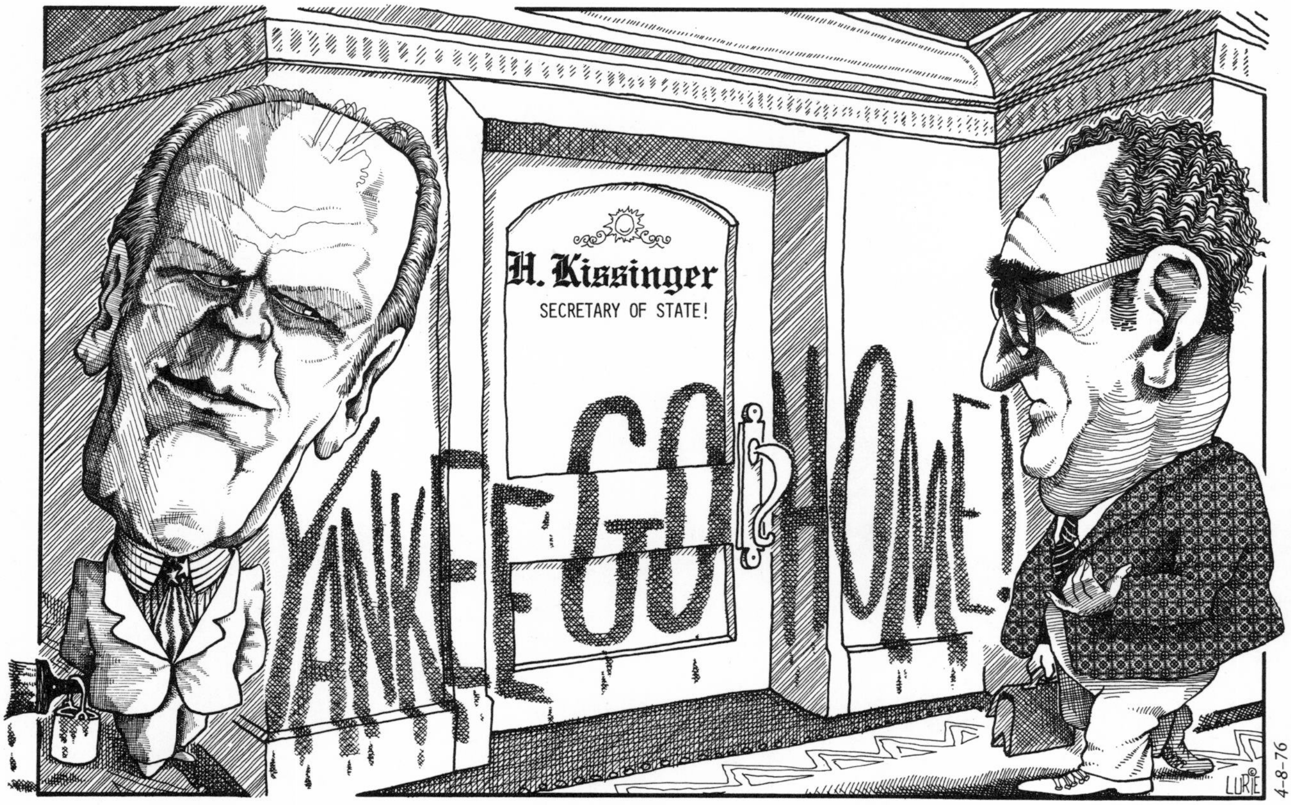
H. Kissinger
SECRETARY OF STATE!
YANKEE GO HOME!
4-8-76
LURIE

''JUST RUMORS, HENRY.''

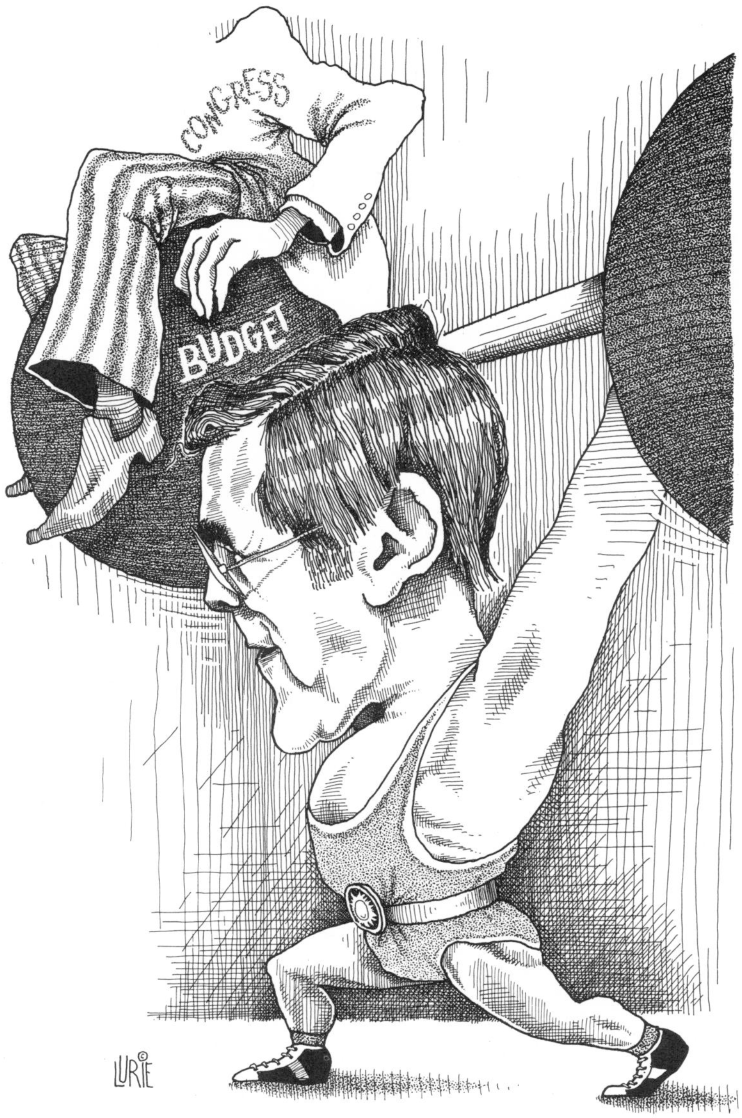
CONGRESS
BUDGET
LURIE

Donald Rumsfeld
Secretary of Defense

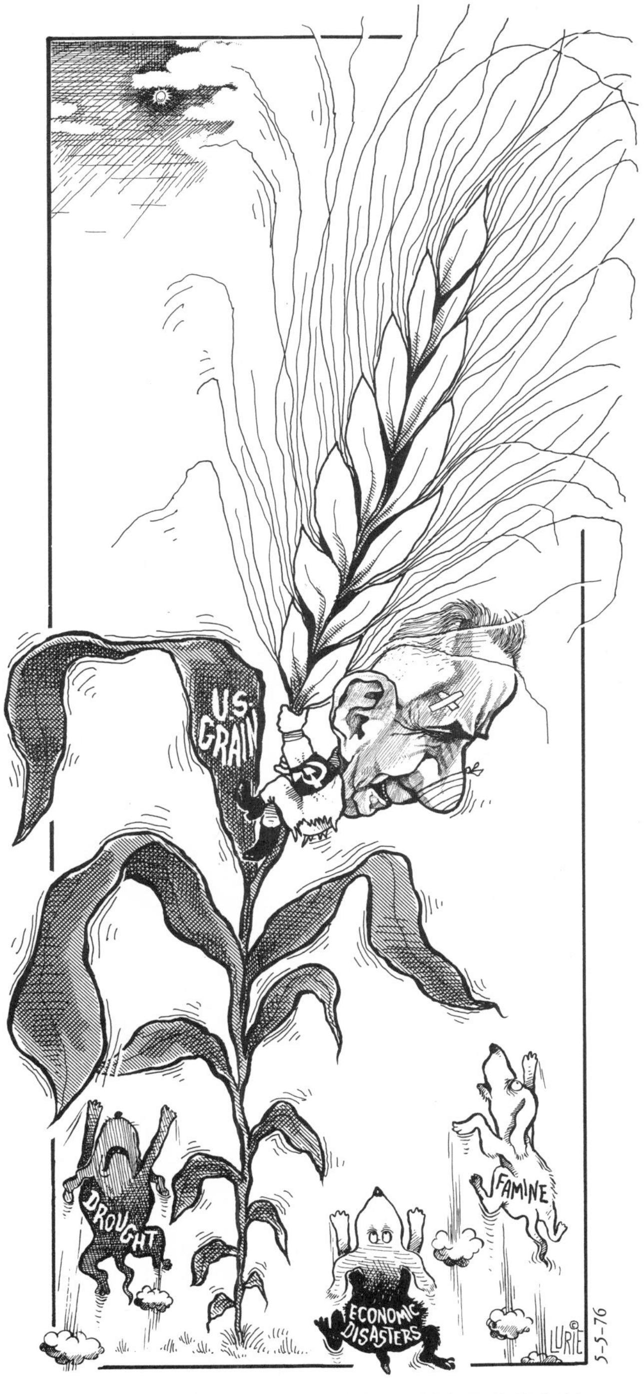
U.S. GRAIN
DROUGHT
FAMINE
ECONOMIC DISASTERS
LURIE
5-5-76

"HA-HA-HA, CAPITALIST DOGS!"

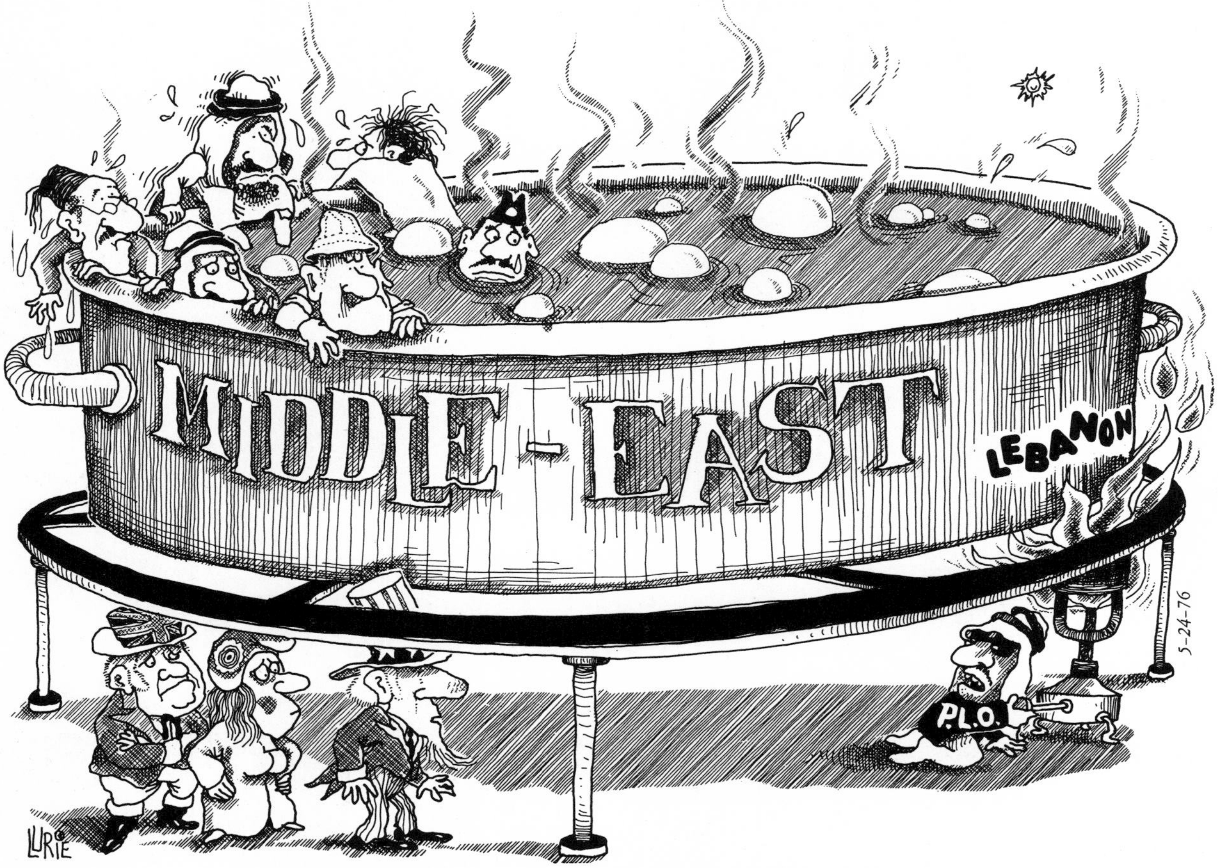
MIDDLE-EAST
LEBANON
P.L.O.
LURIE
5-24-76

"STOP NAGGING—I'M ONLY BOILING *MY* SIDE!"

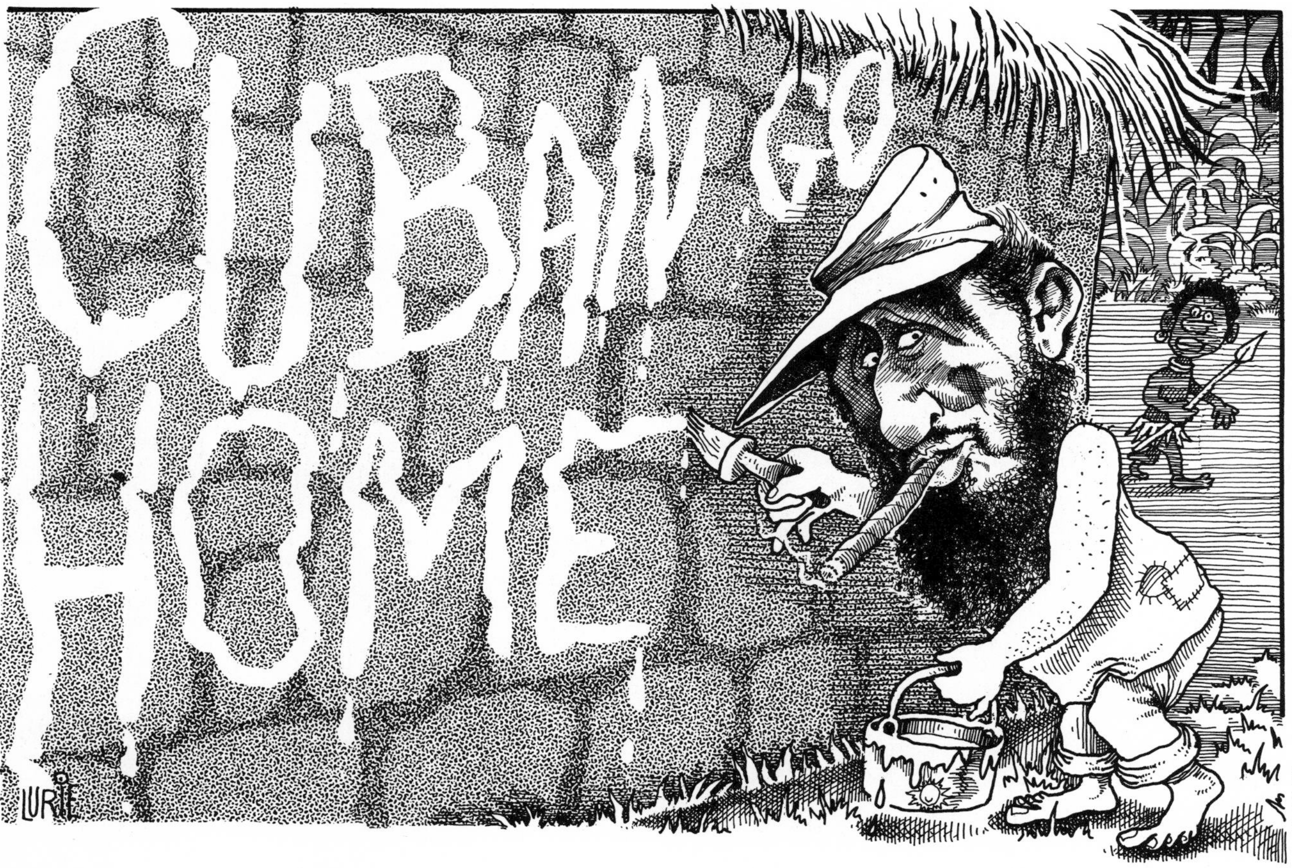
CUBAN GO HOME
LURIE
5-27-76

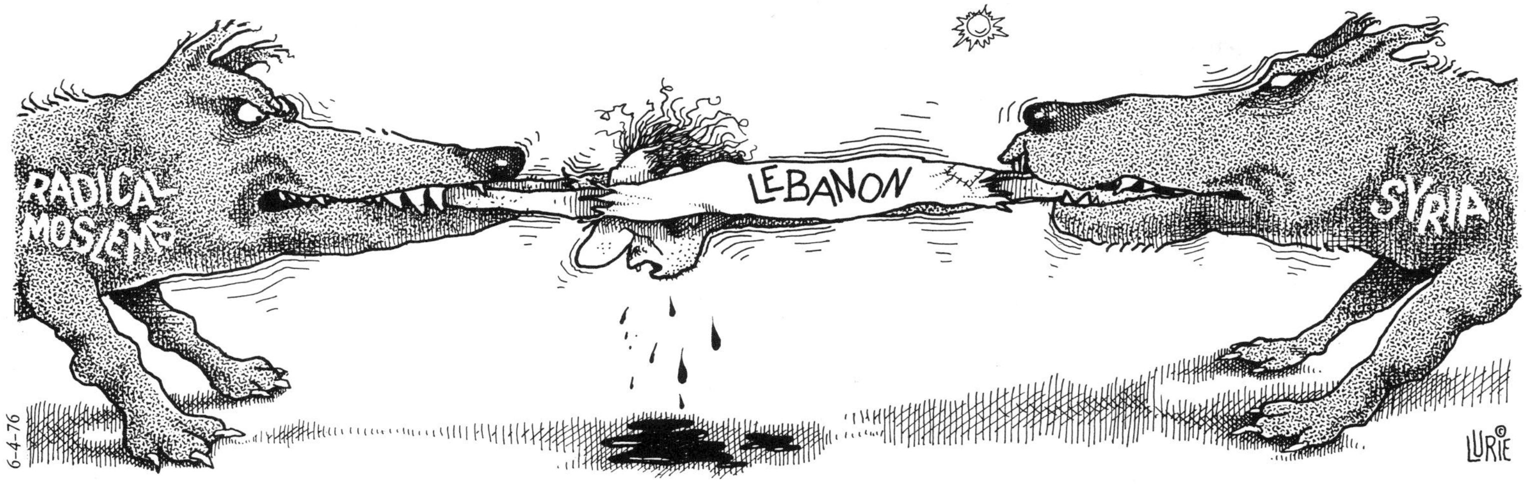
RADICAL MOSLEMS
LEBANON
SYRIA
6-4-76
LURIE©

"I'LL SAVE YOU FROM HIM!"
"NO, *I'LL* SAVE YOU FROM HIM!"

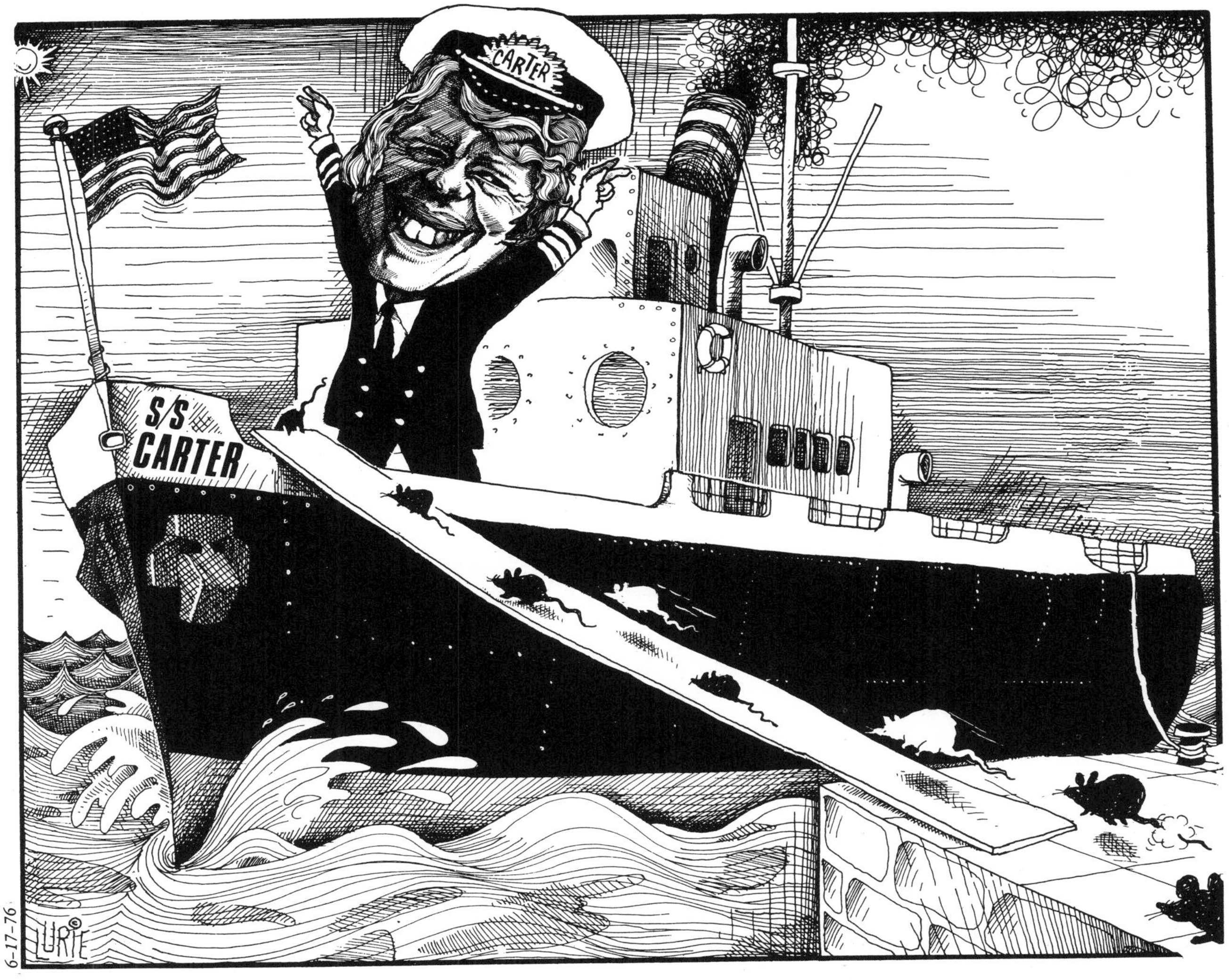
CARTER
S/S CARTER
6-17-76
LURIE©

"WELCOME *BACK* ABOARD, LOYAL SUPPORTERS!"

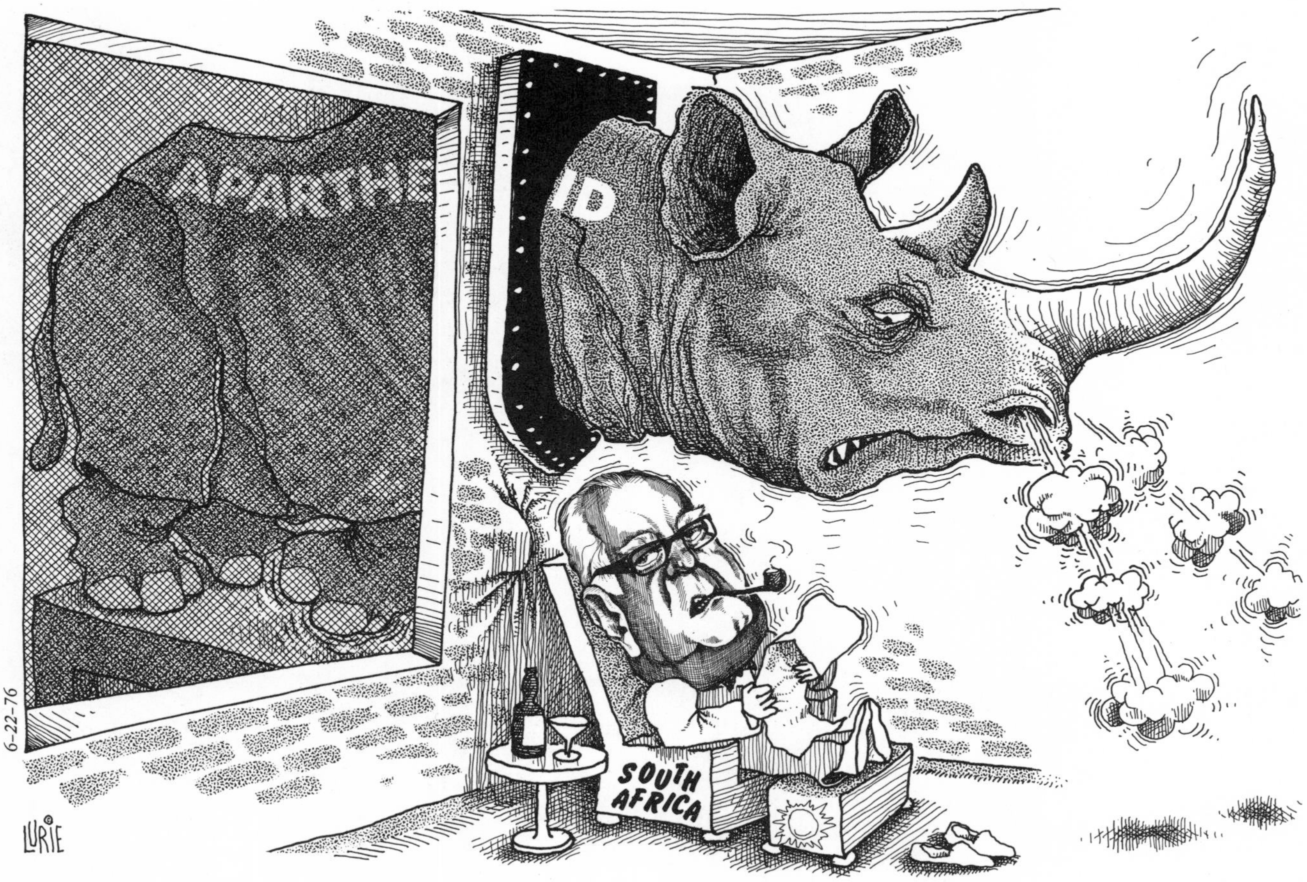
APARTHE
ID
SOUTH AFRICA
6-22-76
LURIE

"NOISES? WHAT NOISES?"

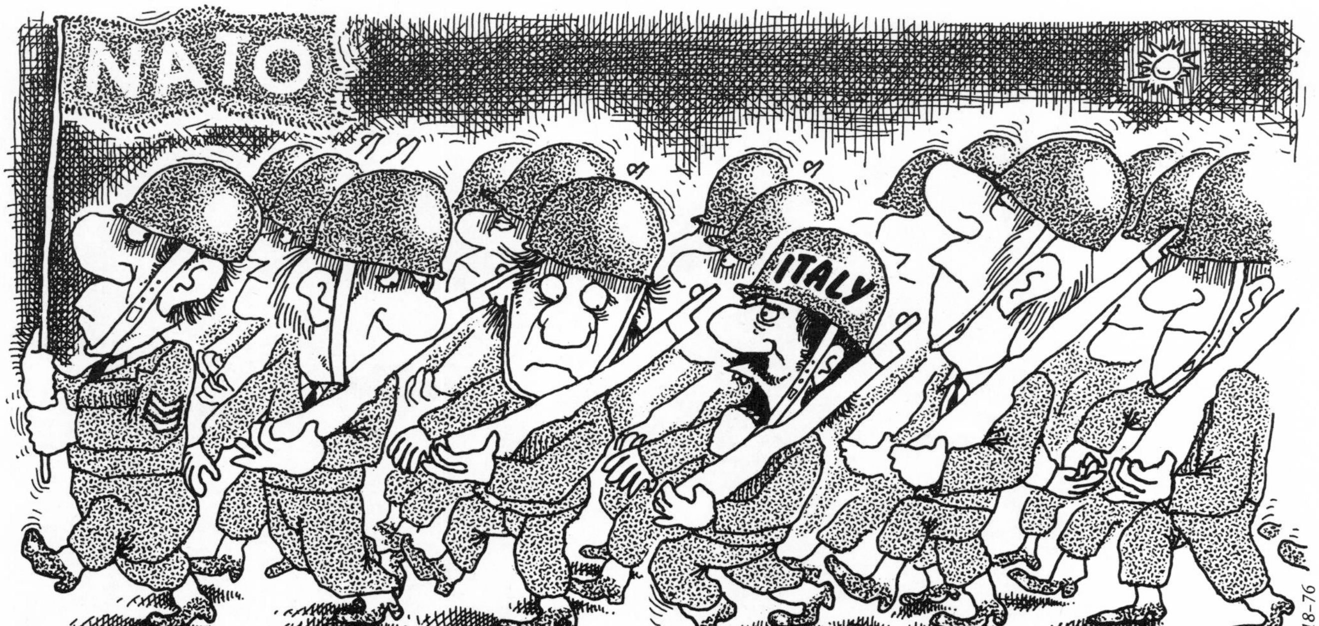
NATO
ITALY
6-18-76
LURIE

"LEFT, LEFT, LEFT–LEFT–LEFT. LEFT, LEFT, LEFT–LEFT–LEFT . . ."

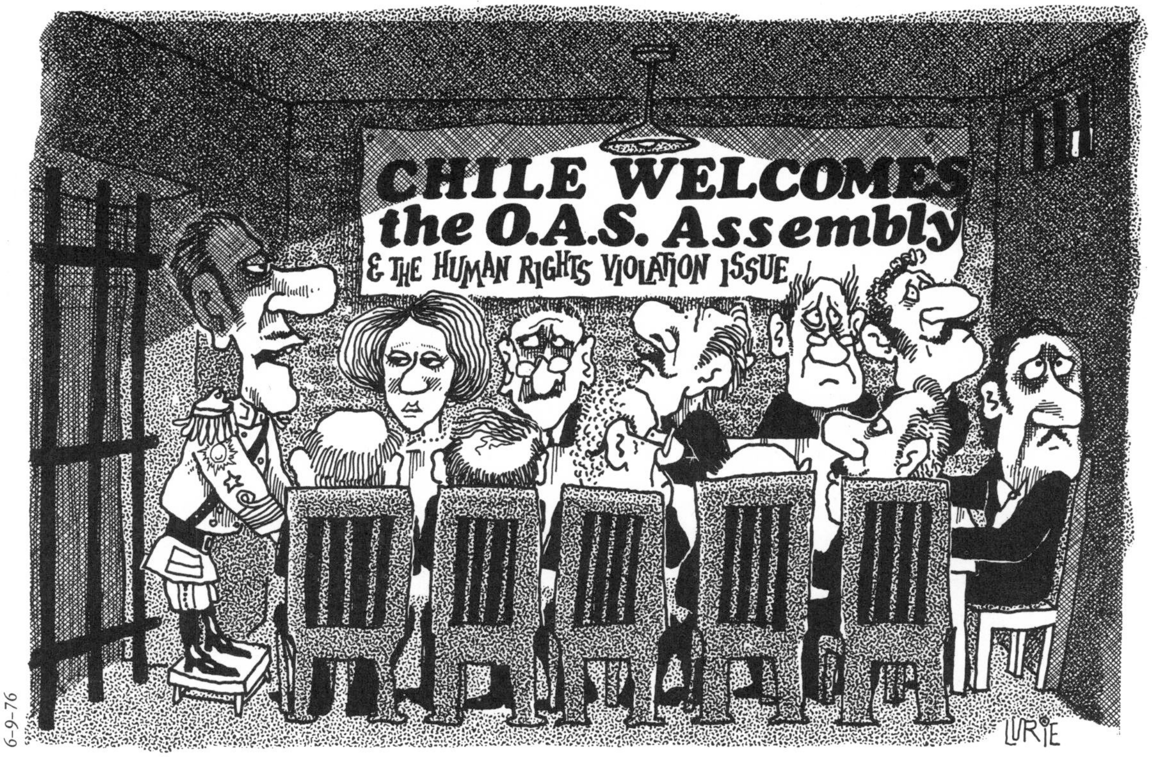
CHILE WELCOMES
the O.A.S. Assembly
& THE HUMAN RIGHTS VIOLATION ISSUE
6-9-76
LURIE

"WE APOLOGIZE FOR THE ACCOMMODATIONS . . .
ALL THE BIGGER CELLS ARE TAKEN."

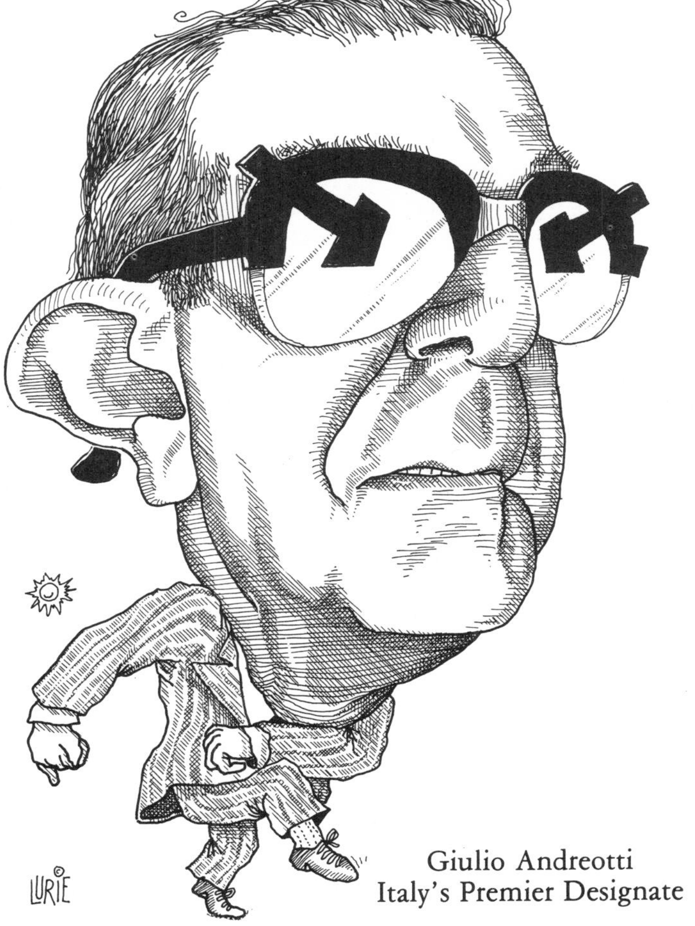
LURIE

Giulio Andreotti
Italy's Premier Designate

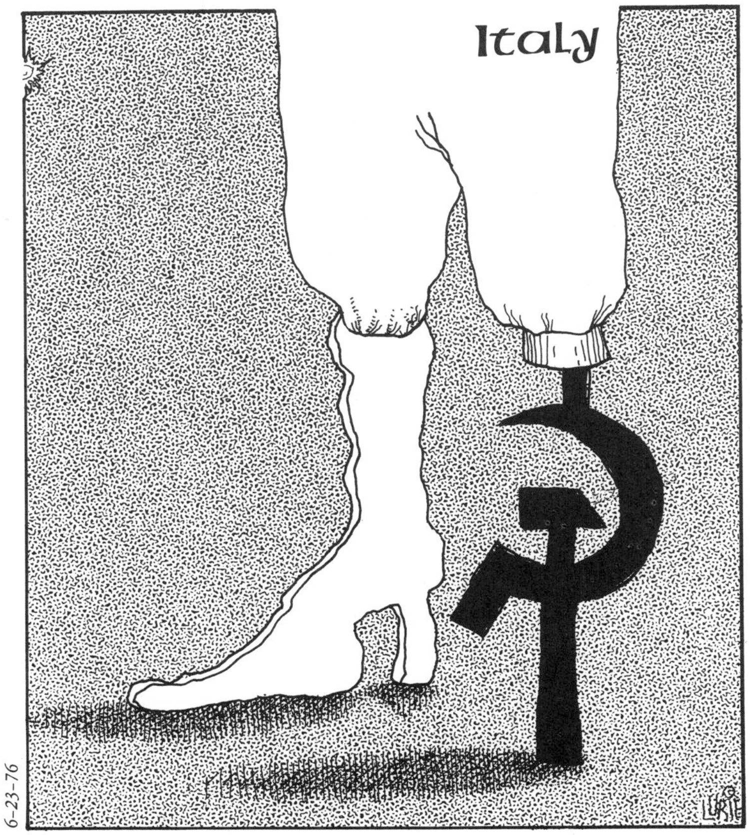
Italy
6-23-76
LURIE

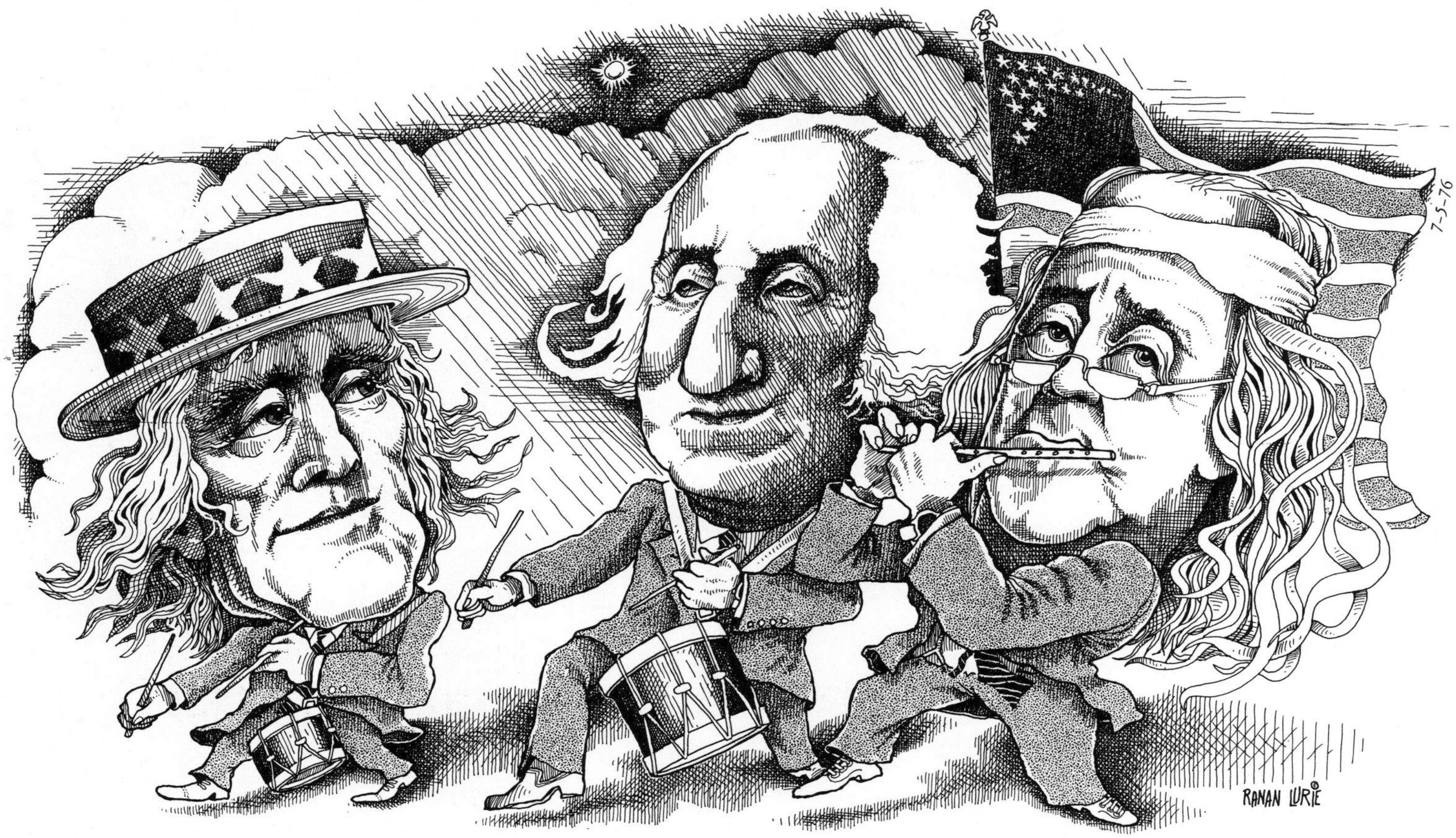
7-5-76
RANAN LURIE

STILL THE BEST SELLING TUNE

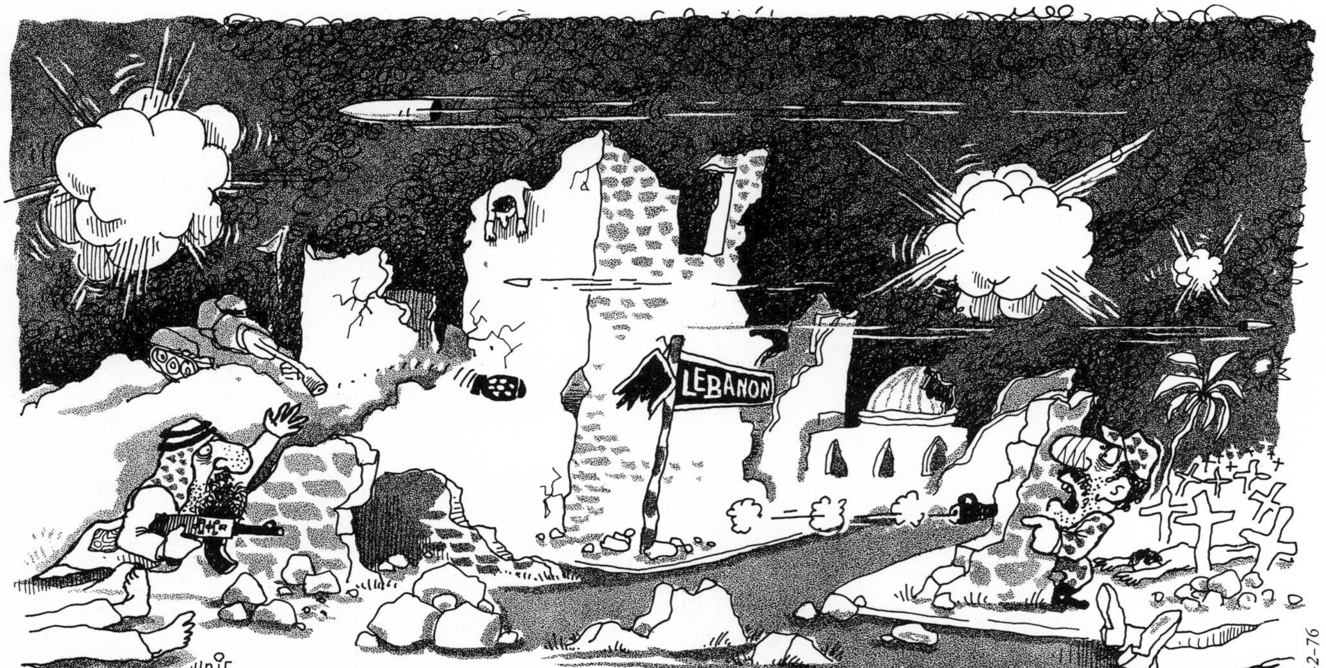
LEBANON
LURIE
7-2-76

"I'M WARNING YOU—DON'T PROVOKE ME INTO A TOTAL WAR!"

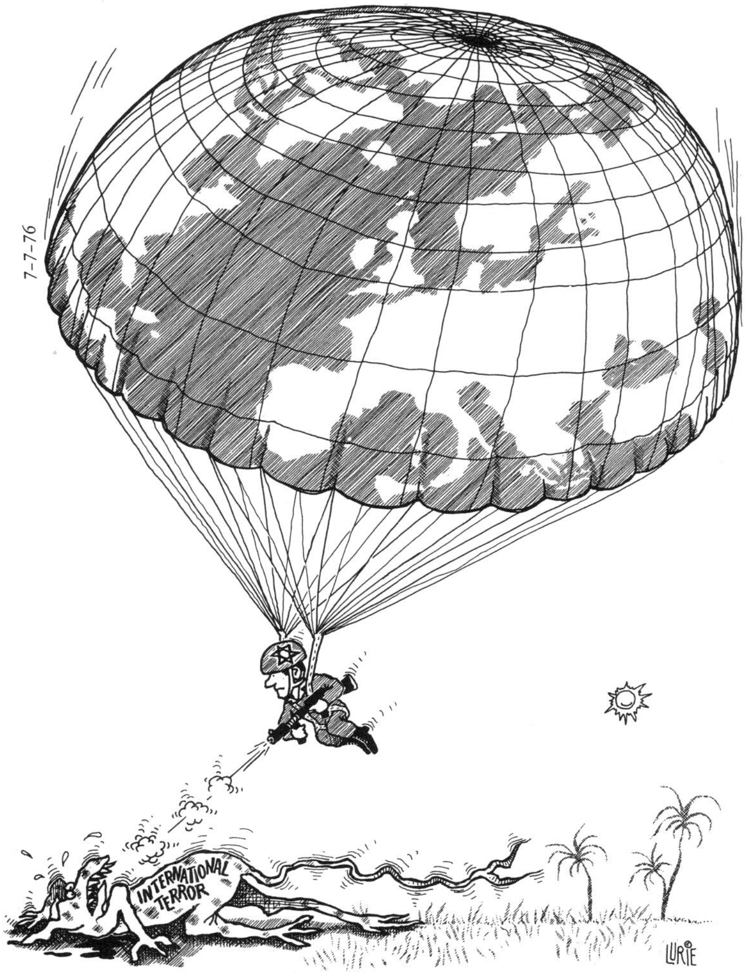
7-7-76
INTERNATIONAL TERROR
LURIE

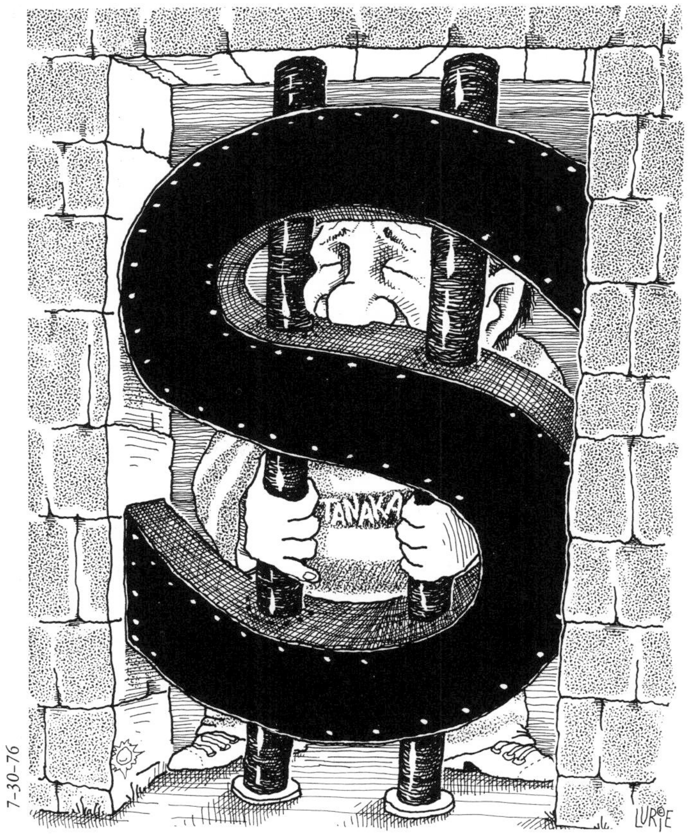
TANAKA
7-30-76
LURIE

THE BUCK STOPS HERE

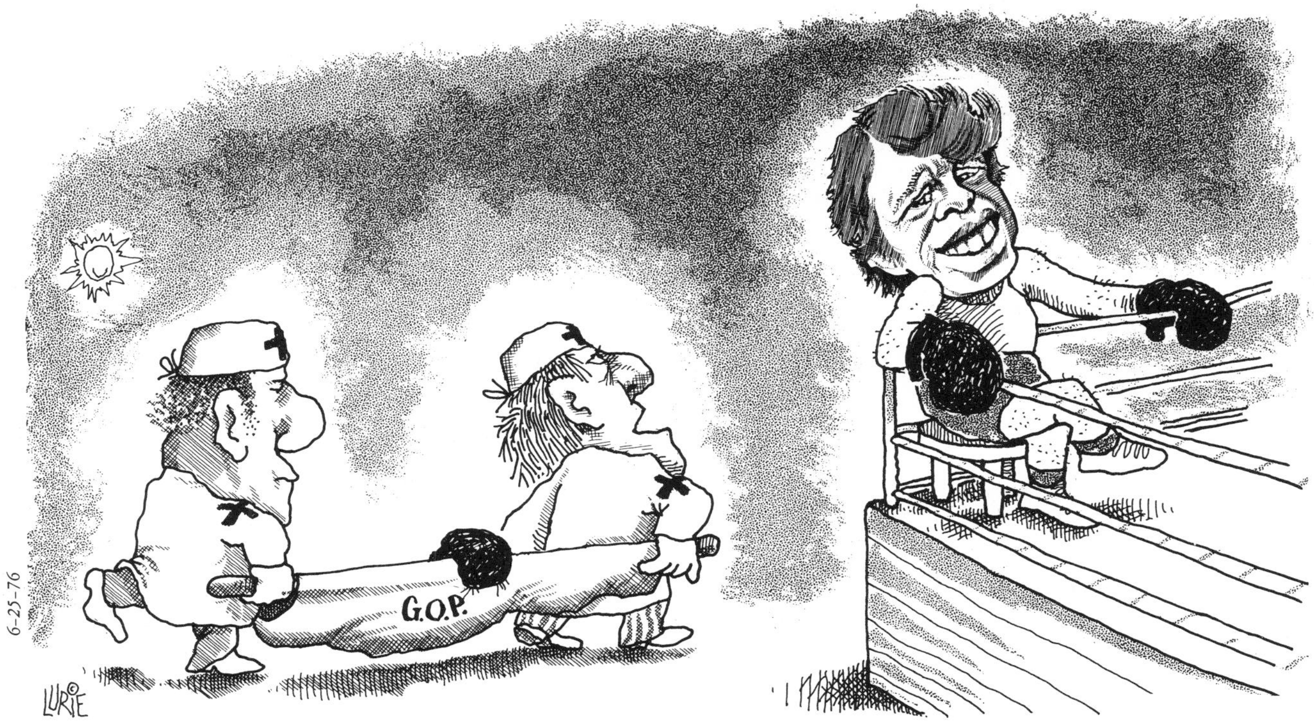
G.O.P.
6-25-76
LURIE

"WE BROUGHT YOUR OPPONENT, MR. CARTER."

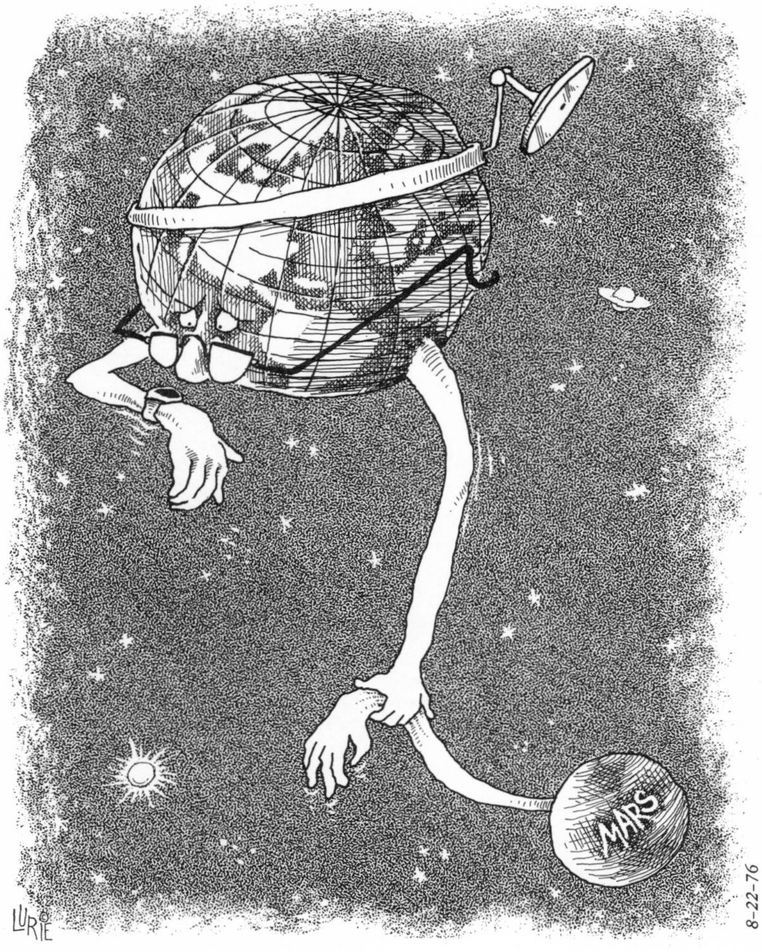
MARS
LURIE
8-22-76

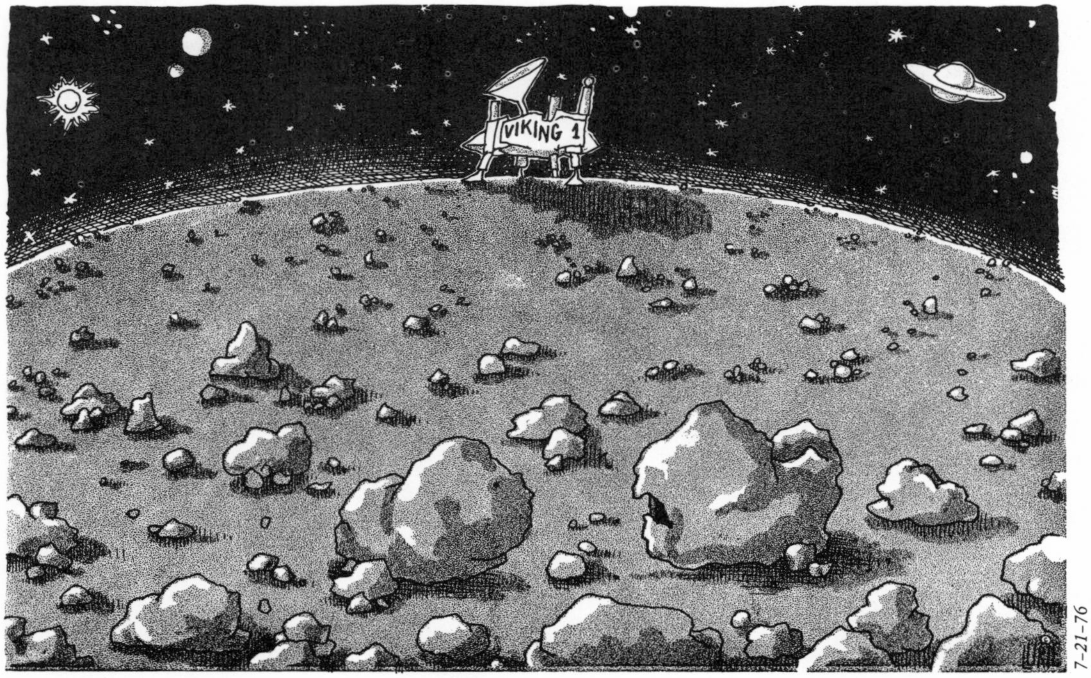
VIKING 1
7-21-76

''DON'T SNEEZE . . .
WITH SOME LUCK THEY MIGHT TAKE US FOR ROCKS!''

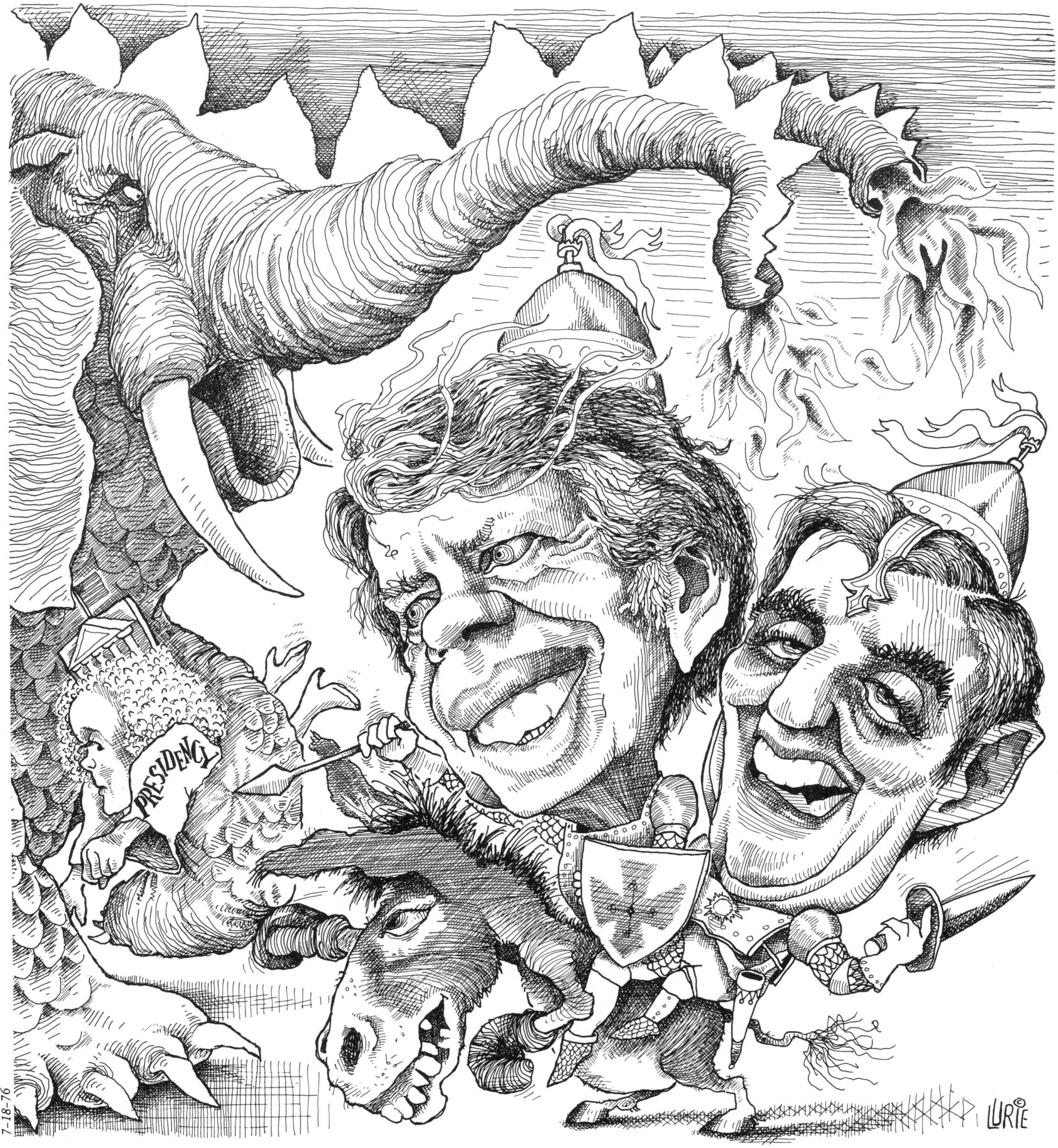
PRESIDENCY
7-18-76
LURIE

ST. CARTER AND THE DRAGON
(OR HOW THE DEMOCRATS LIKE TO VIEW THEIR MISSION)

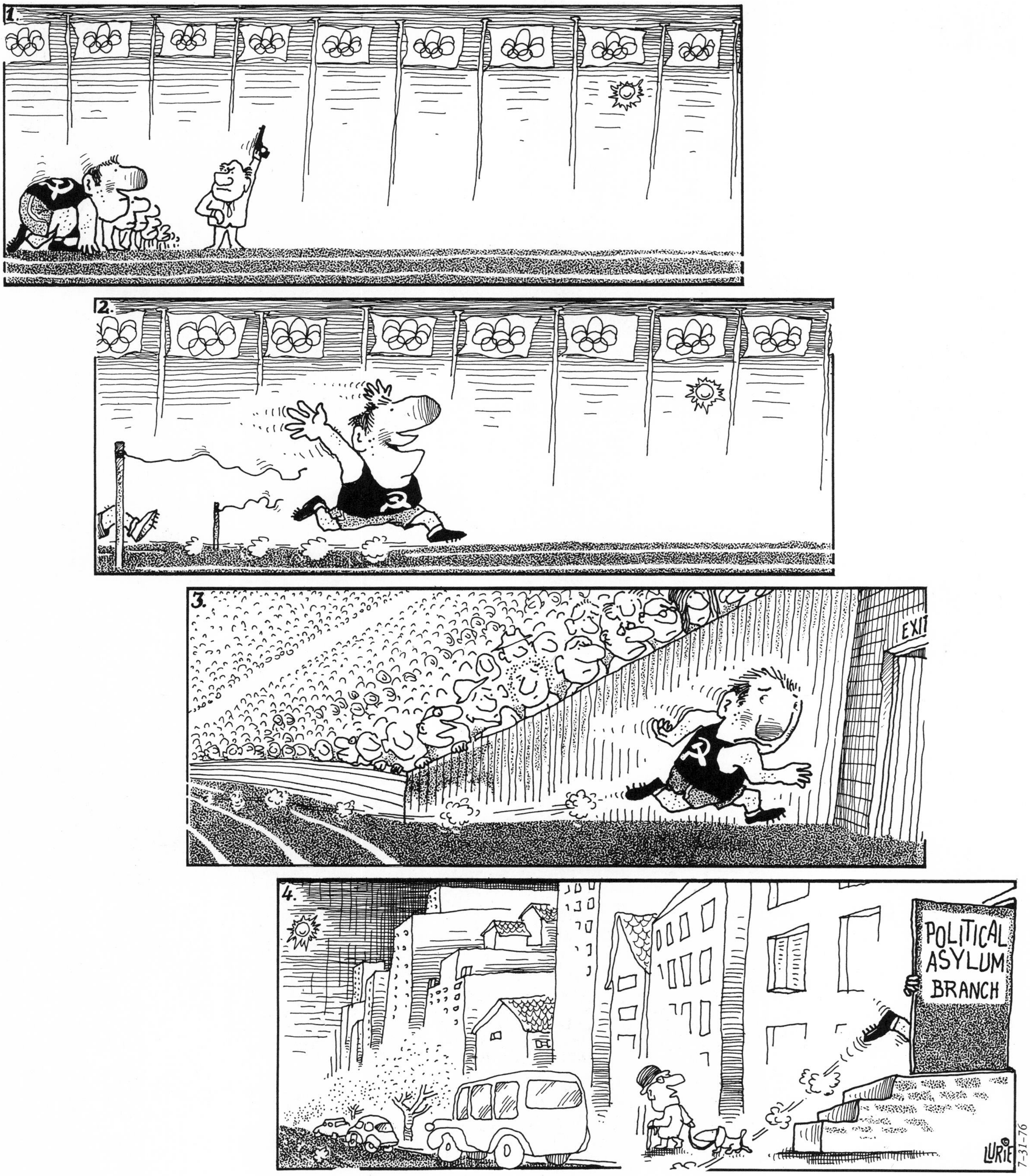
1.
2.
3.
EXIT
4.
POLITICAL
ASYLUM
BRANCH
LURIE
7-31-76

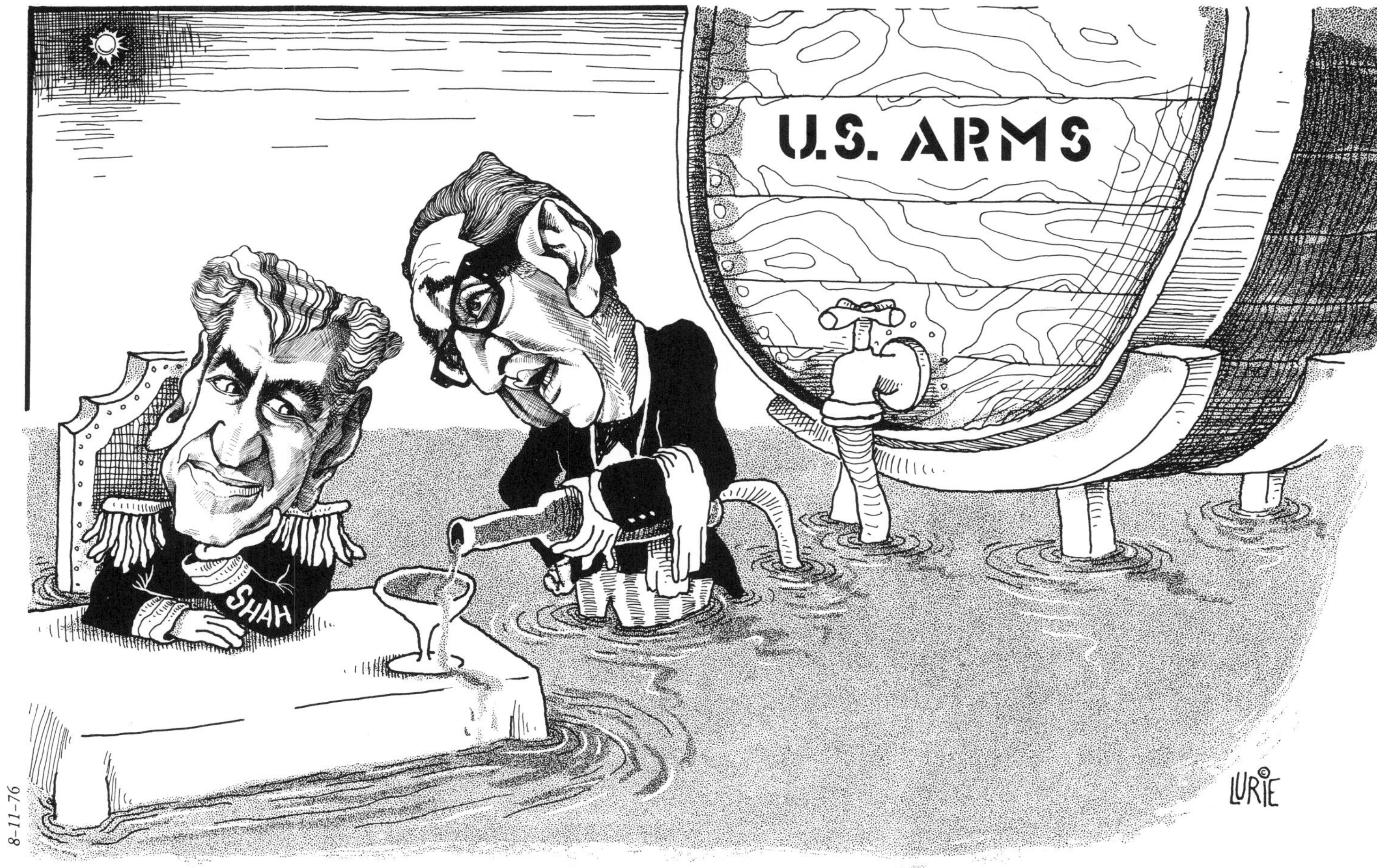
U.S. ARMS
SHAH
LURIE
8-11-76

"SAY WHEN."

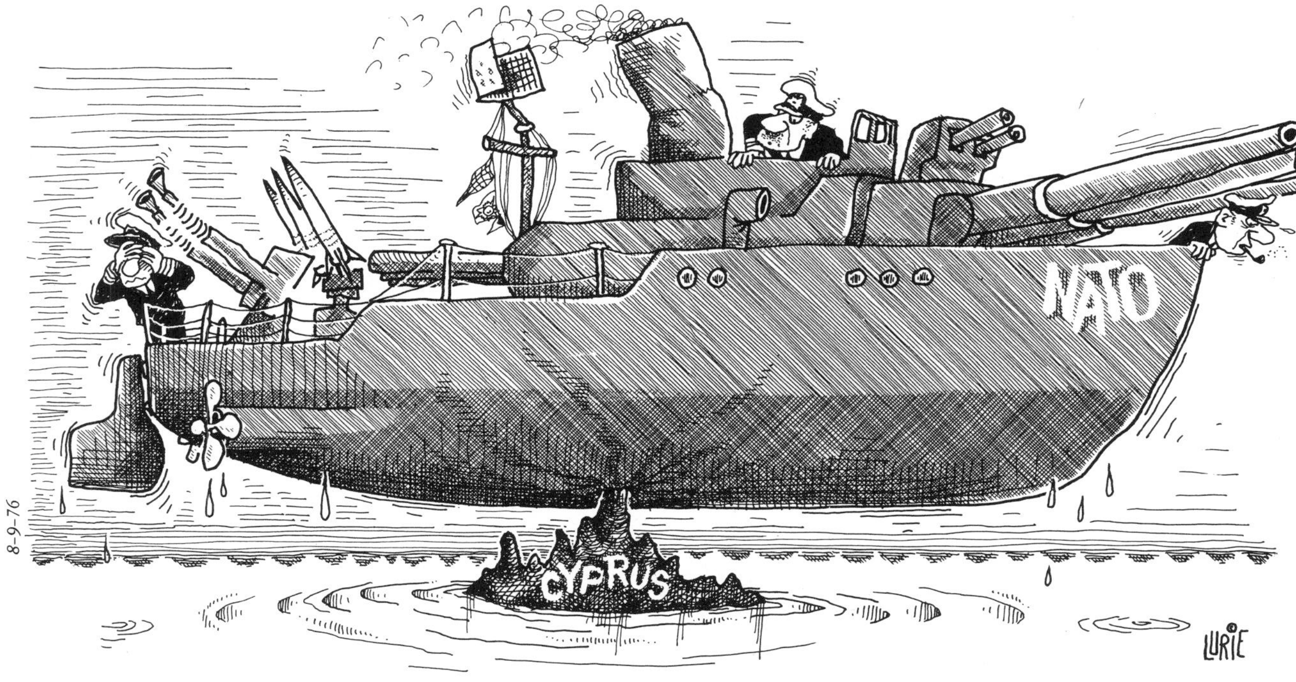
NATO
CYPRUS
LURIE
8-9-76

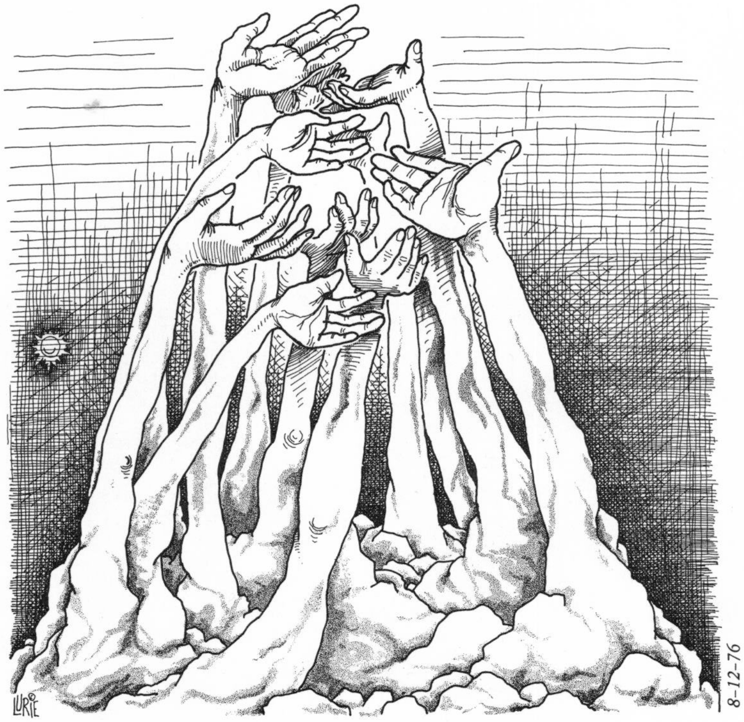
LURIE
8-12-76

THIRD WORLD SUMMIT

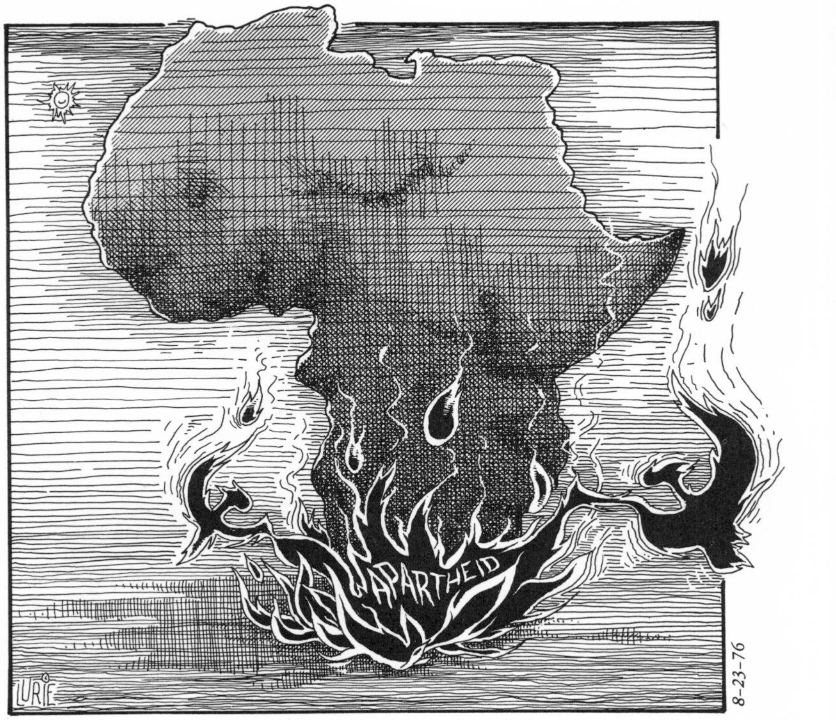
APARTHEID
LURIE
8-23-76

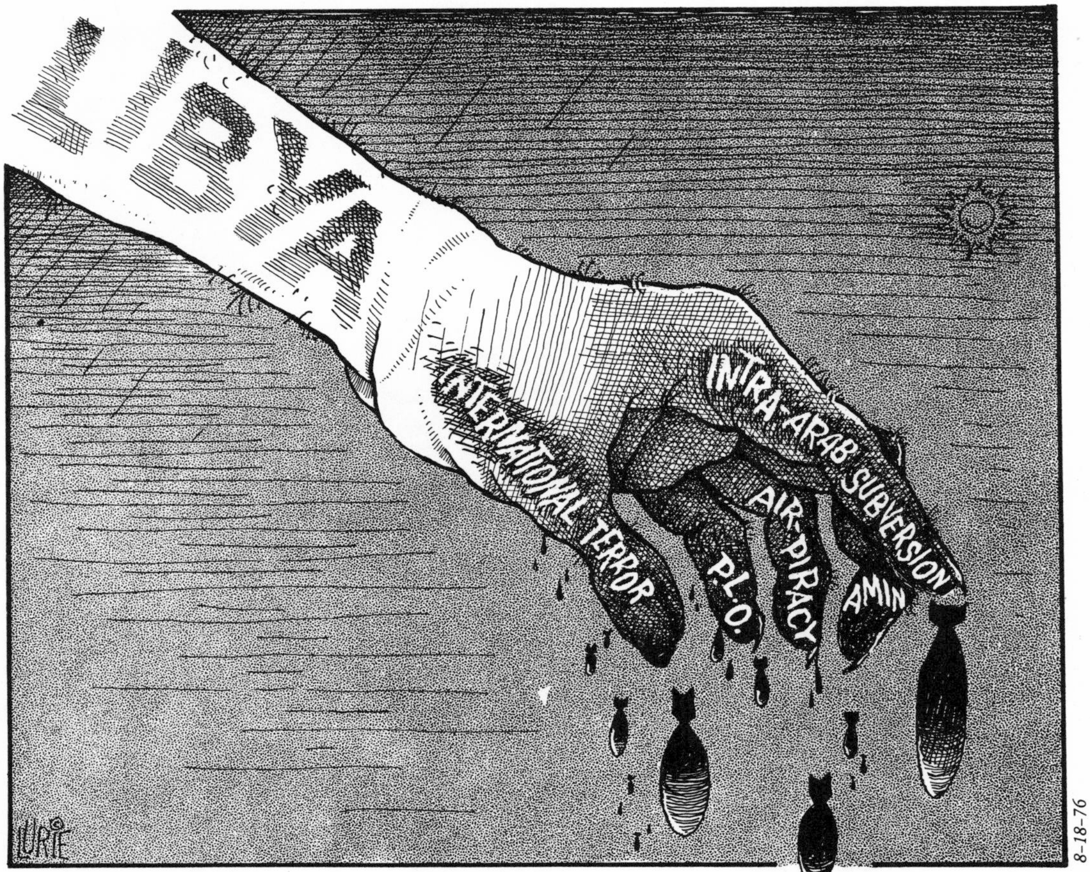
LIBYA
INTERNATIONAL TERROR
P.L.O.
AIR-PIRACY
AMIN
INTRA-ARAB SUBVERSION
LURIE
8-18-76

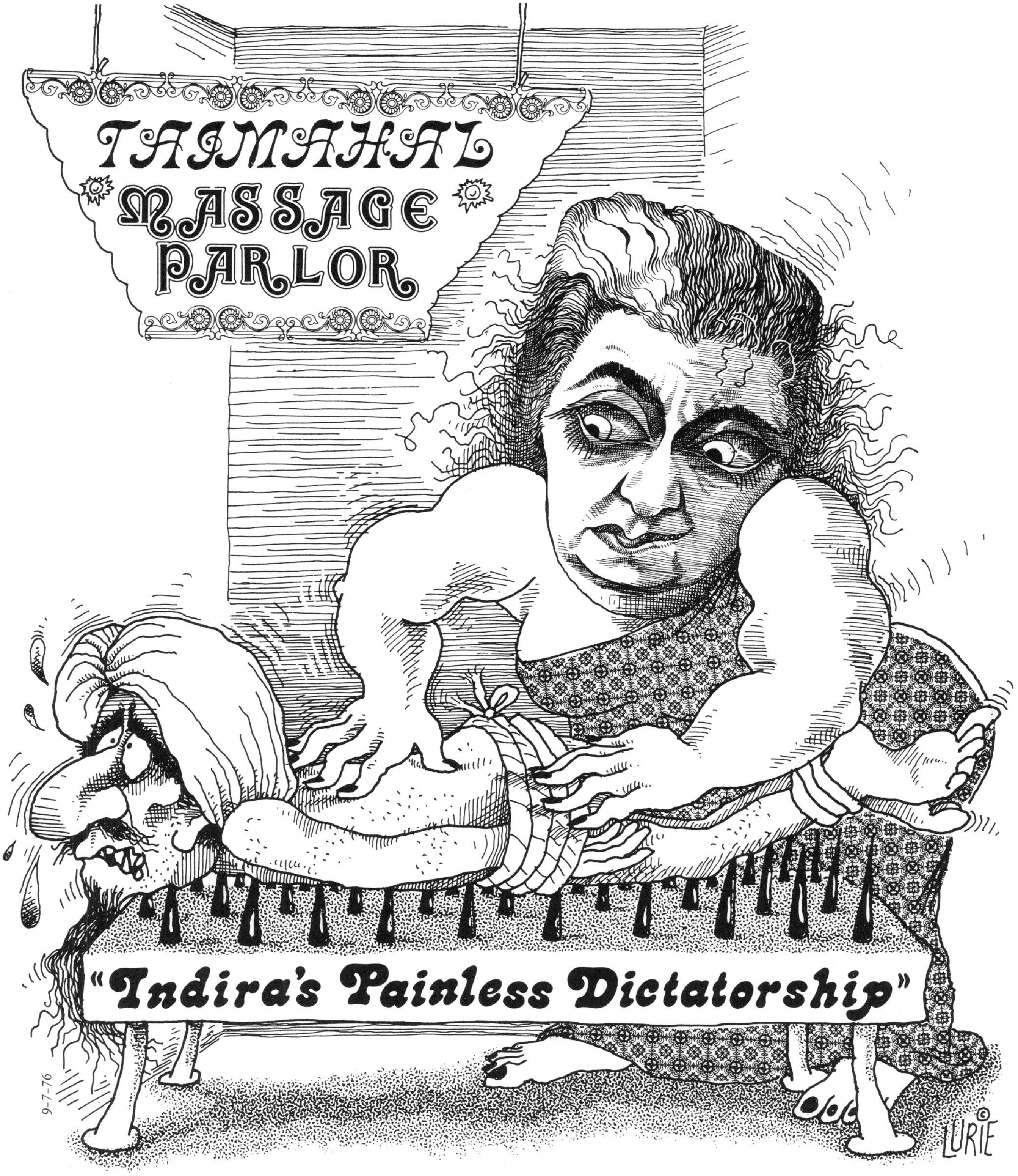
TAJMAHAL
MASSAGE
PARLOR
"Indira's Painless Dictatorship"
9-7-76
© LURIE

''PPPPLEA–S–S–SE D–D–DON'T RU–BBB IT IN . . .''

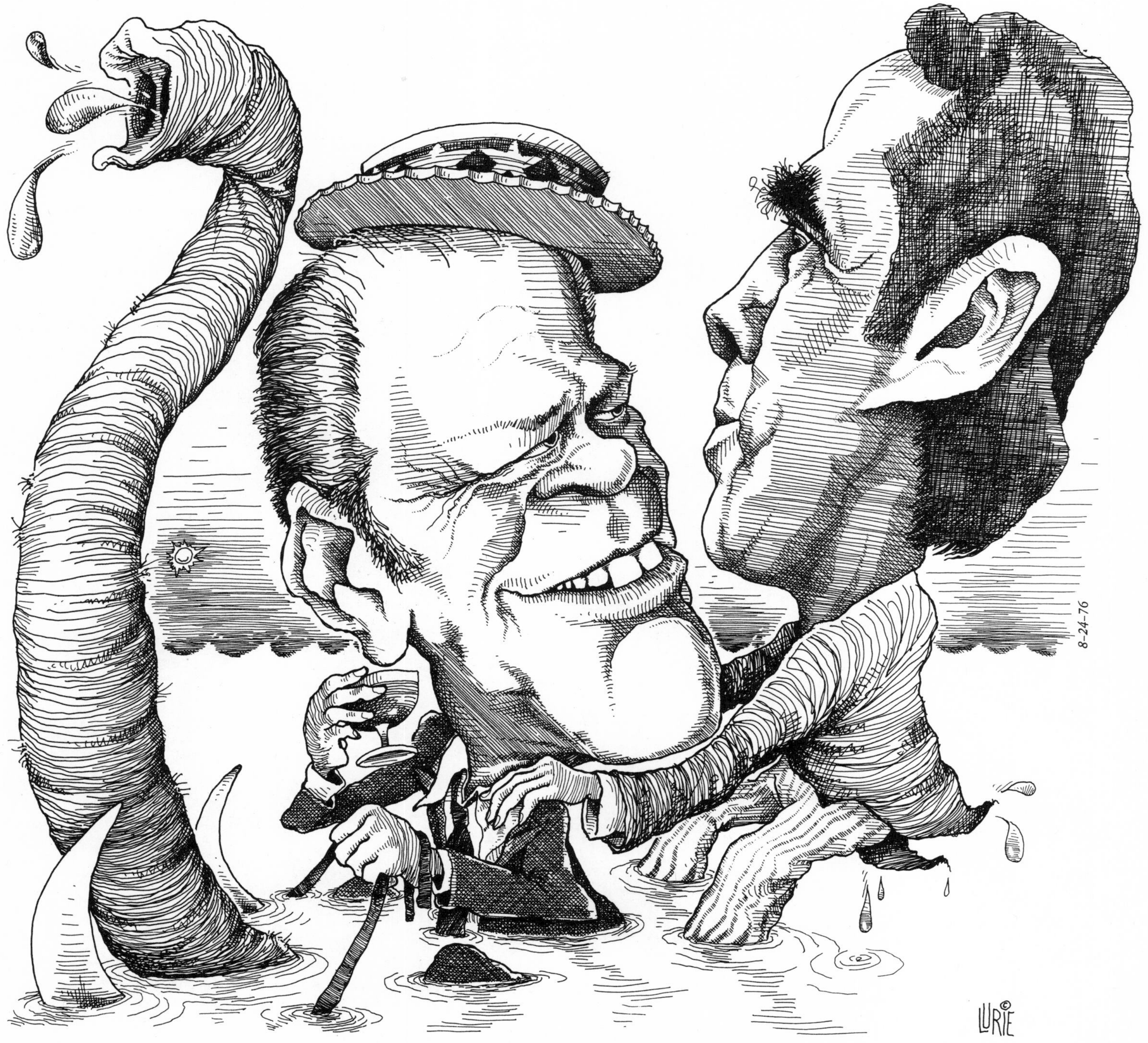
8-24-76
LURIE

"WELCOME ABOARD, SENATOR DOLE!"

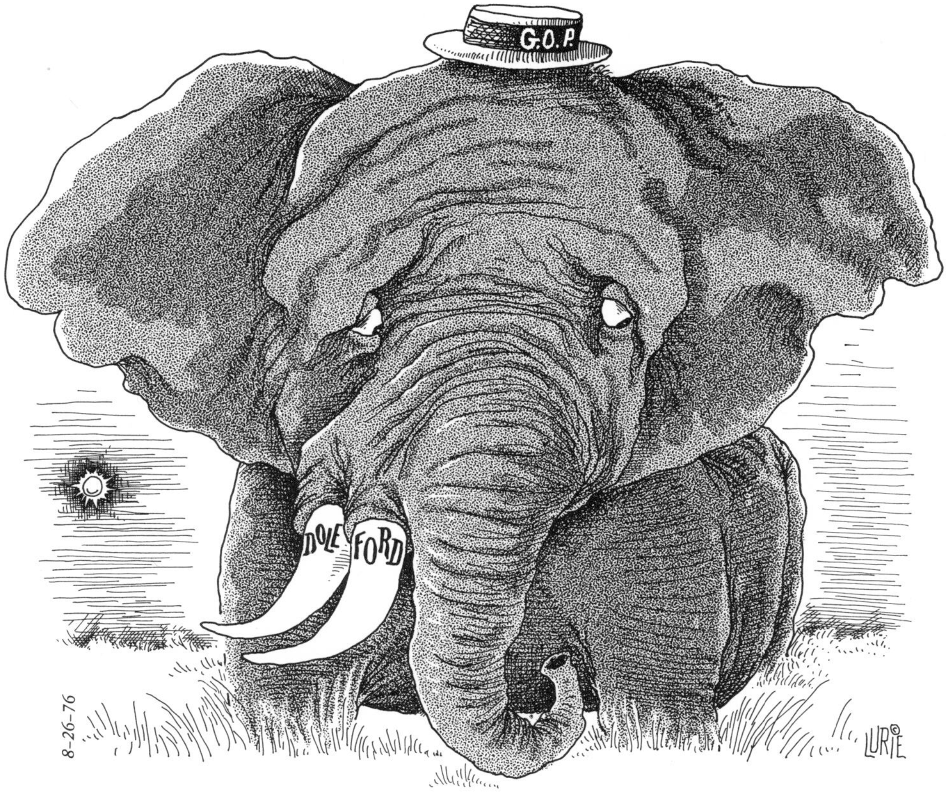
G.O.P.
DOLE
FORD
8-26-76
LURIE

"BUT WHO'LL PROTECT MY LEFT FLANK?"

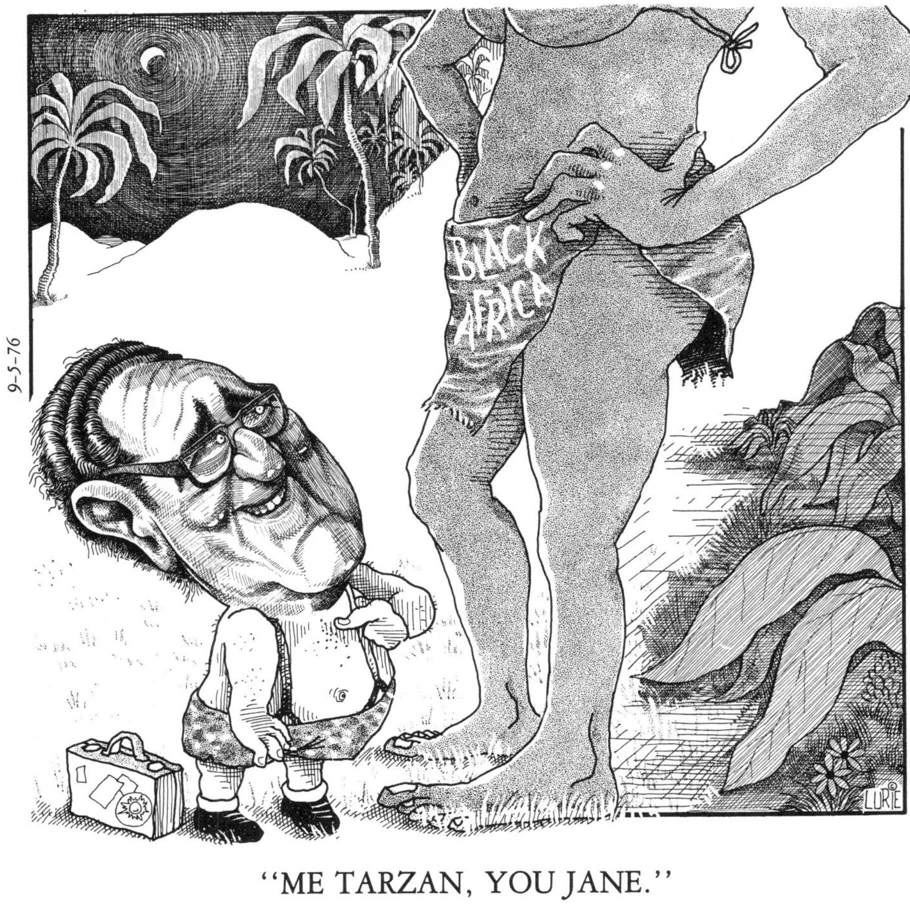
BLACK AFRICA
9-5-76
LURIE

"ME TARZAN, YOU JANE."

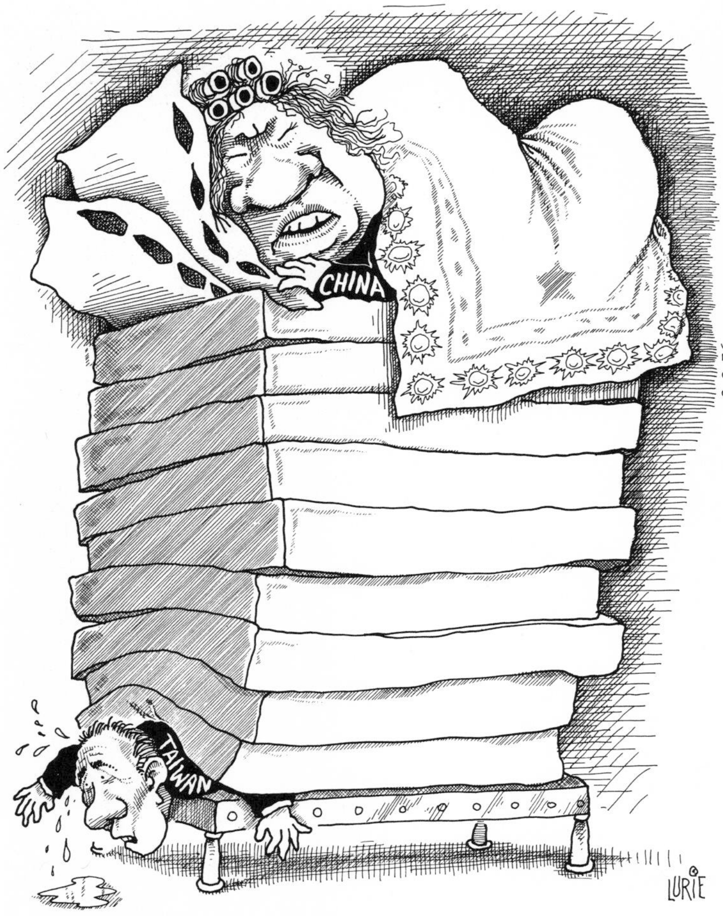
CHINA
TAIWAN
8-8-76
LURIE

THE RED PRINCESS AND THE PEA

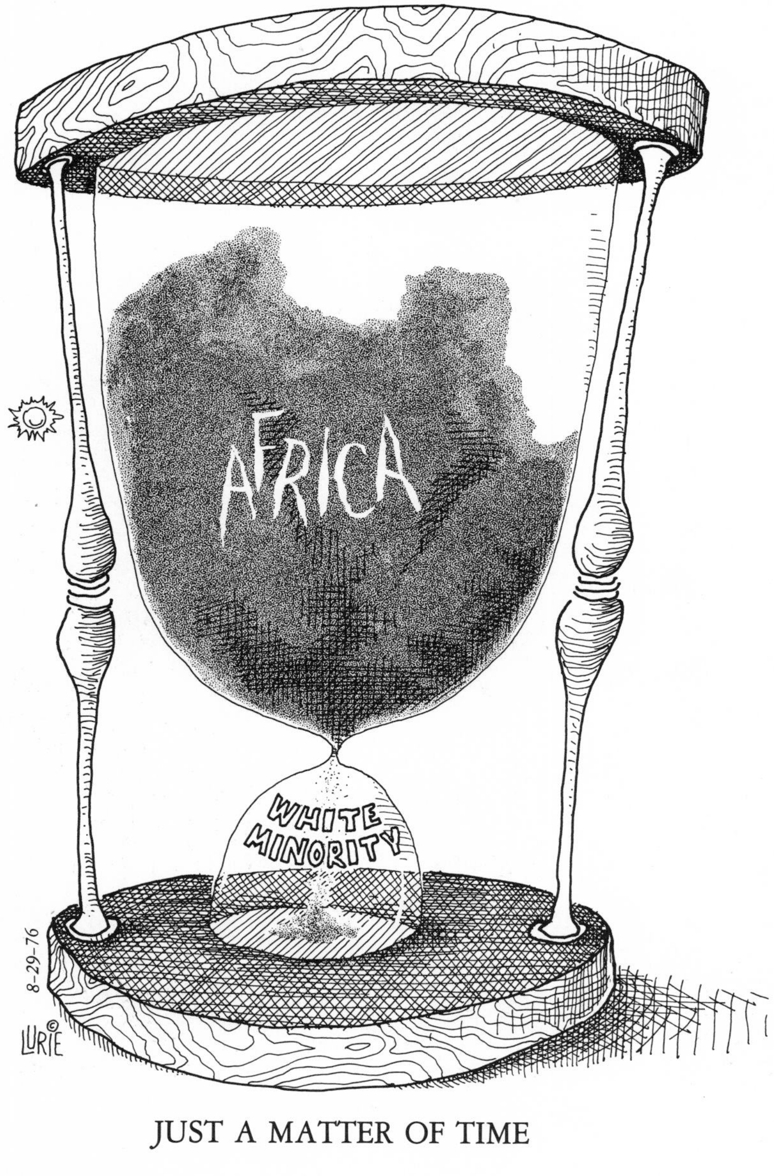
AFRICA
WHITE MINORITY
8-29-76
LURIE

JUST A MATTER OF TIME

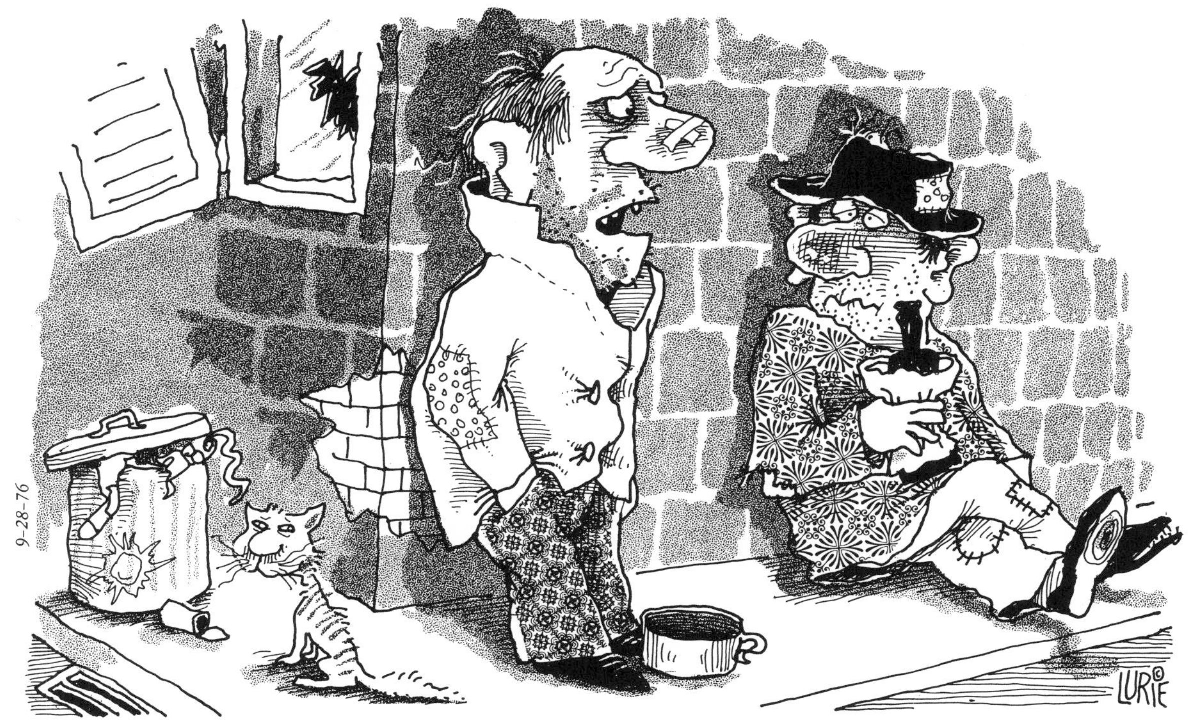
9-28-76
LURIE

"CARTER WANTS TO IMPOSE MORE TAXES ON US
AND GIVE THEM TO THE POOR!"

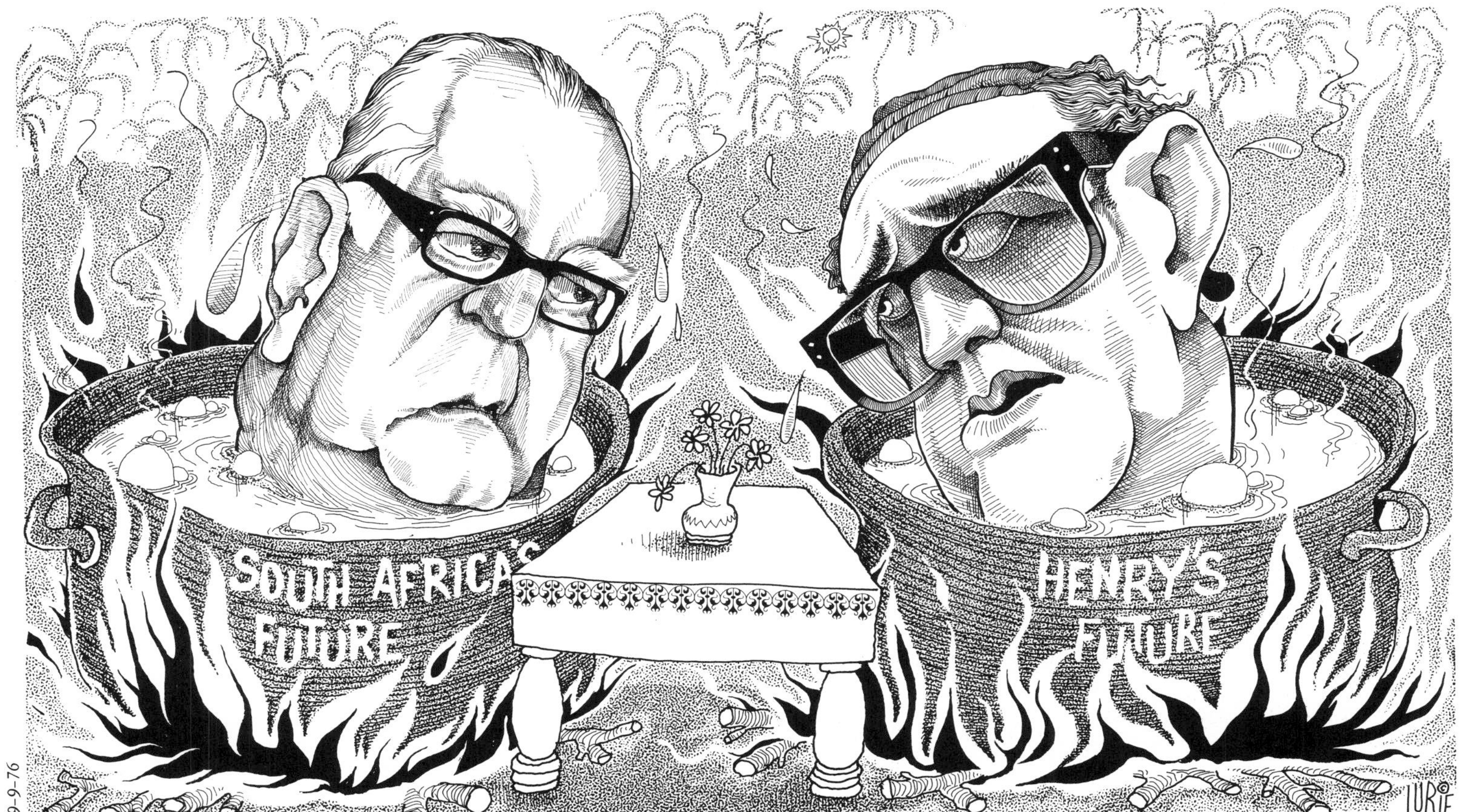
SOUTH AFRICA'S FUTURE
HENRY'S FUTURE
9-9-76
LURIE

HEATED NEGOTIATIONS

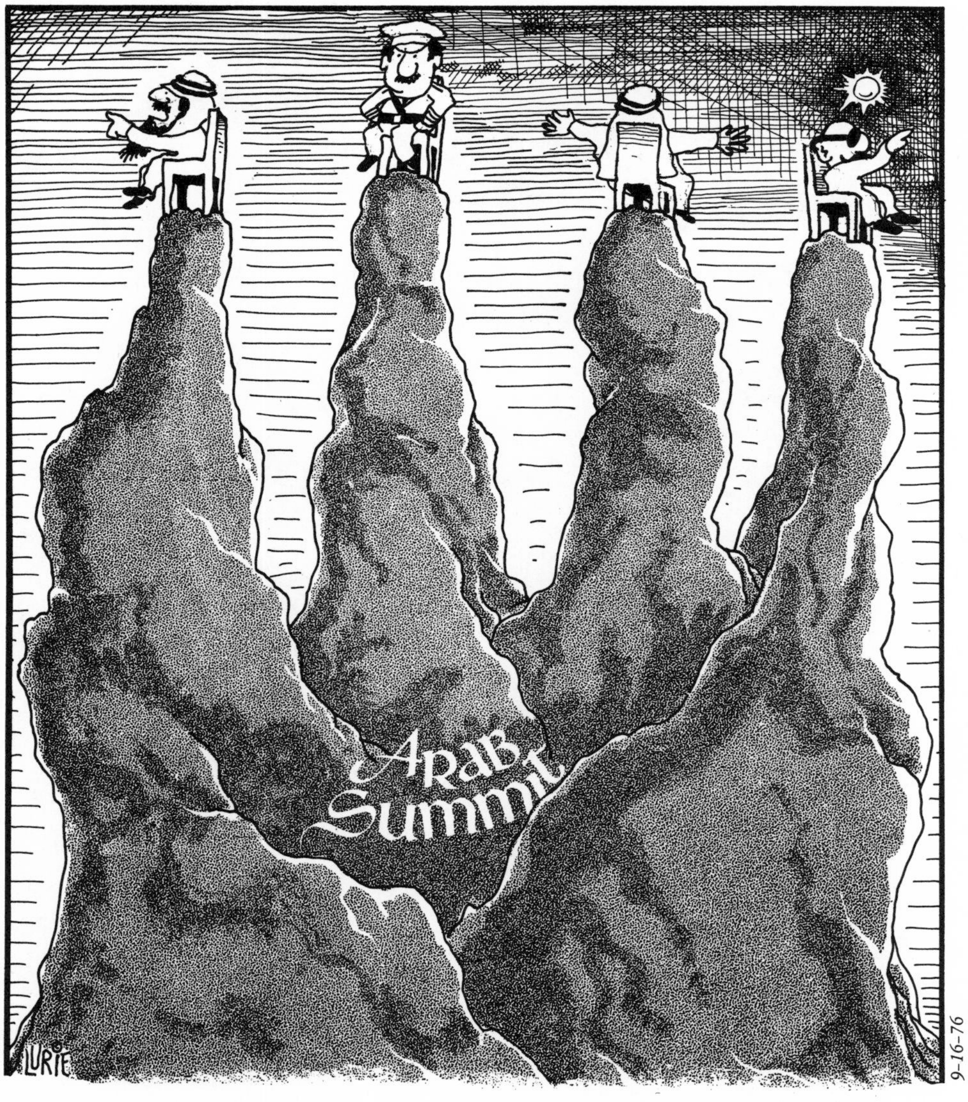
ARAB Summit
LURIE
9-16-76

FOREIGN POLICY DEBATES
FORD
10-15-76
FOREIGN
DEBATES
FORD

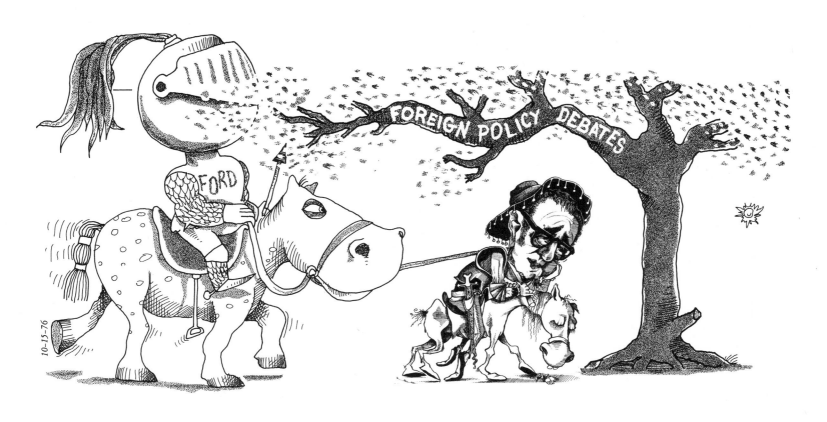

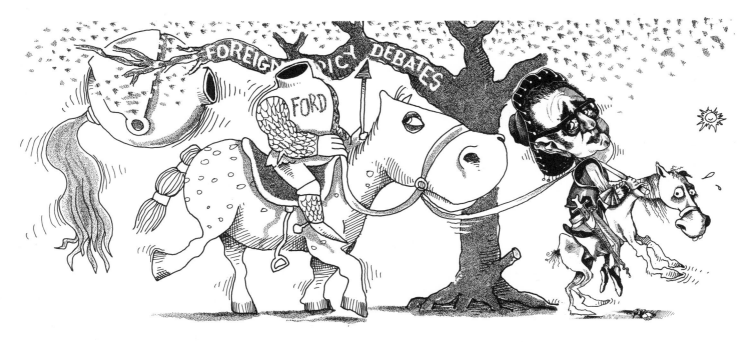

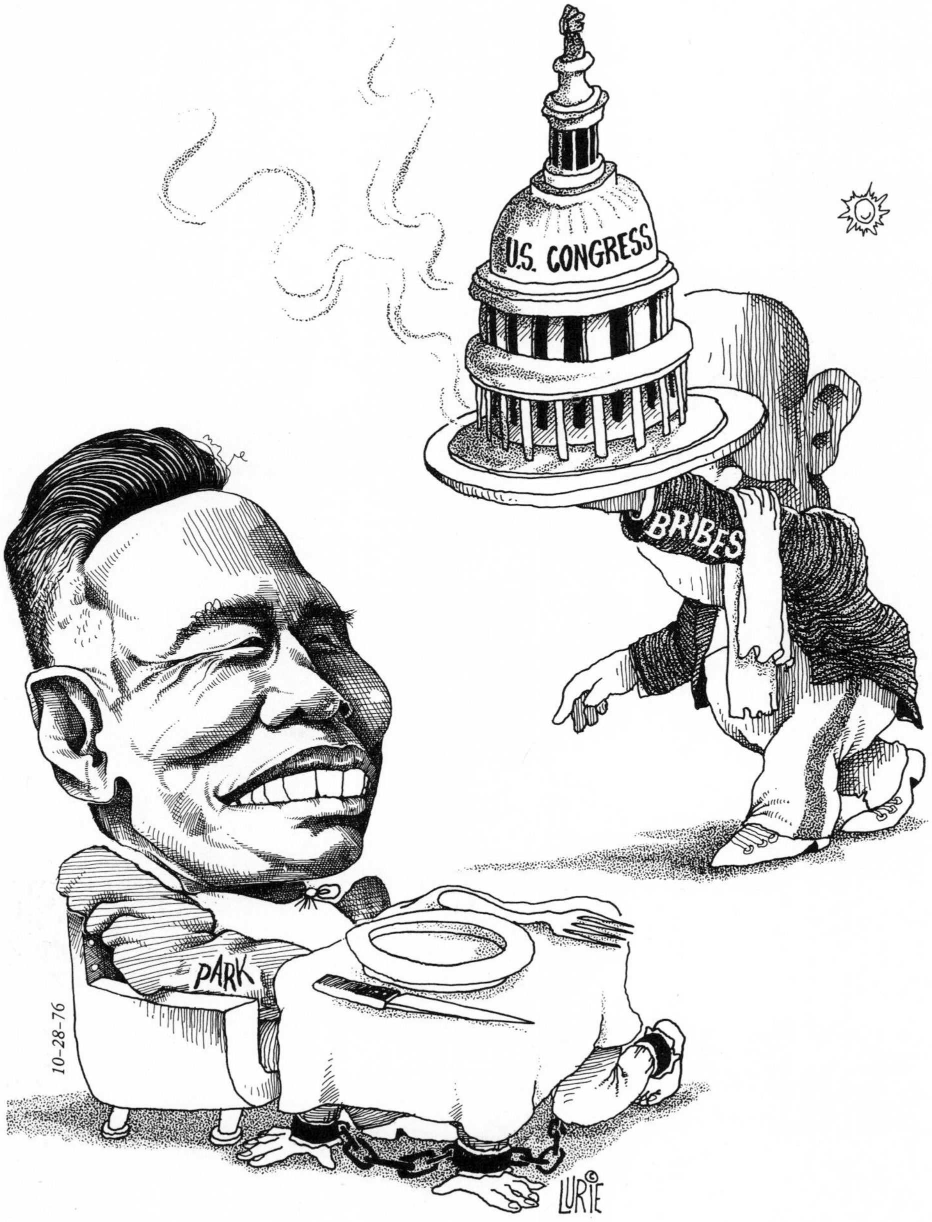
U.S. CONGRESS
BRIBES
PARK
10-28-76
LURIE

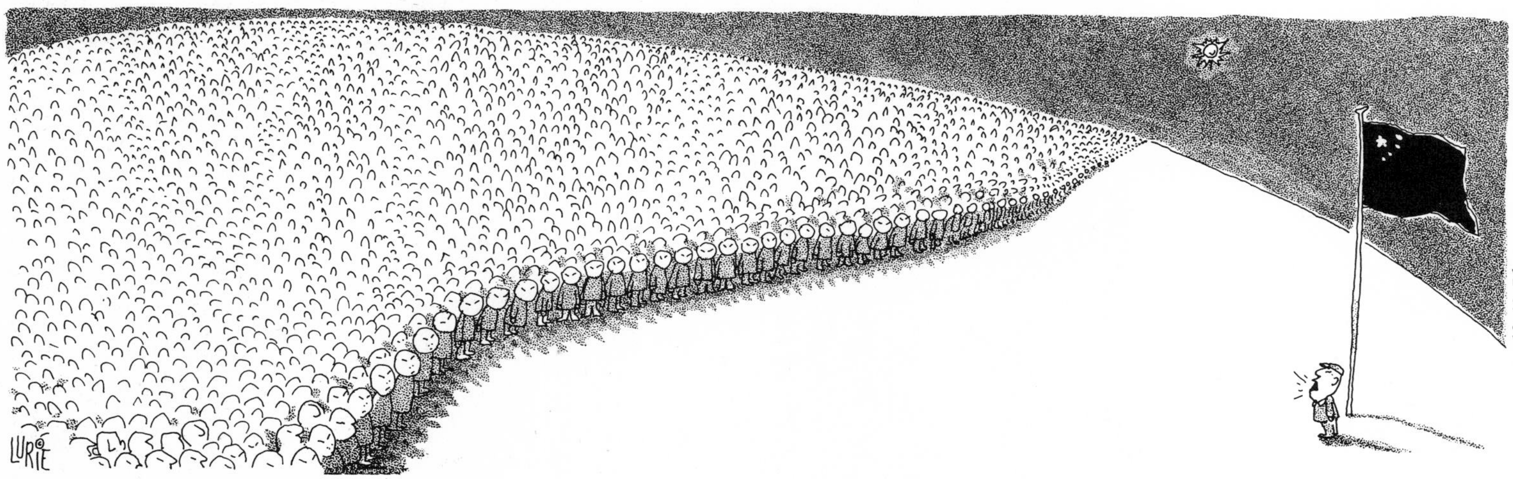
10-19-76
LURIE

"YOU'RE UNDER ARREST!"

10-18-76

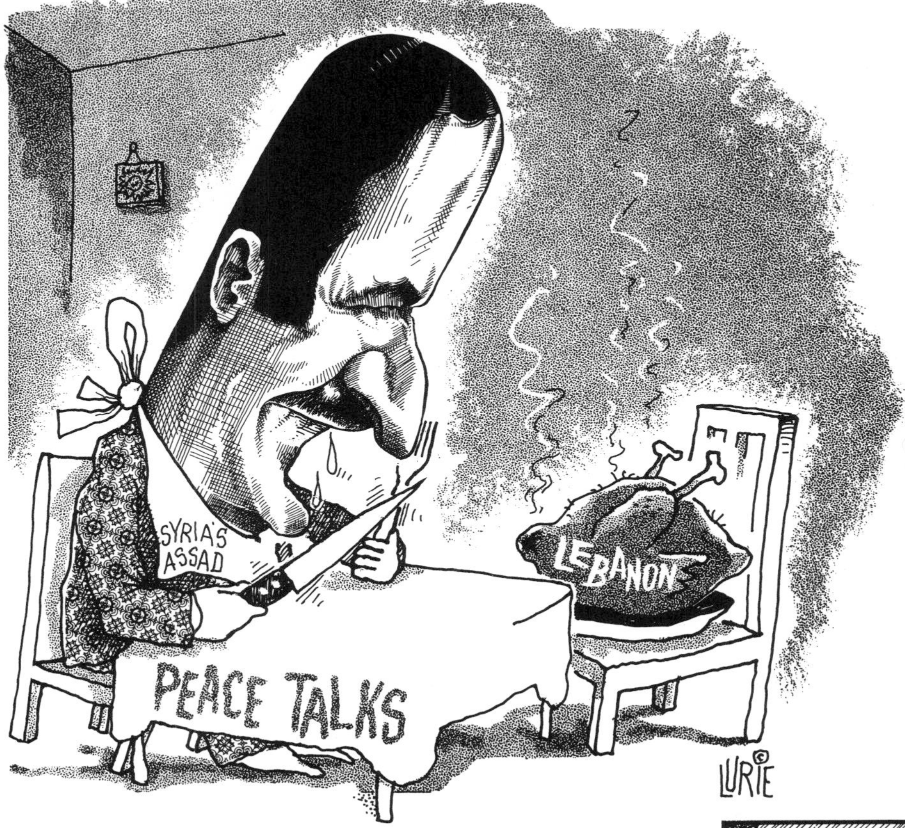
SYRIA'S ASSAD
LEBANON
PEACE TALKS
LURIE©

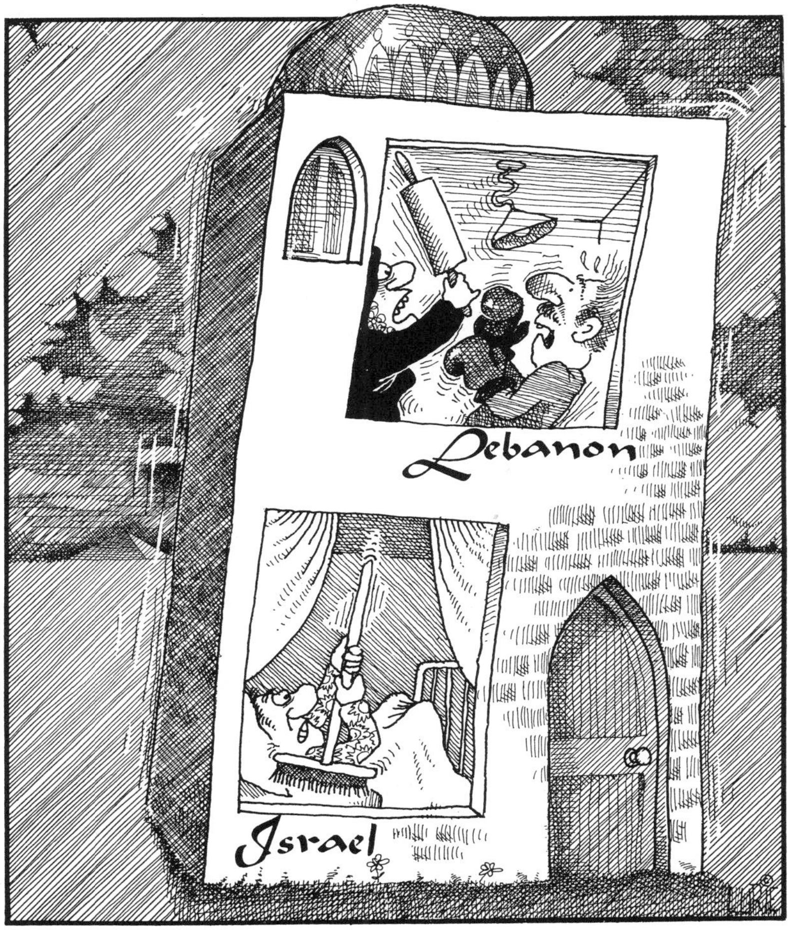
Lebanon
Israel

DAILY NEW
FORD TO N.Y. CITY: DROP DEAD!
N.Y.C. VOTE
SAME TO YOU, FELLA!
11-3-76

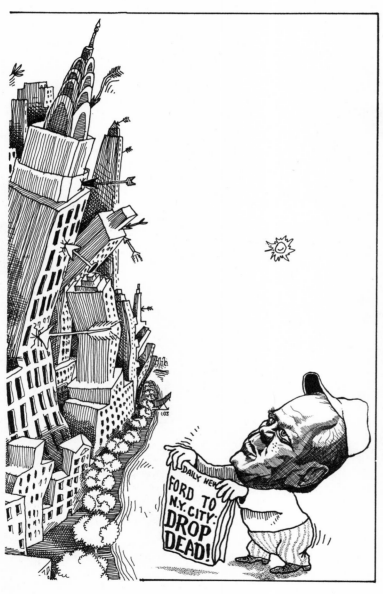

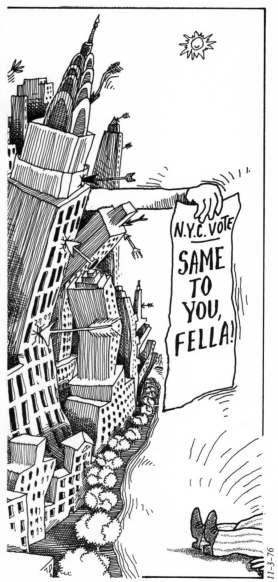

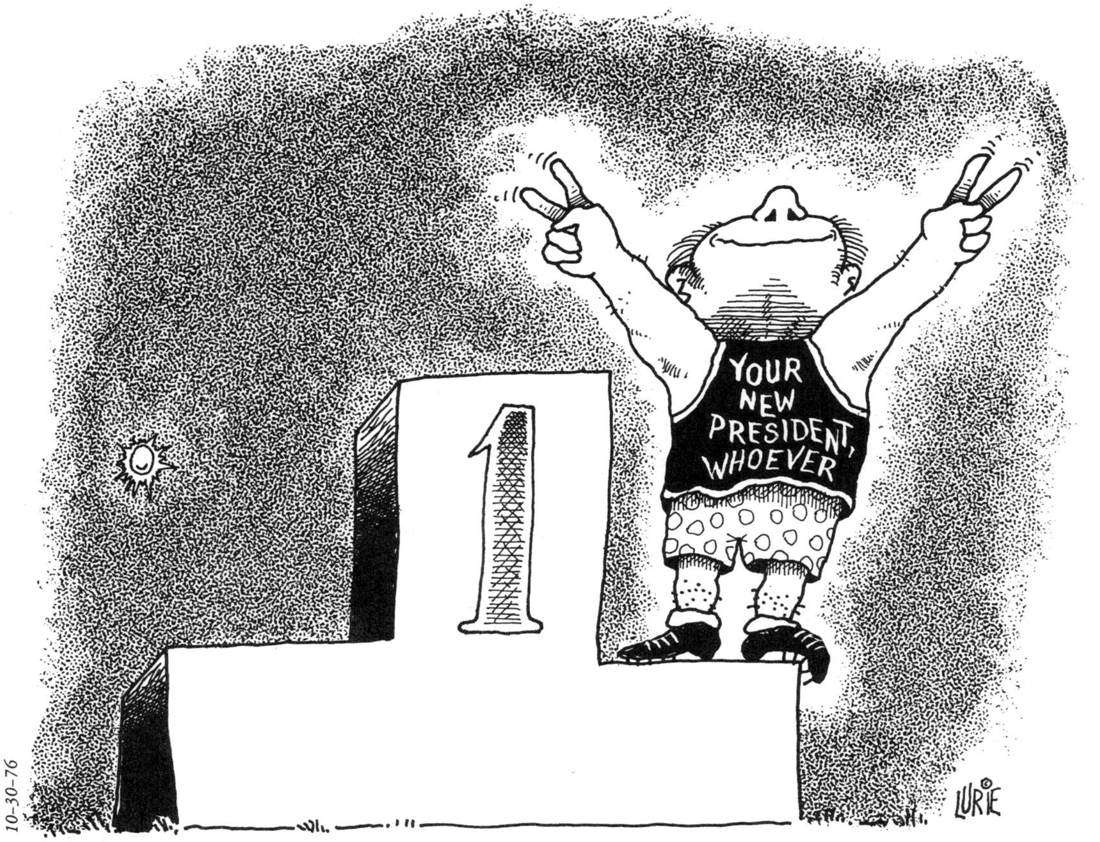
YOUR NEW PRESIDENT, WHOEVER
1
LURIE
10-30-76

OUR PROJECTION OF THE WINNER

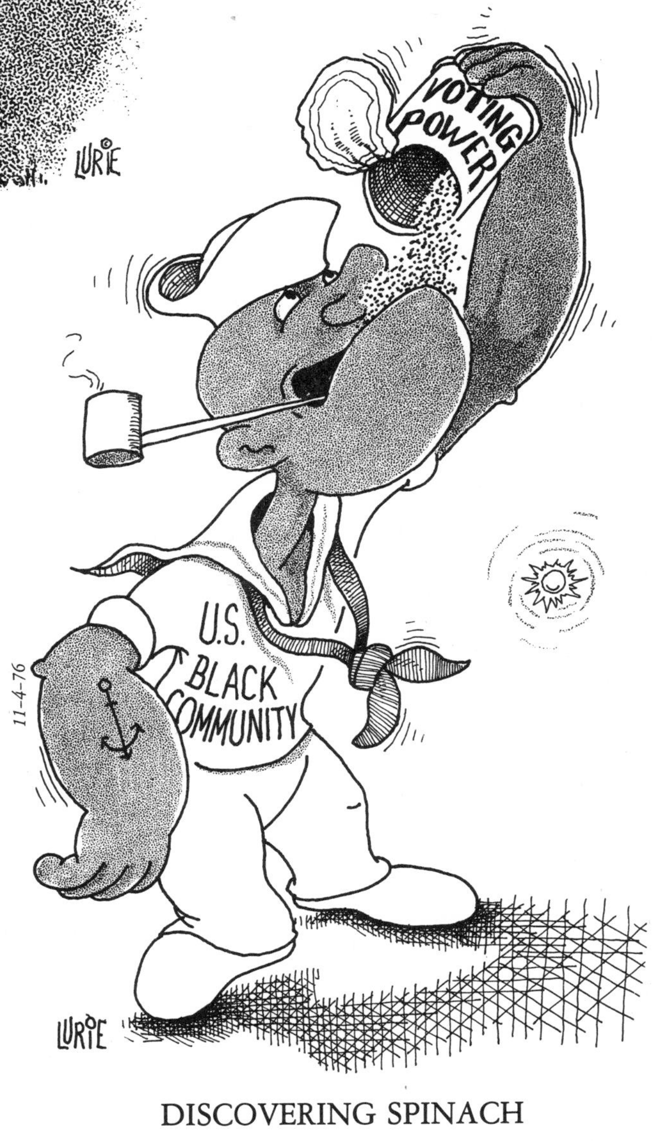
VOTING POWER
U.S. BLACK COMMUNITY
LURIE
11-4-76

DISCOVERING SPINACH

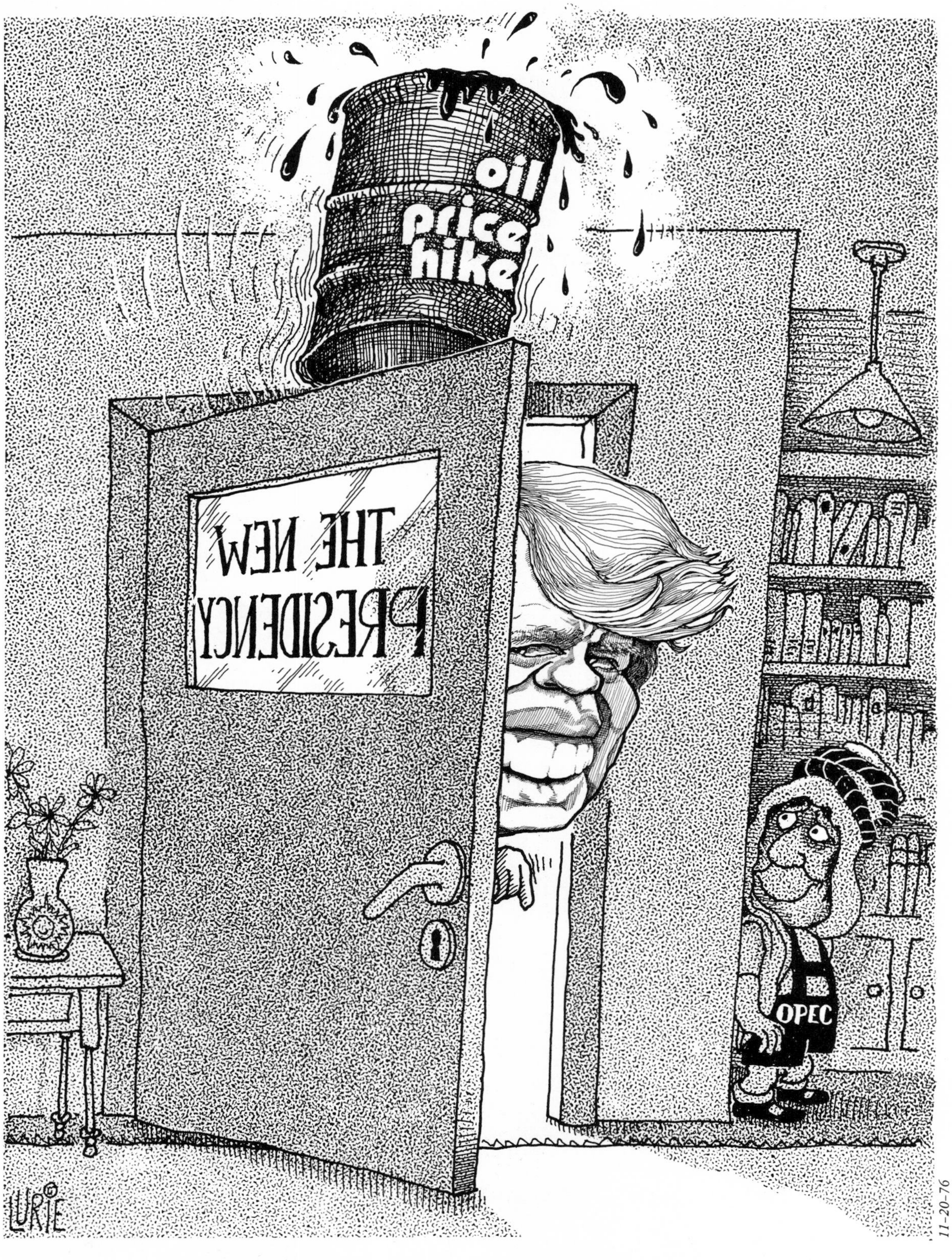
oil
price
hike
THE NEW
PRESIDENCY
OPEC
LURIE ©
11-20-76

WELCOME HOME, CARTER

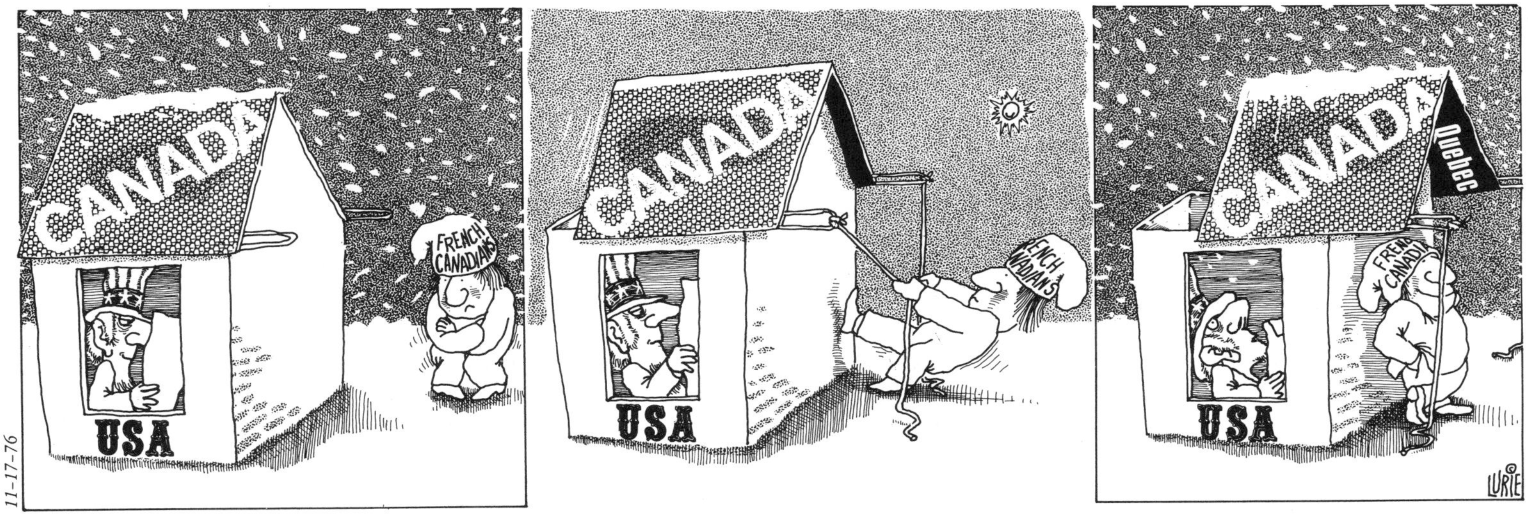
CANADA
FRENCH CANADIANS
USA
CANADA
FRENCH CANADIANS
USA
CANADA
Quebec
USA
LURIE

11-17-76

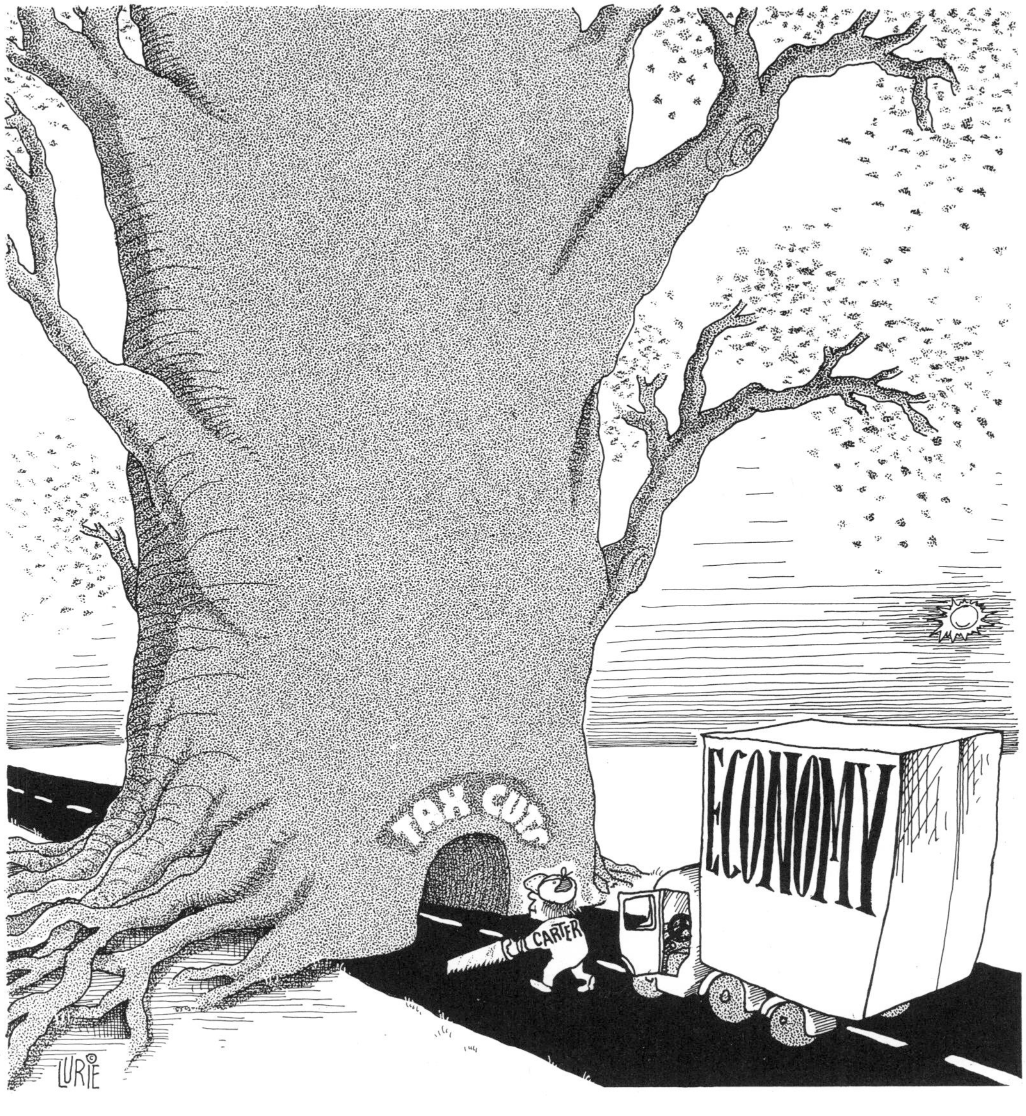
TAX CUTS
ECONOMY
CARTER
LURIE

12-29-76

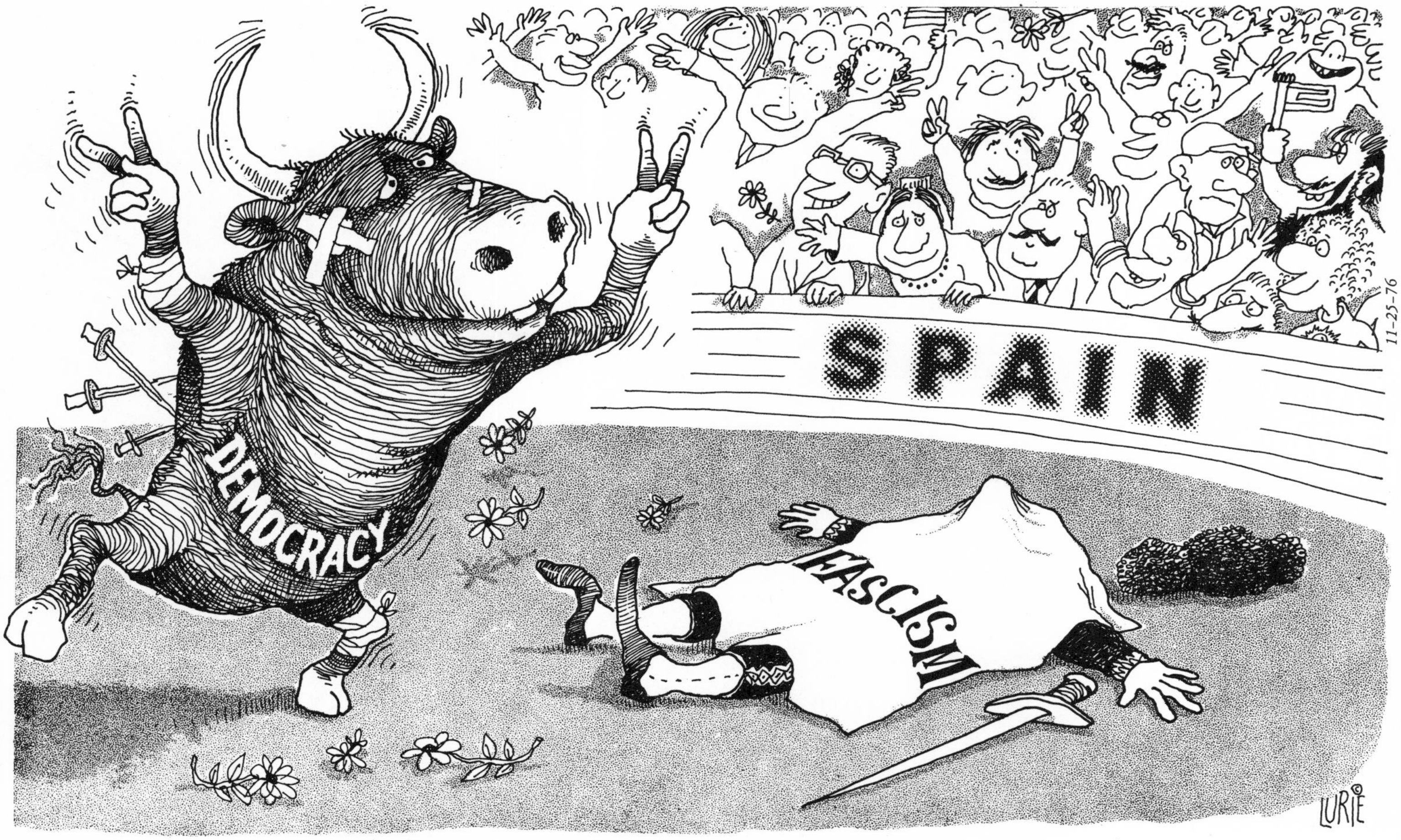
SPAIN
DEMOCRACY
FASCISM
11-25-76
LURIE

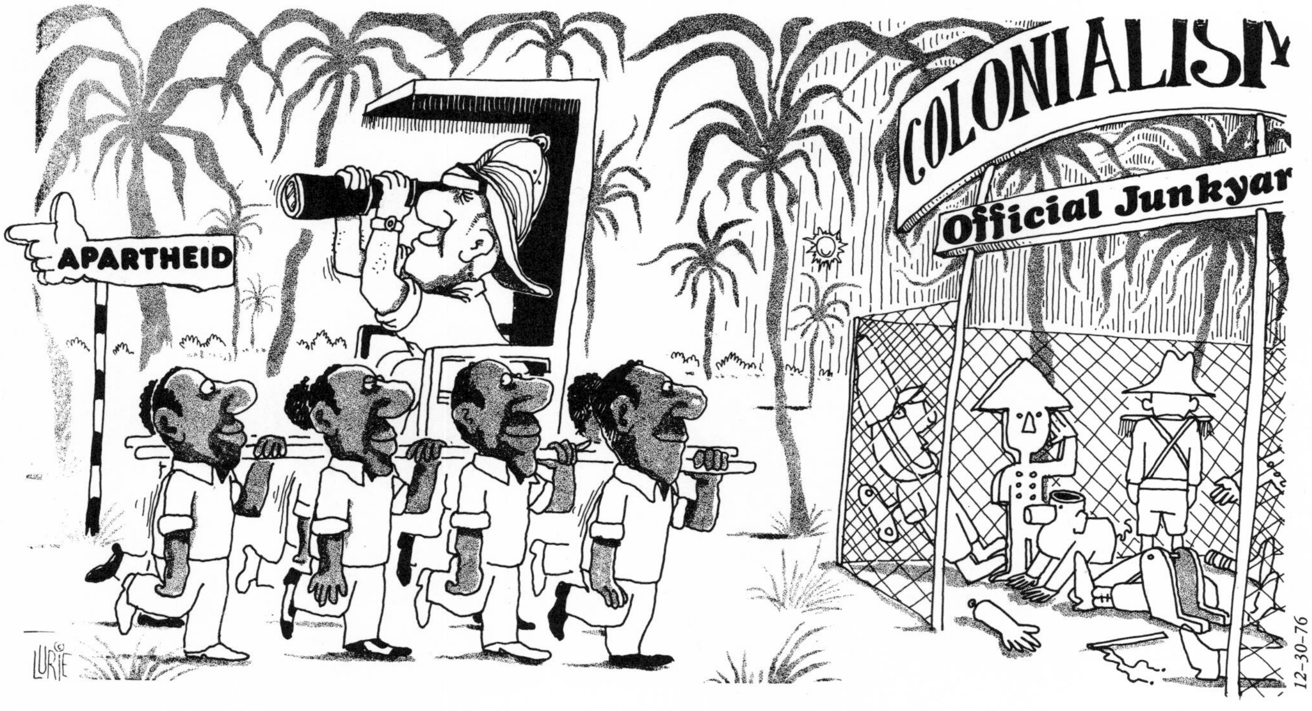
COLONIALISM
Official Junkyar
APARTHEID
LURIE
12-30-76

"CABINET"

12-23-76

LURIE

''ENOUGH BLACK?''

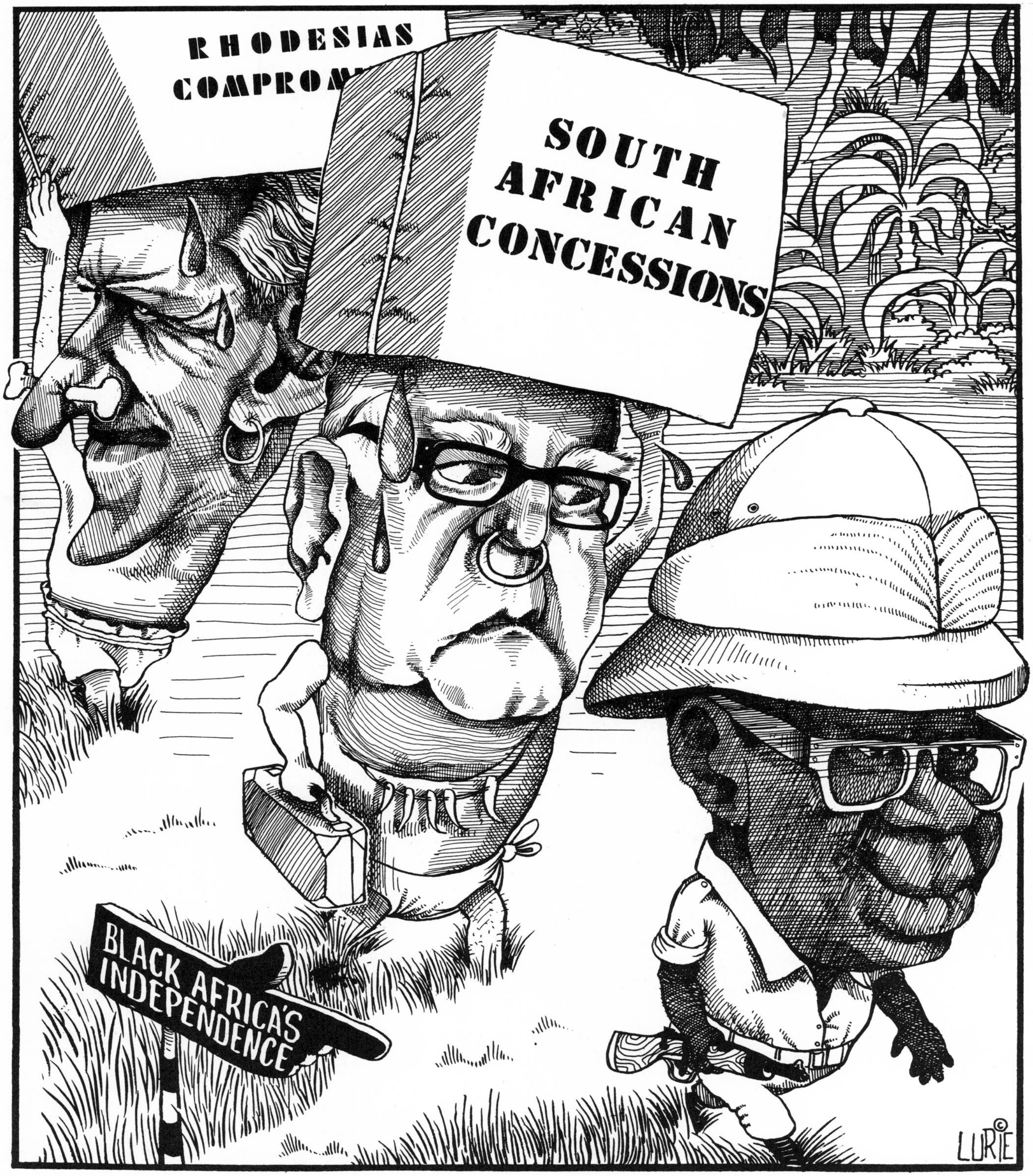
RHODESIAS
COMPROM
SOUTH
AFRICAN
CONCESSIONS
BLACK AFRICA'S
INDEPENDENCE
LURIE©

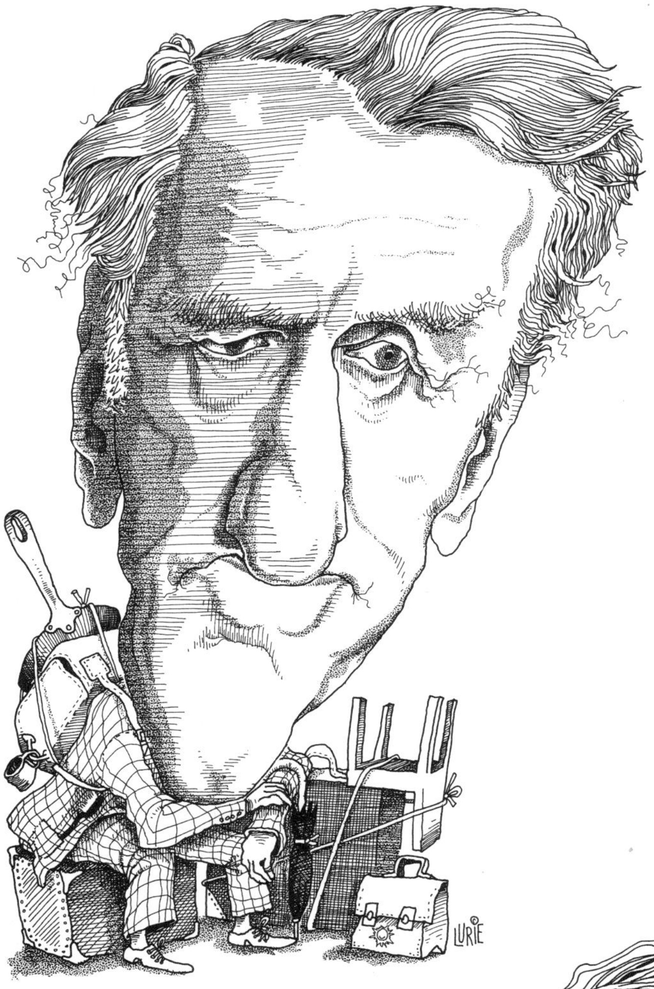
LURIE

Ian Smith
Prime Minister of Rhodesia

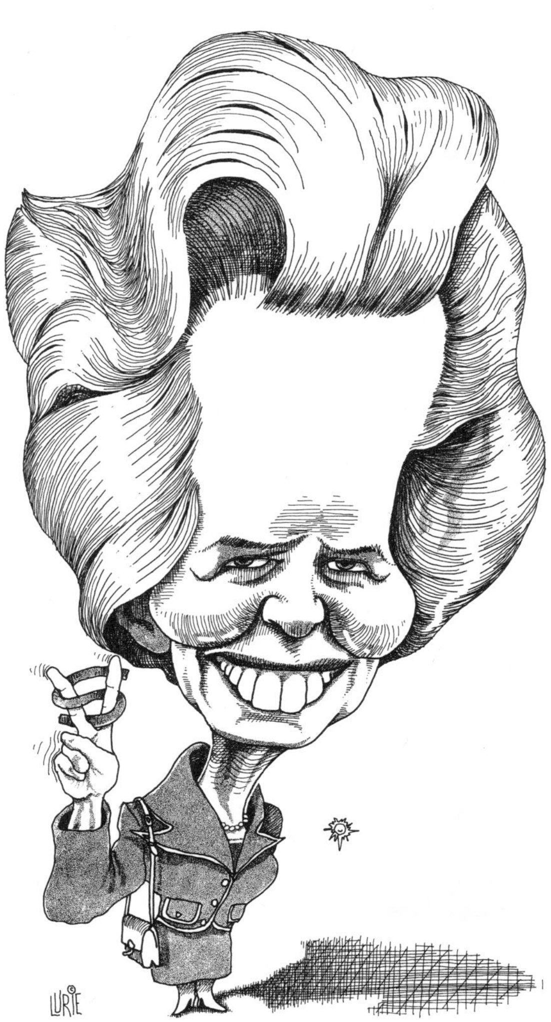
LURIE

Margaret Thatcher
British Opposition Leader

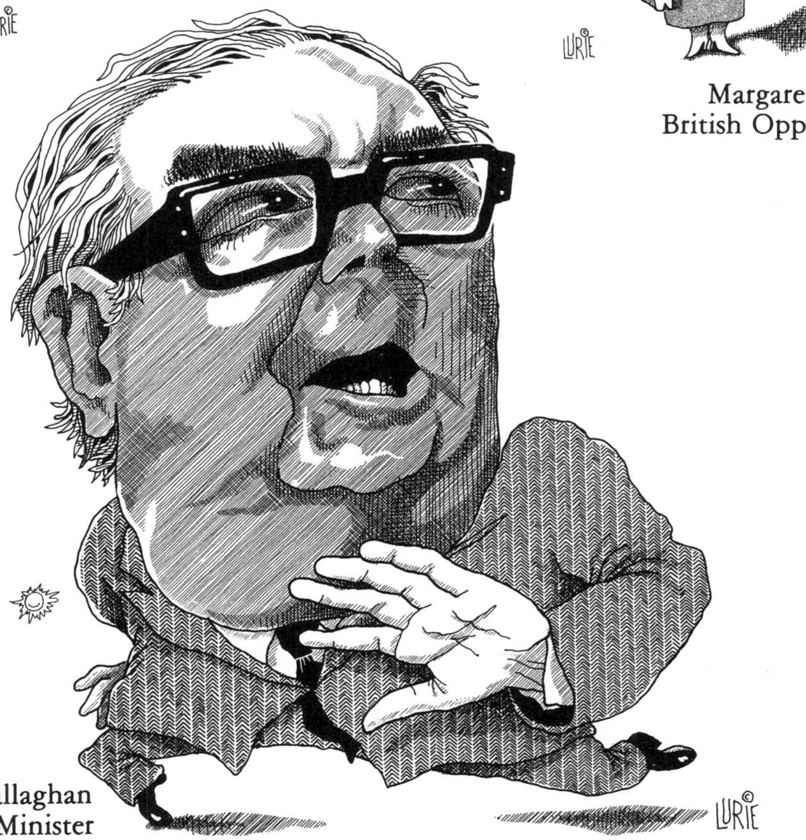
LURIE

Leonard James Callaghan
Britain's Foreign Minister

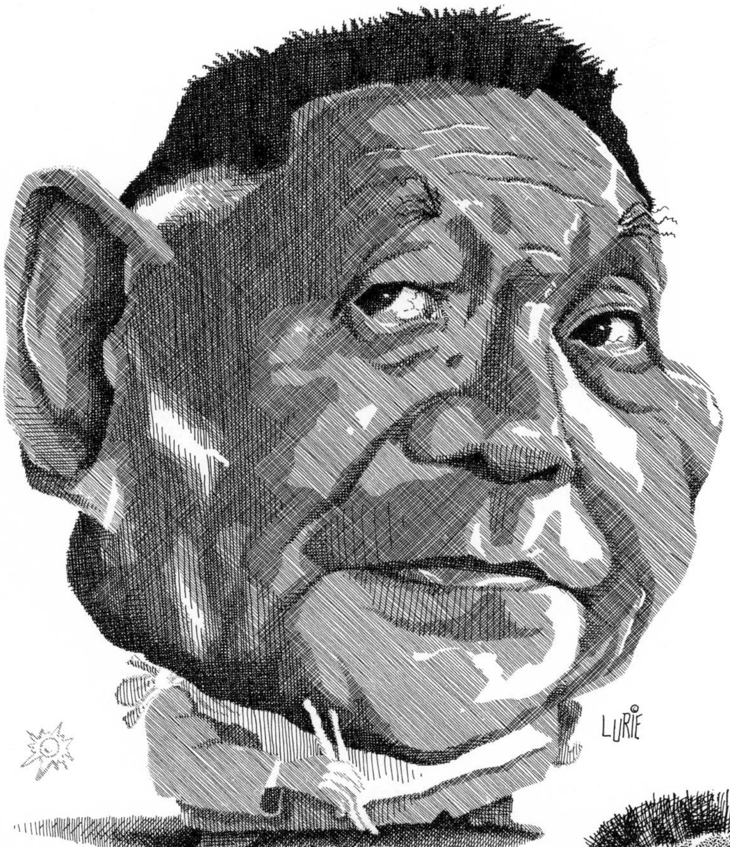
LURIE

Teng Hsiao-ping
China's Future Premier

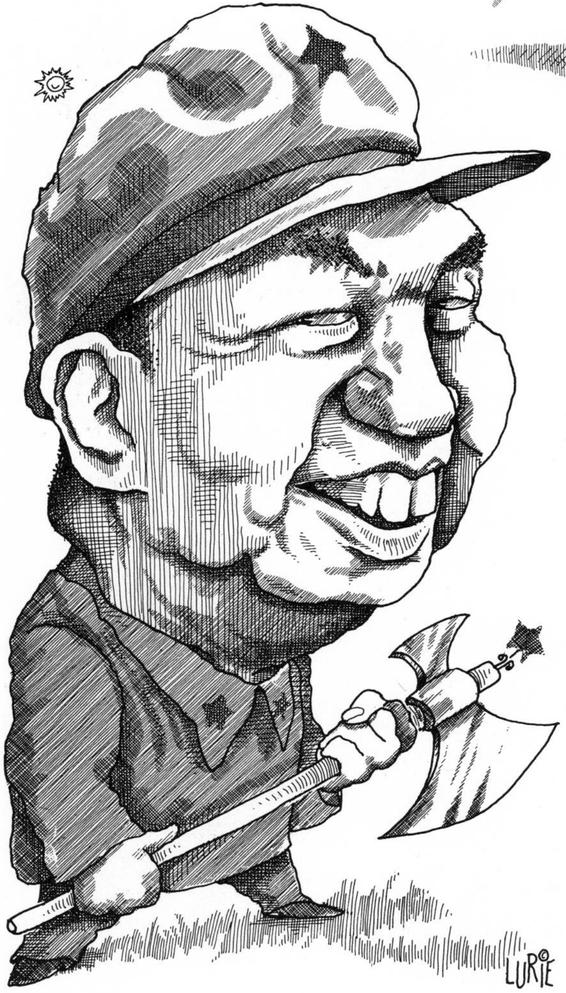
LURIE

Hua Kuo-feng
China's Boss

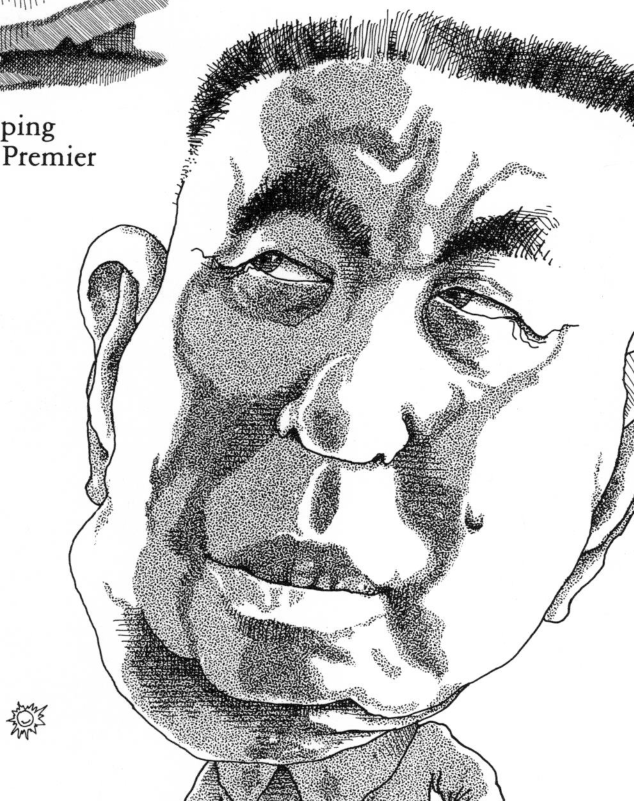
LURIE

Juanita Morris Kreps
New Secretary of Commerce

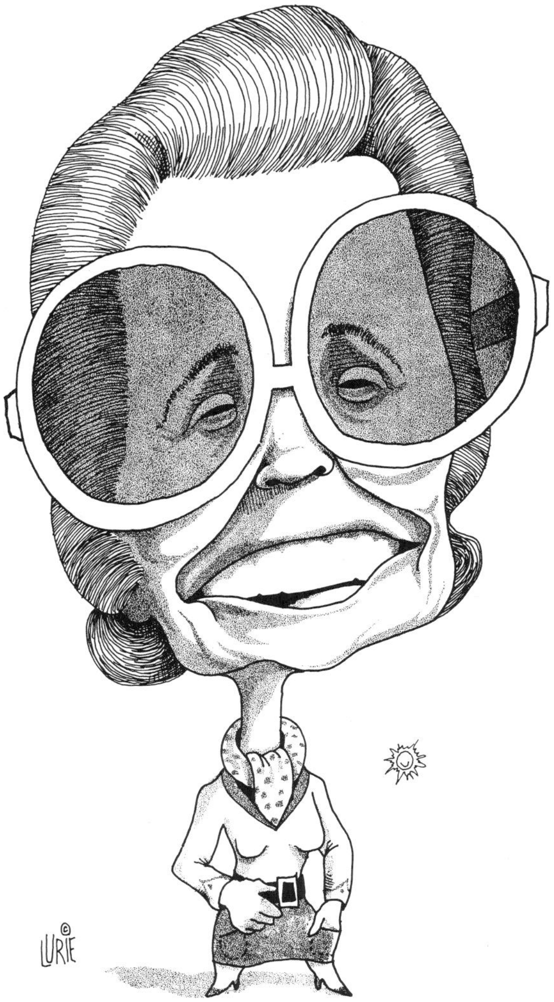
LURIE

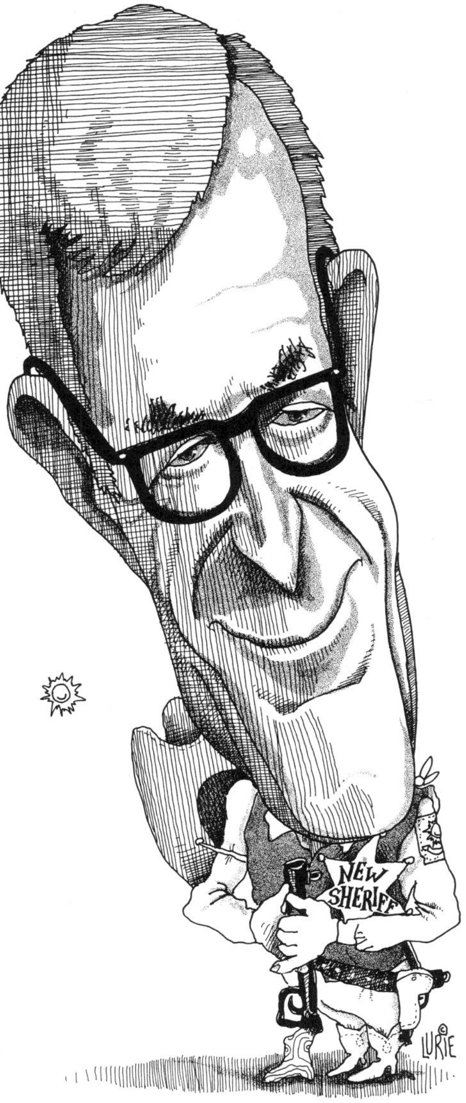
NEW
SHERIFF
LURIE

Dr. Harold Brown
New Secretary of Defense

Griffin Boyette Bell
New Attorney General

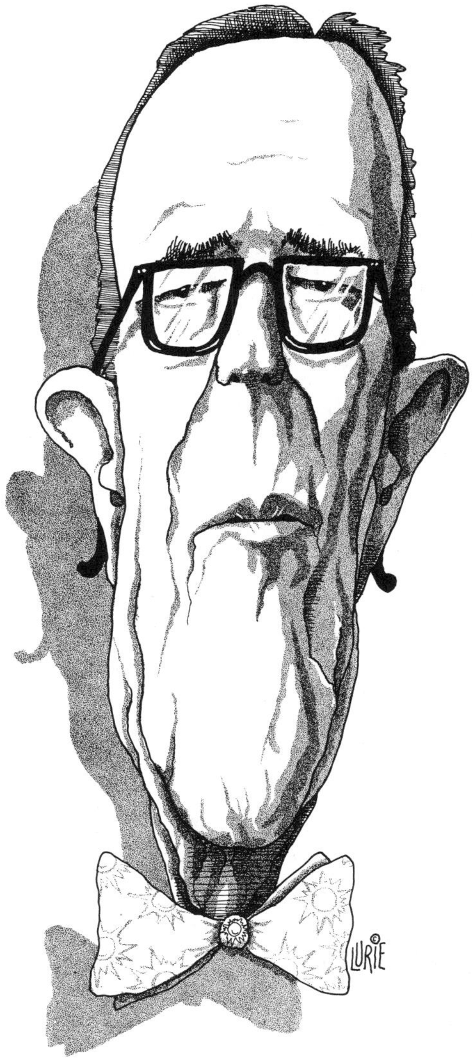
LURIE

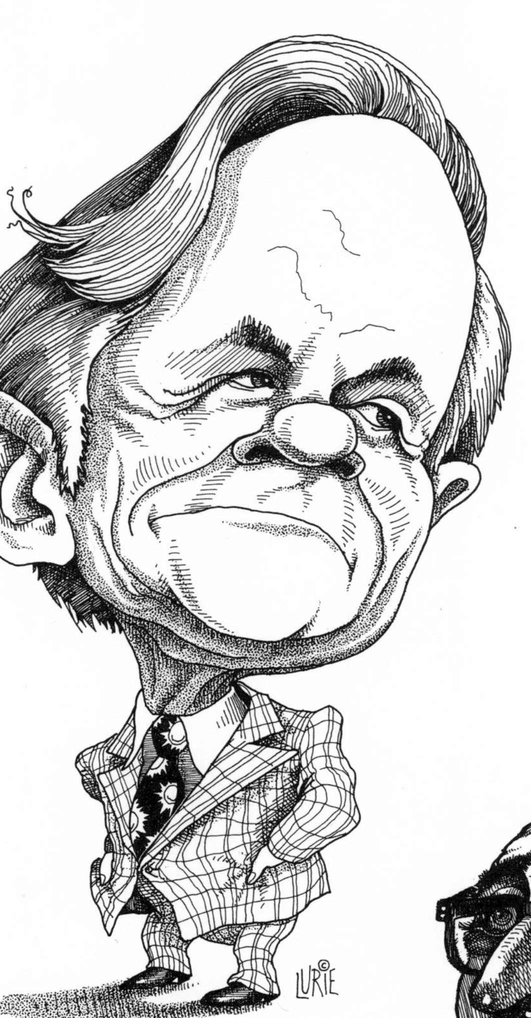
LURIE

Charles Louis Schultze
Chairman of the Council
of Economic Advisers
to President Carter

Arthur Burns
Chairman of the Federal Reserve Board

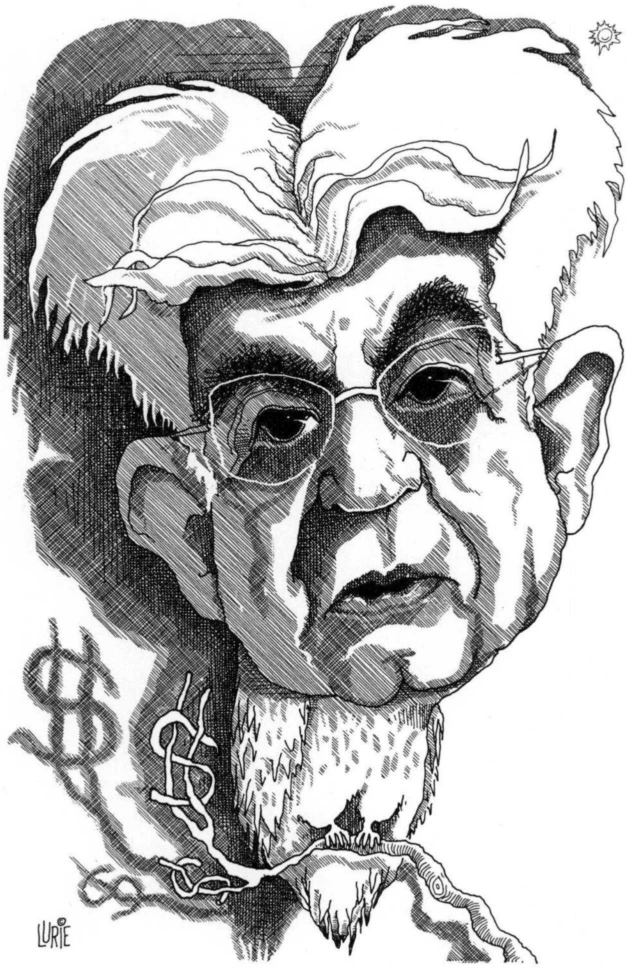
LURIE

Henry

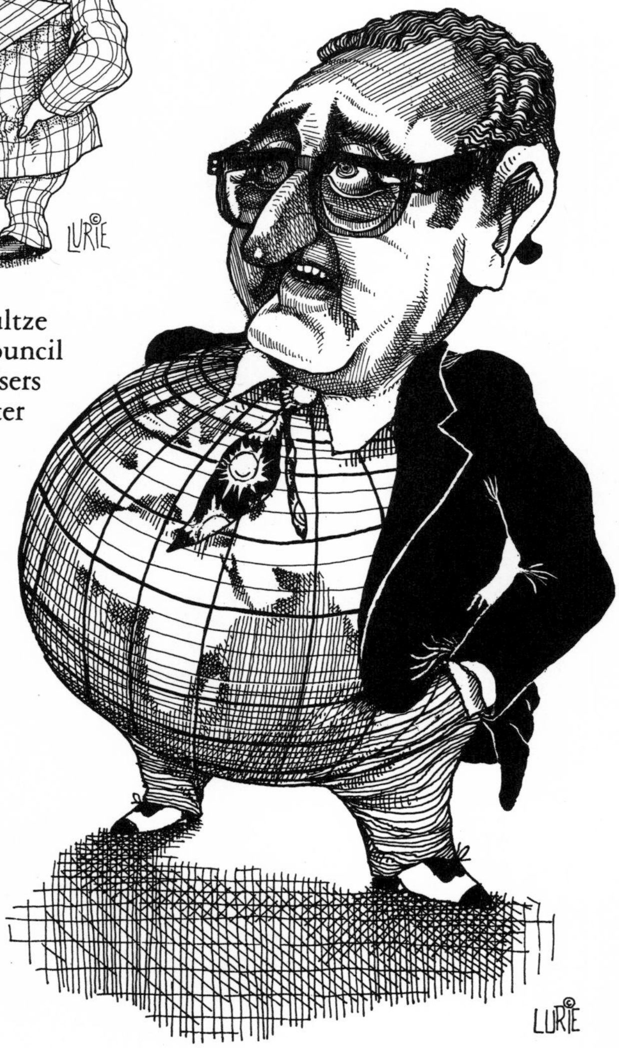
LURIE

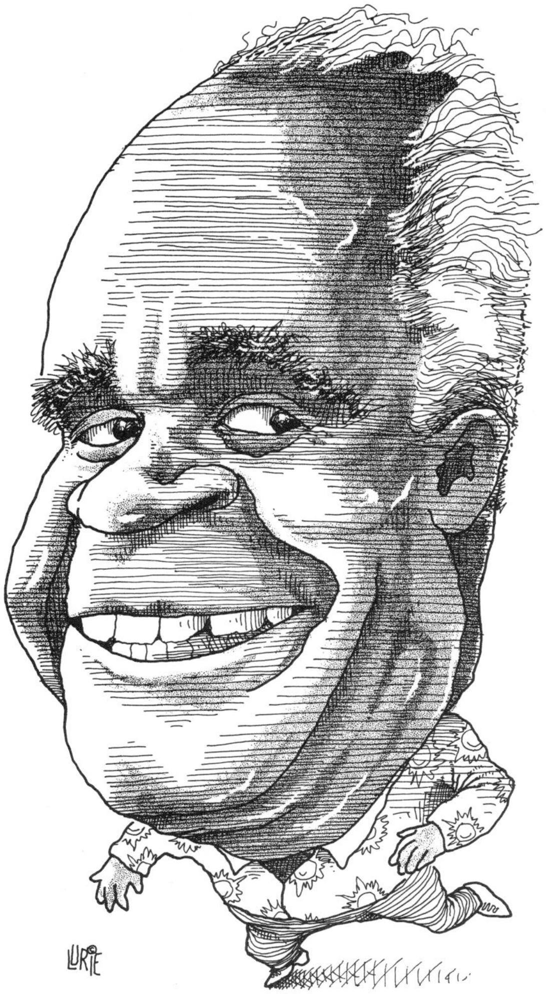

President Kenneth Kaunda
of Zambia

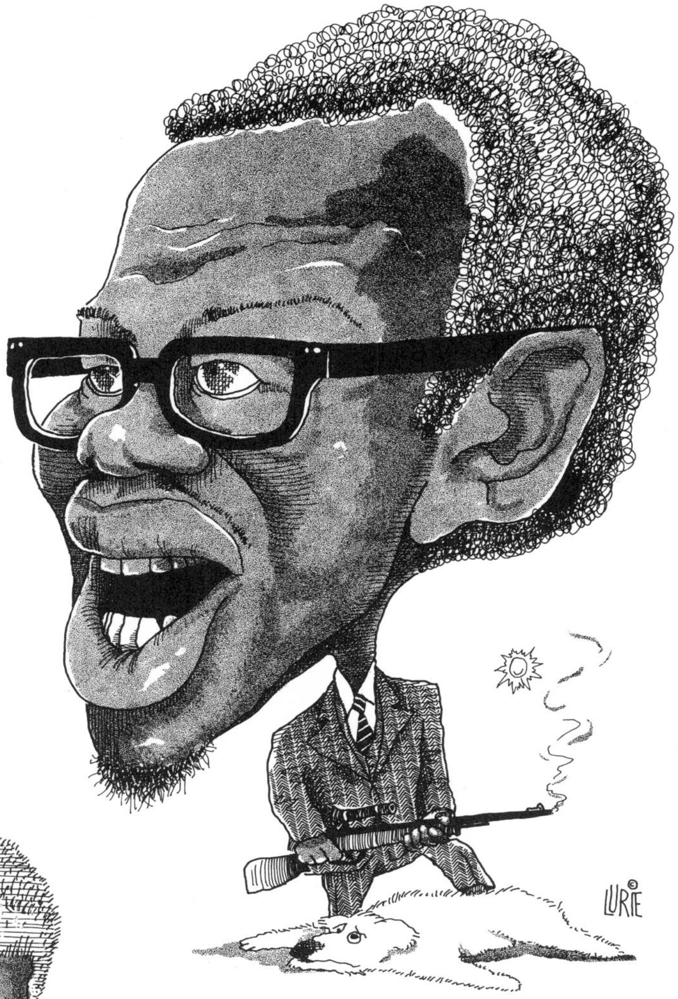

Chief Gatsha Buthelezi
Leader of Black South Africa

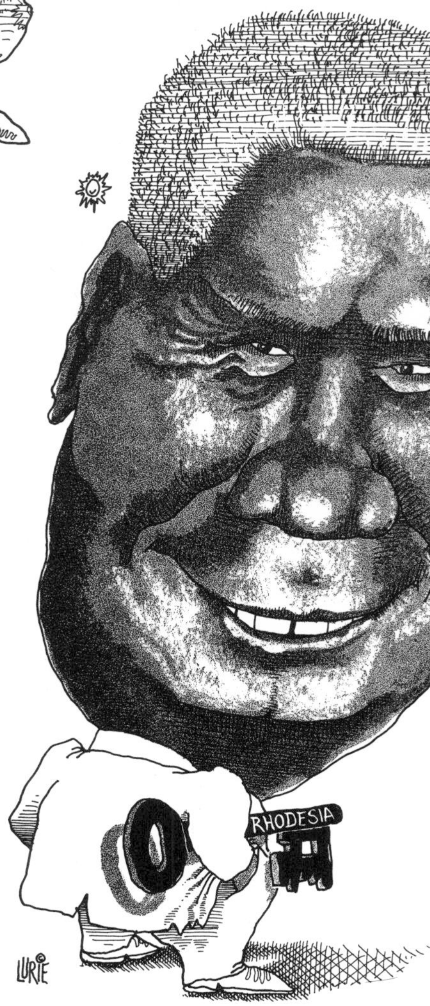
RHODESIA

Joshua Nkomo
Black Rhodesia's Leader

Georges Marchais
French Communist Party Boss

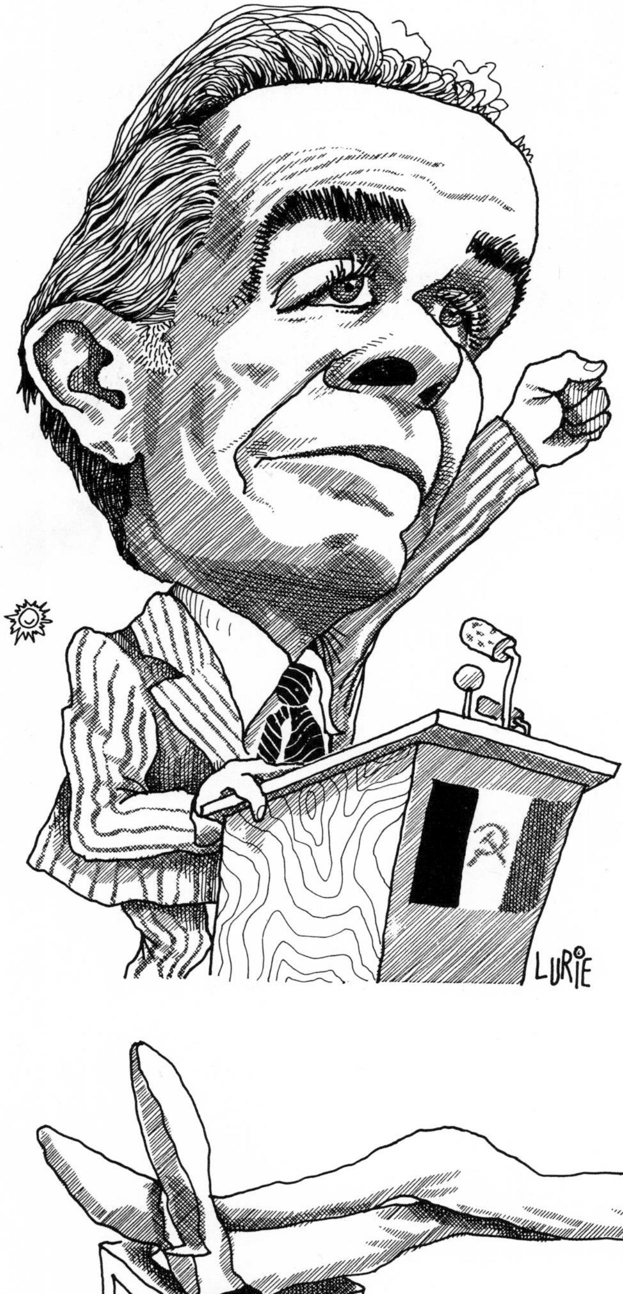
LURIE

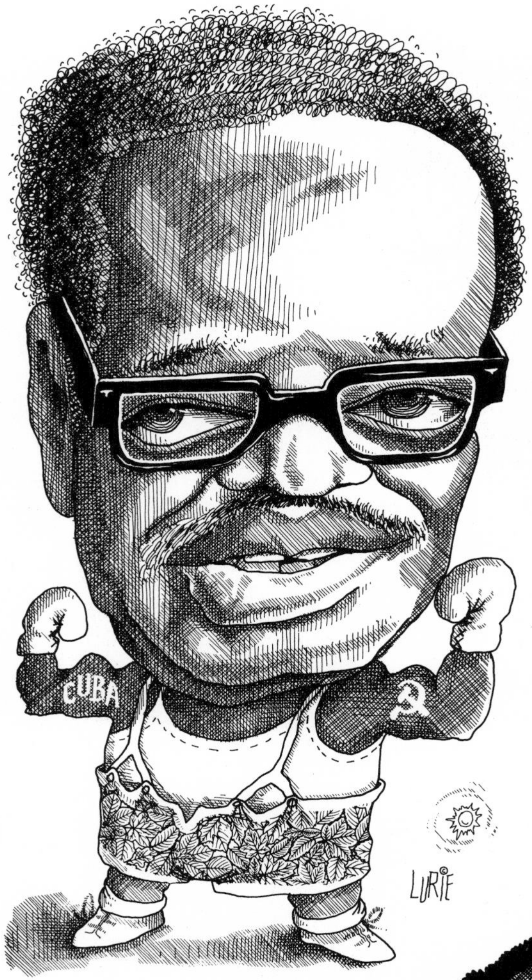
CUBA
LURIE

Agostinho Neto
Angola's MPLA Leader

Holden Roberto
Angola's National Front Leader

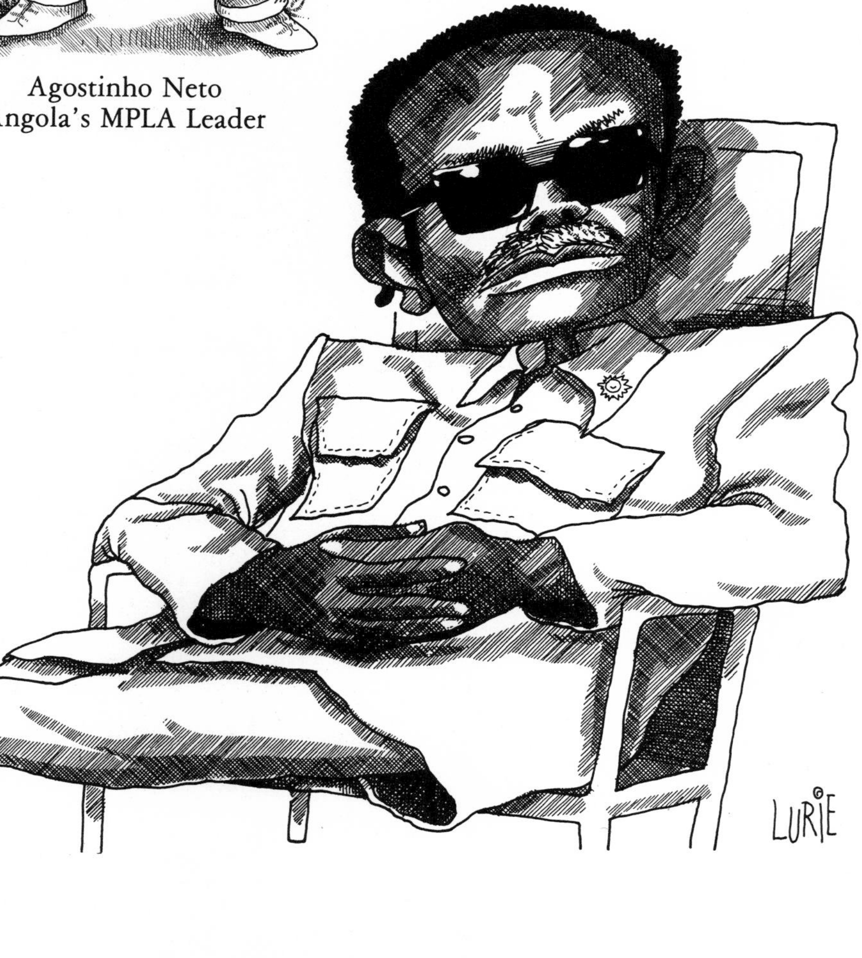
LURIE

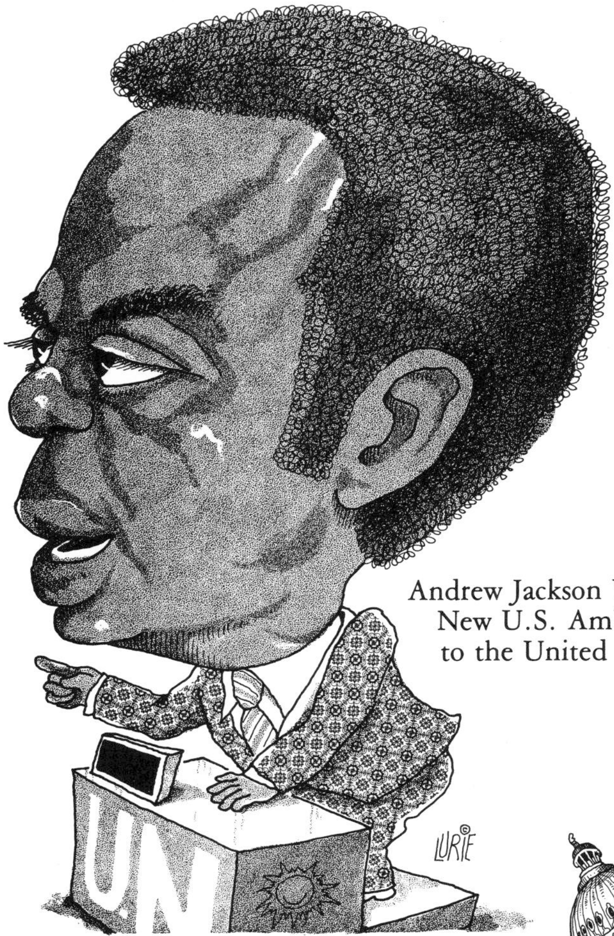
U.N
LURIE

Andrew Jackson Young, Jr.
New U.S. Ambassador
to the United Nations

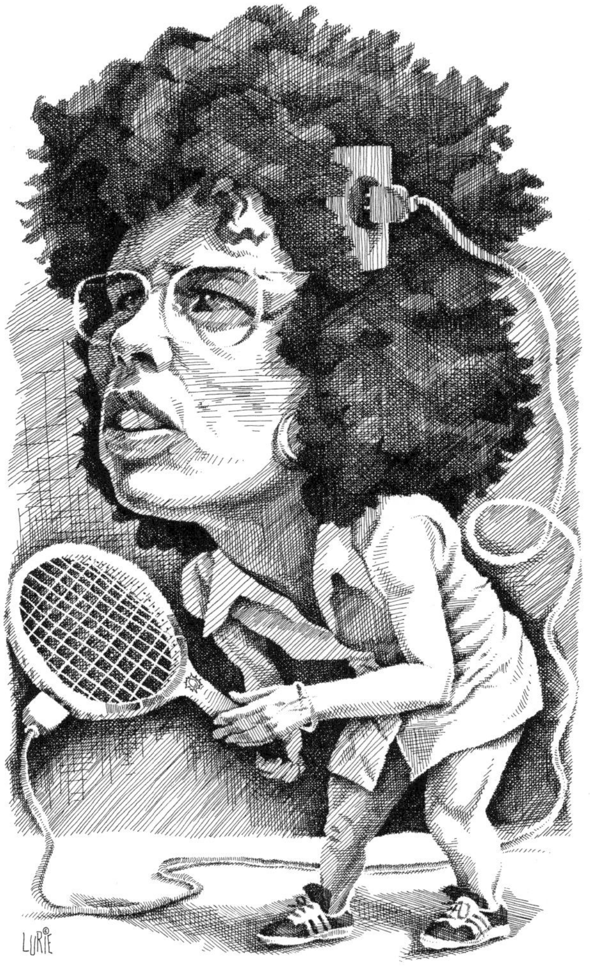
LURIE

Billie Jean King

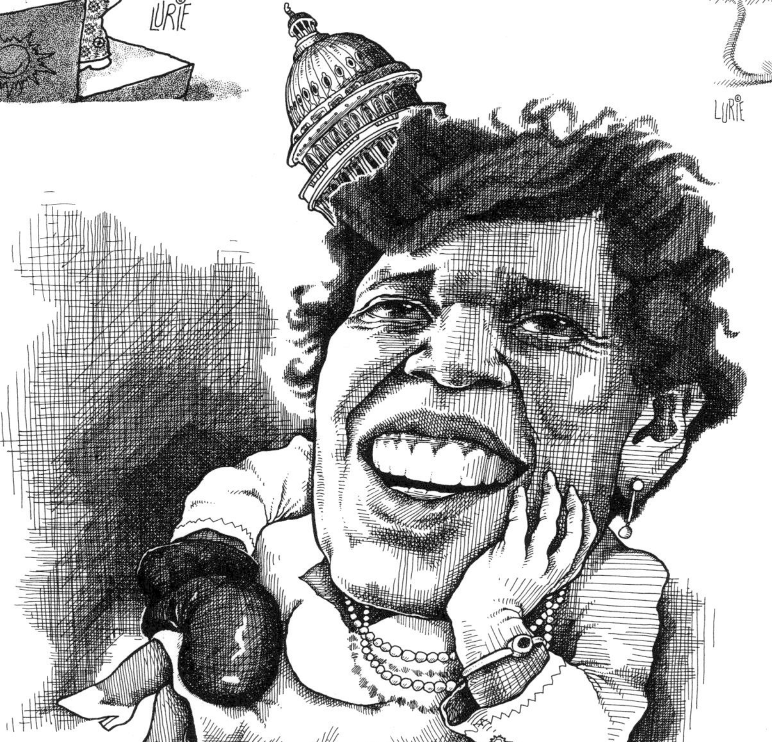
LURIE

Barbara Jordan
Texas State Senator

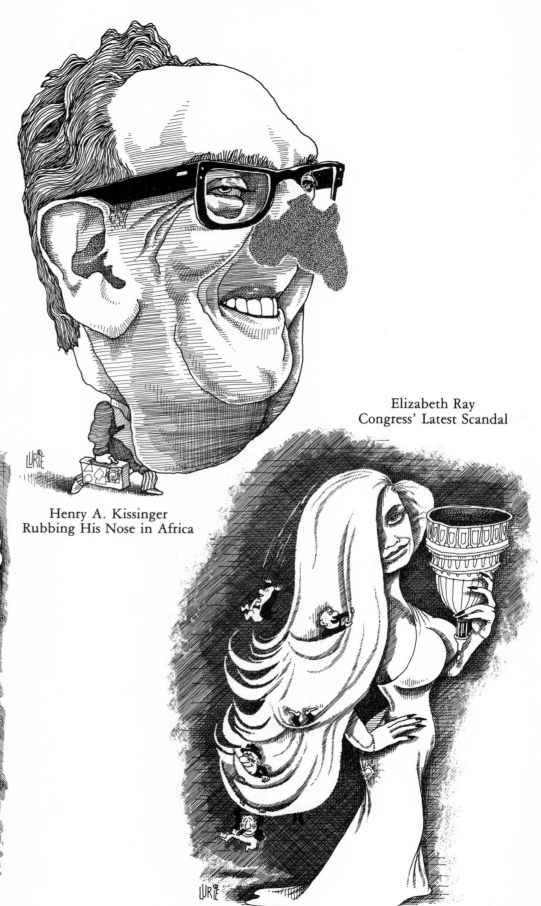

Thomas (Tip) P. O'Neill, Jr.
Next House Speaker

Henry A. Kissinger
Rubbing His Nose in Africa

Elizabeth Ray
Congress' Latest Scandal

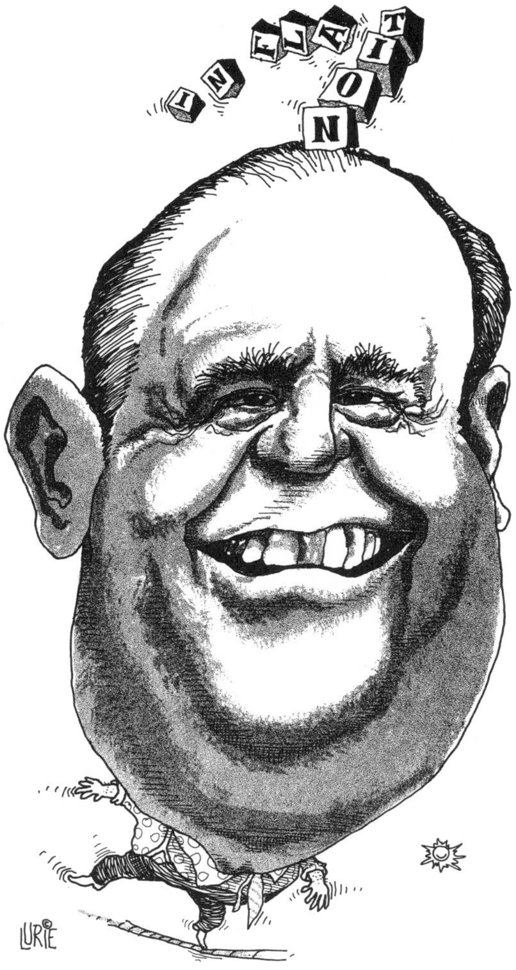
INFLATION
LURIE

Raymond Barre
New Prime Minister of France

Thorbjorn Falldin
Next Prime Minister of Sweden

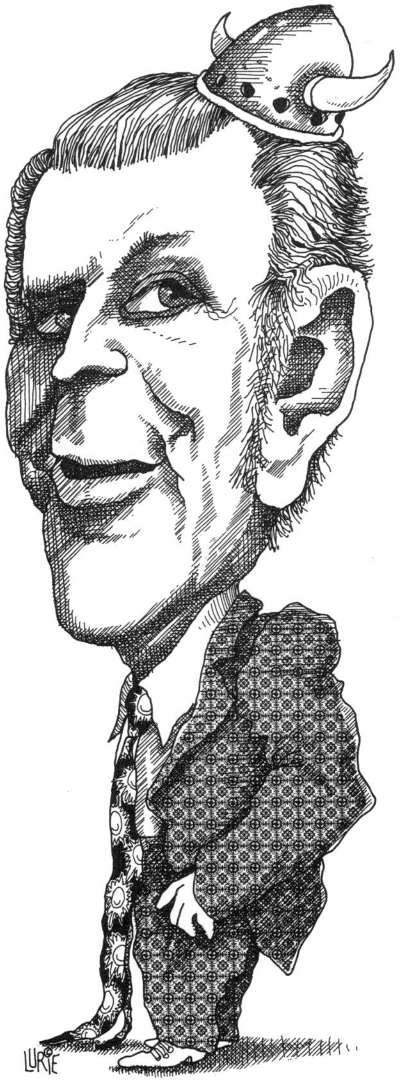
LURIE

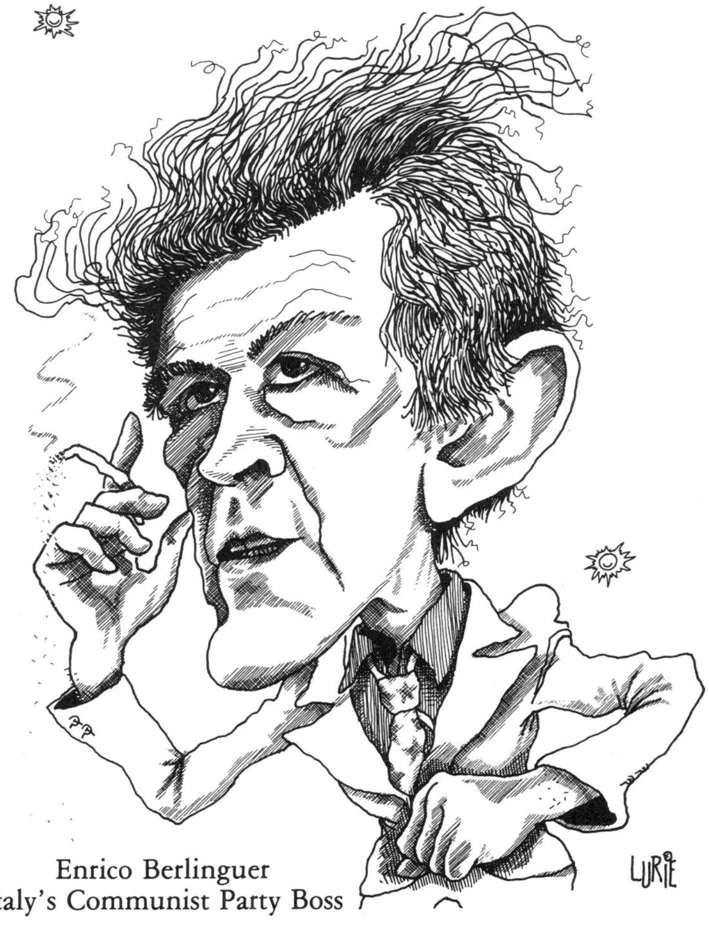
LURIE

Enrico Berlinguer
Italy's Communist Party Boss

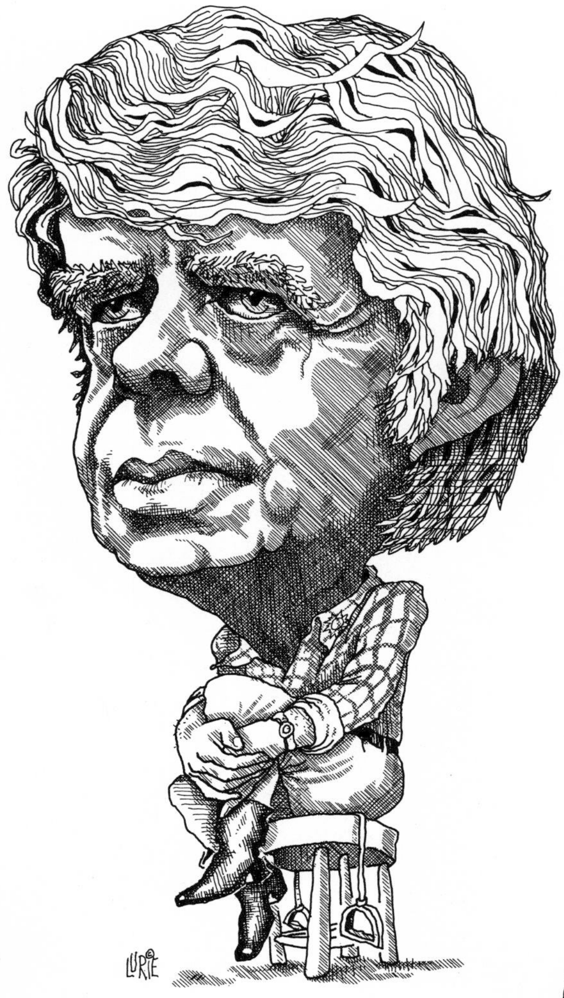
LURIE

Jimmy Carter

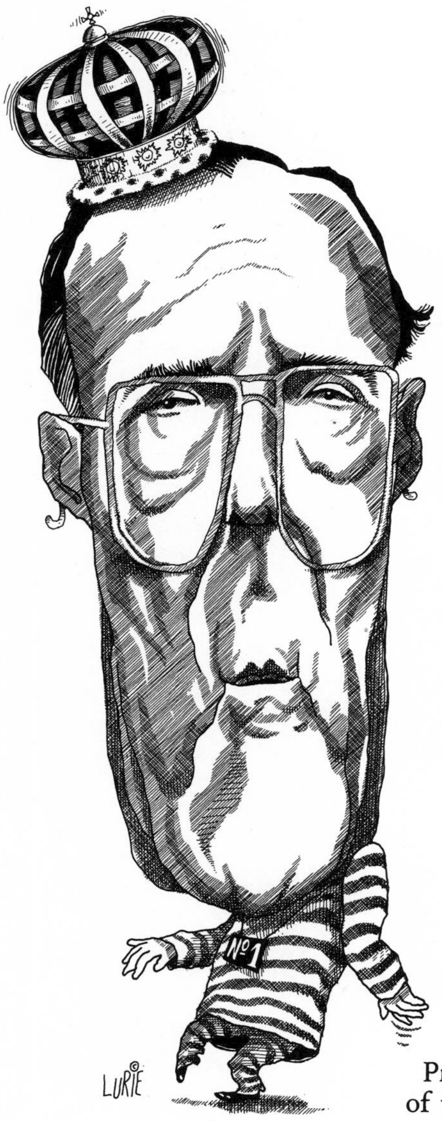
No1
LURIE

Prince Bernhard
of the Netherlands

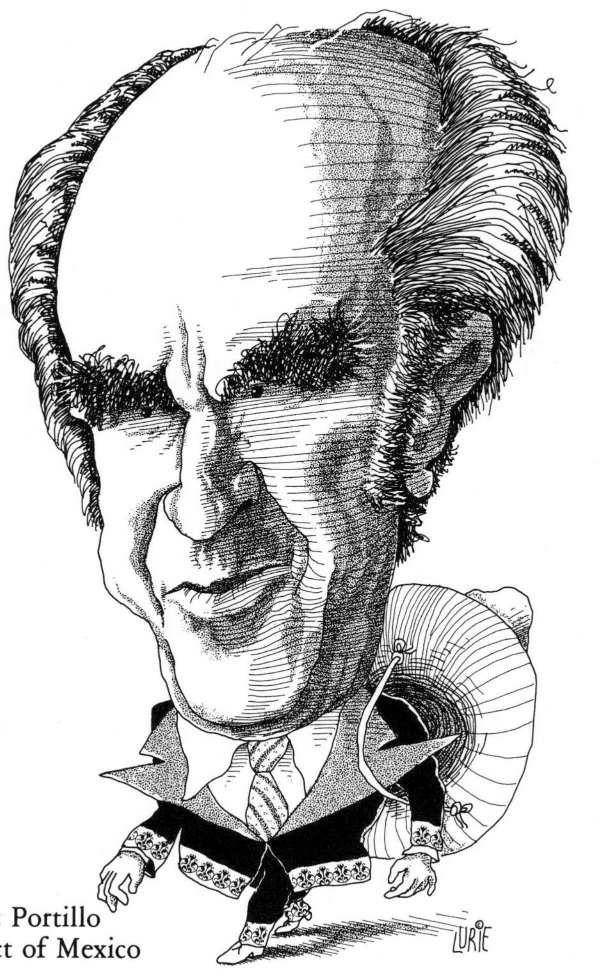
LURIE

Jose Lopez Portillo
President Elect of Mexico

LURIE

Suleyman Demirel
Prime Minister of Turkey

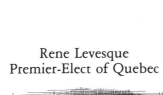

Rene Levesque
Premier-Elect of Quebec

LURIE

ECONOMY
LURIE

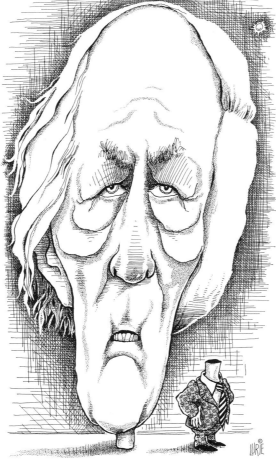

Lt. General Jorge Rafael Videla
Argentina's Boss

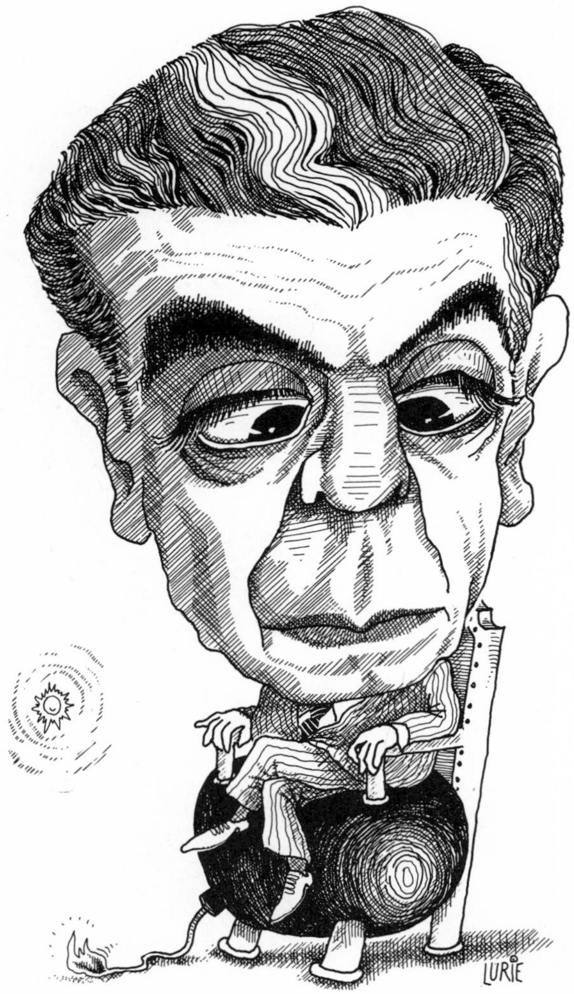
LURIE

Elias Sarkis
New President of Lebanon

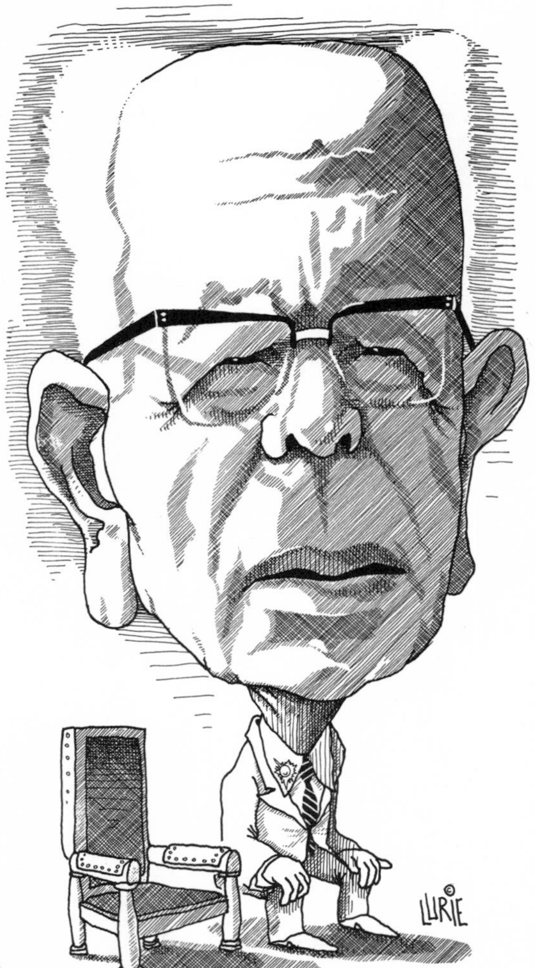
LURIE

President Suleiman Franjieh
of Lebanon

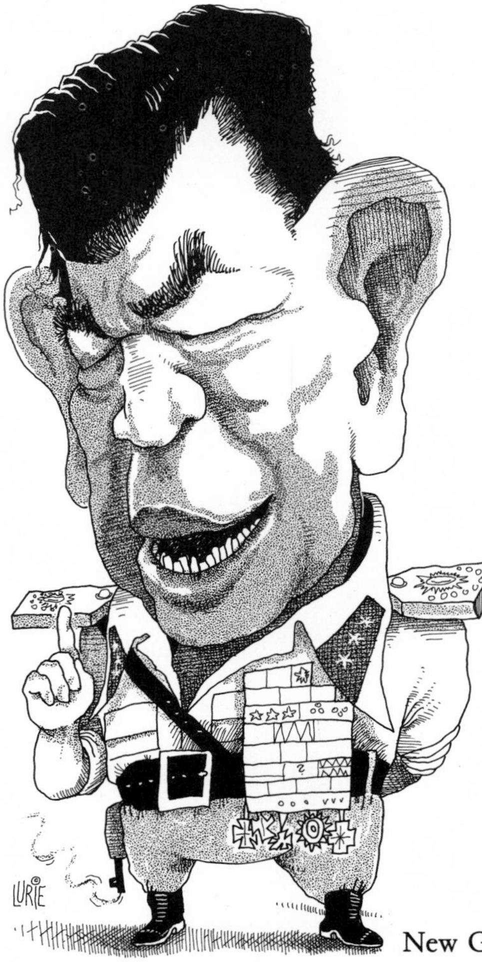
LURIE

Sa-ngad Chaloryu
New Government Chief of Thailand

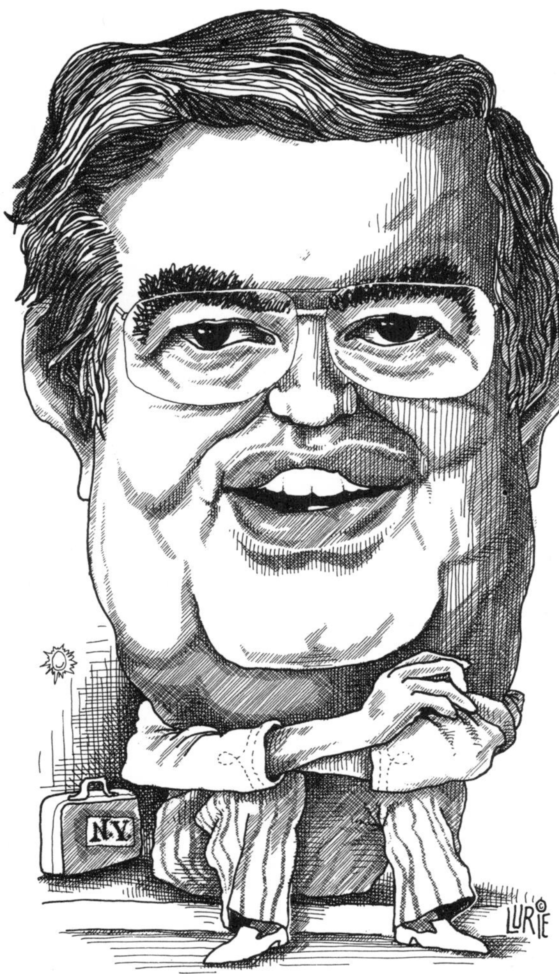
N.Y.
LURIE

Frank Church
Democratic Presidential Candidate

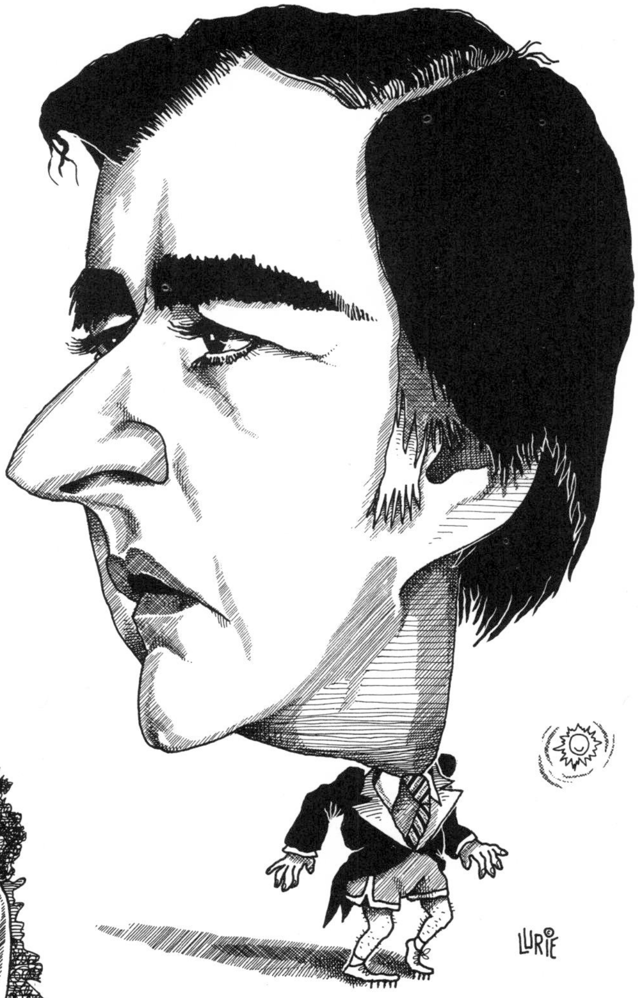
LURIE

Jerry Brown
Democratic Presidential Candidate

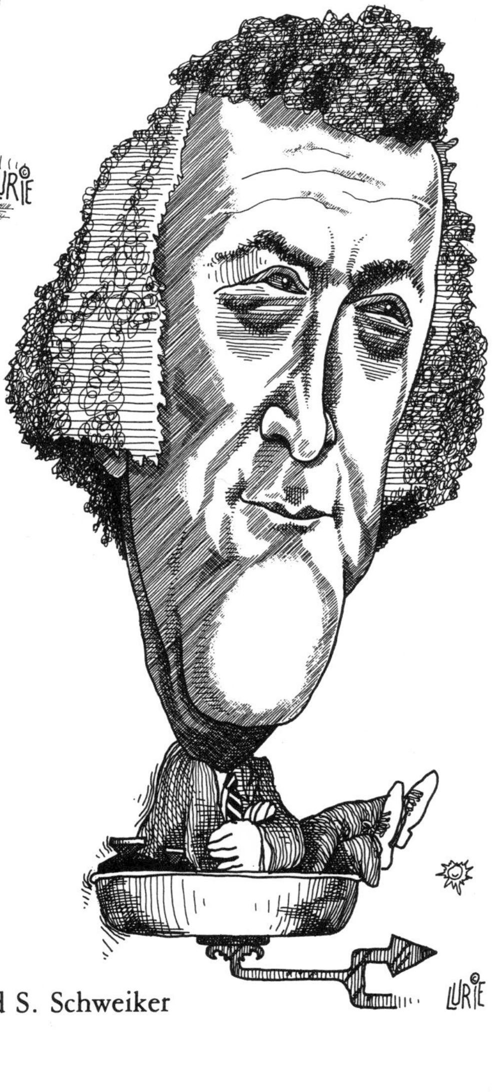
LURIE

Senator Richard S. Schweiker

LURIE

Henry M. Jackson
Presidential Candidate

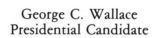

George C. Wallace
Presidential Candidate

WALLACE FOR '76
ACE FOR '72
FOR '68
'64
LURIE

NOMINATION
MY HOPES
LURIE

Hubert H. Humphrey
Potential Presidential Candidate

LURIE

R. Sargent Shriver
Presidential Candidate

Morris K. Udall
Presidential Candidate

PROGRAMS
LURIE

Fred R. Harris
Presidential Candidate

BIG BIZ
LURIE

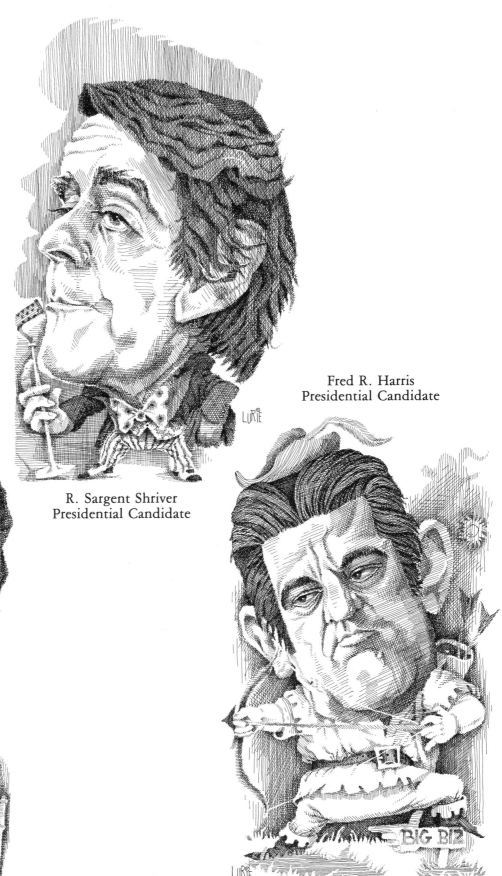

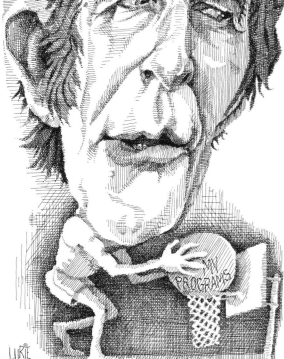

1977

"I highly appreciate the moral and professional motives which led you to create your fantastic cartoons, especially those that firmly support my peace drive, which I embarked upon to restore permanent peace and stability in the Middle East. Such cartoons, coming from a person like you, are very important in backing the peace.

"I have the pleasure to welcome you in Egypt at any time that you deem convenient."

Mohammed Anwar El Sadat

Lurie: ON ANWAR SADAT

I believe the boldest political action of the seventies was Anwar Sadat's move toward peace with Israel at the end of 1977. Simultaneously, he salvaged the sinking Egyptian economy and brought Egypt back into the Western camp in an attempt to regain, piece by piece, the Sinai. A wise move, from every point of view. The benefits: the Nobel Peace Prize; the admiration of the world, and especially the free world; the recognition of Egypt as one of the major U.S. allies in the Middle East.

While preparing for my interview with Sadat in Cairo, I met several Egyptian generals, journalists, artists, taxi drivers, and tourist guides who had been convinced by their countries closed-circuit information machine that during the October War, Israel was saved from the wrath of Egypt by the Americans.

When I interviewed Sadat I mentioned this to him, "reminding" him that it was actually the Israelis who surrounded the Egyptian Third Army, and that only because the U.N. convoys were allowed by the Israelis to cross over to the Egyptian Army were his soldiers saved from starvation or surrender. He, to my astonishment, said, "The Israeli invasion of the Suez West Bank was a fiasco. I was planning to destroy all their tanks within two hours. I informed Kissinger of my intentions, and he threatened me with the intervention of American forces—they would join the Israelis against us. So I decided to refrain."

"Why did you have to ask for Kissinger's permission?" I asked.

A lengthy murmur and shoulder-shrugging was the answer to my question, as if to say that he felt he had had to do so. What worried me more than anything else was that Sadat believed his version of the events.

When I returned to New York, I called Kissinger's office, informed him about the new information that Sadat gave me, and asked for Kissinger's comments. After 24 hours, his office called and left a message: "Mr. Kissinger's comment is 'no comment.'"

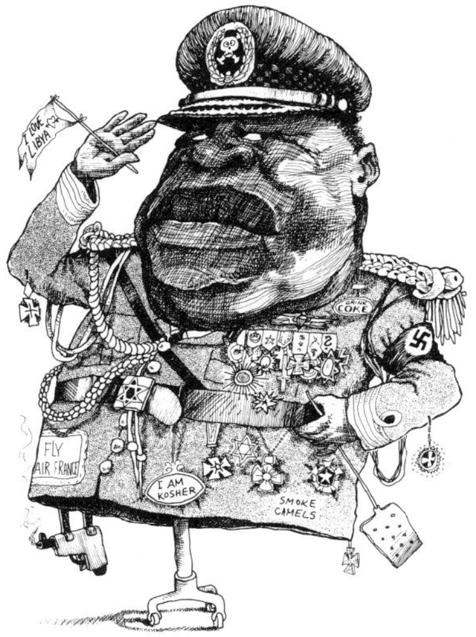
I LOVE LIBYA
DRINK COKE
FLY AIR FRANCE
I AM KOSHER
SMOKE CAMELS

"Why do you do such drawings of me? You must understand my position as a leader of a country full of problems. Your cartoons cause me a lot of anguish and embarrassment, since my ambassadors sent me them from every country. Aren't you ashamed of yourself?"

Idi Amin
(when still President of Uganda)

Lurie: ON THE INTERNATIONAL CARTOONIST

Is it easier to develop cartoons about national and international events rather than local ones? First, there is no such thing as an easy or hard way to develop a cartoon. The important question is whether the political cartoonist has anything to say, to comment on, to predict or project about a given situation. The situation can involve a Mr. Smith or Mr. Helmut Schmidt or a Carter or a Reagan. However, as an internationally syndicated cartoonist I have to be sure that my cartoons will be relevant to readers in Boston, Hong Kong, Indonesia, London, Paris, Bonn, South Africa, Zambia, and so forth. A cartoon on pot holes in New York City would amuse my readers on Long Island who read *Newsday* but be of little interest to readers in Tel Aviv.

On the other hand, working closely with a specific newspaper makes you focus your attention on those specific readers. Many times I'm asked if it is proper for me to criticize local politicians or situations when I have lived in the locality for only a short time. My answer is that I am like a driver who has an international driver's license. Once that driver gets into his car, the host newspaper, he also makes sure that he gets a good road map by picking the brains of his colleagues at the newspaper and reading and studying relevant material.

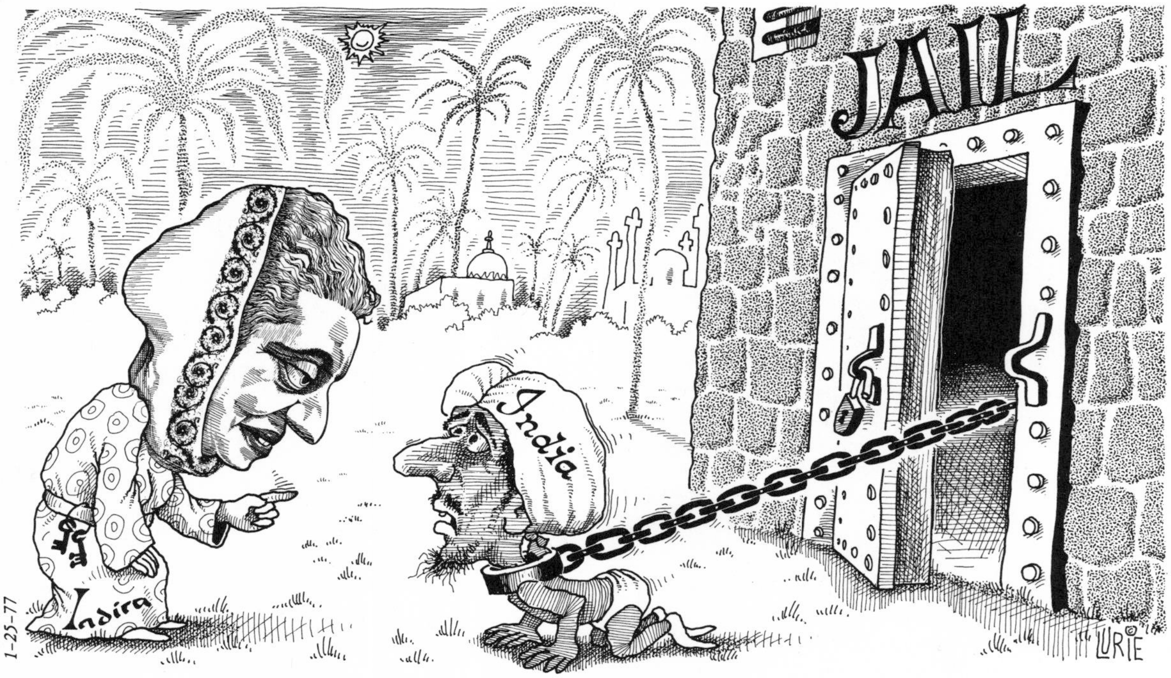
JAIL
India
Indira
1-25-77
LURIE

"SEE, I PROMISED I'D LET YOU OUT!"

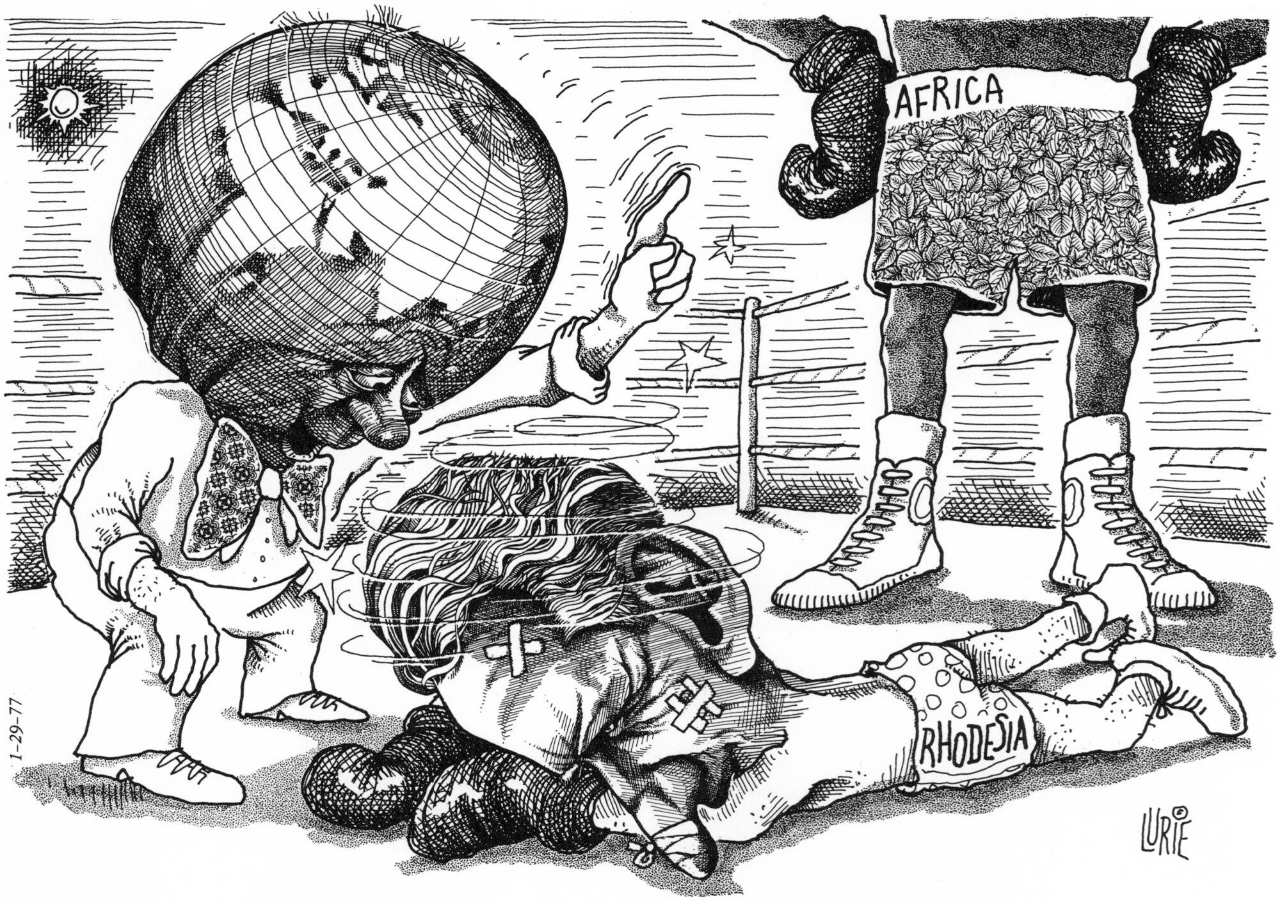
AFRICA
RHODESIA
1-29-77
LURIE

"ONE THOUSAND TWO HUNDRED FIFTY THREE . . .
ONE THOUSAND TWO HUNDRED FIFTY FOUR . . ."

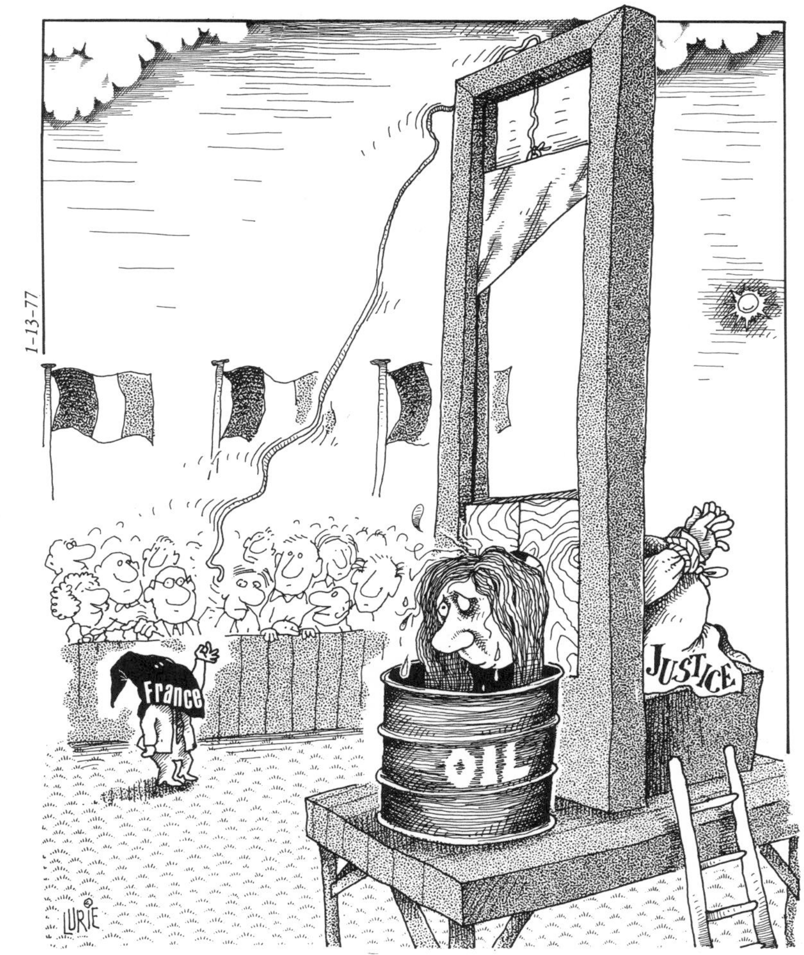
1-13-77
France
OIL
JUSTICE
LURIE

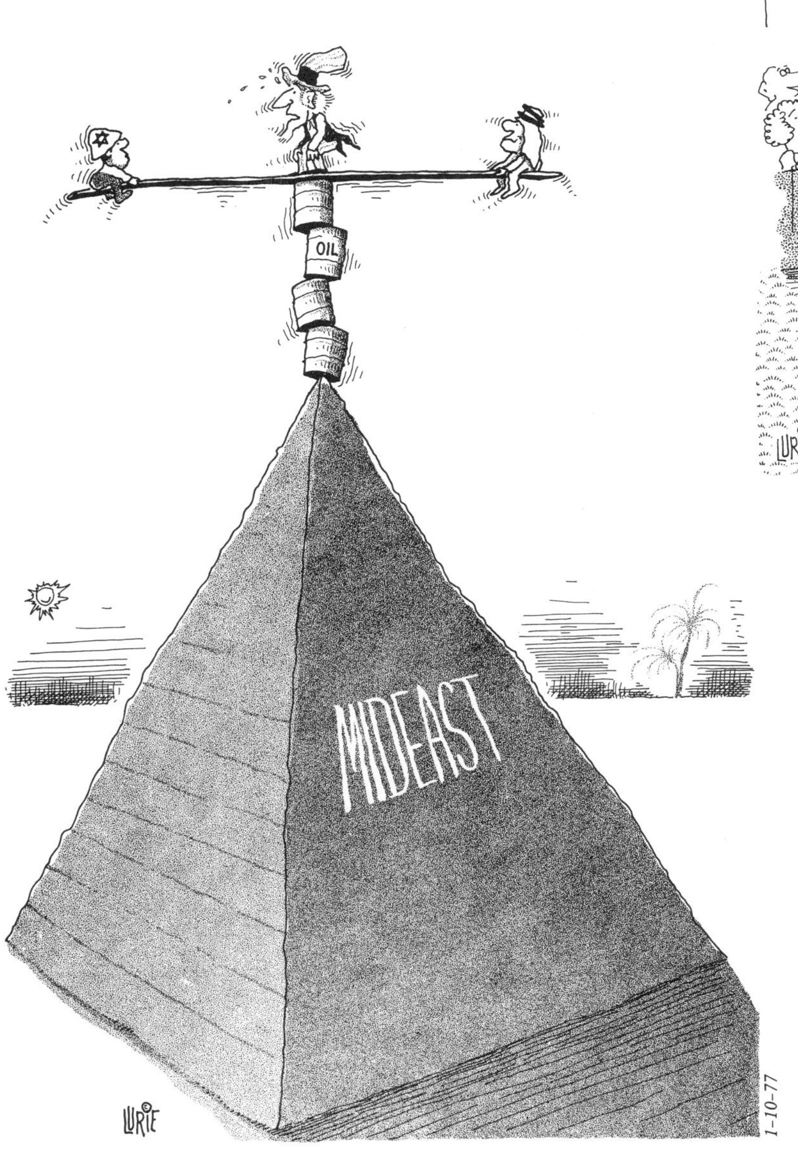
OIL
MIDEAST
LURIE
1-10-77

"N-NOW NOW . . . WE D-DON'T WANT TO M-M-MAKE ANY F-FUNNY MOVES, D-DO WE?!"

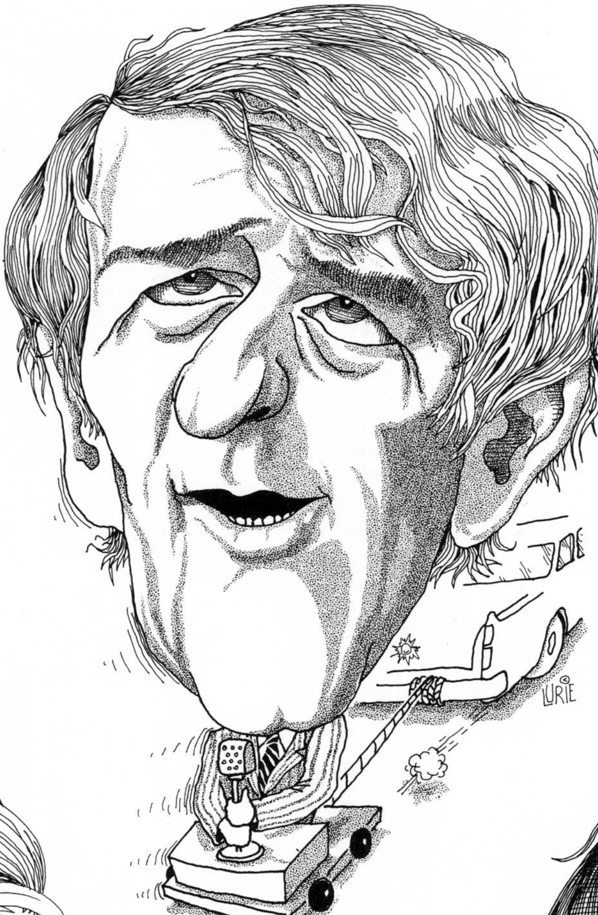
LURIE

Jody Powell
President's Press Secretary

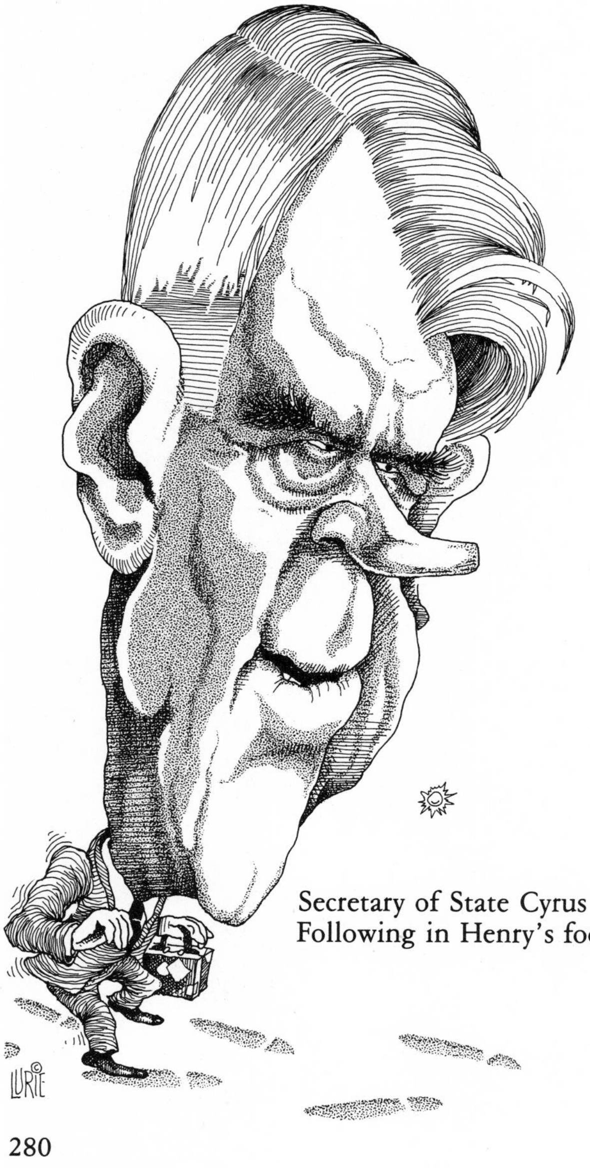
LURIE

Secretary of State Cyrus Vance
Following in Henry's footsteps

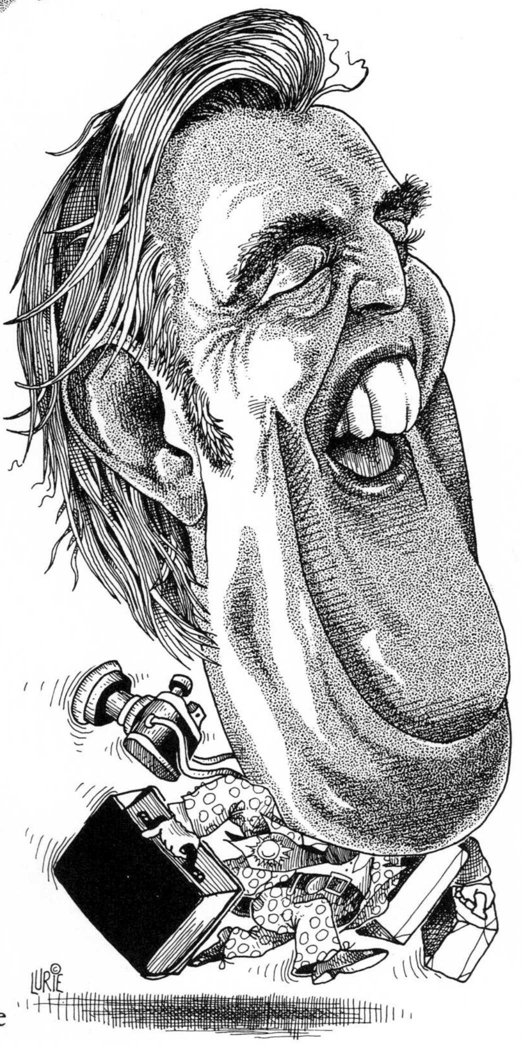
LURIE

Vice President Walter Mondale

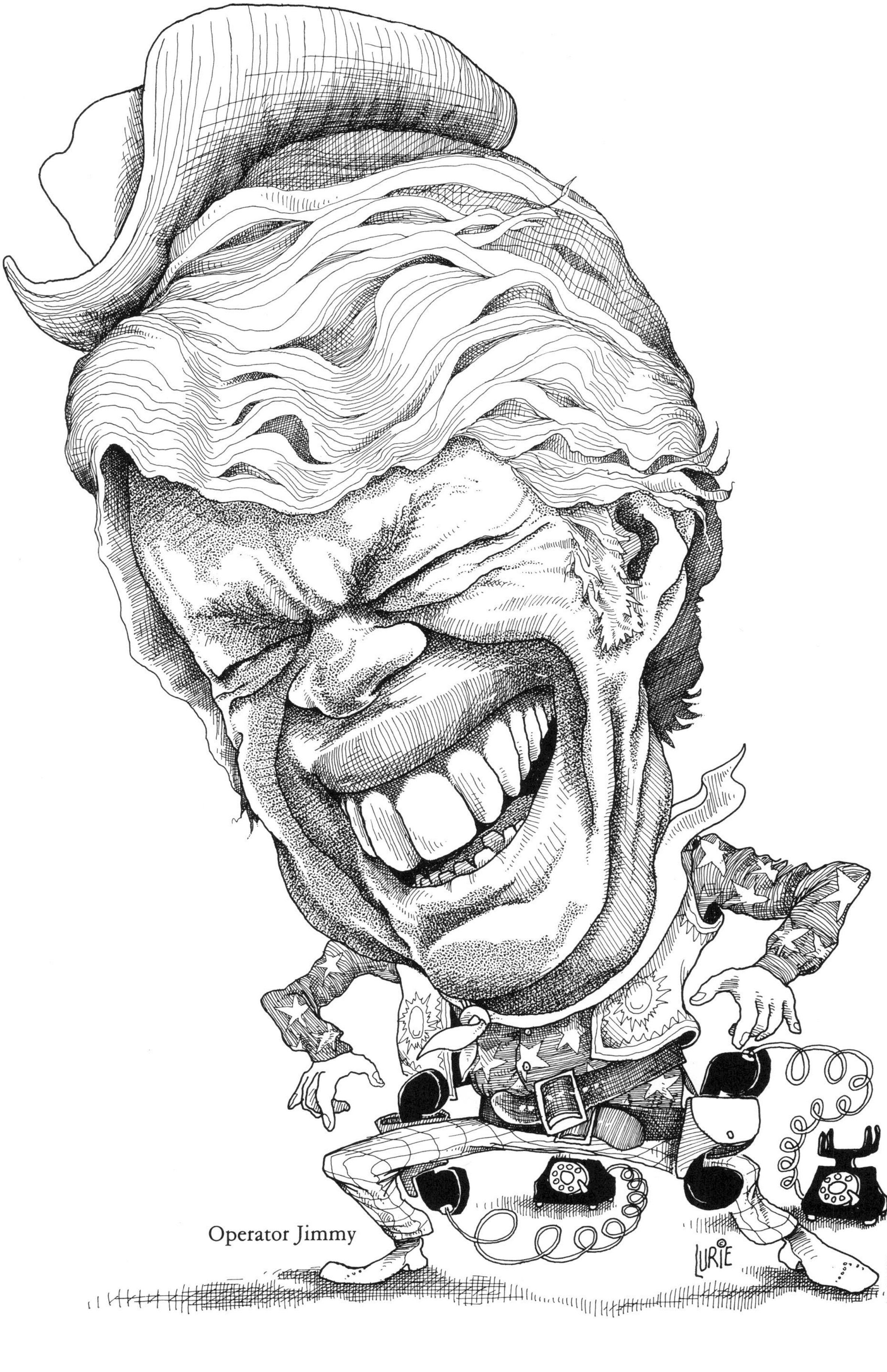
LURIE
2-23-77
Operator Jimmy

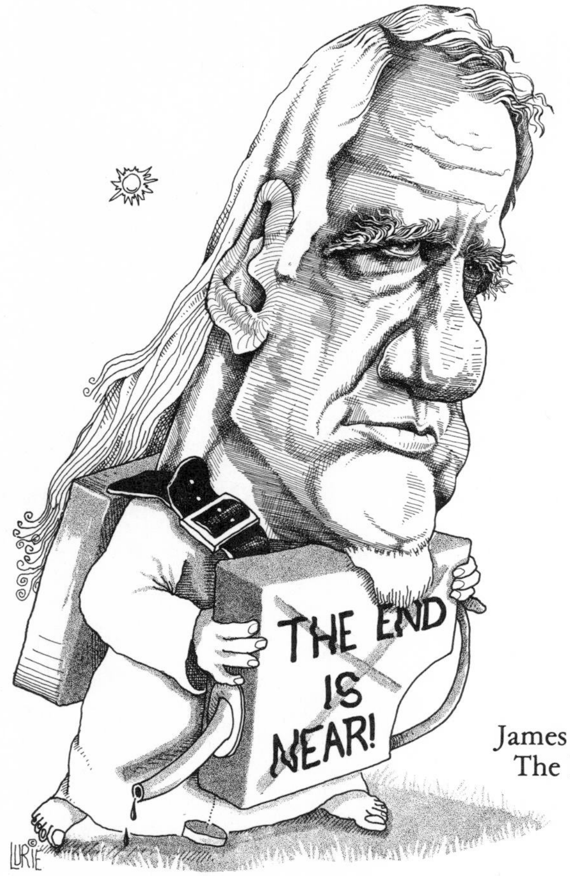
THE END IS NEAR!
LURIE

James Schlessinger
The Fuel Savior

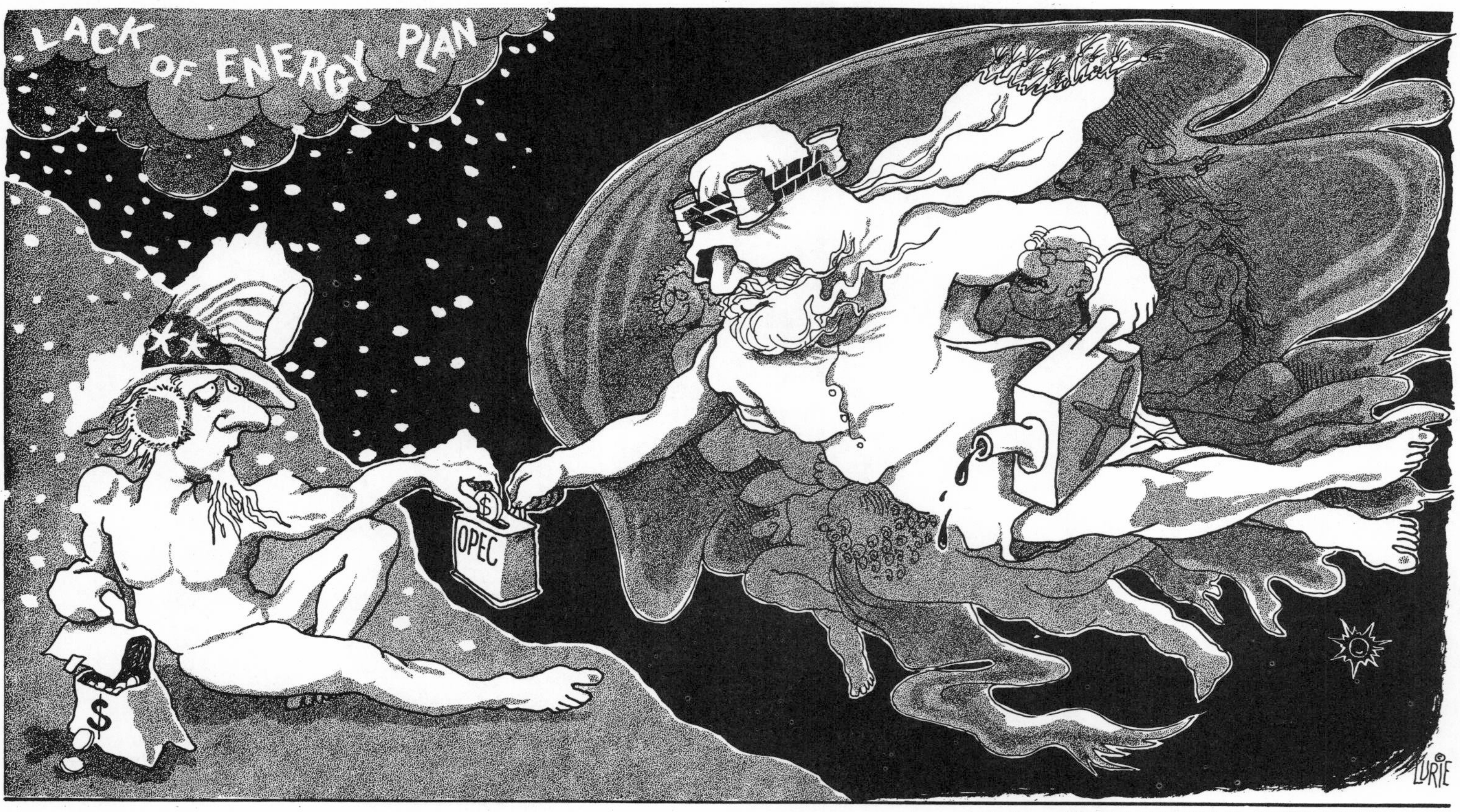
LACK OF ENERGY PLAN
OPEC
$
LURIE

2-11-77 *(WITH APOLOGIES TO MICHELANGELO - R.L.)*

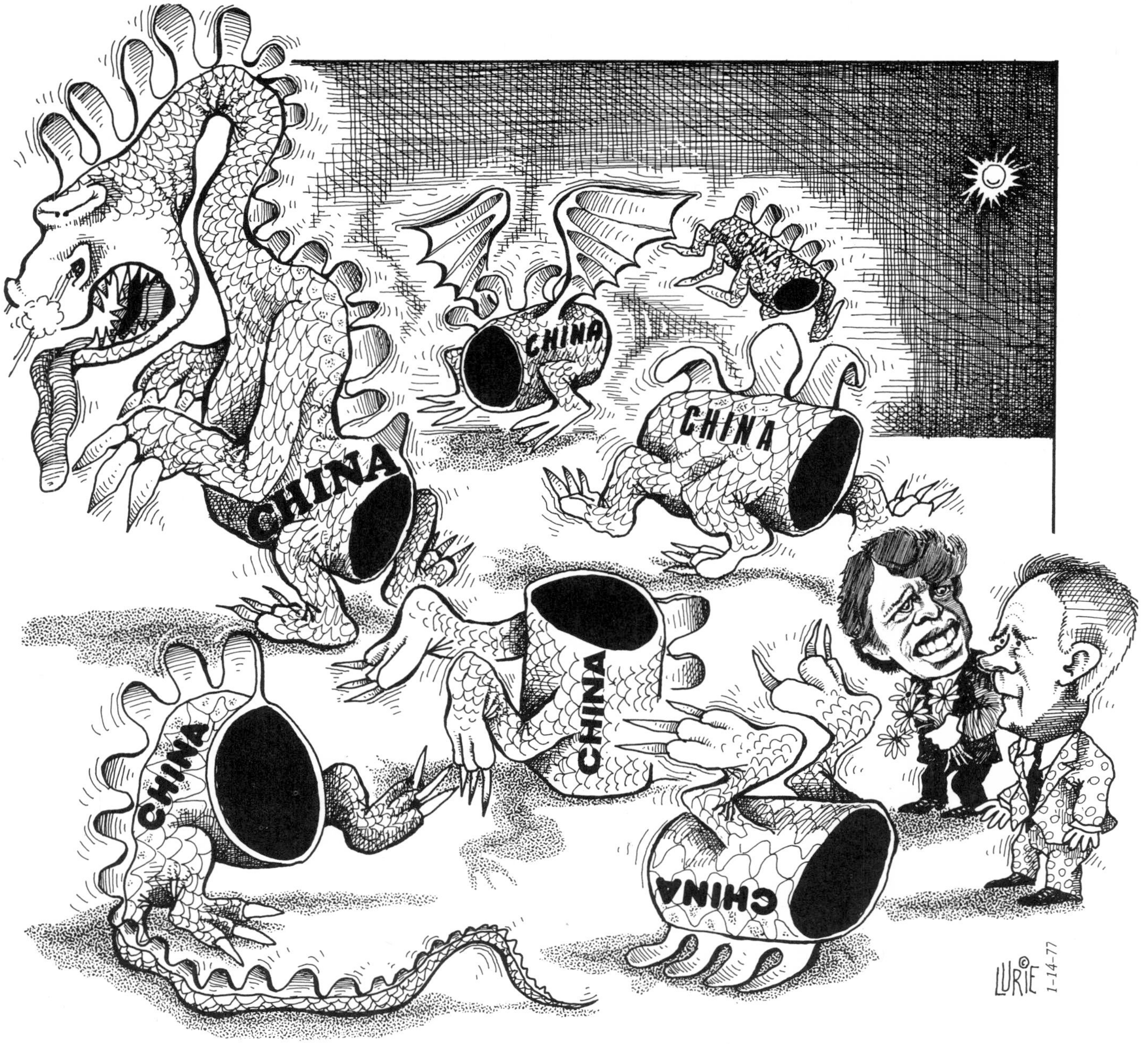
CHINA
CHINA
CHINA
CHINA
CHINA
CHINA
CHINA
LURIE ©
1-14-77

"LOOKS AS IF WE CAME IN THE MIDST OF A FAMILY FEUD, CYRUS."

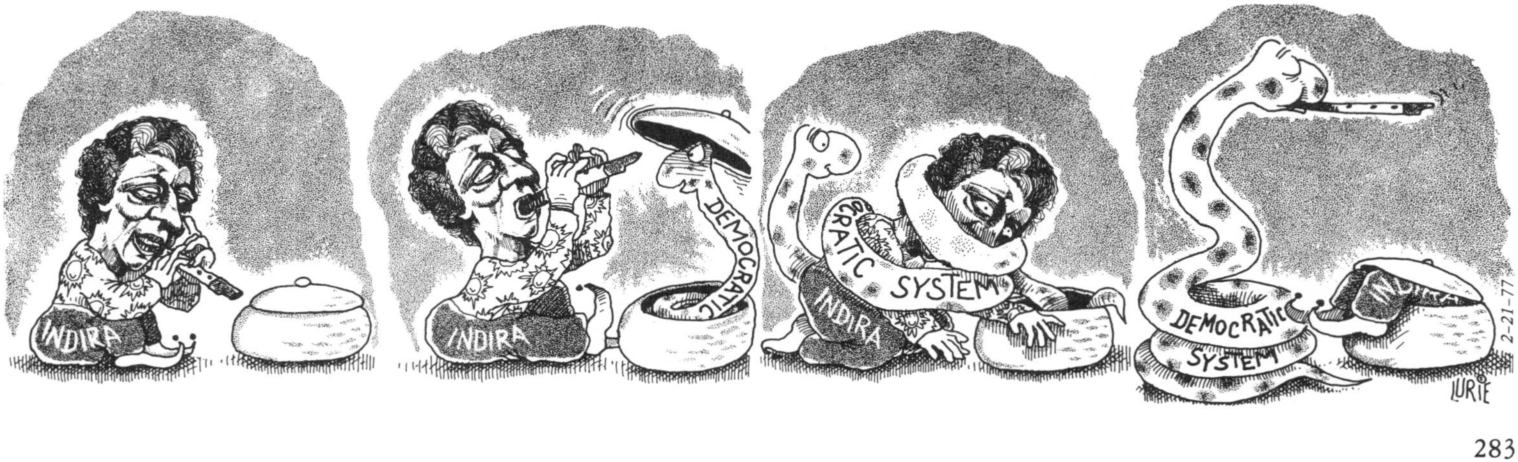
INDIRA
INDIRA
DEMOCRATIC
INDIRA
SYSTEM
DEMOCRATIC
SYSTEM
2-21-77
LURIE ©

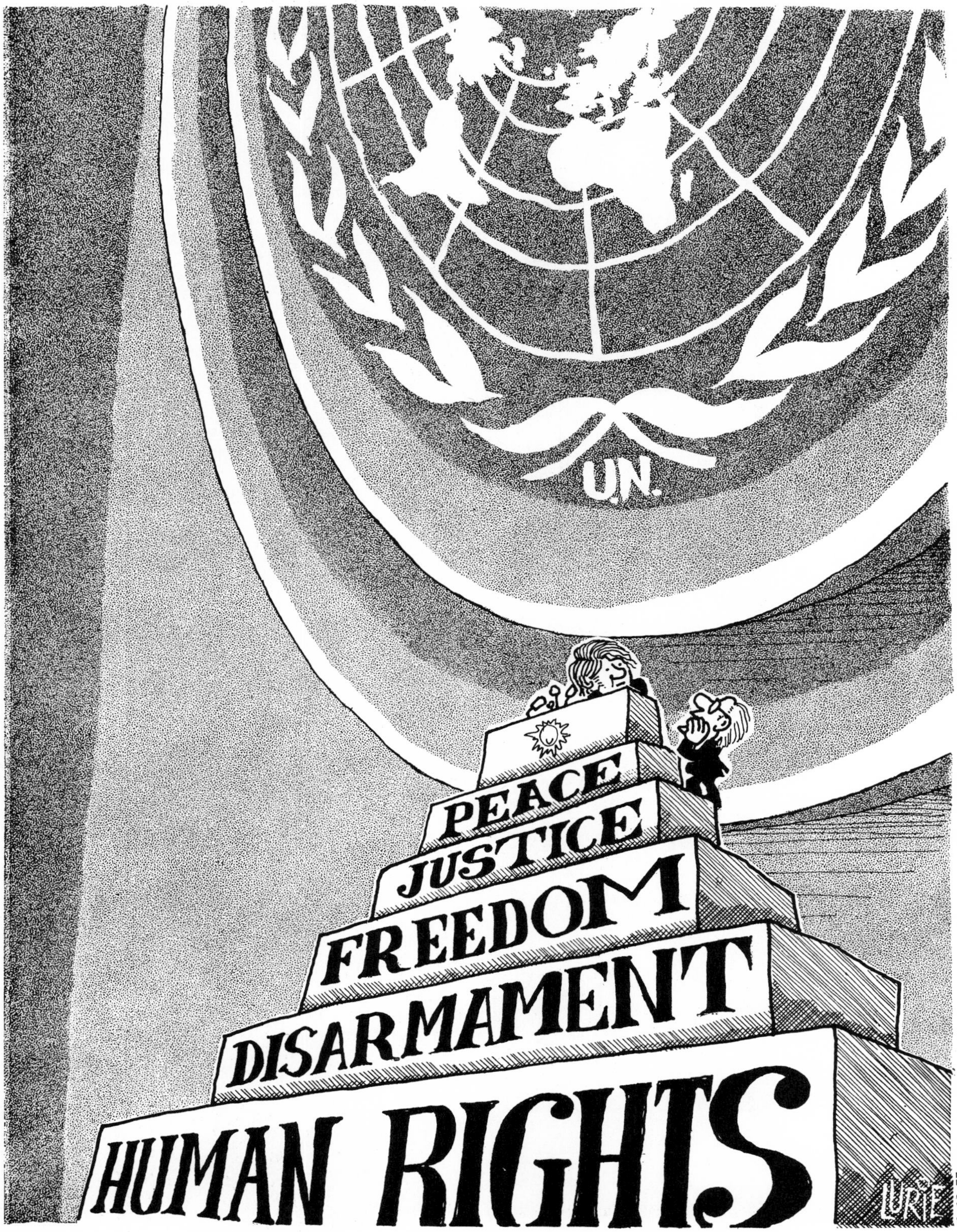
U.N.
PEACE
JUSTICE
FREEDOM
DISARMAMENT
HUMAN RIGHTS
LURIE
3-18-77

"BETTER SPEAK STRONGLY, PRESIDENT CARTER—
IT'S HARD TO HEAR YOU FROM SUCH HEIGHTS!"

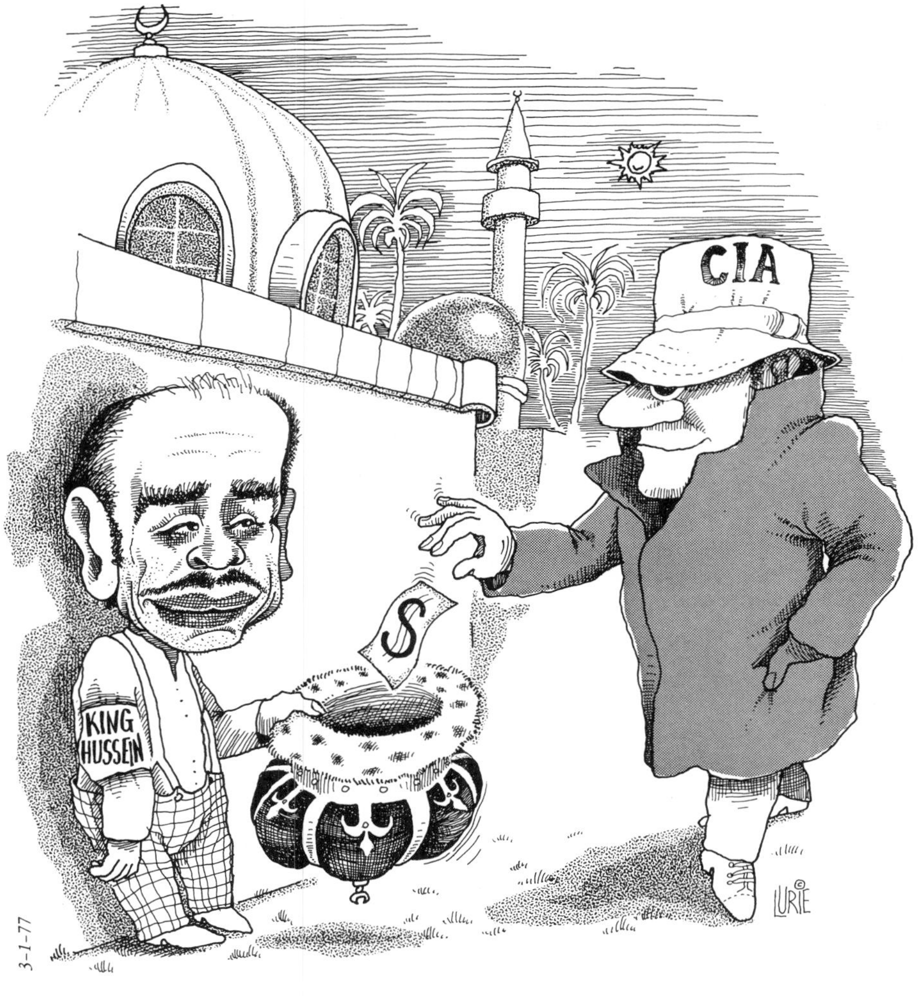
CIA
KING HUSSEIN
$
LURIE
3-1-77

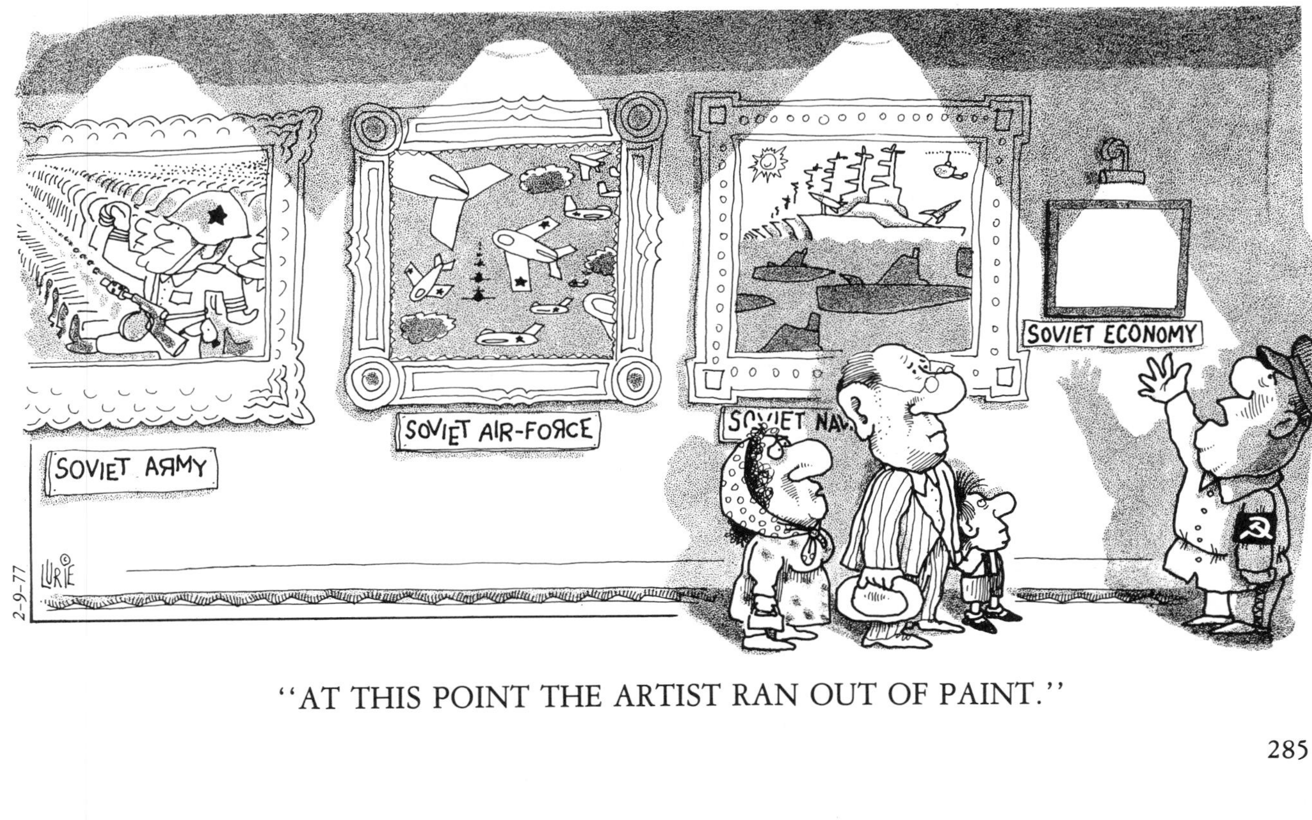
SOVIET ARMY
SOVIET AIR-FORCE
SOVIET ECONOMY
LURIE
2-9-77

"AT THIS POINT THE ARTIST RAN OUT OF PAINT."

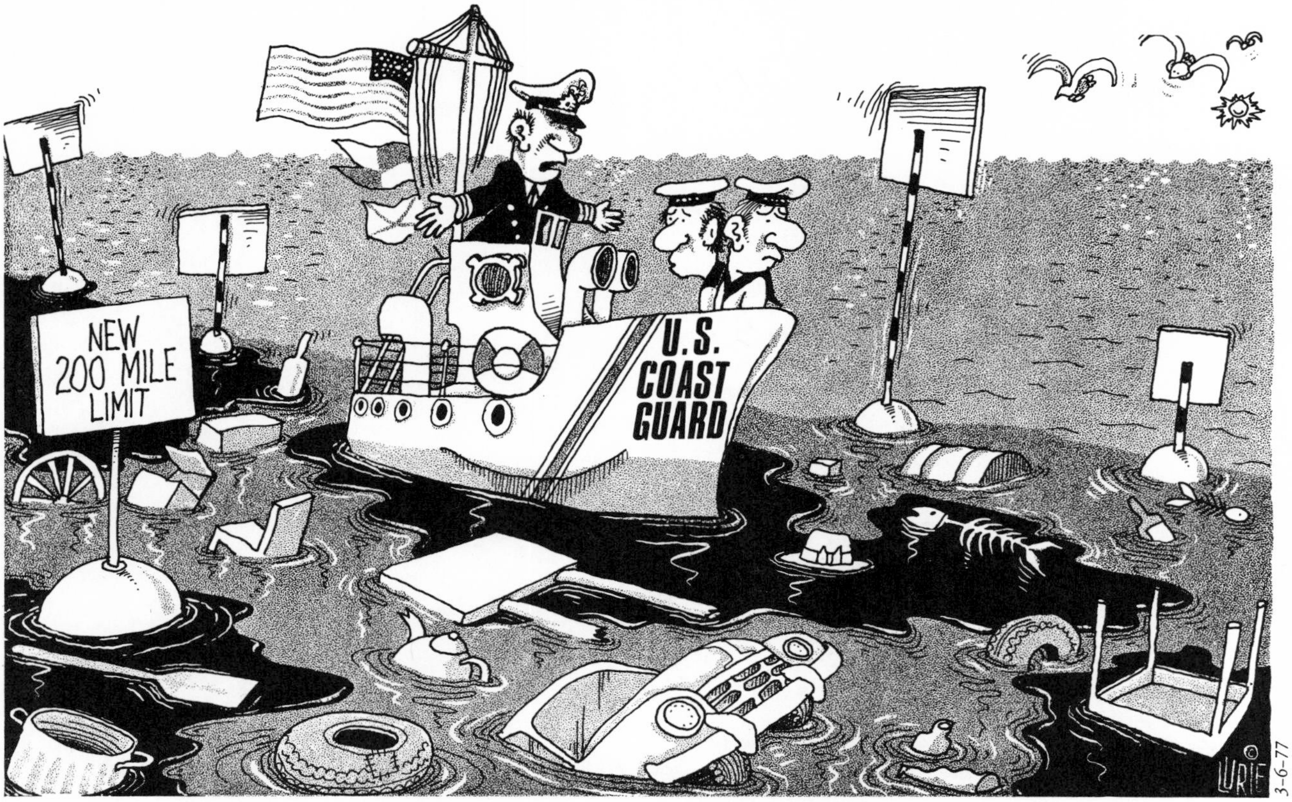
NEW
200 MILE
LIMIT
U.S.
COAST
GUARD
LURIE
3-6-77

"FORTUNATELY, WE HAVE NO PROBLEM DETERMINING WHERE OUR WATERS BEGIN . . ."

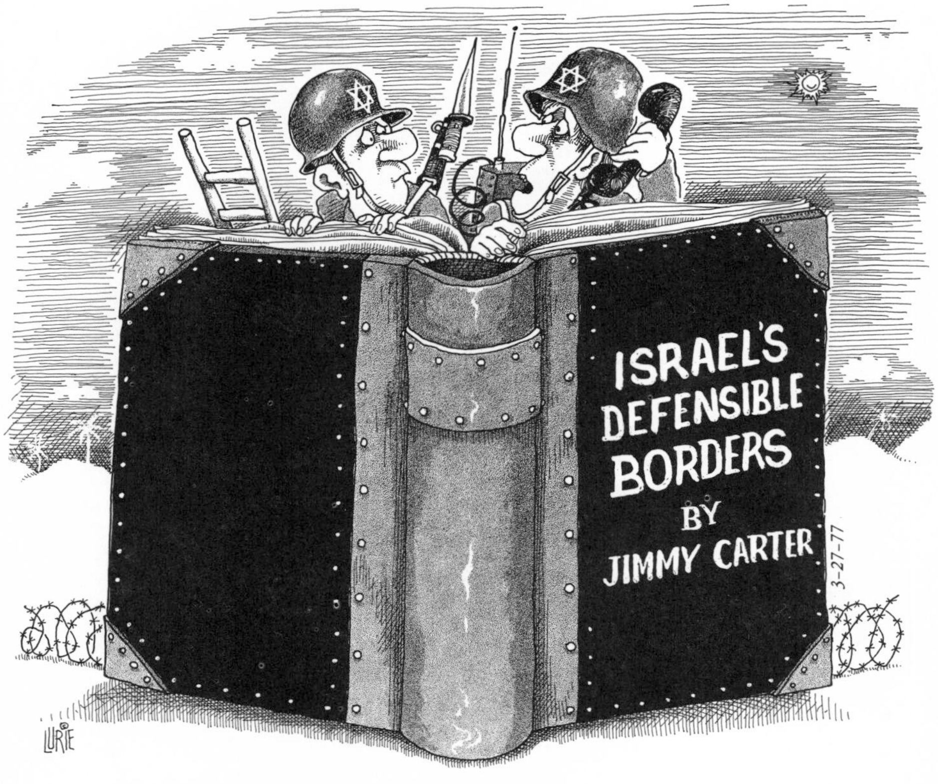
ISRAEL'S
DEFENSIBLE
BORDERS
BY
JIMMY CARTER
3-27-77
LURIE

"HOLY MOSES! NOW CARTER WANTS TO REPLACE THE HARDCOVER WITH A PAPERBACK!"

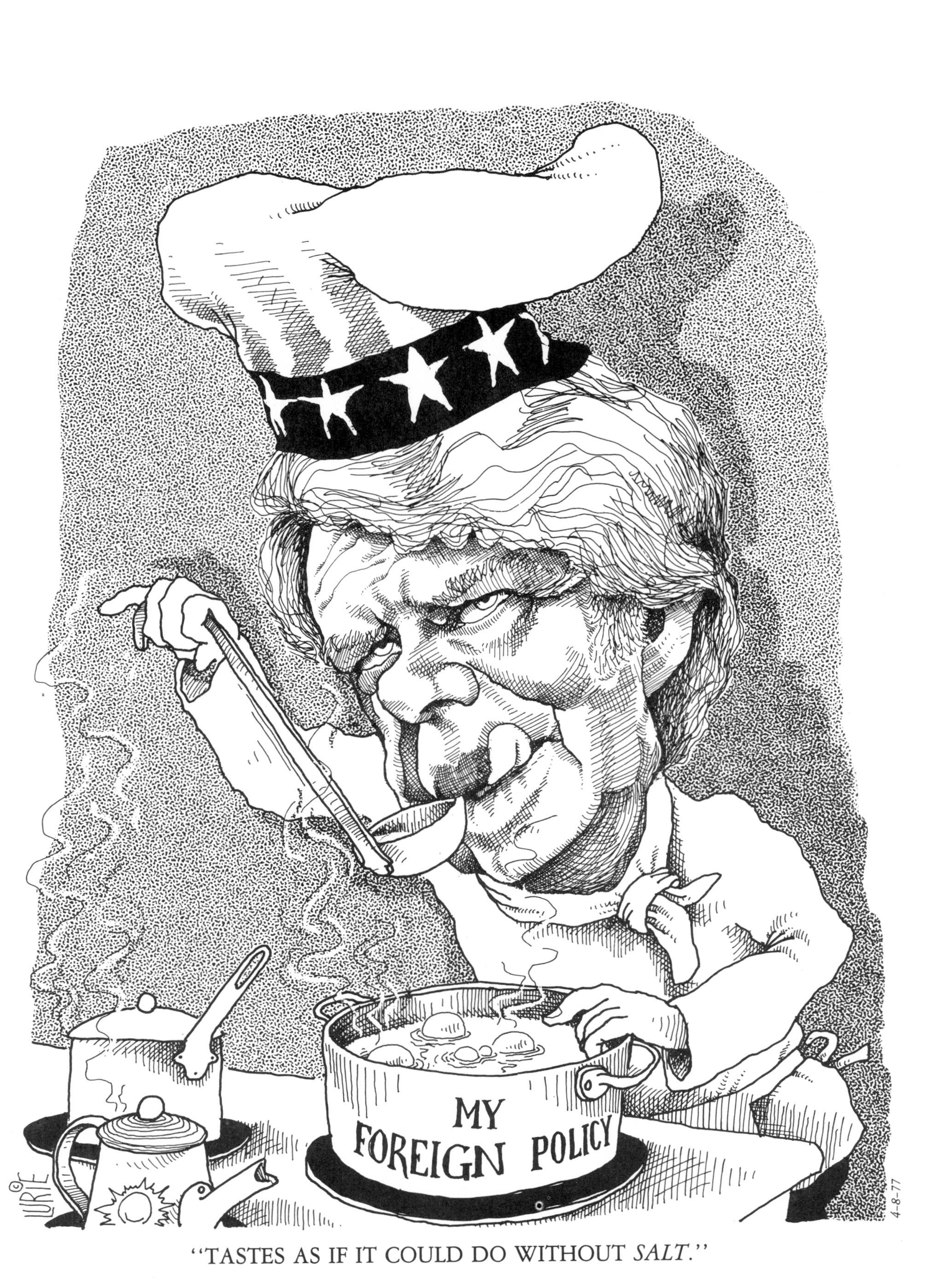
MY
FOREIGN POLICY
LURIE ©
4-8-77

"TASTES AS IF IT COULD DO WITHOUT *SALT*."

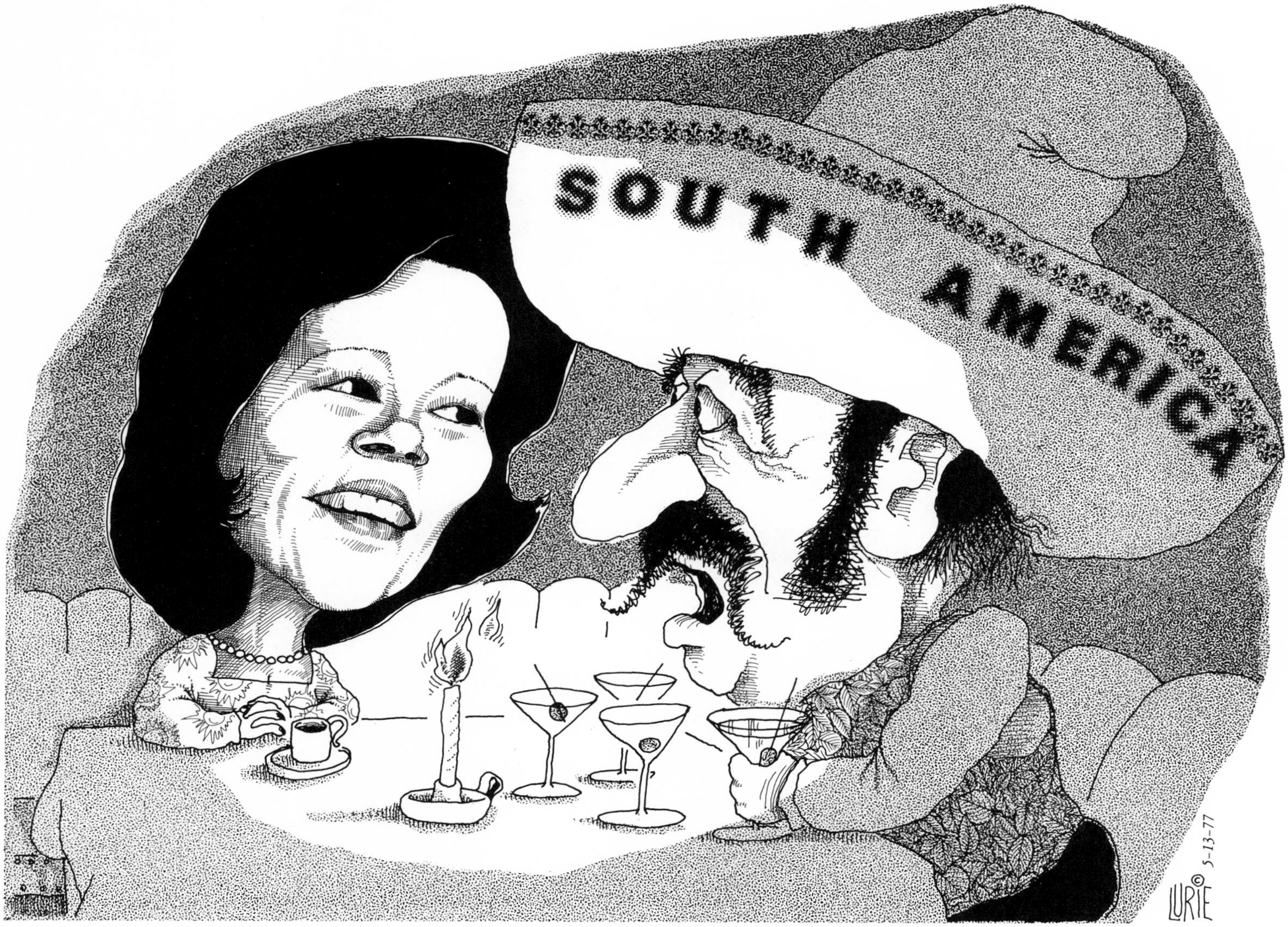
SOUTH AMERICA
LURIE
5-13-77

''YOUR HUSBAND DOESN'T UNDERSTAND ME, ROSALYNN.''

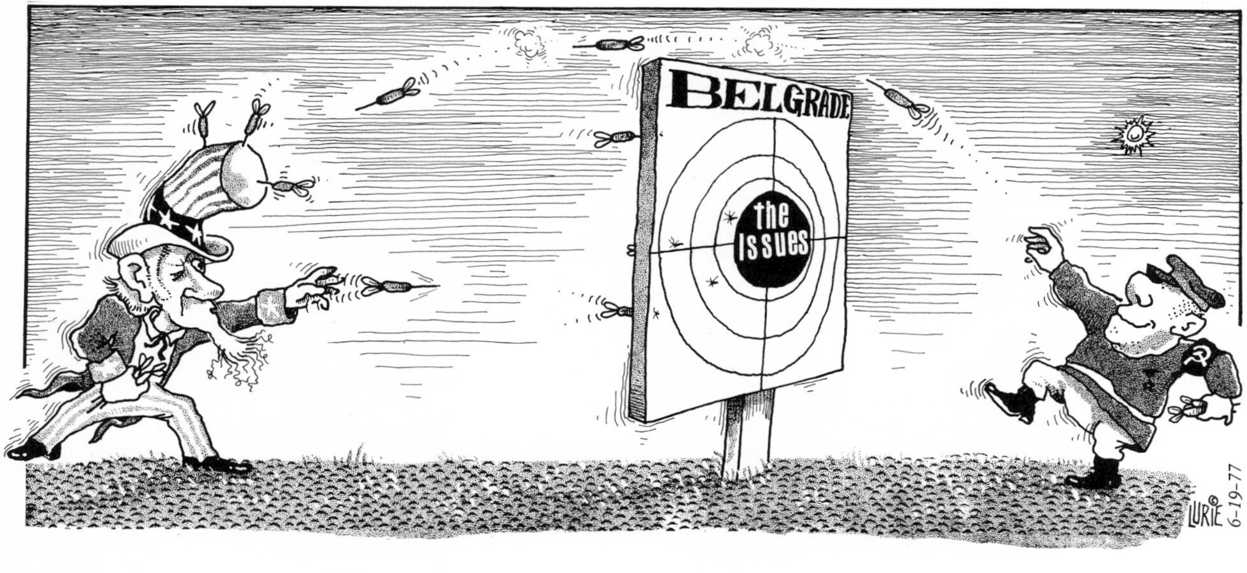
BELGRADE
the issues
LURIE
6-19-77

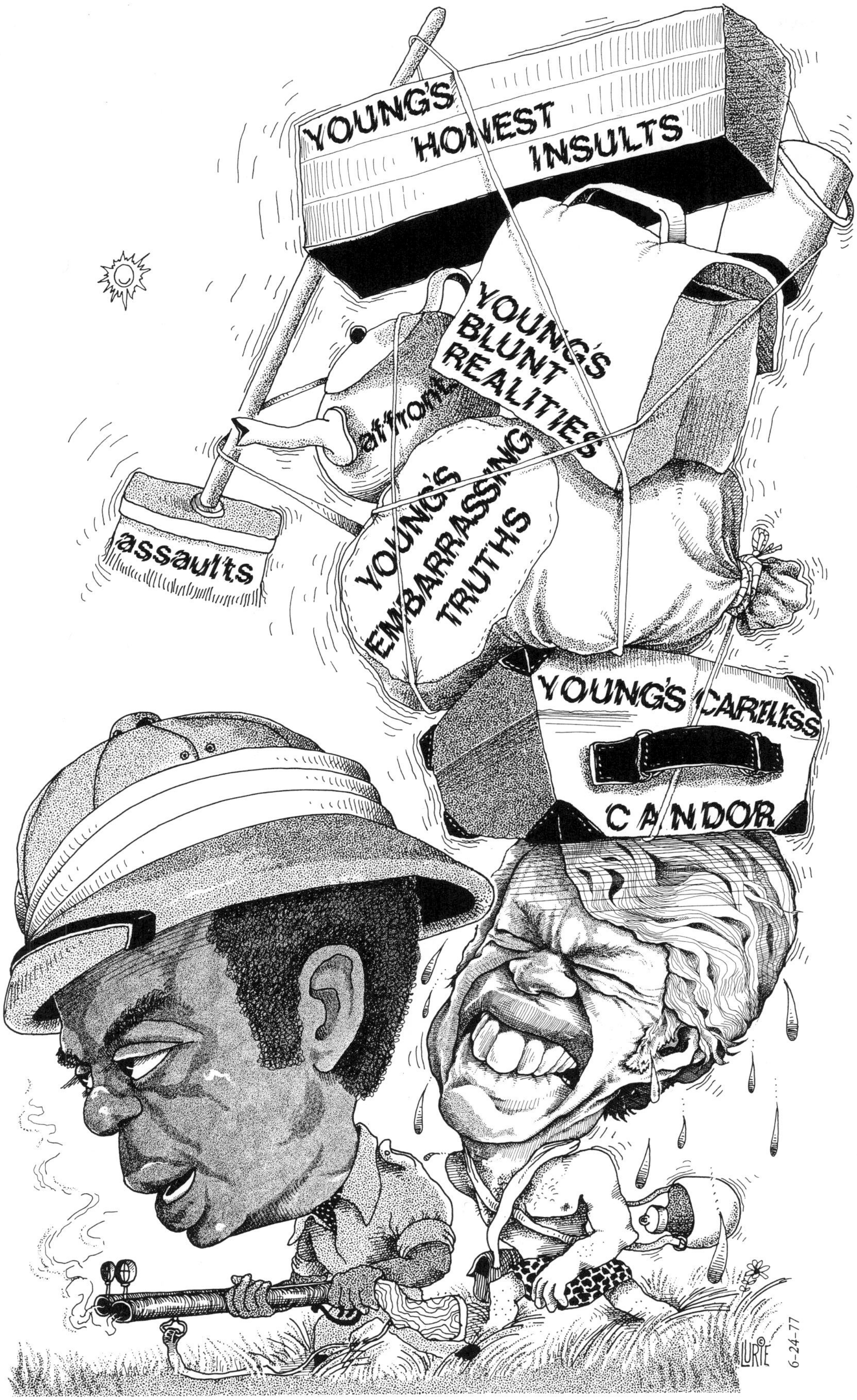
YOUNG'S HONEST INSULTS
YOUNG'S BLUNT REALITIES
affront
YOUNG'S EMBARRASSING TRUTHS
assaults
YOUNG'S CARELESS CANDOR
LURIE
6-24-77

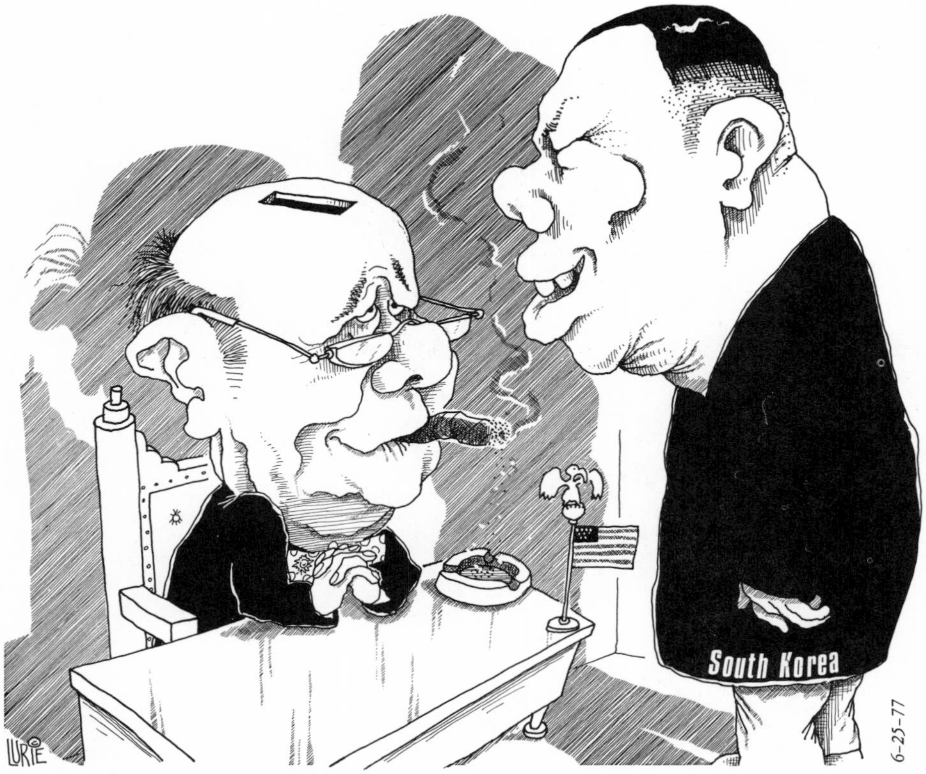
South Korea
LURIE
6-25-77

"WE APPRECIATE OPEN-MINDED CONGRESSMEN!"

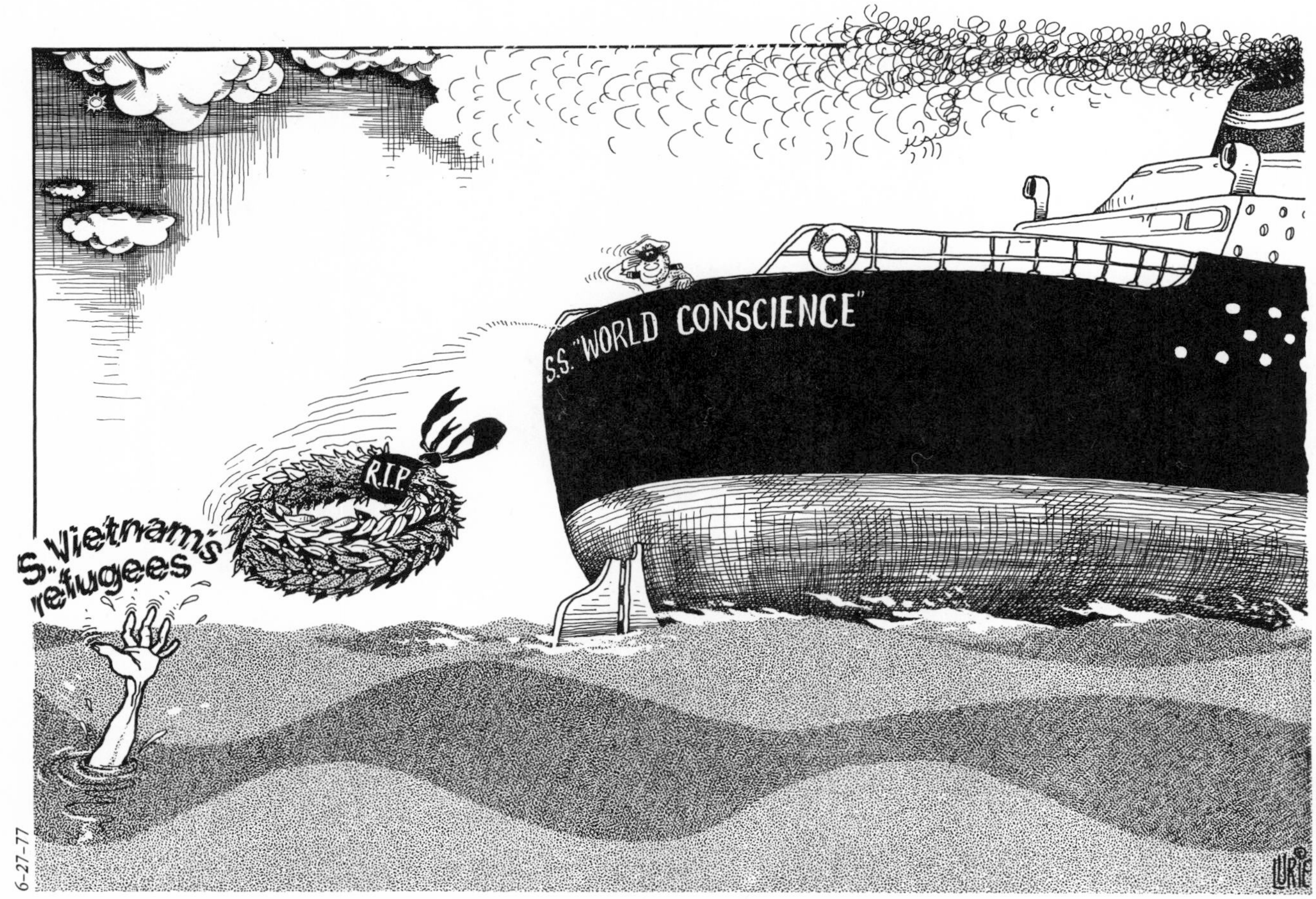
S.S. "WORLD CONSCIENCE"
R.I.P.
S. Vietnam's refugees
6-27-77
LURIE

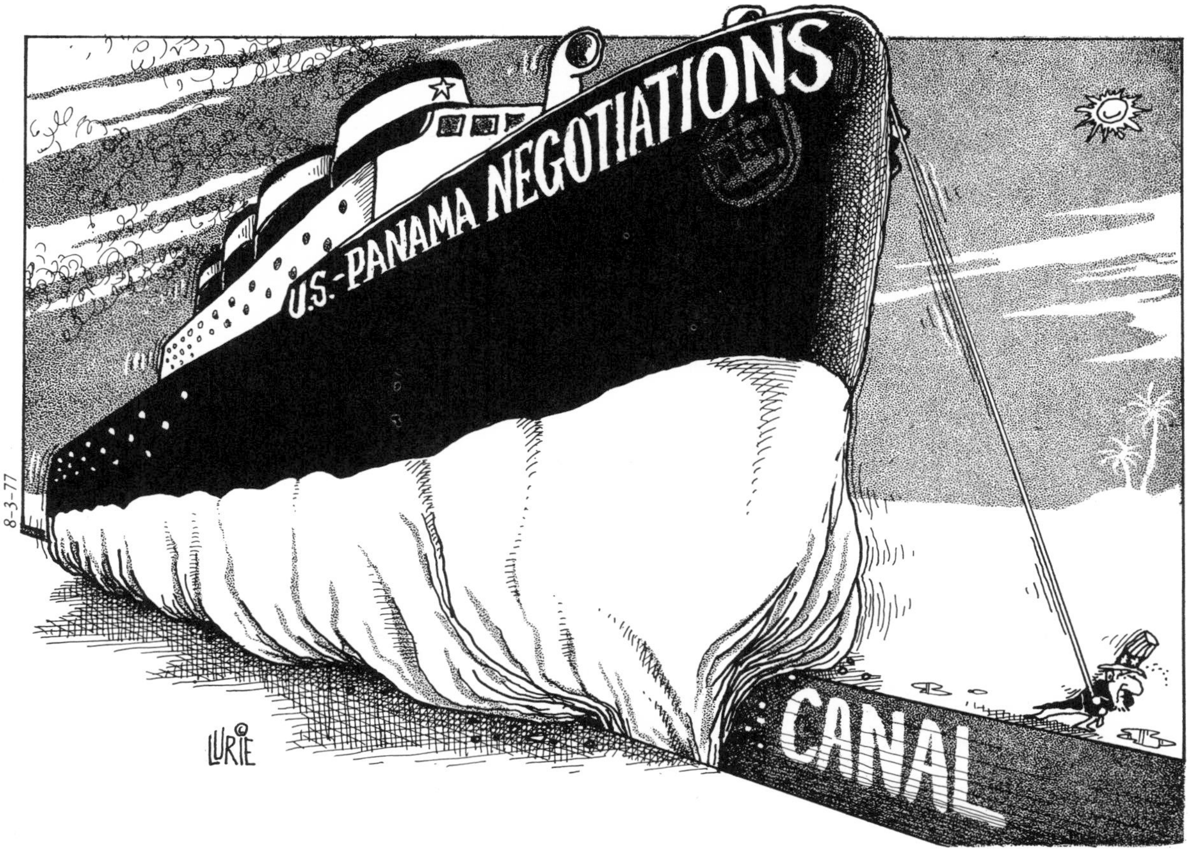
U.S.-PANAMA NEGOTIATIONS
CANAL
LURIE
8-3-77

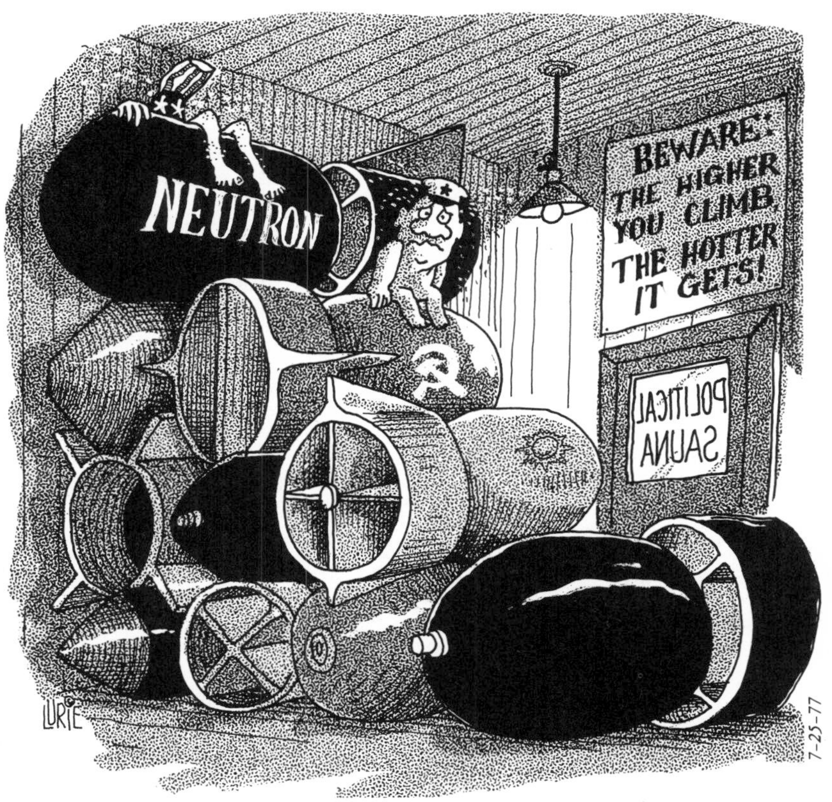
NEUTRON
BEWARE: THE HIGHER YOU CLIMB, THE HOTTER IT GETS!
POLITICAL SAUNA
LURIE
7-25-77

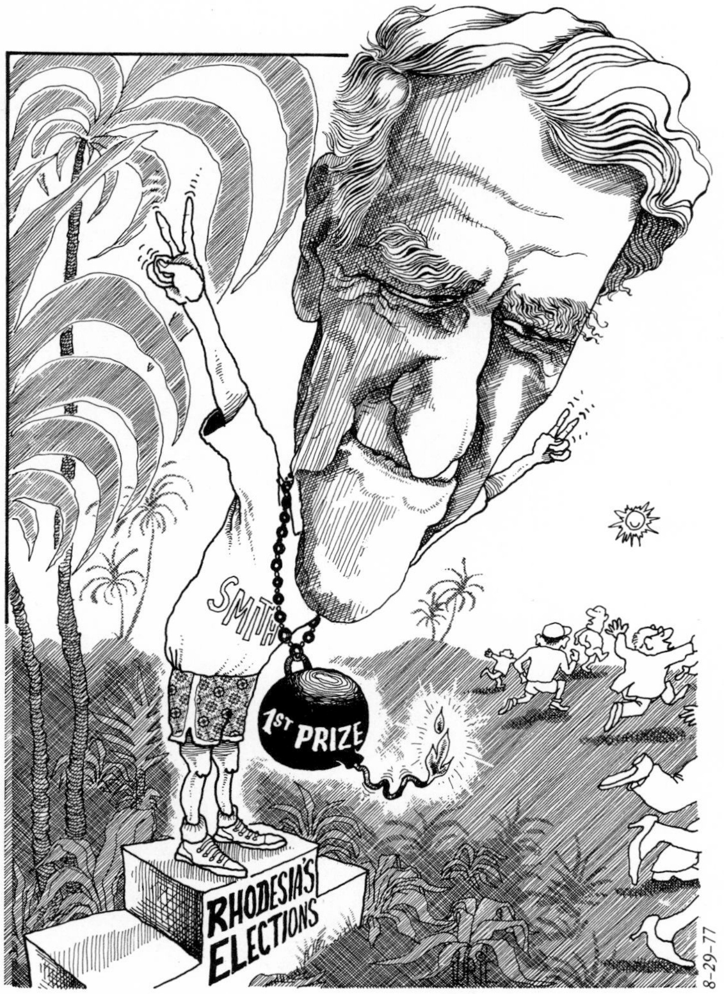
SMITH
1ST PRIZE
RHODESIA'S ELECTIONS
LURIE
8-29-77

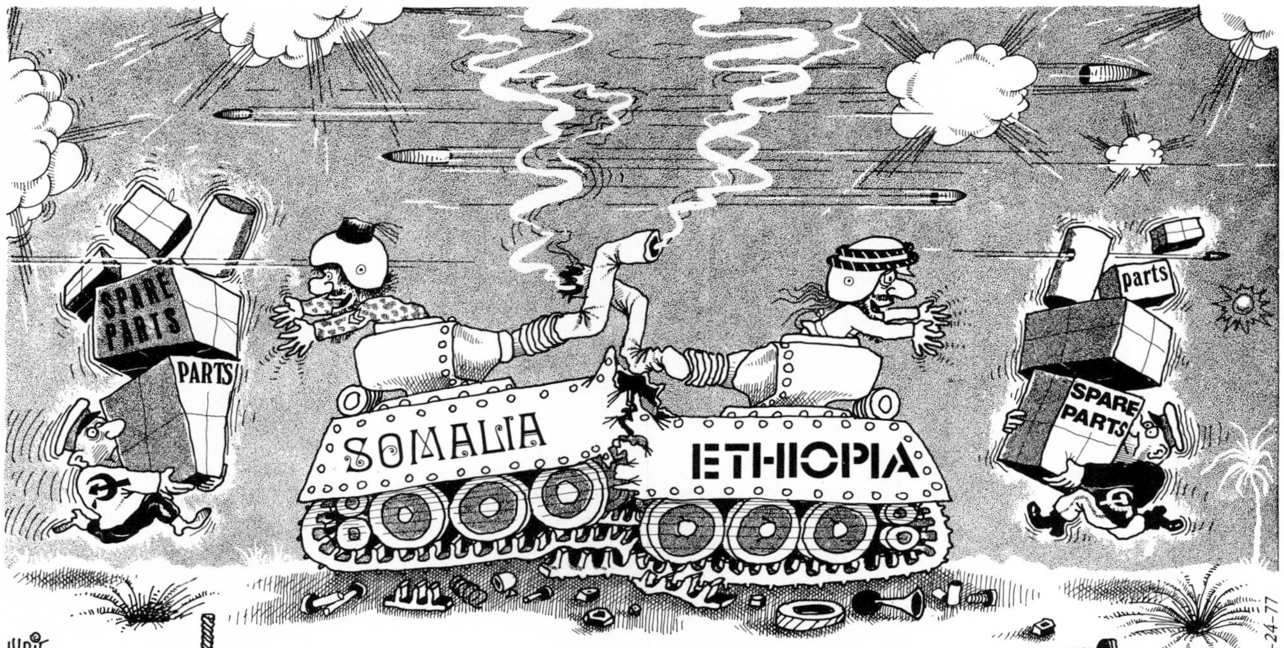
SPARE PARTS
PARTS
SOMALIA
ETHIOPIA
parts
SPARE PARTS
LURIE
8-24-77

"THANK ALLAH FOR SUCH AN ALLY!"
"THANK ALLAH FOR SUCH AN ALLY!"

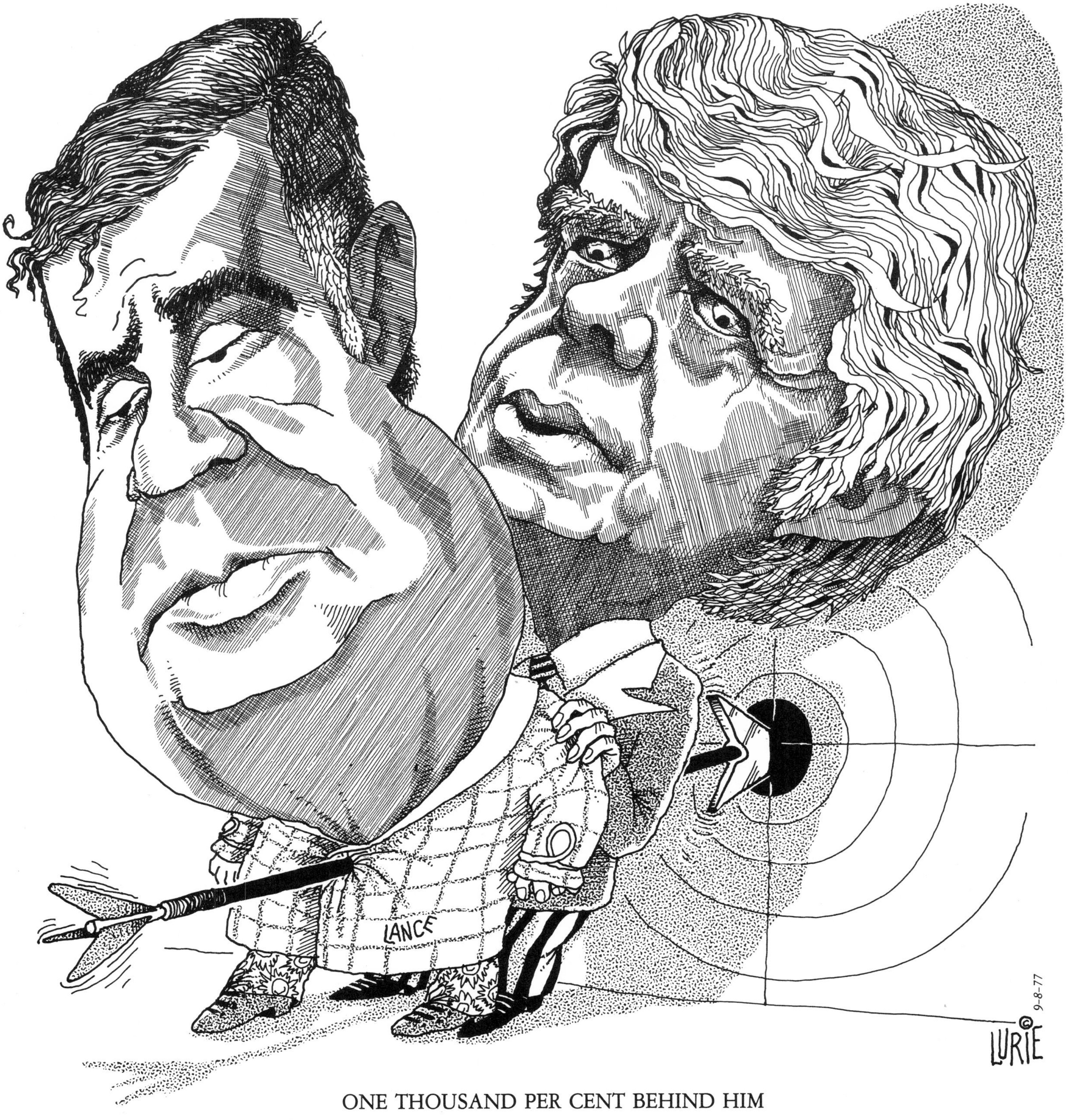
LANCE
9-8-77
©
LURIE

ONE THOUSAND PER CENT BEHIND HIM

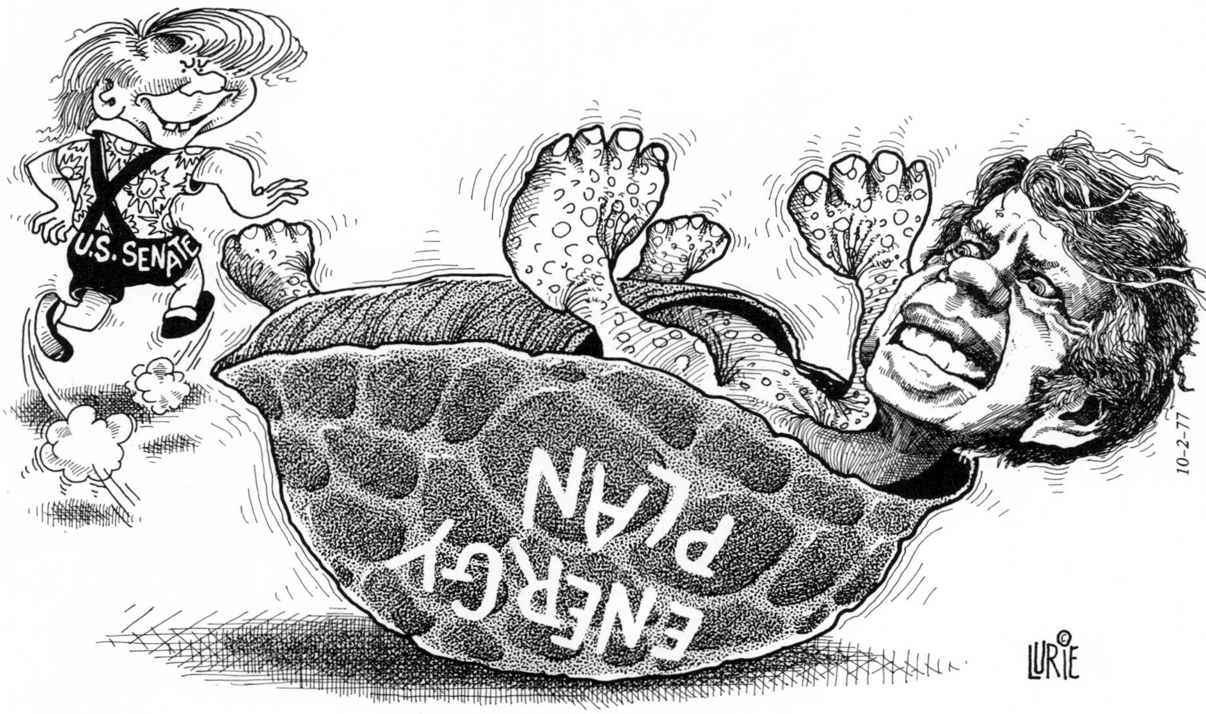
U.S. SENATE
ENERGY PLAN
10-2-77
LURIE

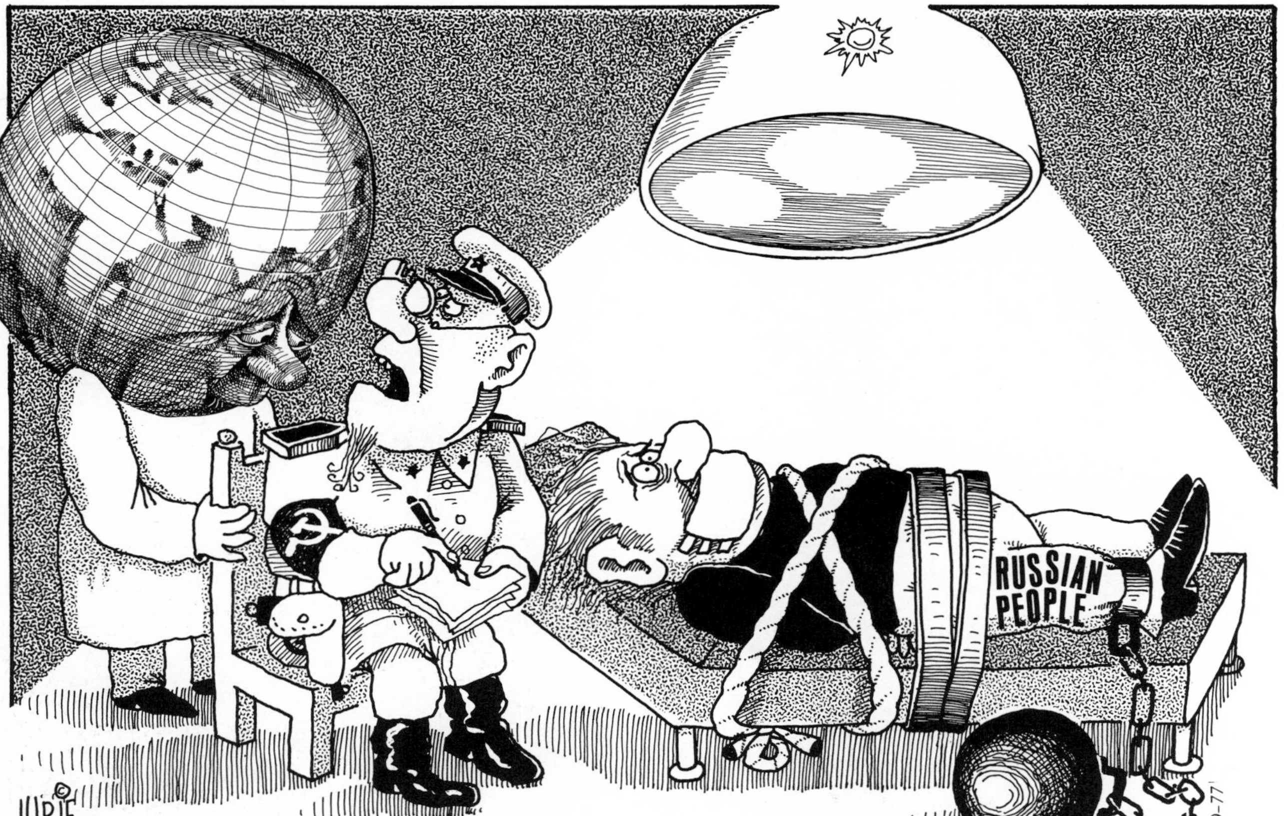
RUSSIAN PEOPLE
LURIE
9-9-77

"CAN'T YOU SEE I'M TRYING TO ANALYZE
HIS PARANOIA COMPLEXES?"

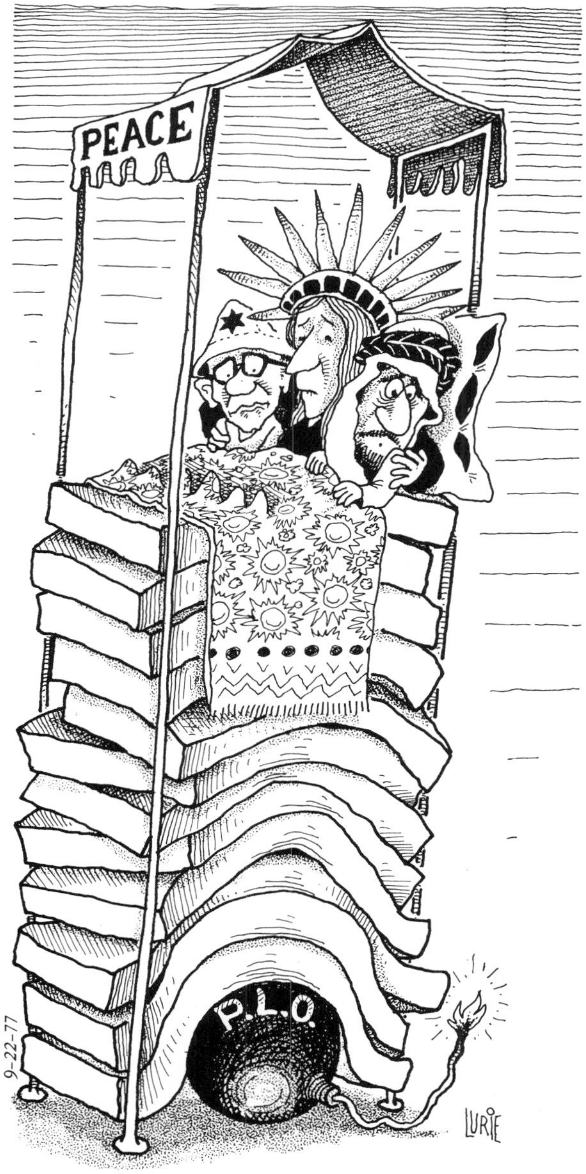
PEACE
P.L.O.
9-22-77
LURIE

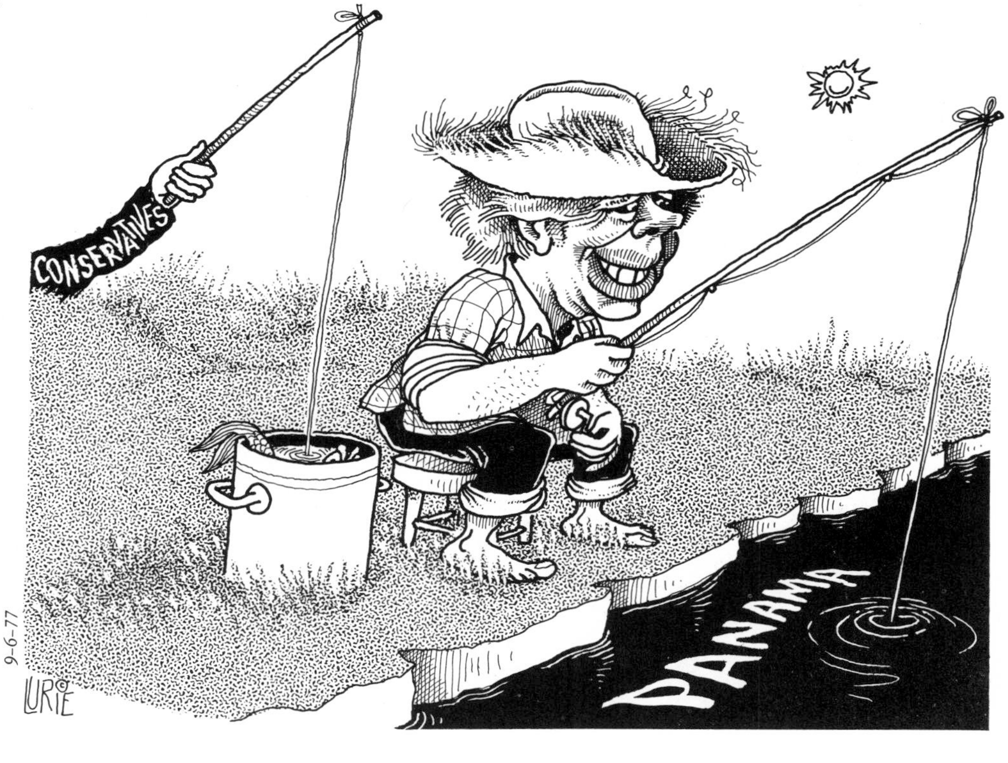
CONSERVATIVES
PANAMA
9-6-77
LURIE

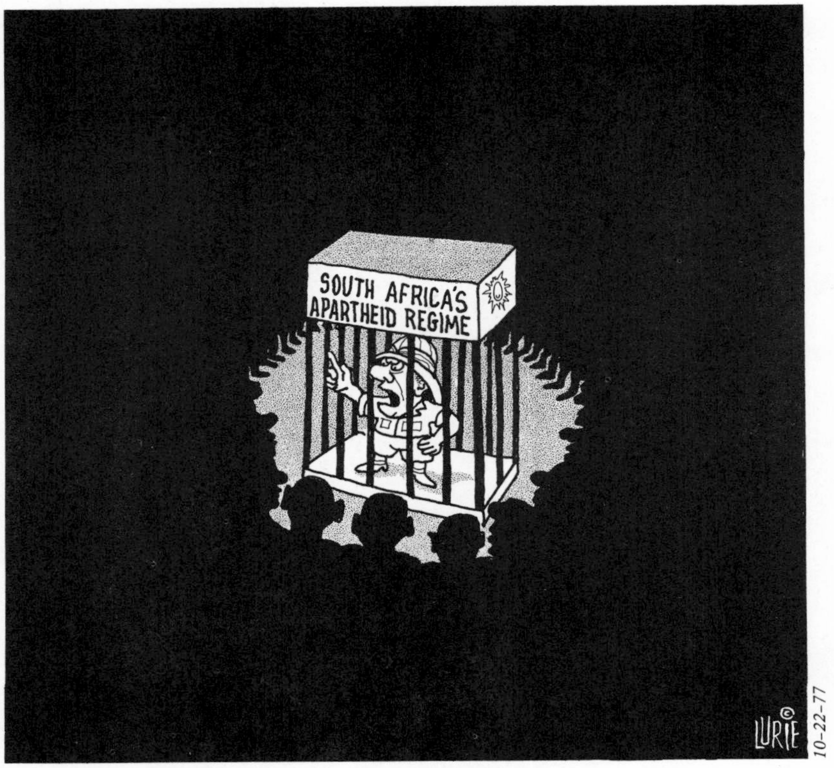
SOUTH AFRICA'S
APARTHEID REGIME
LURIE ©
10-22-77

"SEE, I WARNED I WOULD PUT YOU BEHIND BARS!"

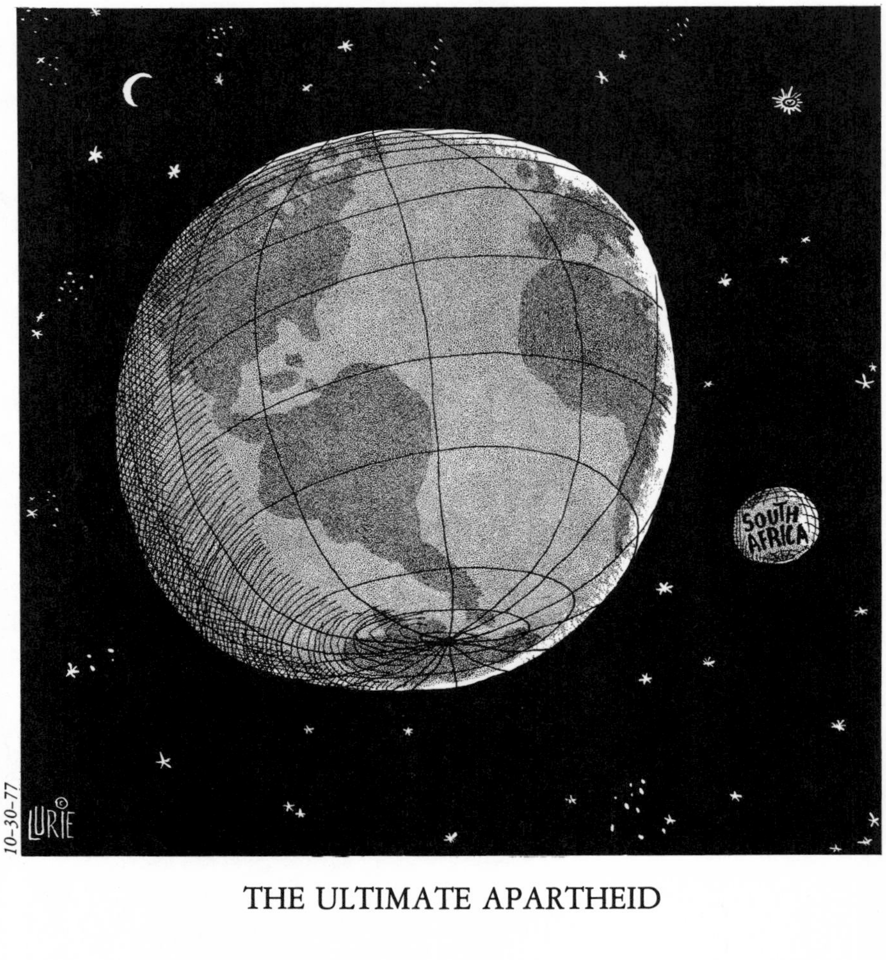
SOUTH
AFRICA
LURIE ©
10-30-77

THE ULTIMATE APARTHEID

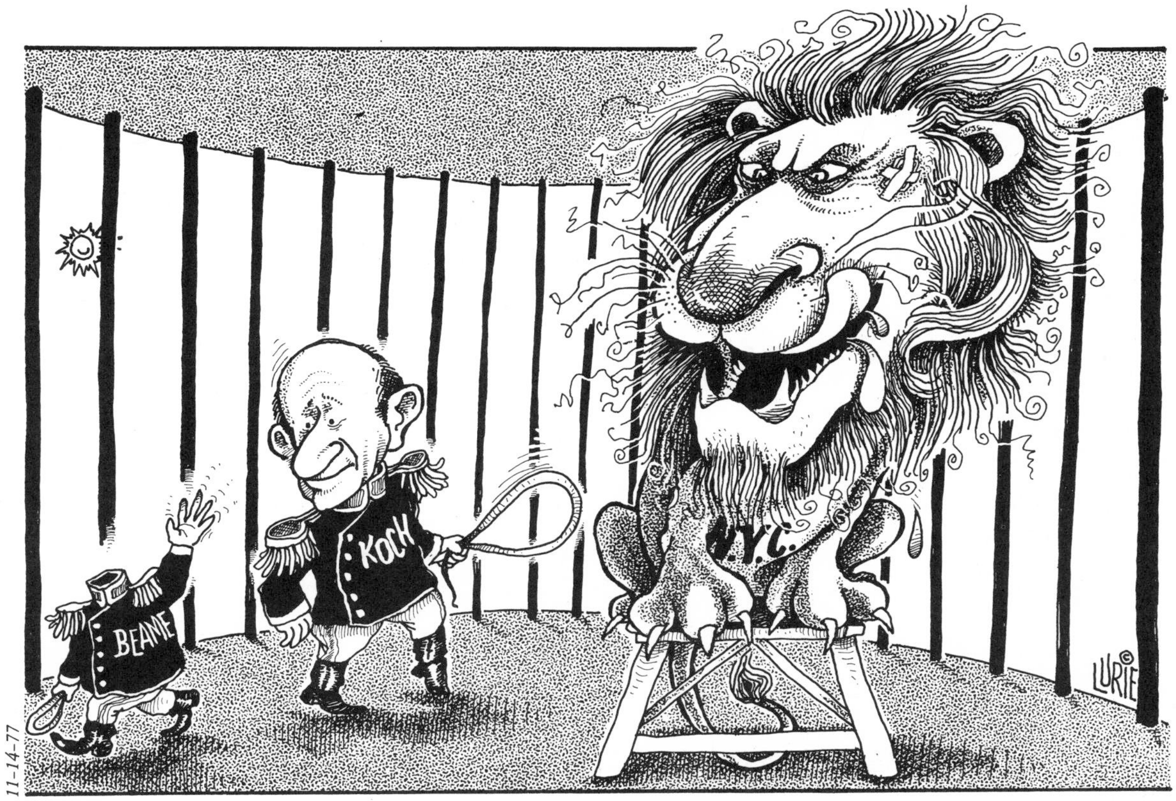
BEAME
KOCH
N.Y.C.
LURIE
11-14-77

"CONGRATULATIONS ON YOUR NEW JOB!"

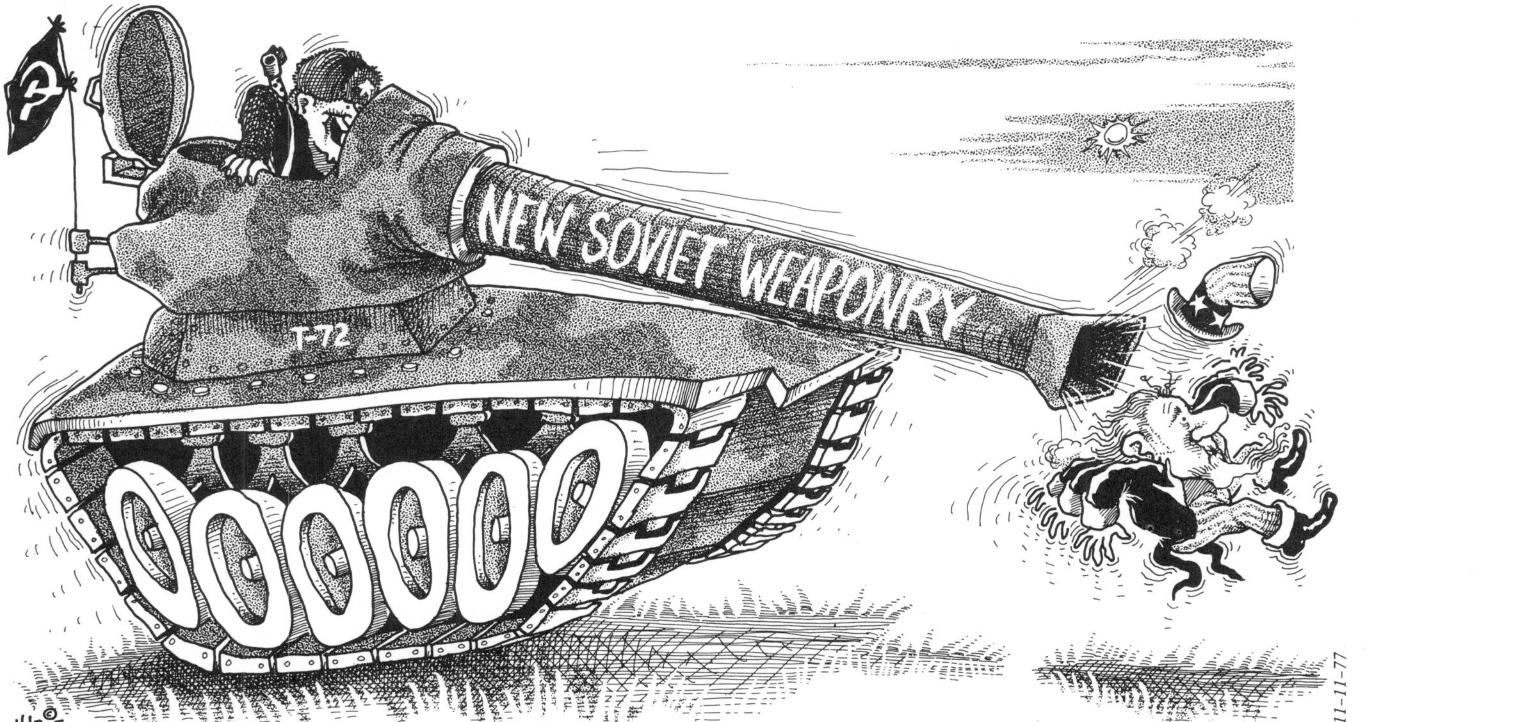
NEW SOVIET WEAPONRY
T-72
LURIE
11-11-77

"PEACE!"

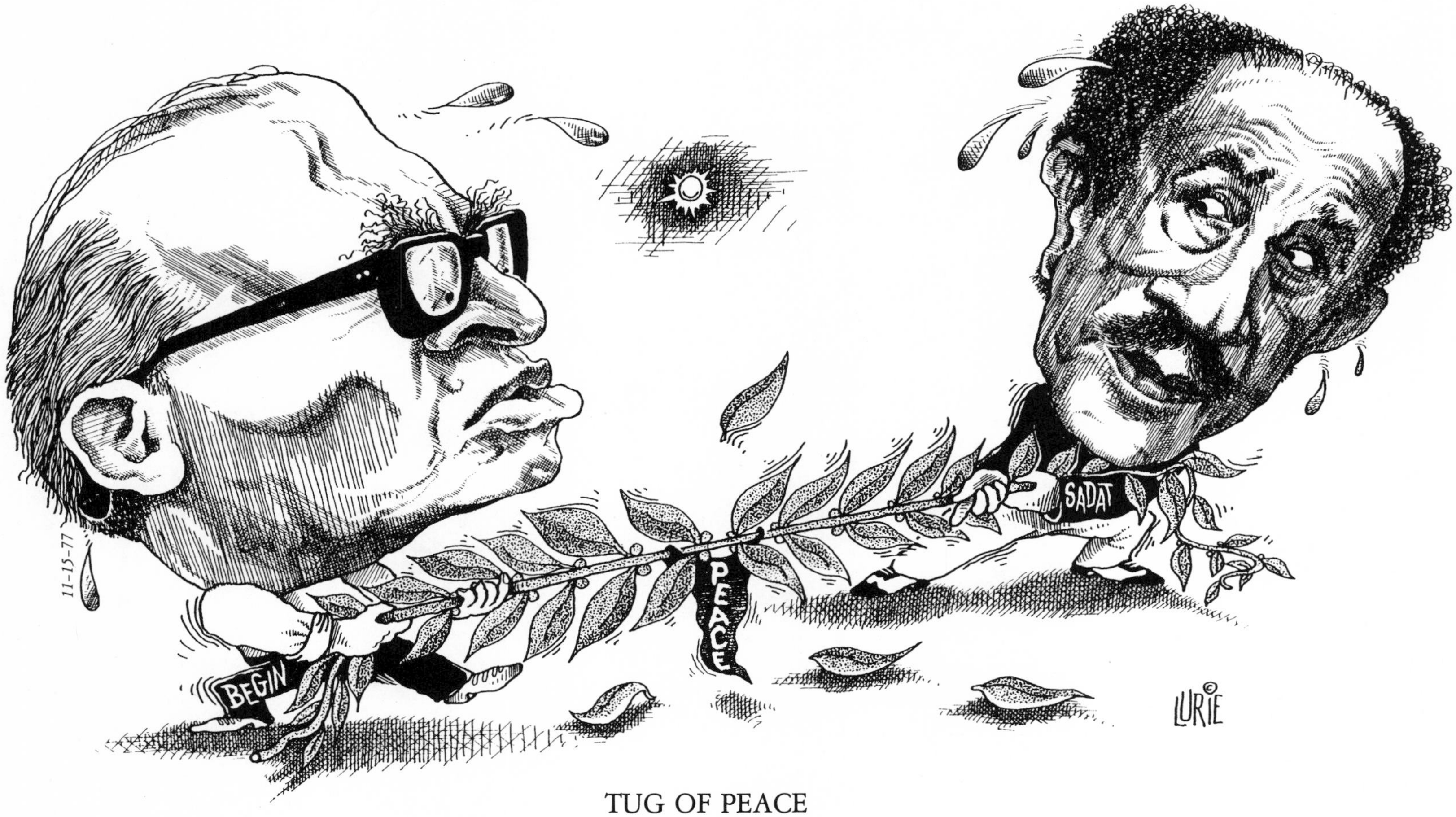
11-15-77
PEACE
BEGIN
SADAT
LURIE©

TUG OF PEACE

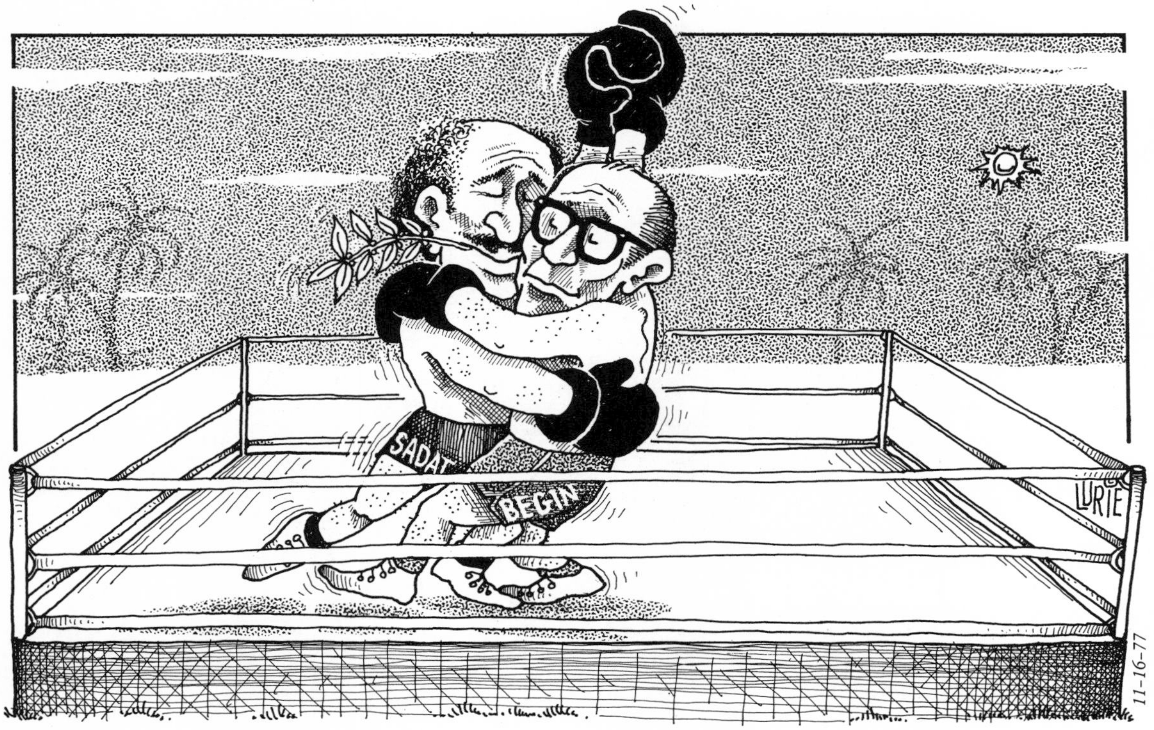
SADAT
BEGIN
LURIE
11-16-77

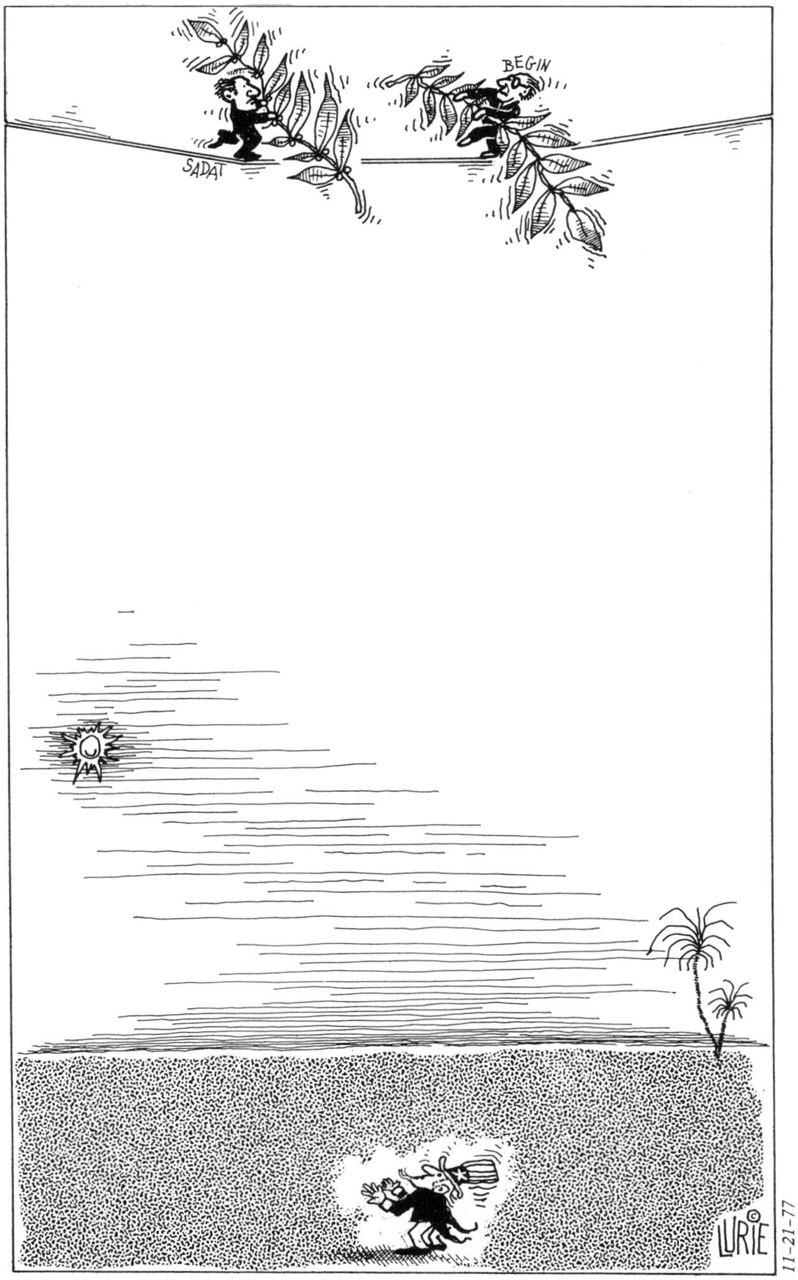
BEGIN
SADAT
LURIE
11-21-77

peace
LURIE
11-22-77

"S H A D E!"

Cairo Summit
Tripoli Summit
LURIE NEWSDAY
12-5-77

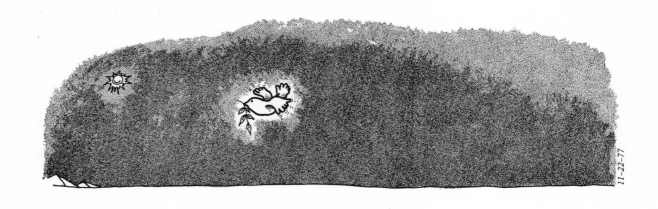

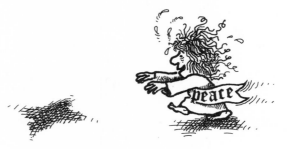

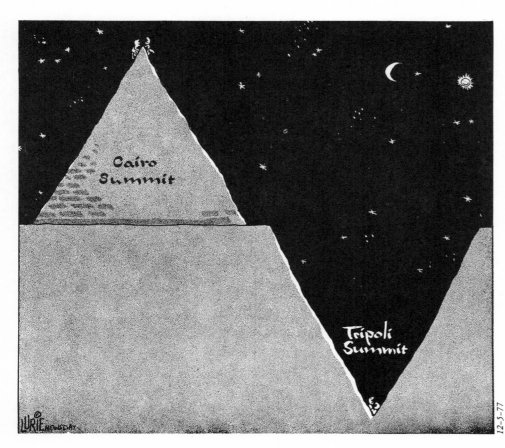

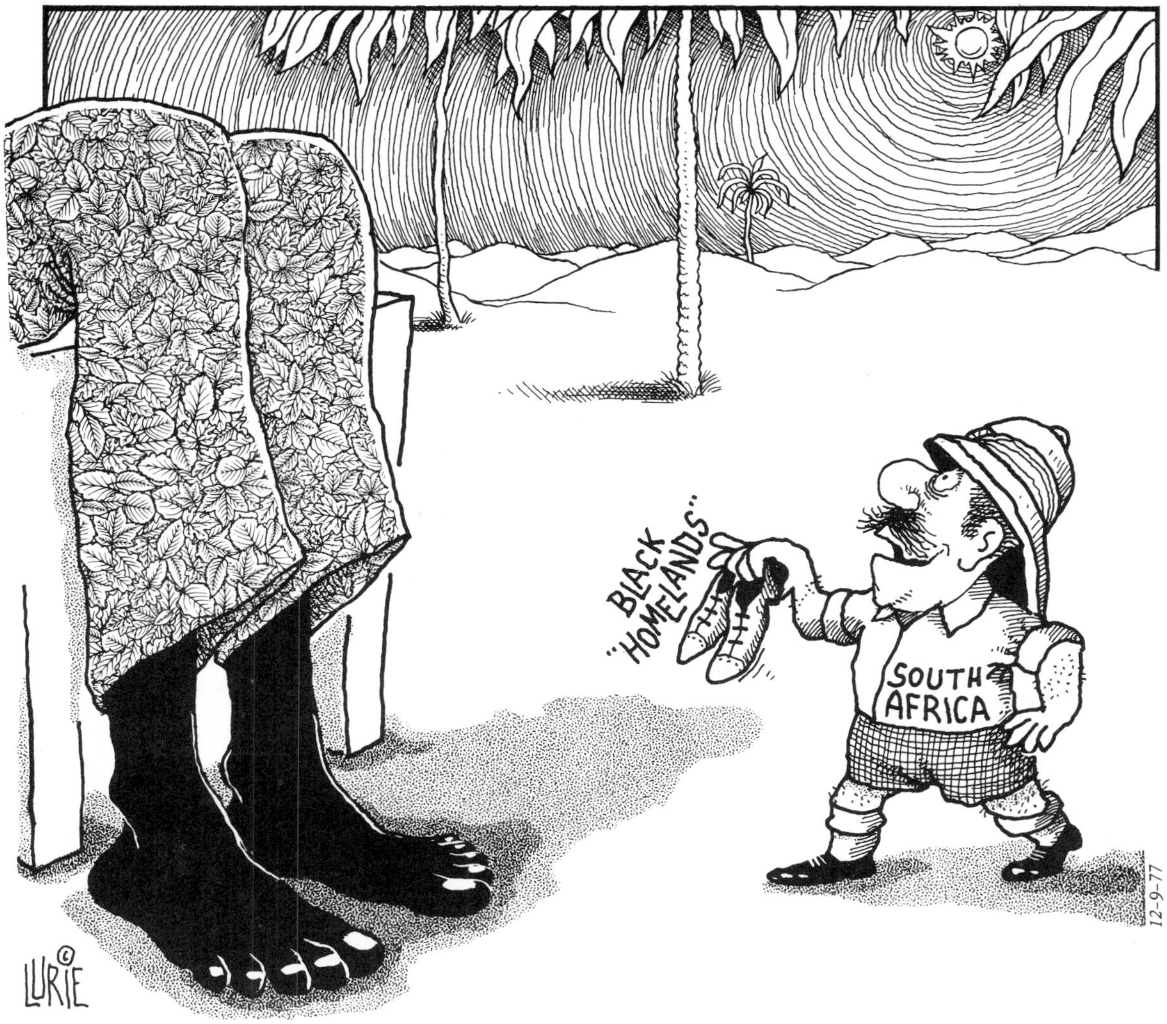
"BLACK HOMELANDS"
SOUTH AFRICA
12-9-77
LURIE©

"YOU'LL ENJOY THEM . . . I CUSTOM MADE THEM TO MY SIZE!"

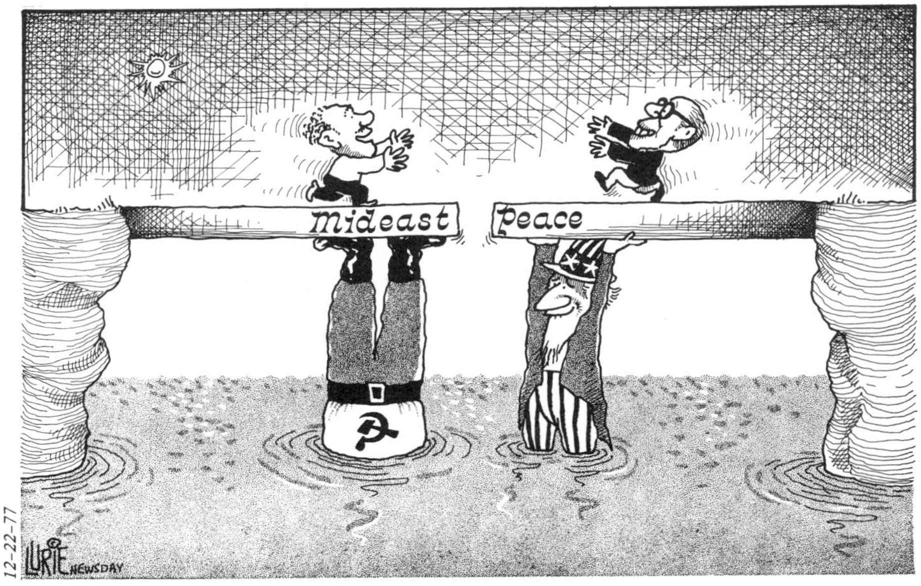
Mideast
Peace
12-22-77
LURIE NEWSDAY

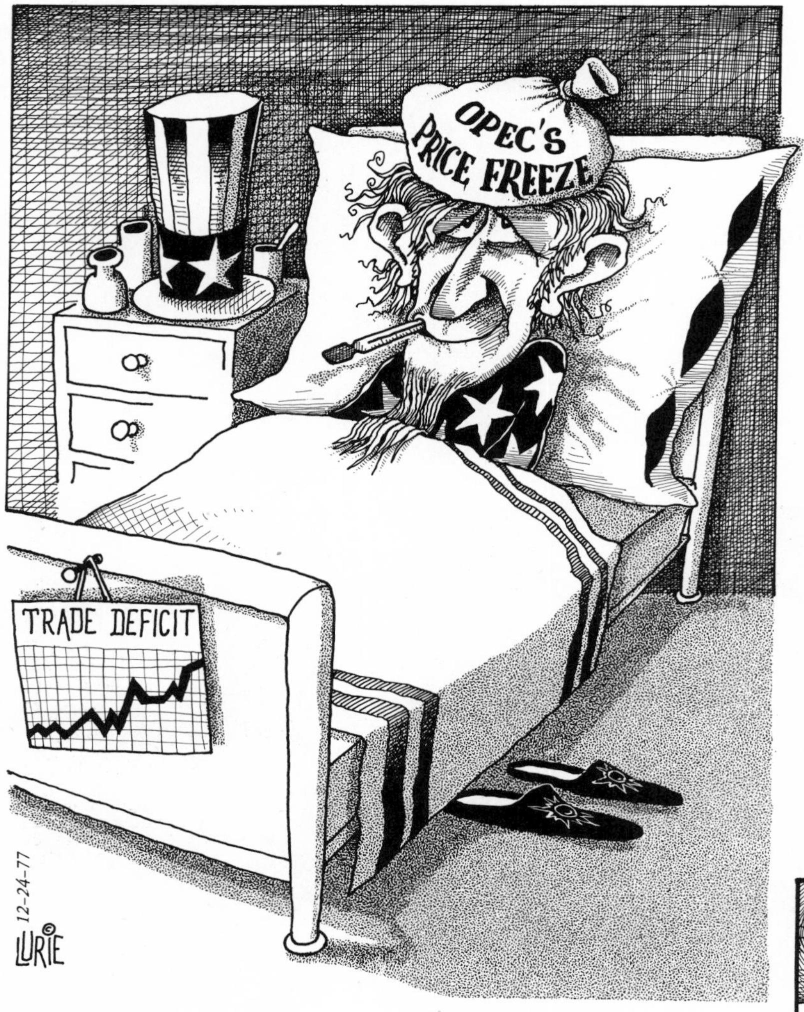
OPEC'S PRICE FREEZE
TRADE DEFICIT
12-24-77
LURIE

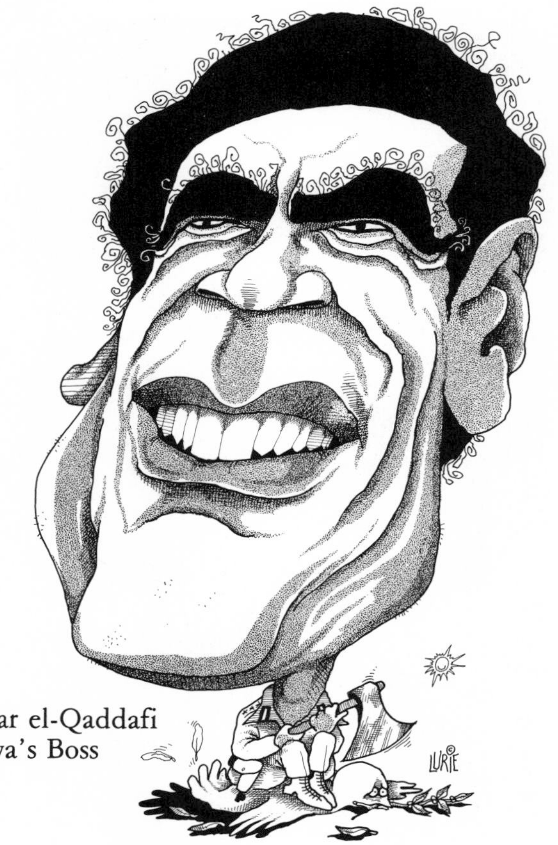
LURIE

Muammar el-Qaddafi
Libya's Boss

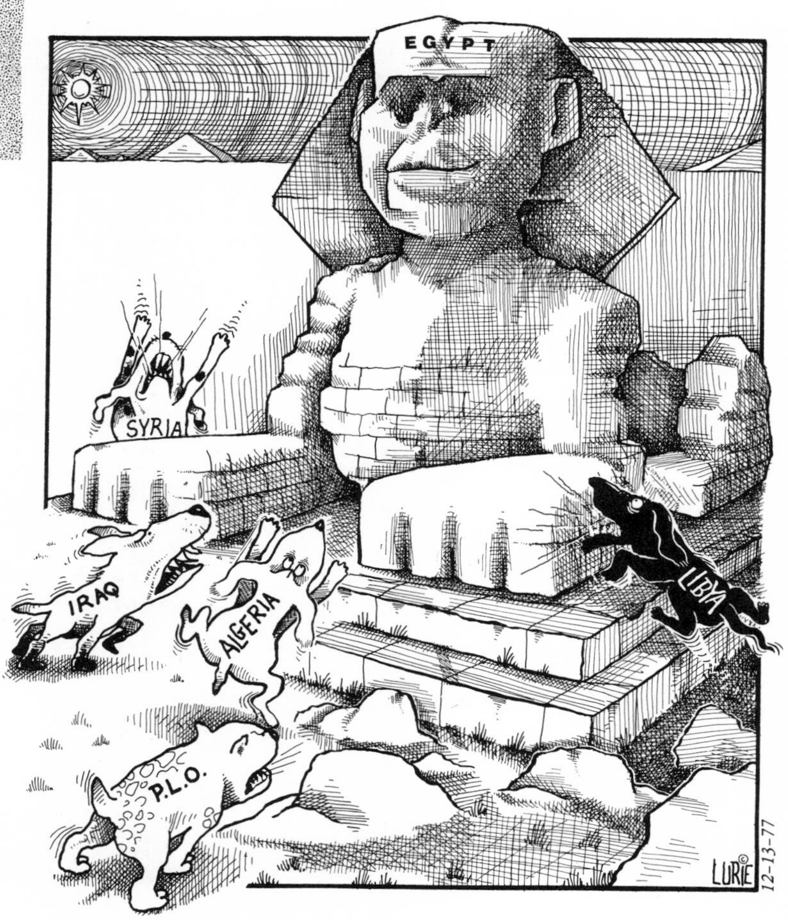
EGYPT
SYRIA
IRAQ
ALGERIA
LIBYA
P.L.O.
LURIE
12-13-77

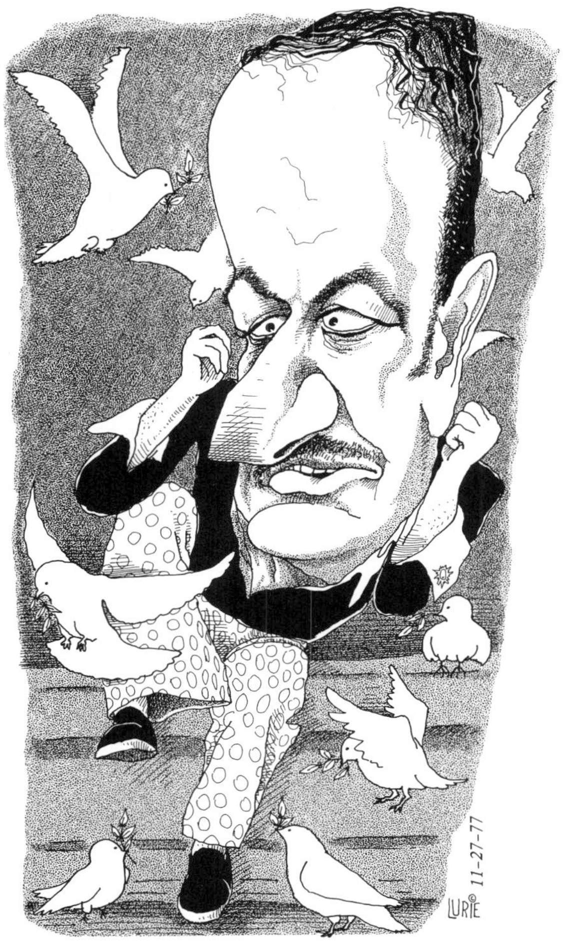
11-27-77
LURIE

President Assad of Syria

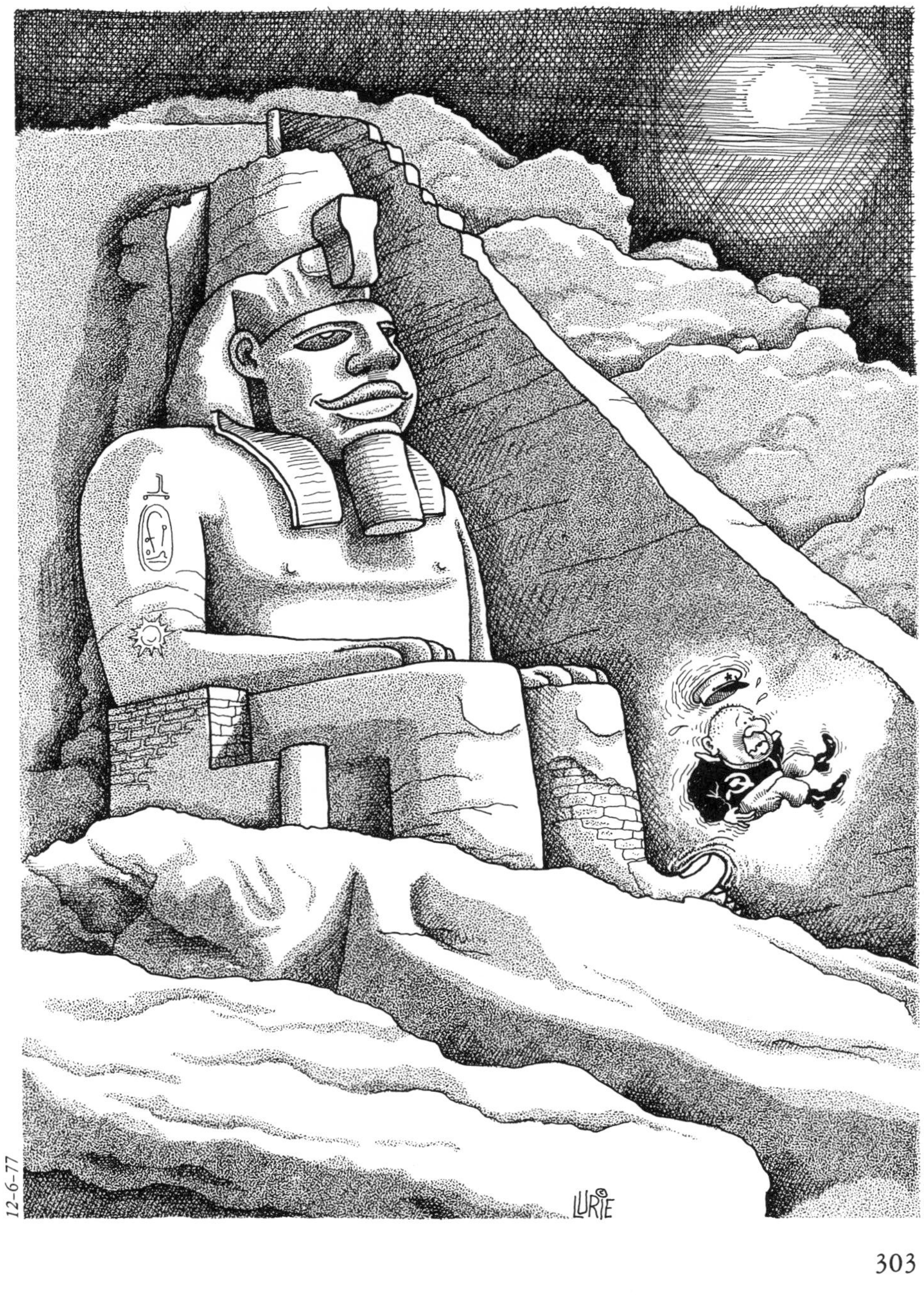
12-6-77
LURIE

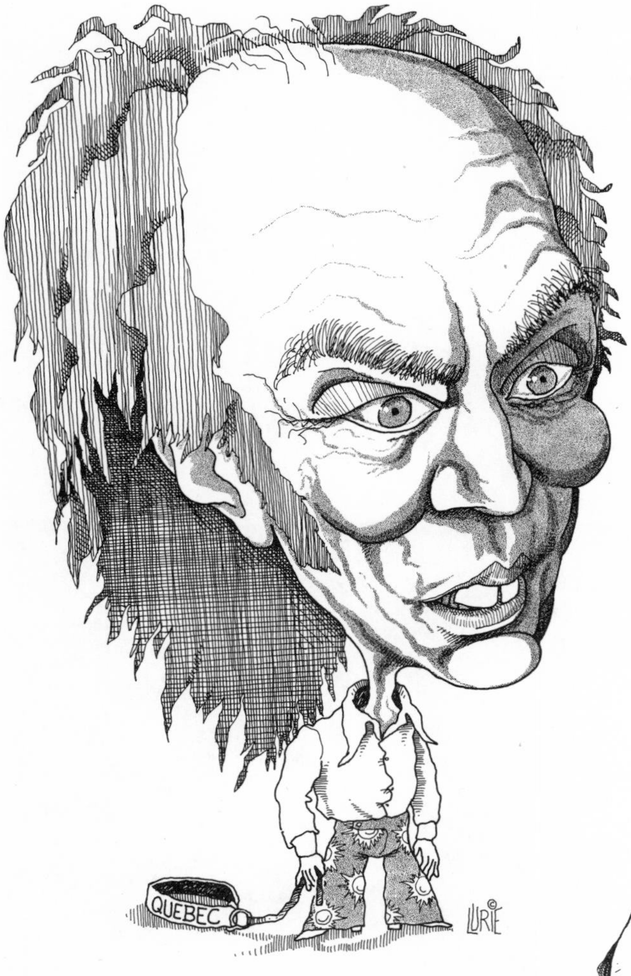
QUEBEC
LURIE

Pierre Trudeau
Canadian Prime Minister

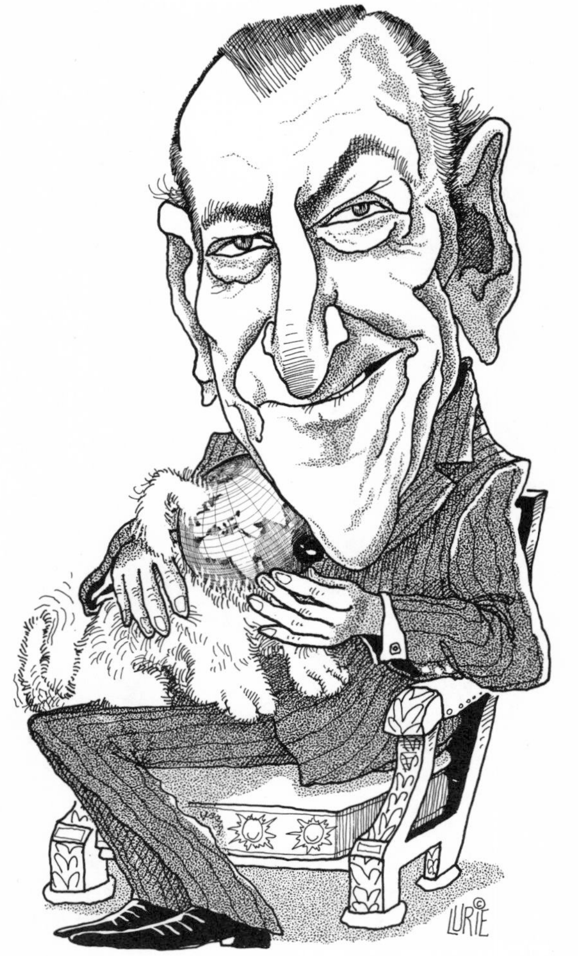
LURIE

Kurt Waldheim
United Nations Secretary-General

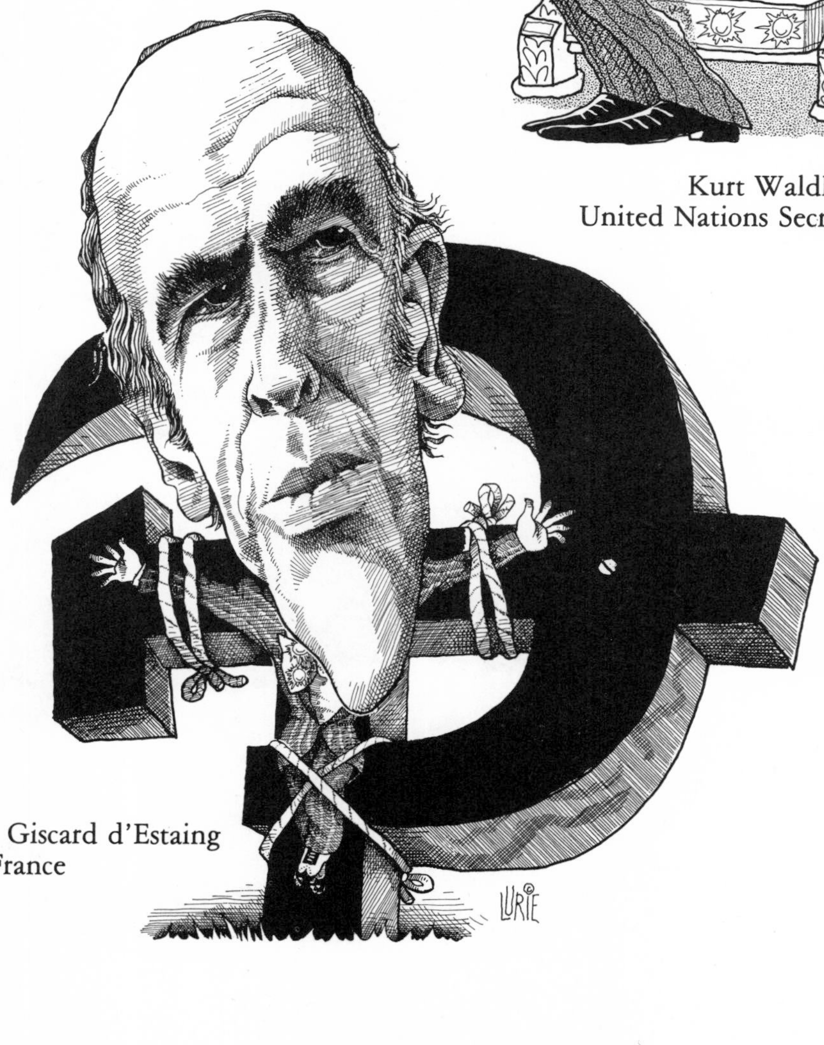
LURIE

President Valery Giscard d'Estaing
of France

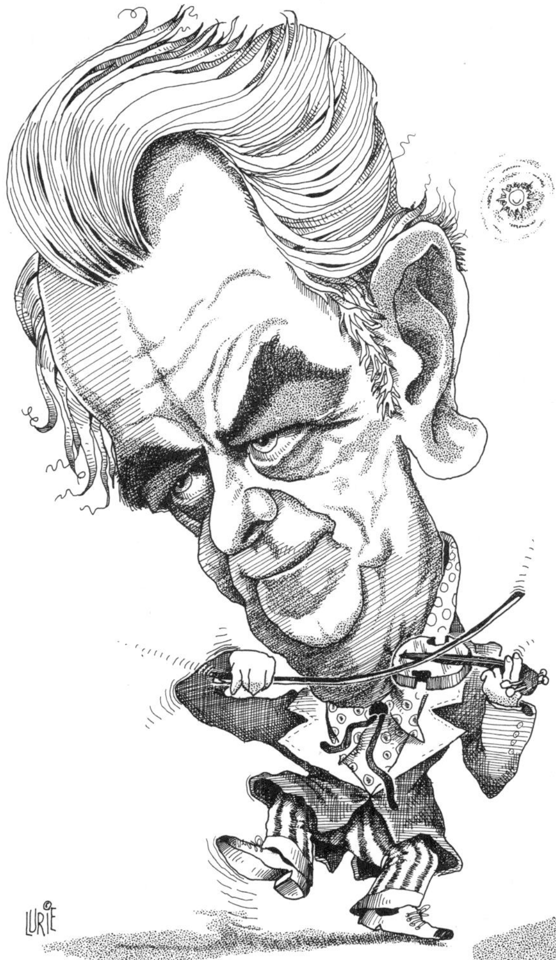
LURIE

Robert C. Byrd
Senate's Majority Leader

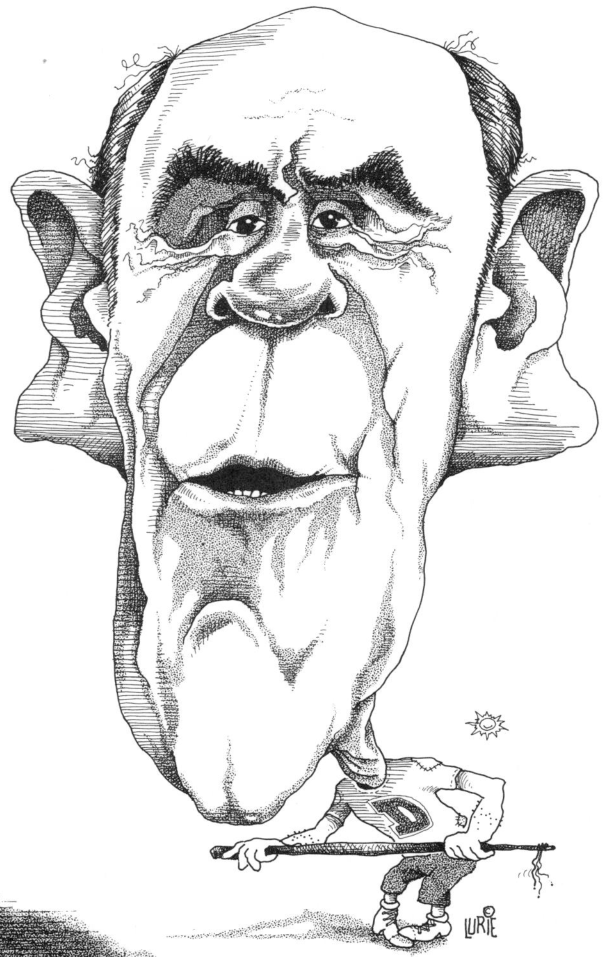
LURIE

Alan B. Cranston
Senate Democratic Whip

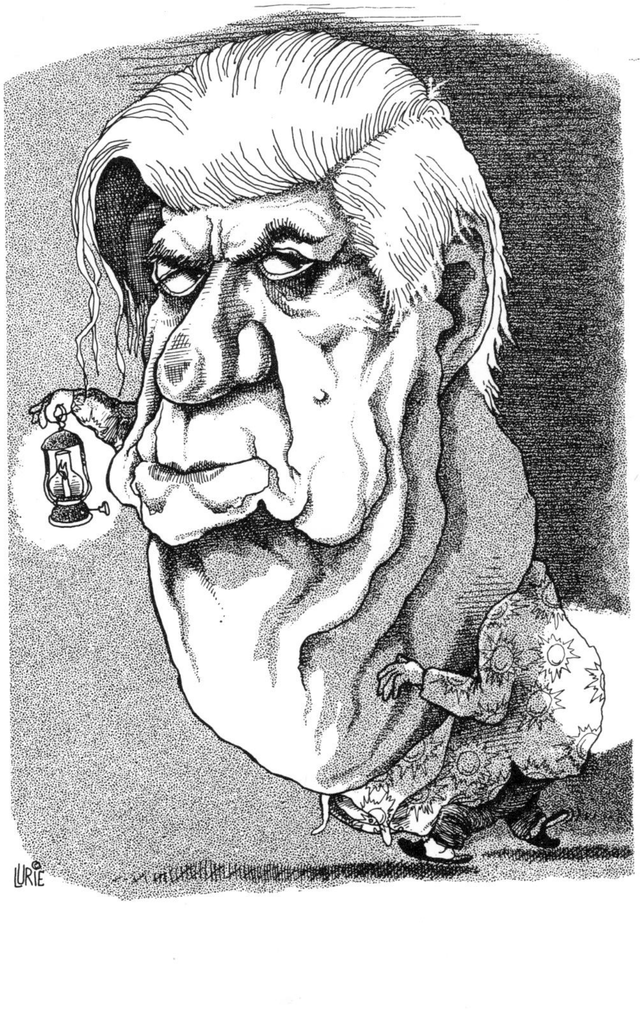
LURIE

Thomas P. (''Tip'') O'Neill, Jr.
House Speaker Under Pressure

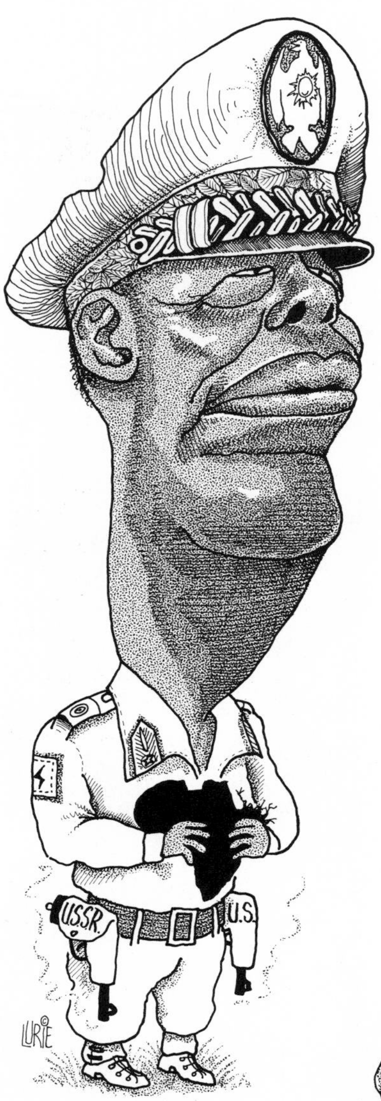
U.S.S.R.
U.S.
LURIE

President Mohammed Siad Barre
of Somalia

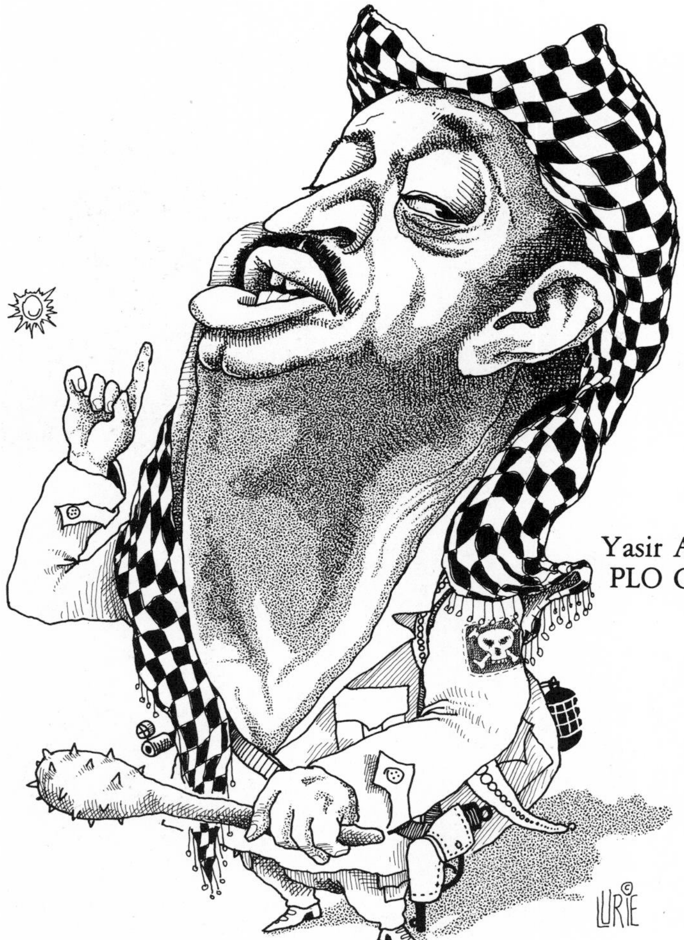
LURIE

Yasir Arafat
PLO Chief

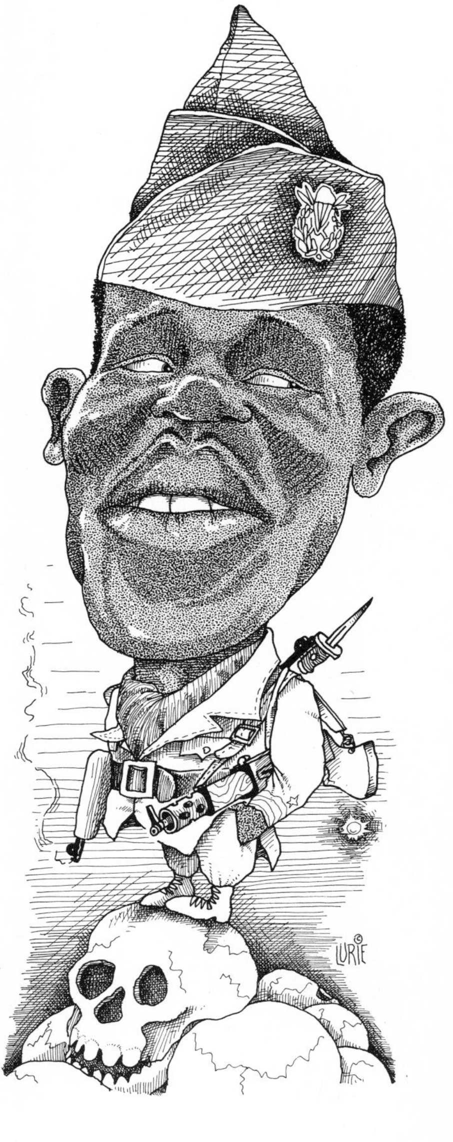
LURIE

Mengistu Haile Mariam
New Ruler of Ethiopia

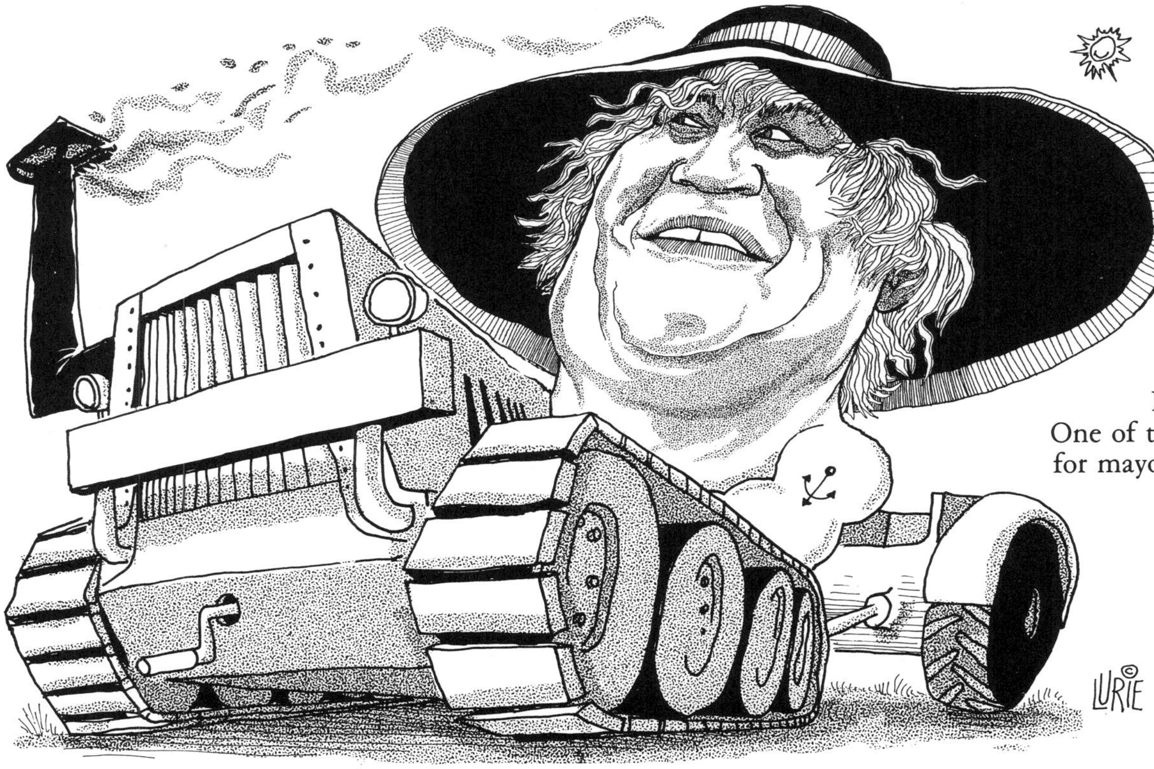
LURIE

Bella Abzug
One of the major contenders
for mayor of New York City

Paul C. Warnke
U.S. Chief Arms Negotiator

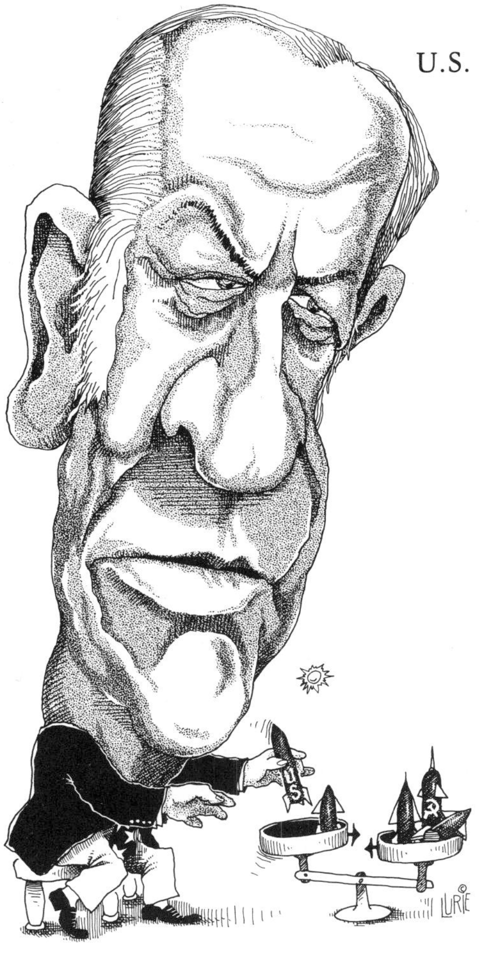
LURIE

Congressman Edward I. Koch
One of the major contenders
for mayor of New York City

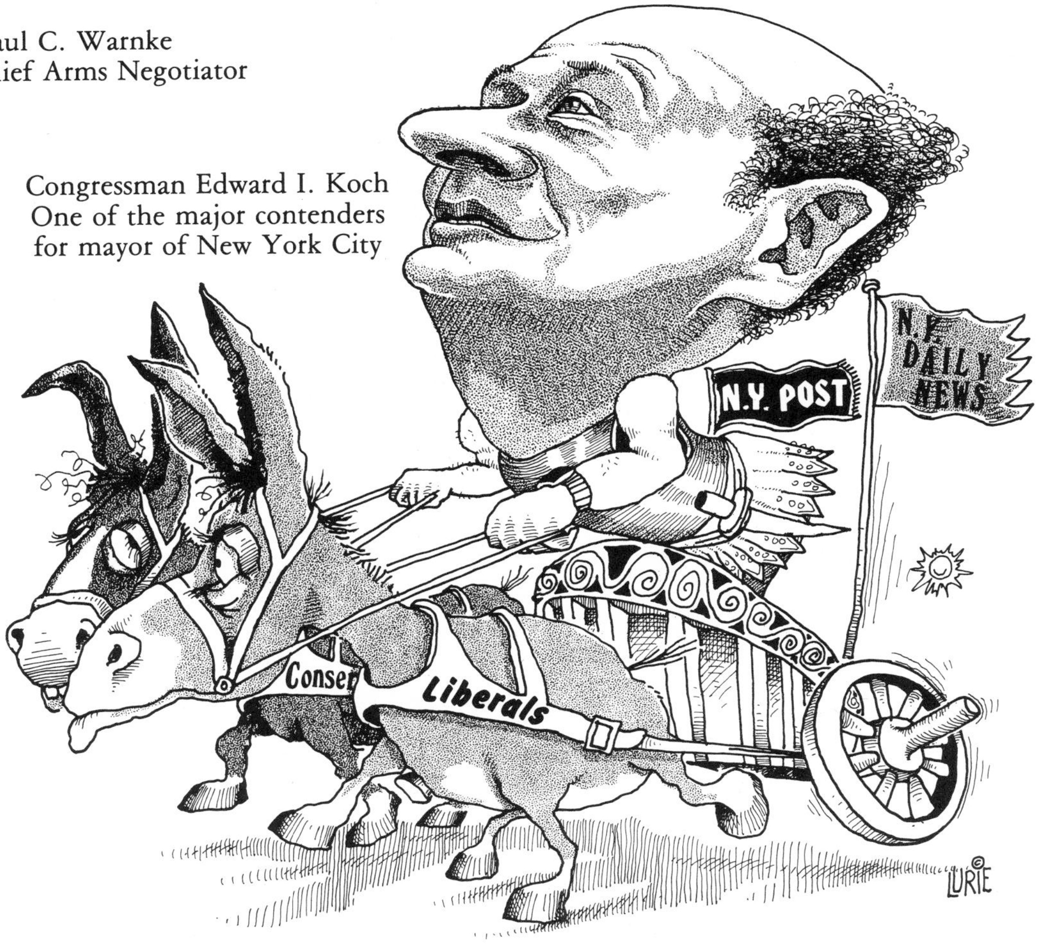
N.Y. POST
N.Y. DAILY NEWS
Conser
Liberals
LURIE

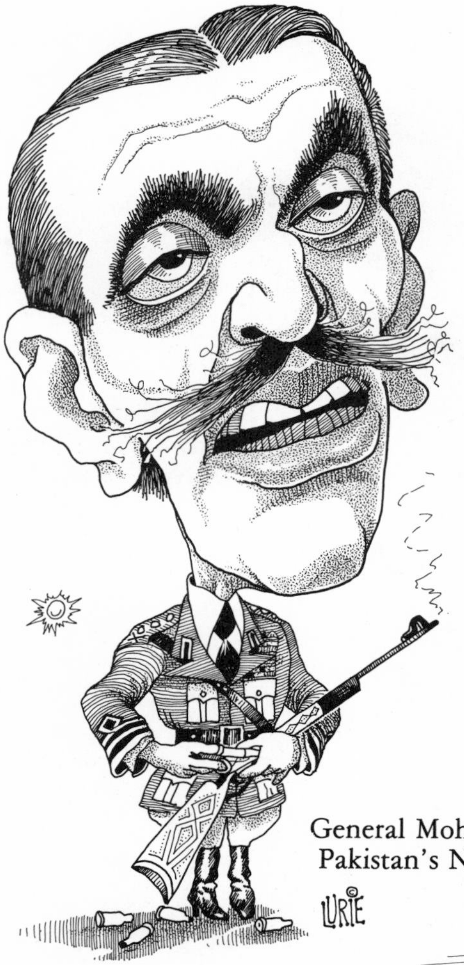
LURIE

General Mohammed Zia ul-Haq
Pakistan's New Military Leader

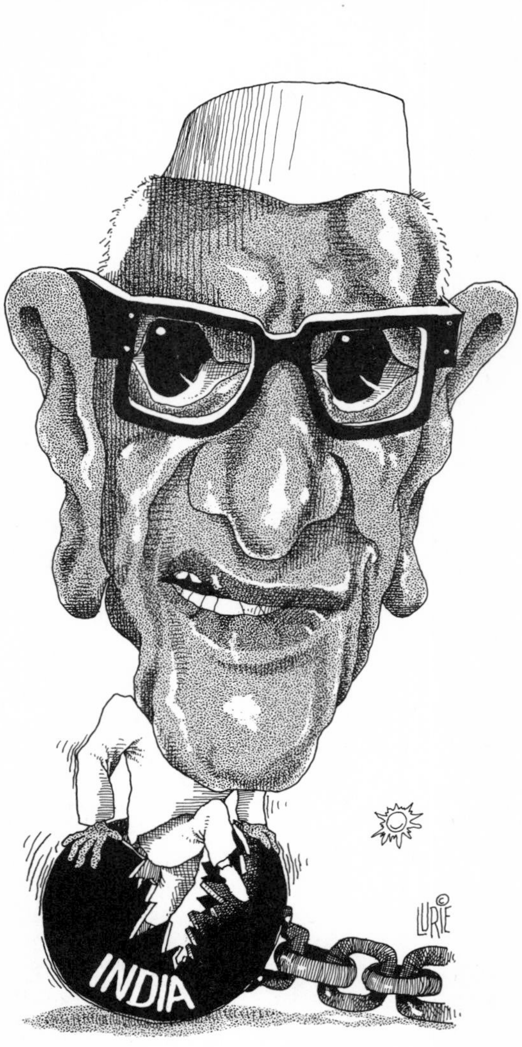
INDIA
LURIE

Prime Minister Morarji Desai
of India

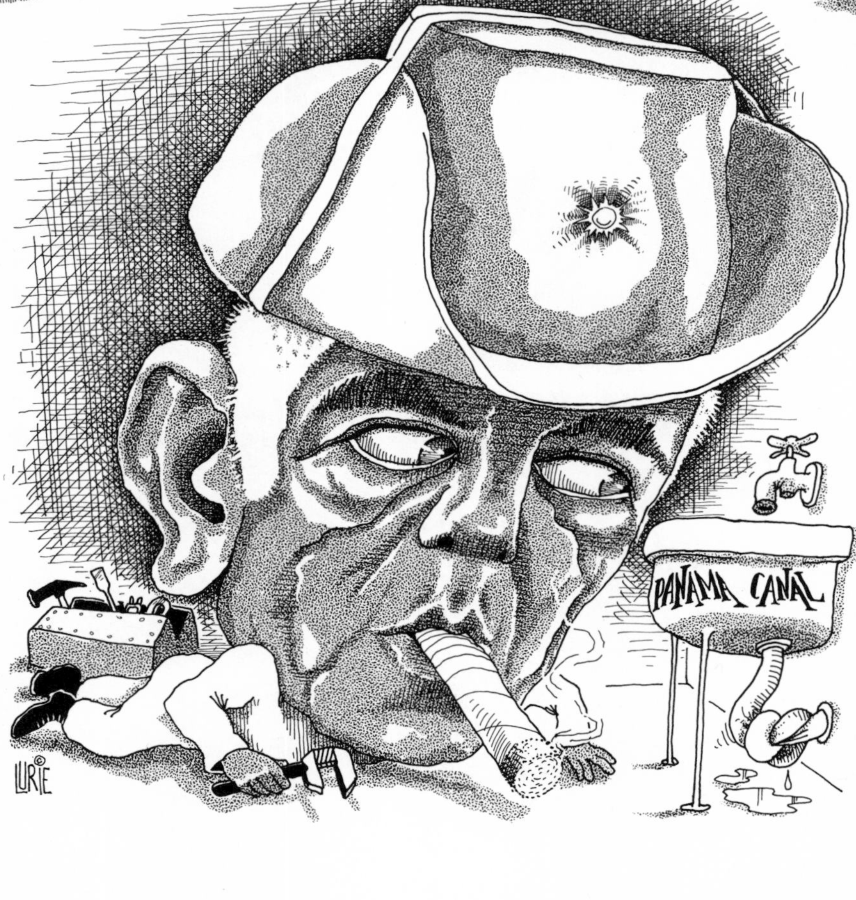
PANAMA CANAL
LURIE

General Omar Torrijos
Ruler of Panama

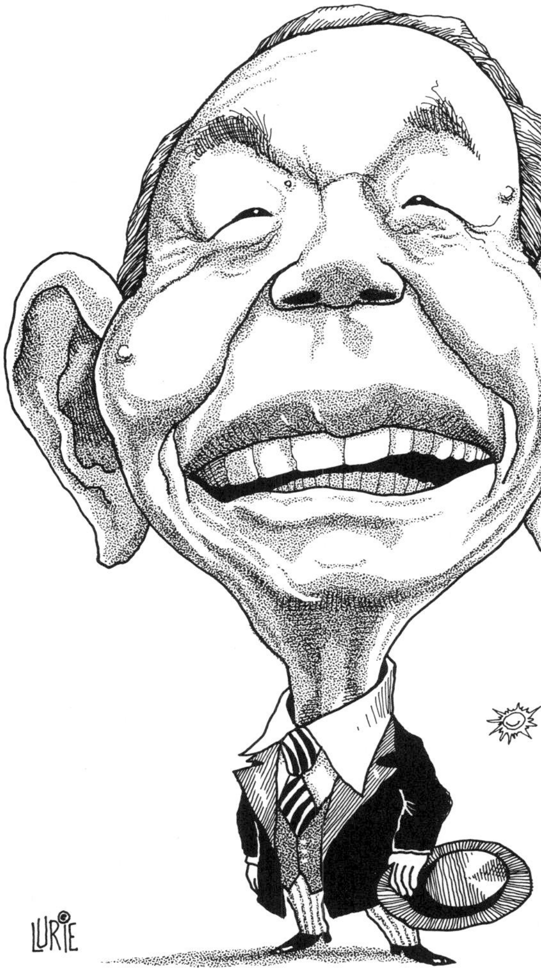
LURIE

Premier Takeo Fukuda
of Japan

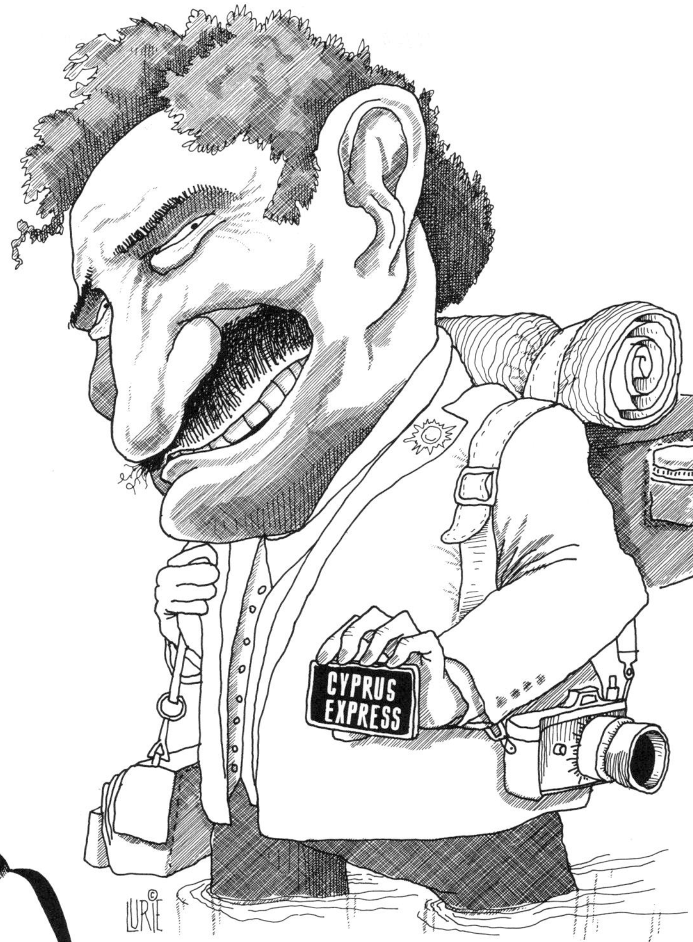
CYPRUS
EXPRESS
LURIE

Bulent Ecevit
Turkey's New Leader

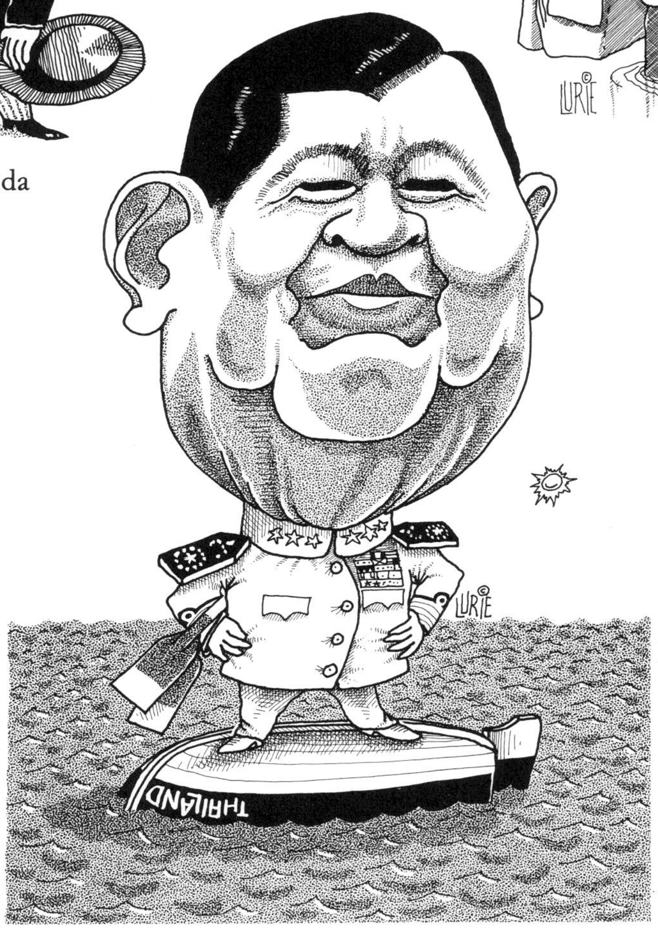
LURIE
THAILAND

Admiral Sa-ngad Chaloryu
Head of Thailand's
Ruling Military Junta

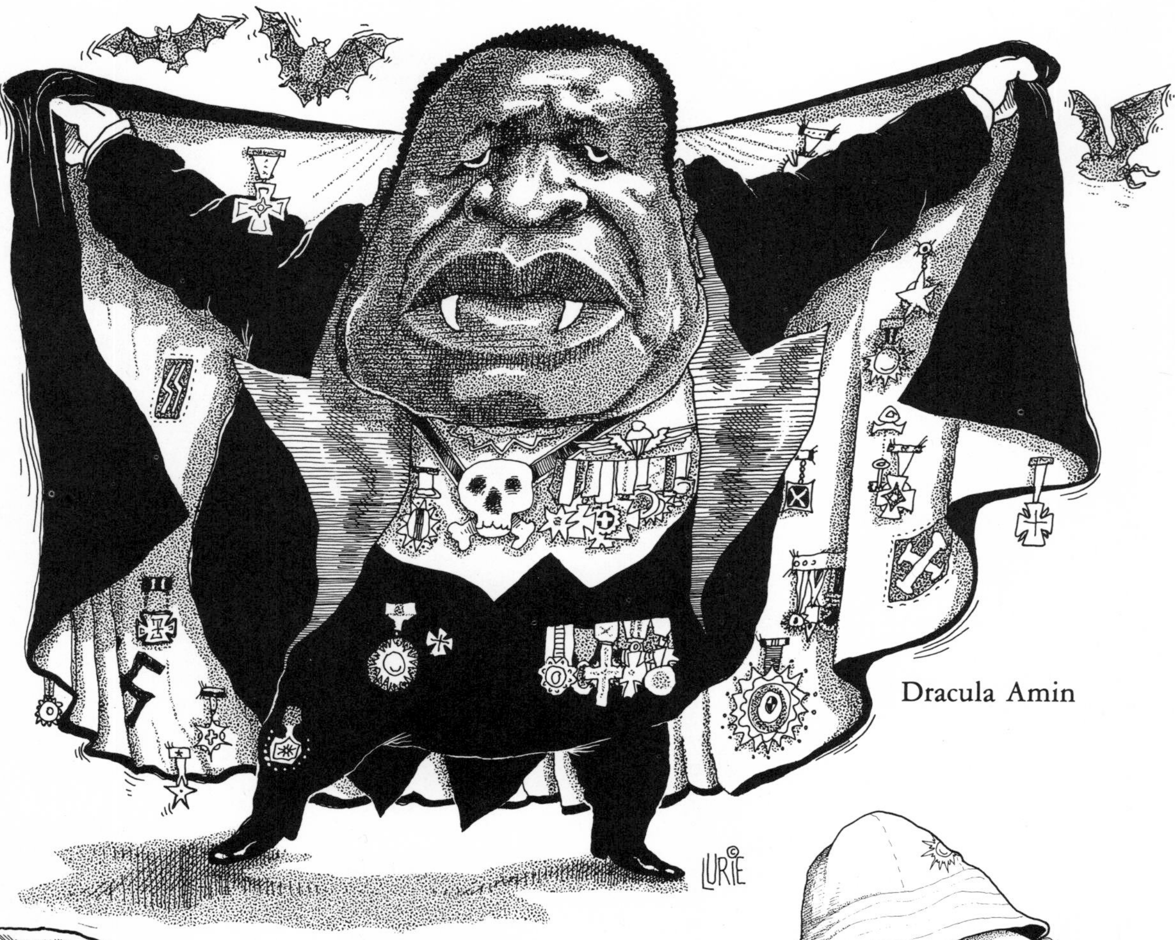
LURIE

Dracula Amin

Prime Minister Menachem Begin
of Israel

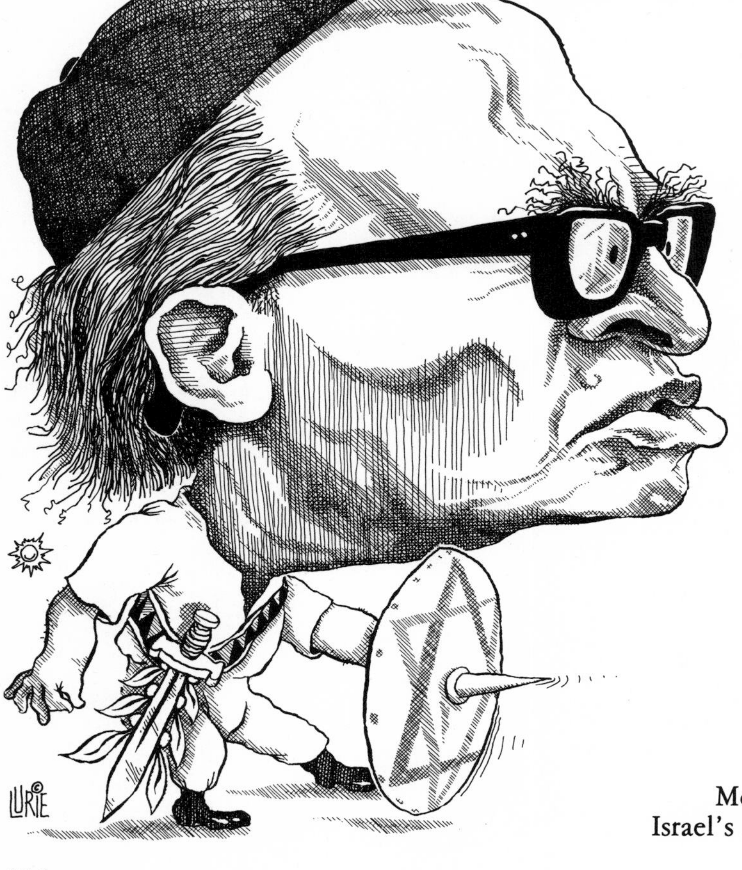
LURIE

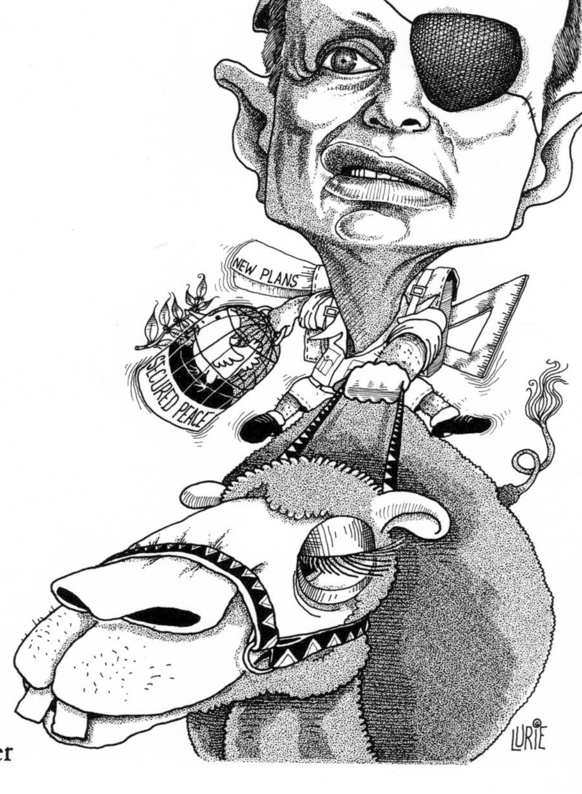
NEW PLANS
SECURED PEACE
LURIE

Moshe Dayan
Israel's Foreign Minister

Brock Adams
Secretary of Transportation

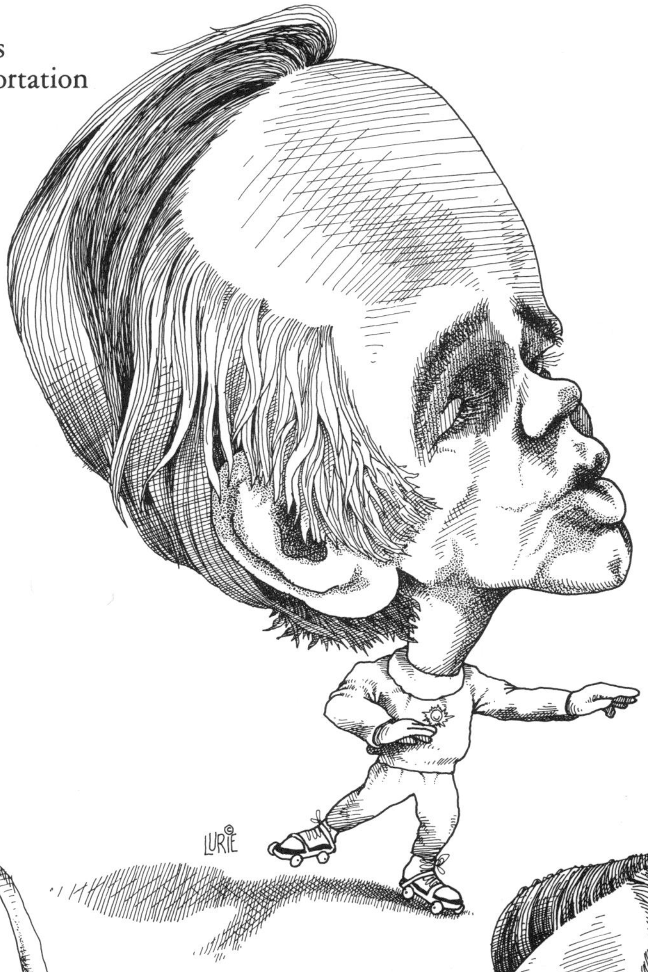
LURIE

Robert S. Bergland
Secretary of Agriculture

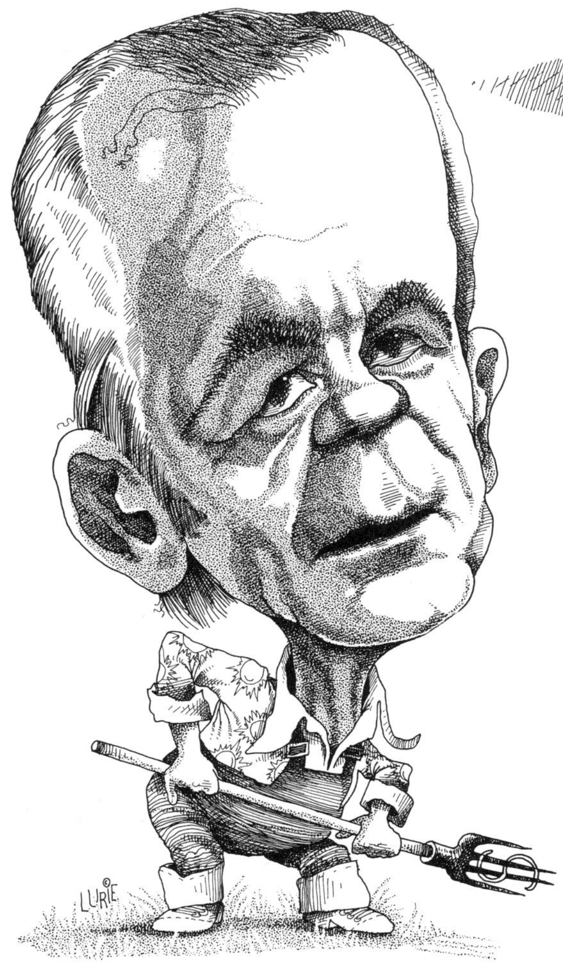
LURIE

Admiral Stansfield Turner
New CIA Skipper

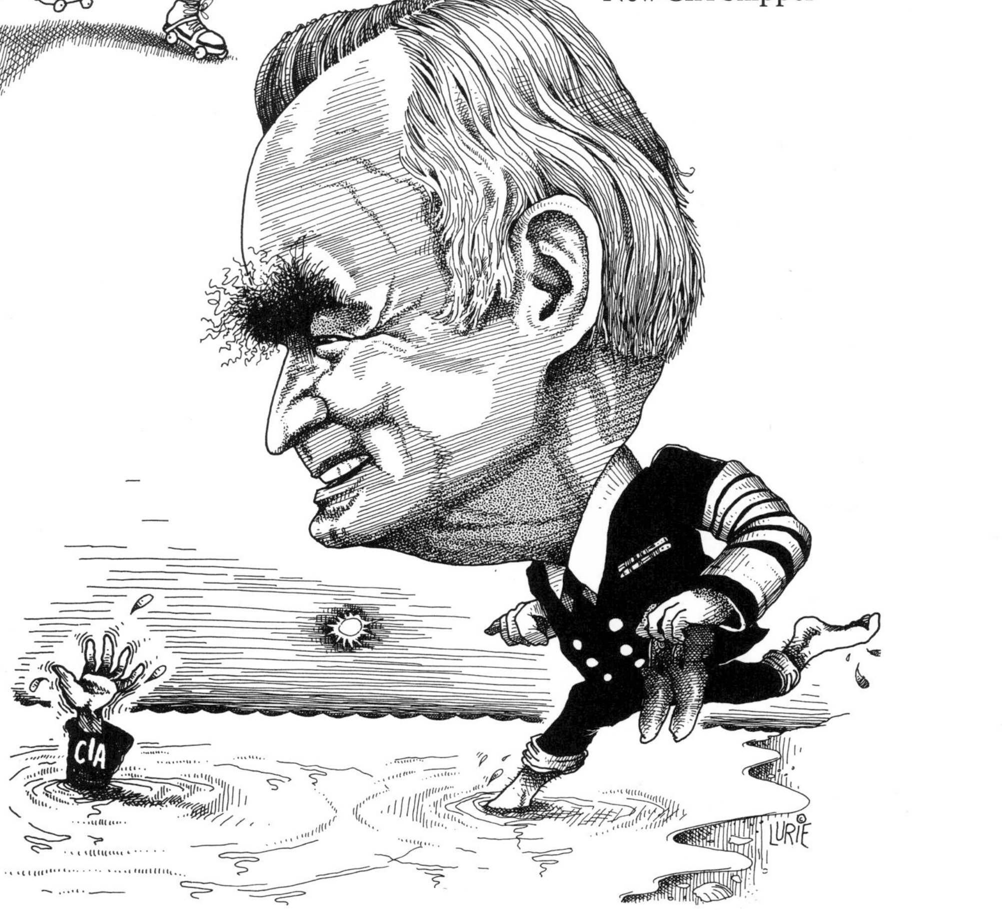
CIA
LURIE

1978

Lurie: ON GAMES AS METAPHORS

I frequently use games as metaphors. The cartoonist naturally tends to feel more comfortable with metaphors he understands from personal experience. I play a lot of tennis, I swim a lot, I used to be on track and field teams. On the other hand, I have never played billiards; yet I occasionally use that game as a metaphor. I did not grow up in America and therefore am not too familiar with baseball, so it does not occur to me to use that metaphor.

Politics does resemble a game—more than anything else, chess. You see how moves are planned ahead and how one move can affect the pawns or knights or bishops on the other side of the globe. The confrontation element in games is definitely present in politics.

People understand game metaphors because they have seen the games so many times on television or in the arena, or, with some luck, they have even participated in them.

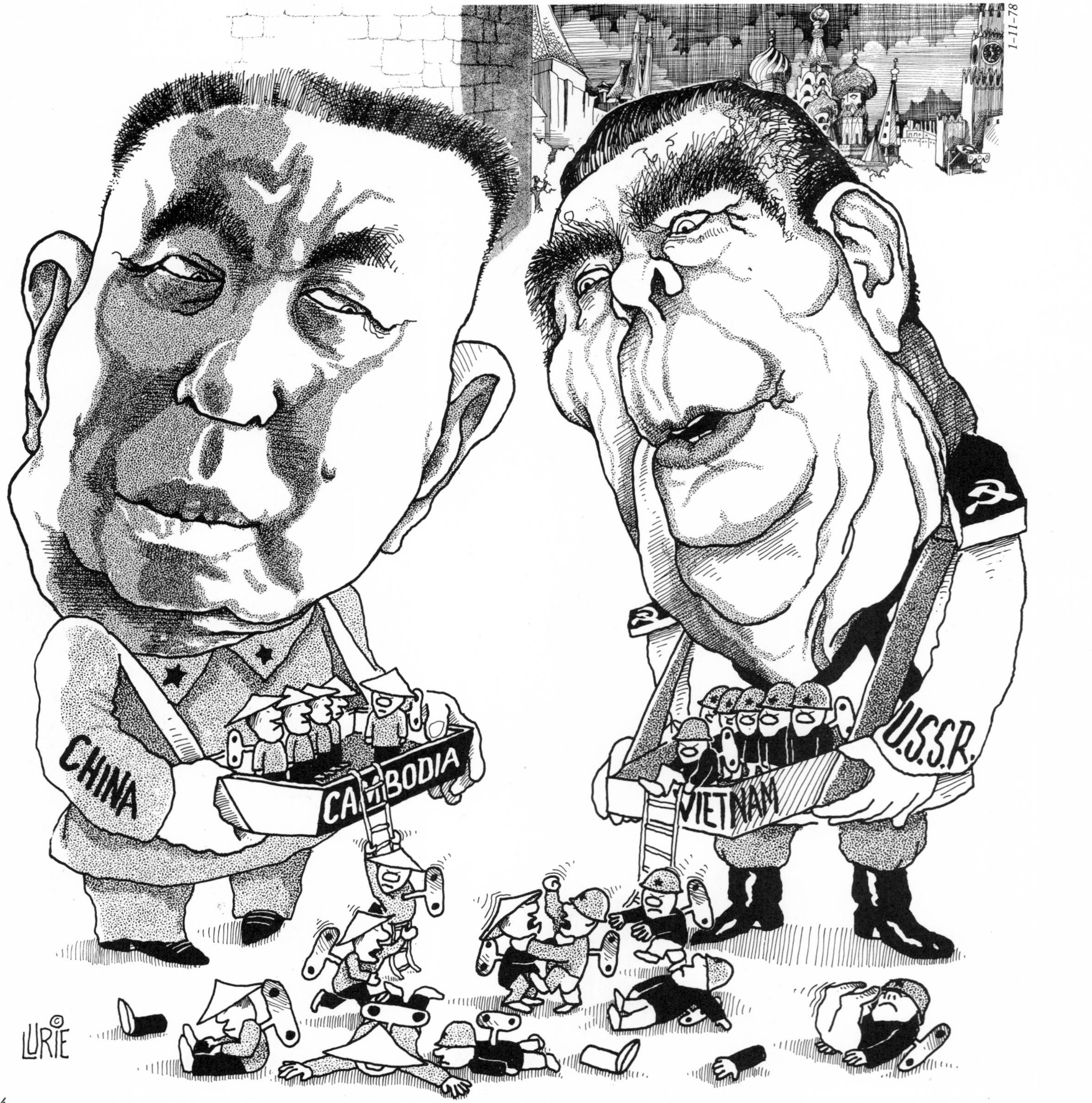
1-11-78
CHINA
CAMBODIA
VIETNAM
U.S.S.R.
LURIE

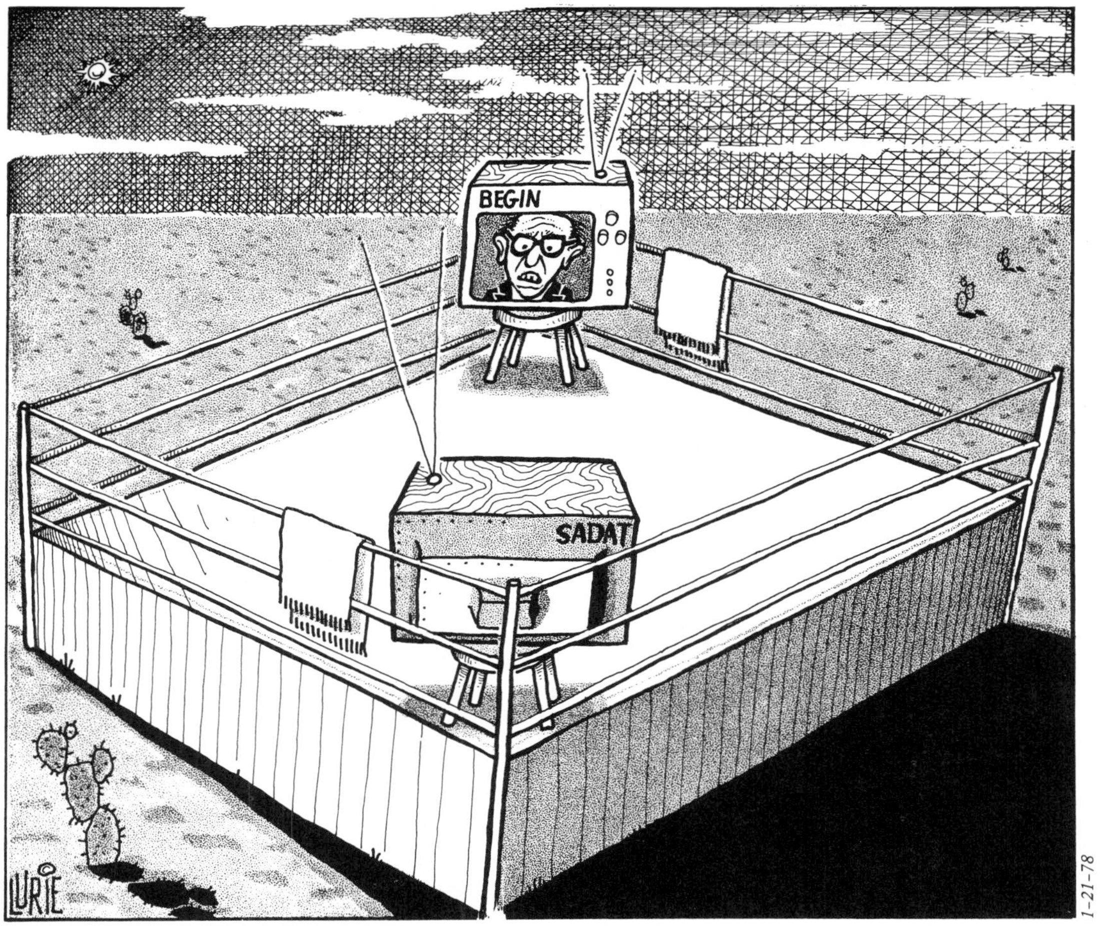
BEGIN
SADAT
LURIE
1-21-78

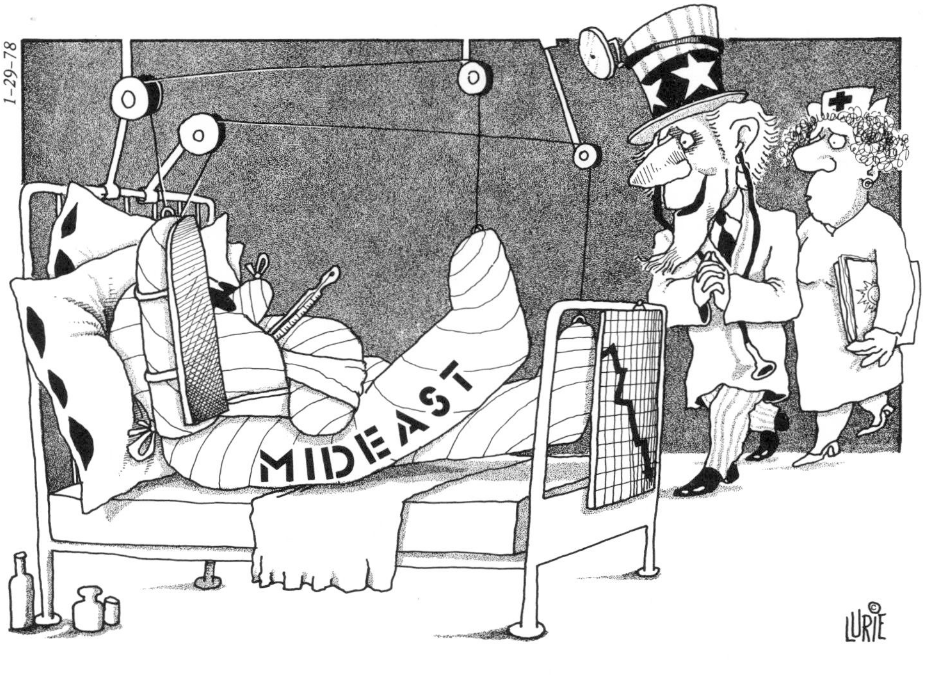
1-29-78
MIDEAST
LURIE

"WELL, WELL—YOU DO LOOK BETTER TODAY!"

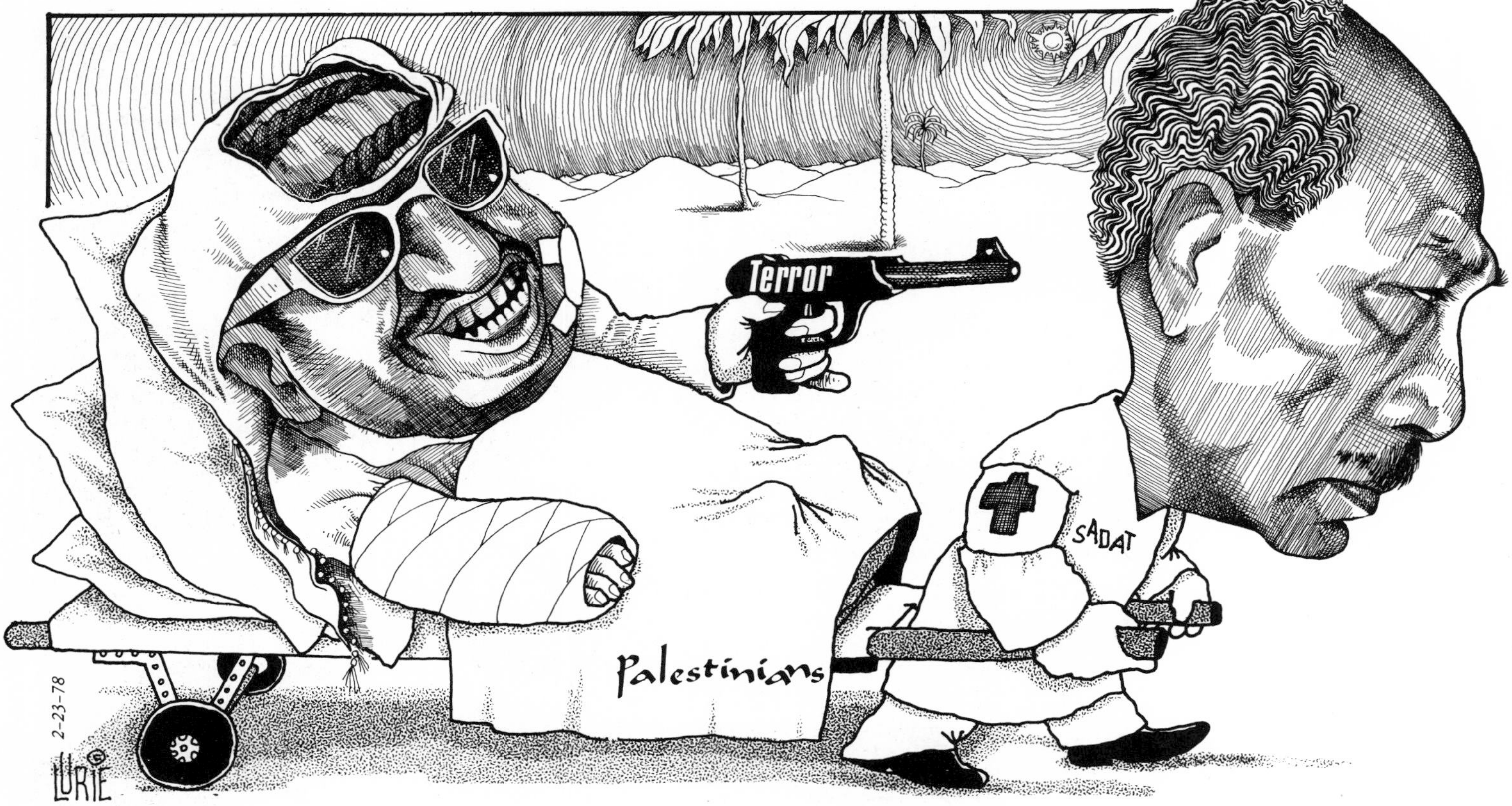
Terror
SADAT
Palestinians
2-23-78
LURIE

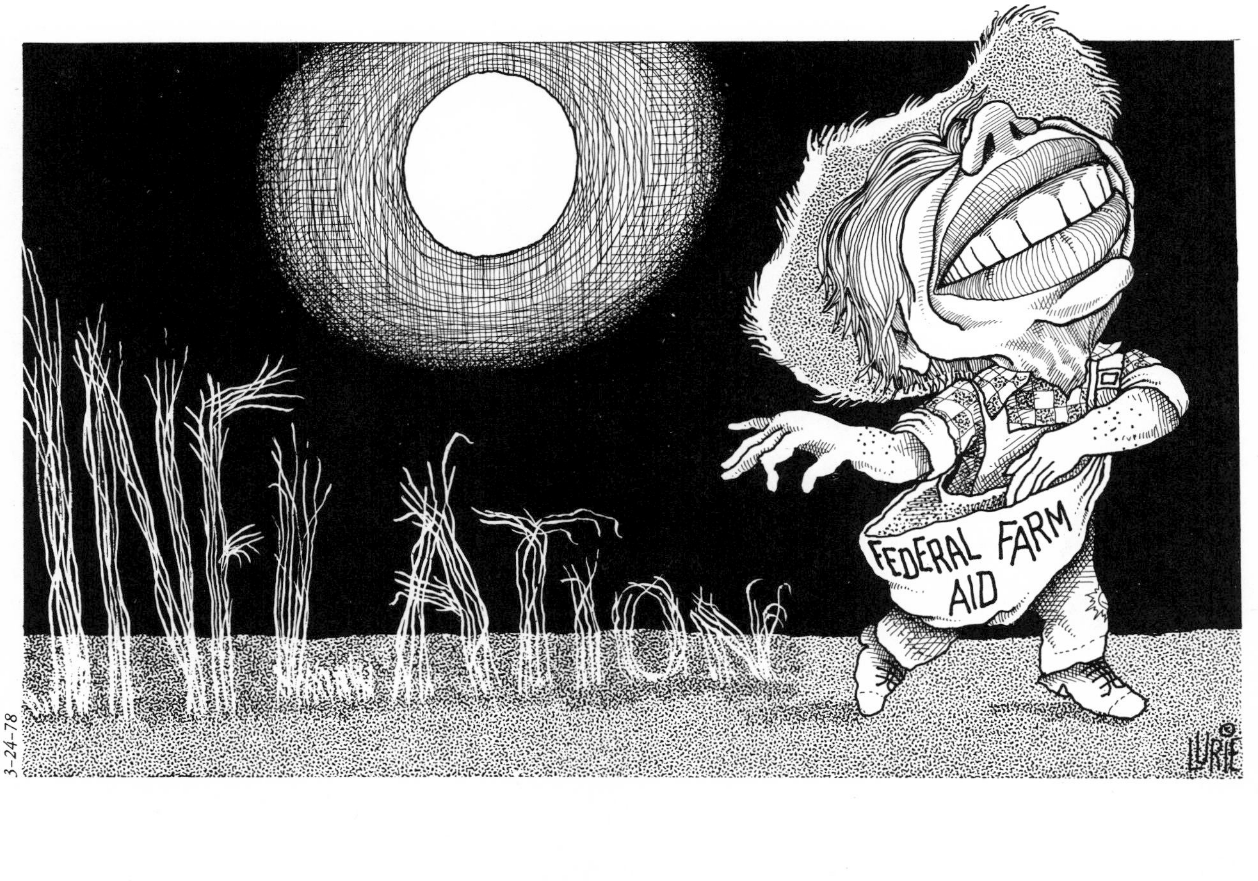
INFLATION
FEDERAL FARM AID
3-24-78
LURIE

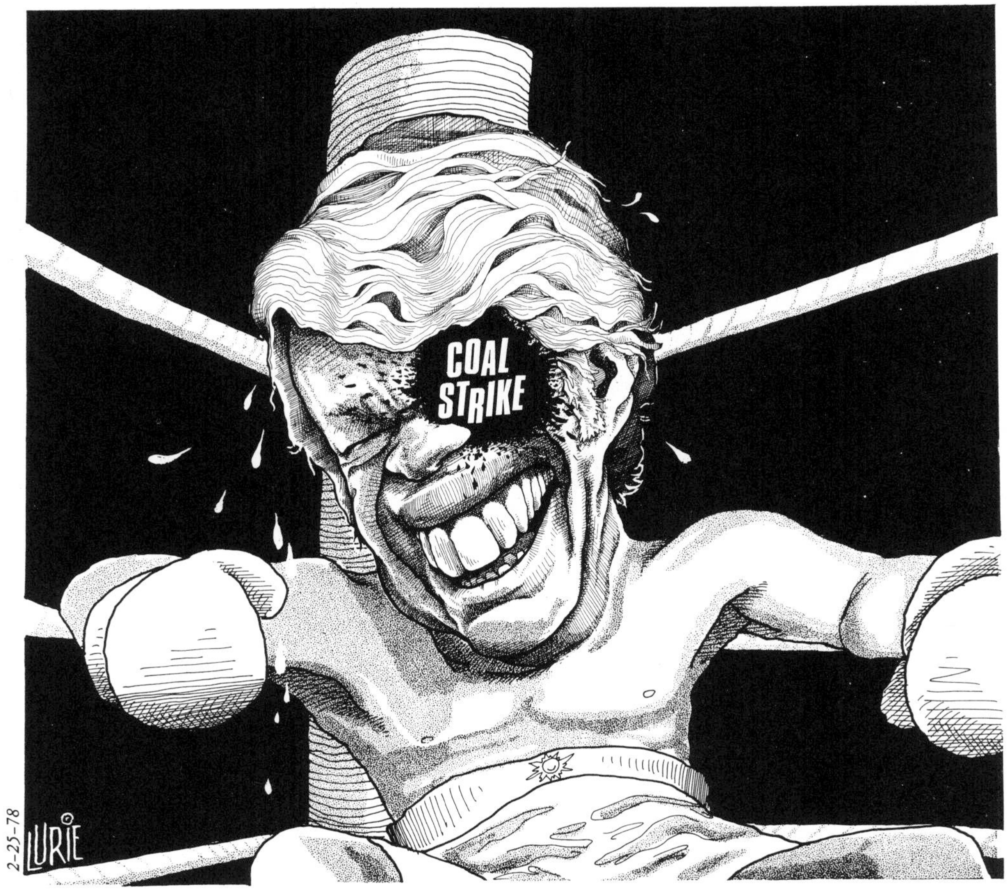
COAL
STRIKE
2-25-78
LURIE

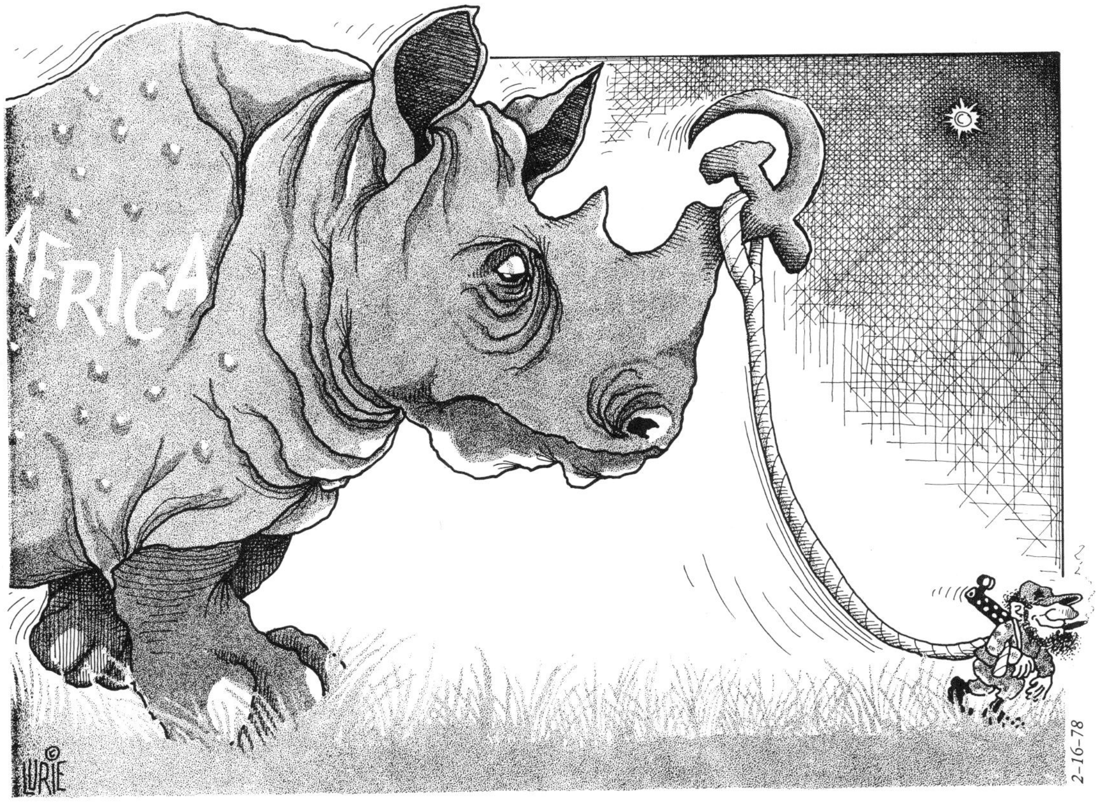
AFRICA
2-16-78
LURIE

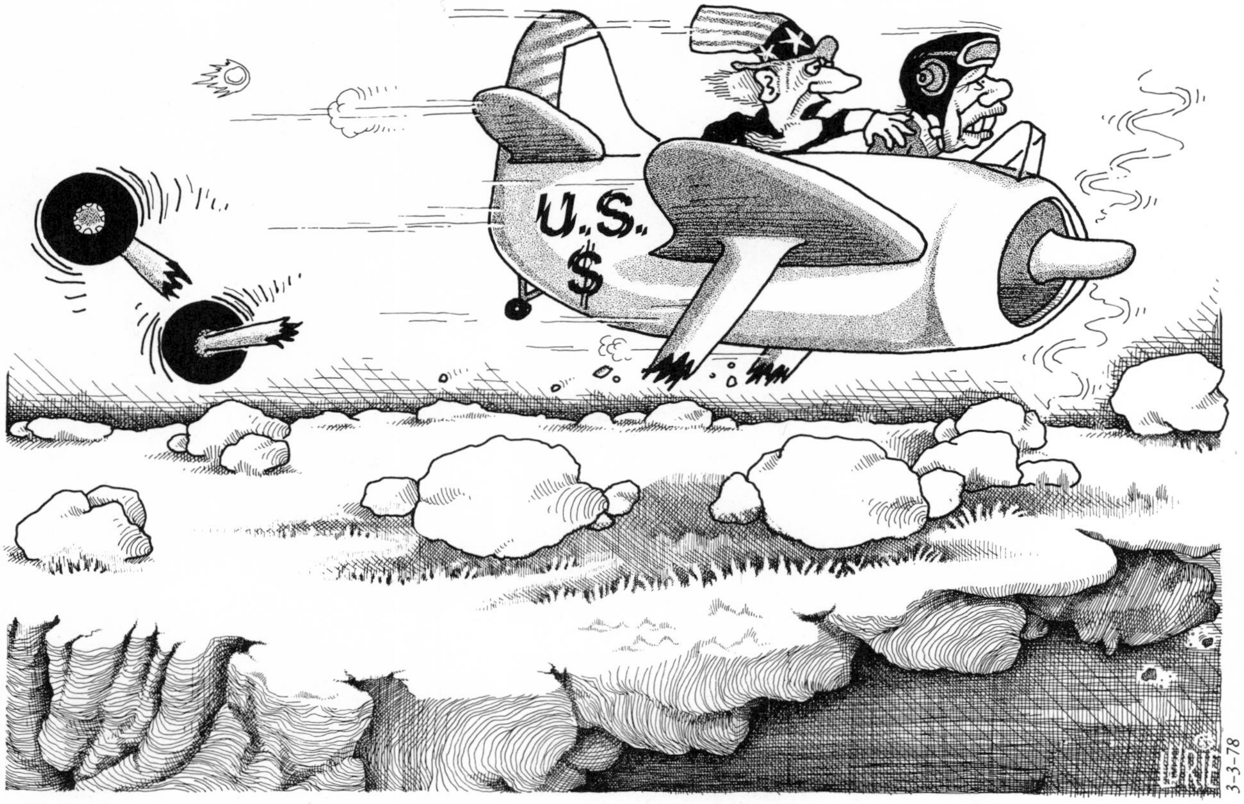
U.S.
$
LURIE
3-3-78

"ENOUGH LOW FLYING, MR. PRESIDENT . . . TRY TO LAND!"

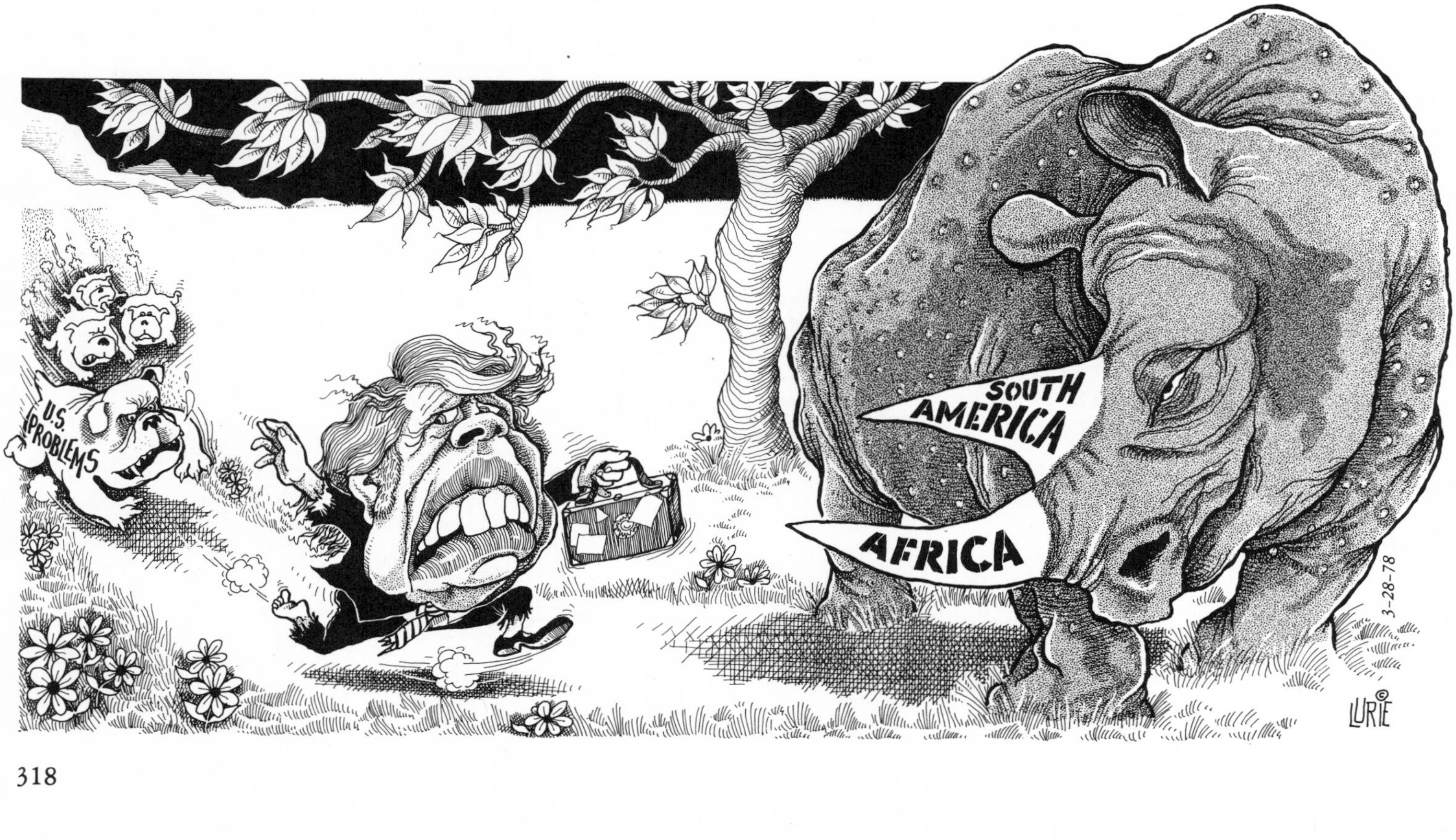
U.S. PROBLEMS
SOUTH AMERICA
AFRICA
3-28-78
LURIE

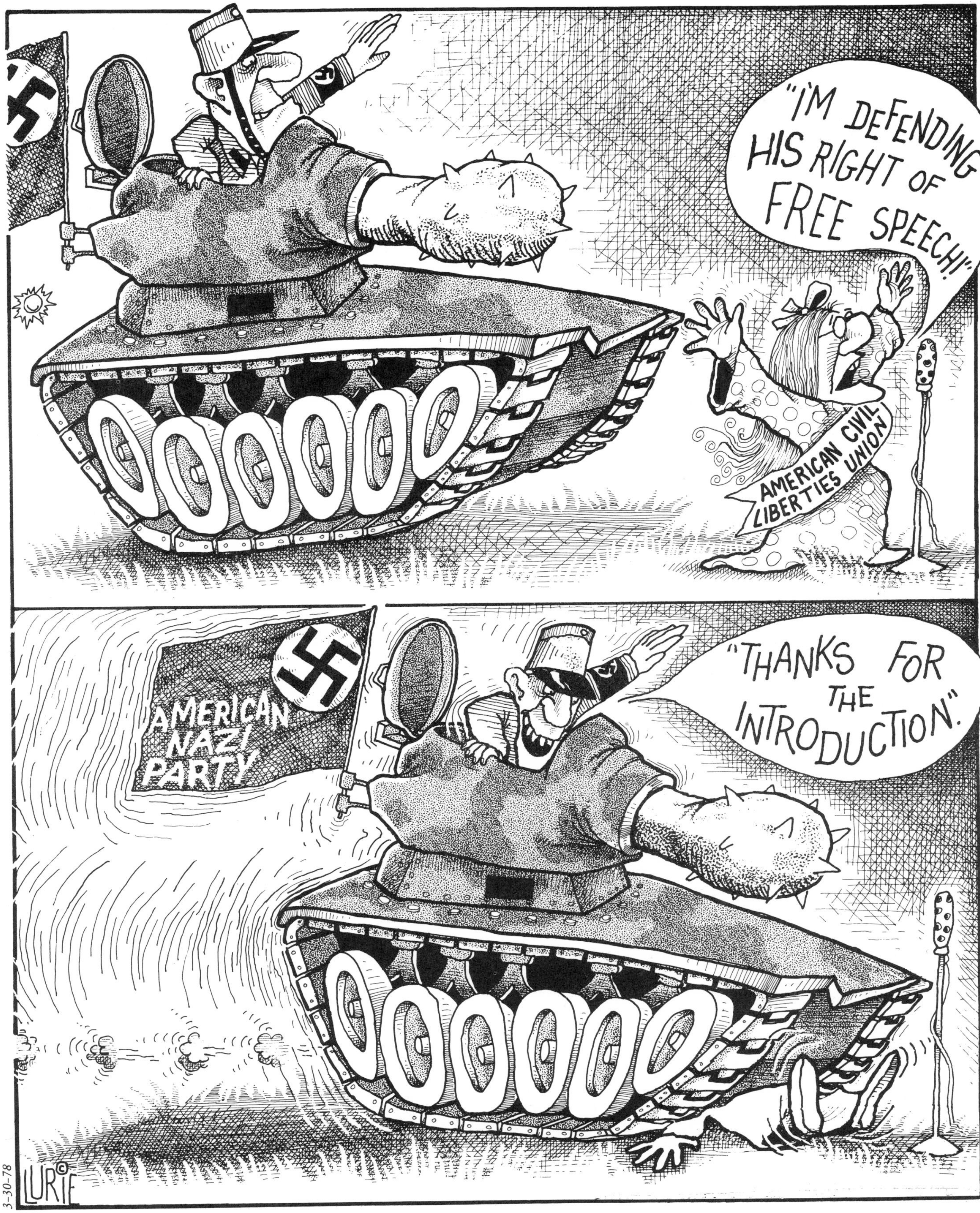
"I'M DEFENDING HIS RIGHT OF FREE SPEECH!"
AMERICAN CIVIL LIBERTIES UNION
AMERICAN NAZI PARTY
"THANKS FOR THE INTRODUCTION."
3-30-78
LURIE©

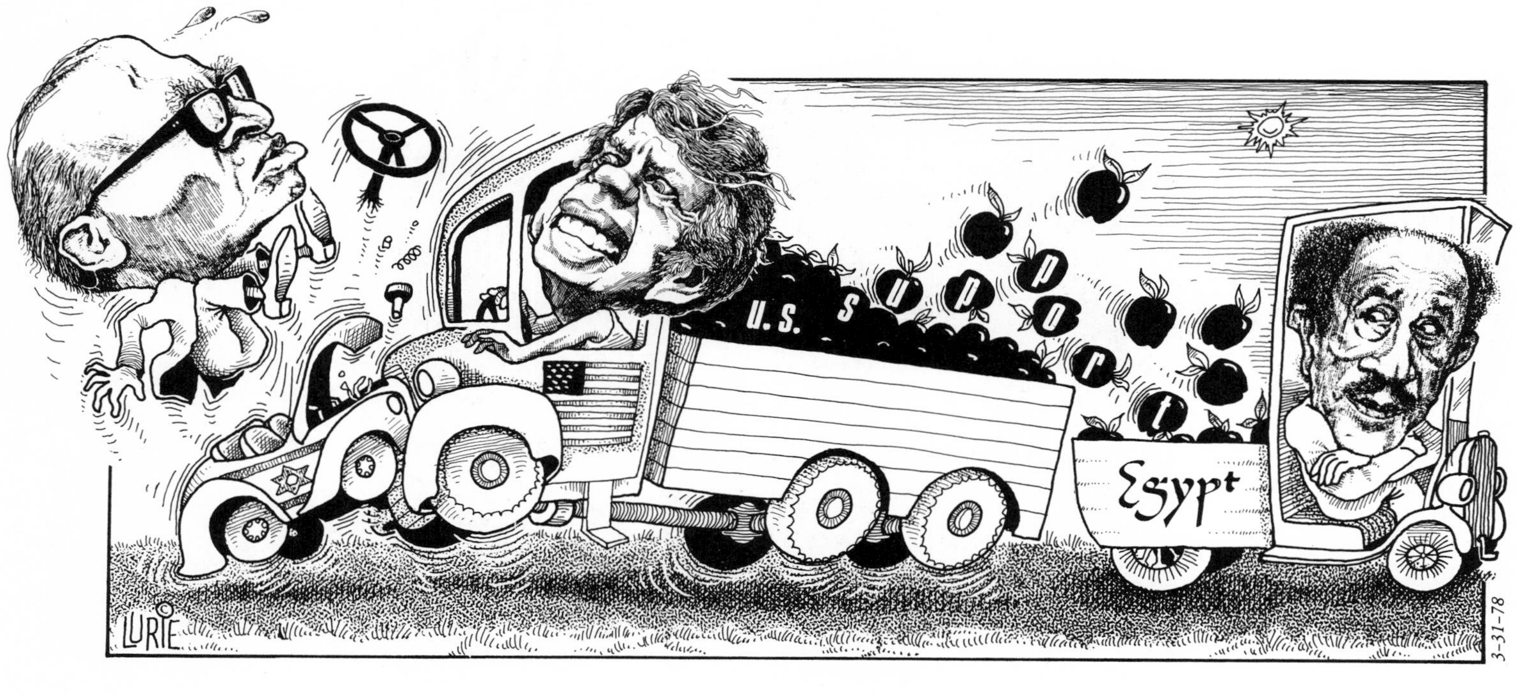
U.S. support
Egypt
LURIE
3-31-78

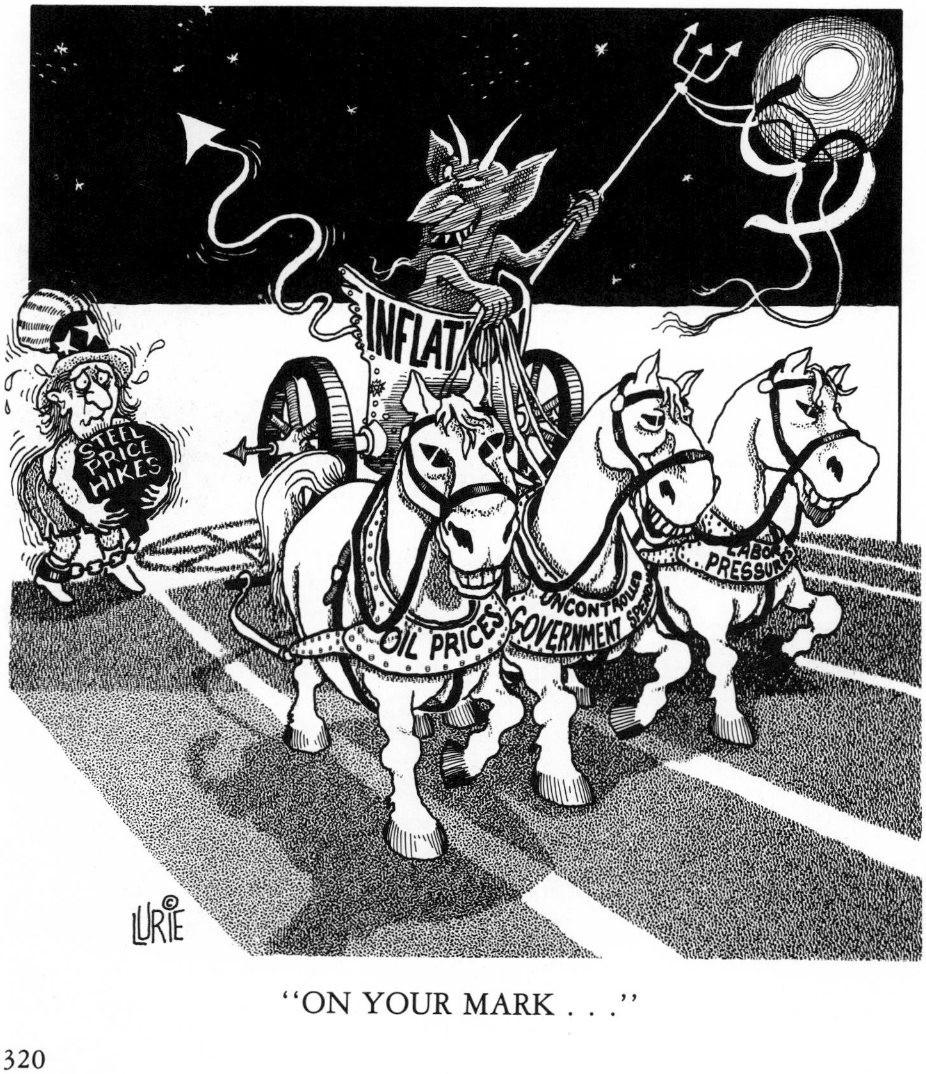
INFLATION
STEEL PRICE HIKES
OIL PRICES
UNCONTROLLED GOVERNMENT SPENDING
LABOR PRESSURE
LURIE
4-1-78

"ON YOUR MARK . . ."

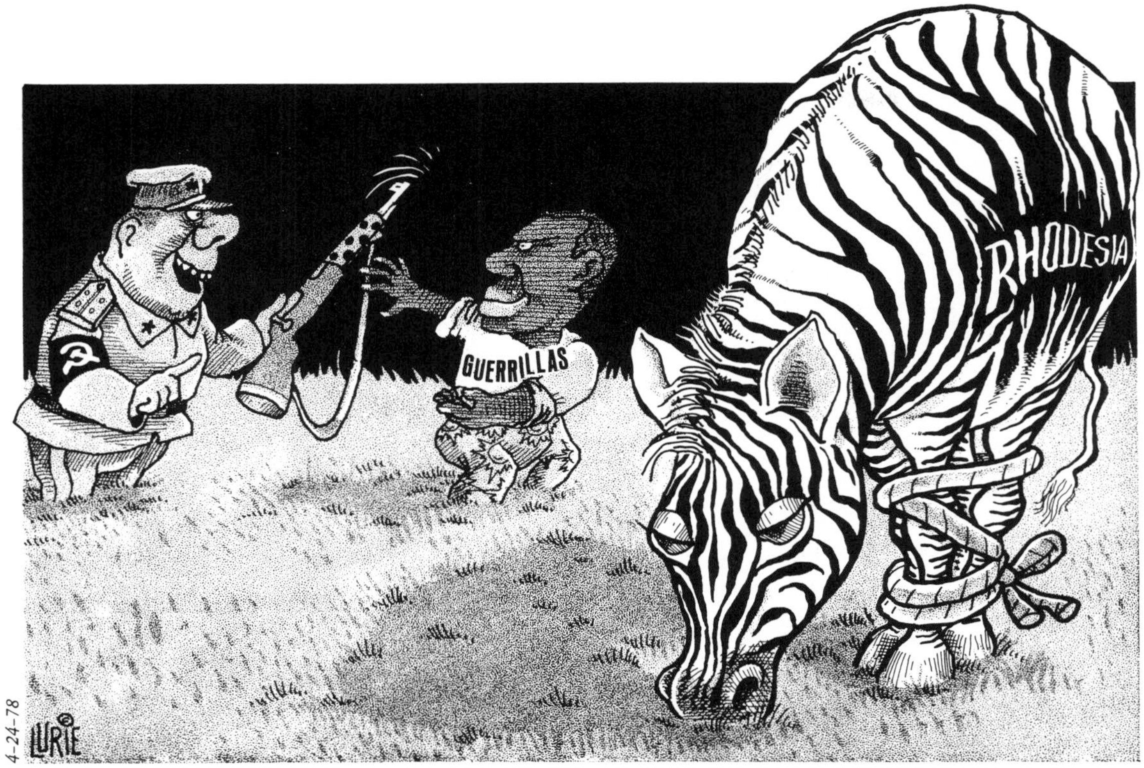
GUERRILLAS
RHODESIA
4-24-78
LURIE

"REMEMBER, YOU PROMISED TO SHOOT AT THE WHITE PARTS ONLY!"

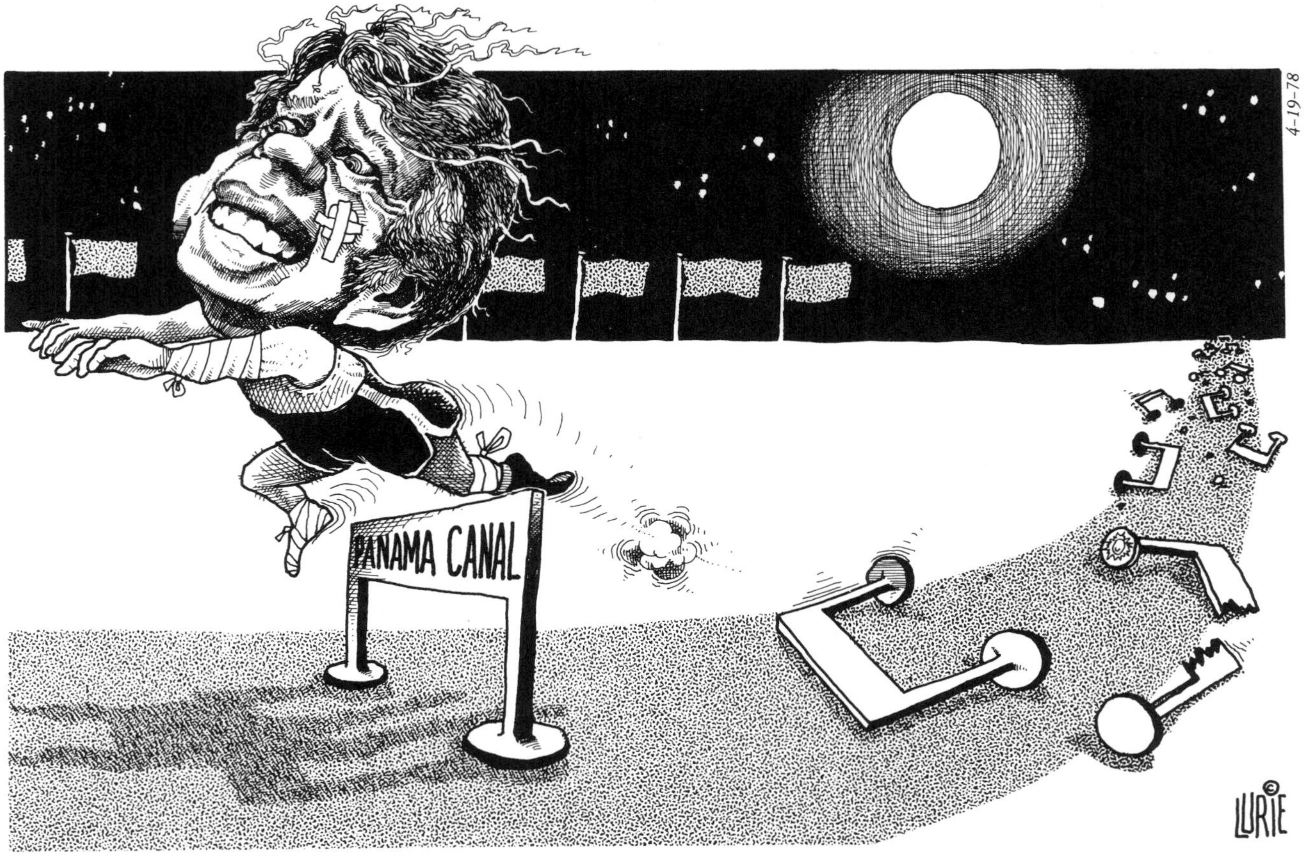
PANAMA CANAL
4-19-78
LURIE

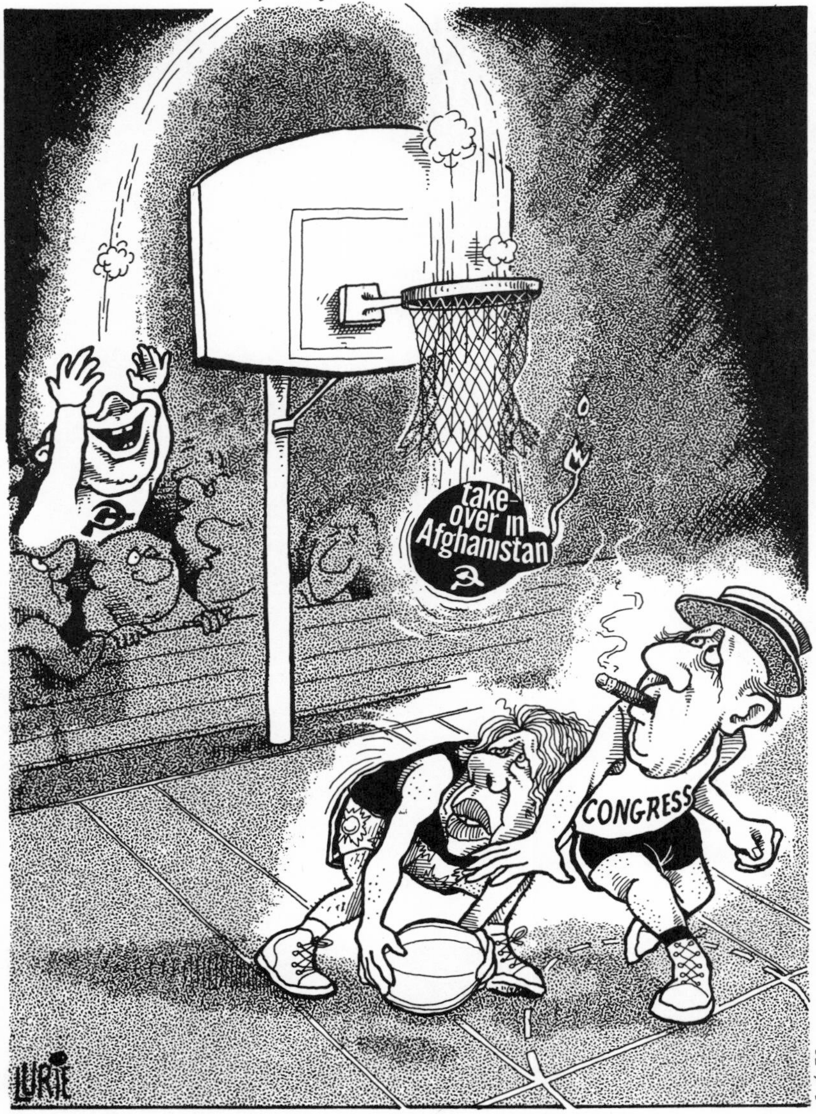
take-over in Afghanistan
CONGRESS
LURIE
5-4-78

"OOPS!"

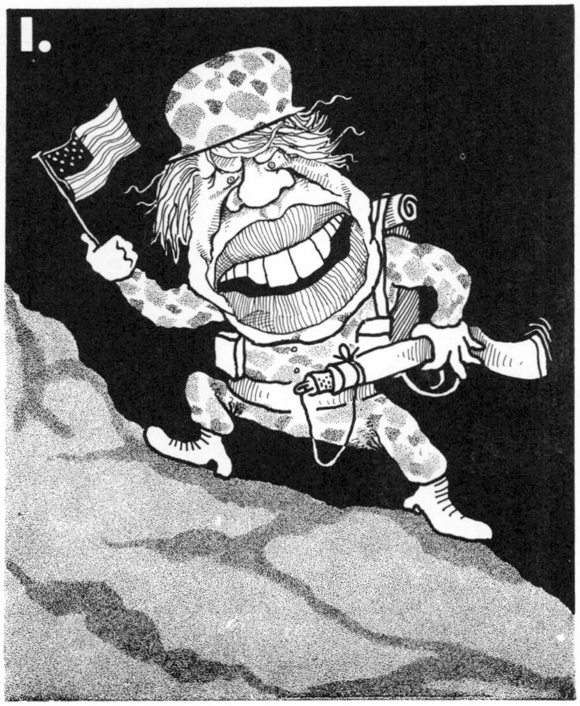
1.

1977: "OUR ENERGY SITUATION IS EQUIVALENT TO WAR!"

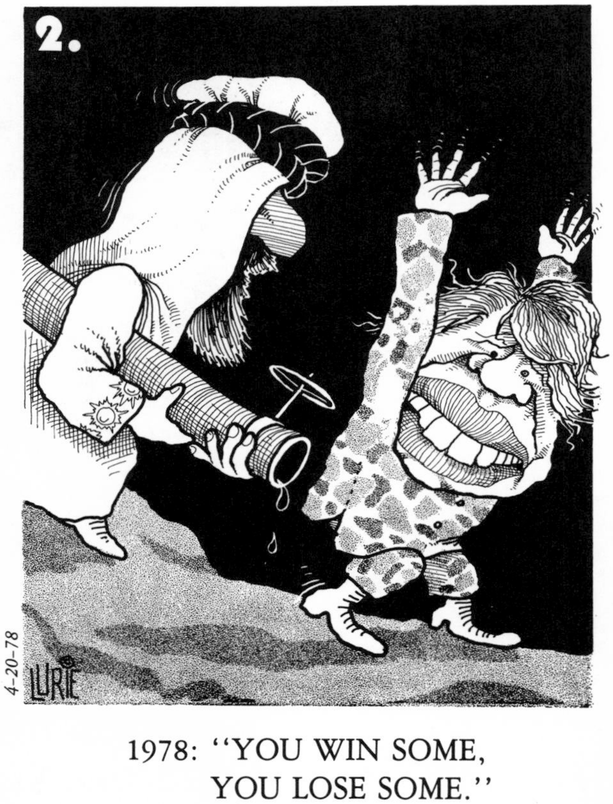
2.
4-20-78
LURIE

1978: "YOU WIN SOME, YOU LOSE SOME."

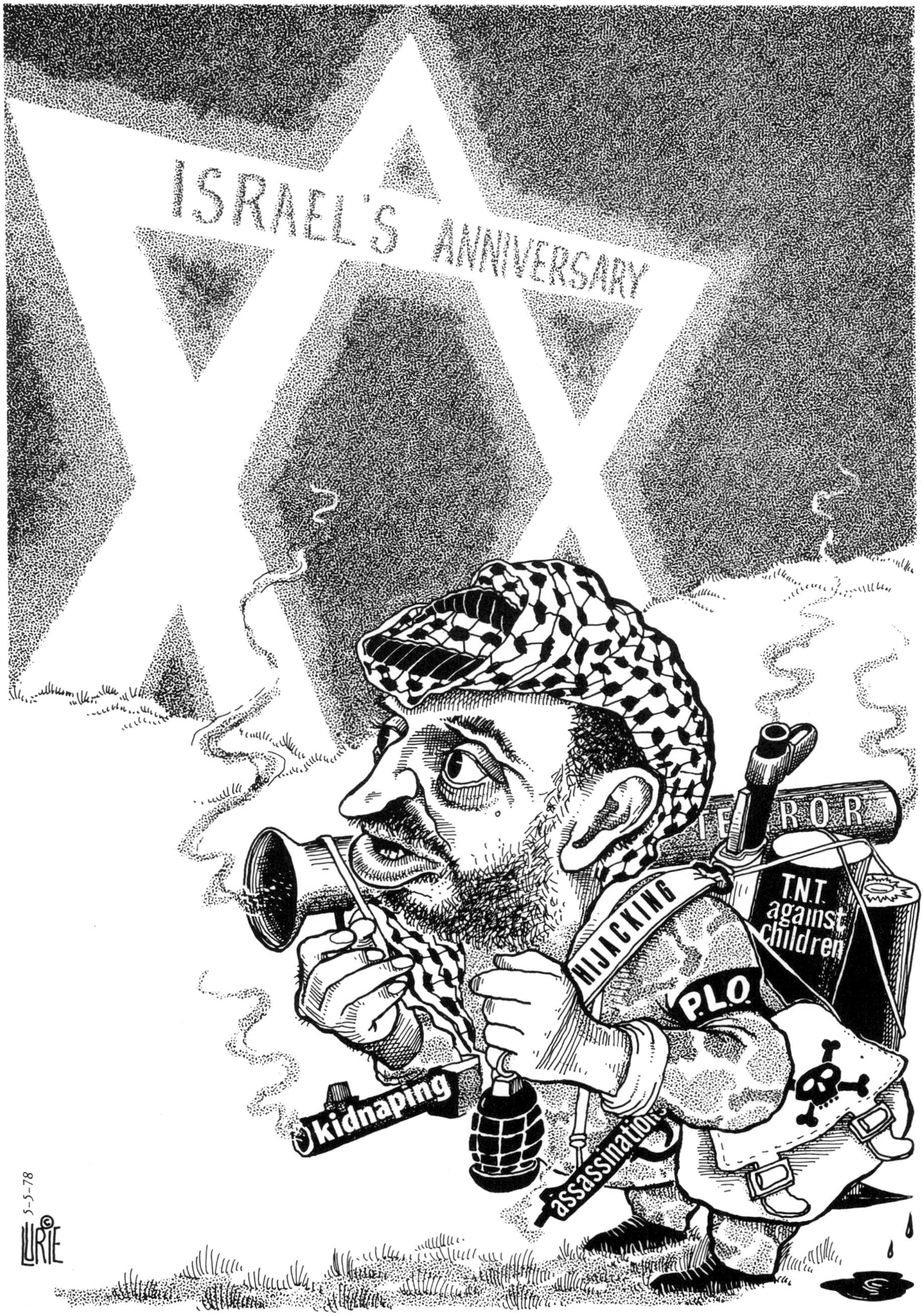
ISRAEL'S ANNIVERSARY
TERROR
T.N.T. against children
HIJACKING
P.L.O.
kidnaping
assassinations
5-5-78
LURIE

"I DON'T TRUST ANYONE OVER THIRTY!"

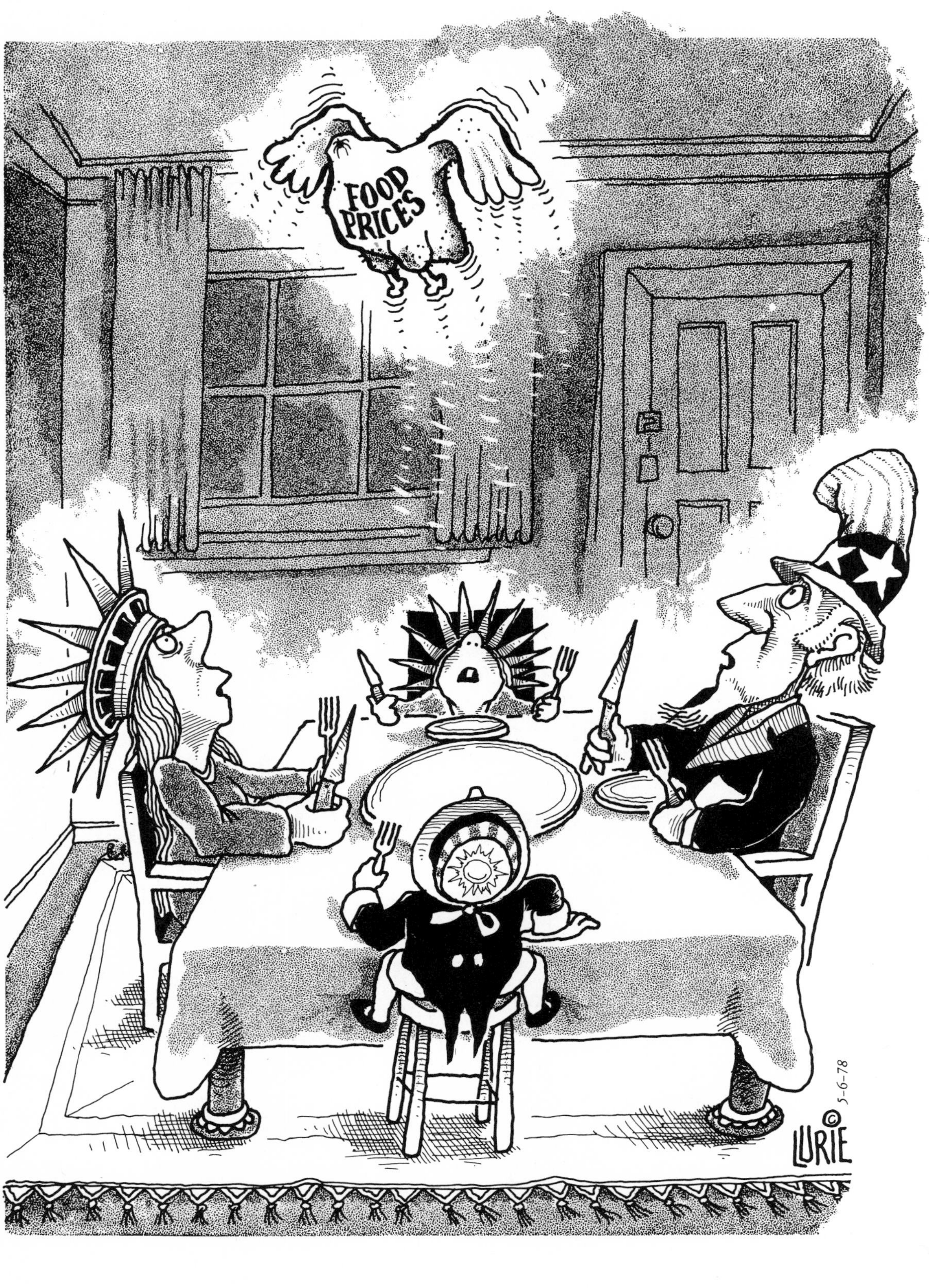
FOOD PRICES
5-6-78
LURIE

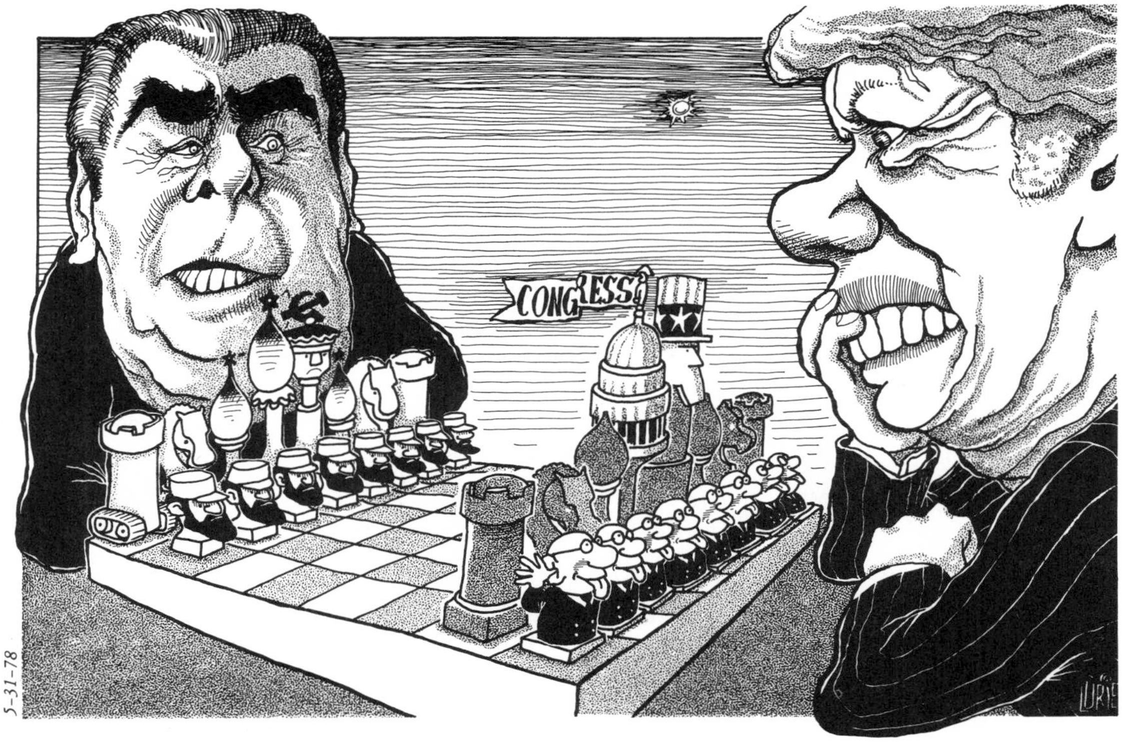
CONGRESS
5-31-78
LURIE

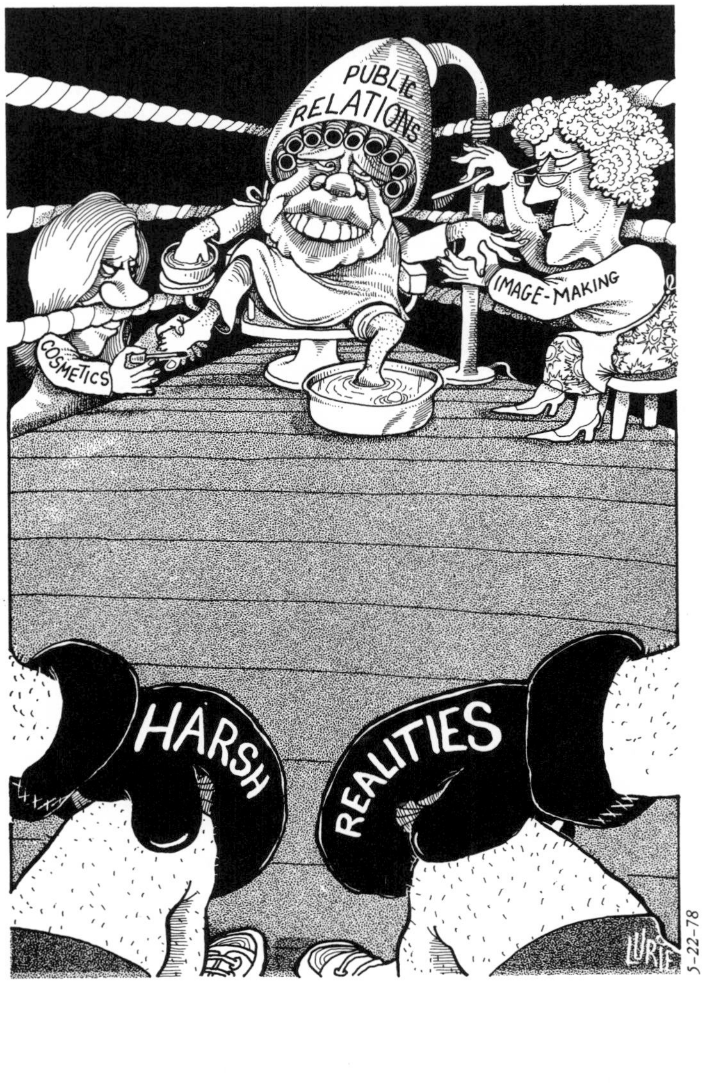
PUBLIC RELATIONS
IMAGE-MAKING
COSMETICS
HARSH
REALITIES
5-22-78
LURIE

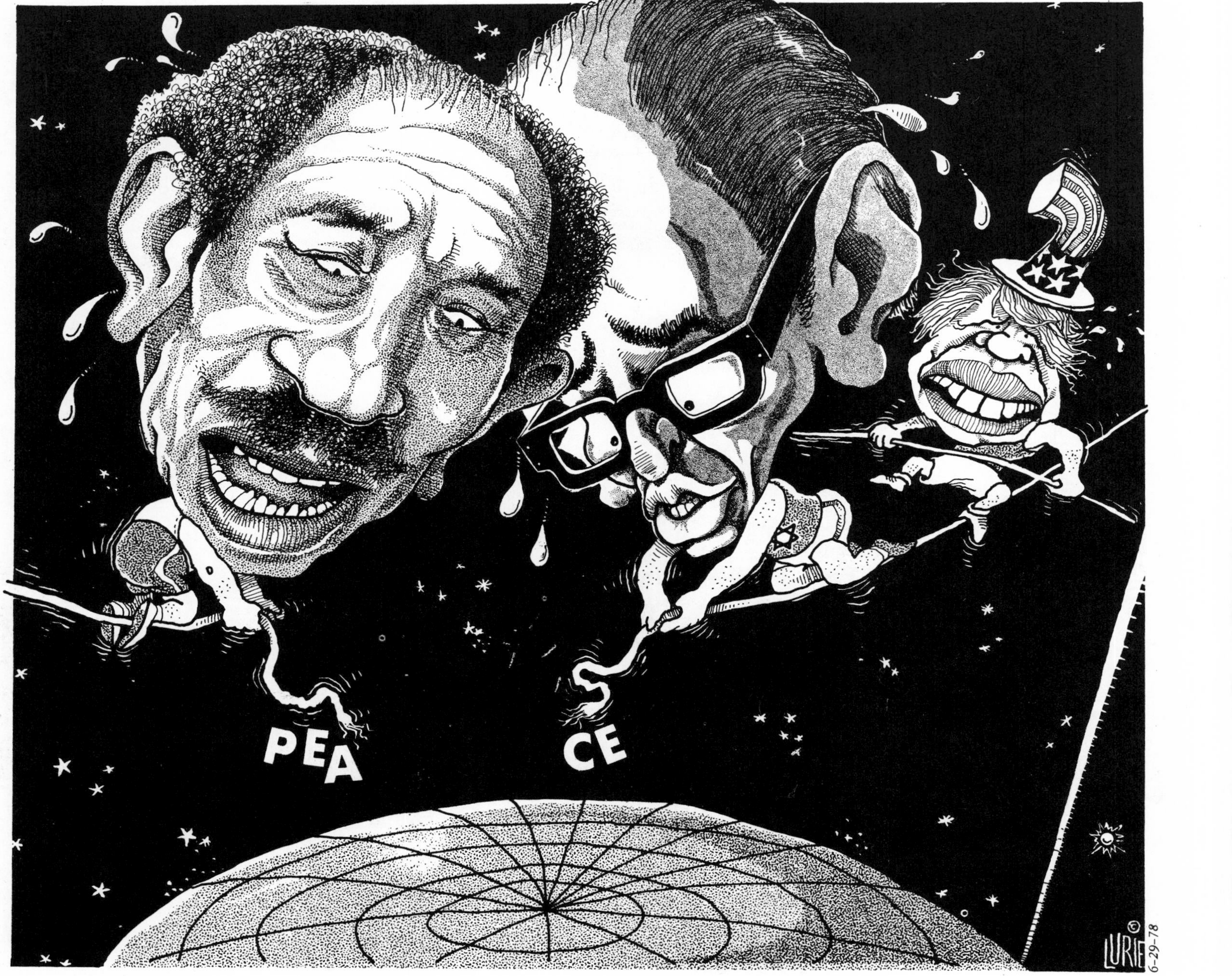
PEA
CE
LURIE
6-29-78

"TIE IT FAST—WE'RE ALL ON THE SAME ROPE!"

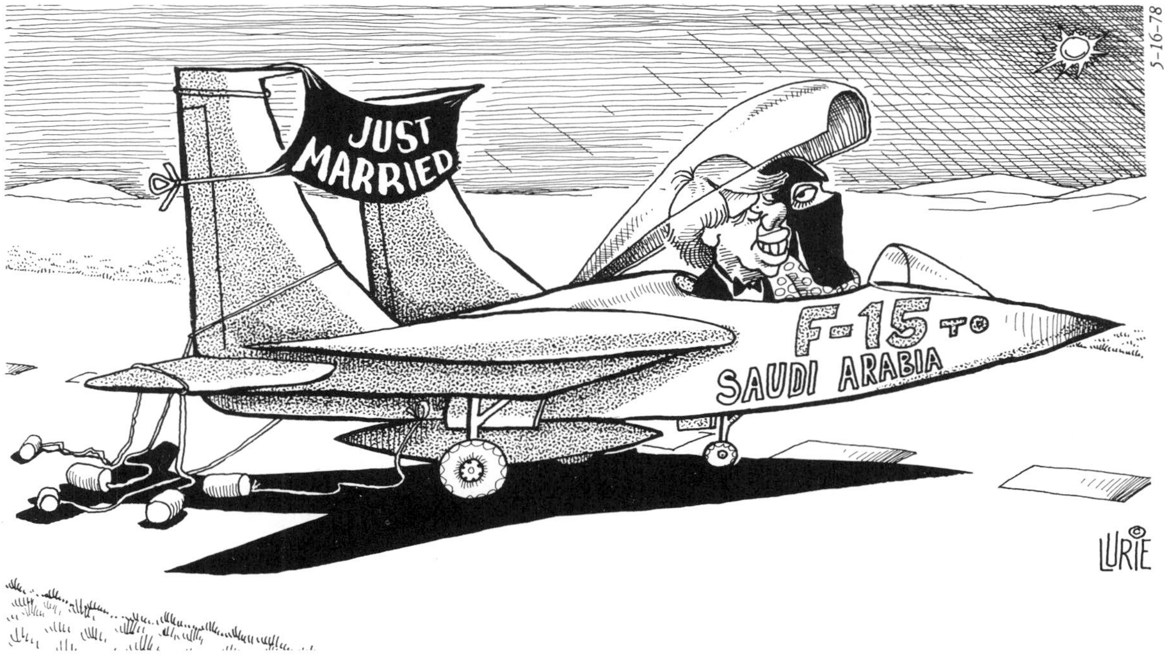
5-16-78
JUST MARRIED
F-15 TO
SAUDI ARABIA
LURIE

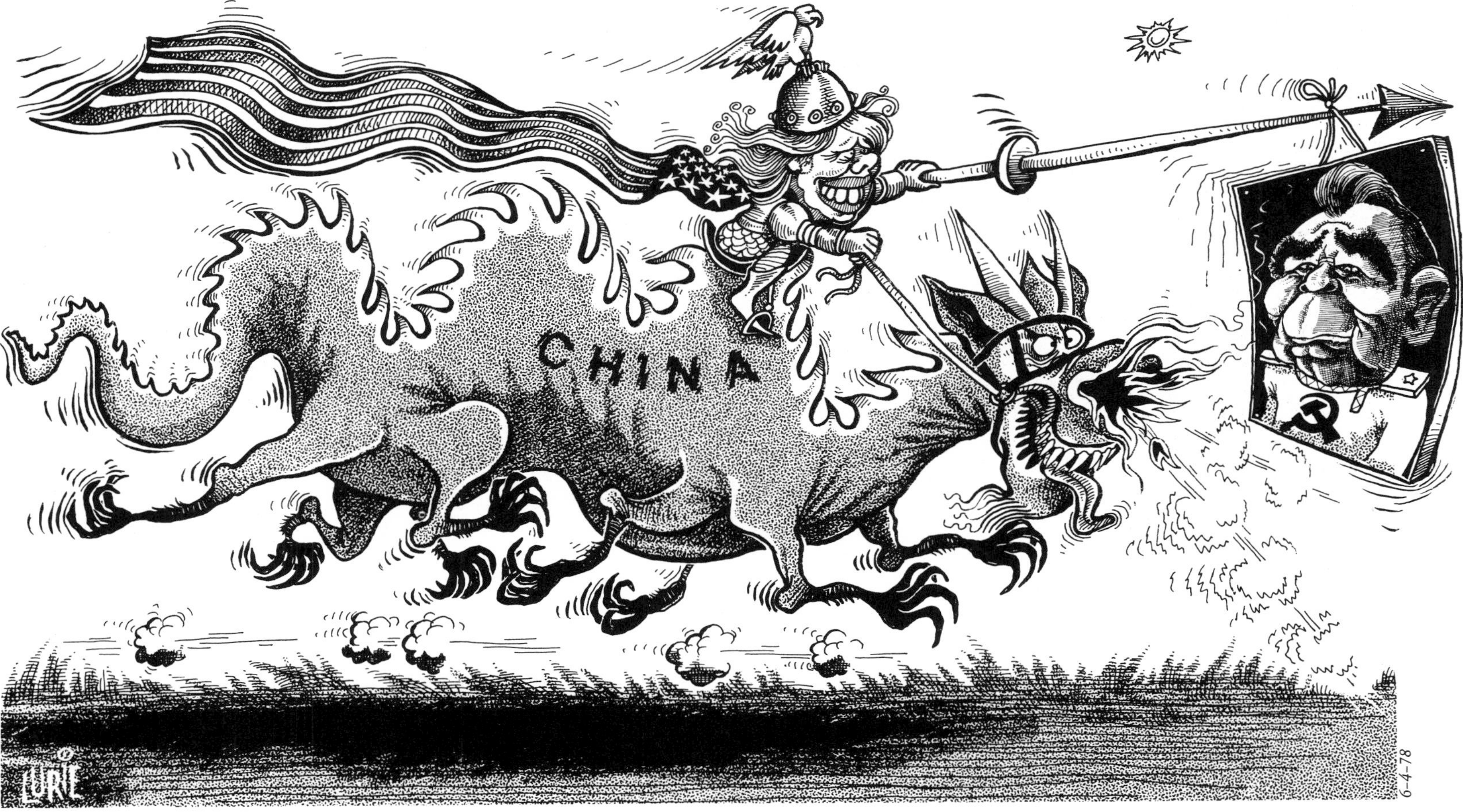
CHINA
LURIE
6-4-78

TAX REVOLT
Mr. politician
Mr. politician
TAX REVOLT
LURIE
6-30-78

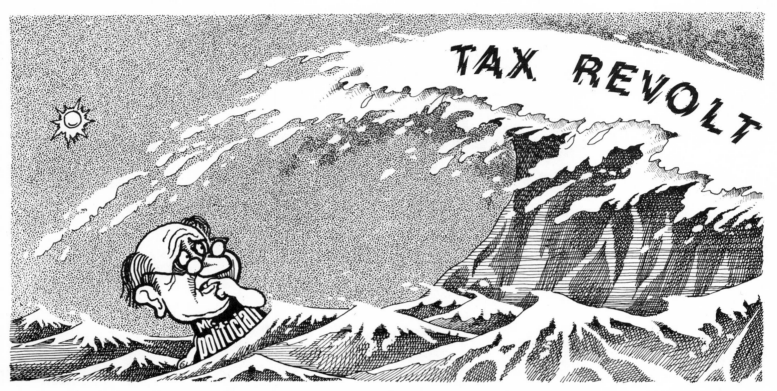

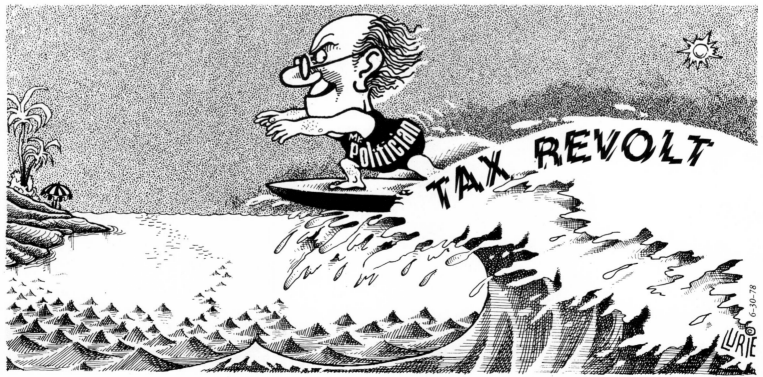

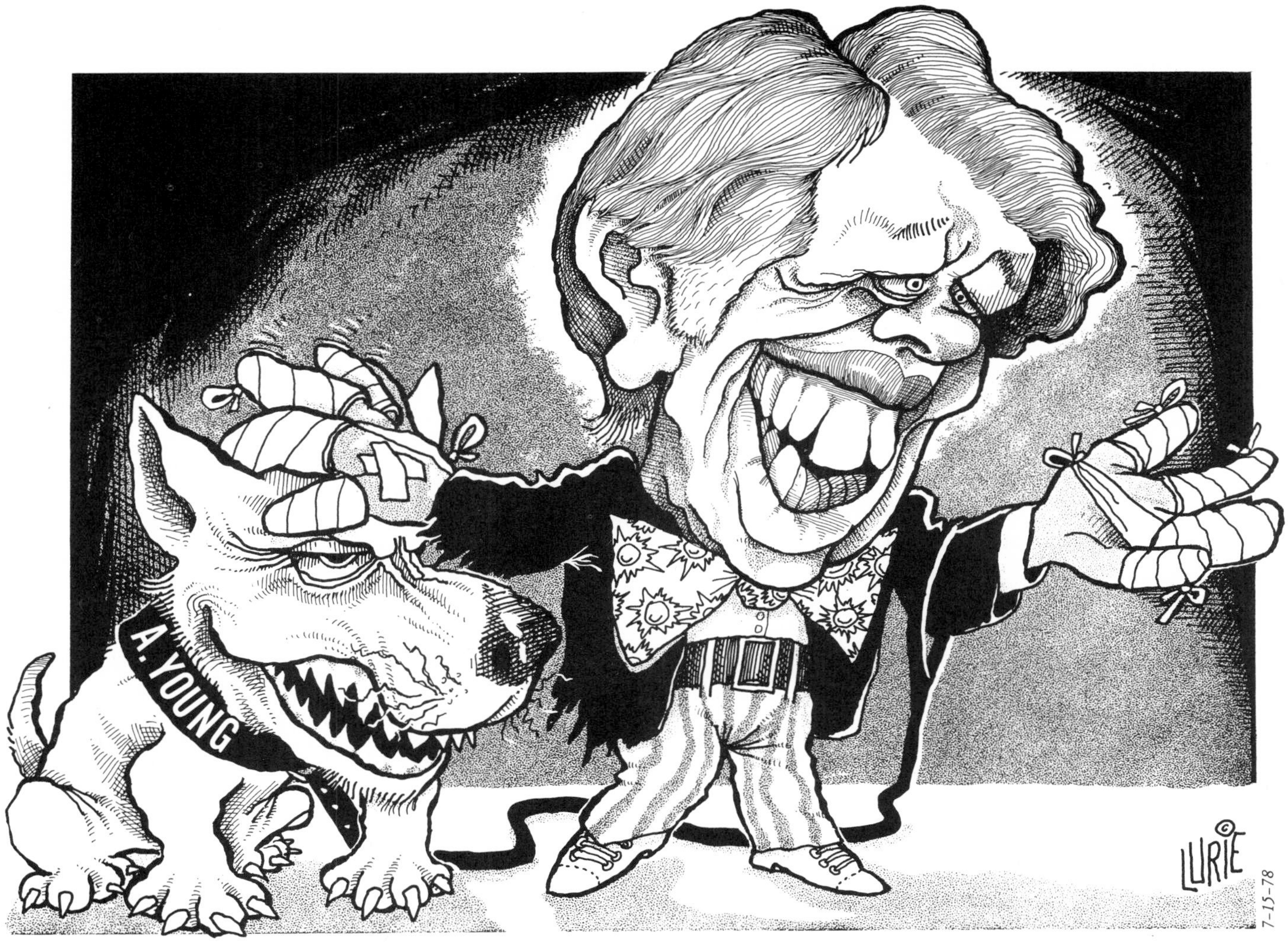
A. YOUNG
LURIE
7-15-78

"DON'T WORRY—HE EATS OUT OF MY HAND! . . ."

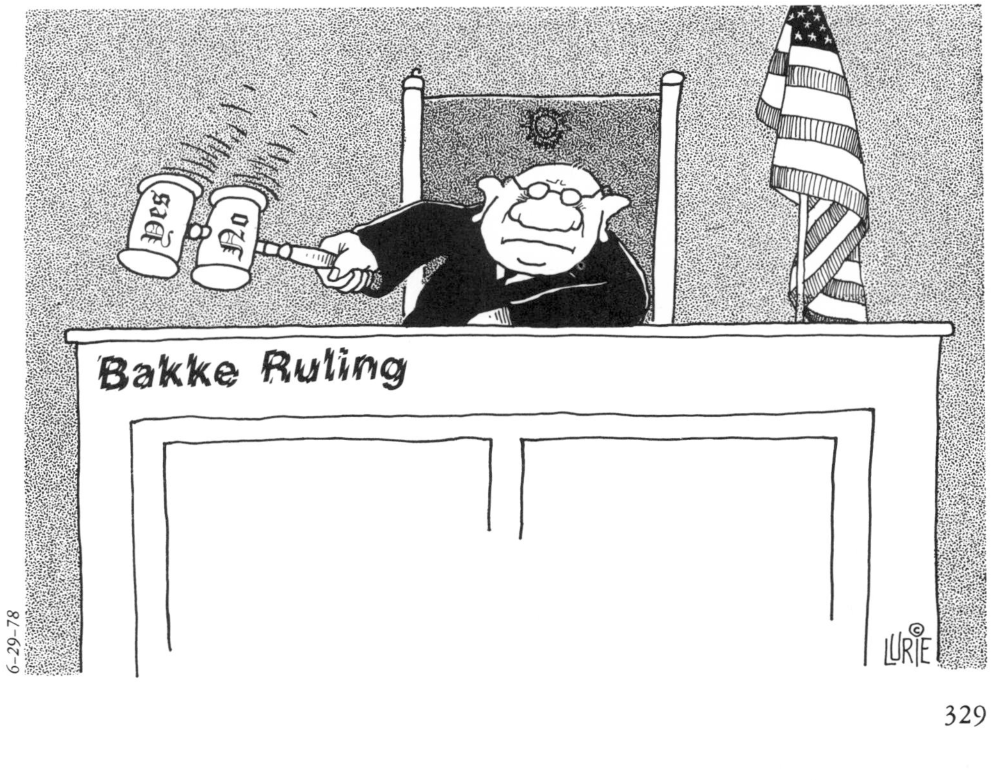
Yes
No
Bakke Ruling
6-29-78
LURIE

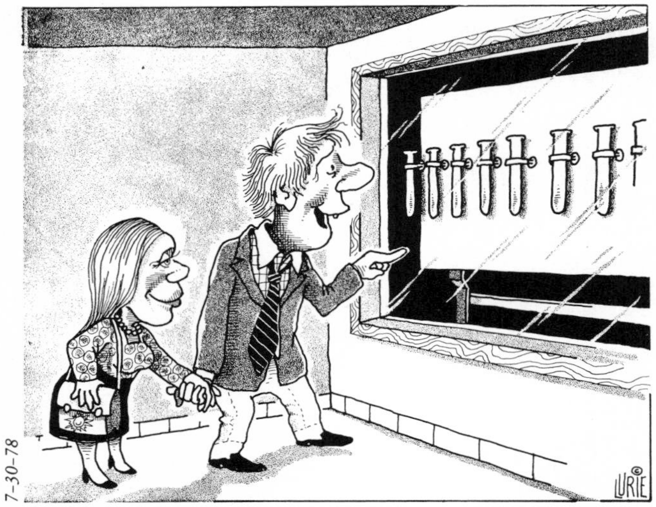
7-30-78
LURIE

''OURS IS THE PRETTIEST!''

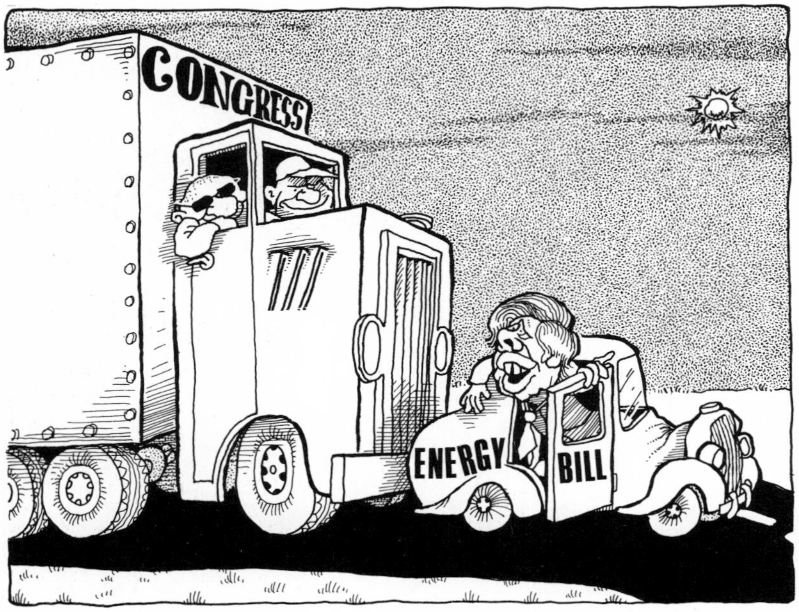
CONGRESS
ENERGY
BILL

''ALL I NEED IS A LITTLE PUSH, GUYS.''

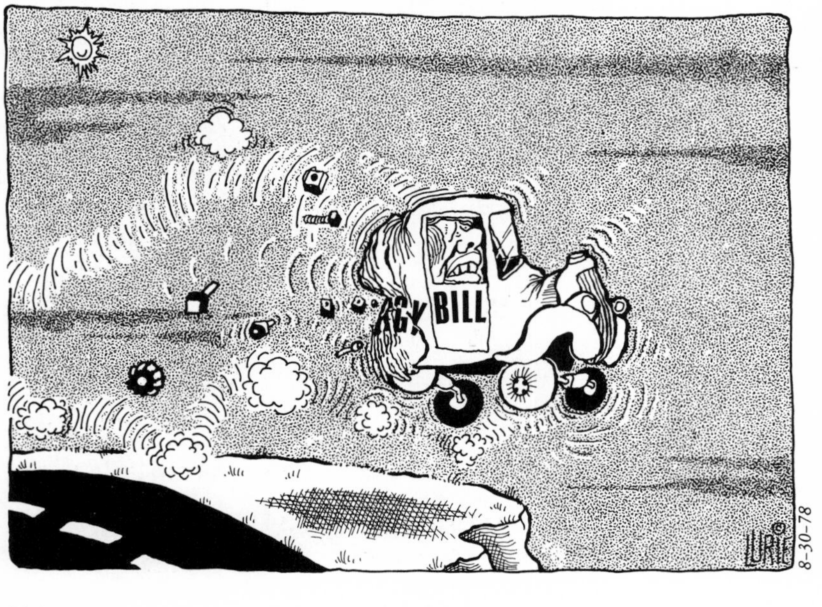
BILL
LURIE
8-30-78

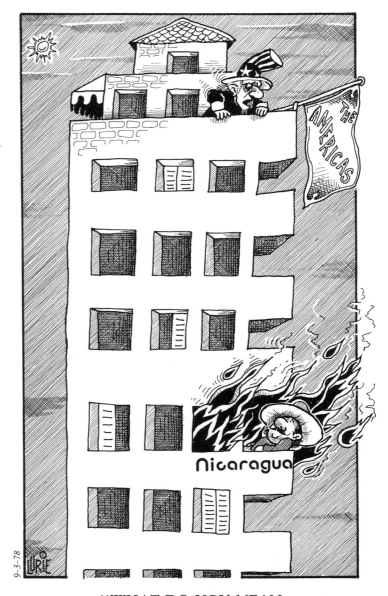

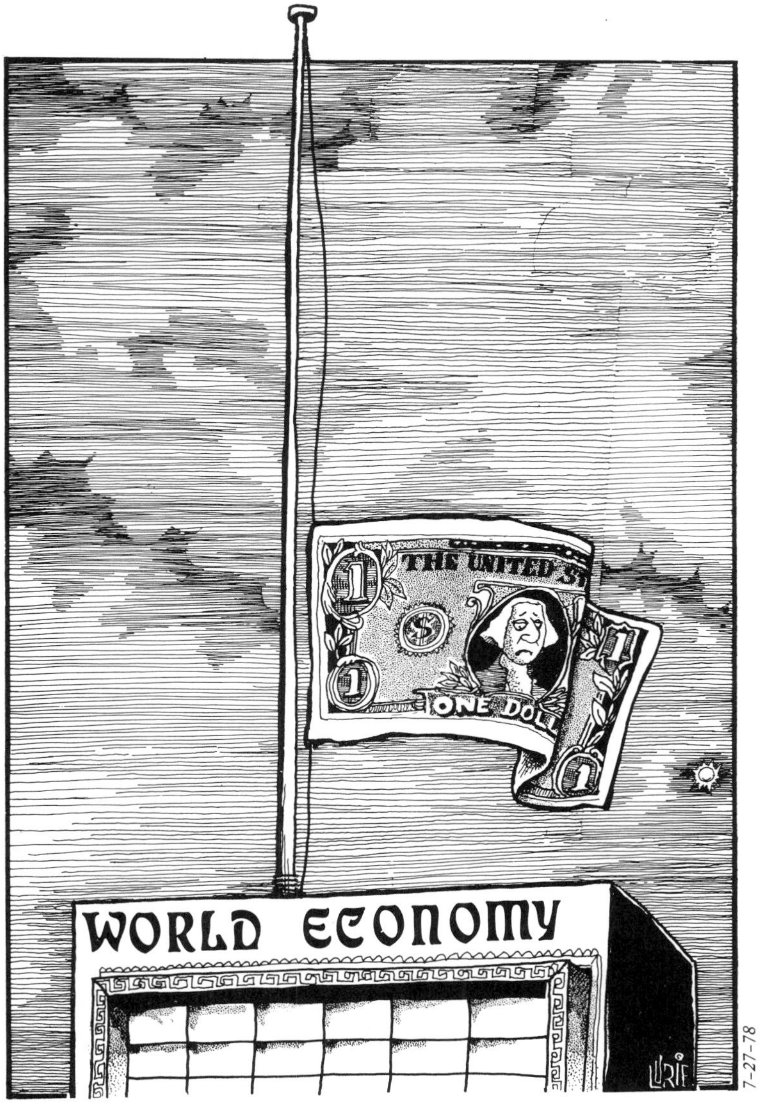

THE UNITED ST
ONE DOLL
WORLD ECONOMY
LURIE
7-27-78

FLYING LOW

THE AMERICAS
Nicaragua
9-3-78
LURIE

"WHAT DO YOU MEAN
'THAT'S NONE OF MY BUSINESS'?"

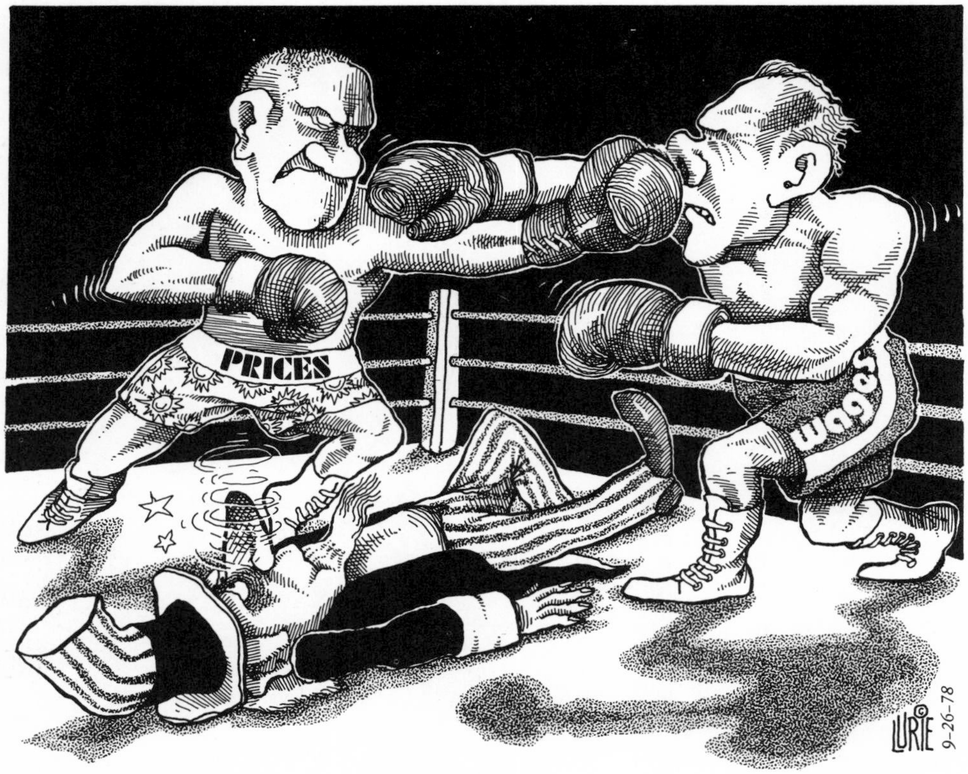
PRICES
WAGES
LURIE©
9-26-78

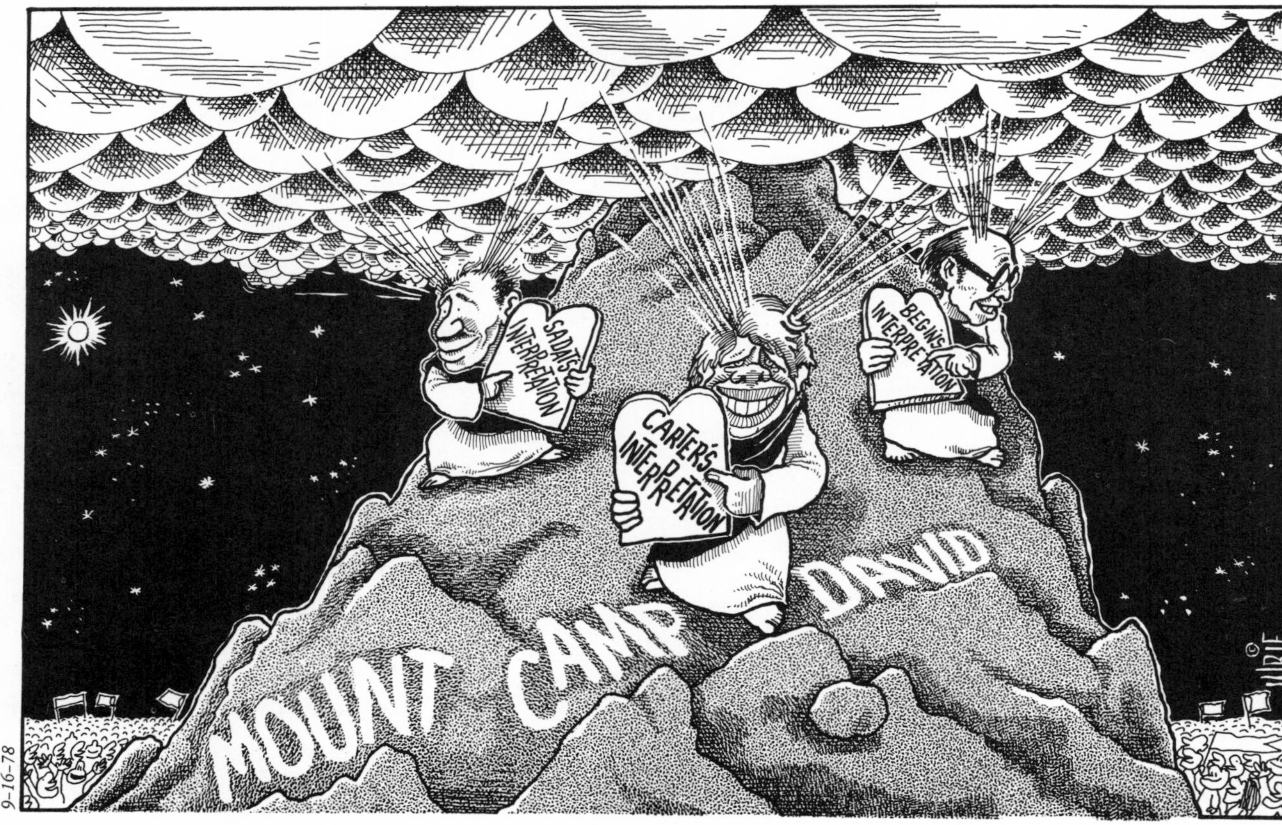
SADAT'S INTERPRETATION
CARTER'S INTERPRETATION
BEGIN'S INTERPRETATION
MOUNT CAMP DAVID
LURIE©
9-16-78

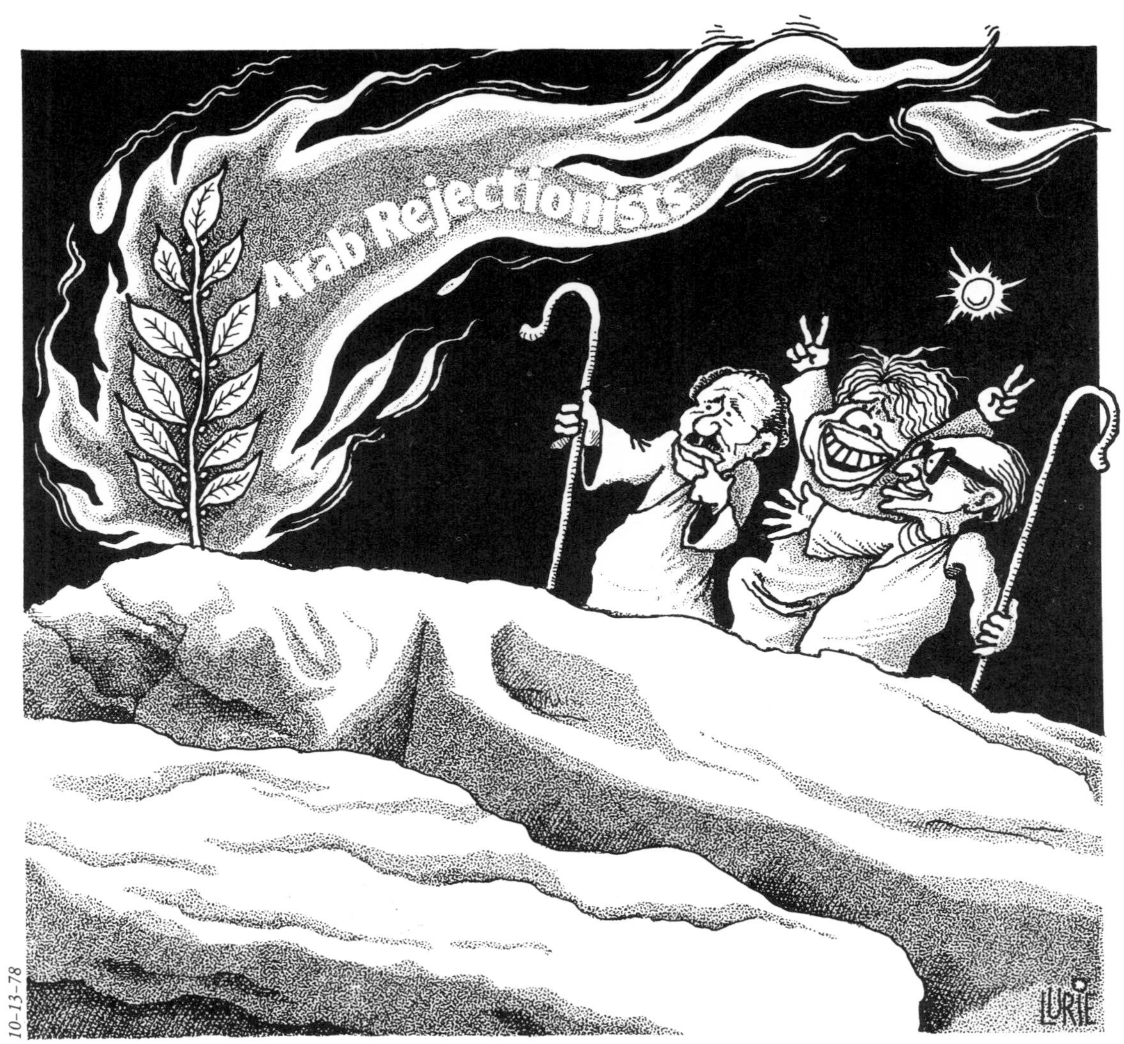
Arab Rejectionists
10-13-78
LURIE

". . . AND THE BUSH WAS NOT CONSUMED." (EXODUS 3, 2)

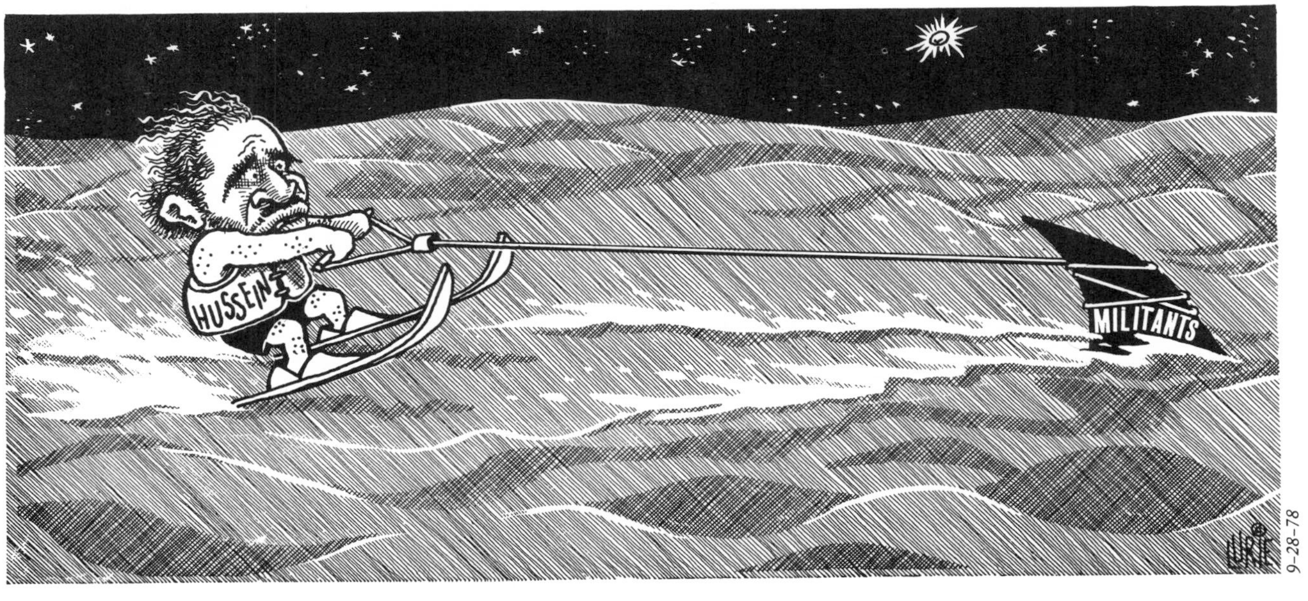
HUSSEIN
MILITANTS
LURIE
9-28-78

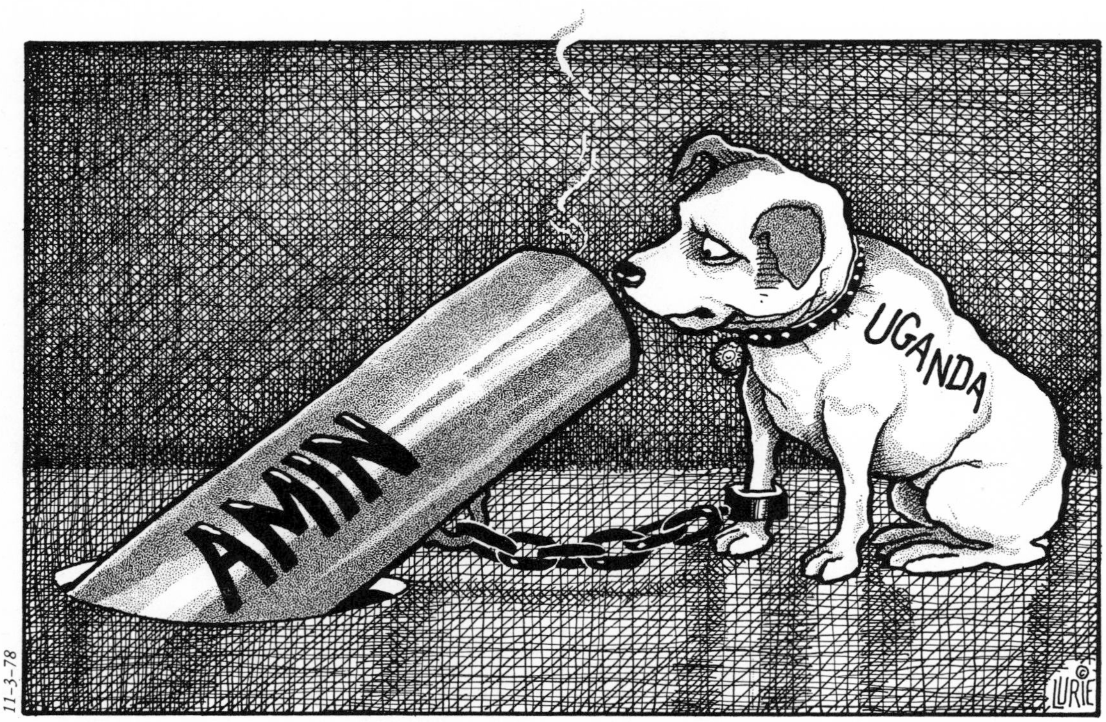
AMIN
UGANDA
11-3-78
LURIE

HIS MASTER'S VOICE

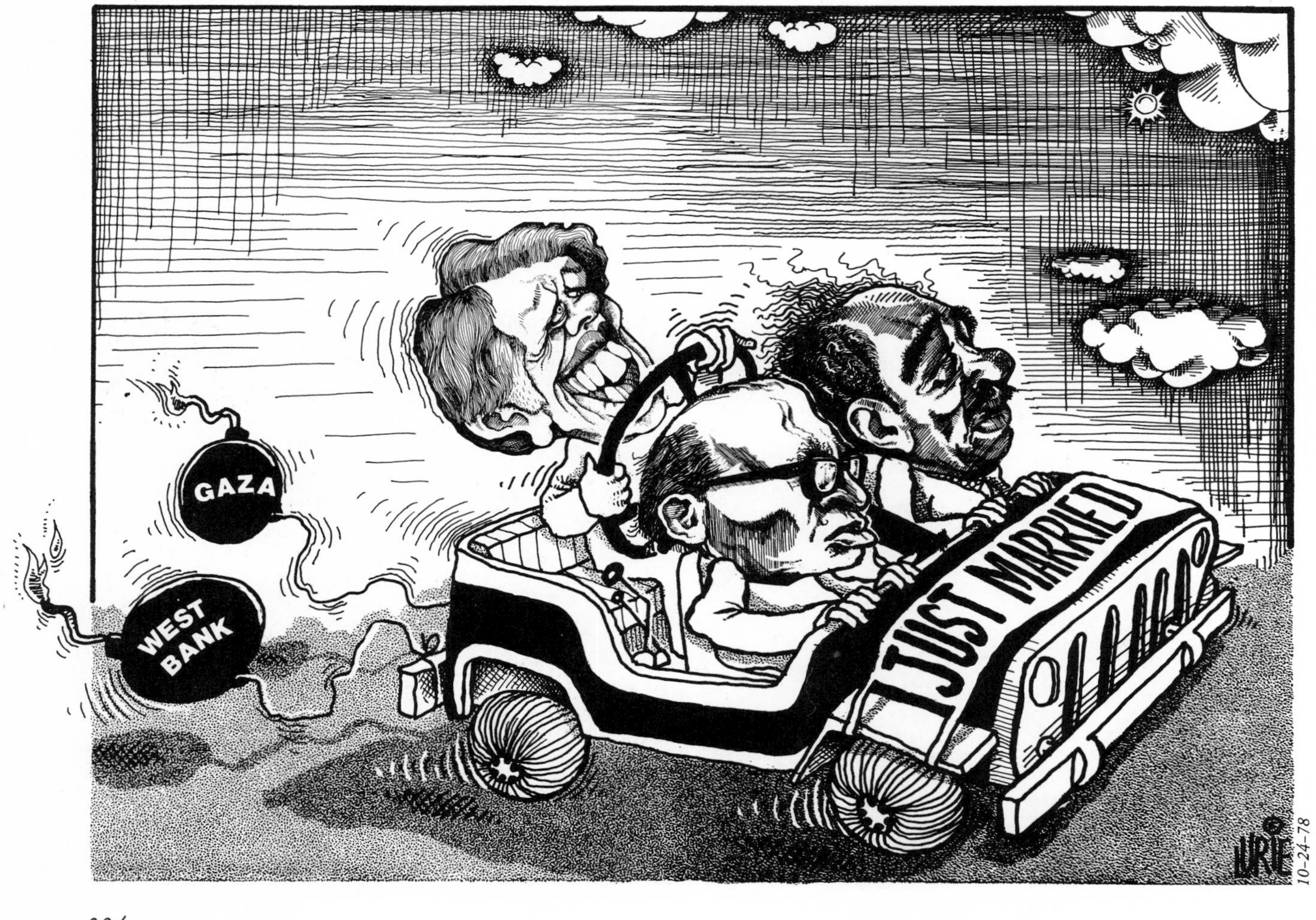
GAZA
WEST BANK
JUST MARRIED
LURIE
10-24-78

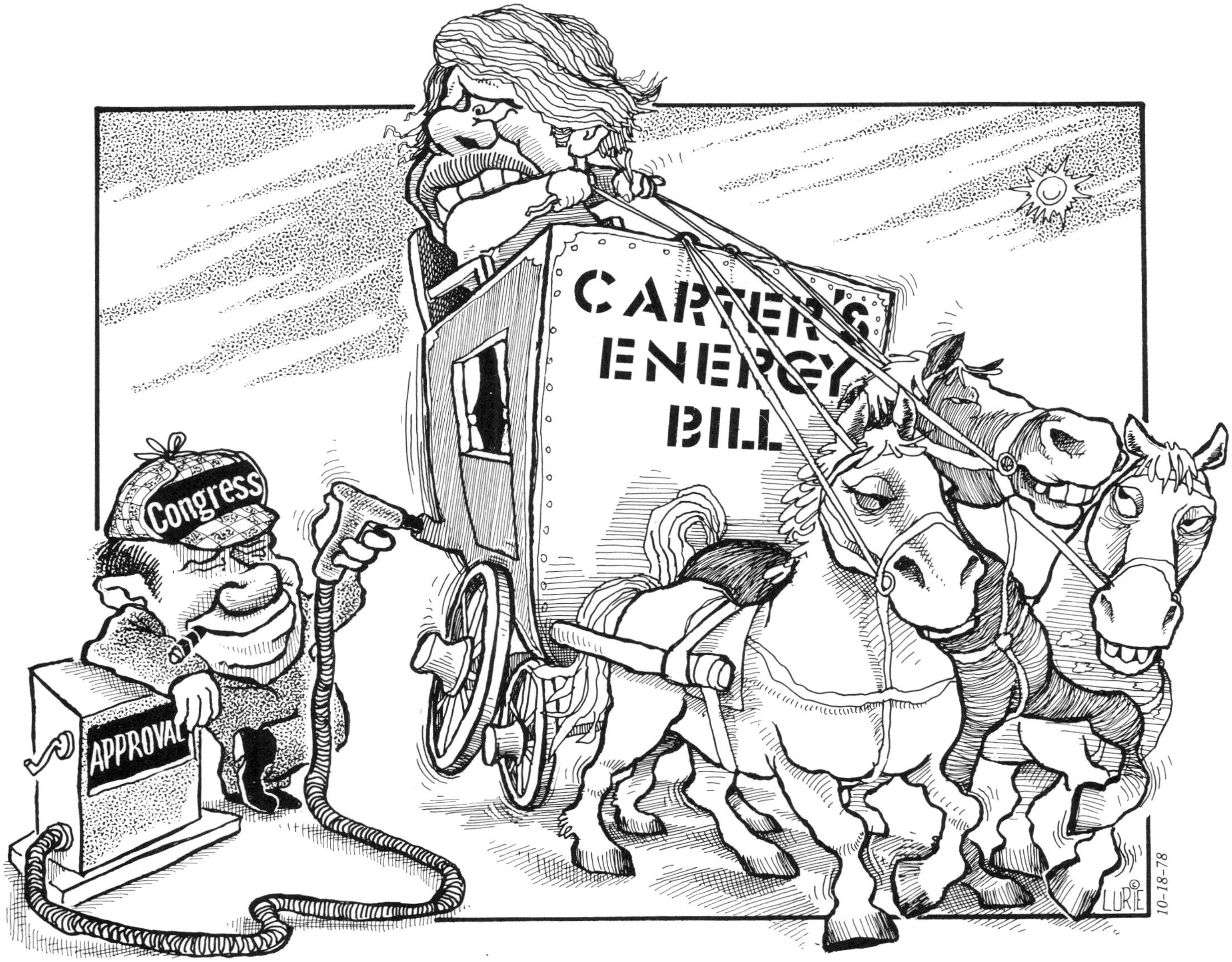
CARTER'S ENERGY BILL
Congress
APPROVAL
LURIE©
10-18-78

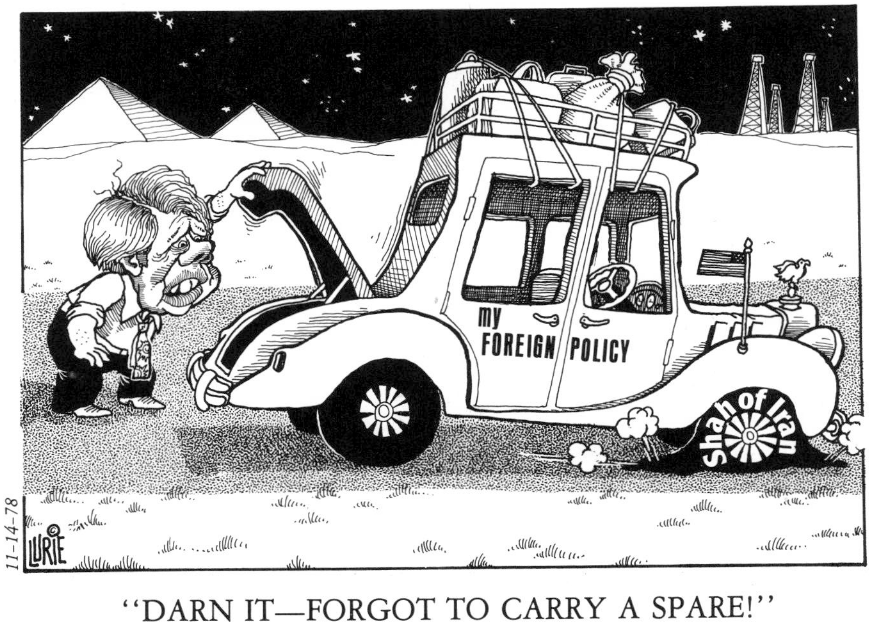
my FOREIGN POLICY
Shah of Iran
11-14-78
LURIE©

"DARN IT—FORGOT TO CARRY A SPARE!"

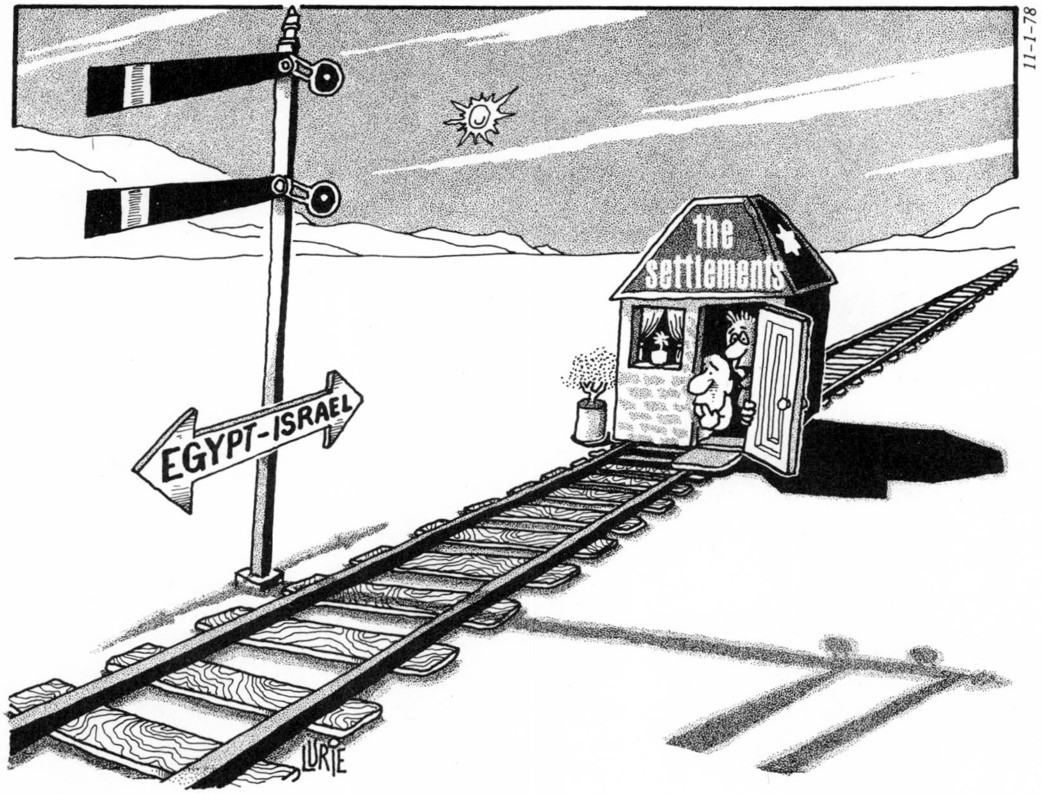
11-1-78
the settlements
EGYPT-ISRAEL
LURIE

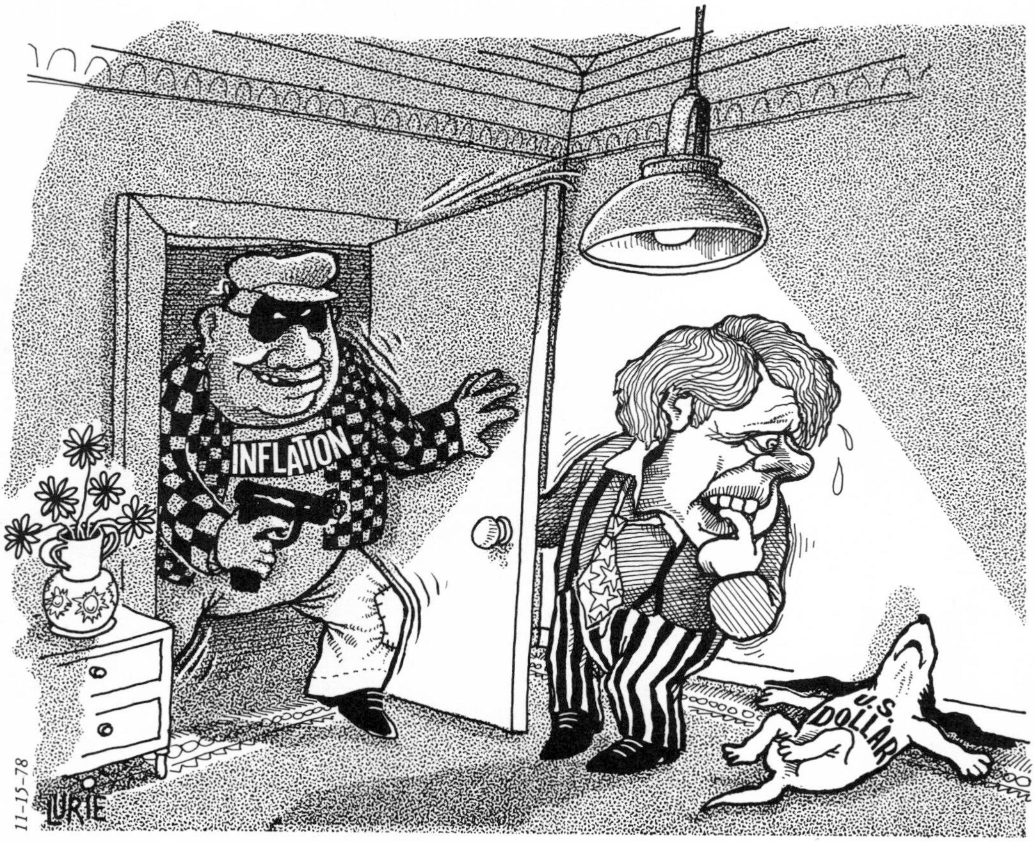
INFLATION
U.S. DOLLAR
11-15-78
LURIE

"A FINE TIME TO PLAY DEAD!"

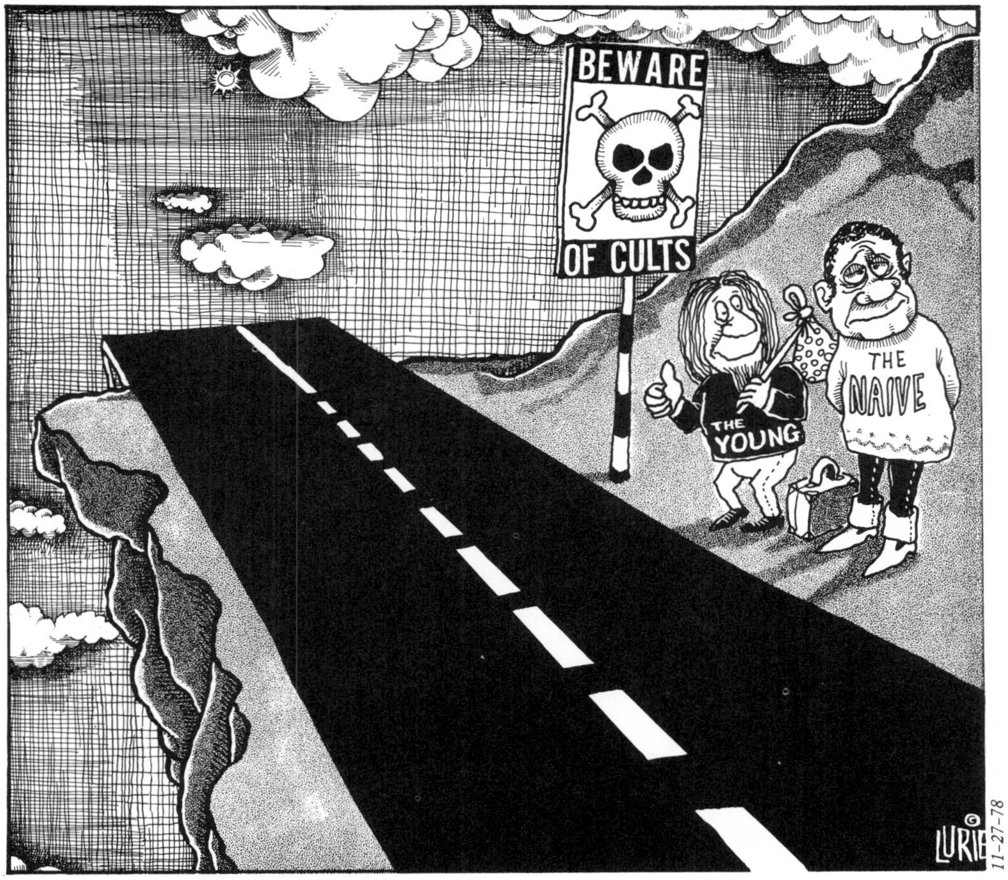
BEWARE
OF CULTS
THE YOUNG
THE NAIVE
LURIE
11-27-78

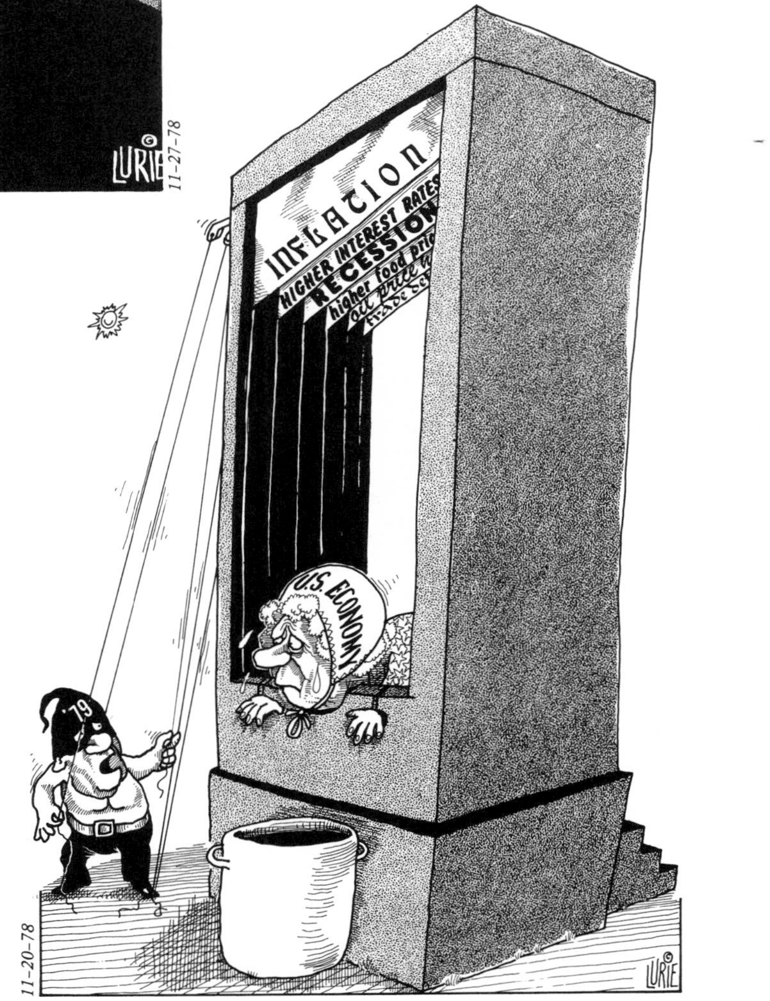
INFLATION
HIGHER INTEREST RATES
RECESSION
U.S. ECONOMY
'79
11-20-78
LURIE

"WHICH DO YOU PREFER FIRST?"

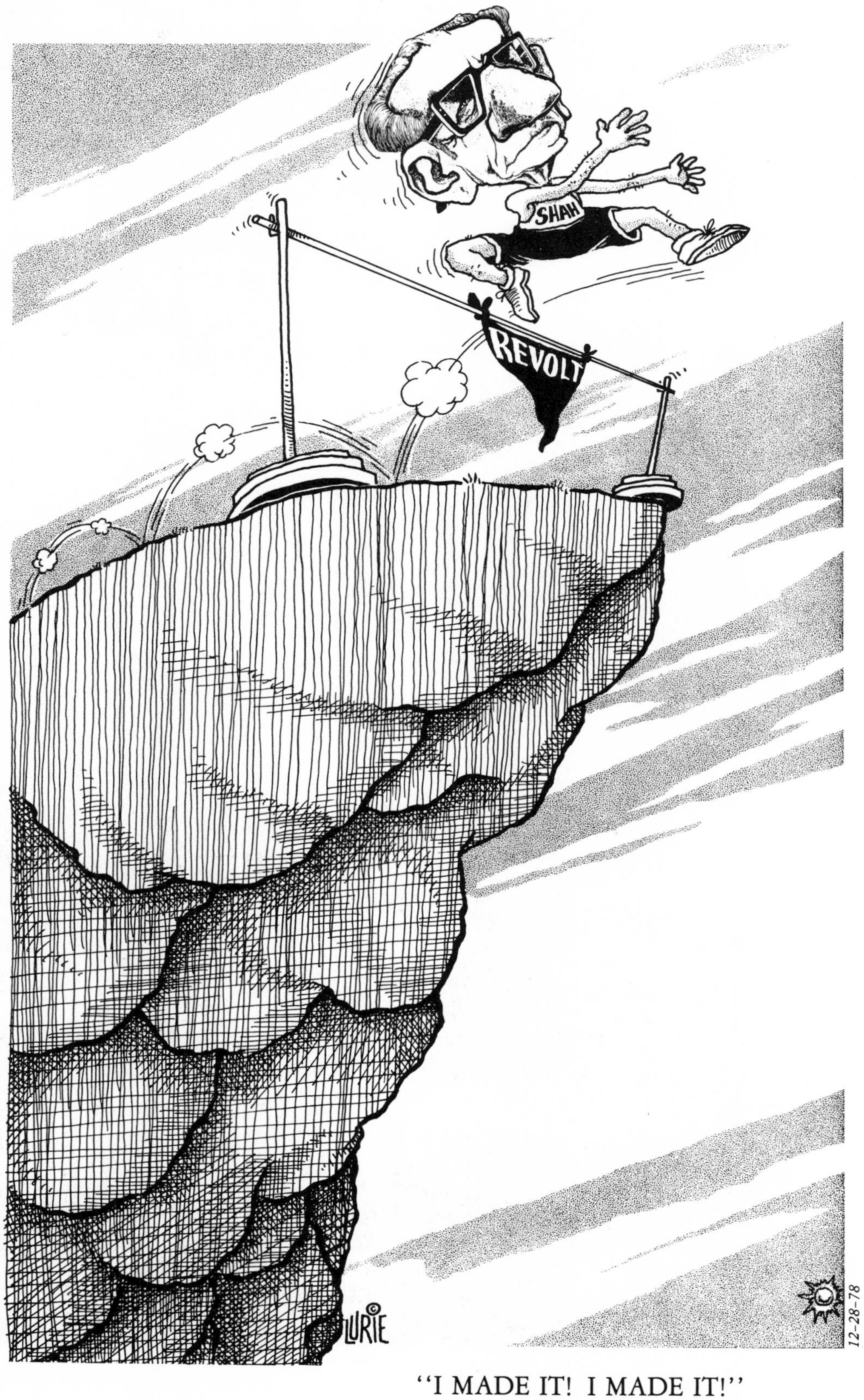
SHAH
REVOLT
LURIE
12-28-78

"I MADE IT! I MADE IT!"

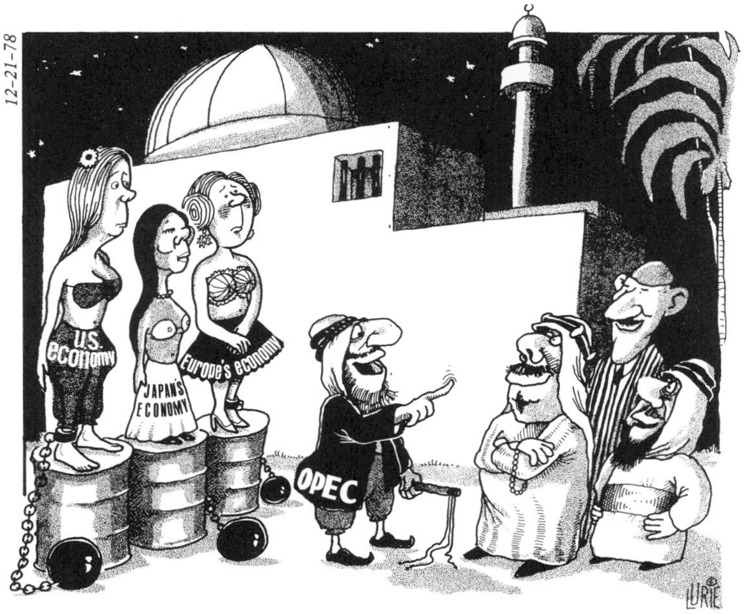
12-21-78
U.S. economy
JAPAN'S ECONOMY
Europe's economy
OPEC
LURIE

". . AND NOT ONLY *T H A T,* BUT THEY ALSO COOK, CLEAN, DRIVE . . ."

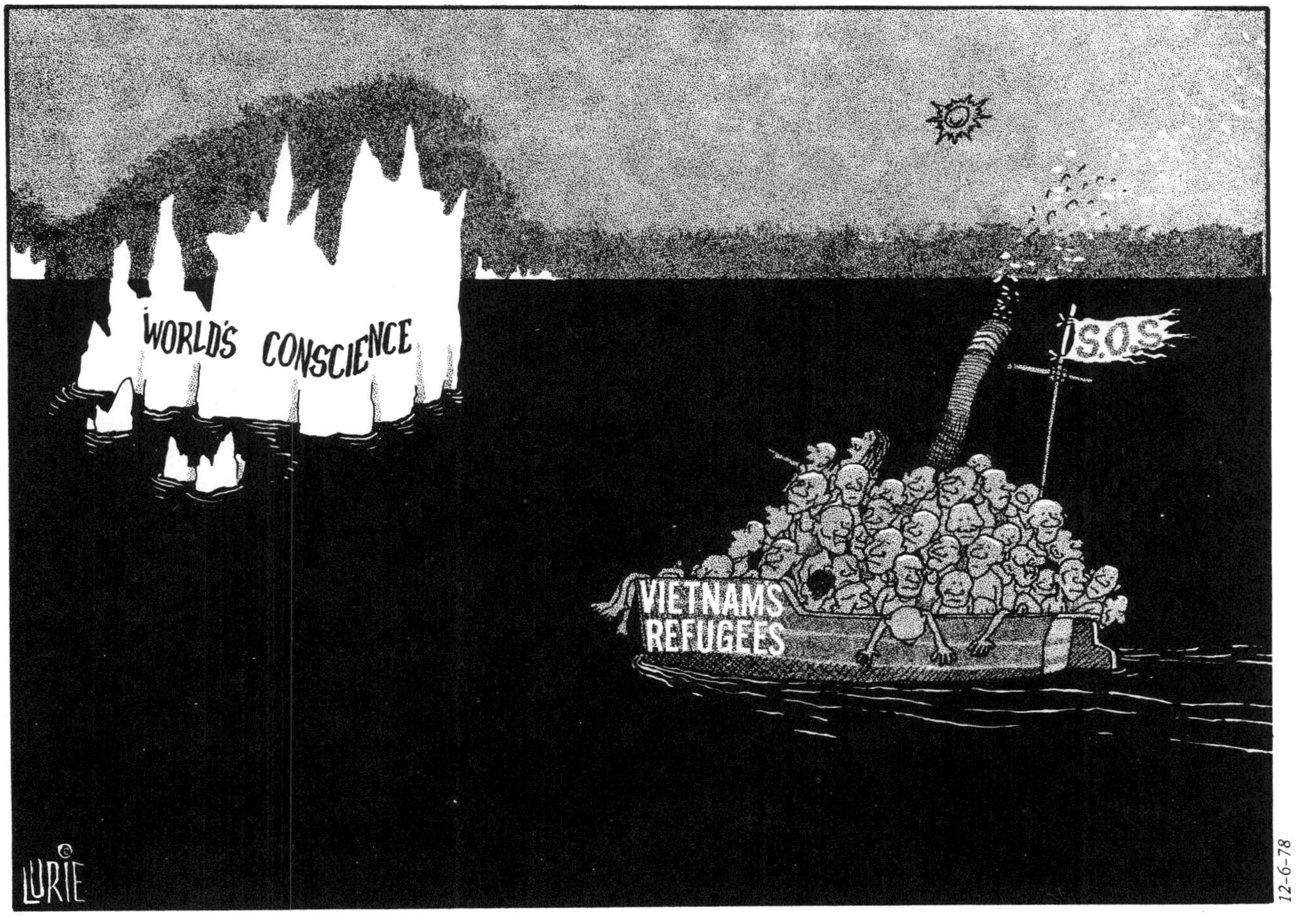
WORLD'S CONSCIENCE
S.O.S
VIETNAMS REFUGEES
LURIE
12-6-78

"NO, SON. THAT'S NOT LAND"

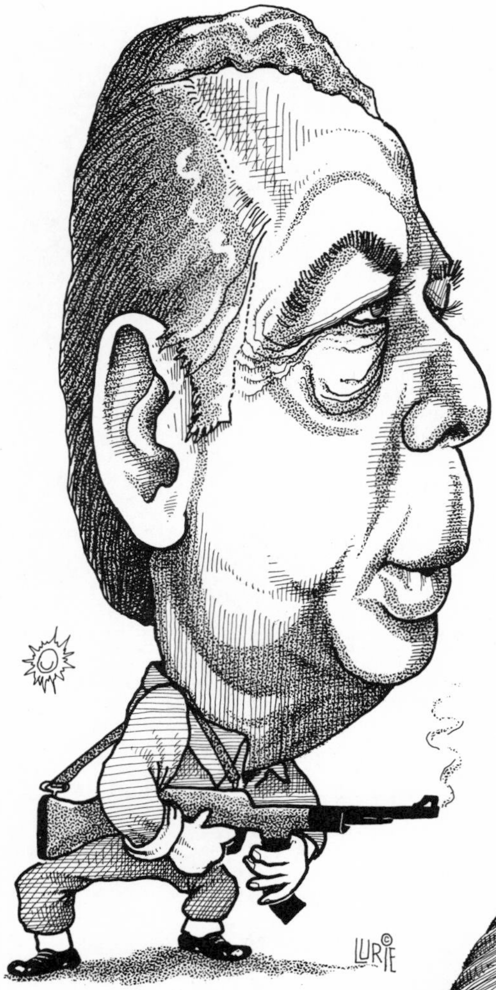
LURIE©

President Spyros Kyprianou
of Cyprus

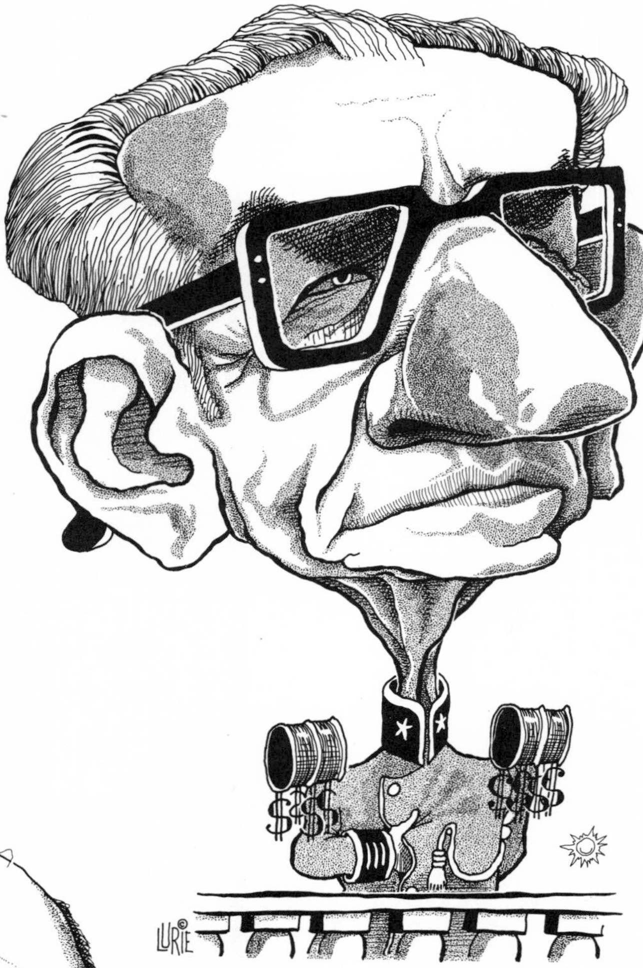
$$$
$$$
LURIE©

Shah of Iran
Mohammed Riza Pahlevi

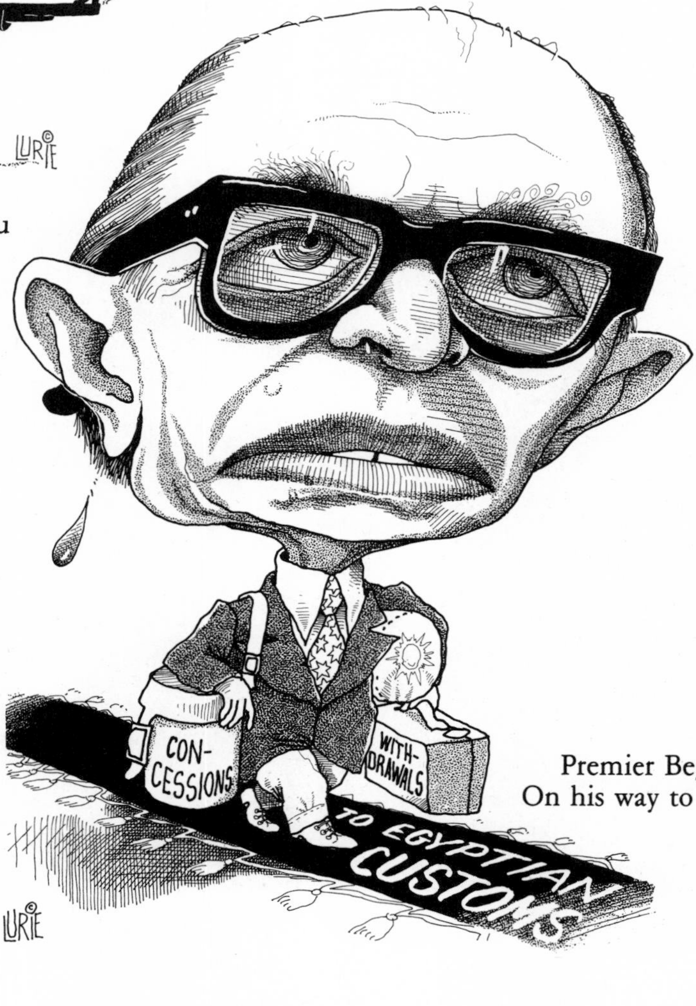
CON-
CESSIONS
WITH-
DRAWALS
TO EGYPTIAN
CUSTOMS
LURIE©

Premier Begin
On his way to Egypt

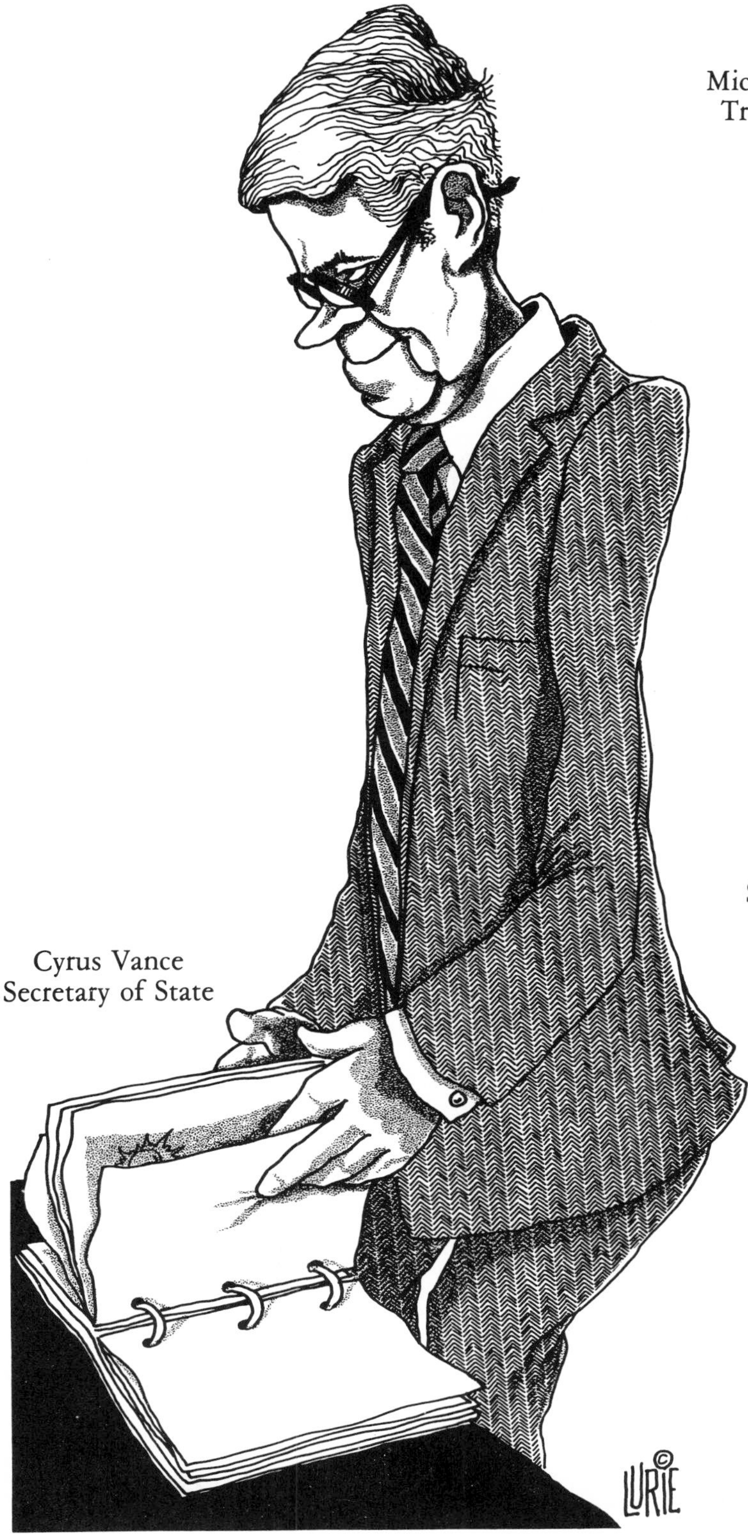
LURIE
Cyrus Vance
Secretary of State

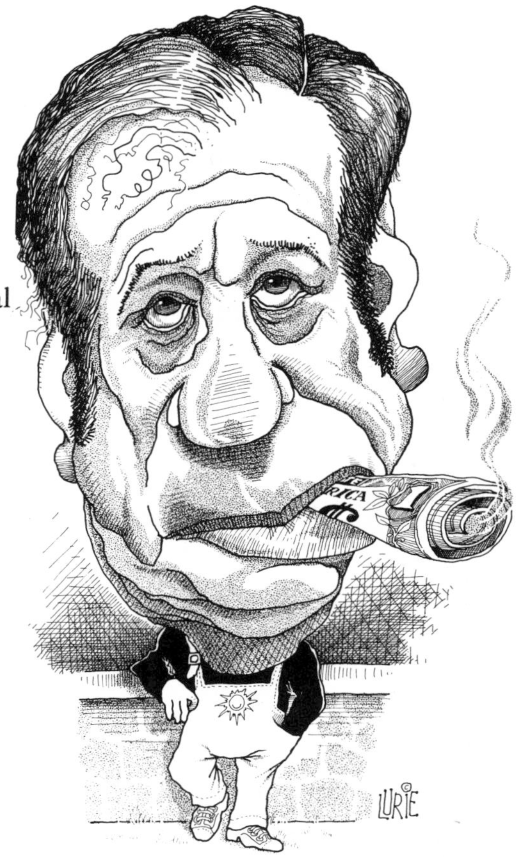
LURIE
Michael Blumenthal
Treasury Secretary

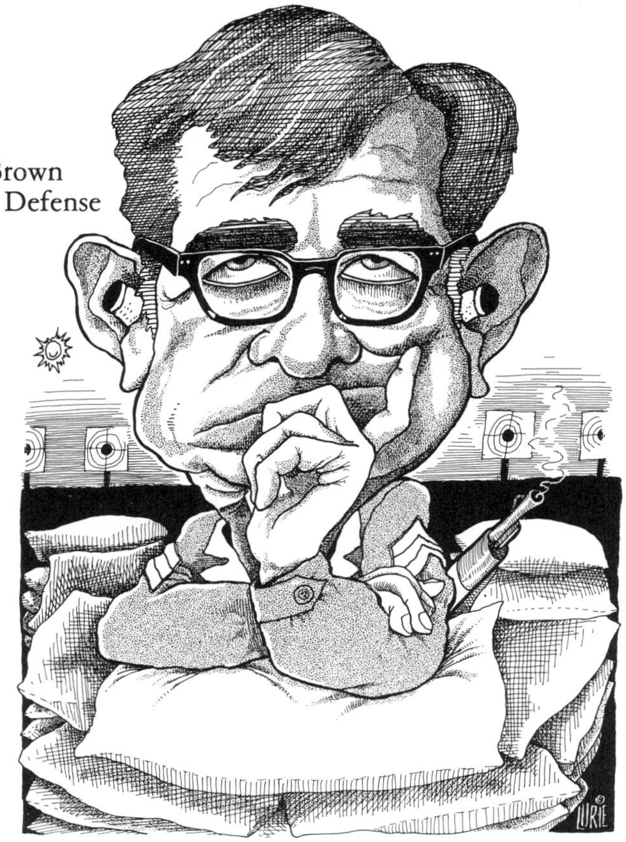
LURIE
Harold Brown
Secretary of Defense

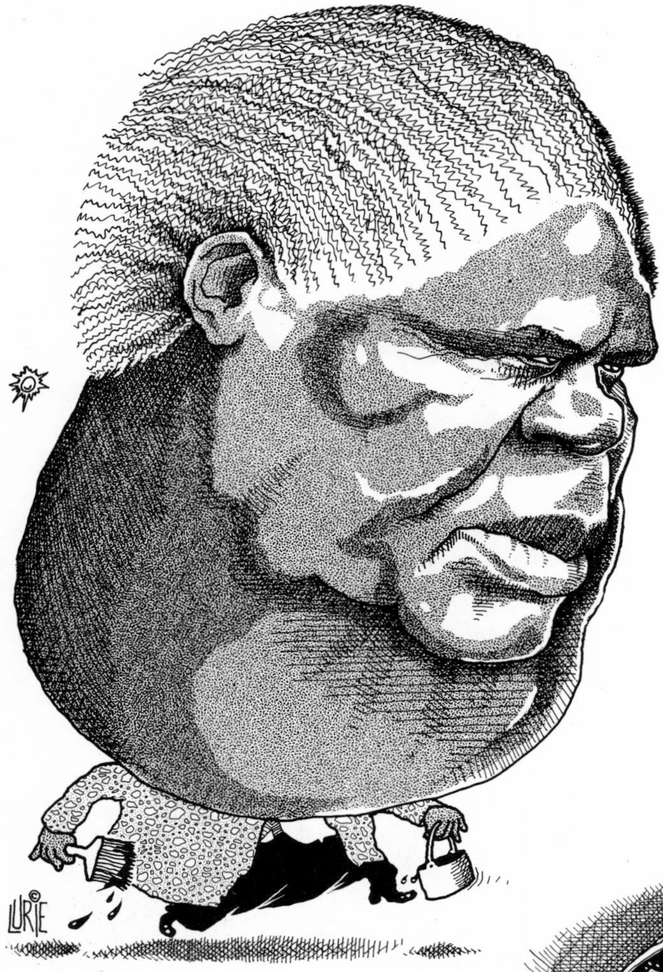

Joshua Nkomo
Rhodesia's Patriotic Front Co-Leader

President Mobutu Sese Seko
of Zaire

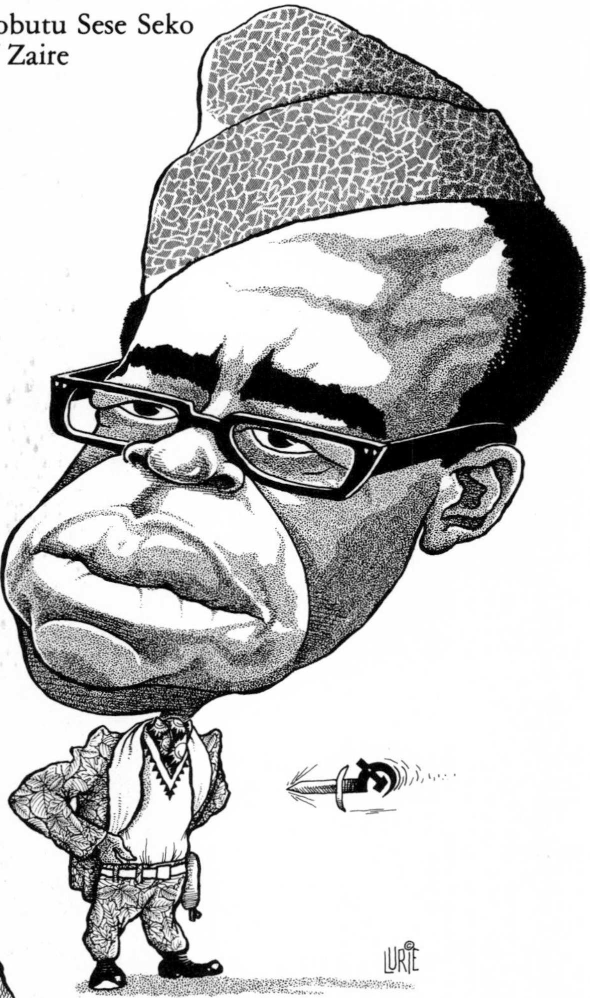

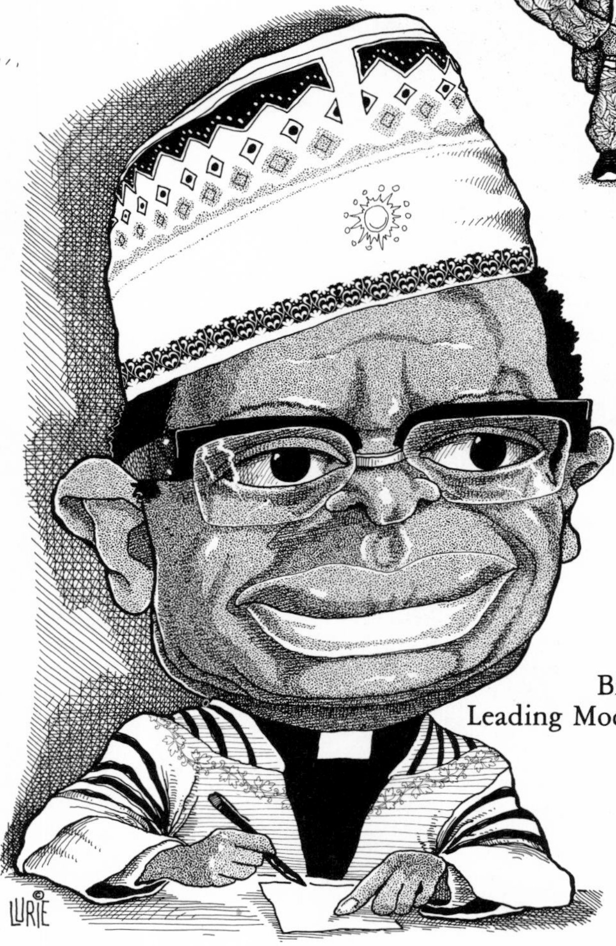

Bishop Abel Muzorewa
Leading Moderate Among Rhodesia's Blacks

Lieutenant General
Fred W. K. Akuffo
New Ruler of Ghana

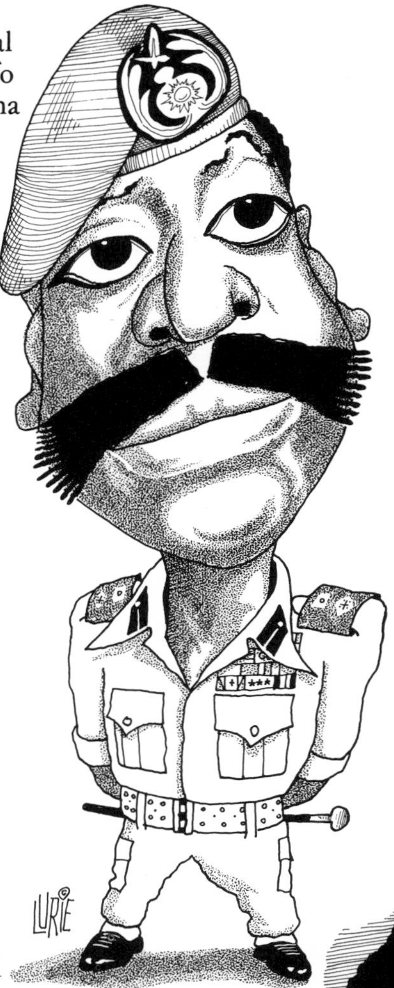
LURIE

President Kenneth Kaunda
of Zambia

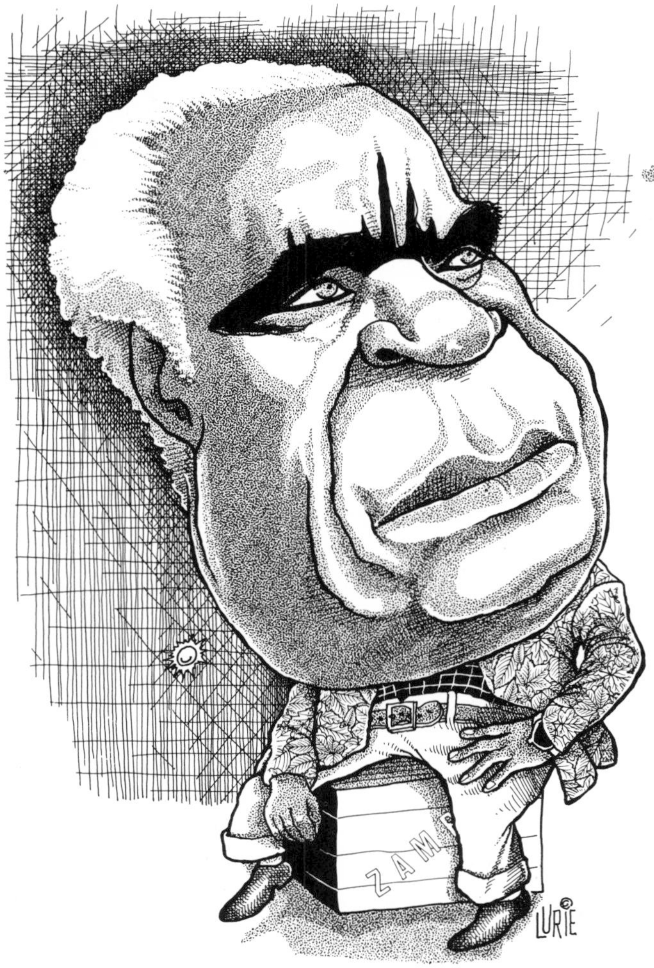
ZAM
LURIE

Sam Nujoma
Namibian Leader

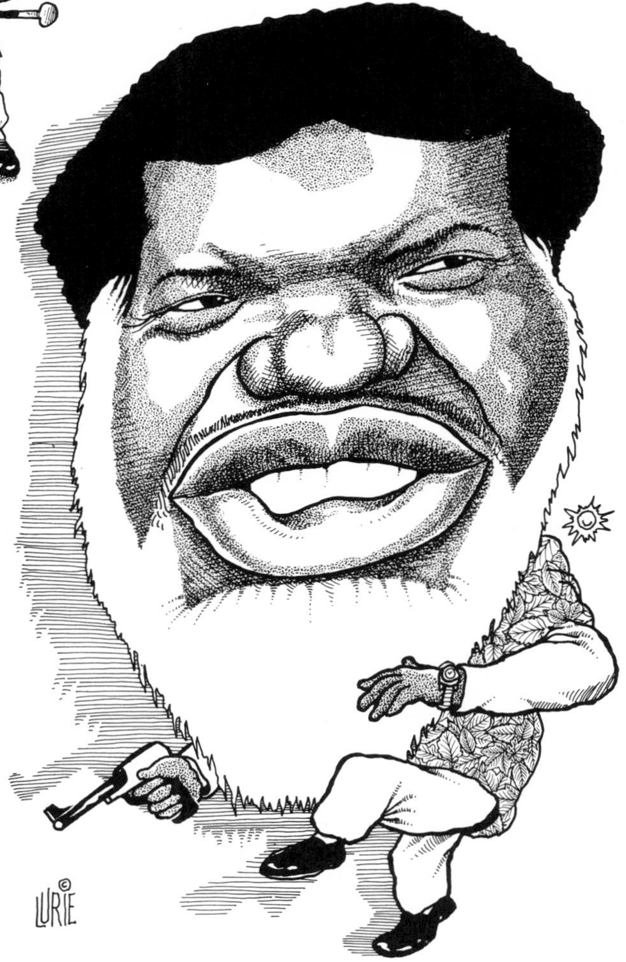
LURIE

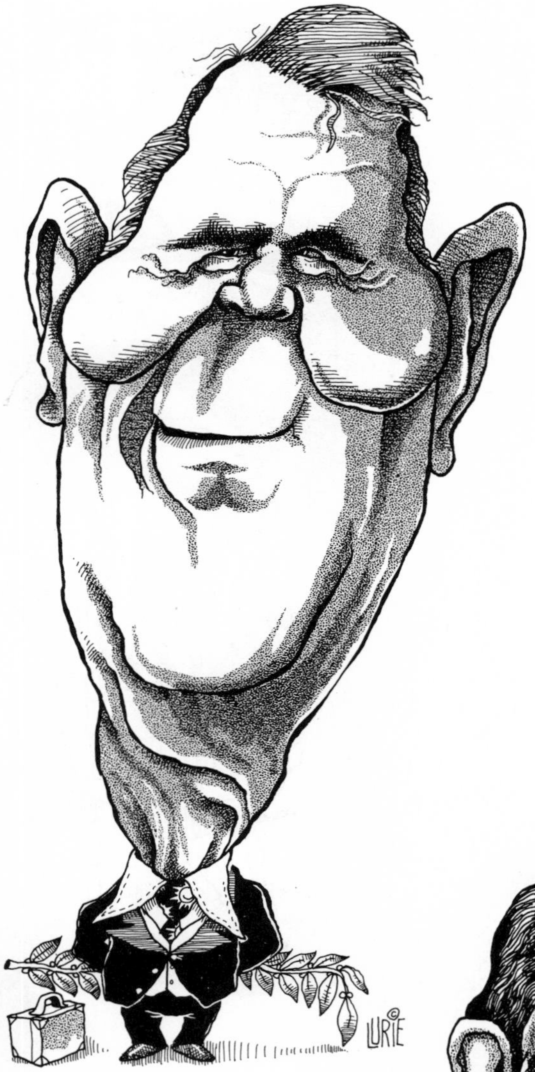
LURIE

Cyrus R. Vance
Secretary of State

William H. Webster
Carter's Nominee for FBI Director

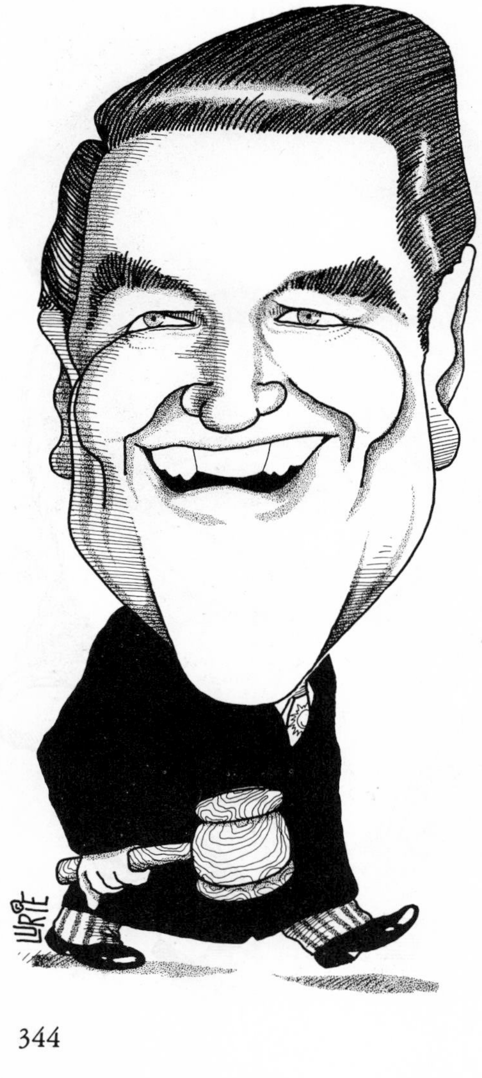
LURIE

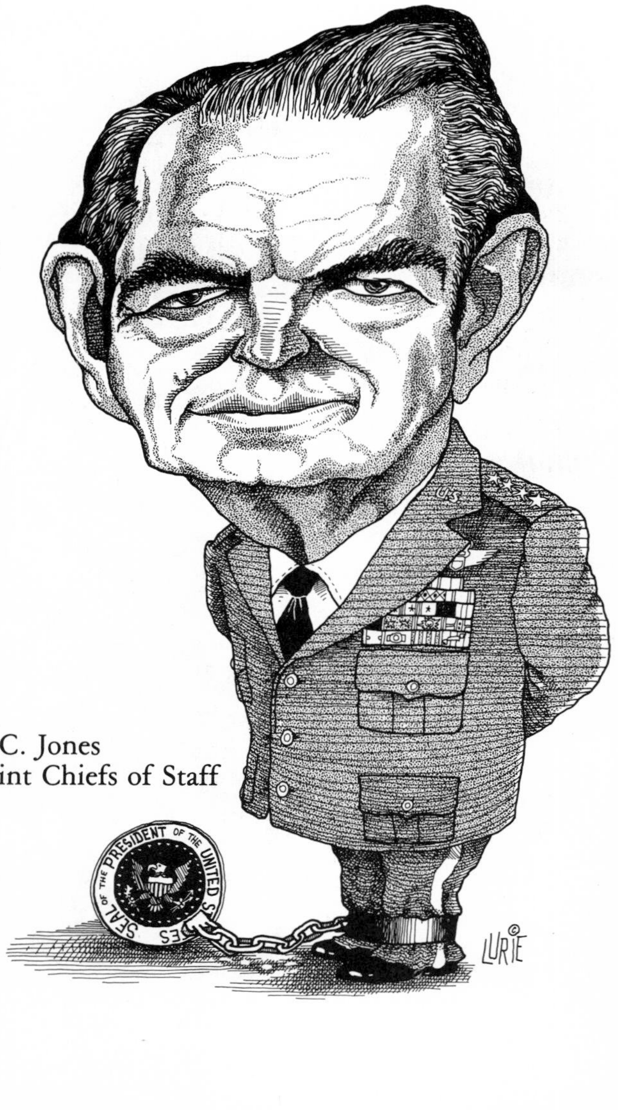
LURIE

General David C. Jones
Next Chairman of the Joint Chiefs of Staff

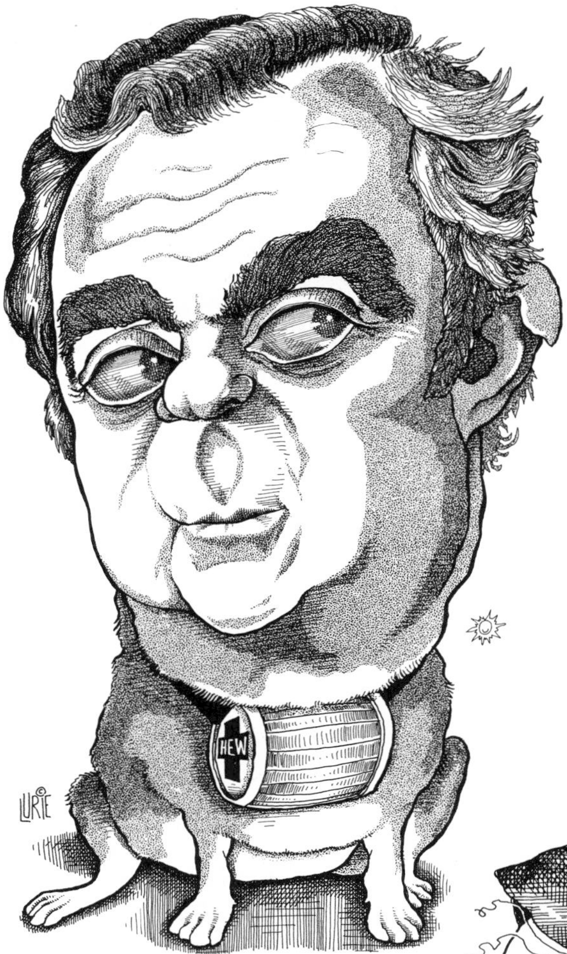
HEW
LURIE

Joseph A. Califano, Jr.
Secretary of Health,
Education & Welfare

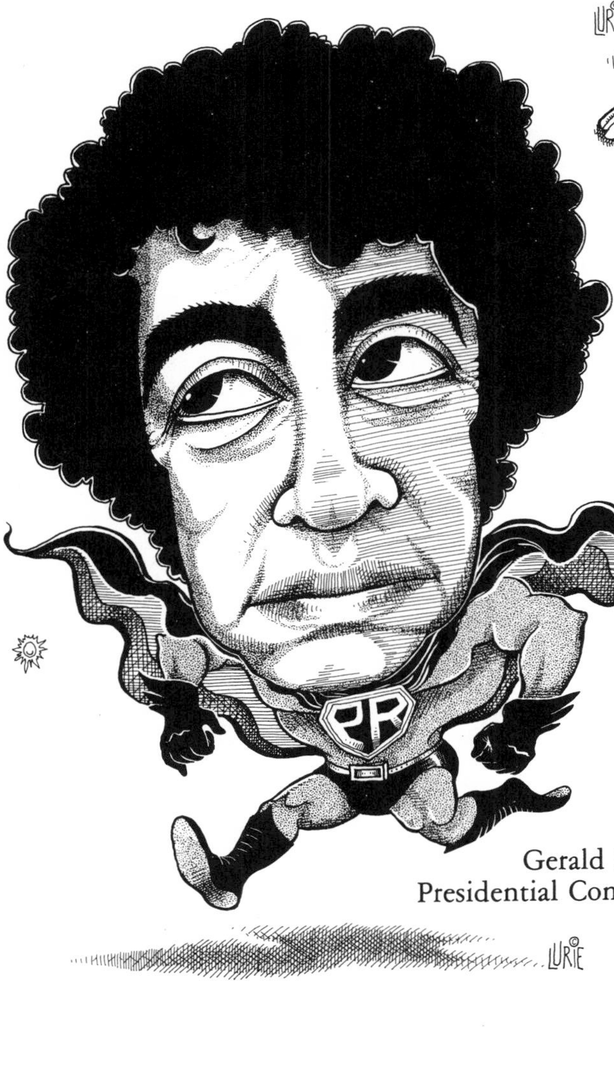
PR
LURIE

Gerald Rafshoon
Presidential Communication Aide

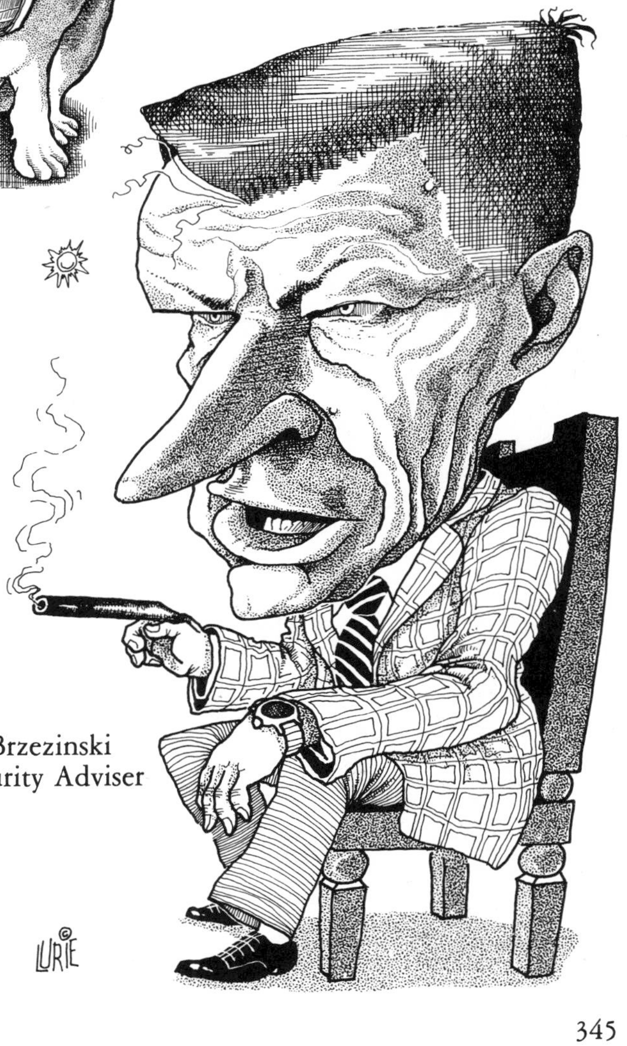
LURIE

Zbigniew Brzezinski
National Security Adviser

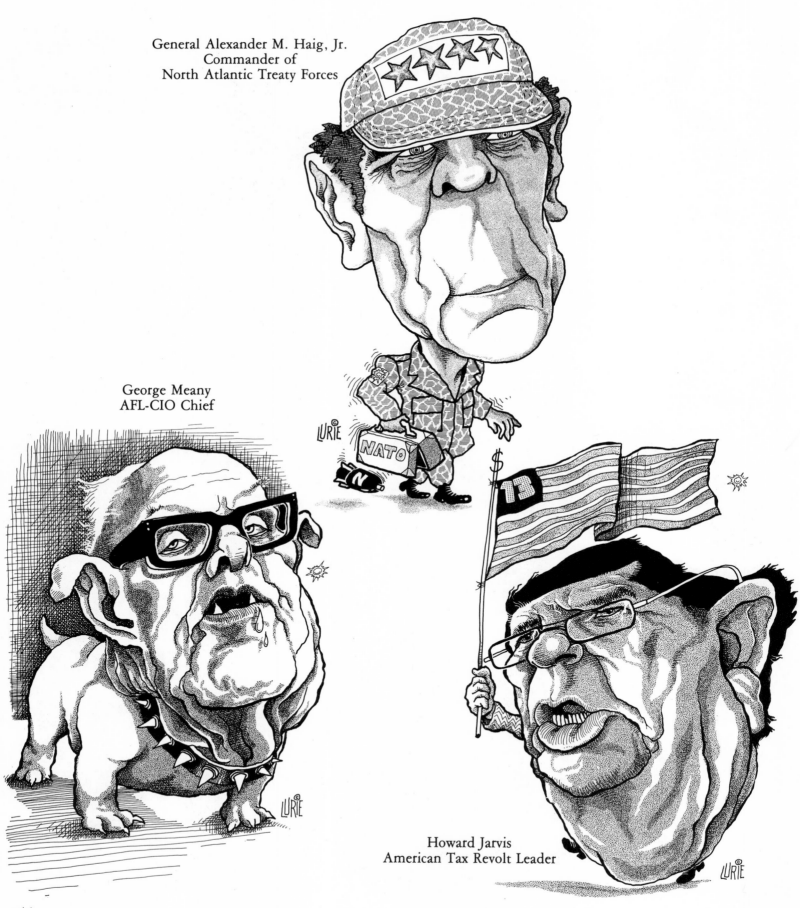

General Alexander M. Haig, Jr.
Commander of
North Atlantic Treaty Forces

NATO
N
LURIE

George Meany
AFL-CIO Chief

LURIE

$
13
LURIE

Howard Jarvis
American Tax Revolt Leader

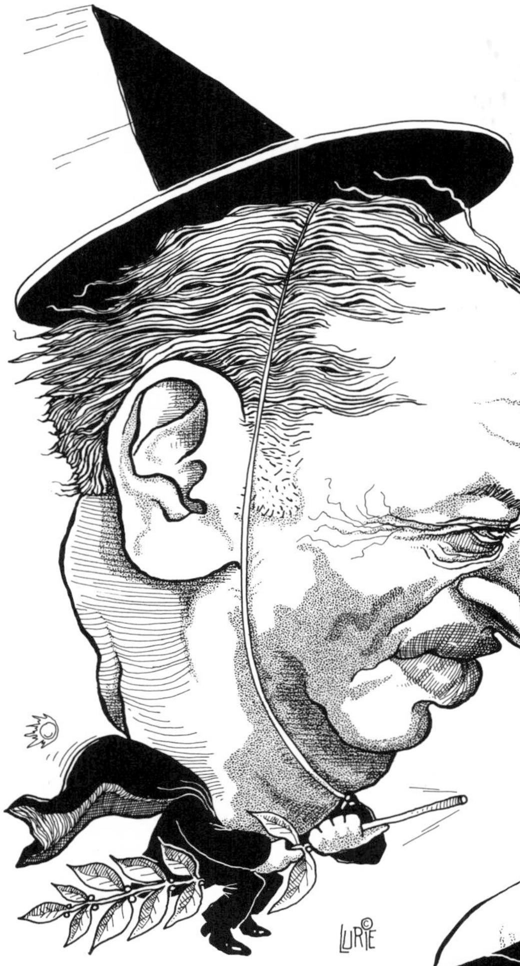
LURIE

Bruno Kreisky
Chancellor of Austria

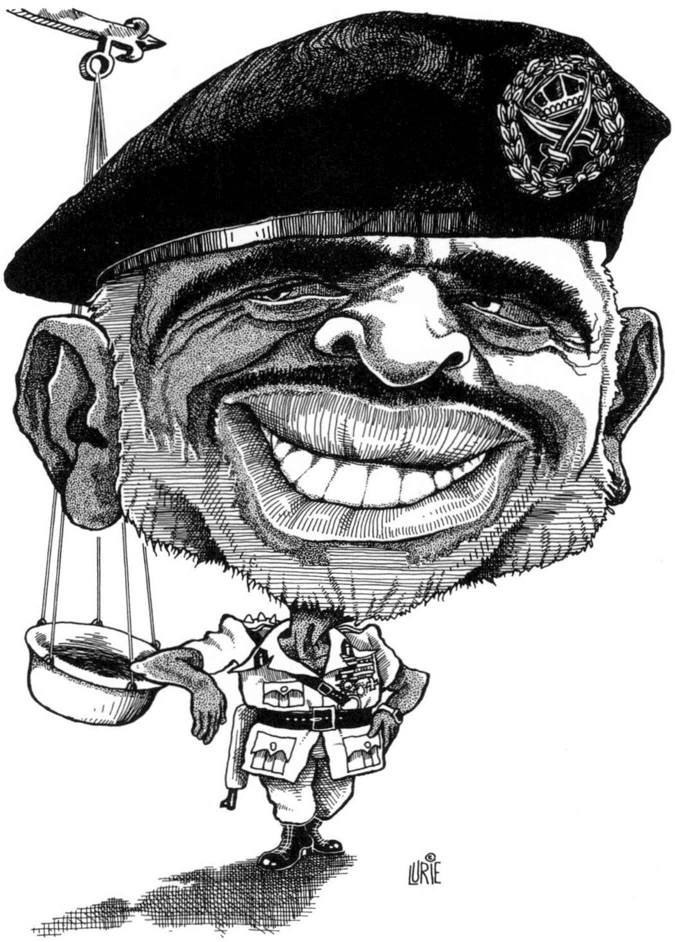
LURIE

King Hussein
of Jordan

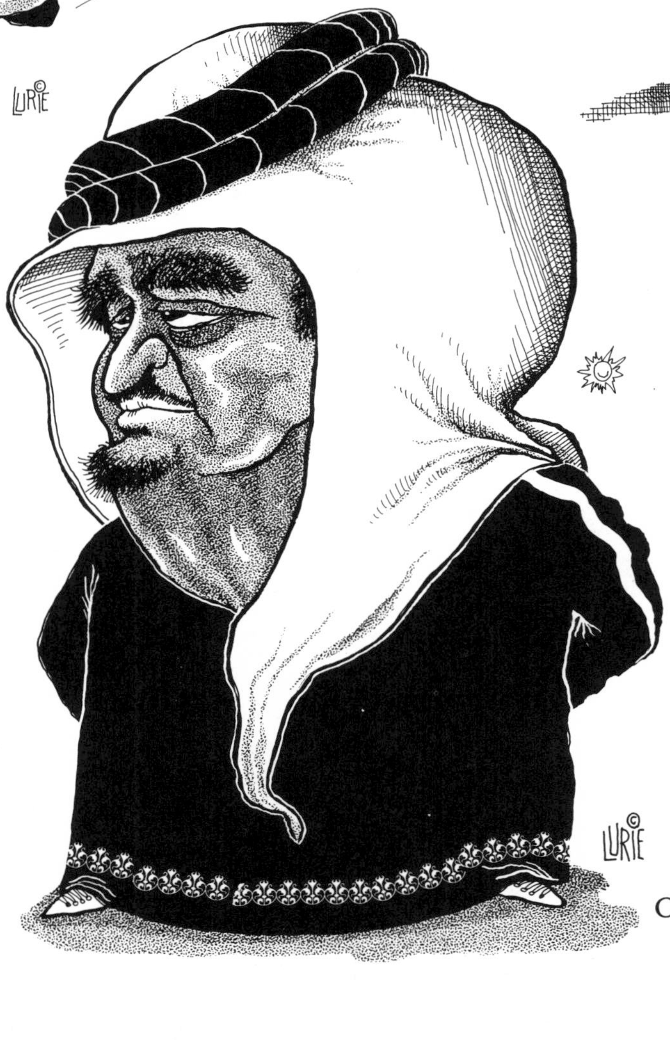
LURIE

Crown Prince Fahd
of Saudi Arabia

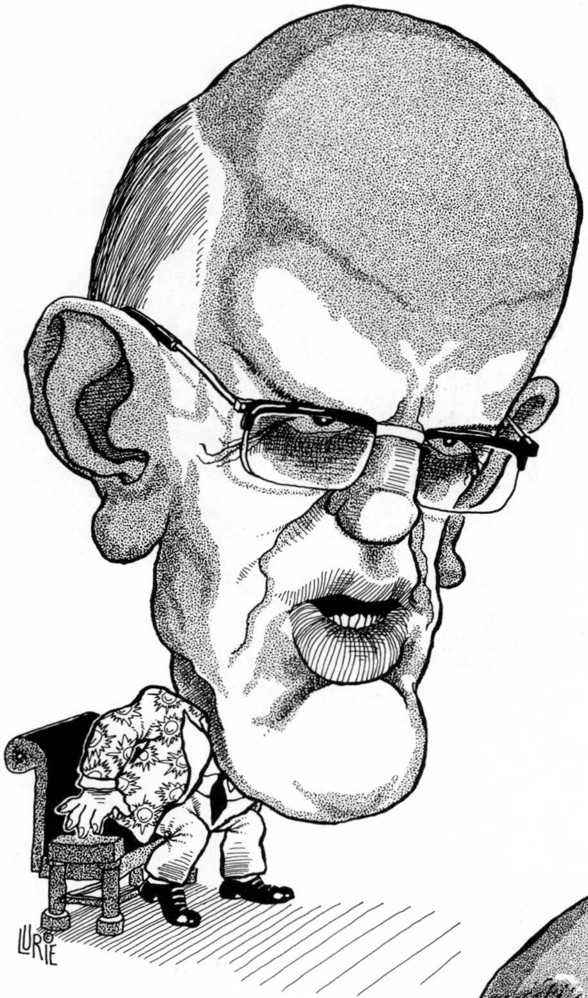
LURIE

Pieter Botha
South Africa's
New Prime Minister

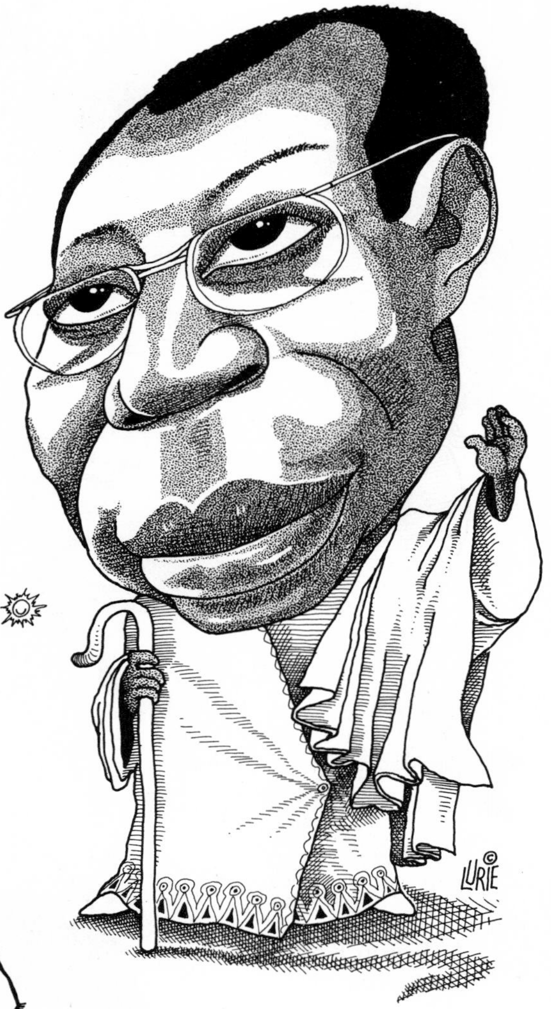
LURIE

President Leopold Sedar Senghor
of Senegal

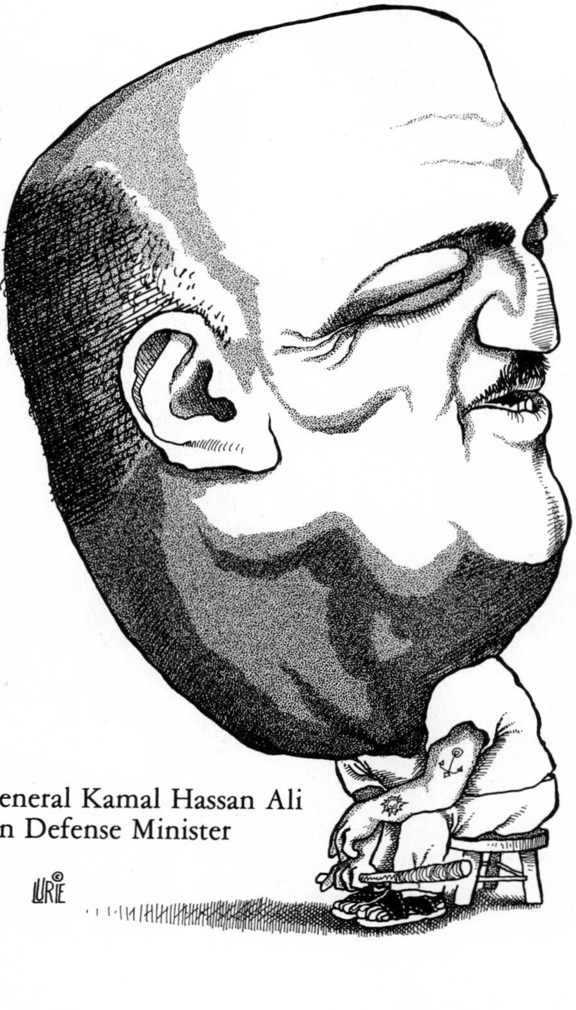
LURIE

Lieutenant General Kamal Hassan Ali
Egyptian Defense Minister

Hua Kuo-feng
China's Boss

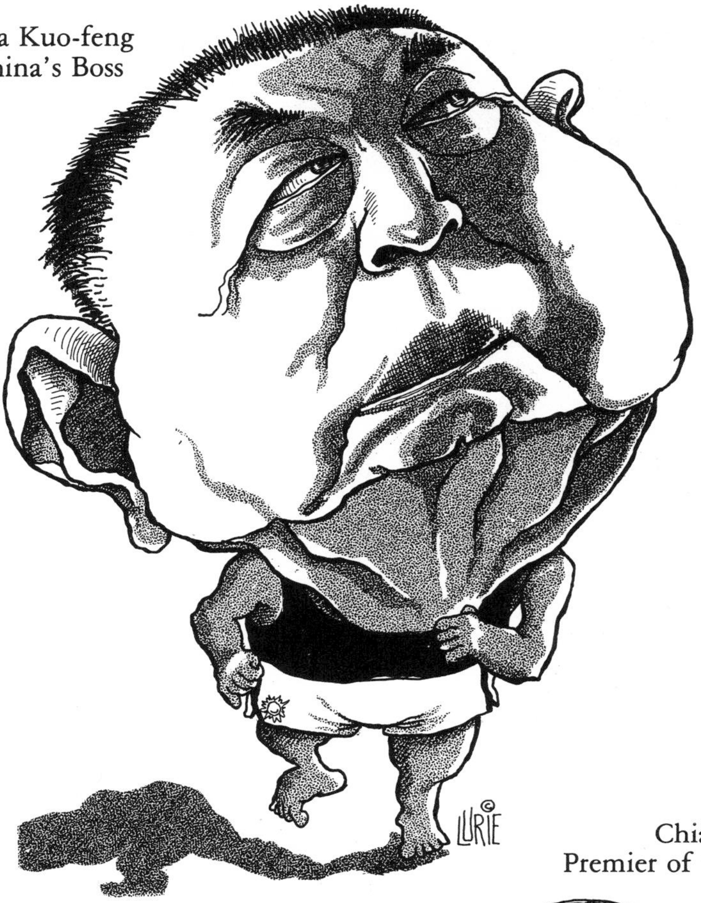
LURIE

Teng Hsiao-ping
China's Vice Premier

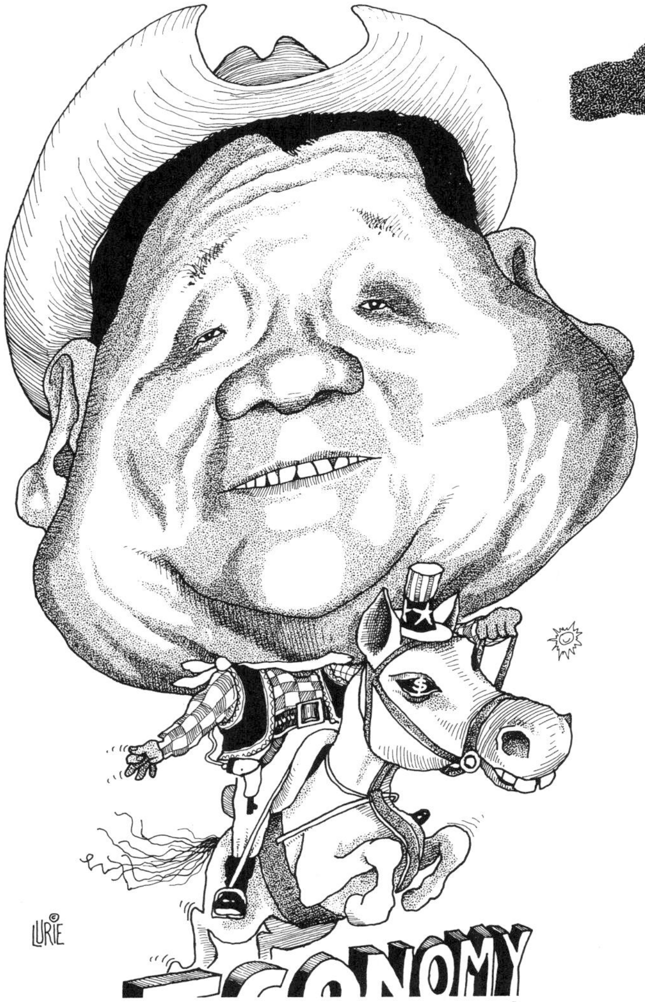
LURIE

Chiang Ching-kuo
Premier of the Republic of China

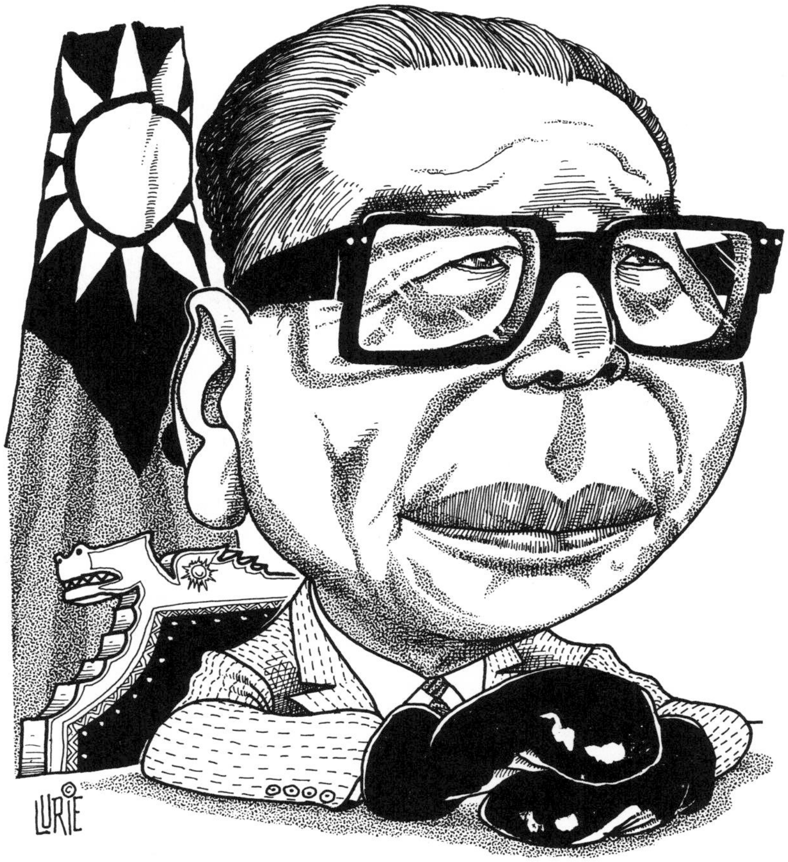
LURIE

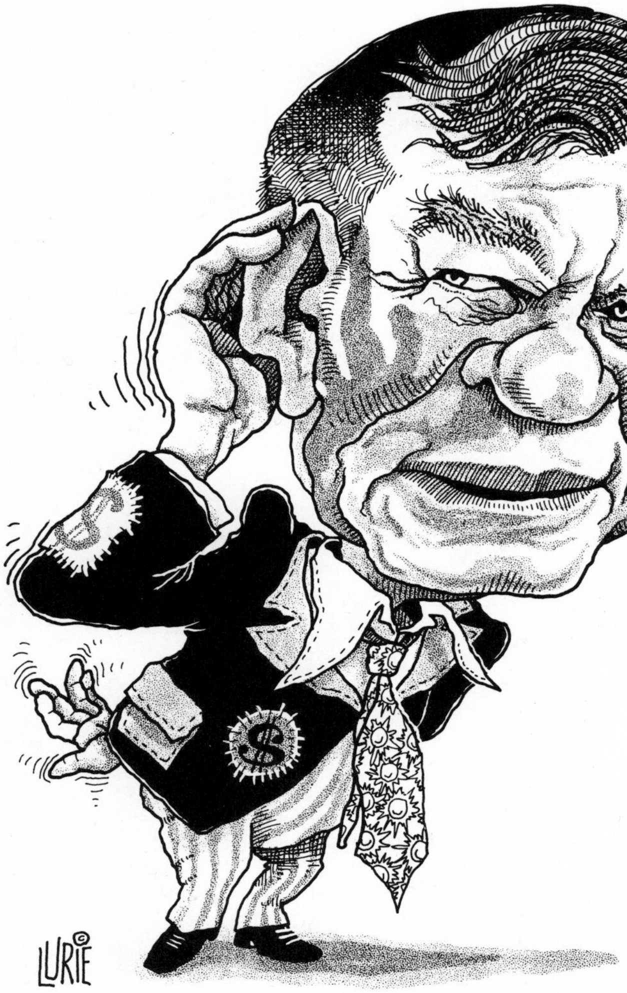
LURIE

Senator Herman Talmadge

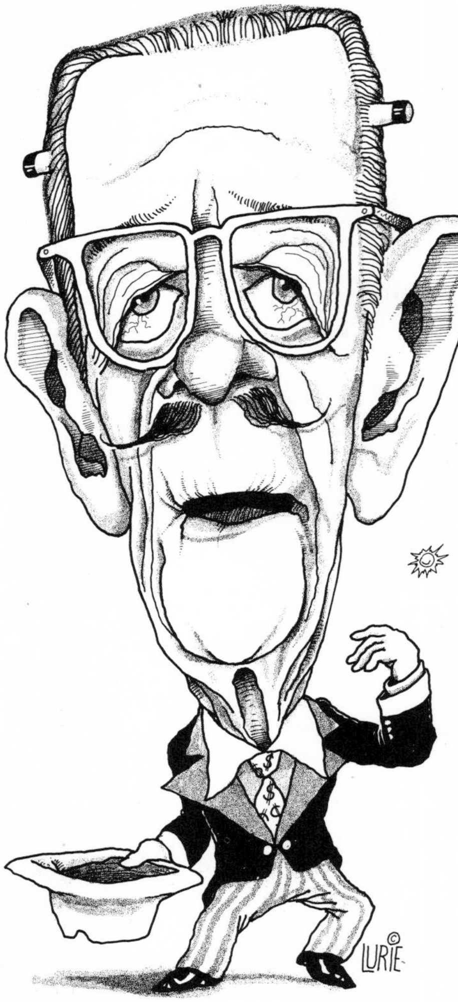
LURIE

Representative Daniel Flood

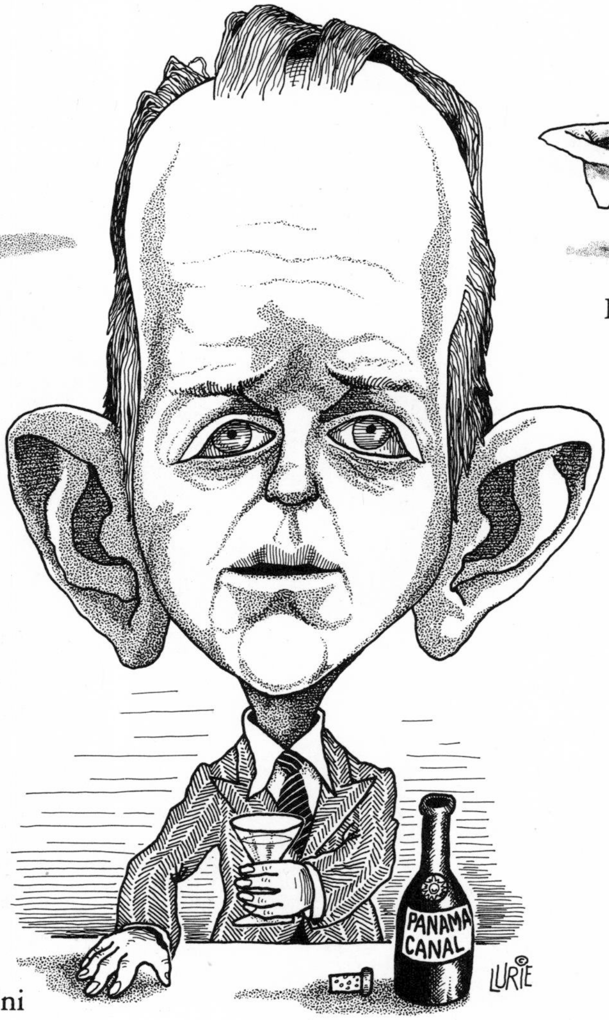
PANAMA
CANAL
LURIE

Senator Dennis Deconcini

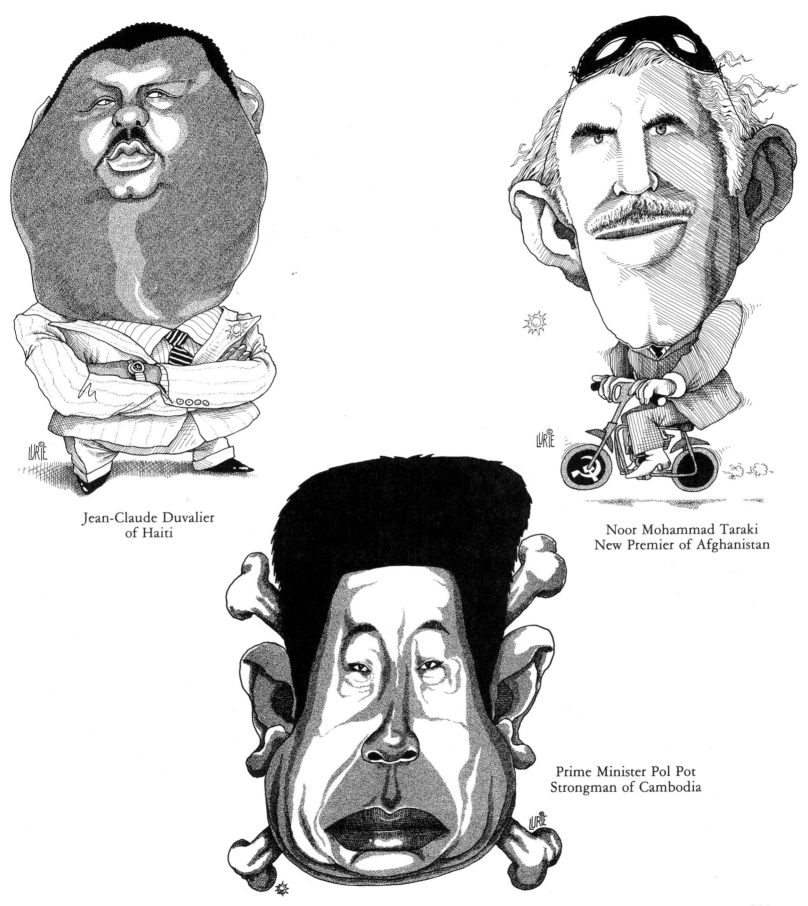

Jean-Claude Duvalier
of Haiti

Noor Mohammad Taraki
New Premier of Afghanistan

Prime Minister Pol Pot
Strongman of Cambodia

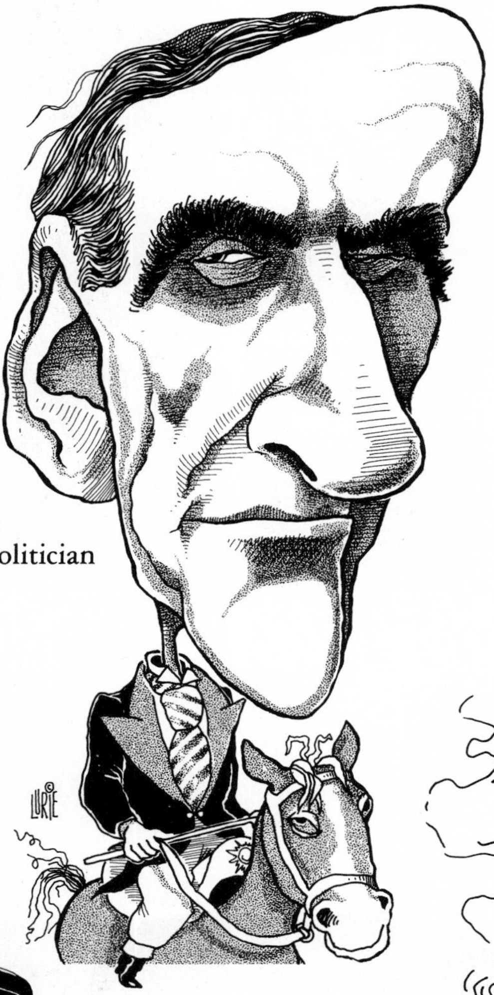
LURIE

Jeremy Thorpe
British Controversial Politician

Mohammed Riza Pahlevi
Shah of Iran

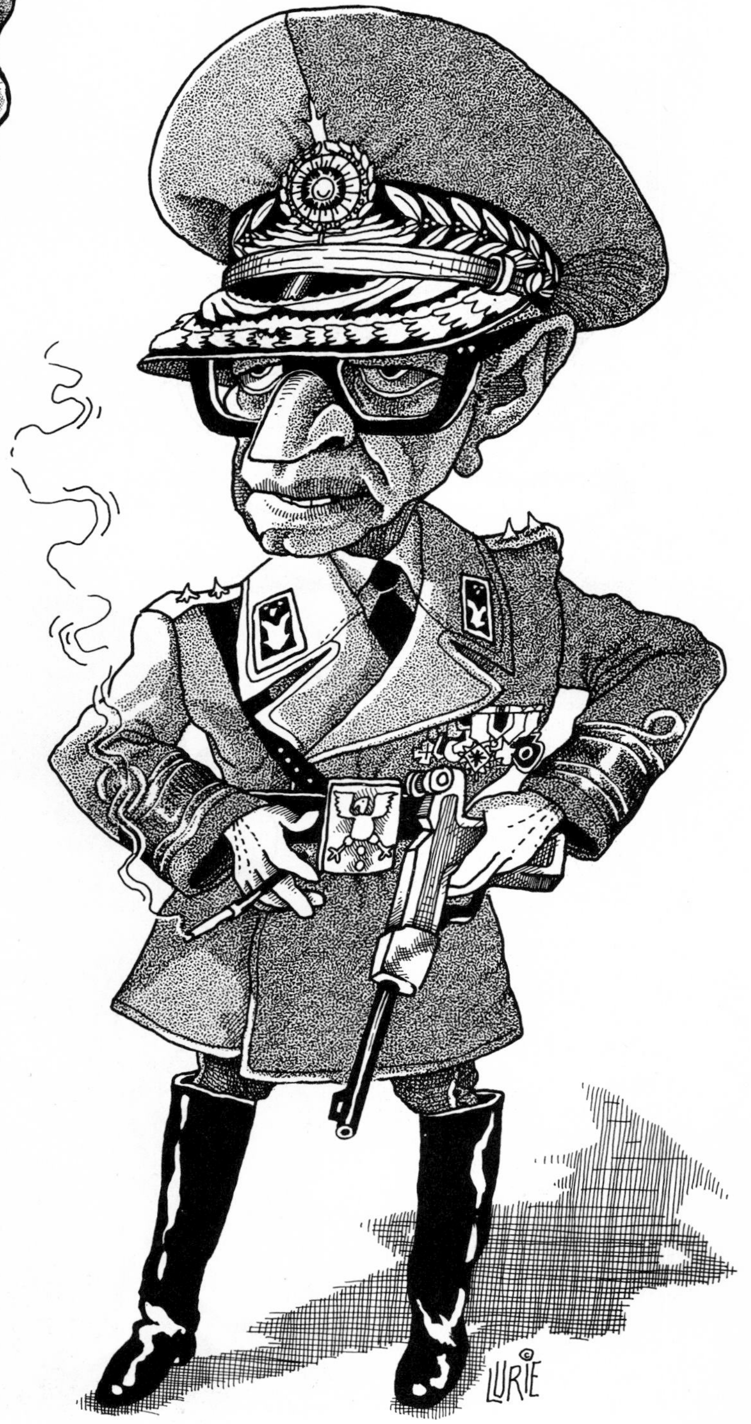
LURIE

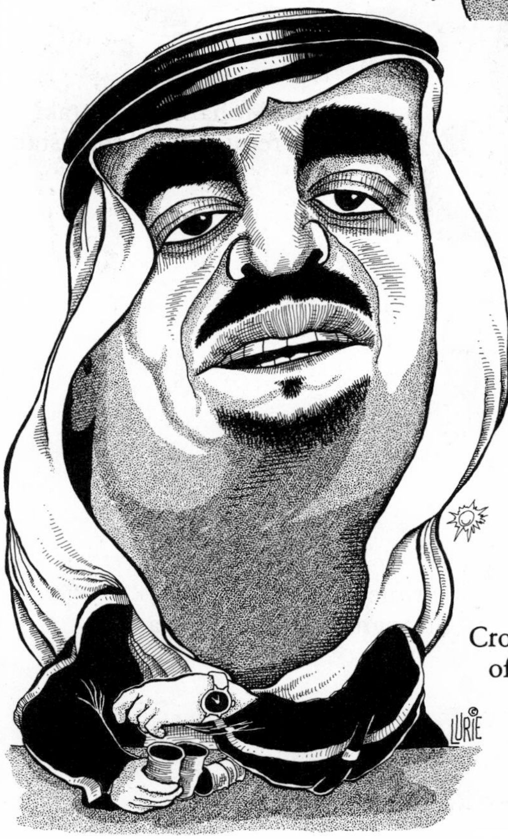
LURIE

Crown Prince Fahd
of Saudi Arabia

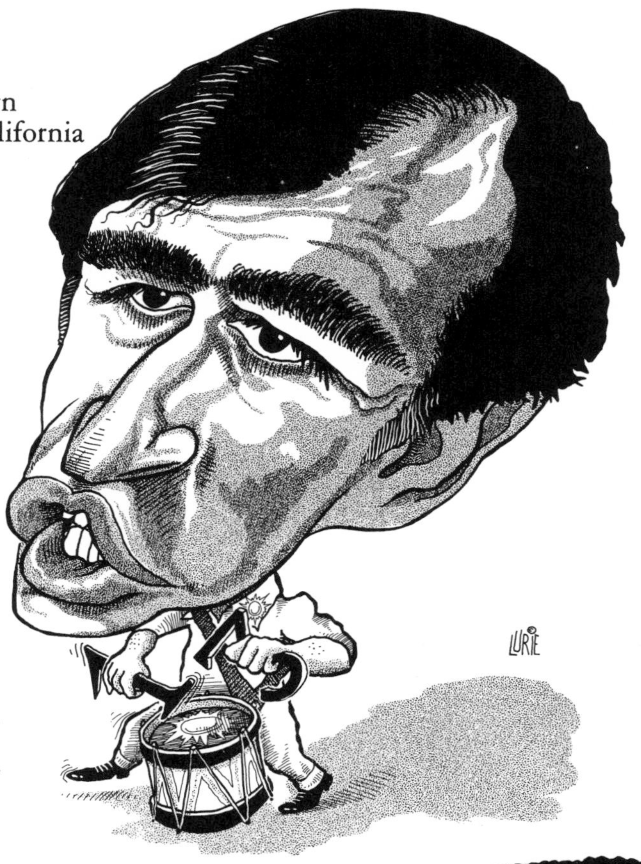
LURIE

Jerry Brown
Governor of California

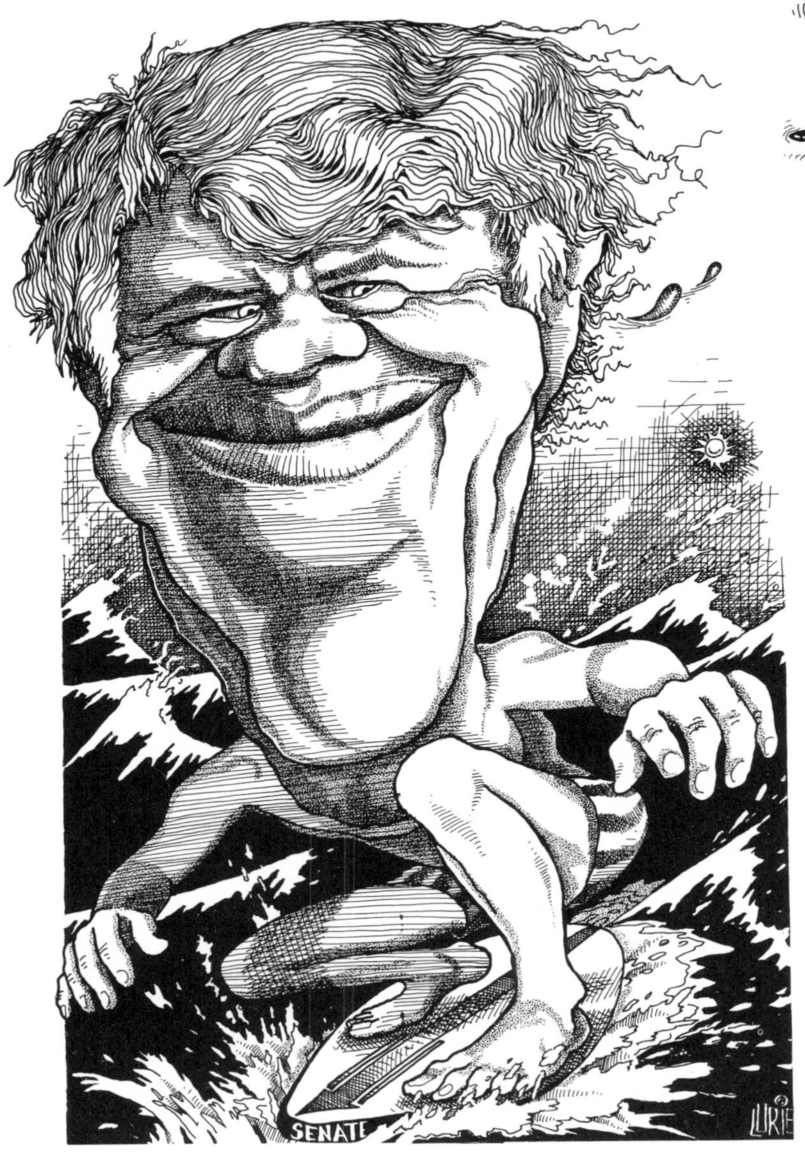
SENATE
LURIE

President Carter

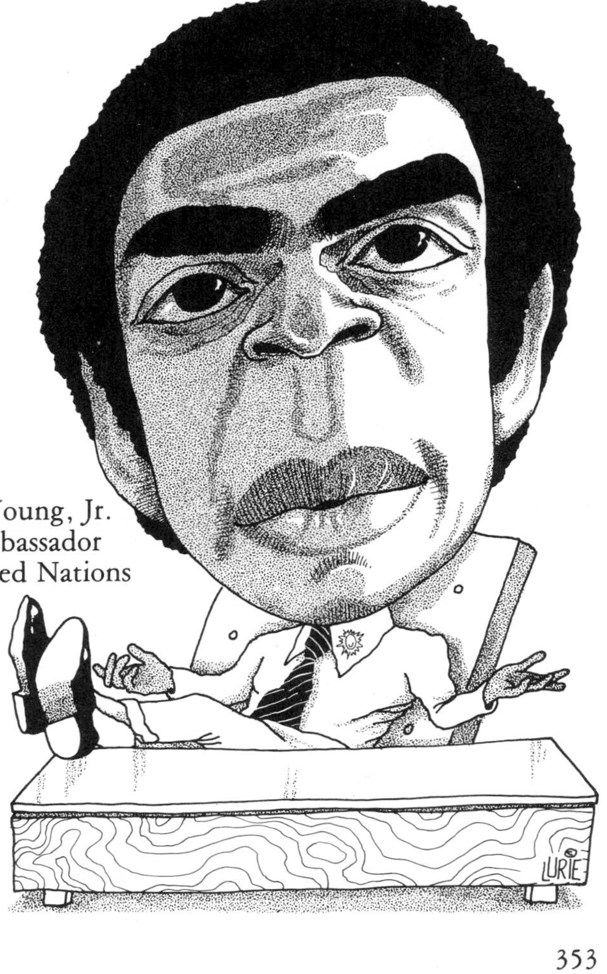
LURIE

Andrew Young, Jr.
U.S. Ambassador
to the United Nations

1979

Lurie: ON THE INTERNATIONAL CARTOON

The real power of the political cartoon is that it can be understood by people of different cultures who speak different languages. The political cartoon is the Esperanto of the media.

Humor does, of course, vary from country to country. British humor is not always appreciated by Americans, for instance. But I believe that a good American cartoon definitely can appeal to readers in Britain or Germany or France or Nigeria or South America. The very nature of American humor evolved through coping with and catering to at least a hundred different ethnic groups during the last two hundred years. However, the British or the Germans—much more homogeneous groups—are in a way stuck within their own humor limitations. They have difficulty finding audiences outside their own societies.

Also, American society enabled humor to spread out and reach a tremendous percentage of the population in contrast to England, for instance. With their very strong class structure, the British have mutually exclusive levels of humor. There the kind of humor that you see in the cartoons of the *Sunday London Times* is not appreciated by the London Cockney.

Lurie: ON THE CARTOON AS AN EDITORIAL

There is a classic tendency for newspaper editors to think that they are editing well if the cartoons on the editorial page happen to match the main editorial or any of the other editorials. In my opinion, an editorial cartoon is a complete editorial in and of itself. If the cartoon deals with a subject that is not otherwise mentioned on the editorial page, that simply gives the reader a broader range of subjects.

Of course, the editorial cartoon may repeat the general theme of an editorial text or, God forbid, may contradict it, in which case everyone is in trouble. However, there is no good reason for an editorial cartoon to follow the text unless the cartoonist is simply an illustrator for written editorials. Probably no editorial cartoonist would ever admit that he is a mere illustrator.

The real editorial cartoonist is an opinion maker, and the cartoons make a complete statement and are independent from any text. The only difference between the editorial writer and the editorial cartoonist is that the editorial writer does not know how to draw.

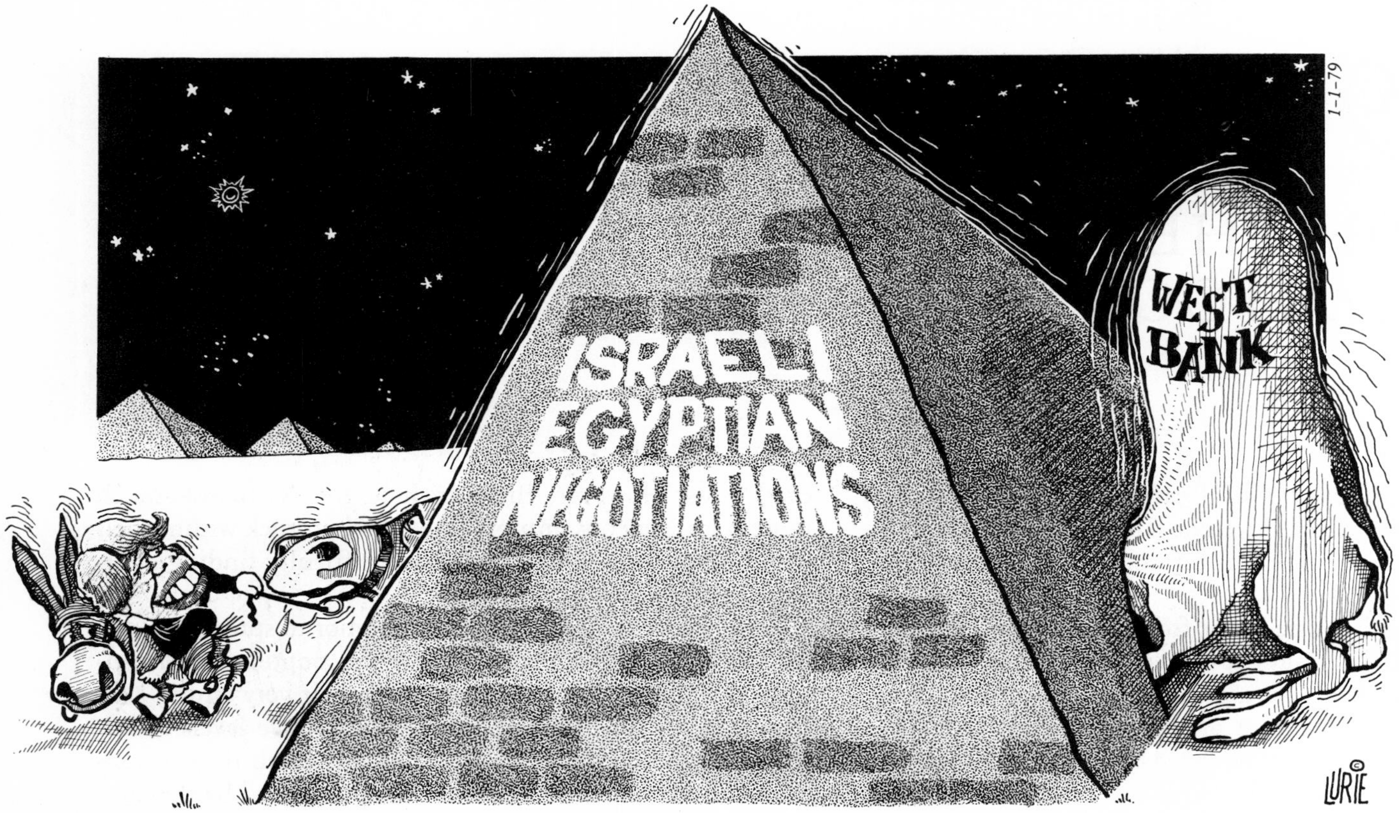
1-1-79
ISRAELI
EGYPTIAN
NEGOTIATIONS
WEST
BANK
LURIE

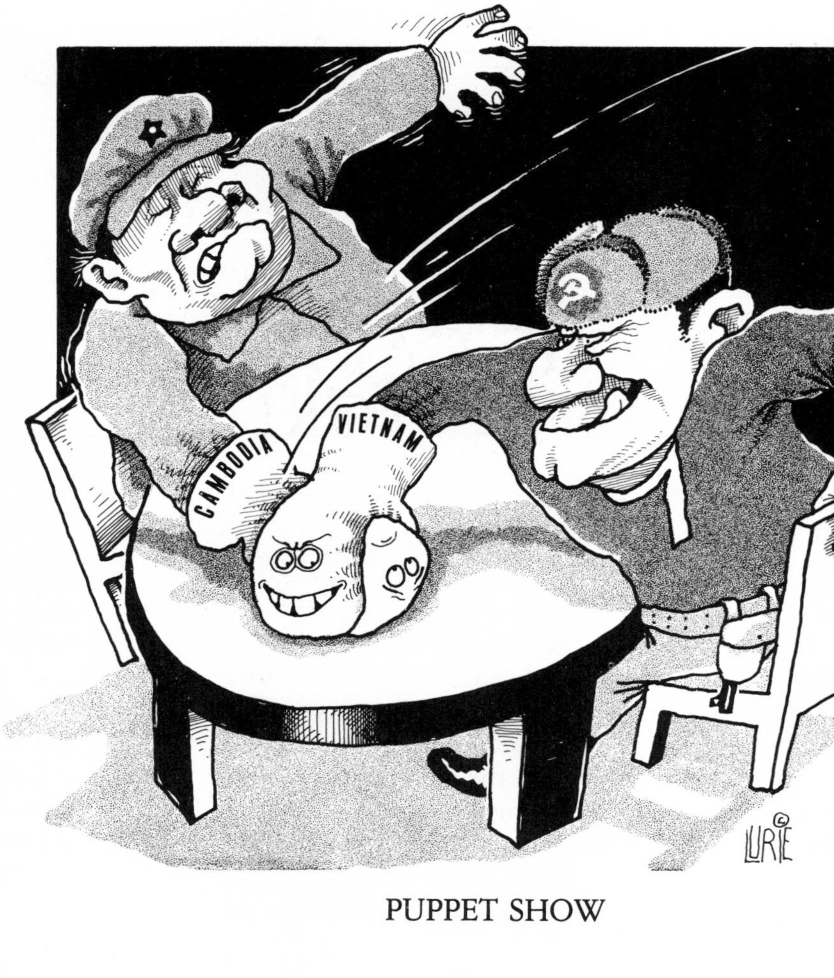
1-8-79
CAMBODIA
VIETNAM
LURIE

PUPPET SHOW

PALESTINIAN PROBLEM

1-19-79

LURIE

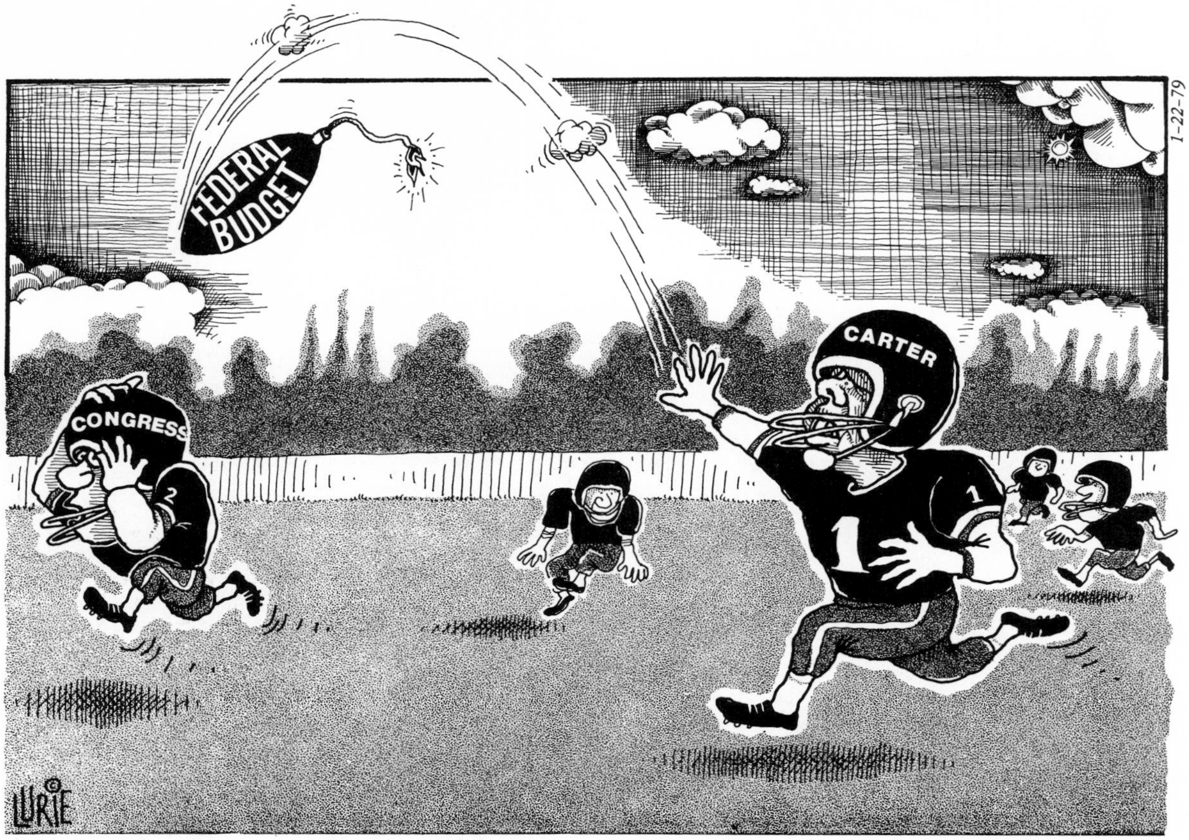
1-22-79
FEDERAL BUDGET
CARTER
CONGRESS
LURIE

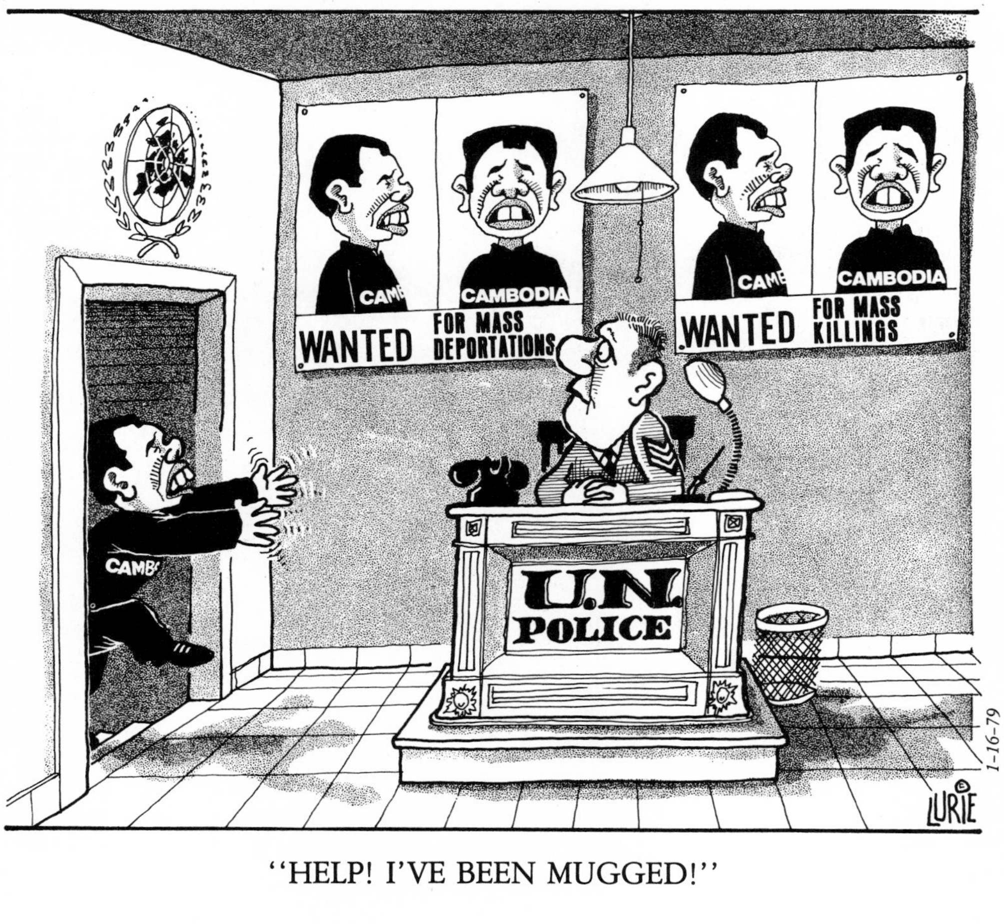
1-16-79
WANTED
FOR MASS DEPORTATIONS
CAMBODIA
WANTED
FOR MASS KILLINGS
CAMBODIA
U.N.
POLICE
LURIE

''HELP! I'VE BEEN MUGGED!''

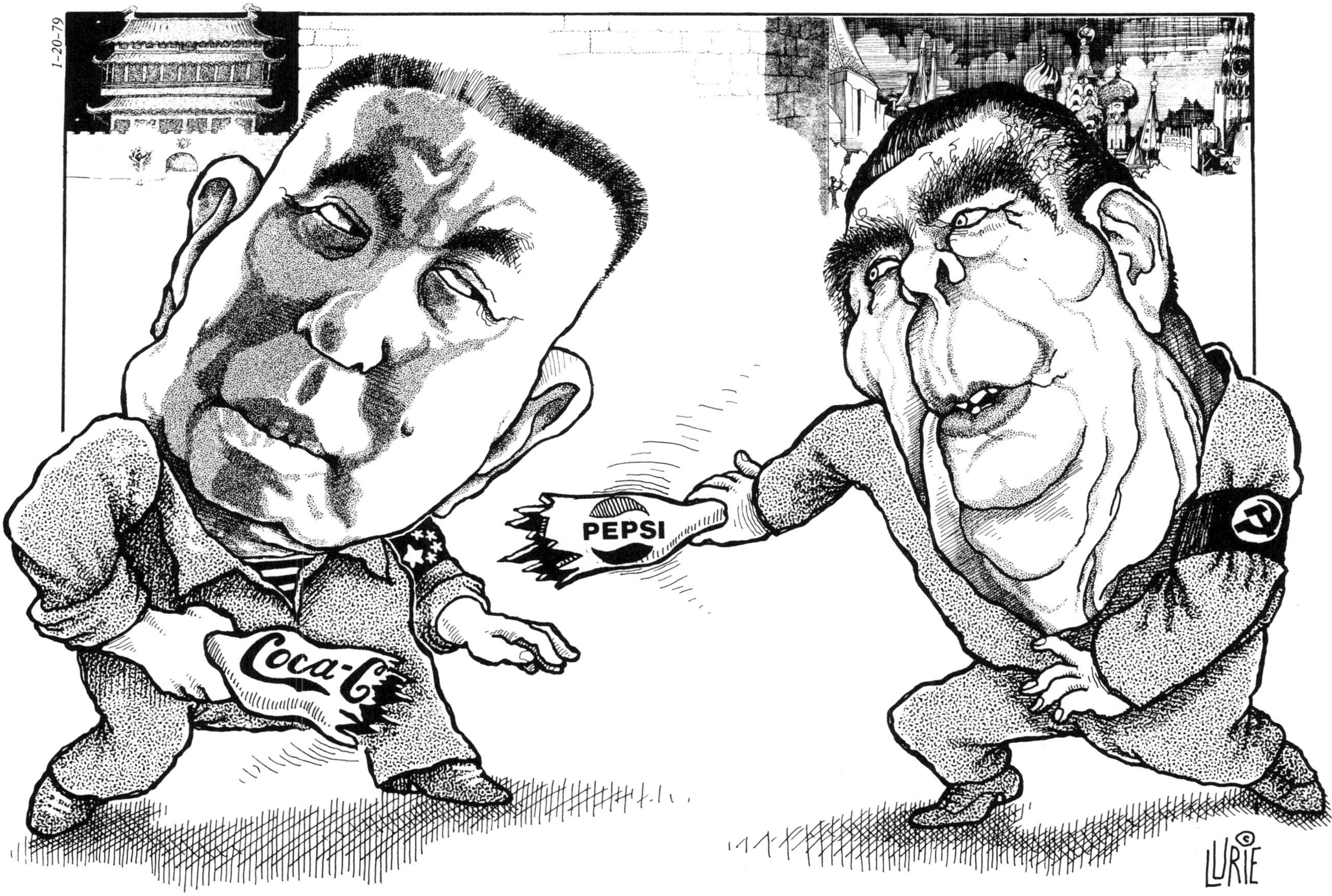
1-20-79
PEPSI
Coca-C
LURIE

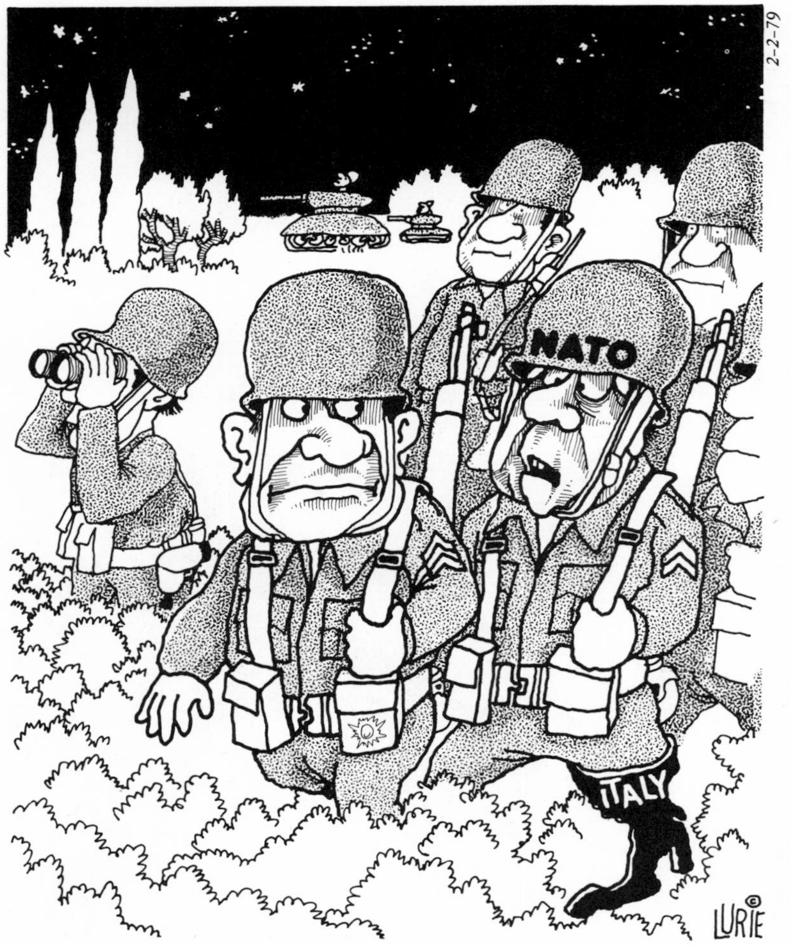
2-2-79
NATO
ITALY
LURIE

''MY FEET ARE KILLING ME!''

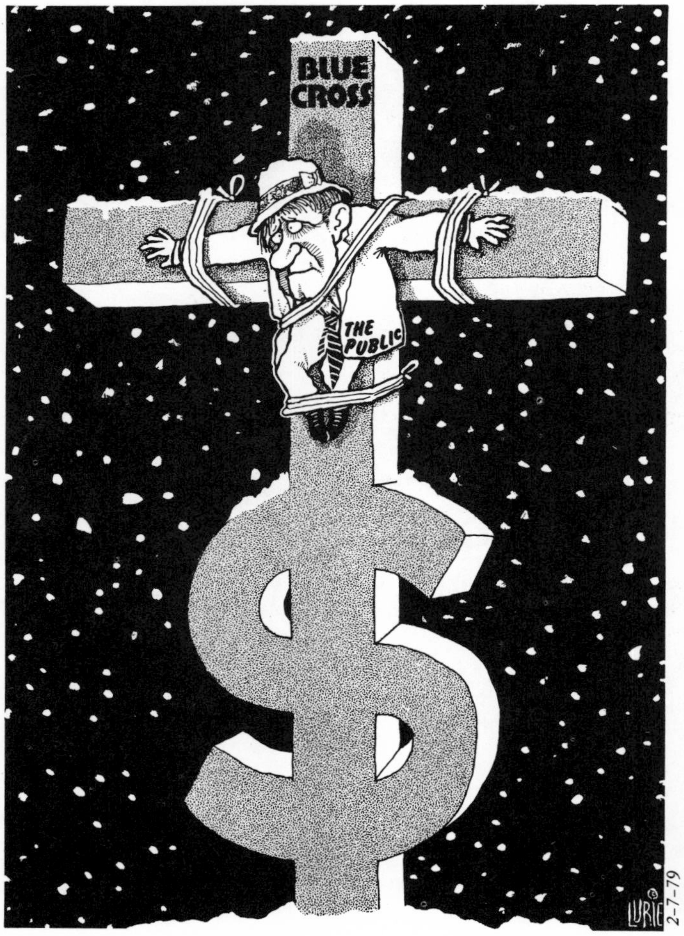
BLUE
CROSS
THE
PUBLIC
LURIE
2-7-79

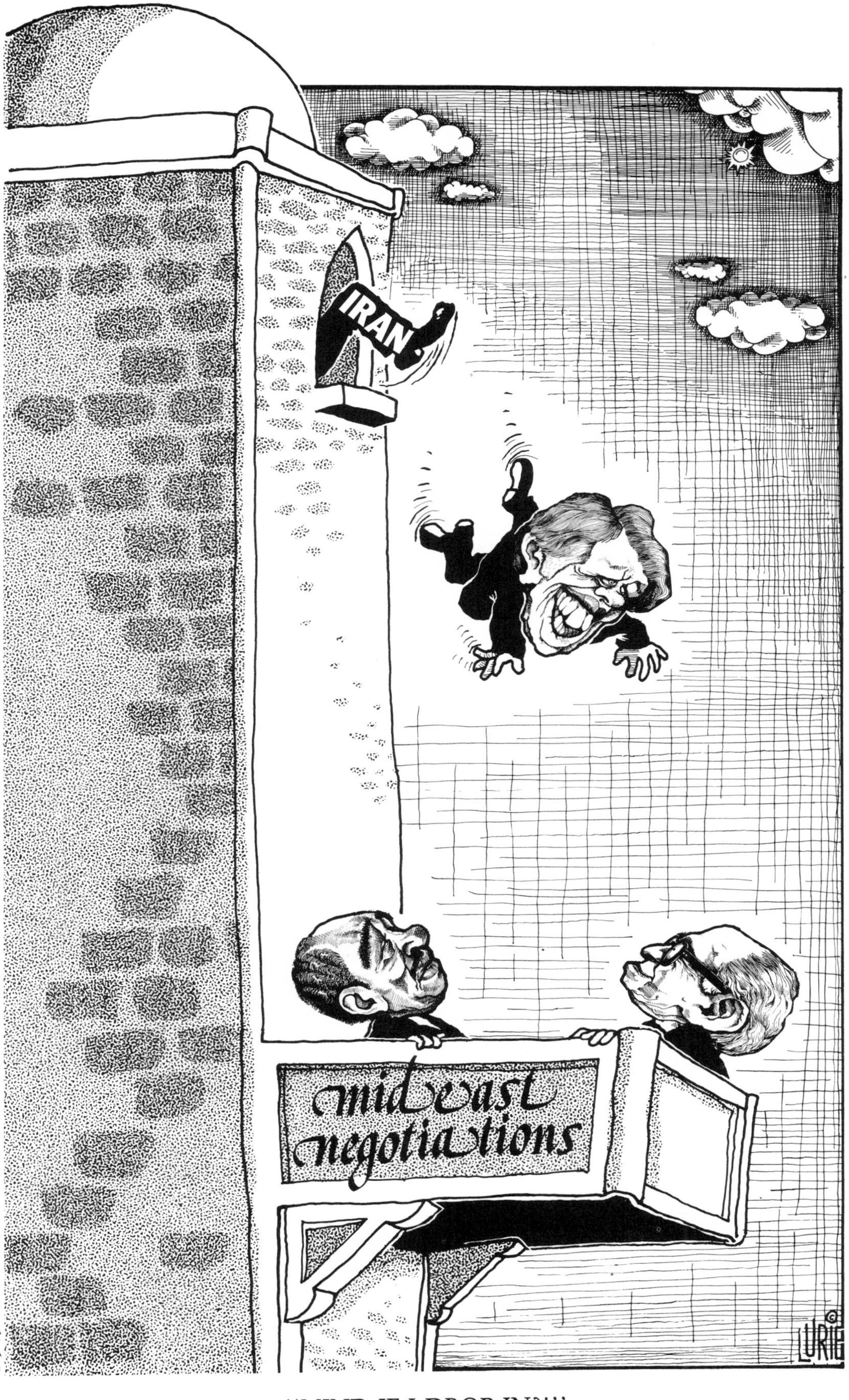
IRAN
mideast negotiations
2-9-79
LURIE

"MIND IF I DROP IN?!"

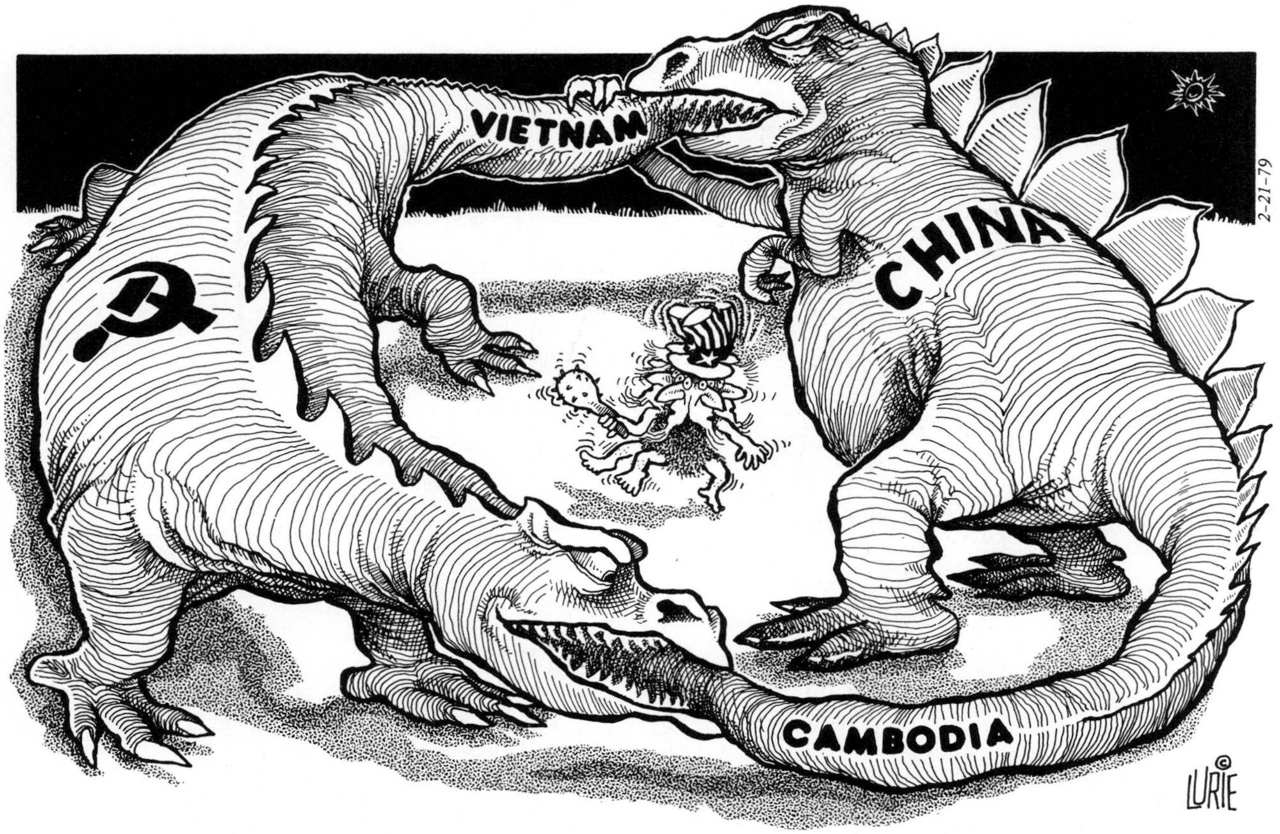
VIETNAM
CHINA
CAMBODIA
2-21-79
LURIE

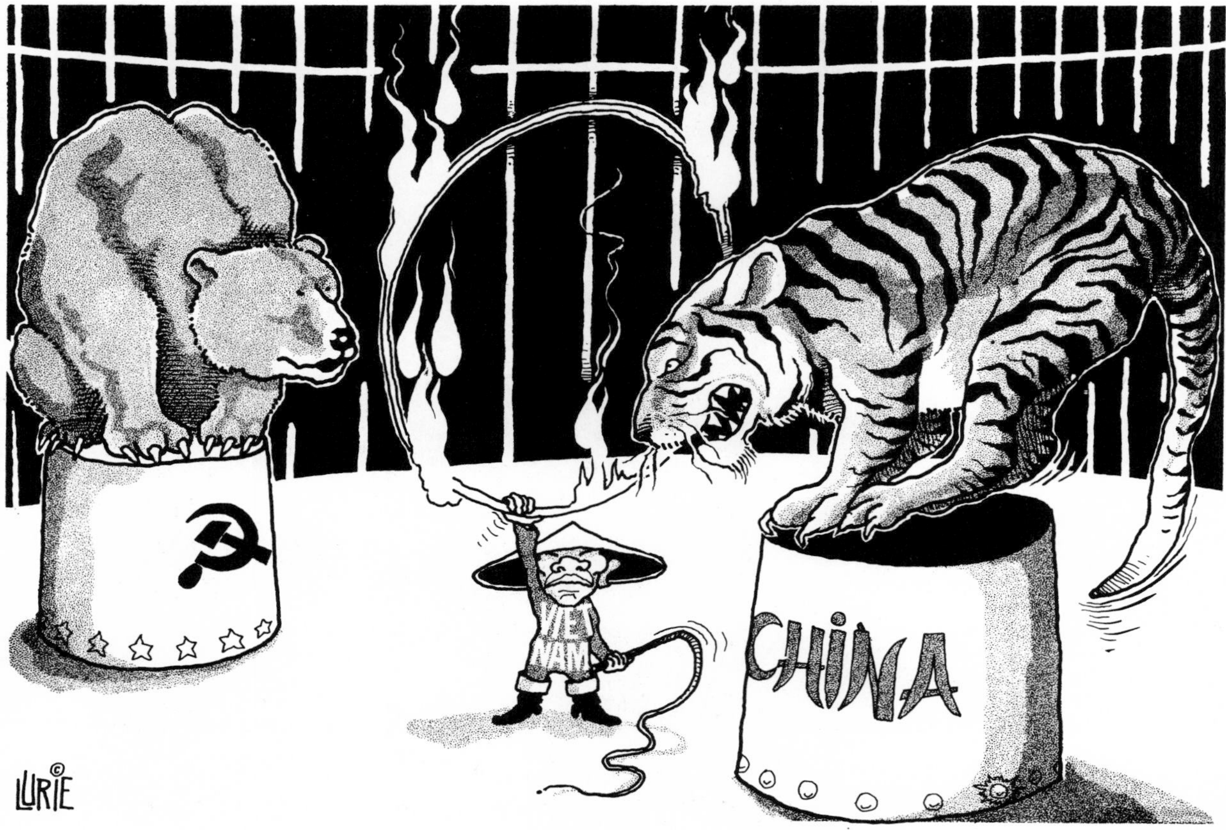
2-26-79
VIET
NAM
CHINA
LURIE

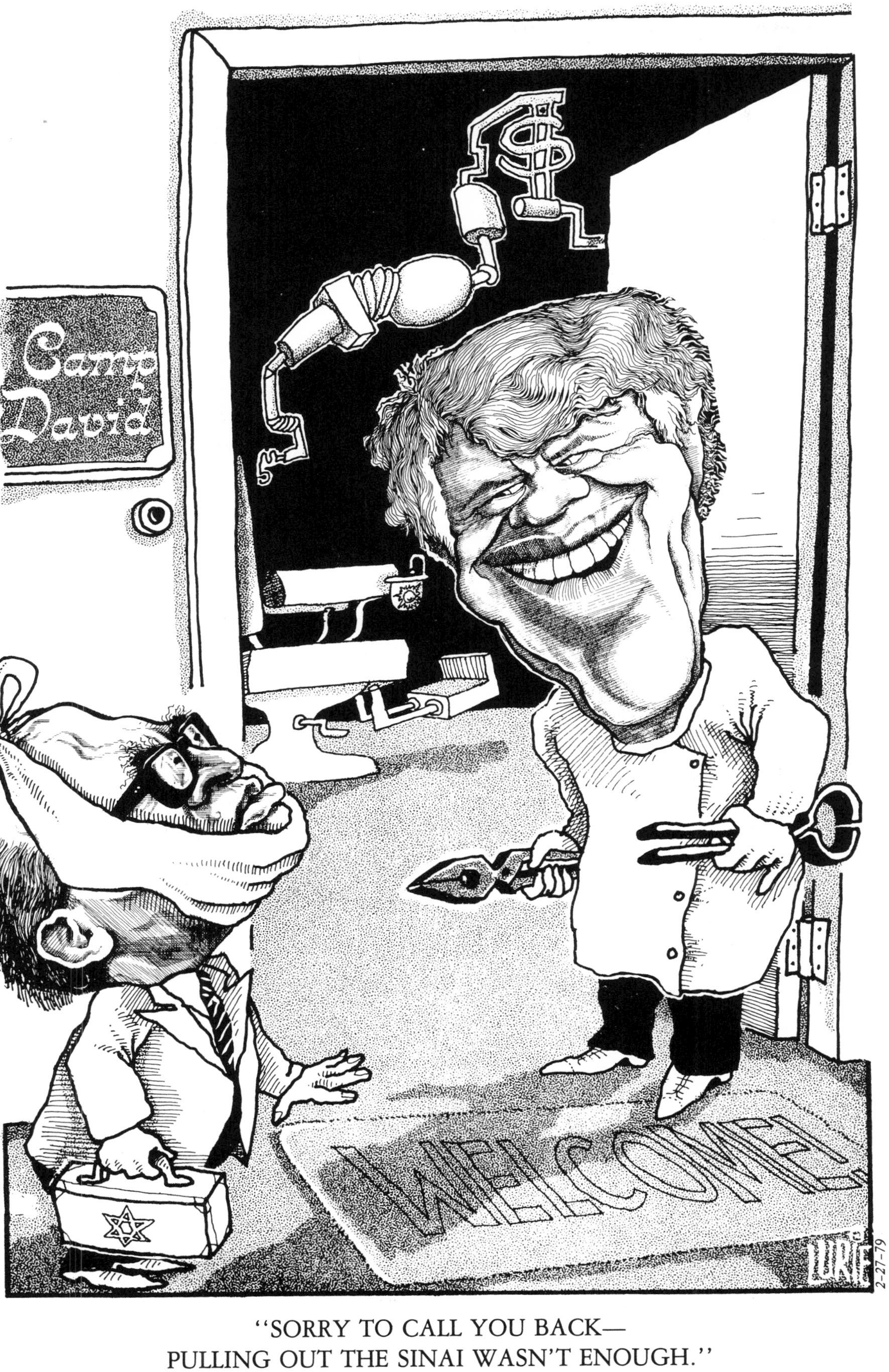
Camp David
WELCOME!
LURIE
2-27-79

"SORRY TO CALL YOU BACK—
PULLING OUT THE SINAI WASN'T ENOUGH."

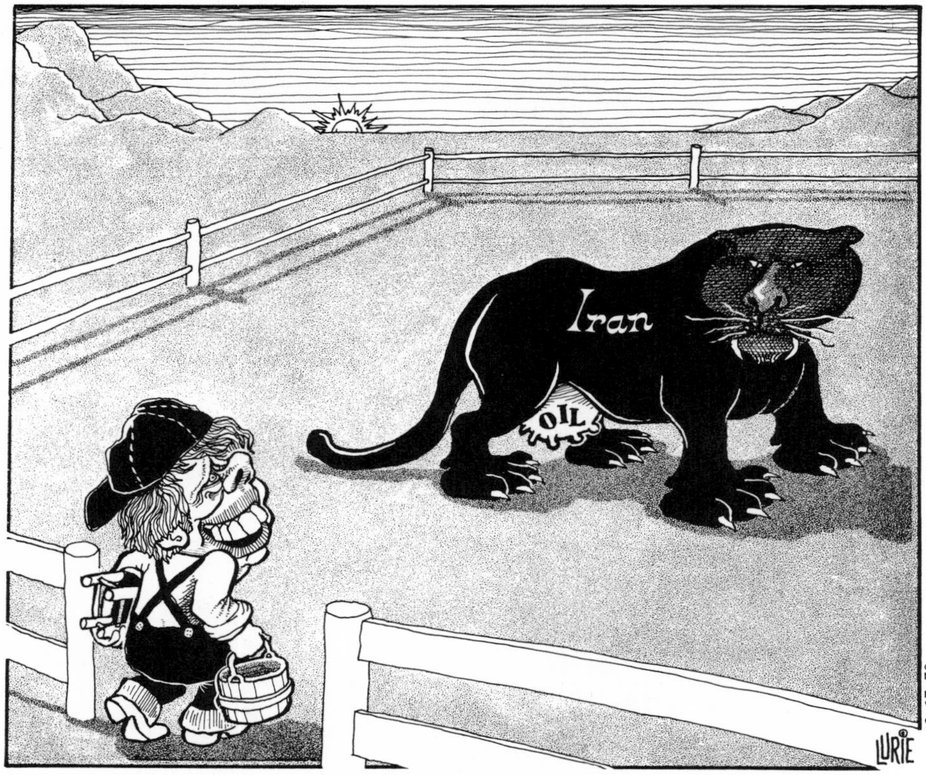
Iran
OIL
2-17-79
LURIE

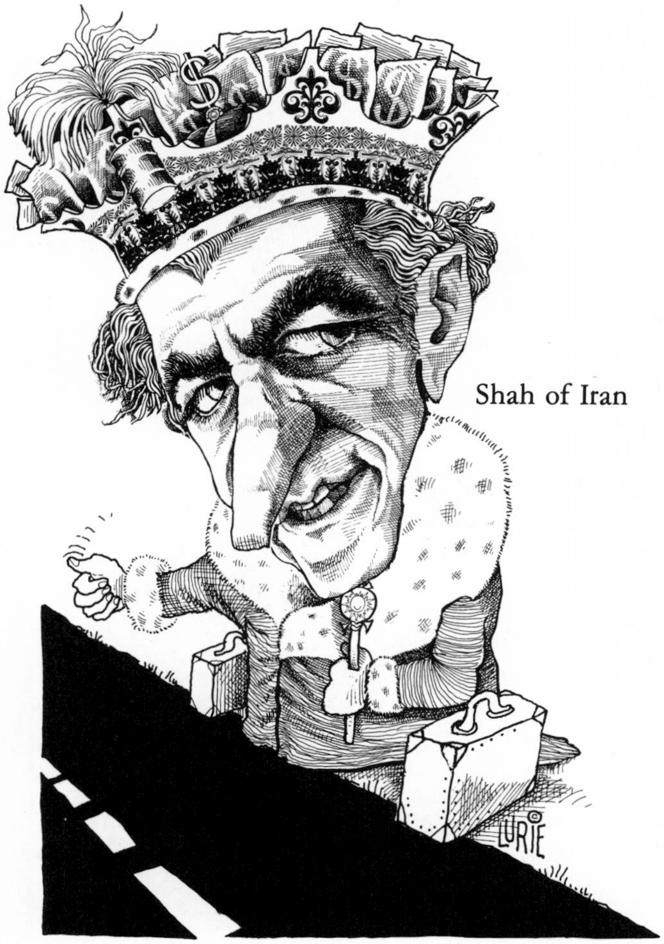
LURIE
Shah of Iran

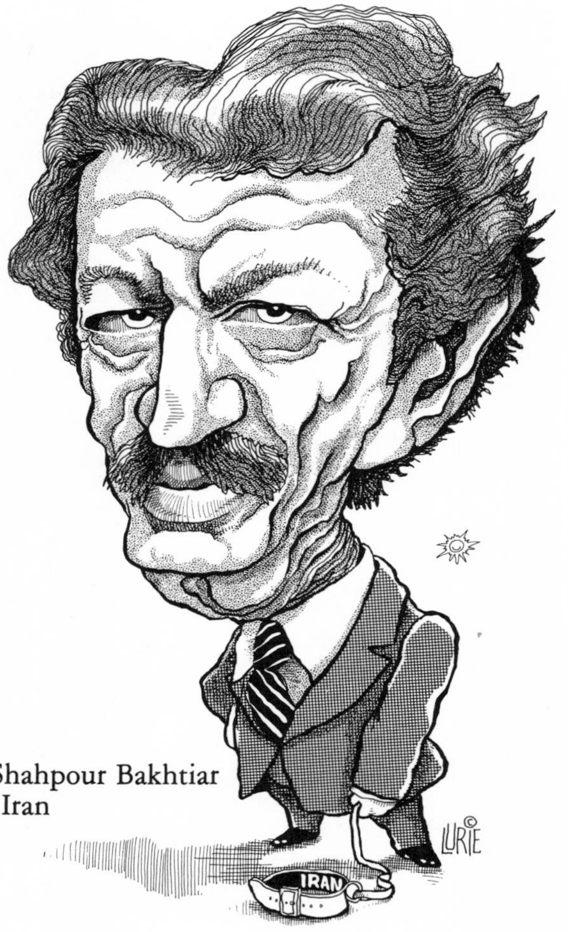
IRAN
LURIE
Prime Minister Shahpour Bakhtiar
of Iran

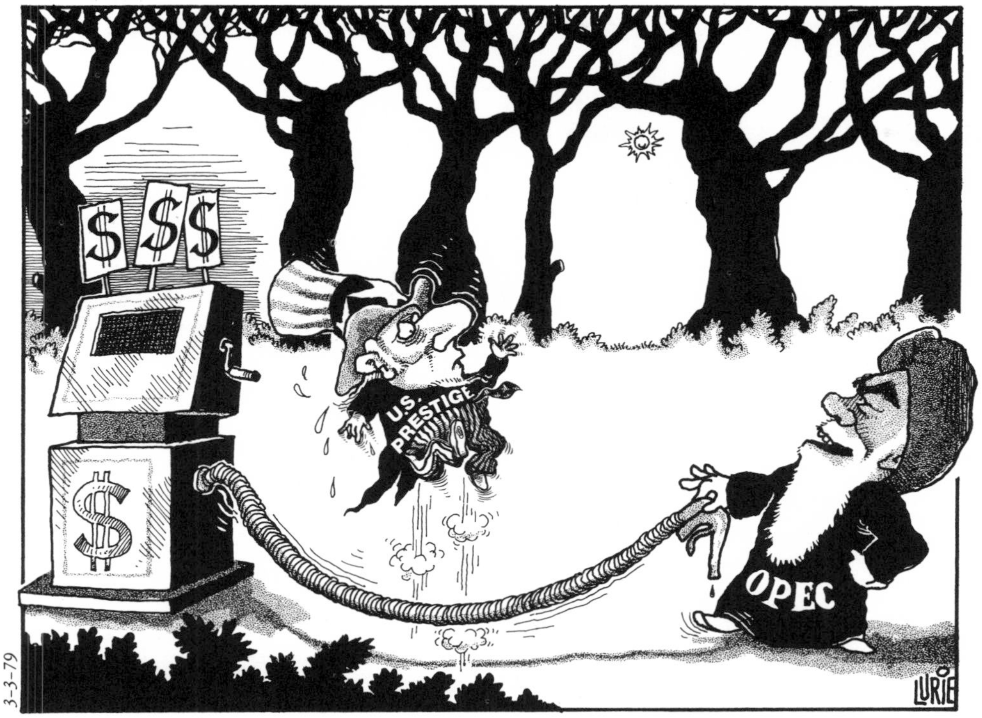
$$$
$
U.S. PRESTIGE
OPEC
3-3-79
LURIE

"GREAT WORK—YOU'RE LOSING WEIGHT RAPIDLY!"

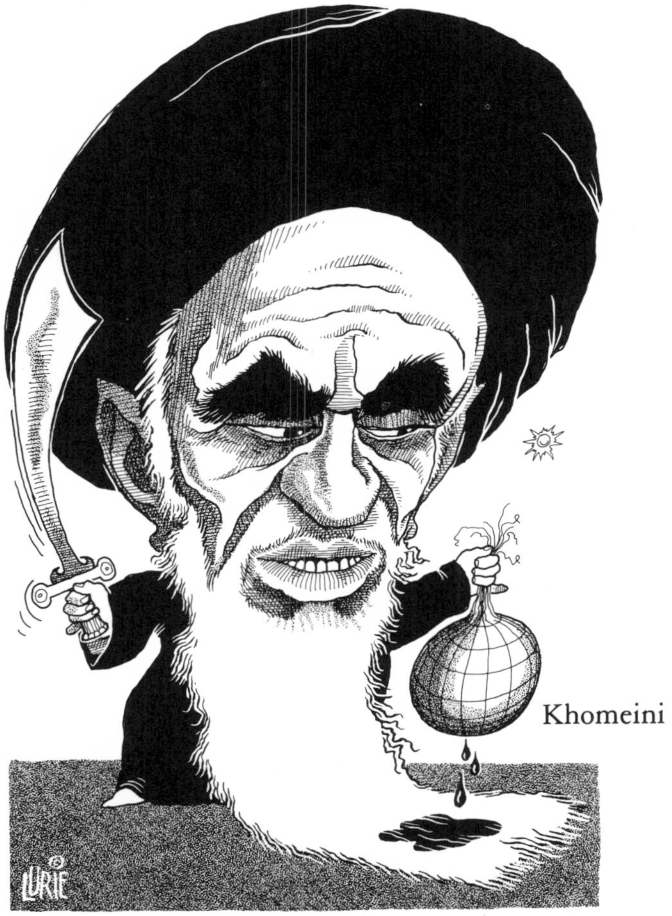
LURIE

Khomeini

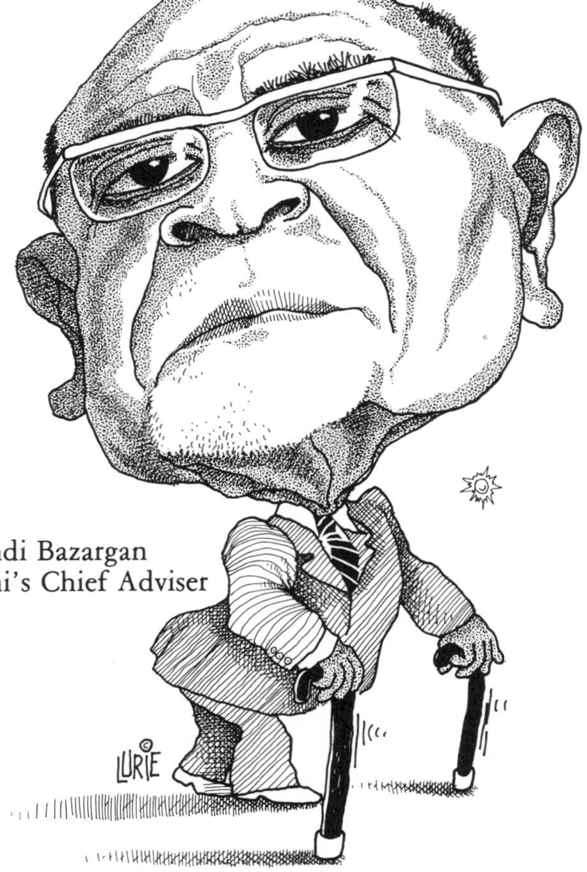
LURIE

Mehdi Bazargan
Khomeini's Chief Adviser

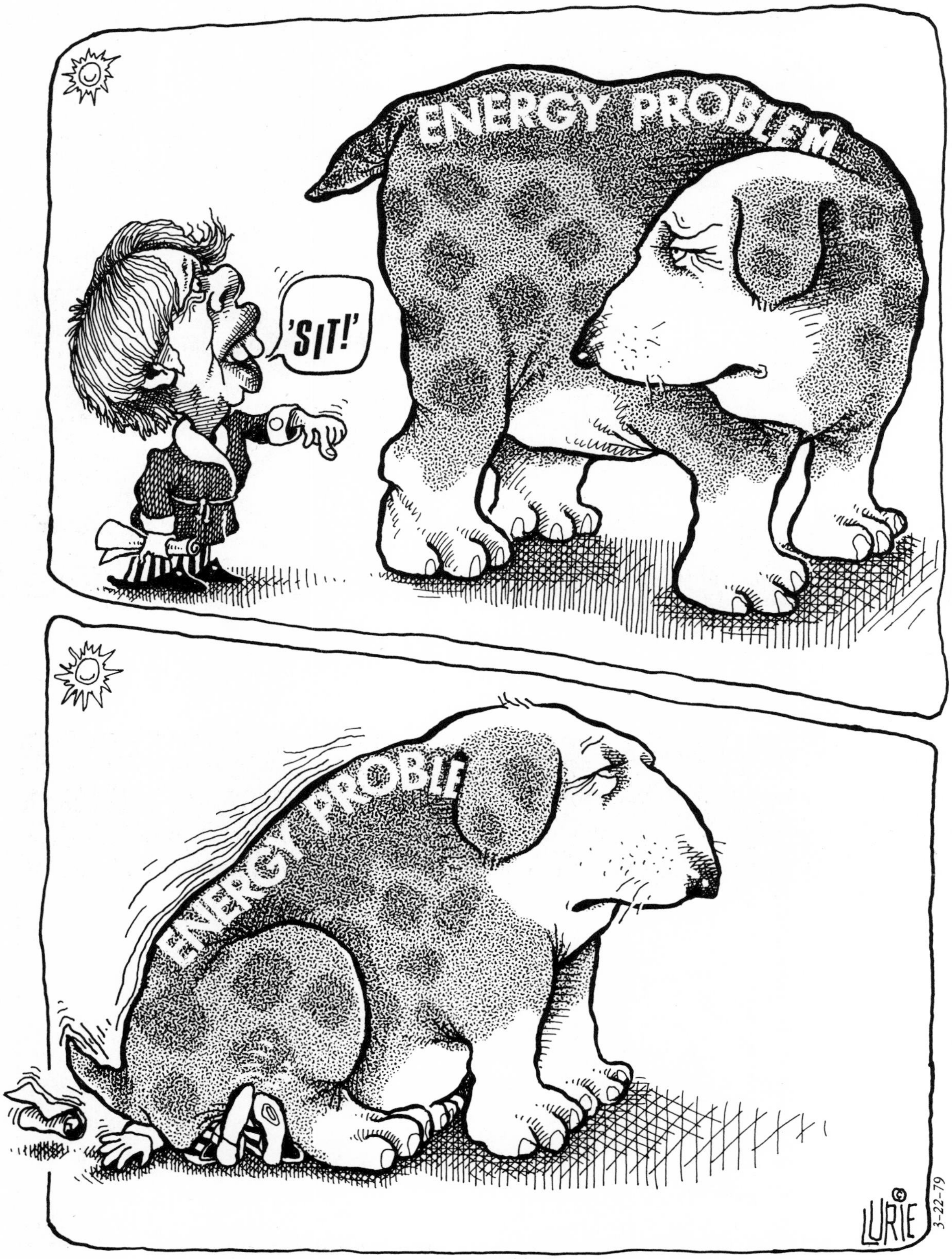
ENERGY PROBLEM
'SIT!'
ENERGY PROBLE
LURIE
3-22-79

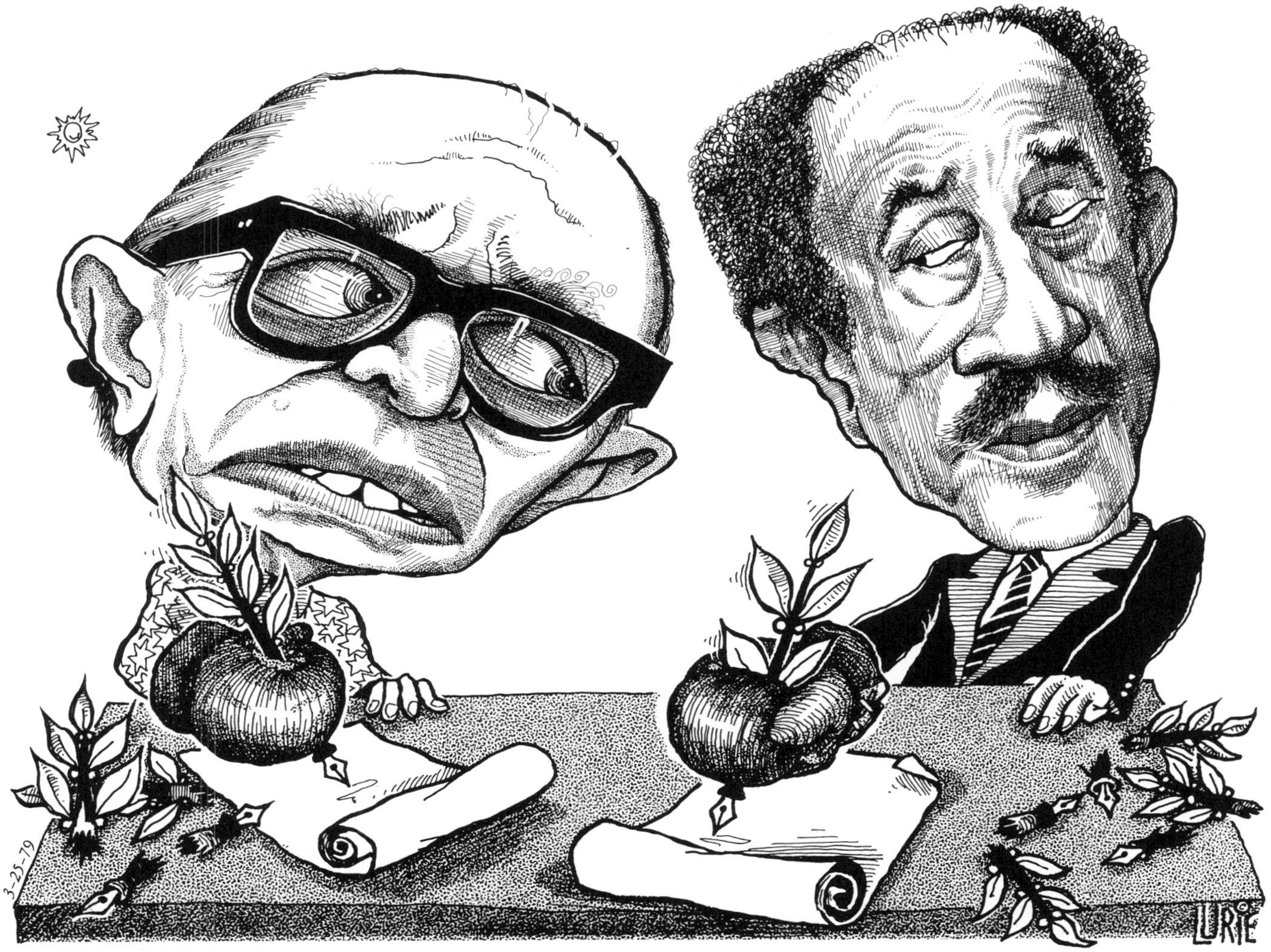
3-25-79
LURIE

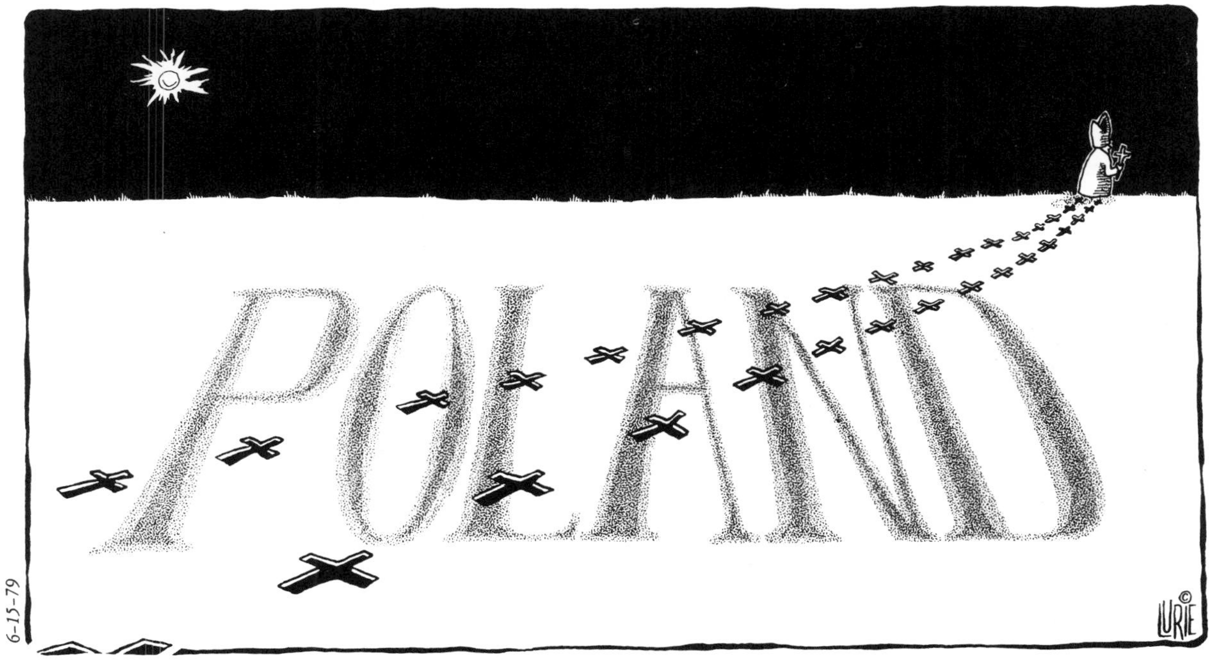
POLAND
6-15-79
LURIE ©

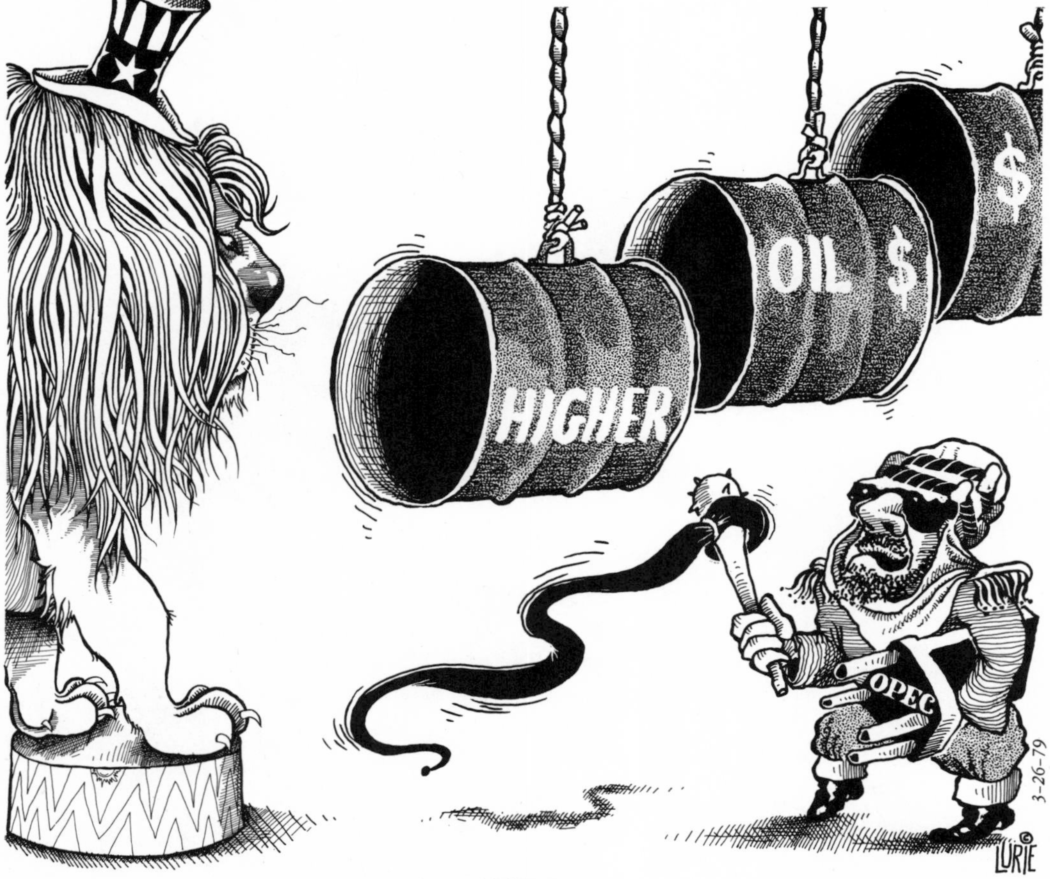
HIGHER
OIL
$
$
OPEC
3-26-79
LURIE

"JUMP!"

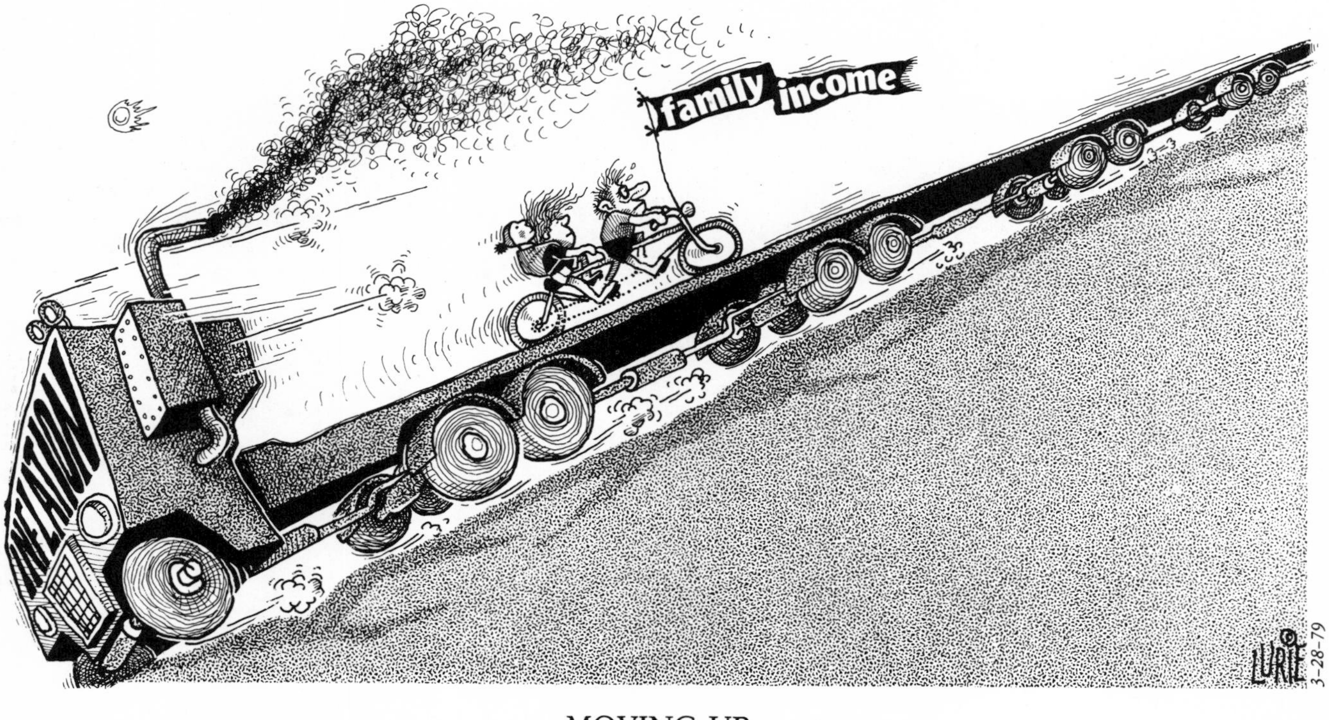
family income
INFLATION
LURIE
3-28-79

MOVING UP

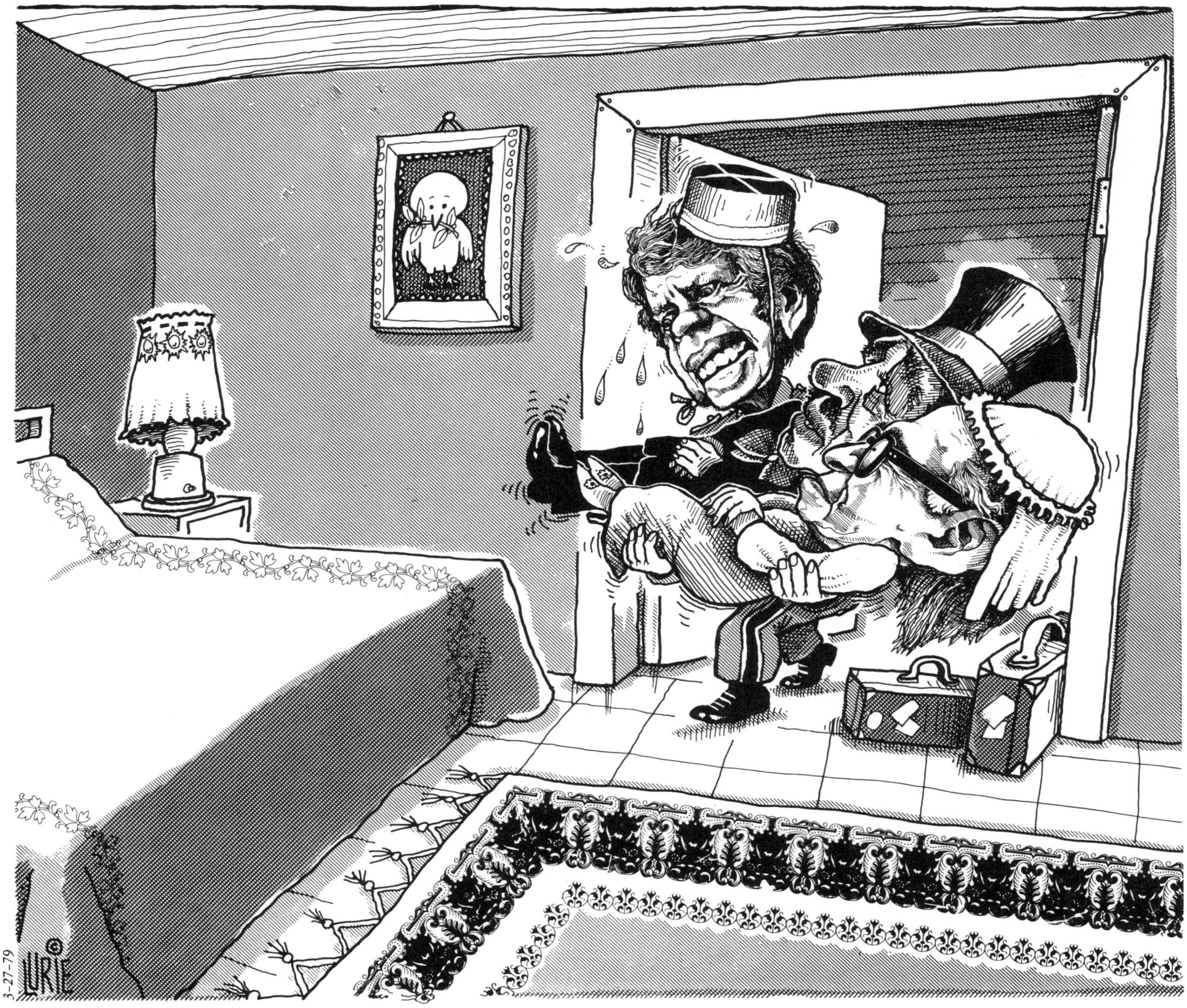
LURIE ©
3-27-79

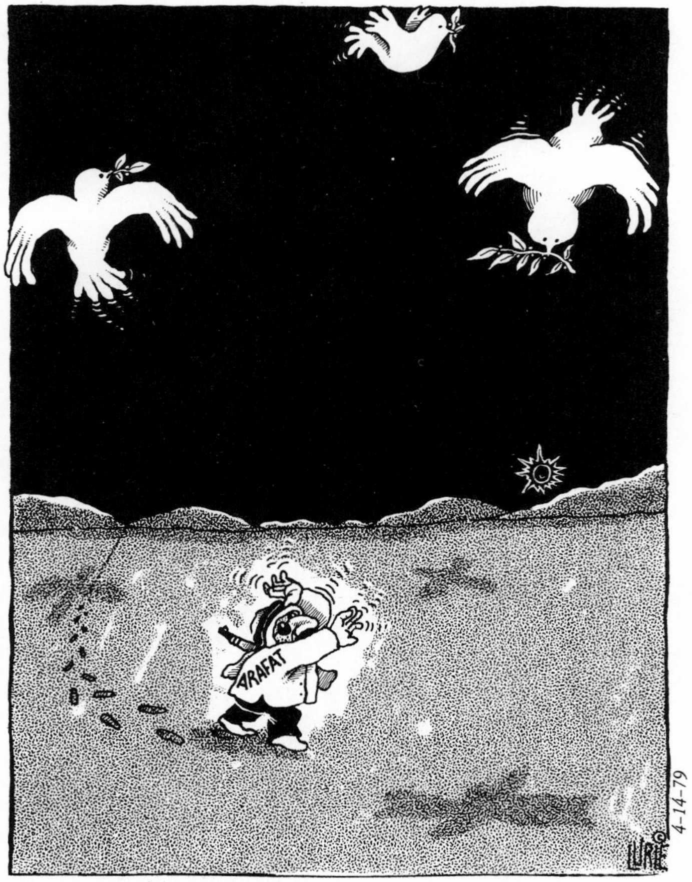
ARAFAT
4-14-79
LURIE

"THESE VULTURES ARE OUT TO GET ME!"

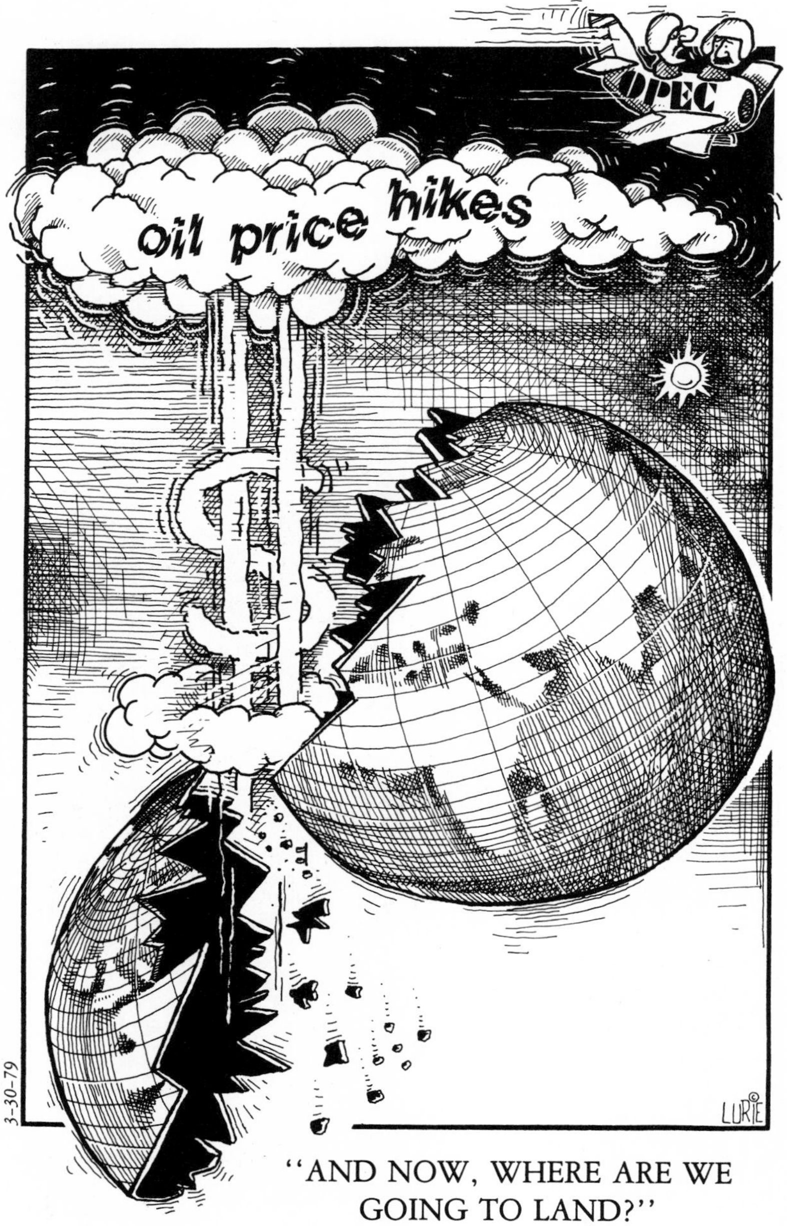
OPEC
oil price hikes
3-30-79
LURIE

"AND NOW, WHERE ARE WE GOING TO LAND?"

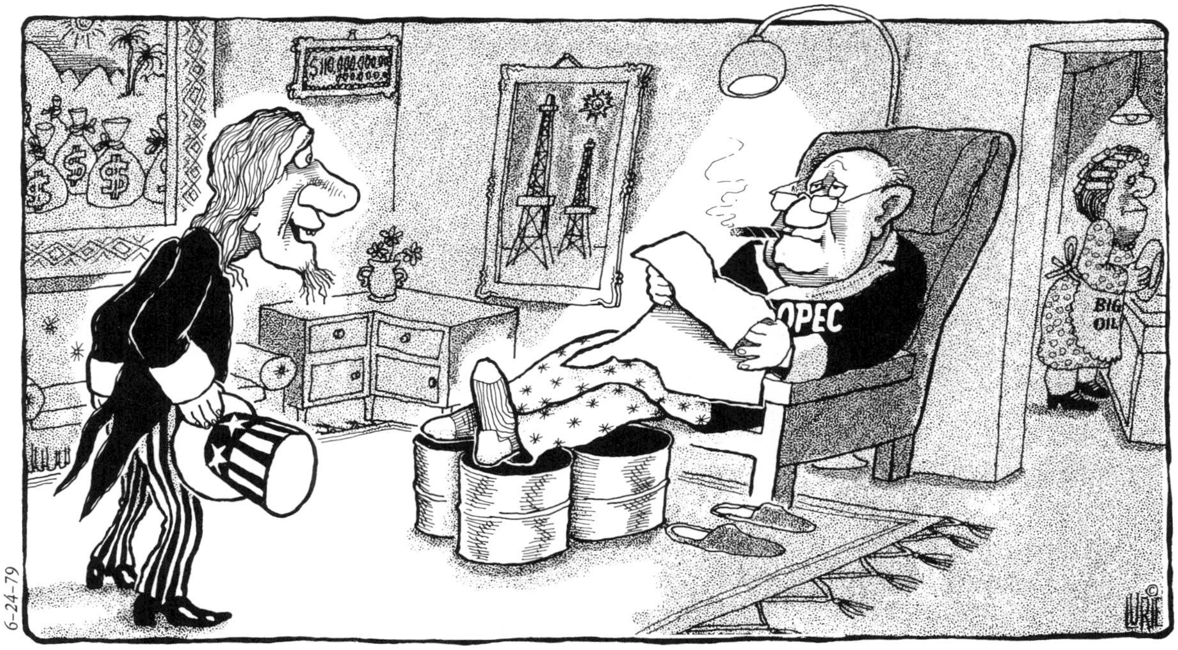
OPEC
BIG OIL
6-24-79
LURIE ©

"CAN I USE THE CAR TONIGHT, POP?"

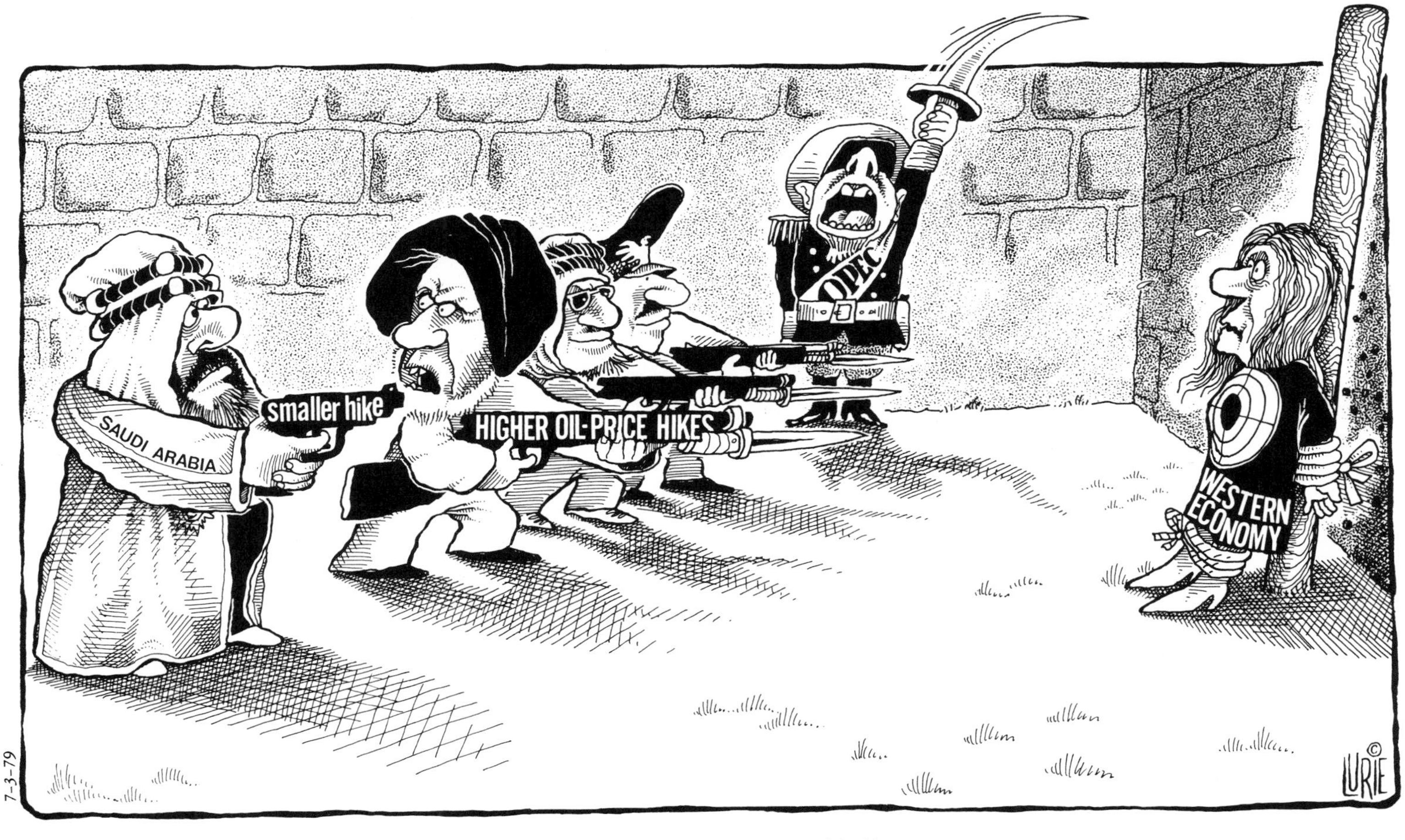
SAUDI ARABIA
smaller hike
HIGHER OIL-PRICE HIKES
OPEC
WESTERN ECONOMY
7-3-79
LURIE ©

"MR. NICE GUY, HA?!"

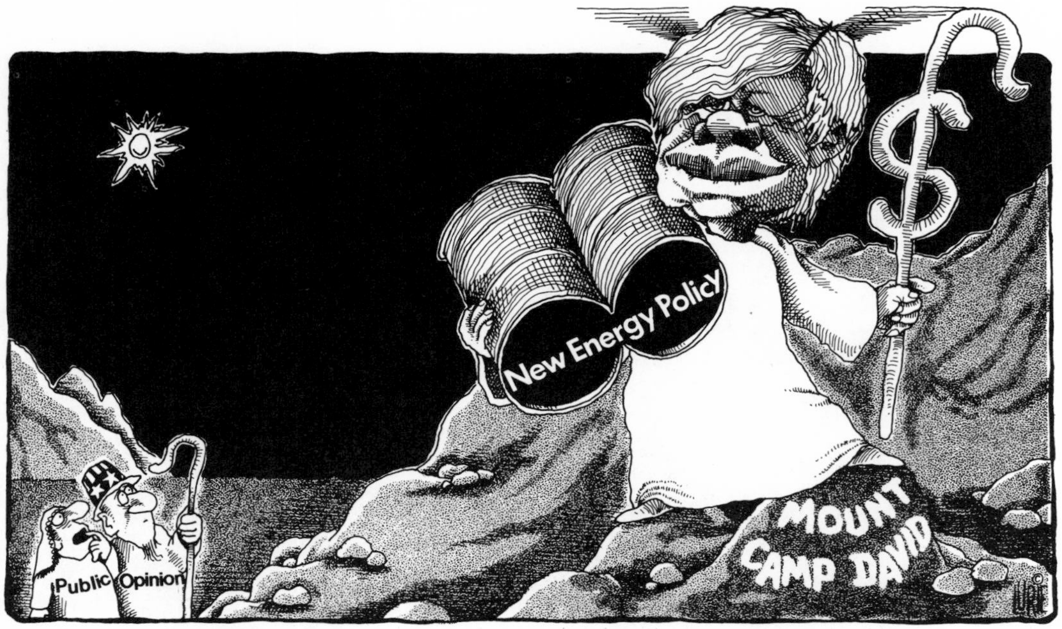
New Energy Policy
MOUNT CAMP DAVID
Public Opinion

''FROM THE WAY HE'S CARRYING THEM,
THEY DON'T LOOK TOO HEAVY.''

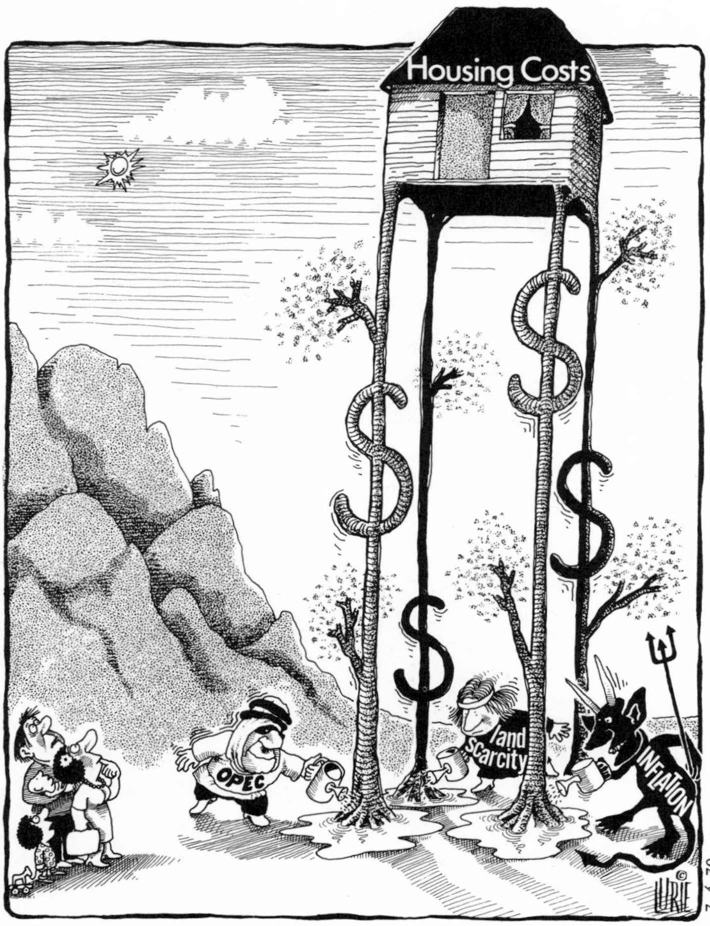
Housing Costs
Land scarcity
OPEC
INFLATION
7-4-79

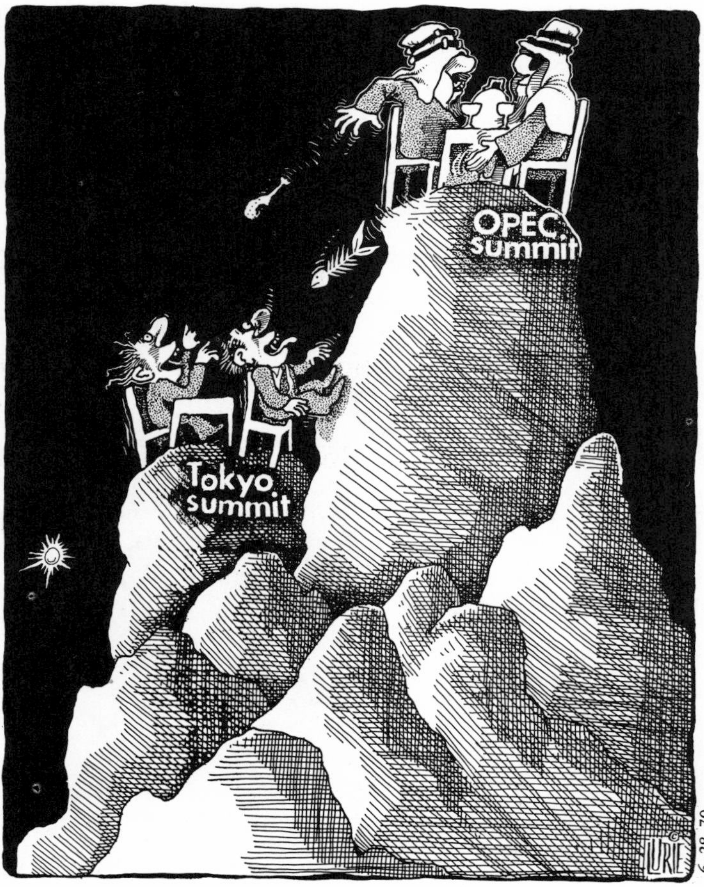
OPEC summit
Tokyo summit
6-28-79

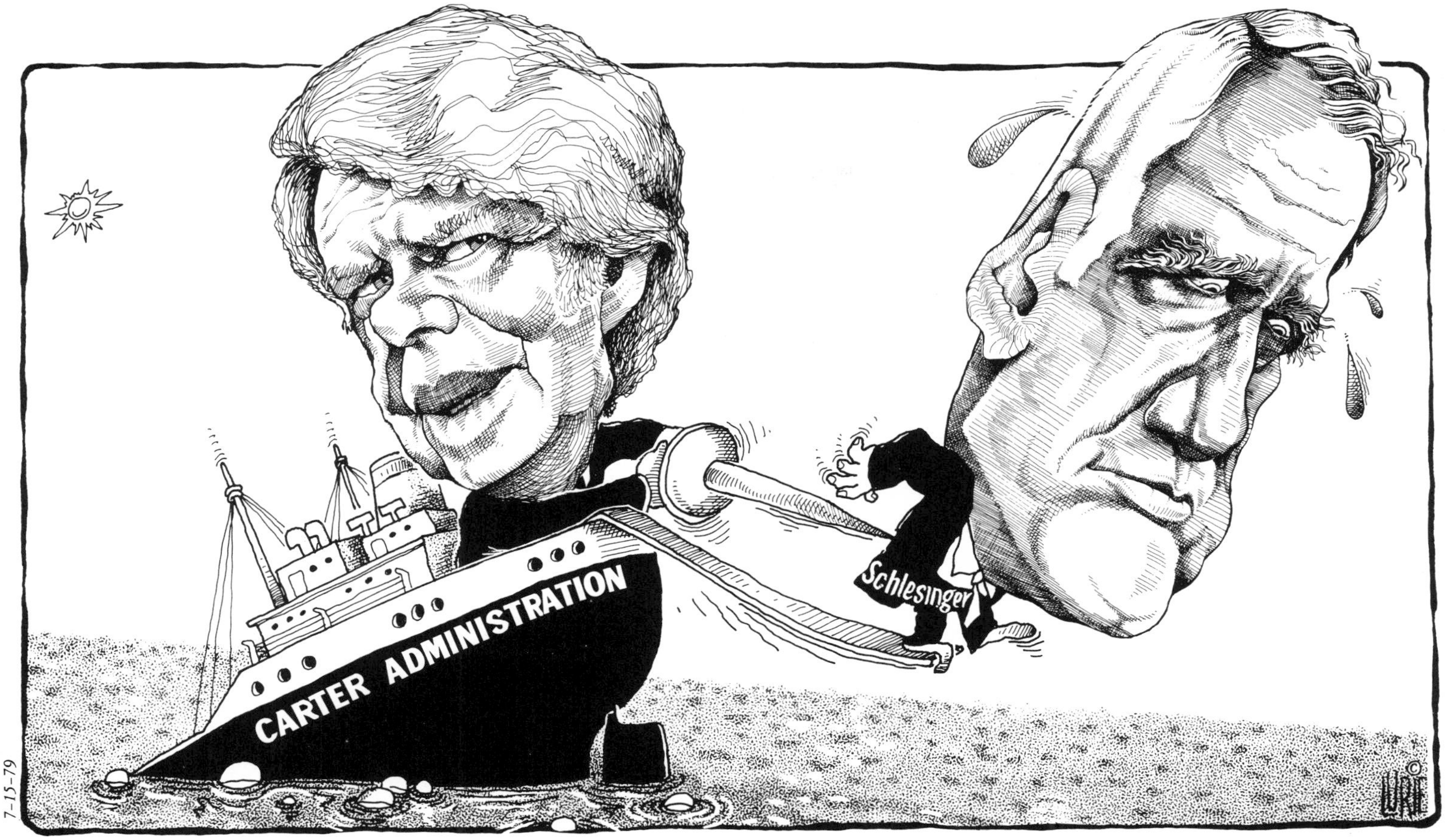
CARTER ADMINISTRATION
Schlesinger
LURIE ©

7-15-79

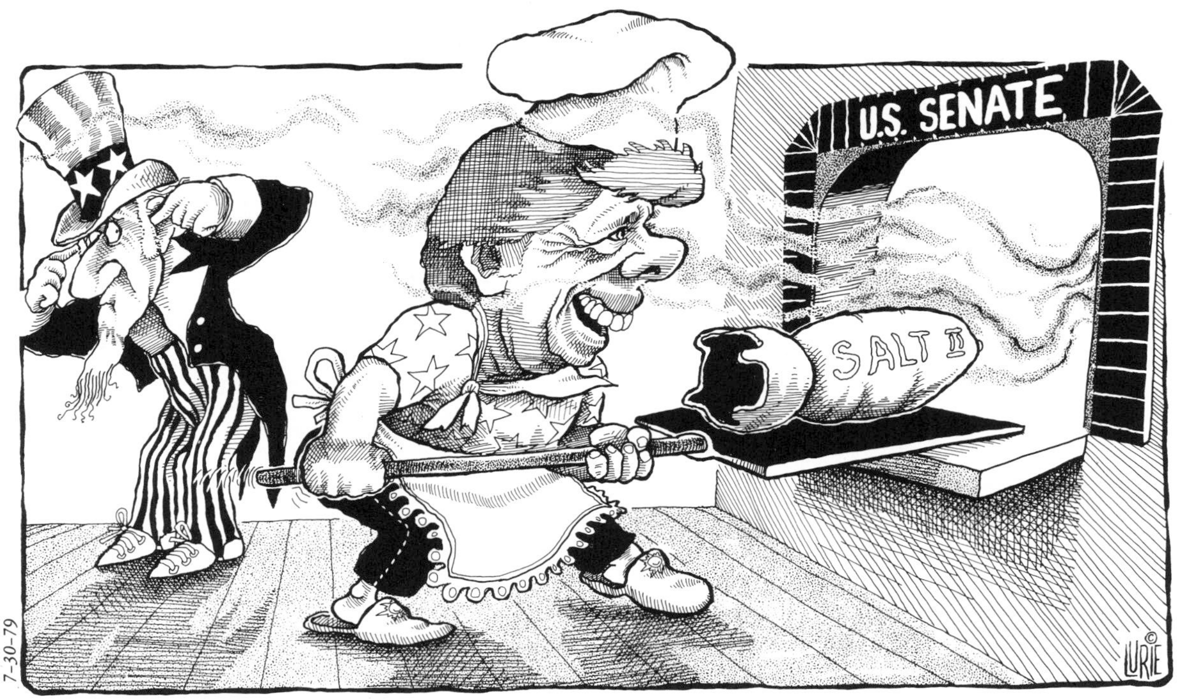
U.S. SENATE
SALT II
LURIE ©

7-30-79

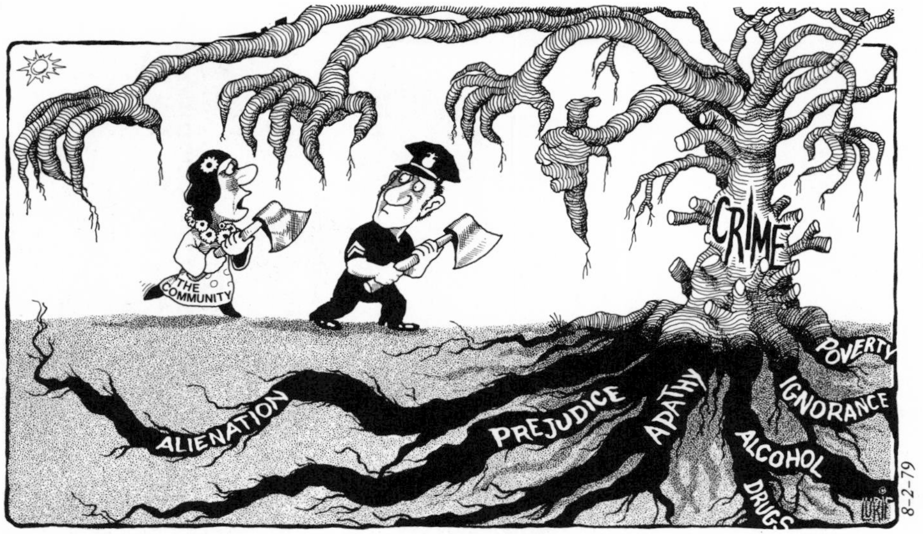
CRIME
THE COMMUNITY
POVERTY
IGNORANCE
ALIENATION
PREJUDICE
APATHY
ALCOHOL
DRUGS
8-2-79

"SHOULDN'T WE START WITH THE ROOTS?!"

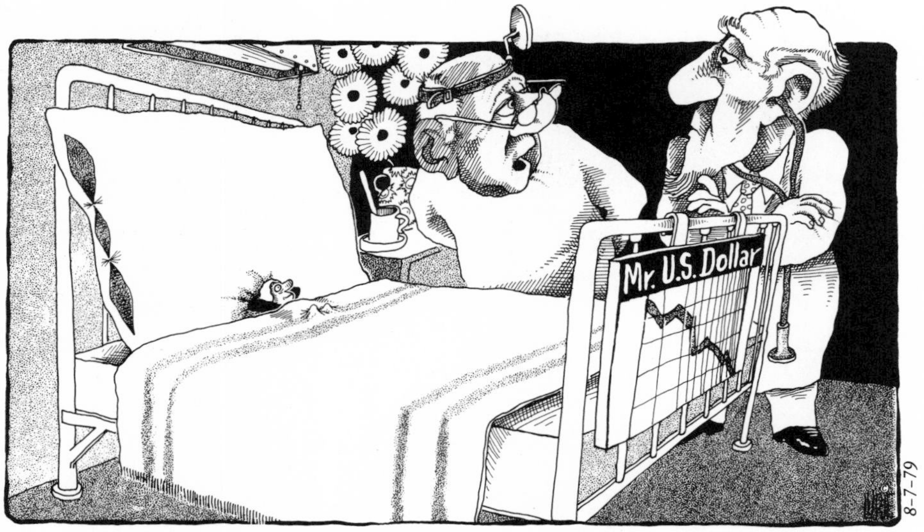
Mr. U.S. Dollar
8-7-79

"ASIDE FROM BECOMING SMALLER AND SMALLER, HE FEELS GREAT."

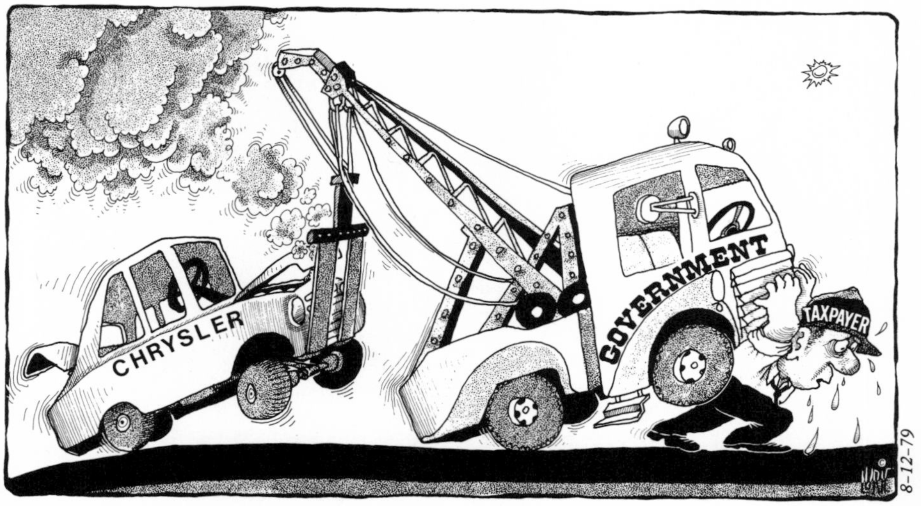
CHRYSLER
GOVERNMENT
TAXPAYER
8-12-79

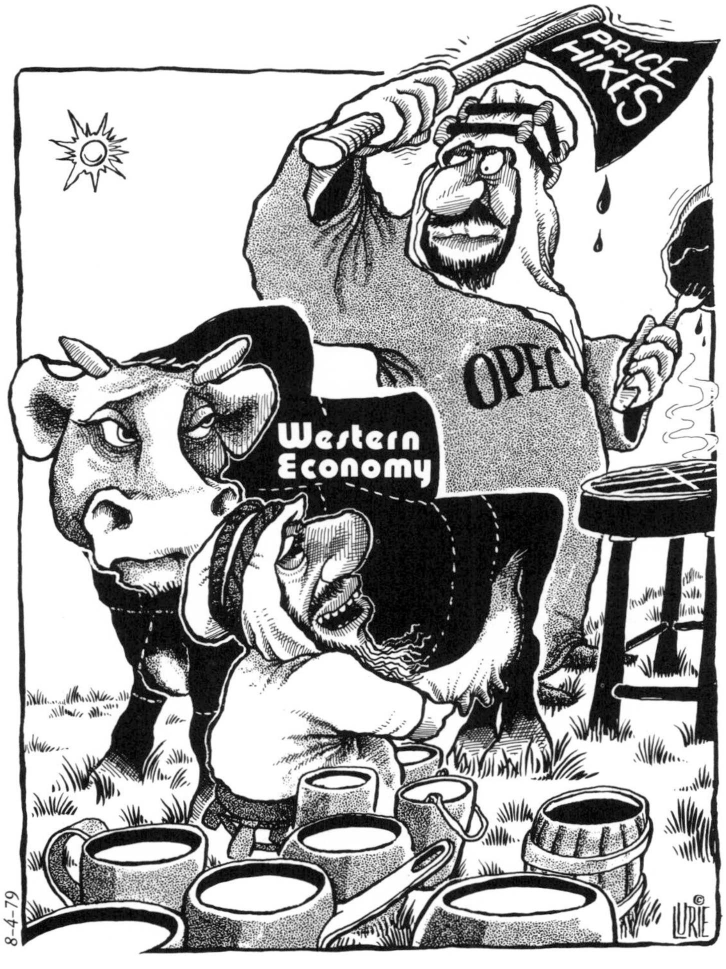
PRICE HIKES
OPEC
Western Economy
8-4-79
LURIE

"CUT SLOWER—
THERE'S STILL LOTS OF MILK LEFT!"

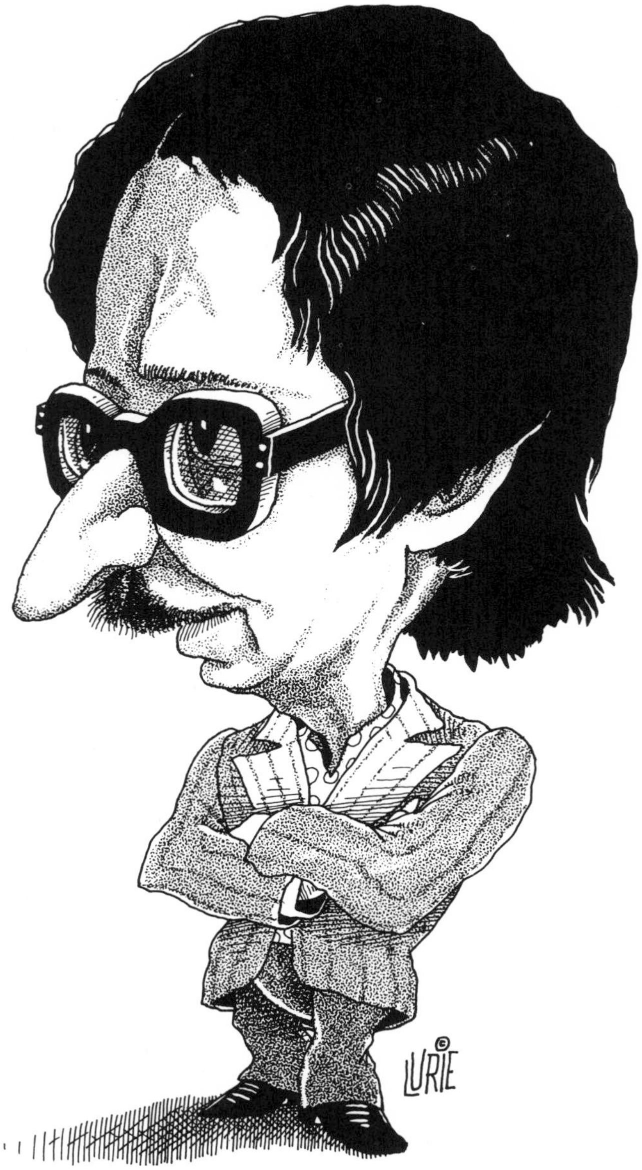
LURIE

Abol Hassan Bani-Sadr
Acting Foreign Minister of Iran

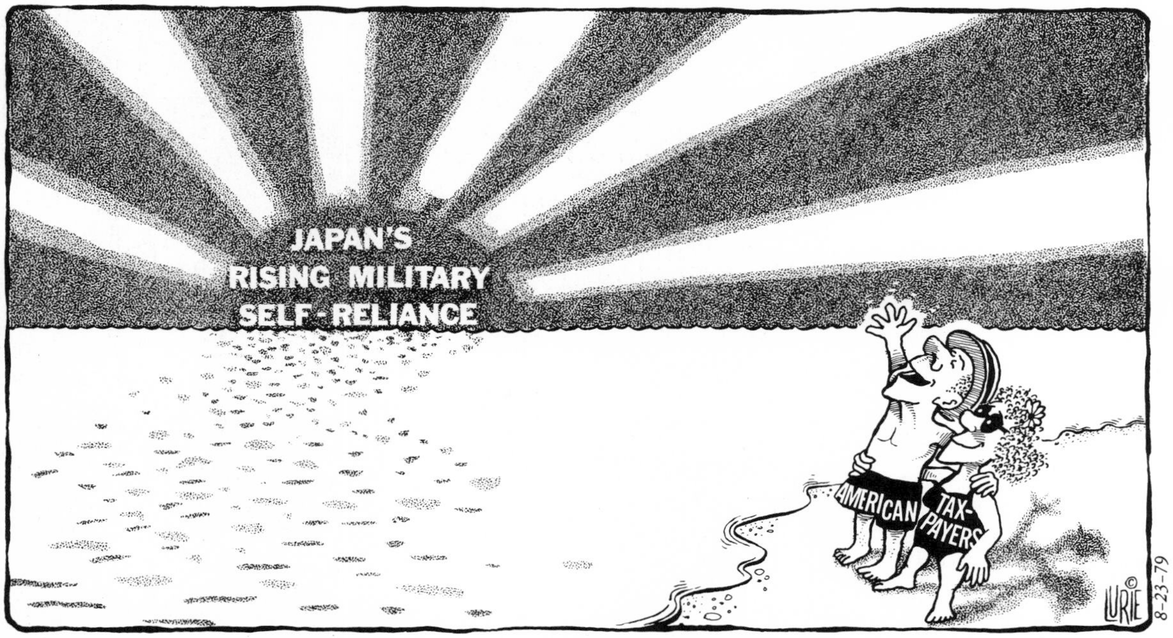
JAPAN'S
RISING MILITARY
SELF-RELIANCE
AMERICAN
TAX-PAYERS
LURIE ©
8-23-79

"AFTER 34 COLD YEARS, WE DESERVE THIS SUNNY VACATION!"

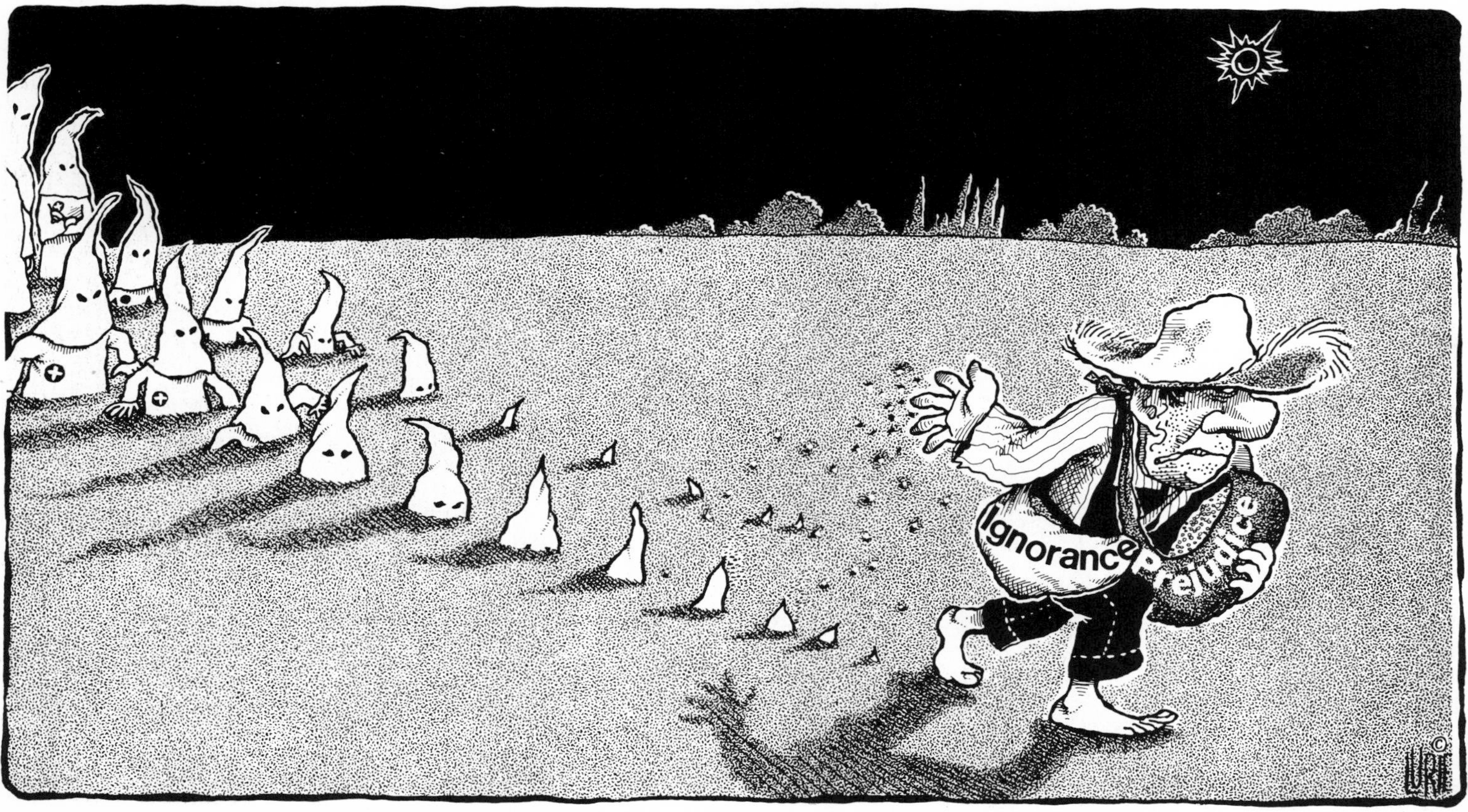
Ignorance
Prejudice
LURIE ©
8-18-79

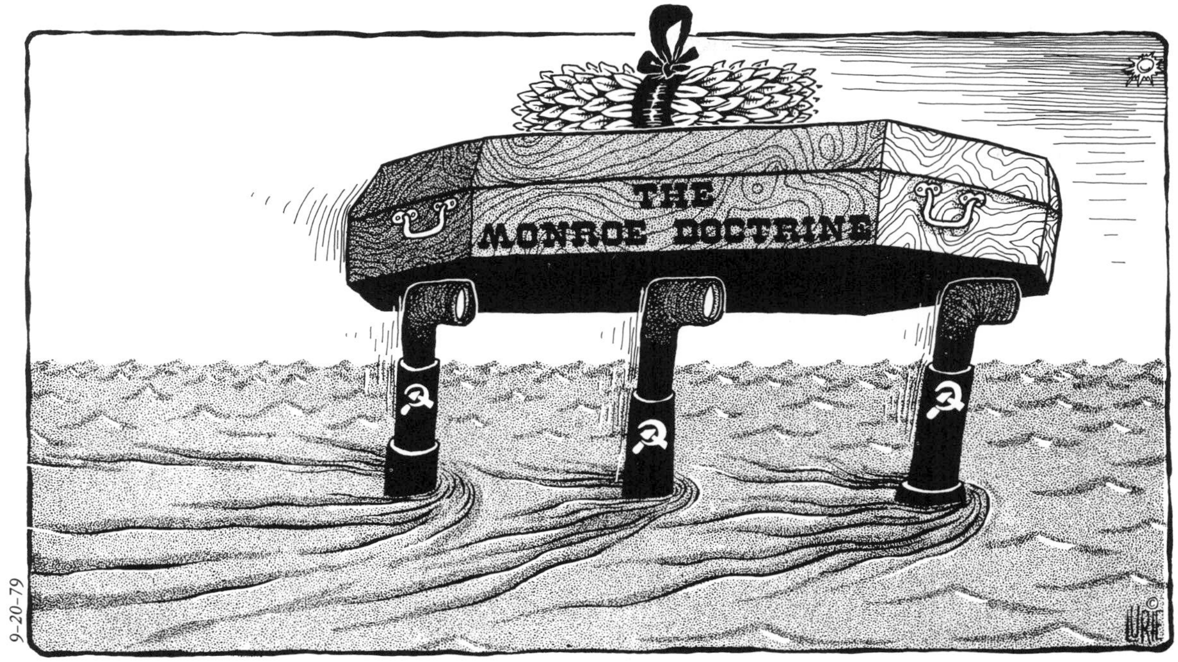
THE
MONROE DOCTRINE
9-20-79
LURIE ©

SEA BURIAL

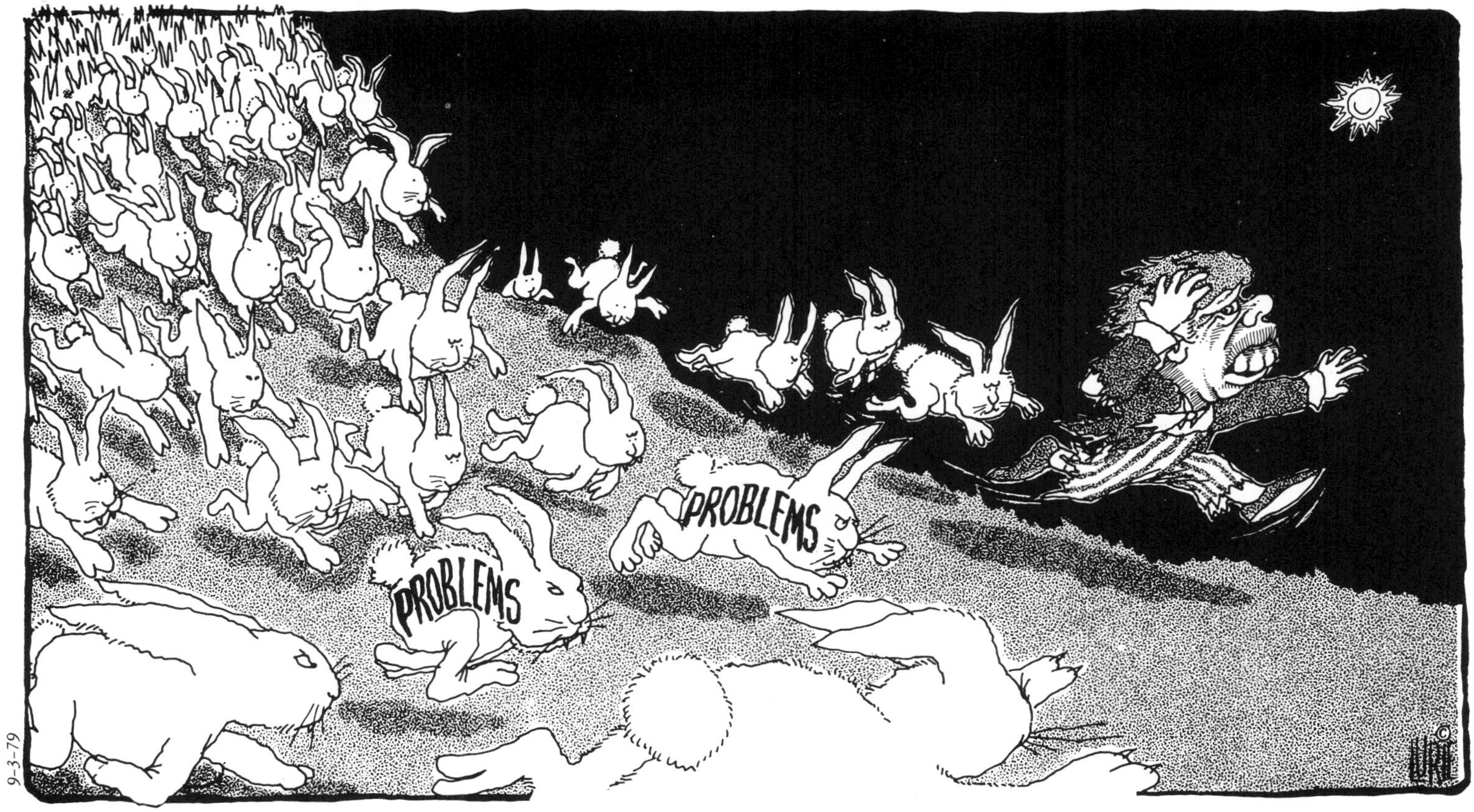
PROBLEMS
PROBLEMS
9-3-79
LURIE ©

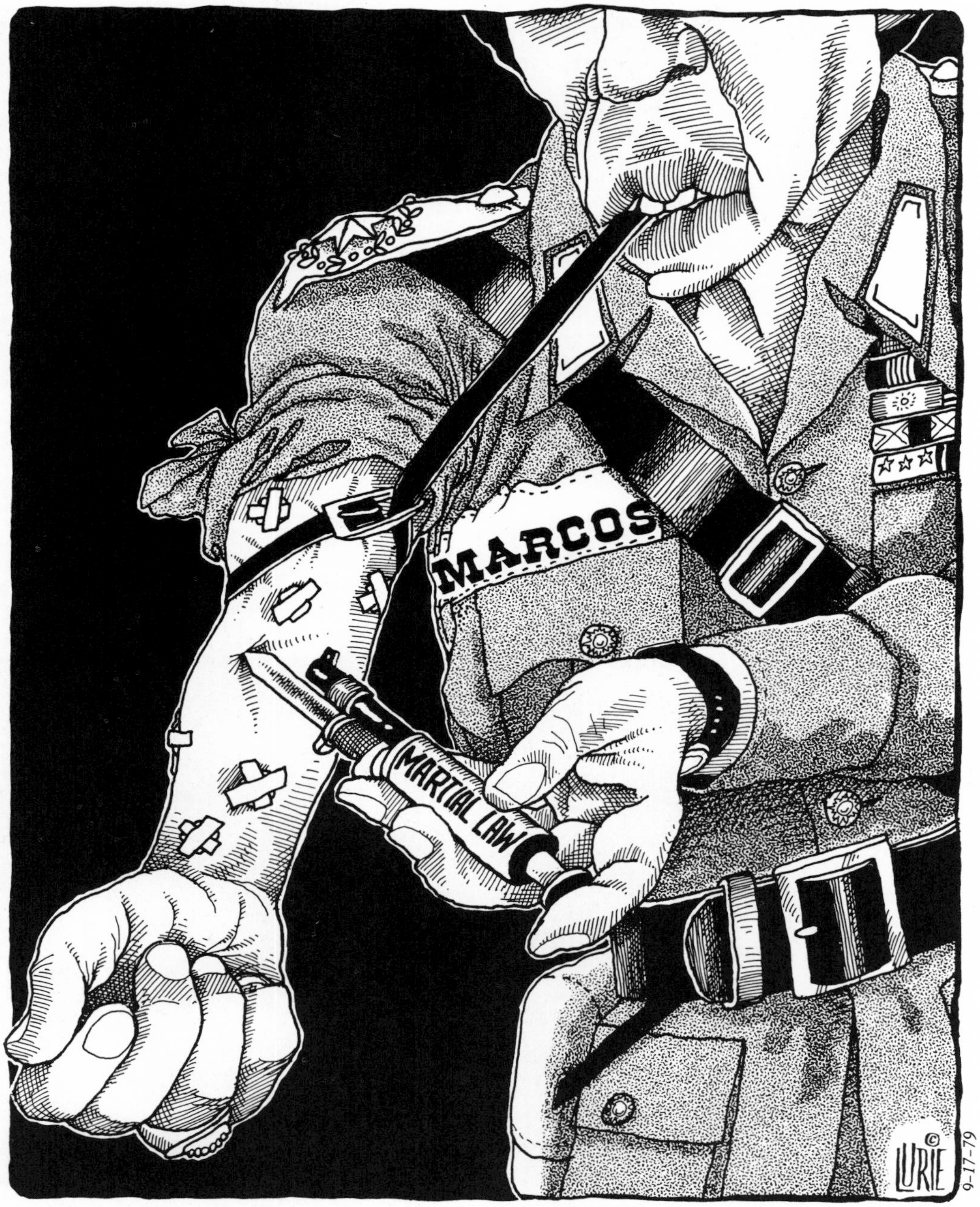
MARCOS
MARTIAL LAW
LURIE
9-17-79

THE ADDICT

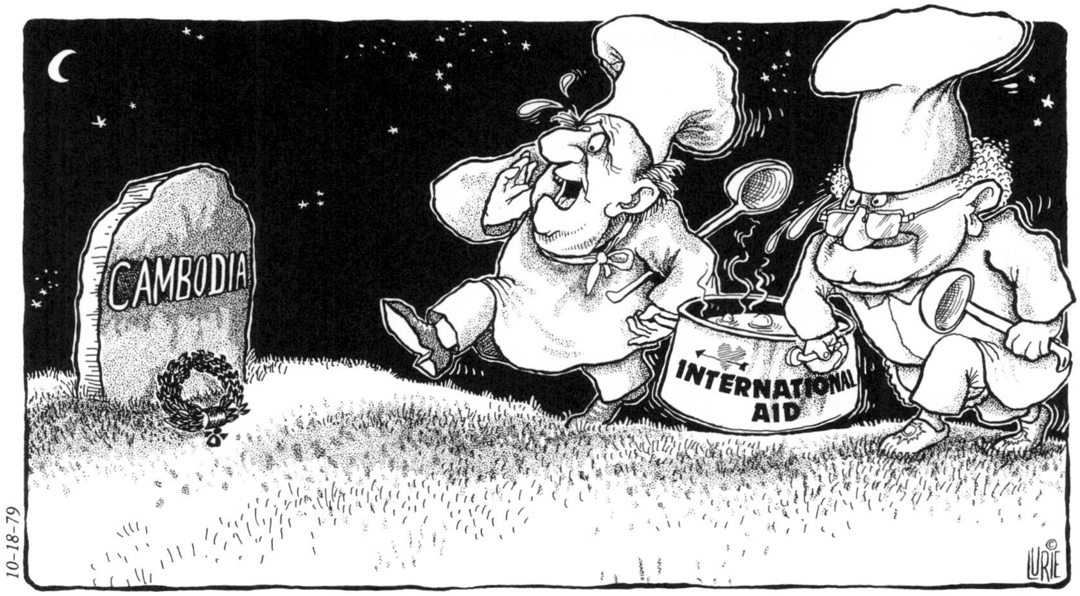
CAMBODIA
INTERNATIONAL AID
10-18-79
LURIE ©

"SORRY FOR BEING SOMEWHAT LATE . . ."

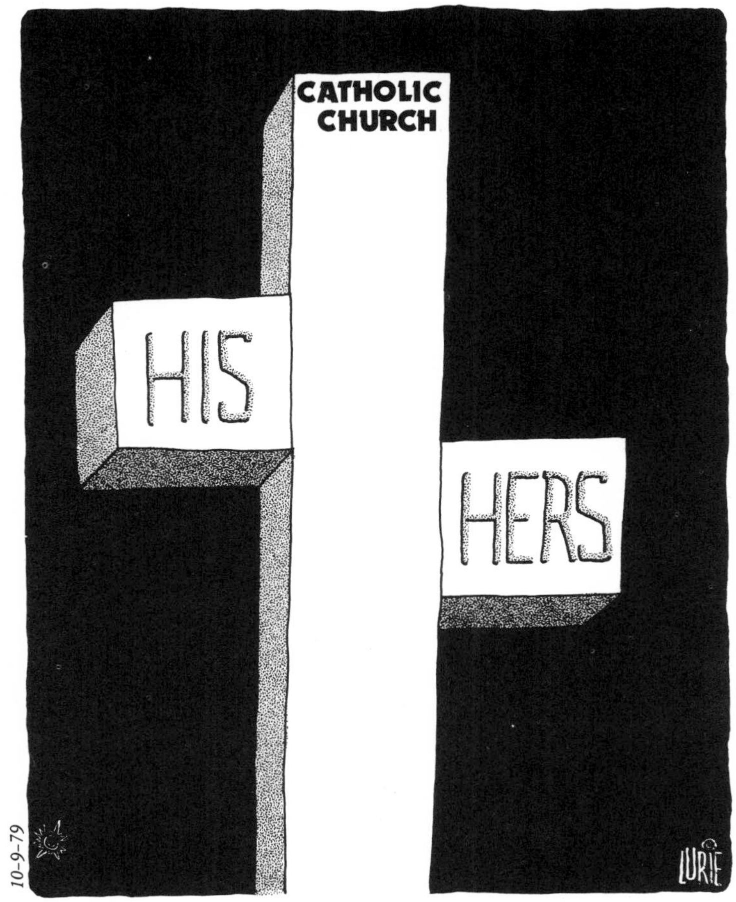
CATHOLIC CHURCH
HIS
HERS
10-9-79
LURIE ©

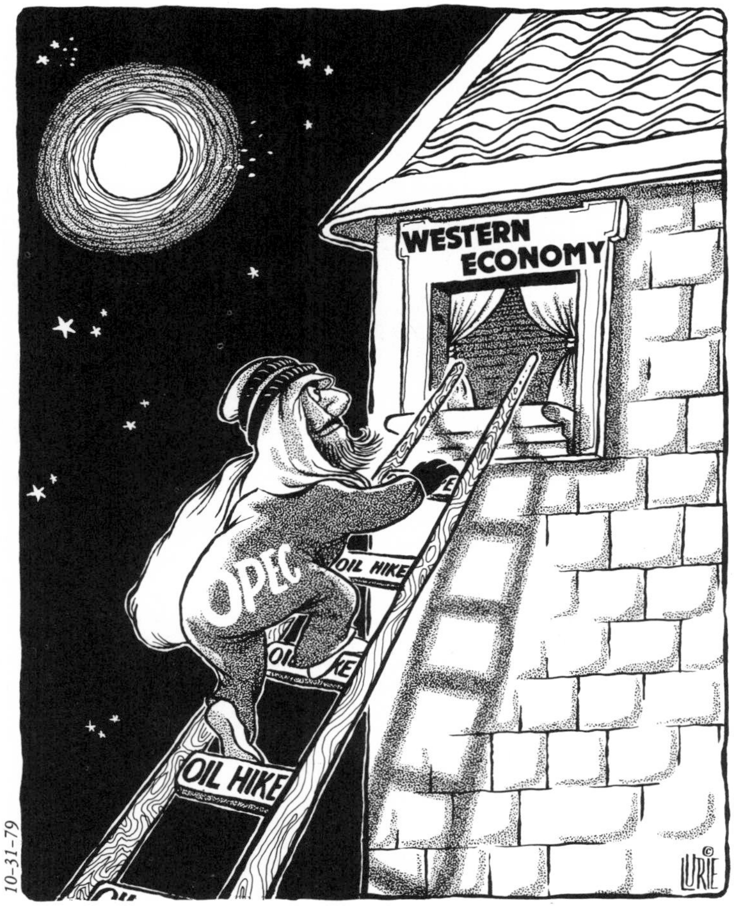
WESTERN ECONOMY
OPEC
OIL HIKE
OIL HIKE
10-31-79
LURIE ©

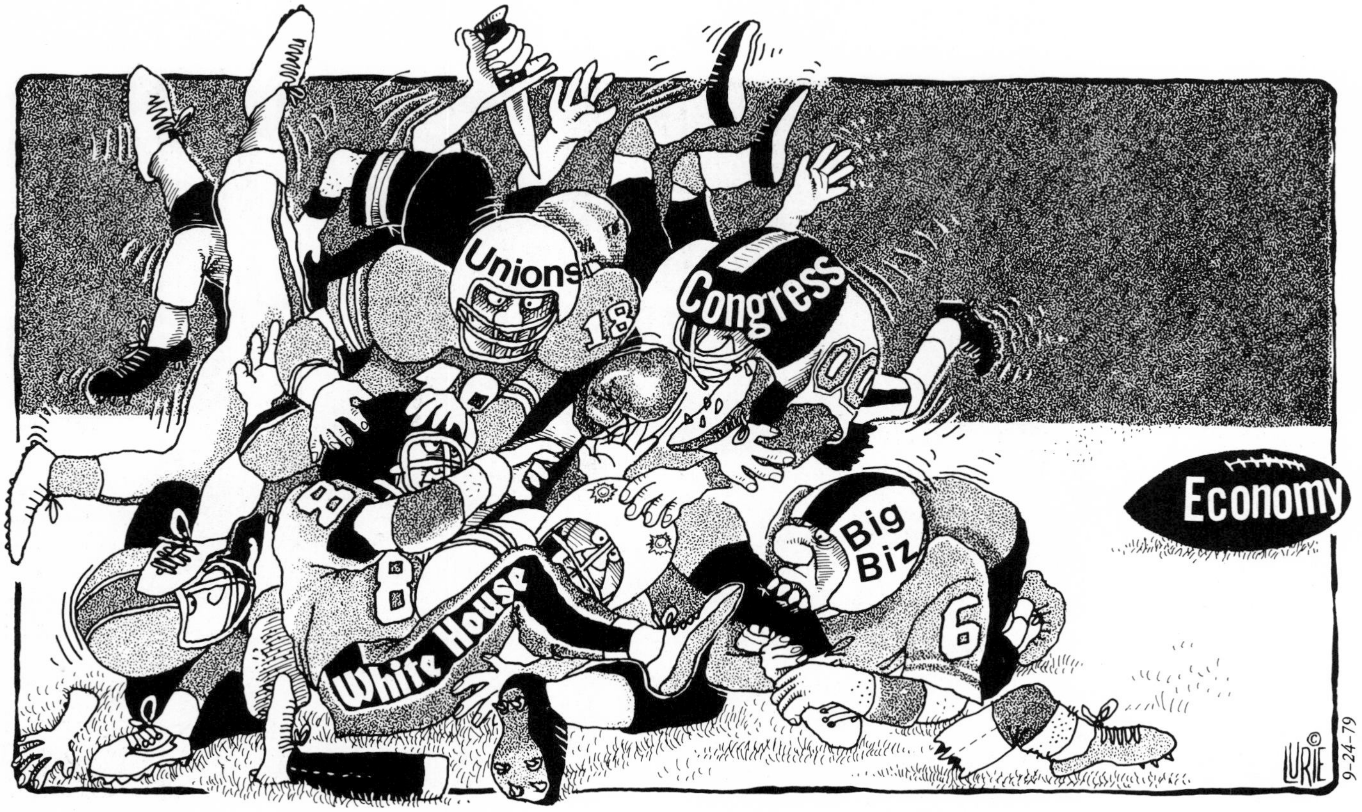

Unions
18
Congress
White House
8
Big Biz
6
Economy
LURIE ©
9-24-79

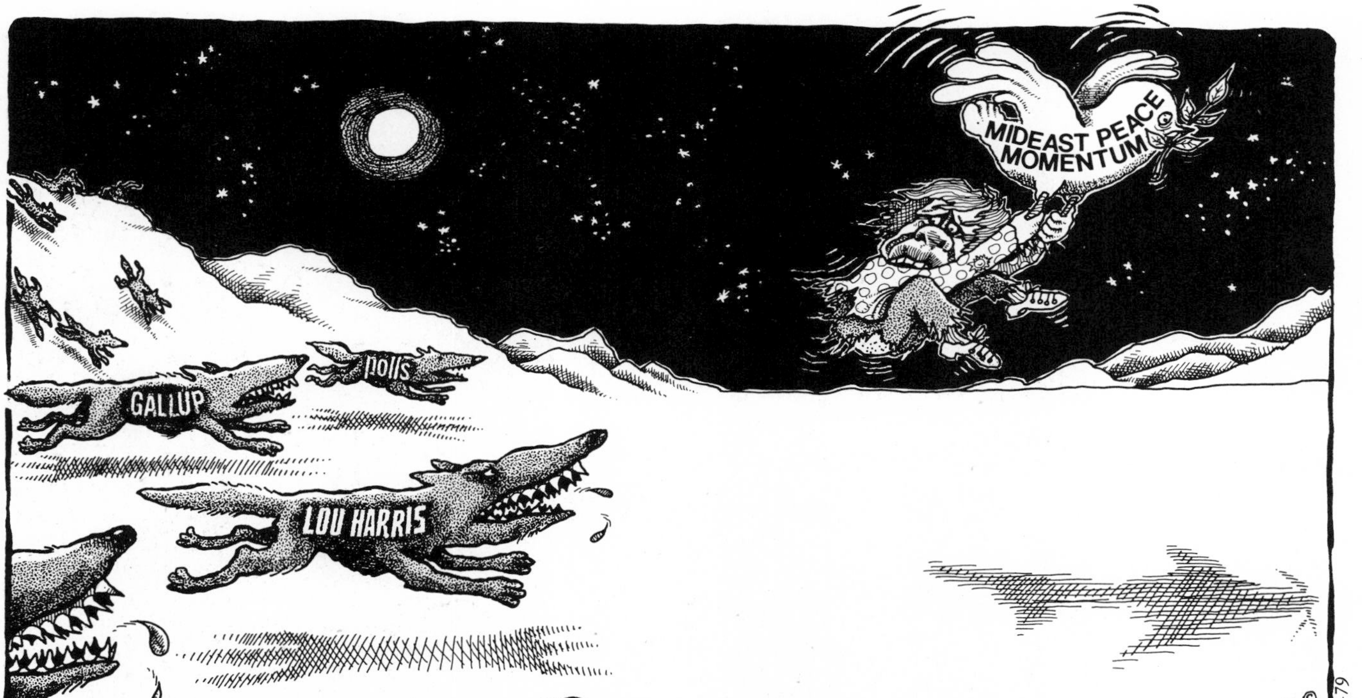

MIDEAST PEACE MOMENTUM
GALLUP
polls
LOU HARRIS
LURIE ©
9-21-79

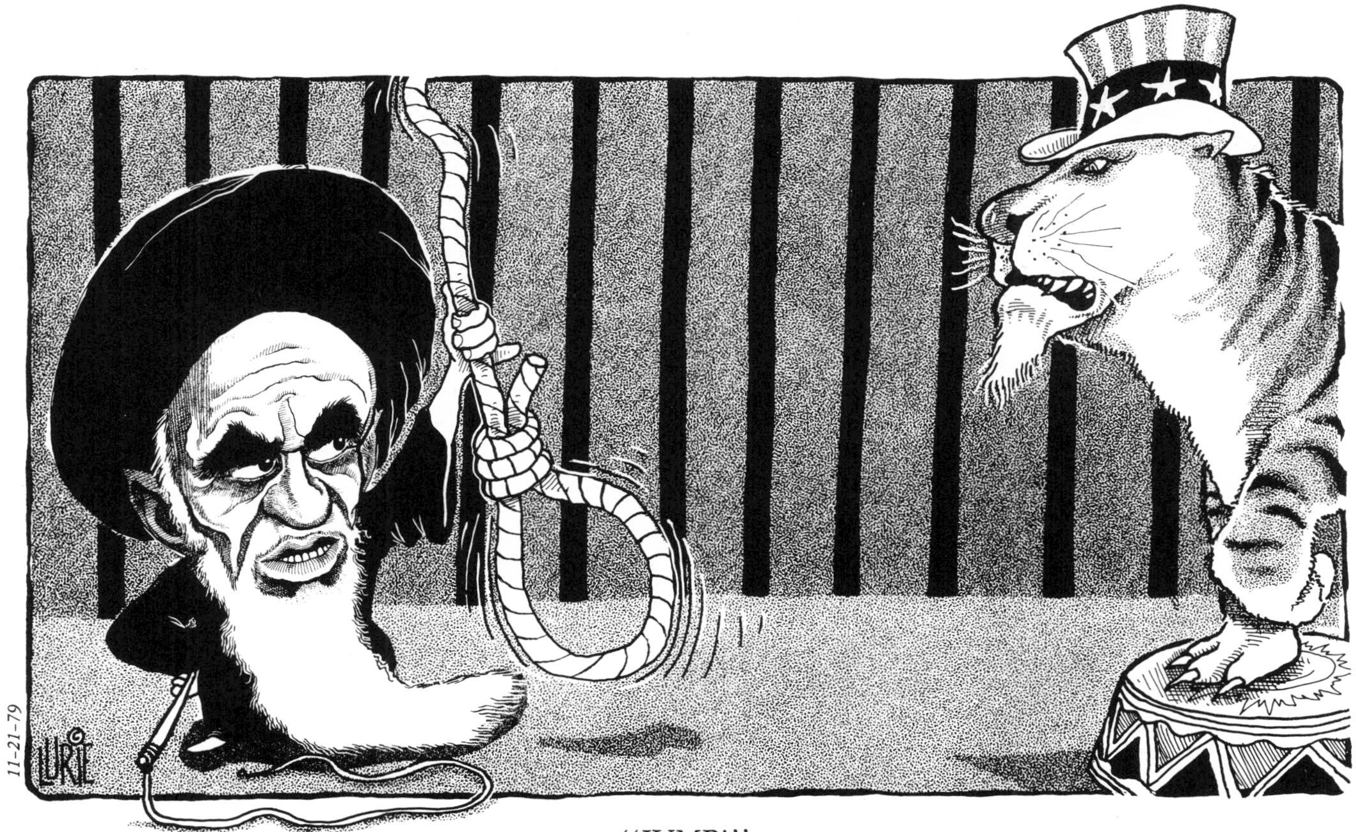
11-21-79
LURIE

"JUMP!"

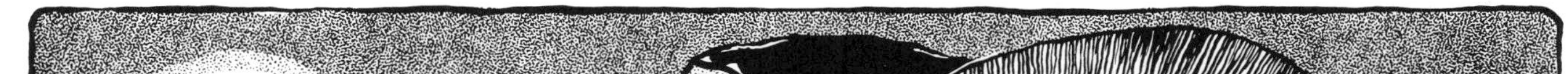
RACISM
KKK
11-9-79
LURIE

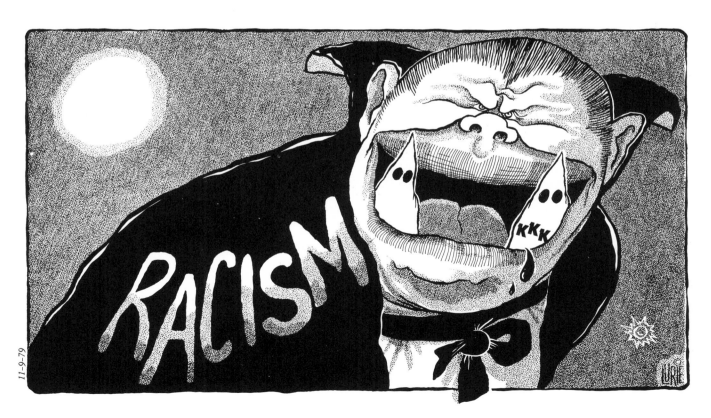

11-12-79
LURIE ©

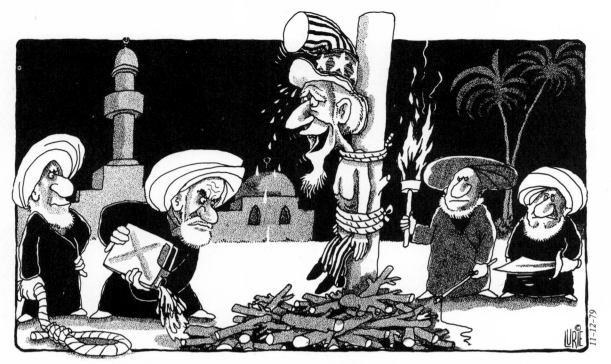

"I'LL BE DELIGHTED TO SET UP A MEETING, AND NEGOTIATE, AT OUR MUTUALLY AGREED-UPON CONVENIENCE, GUYS."

ECONOMIC & POLITICAL
DISASTERS
west bank settlements
LURIE ©
11-5-79

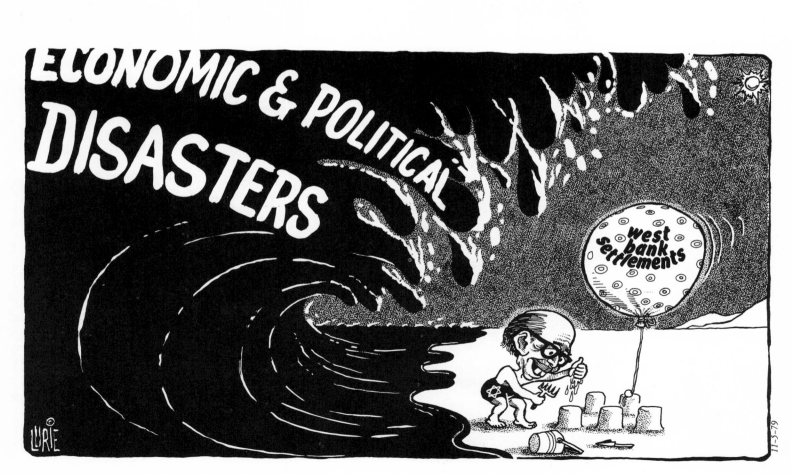

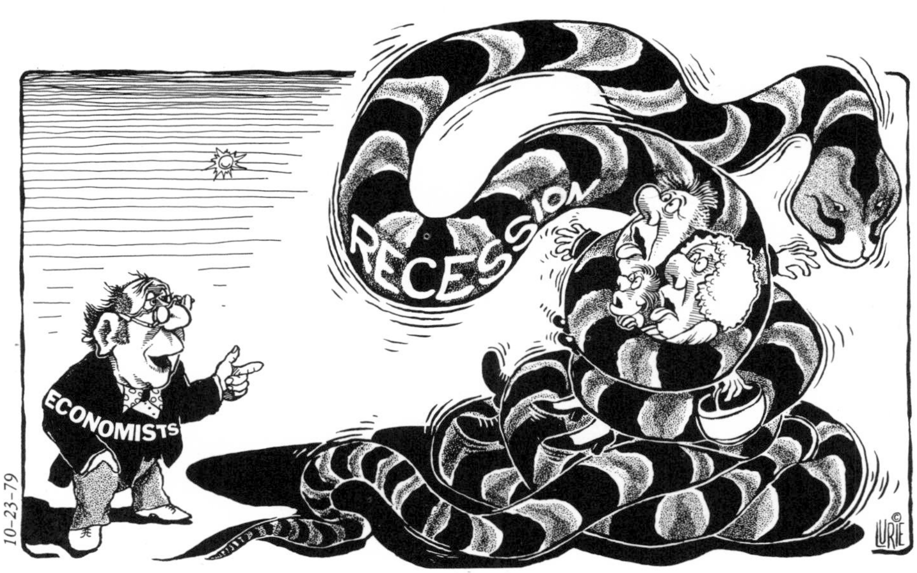
RECESSION
ECONOMISTS
10-23-79
LURIE©

"YOU SHOULD CONSIDER YOURSELF LUCKY—
HE'S NOT POISONOUS!"

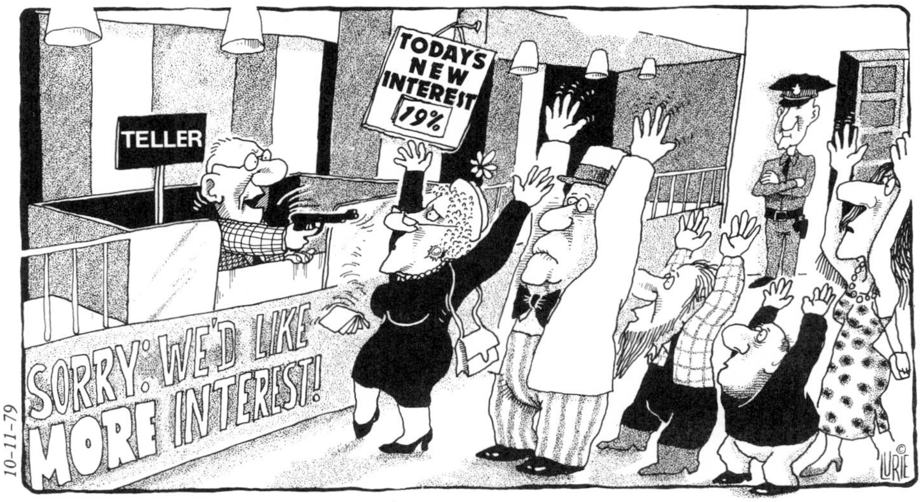
TELLER
TODAYS NEW INTEREST
19%
SORRY: WE'D LIKE
MORE INTEREST!
10-11-79
LURIE©

"THIS IS A HOLDUP!"

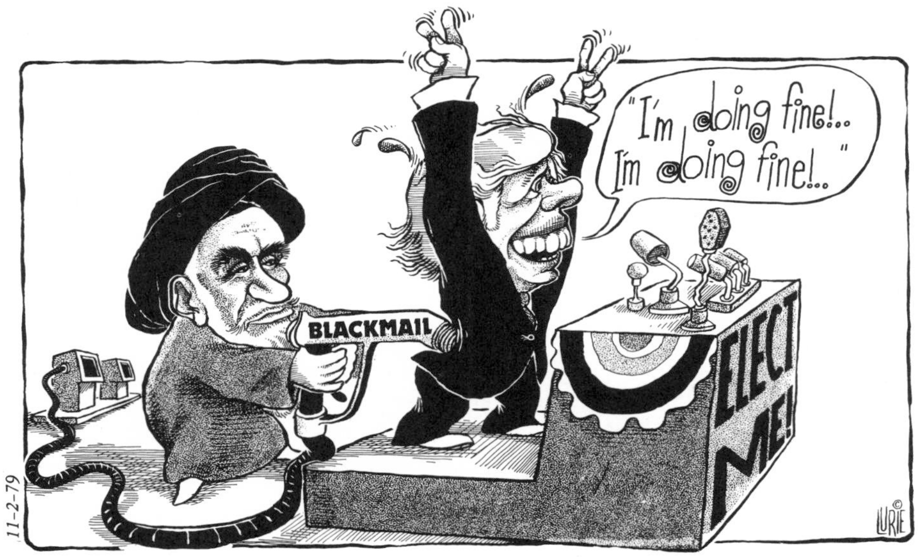
"I'm doing fine!..
I'm doing fine!..."
BLACKMAIL
ELECT ME!
11-2-79
LURIE©

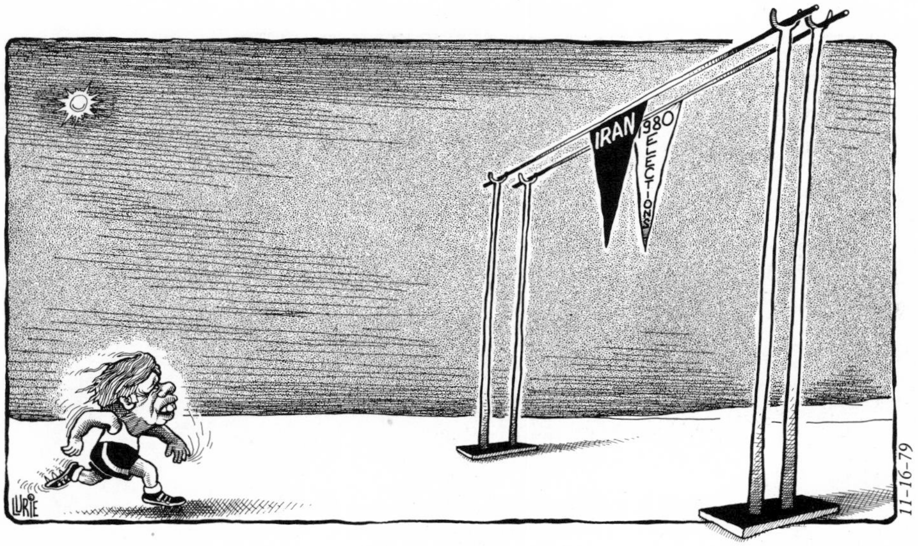
IRAN
1980 ELECTIONS
LURIE
11-16-79

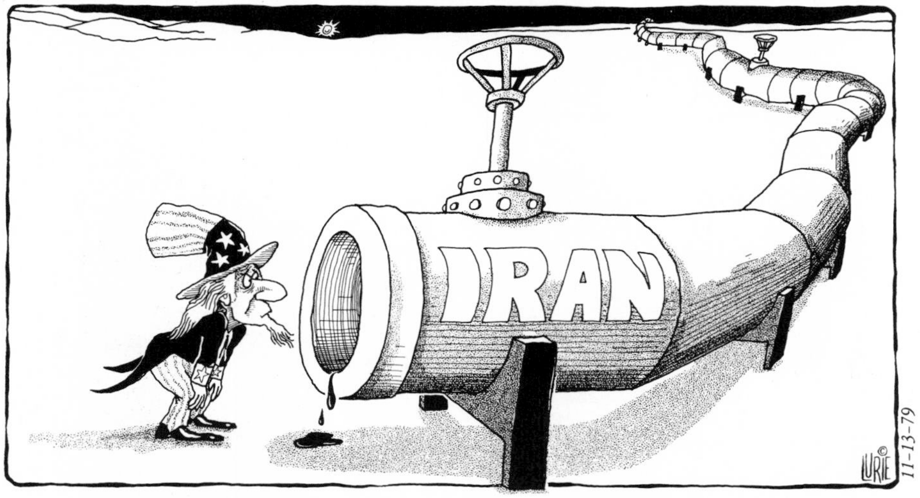
IRAN
LURIE
11-13-79

NO LIGHT AT THE END OF THE TUNNEL

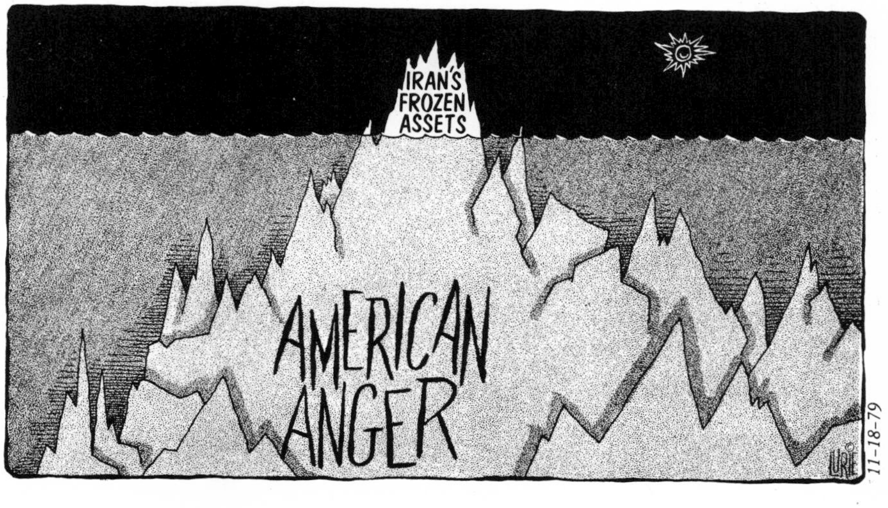
IRAN'S FROZEN ASSETS
AMERICAN ANGER
LURIE
11-18-79

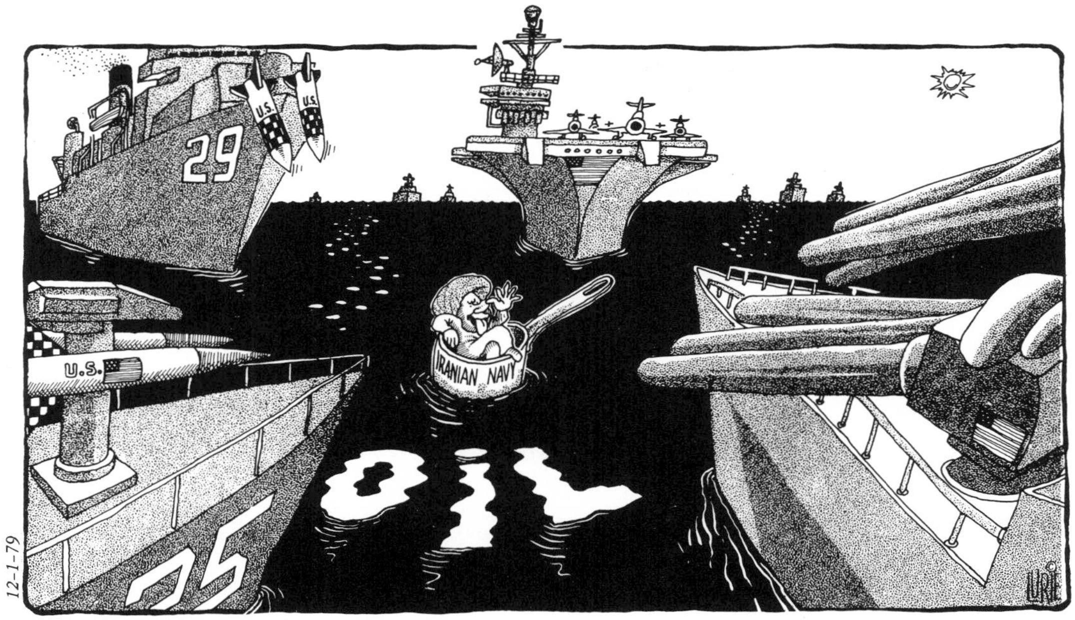
29
U.S.
U.S.
IRANIAN NAVY
OIL
U.S.
25
12-1-79
LURIE

FLAMMABLE SITUATION

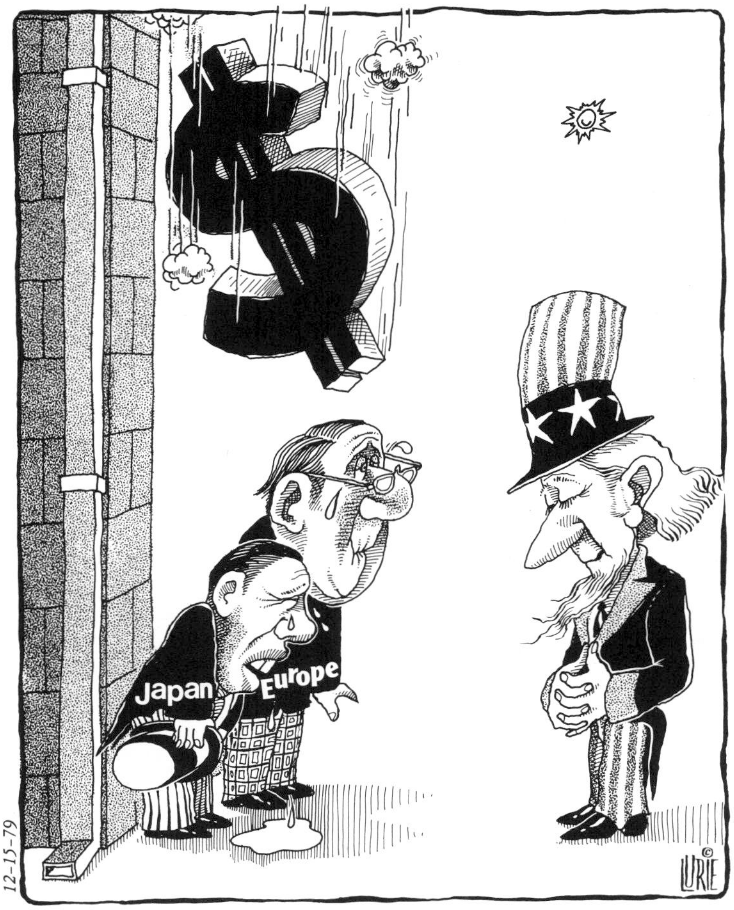
Japan
Europe
12-15-79
LURIE

"CONDOLENCES FOR THE FALL OF YOUR DOLLAR."

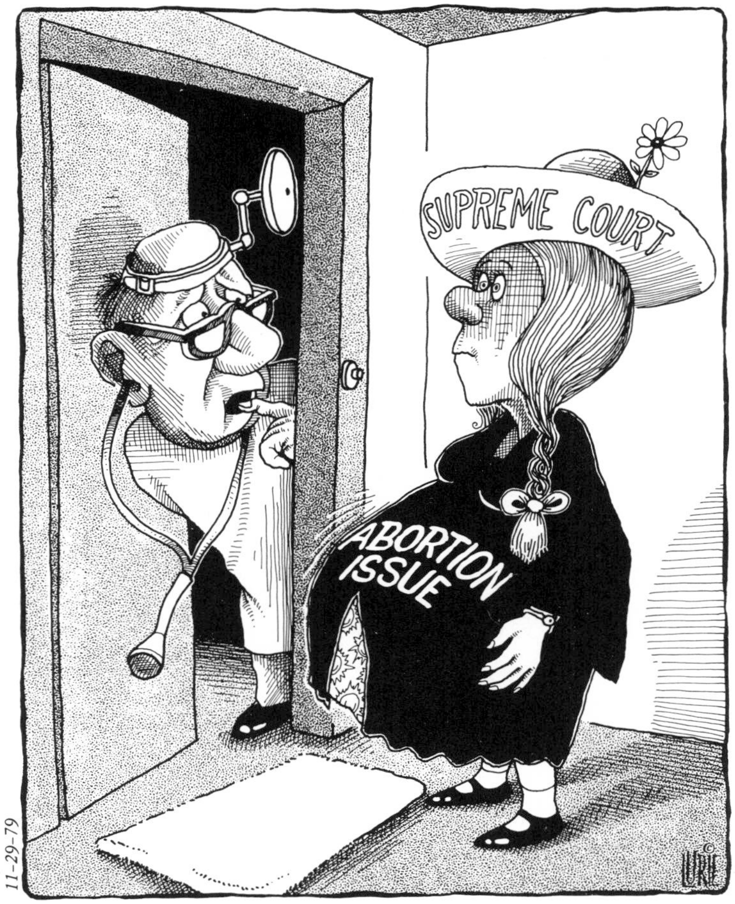
SUPREME COURT
ABORTION ISSUE
11-29-79
LURIE

"AGAIN?"

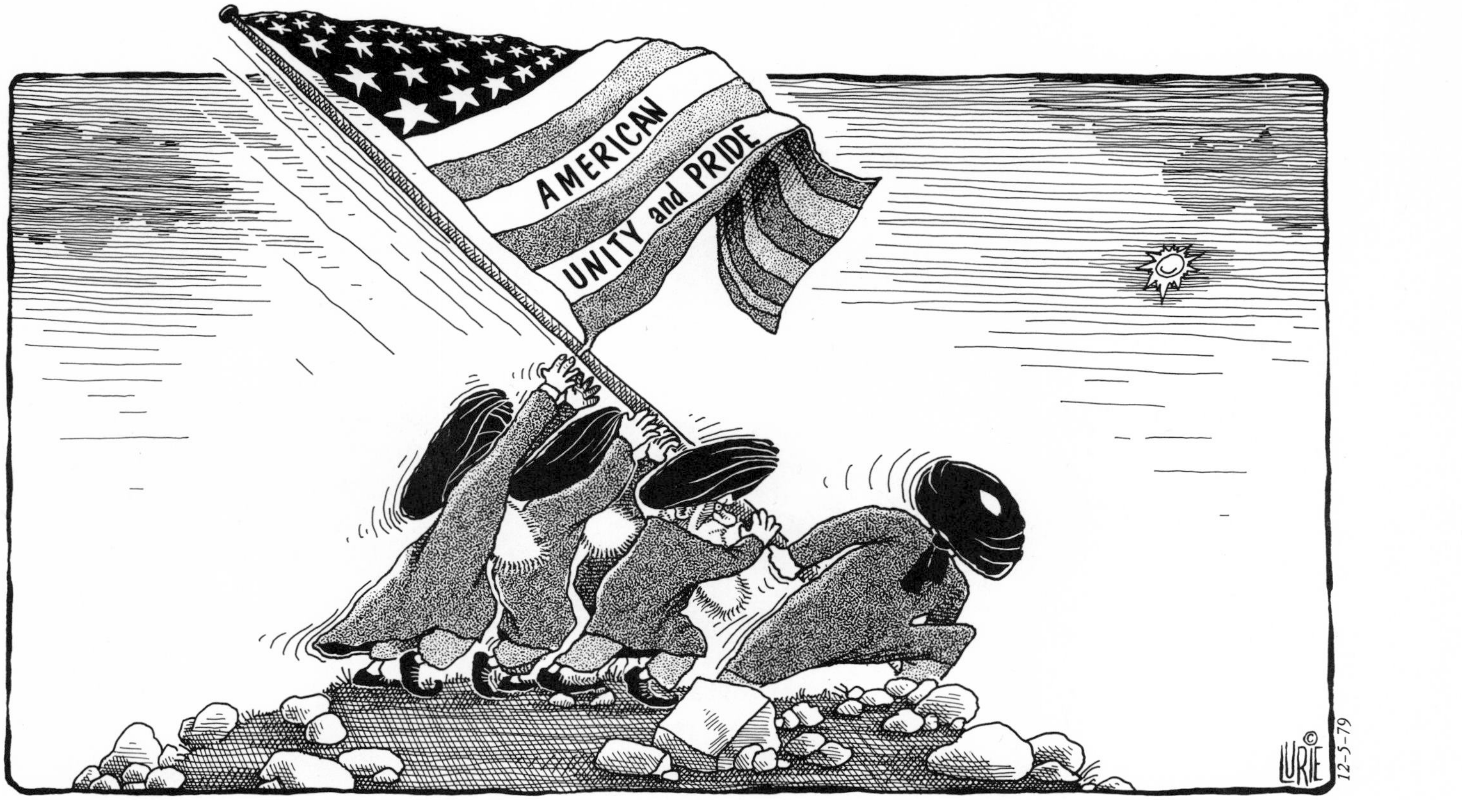
AMERICAN
UNITY and PRIDE
LURIE ©
12-5-79

RESTORING OLD GLORY

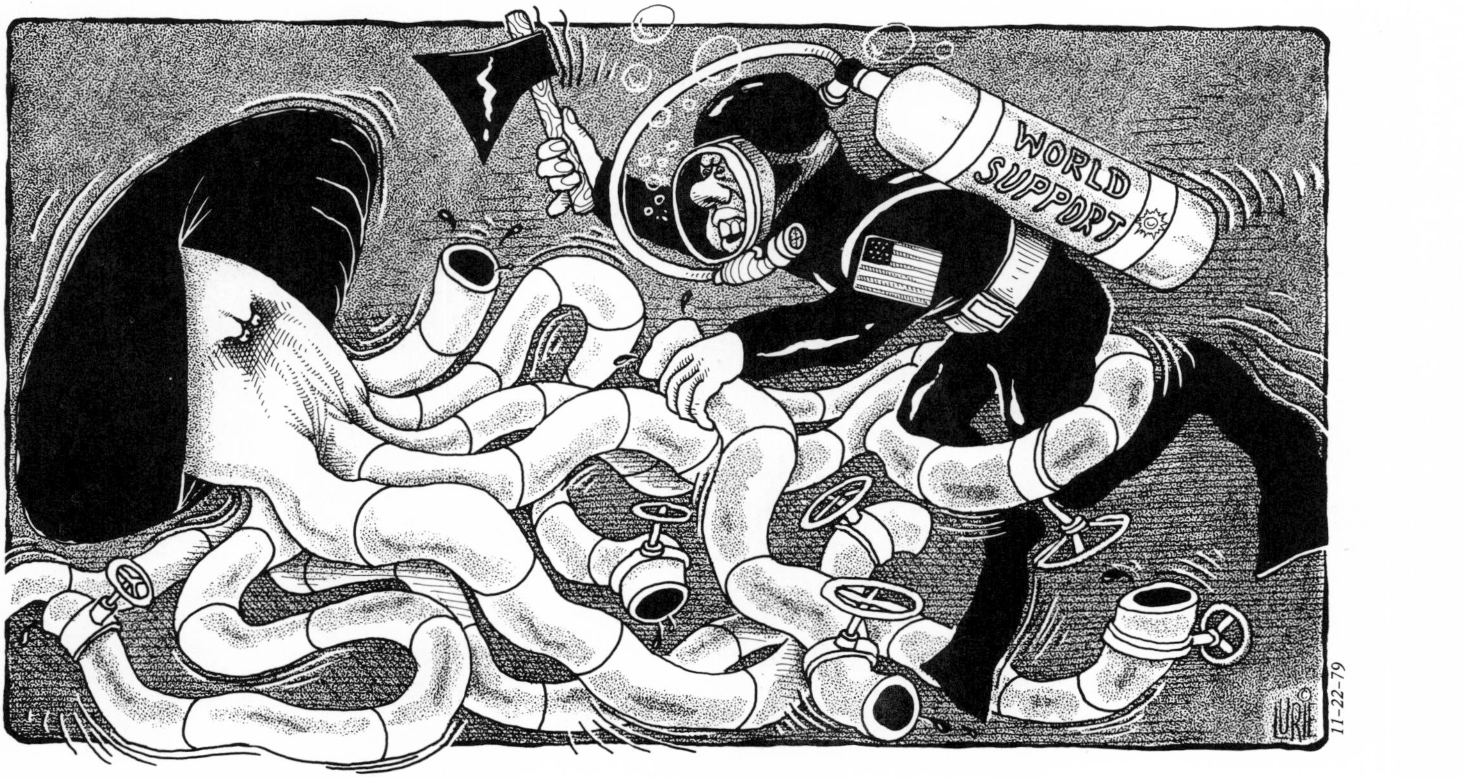
WORLD SUPPORT
LURIE ©
11-22-79

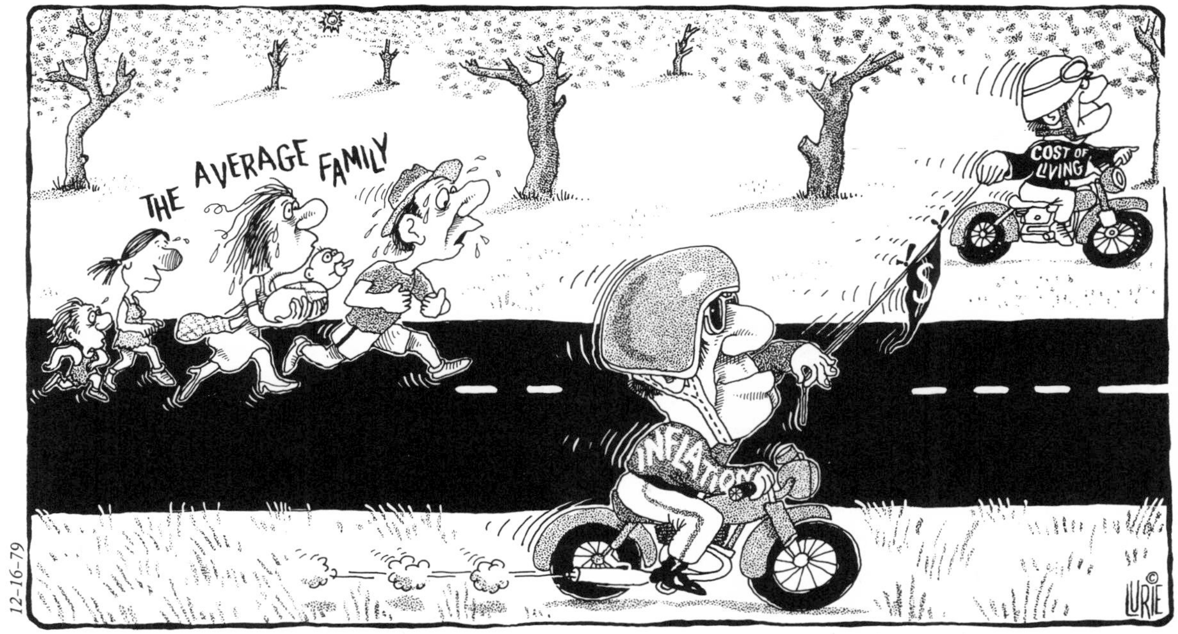
THE AVERAGE FAMILY
COST OF LIVING
INFLATION
$
12-16-79
LURIE ©

THE MARATHON RUNNERS

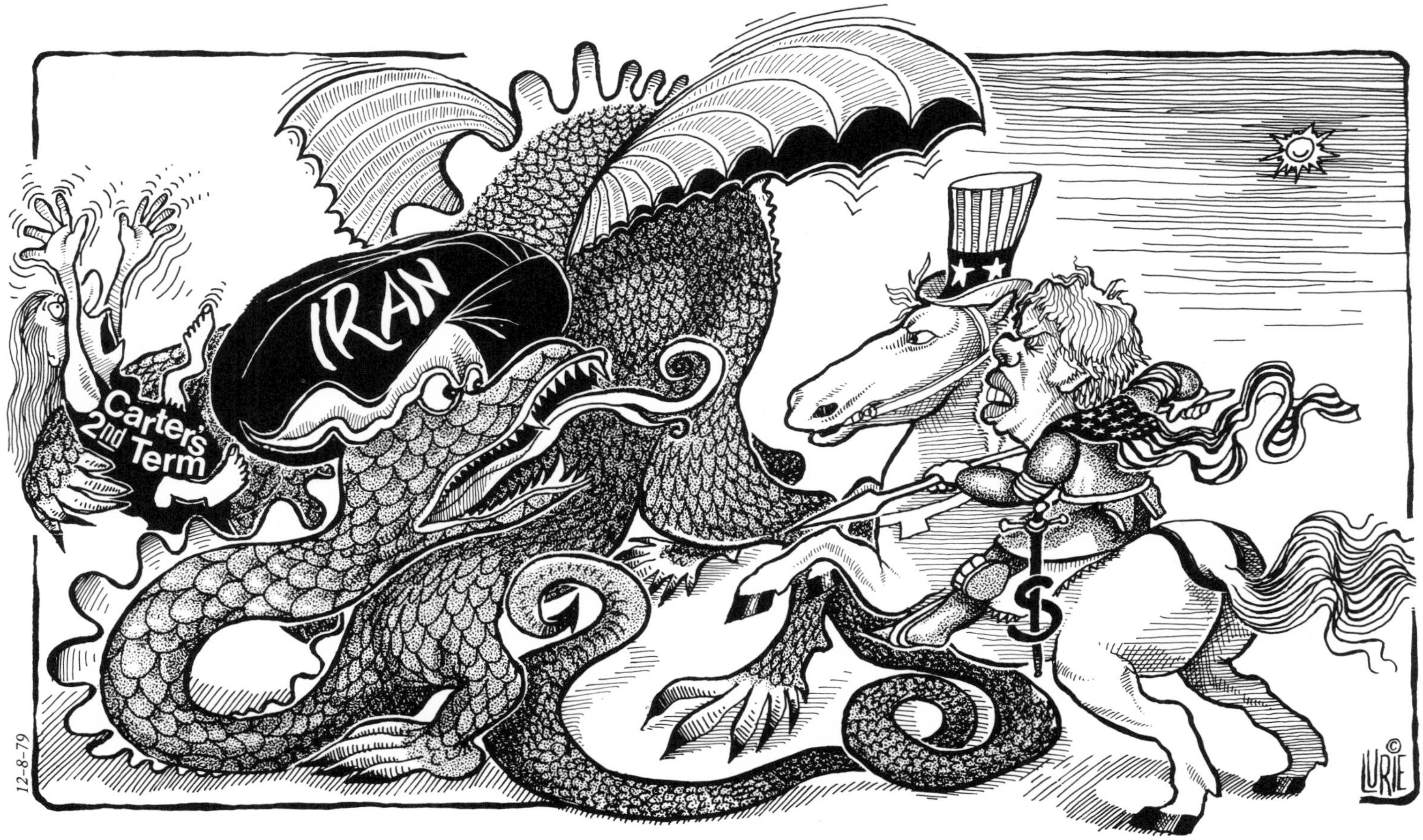
IRAN
Carter's 2nd Term
$
12-8-79
LURIE ©

51ST HOSTAGE

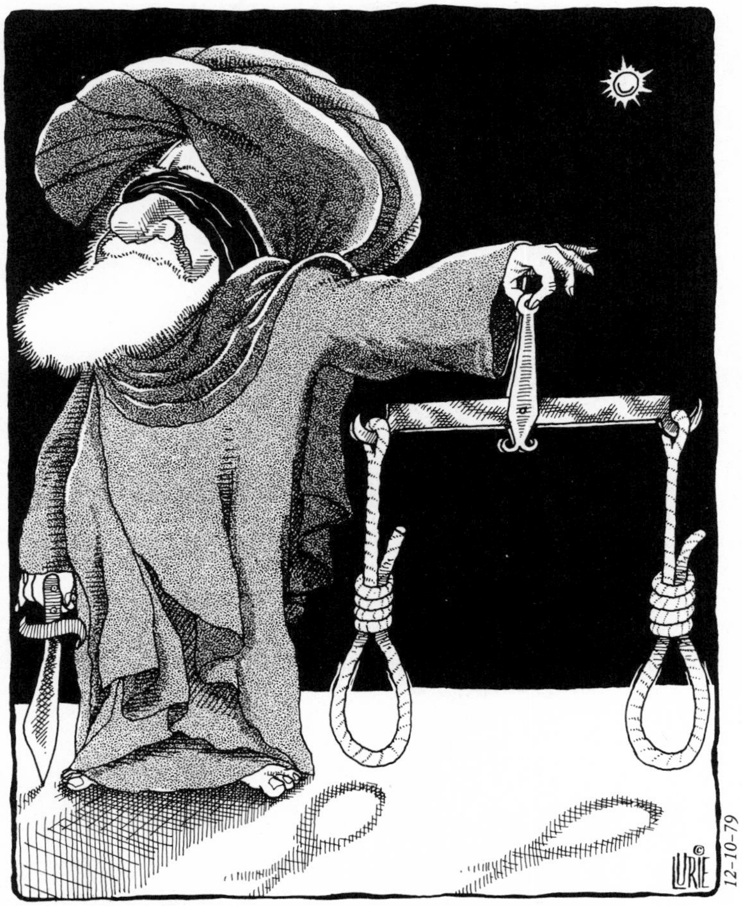
LURIE
12-10-79

IRANIAN SCALES OF JUSTICE

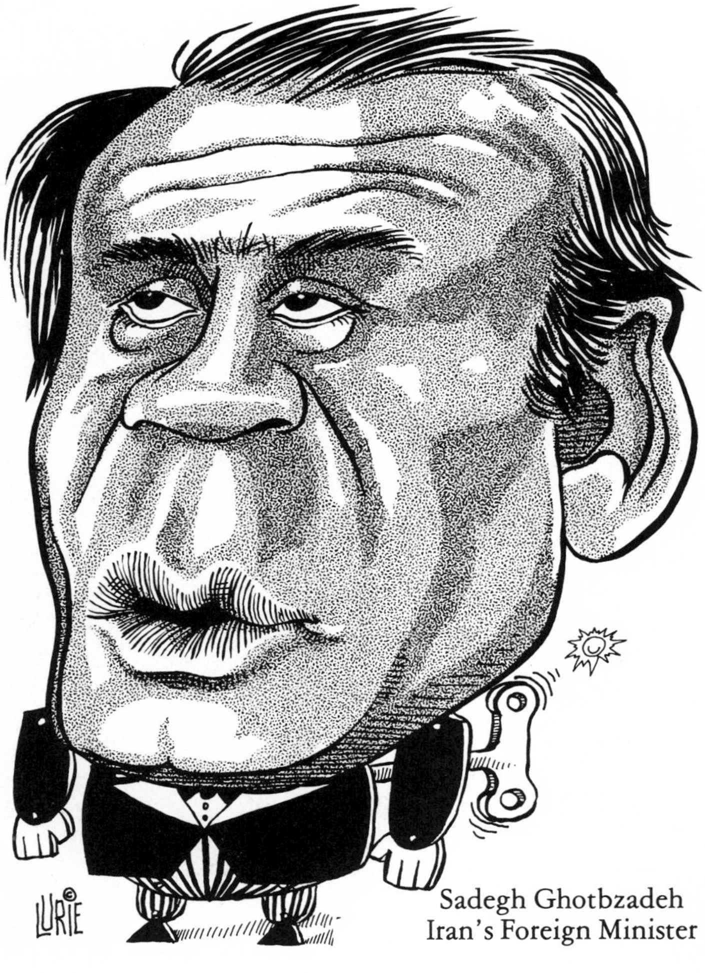
LURIE

Sadegh Ghotbzadeh
Iran's Foreign Minister

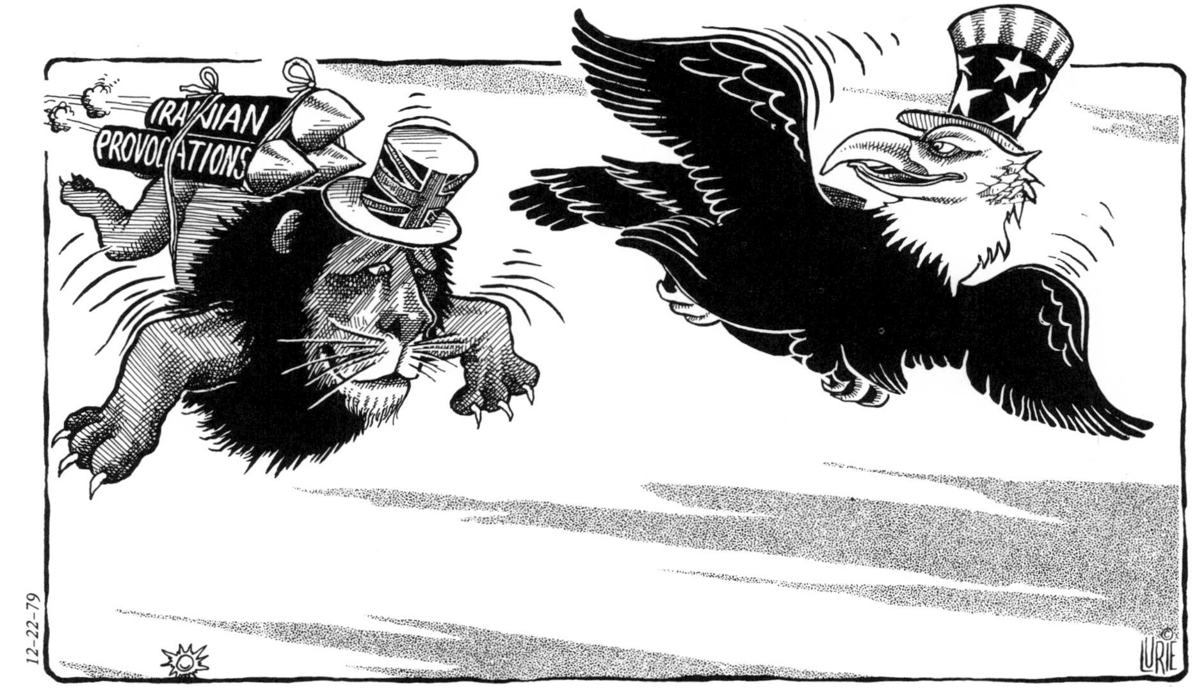
IRANIAN
PROVOCATIONS
12-22-79
LURIE

"SEE? WITH THE PROPER INCENTIVE *ANYONE* CAN FLY!"

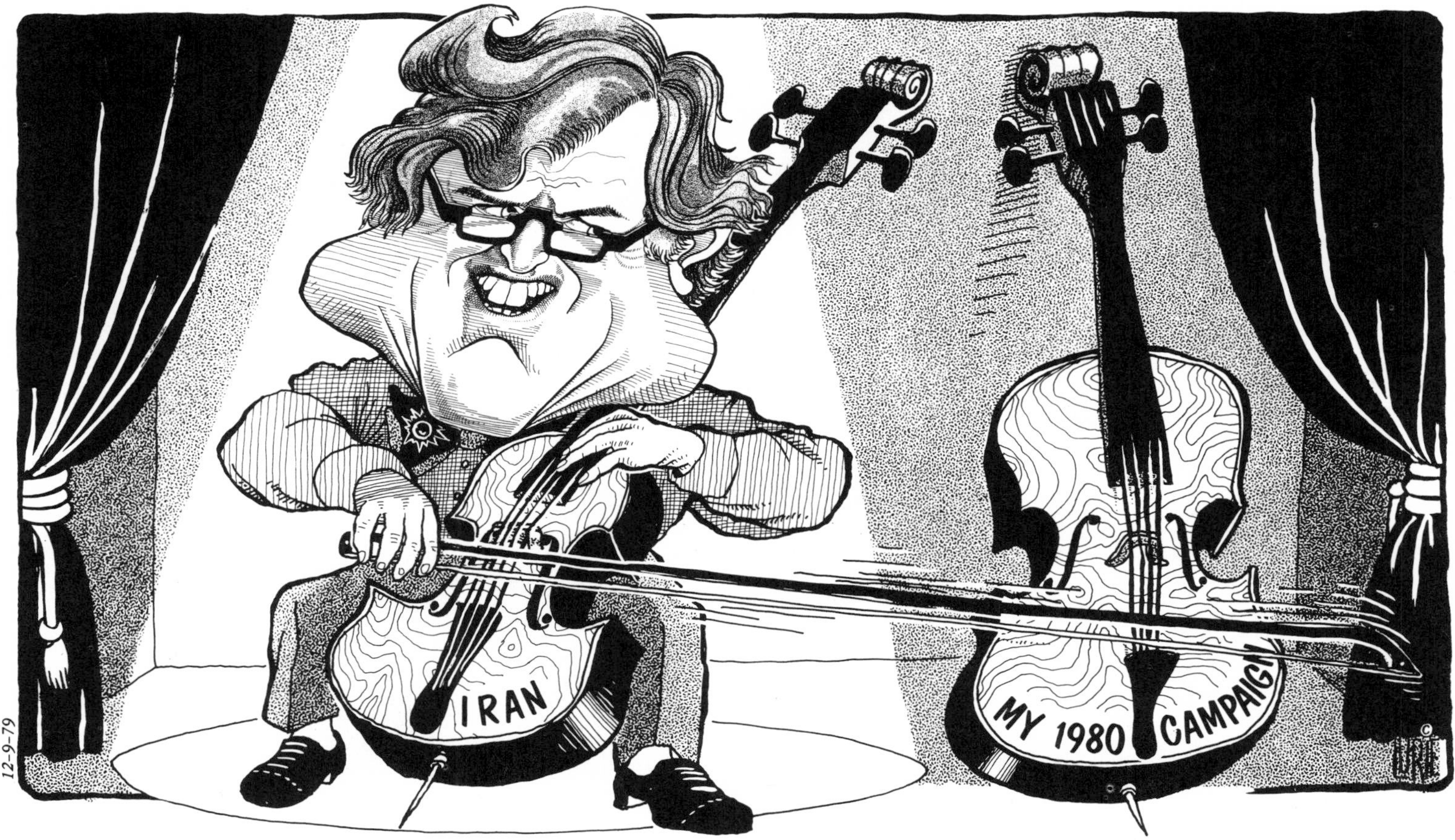
IRAN
MY 1980 CAMPAIG
12-9-79
LURIE

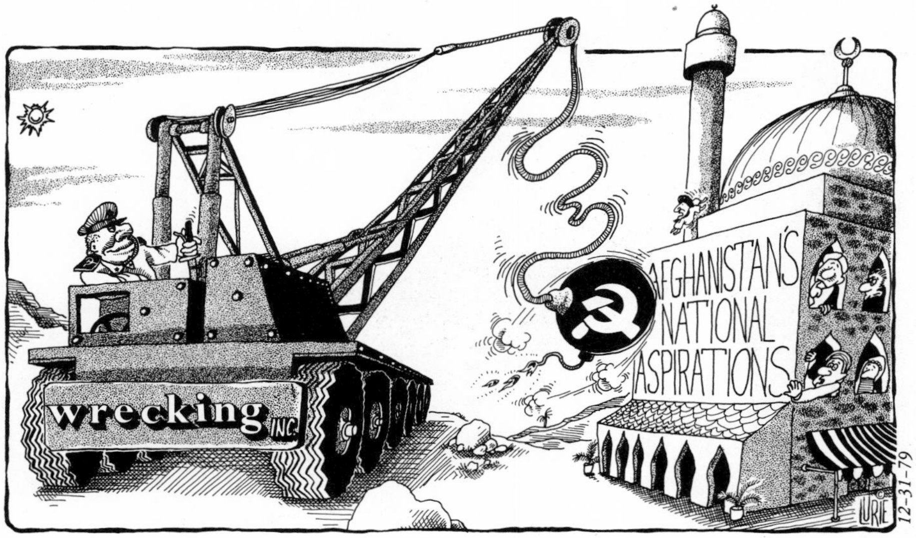
wrecking INC.
AFGHANISTAN'S NATIONAL ASPIRATIONS
LURIE
12-31-79

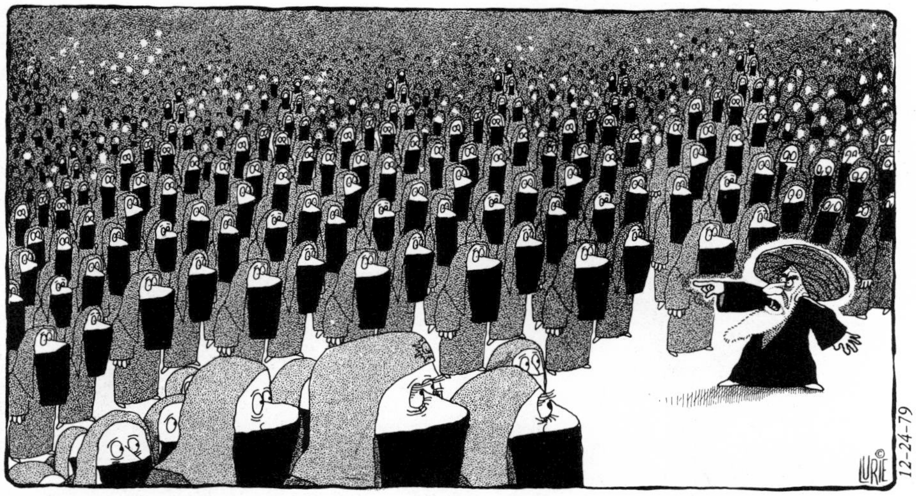
LURIE ©
12-24-79

"THERE IS A DISGUISED CIA AGENT AMONG YOU!"

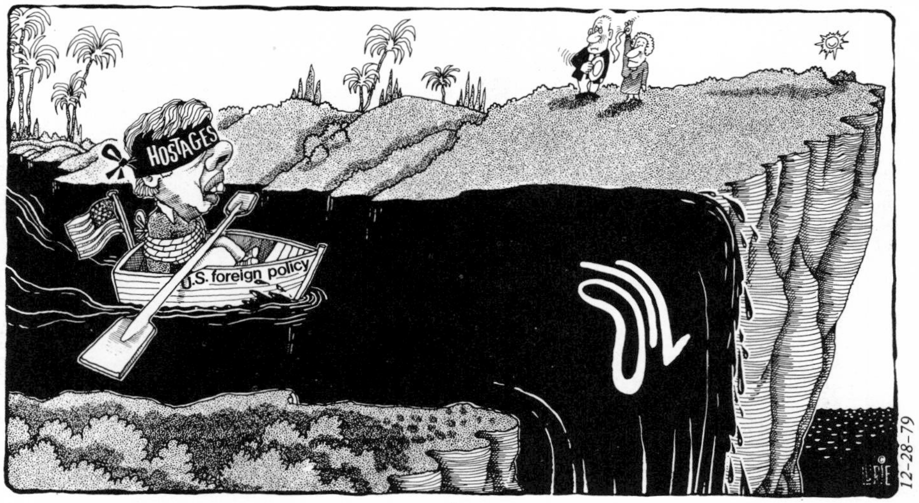
HOSTAGES
U.S. foreign policy
LURIE
12-28-79

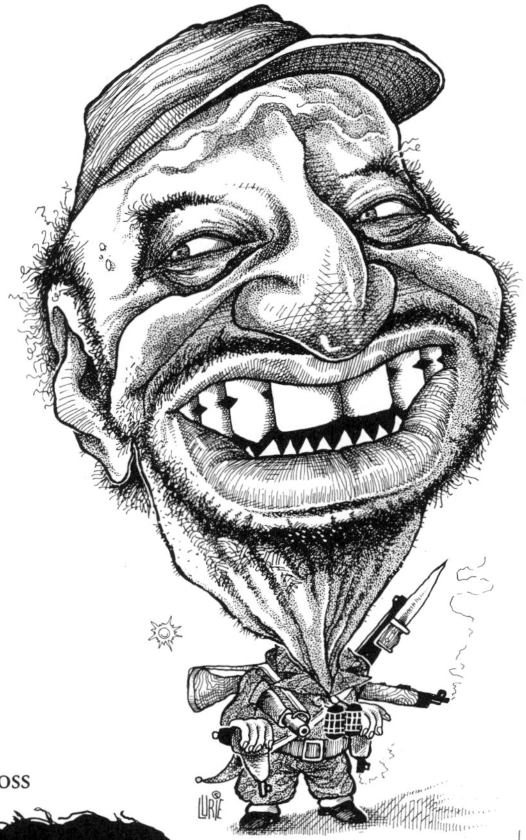
LURIE

Yasir Arafat
PLO Boss

Heng Samrin
Cambodia's New Boss

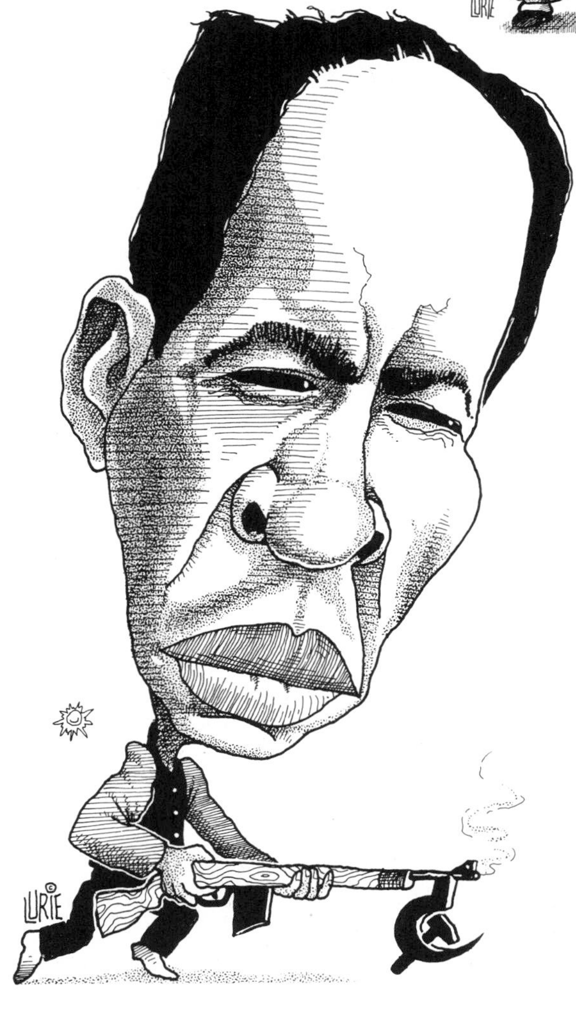
LURIE

Ayatollah Khomeini

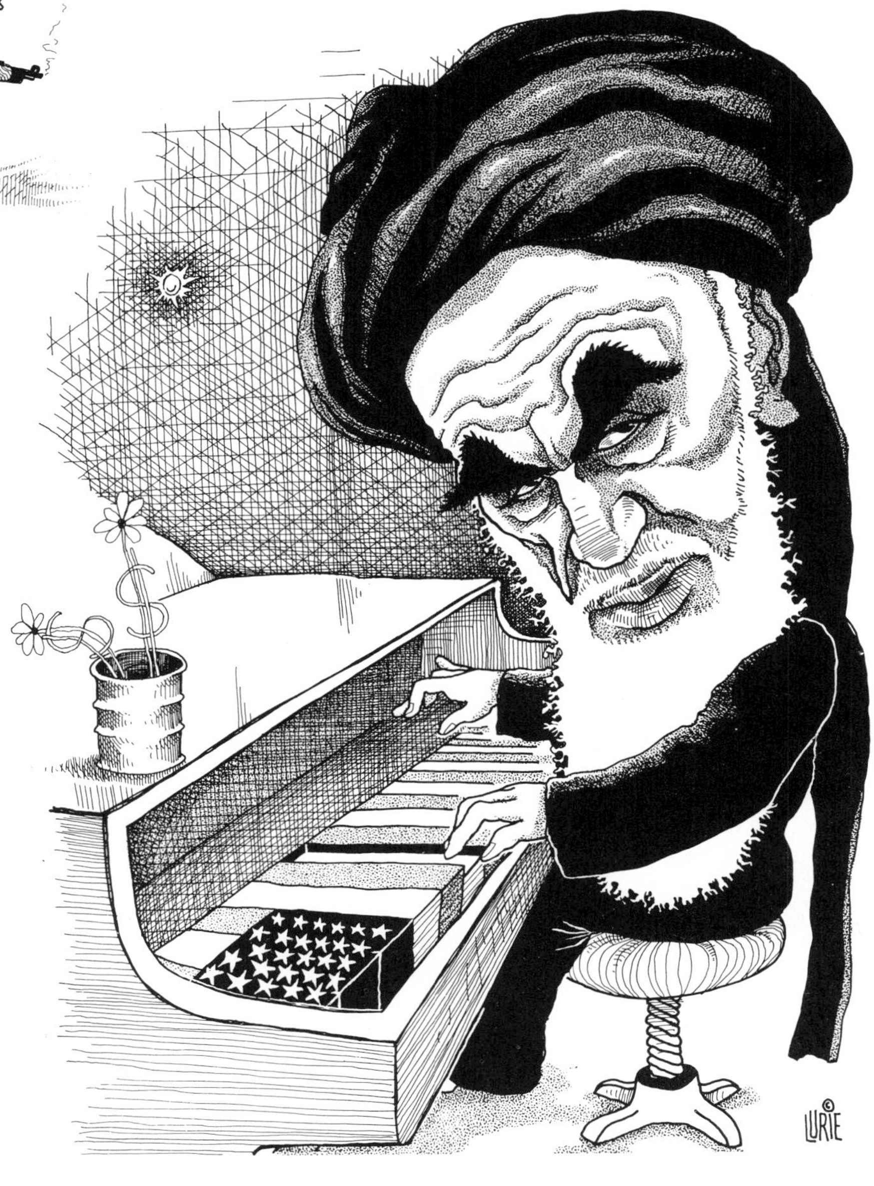
LURIE

Prime Minister
Mustafa Khalil of Egypt
Leading Egypt's Peace Negotiations

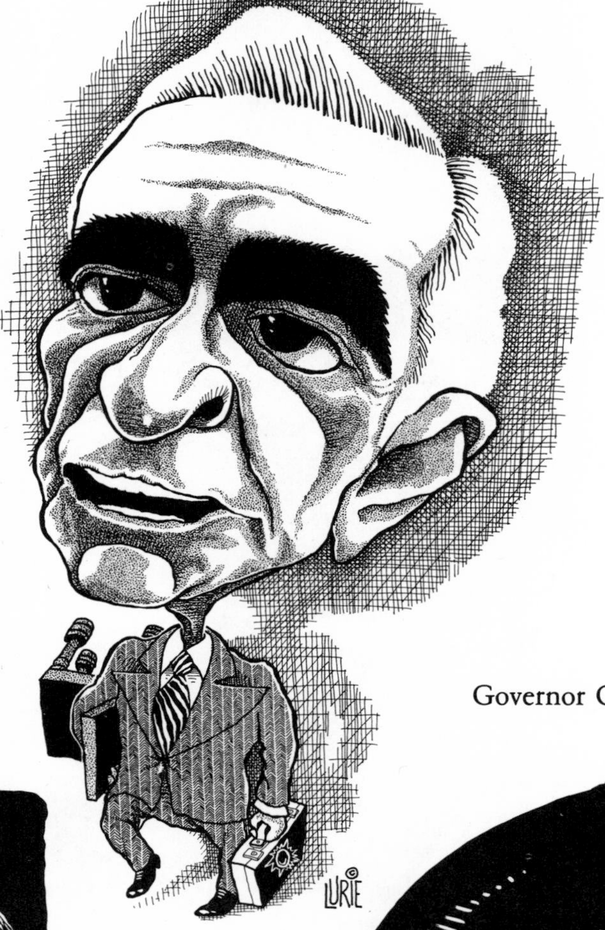
LURIE

Prime Minister Masayoshi Ohira
of Japan

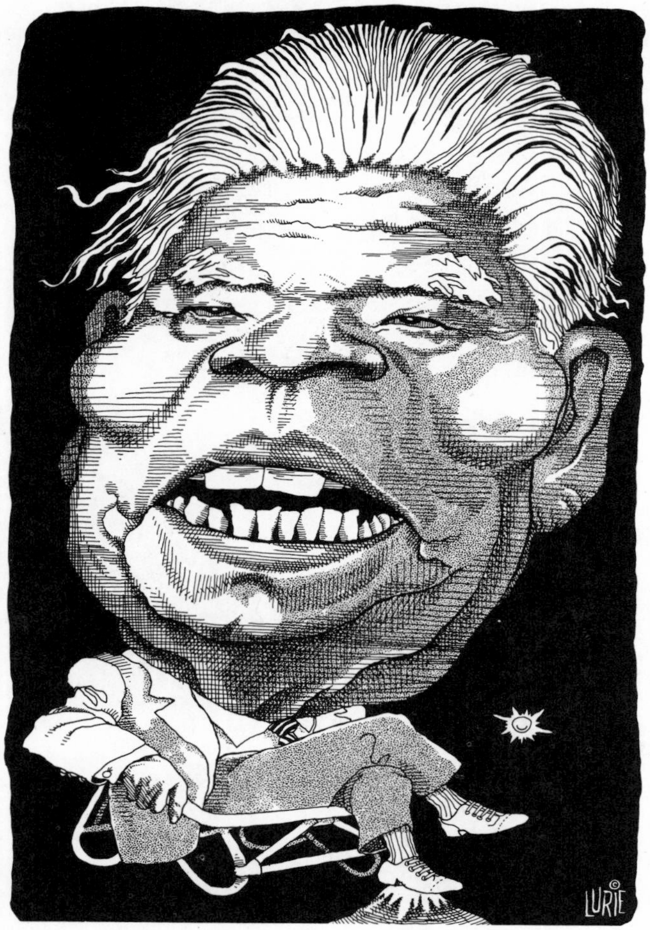
LURIE

Governor George Ryoichi Ariyoshi
of Hawaii

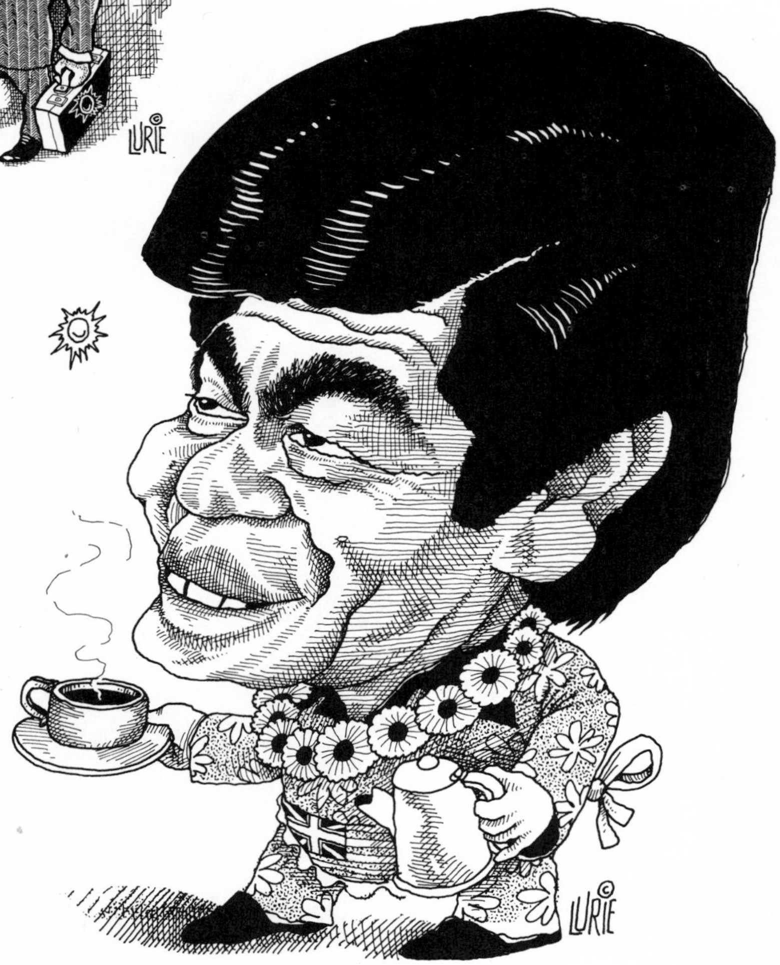
LURIE

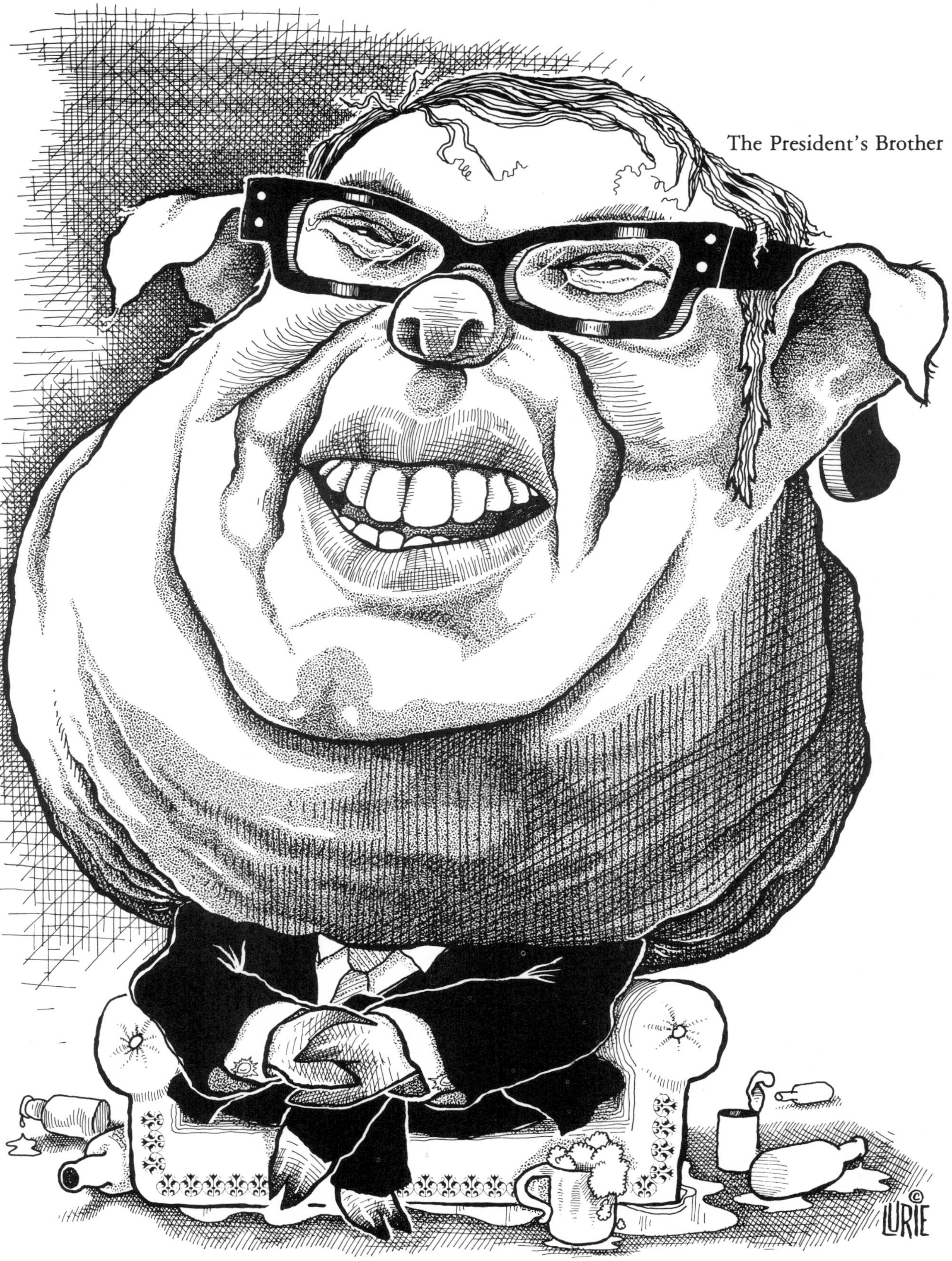
LURIE
The President's Brother

President Carter

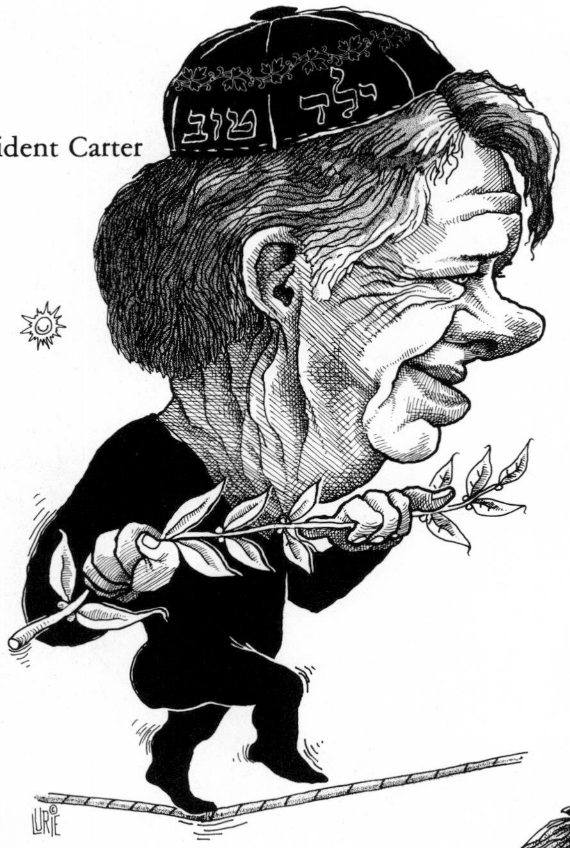

ילד טוב
LURIE

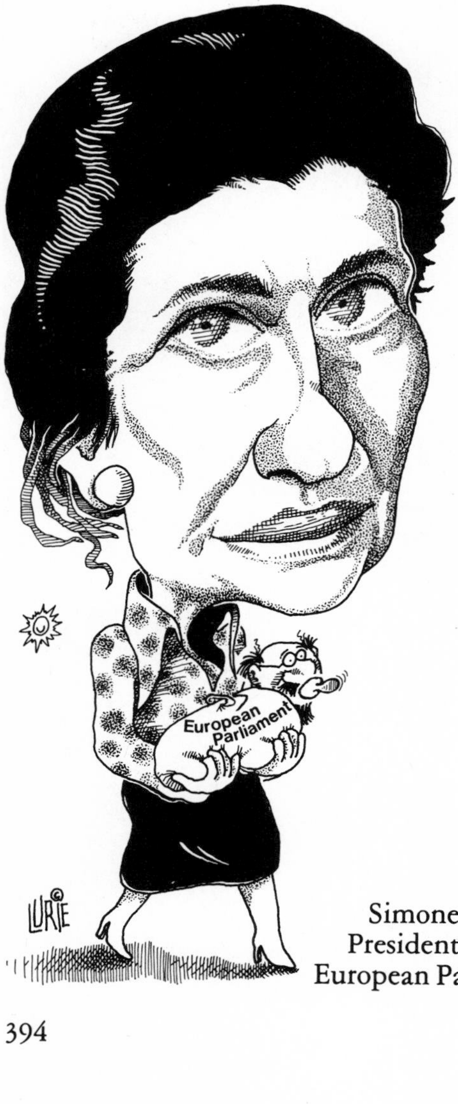

European Parliament
LURIE

Simone Veil
President of the
European Parliament

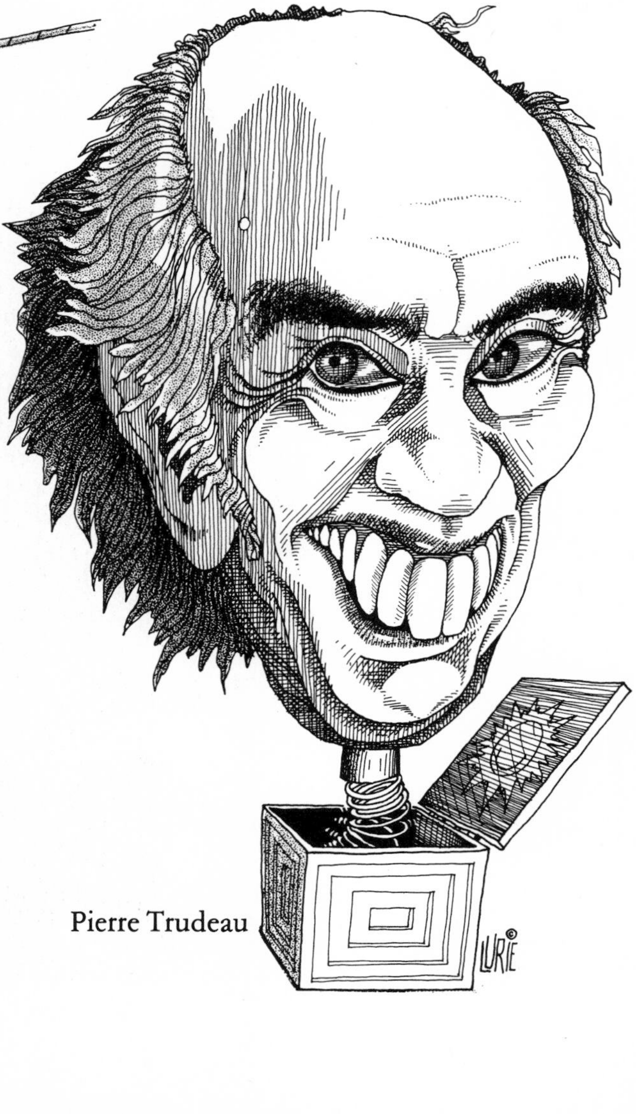

LURIE

Pierre Trudeau

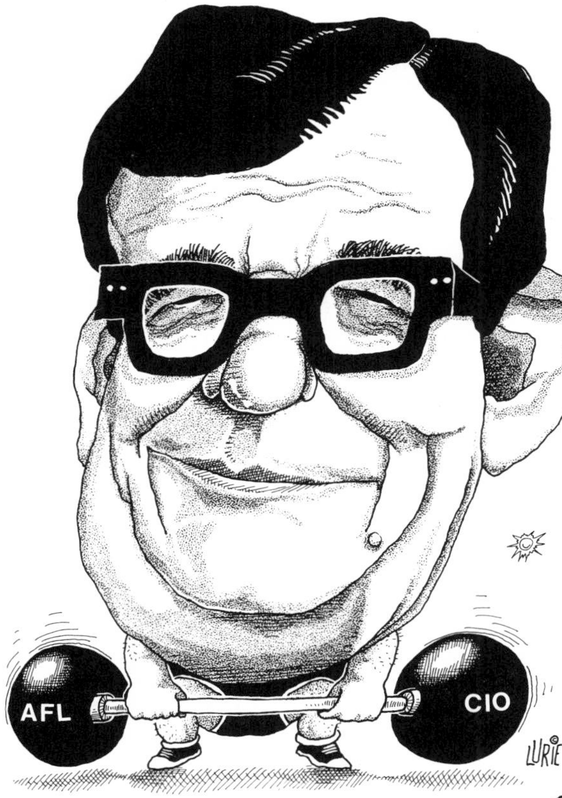
AFL
CIO
LURIE

Lane Kirkland
New AFL-CIO Boss

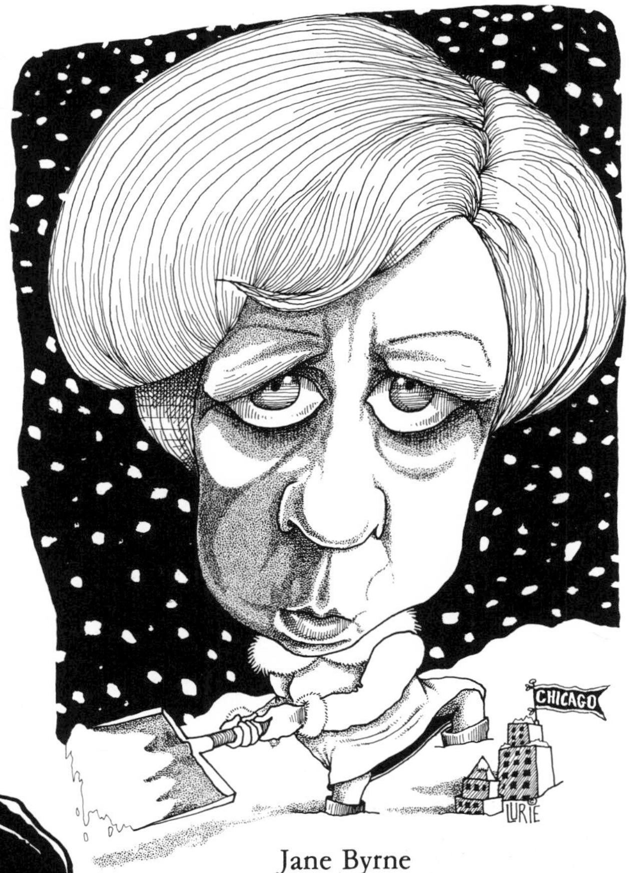
CHICAGO
LURIE

Jane Byrne
Chicago Mayoral Nominee

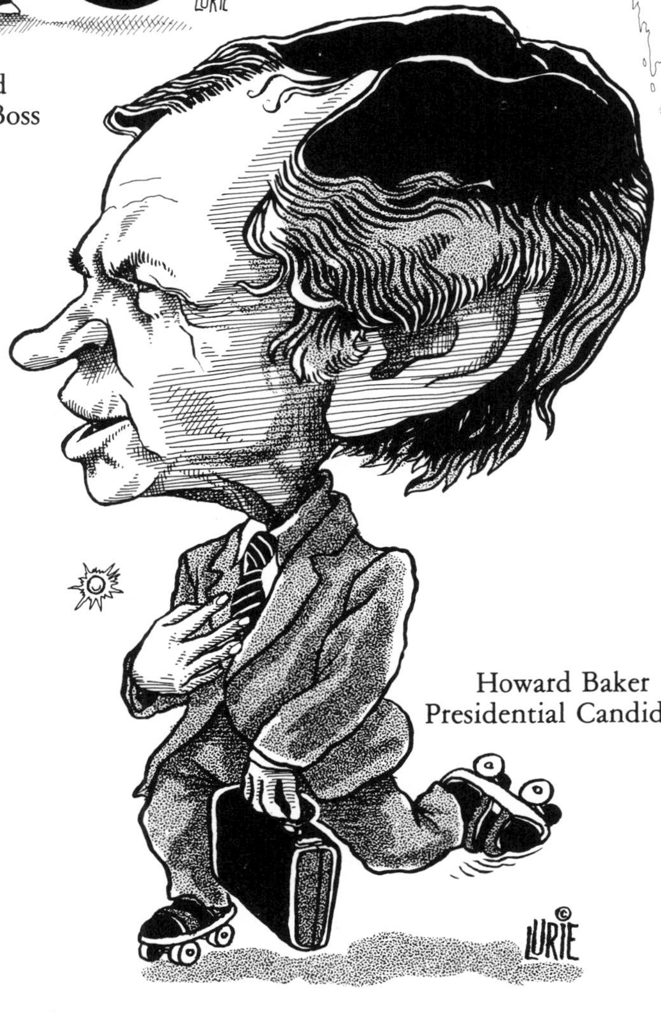
LURIE

Howard Baker
Presidential Candidate

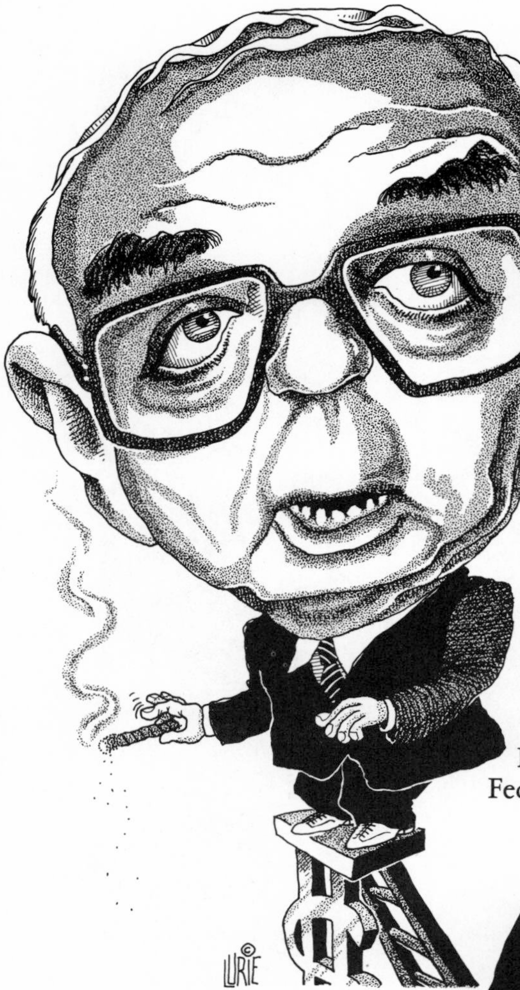

Paul Volcker
New Head of the
Federal Reserve Board

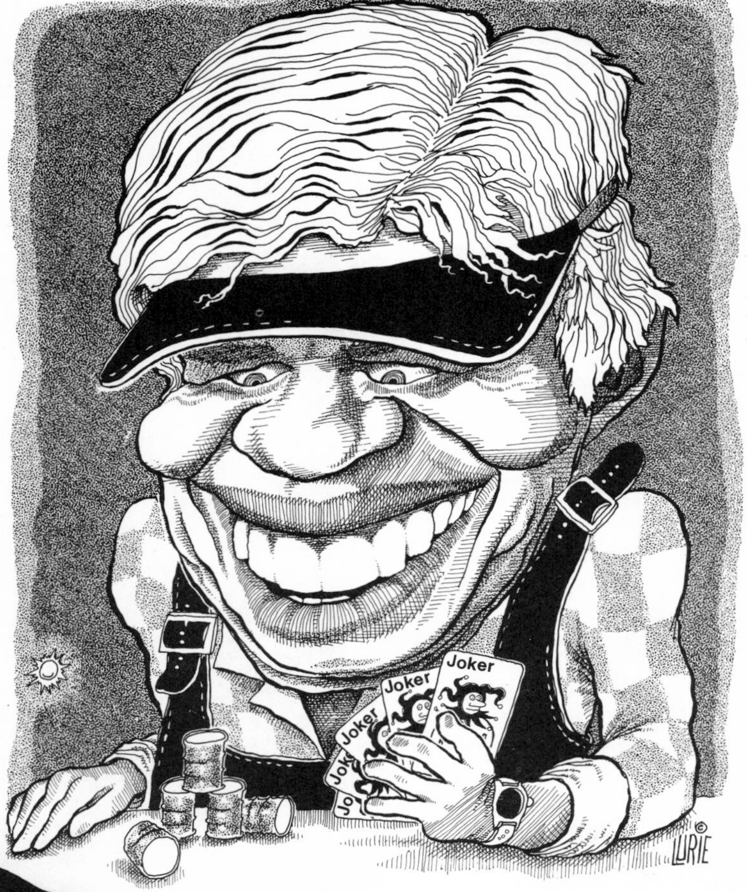
Joker
Joker
Joker
Joker

American Poker:
the New Cabinet

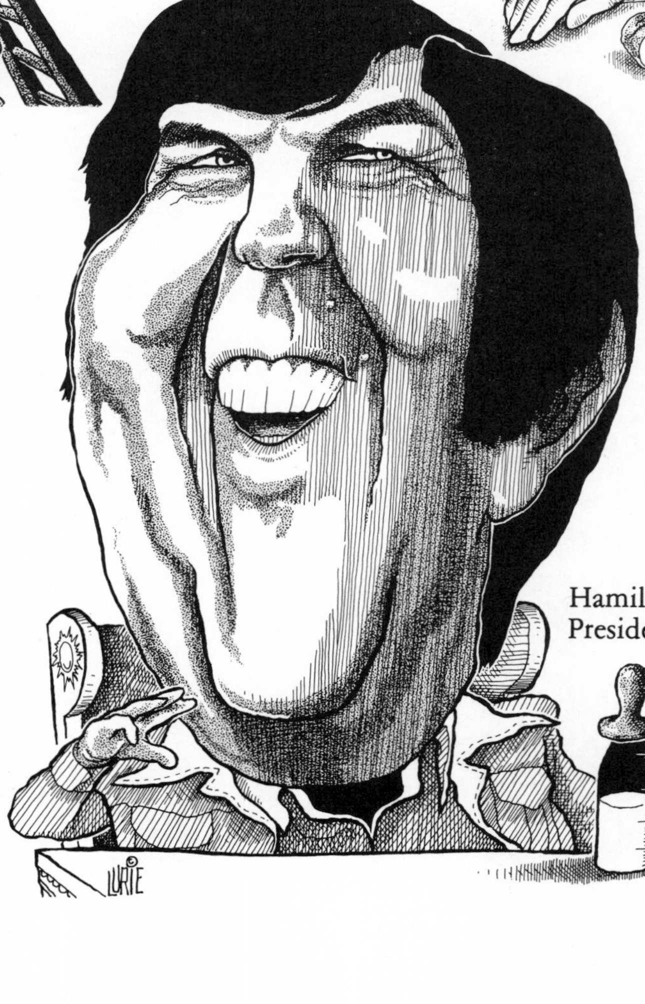

Hamilton Jordan
Presidential Aide

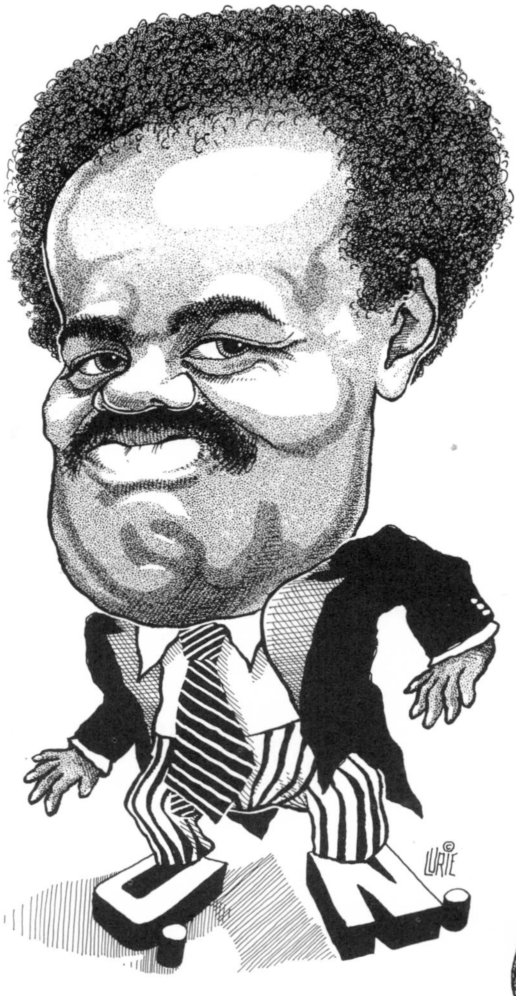
LURIE

Donald McHenry
U.S. Ambassador
to the United Nations

Leonard Woodcock
U.S. Ambassador-Designate
to China

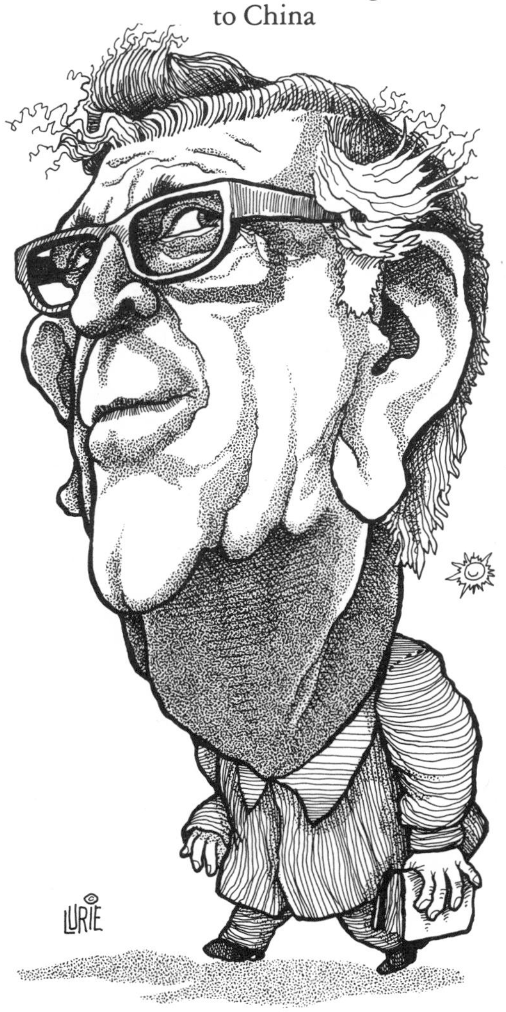
LURIE

General Bernard W. Rogers
Commander-in-Chief,
U.S. European Command

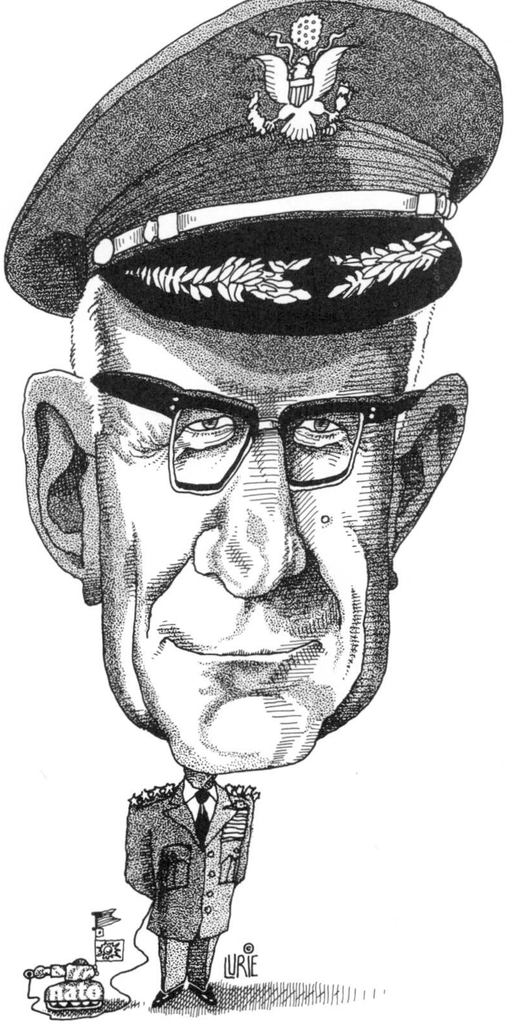
nato
LURIE

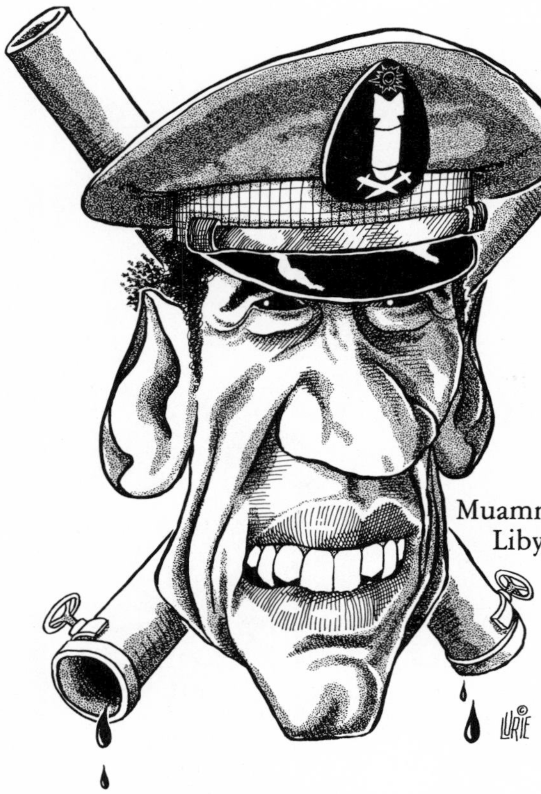
LURIE

Muammar el-Qaddafi
Libyan Dictator

Lieutenant General Olusegun Obasanjo
Nigeria's Strong Man

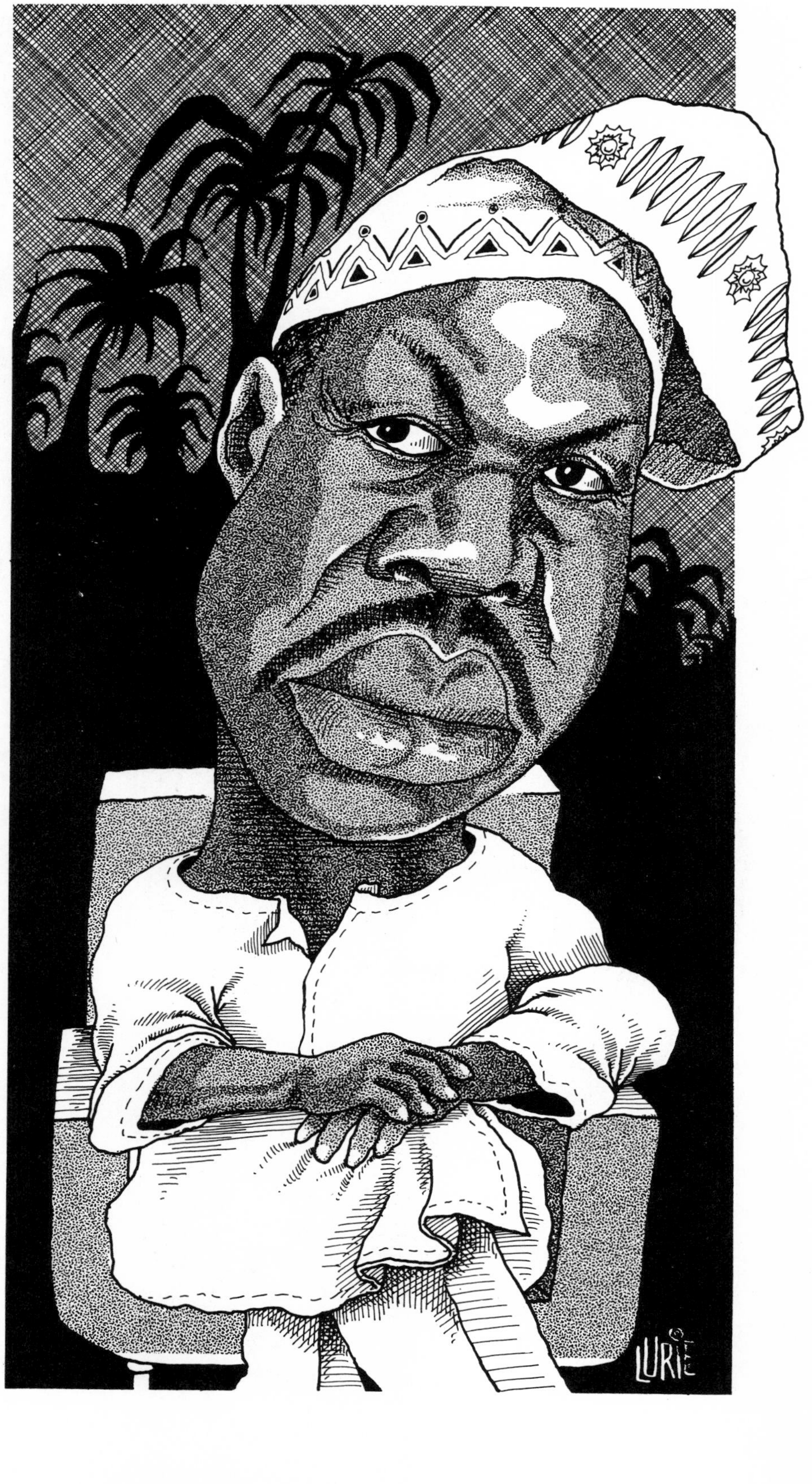
LURIE

Colonel Benjedid Chadli
President of Algeria

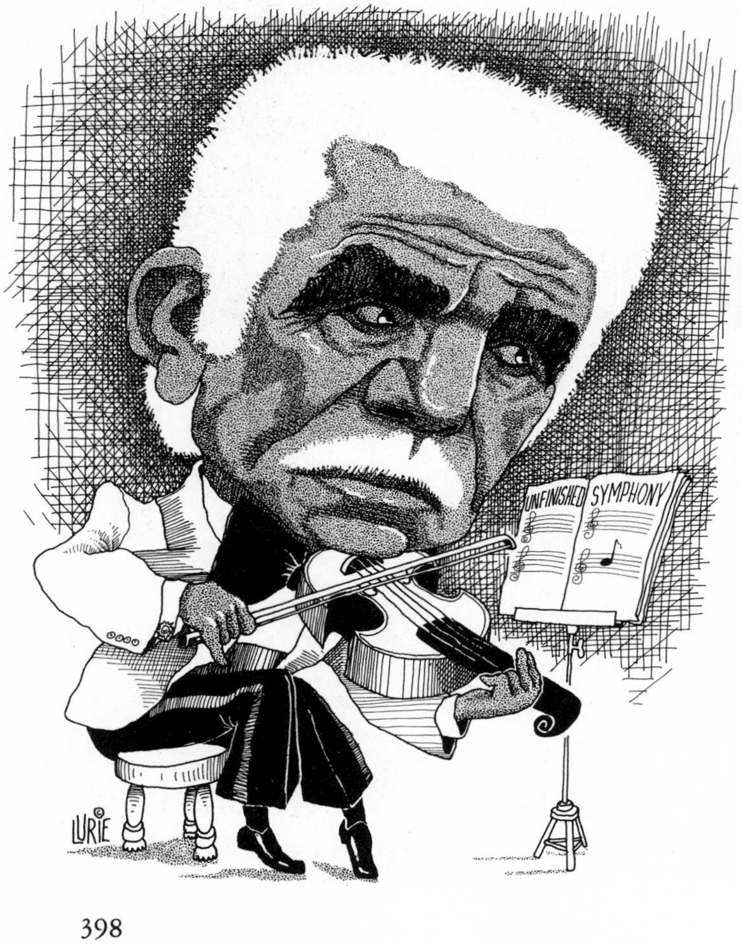
UNFINISHED
SYMPHONY
LURIE

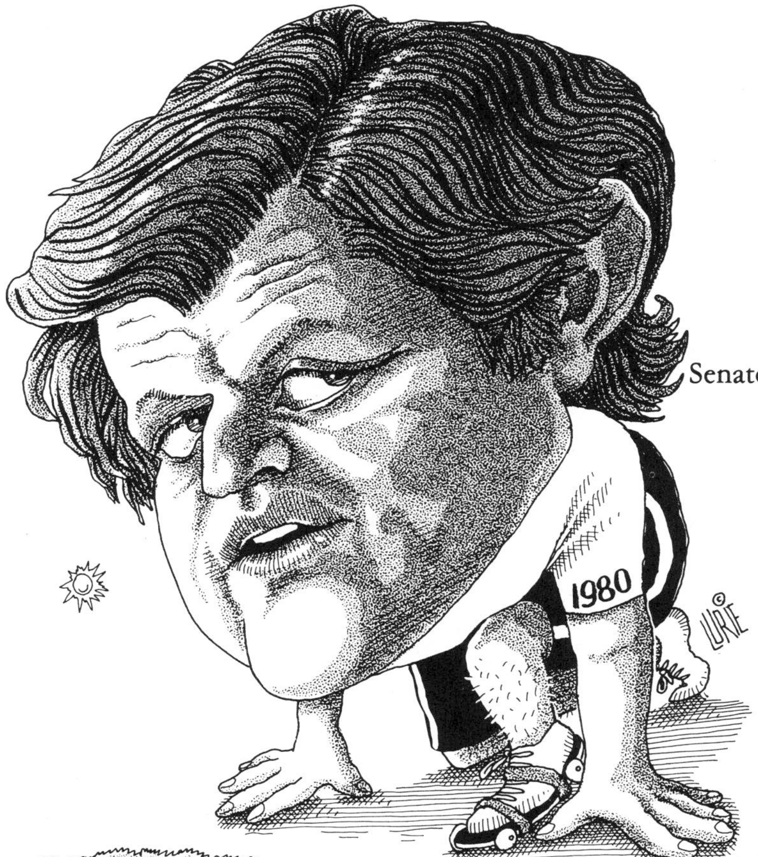
1980
LURIE ©

Senator Edward Kennedy

Reverend Jesse Jackson
Black Civil Rights Leader

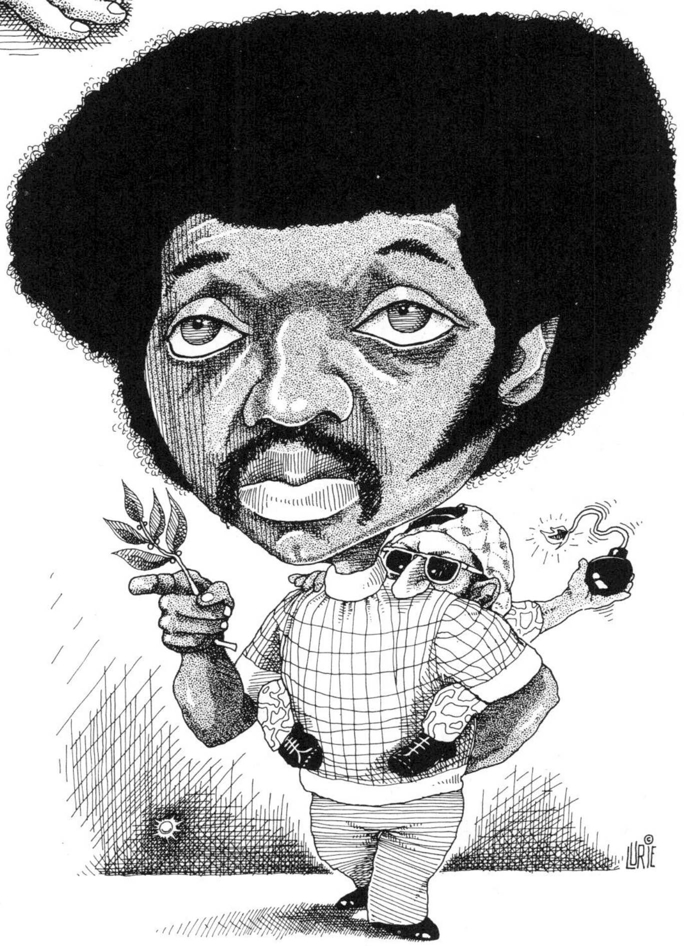
LURIE ©

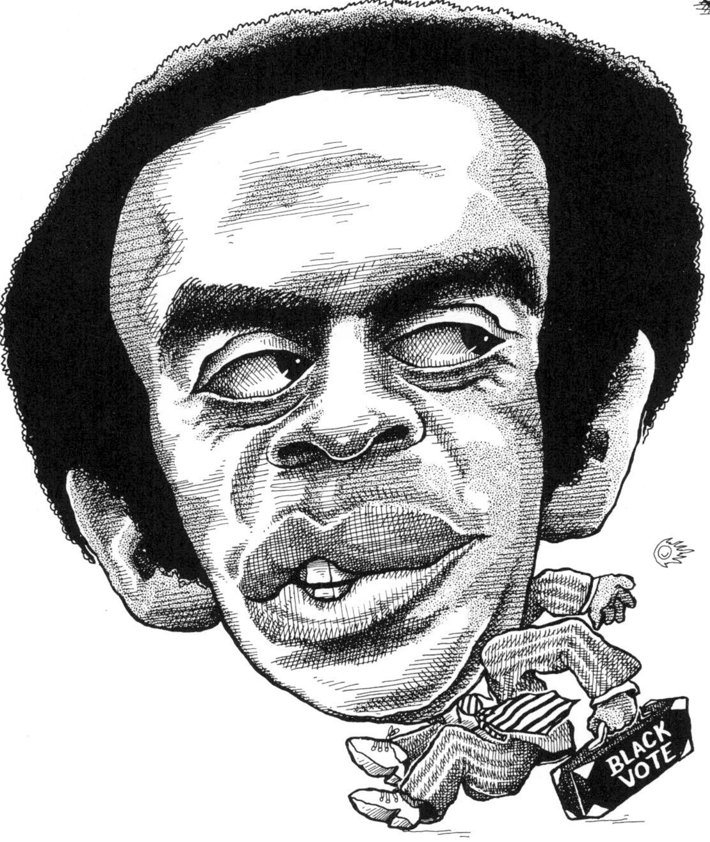
BLACK VOTE
LURIE ©

Ex-Ambassador Andrew Young

1980

Thurston Twigg-Smith: ON LURIE

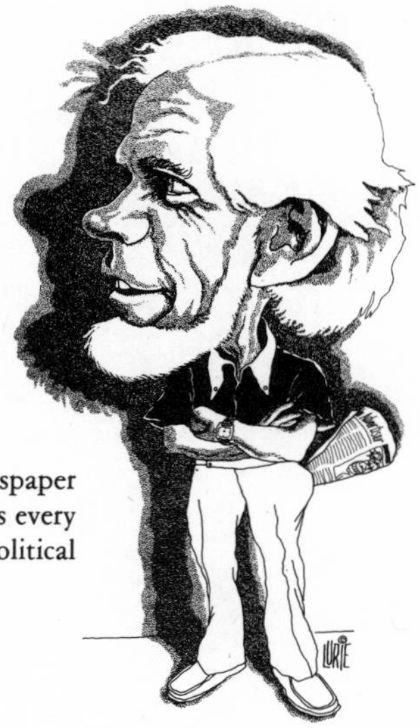

Thurston Twigg-Smith is the publisher of the *Honolulu Advertiser,* the newspaper which invited Ranan Lurie to come over for a stint of one year. Lurie moves every year or two to a different capital in the world so that he can broaden his political range and contacts. Lurie considers Honolulu the capital of the Pacific basin.

When *The Advertiser* brought Ranan Lurie to Honolulu to start a one-year stint on April 1, 1979, as its editorial page cartoonist, there was no thought in anyone's mind that the year would be one we'd remember a long time. But that's the way it turned out.

The idea of an international cartoonist turning his pen to caricatures of local personages seemed harmless enough. Little did the staffers of this daily newspaper know that a different world of cartooning was about to unfold around them.

Ran Lurie doesn't treat cartooning as a way to get laughs, or even smiles. He punches to kill in his carefully modulated drawings. Prior to coming to Honolulu, Lurie was the equivalent of long-range, heavy artillery. He dropped his explosive messages on subjects a considerable distance from his home base. The front line was pretty far away.

Not so when a cartoonist does his thing on the local scene. Making victim the man next door, so to speak, is quite different from slaying a dragon across the ocean. The readers generally know the subject as well as they know themselves. And the hard-hitting cartoon Lurie pens is harder to accept without a jolt.

None of this made much difference to Lurie, and it shouldn't have. His success depends on complete objectivity, complete independence from embroilment with the subjects of his often malevolent blackness. And therein lies his strength.

It wasn't what *The Advertiser* thought it was getting, but it certainly made life interesting for *Advertiser* editors and readers alike. For his cartoons bring strong reaction; there is no middle ground. The viewer becomes either a fan or a detractor, although even in the latter case the readers never challenged the professionalism, the perception inherent in his work.

For Lurie, the interplay at the local level was a new experience important to his long-range goal of the compleat cartoonist. As an international artist, he'd never experienced the different demands of daily newspapering, and it was strange for him to adjust to the hopes of an editor with local needs and problems on his mind.

The professional in Lurie demanded that he respond without yielding his independence of opinion: the paper would run both local and international cartoons, and the local ones would also run them with the familiar slug: "Lurie's Opinion."

The professional interchange with the requirements of a local press was a learning experience for Lurie, he admits. Without question it was a learning experience for the local staff. The awesome worldliness of a man who states that his work is a "noble and important profession," and who acts and believes every bit of the part, was a source of constant wonder for the staffers who passed his office or who had occasion to come in contact with him. Rarely unbending, aloof in spite of his protestations to the contrary, Lurie earned the grudging admiration of his colleagues early in the game.

He made his impact on the community in more ways than through his daily efforts on the editorial page—occasionally on the front page, and, on other occasions when his opinion clashed with the paper's, on the "op ed" page.

Lurie had a one-man show at Honolulu Academy of Arts, and that event, eight months after his arrival, was a great success. A reviewer for *The Honolulu Star-Bulletin* called it an "extraordinary treat." She went on to say that

For those with acute memory of recent political history, both domestic and international, the chronologically arranged exhibition justifies Lurie's reputation for uncanny powers of prediction.

Much has been said about placing Lurie and others in the long tradition of satirical social commentary along with such major artists as Hogarth, Goya and Daumier. While this may be a response to the question ''Is this art?'' establishing a professional provenance for Lurie is much more problematic, for reasons which have less to do with the nature of the work itself than with the changed role of such commentators in society.

The mirror Lurie holds to recent history is fascinating but never flattering, the reflections complex but rarely compassionate. For better or worse, Lurie's work significantly alters our perception and interpretation of current political reality.

Being this close to such a powerful personality was a rare experience for members of the Honolulu press corps. The contact, now established, will continue as Lurie from afar punches away at the patterns of human behavior. Who knows, as he skillfully and deftly works away at his next desk in Bonn, capital of West Germany—and nobody works any longer and harder than Ran Lurie—some person or event in Hawaii may stir a memory of a local personage once jabbed from nearby, and set off a powerhouse blow that will come from afar to prick the ego, expose a flaw of some future Hawaii politico. At that point the transition from world cartoonist to local cartoonist to world cartoonist again will have come full circle.

T. Twigg-Smith

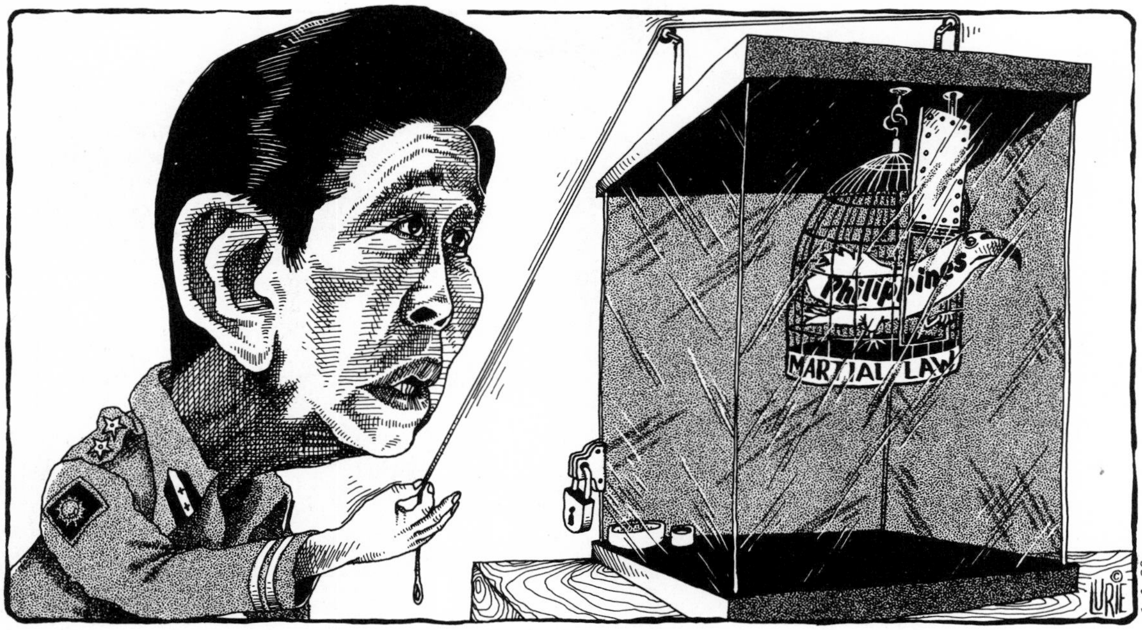
Philippines
MARTIAL LAW
LURIE ©
1-3-80

SET FREE

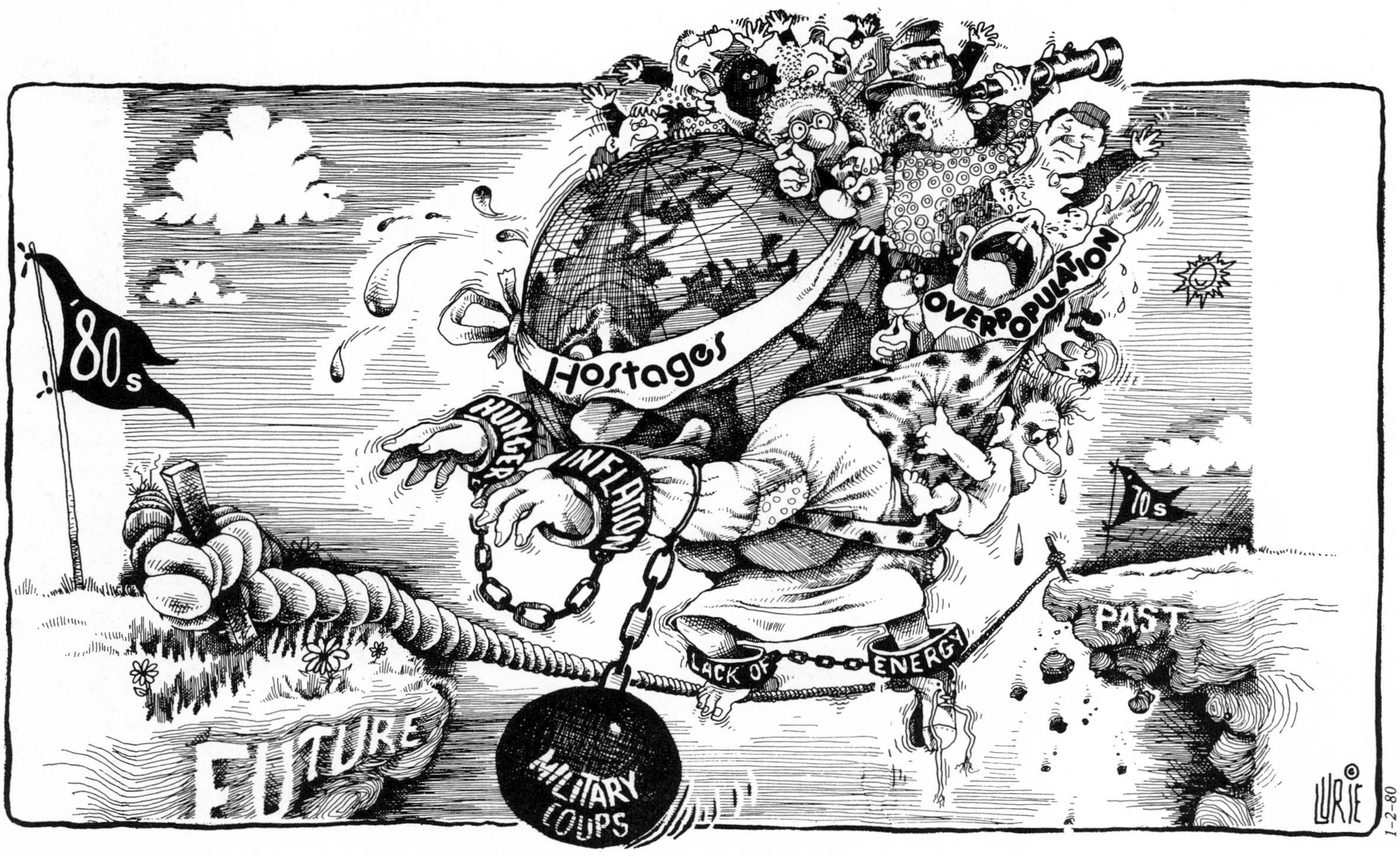
'80s
Hostages
OVERPOPULATION
HUNGER
INFLATION
LACK OF
ENERGY
'70s
PAST
FUTURE
MILITARY COUPS
LURIE ©
1-2-80

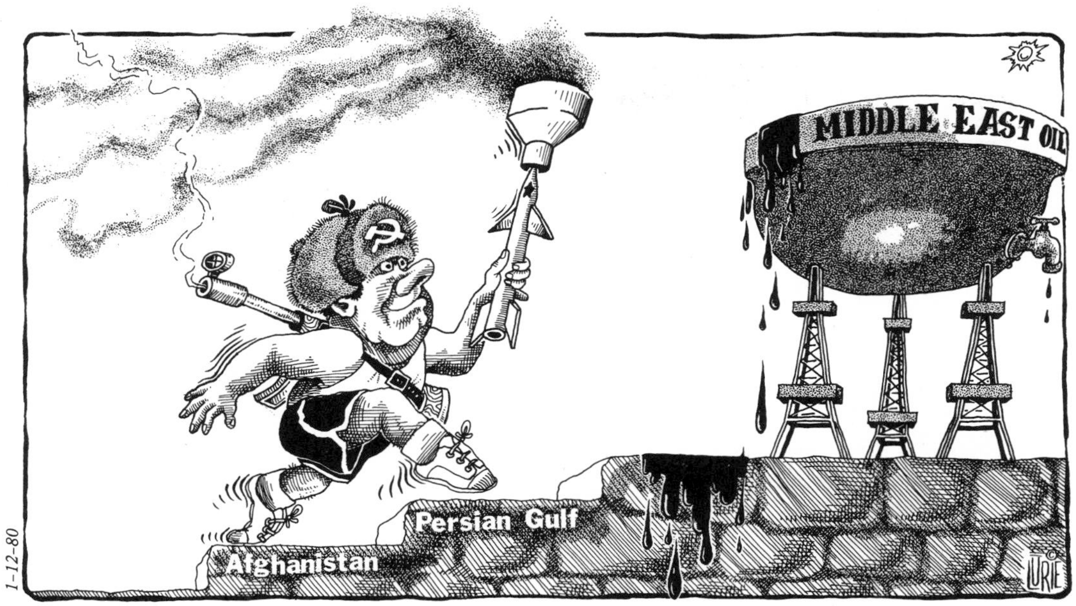
MIDDLE EAST OIL
Persian Gulf
Afghanistan
1-12-80
LURIE

RUSSIAN OLYMPICS

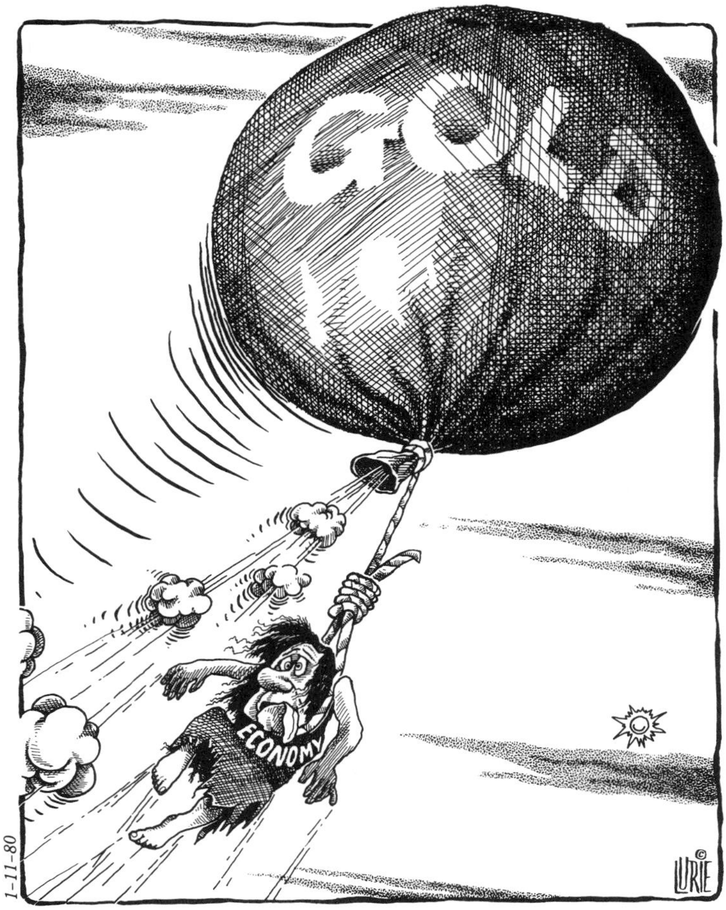
GOLD
ECONOMY
1-11-80
LURIE

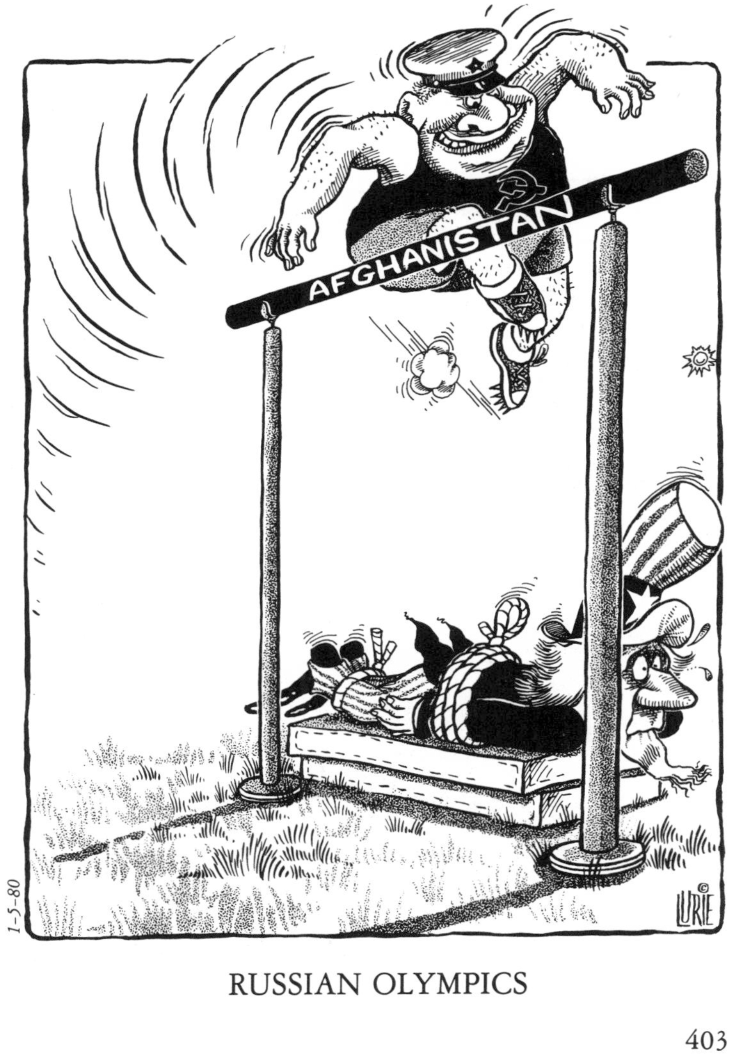
AFGHANISTAN
1-5-80
LURIE

RUSSIAN OLYMPICS

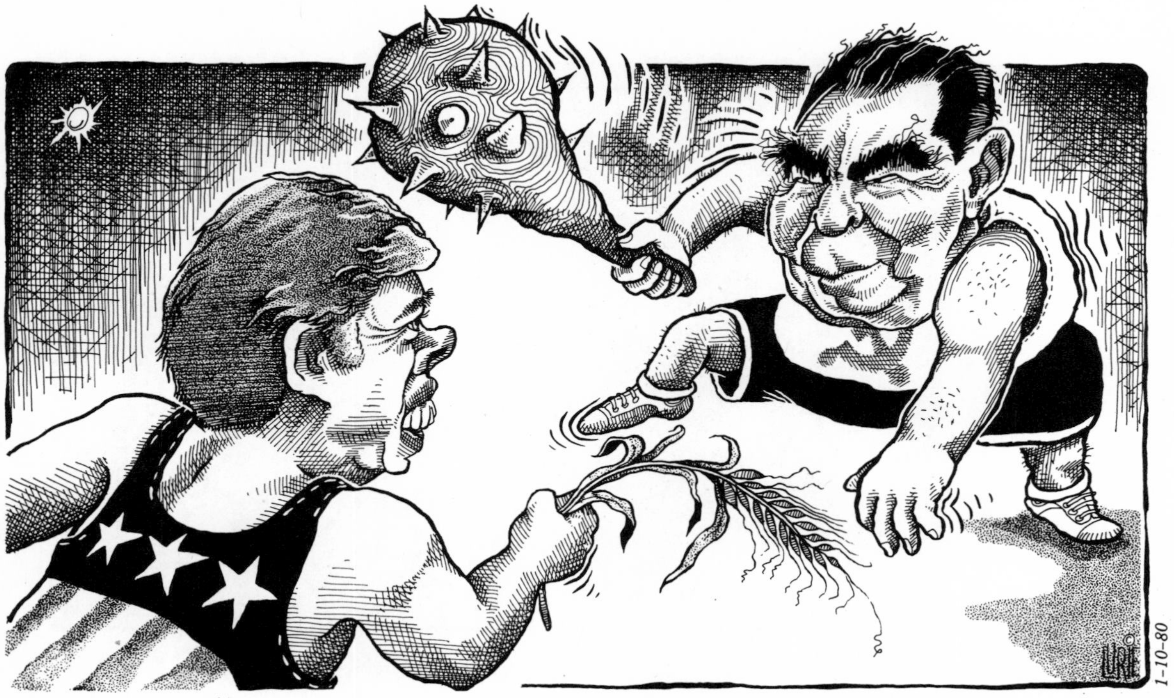
LURIE ©
1-10-80

RUSSIAN OLYMPICS

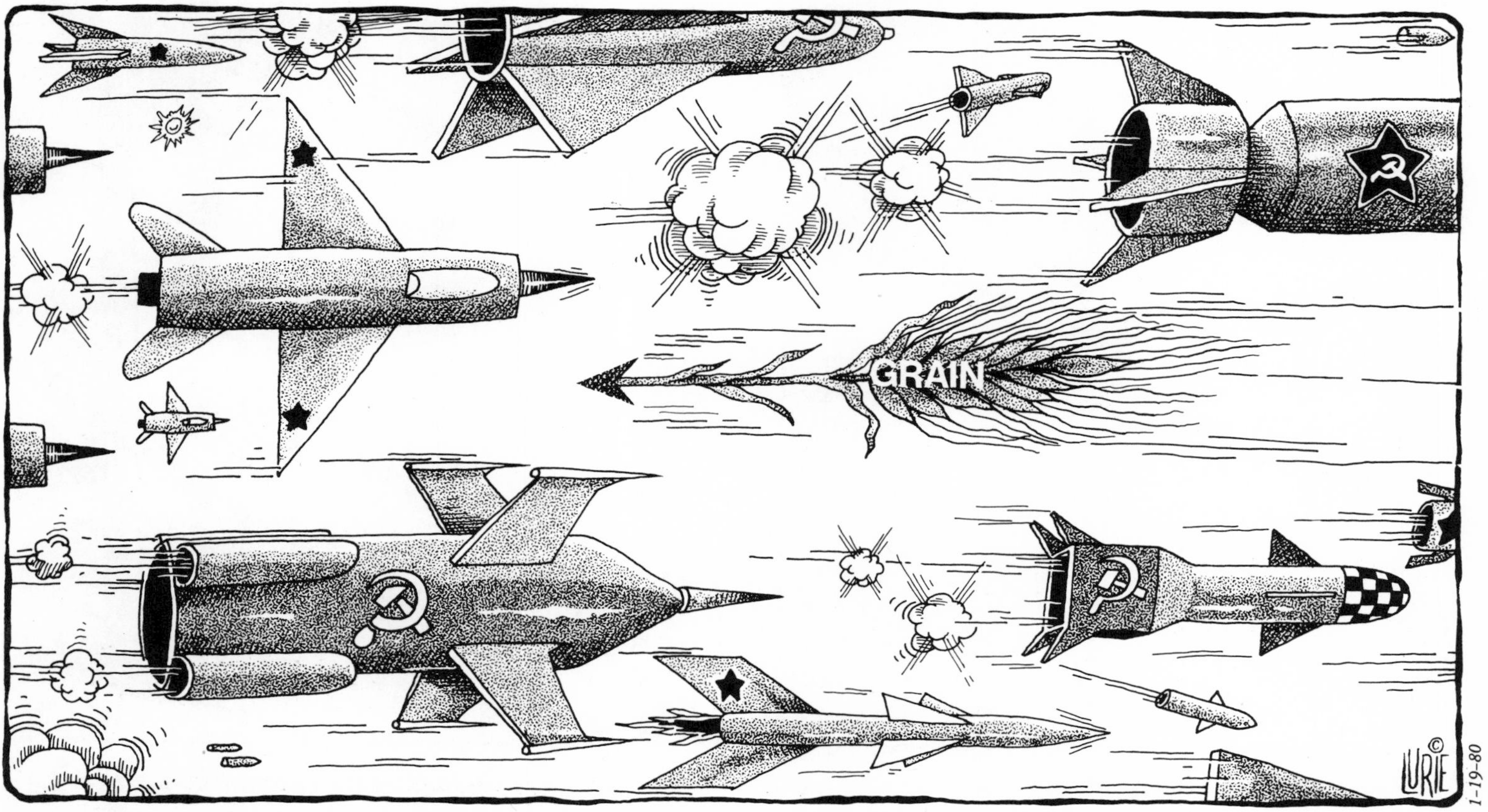
GRAIN
LURIE ©
1-19-80

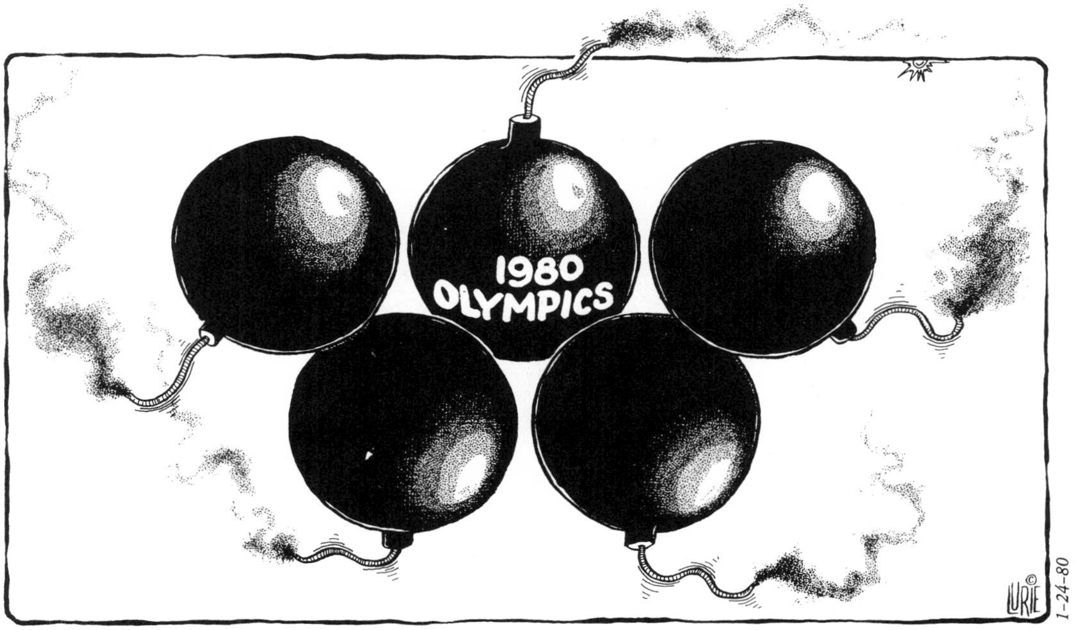
1980
OLYMPICS
LURIE©
1-24-80

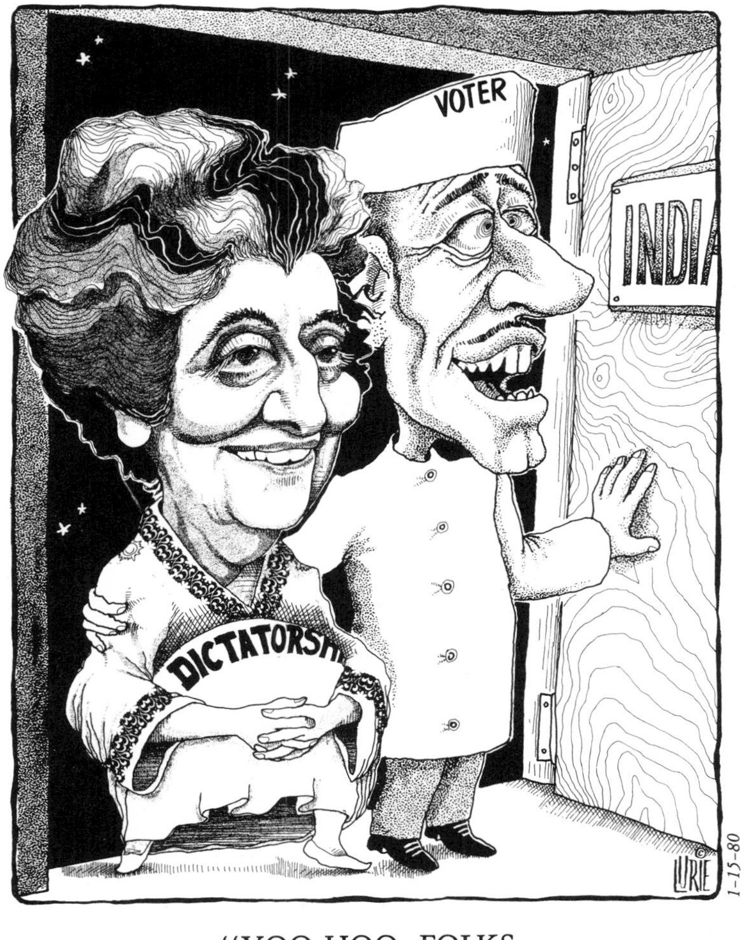
VOTER
INDIA
DICTATORSH
LURIE©
1-15-80

"YOO-HOO, FOLKS,
GUESS WHO'S COMING TO DINNER?"

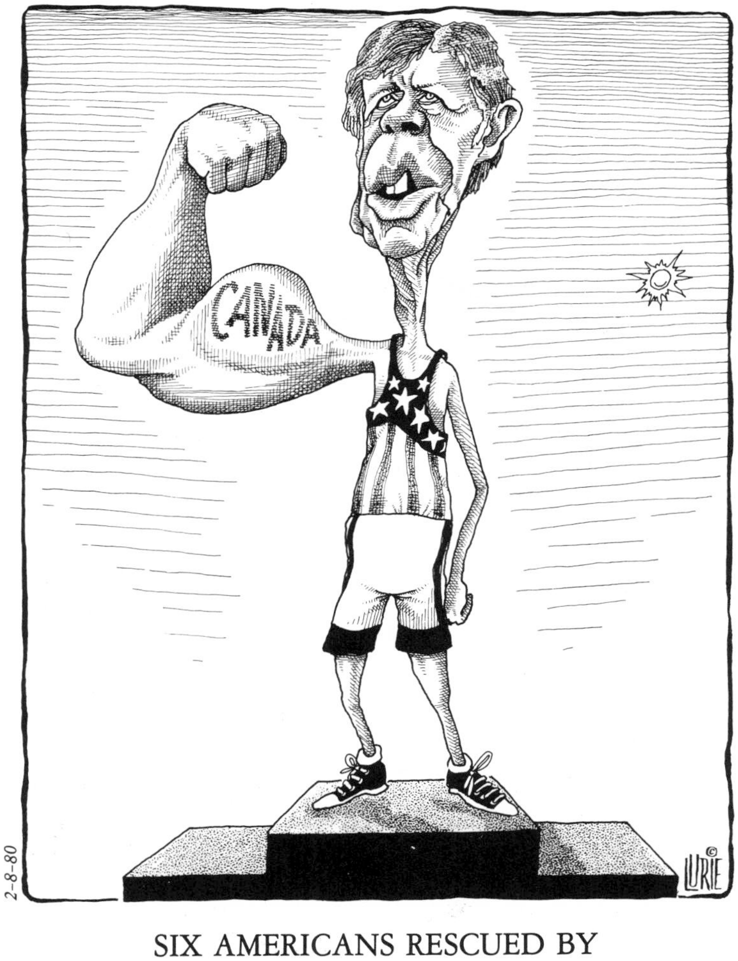
CANADA
LURIE©
2-8-80

SIX AMERICANS RESCUED BY
CANADIAN EMBASSY IN IRAN

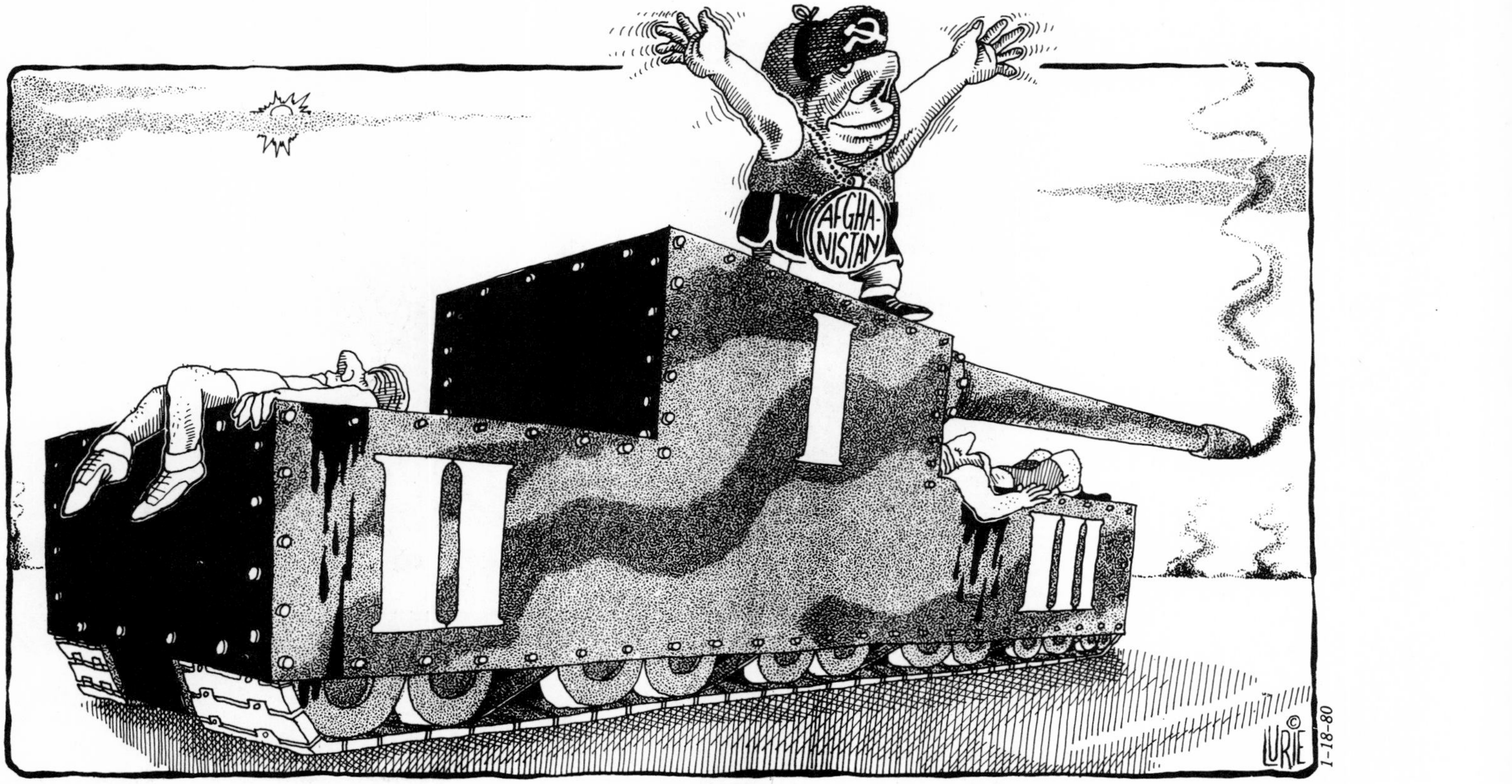
AFGHA-NISTAN
I
II
III
LURIE ©
1-18-80

RUSSIAN OLYMPICS

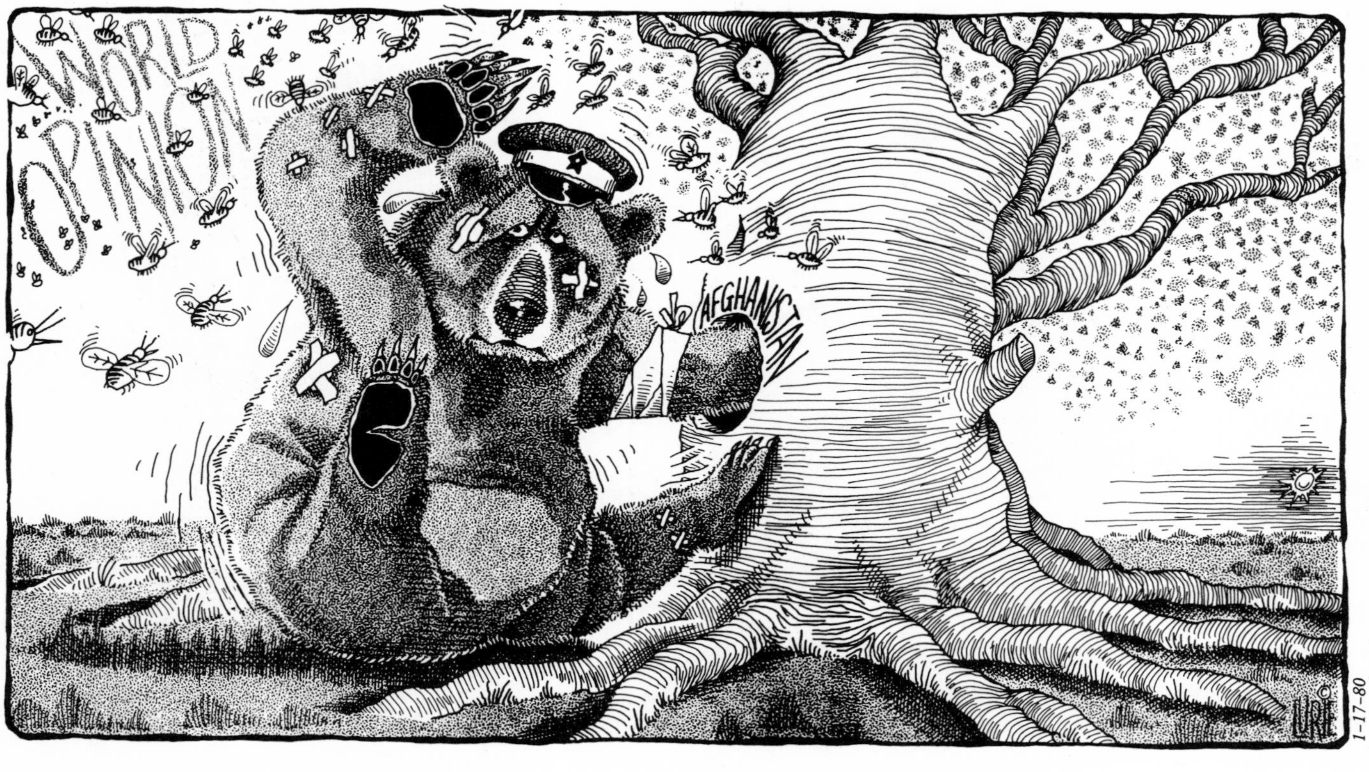
WORLD OPINION
AFGHANISTAN
LURIE ©
1-17-80

"HI THERE! I'M IRAN'S NEW PRESIDENT!"

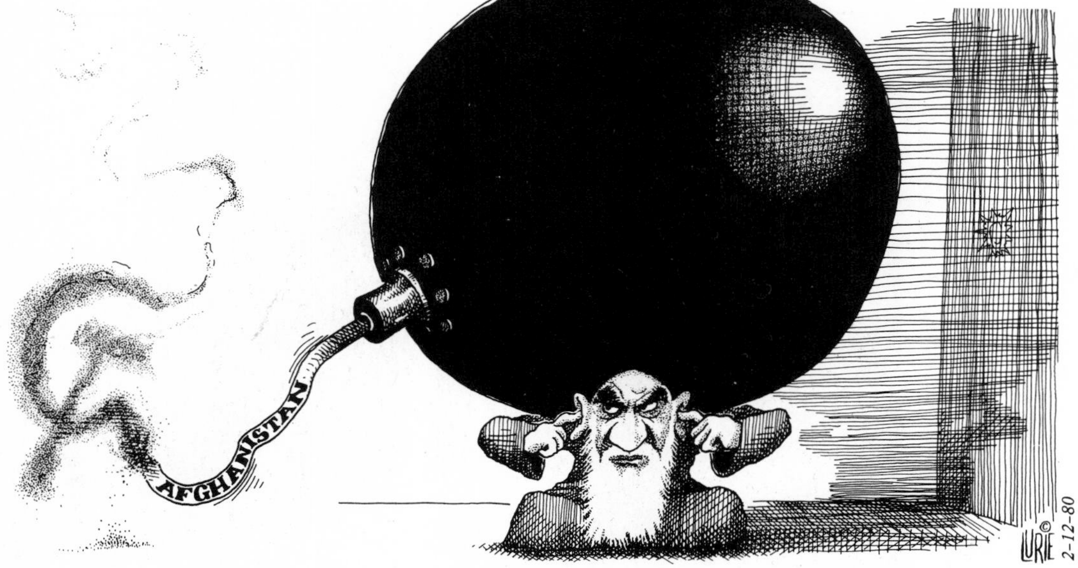
AFGHANISTAN
LURIE ©
2-12-80

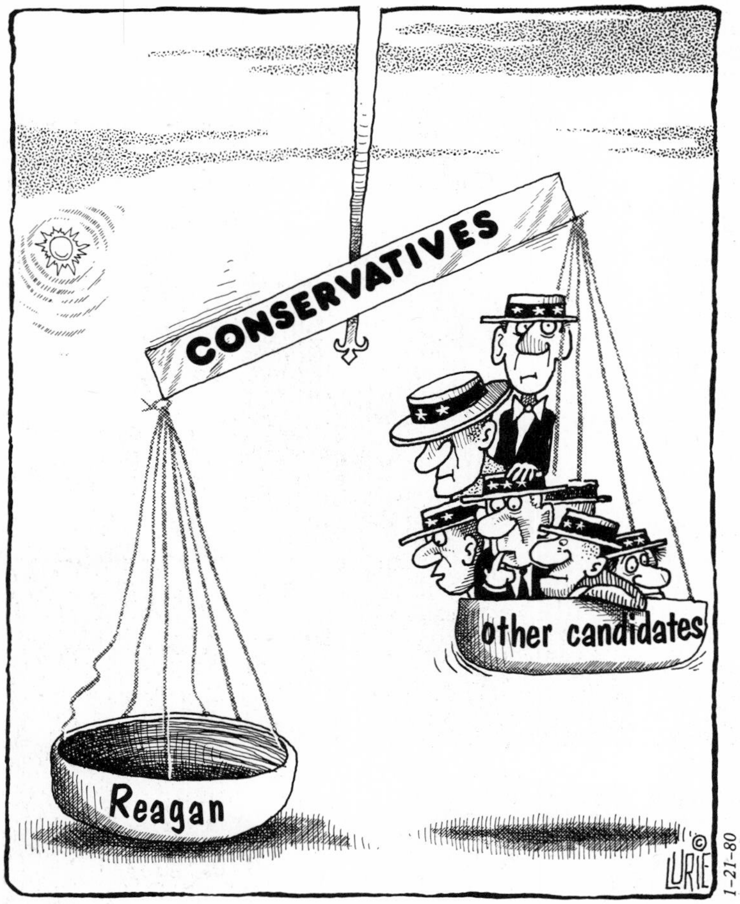
CONSERVATIVES
other candidates
Reagan
LURIE ©
1-21-80

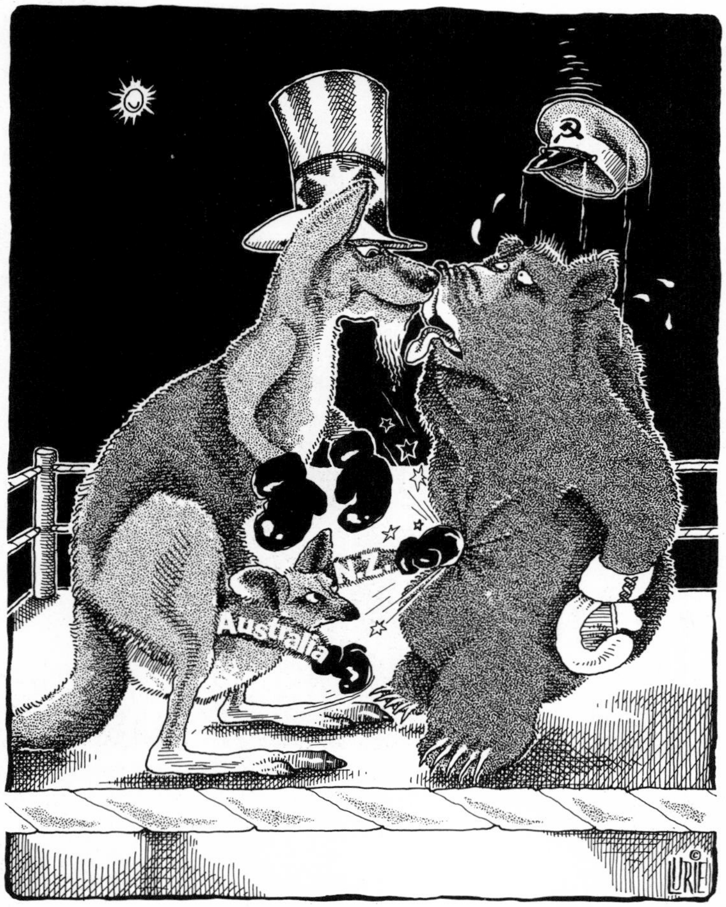
N.Z.
Australia
LURIE ©

OLYMPIC BOXING

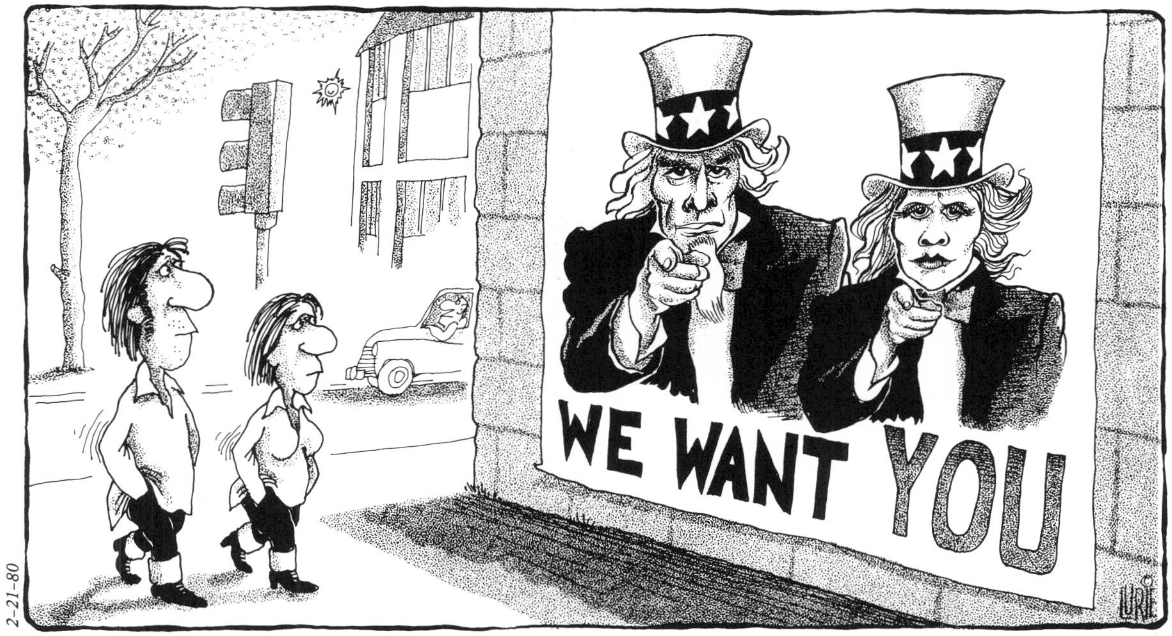
WE WANT YOU
2-21-80
LURIE

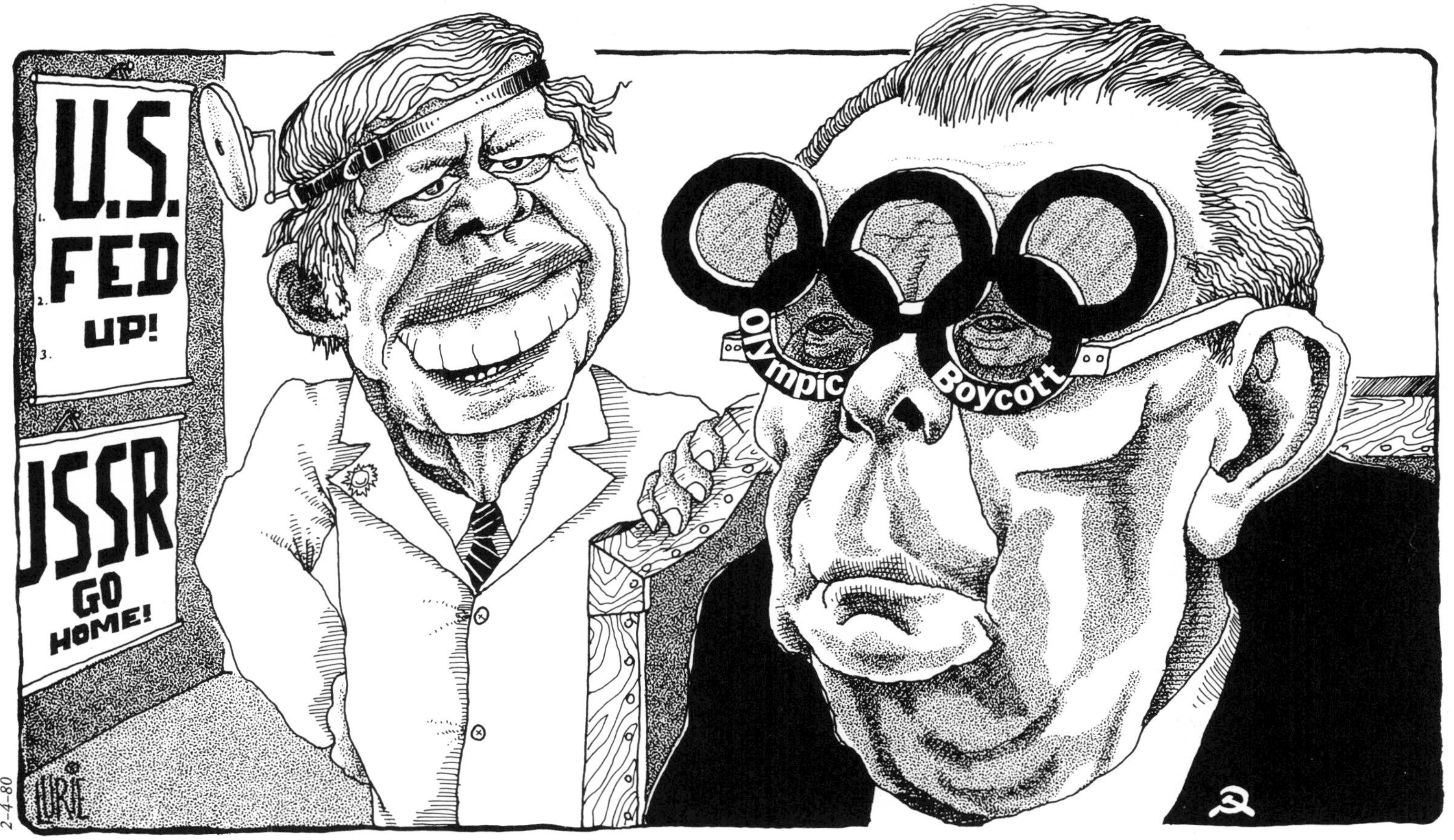
U.S.
FED
UP!
USSR
GO
HOME!
Olympic
Boycott
2-4-80
LURIE

"SEE THE WRITING ON THE WALL NOW?!"

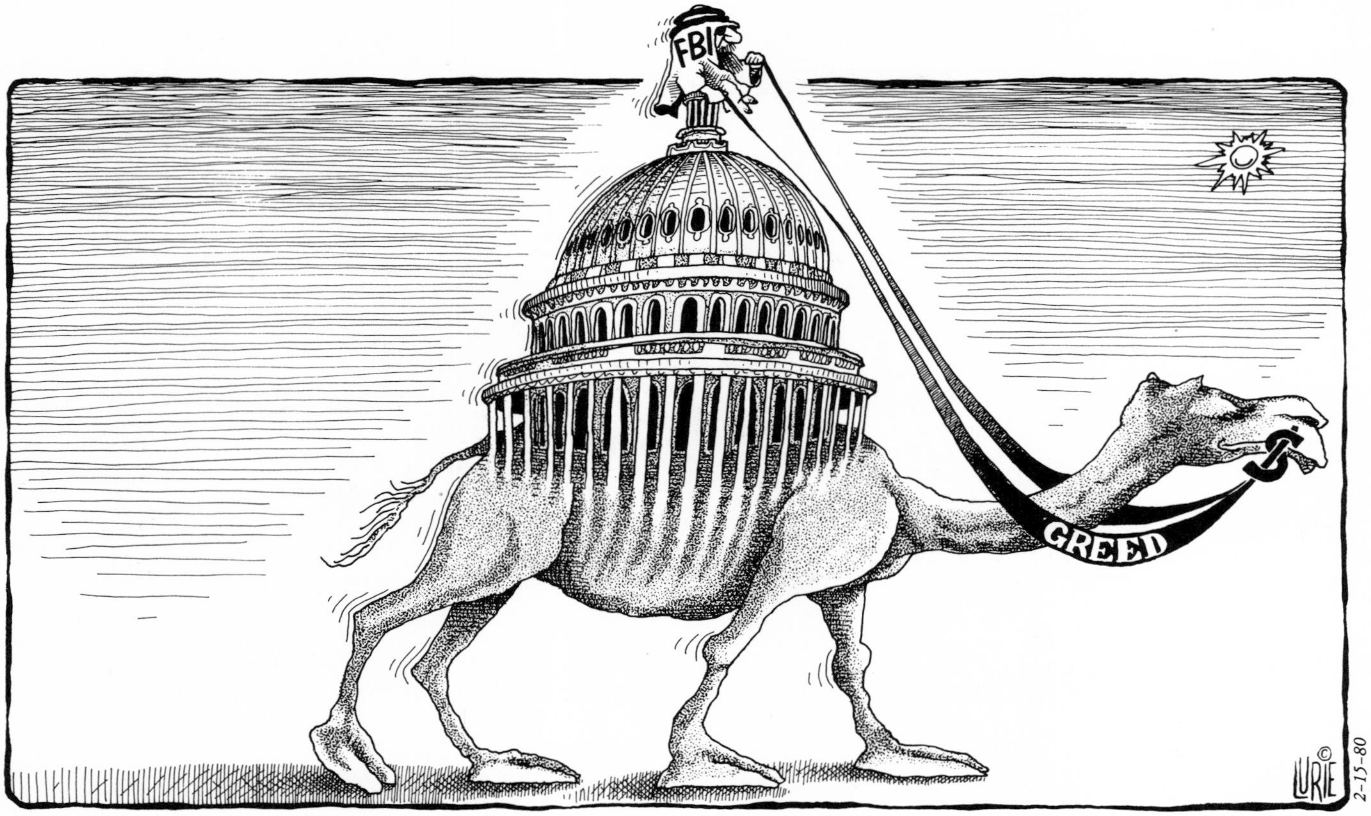
FBI
GREED
LURIE ©
2-15-80

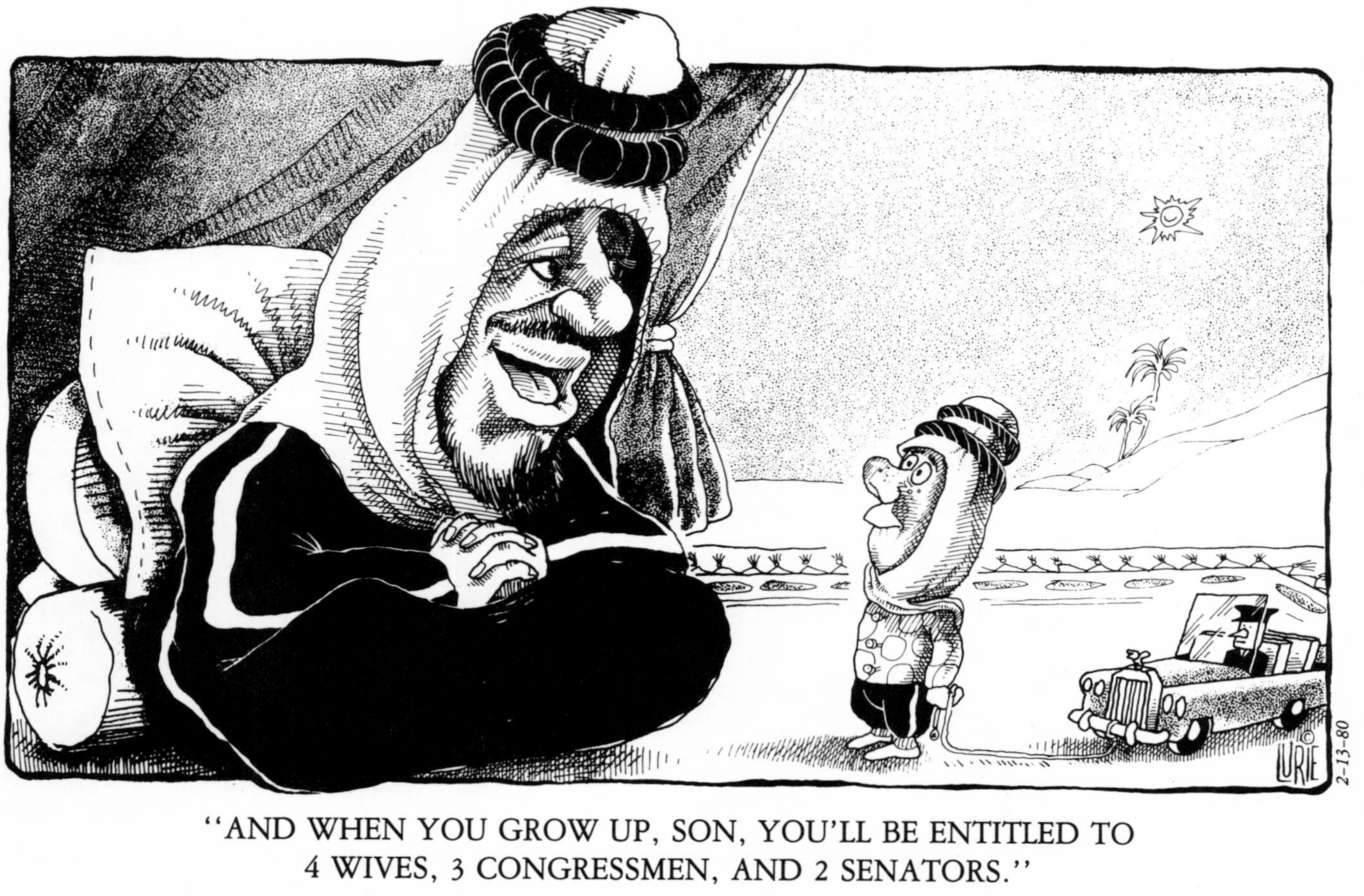
LURIE ©
2-13-80

"AND WHEN YOU GROW UP, SON, YOU'LL BE ENTITLED TO 4 WIVES, 3 CONGRESSMEN, AND 2 SENATORS."

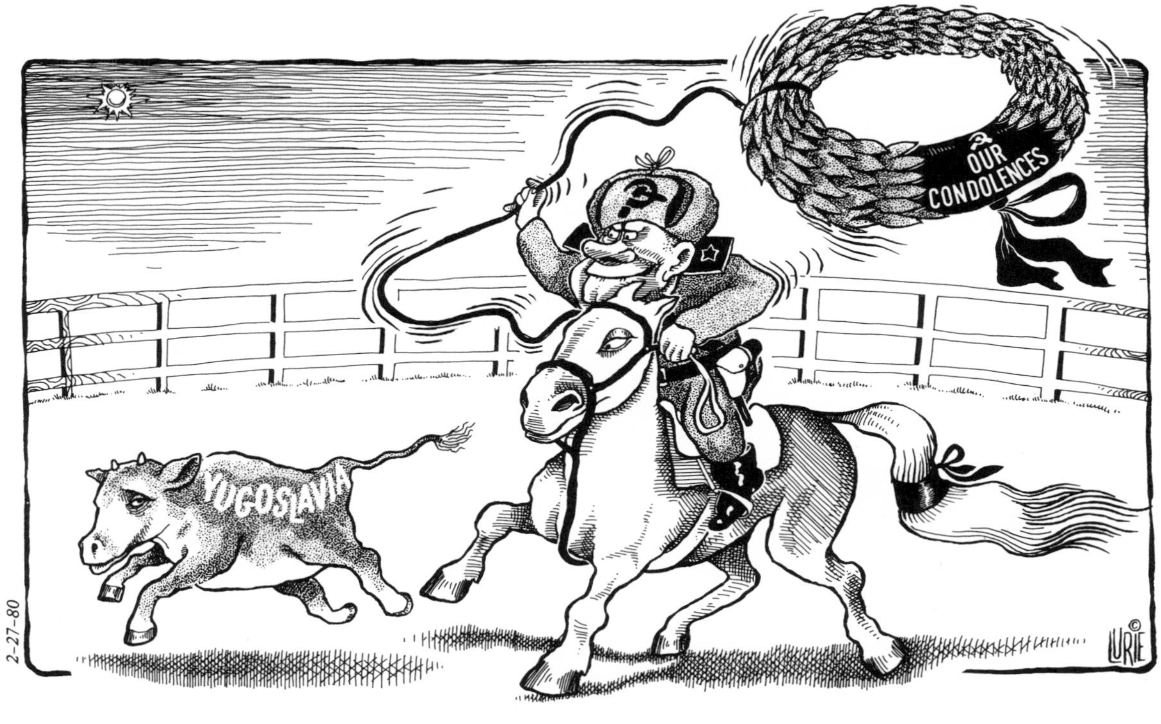

OUR CONDOLENCES
YUGOSLAVIA
2-27-80
LURIE©

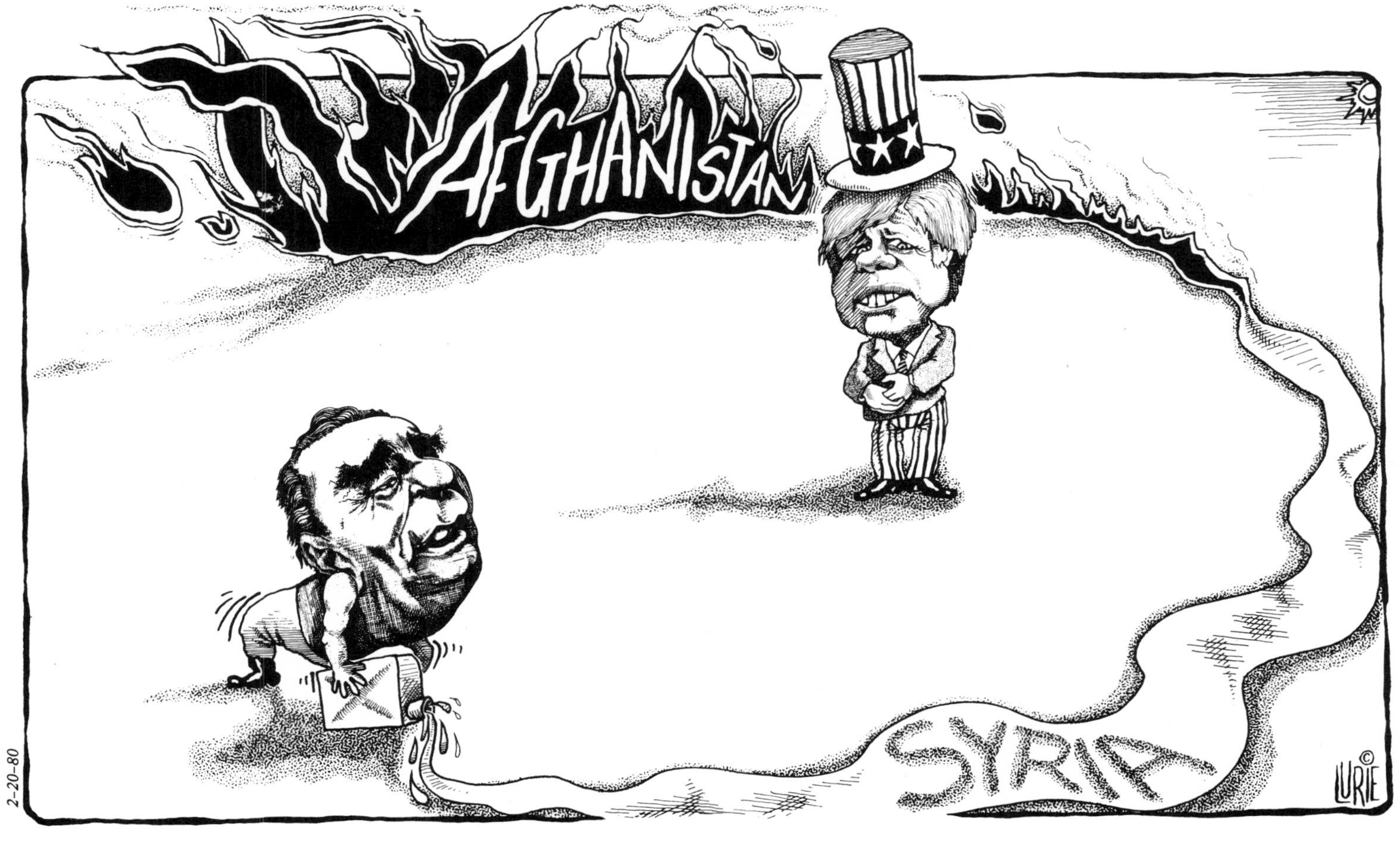

AFGHANISTAN
SYRIA
2-20-80
LURIE©

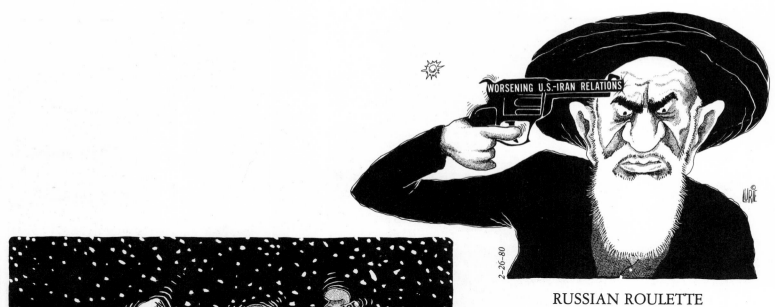

WORSENING U.S.-IRAN RELATIONS
LURIE
2-26-80

RUSSIAN ROULETTE

Kennedy
Brown
Carter
MAINE
LURIE
2-22-80

"I WON!"

INFLATION
LURIE
3-13-80

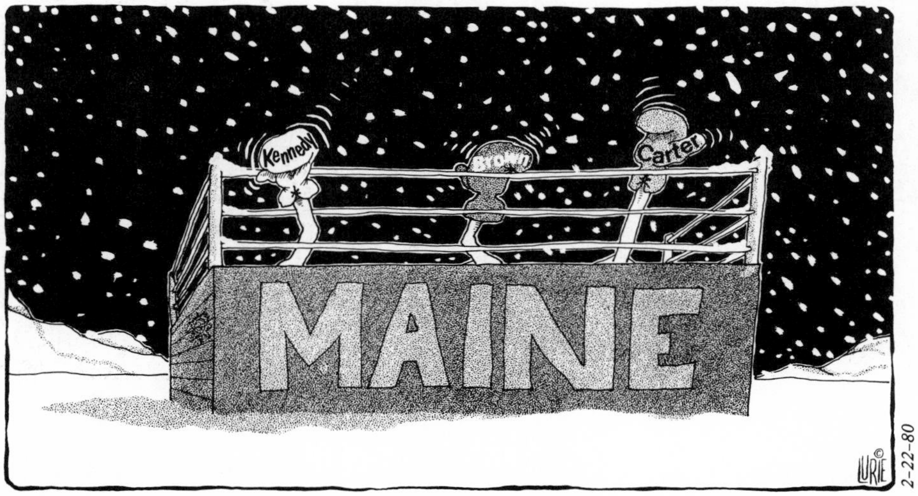

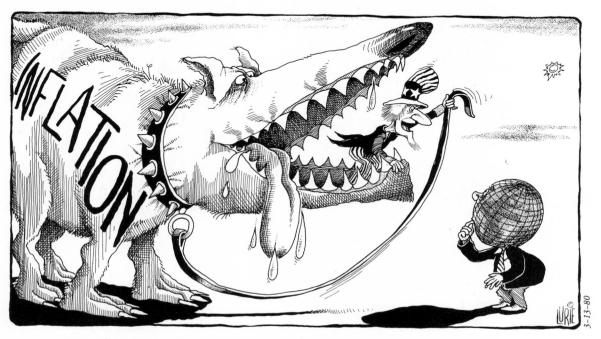

"DON'T WORRY—I'M HOLDING HIM ON A TIGHT LEASH!"

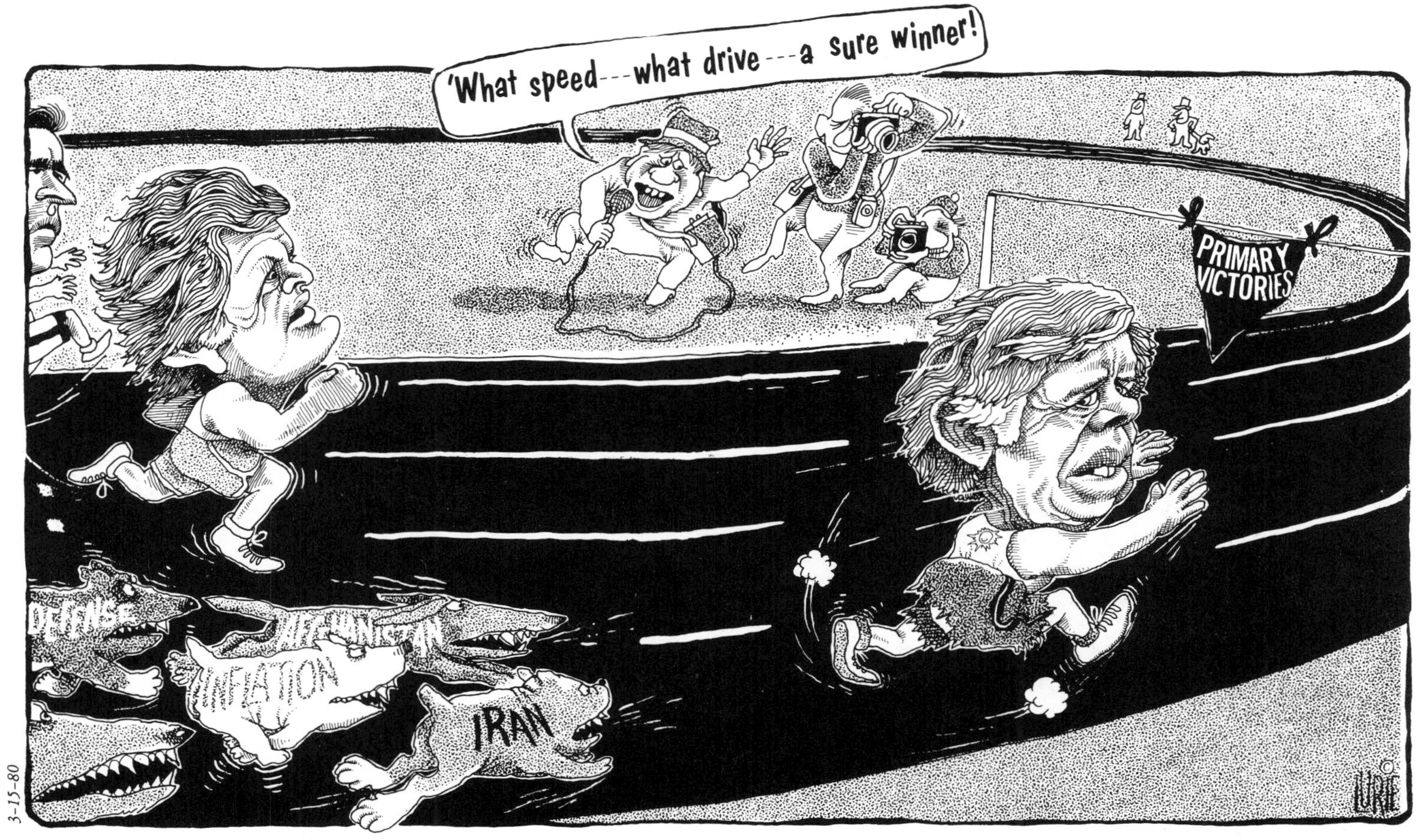
'What speed---what drive---a sure winner!
PRIMARY VICTORIES
DEFENSE
AFGHANISTAN
INFLATION
IRAN
LURIE
3-15-80

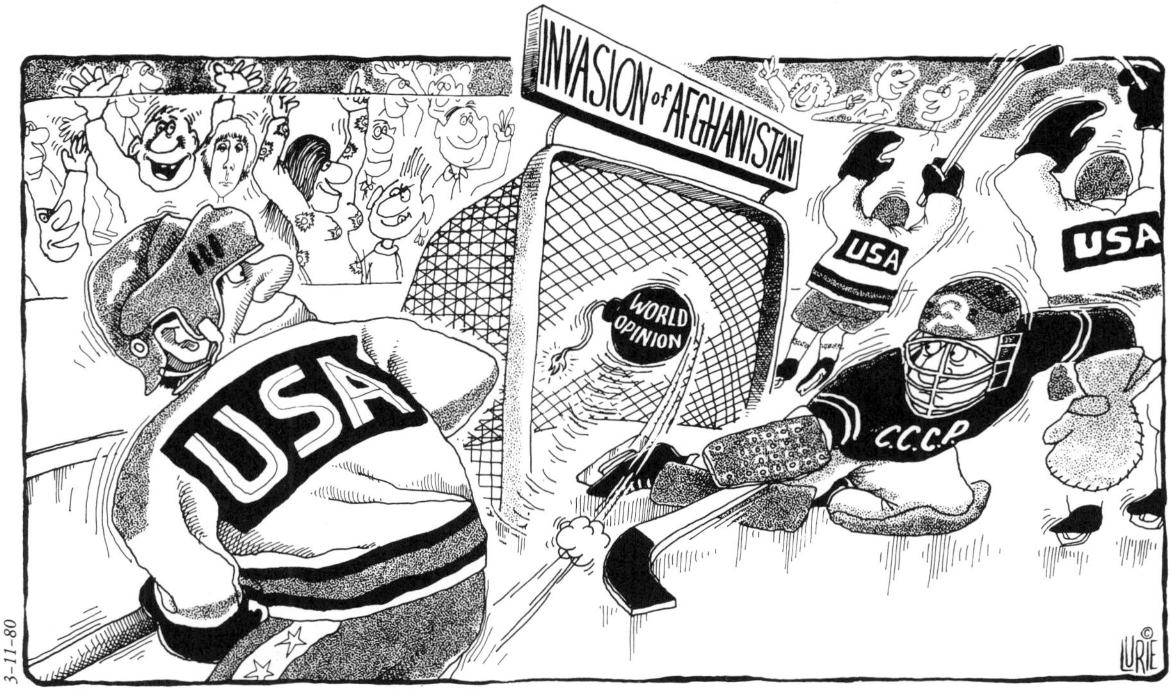
INVASION of AFGHANISTAN
WORLD OPINION
USA
USA
USA
C.C.C.P.
LURIE
3-11-80

1–0

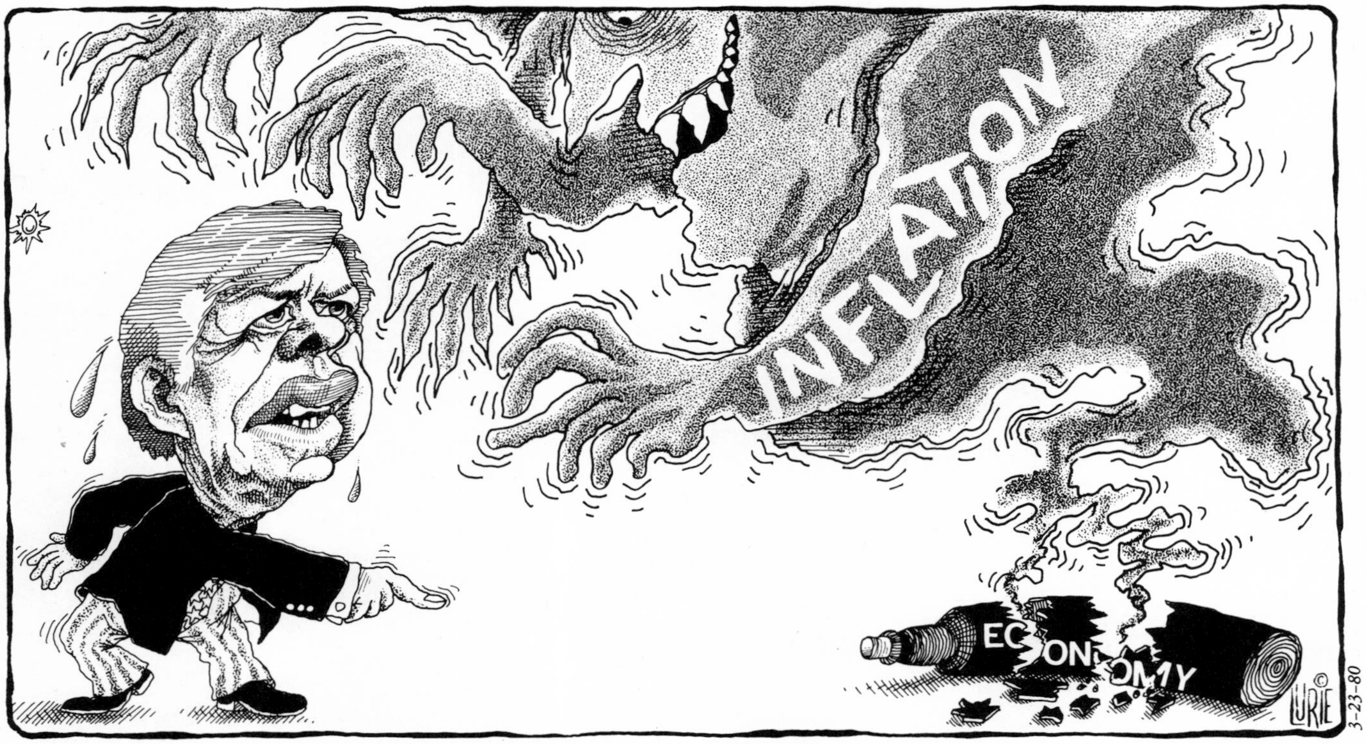
INFLATION
EC ON OMY
LURIE
3-23-80

"RETURN TO YOUR BOTTLE!"

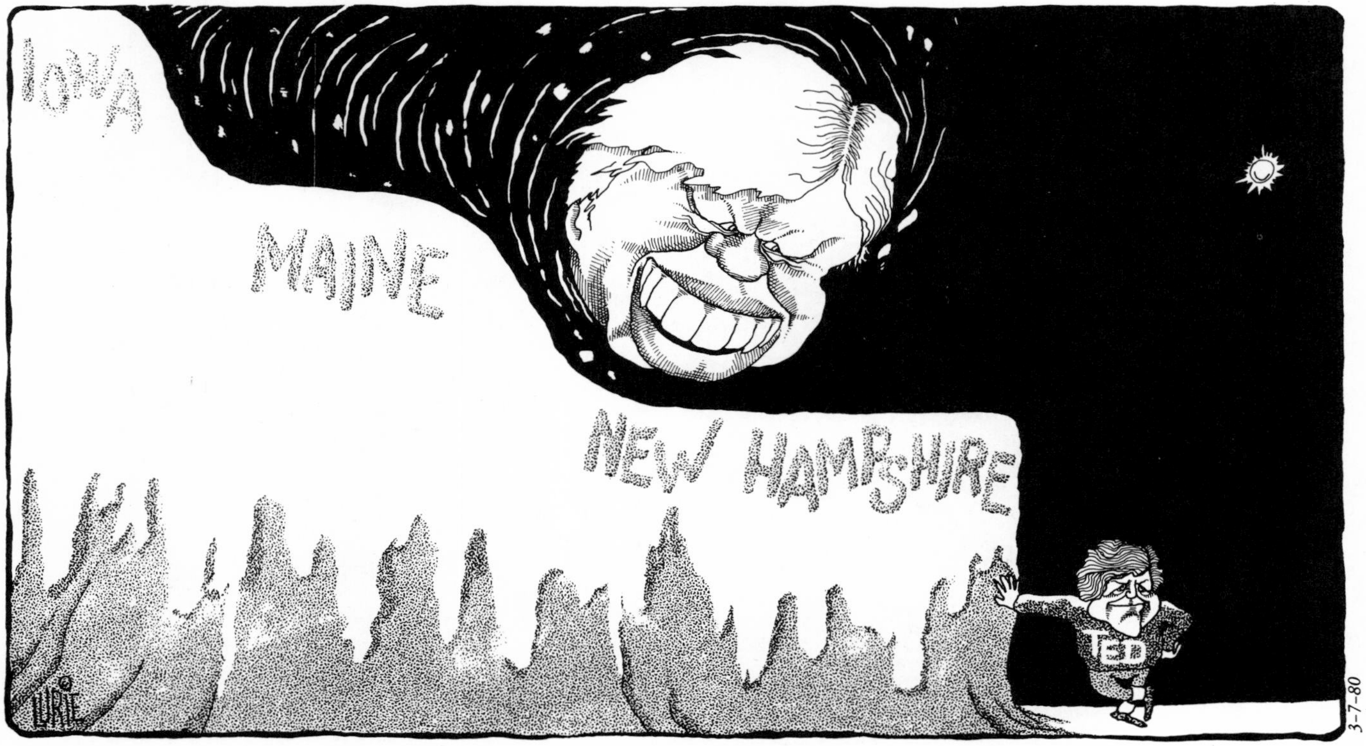
IOWA
MAINE
NEW HAMPSHIRE
TED
LURIE
3-7-80

SNOWBALLING

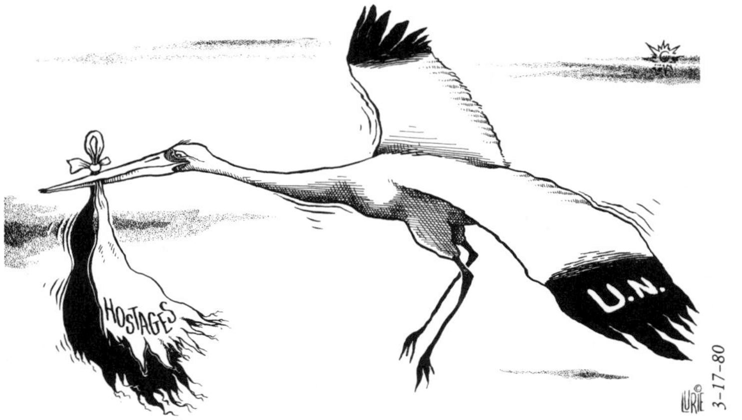
HOSTAGES
U.N.
3-17-80
LURIE

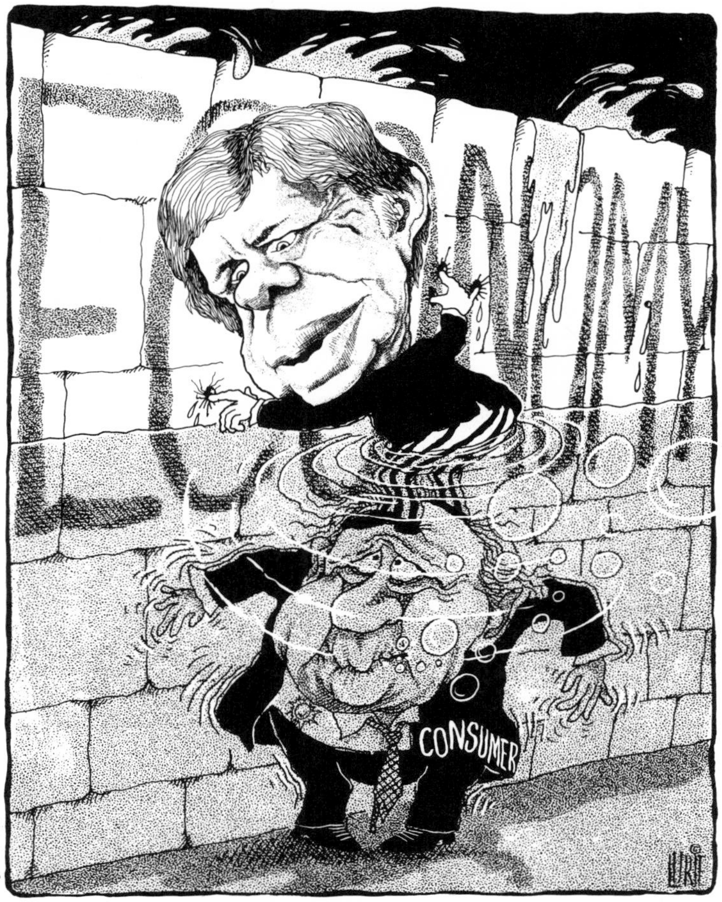
CONSUMER
3-28-80
LURIE

"RELAX . . . THESE THINGS TAKE TIME!"

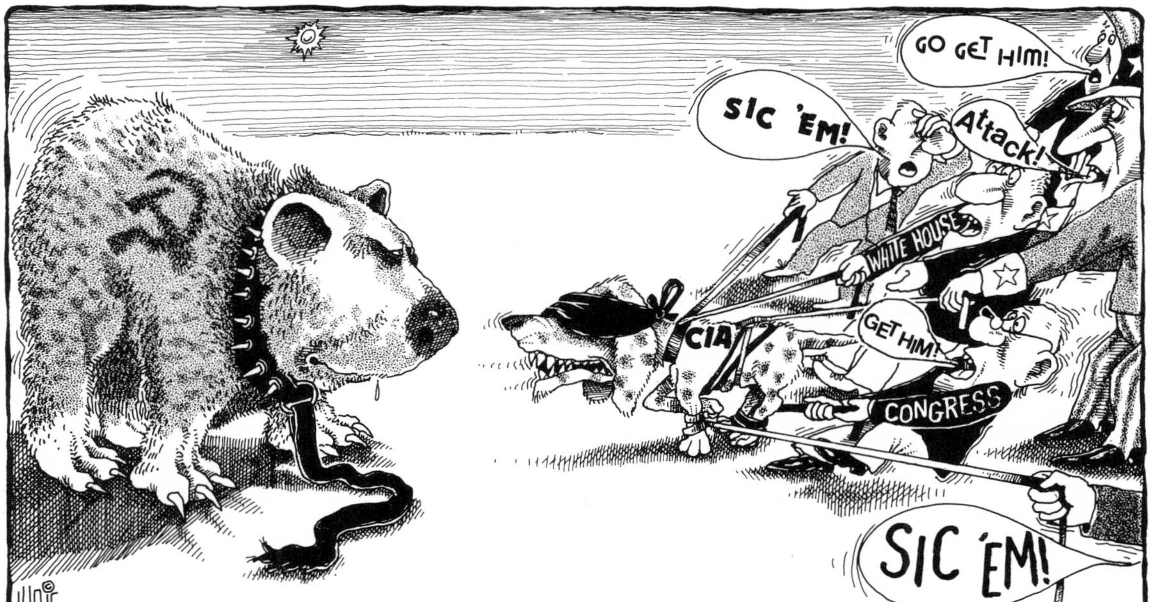
GO GET HIM!
SIC 'EM!
Attack!
WHITE HOUSE
CIA
GET HIM!
CONGRESS
SIC 'EM!
LURIE
3-21-80

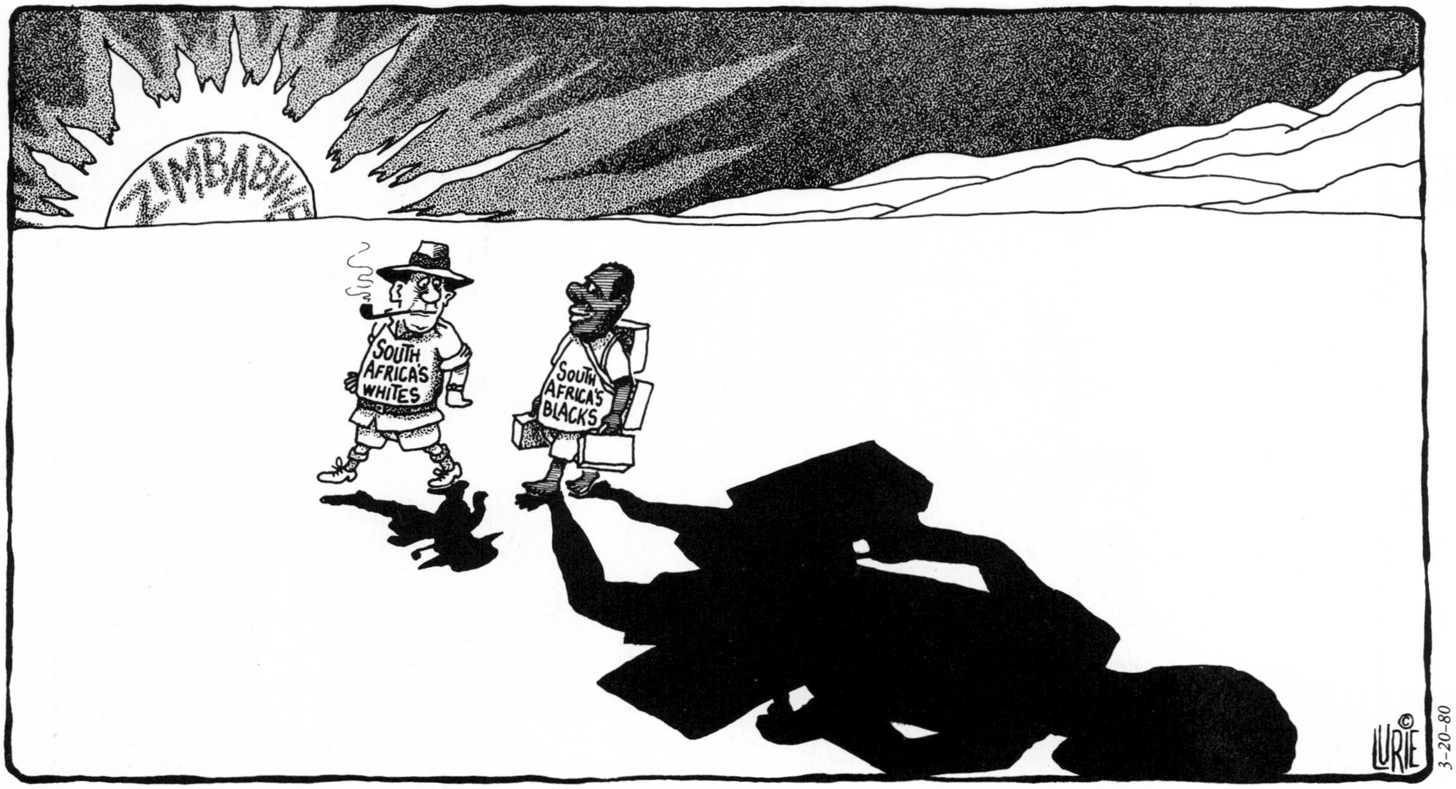
ZIMBABWE
SOUTH AFRICA'S WHITES
SOUTH AFRICA'S BLACKS
LURIE ©
3-20-80

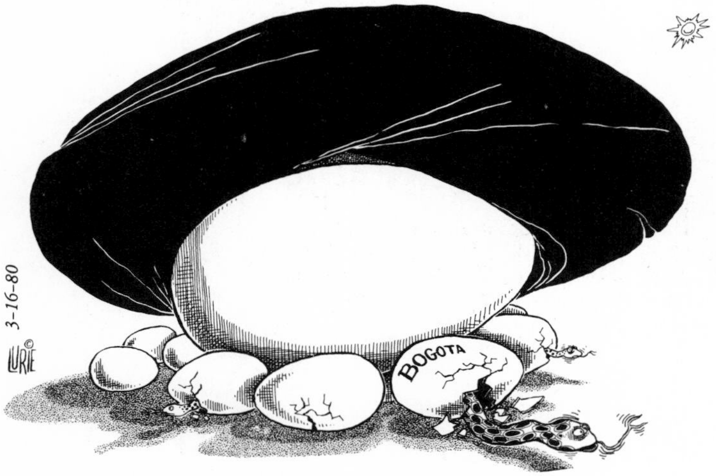
3-16-80
LURIE
BOGOTA

HATCHING

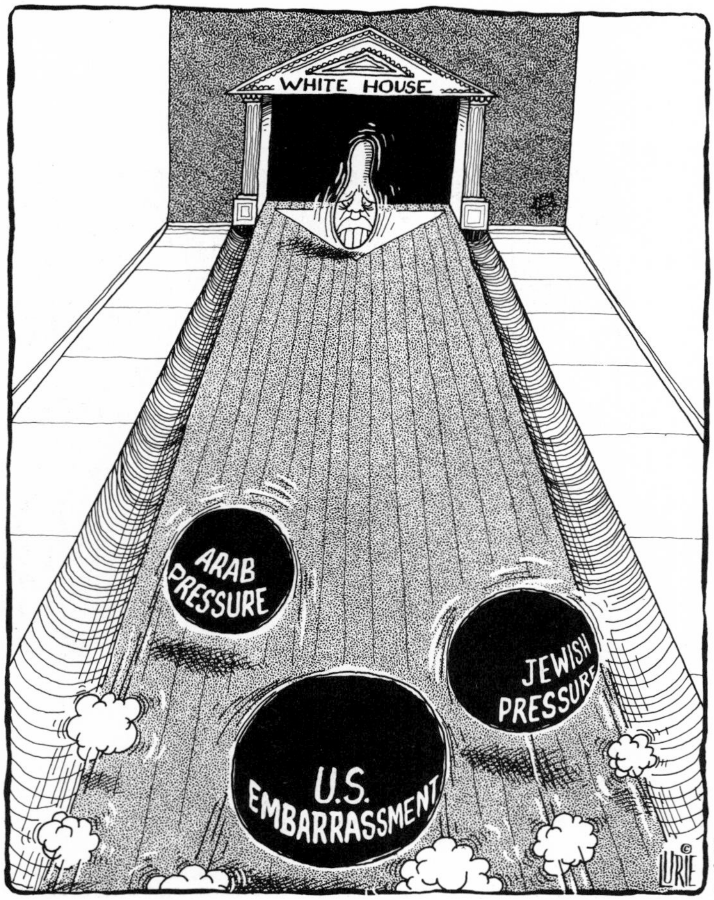
WHITE HOUSE
ARAB PRESSURE
JEWISH PRESSURE
U.S. EMBARRASSMENT
LURIE ©
3-6-80

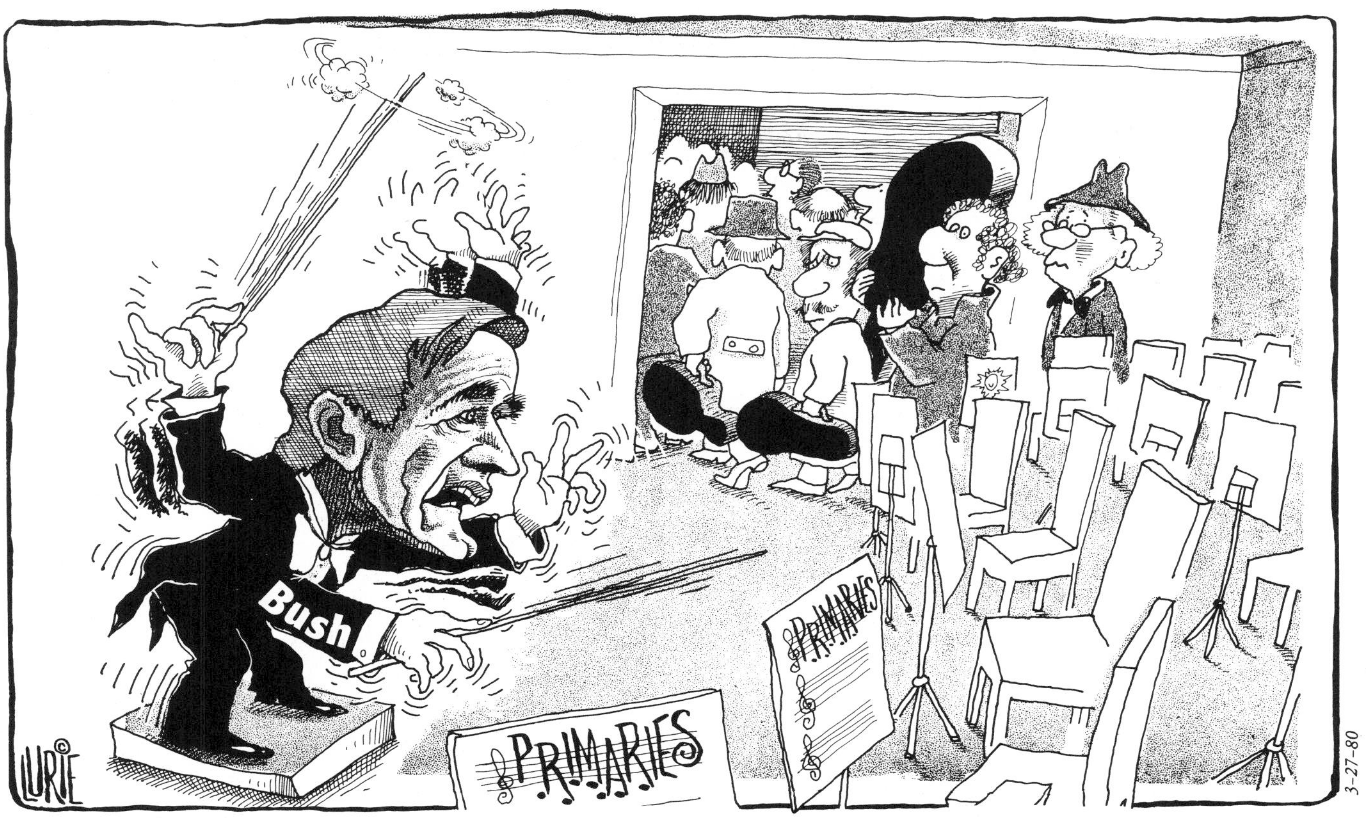
Bush
PRIMARIES
PRIMARIES
LURIE©
3-27-80

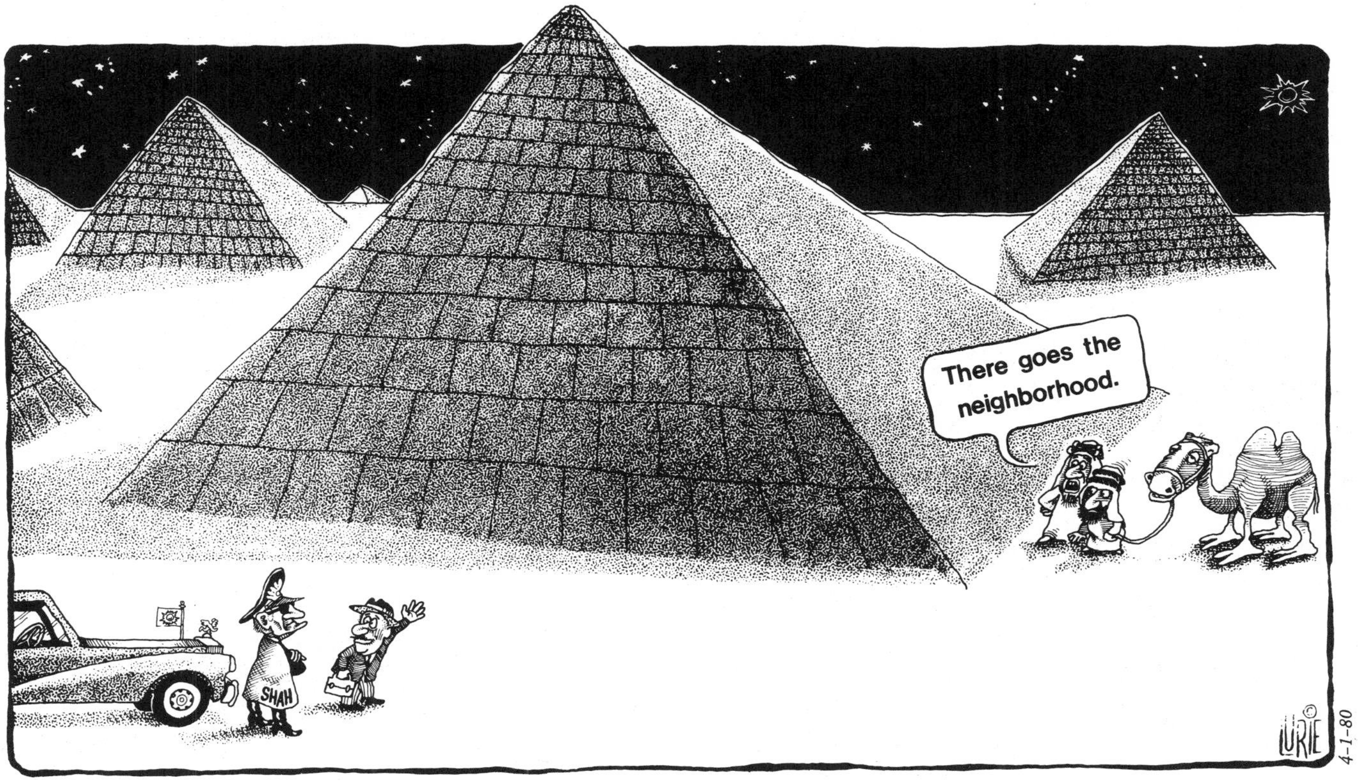
There goes the neighborhood.
SHAH
LURIE©
4-1-80

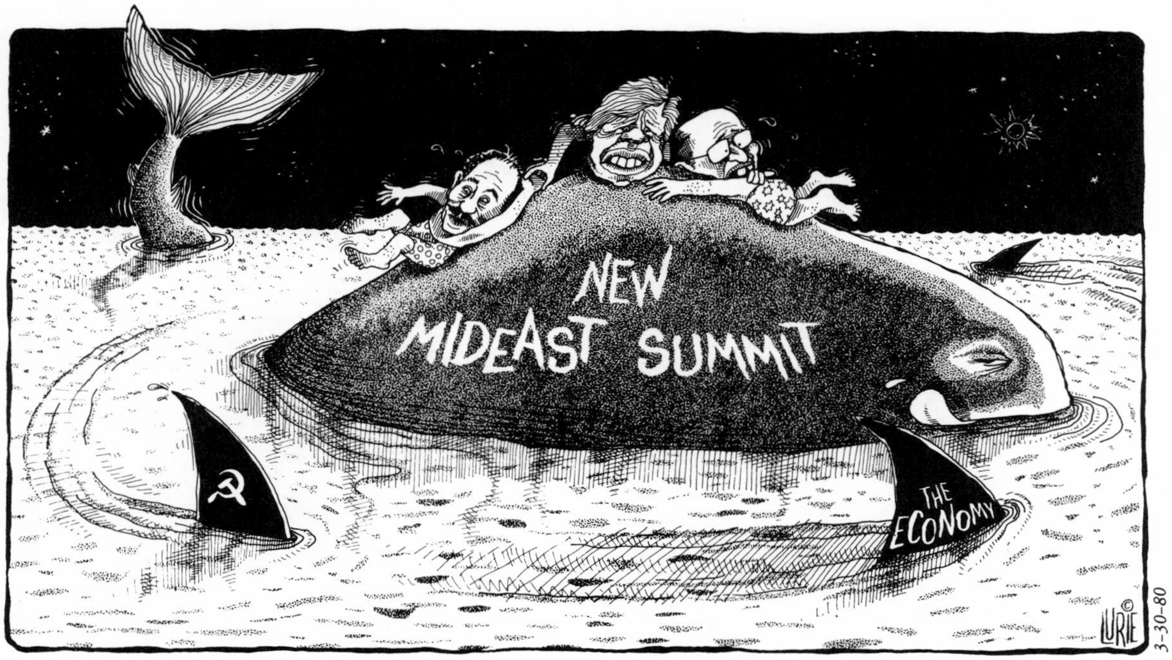
NEW
MIDEAST SUMMIT
THE
ECONOMY
LURIE ©

3-30-80

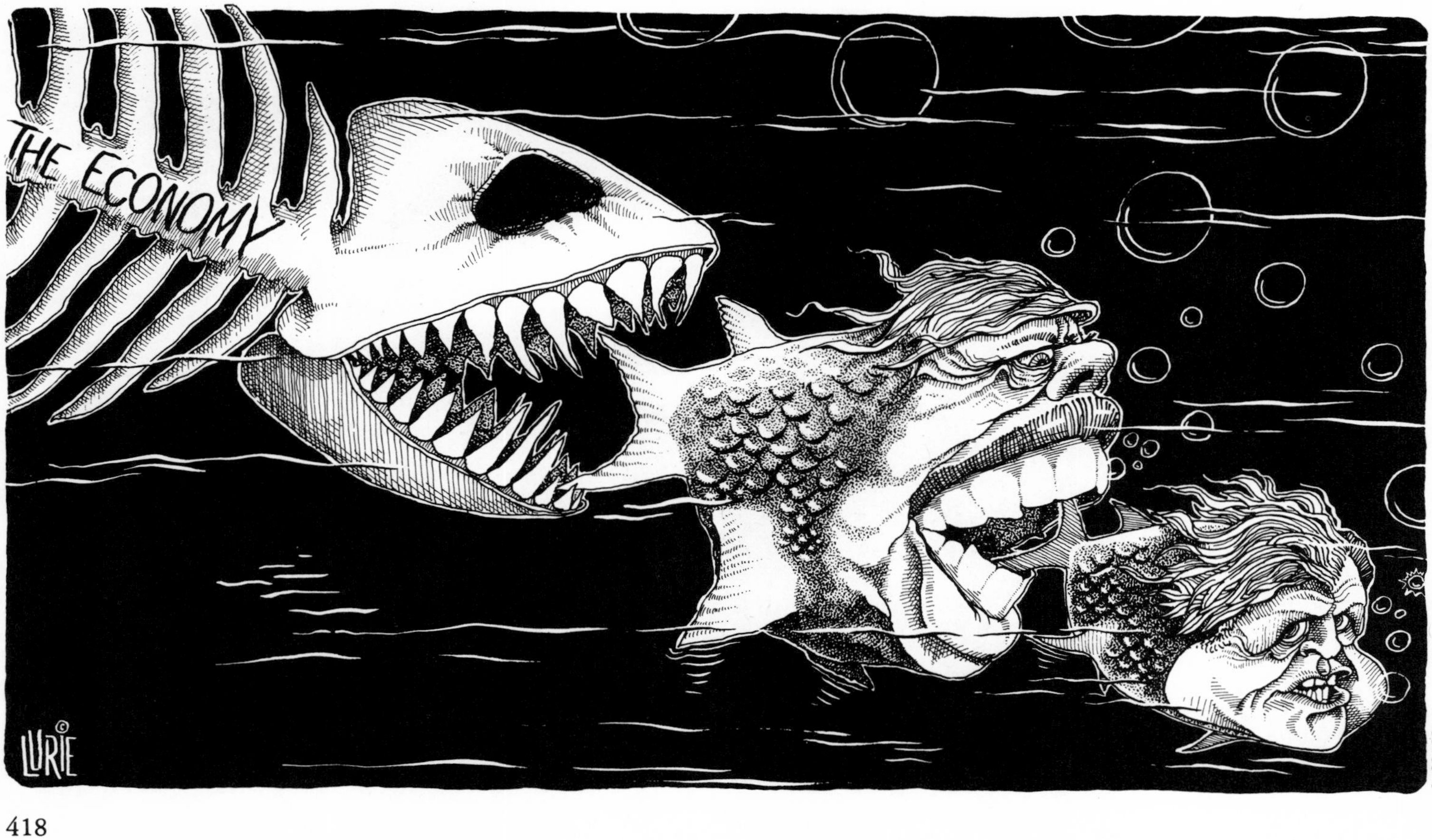
THE ECONOMY
LURIE ©

3-29-80

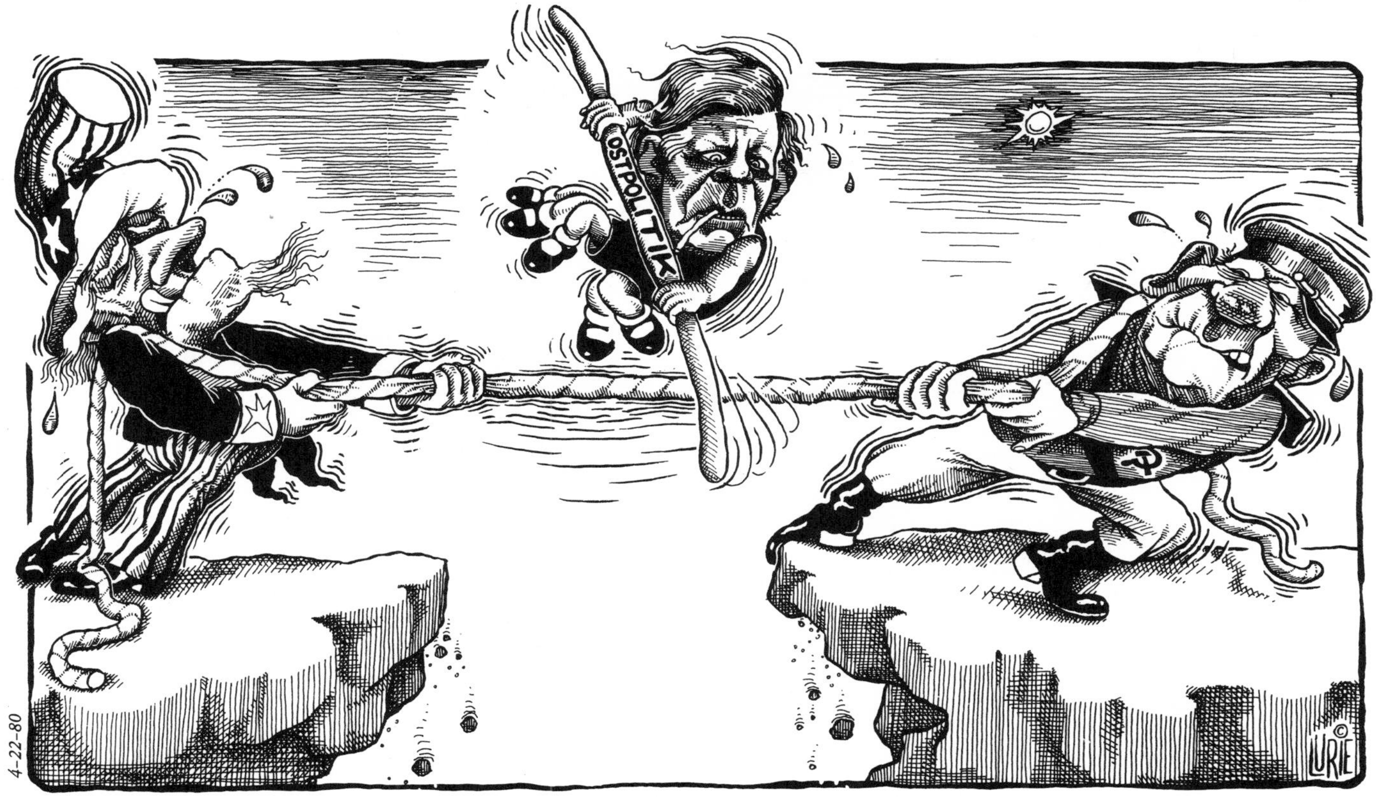
OSTPOLITIK
4-22-80
LURIE ©

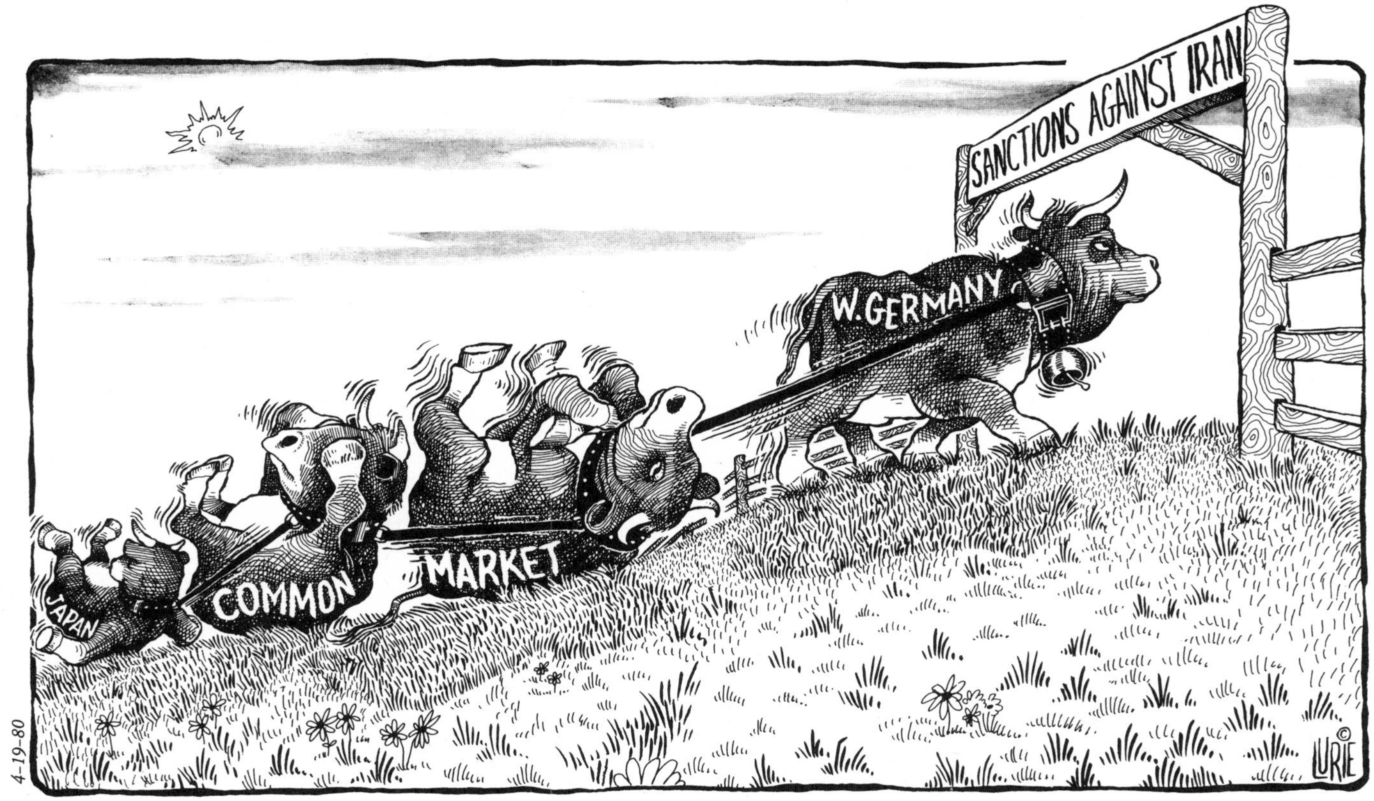
SANCTIONS AGAINST IRAN
W. GERMANY
COMMON
MARKET
JAPAN
4-19-80
LURIE ©

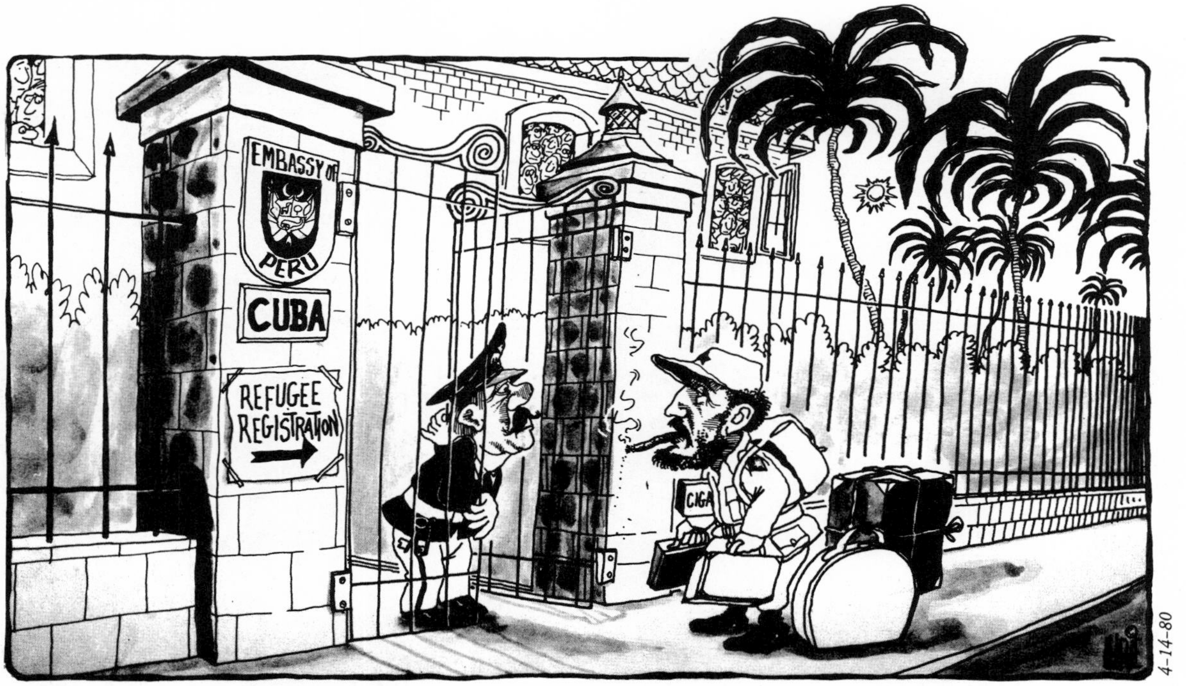
EMBASSY OF
PERU
CUBA
REFUGEE
REGISTRATION
4-14-80

"WILL YOU ACCEPT ONE MORE?"

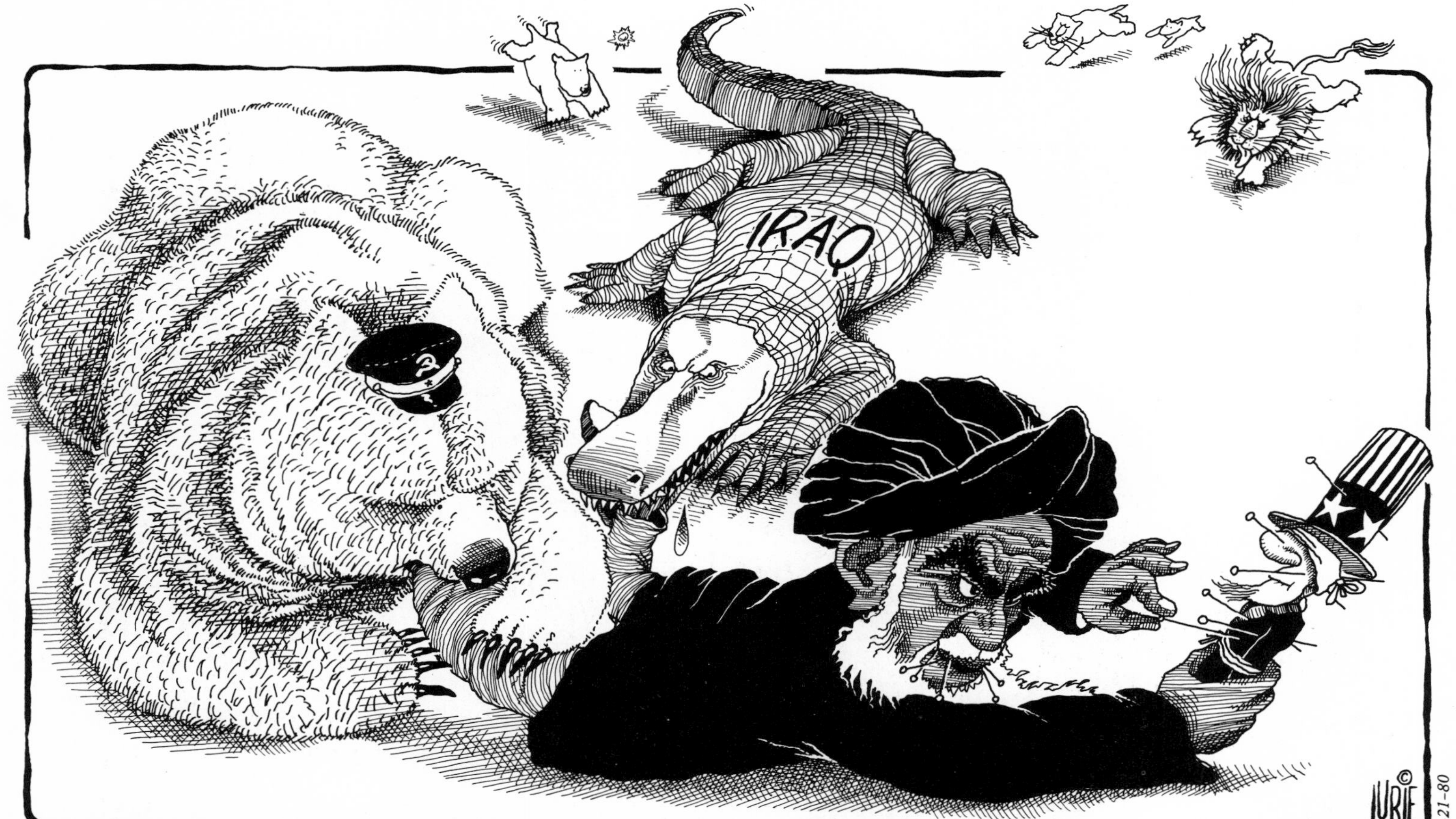
IRAQ
LURIE ©
4-21-80

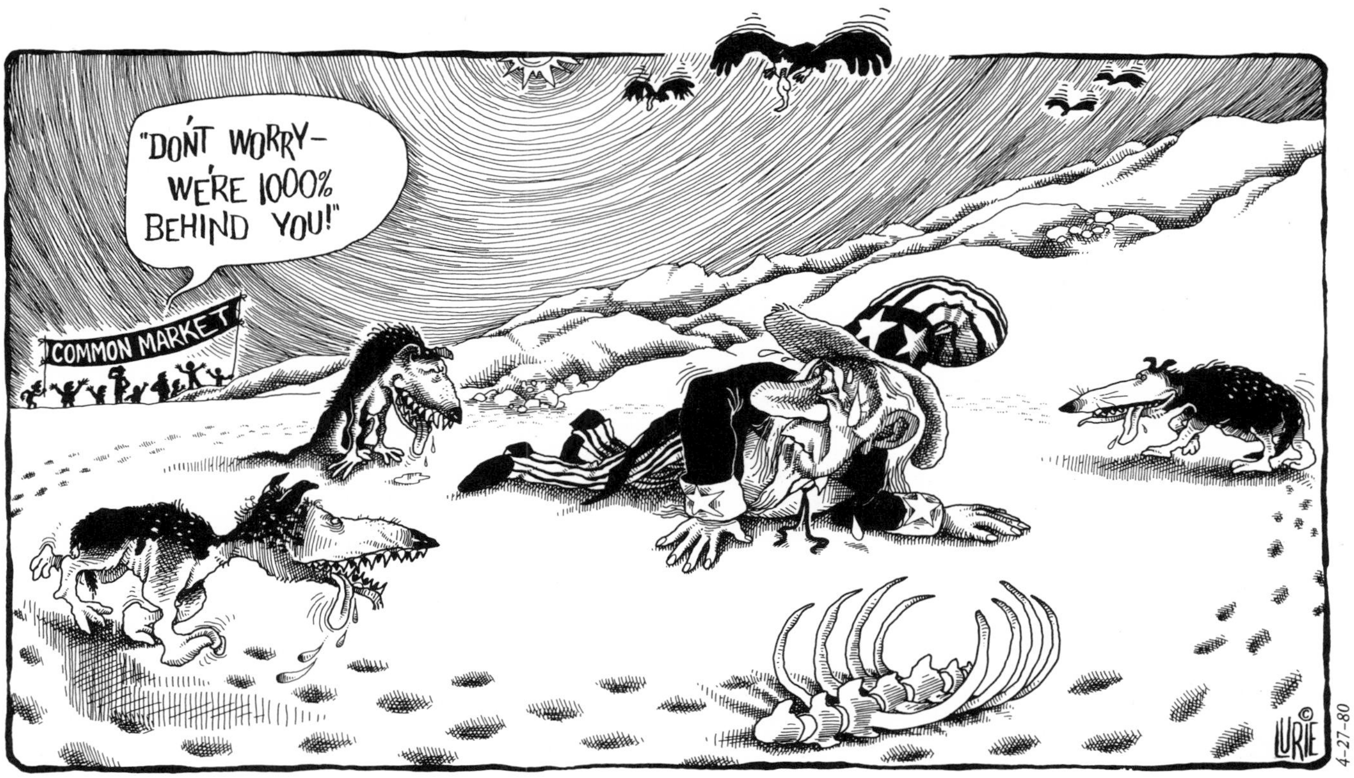
"DON'T WORRY—
WE'RE 1000%
BEHIND YOU!"
COMMON MARKET
LURIE ©
4-27-80

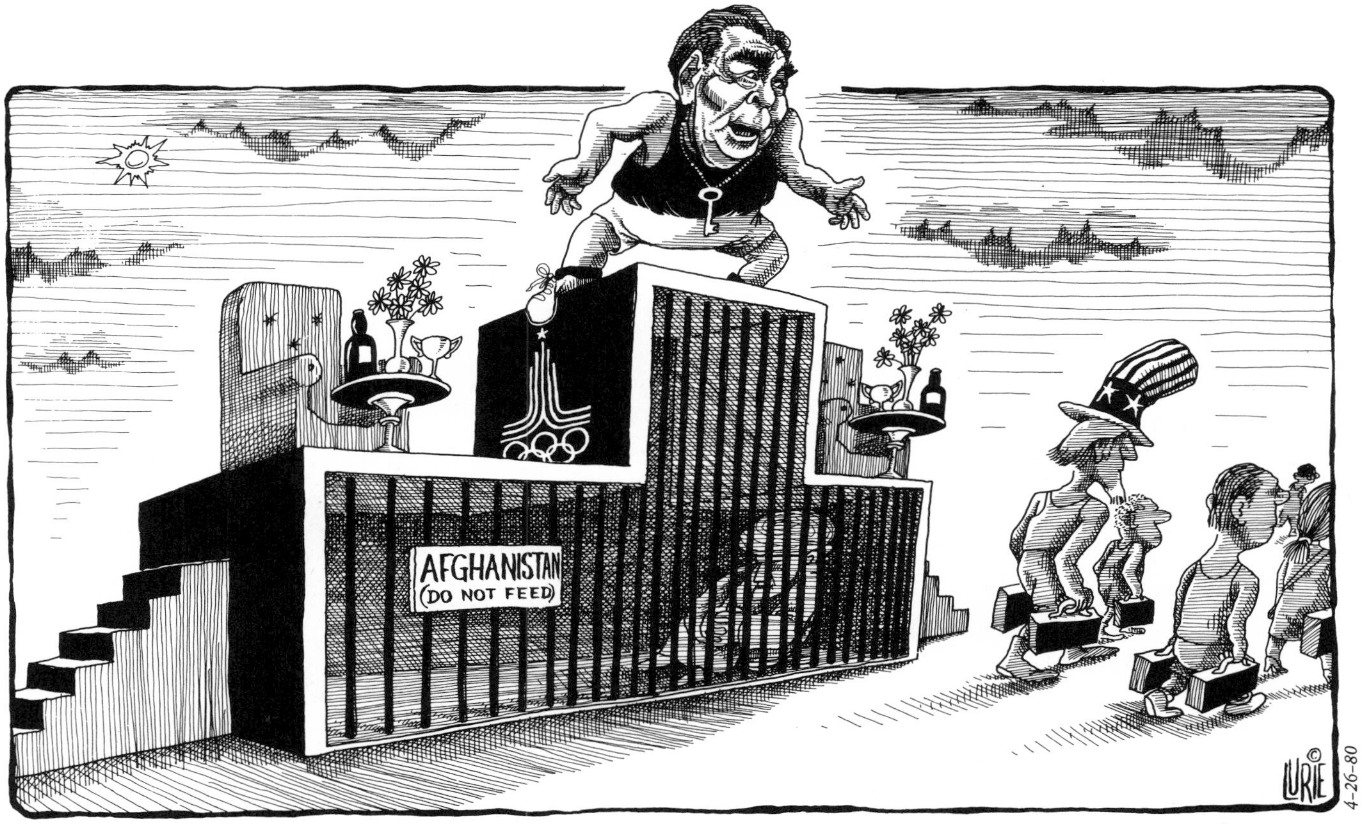
AFGHANISTAN
(DO NOT FEED)
LURIE ©
4-26-80

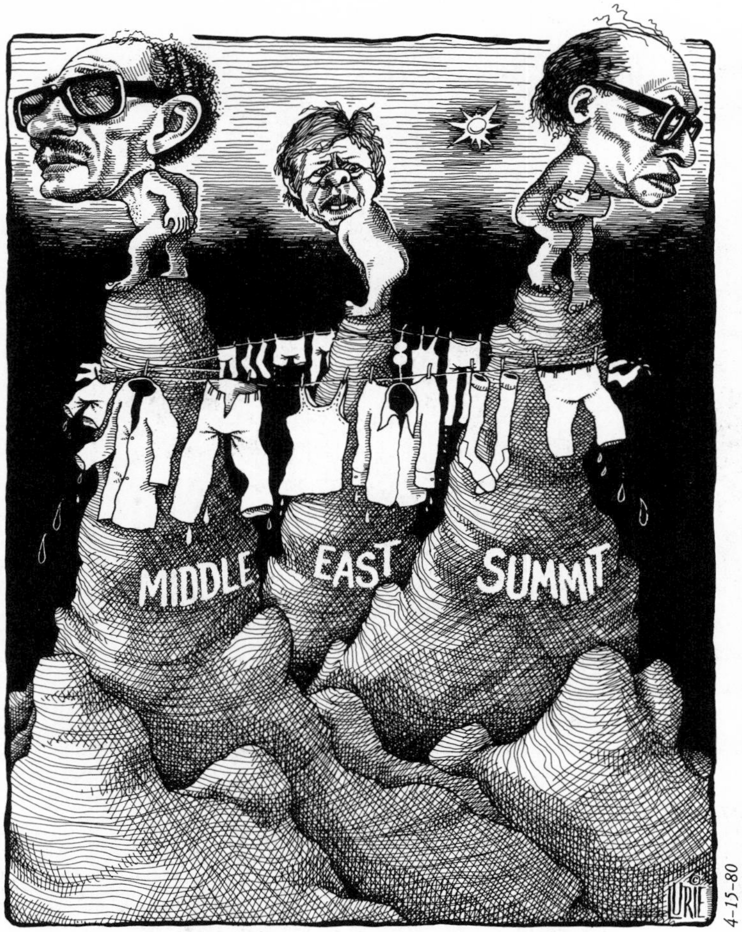
MIDDLE
EAST
SUMMIT
LURIE
4-15-80

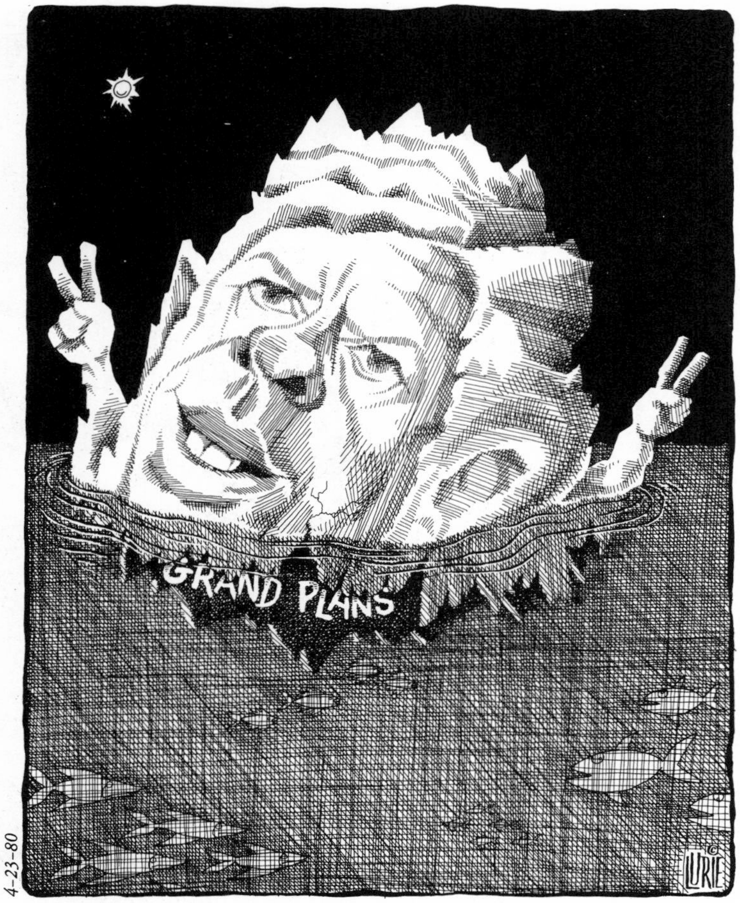
GRAND PLANS
LURIE
4-23-80

TIP OF THE ICEBERG

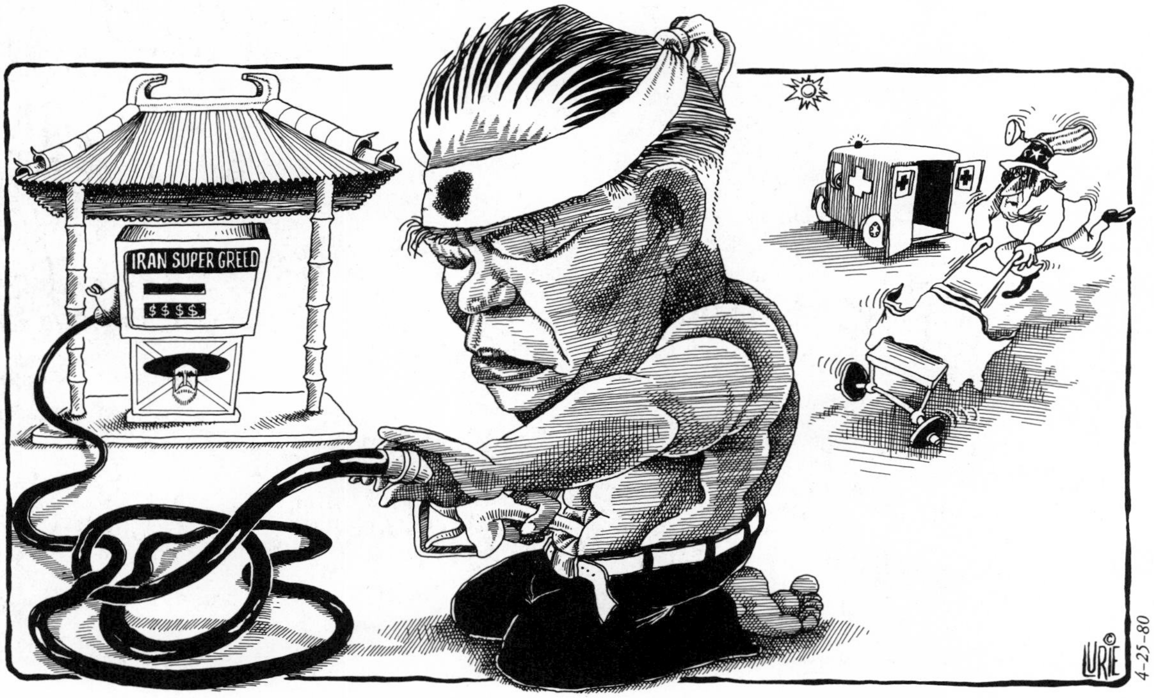
IRAN SUPER GREED
$$$$
LURIE
4-25-80

JAPAN REFUSES IRAN'S PRICE-HIKE DEMANDS

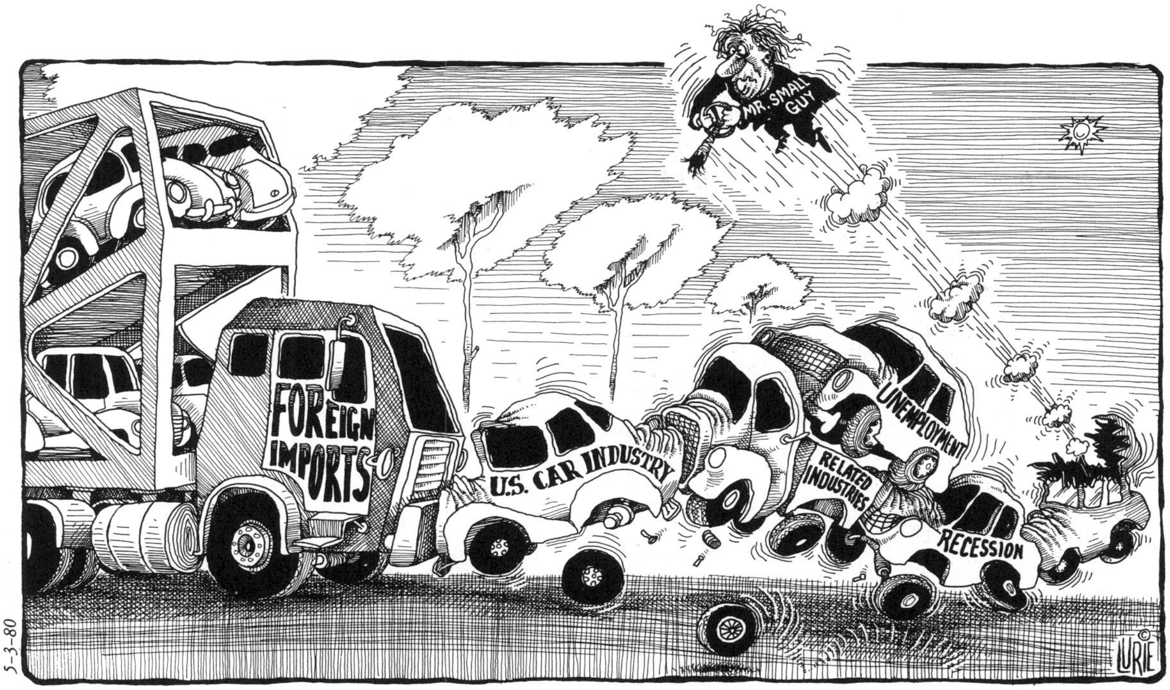
MR. SMALL GUY
FOREIGN IMPORTS
U.S. CAR INDUSTRY
RELATED INDUSTRIES
UNEMPLOYMENT
RECESSION
5-3-80
LURIE ©

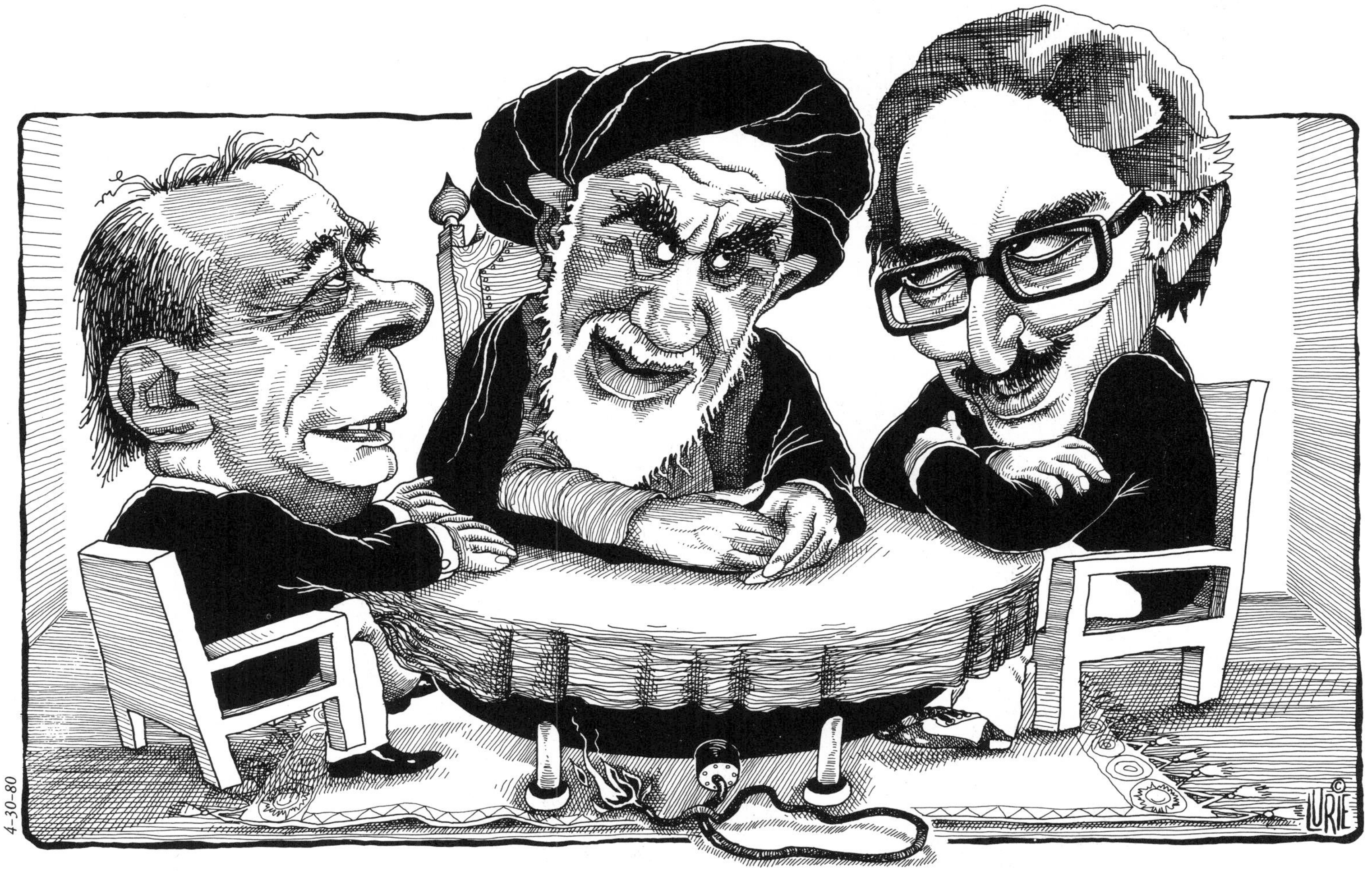
4-30-80
LURIE ©

"I'M SURE THE AMERICANS REALIZE THEY RAN OUT OF TRICKS."

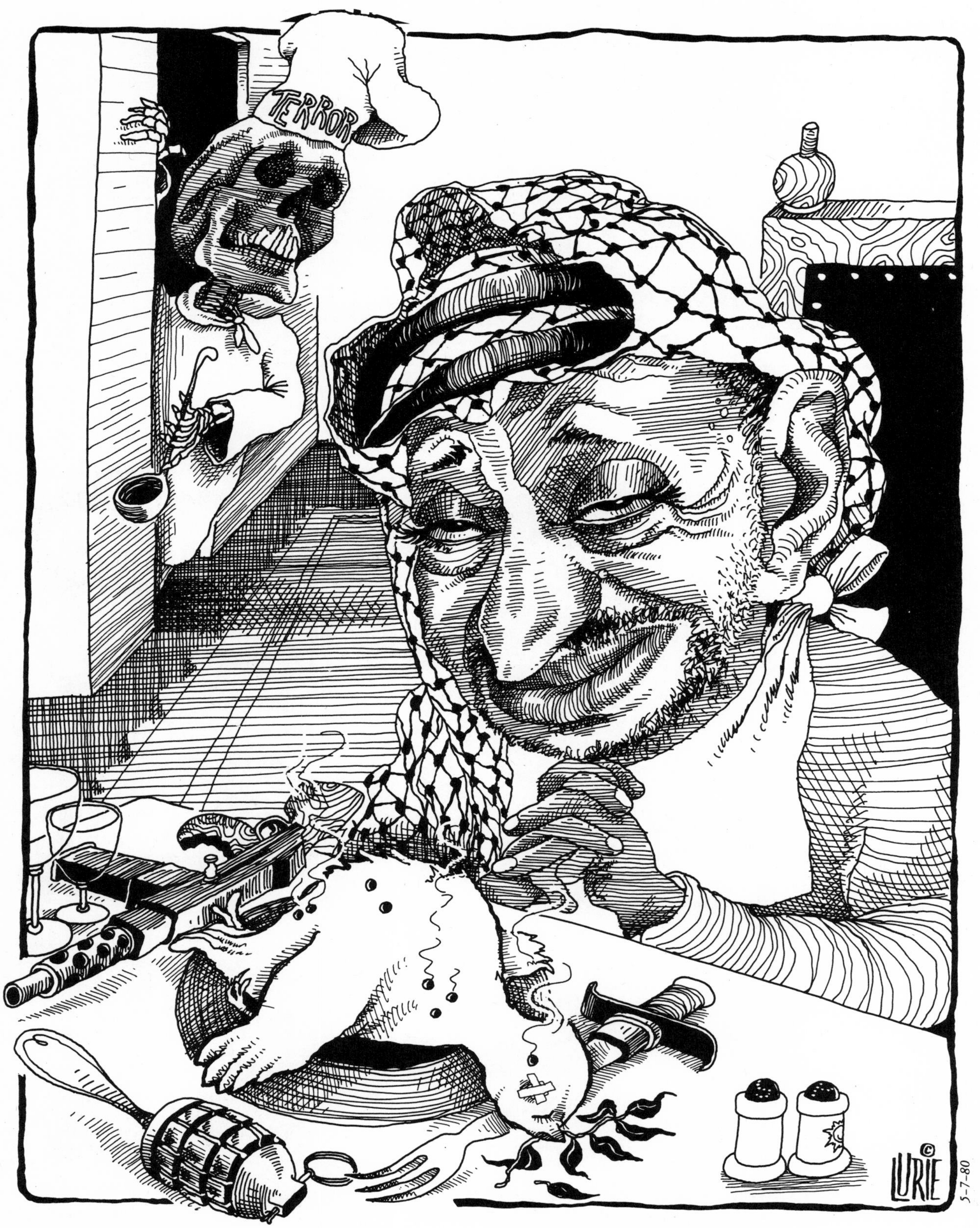
TERROR
LURIE ©
5-7-80

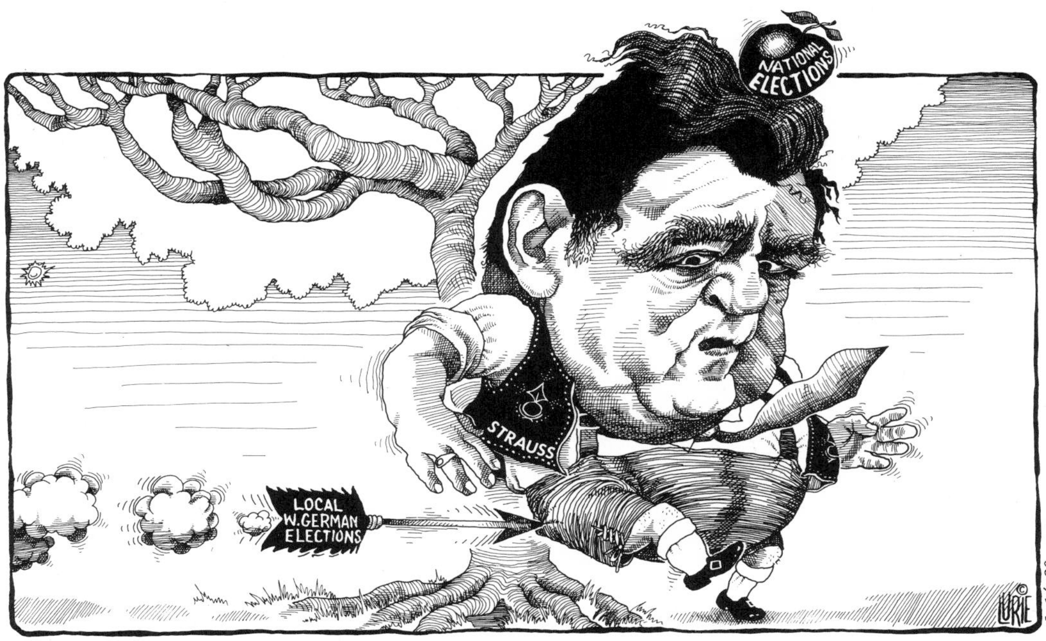
NATIONAL ELECTIONS
STRAUSS
LOCAL W. GERMAN ELECTIONS
LURIE ©
5-14-80

"OUCH!!"

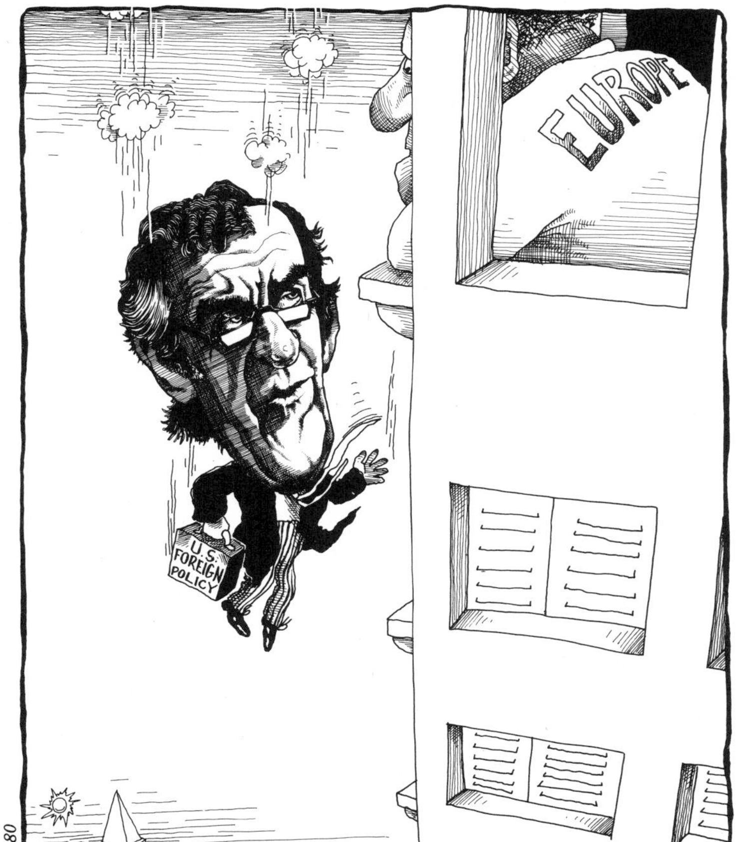
EUROPE
U.S. FOREIGN POLICY
5-15-80
LURIE ©

"JUST THOUGHT I'D DROP BY."

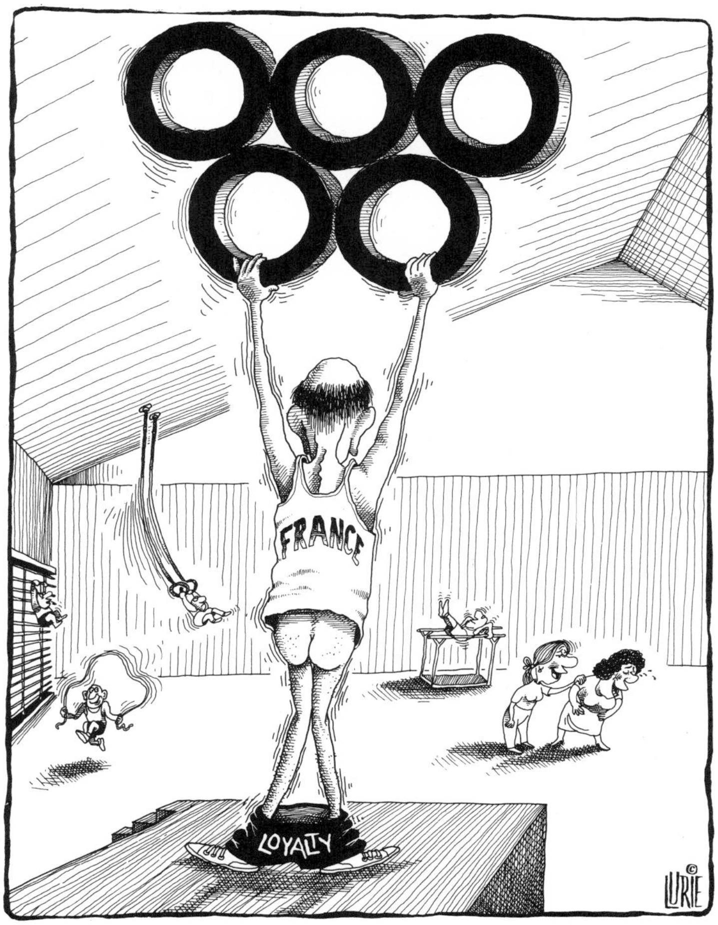
FRANCE
LOYALTY
LURIE ©

"WHAT DID YOU EXPECT?"

TITO
5-6-80
LURIE ©

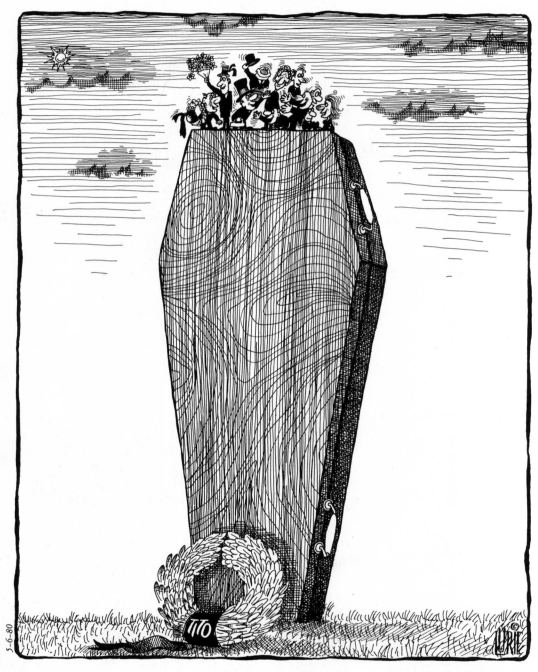

THE SUMMIT

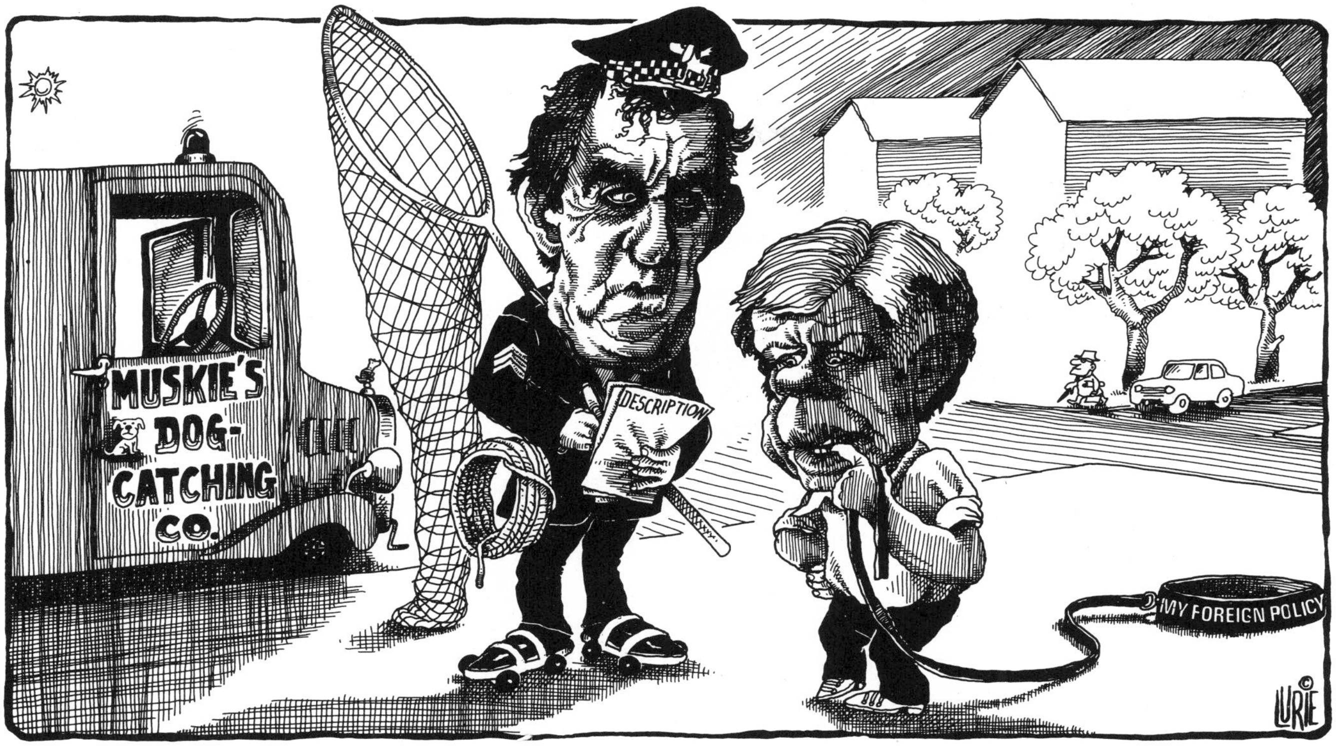
MUSKIE'S DOG-CATCHING CO.
DESCRIPTION
MY FOREIGN POLICY
LURIE ©
5-4-80

''WELL—IT HAS FOUR LEFT FEET, IT IS BLIND, IT IS DEAF . . .''

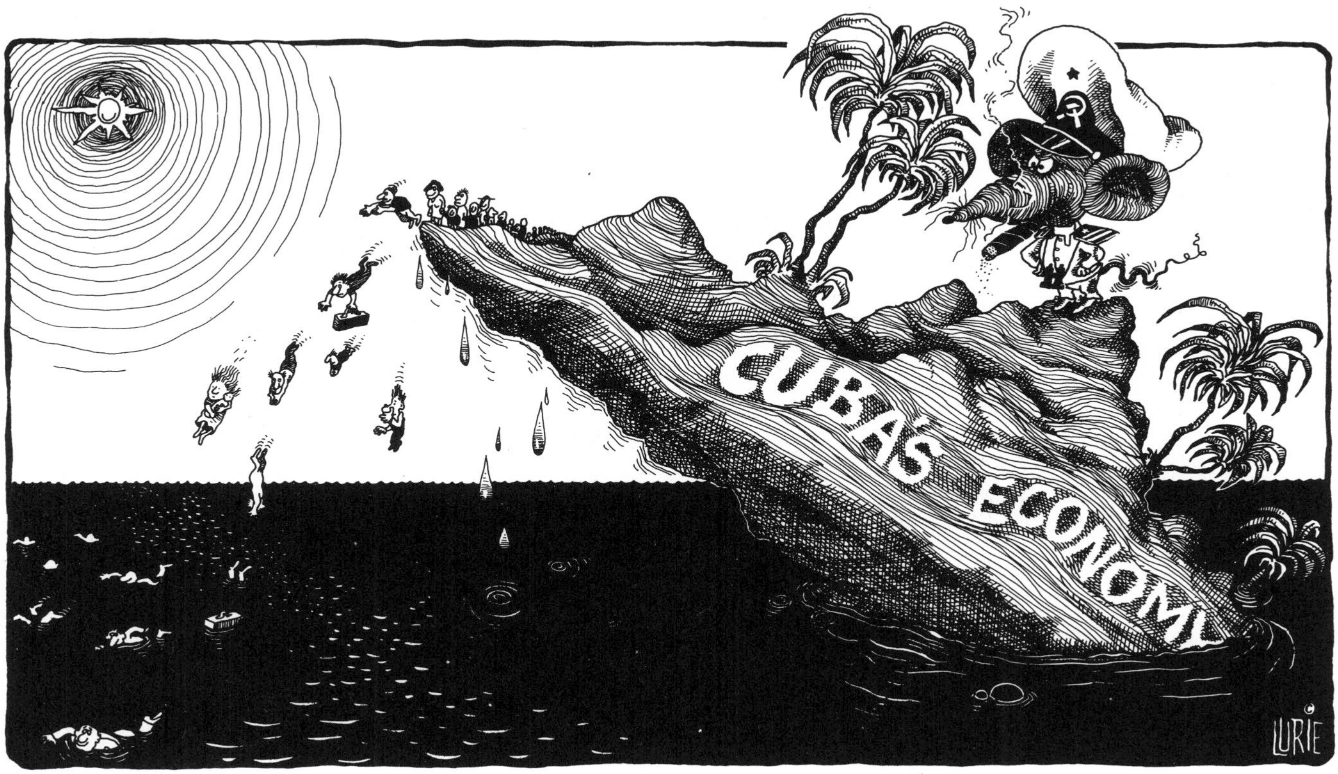
CUBA'S ECONOMY
LURIE
5-9-80

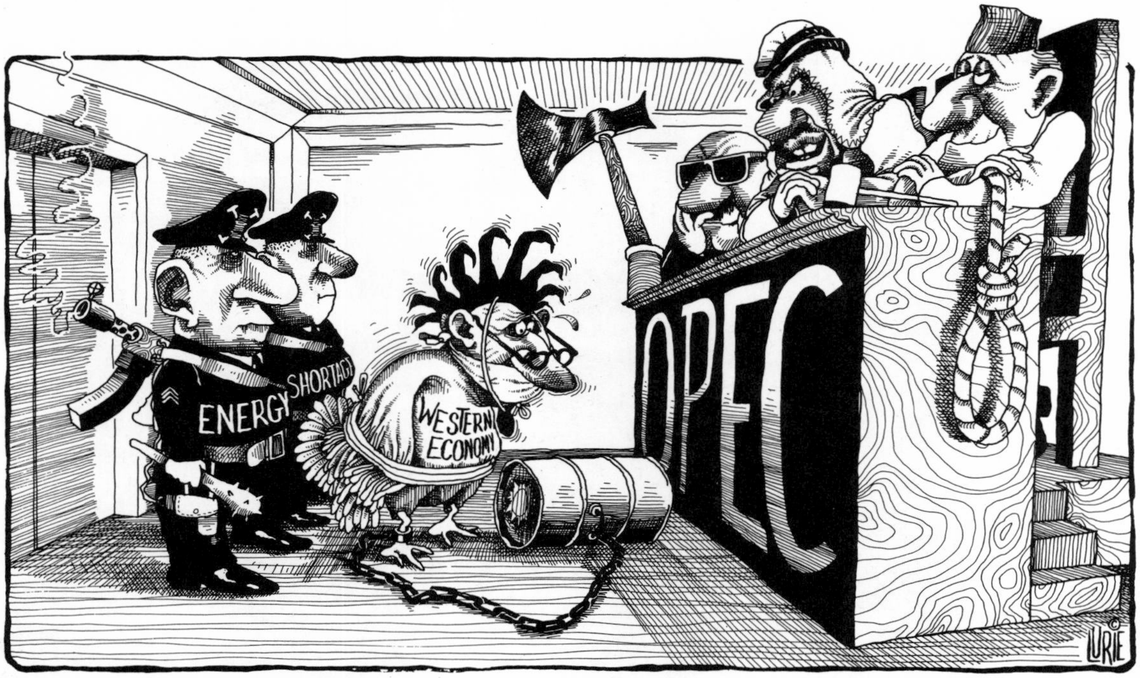
ENERGY
SHORTAGE
WESTERN ECONOMY
OPEC
LURIE
5-10-80

"SO YOU'VE NOT FILLED YOUR QUOTA OF GOLDEN EGGS FOR MAY."

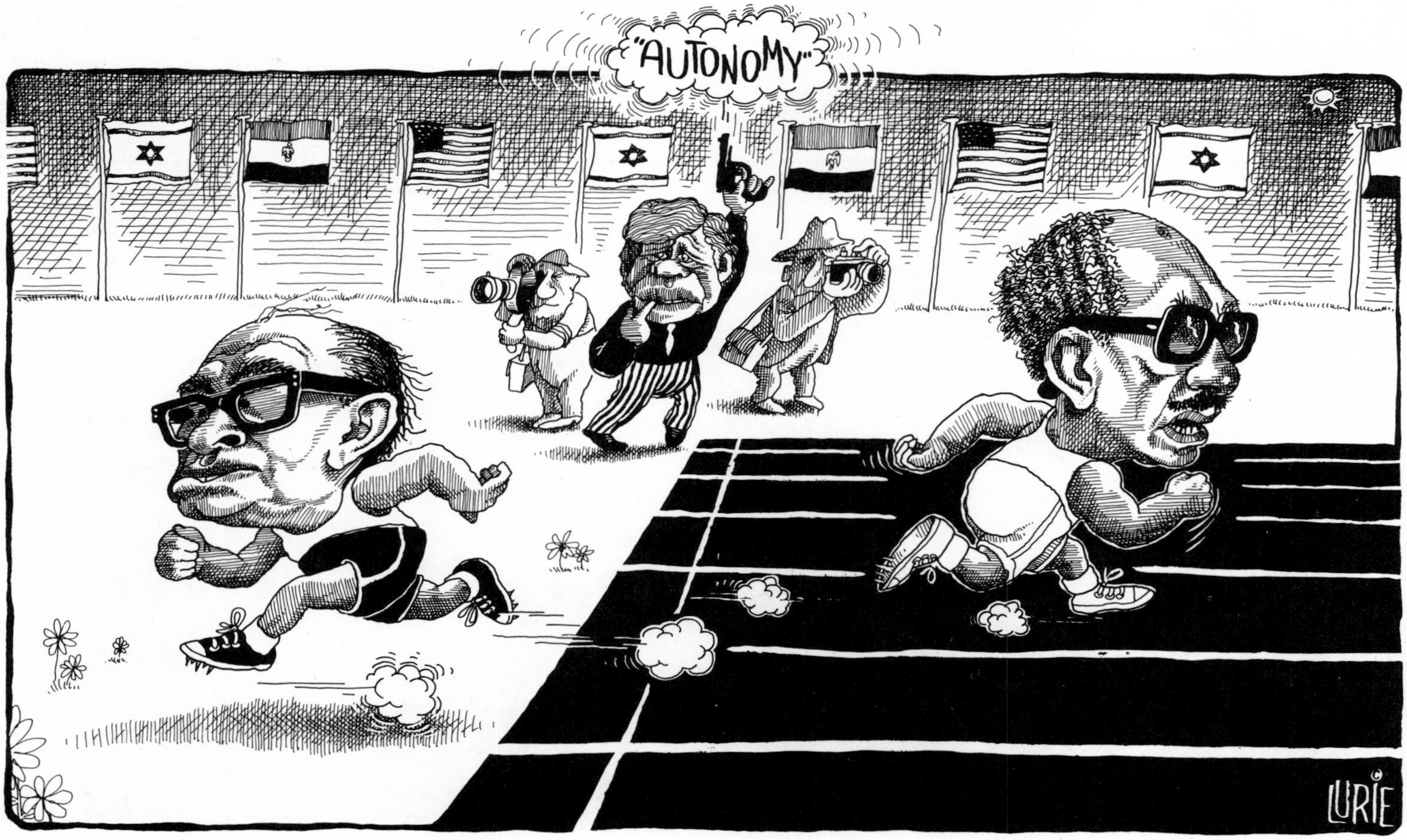
"AUTONOMY"
LURIE

President Abel Hassan Bani Sadr
of Iran

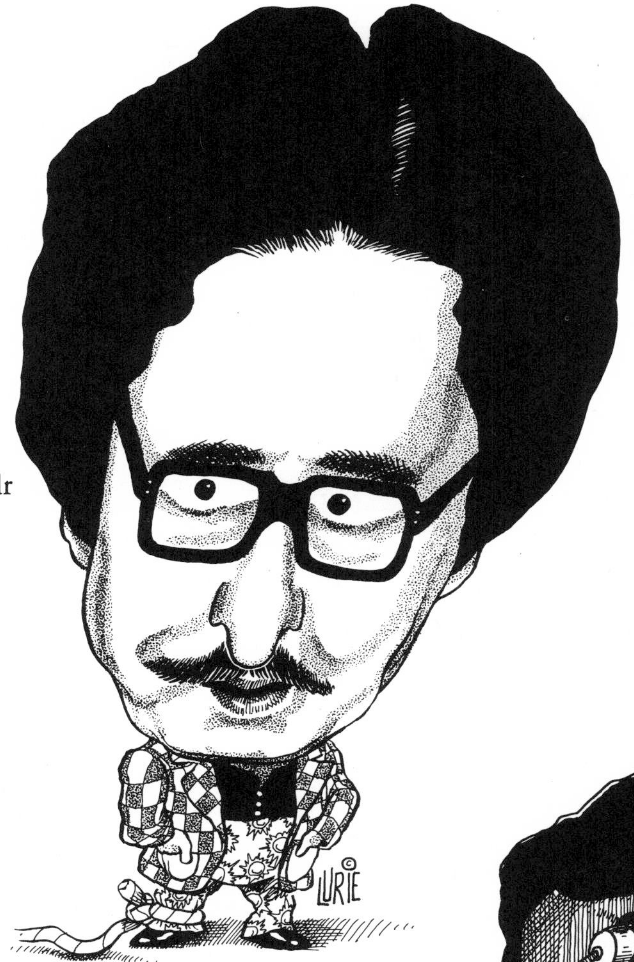
LURIE

Donald F. McHenry
U.S. Ambassador to the United Nations

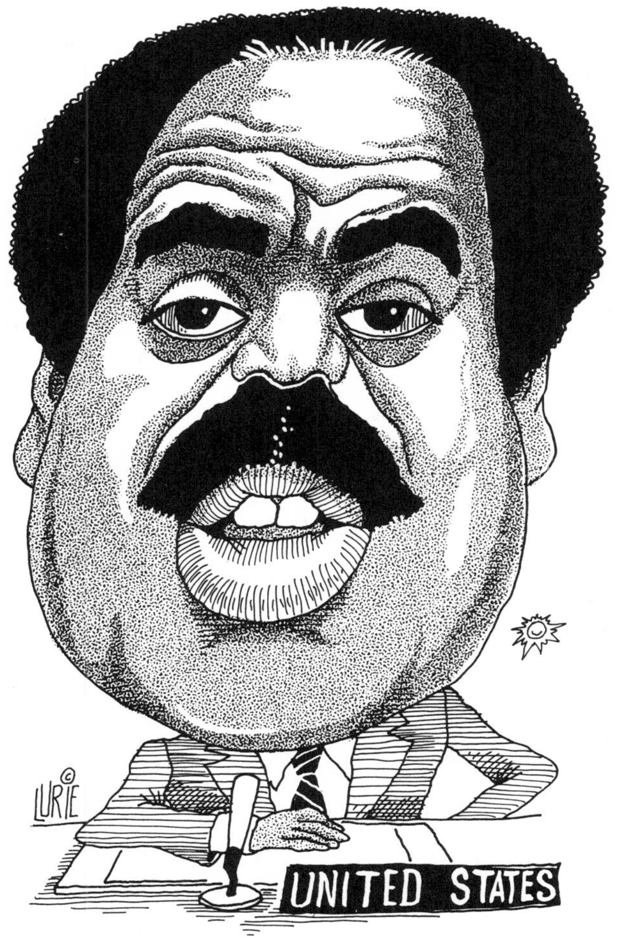
LURIE
UNITED STATES

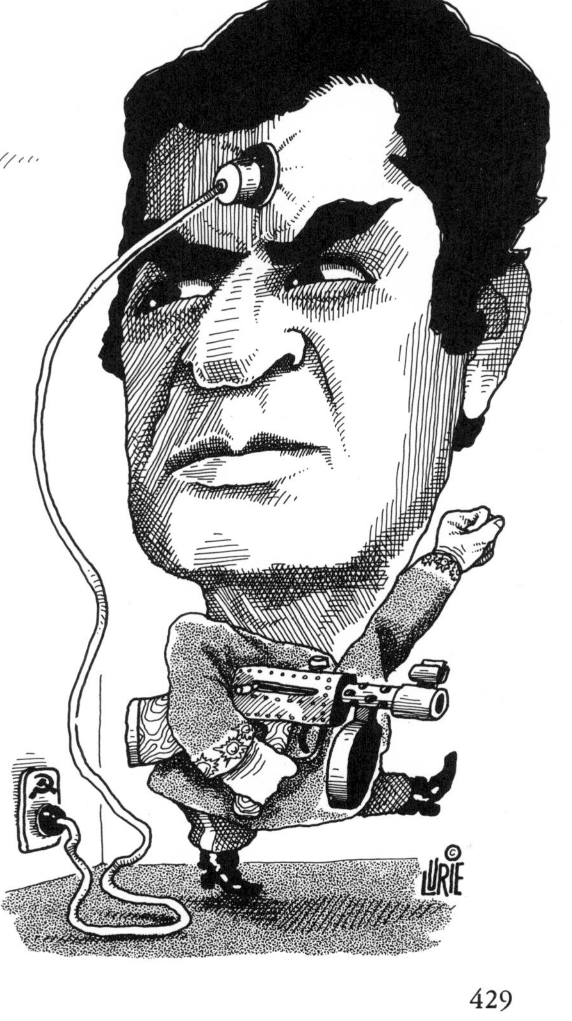
LURIE

Babrak Karmal
Afghanistan's Boss

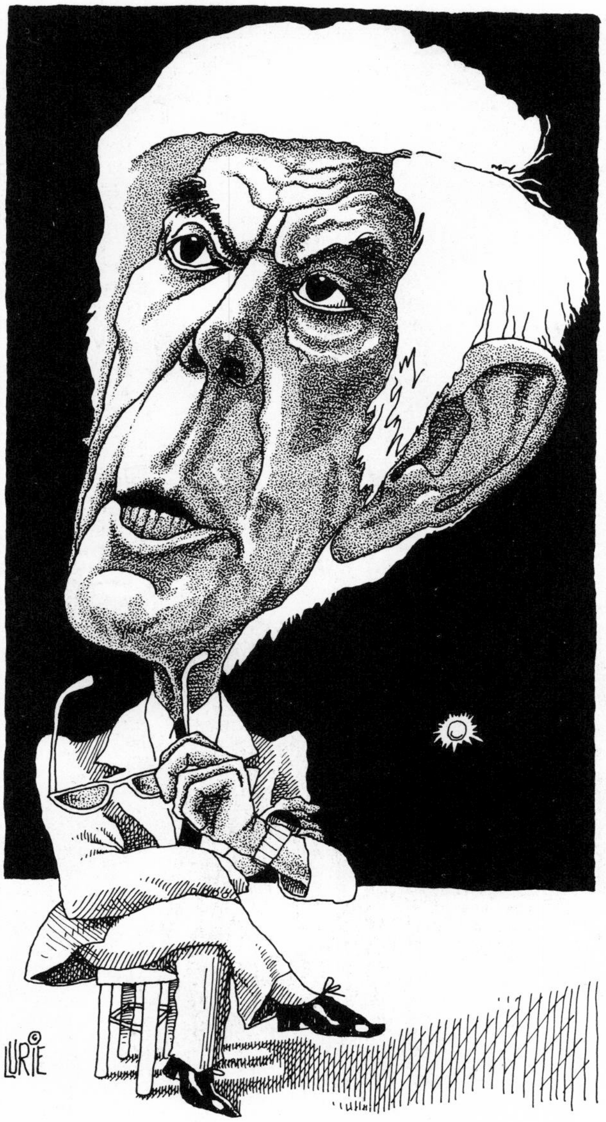
LURIE

Representative John Anderson
Presidential Candidate

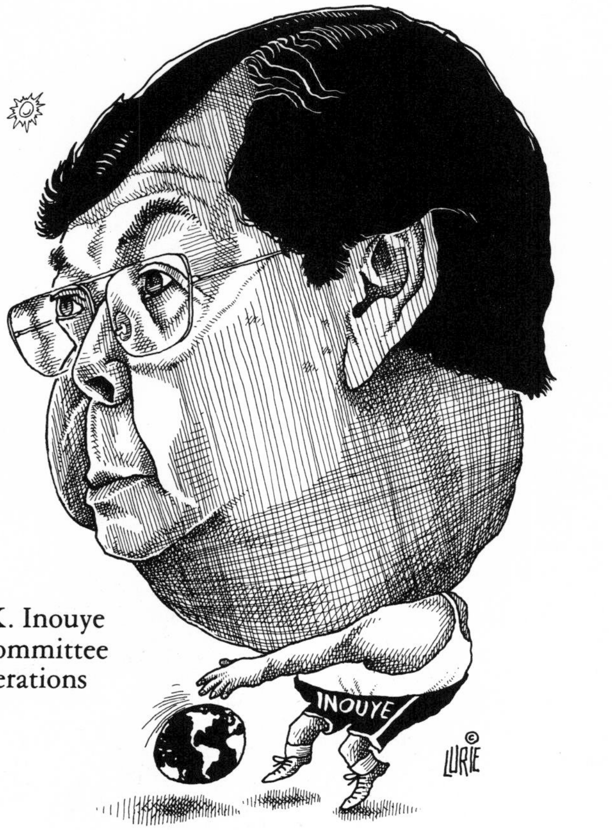
INOUYE
LURIE

Senator Daniel K. Inouye
Chairman, Subcommittee
on Foreign Operations

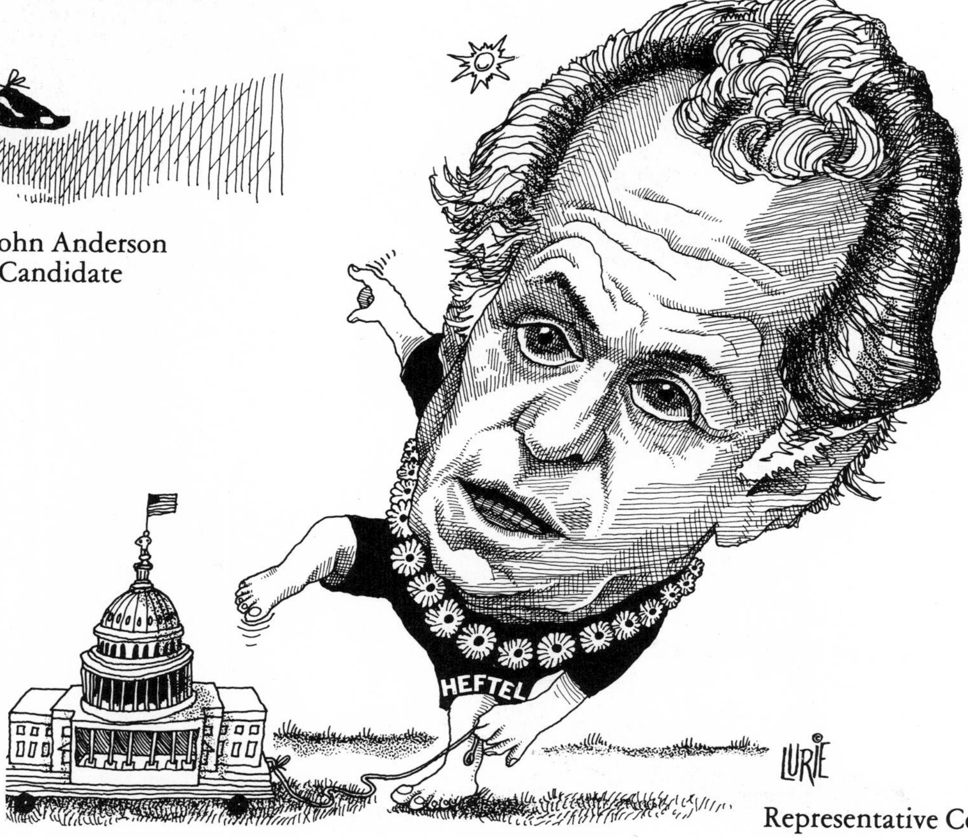
HEFTEL
LURIE

Representative Cecil K. Heftel

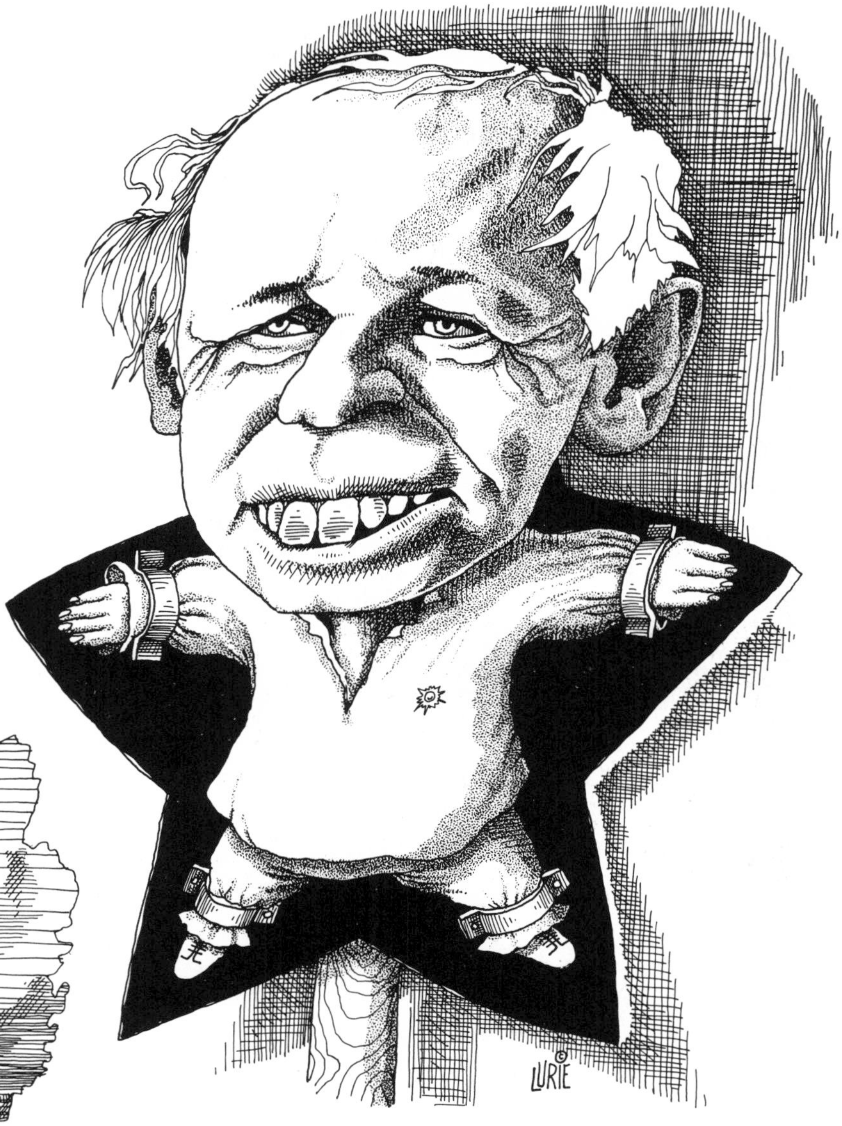
LURIE©

Andrei Sakharov
Russian Dissident Leader

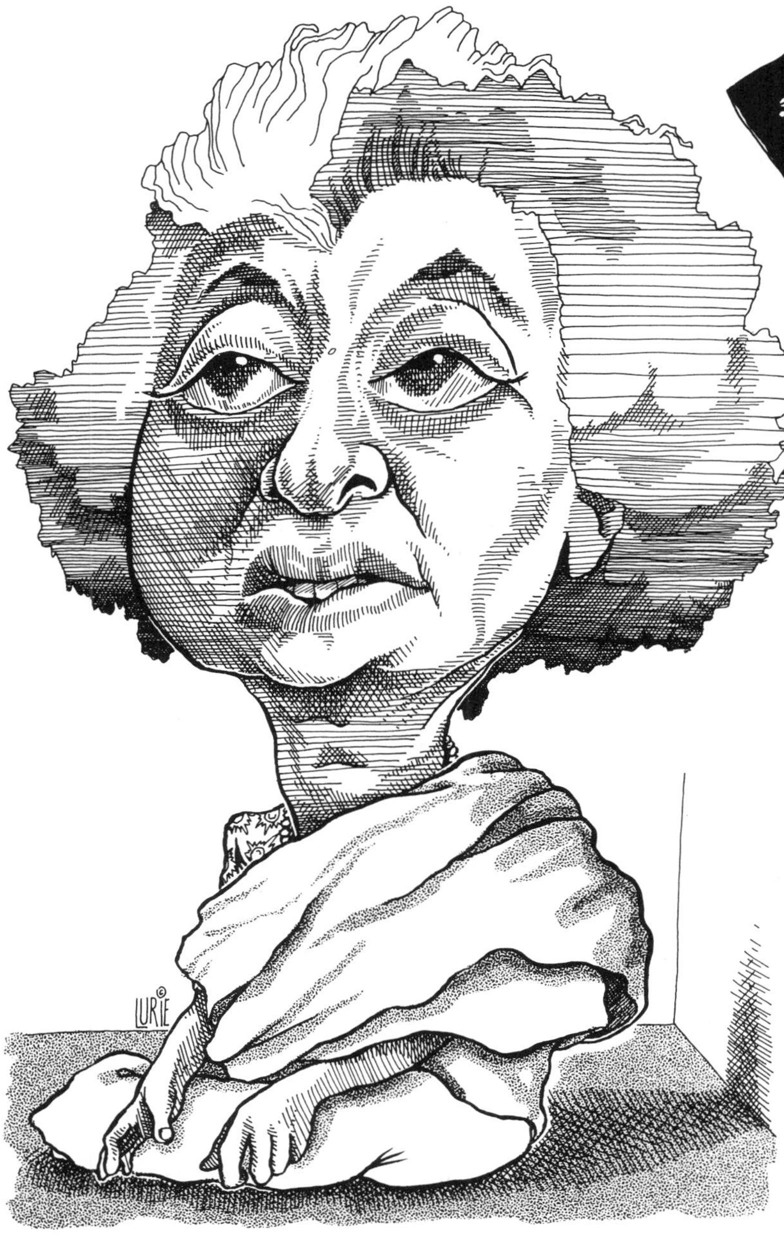
LURIE©

Indira Gandhi

Dmitri Ustinov
Soviet Defense Minister

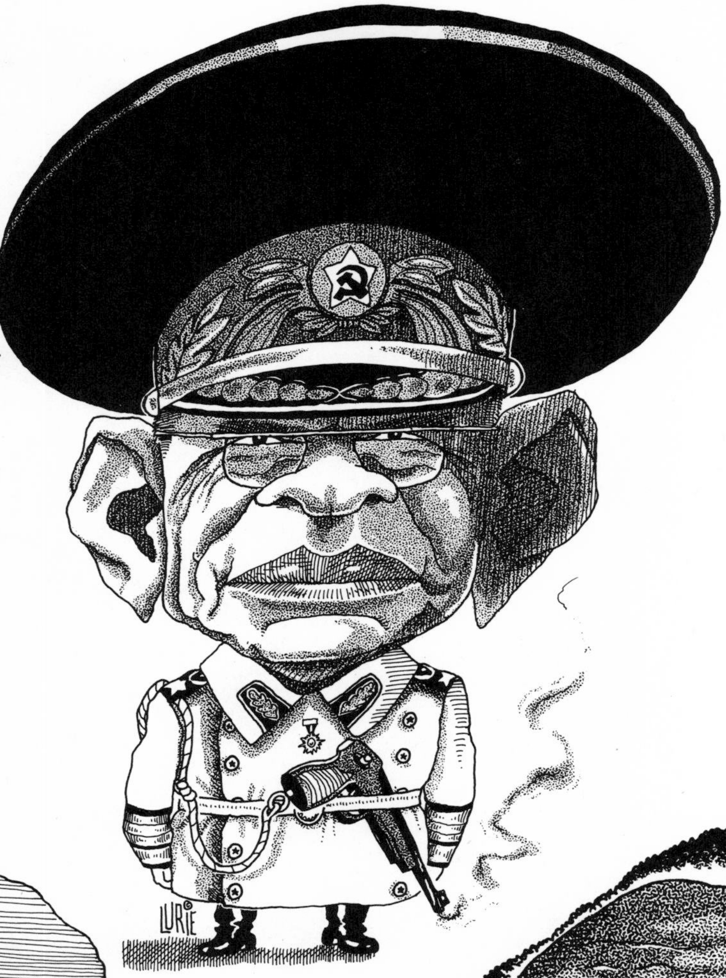
LURIE

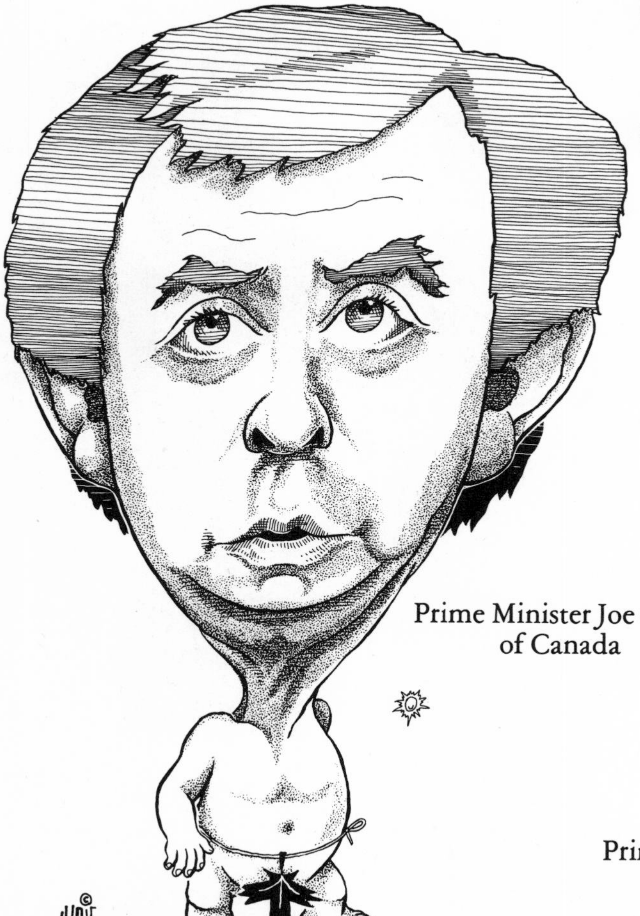
LURIE

Prime Minister Joe Clark
of Canada

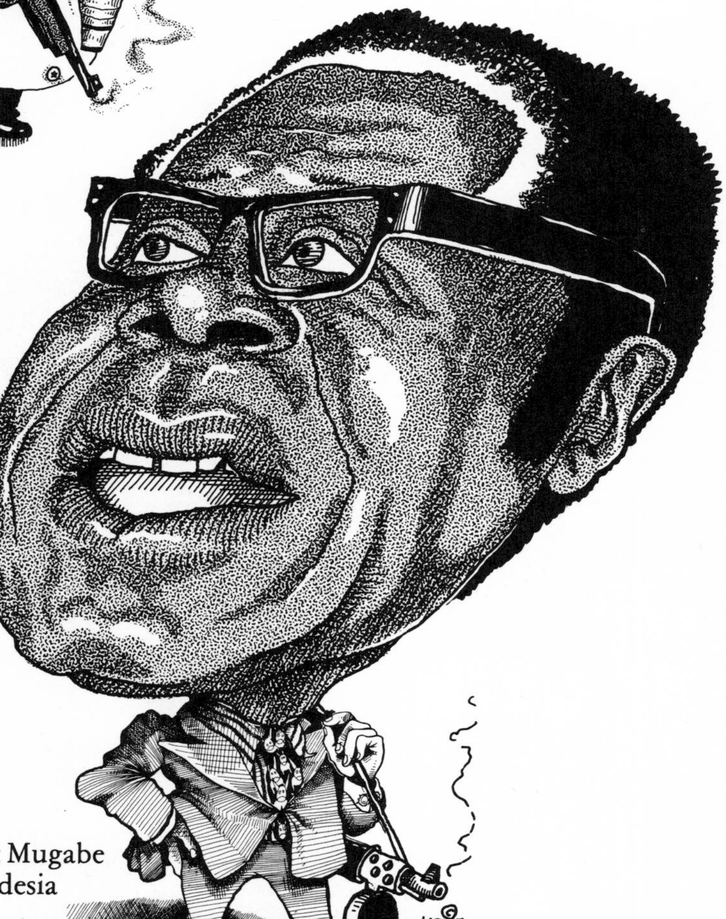
LURIE

Prime Minister Robert Mugabe
of Zimbabwe Rhodesia

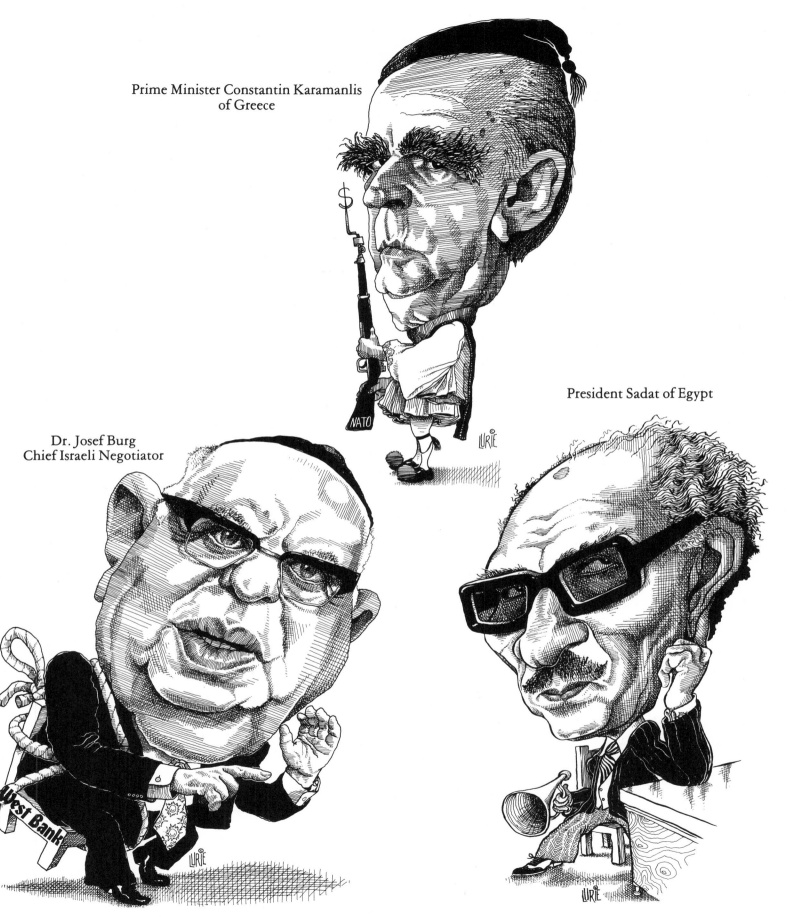

Prime Minister Constantin Karamanlis
of Greece

$
NATO
LURIE

Dr. Josef Burg
Chief Israeli Negotiator

West Bank
LURIE

President Sadat of Egypt

LURIE

Queen Beatrix of the Netherlands

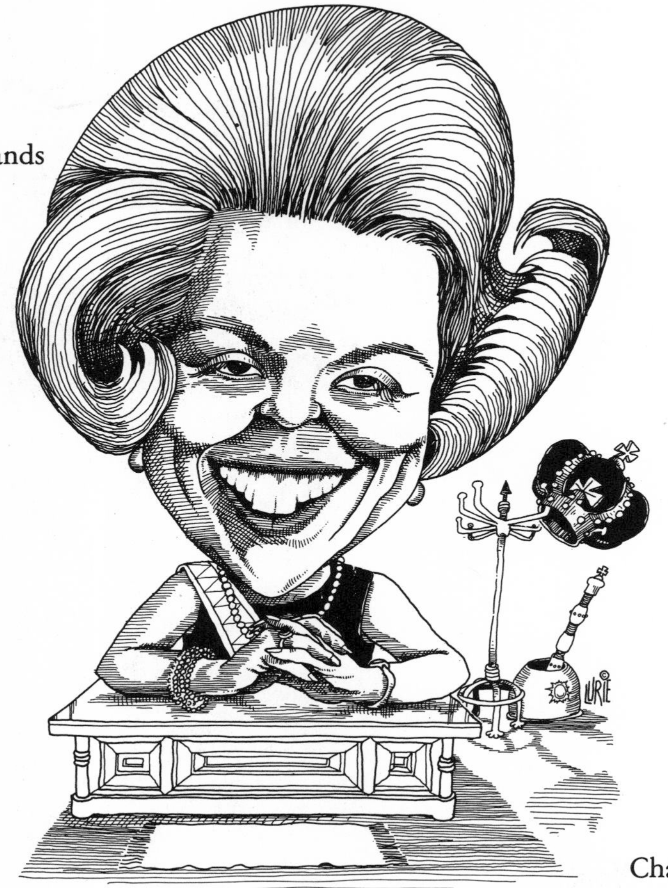
LURIE

Prime Minister Thorbjörn Fälldin
of Sweden

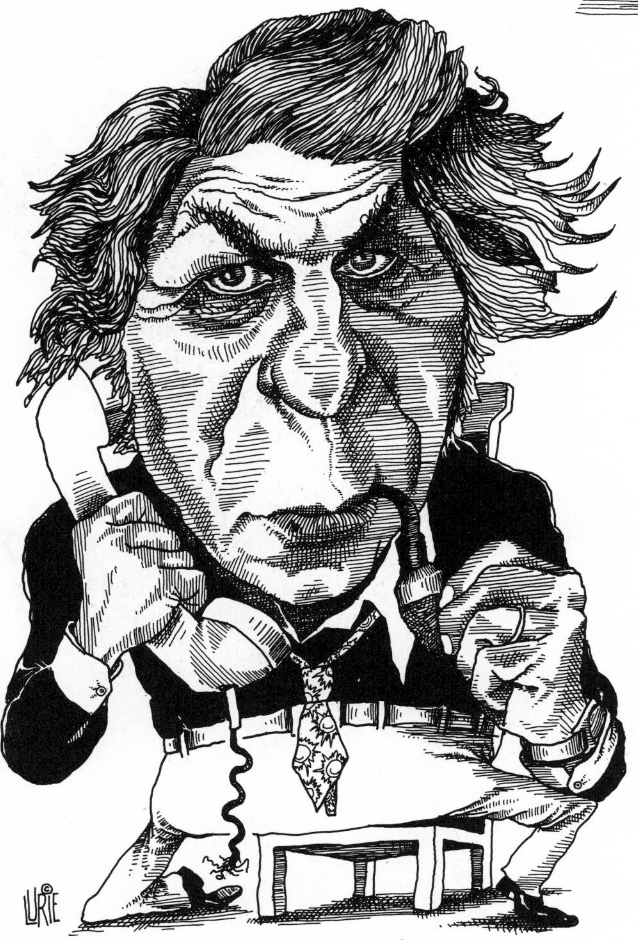
LURIE

Chancellor Helmut Schmidt
of West Germany

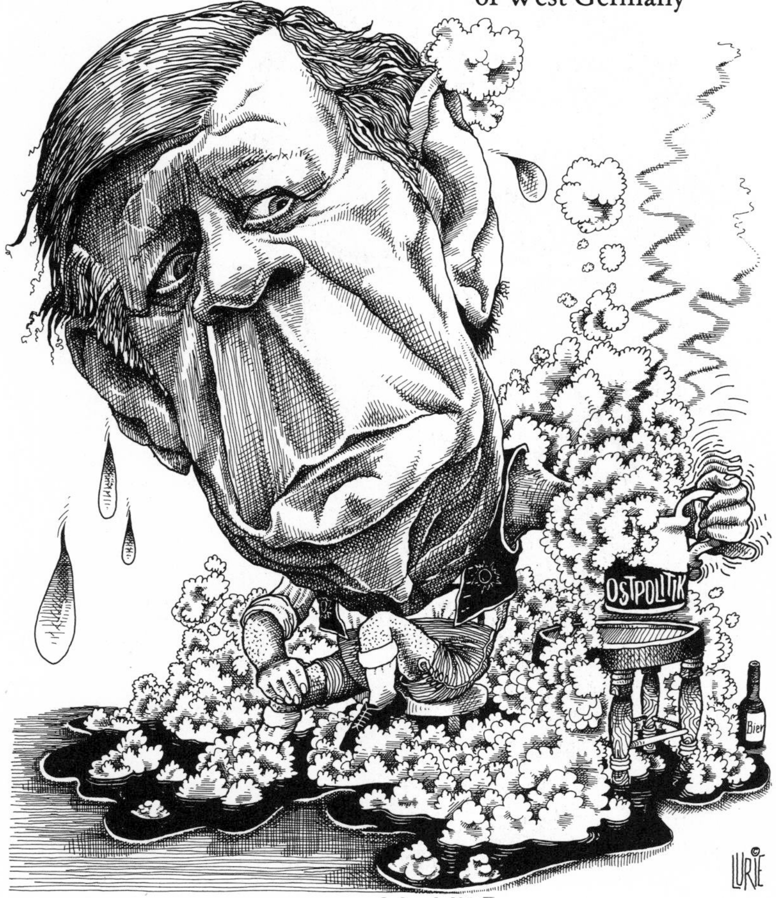
OSTPOLITIK
Bier
LURIE

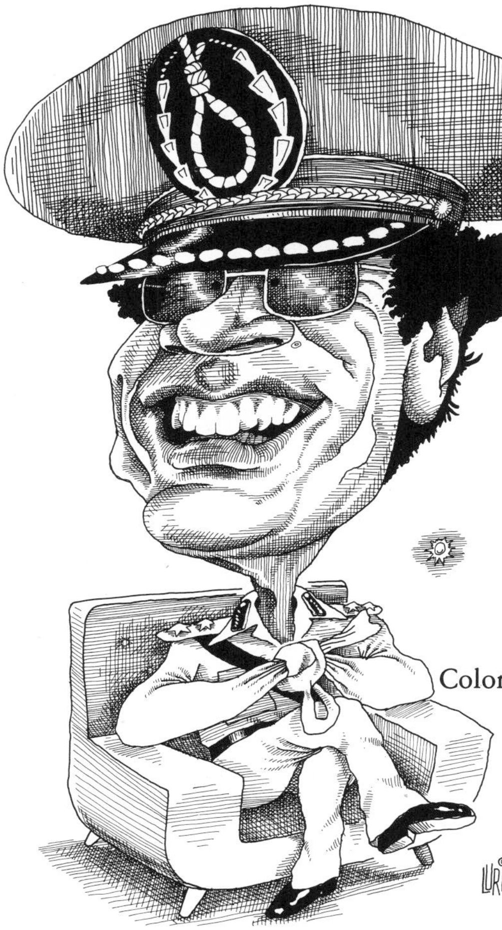
LURIE

Colonel Qaddafi of Libya

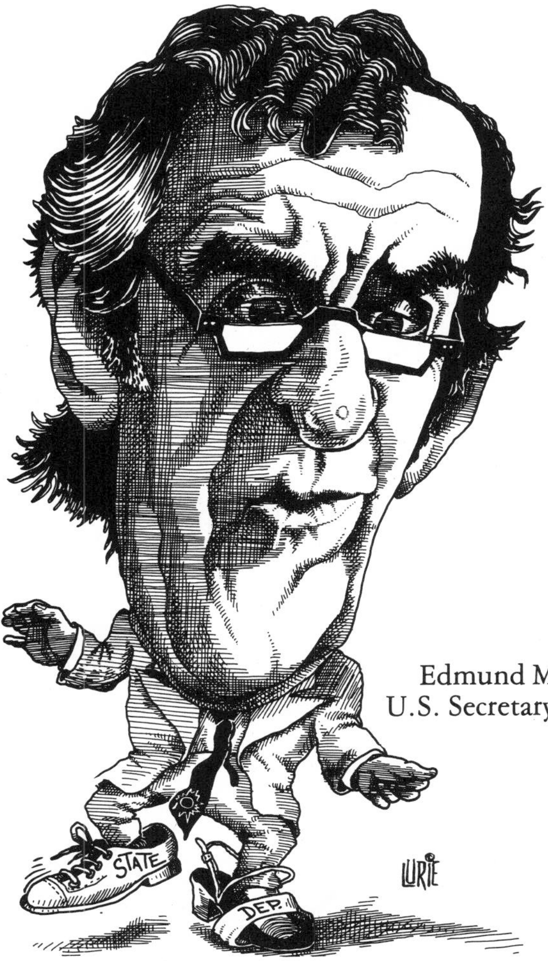
STATE
DEP.
LURIE

Edmund Muskie
U.S. Secretary of State

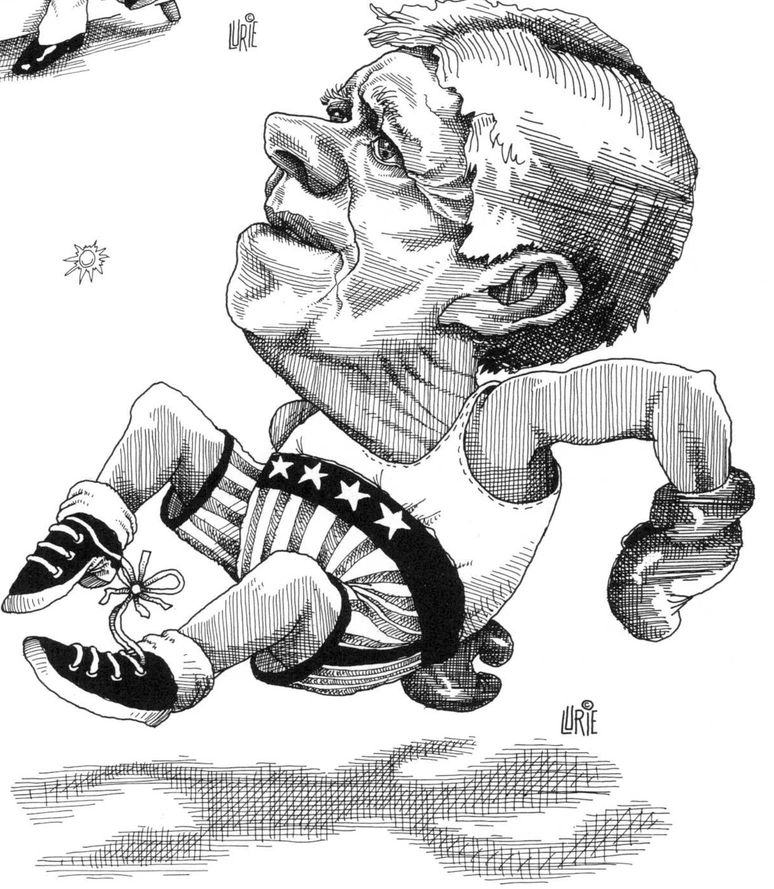
LURIE

Production Notes

This book was typeset on the
Unified Composing System
by The University Press of Hawaii.

The text and display typeface is
Garamond No. 49.

Offset presswork and binding were
done by Kingsport Press, Inc.